The Oxford Paperback Crossword Dictionary

Compiled by
Market House Books Ltd

OXFORD
UNIVERSITY PRESS

OXFORD

UNIVERSITY PRESS

Great Clarendon Street, Oxford OX2 6DP

Oxford University Press is a department of the University of Oxford.
It furthers the University's objective of excellence in research, scholarship
and education by publishing worldwide in

Oxford New York

Athens Auckland Bangkok Bogotá Buenos Aires Calcutta
Cape Town Chennai Dar es Salaam Delhi Florence Hong Kong Istanbul
Karachi Kuala Lumpur Madrid Melbourne Mexico City Mumbai
Nairobi Paris São Paulo Singapore Taipei Tokyo Toronto Warsaw

with associated companies in Berlin Ibadan

Oxford is a registered trade mark of Oxford University Press
in the UK and in certain other countries

Published in the United States
by Oxford University Press Inc., New York

© Oxford University Press 1998

Database right Oxford University Press (maker)

First published in paperback 2000

British Library Cataloguing in Publication Data

Data available

Library of Congress Cataloging in Publication Data

Data available

ISBN 0-19-861249-4

1 3 5 7 9 10 8 6 4 2

Typeset by
Market House Books Ltd.
Printed in Great Britain
on acid-free paper by
TJ International Ltd, Padstow

PREFACE

The *Oxford Crossword Dictionary* is the ideal resource for anyone who enjoys solving crosswords or playing word games. The dictionary comprises lists of words arranged according to the number of letters that they contain.

These word lists provide the reader with a much quicker, easier, and clearer way of finding words of a given length than a traditional dictionary. The listing of words and phrases by the number of letters they contain enables the reader to look for words with the required number of letters, rather than painstakingly picking out words of the appropriate length from a purely alphabetical sequence. The removal of all definitions and explanations means that the reader can locate words at a glance and can scan the lists for particular letter combinations. Within each numerical group the words are arranged alphabetically.

The word lists were created by a series of computer programs, using electronic versions of the *New Shorter Oxford English Dictionary* and the *Concise Oxford Dictionary*. Variant spellings, such as *judgement* and *judgment*, have been included where possible, as have irregular inflections of verbs and plural forms of nouns. Some regular plurals or inflections have also been included when the correct form may not be immediately obvious, e.g. *alibis* has been included to show that the plural of *alibi* is not *alibies*. Orthographic variants, including capitalized and lower case forms (e.g. *Post Office* and *post office*), hyphenated, solid, and broken forms (e.g. *rally-cross* and *rallycross*, *shut down* and *shutdown*) also appear in the lists to allow for the different rules and regulations of various word games and to help crossword solvers who are looking for multiple-word phrases rather than single words. Widely used and well-known abbreviations, such as *AIDS*, appear in the lists. For completeness, formal, informal, taboo, dialect, archaic, and derogatory words have been included – but without labels, as these would have made the lists difficult to read. The source dictionaries provide information about the meaning and usage of the listed words.

ACKNOWLEDGEMENTS

Computerization
Dr John Daintith

Compiled and Typeset by
Market House Books Ltd, Aylesbury

Source Dictionaries
The New Shorter Oxford English Dictionary
The Concise Oxford Dictionary

CONTENTS

TWO LETTERS

aa	ax	dy	fe	hy	ky	na	om	po	te	wa
ab	ay	ea	fo	id	la	ne	on	pu	ti	we
ac	ba	ee	fu	ie	le	né	oo	qi	to	wo
ad	be	ef	fy	if	li	ni	op	ra	ug	wy
ae	bi	eh	ga	in	lo	no	or	re	uh	xi
af	bo	el	ge	io	lü	nu	os	ri	um	xu
ah	bu	em	go	is	ly	ob	ot	sa	un	ya
ai	by	en	gy	it	ma	od	ou	se	up	yd
ak	ca'	er	ha	iv	me	oe	ow	sh	ur	ye
am	ce	es	he	ja	mi	of	ox	si	us	yi
an	da	et	He	jo	mo	oh	oy	so	ut	yo
ar	de	ew	hi	ka	Mr	oi	oz	st	uz	yu
as	di	ex	hm	ki	Ms	OK	pa	su	va	za
at	do	ey	ho	ko	mu	ol'	pe	sy	vi	zi
aw	Dr	fa	hu	ku	my	ol	pi	ta	vo	zo

THREE LETTERS

aam	asp	bro	cut	dos	erm	fud	hab	I Am	jut
aba	ass	bub	cwm	do's	ern	fug	had	ice	kab
abb	ate	bud	dab	DOS	err	fum	hae	icy	kae
a-be	Ate	bug	dad	dot	ess	fun	hag	ide	kai
abo	auk	bum	dae	DoT	est	fur	hah	iff	kat
aby	aul	bun	dag	dow	eta	gab	haj	ike	kay
ace	aum	bur	dah	Dow	eth	gad	ham	ilk	kea
ach	ava	bus	dai	dry	eve	gag	han	ill	ked
act	ave	but	dak	dub	ewe	gah	hào	I'll	kef
add	awa'	buy	dal	dud	eye	gal	hap	imp	keg
ado	awe	bye	dam	due	fab	gam	has	inf	kel
aft	awl	cab	dam'	dug	fad	gap	hat	ink	ken
aga	awn	cad	dan	dun	fag	gar	hau	inn	kep
Aga	axe	caf	Dan	duo	fah	gas	haw	ion	ket
age	aye	cal	Dao	dup	fam	gat	hay	IOU	kex
ago	baa	Cal	dap	dux	fan	gay	he'd	ire	key
agy	bab	cam	das	dye	far	ged	heh	irk	kid
aha	bad	can	dat	dyn	fat	gee	hem	ism	kif
aid	bag	cap	DAT	dzo	fax	gel	hen	ist	kin
ail	bah	car	daw	ean	fay	gem	hep	ita	kip
aim	bal	cat	day	ear	fed	gen	her	it'd	Kir
air	bam	caw	deb	eat	fee	geo	he's	ite	kit
ais	ban	cay	dee	eau	fei	get	het	it's	koa
ait	bap	cel	def	ebb	fem	gey	hew	its	kob
aka	bar	cep	del	ecu	fen	ghi	hex	I've	KO'd
ake	bat	cha	dem	écu	fes	gib	hey	ivi	koi
à la	baw	chi	den	edh	fet	gid	hic	ivy	kop
ala	bay	CIA	dew	eel	feu	gie	hid	jab	kos
alb	bed	CID	dey	Eem	few	gif	hie	jag	kou
ale	bee	cig	dha	e'en	fey	gig	him	Jah	kra
all	beg	clo'	dib	e'er	fez	gim	hin	jak	kya
alp	bel	clo	did	eff	fib	gin	hip	jam	kyd
alt	ben	cob	die	eft	fid	gio	his	Jap	kye
aly	ber	cod	dif	egg	fie	gip	hit	jar	kyu
amp	bet	cog	dig	ego	fig	git	hmm	jat	lab
amu	bey	col	dim	eid	fin	gnu	hob	jaw	lac
ana	bib	con	din	Eid	Fin	goa	hoc	jay	lad
and	bid	coo	dip	eik	fip	gob	hod	jee	lag
ane	big	cop	dis	eke	fir	god	hoe	jer	lah
ani	Bim	coq	dit	eld	fit	God	hog	jes	lai
ann	bin	cor	div	elf	fix	gog	hom	jet	lam
an't	bio	cos	dix	elk	fiz	gom	hon	Jew	lap
ant	bit	cot	DIY	ell	flu	goo	hoo	jib	lar
any	biz	cow	diz	elm	fly	gos	hop	jig	lat
A-OK	boa	cox	dob	eme	fob	got	hot	jit	lav
ape	bob	coy	doc	emu	foe	goy	how	job	law
aps	bod	coz	dod	end	fog	gra	hoy	Job	lax
apt	bog	cro	doe	ene	foh	gul	hub	jod	lay
arb	boh	cru	dog	Eno	fop	gum	hud	joe	lea
arc	boo	cry	doh	ens	for	gun	hue	Joe	led
ard	bop	cub	dol	eon	fou	gup	hug	jog	lee
are	bot	cud	dom	ept	fox	gur	huh	jot	leg
ark	bow	cue	Dom	era	foy	gut	hui	jow	lei
arm	Bow	cum	don	ere	Fra	guv	hum	joy	lek
art	box	cun	doo	erf	fro	guy	hun	jug	Leo
ash	boy	cup	dop	erg	fry	gym	hup	jun	lep
ask	bra	cur	dor	erk	fub	gyp	hut	jus	les

let	met	new	ole	pic	raw	saj	spy	tog	vav	wyn
leu	meu	nib	olm	pie	rax	sal	sty	tom	vee	yad
lev	mew	nid	one	pig	ray	sam	sub	Tom	veg	yag
lew	mho	nig	oof	pik	reb	san	sud	ton	vet	yah
ley	mic	nil	ooh	pin	rec	sap	sue	too	vex	yak
lez	mid	nim	ook	pip	red	sat	sug	top	via	yam
lib	mig	nip	ope	pir	ree	sav	suh	tor	vic	yap
lid	mil	nis	opp	pit	ref	saw	suk	tot	vie	yar
lie	mim	nit	opt	più	reg	sax	sul	tou	vim	yas
lig	min	nix	ora	pix	rei	say	sum	tow	VIP	yaw
lil	Min	noa	orb	ply	rem	sea	sun	toy	vis	yay
lin	Mir	nob	orc	poa	rep	sec	sup	tri	viz	yea
lip	mis	nod	ore	pod	res	see	suq	try	voe	yed
lis	mit	nog	øre	poh	ret	seg	sus	tsk	vol	yeh
lit	mix	Noh	öre	poi	rev	sei	swy	tsu	vow	yen
loa	miz	nor	orf	pol	Rev	sem	tab	tub	vox	yeo
lob	Mme	nor'	org	pom	rew	sen	tad	tue	vug	yep
lod	moa	not	ork	Pom	Rex	ser	tag	tug	vum	yer
log	mob	now	orl	poo	rhe	set	tai	tui	wad	yes
loo	moc	nox	ort	pop	rho	sew	taj	tum	wag	yet
lop	mod	noy	ory	Pop	ria	sex	tam	tun	wai	yew
lor	Mod	nth	oss	pos	rib	sey	tan	tup	wan	yex
lot	mog	nub	ouf	pot	rid	sez	Tao	tur	wap	yez
low	moi	nud	our	pou	rig	she	tap	tut	war	Yid
lox	mol	nug	out	pow	rim	sho	tar	tux	was	yin
loy	mom	num	ova	pox	rin	shy	tat	twa	wat	yip
lud	mon	nun	owe	pre	rio	sib	tau	two	wau	yiz
lug	moo	nut	owl	pro	rip	sic	tav	tye	waw	yob
lum	mop	nye	own	pry	ris	sif	taw	uff	wax	yod
lur	mor	oaf	owt	psi	rit	sig	tax	ufo	way	yoi
luv	mos	oak	pac	pst	riu	sin	taz	UFO	web	yok
lux	mot	OAP	pad	pub	rob	sip	tea	ugg	we'd	yon
lye	MOT	oar	pah	pud	roc	sir	tec	ugh	wed	you
maa	mou	oat	pal	pug	rod	sis	ted	uke	wee	yow
mab	mow	oba	pan	pul	roe	sit	Ted	uki	wem	yuh
mac	moz	obe	pap	pun	rog	six	tee	ule	wen	yuk
mad	Mrs	obi	par	pup	roo	ska	teg	ult	wet	Yuk
mag	mud	obo	pas	pus	rot	ski	tej	ulu	wey	yum
mah	mug	obs	pat	put	rov	sky	ten	ump	who	yup
mai	mum	oca	pav	puy	row	sly	ter	umu	why	yus
mam	mun	och	paw	pya	rub	sny	tew	uni	wig	zac
man	mux	odd	pax	pye	rud	sob	tex	unk	win	zad
map	mya	OD'd	pay	pyx	rue	soc	tha	ure	wis	zag
mar	nab	ode	pea	qat	rug	sod	the	uri	wit	zap
mas	nae	OD's	peb	Qin	rum	soe	tho	urn	wiv	zat
mat	nag	o'er	pec	qua	run	sog	tho'	urs	wiz	zax
maw	nah	off	ped	Qum	rut	soh	thy	use	woa	zea
max	nan	oft	pee	rab	rux	sol	tic	ush	woe	zed
may	nap	oga	peg	rad	rya	Sol	tid	uta	wog	zee
May	nar	ogi	Peg	rag	rye	son	tie	ute	wok	zek
med	nat	ohm	pen	rah	ryo	sop	tig	uva	won	Zen
Med	naw	oho	pep	rai	ryu	SOS	til	Uzi	woo	zho
mee	nay	oik	PEP	raj	sab	sot	Tim	vac	wop	zig
meg	neb	oil	per	Raj	sac	sou	tin	vag	wot	zip
Meg	ned	oka	pes	ram	sad	sov	tip	van	wow	zit
mel	neg	OK'd	pet	ran	sae	Sov	tit	var	woy	ziz
mem	nek	oke	pew	rap	sag	sow	tiz	vas	wro	zoa
men	nep	OKs	phi	ras	sah	soy	toa	vat	wry	zoo
Meo	net	OK's	pho	rat	sai	spa	tod	VAT	wuz	zug
mer		old	pia	rav			toe	vau	wye	

FOUR LETTERS

abba	aiel	anna	auto	bare	beta	blow	boun	bund
Abba	aile	anoa	Avar	barf	bevy	blub	bout	bung
abbé	Aino	anon	aven	bark	Bhil	blue	bove	bunk
abed	ain't	ansa	aver	barm	bhoy	blur	bowl	bunt
abet	Ainu	anta	avid	barn	bias	Boal	boxy	buoy
Abib	airt	ante	avow	Bart	bibb	boar	boyo	BUPA
able	airy	anti	away	base	bibi	boat	boza	burb
ably	aith	anus	a wee	bash	bice	bock	bozo	burd
abob	ajar	aoul	awny	bask	bide	bode	brab	bure
Abos	ajee	apex	AWOL	bass	bidi	body	brad	burg
abox	ajog	APEX	awry	bast	bien	Boer	brae	burh
abri	Akan	apse	axal	bate	bier	boff	brag	burk
ABTA	akee	apso	axel	bath	biff	bogy	brak	burl
abut	akin	Apus	axes	bats	biga	boho	bran	burn
ACAS	alan	aqua	axil	batt	bigg	Bohr	bras	burp
acer	Alan	aquo	axis	batz	bike	boil	brat	burr
ache	alap	Arab	axle	baud	bile	boke	braw	buru
achy	alar	arak	axon	bawd	bilk	boko	bray	bury
acid	Alar	Aran	ayah	bawl	bill	bola	bred	bush
acme	alas	arch	ayle	bawn	Bill	bold	bree	busk
acne	alba	area	ay me	baze	bind	bole	brei	buss
acre	alec	ared	ayre	bead	bine	bolk	bren	bust
acyl	alee	areg	azan	beak	bing	boll	Bren	busy
Adam	aley	Argo	baa'd	beal	bink	bolo	brer	butt
Adar	alfa	Argy	Baal	beam	bint	bolt	bret	buys
a-day	alga	aria	baas	bean	biog	boma	brew	buzz
adit	alit	arid	baba	bear	bird	bomb	brey	byes
adry	alky	aril	babe	be at	biri	bond	Brie	BYOB
adze	ally	army	Babi	beat	birk	bone	brig	byre
aeon	alma	arow	babu	beau	birl	bong	brim	byte
aery	alme	arra	baby	beck	biro	bonk	brio	caba
afar	alms	arse	bach	Bedu	Biro	bony	brit	cack
Afar	alod	arty	Bach	Beeb	birr	boob	Brit	cade
affy	aloe	arum	back	beef	bise	book	brod	cadi
Afro	alow	arvo	bade	been	bish	bool	brog	cady
agal	also	aryl	bael	beep	bisk	boom	broo	cafe
agar	alti	asci	baff	beer	bite	boon	brow	café
agba	alto	asea	baft	beet	bitt	boor	brrr	caff
aged	alum	ashy	baht	Befa	blab	boos	Brum	cage
agee	amah	as if	bail	bego	blad	boot	brut	cagy
agen	Amal	as is	bait	bein	blae	bora	Brut	caid
ager	ambo	as of	bake	Beja	blag	Bora	Bual	cain
agey	amel	Asti	bald	belk	blah	bord	bubo	Cain
agha	amen	as to	bale	bell	blat	bore	buck	cake
agin	Amex	atap	balk	belt	blay	born	bude	caky
agio	amid	at it	ball	bema	bleb	bort	buer	calf
aglu	amil	atom	balm	be me	bled	bosa	buff	calk
agma	amir	atop	Balt	Bemi	blee	bose	buhl	call
agog	ammo	A to Z	banc	bend	bleu	bosh	buhr	calm
agon	amok	atta	band	bene	blew	bosk	buit	calx
agro	Amoy	atwo	bane	bent	bley	bo's'n	bulb	came
ague	amyl	aula	bang	be of	blik	boss	bulk	camp
ahem	anal	auld	bani	bere	blin	bote	bull	cane
ahey	anew	aune	bank	berg	blip	both	bult	cang
ahoy	anil	aung	barb	berk	blob	bott	bumf	cant
aide	anis	aunt	Barb	berm	bloc	bouk	bump	can't
AIDS	ankh	aura	bard	best	blot	boul	Buna	cany

cape	choc	coin	crag	dade	deli	dive	dowd	duro
cap'n	chon	coir	cram	dado	dell	divi	dowf	dusk
capo	chop	coke	cran	daff	deme	dizz	dowl	dust
carb	chou	Coke	crap	daft	demi	doab	down	duty
card	Chou	cola	craw	dago	demn	doat	dowt	dyad
care	chow	cold	cray	Dáil	demo	dobe	doxy	Dyak
carf	chub	cole	cred	dais	Demo	do by	doze	dyer
cark	chug	coli	cree	dale	demy	doby	dozy	dyke
carl	chum	colk	Cree	dalt	dene	dock	drab	dyne
carp	Chün	coll	crew	Dama	denn	doct	drac	dyss
carr	chut	colt	crib	dame	dent	dodo	drag	dzho
cart	ciao	Colt	crim	damn	deny	doek	dram	each
case	ciel	coly	crin	damp	dere	doer	drap	earl
cash	cill	coma	crip	Dane	derm	does	drat	earn
cask	cine	comb	cris	dang	dern	doff	draw	ease
cass	cinq	come	crit	dank	derv	doge	dray	east
cast	cion	comp	croc	daps	desk	dogy	dree	easy
cate	ciré	coms	croo	Dard	dewy	do in	dreg	eath
cauk	cist	cone	crop	dare	dexy	do it	drek	eats
caul	cite	coni	crow	darg	dhak	doit	drew	eaux
cava	city	conk	crub	dark	dhal	dojo	drey	eave
cave	cive	conn	crud	darl	dhan	doke	drib	ebon
cavy	clad	cony	crue	darn	dhar	dole	drie	ecad
cawk	clag	coof	crum	dart	dhol	dolk	drip	ecce
cawl	clam	cook	crus	dash	dhow	doll	drog	echo
caza	clan	cool	crut	data	DHSS	dolt	drop	echt
cede	clap	coom	crux	date	dial	dome	drow	ecru
cedi	claw	coon	cube	dato	Dian	domy	drub	ecus
ceil	clay	co-op	cuck	daub	dibs	dona	drug	Edam
cell	cled	coop	cued	daud	dice	done	drum	Edda
celt	clee	coos	cues	daut	dick	dong	duab	eddo
Celt	clef	coot	cuff	davy	Dick	donk	duad	eddy
cent	cleg	cope	Cuff	Davy	dict	don't	dual	Eden
cere	clem	cops	cuke	dawg	dido	dool	duan	edge
CERN	clew	Copt	cull	dawk	didy	doom	duar	edgy
cero	clip	copy	culm	dawn	died	do on	dubs	edit
cert	clit	cord	cult	dawt	dies	door	duce	eely
cess	clod	core	Cuna	days	diet	dopa	Duce	Efik
cest	clog	corf	cunt	daze	diff	dope	duck	EFTA
cete	clop	cork	curb	dazy	digs	dopy	duct	egad
chad	clot	corm	curd	D-Day	dika	doré	dude	eggy
Chad	clou	corn	cure	dead	dike	dork	duel	egos
chah	clow	cose	curé	deaf	dikh	dorm	duet	eigh
chak	cloy	cosh	curf	deal	dill	dorp	duff	eild
chal	club	coss	curl	dean	dime	dorr	duke	eith
cham	clue	cost	curn	dear	dine	dort	dukw	ekka
chap	coak	cosy	curr	deas	ding	dory	dule	elan
char	coal	cote	curt	debt	dink	dose	dull	élan
chat	coat	coth	cush	deck	dint	dosh	duly	elft
chaw	coax	Coué	cusk	deco	diol	doss	duma	elhi
chay	cobb	coul	cusp	Deco	dire	dost	Duma	elks
chef	coca	coup	cuss	deed	dirk	dote	dumb	elmy
chew	cock	cove	cute	deem	dirl	doth	dump	else
chez	coco	cowl	cyan	deep	dirt	do to	dune	Elul
chic	coda	cowp	cyma	deer	disa	doty	dung	emic
chid	code	cowy	cyme	deft	disc	douc	dunk	emir
chin	coed	coxa	cyst	defy	dish	doum	dunt	emit
Chin	coff	Cox's	cyul	degu	disk	do up	duos	Emmy
chip	coft	coxy	czar	deid	diss	doup	dupe	empt
chir	coho	coze	dace	deil	dita	dour	dura	enol
chit	coif	cozy	dada	dele	dite	dout	dure	enow
chiv	coil	crab	Dada	delf	diva	dove	durn	envy

eoan	fall	filé	foil	fuzz	genu	gnar	Gram	hadj
épée	falx	fill	foin	fyke	germ	gnat	gran	haem
epic	fame	film	fold	fyrd	gest	gnaw	gray	haet
epos	fane	filo	folk	gaby	geta	GNVQ	Gray	haff
EPOS	fang	fils	fond	gade	gett	goad	gree	haft
ergo	Fang	find	font	gaed	geum	goaf	grew	ha-ha
ergs	fard	fine	food	Gael	ghan	goal	grex	haik
eria	fare	fink	fool	gaff	ghap	Goan	grey	hail
erne	farl	Finn	foot	gaga	ghat	go at	grid	hain
Eros	farm	fino	forb	gage	ghee	goat	grig	hair
Erse	faro	fire	ford	Gaia	Gheg	gobo	grim	hait
erst	fart	firk	fore	gain	gibe	go by	grin	haji
Esau	fash	firm	fork	gait	gift	go-by	grip	hajj
Esky	fast	firn	form	gala	GIFT	goby	grit	haka
esne	fate	fisc	fort	gale	GIGO	goer	grog	hake
esox	faun	fish	foss	gall	Gila	goes	grok	hale
espy	faux	fisk	foul	galt	gild	goff	grot	half
ESRC	fave	fist	four	gamb	gill	go-go	grow	hall
etch	fawn	fitz	fowl	game	Gill	Gogo	grub	halm
etic	faze	five	foxy	gamp	gilt	go in	grue	halo
etin	feak	fixt	frab	gamy	gimp	go it	grum	halt
etna	feal	fizz	frae	gang	ging	goky	Grus	hame
Eton	fear	flab	frap	gant	gink	gola	guan	hand
etui	feat	flag	frat	gaol	gird	Gola	guar	hang
étui	feck	flak	Frau	gaon	girl	gold	gufa	hank
euge	feeb	flam	fray	gape	girn	golf	guff	Hans
euro	fee'd	flan	free	garb	giro	Gond	guga	hapu
Euro	feed	flap	fret	gare	girr	gone	guib	hard
even	feel	flat	frib	gari	girt	gong	guid	hare
ever	feer	flaw	frig	garn	gise	gonk	gula	hark
evil	feet	flax	frim	Garo	gism	gony	gule	harl
evoe	fegs	flay	frit	gash	gist	good	gulf	harm
ewer	fehi	flea	friz	gasp	gite	goof	gull	haro
ewry	Fehm	fled	froe	gate	gith	goog	gulp	harp
exam	feis	flee	frog	gatt	give	gook	gump	harr
exec	fell	fleg	from	GATT	givy	gool	gunk	hart
exes	felt	Flem	frot	gaud	gizz	go on	Gunn	hash
exit	feme	flet	frow	gauk	glad	goon	Günz	hask
exon	fend	flew	frug	Gaul	glam	goop	gurk	hasp
Expo	fent	flex	frum	gaum	gled	goor	gurl	hast
exta	feod	fley	fruz	gaup	glee	gore	gurn	hate
eyas	fere	flic	FT-SE	gaur	gleg	gorm	guru	hath
eyed	ferk	flim	fuci	gave	glei	gorp	gush	haul
eyer	fern	flip	fuck	Gawd	glen	gory	gust	haut
eyes	fess	flit	fuel	gawk	glet	gosh	guts	have
eyot	fest	flix	fuff	gawn	glew	goss	guze	hawk
eyra	feta	floc	fufu	gawp	gley	Goss	gwan	haze
eyre	fête	floe	fugu	gaze	glia	gote	gybe	hazy
face	feud	flog	full	GCHQ	glib	Goth	gyle	head
fack	feus	flop	fume	GCSE	glim	go to	gymp	heal
fact	Fian	flot	fumy	gean	glit	go up	gyne	heap
facy	fiar	flow	fund	gear	glob	gour	gypo	hear
fade	fiat	flub	funk	geck	glom	gout	gyps	heat
fado	fice	flue	furl	geed	glop	gove	gyre	hebe
fady	fico	flus	fury	geek	glow	gowk	gyri	Hebe
faff	Fido	flux	fusc	Geez	glue	gowl	gyro	heck
faik	fief	flys	fuse	geld	glug	gown	gyte	heed
fail	fiel	foal	fusk	gelt	glum	goys	gyve	heel
fain	FIFA	foam	fuss	gena	glut	grab	haaf	heft
fair	fife	foci	fust	gene	G-man	grad	haar	he he
fake	fike	fogy	futz	gens	G-men	Graf	hack	heil
fa-la	file	föhn	fuze	gent	gnap	gram	hade	heir

heit	hoki	hurr	info	jawy	jube	keno	knot	lady
HeLa	hoky	hurt	in it	jazz	juck	kent	know	laen
held	hold	hush	Inka	jean	judo	Kent	knub	Lahu
hele	hole	husk	inky	jeep	Judy	kepi	knur	laic
he'll	Holi	huso	inly	Jeep	juga	kept	knut	laid
hell	holl	huss	in on	jeer	ju-ju	kerb	koan	laik
helm	holm	hutt	in re	Jeez	juju	kerf	kobo	lain
help	holp	Hutu	INRI	jeff	juke	kern	koel	lair
heme	hols	huzz	inro	Jehu	July	kero	kohl	Laïs
hemp	holt	hwyl	inti	jell	jump	kest	koji	lait
hent	holy	Hyde	into	jeon	june	keta	koko	lake
herb	homa	hyla	Inuk	jerk	June	kewl	kola	lakh
herd	home	hyle	iota	jert	junk	kexy	Koli	laky
here	homo	hymn	ipoh	jess	Juno	keys	kolm	la-la
herl	Homo	hyne	IRBM	jest	jupe	khad	kolo	lall
herm	homy	hype	irid	Jesu	Jura	khan	Koma	lama
hern	hone	hypo	iris	jeté	jury	khat	Komi	lamb
hero	hong	hyst	iron	Jewy	just	khet	kona	lame
Herr	honk	hyte	I say	jiao	jute	khor	Kond	lamé
hers	hood	IAEA	ISBN	jibe	Jute	khud	kono	lamp
hest	hoof	iamb	ISDN	jiff	juve	kibe	Kono	land
hewn	hook	Iban	I see	jill	jynx	kiby	kook	Land
hick	hoon	ibex	isel	Jill	kade	kick	kopi	lane
hide	hoop	ibis	isle	jilt	kadi	kief	kora	lank
hied	hoot	IBRD	isn't	jimp	kagu	kier	Kora	lant
hies	hope	ICBM	I spy	Jina	Kahn	kike	kore	lanx
hi-fi	Hopi	iced	itch	jing	kaid	kill	kori	Lapp
high	hopo	icky	item	jink	kail	kiln	koru	lard
hike	hora	icon	iter	jinn	kaim	kilo	kosh	lare
hila	Hori	idea	Itie	jinx	kain	kilt	koto	larf
hili	horn	idee	itis	jism	kaka	kina	krab	lari
hill	hose	idem	it'll	jist	kaki	kind	Krag	lark
hilo	hoss	ides	itty	jiva	kale	kine	kran	larm
hilt	host	idle	iwis	jive	kali	king	kray	larn
himp	hour	idli	ixia	jizz	kama	kink	Krio	lary
hind	Hova	idly	izba	Joan	Kama	kino	kris	lase
hing	hove	idol	izle	jock	kame	kips	Kroo	lash
hint	howe	idyl	Ivan	Jock	kana	kirk	krug	lask
hipe	howk	iffy	jack	Jodo	kang	kirn	Kuan	lass
hire	howl	if so	Jack	jods	kans	kish	Kuba	last
hish	hoya	Igbo	jacu	joes	kaon	kiss	kudo	late
hisn	huck	iiwi	jade	joey	kapa	kist	kudu	lath
hiss	huer	ikat	jady	Joey	karo	kite	kuei	lati
hist	huff	ikey	jail	john	kart	kith	kuge	laud
hive	huge	ikky	Jain	John	kati	kiva	kuki	Laue
hiya	Hugo	ikon	jake	join	kava	kive	Kuki	lava
hizz	huhu	ilea	jama	joke	kaya	kiwi	kuku	lave
HMSO	huia	ilex	jamb	joky	kayo	ki-yi	kula	lawk
hoar	huke	ilia	jams	jole	kaza	Klan	Kuna	lawn
hoax	hula	ilka	jane	jolt	keck	klep	kura	laws
hobo	hule	illy	Jane	Joly	keek	klik	Kurd	laxy
hock	hulk	ilot	jann	jong	keel	klip	kuri	laze
hoed	hull	imam	jape	jook	keen	klop	kuru	Laze
hoer	huma	IMAX	jarl	joro	keep	knab	kuta	lazy
hoes	hump	imfe	jasp	josh	keif	knag	kyat	lead
hoey	hung	immy	jati	joss	keld	knap	kyle	leaf
hogg	hunk	impi	jato	joub	kell	knar	kype	leak
hogo	hunt	in at	jauk	jouk	kelp	knee	kyte	leal
ho ho	Hupa	Inca	jaup	jour	kelt	knew	lace	leam
hoik	hupp	inch	Java	Jove	Kelt	knit	lack	lean
hoit	hure	indy	Jawi	jowl	kemb	knob	lacy	leap
hoke	hurl	Indy	jawp	juba	kemp	knop	lade	lear

leat	limn	lord	lyse	matt	midi	moko	mums	Nara
lech	limo	lore	ma'am	maty	Midi	Moko	mu-mu	narc
Lech	limp	lorn	maar	maud	MIDI	mola	mung	nard
lect	limy	lors	maas	maul	mids	mold	muni	nare
leek	line	lory	mace	maum	mien	mole	munt	nark
leep	ling	lose	Mace	maun	miff	moll	muon	narp
leer	link	losh	Mach	maux	mike	molt	mura	narr
lees	Link	loss	mack	mawk	Mike	moly	mure	nary
leet	linn	lost	made	mawm	mild	mome	murk	NASA
left	lino	lote	mado	maxi	mile	Momi	murl	NATO
legh	lint	loth	Maga	maya	milk	mona	murr	nave
Lego	liny	loti	mage	Maya	mill	Mond	musa	navy
lehr	lion	loto	magg	mayo	milo	mong	muse	naze
leir	lira	loud	magi	maze	milt	monk	mush	Nazi
lekë	lire	loup	maid	mazy	mime	mono	musk	neal
Lekh	lirk	lour	mail	MDMA	mimi	mons	muso	neap
lend	liry	lout	maim	mead	mimp	mood	muss	near
lene	lisk	love	main	meal	mina	Moog	must	neat
leno	lisp	lowe	mair	mean	mind	mool	muta	neck
lens	Lisp	lown	majo	mear	mine	moon	mute	need
lent	liss	lowy	make	meat	ming	Moon	muti	Néel
Lent	list	Loxa	mako	mech	Ming	moop	mutt	neem
Leos	Lisu	Lozi	male	Mede	mini	moor	muzz	neep
lere	lite	luau	mali	meed	mink	Moor	myal	ne'er
lerp	Lite	Luba	Mali	meek	mint	moos	myna	neif
lese	lith	lube	mall	meet	minx	moot	myst	nema
less	live	luce	malm	mega	miny	mope	myth	nemo
lest	load	luck	malt	mela	mire	mopy	myxa	nene
let's	loaf	lucy	Malt	meld	mirk	mora	myxo	neon
Lett	loam	ludo	mama	mell	mirl	more	myxy	nerd
leud	loan	lues	mamo	melo	miro	morn	naam	nerf
leva	lobe	luff	mana	melt	mirr	Moro	naan	nerk
levi	lobo	luge	mane	meme	miry	mort	naat	nese
levs	loch	luke	mani	memo	mise	moss	nabe	nesh
levy	loci	lull	mank	mend	miso	most	nabi	ness
lewd	lock	lulu	Manu	meng	miss	mosy	nabs	nest
liar	loco	lump	Manx	meno	mist	mota	naff	nete
lias	lode	luna	many	menu	misy	mote	naga	nett
lice	lodh	lune	mape	meow	mite	moth	Naga	neum
lich	lo-fi	lung	mara	merc	mitt	moto	Nago	névé
lick	loft	lunk	Mara	merd	mity	mott	naib	news
Lide	loge	lunt	marc	mere	mixy	Motu	naïf	newt
lido	logo	luny	mard	Meru	Mizo	moue	naik	newy
lied	logy	lure	mare	mesa	Mlle	moul	nail	next
lief	loid	lurk	marg	mese	m'lud	moup	nain	nibs
lien	loin	lush	Mari	mesh	Mmes	move	naio	nice
lier	loir	lusk	mark	mess	moan	mown	Nair	Nice
lies	loll	lust	marl	meta	moar	moxa	naïs	nick
lieu	Lolo	lute	marm	Meta	moas	moya	nait	Nick
life	loma	luth	Mars	mete	moat	moze	Naja	nide
lift	Loma	lutz	mart	meth	mock	mozz	nake	nidi
Lifu	lone	luxe	marv	meum	moco	Mr Lo	nala	nief
like	long	lwei	Mary	mewl	mode	much	Nama	niet
lila	Lonk	lyam	mase	mews	Mods	muck	name	Nife
lill	loof	lych	mash	mewt	mogo	muff	nana	niff
Lilo	look	lyke	mask	mezz	Moho	muga	nant	nigh
Li-lo	loom	lyme	mass	mhos	Mohs	mugo	naoi	Nile
lilt	loon	Lyme	Mass	Miao	moil	muid	naos	nill
lily	loop	lynx	mast	mias	moit	mule	naow	nimb
Lima	loot	Lyon	mate	mica	mojo	muli	napa	nine
limb	lope	lyra	maté	mice	moke	mull	Napa	nipa
lime	lora	lyre	math	mick	moki	mump	nape	nisi

nite	Nyon	omen	ouph	parp	perp	pirn	Pong	prut
Noah	oafo	omer	ourn	parr	Perp	pirr	pons	psst
noax	oafs	omie	ours	pars	pert	pish	pont	ptui
nock	oaky	omit	oust	part	perv	piss	pony	puce
noda	oary	omul	outa	pash	peso	pita	poof	puck
node	oast	once	outy	pass	pess	pith	pooh	pudu
nodi	oath	oner	ouzo	past	pest	pito	pook	puer
noel	oaty	one's	oval	pata	Pete	pity	pool	puff
Noel	obbo	on it	oven	pate	peth	pium	poon	puha
Noël	obex	only	over	pâté	pevy	pivo	poop	puja
noem	obey	on to	ovum	path	pewl	pixy	poor	puka
noes	Obie	onto	Owen	paua	pewy	pize	pope	puke
nogg	obis	on to	owly	Paul	pfft	plan	pops	puku
no go	obit	onus	oxen	pave	pfui	plap	pore	pula
noia	oboe	onyx	oxer	pavé	phew	plat	pork	pule
noil	obol	oo-er	oxic	Pavo	Phil	play	porn	puli
noir	obus	oofy	Oxon	pavy	phit	plea	Poro	pulk
noll	oche	ooid	oyer	pawa	phiz	pleb	porr	pull
nolt	odal	ooky	oyes	pawk	phon	pled	port	pulp
noma	Oddi	oons	oyez	pawl	phoo	plet	pory	puly
nome	odds	oont	paca	pawn	phos	plew	pose	puma
none	odea	oops	pace	PAYE	phot	plié	posé	pump
nong	odic	Oort	pack	PCAS	phut	plim	posh	puna
no-no	odor	ooze	paco	peag	piai	plod	poss	pung
non-U	odyl	oozy	pact	peai	pial	plop	post	punk
nook	OECD	opah	pacu	peak	pian	plot	posy	punt
noon	ofay	opal	pacy	peal	Piat	plow	pote	puny
noop	offa	OPEC	pada	pean	pica	ploy	pott	pupa
nope	off'n	Op-Ed	padi	pear	pice	plud	Pott	pure
nork	o for	open	paff	peat	pick	plug	pouf	puri
norm	ogam	oppo	page	peba	pict	plum	poui	purl
Norn	ogee	opry	paha	peck	Pict	plup	pour	purr
nose	Ogen	opto	paho	pect	pied	plus	pout	purt
nosh	ogle	opus	paid	pede	pier	pneu	pouw	push
nosy	Ogpu	oral	paik	peed	piet	pnyx	poxy	puss
nota	ogre	orby	pail	peek	piff	pobs	prad	pute
note	ohia	orca	pain	peel	pika	pock	pram	putt
not-I	OHMS	ordo	pair	peen	pike	poco	prat	putz
nott	oh-oh	Oreo	pais	peep	piki	podo	prau	puya
noun	oh-so	orey	Paki	peer	piky	poem	pray	pyet
nous	oick	orfe	pala	pees	pile	poet	pree	pyot
nova	OIEO	orgy	pale	pego	pili	poge	preg	pyre
nown	oily	orle	pali	Pegu	pill	pogo	prem	pyro
nowt	oink	orlo	Pali	pein	Pils	pogy	prep	qadi
nowy	oint	or no	pall	peke	pily	poil	pres	Qing
noxa	OIRO	orra	palm	pele	Pima	poke	prex	quab
Nuba	okay	or so	palp	Pele	pimp	poky	Prex	quad
nubk	Okie	oryx	paly	pelf	piña	pole	prey	quag
nude	okra	osar	pamé	pell	pind	Pole	prez	quai
Nuer	okta	ossa	pand	Pell	pine	polk	prig	quar
nuff	Okun	Ossa	pane	pelt	ping	poll	prim	quat
nuke	olam	osse	Pane	pend	pink	Poll	proa	quay
null	olde	otic	pang	penk	Pink	polo	prob	quel
numb	olea	otto	Pano	pent	pint	polt	prod	quey
nunk	oleo	Otto	pant	peon	piny	poly	Prod	quid
NUPE	olid	ouch	papa	pepo	pion	Poma	prof	quim
nurd	olim	oued	para	perc	pipa	pome	prog	quin
nurk	olio	ough	Pará	père	pipe	Pomo	prom	quip
nurl	olla	ould	pard	peri	pipi	pomp	prop	quit
nuts	olpe	ouma	pare	perk	pipy	pond	pros	quiz
Nuzi	Oman	oung	park	perm	pire	pone	Prot	quod
nyet	omee	oupa	parm	pern	pirl	pong	prow	quop

raad	reel	roar	ruds	sapo	self	shor	skil	snod
race	reem	robe	rued	sard	sell	shot	skim	snog
rack	reen	rock	rues	Sard	sema	show	skin	snot
racy	reft	rode	ruff	sari	seme	shox	skip	snow
RADA	rego	roed	ruga	sark	semé	Shri	skis	snub
raff	reif	roes	ruin	Sart	semi	shul	skit	snug
Rafi	Reil	roid	rukh	sash	semp	shun	skol	snum
raft	rein	roil	rule	sass	sena	shut	skua	snye
raga	rely	roke	ruly	sate	send	shwa	skun	soak
rage	rems	roky	rump	saté	sene	sial	Skye	soam
ragi	rend	role	rune	sati	senn	sice	slab	soap
raia	reng	rôle	rung	Sauk	sent	sich	slag	soar
raid	rent	Rolf	runo	save	seps	sick	slam	so as
raik	repo	roll	runt	sawn	sept	sida	slap	Soay
rail	repp	Roma	rupp	saxe	sera	side	slat	soba
rain	rerd	Rome	rupt	Saxe	Serb		Slav	soca
rait	rere	romp	rurp	SAYE	SERC	sidi	slaw	sock
raja	rest	rond	ruru	says	sere	sidy	slay	soda
rake	rete	rone	rusa	scab	serf	sies	sled	sody
raki	reub	Rong	ruse	scad	Seri	sift	slew	sofa
raku	re-up	rood	rush	scag	sesh	sigh	sley	soft
rale	rhea	roof	rusk	scam	sess	sign	slid	soga
rame	rhus	rook	Russ	scan	seta	sijo	slim	soho
rami	rial	room	rust	scar	SETI	sika	slip	Soho
ramp	RIBA	roon	ruth	scat	Seto	sike	slit	soil
rams	rice	roop	rutt	scaw	sett	Sikh	slob	soke
Rana	rich	root	ryot	scob	sewn	sild	sloe	sola
rand	rick	rope	rype	scop	sext	sile	slog	sold
rang	ride	ropy	sabe	scot	sexy	silk	slop	sole
rani	riel	ro-ro	sack	Scot	SGML	sill	slot	soli
rank	rife	rort	sade	scow	shab	silo	slow	solo
rant	riff	Rory	safe	scry	shad	silt	slub	Solo
rape	Riff	rose	saga	scud	shag	sima	slud	soma
rapt	rift	rosé	sage	scug	shah	simi	slue	some
rare	riga	ross	SAGE	scum	sham	simp	slug	sone
rase	Riga	Ross	sago	scun	shan	sind	slum	song
rash	rile	rosy	sagy	scur	Shan	sine	slup	Song
rasp	rill	Rosy	sa-ha	scut	shat	sing	slur	sook
rass	rima	rota	Saho	scye	shaw	sinh	slut	sool
rata	rime	rote	saic	SDLP	shay	sink	smay	soon
rate	rimu	roti	said	seah	Shay	sion	smew	soop
rath	rimy	roto	sail	seal	shea	Sion	smig	soor
rauk	rind	roué	sain	seam	she'd	sipe	smir	soot
rave	rine	rouf	sais	sean	shed	sire	smit	sope
rayl	ring	rouk	Saka	SEAQ	shen	sisi	smog	soph
raze	rink	roun	sake	sear	shep	siss	smon	sora
razz	riot	roup	saki	seat	she's	sist	smug	sorb
read	ripe	rous	sala	seau	shew	site	smur	Sorb
real	rise	Rous	sale	seax	shhh	sith	smut	sord
ream	risk	rout	salp	sect	Shi'a	sitt	snab	sore
rean	risp	roux	salt	seed	Shia	Siva	snag	sori
reap	Riss	rove	SALT	seek	shim	size	snap	sorn
rear	rite	rown	same	seel	shin	sizy	snax	sort
reck	ritz	rowy	Sami	seem	Shin	sizz	sneb	so so
reco	riva	RSPB	samp	seen	ship	skag	sned	soss
rect	rive	RSVP	sand	seep	shit	skat	sneg	SOSs
redd	riza	rube	sane	seer	shiv	sked	snew	Soto
rede	RNLI	ruby	sang	sego	shod	skeg	snib	souk
redo	RNZN	ruck	sank	seif	shoe	skeo	snig	soul
reed	road	rudd	sans	seir	shog	skep	snip	soum
reef	roam	Rudd	Sant	Sekt	shoo	skew	snit	soup
reek	roan	rude	sapa	sele	shop	skid	snob	sour

sowl	stut	syne	T-bar	tiao	toga	tram	tute	upgo
sown	stye	syph	tcha	tiar	to go	trap	tutu	up in
sowp	Styx	taal	tea'd	tice	togt	tray	Tuva	up on
soya	suba	tabi	teak	tich	to-ho	tree	TVEI	upon
spad	such	tabl	teal	tick	toil	tref	twat	upta
Spad	suck	tabu	team	Tico	toit	trek	tway	up to
spae	sudd	tach	tear	tide	Tojo	trem	twee	UPVC
spag	suds	tack	teat	tidy	toke	tret	twig	upya
spam	sued	taco	tech	tied	toki	trey	twin	ural
Spam	suer	tact	teed	tief	toko	Trib	twit	Ural
span	sues	ta-da	teem	t'ien	tola	trie	twos	urao
spar	suet	tael	teen	tier	told	trig	tyee	urbs
spat	Sufi	Taff	teer	tiff	tole	trim	tyer	Urdu
spay	sugi	taft	tees	tift	toll	trin	tyke	urdy
spaz	suid	tahr	teff	tige	tolt	trio	tyle	urea
spec	suit	Taig	TEFL	tika	tolu	trip	tymp	urge
sped	suke	tail	tegu	tike	tomb	tris	tyne	uric
spet	sukh	tait	tehr	tiki	tome	trod	type	uroo
spew	sulk	taka	teil	tile	tomo	trog	typo	Ursa
spey	sull	take	tele	till	tone	tron	tyre	Uruk
spic	Sulu	tala	tell	tilt	tong	trot	tyro	urus
spin	sumi	talc	temp	time	toni	Trot	tzar	used
spit	sumo	tale	tend	tind	tonk	trow	UB40	user
spiv	sump	tali	tent	tine	tony	troy	UCAS	USSR
spot	sung	talk	tepa	ting	Tony	trub	UCCA	utas
SPQR	Sung	tall	term	t'ing	tooa	true	ucky	uvea
spry	suni	tame	tern	Ting	took	trug	udad	uver
spud	sunk	tamp	terp	tink	tool	tsar	udal	vade
spue	sunn	tana	terr	tint	toom	tsps	udon	vagi
spun	sunt	tang	TESL	tiny	toon	tsun	Uduk	vail
spur	supe	Tang	Teso	tipi	toot	tuan	UEFA	vain
SSSI	supp	tanh	test	tipt	tope	tuba	ufer	vair
stab	sura	tank	tête	tire	toph	tube	ufos	vale
stac	surd	tant	Teut	tirl	topi	tuck	UFOs	vamp
stad	sure	Taos	Tewa	tiro	topo	tuel	Ugli	vane
stag	surf	tapa	text	tirr	tops	tufa	ugly	vang
stap	suss	tape	Thai	tite	tora	tuff	uh-uh	vara
star	susu	tapu	than	titi	torc	tuft	ukky	vari
stat	Susu	ta-ra	thar	tivy	tore	tule	ulli	vary
stay	Svan	tara	that	Tiwa	tori	tulp	ulna	vasa
steg	swab	tare	thaw	Tiwi	torn	Tulu	ulto	vase
stem	swad	tarn	thee	tizz	toro	tu-mo	ulva	vast
Sten	swag	taro	the I	toad	torp	tump	umbo	veal
step	swam	tarp	them	to a T	torr	tuna	umph	Veda
stet	swan	tars	then	Toba	tort	tunc	umps	veed
stew	swap	tart	thet	tobe	Tory	tund	unal	veep
stey	swat	tash	thew	to-be	tosa	tune	unau	veer
stim	Swat	task	they	toby	Tosa	tung	unbe	vega
stir	sway	tass	thig	Toc H	tosh	tunk	unci	veil
stoa	swee	Tass	thin	tock	Tosk	tuny	unco	vein
stob	swig	ta-ta	thir	toco	toss	Tupi	undo	vela
stød	swim	tate	this	Toda	tost	turb	undy	Vela
stog	swiz	tatu	thon	to-do	tote	turd	unio	veld
stop	swob	taum	thou	tody	toto	turf	unis	vell
stot	Swoe	taut	thow	toea	toup	turk	unit	vena
stow	swop	tave	thra	toed	tour	Turk	Unix	vend
stub	swot	tawa	thro	toes	tout	turm	unky	vent
stuc	swum	tawm	thru	toey	town	turn	unto	veny
stud	syce	tawn	thud	toff	towy	turr	upas	verb
stug	syed	taws	thug	toft	toze	tush	up at	verd
stum	syke	taxa	thus	Toft	trac	tusk	up-by	vers
stun	sync	taxi	tial	tofu	trad	tuss	up-do	vert

very	voom	warp	wept	will	worn	yare	yoga	zarf
Very	vote	wart	we're	wilt	wort	yark	yogh	Zarp
vest	vour	wary	were	wily	wove	yarm	yogi	Z-bar
veto	vril	wase	wert	wimp	WRAC	yarn	yo-ho	Z-bed
vial	vuln	wash	west	WIMP	WRAF	yate	yoke	zeal
vibe	Waac	wasm	weta	wind	wrap	yaup	yole	zebu
vice	Waaf	wasp	we've	wine	wraw	yawl	yolk	zein
Vici	waal	WASP	Weyl	wing	wray	yawn	yomp	zeme
vide	wack	wast	wham	wink	wree	yawp	yond	Zend
vier	wade	wath	whap	wino	wren	yaws	yoni	zerk
Viet	wadi	watt	what	winy	Wren	yawy	yont	zero
view	wady	waul	whau	wipe	wrig	Y-cut	yoop	zest
viff	waff	waur	whee	wire	writ	yeah	yopo	zeta
viga	waft	wave	when	wiry	WRNS	yean	yore	Zeus
vila	wage	wavy	whet	wise	wrot	year	york	zeze
vild	waif	wa-wa	whew	wish	wuff	yech	York	zhos
vile	wail	wawl	whey	wisp	wump	yeep	yote	Zhou
vill	wain	waxy	whid	wist	Würm	yegg	you'd	ziff
vina	wait	weak	whig	wite	wuss	yeld	your	zinc
vine	waka	weal	Whig	with	wych	yelk	yous	zine
vink	wake	wean	whim	wive	wynd	yell	yowe	zing
vino	wald	wear	whin	wi-wi	wynn	yelm	yowl	zino
vint	wale	weed	whio	woad	wype	yelp	yo-yo	Zion
viny	walk	week	whip	wo ho	wyte	yeow	yuan	zipp
viol	wall	weel	whir	woke	X-cut	yere	Yuan	zita
virl	walm	ween	whit	wold	Xmas	yerk	yuca	ziti
visa	walt	weep	Whit	wolf	x-ray	yern	yuck	zizz
vise	waly	weer	whiz	womb	xylo	yesk	Yüeh	zoco
visé	wame	weet	whoa	wong	yaas	yeso	yuft	zoea
viss	wand	weft	who'd	wonk	yack	yest	Yugo	zoic
vita	wane	weid	whom	wont	yagé	yeti	Yuit	zoid
Vita	wang	weil	whoo	won't	Yagi	yett	yuke	zona
viva	wank	weir	whop	wood	yair	yeuk	Yuki	zone
vive	want	weka	whys	Wood	Yakö	yé-yé	yuky	zonk
vizy	wa'n't	weld	wich	woof	Yale	yike	yule	zoom
vlei	waqf	welk	wick	wool	y'all	yill	Yule	zoon
voce	warb	we'll	wide	woon	Yami	yips	Yuma	zoot
vogt	ward	well	Wien	woos	Yana	yite	yump	zori
void	ware	wels	wife	wops	yang	ylem	yuro	zouk
vola	wari	welt	wift	word	yank	ylid	yurt	zubr
vole	wark	wely	wild	wore	Yank	YMCA	YWCA	Zulu
volk	warm	wend	wile	work	yapp	yock	zack	Zuñi
volt	warn	went	wili	worm	yard	yodh	zany	zyme

FIVE LETTERS

abaca	acrid	afore	akkra	aloha	anent	après	arsis
abaci	acrow	afoul	aknee	alone	angel	April	arson
aback	act as	afrit	alack	along	anger	apron	artel
abaft	actin	Afros	aland	aloof	angle	apsis	Artex
abaht	act on	after	alant	aloud	Angle	aptly	artic
abase	acton	again	alarm	alpha	Anglo	araba	artsy
abash	actor	agama	alary	altar	angon	Araby	arval
abask	agama	agami	alate	alter	angry	arage	arvos
abate	act up	agape	album	altho'	angst	arain	Aryan
abaya	acute	agasp	alcid	altos	Angus	arbor	asail
Abaza	adage	agate	aldea	altus	anigh	arced	ASCII
abbey	adapt	agave	alder	alula	anile	archy	ascon
abbot	a-days	agaze	Aldis	alure	anima	arder	ascot
abeam	addax	agent	aldol	alway	animé	aread	ascus
abear	added	agger	aleck	amain	anion	areal	asdic
abeat	adder	aggri	aleft	amand	anise	arear	Asdic
abele	add in	aggro	aleph	amang	anker	areca	ASEAN
abeng	addle	aggry	alert	amasi	ankle	arena	as for
aberr	add-on	agila	Aleut	amass	ankus	arene	ashen
abhor	add to	agile	alfin	Amati	annal	aren't	ashet
abide	add up	aging	algae	amaze	annex	arête	as how
abled	adeem	agios	algal	amber	annoy	argal	Asian
abler	adept	agist	algid	ambit	annul	argan	aside
abnet	à deux	aglet	algin	amble	anode	Argie	A-side
abode	ad hoc	agley	Algol	ambon	anole	argil	asile
aboil	adieu	agloo	algum	ambos	anomy	argle	asker
A-bomb	adios	aglow	alias	ambry	antae	argol	askew
aboon	ad lib	Agnus	alibi	ameba	anted	argon	Aslef
abord	adman	a gogo	Alice	ameer	anter	argot	as-new
abort	admen	à gogo	alick	amend	antes	argue	asoak
about	admin	agone	a lick	amene	antic	Argus	aspen
above	admit	agony	alien	ament	anti-g	Arhat	asper
ab ovo	admix	agora	align	amice	antis	Arian	as per
Abram	adobe	agree	alike	amide	antra	ariel	aspic
abrim	adopt	agrin	aline	amigo	antre	Aries	aspre
abrin	adore	agued	A-line	amine	antsy	arise	assai
Abuna	adorn	aguti	alive	amino	anvil	Arita	Assam
abune	adown	ahead	alkie	Amish	Anzac	arity	assay
abura	adoze	aheap	alkyd	amiss	Anzus	arjun	asses
abuse	adrad	ahigh	alkyl	amity	aorta	arles	asset
abuzz	ad rem	ahind	Allah	amnia	apace	Armco	as sin
abysm	adrip	ahold	allay	amnio	apart	armed	assot
abyss	aduki	ahull	allel	amole	apeak	armet	aster
acari	adult	ahunt	Allen	among	apert	armil	astir
accra	adunc	aider	alley	amora	apery	armor	Astis
ace it	adust	aimer	all in	amort	aphid	aroar	as was
acerb	adyta	aioli	allis	amour	aphis	aroid	asway
acidy	aegis	aïoli	allod	amper	apian	aroma	as who
acini	aerie	airer	allot	ample	apish	arose	aswim
ackee	afanc	aisle	allow	amply	a-poop	arrah	as yet
acned	afara	aitch	alloy	ampul	aport	arras	asyle
acock	afear	aiver	all up	amuck	a-pout	array	at all
acold	affix	Akali	allus	amuse	appal	arrha	ataxy
acone	afire	akara	allyl	ancon	apple	arris	at bat
acorn	aflat	akela	almah	and if	apply	arrow	at bay
acral	aflow	Akela	almug	anear	appro	arsed	A-team
acred	afoot	Akita	aloft	anele	appui	arses	A tent

athel	awful	balmy	beach	bench	binal	bloom	boosa
atilt	awing	baloo	beady	bendy	Binet	bloop	boost
atlas	awned	balsa	beaky	benet	binge	blore	boosy
at law	awner	Balti	be-all	Benin	bingo	blown	booth
atman	awoke	banal	beamy	benne	bingy	blowy	boots
atole	awork	banco	beano	benni	binit	blued	booty
atoll	axial	bandy	beard	benny	biome	bluer	booza
atomy	axile	bangy	beast	benty	biota	blues	booze
at one	axing	bania	beath	be off	biped	bluet	boozy
atone	axiom	banjo	beaty	beray	birch	bluey	Borah
atony	axion	banky	beaus	beret	birle	bluff	borak
atopy	axled	banns	beaut	bergy	biros	blunt	borax
atour	ayont	Bantu	beaux	berob	birse	blurb	boree
at par	Azeri	barbe	bebop	beroe	birth	blurt	borel
atria	azide	bardi	bedad	berry	bison	blush	borer
atrip	azine	bardy	beddy	berth	bitch	board	boric
at sea	azoic	barge	bedel	beryl	biter	boart	borne
attap	azole	barky	bedew	besaw	bitsy	boast	borné
attar	azote	barmy	bedim	besee	bitts	bobac	boron
atter	azoth	baron	bedip	beset	bitty	bobak	boser
attic	Aztec	barre	bedye	besom	bivvy	bobby	bosey
Attic	azuki	barré	beech	besot	bixin	bob of	boshy
at war	azure	barry	beedi	betel	black	bocca	bosie
aucht	azury	barse	beefs	Betsy	Black	Boche	bosky
audio	azyme	basal	beefy	Betty	blade	boden	bosom
audit	baaed	basan	beery	bevel	blady	boder	boson
augen	Baath	bases	beeve	bever	blahs	bodge	bossy
auger	babby	basha	befit	bevil	blain	bodin	bo'sun
Auger	babel	basho	befog	bevvy	blame	bodle	bosun
aught	babul	basic	be for	bewig	bland	Boehm	botch
augur	bacca	BASIC	befur	bewit	blank	boffo	botel
aulic	bacco	basil	begad	bezel	blare	bogey	bothy
aumil	baccy	basin	begah	B-film	blart	boggy	botty
aunty	backy	basis	began	B flat	blasé	bogie	bouge
aurae	bacon	bason	begat	bhaji	blast	bogle	bough
aural	baddy	basse	begem	bhang	blate	bogue	boule
auras	badge	bassi	beget	Bheel	blatt	bogus	boult
auric	badly	basso	begin	Bhora	blaud	bohea	bound
aurin	bad of	baste	begob	bhusa	blaze	bohos	bourd
autos	BAFTA	basto	begot	Bible	bleak	boier	bourg
auxin	bagel	Batak	begum	bicky	blear	boing	bourn
avail	baggy	batch	begun	biddy	bleat	boist	bouse
avast	bags I	bated	beige	bidet	bleck	bokay	bovid
avens	bag up	batey	being	bidri	bleed	bolar	bowel
avert	Baha'i	bathe	beisa	bid up	bleep	bolas	bower
avgas	Ba-ila	baths	bejel	bield	blend	boldo	bowet
avian	bairn	batik	belah	bifid	blent	bolus	bowie
avine	baity	baton	belap	bigha	bless	bombe	Bowie
aviso	baize	Batta	belar	bight	blest	bonce	bow-on
avoid	Bajan	batty	belay	bigly	blimp	boned	bowse
awabi	Bajau	Batwa	belch	bigot	blind	boner	boxen
AWACS	bajra	bauch	belee	bijou	blink	bongo	boxer
await	baked	bauds	belie	biker	bliny	bonny	Boxer
awake	baken	baulk	belle	bikie	blirt	bonus	boyar
awald	baker	Baumé	belly	bikky	bliss	bonze	boyer
award	balao	bavin	below	bilbo	blite	booay	boyos
aware	balas	bawdy	bemad	bilby	blitz	booby	bozos
awash	baldy	bayed	be man	bilge	bloat	booed	braai
aways	baler	bayou	Bemba	bilgy	block	booer	brace
a week	balky	bazan	Bembo	billy	bloke	booky	brach
aweel	balls	bazil	be mum	bimbo	blond	boomy	brack
aweto	bally	bazoo	benab		blood	boong	bract

Bragg	brugh	busby	calla	catch	chase	cholo	clart
braid	Bruin	buses	calmy	cater	chasm	chomp	clary
brail	bruit	bushy	Calor	catty	chawl	chook	clash
brain	brume	busky	calve	cauda	cheap	choom	clasp
brake	brung	bussu	calyx	cauld	cheat	chopt	class
braky	brunt	busty	caman	caulk	check	chord	clast
brand	brush	butch	camas	cause	cheek	chore	clave
brank	brusk	butea	camel	caval	cheep	chose	clead
brant	brute	butle	cameo	cavea	cheer	chota	cleam
brash	B-side	butte	campo	cavel	Cheka	chott	clean
brass	B-tree	butty	campy	caver	chela	chout	clear
brast	bubal	butut	CAMRA	cavie	chelp	choux	cleat
brava	bubby	butyl	camus	cavil	chena	chowk	cleck
brave	buchu	buxom	canal	C clef	chert	choya	cleed
bravo	bucko	buyer	can-do	CD-ROM	chess	Chubb	cleek
brawl	budda	buy-in	candy	cease	chest	chuck	cleft
brawn	buddy	buy it	caner	cebid	chevy	chufa	cleik
braxy	budge	buy up	canid	cecum	chewy	chuff	clepe
braze	buffe	buzzy	Canis	cedar	Chian	chula	clerk
bread	buffo	bwana	canna	cedis	chica	chump	cleuk
break	buffy	by air	canny	ceiba	chich	chunk	cleve
bream	buggy	by-end	canoe	celeb	chick	churl	click
breck	bught	by far	canon	cella	chide	churn	cliff
brede	Bugis	by gad	cañon	cello	chief	churr	clift
breed	bugle	by God	canst	celom	child	chuse	climb
breek	build	by gum	canto	cense	chile	chute	clime
breme	built	by hap	canty	cento	Chile	chyle	cline
brent	buist	by-law	caped	ceorl	chili	chyme	cling
brerd	bulge	by sea	caper	ceral	Chili	cibol	clink
Brett	bulgy	byssi	caple	cerci	chill	cicad	clint
breve	bulky	byway	capon	ceric	chimb	cicer	clipe
briar	bulla	Caaba	capos	cerin	chime	cider	clipt
bribe	Bulli	cabal	capot	certy	chimp	cigar	cloak
brick	bully	caban	cappa	ceryl	china	ciggy	cloam
bride	bumbo	cabas	Capri	Cetus	China	cilia	clock
brief	bumph	cabby	capsa	cetyl	chine	cimex	cloff
brier	bumpy	caber	capul	chace	chiné	cinch	cloke
brill	Buna N	cabin	caput	chack	Ching	cinct	cloky
brine	bunce	cable	carat	chaco	chink	circa	clomb
bring	bunch	cabob	cardi	chafe	Chink	Circe	clomp
brink	bunco	cabri	cardo	chaff	chino	circs	clone
briny	bundu	cacao	cardy	chaft	Chips	cirri	clonk
brish	bungy	cache	carer	Chaga	chirk	cisco	cloop
brisk	bunko	cacky	caret	chain	chirl	cissy	cloot
britt	bunny	cacti	carex	chair	chirm	citer	close
broad	bunty	caddy	carga	chalk	chirp	civet	closh
Broca	bunya	cadet	cargo	chama	chirr	civic	clote
broch	buran	Cadet	Carib	champ	chirt	civil	cloth
brock	burgh	cadew	carle	chang	chiru	civvy	cloud
broil	burin	cadge	carny	chank	chive	clack	clour
broke	burka	cadgy	carob	chant	chivy	clade	clout
brome	burke	cadre	carol	chaos	chizz	claes	clove
bromo	burly	Cafod	carom	chape	chock	claik	clown
bronc	burnt	cagey	carpi	chaps	choco	claim	cloze
Bronx	buroo	cahow	carry	chara	choga	clame	cluck
brood	burra	caird	carse	chard	choil	clamp	clued
brook	burro	cairn	carsy	chare	choir	clang	clues
brool	burru	cajan	carte	chark	choke	clank	clump
broom	burry	Cajun	carve	charm	choko	clapt	clung
brose	bursa	calid	caser	charr	choky	Clare	clunk
broth	burse	calif	casse	chart	chola	Clark	Cluny
brown	burst	calix	caste	chary	choli	claro	clype

coach	conte	cower	crone	cuppy	dandy	Dehua	dicky
coact	Conté	cowey	cronk	curby	Danic	de-ice	dicot
coaly	conto	cowle	crony	curch	danio	deify	dicta
coapt	conus	cowry	crood	curdy	danky	deign	dicty
coarb	cooed	coxae	crook	curer	dante	deism	diddy
coast	cooee	coxal	croon	curia	Darby	deist	didn't
coath	cooer	coyer	cropt	Curia	darcy	deity	didos
coati	coo-er	coyly	crore	curie	dared	dekko	didst
cobby	cooey	coypu	cross	curio	darer	delay	die-in
cobia	cooky	cozen	croup	curly	daric	deled	diene
coble	cooly	crack	crove	curny	Darii	delft	Digby
COBOL	coomb	craft	crowd	curry	darky	delis	dight
cobra	coomy	craig	crown	curse	darky	delph	dig in
cocci	co-opt	crake	croze	curst	dashy	delta	digit
cocky	co-own	cramp	cruck	curve	datal	delve	dig up
cocoa	copal	crane	crude	curvy	dated	demit	dildo
cocos	copek	crang	cruel	cusec	dater	demob	dilly
cocus	copen	crank	cruet	cushy	datok	demoi	dilse
coder	coper	crape	crumb	cutch	datuk	demon	dimer
codex	cop it	craps	crump	cutey	datum	demos	dimly
codon	copra	crapy	crums	cutie	daube	demur	dimmy
cogie	copse	crare	crunk	cut-in	dauby	denar	dimps
cogue	copsy	crash	crunt	cutin	dault	de-net	dinar
cohoe	coque	crass	crura	cut in	daunt	denim	diner
cohog	corah	crate	cruse	cutis	Davis	dense	dinge
coiff	coral	crave	crush	cutty	davit	den up	dingo
coign	cordy	crawk	crust	cut up	Dayak	depel	dingy
coker	corer	crawl	crwth	cuvée	dayan	depot	Dinka
cokey	corgi	craze	cryer	cycad	dealt	depth	dinky
coley	corks	crazy	crypt	cycle	deary	deray	dinna
colic	corky	creak	cry up	cycli	death	Derby	dioch
colin	corno	cream	CS gas	cyder	deave	de-rig	diode
colly	cornu	credo	Cuban	cylix	debag	derma	dippy
colon	corny	creed	cubby	cymar	debar	derry	dipso
color	corps	creek	cubeb	cynic	debby	desai	dirge
colsa	corse	Creek	cuber	Czech	debel	desex	dirty
colza	Corso	creel	cubic	dabby	debit	de-sex	disco
comae	Corti	creep	cubit	dacha	debug	deter	dishy
comas	cosec	Crees	cucuy	dachs	debus	detin	disna
combe	coset	crêpe	cuddy	daddy	debut	detox	dital
combi	costa	crêpé	cueca	dados	début	detur	ditch
combo	Costa	crept	cue in	daffy	decad	deuce	ditsy
combs	cothe	crêpy	Cuffy	Daffy	decaf	devel	ditto
comby	cotta	cress	Cufic	dagga	Decaf	devil	ditty
comer	couac	crest	cuing	daggy	decal	Devon	ditzy
comes	couba	crève	cuish	Dagon	decan	dévot	divan
comet	couch	cribo	culch	dagos	decay	dewan	divas
comfy	coudé	crick	culet	daily	decky	dewar	dived
comic	cough	cried	culex	dairi	decor	Dewar	diver
comma	could	crier	cully	dairy	décor	Dewey	Dives
Commo	count	cries	culpa	daisy	decoy	dexie	divot
compo	coupe	crime	Cuman	daker	decry	dhand	divvy
Comus	coupé	crimp	cumin	Dakin	decus	dhobi	dixie
conch	coups	crine	cumly	dalek	decyl	dhole	Dixie
condo	court	crisp	cunet	dally	dedal	dhoon	dizen
coney	couth	croak	cu-nim	Dally	deedy	dhoti	dizzy
conga	coven	Croat	cunit	daman	deevy	dhyal	djinn
congé	cover	croci	cunny	damme	defat	Diana	D-mark
congo	covet	crock	cupel	damna	defer	diary	do-all
Congo	covey	croft	Cupid	dampy	degas	diazo	doaty
conic	covin	cromb	cupie	dam up	degum	dicer	dobby
conky	cowan	crome	cuppa	dance	degut	dicey	dobey

dobie	douar	drive	duple	effer	enact	essay	faced
dobro	Douay	droit	duply	E flat	enarm	Essex	facer
doddy	doubt	droke	duppy	egall	ender	ester	facet
dodge	douce	droll	dural	egest	end on	estoc	facia
dodgy	dough	drome	Durex	eggar	endow	estop	facta
dodos	douro	drone	Duroc	egger	endue	ethel	facty
doest	douse	drong	duroy	egret	end up	ether	faddy
doeth	dover	drony	durra	eider	enema	ethic	faded
do for	dovey	droob	durst	eight	enemy	ethos	fader
dogan	dowar	droog	durum	eigne	Enets	ethyl	fadge
doggo	dowdy	drook	durzi	eject	engem	etrog	fados
doggy	dowel	drool	dusky	eking	enjoy	Etrog	faery
dogie	dower	droop	dusty	ekker	ennew	ettle	faggy
dog it	dowie	dropt	Dusun	elain	ennit	étude	Fagin
dogma	dowly	dross	dutch	Elami	ennui	etwee	fagot
Dogra	downy	drouk	Dutch	eland	enorm	etyma	faint
doily	dowry	drove	duvet	elate	enrol	Euler	fairy
doing	dowse	drowk	dwale	elbow	ensky	Eupad	faith
dojos	doyen	drown	dwalm	elder	ensue	euros	faker
Dolby	doylt	Druid	dwang	elect	enter	eurus	fakir
dolce	doyly	drunk	dwarf	elegy	entia	Eusol	false
doler	dozed	drupe	dweeb	eleme	entry	evade	famed
dolia	dozen	druse	dwell	elemi	enure	evens	fanal
dolly	dozer	Druse	dwelt	elfin	enurn	event	fanam
dolma	draba	drusy	dwile	Elian	envoi	evert	Fanar
dolor	drabi	druxy	dwine	elide	envoy	every	fancy
dolos	drach	Druze	dyery	elint	Enzed	Evian	fango
dolus	Draco	dryad	dying	Elint	eosin	evict	fanny
domal	drack	dryas	dyker	elite	epact	evite	fanon
domed	draff	dryer	dykey	élite	ephah	evoke	Fante
dompt	draft	dryly	dzong	elmen	ephod	ewery	Fanti
domus	drail	dryth	eager	elope	ephor	ewest	farad
donah	drain	dry up	eagle	elpee	epiky	ewhow	farce
Donau	drake	dubba	eagre	Elsan	epoch	Ewing	farcy
donee	drama	dubby	eared	elsin	epode	exact	farer
doner	drang	ducal	early	elude	epopt	exalt	Farsi
doney	drank	ducat	EAROM	elute	epoxy	excel	Fasti
donga	drant	duces	earth	elvan	EPROM	ex-con	fatal
donna	drape	duchy	easel	elven	Epsom	excur	fated
donné	drave	ducks	easer	elver	eptly	ex div	Fatha
donor	drawk	ducky	eaten	elves	equal	exeat	fatly
donut	drawl	duddy	eater	e-mail	equid	exert	fatso
do off	drawn	due to	eat-in	email	equip	exies	Fatso
dooms	dread	duggy	eat up	embar	erase	exile	fatty
doomy	dream	dulce	eaved	embay	erbia	exine	fatwa
Doona	drear	dulia	eaves	embed	erect	exist	faugh
do out	dreck	dully	Eblis	ember	ergot	exite	fault
doozy	dreed	dulse	E-boat	Ember	erica	exode	fauna
doper	dreed	dumbo	ebony	embog	eriff	expat	faust
dopey	dreep	dumka	echoy	embow	Ernie	expel	fauve
doria	drees	dummy	éclat	embox	erode	expos	favic
Doric	dreng	dumps	edder	embus	erose	extol	favor
dormy	dress	dumpy	Eddic	emcee	error	extra	favus
dorsa	dried	dunam	edema	emend	eruca	extry	faxed
dorse	drier	dunce	edged	emery	eruct	exude	faxer
dorty	dries	dunch	edger	emmer	erump	exult	fayre
doser	drift	dunga	edict	emmet	erupt	exurb	F clef
dotal	drill	dungy	edify	Emmys	erven	exute	feast
doter	drily	dunno	educe	emony	eskar	eying	feaze
dotey	dring	dunny	educt	emote	esker	eyrie	fecal
dotty	D-ring	duomo	eejit	emove	esraj	fabby	feces
Douai	drink	duper	eerie	empty	esrog	fable	fedai

fedan	filch	flews	foody	fritt	F-word	gawky	ghyll
fed up	filer	flick	foots	fritz	fytte	gayal	giant
feely	filet	flier	footy	Fritz	gabby	gayer	gibby
feeze	filly	flies	foram	frizz	gable	gayly	gibel
feign	filmy	fling	foray	frock	gadid	gazar	giber
feint	filth	flint	forby	frond	gadso	gazer	gibli
feist	final	flipe	force	frons	gaffe	gazob	gibus
felid	finch	flirt	forcy	front	Gaian	gazoo	giddy
fella	finer	flisk	fordo	froom	gaily	G clef	gigot
felly	finew	flite	forel	frore	galah	gebur	gigue
felon	Fingo	float	forex	frory	galax	gecko	GI Joe
felty	finif	flock	forge	frosh	galbe	gee-ho	gilet
femic	finis	flong	forgo	frosk	galea	geeky	gilly
femur	finny	flood	forky	frost	Galen	geese	gilpy
fence	finos	floor	forma	froth	Galla	gee-up	gimme
fendy	fiord	flora	forme	frown	Galle	geeze	gimpy
fenks	firer	flory	formé	frowy	gally	gekko	ginep
fenny	firry	flosh	formy	froze	galon	gelid	ginny
feoff	first	floss	forte	fruit	galop	gelly	ginzo
feral	firth	flota	forth	frump	galvo	gemel	gipon
feria	fishy	flour	forty	frush	Gamay	gemma	gippo
Ferio	fiste	flout	forum	fryer	gamba	gemmy	gippy
ferly	fisty	flown	fossa	fry up	gambe	gemot	gipsy
fermi	fitch	flued	fosse	f-stop	gambo	genal	girba
Fermi	fit in	fluey	fossé	fubar	gamel	genco	girly
ferns	fitly	fluff	found	fubby	gamer	genet	giros
ferny	fit on	fluid	fount	fubsy	gamey	genic	girse
ferry	fitty	fluke	fouth	fucus	gamic	genie	girsh
fesse	fit-up	fluky	fouty	fudge	gamin	genii	girth
festa	fiver	flume	fovea	fudgy	gamma	genin	gismo
fetal	fives	flump	fowls	fugal	gammy	genip	given
fetch	fixed	flung	foxie	fuggy	gamut	genoa	giver
fetid	fixer	flunk	foyer	fugie	Gamza	Genoa	givey
fetor	fixit	fluor	frack	fugle	ganch	genre	gizmo
fetta	fix on	flurr	frail	fugue	ganga	Genro	glacé
fetus	fix up	flush	frame	Fulah	gange	genty	glade
fetwa	fizzy	flute	franc	Fulbe	ganja	genus	glady
feuar	fjeld	fluty	frank	fully	ganzy	geode	glaik
feued	fjord	fly at	Frank	fulth	gaper	geoid	glair
fever	flack	fly-by	frape	fumer	gappy	gerah	gland
feyly	flail	flyer	frass	fumet	garbo	gerbe	glans
f-hole	flair	fly in	frate	fundi	Garda	germy	glare
Fiann	flake	fly on	frati	Fundi	gardy	gesso	glary
fiant	flaky	flype	fraud	fungi	garri	geste	glass
fiber	flame	flyte	frayn	fungo	garth	Getae	glaum
fibre	flamy	foamy	freak	funky	garum	Getan	glaze
fibro	flane	focal	freck	funny	gases	get at	glazy
fibry	flank	focus	freer	furan	gassy	get by	gleam
fiche	flare	fodge	fremd	furca	gatch	Getic	glean
fichu	flary	foehn	freon	furor	gated	get in	gleba
ficus	flash	fogey	Freon	furry	Gatha	get it	glebe
fidge	flask	foggy	frere	furyl	gator	get on	gleby
field	flawn	fogle	fresh	furze	Gatso	get to	gleed
fiend	flaxy	fogou	friar	furzy	gaudy	get up	gleek
fiery	flead	foist	fried	fusee	gauge	ghast	gleet
fifer	fleam	folia	frier	fusil	gault	ghazi	glent
Fifer	fleay	folic	fries	fusky	gaumy	Ghazi	gleyd
fifth	fleck	folie	frill	fussy	gaunt	Ghent	glial
fifty	fleed	folio	frisé	fusty	gauss	ghoor	glide
figgy	fleer	folks	frisk	futon	gauze	ghost	gliff
fight	fleet	folky	frist	fuzee	gauzy	ghoul	glint
filar	flesh	folly	frith	fuzzy	gavel	Ghuzz	glisk

gliss	golpe	grave	guess	hadal	harle	hemic	H-iron
glist	go mad	gravy	guest	hadda	harpy	hem in	hirst
glitz	gonad	graze	guide	Hades	harre	hemin	hi-spy
gloam	go nap	great	guige	hadji	Harri	hempy	hissy
gloat	Gondi	grebe	guild	hadn't	harry	hence	hitch
globe	goner	grebo	guile	hadst	Harry	henge	hithe
globi	gonna	grece	guilt	had to	harsh	Henle	hit in
globy	gonys	greed	guimp	hafiz	harsk	henna	hit it
glode	gonzo	Greek	guira	haggy	hashy	henny	hit on
glome	goodo	green	guiro	haham	Hasid	henry	hit up
gloom	goody	greet	guise	haick	hasky	Henry	hives
gloop	gooey	grège	guize	Haida	hasn't	he-oak	Hizen
glore	go off	grego	Gulag	haiku	haste	hepar	hoard
glory	goofy	Grepo	gular	haily	hasty	Herat	hoary
gloss	gooly	grice	gulch	hairy	hatch	herby	hoast
glost	goopy	gride	gules	haith	hater	herit	hobby
glout	goose	grief	gulfy	hajji	Hatti	heroa	hobos
glove	goosy	griff	gulix	hakea	haugh	heron	hoboy
gloze	go out	grift	gully	hakim	haulm	herse	hocus
gluck	gopak	grike	gulpy	Hakka	haunt	hertz	hodad
glued	gorah	grill	gumbo	halal	Hausa	Hertz	Hodge
gluer	goral	grime	gumly	halch	hause	het up	hoe in
glues	goree	grimy	gumma	haldi	haute	heuch	hogan
gluey	gorge	grind	gummy	haldu	haven	heugh	hogen
glugg	gorgy	griot	gumph	haler	haver	hevea	ho-hum
glume	gormy	gripe	gum up	halfa	havoc	hewed	hoick
glump	gorry	grist	Gumza	halgh	hawse	hewer	hoise
gluon	gorse	grith	gundi	hallo	hazan	hexad	hoist
glyde	gorsy	grits	gundy	halma	hazel	hexon	Hokan
glyph	gotta	groan	gunge	halon	hazer	hexyl	hokey
gnarl	Gouda	groat	gungy	halos	hazle	hey-ho	hokku
gnarr	Goudy	grody	gunny	halva	H-bomb	H-hour	hokum
gnash	gouge	groin	guppy	halve	heady	hiant	holed
gnaur	goura	groof	Gupta	Haman	heald	hiawa	holer
gnawn	gourd	groom	gurge	hamba	heapy	hided	holey
gnome	gouty	groop	gurly	hamel	heard	hider	holla
go ape	gowan	groot	gurry	hames	heart	hield	hollo
goaty	goyal	grope	gushy	hammy	heath	hi-fis	holly
goave	goyim	gross	gusle	hamza	heave	Higgs	holme
go bad	goyle	group	gussy	hanap	heavy	hight	homer
gobby	grace	grout	gusto	hance	hebra	hi-hat	homey
go big	gracy	grove	gusty	handy	heder	hijra	homie
Gödel	grade	grovy	gutsy	hangi	hedge	Hijra	homos
godet	graff	growl	gutta	hanif	hedgy	hiker	honda
godly	graft	grown	gutty	hanky	heeze	hilar	honey
go dry	grail	gruel	guyot	Hansa	heezy	hillo	honky
goest	Grail	gruff	gwely	hanse	hefty	hilly	honor
goeth	grain	gruft	gwine	Hanse	Heian	hilsa	hooch
goety	graip	grume	gynae	Hants	heiau	hilum	hooer
go far	grama	grump	gynie	hantu	heigh	hilus	hooey
gofer	grame	grunt	gyppo	haoma	heist	himbo	hoofs
go for	gramp	grush	gyppy	haori	heize	hinau	hoofy
gofor	grana	gryke	gypsy	hapax	hekte	Hindi	hoo-ha
go-get	grand	G-suit	gyral	haply	helio	Hindu	Hooke
going	grane	guaap	gyron	happi	helix	Hiney	hooky
golah	grant	guaca	gyros	happy	hello	hinge	hooly
Golah	grape	guaco	gyrus	haram	helly	hinny	Hoopa
goldy	graph	guana	gyver	hards	helot	hippo	hoose
golem	grapy	guano	habit	hardy	helve	hipps	hoosh
goles	grasp	guara	habra	harem	hemal	hippy	hoots
Golgi	grass	guard	háček	harif	he-man	hired	hoove
golly	grate	guava	hacky	harka	he-men	hirer	hooze

hoped	husky	ilium	inked	IUPAC	jeton	julep	kavir
hoper	hussy	illth	inken	ivied	jetty	julio	kayak
hop in	hutch	Iloco	inker	ivies	jewel	julus	Kayan
hop it	hutia	image	in key	ivory	Jewry	Julys	Kazak
Hoppo	Hutus	imago	inkle	ivyed	jezia	jumar	kazoo
hoppy	huzza	Imari	in-law	ixora	jheel	jumbo	kbyte
horae	huzzy	imbed	inlaw	Iyyar	jhula	jumby	kebab
horah	hyawa	imbue	in lay	izard	jibba	jumma	kedge
horal	Hydah	I mean	inlay	jabot	jiffy	jumpy	keech
horde	hydel	imide	inlet	J acid	jihad	junco	keely
horme	hydra	imine	in-lot	Jacko	jildi	jundy	keeve
horny	hydro	immer	in mew	Jacky	jimmy	junky	kefir
horse	hyena	immie	inmix	Jacob	Jimmy	junta	kelch
horst	hying	immit	inner	jaded	jingo	junto	Kelim
horsy	hyleg	immix	innit	Jaffa	jings	jupon	Kelly
hosen	hylic	impel	in-off	jäger	jinny	jural	kelpy
hosta	hymen	impis	in one	jaggy	jippo	jurat	keltz
hotch	Hymie	imply	inorb	jagir	jirga	juror	kempt
hotel	hyoid	impro	in pay	jakes	jiver	jutka	kempy
hotly	hyper	imshi	in pig	Jakun	jivey	jutty	kenaf
hotty	hypha	inact	in pod	jalap	jiwan	juvia	kench
hough	hypna	inajá	in pop	jamah	jizya	juvie	kendo
hound	hypos	inaka	in pup	jaman	jnani	Kaaba	kente
houri	hyrax	in all	input	jambe	Jocko	kaama	Kenya
house	hyson	inane	inrun	jambo	jodel	kacha	kepis
hovel	Hy-spy	inapt	inset	jambu	joeys	Kadet	Kerch
hoven	hythe	inarm	in sum	James	johar	Kafir	kêrel
hover	iambi	in bad	inter	jamma	Johne	Kajar	Keres
how do	I-beam	in bed	intro	jammy	joint	kakar	kerne
howdy	Iblis	in bud	intue	jam-up	joist	kakas	Kerry
howel	icaco	in-bye	in two	janty	jokee	kakur	ketal
howff	ichor	Incan	Inuit	Janus	joker	kalij	ketch
how so	icier	in-car	inula	japan	jokey	kalpa	ketol
how-to	icily	incog	inure	Japan	jokul	Kamba	ketyl
hoyle	icing	incur	inurn	japer	jollo	kamik	kevel
Hoyle	icker	incus	Invar	jarul	jolly	kanga	kevir
huaca	ickle	incut	in wed	jasey	Jolly	kango	keyed
huaco	ictal	index	inwit	jaspé	jolty	kanji	keyer
hubby	ictic	India	iodic	jatos	Jomon	Kansa	key up
huffy	ictus	Indic	ionic	jaunt	Jonah	kanzu	khair
huh-uh	idea'd	indie	Ionic	Javan	Jones	kapok	khaki
hulan	ideal	Indio	Iowan	javel	jonga	kappa	khama
hulky	ident	indri	ipiti	jawan	jonty	kapur	Khasi
hullo	idiom	indue	ippon	jawar	joree	kaput	khaya
hulwa	idiot	Indus	irade	jawed	jorum	karat	kheda
human	idler	inept	Iraqi	jazzy	jotty	karee	Khmer
humic	idola	inert	irate	jeans	jougs	Karen	Khond
humid	idryl	in fee	Irgun	jebel	joule	karma	khoum
humor	idyll	infer	Irish	jehad	joust	Karok	kiaat
humph	ier-oe	in feu	iroko	jelab	jowar	Karoo	kiack
humpy	i' fegs	in few	irony	jello	jowel	karri	kiang
humus	if not	infix	ishan	Jell-O	jower	karst	kiawe
hunch	Igbos	in for	Isiac	jelly	jowly	karsy	kicky
hunks	igloo	infra	Islam	jemmy	jubba	karzy	kiddo
hunky	ileac	in fun	islet	jenny	Judas	Kasha	kiddy
hurly	ileal	ingan	islot	jerid	judge	katel	kikar
Huron	ileum	ingem	Isnik	jerky	jugal	kathi	kikoi
Hurri	ileus	Ingin	issue	jerry	juger	katil	kilim
hurry	iliac	ingle	istle	Jerry	jugum	katti	Kilim
hurst	Iliad	ingot	itchy	Jesse	juice	katun	kilos
husht	Ilian	inion	I-Thou	Jessy	juicy	kauch	kinda
huske	Iliat	Injun	iulus	Jesus	juldy	kauri	kindy

kinep	kofta	kungu	laree	leash	level	lingo	loner
kingy	kohua	Kuo-yu	lares	least	lever	lingy	lones
kinin	koine	Kuril	large	leath	levin	linin	longe
kinky	kojic	kurta	largo	leave	levir	links	long s
kinos	kokam	kurus	larin	leavy	Levis	linky	looby
Kioko	koker	kvass	larix	Leber	lewis	linos	looey
kiore	kokko	kvell	larky	leche	Lewis	linty	looie
kiosk	kokum	kweek	larry	ledge	lewth	linum	looky
Kiowa	Kolam	kwela	Larry	ledgy	lexis	lipid	loony
kipsy	Kolbe	kyack	larum	ledum	lezzy	lippy	loopy
Kirby	Koman	kyang	larva	leech	Lhasa	lisle	loose
kirri	kombé	kyats	laser	Leeds	L-head	lispy	loper
kirsh	kombu	kyles	Lassa	lee ho	liana	liter	loppy
kisan	konak	kylie	lassi	leeky	liane	lithe	loral
Kisii	Kongo	kylin	lasso	leery	liang	litho	loran
Kissi	kooka	kylix	lassy	lefty	liard	lithy	lordy
kissy	kooky	kyloe	lasya	legal	libel	litre	Lordy
Kiswa	kopek	kyped	latch	leger	liber	litui	lored
Kitab	kopje	Kyrie	lated	Leger	Libra	lit up	loris
kithe	koppa	kythe	laten	leggo	licca	lived	lorry
kitty	Koran	laari	later	leggy	licit	liven	lorum
kiver	korin	label	lates	leg it	lidar	liver	losel
kiwis	Korku	labia	latex	legit	lidos	lives	loser
Kizil	korma	labor	lathe	leg-up	lie by	livid	lossy
kleft	Korwa	labra	lathi	lehua	liege	livor	lotic
klick	kotal	laced	laths	leigh	lie in	livre	lotos
klieg	kotos	lacet	lathy	leman	lie to	llama	lotsa
Kling	kotow	lacis	Latin	lemel	lie up	llano	lotta
klong	koura	laddo	laton	lemma	lifer	loach	lotto
kloof	kovsh	laden	latus	lemme	lifey	loamy	Lotto
klops	kraal	lader	lauan	lemna	ligan	loath	lotus
klunk	kraft	Ladik	lauds	lemon	liger	lobar	lough
klutz	krait	Ladin	laugh	lemur	light	lobby	louis
knack	Krama	ladle	laund	lenes	liken	lobed	Louis
knape	krans	lagan	laval	lenis	liker	local	loupe
knarl	kraut	lagen	laver	lenos	Likud	lo-cal	lourd
knaur	Kraut	lager	lavvy	lente	lilac	loche	loure
knave	kreef	lahar	lawdy	lento	Li-los	lochi	louro
knead	kreng	laich	lawks	leone	liman	lochy	loury
kneed	krill	laigh	lawny	leper	limax	locie	louse
kneel	kriti	laika	lawsy	lepid	limba	locky	lousy
knees	Kromo	laird	laxly	lepra	Limba	locos	lovat
knell	krona	lairy	lay at	lepta	limbi	locum	lover
knelt	krone	laity	lay-by	Lepus	limbo	locus	lovey
knick	kroon	laker	layer	lered	Limbu	loden	lowan
knife	Krupp	lakin	lay in	lerky	limen	lodge	lower
knish	kudos	lamba	lay on	lesbo	limer	loess	lowly
knive	kudzu	Lamba	lay to	lesed	limes	lofty	low on
knock	Kufic	lamel	lay up	lessy	Limey	logan	Lowry
Knole	kugel	lamia	lazar	leste	limit	loggy	loxia
knoll	kukri	lamin	Lazic	let at	limma	logia	loyal
Knoop	kukui	Lamut	l-dopa	let be	limos	logic	lozen
knorr	kulah	lanai	leach	letch	linac	logie	lubra
knosp	Kulah	lance	Leach	let go	linch	log in	Lucan
knout	kulak	Langi	leady	Lethe	Linde	logit	Lucas
knowe	kulan	Lango	leafy	let in	lindy	log on	Lucca
known	Kulin	lanky	leaky	let on	lined	logos	lucet
knuck	Kuman	lapel	leant	letty	linen	Logos	lucid
knurl	kumis	lappa	leapt	let up	liner	Lohan	lucky
knurr	Kumyk	lapse	learn	levan	liney	Loire	lucre
koala	kunai	larch	leary	levas	linga	lokey	ludic
Kodak	kunbi	lardy	lease	levee	linge	lolly	Ludic

luffa	madar	manse	mavis	merit	minae	moist	motel
Luger	madge	manta	mawky	merle	mince	molal	motet
Lugol	madia	manto	maxim	meros	miner	molar	motey
Luing	madid	manul	Maxim	merou	minge	moldy	mothy
lulav	madly	man up	maxis	merry	mingy	Moler	motif
lulla	maedi	manus	Mayan	mesad	Minié	moley	moton
lumen	Mafia	Maori	Mayas	meshy	minim	molly	motor
lumme	mafic	mapau	maybe	mesic	minis	molto	motte
lummy	mafoo	maple	mayer	meslé	minke	momma	motto
lumpy	Magar	mapou	mayn't	mesne	minol	momme	motty
lunar	magic	mappy	mayor	meson	minor	mommy	mouch
lunch	magma	maqui	mayst	messy	minty	Momus	mould
Lunda	magot	marae	mazar	metae	minus	monad	Mouli
lunel	magus	marah	mazer	metal	MIRAS	monal	moult
lunge	mahal	maral	mazey	metel	mired	monas	mouly
lungi	Mahdi	march	mazut	meter	mirex	mondo	mound
lungy	mahoe	March	Mbuti	metho	mirid	Monel	mount
lupin	mahua	mardy	McCoy	Metho	mirky	money	mourn
lupus	maidy	Maree	mealy	meths	mirth	mongo	mouse
lurch	maiko	mares	means	metic	misdo	Mongo	mousy
lurer	maint	marge	meant	metif	miser	monic	mouth
lurex	maire	margo	meany	metis	misgo	monos	mover
Lurex	maize	maria	mease	Metis	missy	monte	movie
Lurgi	major	Maria	meaty	metol	misty	month	mowed
lurgy	makai	marid	mebbe	me-too	mitch	monty	mower
lurid	makar	marie	mebos	metre	miter	mooch	mowra
lurky	maker	marly	Mecca	metro	mitre	moody	moxie
lurry	makos	marra	medal	meuse	mitry	mooed	moyen
lushy	malar	marri	media	mezzo	Mitty	mooey	Mr Big
lusky	Malay	marry	medic	miaow	mivvy	mooli	M-roof
lusty	maleo	Marse	Medic	miasm	Miwok	moony	Mrs Lo
lusus	Maler	marsh	medio	miaul	mixed	moory	msasa
luter	malic	Marsh	Medoc	micky	mixen	moose	MS-DOS
luton	malik	Marsi	Médoc	micro	mixer	moosh	mtepe
luvvy	malis	marum	meech	Midas	mix in	moped	muchi
lyart	malmy	Marys	meeja	middy	mixis	moper	mucho
lycée	Malta	Masai	meese	midge	mix it	moppy	mucic
lycid	Malto	maser	Meiji	midis	mix up	mopsy	mucid
Lycra	malty	masha	meith	mid-on	mizen	mop up	mucin
lygus	Malvi	mason	melam	midst	Mlles	mopus	mucky
lying	mamba	Massa	Melba	miffy	mneme	moral	mucor
lymph	mambo	massé	melch	might	mobby	morat	mucro
lynch	mamey	massy	mêlée	migma	moble	moray	mucus
Lyons	mamma	masty	melic	migod	mocha	moree	mudar
lyric	mammy	matai	meloe	mikan	Mocha	morel	muddy
Lyrid	Mande	match	melon	mikva	mocky	mores	mufti
lyses	mandy	mater	melos	Milan	modal	morne	muggy
lysin	maneb	matey	melsh	milch	model	morné	mug-up
lysis	maned	mathe	melty	milds	modem	moron	Mujur
Lysol	manes	maths	memos	miler	modii	Moros	mukim
lyssa	manga	matie	menad	miles	Modoc	morph	mukti
lythe	mange	matin	mench	milia	modom	morra	mulch
lytic	mango	matje	Mende	milko	moggy	morse	mulct
lytta	mangy	matlo	Mendi	milky	mogra	Morse	muled
macaw	mania	matra	mends	mille	mogul	Mosan	Mules
macca	manic	matte	mensa	Mills	Mogul	Mosel	muley
macer	manis	matzo	mense	milpa	mohel	Moses	mulga
macho	manky	mauby	mensh	miltz	mohur	mosey	mully
macle	manly	mauma	mento	mimeo	mohwa	Mossi	mulsh
Màcon	manna	maund	mercy	mimer	Moine	mosso	mummy
macro	manny	mauve	merel	mimic	moire	mossy	mumps
madam	manor	maven	merge	mimsy	moiré	moted	mumsy

munch	nadir	Ndama	nieve	no joy	nudge	offer	on ice
Munda	naevi	neath	niffy	nokes	nudie	OFFER	onion
munga	Naffy	neato	nifle	no kid	Nujol	off of	onium
mungo	naggy	nebel	nifty	nolle	nulla	Ofgas	onlap
mungy	nagor	neddy	Niger	nomad	nullo	of his	onlay
munja	nahal	needs	nigga	no man	nully	of kin	on lee
Munro	naiad	needy	night	no-mar	numby	Oflag	onlie
mural	naice	ne'er a	nigra	nomen	numen	of old	on-off
murex	naieo	neeze	nigua	nomic	Numic	Oftel	on-set
Muria	naily	neger	nikau	nomos	nummy	often	onset
murid	naira	Negri	nilas	nonce	numps	oftly	ontal
murky	naive	negro	Nilot	nonda	nunky	ofuro	on tap
murly	naive	Negro	nimbi	nones	nuque	Ofwat	ontic
Murmi	naked	negus	Nimby	nonet	nurse	ogee'd	on top
murra	naker	Negus	ninja	nonic	nutso	ogeed	oojah
murre	naled	Nehru	ninny	no-nos	nutsy	oggin	ooloo
Murut	NALGO	neigh	ninon	nonyl	nutty	ogham	oomph
musae	Namas	nelia	ninth	nooky	nyala	Oghuz	ootid
Musca	namer	nelly	Niobe	no one	Nyasa	ogive	op-amp
muser	namma	nemic	niopo	noose	nylon	ogler	op art
muset	nance	neoza	nippy	nopal	nymph	ogmic	opepe
musha	nancy	neper	Nippy	noria	nyssa	oh boy	opera
mushy	Nandi	neral	NIREX	norma	Nzima	Ohian	opihi
music	Nanga	neram	Nisan	Norna	oaken	ohmic	opine
musky	nanna	nerdy	nisei	Norse	oakum	ohone	opium
musos	nanny	nerka	nisin	Norsk	oared	oidia	oppos
mussy	Nants	nerol	Niska	north	oasis	oiled	opsin
musth	Nantz	nerts	Nissl	nosed	oaten	oiler	optic
musty	napoh	nerve	nisus	noser	oater	oil in	opt in
mutch	napoo	nervy	nital	nosey	oaths	oil up	orach
muted	nappa	net of	nitch	noshi	Obaku	ojime	oracy
mutha	Nappa	netty	niter	no sir	obang	okapi	orage
mutic	nappe	neuma	nitid	no sky	obeah	OK'ing	orang
muton	nappy	neume	niton	notae	obeli	oktas	orans
muzak	naras	nevel	nitre	notal	obese	olate	Oraon
Muzak	narco	never	nitro	notam	obley	olden	orate
muzzy	nares	nevus	nitta	notch	obole	older	orbed
mvule	narks	nevvy	nitty	noted	Occam	oldie	orbic
Mwami	narky	Newar	nival	noter	occur	oldly	orbit
myall	narra	newel	nixie	not-go	ocean	oleic	orcin
my eye	nasal	newie	nix on	not on	ocher	olein	order
my God	Nasca	newly	Nizam	not on	ochre	olent	oread
my hat	Nasho	newsy	nobby	notum	ochry	oleum	orful
Mylar	Nasik	nexal	Nobel	nouny	ocker	oleyl	organ
my man	nassa	nexus	noble	nouse	ocote	olios	orgic
mynah	nasty	ngaio	nobly	novae	ocrea	oliva	orgie
myoma	nasus	Ngala	no bon	novas	octad	olive	orgue
myope	natal	Ngoko	nocht	novel	octal	Olmec	oribi
myopy	Natal	Ngoni	nodal	no way	octet	ology	oriel
my own	natch	Nguni	noddy	noway	octic	Omaha	O-ring
myrrh	nates	ngwee	nodum	nowed	octyl	Omani	Orion
mysid	nathe	niata	nodus	nowel	oculi	omasa	Oriya
mysis	natty	nicad	noema	Nowel	oddly	ombre	Orlon
my son	naunt	Nicam	noeme	no-win	odeon	ombré	orlop
mythi	naval	nicey	no end	noxal	odeum	omega	ormer
NAAFI	navel	niche	Nogai	noyau	OD'ing	ommin	orpin
nabal	navew	nicol	Nogay	NSPCC	odist	oncer	orris
nabla	navvy	Nicol	no-hit	n-type	odium	on cue	ortet
nabob	nawab	nidge	nohow	nubby	odour	on dit	ortho
nache	nazar	nidor	noint	nubia	of all	on end	or two
nacho	Nazca	nidus	noise	nucha	offal	one-up	Osage
nacre	Nazis	niece	noisy	nuddy	offen	ongon	Oscan

Oscar	Ozark	pared	peace	pesta	pilei	plate	pokie
osier	ozena	paren	peach	pesto	piler	Platt	Polab
osmic	ozone	parer	péage	pesty	piles	platy	polar
osmol	Ozzie	pareu	peaky	petal	pilot	playa	poler
osone	pacay	parge	Peano	peter	pilus	plaza	poley
ossia	pacer	pargo	pearl	petit	Piman	plead	polio
Ossie	pacey	Paris	peart	petre	pinax	pleat	polis
ostia	pacha	parka	pease	petty	pinch	plebe	polje
otary	paddy	parky	peasy	Peulh	pinda	pleck	polka
other	Paddy	parle	peaty	pewee	piner	plene	pollo
Otomi	padge	parma	pecan	pewit	piney	pleon	polly
otter	padre	Parma	pecia	phage	pingo	plica	Polly
oubit	paean	parol	pecky	phare	pinic	plied	polyp
ouens	paeon	parry	pedal	phase	pinko	plier	polys
ought	pagan	parse	pedee	phasm	pinky	plies	Pomak
Ouija	paged	Parsi	pedes	pheer	pinna	pliés	pommé
oumer	pager	party	pedia	pheme	pinny	plink	pommy
ounce	Paget	pasan	pedon	phene	piñon	ploce	Pommy
ourie	pagle	Pasch	pedro	pheno	Pinot	plock	Ponca
ousel	pagne	paseo	pee em	pheon	pinta	plonk	ponce
out-by	paint	pasha	peent	phial	pinto	plore	poncy
outdo	paisa	pashm	peeoy	phlox	pin-up	plosh	Pondo
outen	paise	pasmo	peepy	phoca	pious	plote	pondy
outer	Pakis	passé	peery	phone	pipal	Plott	ponga
outgo	pa-kua	pasta	peeve	phono	piped	plotz	pongo
outly	palae	paste	peggy	phony	piper	plout	pongy
out of	palar	pasty	peg on	phoss	pipit	pluck	ponor
outré	palas	patas	peise	photo	pippy	pluff	ponty
outro	palea	patch	pekan	phwat	pique	plumb	pooch
outta	paled	pated	pekea	phyla	piqué	plume	pooey
out to	palla	patée	Pekin	phyle	piqui	plump	poofy
ouzel	pally	patel	pekoe	piani	pirog	plumy	pooja
ouzos	palmy	paten	pelta	piano	Pisan	plunk	pooka
ovary	palpi	pater	penal	pians	pisco	plush	Poole
ovate	palps	paths	pence	Piast	pissy	plute	pooly
overt	palsa	patil	penes	piccy	piste	Pluto	Poona
ovest	palsy	patio	pengö	pichi	pitch	poach	poopy
ovine	pamby	patly	penis	picky	pithy	pobby	pooty
ovism	panch	Patna	penne	picot	piton	pocan	poove
ovist	panda	patsy	penni	pi-dog	pitot	poché	poppa
ovoid	pandy	patty	penny	piece	pitso	pocky	poppy
ovoli	Pandy	Pauli	pensy	pietà	pitta	podal	popsy
ovolo	panel	pause	peola	Pietà	piuri	poddy	pop-up
ovule	panga	pauxi	peony	piety	pivot	podex	poral
o' will	panic	pavan	pepos	piezo	pixel	podge	porch
owing	panji	paven	peppy	piggy	pixie	podgy	pored
owler	panne	paver	Pepsi	pight	Piyut	podia	porer
owlet	pansy	pavia	perai	pig it	pizer	poena	porge
owner	panto	pavid	perch	pigmy	pizza	poesy	porgy
ownio	pants	pavis	Percy	pi jaw	place	pogey	poria
own up	panty	pavvy	perdu	pikau	plack	pogge	porin
owzat	paolo	paw at	peril	piked	plage	pogos	porky
ox-bot	papal	pawky	peris	pikel	plaid	pogue	porno
oxbow	papas	pawne	perky	piker	Plaid	poilu	porny
ox-eye	papaw	payas	perle	pikey	plain	poind	porta
Oxfam	Papaw	payed	perry	pikia	plait	point	Porte
oxide	paper	payee	per se	pilaf	plane	poire	porty
oxime	pappi	payer	perse	pilau	plank	poise	posca
oxine	pappy	pay in	perve	pilaw	plano	pokal	posed
oxlip	parch	payor	pervy	pilch	plant	poked	poser
ox-ray	parcy	pay up	pesky	pilea	plash	poker	posey
oxter	pardi	p-code	pesos	piled	plasm	pokey	posho

posit	prion	pulao	quack	racon	rauli	reest	retia
Posix	prior	puler	Quadi	radar	raupo	reeve	retie
posse	prise	pulik	quaff	radii	ravel	refan	re-tin
possy	prism	pulka	quail	radio	raven	refer	re-tip
posty	priss	pulli	quake	radix	raver	reffo	retro
potch	privy	pulpy	quaky	radly	ravin	refit	retry
poter	prize	pulse	quale	radon	rawin	refix	reune
pot on	pro-am	pulza	qualm	raffy	rawky	refry	reuse
potoo	probe	Punan	quant	rafty	rawly	regal	revel
potro	proby	punch	quare	ragee	rayed	Regge	revet
potsy	prodd	punga	quark	rager	rayon	reggo	revue
potto	proem	pungy	quarl	ragga	razee	regma	re-wet
potty	proke	Punic	quart	raggy	razer	regur	re-win
pot up	prole	punji	quash	rainy	razoo	rehab	rhamn
pouch	proly	punky	quasi	raise	razor	Reich	rheid
poulp	promo	punny	quass	raita	razzo	reify	rheme
poult	prone	punto	quave	rajah	R-boat	reign	rheum
pound	prong	punty	quawk	Rakah	reach	reink	rhine
pouty	pronk	pupae	quean	rakel	react	reins	Rhine
powan	proof	pupal	queen	raker	re-act	reive	rhino
power	proot	pupil	queer	rakis	ready	rejig	rhodo
pozzy	prore	puppy	quell	ralli	realm	rekey	rhody
praam	prosa	purau	queme	rally	Realo	relax	rhomb
prahu	prose	purée	quere	ramal	reamy	relay	Rhône
praia	pross	purge	querl	Raman	rearm	re-lay	rhumb
prana	prosy	Purim	quern	rambo	re-ask	relet	rhyme
prang	proud	purry	query	Rambo	reasy	re-let	rhyta
prank	prove	purse	quest	ramen	reata	relic	riant
p'raps	provo	pursy	queue	ramet	reate	relit	riata
prase	Provo	purty	quick	ramie	reave	reman	ribby
prate	prowl	Purum	quies	ramin	rebab	remen	ribes
pratt	proxy	pushy	quiet	rammy	reban	remex	ribit
Pratt	prude	pussy	quiff	ramon	re-bar	remit	ricer
prawn	prune	put at	quile	ramps	rebbe	remix	ricey
praya	prunt	put by	quill	ramus	rebec	renal	richy
predy	pryan	putid	quilt	rance	rebel	renew	ricin
preen	pryce	put in	quina	ranch	rebid	renga	rided
prego	pryse	put on	quint	R and R	rebud	renin	ridel
preon	psalm	putti	quipu	randy	rebus	repat	rider
pre-op	pseud	putto	quire	ranee	rebut	repay	ridge
press	pshaw	put to	quirk	range	rebuy	repel	ridgy
prest	psoas	putto	quirl	rangé	recap	repin	riffy
prexy	psora	putty	quirt	rangy	recce	repla	rifle
Prexy	psych	put-up	quite	ranid	recco	reply	rifty
prial	P trap	pygal	quits	ranny	recon	repot	right
prian	p-type	pygmy	quoin	ranty	recta	repro	rigid
price	pubes	pylon	quoit	raper	recti	reran	rigol
prick	pubic	pylor	quoll	raphe	recto	re-row	rigor
pricy	pubis	pyoid	Quorn	rapid	recur	rerun	riley
pride	pucka	pyral	quota	rarer	recut	resam	Riley
pridy	puddy	pyran	quote	Rarey	redan	resat	rille
pried	pudge	Pyrex	quoth	raspy	reddy	resaw	rilly
prier	pudgy	pyrus	Qur'an	rasse	redia	resee	rimed
pries	pudic	pyxie	Quran	Rasta	redid	reset	rimer
prill	pudor	pyxis	qursh	ratal	redly	resew	rindy
prima	pudsy	pzazz	rabat	ratan	redox	Resht	riner
prime	puffy	Qajar	rabbi	ratch	red 'un	resin	ringe
primi	puggy	Qiana	rabic	ratel	redux	resit	ringy
primo	pugil	qibla	rabid	rater	reedy	resol	Rinne
primp	puker	qibli	Racah	rathe	reefy	resow	rinse
prink	pukey	qirsh	racer	ratio	reeky	resty	Rioja
print	pukka	Q-ship	rache	ratty	reely	retch	ripen

rip up	roral	rumbo	sakes	saraf	scalp	scrod	señor
risen	rorty	rumen	sakis	Saran	scaly	scrog	sensa
riser	rosed	rumex	Sakta	saree	scamp	scrow	sense
rishi	roset	rum go	Sakti	sarge	Scand	scrub	sente
risky	Roshi	rummy	salad	sargo	scant	scrum	sepal
rithe	Rosie	rumor	salal	Sarik	scape	scuba	sepia
ritzy	rosin	rumpo	Salem	sarin	scapi	scudo	Sepik
rival	RoSPA	rumpy	salep	saris	scare	scuff	sepoy
rived	rotal	run at	salic	sarky	scarf	scull	septa
rivel	roter	runch	Salic	Sarn't	scari	sculp	serac
riven	rotge	runic	salie	sarod	scarn	scurf	serai
river	roton	run in	Salii	saron	scarp	scuse	seral
rivet	rotor	runny	salix	saros	scart	scuta	Serax
riyal	rotta	run on	salle	sarpo	SCART	scute	Seres
RNase	Rouen	runot	sally	sarsa	scary	scuzz	serge
roach	rouge	run to	Sally	Sarsi	scaum	Scyth	Seric
roast	rough	runty	salmi	Sarum	scaup	seamy	serif
robed	rouky	run up	salol	sarus	scaur	Sebat	serin
robin	round	rupee	salon	Saryk	scena	Sebei	serir
roble	roupy	rupia	salpa	sarza	scend	sebum	seron
robot	rouse	rural	salsa	Sasak	scene	secco	serow
robur	roust	rusha	salse	sasin	scent	secko	SERPS
roche	route	rushy	salta	sassy	schiz	sedan	serra
Roche	routh	rusma	salto	satai	schmo	Seder	serry
rocky	rover	rusty	salty	Satan	schol	sedge	serum
rodeo	rowan	rutin	salud	satay	schwa	sedgy	serve
rofia	rowdy	rutty	salve	satem	sci-fi	sedra	servo
rogan	rowed	ruvid	salvo	satin	scion	sedum	setae
roger	rowel	rymer	Salvo	satis	scoff	seech	setal
Roger	rowen	Saale	salvy	satyr	scoke	seedy	set by
rogue	rower	sabal	samaj	sauba	scold	see-er	set in
rohun	rowet	saber	Samal	sauce	scone	seege	set on
roily	row in	sabin	saman	sauch	scoop	see-ho	seton
roker	rowty	Sabir	samba	saucy	scoot	seely	set to
rolag	royal	sable	sambo	Saudi	scopa	see to	set up
roleo	royet	sably	Sambo	saugh	scope	segar	seven
rolly	RSPCA	sabot	samel	sault	scops	segos	sever
romal	ruana	sabra	samey	sauna	scopy	segue	Sevin
roman	rubby	sabre	samfu	saury	score	Sehna	sevum
Roman	rub in	sacky	sammo	sauté	scorn	seine	sewan
Romeo	rubio	sacra	sammy	saver	scorp	seise	sewed
romer	ruble	sacre	Sammy	savin	scote	seism	Sewee
rompy	rub on	sadhu	Samos	savor	Scots	seity	sewen
ronde	rubor	sadic	sampi	savoy	scoup	Seitz	sewer
rondo	rub up	sadly	sanad	Savoy	scour	seize	sewin
Roneo	ruche	sadza	sanct	savvy	scout	selah	sew-on
Ronga	rucky	Sagan	Sande	sawed	scove	Selah	sew up
ronge	rudas	sagey	sandy	sawer	scowl	selch	sexed
ronin	ruddy	saggy	Sandy	Saxon	scrab	selfs	sexer
Ronuk	rudie	sagos	sanga	sayer	scrag	selky	sexto
roofs	Rufai	sagum	Sanga	say no	scram	sella	seyal
roofy	ruffe	sahel	Sango	say on	scran	selva	shack
rooky	ruffy	sahib	Sanio	says I	scrap	selve	shade
roomy	rugal	Sahli	Sanka	say-so	scrat	semée	shads
roosa	rugby	saiga	sanko	S-band	scraw	semen	shady
roose	Rugby	saint	Sansi	S-bend	scray	semic	shaft
roost	ruggy	Saite	Santa	scads	scree	semis	shahi
roots	ruing	saith	santo	scaff	screw	semon	shail
rooty	ruise	Saiva	sapan	scala	scrib	semul	shake
roper	ruler	Sakai	sapid	scald	scrim	sengi	shako
ropey	rumal	Sakel	sapor	scale	scrin	senna	shaky
roque	rumba	saker	sappy	scall	scrip	Senoi	shale

shall	shirr	shuck	sisal	Skoda	slopy	sneap	solen
shalt	shirt	shude	sisel	skoob	slosh	sneck	soler
shaly	shish	shuka	sissy	skosh	slote	sneer	soles
shama	shite	shunt	sitar	skulk	sloth	snell	sol-fa
shame	shiur	shura	sit by	skull	slove	snick	solid
Shang	shiva	shush	sitch	skunk	sloyd	snide	solod
shank	Shiva	shute	sited	skyer	sluff	snidy	Solon
shan't	shive	shuto	sithe	skyey	sluit	sniff	solos
shant	shlub	shyer	sit in	slack	slump	snift	solum
shape	Shluh	shyly	Sitka	slade	slung	snipe	solus
shard	shmoo	siafu	sit on	slaik	slunk	snipy	solve
share	shoad	sibyl	sit-up	slain	slurb	snirt	solvi
shark	shoal	Sican	situs	slake	slurp	snite	somal
sharm	shoat	sicca	Sivan	slaky	slush	snock	Soman
sharn	shoch	Sicel	sixer	slamp	slyer	snoek	somma
sharp	shock	sicko	sixmo	slane	slyly	snoff	sonar
shave	shode	sicle	sixte	slang	slype	snoke	sondo
shawl	shoed	sided	sixth	slank	smack	snood	sonic
shawm	shoer	sider	sixty	slant	smaik	snook	sonly
shchi	shoes	Sidhe	sizar	slash	small	snool	Sonne
sheaf	shoey	sidle	sized	slate	smalt	snoop	sonny
shear	shogi	sidra	sizer	slath	smarm	snoot	sonse
sheat	shoji	Sidur	skaff	slaty	smart	snore	sonsy
sheel	shola	siege	skail	slave	smash	snork	sooey
sheen	sholt	Siena	skald	slawk	smaze	snort	soosy
sheep	sholy	sieur	skank	slead	smear	snous	sooth
sheer	Shona	sieve	skarn	sleak	smeek	snout	sooty
sheet	shone	sight	skate	slean	smell	snowy	Sophy
sheik	shonk	sigil	skean	sleat	smelt	snuck	sopor
sheld	shood	sigla	skeel	sleck	smift	snuff	soppy
shelf	shook	sigma	skeer	sleek	smile	snurt	soral
she'll	shool	siket	skeet	sleep	S-mine	soapy	Sorbo
shell	shoon	Silbo	skein	sleet	smirk	soave	sorel
shelt	shoos	silen	skelf	slent	smirr	Soave	sorgo
Shema	shoot	silex	skell	slept	smite	sobby	sorry
shend	Shope	silky	skelm	slice	smith	sober	sorus
sheng	shore	silly	skelp	slick	smock	socii	sorva
shent	Shore	silos	skelt	slide	smoke	socko	sotch
Sheol	shorn	silty	skene	slied	smoko	socks	Sotho
sherd	short	silva	Skene	slift	smoky	socle	sotie
sheth	shots	silyl	skerm	slily	smolt	sodar	sotol
sheva	shott	simar	skete	slime	smoor	soddy	sough
shewa	shout	simba	skewy	slimy	smoot	sodic	souly
shewt	shove	simpy	skice	sline	smore	Sodom	sound
Shias	Showa	simul	skied	sling	smote	soe'er	soupy
shice	shown	since	skier	slink	smout	sofa'd	souse
shick	showy	sinew	skies	slipe	smush	so far	south
shide	shoyu	singe	skiff	slish	snack	Sofar	sowar
shied	Shqip	Singh	skift	slite	snafu	softa	sowed
shiel	shrab	Sinic	skill	slive	snail	softy	sowel
shies	shrag	sinky	skimp	slize	snake	soggy	sower
shift	shram	Sinon	skink	slock	snaky	soily	sowff
Shiga	shrap	sinus	skint	sloff	snape	soken	sowth
shiko	shred	Sioux	skire	sloid	snaps	Sokol	space
shill	shrew	sipid	skirl	sloka	snare	solah	spack
Shina	shrim	siree	skirp	sloke	snarf	solan	spacy
shine	shrip	siren	skirr	slomo	snark	solar	spade
shiny	shrub	sirex	skirt	slonk	snarl	Solas	spahi
shipo	shrug	sirih	skish	sloom	snash	soldi	spake
shire	shtik	siris	skite	sloop	snath	soldo	spald
shirk	shtup	siroc	skive	sloot	snead	solea	spale
shirl	shuba	sirup	skoal	slope	sneak	soled	spall

spalt	spitz	stagy	still	strut	sump'n	swipe	Tajik
spane	Spitz	staid	stilt	stuck	sumpy	swire	taken
spang	splat	stain	stime	study	sum up	swirl	taker
spank	splay	stair	stimy	stufa	sunck	swish	takht
spare	splet	stake	sting	stuff	sunly	Swiss	takin
spari	splib	stale	stink	Stuka	Sunna	swith	takyr
spark	splif	stalk	stint	stull	Sunni	swive	talak
spart	split	stall	stipe	stulm	sunny	swizz	talaq
spasm	Spode	stamp	stire	stuma	sunup	swoln	talar
spate	spoil	stand	stirk	stumm	sun-up	swoof	talcy
spath	spoke	stang	stirp	stump	super	swoon	talea
spaug	spoky	stank	stith	stung	supra	swoop	tales
spave	spong	staph	stive	stunk	surah	sword	talha
spawl	spoof	stare	stivy	stunt	surai	swore	talik
spawn	spook	stark	stoai	stupa	sural	sworn	talky
spazz	spool	Stark	stoas	stupe	Surat	swung	tally
speak	spoom	starn	stoat	sturb	surfy	sybow	talma
spean	spoon	starr	stock	sture	surge	sycee	talon
spear	spoor	start	stoep	sturt	surgy	sycon	talpa
speck	spore	START	stogy	stuss	surly	Sylow	taluk
specs	Spork	stary	Stoic	styan	surma	sylph	taluq
spect	sport	stash	stoit	styca	surra	sylva	talus
speed	s'pose	Stasi	stoke	styes	sushi	synch	tambo
speel	sposh	state	stola	style	sussy	synod	tamer
speer	spout	stats	stole	styli	sutra	synth	Tamil
speir	sprag	stave	stolo	stylo	Sutra	Syrah	Tamla
speld	sprat	stead	stoma	styme	swack	syrma	tammy
spele	spray	steak	stomp	suade	swage	syrop	tanga
spelk	spree	steal	stone	suant	swain	syrup	tangi
spell	spret	steam	stonk	suave	swale	sysop	tango
spelt	sprew	stean	stony	subah	swami	tabac	tangy
spend	sprig	stech	stood	subby	swamp	tabby	tania
spent	sprit	steed	stook	suber	swamy	tabes	tanka
speos	sprod	steek	stool	Subud	swang	tabid	Tanka
sperm	sprog	steel	stoop	sucky	swank	tabla	tanky
spewy	sprot	steen	stoor	sucre	Swapo	table	tanna
sphex	sprue	steep	stope	Sudan	sward	taboo	tansy
spial	spule	steer	store	Sudra	sware	tabor	tante
spica	spume	stegh	stork	sudsy	swarf	tabun	tanto
spice	spumy	stein	storm	suede	swarm	Tabun	tanya
spick	spunk	stela	story	Suess	swart	tabus	tapas
spicy	spurn	stele	stoss	suety	swash	tacan	taper
spied	spurt	stelk	stoun	Sueve	swath	tacet	tapet
spiel	sputa	stell	stoup	Sufic	Swati	tache	tapia
spier	squab	stend	stour	Sufis	swats	tacho	tap-in
spies	squad	steno	stout	sugan	Swazi	tacit	tapir
spiff	squat	stent	stove	sugar	sweal	tacky	tapis
spike	squaw	stere	Strad	suing	swear	tacos	tapit
spiky	squeg	stern	stram	suint	sweat	taddy	tappa
spile	squib	stewy	strap	suite	Swede	taele	tapul
spill	squid	Steyr	straw	suity	sweep	taffy	tap up
spilt	squit	stich	stray	sukey	sweer	Taffy	tardy
spina	squiz	stick	strep	sulci	sweet	tafia	tarfa
spine	squop	Stick	strew	sulfa	swell	Tafia	targa
spink	sqush	stied	stria	sulky	swelt	tagma	targe
spiny	srang	sties	strid	sulla	swept	tagua	taroc
spire	sruti	stife	strig	sully	swift	taiga	taros
spirt	stack	stiff	strip	sumac	swill	taiko	tarot
spiry	stade	Stift	strop	sumen	swine	Taino	tarry
spiss	stadt	Stijl	strow	sumi-e	swing	taint	tarse
spite	staff	stilb	stroy	summa	Swing	taipo	tarsi
spits	stage	stile	strum	sumph	swink	Taita	tarty

tarve	telic	thack	Thule	tipsy	tonto	toyte	trite
Taser	telly	thaft	thumb	tip-up	ton-up	trace	troat
tasse	tembe	Thais	thump	tired	tonus	track	Troic
tasso	tembo	thali	thunk	tiros	tooth	tract	troll
taste	Tembu	thana	thuya	tirve	toots	trade	tromp
tasto	Temne	thane	Thyad	Tisri	to pay	tragi	trona
tasty	Tempe	thang	thyme	tisso	topaz	traik	tronc
Tatar	tempi	thank	thymi	Titan	topee	trail	tronk
tater	tempo	tharm	thymy	titar	toper	train	troop
tatie	tempt	that's	tiang	titch	tophe	trait	trope
tatou	temse	thawy	tiara	titer	tophi	tra-la	tropo
tatty	tenas	thebe	tiare	tithe	topic	trama	troth
taula	tench	theca	Tibet	titis	topis	tramp	trout
taunt	tendo	theek	tibia	title	topoi	trank	trove
tauon	tenet	theft	tical	titre	topos	trans	truce
taupe	tenia	thegn	ticca	titty	toppy	trant	truck
tavel	tenko	theik	ticer	ti-tzu	topsy	trape	trued
Tavel	tenné	their	ticky	tizzy	top up	trapp	truer
Tavgi	tenno	theme	tidal	tjalk	toque	traps	trues
tawer	tenny	theor	tiddy	toado	Torah	tra-ra	truff
tawie	tenon	theow	tided	toady	torba	trash	trull
tawny	Tenon	there	tidge	toast	torch	trass	truly
tawse	tenor	therm	tie-in	tober	toric	tratt	trump
taxed	tenpo	these	tie-on	today	torii	trave	trunk
taxer	tense	thesp	tie to	toddy	torma	trawl	truss
taxes	tenth	theta	tie-up	todea	torni	tread	trust
taxis	tenty	thete	tiffy	to-dos	torry	treat	truth
taxol	tepal	thewy	tifle	toe-in	torse	treed	try in
taxon	tepee	they'd	tiger	toffy	torsk	treen	tryma
taxor	tepid	thick	tiggy	to-fro	torso	trees	try me
tayra	terai	thief	tight	toga'd	torte	treet	try-on
tazza	terap	thigh	tigon	toged	torus	treey	tryst
T-bone	terce	thilk	Tigre	toggy	torve	trefa	tsama
tbsps	Terek	thill	Tigua	toghe	to see	treff	tsine
T-cell	teres	thine	tikka	togue	toshy	trend	Tsing
tchin	tereu	thing	tilak	toich	tosyl	tress	T-stop
teach	terga	Thing	tilde	toile	total	trest	tsung
teaed	terna	think	tiled	toils	totem	tretc	tuart
teals	terne	thiol	tiler	toise	toter	trews	tubae
teart	terra	third	tilly	tokay	totsy	treys	tubal
teary	terry	thirl	tilma	Tokay	totty	triac	tubas
tease	terse	thoft	tilth	token	totum	triad	tubby
teasy	tesla	thole	timar	tokus	touch	trial	tubed
Tebet	TESOL	tholi	timbo	Tolai	tough	trian	tuber
techy	TESSA	thong	timer	to let	tourn	trias	tucum
Tecla	testa	thorn	times	tolyl	touse	tribe	Tudeh
teddy	testy	thorp	timid	toman	tousy	trice	Tudor
teend	tetch	those	Timon	tombo	towai	trich	tufty
teens	tetel	thous	timor	tommy	towan	trick	tuggy
teeny	Teton	thraw	Timor	Tommy	towel	tried	tuile
teeth	tetra	three	timps	tonal	to wed	trier	tuism
teety	tetty	threw	tinct	tondi	towel	tries	tukul
tee up	tetur	thrid	tinea	tondo	tower	trifa	tulip
te-hee	tevel	thrin	tined	toned	to wit	trike	tulle
Tê-hua	Tevet	thrip	tinge	tonel	towny	trill	tulsi
Teian	tewel	throb	tinny	toner	towse	trine	tuman
teind	tewit	throe	tinto	toney	towsy	Trini	tumbu
tekke	te-wit	throw	tinty	tonga	towzy	trink	tumid
Tekke	tewly	thrum	tip-in	Tonga	toxic	triol	tummy
telco	Texan	thuck	tip-it	tongs	toxin	trios	tumor
telex	Texas	thuja	tiple	tonic	toyer	tripe	tumpy
telia	Texel	thula	tippy	tonne	toyon	trist	tunal

tunas	typer	undig	upcut	vacat	venue	viva'd	wahey
tuner	typey	undub	up-dip	vaccy	Venus	vivas	wahoo
tuney	typha	undue	updry	vacky	Verel	vivat	waily
tunic	typic	undug	upend	vacua	verge	vivax	waist
tunku	typos	unfed	up-end	vagal	Verné	viver	waive
tunny	tyred	unfit	up for	vague	verse	vives	waked
tupan	Tyson	unfix	uplay	vagus	verso	vivid	waken
tupik	Ubaid	ungag	upled	vairy	verst	vixen	waker
Tupis	U-bend	ungay	upped	vakky	vertu	vizor	wakon
tuque	ubity	unget	upper	valet	verve	VJ day	waldo
turba	U-boat	ungod	uppie	valid	Vesak	Vlach	waler
turbo	Ubykh	ungot	upset	valor	Vespa	V-moth	Waler
turca	UCATT	ungum	upter	valse	vesta	V-neck	walia
turco	Uchee	unhad	uptie	value	vetch	vocab	walla
Turco	udder	unhat	up top	valva	veuve	vocal	wally
turfs	Ugric	unhid	uraei	valve	vexed	vodka	walty
turfy	uh-huh	unhip	urali	vampy	vexer	vodun	waltz
Turki	uhlan	unhit	urari	vanda	viand	vogie	wamus
turps	Uhuru	unify	urate	vaned	vibes	vogue	wanax
tusky	Uigur	union	urban	vapid	vibex	Vogul	wandy
tutee	UKAEA	unite	urbic	vapor	vicar	voice	waned
tutor	ukase	unity	urdee	vappa	Vicat	voile	waney
Tutsi	ukeke	unjam	ureal	vardo	Vichy	volar	wanga
tutti	ukemi	unkey	uredo	vardy	vicus	volet	wanky
tutty	ulcer	unkid	urent	varec	video	volta	wanle
twain	ulema	unkie	ure-ox	vario	viewy	volte	Wan-Li
Twana	ulmic	unlap	urger	varix	vigia	volva	wanly
twang	ulmin	unlaw	urial	varna	vigil	volve	wanna
twank	ulnae	unlay	uriei	varus	vigor	vomer	wanst
tweak	ulnar	unled	urine	varve	villa	vomit	wanta
tweed	ulnas	unlet	urisk	vasal	ville	votal	wanty
tweek	ultra	unlid	urnal	vased	villi	voter	wanze
tweel	ululu	unlit	urned	vasty	vinal	Votic	Warao
Tween	umbel	unman	Urnes	Vater	vinca	vouch	Waraw
tweer	umber	unmet	ursal	vates	Vinča	vowed	warby
tweet	umbos	unmix	ursid	vatic	vinea	vowel	waree
twerp	umbra	unpeg	urson	vatje	viner	vower	warth
twice	umbre	unpen	urubu	vaude	vinew	vozhd	warty
twick	umiak	unpin	urucu	vault	vinic	vraic	Washo
twill	umpty	unput	usage	vaunt	vinny	vroom	washy
twine	Unami	unray	usen't	V belt	vinyl	vrouw	wasn't
twing	Unani	unrig	use up	vealy	viola	V-sign	waspy
twink	unapt	unrip	Ushak	vease	viper	vuggy	WASPy
twiny	unarm	unsaw	usher	VE day	viral	vulgo	waste
twire	unary	unsay	usine	Vedda	vireo	vulva	wasty
twirk	unbag	unsee	us lot	Vedic	virga	vurry	watap
twirl	unban	unset	usnea	vedro	Virgo	vygie	watch
twirp	unbar	unsew	usnic	veena	virid	vying	water
twist	unbed	unsex	usnin	veery	virtu	wacke	waugh
twite	unbid	unshy	ustad	vegan	virus	wacko	waulk
twoer	unbit	unsin	usual	vegie	visa'd	wacky	waved
two-up	unbox	unson	usurp	Vehme	visas	waddy	wavel
twyer	uncap	untie	usury	veiny	visit	wader	waver
tyger	uncia	until	uteri	velar	visna	wadge	Waves
tyhee	uncle	unuse	utile	veldt	visne	wadis	wavey
tying	uncos	unweb	utrum	velic	vison	wafer	waxed
tyled	uncus	unwed	utter	velly	visor	wafty	waxen
tyler	uncut	unwet	U-turn	velum	vista	waged	waxer
typal	undam	unwig	uvala	venal	vital	wagel	way in
type A	undee	unwon	uveal	Venda	vitex	wager	way-up
type B	under	unzip	uvula	venge	vitry	Wagga	wazir
typed	undid	upbow	Uzbek	venom	vitta	wagon	Wazir

weaky	wheal	widdy	wodge	wrest	yahoo	yojan	Z-axis
weald	wheat	widen	wodgy	wrick	yajna	yoked	zazzy
Weald	wheek	widow	woe to	wride	yakka	yokel	Z-bend
we-all	wheel	width	woken	wrier	Yakut	yoker	zebec
weany	wheen	wield	Wolff	wrily	Yalie	yokes	zebra
weary	wheep	wifey	wolfy	wring	yandy	yolky	zendo
weave	wheft	wifie	wolly	wrist	yaply	Yomud	Zener
webby	whelk	Wigan	Wolof	write	yapok	yonks	zero G
weber	whelm	wiggy	wolve	wroke	yapon	you'll	zeros
Weber	whelp	wight	woman	wrong	yappy	young	zeste
wedge	where	wilco	womby	wrote	Yaqui	you're	zesty
wedgy	whewl	wildy	women	wroth	yarak	yourn	zibet
weeds	which	wilga	womyn	wrung	yauld	yours	zibib
weedy	whiff	willi	wonga	wryer	yawny	yourt	Ziehl
weeny	whift	willy	wongi	wryly	Y-axis	youse	zilch
weepy	while	Wilms	wonky	wumph	yayla	youth	Zimba
weese	whimp	wimpy	wonts	wurra	Yayoi	you've	zinco
weest	whine	Wimpy	woody	wurst	yclad	yowie	zineb
weeze	whing	wince	wooed	Wurtz	yealm	yowza	Zingg
wefty	whiny	winch	wooer	wussy	yearn	yo-yos	zingo
weigh	whirl	windy	woofy	wuzzy	yeast	ypent	zingy
weird	whirr	wined	woold	Wyatt	yechy	yrast	Zippo
weism	whish	winer	wooly	X-acto	yedda	ytter	zippy
welch	whisk	winey	woopy	X-axis	yeddo	yucca	zip-up
Welch	whisp	wingy	woosh	xebec	Yeddo	Yuchi	ziram
welly	whiss	winky	wootz	xenia	yeeow	yucky	zizel
welsh	whist	winny	woozy	xenic	Yekke	yukky	zizzy
Welsh	white	winos	wordy	xenon	yelek	Yukon	Z line
wench	White	winze	worky	Xeres	Yenan	yulan	zloty
wenge	whity	wiped	world	xeric	yenta	yuloh	zocle
wen li	whizz	wiper	wormy	Xerox	yentz	Yuman	zoeal
wenny	whole	wired	worry	Xhosa	yerba	yummy	Zohar
wersh	whomp	wirer	worse	xoana	yerra	Yunca	zoite
Wesak	whoof	wirey	worst	xylan	yerse	Yupik	zonal
westy	whoom	wirra	worth	xylem	yes-no	yuppy	zonda
wetly	whoop	wiser	wough	xylol	yesty	Yurak	zoned
wevet	whore	wisha	would	xylyl	yeuch	Yurok	zoner
whack	whorl	wisht	wound	xysma	yewen	Yuruk	zonky
whale	whort	wispy	woven	xysti	yield	yusho	zooid
whame	whory	witan	wowee	yabba	yikes	zabra	zooks
whang	whose	witch	wrack	yabby	yipes	Zahal	zoomy
whare	whoso	withe	wramp	ya boo	yoaks	zaire	zooty
wharf	whuff	withy	wrang	yaboo	yobbo	zakat	zoris
wharl	whump	witty	wrapt	yacca	yobby	zaman	zorro
whata	whush	wives	wrath	yacht	yodel	zambo	zowie
what'n	why so	Wiyot	wrawl	yacka	yogic	zamia	Z-plan
whaup	Wicca	wizen	wreak	yager	yogin	Zande	zygal
wheak	Widal	wizzo	wreck	yagna	yogis	zappy	zymin

SIX LETTERS

abacus	accrue	Adonai	agaric	alanna	all-red	amtrac	anonym
abanet	accuse	Adonic	agedly	alarum	all set	amtrak	anorak
abaser	acedia	Adonis	age gap	Alaska	all the	amulet	anoxia
abater	acetal	adoral	ageing	alated	allude	amusee	anoxic
abatis	acetic	adorer	ageism	albata	allure	amuser	answer
abator	acetyl	adream	ageist	albedo	all wet	Amytal	anthem
abbacy	achate	adrift	agency	albeit	Almain	anabas	anther
abbate	achene	adroit	agenda	albert	Almayn	anadem	antler
abbess	achkan	adsorb	age-old	albino	almery	anally	antlia
abbeys	Acholi	adsuki	aghast	Albion	almond	analog	antral
abduce	acidic	advect	aglare	albite	almost	ananas	antrum
abduct	acidly	advene	agleam	albugo	alnage	anarch	anuran
abeigh	acinar	advent	aglyph	alcade	alpaca	anatta	anuria
abelia	acinus	Advent	agnail	alcaic	alpeen	anatto	anuric
abided	ack-ack	adverb	agnate	alcove	alphin	anbury	any day
abider	ackers	advert	agnise	Aldine	alpine	anchor	anyhow
a bit of	acmite	advice	agnize	aldose	Alpine	Ancona	anyone
abject	acquit	advise	agogic	aldrin	alsike	and all	any way
abjure	acrawl	adviso	agonal	alegar	Altaic	Andean	anyway
Abkhaz	acrook	advoke	agones	alerce	altern	and how	Aonian
ablate	across	adytum	agonic	A level	aludel	Andrew	aorist
ablaut	act for	adzuki	agorot	alevin	alumna	aneath	aortal
ablaze	acting	aecial	agouti	alexia	alumni	anemia	aortas
ablest	action	aecium	agreed	alexic	alvine	anemic	aortic
ablins	active	aedile	agreer	alexin	always	anergy	aoudad
ablism	actory	Aegean	agrees	Alfvén	alwise	angary	Apache
abloom	act out	Aeolic	agrimi	algate	amadou	angely	apathy
ablush	actual	aeonic	aguila	Al-Hadj	amatol	angili	apeman
ablute	acuate	aerate	aguish	alhagi	amazed	angina	apemen
Abnaki	acuity	aerial	ahimsa	alhaji	Amazon	angled	aperçu
aboard	acumen	aerobe	a-horse	Al-Hajj	ambari	angler	A per se
aboral	acuter	aerugo	aidant	alibis	ambash	Anglic	apexes
aborti	adagio	aether	aidful	alible	ambler	Anglos	apheta
abound	Adamic	affair	aiglet	aliene	ambury	angola	aphony
abrade	adance	affect	aikido	alight	ambush	angora	aphtha
abrase	adatom	affeer	ailing	alisma	amebic	anicut	apiary
abroad	addend	affine	aimful	alkali	amends	anilic	apical
abrook	addict	affirm	air bag	alkane	amenta	animal	apices
abrupt	addled	afflux	air-bed	alkene	aments	animus	apiece
abseil	adduce	afford	Airbus	alkies	amerce	anisic	aplite
absent	adduct	affray	air-dry	alkine	amical	anisyl	aplomb
absorb	Adélie	affuse	airgun	alkyne	amidic	anklet	apnoea
absurd	adhere	Afghan	airier	all but	amidst	anlace	apodal
abulia	adhort	afield	airily	all-day	amigos	anlage	apodan
abuser	adieus	aflame	airing	allege	ammine	anlaut	apogee
abzyme	adieux	aflare	airish	allele	amnion	annals	apolar
acacia	adipic	afloat	airman	allene	amnios	annate	aporia
acajou	adject	afocal	airmen	allers	amoeba	anneal	appale
acarid	adjoin	afraid	air sac	alleys	amomum	annexe	appeal
acarus	adjure	A-frame	airway	all for	amoral	annual	appear
accede	adjust	afreet	aisled	allice	amount	annuli	append
accent	adless	afresh	aixies	allied	ampere	anodal	apples
accept	admass	afront	akasha	allies	ampler	anodic	applot
access	admire	afters	ake-ake	allium	ampule	anoint	apport
accloy	adnate	Agadic	aketon	all one	amrita	anomer	appose
accord	adnexa	agamic	akimbo	all out	amster	anomic	apsara
accost	adoing	agamid	alalia	all-pro	amtman	anomie	aquake

Aquila	arolla	aspect	athrob	auntly	Azeris	bajada	bare of
aquose	aromal	aspire	at last	au pair	azo dye	bakery	barfam
Arabic	around	asport	atlatl	aurata	azolla	baking	barfly
arabis	arouse	asquat	at most	aurate	azonal	Balaam	bargee
arable	aroynt	assail	at need	aureus	azonic	balata	barish
Arahat	arpent	assart	at odds	aurify	azygos	balboa	barite
aralia	arrack	asself	atomic	Auriga	babaco	baldie	barium
Aranda	arrand	assent	atonal	aurist	babble	baldly	barken
Aranta	arrant	assert	at once	aurora	babied	baleen	barker
Arawak	arrear	assess	atoner	aurous	babies	Balkan	barkey
arbour	arrect	assify	atonic	Aussie	babify	balk of	barkle
arbute	arrent	assign	atopic	Auster	babish	ballad	barkum
arcade	arrest	assish	at outs	Austin	Babism	ballan	barley
Arcady	arride	assist	at play	auteur	Babist	baller	barlow
arcana	arrive	assize	at rest	author	Babite	ballet	barman
arcane	arroba	assoil	atrial	autism	babool	ballot	barmen
archei	arrowy	assort	at risk	autumn	baboon	ballsy	barnet
archer	arroyo	as such	atrium	avania	babyfy	Balmer	barney
Arches	arshin	assume	Atsina	avatar	baccer	Baloch	Barnum
Archie	arsine	assure	at stud	avaunt	backed	balsam	Baroco
archil	artery	astare	at suck	avener	backen	balter	Barolo
archly	artful	astart	attach	avenge	backer	Baltic	barony
archon	artify	asteer	attack	avenue	backet	bamboo	barque
arcing	artist	astern	attain	averse	back of	banana	barras
Arctic	Arunta	as that	atteal	Avesta	back up	banate	barred
arcual	as a man	asthma	attend	aviary	backup	bandar	barrel
ardent	Asante	astony	attent	aviate	Backus	bander	barren
ardour	ascend	astoop	attery	avidin	badass	bandit	barret
areola	ascent	astral	attest	avidly	badder	bandog	barrio
areole	aseity	astray	at that	avocet	baddie	banger	barrow
argali	as from	astrut	attire	avouch	bad egg	banghy	Barsac
Argand	as good	astute	at tops	avowal	badger	bangle	barter
argent	a shade	aswarm	attorn	avower	bad hat	bang on	barton
Argive	ashake	asweat	attrit	avowry	badian	bang-up	bar two
argosy	ashame	as well	attune	avoyer	Badian	banian	baryon
argued	A sharp	aswing	atwain	avulse	bad job	banish	baryta
arguer	ash-bin	aswirl	atweel	awaken	bad law	banjax	baryte
argues	ashcan	aswoon	atween	awaker	bad lot	banjos	basalt
argufy	as hell	asylum	at will	aweary	badman	banker	basely
argute	ashery	atabal	atwist	aweigh	baetyl	banket	bashaw
argyle	ashine	at a jar	atwixt	awheel	baffle	bank on	basher
aridly	ash-key	ataman	at work	awheto	bagful	bannat	basket
aright	ashlar	ataunt	atypia	awhile	bagged	banned	basnet
ariose	ashore	atavic	aubade	awhirl	bagger	banner	Basque
arioso	ashpan	ataxia	auburn	awmous	baggit	bantam	basset
arisen	ash-pit	ataxic	aucuba	awning	bag job	banter	bassus
arista	ashram	at best	audile	awoken	bagman	Bantus	basten
aristo	Ashura	at call	audion	awrong	bagmen	banyan	baster
arkite	asilid	at cost	au fait	axeman	bag-net	banzai	baston
arkose	asilus	at ease	au fond	axemen	bagnio	baobab	basuco
armada	as it is	a tempo	Augean	axenic	bag-wig	barbal	Basuto
armful	askant	at foot	augend	axiate	bahada	barbed	batata
armies	askari	at full	augite	axilla	Baha'is	barbel	batboy
arming	asking	at gaze	augury	axonal	Bahasa	barber	batchy
armlet	ask out	at hack	august	axonic	Bahutu	barbet	bateau
armory	a skull	athame	August	axopod	bailee	barbie	bather
armour	aslant	at hand	auklet	axtree	bailer	Barcoo	bathos
armpit	asleep	at heel	aumail	axunge	bailey	bardee	bating
armure	aslope	Athoan	aumbry	aye aye	bailie	bardic	batman
Arnaut	as many	at home	auncel	Aymara	bailor	bareca	batmen
arnica	asmoke	athort	aunter	azalea	Bairam	barège	batoon
aroint	as much	at host	auntie	Azande	baiter	barely	battel

batten	bedaub	behoof	berlin	biceps	birder	blowen	boiled
batter	bedaze	behove	Berlin	bicker	birdie	blower	boiler
battle	bedbug	behung	bertha	bidden	bireme	blow in	boil-up
battue	bedded	beigel	Bertha	bidder	birkie	blow on	bolden
bauble	bedder	bejant	besang	bide by	birley	blowse	boldly
bauera	bedeck	bekiss	beseem	bident	birsle	blowth	bolero
baulky	bedell	beknow	beseen	biding	bisect	blow up	bolide
bauson	bedene	belate	beside	bieldy	bishop	blowze	bollen
bawbee	bed-hop	belaud	besing	Bielid	bisket	blowzy	bollix
bawdry	bedlam	beldam	besmut	biface	bisque	bludge	bollux
bawler	bedlar	belfry	besnow	biffin	bister	bluely	Bolshy
bawley	bedpan	Belgae	besoil	bifold	bistre	bluest	bolson
bawson	bedral	Belgic	bespot	biform	bistro	bluesy	boltel
baxter	bedrid	Belgie	bestar	bigamy	bitchy	blueys	bolter
bayard	bedrop	Belial	bested	Big Ben	biting	bluggy	bolt on
bayman	bedsit	belief	bester	big bud	bitmap	bluing	bombax
bay rum	Beduin	belier	bestir	big bug	bitten	bluish	bombed
bazaar	bedull	belike	bestow	big cat	bitter	bluism	bomber
bazoom	bedust	belive	bestud	big end	biuret	blunge	bombyx
bazuco	beebee	belled	besung	biggen	bivium	blurry	bon-bon
beachy	beechy	bellow	be sure	bigger	blacky	blusht	bonded
beacon	beefer	bellum	betake	biggie	bladed	blushy	bonder
beaded	bee-fly	be long	bethel	biggin	blague	B-movie	bonduc
beadle	beef up	belong	betide	big gun	blakey	boatel	boneen
beagle	bee-gum	belord	bêtise	big lie	blamed	boater	boneta
beaked	bee man	belote	betony	big pot	blamer	boatie	bone up
beaker	been-to	belove	betook	big toe	blanch	bobbed	bongos
be a man	beeper	belted	betrap	big top	blanco	bobber	bonham
beamed	beer-up	belter	betray	bigwig	blanky	bobbin	bonier
beamer	beesty	belt up	betrim	Bihari	blasty	bobble	bonify
beanie	beetle	beluga	betted	bikini	blatta	bobbly	boning
beanos	beeves	be made	better	bilbos	blazed	bobcat	bonism
be a pup	beezer	bemata	bettor	bilker	blazer	bob-fly	bonist
beardy	befall	bemaul	beurré	billed	blazon	bob for	bonito
bearer	befell	bemean	bevies	billet	bleach	boblet	bon mot
bear on	befile	bemire	bewail	billie	bleaky	bob-wig	bonnet
bear up	befoam	bemist	beware	billon	bleary	bocage	bonnie
beaten	befool	bemoan	beweep	billow	blebby	bodach	bonobo
beater	before	bemock	bewest	billy-o	blench	bodega	bonsai
beat in	befoul	bemoil	Bewick	bimbos	blende	bodger	bonxie
beat it	befrog	bemuse	be with	bimeby	blenny	bodgie	bonzer
beat-up	beggar	bender	bewrap	binant	blerry	bodice	boo-boo
Beaumé	begged	Bengal	bewray	binary	blight	bodied	booboo
Beaune	begift	benign	beylik	binate	blimey	bodies	boodie
beauty	begild	bennet	beyond	bin-bag	blinis	bodily	boodle
beaver	begird	benumb	bezant	binder	blirry	boding	boogie
Beaver	begirt	benzil	bezoar	bindle	blirty	bodkin	boohai
be away	begnaw	benzin	bezzle	bind up	blithe	Bodley	boohoo
becall	beg off	benzol	bhajis	bin-end	blivit	Bodoni	boojum
becalm	be gone	benzyl	bharal	bingee	blobby	boffin	booker
became	begone	be on at	bhisti	binghi	blocky	Bofors	bookie
becard	be good	be on to	bhoosa	bingle	blodge	bogeys	book in
becket	begunk	bepelt	Bhotia	biniou	blonde	bog fir	booksy
beckon	behalf	bepity	Bhutia	binman	bloody	bogged	book up
beclad	behang	bepuff	biased	binmen	blooey	boggle	boomer
beclip	Behari	be pulp	bibbed	binned	bloomy	bogies	booted
beclog	behave	berate	bibber	biogas	blooth	bog oak	bootee
become	behead	Berber	bibble	bionic	blotch	bog off	Boötes
becurl	beheld	bereft	bibira	biopic	blotto	bogong	boozed
bedaff	behest	Bergan	biblic	biopsy	blotty	bog ore	boozer
bedark	behind	Bergen	biblus	biotic	blouse	Bohora	bo-peep
bedash	behold	berime	bicarb	biotin	blowed	bohunk	bopped

bopper	bow out	bridge	budget	burden	buttie	caddie	camois
borage	bow-saw	bridle	budgie	bureau	butt in	caddis	camper
borane	bowsaw	briery	budlet	burgee	buttle	caddle	cample
borate	bowser	brieve	buffed	burger	button	caddow	campoo
bordar	bow tie	bright	buffel	burgle	butyne	cadent	campus
bordel	bow-wow	brigue	buffer	burgoo	buying	cadger	Canaan
border	bowyer	brimmy	buffet	burgul	buy off	caecal	Canada
boreal	boxcar	briony	buffle	burhel	buyout	caecum	canapé
borean	boxful	brisky	buffos	burial	buy out	Caelum	canard
Boreas	box-gum	britch	bugged	Buriat	buyout	Caesar	canary
boreen	boxier	Briton	bugger	buried	buzzer	cafard	canaut
boride	boxing	broach	bugler	burier	by-blow	caffle	cancan
boring	box pew	broché	buglet	buries	bye-bye	Caffre	cancel
borish	boyish	brogan	bugong	burlap	bye-law	cafila	cancer
borrel	boyism	brogue	bukshi	burler	by fits	caftan	candid
borrow	bracer	broken	bulbar	burley	by-form	cagier	candle
borsch	bracky	broker	bulbed	Burley	bygone	cagily	canful
borzoi	brahma	brolga	bulbil	Burman	by half	cagmag	cangia
bosbok	Brahma	brolly	bulbul	burned	by hand	cahoot	cangue
bosher	Brahmi	bromic	bulgar	burner	by Jove	cahoun	canine
bosker	Brahmo	bronco	Bulgar	burnet	by land	caiman	caning
bosket	Brahui	bronze	bulgur	burn in	by-lane	caique	canker
bosomy	brainy	bronzy	bulked	burn up	byline	cajang	canned
bosset	braird	brooch	bulker	bur oak	by much	cajole	cannel
Boston	braise	broody	bulkin	burpee	by name	calalu	canner
botany	branch	broomy	bulk up	burras	byname	calash	cannon
Botany	brandy	broose	buller	burros	bypass	calcar	cannot
botchy	branks	brothy	bullet	burrow	bypast	calces	canoed
botfly	branle	brough	bullsh	bursae	bypath	calcic	canoes
bother	branny	browed	bumbag	bursal	byplay	calean	canola
bothie	brashy	browis	bum-bee	bursar	by post	calice	canopy
botony	brassy	browny	bumble	bursas	byrlaw	calico	Cantab
bo tree	bratty	browse	bumboy	burton	byrnie	caliph	cantal
bottle	braver	browst	bumkin	Buryat	by road	calker	Cantal
bottom	bravos	browsy	bummed	busbar	byroad	calkin	cantar
boucan	brawly	brucia	bummel	busboy	by-room	callee	canter
bouclé	brawny	bruise	bummer	bushed	by rote	caller	canthi
boudin	brayer	brumal	bumper	bushel	by rule	callet	cantle
bouget	brazen	brumby	bump up	busher	byssal	call in	cantly
bought	brazil	Brummy	bum rap	bushie	byssus	call on	canton
bougie	Brazil	brunch	bunchy	bushwa	by tale	calloo	cantor
boules	breach	brunet	buncos	busier	by-talk	callop	cantos
boulle	breast	brushy	bunder	busily	by-time	callow	Canuck
bounce	breath	brutal	bundle	busker	by-walk	call up	canvas
bouncy	breech	Brutus	bundly	buskin	by wire	callus	canyon
bounty	breedy	bryony	bungee	busman	byword	calmer	canzon
bourne	breeks	bubble	bung-ho	busmen	by-work	calmly	capful
bourse	breeze	bubbly	bungle	bussed	byzant	calory	capias
bouton	breezy	buboes	bunion	busses	cabala	calpac	capite
bovate	bregma	buccal	bunker	busted	Cabala	calque	Caplet
bovine	Brehon	buccan	bunkie	bustee	cabana	caltha	caplin
Bovril	Breton	buccra	bunkum	buster	cabane	calved	capote
bovver	brevet	bucked	bunk-up	bustle	cabbie	calver	capped
bow-arm	brevit	bucker	Bunsen	bust up	cabler	calves	capper
bowery	brewer	bucket	buntal	busway	cablet	camail	capric
bowfin	brewis	buckie	bunter	but and	cabman	camber	caprid
bowing	brew up	buckle	Bunter	butane	cabmen	cambia	Capris
bowler	Briard	buckra	bunton	butene	cacaos	cameos	capryl
bowman	bribee	budded	bunyip	but for	cachet	camera	capsid
bowmen	briber	Buddha	buppie	butler	cachou	camion	captor
bow-net	bricky	buddle	burble	but one	cackle	camise	carafe
bow oar	bridal	budger	burbot	butter	cactus	camlet	carama

carapa	cassab	celled	chappy	chicly	chosen	citrus	cloqué
carbon	cassia	cellos	charas	chided	chough	cityfy	closed
carboy	cassie	Celtic	charge	chider	chouse	civics	closen
cardan	cassis	cembra	chargé	chield	chowry	civism	closer
carder	caster	cement	charka	chigoe	chowse	claggy	closet
cardia	castle	ceneme	Charon	chi-ike	chrism	clammy	clothe
cardie	cast on	censer	charro	chikan	Christ	clamor	cloths
careen	castor	censor	charry	childe	chroma	clanny	clotty
career	cast up	census	charta	Childe	chrome	claque	cloudy
care of	casual	cental	chaser	chiles	chromo	claret	clough
caress	catalo	center	Chasid	chilli	chubby	clarty	cloven
carfax	catchy	centos	chasmy	chilly	chucky	classy	clover
carfox	catena	centra	chasse	chimer	chuddy	clatch	Clovis
carful	catery	centre	chassé	chinar	chuffy	clause	clubby
cargos	catgut	centum	chaste	chinch	chukar	clavel	clucky
carhop	Cathar	cerate	chatty	Chinee	chukka	claver	clue in
Carian	Cathay	cercal	chat up	chinky	chumar	clavis	cluing
caribe	cat-ice	cercus	chauki	Chinky	chummy	clavus	clumps
caries	cation	cereal	chaung	chinny	chum up	clawed	clumpy
carina	catkin	cereus	chaunt	chinos	chunam	clawer	clumse
caring	cat-lap	ceriph	chavel	chinse	chunky	clayen	clumsy
Carley	catnap	cerise	chawer	chintz	church	clayey	clunch
carman	catnip	cerite	chaw up	chin up	churel	cleach	clunky
carnac	catsup	cerium	chazan	chip in	chutty	cleave	clutch
carnal	catted	cermet	Chazar	chippy	chylde	cledge	clypei
carnet	cattle	ceroon	cheapo	chiral	chypre	cledgy	coachy
carney	Cauchy	cerous	checky	chi-rho	cicada	cleeve	coaita
Carnic	caucus	certes	cheder	chirpy	cicala	clench	coaler
carnie	caudal	certie	cheeky	chisel	cicely	cleome	coarse
Carnot	caudex	cerule	cheepy	chital	cicuta	clergy	coated
caroon	caudle	ceruse	cheero	chitin	cidery	cleric	coatee
carpal	caught	cervid	cheers	chiton	cierge	clerid	coatis
carpel	caules	cervix	cheery	chitty	cigala	cletch	coaxer
carper	caulis	Cesare	cheese	chiule	cigary	cleuch	cobalt
carpet	Caurus	cesium	cheesy	chivvy	cilery	clever	cobber
carpus	causal	cesser	chelae	choana	cilice	clevis	cobble
carrel	causer	cestus	chelas	choate	cilium	cliche	cobbly
carrom	causey	cetane	chemic	chocho	cimbia	cliché	cobbra
carrot	cautel	Ceylon	chemmy	chocka	cinder	clicky	cobnut
carsey	cauter	cha-cha	chenar	choice	cinema	client	Coburg
cartel	cavass	chacma	cheque	choise	cingle	cliffy	cobweb
carter	caveat	chadar	chequy	choker	cinque	clifty	coccal
cartle	cave in	Chadic	cherry	chokey	cipher	climax	coccid
carton	cavern	chador	cherty	chokos	cippus	clinal	coccus
carval	caviar	chaeta	cherub	chokra	circar	clinch	coccyx
carvel	cavies	chafer	chesil	choler	circle	clingy	Cochin
carven	caving	chaffy	chesty	cholic	circus	clinic	cockal
carver	cavity	chagal	chetty	cholis	cirque	clinty	cocker
Carver	cavort	chagan	chevet	cholla	cirrus	clip-on	Cocker
carzey	cayman	Chagga	chevin	chomer	cisoid	clippy	cocket
casbah	Cayuga	chaise	chevra	choola	cistus	clique	cockle
casein	Cayuse	chakra	chèvre	choose	citess	clitch	cockly
casern	ceboid	chalan	chewer	choosy	cither	clitic	cocksy
cashel	cecity	chalet	chew on	chopin	citied	clivia	cock up
cashew	cedarn	chalky	chiack	choppy	cities	cloaca	cocoas
cash in	cedent	chalon	chiaus	chop up	citify	cloche	cocoon
cash up	cedrat	chamar	chibol	choral	citole	cloddy	codded
casing	Ceefax	chance	chic-er	chorda	citral	cloggy	codder
casino	Cefaut	chancy	chicha	chorea	citric	clonal	coddle
casket	celery	change	chichi	choree	citril	clonic	codger
Caslon	celiac	chanty	chi-chi	choric	citrin	clonus	codify
casque	cellar	chapel	chicle	chorus	citron	cloose	codlin

cod war	comfit	coolie	corves	cowman	creeve	cruxes	cupule
coelom	Comice	cool it	corvid	cowmen	creish	cry aim	curacy
coerce	coming	coolly	Corvus	co-work	cremor	crying	curare
coeval	comity	coolth	corymb	cow-pad	crenel	cry off	curate
coffee	commie	cooper	coryza	cow-pat	creole	crypta	curbed
coffer	Commie	cooter	cosher	cowpea	Creole	crypto	curber
coffin	commis	cootie	cosier	cow pen	crêpey	C sharp	curded
coffle	commit	copalm	cosily	cowpox	crêpon	C sol fa	curdle
cogent	commix	copeck	cosine	cowrie	cresol	cuatro	curdly
cogged	common	copied	cosmea	cow-run	cresyl	cubage	cure of
cogger	commot	copier	cosmic	cowson	Cretan	cubbed	curfew
coggie	comose	copies	cosmos	coydog	cretic	cubica	curial
coggle	comous	coping	cosset	coyest	cretin	cubism	Curial
coggly	compel	copita	cossid	coyish	crewel	cubist	curing
cogito	comply	cop out	cossie	coynye	cribos	cuboid	curios
cognac	compos	copped	costae	coyote	crikey	cuckoo	curist
co-head	Comsat	copper	costal	coypus	crimes	cucujo	curium
coheir	concha	copple	co-star	cozzie	crimpy	cudden	curled
cohere	conche	copter	costed	crabby	crinal	cuddie	curler
cohorn	conchs	Coptic	coster	cracky	crined	cuddle	curlew
cohort	conchy	copula	costly	cradle	crinet	cuddly	curl up
cohosh	concur	coquet	costus	crafty	cringe	cudgel	curple
cohune	condom	corban	coteau	craggy	cripes	cue-bid	cursed
coiffé	condor	corbel	cotext	crakow	crises	cueing	curser
coiled	condos	corbie	cotise	crambo	crisis	cueist	cursor
coiner	coneys	corbin	cotman	cram in	crispy	cue-owl	cursus
coin-op	confab	cordax	cotset	crampy	crista	cuesta	curtal
coital	confer	corded	cottar	crance	critic	cuffed	curtly
coitus	confix	corder	cotted	cranch	croaky	Cuffee	curtsy
coldly	conga'd	cordia	cotter	crania	croche	cuffer	curule
coleta	congas	cordon	cottid	cranky	crocin	cuffin	curved
coleus	congee	coreal	cotton	cranny	crocus	cuisse	curvet
coleys	conger	corgis	cotwal	crants	croove	cuiter	cuscus
collar	congou	corial	coucal	crappy	croppy	cuivré	cushat
collet	conies	corium	couché	crases	crop up	culbut	cushaw
collie	coning	corked	couchy	crasis	crosse	Culdee	cusped
collop	conium	corker	cougar	cratch	crotal	culler	cuspid
collow	conjee	corkir	coulée	crater	crotch	cullet	cuspis
Colmar	conker	cornea	coulie	craton	crotey	cullis	cussed
colony	conman	corned	coulis	cravat	croton	culmen	custom
coloss	conmen	cornel	county	craven	Croton	cultch	custos
colour	conned	corner	coupee	craver	crouch	cultic	cutcha
colter	conner	cornet	coupla	crawly	croupy	cultus	cutely
colugo	connex	cornua	couple	crayer	crouse	culver	cutesy
column	conoid	cornus	coupon	crayon	crowdy	cumber	cut ice
colure	con-rod	corody	courge	crazed	crowed	cumbia	cutler
co-mate	consol	corona	course	crazia	cruces	cumble	cutlet
combat	consul	Corona	cousin	creagh	cruche	cumbly	cut-off
combed	contra	corozo	coutel	creaky	cruddy	cumene	cut-out
comber	conure	corpse	couter	creamy	cruise	cummer	cutted
combie	convex	corpsy	coutil	crease	cruive	cummin	cuttee
combos	convey	corpus	co-vary	creasy	crumbs	cumuli	cutter
come at	convoy	corral	covent	create	crumby	cuneal	cuttle
come by	conyza	corrie	covert	creave	crumen	cunjee	cuttoe
comedo	coobah	corsac	covess	crèche	crummy	cunjie	cyanic
comedy	cooeed	corsak	coveys	credal	crunch	cunner	cyanin
come in	cooees	corser	coving	credit	crural	cupful	cyathi
comely	cookee	corset	cowage	credos	crusie	cupola	cyborg
come of	cooker	Cortes	coward	creeky	Crusoe	cupped	cyclas
come on	cookie	cortex	cowboy	creepy	crusta	cupper	cycler
come to	cook up	corvée	cowish	creese	crusty	cupric	cyclic
come up	cooler	corver	cowled	creesh	crutch	cup-tie	cyclin

Cyclon	dammer	day-bed	deener	demure	détenu	dicken	dinner
Cyclop	dammit	daybed	deepen	denary	detest	dicker	diodon
cyclus	damned	day-boy	deepie	denest	detour	dickey	dioecy
cygnet	damner	day-fly	deeply	dengue	de trop	dickin	diosma
Cygnus	damnum	Day-Glo	deeshy	denial	Dettol	dictum	diotic
cymbal	dampen	day off	deface	denied	detune	didder	dioxan
cymene	damper	day out	defalk	denier	deuced	diddle	dioxin
cymoid	damply	day owl	defame	denies	deutan	didoes	diplex
cymose	damsel	dazzle	defang	denned	devall	didric	diploe
Cymric	damson	deacon	defeat	dennet	devast	die off	dip-net
cynism	danaid	deaden	defect	denote	devein	die out	dipody
cyphel	dancer	deadly	defend	de novo	devest	diesel	dipole
cypher	dander	dead on	defial	densen	device	diesis	dip out
cy pres	Dandie	deafen	defied	dental	devise	dieted	dipped
cypris	dandle	deafly	defier	dented	devoid	dieter	dip pen
cystic	danger	dealer	defies	dentex	devoir	dietic	dipper
cystid	dangle	deaner	defile	dentil	devote	differ	dipsas
cytase	dangly	dearie	define	denude	devour	digamy	dipsos
cytoid	Daniel	dearly	deflex	deodar	devout	digest	diquat
dabbed	Danish	dear me	deform	depark	Dewali	digger	dirdum
dabber	Danism	dearth	defray	depart	dewani	diglot	direct
dabble	Danite	deasil	deftly	depend	dewbow	dig out	direly
daboia	dankly	deathy	defuse	deperm	dew-cup	digram	dirham
da capo	Danzig	debark	dégagé	depict	dewier	digyny	dirndl
Dacian	daphne	debase	degras	deploy	dewily	diiamb	disard
dacite	dapped	debate	degree	depone	De-Witt	dik-dik	disarm
dacker	dapper	debeak	degust	deport	dewlap	dikkop	disbar
dacoit	dapple	debile	dehair	depose	deworm	diktat	disbud
Dacron	Dardan	deblur	dehorn	depure	dew-ret	dilate	discal
dactyl	Dardic	debord	dehort	depute	dexter	dildos	discos
dadder	daring	debris	de-icer	deputy	Dexter	dilogy	discus
daddle	darken	debtee	deific	derail	dhaman	dilute	disdar
daedal	darkey	debtor	deisal	derate	dhamma	dimble	disher
daemon	darkie	debunk	deixis	deride	dhania	dimity	dish up
daffle	darkle	decade	deja vu	derive	dharma	dimmed	dismal
daftie	darkly	decaff	déjà vu	dermal	dharna	dimmer	disman
daftly	darned	decamp	deject	dermic	Dharuk	dim out	dismay
dag-boy	darnel	decane	de jure	dermis	dhobey	dimple	disome
dagesh	darner	decani	dekink	derout	dhobis	dimply	disorb
dagged	daroga	decant	dekkos	derris	dholak	dimpsy	disour
dagger	darter	deceit	delate	desalt	dholuk	dim sim	disown
daggle	dartle	decent	delect	descry	dhoney	dim sum	dispel
daggly	dartos	decern	delete	deseed	dhotis	dim-wit	dissed
dagoba	dartre	Decian	Delian	desert	dhurna	dimwit	distad
dagoes	Darwin	decide	delict	design	dhurra	din-din	distal
dahlia	dashed	decile	delire	desire	dhyana	dindle	distil
daidle	dasher	decima	delish	desist	diacid	dinero	disuse
daiker	dassen	decked	delope	desize	diadem	dinful	diswig
daimio	dassie	decker	Delphi	desman	diadic	dinger	ditchy
daimon	dastur	deckie	delude	desmid	dialer	dinges	dither
daimyo	datary	deckle	deluge	desorb	dialog	dinghy	ditone
dainty	datcha	decoct	de luxe	despan	dial up	dingle	dittay
dakhma	dating	decode	delver	despin	diaper	dingly	dittos
Dakota	dation	decoke	demand	despot	diapir	dingos	Divali
dalasi	Datisi	decore	demark	despun	diarch	dingus	dive in
dalles	dative	decree	demean	des res	diatom	dining	divers
dalton	datura	decury	dement	detach	dibbed	dinkel	divert
damage	dauber	dedans	demise	detail	dibber	dinkey	divest
Damara	dauncy	deduce	demiss	detain	dibble	dinkie	divide
damask	Davies	deduct	demist	detant	dibbuk	dinkly	divine
dammar	dawdle	deejay	démodé	detect	dicast	dinkum	diving
dammed	dawing	deemer	demote	detent	dicier	dinned	Diwali

diwani	doline	dorsel	draunt	dry-ski	durant	ectype	eldern
djibba	dolium	dorser	drawee	dry way	durbar	eczema	eldest
D-layer	dollar	Dorset	drawer	duadic	duress	Eddaic	elding
doable	dollop	dorsum	draw in	dually	durgah	eddied	elegit
do a guy	dolman	dorter	drawly	dubash	Durham	eddies	elenge
do alms	dolmas	dosage	draw on	dubbed	durian	eddish	eleven
doater	dolmen	do-se-do	draw up	dubber	during	eddoes	elevon
do a ton	dolose	do-si-do	dreamt	dubbin	durned	Edenic	elfish
do away	dolour	dossal	dreamy	ducape	durrie	edge-on	elicit
dobbed	dolous	dossel	dreary	ducker	durwan	edgier	elisor
dobber	domain	dosser	dredge	duckie	durzis	edgily	elixir
dobbie	doment	dossil	dreepy	duck up	dusken	edging	El Niño
dobbin	domett	dotage	dreggy	ductor	duskly	edible	elodea
dobson	domina	dotard	dreich	ductus	dustak	Edipal	Elohim
Doccia	domine	dotate	dreigh	dudeen	duster	edited	eloign
docent	domino	do time	drench	dudess	dust-up	editor	eloper
Docete	domite	dotish	dressy	dudish	Dutchy	Edward	Elster
docile	donary	dotkin	dretch	dueful	dutied	eejity	eluant
docity	donate	dot-map	driech	duello	duties	eelery	eluate
docken	dongle	dotted	driegh	duende	duyker	Eemian	eluder
docker	donjon	dottel	driest	duenna	dwarfs	eerier	eluent
docket	donkey	dotter	drieth	duetto	dwarfy	eerily	elvish
doctor	donned	dottle	drifty	duffel	dweeby	efface	elytra
dodder	donnée	douane	drinky	duffer	dyadic	effect	embale
doddie	donner	double	drippy	duffle	dybbuk	effeir	emball
doddle	donnot	doubly	drivel	duff up	dyeing	effete	embalm
dodgem	donsie	doucet	driven	dufter	dynamo	effigy	embank
Dodgem	donzel	douche	driver	dugong	dynast	effing	embark
dodger	doocot	doucin	drogue	dugout	dynode	efflux	embind
dodkin	doodad	dought	drolly	duiker	dyvour	efform	emblem
dodman	doodah	doughy	dromic	duk-duk	eaglet	effort	emblic
dodoes	doodle	dourly	dromoi	dukely	earful	effund	embody
do down	doofer	dourra	dromos	dukery	earing	effuse	emboli
doesn't	Doolan	douser	droner	dulcet	ear-lap	efreet	emboly
doffer	doolie	douter	drongo	dulcin	earlet	EFTPOS	emboss
dogana	doomer	dovish	drooby	dumble	earner	egally	embrue
dogate	doonga	do-well	droopy	dumbly	earthy	Egeria	embrya
dog box	doored	do with	drop in	dumbos	earwax	egesta	embryo
dogdom	doovah	dowlas	drop it	dumb ox	earwig	egg-box	emceed
dog-ear	do over	downed	drop on	dumdum	ease in	eggcup	emcees
dog-end	doo-wop	downer	droppy	dum-dum	easier	eggery	em dash
dog-fly	doozer	down to	dropsy	dummel	easily	eggier	emerge
dog-fox	doozie	dowser	drop to	dumper	eassel	eggler	emerse
dogged	dopant	dowset	drossy	dump on	easter	egg-nog	emesis
dogger	dopier	doxies	drouth	dumpty	Easter	egoism	emetic
doggie	dopily	doyley	drover	dun-bar	easy on	egoist	emigre
dog-leg	Dopper	dozier	drowse	Dundee	eatage	egoity	émigré
dogleg	doppie	dozily	drowsy	dunder	eatery	egress	émigré
dogman	dorado	dozzle	drudge	dunite	eathly	eident	emodin
dogmen	dor-bee	drabby	druggy	dunker	eating	eidola	emoter
dog-nap	dor-bug	drably	drumly	Dunker	eat off	eighth	empale
do-good	Dorcas	drachm	drummy	dunlin	eat out	eighty	empery
do gree	dor-fly	draffy	drum up	Dunlop	eaving	either	empest
Dogrib	Dorian	drafty	drupel	dunned	écarté	ejecta	empire
dog tag	dories	dragée	dry-bob	dunner	echini	eke out	employ
doiled	Dorise	drag in	dry fly	dunter	echium	ektene	emptin
doited	Dorism	dragon	dry ice	duomos	echoer	elance	Empusa
do kief	Dorize	drag up	drying	dupery	echoes	elapid	em quad
dolcan	dormer	Dralon	dryish	dupion	echoey	elapse	em rule
dolent	dormie	draper	dry out	duplet	echoic	elater	emu-bob
doless	dorsad	dratch	dry rot	duplex	éclair	E-layer	emulge
dolina	dorsal		dry run	durain	ectene	elchee	enable

enamel	enough	epoché	étrier	exogen	faffle	fasola	Fenian
enamor	en quad	eponym	etymon	exoner	fag end	fasten	fenman
enarch	enrage	epopee	Euboic	exonic	fagged	faster	fennec
en bloc	enrank	epulis	euchre	exonym	fagger	fastly	fennel
encage	enrapt	equant	Euclid	exopod	faggot	fat cat	fenner
encamp	enrich	equate	eucone	exotic	fag hag	fat hen	ferash
encase	enring	equine	Eudist	expand	fagoty	father	ferfel
encash	enrobe	equity	eulogy	expect	failed	fathom	ferial
encave	enroot	eraser	eunomy	expede	failer	Fatiha	ferine
encell	en rule	erbium	eunuch	expend	faille	fatism	ferity
encode	enseal	erenow	eureka	expert	fainly	fatist	ferlie
encoop	enseam	ere yet	Euro-MP	expire	faints	fatted	Fermat
encore	enserf	Erinys	Europe	expiry	fainty	fatten	fermis
encyst	ensete	erlang	eutaxy	expone	fairly	fatter	ferrel
end-all	ensign	ermine	evader	export	fajita	faucal	Ferrel
en dash	ensile	Erotes	evanid	expose	fakery	fauces	ferret
endear	ensoul	erotic	eve-jar	exposé	falces	faucet	ferric
ending	ensued	errand	even as	ex post	falcon	faulty	ferula
endite	ensuer	errant	evener	exsect	fal-lal	faunal	ferule
endive	ensues	errata	evenly	exsert	fallen	faunas	fervid
end-man	ensure	ersatz	even so	extant	faller	fausen	fervor
endrin	entail	erucic	even up	extend	fall in	fautor	Fesapo
end run	entame	eryngo	everly	extent	fall on	favela	fescue
Endura	entera	Esalen	ever so	extern	Fallot	favism	festal
endure	entice	escape	evilly	extine	fallow	favour	fester
enduro	entify	escarp	evince	extirp	fall to	fawner	fetial
enemas	entire	eschar	Evipan	extort	falset	fawn on	fetish
energy	entity	eschew	evoker	extund	falter	fealty	fetter
enerve	entoil	escort	evolve	ex-voto	famble	feared	fettle
enface	entomb	escrod	evulse	eye-cup	family	fearer	feudal
en fête	entone	escrow	evzone	eyecup	famine	featly	feuing
enfile	entrap	escudo	Evzone	eyeful	famish	fecial	fewmet
enfold	entrée	Eskies	ewerer	eyeing	famose	fecket	fewter
engage	enurny	Eskimo	exacta	eyelet	famous	feckly	fezzed
engagé	enveil	espial	examen	eyelid	famuli	fecula	fezzes
engaol	envein	espied	ex ante	eye-pit	fandom	fecund	fiacre
engild	envied	espies	exarch	Eyetie	fanega	fedora	fiancé
engine	envier	esprit	excamb	Fabian	fanged	feeble	fiants
engird	envies	essart	excave	fabism	fangle	feebly	fiasco
engirt	enwall	Essene	exceed	fabled	fan-jet	feeder	fibbed
englut	enwind	essive	except	fabler	fanned	feed up	fibber
englyn	enwomb	essoin	excess	Fablon	fanner	feeler	fibred
engore	enwood	estate	excide	fabric	fantad	feerie	fibril
engram	enwrap	esteem	excise	facade	fan-tan	fegary	fibrin
engulf	enzyme	estral	excite	façade	Fantis	feijoa	fibros
enhalo	Eocene	estray	excuse	facete	fantod	Feinne	fibula
enigma	eolian	estrin	excyst	face up	faquir	feints	fiches
enisle	Eolian	etalon	exedra	facial	farcer	feirie	fickle
enjail	eolith	etaoin	exempt	facies	far cry	feisty	fickly
enjamb	Eonism	etcher	exequy	facile	farded	feline	fiddle
enjoin	Eonist	eterne	exergy	facing	fardel	fellah	fiddly
enknot	eparch	ethane	Exeter	factor	farina	feller	fidfad
enlace	epaule	ethene	exeunt	factum	faring	felloe	fidget
enlink	épéist	ethics	exhale	facula	farman	fellow	fie-fie
enlist	ephebe	ethide	exhort	facund	farmer	felony	fierce
enlock	ephyra	ethine	exhume	faddle	far-off	felsic	fiesta
enmesh	epical	Ethiop	exilic	fade-in	far out	felter	Figaro
enmity	epilog	ethnic	exited	fading	farrow	female	figged
ennead	epimer	ethrog	exitus	faecal	farter	femora	fighty
enolic	epipod	ethyne	Exmoor	faeces	fasces	femurs	figura
enosis	Epirot	etoile	Exocet	Faenza	fascet	fencer	figure
enotic	epizoa	etrier	exodus	faerie	fascia	fender	Fijian

filaze	fitted	floose	folate	fortes	frisée	funker	galega
filial	fitten	floozy	folder	fortis	Frisic	funkia	galena
filing	fitter	floppy	fold in	forwhy	frisky	funnel	Galibi
filled	fitton	florae	fold up	fossae	frivel	fun run	galiot
filler	fixate	floral	foliar	fossed	frivol	furcal	galium
fillet	fixing	floras	folios	fossil	frizzy	furfur	galled
fill in	fixity	floret	foliot	fossor	Fröbel	furied	gallet
fillip	fixure	florid	folium	foster	froggy	furies	galley
fillis	fizgig	florin	folkie	fother	froise	furner	gallic
fill-up	fizzer	flossy	folksy	fought	frolic	furore	Gallic
filmic	fizzle	flotel	folles	Foulah	frosty	furphy	Gallio
filter	flabby	floury	follis	foully	frothy	furred	gallon
filthy	fladge	flower	follow	foul-up	frough	furrin	gallop
fimble	flaggy	flow-on	Folsom	fourth	froust	furrow	gallus
finale	flagon	fluent	foment	fouter	frowst	fusain	Galois
finder	flaked	fluffy	fondle	foutre	frowsy	fusile	galoot
find up	flaker	fluked	fondly	foveae	frowzy	fusion	galore
finely	flambé	flunky	fondue	foveal	frozen	fusoid	galosh
finery	flamen	flurry	fonduk	fowler	frugal	fusser	galpon
fine up	flamer	flushy	fontal	foxery	fruity	fustet	Galton
finger	flanch	fluted	foodie	fox-fur	frumpy	fustic	gamash
finial	flange	fluter	foo-foo	foxier	frushy	futile	gambit
finick	flappy	flutey	footed	foxily	frusta	futtah	gamble
finify	flaser	fly ash	footer	foxing	frutex	future	gambol
fining	flashy	fly boy	footie	Foxite	frypan	fu yung	gamely
finish	flatly	fly cop	foot it	fox-red	fry-pan	fuzzle	gamete
finite	flatty	flyest	footle	fracas	F sharp	fylfot	gamgee
finity	flatus	fly-fan	foozle	fraena	fucate	gabbed	gamier
finkle	flaunt	flying	forage	fraise	fucker	gabber	gamily
finlet	flavin	flyman	for aye	framed	fuck up	gabble	gamine
finnan	flavor	fly-net	forbad	framer	fucoid	gabbro	gaming
finned	flawed	fly-nut	forbid	frappé	fuddle	gabion	gammer
finner	flaxen	fly off	forbye	fratch	futtle	gabled	gammon
Finnic	flayer	fly out	forced	frater	fugato	gablet	gamont
finnip	F-layer	fly-rod	forcer	fratry	fugged	Gaboon	ganbei
finnoc	flèche	flysch	foredo	Frauen	fuggle	gadbee	gander
finnow	fledge	flyter	forego	fraxin	fugued	gadded	gangan
fin-ray	fledgy	fly-tip	forest	frazil	fugues	gadder	ganger
Finsen	fleece	flyway	forfex	freaky	führer	gadfly	gangle
finsko	fleech	foamed	for fun	freath	Fulani	gadget	gangly
fiorin	fleecy	fobbed	forger	freely	fulcra	gadman	gangue
fipple	flench	fob off	forget	freest	fulfil	gadoid	gang up
fire up	flense	fo'c'sle	forgot	free up	fulgid	Gaelic	gannet
firing	fleshy	fo'c's'le	forint	freeze	fulgor	gaffer	ganoid
firker	fletch	fodder	forked	freezy	Fulham	gaffle	ganoin
firkin	fleury	fodgel	forker	French	fuller	gagaku	gansel
firlot	flewed	foeman	formal	frenum	full up	gag-bit	gansey
firman	flewet	foetal	format	frenzy	fulmar	gagged	gantry
firmly	flexed	foetid	formée	fresco	fulvid	gagger	gaoler
fiscal	flexor	foetor	former	fretty	fulyie	gaggie	gaping
fiscus	flight	foetus	formic	friary	fumado	gaggle	gapped
fisgig	flimsy	fog-bow	formol	fribby	fumage	gag man	garage
fisher	flinch	fog-dog	formyl	Friday	fumble	gaiety	Garand
fishes	flinty	fogeys	fornix	fridge	fumish	gaijin	garble
fissle	flirty	fogged	for now	friend	fumose	gainer	garçon
fisted	flisky	fogger	forold	frieze	fumous	gainly	garden
fistic	flitch	fogies	for one	friezy	fundal	gainst	gardie
fistle	floaty	fogman	forpet	fright	fundus	gaited	garget
fitché	flocci	fogram	forpit	frigid	funest	gaiter	gargle
fitchy	flocht	foible	forrel	frilly	fungal	galago	garish
fitful	flocky	foison	forrit	fringe	fungic	galaxy	garled
fit out	floody	foisty	forset	fringy	fungus	galeae	garlic

garner	gee-hup	gherao	glacis	gneeve	goniff	goyish	Griqua
garnet	geeing	ghetto	gladly	gneiss	gonion	grabby	grisly
Garnet	geelum	ghibli	glaire	gnomic	gonoph	graben	grison
garret	geezer	Ghilji	glairy	gnomon	goober	graced	gritty
garron	geggie	gholam	glaive	gnosis	gooder	gradal	grivet
garrya	geisha	ghoont	glance	goalie	goodie	grade A	Grizel
garter	gelada	ghosty	glassy	goanna	goodly	graded	groats
garuda	gelate	ghurry	glaver	goatee	good-oh	grader	Gro-bag
gasbag	gelder	giaour	glazed	go at it	good on	gradin	grocer
Gascon	gelled	gibber	glazen	go away	goofer	gradus	groggy
gas gun	Gemara	gibbet	glazer	go awry	goof-up	Graham	groomy
gashed	Gemini	gibbon	gleamy	go back	goofus	graine	groose
gashly	gemmae	gibier	glease	go bail	googly	grainy	groove
gasify	gemman	giblet	gledge	go bang	googol	graith	groovy
gasket	gemmed	Gibson	gleety	gobang	goo-goo	gramma	groper
gaskin	gemmen	giddap	glegly	gobbed	gooier	gramme	groser
gaslit	gemmer	giddup	gleyde	gobbet	gooily	Grammy	groset
gasman	gender	Gideon	gleyed	gobble	goolie	grampy	grossy
gasmen	geneat	gidgee	glibly	gobdaw	goonda	grange	grotto
gas oil	genera	gifted	glider	gobies	gooney	granma	grotty
gasper	geneva	giftie	glioma	gobiid	gooroo	granny	grouch
gassed	Geneva	gigged	glissé	goblet	gooses	Granth	ground
gasser	genial	giggle	glitch	goblin	goosey	granum	grouse
gasses	Genist	giggly	glitzy	gobony	go over	grapey	grouty
gaster	genius	giglet	global	go bung	gopher	graphy	groved
gateau	genned	gigman	globed	go bush	go phut	grappa	grovel
gather	gennel	gigolo	globin	go bust	gopura	grassy	grovet
Gathic	gennet	gilded	globus	go-cart	Gordon	grater	growan
gating	Genoan	gilder	glomus	God-box	gorged	gratin	grower
gatten	genome	gilgai	gloomy	goddam	gorger	gratis	growly
gatter	gentes	gilguy	gloopy	godkin	gorget	graved	grow on
gauche	gentil	gilled	gloppy	godlet	Gorgio	gravel	growth
gaucho	gentle	giller	gloria	God-man	gorgon	graven	grow up
gauger	gently	gillie	Gloria	go down	gorier	graver	groyne
Gaulic	gentoo	Gilyak	glossy	godown	gorily	graves	grubby
gaulin	Gentoo	gimbal	glover	godson	goring	Graves	grub up
gaulty	gentry	gimbri	glower	godwit	gosain	gravid	grudge
gaupus	genual	gimlet	glucan	God wot	Goshen	grazer	gruffy
gavage	geodic	gimmal	gluier	go easy	go sick	grazet	grugru
gavial	geonim	gimmer	gluily	goetic	go slow	grease	grumly
gawker	George	ginger	gluing	goffer	go some	greasy	grumph
gawper	gerbil	gingko	gluino	goggie	go sour	greave	grumpy
gawpus	gerent	ginkgo	gluish	goggle	gospel	grebos	Grundy
gay cat	german	ginned	glulam	goggly	gossan	greedy	grunge
gay dog	German	ginnel	glumly	goglet	gossip	greeny	grungy
gaydom	germen	ginner	glummy	go gold	gotcha	greety	Grunth
gayest	germin	gipser	glumpy	go hang	Gotham	gregal	grutch
gayety	germon	girded	glunch	go home	Gothic	greyly	guaiac
Gay Lib	gersum	girder	glutch	Goidel	go to it	gricer	guanay
gazabo	gerund	girdle	glutei	go into	gotten	griece	guango
gazebo	gestic	girlie	gluten	goitre	gouger	grieve	guanos
gazook	get gay	girnel	glycan	go-kart	goujon	griffe	guardo
gazump	get his	giroes	glycin	golden	go upon	gri-gri	guardy
geared	get off	girran	glycol	golfer	gourbi	grille	guarea
gear up	get-out	gismos	glycyl	go live	gousty	grillo	guarri
geason	getter	gitana	gnamma	gollan	goutte	grilse	gubbin
gebang	get wet	gitano	gnap at	gollop	govern	grimly	Gubbio
geckos	gewgaw	Giunta	gnarly	golosh	gowany	gringa	gubble
gedact	geyser	give in	gnatoo	gomuti	go well	gringo	guddle
geddit	gharry	give me	gnatty	go near	go west	griper	Guebre
geed-up	ghazal	give up	gnawed	gone on	go with	grippe	Guelph
gee-gee	Ghazis	giving	gnawer	gonger	gowpen	grippy	guemal

guenon	gusset	halawi	harass	header	hepcat	Higher	hoeing
guffaw	gustos	halely	harbor	head-on	hepped	highly	hogged
guffer	gutful	haleru	hard by	head up	hepper	high-up	hogger
guggle	Gutian	halide	harden	healer	heptad	hijack	hogget
guglia	gut-rot	halite	harder	health	heptyl	Hilary	hoggin
guider	gutser	hallal	hardly	heaped	herald	hilted	hog gum
Guider	gutted	halloo	hard on	heaper	Herati	hinaki	hognut
guidon	gutter	hallos	hard up	hearer	herbal	hincty	hog-pen
guilty	gut-tie	hallow	hareld	hearse	herbed	hinder	hog-tie
guimpe	guttle	hallux	harken	hearst	herber	Hindki	hoicks
guinea	guttur	haloes	harker	hearth	herder	Hindoo	hokier
Guinea	guttus	halter	Harlem	hearty	herdic	Hindus	holcus
guinep	gutzer	halvah	harlot	heated	hereat	hinged	hold by
guinzo	guvner	halver	harman	heater	hereby	hingle	holden
guiser	guyver	halves	harmel	heathy	herein	hinnie	holder
guitar	guzzle	hamada	harper	heaume	hereof	hinoki	hold in
guiver	gymnic	hamate	Harris	heaved	hereon	hint at	hold it
gulden	gympie	hamble	harrow	heaven	Herero	hinter	hold on
Gullah	gypped	Hamite	hartal	heaver	heresy	hip-cat	hold up
gullet	gypsum	hamlet	Harvey	hebete	hereto	hip hop	hole up
gulley	gyrase	Hamlet	haslet	hebona	heriot	hipped	holier
gulose	gyrate	hammal	Hassid	Hebrew	hermit	hipper	holily
gulper	gyrene	hammam	hassle	Hebrid	hernia	hippic	holing
gulpin	gyrine	hammed	hasten	Hecate	heroes	hippie	holism
Gumban	gyrose	hammer	hatbox	heckle	heroic	hippos	holist
gumbos	gyrous	hammle	hatful	hectic	heroin	hippus	holla'd
gum-gum	gyttja	hamose	hatpin	hector	herola	Hirado	hollas
gum ivy	habara	hamous	hatred	heddle	heroon	Hirato	holler
gum lac	habile	hamper	hatted	hedger	her own	hirmos	hollin
gumlah	hab-nab	hamsin	hatter	hee-haw	herpes	hirola	holloa
gummas	haboob	hamuli	Hattic	heeled	Herren	hirple	hollos
gummed	hachis	Hanafi	haught	heeler	Hesped	hirsel	hollow
gummer	hackee	handed	Hau Hau	hegira	Hesper	hirsle	holmia
gunate	hacker	hander	hauler	Hegira	Hesvan	his own	holoku
gun dog	hackia	hand-in	haunch	he-goat	hetero	hispid	holpen
gung-ho	hackie	handle	Hausas	heifer	hetman	hisser	homage
gunite	hackle	hand on	hausen	height	hetmen	hister	hombre
gunman	hackly	hangar	haüyne	heimin	heurte	hi-tech	homely
gunmen	hadada	hang-by	Havana	Heinie	hewgag	hither	homier
gunned	haddie	hanged	have it	hejira	hexane	Hitler	homily
gunnel	Hadean	hanger	haven't	Hejira	hexite	hit man	homing
gunner	Hadith	hangie	have on	heliac	hexode	hit men	hominy
gunnis	hadron	hang in	have to	heling	hexone	hit-out	homish
gun-pit	haemal	hang me	have up	helion	hexose	hitter	honcho
gunsel	haemic	hang on	havier	helium	hey-day	hive up	honest
gun-shy	haemin	hangul	having	heller	heyday	hoagie	honeys
Gunter	haffet	hang up	haw-haw	helluo	hiaqua	hoarse	honied
gunyah	hafter	haniwa	hawked	helmed	hiatal	hoaxer	honker
guppie	hagged	hanjar	hawker	helmet	hiatus	hobbit	honour
gurges	haggis	hanjee	hawkit	helper	hiccup	hobble	Honved
gurgle	haggle	hanker	hawser	help up	hickey	hobday	hooded
gurgly	Haidas	hankie	haybag	hemina	hickle	hob-nob	hoodie
gurjun	haikal	hansel	haybox	hemmed	hidage	hobnob	hoodoo
Gurkha	hailer	Hansen	haymow	hemmel	hidden	hoboes	hoofed
gurner	hairdo	hansom	hayrif	hemmer	hi-de-hi	hocket	hoofer
gurnet	haired	hantle	hazard	hempen	hi-de-ho	hockey	hoof it
gurney	hairen	happed	hazier	henbit	hide up	hodden	hoo-hoo
gurrag	hairif	happen	hazily	hen-egg	hiding	ho-de-ho	hookah
gurrah	hajeen	happis	hazing	Henoch	hieing	hodful	hooked
Gurung	hakama	hapten	hazzan	hen-run	hiemal	hodman	hooker
gusher	hakeem	haptic	H-block	henrys	higgle	hodmen	hookey
guslar	halala	hapuku	headed	hep-cat	higher	hoeful	Hookey

hook it	hourly	hunsup	ibexes	I'm easy	incend	in form	in-milk
hook-up	housel	hunted	Ibibio	imidic	incept	inform	in mode
Hoolee	housey	hunter	ibises	immane	incest	infula	inmost
hooley	howdah	hunt up	Ibizan	immerd	inched	in full	in name
hooped	howdie	hunyak	Icarus	immesh	incher	infuse	innate
hooper	howe'er	hurdie	ice age	immote	incide	in gage	in need
hoop-la	how far	hurdle	ice axe	immund	incise	ingaol	inness
hoopla	howish	hurkle	ice-bag	immune	incite	ingate	inning
hoopoe	howler	hurler	icebox	immure	inclip	in gear	in nuce
hooray	howlet	Hurler	ice cap	impack	income	in germ	Innuit
hooroo	how now	hurley	ice fog	impact	incubi	ingest	inogen
hootch	how way	hurrah	iceman	impair	incult	ingine	inosic
hooter	howzat	hurray	icemen	impala	in curl	in goal	inower
hooved	hoyden	hurroo	Icenic	impale	incuse	in good	in pain
Hoover	hoyman	hurter	ice pan	impall	incyst	ingram	in pale
hooves	Hubble	hurtle	I Ching	impark	indaba	in gree	in part
hop-dog	hubbub	hushed	icicle	imparl	indart	ingulf	in pawn
hop-fly	hub-cap	hush up	iciest	impart	indebt	Ingush	in pile
hop off	hubcap	husked	iconic	impave	in deed	inhale	in play
hopped	hubris	husker	Idaean	impawn	indeed	in hand	in rags
hopper	huchen	huskie	ideate	impede	indene	inhaul	inroad
hoppet	huckle	huspil	idiocy	impend	indent	in heat	inroot
hopple	huddle	hussar	idlest	impest	Indian	inhell	inrush
Hoppus	huerta	hustle	idolum	imphee	indict	inhere	in salt
hop toy	huffer	hutted	i' faith	impish	Indies	in hock	insane
horary	huffle	hutung	iffier	import	indign	inhume	insect
horkey	hugely	Huxham	iffish	impose	indigo	inimic	in seed
hormic	hugged	huzoor	if only	impost	indite	inisle	insert
horned	hugger	Hyades	if that	impros	indium	injail	in show
hornen	huggle	hyaena	ignify	improv	in dock	inject	in-side
horner	Hughie	hya-hya	ignite	impugn	indole	in jest	inside
hornet	huldee	hyalin	ignomy	impure	indoor	in-joke	in silk
horn in	hulver	hybrid	ignore	impute	indraw	injure	insist
horrid	humane	hybris	iguana	in a fog	indrew	injury	in situ
horror	humate	hydria	I guess	in a hat	indris	ink-cap	insole
horsey	humble	hydric	Ilamba	in a low	induce	inkier	insoul
horsie	humbly	hydrol	Ilanun	inanga	induct	in kind	inspan
hortal	humbug	hydros	Il Duce	inarch	indult	inkish	instal
hosier	Humean	Hydrus	Illano	in arms	induna	inknot	instar
hostel	humect	hyemal	ill-got	in a row	inface	inkosi	in step
hostie	humeri	hygeen	illipe	in a rut	in fact	ink out	instep
hot air	humhum	Hygeia	illish	in a way	infall	ink-pad	instil
hotbed	Humian	Hyksos	illite	in banc	infame	inkpot	in suit
hotcha	humify	hymnal	I'll say	in bank	infamy	inlaid	insula
hot dog	Humism	hymner	I'll see	in bend	infant	in-lamb	insult
hotdog	Humist	hymnic	illude	inbent	infare	inland	insure
hot key	humite	hypate	illume	inbind	in fawn	in lane	in sync
Hotnot	humlie	hyphae	illupi	in bond	in fine	inlaut	intact
hotpot	hummed	hyphal	ill use	inborn	infect	in leaf	in tail
hot rod	hummel	hyphen	imaged	inbred	infeed	inleak	intake
hot tap	hummer	hypnum	imager	in bulk	infeft	inlier	intend
hotted	hummum	hypoid	imagic	Incaic	in fess	in lieu	intent
hotter	hummus	hypped	imagos	in calf	infest	in life	intern
hottie	humour	Hyrcan	imaret	incall	in file	in-line	in that
hot tip	humous	hyssop	imbark	incame	infill	inlook	intill
hot tub	humped	hyther	imbibe	incant	in fine	in love	intima
hot war	humper	iambic	imbibe	in care	infirm	in luck	in time
Houdan	humpty	iambus	imbrex	incarn	in fits	in mask	intine
hougan	hunger	Iatmul	imbrue	in case	inflow	in mass	in-toed
houp-la	hungry	iatric	imbued	incase	in flue	inmate	intone
houred	hunker	Ibanag	imbues	in cash	influx	inmeat	in toto
houris	hunkey	iberis	imbuya	incede	infold	in mesh	in-town

in-tray	Irishy	jaguar	jet set	join up	jump on	Kansan	kelter
in trim	iritic	Jahveh	jet ski	jojoba	jump to	Kansas	Keltic
intron	iritis	jailer	jetted	Jokari	jump up	kantar	kelvin
intros	irokos	Jaipur	jetton	jokery	juncos	kanuka	Kelvin
intuit	ironed	jalopy	Jetway	jokily	jungle	Kanuri	kempas
in tune	ironen	jam jar	Jew boy	jokist	jungly	kaolin	kemper
in turn	ironer	jammed	Jewess	jolley	Junian	kaonic	Kendal
inturn	ironic	jammer	Jewish	Jollof	junior	Kaposi	keneme
in tway	iron-on	jamoon	Jewism	jollop	junker	kappie	Kenite
in type	irrupt	jampan	jezail	jolter	junket	karaka	kenned
inulin	Isabel	jangle	jibbah	jonick	junkie	karamu	kennel
inunct	Isaian	jangly	jibbed	jonnop	jupati	karana	kentia
Inupik	isatin	janker	jibber	jordan	jurant	karate	kentum
invade	ischia	jansky	jib-guy	Jordan	juried	karaya	Kenyah
in vain	island	japery	jicama	jorram	juries	karela	Kenyan
invein	isobar	japish	jiffle	Joseph	juring	karkun	kephir
invent	isogam	jarful	jigged	josher	jurist	Karman	Kepler
invert	isogon	jargle	jigger	Joshua	just as	karmic	kereru
invest	isohel	jargon	jigget	joskin	just it	kaross	kerfed
in view	isolex	jarool	jiggle	josser	justle	karree	Kerman
invite	isolog	jarrah	jiggly	jostle	justly	Karren	kermes
in vivo	isolux	jarred	jig-jig	jotted	just so	karris	kermis
invoke	isomer	jarvey	jigman	jotter	Jutish	Karroo	kerned
in-wale	isopod	jasmin	jigsaw	jounce	jutted	karsey	kernel
inwall	Israel	jasper	jillet	joundy	jyrene	kartel	kernos
inward	issued	jaspis	Jiminy	journo	Kabaka	kasbah	kerria
inwarp	issuer	jassid	jimjam	jovial	kabane	Kashan	kersey
in wear	issues	Jataka	jimply	Jovian	kabuki	Kathak	Kertch
inwick	isthmi	jaunce	jimson	jowari	Kabuli	katipo	ketene
inwind	italic	jaunty	jingle	jowled	Kabyle	kauris	ketone
in wine	Italic	javver	jingly	jowler	Kachin	kausia	kettle
in with	it says	jaw-jaw	jinker	joyant	Kaffir	kavass	Keuper
inwith	itself	Jaycee	jinnee	joyful	kaftan	kawass	Kevlar
inwork	itzebu	jazzbo	jipper	joyous	kahili	kayles	kewpie
inwove	ivy-tod	jazzer	jirene	joy-pop	kahuna	kayoed	keyaki
inwrap	ixodid	jazz up	jirine	Judaic	kaikai	kayoes	key man
inyala	Izarra	J-cloth	jitney	judder	kainga	Kazakh	key map
inyoke	Izzara	J-curve	jitter	Judean	kainic	kebbie	keypad
iodate	izzard	jeaned	Jivaro	judger	kaiser	keckle	key-way
iodide	jabbed	jeerer	joanna	Judies	Kaiser	keddah	keyway
iodine	jabber	jeerga	jobbed	judoka	k'ai shu	keeker	khadar
iodise	jabble	Jeeves	jobber	jugate	kaizen	keeled	khadir
iodism	jabers	jejune	jobbie	jugful	kajang	keeler	khakis
iodize	jabiru	Jekyll	jobble	jugged	kakaki	keelie	khalif
iolite	jacana	jelick	job lot	juggle	kakapo	Keemun	khalsa
ion gun	jaçana	Jemima	job off	jug-jug	kaleej	keener	khanda
Ionian	jacent	jennet	Jocism	juglet	kalgan	keenly	khanga
ionise	jackal	jerbil	Jocist	juiced	kalmia	keen on	Khanty
Ionism	jacked	jerboa	jocker	juicer	Kalmyk	keep at	khanum
ionium	jacker	jereed	jockey	jujube	kalong	keeper	khapra
ionize	jacket	jerker	jocose	Julian	kamahi	keep in	kharif
Ionize	Jackey	jerkin	jocund	jumart	kamala	keep on	Kharri
ionone	jack in	jerque	jogged	jumbal	kamash	keep to	Khatti
ipecac	jacksy	jersey	jogger	jumbie	kameez	keep up	Khazar
Iranic	jack-up	Jersey	joggle	jumble	kanaka	Keftiu	Khlyst
Iraqis	Jacobi	jessed	joggly	Jumble	kanari	kegler	Khotan
ireful	jadish	Jessie	jog-jog	jumbly	kanban	Kekchi	Khurri
irenic	jaeger	jester	johnny	jumbos	Kanjar	Kekulé	Khyber
iridal	Jaeger	Jesuit	Johnny	jument	kankar	keloid	kiaugh
irides	jagged	jet age	joiner	jump at	kankie	kelper	kibble
iridic	jagger	jet lag	join in	jumped	kanoon	kelpie	kibitz
irised	jaggie	jetsam	jointy	jumper	kan-pei	kelson	kiblah

kiboko	kit-car	kopeck	laagte	lament	laster	lazuli	leguan
kibosh	kit-cat	koppel	labakh	lamina	Lastex	leachy	legume
kickee	Kit-cat	koppie	labial	lamish	lastly	leaded	lemans
kicker	kit-fox	Korana	labile	lamium	lateen	leaden	lemony
kick in	kitful	kordax	labium	Lammas	lately	leader	Lenape
kick on	kitsch	Korean	lablab	lammed	La Tène	lead-in	lenate
kick up	kitset	korero	labour	lammie	latent	lead on	lender
kidang	kitted	korkir	labral	Lamout	latest	lead up	length
kidded	kittel	koruna	labret	lampas	lathen	leafed	Lengua
kidder	kitten	Koryak	labrum	lamper	lather	leafit	lenify
kiddie	kittle	kosher	labrys	lanate	lathis	league	lenite
kiddle	kittly	kotuku	lac-dye	lanced	Latian	leaker	lenity
kiddos	kittul	kotwal	lacery	lancer	latigo	leally	lensed
kidlet	klatch	koulan	lace-up	lances	Latina	lealty	Lenten
kidnap	klaxon	kouros	laches	lancet	latine	leaned	lentic
kidney	Klaxon	kowhai	lacier	landau	Latino	leaner	lentil
kidult	klepht	kowtow	lacily	landed	latish	leanly	lentor
kidvid	klepto	kraken	lacing	lander	lative	lean on	Leonid
kiekie	klippe	kramat	lacker	Länder	latomy	lean-to	leopon
kierie	klooch	kronen	lackey	land on	latoun	leap at	Lepcha
Kievan	kludge	kroner	lactam	Landry	latria	leaped	lepper
kijang	klutzy	kronor	lactic	land to	latron	leaper	lepton
Kikuyu	Kluxer	kronur	lactim	land up	latten	learnt	lerret
kilhig	K-meson	K-shell	lactol	langur	latter	leasee	lesbic
kilian	knacky	kubong	lactyl	lankly	lauder	leaser	lesion
killas	knaggy	Ku Klux	lacuna	lanner	Laufen	leasor	lessee
killer	knarry	kukris	lacune	lanose	laughy	leasow	lessen
kilted	knawel	kukupa	ladang	lanugo	launce	leaved	lesser
kilter	Kneipp	Kullah	ladder	lap-dog	launch	leaven	lesses
kiltie	knevel	Kultur	laddie	lapdog	laurel	leaver	less of
kimchi	knicks	kumara	la-di-da	lapful	lauric	leaves	lesson
kim-kam	knifer	kumbuk	ladies	lapiés	lauryl	lebbek	lessor
kimmer	knifey	kumera	ladify	Lapita	lauter	leccer	let fly
kimnel	knifie	kumiss	lading	Lapith	lavabo	lecher	lethal
kimono	knight	kumkum	ladino	lap-lap	lavage	Lecher	lethed
kinase	knitch	kümmel	Ladino	lapped	laveer	lechwe	lether
kincob	knit up	kumpit	ladler	lapper	lavish	lecker	let lie
kindle	knives	kung fu	ladyfy	lappet	law-day	lectin	let-off
kindly	knobby	kunkur	laetic	lappie	lawful	lector	let-out
kind of	knolly	kurgan	lagena	lapser	lawing	ledged	let rip
kineme	knotty	Kurnai	lag-end	laptop	lawman	ledger	letted
kinety	know as	kurper	lagged	larder	lawmen	leegte	letter
king it	knower	kurtha	lagger	lardon	lawned	leetle	Lettic
kingly	know of	Kurukh	laggin	largen	lawyer	leeway	let wit
kinjal	knurly	kuruma	lagoon	largos	laxist	leftie	leucon
kinkey	kobang	Kurume	Lahnda	lariat	laxity	legacy	levade
kinkle	kobold	kurvey	laical	larker	Laxton	legate	levain
kipped	Kodiak	Kushan	Laïdes	Larmor	lay-bed	legato	levant
kipper	kokako	Kutani	laidly	larnax	lay-bys	leg-bye	Levant
kippin	kokila	kutcha	laid up	larrup	lay-day	legend	leveed
kipsie	kokopu	kutira	laithe	larvae	lay-fee	leggat	levers
Kirman	kolach	kuttar	lakish	larval	laying	legged	Levers
kirpan	Kolami	Kuvasz	Lakist	larynx	lay low	legger	levied
kirsch	Komodo	kvetch	Lakota	lascar	layman	legget	Levied
kirtan	konaki	kvutza	lalang	Lascar	laymen	legion	levier
kirtle	Kongos	kwacha	Lallan	lashed	lay off	legist	levies
kishke	kongsi	kwanga	Lallan	lasher	lay out	leglen	Levite
Kislev	konini	kwanza	lambaic	lash-up	layout	leglet	levity
kismet	konjak	kybosh	Lambeg	lasket	Laysan	leg man	lewdly
kissar	koodoo	kyogen	lamber	lasque	lazier	legman	lexeme
kisser	koodos	Kyrgyz	lambie	lassie	lazily	legmen	Leyden
kitbag	kootie	laager	lamely	lassos	lazule	leg-pad	Leydig

liable	limner	litmus	loggia	louden	lupous	made up	maleic
liaise	limnic	litten	Logian	loudly	lurdan	madman	malgas
libate	limous	litter	logier	lounge	luring	madmen	Malian
libber	limper	little	logion	lourie	lurker	madras	Malibu
libbet	limpet	littly	log jam	louser	Lushai	Madras	malice
Lib Dem	limpid	lituus	log-log	louses	lusher	madtom	malign
libero	limply	Litvak	log-man	louver	lushly	maduro	Maliki
libido	limpsy	live in	log-off	louvre	Lusian	maenad	malism
Lib-Lab	linage	lively	log-out	lovage	lusory	Maffia	malist
libral	linden	livery	loined	love-in	luster	maffle	malkin
Libran	lineal	live to	loiter	lovely	lustly	magcon	mallam
Libyan	linear	livier	loligo	love-up	lustra	magged	mallee
lichee	line-up	living	Lolita	loveys	lustre	Maggid	mallei
lichen	lingam	livret	loller	loving	luteal	maggie	mallet
licken	lingel	livyer	lollop	lowboy	lutein	maggot	mallow
licker	linger	lizard	loment	low-cut	luting	magian	maloca
lictor	lingle	Lizzie	London	low-end	lutino	magilp	maloti
lidded	lingos	llanos	lonely	lowish	lutist	maglev	Malozi
lidden	lingot	Lloyd's	longan	low-key	lutite	magmas	malted
liddle	lingua	loaded	longer	low men	luvvie	magnet	malter
Liebig	linhay	loaden	longie	lownly	Luwian	magnon	maltha
lieder	linier	loader	longly	L-plate	luxate	magnox	maltol
liefly	lining	loadum	long on	lubber	luxury	Magnox	mambos
lieger	linish	load up	lontar	Lubish	Lyaeus	magnum	Mamluk
lie low	linked	loafer	loofah	lubric	lycaon	magpie	mammae
lie off	linker	loanee	loogan	Luccan	Lyceum	maguey	mammal
lierne	link up	loaner	looked	lucent	lychee	Magyar	mammee
lifter	linnet	loasis	looker	lucern	Lycian	mahant	mammer
lift-on	linsey	loathe	look-in	lucida	lycium	Mahdis	mammet
lift-up	Linson	loathy	lookit	Lucina	lyctid	mahout	Mammon
Lifuan	lintel	loaves	look on	Lucite	lyctus	Mahsud	mamoty
ligand	linter	lobate	look up	luckie	Lydian	mahwah	mampus
ligase	lintie	lobbed	loomer	lucuma	lydite	maidan	mamzer
ligate	linton	lobing	looney	lucumo	Lylian	maiden	manage
ligged	lionel	lobule	loonie	Ludian	lymphy	maigre	manaia
ligger	lionet	locale	looped	luetic	Lyngby	maihem	mañana
lights	lionly	locant	looper	lugged	lyrate	mailed	man-ape
lignin	lipase	locate	loop-in	luggee	lyrism	mailer	man-boy
lignum	lipoic	lochan	loosen	lugger	lyrist	mail-in	manche
ligula	lipoid	lochia	looser	luggie	lysate	maille	Manchu
ligule	lipoma	lochus	looter	lukiko	lysine	maimai	mancia
ligure	lipped	locked	lop-ear	lullay	lyxose	maimed	mancus
like as	lippen	locker	lopped	lumbar	Maasai	maimer	Mandan
likely	lipper	locket	lopper	lumber	mabele	Mainer	man-day
like so	lippet	lock in	loquat	lumens	macaco	mainly	mandil
liking	liquid	lock on	lorate	lumina	macana	Maioli	mandor
likuta	liquor	lock-up	lorcha	lumine	machan	Majlis	manege
lilied	lirate	locoed	lordly	lummox	machos	majoon	manège
lilies	Lisbon	locoes	loreal	lumped	Mackay	make do	maness
lilipi	lisper	locoum	Lorenz	lumpen	mackle	make in	manful
lilium	lissom	locule	lorica	lumper	macled	make it	mangel
Lillet	listed	loculi	lories	lunacy	macock	make of	manger
limail	listel	locust	loriot	lunary	macron	make on	mangey
limbal	listen	lodged	losing	lunate	macula	make up	mangle
limbed	lister	lodger	losset	lunged	macule	making	man-god
limber	litany	loerie	lostly	lunger	Madame	makoré	mangos
limbic	litchi	lofted	lost to	lungis	madcap	makuta	maniac
limbos	lither	lofter	lotion	lunker	madded	makutu	manify
limbus	lithia	loggat	lot-man	lunula	madden	malady	Manila
Limeys	lithic	logged	lotong	lunule	madder	Malaga	manioc
limier	Lithol	logger	lotted	lupine	maddle	malate	manism
limmer	lithos	logget	louche	lupoid	made of	Malawi	manito

manjak	marled	matter	medick	menton	micher	minify	mizzle
manjee	marler	mattie	medico	mentor	mickey	minima	mizzly
mankin	marlin	mature	medina	mentum	mickle	minimi	mnemic
man-mad	marmem	matzos	Medina	menudo	Micmac	mining	mnemon
mannan	marmot	maudle	medine	menuet	micron	minion	moaner
manned	maroon	maugre	Medise	menura	micros	minish	mobbed
manner	marque	mauler	Medism	menzil	mictic	minium	mobber
mannie	marram	mauley	medium	merbau	mid-age	minnie	mobbie
manoao	marred	maulvi	medius	mercer	mid-air	Minnie	mob cap
manool	marrer	mau-mau	Medize	merely	midday	minnow	mobile
manqué	marron	Mau Mau	medlar	merese	midden	Minoan	Möbius
man-rem	marrot	maumet	medley	merest	midder	minted	mob law
man-sty	marrow	maunch	medusa	mergee	middie	minter	mocamp
mantel	marshy	Maundy	meeken	merger	middle	Minton	mocker
mantic	Marsic	Mauser	meekly	mering	midear	minuet	mocket
mantid	martel	Mavors	meemie	merino	midget	minute	mock-up
mantis	marten	mawkin	meeten	merise	midgut	minyan	mocock
mantle	Martha	maxima	meeter	merkin	mid-leg	Minyan	mod con
Manton	martin	maxina	meetly	merled	mid-off	miombo	Model T
mantra	Martin	maxixe	meet up	merlin	midrib	miosis	modena
mantri	martyr	May-bug	megass	merlon	mid-sea	miotic	modern
mantua	marudi	mayday	Megger	Merlot	mid-sky	mirage	modest
manual	marula	May Day	megilp	merman	midway	miragy	modify
manuka	marvel	May dew	megohm	mermen	Miehle	mirror	modish
manure	marver	mayest	megrim	merops	mielie	misact	modius
manway	Masais	mayfly	mehari	merrie	mighty	misaim	module
manzil	masala	mayhap	mehtar	merula	mignon	miscue	moduli
Maoism	mascle	mayhem	meinie	mescal	mihrab	misdid	modulo
Maoist	mascon	maying	meisie	meself	mikado	misère	moffie
maomao	mascot	mayory	melano	meshed	Mikado	misery	moggie
Maoris	mashed	May-pop	melded	mesiad	milady	misfit	Moghul
Mao-tai	masher	maythe	melder	mesial	milage	mishap	mogote
map-net	mashie	mazame	melena	mesode	milden	mishit	mohair
map out	masked	mazard	Melian	messan	mildew	mishla	Mohave
mapped	masker	mazier	melick	messer	mildly	misken	Mohawk
mapper	maslin	mazily	meline	Messer	milieu	miskey	Mohock
maquis	masque	mazout	mellah	messin	miling	mislay	mohohu
Maquis	massed	mazuma	mellay	Messrs	milium	misled	moider
maraca	masser	meadow	mellow	mess-up	Milium	missal	moiety
marage	Massic	meager	melody	mestee	milken	missay	moiled
maraud	massif	meagre	meloid	metage	milker	missee	moiley
marble	Massim	mealer	melter	metake	milkie	missel	moisty
marbly	massoy	mealie	melton	Metaxa	milled	misset	Mojave
Marcan	mastax	meaner	melvie	meteor	miller	missie	moksha
marcel	masted	meanie	member	methel	Miller	missis	Molale
marcid	master	mean it	memoir	method	millet	missus	molary
marcor	mastic	meanly	memory	methos	Millon	misted	molded
marcot	matapi	measle	menace	methyl	milord	mister	molder
margay	matata	measly	ménage	métier	Milori	mistle	molest
margin	matico	meatal	menald	metope	milter	mistry	molies
Marial	matier	meatus	mendee	Metran	Milton	misuse	moline
Marian	matily	mecate	mender	metric	mimbar	mithan	moling
marina	matins	Meccan	mendhi	metrop	mimosa	mither	mollie
marine	matipo	Meckel	meneer	metros	Minaic	mitral	moloch
marish	matlow	medano	menhir	mettle	minbar	mitred	Moloch
Marist	mat-man	meddle	menial	Mewari	mincer	mitted	molten
marked	matoke	medfly	meninx	Mewati	minded	mitten	molter
marker	matric	mediae	mennal	mézair	Mindel	mixing	mombin
market	Matric	medial	mensal	mezuza	minder	mixite	moment
markka	matrix	median	mensch	miacid	Minean	Mixtec	momism
Markov	matron	Median	menses	mia-mia	minery	Mizpah	mommet
mark up	matted	Medici	mental	miasma	mingle	mizzen	mompei

momser	morkin	move it	multum	mutism	naiads	nebula	new boy
momzer	mormal	move on	mumble	mutter	naiant	nebule	new bug
monack	Mormon	move up	mummed	mutton	naïdes	nebulé	Newfie
monaul	mornay	moving	mummer	mutual	naïfly	nebuly	newing
Monday	Mornay	mowhay	mummia	mutuel	nailed	necked	newish
moneme	morose	mowing	mumper	mutule	nailer	necker	new law
moneys	morpho	mozzie	Munchi	mutuum	nail up	nectar	new man
mongan	morris	mozzle	Munich	muu-muu	namely	need-be	new one
monger	Morris	mpingo	munity	muvule	naming	needer	newsie
Mongol	morrow	Mr Chad	munshi	muvver	nanism	needle	newton
monial	morsel	Mrs Mop	Munshi	muzhik	nannie	needly	Newton
monied	mortal	mucate	munsif	muzzed	nanoid	needn't	nextly
monies	mortar	much as	muntin	muzzle	Nansen	nefast	next to
monish	Morton	muchly	muonic	my aunt	napalm	negate	ngaios
monism	morula	mucify	murage	my-dear	napery	neifty	Ngbaka
monist	mosaic	mucker	Murano	myelin	napkin	neinei	niacin
monkey	Mosaic	muck in	murder	myelon	Naples	nekton	Niamid
monkly	moseys	muckle	murein	my foot	napped	nelson	nibbed
monoao	moshav	muckna	murena	mygale	napper	Nelson	nibble
monody	mosker	muck-up	murine	my lady	nardoo	nembie	nibful
monoid	Moslem	mucoid	murmur	my life	nardus	Nemean	niblet
monops	mosque	mucosa	murphy	my lord	narial	Nenets	Nibmar
monose	Mossad	mucose	Murphy	my oath	narker	neo-con	nicely
montan	mossed	mucous	murram	myogen	nark it	neoned	Nicene
Montem	mosser	mud box	Murray	myopia	narrow	Nepali	nicety
moocha	mossie	mudcat	murrey	myopic	Nasara	nepeta	niched
moo-cow	mossoo	mud dab	murrha	myosin	nasion	nephew	nicher
moolah	mostly	mudder	musang	myosis	Nassau	nepman	nicish
mooley	mothed	muddie	muscae	myotic	nastic	Neread	nickar
moolvi	mother	muddle	muscat	myriad	nasute	nereid	nickel
moomba	motile	muddly	muscid	myrica	natant	Nereid	nicker
mooned	motion	mud eel	muscle	myrrhy	natica	nereis	nickey
mooner	motive	mud-hen	muscly	myrtle	nation	nerine	nicolo
moonga	motley	mud hog	museum	myself	native	Nerita	nidget
Moonie	motmot	Mudjur	musher	Mysian	natron	nerite	nidify
moon-up	motory	mud pie	mushie	Mysore	natter	nerium	niding
mootah	Motown	muduga	musico	mysost	nature	Nernst	nidiot
mooter	mottle	muesli	musing	mystic	naught	neroli	nid-nod
mopane	mottos	muffed	musion	mythic	nausea	nerval	nielli
mopery	Motuan	muffin	musive	mythoi	nautch	nerved	niello
mopier	motuca	muffle	musked	mythos	nautic	neshly	nievie
mopily	mouche	mugful	muskeg	mythus	Navaho	Nesite	niffer
mopish	mought	mugged	musket	my word	navaid	Nessus	nigger
Moplah	moujik	muggee	muskie	Myxine	Navajo	nester	niggle
mopoke	mouldy	mugger	musk ox	myxoid	naveta	nestle	niggly
mopped	moulin	mugget	muskwa	myxoma	navies	Nestor	nigguh
moppet	moulvi	muggle	Muslim	myzont	Naxian	netful	nighly
moppie	moundy	Mughal	muslin	nabbed	nay-say	nether	nights
morale	mourne	mukluk	musmon	nabber	naysay	net net	nighty
morass	mouser	muktuk	mussal	nabbie	Nazify	netted	nig-nog
morbid	mouses	muleta	mussel	nabism	Nazism	netter	nihang
moreen	mousey	mulier	must-be	nachas	nealie	nettle	Nikkei
Morenu	mousie	mulish	mustee	naches	neanic	nettly	nilgai
more of	mousle	mullah	muster	nachos	near by	net ton	nimbed
more so	mousmé	mullen	mustn't	nacket	nearby	neural	nimble
morgan	mousse	muller	mutant	nacred	near go	neuric	nimbly
Morgan	moutan	Muller	mutase	Na-Dene	nearly	neuron	nimbus
morgay	mouths	Müller	mutate	naevus	neaten	neuter	niminy
morgen	mouthy	mullet	mutely	nagana	neatly	New Age	nimmer
morgue	mouton	mulley	mutine	nagged	nebbuk	Newari	Nimrod
morion	movant	Mulozi	muting	nagger	neb-neb	Newark	nincom
morish	move in	multip	mutiny	naggle	nebris	New Art	nincum

ninety	non-com	Novial	nutter	oculus	oilcan	one-act	opaque
niobic	non-con	novice	Nutter	odd bod	oil-cup	one-arm	opelet
nipped	non-ego	novity	Nuzian	oddish	oildom	one-bar	opener
nipper	non-fat	no-vote	nuzzer	oddity	oil-gas	one day	open go
nipple	nonius	noways	nuzzle	odd job	oilier	on edge	openly
Nishga	non-net	Nowell	Nyanja	odd lot	oilily	Oneida	open up
Nissen	nonoic	nowhat	nybble	odd man	oilman	oneing	operon
nisses	nonose	nowhen	nympha	odd-odd	oilmen	one-man	ophite
nitery	non-use	no whit	nympho	odds-on	oil-nut	one-off	Ophite
nitric	noodle	nowise	nytril	odelet	oil out	one-one	ophrys
nitron	noodly	now now	oafish	odeums	oil pan	one-pip	opiate
nitryl	nooked	noyade	Oak-boy	Odinic	oil rig	one-two	opiism
nitwit	nookie	noyaux	oak-fly	odious	oil-way	one-way	opiner
Niuean	nooser	nozzle	oaklet	Odissi	Ojibwa	onfall	opioid
Nivose	Nootka	nritta	oak-web	odylic	okapis	on file	oppose
nix out	Noraid	nritya	oarage	oecist	OK-ness	on fire	oppugn
Noahic	Nordic	nuance	oar-lop	oedema	okoume	onflow	optant
no-ball	norite	nubbin	oarman	oekist	olamic	on foot	optate
nobber	normal	nubble	obduct	oeuvre	old age	on form	optics
nobble	norman	nubbly	obdure	of a day	old boy	on hand	optima
nobbly	Norman	Nubian	obeche	off-air	old dog	on heat	optime
nobbut	normed	nubile	obelus	off-cap	oldest	on high	option
nobler	Nornir	nuchal	oberek	offcut	old hat	on hire	opt out
nobody	Norroy	nuclei	obeyer	off day	old ice	on hold	opuses
nocake	Norway	nucule	object	offend	oldish	oniony	orache
nocent	nor yet	nuddle	objure	office	old lag	onlaid	oracle
no chop	nosema	nudely	oblata	offing	old law	on-lend	orally
noctua	nose-up	nudger	oblate	offish	old man	on life	orange
nodded	nosher	nudism	oblige	off-key	old pal	on-line	Orange
nodder	no shit	nudist	oblong	offlap	Old Peg	online	orator
noddle	no-show	nudity	oboist	offlet	Old Tom	on loan	orblet
no dice	nosh-up	nuffin	obolus	off-put	oleate	on mace	orb-web
nod off	no side	nuggar	obsess	off-set	olefin	on oath	orcein
nodose	nosier	nugget	obtain	offset	oleose	onrush	orchid
nodous	nosily	nullah	obtect	of hers	oleous	on sale	orchil
nodule	nosing	numbat	obtest	of late	O level	onsell	orchis
noduli	nosism	numbed	obtund	of mark	olfact	on show	ordain
noesis	no soap	number	obtuse	of mine	olingo	on side	ordeal
noetic	nosode	numbly	obvert	of name	olived	onside	ordure
Noetic	nossir	numdah	occamy	of note	oliver	on-site	Oregon
no fear	nostoc	numina	occult	of ours	Oliver	onsold	or else
no fool	nostos	numnah	occupy	OFSTED	olivet	on song	orenda
nogged	nostra	num-num	ocelli	oftens	ollamh	on spec	orfray
noggin	no such	nuncio	ocelot	of wont	olland	on suss	organa
no-good	notamy	nuncle	ochone	of yore	ollave	on tape	organy
no-iron	notary	nunlet	ochrea	ogdoad	omasum	on time	orgasm
no joke	notate	nuphar	Ockham	ogival	omelet	on tour	orgeat
no-jump	not bad	nuplex	o'clock	ogived	omened	onuses	orgiac
no less	notchy	nuragh	ocracy	Oglala	omenta	on view	orgies
no-load	not hay	nurser	octane	O grade	omertà	onward	orgone
nomade	nother	nursey	Octans	O'Grady	ometer	oocyst	oribis
nomady	notice	nursle	octant	ogress	omnify	oocyte	orient
no mean	notify	nutant	octave	ogrish	omnium	oodles	origin
nomina	no time	nutate	octavo	oh dear	onager	oogamy	oriole
nomism	notion	nut-cut	octode	Ohioan	on bail	oolite	Orisha
no more	not out	nuthin	octoic	ohmage	on call	oolith	orison
non-act	nougat	nutlet	octopi	oh well	oncome	oology	Orissi
nonage	nought	nutmeg	octose	oh yeah	oncost	oolong	Orkney
no-name	nounal	nut oil	octroi	oidium	on deck	oomiak	orl-fly
nonane	novate	nutria	octroy	oikist	ondine	oompah	orming
non-art	novell	nuts to	octuor	oil-box	on-ding	oorali	ormolu
nonary	novena	nutted	ocular	oil can	on duty	oozily	or more

ornate	outing	oxlike	paleae	Papago	Pasdar	Pawpaw	pegged
ornery	outjet	oxtail	Palekh	papain	pasear	paxwax	pegger
orobus	outjut	oxy-arc	palely	papaya	Pashto	pay bed	Pegity
orogen	outlaw	oxy-gas	paling	papery	paskha	paybob	peg-leg
orotic	outlay	oxygen	palish	papess	pass by	pay day	peg out
orphan	outlet	oxygon	palkee	papish	passed	payess	pegtop
Orphic	outlie	oxymel	pallah	papism	passée	pay for	Peguan
orpine	out-lot	oyster	Pallas	papist	passel	paynim	Peguer
orrery	outman	ozaena	palled	pappus	passer	pay off	Peigan
oscine	outnal	Ozalid	pallet	Papuan	passim	payola	Peirce
oscula	output	ozoned	pallia	papula	pass on	pay out	Peking
osiery	outran	ozoner	pallid	papule	pass up	payout	pelade
osmate	outray	ozonic	pallor	papyri	pastel	Pazand	pelage
osmics	outrig	pa'anga	palmar	parade	paster	pazazz	Peléan
osmium	outros	Pablum	palmed	paramo	pastie	pea-bug	pelham
osmole	outrow	paccay	palmer	parang	pastil	peachy	Pelham
osmose	outrun	pacier	palolo	paraph	pastis	pea-cod	pelike
osmund	out-run	pacify	palone	parcel	past it	peagle	Pelion
osprey	outsat	pacing	palpal	parded	pastor	pea-gun	pelite
ossein	outsee	packed	palpus	pardon	pastry	peahen	pellet
Ossete	outseg	packer	palter	parent	pataca	peaked	Pelman
ossify	outset	packet	paltry	parera	pataka	pealer	pelmet
ostend	outsin	packie	pampas	Pareto	patana	peanut	peloid
ostent	outsit	pack in	pamper	parget	patart	pea-pod	pelong
osteon	out-top	pack up	panace	pariah	patchy	pearly	pelota
ostial	outvie	Pac-Man	panada	Parian	patent	peasen	peltae
ostium	outwit	padauk	panama	paries	patera	peavey	pelter
ostler	ovally	padded	Panama	paring	patesi	pebble	peltry
Ostman	Ovambo	padder	panary	parisa	Pathan	pebbly	peludo
Ostmen	ovaria	paddle	pandan	parish	pathic	pechan	pelure
ostomy	ovator	pad eye	pandar	parity	pathos	peck at	pelves
ostrog	over-by	pad-nag	Pandee	parker	patiki	pecked	pelvic
Ostyak	overdo	padouk	pander	parkie	patina	pecker	pelvis
Oswego	overgo	padsaw	pandit	parkin	patine	pecket	pencel
Othman	overly	Paduan	Paneth	parkly	patios	peckle	pencil
otiose	over to	paella	panfan	parlay	patois	pecten	pendle
otitic	ovibos	paeony	pan-fry	parley	patrix	pectic	peneid
otitis	ovisac	paging	panfry	parnas	patrol	pectin	Penest
Ottawa	ovonic	pagoda	panful	parode	patron	pectus	penful
oubaas	ovular	Pahari	Pangan	parody	patted	pedage	pen-gun
oughta	owelty	paiche	pan-ice	parole	pattée	pedalo	penial
ouklip	owl bus	paigle	panisc	paroli	patten	pedant	penide
ouncer	owlery	pai-hua	pankin	parore	patter	pedate	penile
our kid	owl-fly	pai kau	pan-man	parous	pattle	pedder	penman
oursin	owlish	pailou	pan-mug	parpen	patzer	peddle	Penman
ouster	owl jug	pained	pannam	parrel	paucal	pedion	penmen
outact	owl-ray	painty	panned	parrot	paulin	pedlar	penned
outage	oxalic	paired	pannum	parsec	paunch	pedway	penner
outarm	oxalis	pair up	pannus	parsec	pauper	peek-bo	pennet
out-ask	oxalyl	Paiute	Panoan	Parsee	pausal	peeled	penniä
outbid	ox-beef	pajala	pan out	parser	pavage	peeler	pennon
outbuy	oxbird	pakeha	pan-pie	parson	pavane	peenge	pen pal
outcry	ox cart	pakhal	panpot	partan	Pavian	peep-bo	pensée
out-cue	ox-eyed	pakihi	pantec	parted	paving	pee-pee	pensil
outdid	ox-foot	pakora	panter	parter	pavior	peeper	pentad
outeat	Oxford	pak pai	pantie	partly	pavise	peepul	Pentel
outfit	ox-gall	palace	pantle	parton	Pavlov	peerie	penton
outfly	oxgang	Palaic	pantos	parula	pawnee	peever	pentyl
out for	ox-head	palais	pantry	parure	Pawnee	peewee	penult
outfox	oxherd	palank	panyar	parvis	pawner	peewit	penury
outgas	oxhide	palapa	panzer	pascal	paw-paw	peg-bag	peonin
outgun	Oxisol	palate	papacy	Pascal	pawpaw	pegbox	people

pepful	phanal	Picene	pilose	pipped	planet	poddle	pommee
pepino	Phanar	pick at	pilous	pippie	plan on	podeon	pommel
peplos	pharos	picked	pilpul	pippin	Planté	podger	pommer
peplum	phaser	picker	pilule	pip-pip	plaque	podite	pommes
pepped	phases	picket	piment	pipsyl	plashy	podium	pommey
pepper	phasic	pickie	pimple	piqued	plasma	podley	Pommie
pepsin	phasis	pick in	pimply	piques	platan	podsol	Pomoan
peptic	phason	pickle	piñata	piquet	plated	Podunk	Pomona
Pequot	phasor	pick on	pinate	piracy	platen	podura	pompal
peract	phatic	pick up	pin-boy	pirate	plater	podzol	pomped
percid	phenic	picnic	pincer	piraya	platic	poetaz	pom-pom
percur	phenix	picong	pinche	pirned	player	poetic	pompom
perdie	phenol	picory	pindan	pirnie	play on	poetry	pompon
perfay	phenom	picral	pindar	pirrie	play up	poffle	ponask
perfin	phenon	picric	pinder	Pisces	pleach	poggle	poncey
period	phenyl	picryl	pineal	Pisgah	please	pogrom	poncho
perish	Philip	Pictor	Pineau	pisher	plebby	pointy	ponder
periti	Philly	picuda	pinene	pissed	pledge	poised	pondok
Perkin	phizog	piddle	pinery	pisser	pleiad	poiser	ponent
perk up	phlegm	piddly	pineta	piss on	Pleiad	poisha	pongal
Perlon	phloem	pidgin	pin-fit	piss-up	plenar	poison	pongee
Permic	phobia	piecen	pingao	pistia	plener	pokier	pongid
per mil	phobic	piecer	pinger	pistic	plenty	pokily	pongos
permit	phocid	pie-dog	pingle	pistil	plenum	poking	pongyi
pernio	phoebe	piedra	pingos	pistol	pleura	polack	ponies
Pernod	Phoebe	Piegan	pining	piston	pleuro	Polack	pontac
peroba	pholas	pieing	pinion	pitchi	plexal	polari	pontes
per pro	phoner	pielet	pinite	pitchy	plexor	polder	pontic
perron	phoney	pieman	pinken	pit dog	plexus	Polian	Pontic
persea	phonic	piemen	pinker	pithoi	pliant	police	pontil
Persic	phonon	pierce	pinkie	pithos	plical	policy	poodle
person	phooey	pierid	pinkly	pitied	pliers	poling	poonac
pertly	phoria	pieris	pinkos	pitier	plight	polish	Poonah
peruke	phossy	pietas	Pink 'Un	pities	plinth	Polish	pooped
peruse	photic	Piffer	pinlay	pitman	plisky	polite	poo-poo
Pesach	photog	piffle	pin-leg	Pitman	plissé	polity	poor do
pesage	photon	pig-bed	pin-man	pitmen	plodge	polka'd	poorly
Pesaro	photos	pig-bel	pinnae	pitpan	ploidy	polkas	pooter
peseta	phrase	pig-dog	pinnas	pit-pat	plombe	pollam	Pooter
pesewa	phrasy	pigeon	pinnay	pit-saw	plonko	pollan	pootle
peshwa	phreak	pigged	pinned	pitted	plotch	pollee	pop art
pester	pH-stat	piggie	pinner	pitter	plotty	pollen	Popean
pestle	phylae	piggin	pinnet	pit tip	plough	poller	popely
petard	phylic	piggle	pin oak	pituri	plover	pollex	popery
pet-day	phyllo	piglet	pinole	piupiu	plucky	polley	popess
petite	phylum	pignut	pinson	pixies	pluffy	pollie	pop-eye
petrel	physic	pig out	pintid	pizazz	plug in	polloi	pop fly
petrol	physio	pigpen	pintle	pizzle	plumed	polone	popgun
pe-tsai	phytal	pigsty	pintos	placee	plumet	Polong	popish
petted	phytic	pike on	pinule	placer	plummy	polony	Popish
petter	phytin	piking	Pinyin	placet	plumpy	Polony	popism
pettle	phytol	pilaff	pinyon	placid	plunge	polska	poplar
pewage	phyton	pilage	piolet	plagal	plural	polyad	poplin
pewdom	phytyl	Pilate	pionic	plague	plurry	polyol	pop off
pewful	piacle	pile up	piopio	plaguy	plushy	polype	pop-out
pewing	piaffe	pileus	pipage	plaice	pluton	polypi	popped
pewter	pianos	pilfer	pipe in	plaidy	pneuma	pomace	popper
peyote	piazza	pilger	pipery	plaint	poachy	pomade	poppet
peziza	pi-bond	piling	pipe up	planar	pocked	pomato	poppit
pfella	Picard	pillar	piping	planch	pocket	pomeis	popple
phakic	picaro	piller	pipkin	Planck	podded	pomelo	popply
phalli	picein	pillow	pip out	planer	podder	pomeys	popsie

pop-top	pottos	pricer	psocid	pungle	putter	quelea	raddle
porger	potzer	pricey	psyche	punier	puttoo	quelle	radeau
porion	pouchy	pricky	psycho	punily	puture	quench	radial
porism	poudre	priest	psylla	punish	puzzle	quetch	radian
porker	pouffe	primal	psy-ops	punkah	pycnic	queued	radios
porket	pounce	primed	psy-war	punker	pye-dog	queuer	radish
pornie	pounds	primer	PT boat	punkie	pyemia	queues	radium
porose	pourer	primly	pterin	punkin	pygarg	quiche	radius
porous	pouter	primos	ptisan	punned	pyjama	Quiché	radman
porret	powder	primus	ptooey	punner	pyjams	quilly	Radnor
porron	powwow	Primus	ptosis	punnet	pyknic	quince	radome
Porson	poxier	prince	ptotic	puntal	Pylian	quinch	radula
portal	Prague	prinky	ptygma	punter	pylori	Quincy	Raetic
portas	praise	priory	ptyxis	pupate	pyosis	quinia	raffee
ported	prance	priser	pubbed	pupped	pyrene	quinic	raffia
portée	prancy	prismy	pubble	puppet	pyrite	quinoa	raffle
porter	prankt	prison	public	Puppis	pyrola	quinol	rafter
portia	pranky	prissy	pucker	pupton	pyrone	quinsy	rag-bag
Portia	prasad	pritch	puckle	Purana	pyrope	quinte	ragbag
portly	pratal	privet	pudden	purdah	Pythic	quinti	ragged
porule	prater	prizer	pudder	Purdey	python	quinua	raggee
posada	pratie	prober	puddle	puréed	pyuria	quinze	ragger
poseur	praxis	probie	puddly	purées	pyx-box	quirky	raggie
poshly	prayer	probit	pueblo	purely	Qantas	quisby	raggle
posh up	pray-TV	Procne	puffer	purfle	Qatari	quisle	raging
posied	preach	Proddy	puffin	purgee	Q fever	quitch	raglan
posies	pre-act	profer	puff up	purger	qiblah	quite a	ragman
posish	pre-amp	profit	pug-dog	purify	qintar	quiver	ragmen
posnet	preamp	Progne	pugged	purine	Q meter	quizzy	rag-out
posser	precip	prolan	puggle	puriri	quadra	Qumran	ragout
posset	précis	proleg	puisne	purism	quadro	quokka	ragtag
possie	precog	prolix	pujari	purist	quaere	quorum	ragtop
possum	pre-cut	prolly	pukeko	purity	quagga	quotas	raguly
postal	precut	prolog	pukkah	purler	quaggy	quotee	rah-rah
postea	prefab	Prolog	pullen	purlin	quagma	quoter	raider
posted	prefer	promos	puller	purpie	quahog	quotha	railer
poster	prefix	prompt	pullet	purple	quaich	quotum	rail in
postie	preggo	pronto	pulley	purply	quaigh	qwerty	rainer
postil	preggy	pro-ode	pull in	purree	quails	QWERTY	raised
post-op	pre-law	propel	pull-on	purrer	quaint	rabate	raiser
Postum	prelim	proper	pull to	purser	quaiss	rabato	raisin
potage	pre-man	propho	pull up	pursue	quaite	rabbet	Rajput
pot-ale	pre-med	proppy	pullus	purvey	quaker	rabbin	rake in
potash	premed	propyl	pulpal	pusher	Quaker	rabbis	rakery
potato	pre-men	proser	pulper	push-in	qualmy	rabbit	rake up
pot-boy	premie	prosit	pulpit	push it	quango	rabble	raking
poteen	premio	prosty	pulque	Pushtu	quanta	rabies	rakish
potent	premix	protea	pulsar	push-up	Quapaw	raceme	ramada
potful	prenex	pro tem	pulsed	pusill	quarry	rachel	ramage
pot hat	prepay	protic	pulser	pussel	quarte	rachis	ram air
pother	preppy	proton	pultan	pusser	quarto	racial	rambai
pothos	preses	proved	pultun	puszta	quartz	racier	ramble
potion	pre-set	proven	pulwar	puteal	quasar	racily	ram-cat
potleg	presto	prover	pumice	put fly	quatre	racing	Ramean
pot-lid	pre-tax	Provie	pummel	putlog	quatro	racism	ramify
potman	pretor	Provos	pumped	put-off	quaver	racist	Ramism
pot off	pretty	prowed	pumper	put out	queach	rackan	Ramist
pot pie	prevue	pruner	punchy	put-put	queasy	racker	ram-jam
potsie	pre-war	prunus	puncta	putrid	Quebec	racket	ramjet
potted	preyer	prusik	puncti	putsch	queeny	rackle	rammed
potter	Priapi	prying	pundit	putted	queest	rack up	rammel
pottle	priced	pseudo	punger	puttee	quelch	racoon	rammer

rammle	ratbag	rebeck	redden	reflux	relier	report	retama
ramnas	rat-bat	rebend	redder	refold	relies	repose	retard
ramoon	rather	rebind	reddle	refoot	reline	repost	retell
ramose	Rathke	rebody	red dog	re-form	relish	repped	retene
ramous	ratify	reboil	red-ear	reform	relive	repros	retest
ramper	ratine	rebook	redeem	refuel	reluct	repugn	re-time
ramrod	rating	reboot	red elm	refuge	reload	repute	retina
ramtil	ration	rebore	red-eye	re-fund	relume	requit	retire
rancel	ratios	reborn	Red Fed	refund	remade	rerail	retold
rancho	ratite	reboso	red fin	re-fuse	remain	re-rate	retook
ranchy	ratlin	rebozo	red fir	refuse	remake	reread	retool
rancid	ratoon	rebrew	red fog	refute	remand	re-reel	retort
rancio	Ratrac	rebuff	red fox	regain	re-mark	reride	retoss
randan	rat-run	rebuke	red gum	regale	remark	re-rise	retour
randem	rattan	rebunk	red hat	regalo	remast	rerobe	retral
random	rat-tat	rebuoy	red-hot	regard	remede	re-roll	retree
ranger	ratted	rebury	redial	regent	remedy	re-roof	retrim
rangle	ratter	re-bush	red ink	reggae	remeet	resail	retrod
ranine	rattle	recall	red leg	regild	remeid	resait	retros
ranker	rattly	recant	red man	regime	remelt	resale	retted
ranket	ratton	re-case	red mud	régime	remind	resalt	retter
rankle	raunch	recast	Red Ned	Regina	remint	rescue	retube
rankly	rauque	recced	red oak	region	remise	reseal	retune
ransel	ravage	re-cede	redoes	Regius	remiss	reseat	returf
ransom	ravers	recede	redone	regive	remold	réseau	re-turn
ran-tan	ravery	recede	red-out	reg'lar	remora	resect	return
ranter	rave-up	recent	red rag	reglet	remord	reseda	retuse
ranula	ravine	recess	red-raw	regnal	remote	reseed	retype
raphae	raving	recipe	redraw	regret	remove	reseek	Reuben
raphia	ravish	recite	redrew	regrew	rempli	resell	re-urge
rapido	Rawang	reckon	red rot	regrow	remuda	resent	revamp
rapier	raw bar	recoal	red-top	regula	rename	reship	reveal
rapine	rawish	recoat	reduce	reguli	render	reside	revend
rapist	ray-fin	recock	reduct	regulo	renege	re-sign	revent
rap out	ray gun	recoct	reduit	rehang	rengas	resign	reverb
rapped	raylet	recode	redund	rehash	renish	resile	revere
rappee	razant	recoil	reebok	rehear	rennet	resing	Revere
rappel	razing	recoin	re-echo	reheat	rennin	resiny	revers
rappen	razzia	recopy	reechy	reheel	renown	resist	revert
rapper	razzle	record	reeded	rehome	rental	re-site	revery
raptly	reable	recork	reeden	rehung	rented	resite	revest
raptor	reachy	recoup	reeder	Reilly	renter	resize	review
raptus	reader	rectal	re-edit	reiter	renule	reskin	revile
rarefy	read-in	rectly	reefer	Reiter	renvoi	reslay	revise
rarely	read of	rector	reeler	reiver	reopen	resoil	revive
rarest	read up	rectos	re-emit	Rejang	repack	resold	revoke
rarify	reagin	rectum	reeper	reject	repaid	resole	revolt
rariki	realia	rectus	ree-raw	rejoin	repair	resorb	revote
raring	really	recumb	reesed	rekiss	repand	re-sort	revved
rarish	realty	recuse	reesle	reknit	repass	resort	rewake
rarity	reamer	redact	reesty	relade	repast	respin	reward
rasant	reaper	red ant	reeved	re-laid	repave	restem	rewarm
rascal	rearer	red ash	reezed	relaid	repeal	rester	rewash
rasher	reason	redate	reface	reland	repeat	restow	rewind
rashly	reasty	red bat	refect	relata	repent	rest up	rewire
raskol	reaver	red bay	refeed	relate	repick	result	reword
rasper	reback	red box	refill	relend	repine	resume	rework
rassle	rebake	red bud	refine	relent	replan	resumé	rewrap
raster	rebase	redbud	reflag	relevé	replay	résumé	Rexine
rastle	rebate	red bug	reflet	relict	replot	retail	Rexism
Rastus	rebato	redcap	reflex	relied	replum	retain	Rexist
rasure	re-beat	red cat	reflow	relief	repone	retake	reyoke

re-zero	riegel	roachy	rooter	rubbed	run low	sadden	salwar
rezone	riffle	roadeo	rootle	rubber	run mad	sadder	samaan
Rhages	rifled	roader	rootsy	rubble	runnel	saddle	samara
rhagon	rifler	roadie	rooves	rubbly	runner	Sadean	samba'd
rhebok	riggal	roamer	rope in	Rubens	runnet	sadful	sambal
rhenic	rigged	roaned	ropery	rubied	run off	sadism	sambar
rhesis	rigger	roarer	ropier	rubies	run-out	sadist	sambas
rhesus	riggot	roband	ropily	rubify	runrig	saeter	sambok
rhetic	righto	robbed	roping	rub off	runted	safari	Sambos
Rhetic	righty	robber	roquet	rub out	runway	safely	sambuk
rhetor	rigour	robbin	rorter	rubral	rupiah	safety	sambuq
rheumy	rig-out	Robert	rosace	rubric	rupial	Sagbag	sambur
rhexia	rilled	robing	rosary	ruched	rurban	sagely	samely
rhexis	rillet	Rob Roy	roscid	ruckle	ruscus	sagene	Samian
rhinal	Rilsan	robust	roscoe	ruckus	rushee	saggar	samiel
rhinos	rimaye	rochea	roseal	rudder	rushen	sagged	samier
Rhodes	rimier	rocher	rosery	ruddle	rusher	sagger	samite
rhodic	rim man	rochet	Roshis	rudely	rusine	sagina	samiti
rhombi	rimmed	rocker	rosied	rudery	russet	sagoin	samlet
rhotic	rimose	rocket	rosier	rudish	Russia	Sahara	sammen
Rhovyl	rimous	rococo	rosily	rudist	Russic	sahiba	sammie
rhumba	rimple	rodded	rosiny	rudite	Russki	said he	Samoan
rhymer	rinded	rodder	rosser	rueful	Russky	sailed	samosa
rhymic	rindle	rodent	rossie	rueing	rustic	sailer	sampan
rhythm	ringed	rodeos	roster	ruffed	rustle	sail in	sample
rhyton	ringer	rodham	rostra	ruffer	rustly	sailor	Samsam
Rialto	Ringer	rodlet	rotang	ruffle	rustre	saithe	Samsoe
ribald	ringie	rodman	rotary	ruffly	ruther	Saitic	Samson
riband	ring in	rodney	rotate	rufous	rutile	saiyid	sancho
ribbed	ringle	Rodney	rotche	rugate	rutted	Sakian	Sancho
ribber	ring up	roguer	rot gut	rugged	ruttee	sakura	sancta
ribbit	rinser	Roland	rother	rugger	rutter	salaam	sandal
ribbok	Rinzai	roller	rotolo	ruggle	ruttle	salade	sandar
ribbon	Riojan	roll in	rottan	Rugian	Rwanda	salami	sanded
rib-eye	rioter	rollio	rotted	rugosa	Rylean	salary	sander
riblet	riotry	roll on	rotten	rugose	ryokan	Salian	sandhi
ribose	ripely	roll up	rotter	rugous	ryotti	salify	Sandow
Ricard	rip off	Romaic	rottle	rug-rat	Ryukyu	salina	sandur
richen	rip out	romaji	rotula	ruiner	Saanen	saline	sandyx
riches	ripped	Romani	rotund	rule in	Sabaic	Salish	sanely
richie	ripper	Romano	rouble	ruling	sabalo	salita	sangar
richly	ripple	Romany	roucou	rumaki	sabbat	saliva	sanies
ricker	ripply	Romeos	roughy	rumble	sabbed	sallee	sanify
ricket	Rippon	Romish	Rouman	rumbly	Sabean	sallet	sanity
rickey	riprap	Romney	rounce	rumdum	Sabian	sallow	sanjak
rickle	ripsaw	romper	rouncy	rum-jar	sabicu	salmis	Sankey
ricrac	rise to	romp in	roundy	rumkin	sabine	salmon	sannah
rictal	rise up	rondel	rouped	rummer	Sabine	saloon	sannup
rictus	rishis	rondos	rouper	rumour	sabkha	saloop	sanpro
ridded	rishon	ronins	rouser	rum pad	sabled	saltee	sansei
riddel	rising	roo-bar	rousie	rumped	sabred	salten	santal
ridden	risker	roodge	router	Rumper	sacate	salter	Santal
ridder	Risley	roofed	routhy	rumple	sachem	saltie	santir
riddle	risqué	roofer	roving	rumply	sachet	saltly	santon
rident	ritard	rooker	rowage	rumpot	sacked	saltus	Santos
ride-on	ritter	rookie	rowing	rumpus	sacken	saluki	Sanusi
ride up	ritual	rookus	row out	rum-tum	sacker	salute	sapele
ridged	Riu-kiu	roomed	rozzer	rundle	sacket	salver	sapful
ridgel	rivage	roomer	Rualla	run dry	sackie	salvia	saphie
ridger	rivery	roomie	Ruanda	runged	sacral	salvor	Sapiny
riding	rizzar	roomth	rubati	runkle	sacred	salvos	sapota
ridley	r month	rooted	rubato	runlet	sacrum	Salvos	sapour

sappan	saxony	sclera	scutal	secule	senary	sester	shamal
sapped	Saxony	scolex	scutch	secund	senate	sestet	shaman
sapper	sayall	scolia	scutel	secure	Sendai	seston	shamba
sapple	sayest	scoloc	scutty	sedate	sendal	Setine	shamer
sap-rot	saying	sconce	scutum	sedent	sendee	set net	shammy
sap-run	say nay	scoopy	scuzzy	sedged	sender	set off	shamus
sarang	say out	scopae	Scylla	sedile	send in	setose	shandy
sarape	say yea	scorch	scypha	seduce	sendle	set out	Shango
Sarcee	say yes	scorer	scyphi	seeded	send on	settee	shangy
sarcle	sayyid	scores	scythe	seedee	send up	setter	shanny
sardar	scabby	scoria	sea air	seeder	Seneca	settle	shanty
sarees	scaffy	scorse	sea-ape	see fit	senega	set-tos	shaped
sargus	scaife	scotch	sea-ash	see for	senhor	setule	shapen
saried	scalar	Scotch	sea bag	seegar	senile	severe	shaper
sarkar	scaled	scoter	sea-bat	seeing	senior	severy	shapka
sarlac	scaler	scotia	seabed	seeker	seniti	Sèvres	shapoo
sarnie	scaley	Scotic	sea-bug	seemer	senium	sewage	sharer
sarong	scalic	scotty	sea-cat	seemly	sennet	sewery	sharia
Sarouk	scally	Scouse	sea-cob	see off	sennit	sewing	Sharia
sarsen	scampi	scouth	sea cow	see out	señora	sewn-in	sharif
sartin	scance	scovan	sea dog	see red	senryu	sex act	sharka
sartor	scanty	scovel	sea-ear	see-saw	sensal	sex aid	sharky
sashay	scapus	scovin	sea-eel	seesee	Sen-Sen	sexfid	sharny
sashed	scarab	scowly	sea-egg	seethe	sensor	sexful	Sharps
sasine	scarce	scrape	sea fan	see you	sensum	sexier	sharpy
satang	scared	scrapy	sea-fir	Sefton	sentry	sexily	sharry
satara	scarer	scrawl	sea fog	seggie	Senufo	sexism	Shasta
sateen	scarfs	scraze	sea-fox	segoon	sepium	sexist	shaved
satiny	scarpe	screak	sea hen	segued	sepsis	sexpot	shaven
satire	scarry	scream	sea-hog	segues	septal	sextal	shaver
satnav	scarth	screed	sealed	seiche	septet	sextan	shavie
satori	scarus	screef	sealer	seidel	septic	sextar	shazam
satrap	scathe	screel	seaman	seiner	septum	sextet	sheafy
Saturn	scatty	screen	sea-mat	seised	sequel	sextic	sheath
saucer	scazon	screwy	sea-maw	seisin	sequin	sexton	sheave
Saudis	Sceaux	scribe	seamen	seized	serail	sextry	Shebat
sauger	scenic	scried	seamer	seizer	serang	sexual	sheela
saulie	scenty	scries	seamew	seizin	serape	Sézary	sheeny
Saumur	schelm	scrimp	Seanad	sejant	seraph	sferic	sheep-o
saurel	schema	script	seance	sejoin	seraya	Shabak	sheepy
sautéd	scheme	scrive	séance	sekere	serdab	shabby	sheety
savage	Schick	scrobe	sea oak	seldom	serein	shable	Sheika
Savage	Schiff	scroll	sea-owl	select	serene	shabti	sheikh
savant	schism	scroop	sea pen	selion	sereno	shacky	sheila
savate	schist	scrota	sea-pie	Seljuk	serial	shaded	shekel
savine	schitz	scruff	sea-pig	Selkup	Serian	shader	shelfs
saving	schizo	scrump	searce	seller	series	shadow	shelfy
savory	schlep	scrunt	search	sell-in	serine	shaduf	shelly
savour	school	scruto	sea-run	sell on	sermon	Shafii	Shelta
Sawbwa	schoon	scruze	season	sell up	Sernyl	shafty	shelty
sawder	schoot	scryer	seater	selsyn	serosa	shaggy	Shelty
sawfly	schorl	scubas	seaway	selves	serous	shahid	shelve
saw-gin	schout	scuddy	Sebago	Semang	serpaw	shaikh	shelvy
sawing	schuit	sculch	sebkha	semata	serrae	shaken	shenzi
saw-log	Schupo	sculpt	secant	semble	serran	shaker	she-oak
sawney	schuss	scummy	secede	seméed	serums	shakey	sherif
saw-pit	schuyt	scunch	secern	sememe	serval	shakos	Sherpa
saw-set	scient	scunge	secesh	Semite	server	Shakti	sherry
sawyer	sci-fic	scungy	Seckel	semmit	servos	shaley	sherut
saxaul	scilla	scurfy	second	Semple	sesame	shall I	sheugh
saxist	Sciote	scurry	secret	sempre	sesban	shalom	Shevat
saxman	sclaff	scurvy	sector	Semtex	seseli	shalot	shewel

shicer	shradh	sifter	sinker	skilly	sleyer	smelts	snippy
shield	shrank	sigher	sink in	skimpy	sliced	smeuse	snitch
shifta	shrape	sighty	sinned	skinch	slicer	smidge	snitty
shifty	shrdlu	siglum	sinner	skinny	slider	smilax	snivel
Shi'ism	shrewd	signal	sinnet	skip it	slight	smiler	snobby
Shiism	shriek	signed	sinter	skippy	slimly	smilet	Sno-cat
Shi'ite	shrift	signee	sintok	skirty	slimsy	smiley	snodly
Shiite	shrike	signer	Siouan	ski run	slinge	smirch	Snooks
shikar	shrill	signet	sipage	skiter	slinky	smirky	snoopy
shikho	shrimp	sign in	siphon	ski tow	slip-in	smitch	snoose
shikra	shrine	sign on	Sipibo	skiver	slip-on	smiter	snooty
shiksa	shrink	signor	siping	skivie	slippy	smithy	snoove
Shilha	shrive	sign up	sipped	skivvy	slip up	smoggy	snooze
shilpy	shroff	silage	sipper	ski-wax	slitch	smoked	snoozy
shimmy	shroud	silane	sippet	sklent	slithe	smoker	Snopes
shindy	shrove	silene	sipple	skolly	slithy	smokey	snorer
shined	Shrove	sileni	sirdar	Skraup	slitty	smokie	snorty
shiner	shruff	silent	sireen	skreek	sliver	smooch	snotty
shinny	shrunk	silica	Sirian	skreel	Sloane	smooge	snouch
Shinto	shtick	silked	sirkar	skrike	slobby	smooth	snouty
shinty	shtook	silken	sirrah	skuett	slogan	smouch	snubby
shippo	shtoom	silker	Sirrah	skunky	sloosh	smouse	snudge
shippy	shtuck	silkie	sirree	skutch	sloped	smriti	snuffy
Shiraz	shtumm	sillar	siskin	skycap	sloper	smudge	snugly
shirty	shufti	siller	sissoo	skyful	slopey	smudgy	snurge
shisha	shufty	siloes	sister	sky-god	sloppy	smugly	soaken
shit on	shut in	Silozi	sistra	skyish	sloshy	smutch	soaker
shitty	shut it	silure	sitcom	skyjam	slouch	smutty	soaper
shivah	shut to	silvan	sithen	Skylon	slough	Smyrna	soapie
shiver	shut up	silver	sit mum	skyman	slougi	snaggy	soarer
shivey	shyest	silvex	sit out	skyway	Slovak	snaily	sobbed
shivoo	shyish	simial	sitrep	slabby	sloven	snaith	sobber
shlump	shypoo	simian	sitten	slaggy	slower	snakey	so be it
shmear	sialic	simile	sitter	slaked	slowly	snap at	sobeit
shoaly	sialon	simkin	situal	slalom	slow-up	snap-in	sobful
shoddy	sibbed	simlin	situla	slangy	slubby	snap-on	sobole
shoder	sibred	simmer	Sivite	slanty	sludge	snappy	socage
shofar	siccan	simmon	Siwash	slap-up	sludgy	snap up	soccer
shoful	sicken	simnel	sixain	slashy	sluggy	snarer	social
shoggy	sicker	simony	six-gun	slatch	sluice	snarky	socius
shogun	sickie	simool	six-two	slater	sluicy	snarly	socked
shomer	sick-in	simoom	size up	slaver	slum it	snaste	socket
shonda	sickle	simoon	sizing	slavey	slummy	snatch	socman
shonky	sickly	simper	sizzle	Slavic	slumpy	snavel	Socred
shooed	sickos	simple	skaith	Slavon	slurry	snavle	sod-all
shoo-in	sicsac	simply	skance	slayer	slushy	snazzy	sodded
shoppe	sicula	sim-sim	skater	sleave	slutch	sneaky	sodden
shoppy	Sidamo	simson	skates	sleaze	slutty	sneath	sodger
shoran	Sidcot	simurg	skeigh	sleazo	sly dog	sneery	sodian
shorer	sidder	Sinaic	skelet	sleazy	slyest	sneeze	sodide
shorts	siddow	sin bin	skelly	sledge	slyish	sneezy	sodium
shorty	Siddur	Sindhi	skelvy	sleech	smahan	snelly	sod off
shotty	side-on	sindon	skerry	sleeky	smally	sniddy	sodoku
should	siding	sinewy	sketch	sleepy	smalts	snidey	sodomy
shouse	Siebel	sinful	skewed	sleety	smarmy	snidge	soever
shovel	sieger	singer	skewer	sleeve	smarty	sniffy	soffit
shover	sienna	sing-in	ski-bob	sleeze	smatch	snifty	soften
showed	sierra	single	skiddy	sleezy	smeary	snip at	softie
shower	siesta	singlo	skidoo	sleigh	smeech	sniper	softly
show in	siever	singly	Skidoo	sleugh	smeeth	snipes	sogged
show-me	sifaka	sing up	skiing	sleuth	smegma	snipey	soigné
show up	siffle	sinify	ski-ing	S level	smelly	snipey	soiled

soirée	sorner	spawny	splosh	squash	status	stitch	streak
solace	sorrel	spayad	splurt	squatt	staved	stithy	stream
solate	sorren	speary	spodic	squawk	staver	stiver	streck
soldan	sorrow	specie	spoilt	squdge	staves	stoach	streek
solder	sortal	specky	spoked	squdgy	Stavka	stocky	streel
sold on	sorted	speech	spoken	squeak	stayer	stodge	street
solely	sorter	speedo	sponge	squeal	stay in	stodgy	Strega
solemn	sortie	speedy	spongy	squeam	stay on	stogie	strene
solera	sort of	speiss	spooky	squill	stay-up	stoked	stress
soleus	so soon	spence	spoony	squint	steady	stoker	strewn
solidi	Sothic	spense	sporal	squire	steamy	stokes	striae
soling	sotted	sperma	Spörer	squirl	steboy	Stokes	strick
solion	sotter	sperms	sporty	squirm	steely	stoled	strict
solity	souari	spermy	sposhy	squirr	steepy	stolen	stride
sollar	soubah	sperse	spot on	squirt	steeve	stolid	strife
so long	soucar	spetch	spotty	squish	Stefan	stolon	strift
soloth	sought	spewer	spouse	Sranan	stelae	stomal	striga
soloti	souled	sphene	spousy	Stabex	stelar	stomas	strike
solute	souler	sphere	spouty	Stabit	stemma	stomia	strind
Solvay	soulie	sphery	sprack	stable	stemmy	stompy	Strine
solver	Soumak	sphinx	sprain	stably	stench	stoned	string
solvus	souper	spiced	sprang	staboy	stenog	stonen	stripe
Somali	source	spicer	sprawl	stacte	stenol	stoner	stript
so many	sourly	spicey	spread	stadda	stenos	stoney	stripy
sombre	sour on	spider	spreed	stadia	step-in	Stoney	strive
somite	souter	spiffy	sprees	stadic	step it	stooge	stroam
sommer	soviet	spigot	spreeu	staffs	step-on	stoopy	strobe
so much	Soviet	spiked	sprent	staged	steppe	stooth	strode
sonant	sovran	spiker	spring	stager	step up	stop by	stroil
sonata	sowans	spikey	sprink	stagey	stereo	stoper	stroke
sonder	sow bug	spilly	sprint	staggy	steric	stop-go	stroky
sonics	sowbug	spilth	sprite	stainy	sterks	stop in	stroll
sonnet	sowens	spinae	sprity	stairy	sterna	stop on	stroma
sonsie	so what	spinal	spritz	staker	Sterno	stoppo	stromb
sontag	sowing	spinar	sprong	stakey	sterny	stop up	strome
soogan	sowlth	spined	sprote	Stalag	sterol	storax	strong
soogee	sow-pig	spinel	sprout	stalch	sterro	storer	strool
soojee	sozzle	spinet	spruce	staler	steven	storey	stroud
sookey	spaced	spinks	spruik	stalky	stewed	stormy	stroup
sookie	spacer	spinny	spruit	stamen	stibic	stotty	strove
sooler	spacey	spinor	sprung	stance	stické	stound	strown
soon as	spader	spinto	sprunt	stanch	sticky	stoury	struck
sooner	spadix	spin-up	spryer	stanol	Sticky	stoush	struma
soonly	spammy	spiral	spryly	stanza	stieve	stoven	strung
soorma	spandy	spirea	spuddy	stanze	stiffy	stover	strunt
so or so	sparer	spired	spunky	stapes	stifle	stowce	struth
soothe	sparge	spirit	spurge	staple	stigma	stower	Stuart
Sophia	sparid	spital	spuria	starch	stilly	stow it	stubby
sophic	Sparks	spitty	spurii	starer	stilty	stract	stucco
sopite	sparky	spit up	spurry	starey	stinge	strafe	studio
sopped	sparry	spitzy	sputum	starko	stingo	straif	stuffy
sopper	sparse	spivvy	spydom	starry	stingy	straik	stuggy
sorage	sparth	splake	spyism	starve	stinko	strain	stumer
sorbet	sparus	splash	spy out	stases	stinky	strait	stumpy
sorbic	spasmi	spleen	squail	stasis	stinty	strake	stuns'l
sorbus	spasmy	spleet	squali	statal	stipel	straky	stunty
sordes	spatha	splice	squall	stated	stiper	strand	stupid
sordid	spathe	spliff	squama	stater	stipes	strass	stupor
sordor	spauld	spline	squame	Stater	stir in	strata	sturdy
sordun	spaver	splint	square	static	stir it	strath	sturks
sorely	spavie	splirt	squark	stator	stirps	strawn	styany
sorgho	spavin	splore	squary	statue	stir up	strawy	stylar

styler	Sullan	surtax	switch	tagged	tanger	tarsia	teapoy
stylet	sullen	survey	swivel	tagger	tangle	tarsus	tearer
stylos	sullow	surwan	swiver	taglet	tangly	tartan	tear-up
stylus	sulpha	Susian	swivet	tagrag	tangor	tartar	teasel
stymie	sultan	Susie-Q	swoony	taguan	tangos	Tartar	teaser
styrax	sultry	suslik	swoose	tahali	tangun	tarten	teaset
styrol	sumach	sussed	swoosh	tahina	Tangut	tartly	teated
styryl	sumbul	Sussex	swound	Tahiti	tanist	Tarvia	teazel
suable	summae	susurr	Sydney	tahsil	tanjib	Tarzan	teazle
suaeda	summar	sutile	syllab	taiaha	tanker	tasajo	Tebele
subbed	summat	sutler	syllid	t'ai chi	tanned	Tasian	techie
subbie	summed	suttee	sylphy	T'ai Chi	tanner	tasker	techno
sub-deb	summer	suttle	sylvae	taihoa	tannia	Taslan	teckel
subdue	summit	suture	sylvan	tailed	tannic	taslet	tecoma
sub-era	summon	Suzuki	sylvas	tailer	tannie	tassel	tectal
subfeu	sumner	Svarga	symbol	tail in	tannin	tasset	tectum
subgum	Sumner	svelte	syndic	tail on	tannoy	tassie	tedded
subito	sun arc	swaddy	syngas	tailor	Tannoy	Tassie	tedder
subjee	sunbed	swadge	syngen	tailye	Tanoan	tasted	Te Deum
sub-let	sunbow	swaged	synjet	taipan	tan-pit	taster	tedium
sublet	sundae	swager	synoil	taisch	tanrec	tatami	teedle
subman	Sunday	swallo	synroc	takahe	tantra	tatted	tee-hee
submen	sunder	swamis	syntax	take in	tan-vat	tatter	teemer
submit	sundew	swampy	syphon	take it	Tan war	tattie	teener
suborn	sun-dog	Swanee	Syriac	take on	Taoism	tattle	teensy
subsea	sundri	swanky	Syrian	take to	Taoist	tattoo	teenty
subset	sun-dry	swanny	syrinx	take up	taotai	taught	tee off
subtle	sundry	Swaraj	syrtis	taking	tapism	tauric	teepee
subtly	sungem	swardy	syrtos	takkie	taplet	Taurid	Teepol
suburb	sun-god	Swarga	syrupy	talbot	tap out	Taurus	teerer
subway	Sun Gun	swarri	system	talced	tappal	Tau Sug	teesoo
succah	sun-hat	swarry	syzygy	talcum	tapped	tauten	teetar
succor	sunhat	swarth	Szekel	talent	tapper	tautly	teetee
such as	sunken	swarty	Sze Yap	talion	tappet	tautog	teeter
sucken	sunker	swarve	tabard	talked	tap-tap	tavern	teethe
sucker	sunket	swashy	tabbed	talker	tap-too	tawdry	teethy
sucket	sunlet	swatch	tab key	talkie	tarada	tawhai	teevee
suck in	sunlit	swathe	tabled	talk-in	tarama	tawpie	Teflon
suckle	sunned	swaths	tabler	talk of	tarara	taxeme	Tegean
suck up	Sunnis	Swatow	tablet	talk to	tarata	taxied	tegmen
sudary	sunnud	swaver	tabnab	talk up	tar-box	taxies	tegula
sudden	sun-oil	swayed	taboos	tallow	tar-boy	taxine	telcos
Sudder	sun-ray	swayer	taboot	Talmud	tardon	taxman	tele-ad
sudser	sunset	sweaty	tabret	talook	targer	taxmen	teledu
sueded	suntan	swedge	Tabriz	talweg	target	taxwax	telega
Suevic	supawn	sweeny	tabued	tamale	Targui	Taylor	Telegu
suffer	superb	sweepy	tabule	Tamang	Targum	tchick	telial
suffix	sup gum	sweert	tachos	tamanu	tariff	tea bag	telium
Sufism	supine	sweety	tacker	tamari	taring	tea bar	tellen
sugary	supped	swelty	tacket	tamber	tariqa	tea-box	teller
suggan	supper	swerve	tackie	tamein	tarmac	tea boy	tellin
sugged	supple	sweven	tackle	tamely	Tarmac	tea-can	tellow
suited	supply	swifty	tactic	tamine	tarnal	teache	tellus
suiter	surely	swimmy	tactor	tammar	tarock	teacup	telome
suitor	surety	swines	tactus	Tammuz	tarpan	teagle	telson
sukiya	surfer	swinge	tadger	tampan	tar-pit	Teague	Teltag
Sukuma	surfie	swingy	Tadjik	Tampax	tarpon	teaman	Telugu
sulcal	Surlyn	swinny	taenia	tamper	tar-pot	teamer	Temiar
sulcus	surnai	swiper	Taffia	tampon	tarras	teanel	tempeh
sulham	surnap	swipey	tafone	tam-tam	tarred	tea oil	temper
suling	surrey	swirly	tag day	tan-bed	tarrow	tea pad	temple
sulker	Surrey	swishy	tag end	tandem	tarsal	teapot	tempos

tempus	tester	thewed	thyine	timous	titled	Tolman	top off
temura	testes	they'll	thymic	tinaja	titler	tolsel	top out
tenace	testis	they're	thymol	tincal	titman	Toltec	topped
tenant	teston	they've	thymus	tin can	titoki	toluic	topper
Tendai	tetany	Thibet	thyrse	tindal	ti-tree	toluol	toppie
tender	tetchy	thible	thyrsi	tinder	titter	toluyl	topple
tendon	tether	thicko	tibbin	tin ear	tittle	tolzey	topply
tenent	Tethys	thicky	Tibert	tineid	tittup	tomata	topset
tenner	tetrad	thieve	tibiae	tinful	titule	tomato	top ten
tennis	tetryl	thight	tibial	tinger	tityra	tombac	torchy
tennos	tetter	thingy	ticked	tingle	tjaele	tombic	torero
tenour	tettix	thinly	ticken	tingly	tmeses	tomboy	torfle
tenpin	Teuton	thiram	ticker	tin god	tmesis	tom-cat	Torgut
tenrec	tevish	thirst	ticket	tin hat	to a dot	tomcod	Tories
tensed	te-whit	thirty	tickey	tinier	to a man	tomial	tornal
tenser	tewhit	thitsi	tickle	tinily	to arms	tomium	tornus
tenson	tewtaw	thivel	tickly	tining	toasty	tommed	toroid
tensor	Texian	tholoi	tic-tac	tinker	to a tee	to-morn	torori
tented	Tex-Mex	tholos	Ticuna	tinkle	toa-toa	tomtit	torose
tenter	thaive	Thomas	tidbit	tinkly	to bits	tom-tom	torous
tenues	thakin	thorax	tiddle	tinman	to boot	to-name	torpex
tenuis	thakur	thoria	tiddly	tinned	tocher	tonant	torpid
tenure	thaler	thorny	tidier	tinner	tochis	toneme	torpor
tenuto	thalli	thoron	tidily	tinnet	to come	tone up	torque
tenzon	thamin	thorpe	tiding	tinnie	tocsin	Tongan	torret
tepary	Thamud	though	tie-bar	tinpot	to date	tonged	torrid
tepefy	thatch	thrack	tie-dye	tinsel	Todd-AO	tonger	torsel
tephra	that is	thrall	tieing	tinsey	todder	tongue	torsos
tepify	thawer	thrash	tienda	tinted	toddle	tonier	torten
teraph	the act	Thraso	tie-off	tinter	todger	tonify	tortes
terbia	theave	thrave	tie-pin	tipcat	todies	tonish	tortie
tercel	the axe	thrawn	tiepin	tipiti	toe box	tonist	torula
tercer	Theban	thread	tierce	tiplet	toecap	tonite	torvid
tercet	the Bar	threap	tiercé	tip off	toe-end	tonjon	Toryfy
tercio	the boy	threat	tiered	tipped	toeing	tonker	to seek
teredo	the Bye	threep	tierer	tippee	toe-out	tonlet	tosher
Terena	thecae	threne	tie rod	tipper	toe-rag	tonnel	tosser
terete	thecal	thresh	Tietze	tippet	toerag	tonner	toss in
tergal	The Day	threst	tie-wig	Tippex	toe-tip	tonsil	toss up
Tergal	the end	thrice	tiffin	Tipp-Ex	to-fall	tonsor	toston
tergum	the flu	thrift	tiffle	tipple	toffee	too bad	totara
termer	theine	thrill	tigery	tip-tap	togaed	tooler	t'other
termes	theirn	thring	tigger	tiptoe	togate	toolie	tother
termly	theirs	thrips	tiglic	tip-top	togged	tool up	to time
termon	theism	thrive	tiglon	tiptop	toggle	toonie	tot lot
termor	theist	throat	tignon	tipula	to hand	tooter	totora
ternal	the lot	throne	Tigray	tirade	to heel	toothy	totted
ternar	the man	throng	tigron	tirage	to home	tootle	totter
terpen	the Met	throve	tilery	tiring	Toidey	too-too	Tottie
terpin	thenal	thrown	tiling	tirlie	toiler	tootsy	tottle
terrae	thenar	thrump	tiller	tirrit	toilet	topass	toubab
terral	thence	thrums	tillet	tisane	toi-toi	topazy	toucan
Terran	the net	thrush	tillot	Tishri	tokkin	top-cut	touché
terrar	theory	thrust	Tilsit	tissue	to lack	top dog	touchy
terrer	there's	thulia	tilter	tiswas	Toledo	topees	toughe
terret	theses	thumby	tilt-up	titbit	tolite	Top End	tought
territ	thesis	thumri	timbal	titchy	toller	top hat	toughy
terror	the Six	thurse	timber	titely	tolley	Tophet	toupee
terser	the Ten	thusly	timbre	titfer	toll in	tophus	toupet
tertia	thetic	thwack	timely	tither	tol-lol	top-lit	tourer
testae	Thetis	thwart	timing	Titian	tollon	topman	tourte
testee	the Way	thwite	timist	Titian	toll TV	topmen	Tourte

tousle	trendy	troppo	Tudric	turnel	two-one	unawed	unease
tously	trepan	tro-tro	tuffet	turner	two-ply	unbait	uneasy
touter	trepid	trotty	tufted	Turner	two-two	unbank	uneath
touzle	tressy	trotyl	tufter	turn in	two-way	unbare	unedge
towage	trevat	trough	tugged	turnip	Tyburn	unbark	UNESCO
toward	trevis	troupe	tugger	turn on	tycoon	unbelt	uneven
tow bar	triage	trouse	tuggle	turn to	tykish	unbend	uneyed
towery	tribal	trouts	tughra	turn up	tylose	unbind	unface
towhee	tricar	trouty	tugrik	turpid	Tylose	unbitt	unfact
towing	Tricel	trover	tuille	turret	tymbal	unbody	unfain
towkay	trichi	trowel	Tuinal	turron	tymber	unbold	unfair
townee	tricky	trowie	tuk-tuk	turrum	tympan	unbolt	unfast
tow-net	tricot	truant	tulgey	turtle	typhon	unboot	unfeed
townie	triduo	trucks	tulwar	turved	Typhon	unborn	unfelt
townly	triene	trudge	tumbak	turves	typhus	unbran	unfilm
to work	trifid	truest	tumble	Tuscan	typify	unbred	unfine
tow-row	trifle	true to	tumefy	tusche	typist	unbung	unfirm
towser	trigly	truing	tumour	tushed	tyrant	unburn	unfold
towzle	trigon	truish	tum-tum	tuskar	Tyrian	unbury	unfond
toxoid	tri-jet	truism	tumuli	tusked	Tyrode	unbusy	unfool
toybox	triker	trumph	tumult	tusker	tystie	uncage	unform
toy boy	trilby	trunch	tundra	tussac	uakari	uncalm	unfree
toyboy	trillo	trusty	tune in	tussah	Ubangi	uncart	unfurl
toy car	trimer	truths	tune up	tusser	uberty	uncase	ungain
toy dog	tri-mix	truthy	tunful	tussle	ubiety	uncast	ungave
to-year	trimly	try gun	Tungan	tutory	uckers	unchid	ungear
toyful	trinal	trying	Tungar	tutsan	udatta	uncial	ungild
toyish	triode	try out	Tungus	Tutsis	Udmurt	unclad	ungilt
toyman	triose	trypan	tung-yu	tuttis	Udsbud	unclay	ungird
trabea	triped	try-pot	tunica	tut-tut	uffish	unclew	ungirt
tracer	tripey	tsamma	Tunica	tu-whit	UFOish	unclip	ungive
tradal	tripla	tsetse	tuning	tu-whoo	Uganda	unclog	unglad
traded	triple	T-shirt	Tunker	tuxedo	uglier	unclue	unglue
trader	triply	tsk tsk	tunket	tuyere	uglify	uncoat	ungone
tragal	tripod	Tsonga	tunned	tuyère	uglily	uncock	ungood
tragic	tripos	tsores	tunnel	tvorog	Ugrian	uncoil	ungrew
tragus	trippy	tsotsi	tunner	twaite	ugsome	uncool	ungrow
traiky	tripus	T-strap	tupelo	twangy	uguisu	uncord	ungual
traily	Trique	tsuica	Tupian	tweedy	ujamaa	uncork	ungues
traist	triste	Tswana	tuplet	tweely	ulendo	uncowl	unguis
trajet	tristy	T totum	tupped	tweeny	ullage	uncurb	ungula
tramal	trisul	Tuareg	tupsee	tweest	ulnage	uncurl	ungyve
trance	triton	tubage	turaco	tweeze	ulster	undead	unhair
tranky	Triton	tubbed	turban	twelve	Ulster	undeaf	unhand
tranny	trityl	tubber	turbeh	twenty	ultima	undear	unhang
trapes	triune	tubboe	turbid	twicer	ultimo	undeep	unhasp
trappy	trivet	tubful	turbit	twiggy	umbery	undear	unhead
trashy	trivia	tub-gig	turble	twilit	umbles	undern	unheal
trauma	trocar	tubing	turbos	twilly	umbone	undewy	unhear
travel	troche	Tubism	turbot	twiner	umboth	undies	unheld
travis	trochi	Tubist	Turcos	twinge	umbrae	undine	unhele
travoy	trogon	tubman	tureen	twingy	umbral	undock	unhelm
treaty	troika	tubule	Turfan	twinky	umbras	undoer	unhelp
treble	Trojan	tubuli	turfen	twinly	umbril	undoes	un-hero
trebly	trolly	Tucana	turgid	twirly	umfaan	undone	unhewn
trefid	Trombe	tuchun	turgor	twisel	umlaut	undraw	unhide
trefle	trompe	tucked	Turing	twisty	umpire	undrew	unhive
treflé	troner	tucker	turion	twitch	umteen	unduke	unholy
trek ox	troper	tucket	turkey	twitty	unable	undull	unhood
tremie	trophi	tuck in	Turkey	two-bit	unaker	unduly	unhook
tremor	trophy	tucuma	Turkic	two-egg	unakin	undust	unhoop
trench	tropic	Tudory	turned	twofer	unarch	undyed	unhope

unhung	unmown	unsnap	unwork	upsend	Usonan	varsal	Verdea
unh-unh	unnail	unsnib	unworn	upsett	US pint	varved	verdet
unhurt	unneat	unsoft	unwrap	upshot	usuary	varvel	verdin
unhusk	unnest	unsold	unyoke	upside	usurer	vassal	verdoy
Uniate	unopen	unsole	uparch	upsoar	usward	vastly	vergée
UNICEF	unpack	unsoul	upbank	upstay	Utahan	vat dye	verger
unific	unpaid	unsown	upbear	upstir	uterus	vatful	verify
unimer	unpass	unspan	upbeat	uptake	utmost	vat-man	verily
uniped	unpave	unspar	upbind	uptear	utopia	VATman	verism
unipod	unpeel	unsped	upboil	uptick	Utopia	VATmen	verist
unique	unpent	unspin	upbray	up till	utopic	vatted	verity
unisex	unpick	unspit	upbuoy	uptime	U value	vaulty	vermes
unison	unpile	unspun	up-card	uptook	uvulae	vaunty	vermil
UNISON	unplug	Unstan	upcast	uptorn	uvular	vaward	vermin
unital	unpope	unstep	upcome	uptoss	vacant	V-block	vermis
united	unposh	unstop	upcurl	uptown	vacate	vealer	vernal
uniter	unpray	unstow	updart	upturn	vacuum	vectis	Verneh
unjoin	unprop	unsued	update	upwaft	vading	vector	vernix
unjust	unrake	unsuit	updraw	upwake	vadose	Vedism	Verona
unkard	unread	unsung	upfill	upward	vagary	Vedist	verrel
unkeen	unreal	unsunk	upfold	upwarp	V-agent	veejay	versal
unkent	unredy	unsure	upgang	upwash	vagile	vegete	versed
unkept	unreel	untack	upgaze	upwell	vagina	veggie	verser
unkind	unrein	untame	upgrow	upwind	vagous	Vehmic	verset
unking	unrent	untape	uphand	upwing	vagrom	V-eight	versin
unkink	unrest	untent	uphang	up with	vahana	veigle	versor
unkiss	unrich	unthaw	upheap	upwith	vainly	veiled	versos
unknew	unrind	untidy	upheld	uracil	Vaisya	veinal	versus
unknit	unripe	untied	up helm	uraeus	vakeel	veined	vertex
unknot	unrobe	untile	uphill	Uralic	valent	veiner	vertic
unknow	unroll	untine	uphold	uramil	valeta	velate	vervet
unk-unk	unroof	untire	uphroe	Urania	valgus	Velcro	vesica
unlace	unroot	untold	uphurl	uranic	valine	veleta	vesper
unlade	unrope	untomb	upkeep	Uranus	valise	vellon	vessel
unlaid	unrove	untone	upknit	uranyl	Valium	vellum	vestal
unlash	unrule	untorn	up land	uratic	vallar	velour	vested
unlead	unruly	untrim	upland	urbane	valley	velure	vestee
unleaf	unrung	untrod	upleap	Urbino	vallum	velvet	vestry
unleal	unruth	untrue	uplift	urchin	valour	vendee	vetchy
unless	unsack	untuck	uplink	urease	valued	vender	vetoer
unlike	unsafe	untune	upload	uredia	valuer	vendor	vetoes
unlime	unsaid	unturn	uplong	ureide	values	vendue	ve-tsin
unline	unsalt	unused	uplook	uremia	valuta	veneer	vetted
unlink	unsane	unveil	upmost	ureter	valval	venene	vetter
unlive	unsawn	unvest	upness	uretic	valvar	venery	vetust
unload	unseal	unvote	up-pent	urgent	valved	Veneti	vexing
unlock	unseam	unware	upping	urinal	vamper	venger	viable
unloop	unseat	unwarp	uppish	urnful	vandal	venial	viably
unlord	unseen	unwary	uppity	urning	vanish	Venice	viatic
unlost	unself	unweal	up-push	urochs	Vanist	Venite	viator
unlove	unsell	unweft	uprate	uronic	vanity	vennel	vibist
unluck	unsent	unwell	uprear	uropod	vanner	venomy	Vibram
unlute	unsewn	unwept	uprend	ursine	Vannic	venose	vibrio
unmade	unsexy	unwhig	uprest	urtica	vapory	venous	vicine
unmaid	unshed	unwill	uprise	urtite	vapour	vented	victim
unmake	unship	unwily	uprist	urushi	Variac	venter	victor
unmask	unshod	unwind	uproar	usable	varied	ventil	vicuña
unmeek	unshoe	unwise	uproll	usager	varier	venule	vidame
unmeet	unshot	unwish	uproot	usance	varies	venust	videos
unmesh	unshut	unwist	uprose	useful	varlet	Vepsic	vidiot
unmild	unskin	unwive	uprush	useter	varoom	verbal	vidual
unmoor	unslip	unwont	upsara	us-ness	varroa	verbid	vielle

Vienna	vittae	waboom	wampum	waspie	weirdo	whimmy	wilier
view as	Vittel	wacker	wampus	wasser	weirdy	whimsy	wilily
viewer	vivace	wackos	wanded	wasted	welded	whiner	will do
viewly	vivaed	wadded	wander	wastel	welder	whinge	willed
vigent	vivary	wadder	wandle	waster	welked	whingy	willer
vigoro	vively	waddle	wandoo	wastry	welkin	whinny	willet
vigour	vivers	waddly	wangan	watery	welled	whip in	willey
vihara	vivify	wade in	wangle	Watson	wellie	whip on	willie
Viking	vivres	wadies	wanhap	wattap	well-in	whippy	willow
vildly	vizard	wadmal	wanion	wattle	Welshy	whip up	will to
vilely	vizier	wadset	Wankel	Watusi	welted	whirly	willya
Vilene	vizsla	wafery	wanker	waught	welter	whirry	Wilson
vilify	vlakte	waffie	wankle	wavery	Wemyss	whisht	Wilton
vility	vocode	waffle	wanner	wavier	Wendic	whisky	wimble
villan	vocoid	waffly	want ad	wavies	we-ness	whited	wimmin
villus	vocule	wagged	wanted	wavily	wen jen	whiten	wimple
vineal	Vodian	wagger	wanter	wax-end	wen-yen	whitey	Wimpys
vinery	voguer	waggle	wanton	wax-eye	weren't	Whitey	wincer
vin fou	voguey	waggly	wapato	waxier	wessel	whizzo	wincey
vingty	voiced	waggon	wapiti	waxily	Wessex	whizzy	windas
vinify	voicer	Wagogo	wapper	waxing	wester	who-all	winded
vining	voided	Wahabi	wappie	wax-pod	westie	whoe'er	winder
vinney	voidee	wahine	wappit	wayang	Weston	wholly	windle
vinose	voider	wah-wah	waragi	waylay	wet bar	whomso	wind on
vinous	Volans	waiata	war bag	wayman	wet-bob	whoops	window
vintem	volant	wailer	warble	way off	wet fly	whoosh	wind up
vintry	volary	wainer	War Box	way-out	wether	whorer	winery
Vinyon	volcan	waiter	war cry	weaken	wet rot	whosis	Wingco
violer	volens	wait on	warday	weakie	wetted	whydah	winged
violet	volent	wait up	warded	weakly	wetter	why-not	winger
violin	volley	waiver	warden	wealth	wet way	Wiccan	winier
violon	volume	Wai-Wai	warder	weanel	whacko	wicked	wink at
vipoma	voluta	wakame	war-dog	weaner	whacky	wicker	winker
virago	volute	Wakash	warely	weanie	whaler	wicket	winkle
virent	volvox	wake to	warful	weapon	whales	wicopy	winner
vireos	vomica	wake-up	war gas	wearer	whally	widdle	winnow
virgal	vomity	waking	war-god	wear on	whammo	widely	winrow
virger	voodoo	Walach	warier	weasel	whammy	widger	winsey
virgie	vorago	Walian	warily	weaver	wharfs	widget	winter
virgin	vorant	waling	Waring	weazen	wharve	widgie	wintle
Virgos	vortex	walker	war-man	webbed	what ho	widish	wintry
virial	votary	Walker	warmer	web-fed	what if	wieldy	Wintun
virile	Vo-Tech	walk in	warmly	Webley	what of	wiener	wipe up
virino	voteen	walk it	warmth	wedded	whatso	wienie	wirble
virion	vote in	walk-on	warm up	wedeln	wheaty	wifely	wire in
viroid	voting	walk up	warner	wedged	wheely	Wiffle	wirier
virola	votive	wallah	warped	wedger	wheeze	wifish	wirily
virole	Votyak	walled	warper	wedgie	wheezy	wigeon	wiring
virose	vowess	waller	warple	weeded	whelky	wigged	wirrah
virous	vox pop	wallet	warred	weeder	whelve	wiggle	wisdom
virtue	voyage	wallie	warree	weekly	whenas	wiggly	wisely
visaed	voyeur	wallis	warren	weenie	whence	wighty	wisent
visage	vuelta	wallop	Warren	weeper	whenso	wiglet	wise to
viscid	Vulcan	wallow	warrer	weepie	wherry	wigsby	wished
viscin	vulgar	wallum	warsle	weeshy	wheyey	wig-wag	wisher
viscus	vulgus	walnut	warted	weever	whidah	wigwag	wishly
Vishnu	vulpic	walrus	wasabi	weevil	whiffy	wigwam	wissel
visile	vulval	walter	washed	wee-wee	whiles	wilder	Wistar
vision	vulvar	wamara	washen	wei ch'i	whilie	wildie	witchy
visual	vulvas	wamble	washer	weight	whilly	wildly	witful
vitric	Vynide	wambly	washin	Weimar	whilom	wilful	withal
vitrum	wabbit	wampee	wash up	weiner	whilst	wilgie	withen

wither	woomph	wrothy	yakuza	yen hop	yorker	zareba	zither
withes	woopie	wryest	yaller	yenned	Yorker	zariba	zlotys
within	worder	wubbit	yammer	yen-yen	Yorkie	zealot	zocalo
with it	wordly	wurley	Yankee	yeoman	Yoruba	zearat	zodiac
with us	worked	wurzel	Yanqui	yeomen	you-all	zeatin	zoftig
Witney	worker	wuther	yantra	yepsen	you bet	zebeck	Zogist
witted	work in	wu ts'ai	yaourt	yerbal	you lot	zebras	Zoilus
witter	work it	wyvern	yapped	yes-man	you see	zedonk	zombie
Wittig	work on	Xanadu	yapper	yes-men	youths	Zeeman	zonate
wittol	work to	X chair	yappet	yes sir	youthy	zenana	Zonian
wivern	work up	xenial	yaqona	yessir	yowler	Zendic	zoning
wizard	wormed	xenium	yarder	yessum	yow-yow	Zendik	zonite
woader	wormer	xeroma	Yardie	yester	yo-yoed	zenick	zonked
wobble	wornil	X-frame	yarely	yether	yo-yoer	Zenist	zonkey
wobbly	worrit	Xhosas	yarooh	Yezidi	yo-yoes	zenith	zonula
woeful	worsen	xoanon	yarran	yieldy	Y-plate	Zenker	zonule
Wogdon	worser	X-plate	yarrow	yikker	Y track	zephyr	zonure
woggle	worthy	x-rated	yatter	yipped	yttria	zereba	zooman
wolfer	wortle	X-rated	yaupon	yippee	yuckle	zeroth	zootic
wolver	woubit	xylary	yautia	yippie	Yukawa	zester	zorino
wolves	wounds	xylene	yaw-haw	Yishuv	yumpie	zeugma	zoster
wombat	woundy	xylose	yawler	Yizkor	yum-yum	ziarat	Zouave
wombed	wowser	xystus	yawner	ylidic	yuppie	ziczac	zounds
womble	wow-wow	yabber	yawper	yobbos	zacate	zigged	Zou-Zou
wompoo	wraith	yabbie	Yazidi	yogini	zaffre	zigzag	zoysia
wonder	wrap up	yachty	yclept	yogism	zaftig	zillah	zufolo
wongai	wrasse	yacker	Y cross	yogurt	zagged	Zimmer	Zuñian
wonner	wrathy	yaffle	yeared	yo-ho-ho	zaguan	zincic	Zurich
wonted	wraxle	Yagara	yearly	yoicks	zambra	zincos	zydeco
wonton	wreath	yah boo	yea-say	yoi-yoi	zambuk	Zindiq	Zydeco
wooded	wrench	Yahgan	yeasty	yoking	zander	zingel	zygite
wooden	wretch	Yahudi	yedder	Yokuts	zanier	zinger	zygoma
wooder	wriest	Yahveh	yeehaw	yolked	zanily	zinnia	zygote
woodie	wright	Yahweh	yeeuch	yomper	Zantac	zip bag	Zyklon
woodly	wristy	yakdan	ye gods	yom tov	Zapata	zip gun	zymase
woodsy	writee	Yakima	Yehudi	yonder	zap gun	zip-out	Zyrian
woofer	writer	yakked	yeller	yonker	zapote	zipped	zythum
wooled	writhe	yakker	yellow	yonnie	zapped	zipper	
woolen	wroken	yakkha	yelper	yoo-hoo	zapper	zip-top	
woolly	wrongo	yaksha	Yemeni	yordim	zarape	zircon	

SEVEN LETTERS

Aaronic	abustle	acouchi	ad litem	agamous	airfoil	al dente
abacist	abuttal	acquest	admiral	agarose	airglow	alecost
aback of	abutted	acquire	admirer	agelast	airhead	ale-hoof
abacost	abutter	acquist	adnexal	ageless	air-hole	alembic
Abaddon	abysmal	acreage	Adonian	age-long	airiest	alength
abalone	abyssal	acridid	adonize	age-mate	air-kiss	alerion
abandon	academe	acridly	adoptee	agendas	air lane	alertly
abate of	academy	Acrilan	adopter	agendum	airless	aleuron
abattis	Academy	acrobat	adorant	ageusia	airlift	alewife
abature	Acadian	acrogen	adoring	Aggadah	air-lift	ale-wort
abaxial	acarine	acronym	adorner	aggrace	airlike	alfalfa
Abbasid	acaroid	acrylic	adrenal	aggrade	airline	alfaqui
abdomen	acausal	actable	adulate	aggress	airlock	alferez
abelian	accidie	act a lie	adulter	aggroup	airmail	Alfisol
Abenaki	accinge	act-drop	adultly	agilely	air mile	alforja
abetted	acclaim	actinia	advance	agility	airmiss	algebra
abetter	accompt	actinic	adverse	agister	air-pipe	alginic
abettor	account	actinon	advised	agistor	airplay	Ali Baba
abeyant	accrete	actress	advisee	agitant	airport	alibied
abide by	accrual	act-tune	adviser	agitate	air pump	alidade
abiding	accrued	actuary	advisor	agitato	air raid	alienee
abietic	accruer	actuate	advowee	agnamed	airship	alienor
abigail	accrues	act up to	aeolian	agnatic	air-shot	aliform
ability	accurse	acushla	Aeolian	Agnoite	air show	aliment
abiotic	accurst	acutely	aeonial	agnomen	airsick	alimony
a bit hot	accusal	acutest	aeonian	agnosia	airside	aliquot
abjurer	accused	acyclic	aerated	agnosic	airtime	a little
ablator	accuser	acylate	aerator	agonies	air-time	alive oh
able for	ace-high	adagial	aerobat	agonise	airward	Al-kaaba
ablcism	acerbic	adagios	aerobic	agonism	airwave	alkalic
abolish	acerbly	adamant	aerosol	agonist	ajutage	alkalis
abomasa	acerose	adamite	Aesopic	agonize	a kind of	alkanet
abortee	acetate	Adamite	aestive	a good 'un	akvavit	alkanna
abortus	acetify	adangle	aetatis	agraffe	Aladdin	Alkoran
abought	acetone	adapter	a far cry	agrapha	alameda	alkoxyl
aboulia	acetous	adaptor	afar off	aground	Alamire	allayer
aboulic	Achaean	adaxial	a fat lot	ahead of	à la mode	all ears
abrader	Achaian	adazzle	afeared	a-height	alamort	alleged
Abraham	acharya	addenda	affable	ahunger	alanine	alleger
abreact	Achates	address	affably	ahungry	alapana	allegro
abreast	Acheron	adducer	affaire	aiblins	Alaskan	allelic
abridge	achieve	adenine	affairé	aidable	Alastor	allergy
abroach	achiral	adenoid	affiant	aidance	albedos	alleyed
abscess	achylia	adenoma	affinal	aidless	albinos	all eyes
abscind	acicula	adeptly	affined	aileron	albitic	allgood
abscise	acid air	adherer	affixal	ailette	albumen	all hail
absciss	acid dye	adhibit	affixer	ailment	albumin	all-heal
abscond	acidify	adiabat	afflate	aim high	alcaide	allicin
absence	acidise	adipose	afflict	aimless	alcalde	all-male
absinth	acidity	adipous	afforce	air-ball	alcanna	allness
absolve	acidize	adivasi	affront	airbase	alcayde	allonge
absorpt	acinous	Adivasi	afghani	air-bell	alcazar	all over
abstain	ack emma	adjoint	aflaunt	air-cell	alchemy	allower
abubble	aclinic	adjourn	aflower	aircrew	alchera	alloxan
a-burton	acolyte	adjudge	African	airdrop	alcohol	allseed
abusage	aconite	adjunct	against	air-drop	Alcoran	all-star
abusive	acorned	adjutor	Aga Khan	airflow	alcoved	all that

all this	amentum	anchusa	anodize	aphetic	Arabian	armlock
all-time	Amerind	ancient	anodyne	aphides	arabica	armoire
all told	Ameslan	ancilla	anoesis	aphonia	Arabise	armorer
allurer	Amharic	ancones	anoetic	aphonic	Arabism	armoury
alluvia	amiable	ancress	anomaly	aphotic	Arabist	armrest
all work	amiably	Andaman	anopsia	Apician	Arabize	army ant
allylic	amianth	andante	anormal	apiculi	arachis	arnatta
almadia	amidine	AND gate	anosmia	a-pieces	Aramaic	arnotto
almanac	amildar	andiron	anosmic	apishly	Aramean	arousal
almirah	aminded	and more	another	aplanat	araneid	arouser
almoign	amirate	and only	ansated	aplasia	Arapaho	arraign
almondy	ammeter	android	antacid	aplenty	araroba	arrange
almoner	ammonal	and so on	antapex	aplitic	aration	arrased
almonry	ammonia	and such	ant-bear	apnoeic	Arawaks	arrayal
almsfee	amnesia	and that	antbird	apocope	arbiter	arrayer
almsman	amnesic	anemone	antefix	apodeme	arblast	arrears
a load of	amnesty	anergic	ant eggs	apodous	arboral	arriage
aloetic	amniote	aneroid	antenna	apogamy	arboret	arrival
alonely	amoebae	aneurin	antheap	apogeal	arbutus	arriver
alongst	amoebas	angareb	ant-heap	apogean	arcaded	arrowed
aloofly	amoebic	a new one	anthill	apojove	Arcadia	arroyos
Alp-horn	amongst	angekok	Anthony	apology	Arcadic	arsenal
already	amoraic	angelet	anthrax	apolune	arcanum	arsenic
alright	amorino	angelic	anticly	apomict	archaic	art deco
Alsatia	amorist	angelin	antigen	apoplex	Archean	art form
al segno	Amorite	angelot	anti-god	apostil	archery	arthame
also-ran	amoroso	angelus	antilog	apostle	archeus	article
Altaian	amorous	angerly	antique	apothem	arch-foe	artisan
alterer	amorphy	Angevin	antlike	apparat	arching	artiste
althaea	amosite	anginal	ant-lion	apparel	archive	artizan
Althing	amotion	angioma	antonym	appeach	archlet	artless
althorn	amphora	Anglian	Antwerp	appease	archway	artsier
alto sax	amplest	anglice	anxiety	applaud	arc lamp	artsman
alumina	amplify	Anglify	anxious	applial	arc sine	artwork
alumnae	ampoule	Anglist	anybody	applied	arcuate	art work
alumnus	ampster	Angolan	any more	applier	ardency	arugula
alunite	amptman	angrier	anymore	applies	arduous	as a gift
alveary	ampulla	angrily	any road	appoint	areally	as a rule
alveole	amputee	anguine	any time	appress	areaway	ascarid
alveoli	amusing	anguish	anytime	apprise	arenite	ascaris
alyssum	amusive	angular	anyways	apprize	arenose	ascesis
amalgam	amylase	anhinga	anywhen	approof	areolae	ascetic
amasser	amylene	anilide	anywise	approve	areolar	ascites
amateur	amyloid	aniline	apaches	appulse	Aretine	ascitic
amative	amylose	anility	Apaches	apraxia	arguing	asclent
amatory	anacard	animate	apagoge	apricot	argyria	ascribe
a matter	anaemia	animism	apanage	a priori	aridify	ascrive
amazing	anaemic	animist	aparejo	aproned	aridity	asepsis
ambages	anagoge	anionic	apatite	apropos	arietta	aseptic
ambassy	anagogy	aniseed	a peck of	aprotic	ariette	asexual
ambatch	anagram	anisole	apelike	apsidal	Arimasp	as far as
ambient	anality	annates	apeling	apsides	ariosos	ashamed
ambones	analogy	annatto	Apelles	apteryx	aripple	Ashanti
amboyna	analyse	annelid	apepsia	aptness	arkosic	A-shaped
ambries	analyst	annicut	apertly	Apulian	armband	Asherah
ambroid	analyze	annotto	aphakia	aquaria	arm-bone	ash-grey
ambs-ace	Anamese	annoyer	aphakic	aquatic	armfuls	ash-hole
ameboid	anapsid	annuity	aphasia	aquavit	armhole	ashiver
amender	anarchy	annular	aphasic	aqueous	armiger	ashling
amenity	anatase	annulet	aphelia	aquifer	armilla	ashtray
amental	anatomy	annulus	aphemia	aquiver	armless	ash tree
amentia	anchovy	anodise	aphesis	Arabdom	armlike	ashweed

ash-wood	Atebrin	audible	awarder	back-way	balling	barge in
Asianic	atelier	audibly	a wee bit	baclava	ballist	bar-girl
Asiarch	Atellan	audient	aweless	baconer	ballium	barilla
Asiatic	Atenism	audited	awesome	baculum	ballock	bar-keel
asinine	Aterian	auditor	awfully	bad call	balloon	barkeep
askance	at fault	aufgabe	awkward	bad coin	balls up	bar line
askaris	at first	augitic	awl-bird	bad debt	balmier	barmaid
asklent	at grade	augment	awlwort	baddest	balmily	barmier
AS level	at grass	augural	awnless	baddies	balneal	barmily
asocial	at grips	augurer	axe-head	baddish	baloney	barmkin
as of now	athanor	auguste	axially	bad form	balsamy	barmote
a sort of	at heart	aulnage	axillae	badland	Baluchi	Barnaby
asperge	atheise	aunties	axillar	badling	bambini	barneys
asperse	atheism	aurally	axinite	bad luck	bambino	barngun
asphalt	atheist	aureate	axolotl	badmash	banally	barnlot
asphyxy	atheize	aureity	axoneme	bad mood	bandage	bar none
aspirer	atheous	aurelia	Aymaras	badness	band-aid	barn owl
aspirin	athirst	aureola	azarole	bad news	Band-Aid	barocco
asprawl	athlete	aureole	azelaic	bad show	bandbox	baronet
aspread	athrill	auricle	Azilian	baffler	bandeau	baroque
asquint	athrong	aurochs	azimuth	Baganda	bandied	Barotse
assagai	athwart	aurorae	azotize	bagarre	bandier	barrace
assault	atingle	auroral	Aztecan	bagasse	bandies	barrack
assayer	atiptoe	auroras	azulene	bagfuls	banding	barrage
assegai	atishoo	auscult	azuline	baggage	bandits	barrico
assever	at issue	auslaut	azurine	baggier	bandlet	barrier
ass-head	at large	auspice	azurite	baggily	bandore	barring
asshole	at least	austere	azygous	bagging	bandsaw	bar-room
assizer	at night	austral	Azymite	bag lady	band-saw	barruly
assizor	at nurse	autarch	baa-lamb	baglike	baneful	bar soap
asslike	atomies	autarky	Baalism	bagnios	bangled	bartsia
assuage	atomise	autobus	Baalist	bagpipe	bang off	barwood
assumer	atomism	autocar	Baalite	bagwash	bang out	barytes
assumpt	atomist	autocue	babassu	bagworm	banjoes	barytic
assured	atomize	Autocue	babbitt	Bahadur	banking	baryton
assurer	at pause	automat	Babbitt	Baha'ism	banksia	bascule
assuror	at peace	autonym	babbler	Bahaism	banning	base hit
astable	at point	autopsy	babiche	Bahaist	bannock	baseman
astatic	at press	autumny	Babygro	Bahiric	banquet	basenji
asteism	at quiet	auxesis	babyish	bailage	banshee	base pay
astilbe	atresia	auxetic	babyism	baileys	banteng	bashful
astound	atresic	Avarian	Babylon	bailiff	Banting	bashing
astrain	atretic	avarice	babysit	baillie	banzuke	Bashkir
astrand	a trifle	ave-bell	Bacardi	bail out	baptise	bashlik
astream	atriums	avellan	baccate	bailout	baptism	basilar
astrict	at roost	avenger	Bacchic	bairnly	baptist	basilic
astride	atrophy	average	Bacchus	baittle	baptize	basinet
astroid	at sight	Avernal	Bachian	baklava	baracan	Baskish
astylar	at speed	averred	bacilli	balance	Barbara	basmati
asudden	at squat	Avestan	backbar	balcony	Barbary	Basotho
asunder	at stake	Avestic	back emf	baldies	barbate	basqued
as usual	at table	aviator	back-end	balding	barbell	bass-bar
atactic	attaboy	avicide	backhoe	baldish	barbery	bassist
ataghan	attaché	avidity	backing	baldric	barbola	bassman
at a heat	attaint	avionic	backlit	baleful	Barbour	bassoon
at a loss	attempt	avocado	backlog	bale out	barbule	bastard
at an end	at times	avodiré	back off	baleout	barchan	bastide
at a push	attract	avoidal	back out	balkier	bar code	bastile
ataraxy	attrite	avoider	back-pay	ballade	bardies	bastion
at a time	at worst	avowant	back row	ballast	bardish	bastite
atavism	auberge	awaiter	back-saw	ballata	bardism	bateaux
at a word	auction	awake to	back-set	ballboy	bargain	batfish

bat flea	bearpit	beer-jug	benison	betaken	bigness	Bismark
Bath bun	bear-pit	beer mat	benomyl	beta ray	bigoted	bismite
bathing	beastie	beer-off	benorth	betcher	bigotry	bismuth
bath mat	beastly	beeswax	benthic	Beth Din	big shot	bistort
bathtub	beatbox	beetled	benthos	bethink	big show	bistred
bath-tub	beatify	be fixed	benting	bethump	big talk	bistros
bathyal	beating	be for it	benzene	bethump	big time	bitless
batiste	beatnik	beggary	benzine	betimes	big tree	bitonal
bat-mule	beat off	begging	benzoic	betitle	bike boy	bit part
batsman	beat out	beghard	benzoin	betoken	bikeway	bittern
batsmen	beaufin	begin at	benzole	betroth	bikkies	bittier
battels	beauish	begin on	benzoyl	betting	bilayer	bittily
battery	beau-pot	begloom	Beothuk	bettong	bilboes	bittock
battier	beavers	begonia	bepaint	betulin	bi-level	bitumen
battily	bebeeru	begorra	bequest	between	biliary	bitwise
batting	bebleed	begrace	be quick	betwixt	bilimbi	bivalve
battler	beblood	begrime	be quiet	bevilly	bilious	bivious
batture	be brief	beguile	bereave	bevvies	billard	bivouac
battuta	because	beguine	beretta	bewitch	billeté	bizarre
batwing	becharm	behight	bergylt	bezanty	billies	blabbed
bauchle	becloud	beignet	berhyme	bezique	billion	blabber
baudkin	becross	bejasus	be rid of	bez tine	billowy	blacken
Bauhaus	becrown	bejesus	Bermuda	bhangra	bilobed	blacker
bausond	bedding	bejewel	Bernese	bheesty	biltong	blackly
bauxite	bedevil	be judge	berried	Biafran	bimanal	black up
bavaroy	bedfast	beknave	berries	biasing	bi-media	bladder
baviaan	bedgown	belated	berserk	bias-ply	bimetal	blagged
bawcock	bedhead	Belauan	besaiel	biassed	bimodal	blagger
bawdier	bed-head	belcher	besaint	biaxial	bindery	blakeys
bawdily	bedight	beldame	besayle	bibasic	binding	blandly
bawl out	bedizen	Belgian	beseech	bibbing	binging	blanked
bawneen	bedload	belibel	beshade	bibbler	binning	blanket
bay leaf	Bedouin	believe	beshine	bib-cock	binocle	blankly
bayonet	bedpost	bellboy	beshrew	bibelot	biochip	blarney
bay salt	bedrest	bell-boy	besides	biblist	biocide	blasted
bay tree	bedrock	Belleek	besiege	bicycle	biodata	blaster
baywood	bedroll	bell-hop	beslave	bidarka	bioherm	blatant
bazooka	bedroom	bellied	besmear	biddery	biology	blather
be about	bedside	bellies	besmoke	biddies	biomass	blatter
beached	bedsock	bell jar	besouth	bidding	bionics	blawort
beadier	bedsore	bellman	bespake	bid fair	biotech	blaze up
beadily	bedtick	bellmen	bespeak	biennia	biotite	blazing
beading	bedtime	Bellona	bespeck	bifidly	biotope	bleakly
beadlet	be dying	bellows	bespell	bifilar	biotype	bleater
bead-rim	bee-balm	beloved	bespoke	bifocal	bipedal	bleeder
beagler	bee-bird	Beltane	besport	bifront	biplane	bleeper
beakful	beechen	belting	bespout	big band	bipolar	blellum
beamish	beefalo	beltman	bestain	big bang	biprism	blemish
beam sea	beefier	beltmen	best boy	big bore	birchen	blender
beanbag	beefily	belt out	best buy	big deal	bircher	blesbok
bean-bag	beefing	beltway	bestead	bigener	Bircher	blessed
beanery	beef tea	belying	best end	Bigfeet	bird dog	blesser
be a pair	bee-glue	bemazed	bestest	Bigfoot	birdied	bless me
be a pulp	beehive	bencher	bestial	big game	birdies	blether
bear-cat	beeline	bendlet	bestick	biggest	birding	blewits
bearded	bee-moth	beneath	bestill	bigging	birdman	Blighty
beardie	been and	benefic	best man	biggish	biretta	blinder
bear-hug	beerage	benefit	bestorm	biggity	biriani	blindly
bearing	beer-boy	Benelux	bestrew	big-head	birling	blind me
bearish	beer gut	Bengali	be stuck	bighorn	biryani	blind to
bear off	beerier	benight	bestuck	big idea	biscuit	blinker
bear out	beerily	Benioff	betaine	big name	Bislama	blintze

blipped	boating	boluses	bordage	bow line	brassie	brisken
blister	boatman	bombard	bordure	bowline	brassil	brisket
blither	boatmen	bombast	boredom	bowling	brastle	briskly
blitter	Bobadil	bomb bay	Bornean	bowl out	brattle	bristle
bloated	bobajee	bombing	borneol	bowshot	bravado	bristly
bloater	bob a job	bomblet	bornite	bowtell	bravely	Bristol
blocker	bobance	bombora	boronia	bow wave	bravery	brisure
block in	bob a nob	bonaght	borough	bowyang	bravoes	Britain
block up	bobbery	bonanza	Borstal	boxcalf	bravura	British
Blondin	bobbies	bonasus	borstch	box coat	brawler	brittle
blooded	bobbing	bondage	bortsch	box-fish	brawner	brittly
bloomed	bobbish	bonding	boscage	boxfuls	brazier	britzka
bloomer	bobbled	bondman	boskage	box-haul	breachy	broaden
blooper	bobotie	bone-ash	Bosniac	boxiana	breaden	broadly
blossom	bobsled	bone dry	Bosnian	boxiest	breadth	brocade
blotchy	bob-sled	bone-oil	bosomed	box kite	breaker	brocard
blot out	bobstay	boneset	bosquet	boxlike	break in	brochan
blotted	bobtail	bonfire	bossage	boxroom	break of	brocked
blotter	bob-wire	bongoes	bossier	box-seat	break up	Brocken
blouson	Bocardo	boniest	bossily	box tree	breakup	brocket
blow-dry	bocasin	bonitos	bossism	boxwood	breasty	brockit
blowfly	boccaro	bonjour	boss-man	boycott	breathe	brodder
blowgun	bocking	bonkers	bostryx	boyhood	breathy	brodkin
blowier	bodeful	bonnail	Boswell	boykins	breccia	Broeder
blowing	bodikin	bonnier	botanic	boylike	brecham	broggle
blow job	body bag	bonnily	botargo	brabble	breeder	brogued
blow off	Boeotic	bontbok	botcher	braccio	breed in	broider
blow out	Boer War	bonzess	bothies	brachet	Breguet	broiler
blubbed	boffola	boobies	botling	brachia	brekker	broking
blubber	bogbean	boobook	bottine	bracing	brekkie	bromate
blucher	bog-bean	boodler	bottled	bracken	Bren gun	bromide
bludger	boggard	boogied	bottler	bracker	bretzel	bromine
blue bag	boggier	boogies	bottony	bracket	brevier	bromism
blue box	bogging	boohoos	botulin	bradawl	brevity	bromize
bluecap	boggler	bookend	boudoir	bradoon	brewage	bronchi
blue eye	bog-hole	book-end	boughed	bragged	brewery	broncho
blue fly	bog iron	bookful	bouilli	bragger	brewing	broncos
bluegum	bog-land	booking	boulder	bragget	bribery	brooder
blueing	bog moss	bookish	boulter	brahman	brickie	broomie
blueish	Bogomil	booklet	bouncer	Brahman	brickle	brothel
blueism	bog pine	bookman	bounded	brahmic	bricole	brother
blue jay	bog-rush	bookmen	bounden	brahmin	bridler	brought
blue rod	bog-trot	book-shy	bounder	Brahmin	bridoon	browden
blue-sky	bogusly	Boolean	bound to	braider	briefly	brownie
blue tit	bogyman	boom box	bound up	braid of	briered	Brownie
bluffer	bogymen	booming	bouquet	Braille	brigade	brownly
bluffly	Bohemia	boomlet	bourbon	brained	brigand	browser
blunder	boilery	boonies	Bourbon	braless	brimful	bruchid
blunger	boiling	boorish	bourder	bramble	brimmed	brucine
bluntly	boil-off	booster	bourdon	brambly	brimmer	brucite
blur out	Bokhara	bootboy	bourock	Bramley	brinded	bruckle
blurred	boleros	bootery	bourrée	branchy	brindle	bruiser
blusher	boletus	bootleg	boutade	branded	Brinell	brulzie
bluster	bolivar	boot-top	bow down	brander	bringer	Brummie
boarder	bollard	booze-up	bow-fast	brangle	bring in	brumous
boardly	bollock	boozier	bow-hand	bran-new	bring on	brushed
boarish	bologna	boozily	bowhead	bran-pie	bring to	brusher
boaster	Bologna	bopping	bowhunt	bran tub	bring up	brush up
boatage	boloney	bopster	bowlder	brashly	brinish	brusque
boat-axe	Bolshie	boracic	bow-legs	brasque	brinjal	brustle
boat-fly	bolster	borasco	bowless	brassed	brioche	brutely
boatful	bolting	Borazon	bowlful	brassey	briquet	brutify

brutish	bullous	burster	by a nose	caesura	calvish	canteen
brutism	bullpen	burthen	bycoket	cafe-bar	calvity	canthus
bruvver	bull-pup	bur-weed	bye-byes	café-bar	calyces	cantina
bruxism	bulrush	burying	bye-line	cagiest	calycle	canting
bubbler	bulwark	busbied	by force	cagoule	calypso	cantlet
bubonic	bumbaze	busbies	bygoing	cahoots	calyxes	cant off
buccaro	bumbler	buscarl	by golly	Cainite	calzone	cantred
buckeen	bumboat	bush-cat	by heart	Cairene	camaron	cantrip
buckeye	bum-boat	bush cow	by jingo	caisson	cambial	canvass
bucking	bummalo	bush-eel	byliner	caitiff	cambist	can wait
buckish	bumming	bush-fly	by night	cajeput	cambium	canzona
buckler	bumpety	bush hen	by order	cajoler	cambrel	canzone
buckoes	bumpier	bushido	by-place	cajuput	cambric	capable
buckram	bumpily	bushier	by right	cakelet	camelry	capably
buck-saw	bumping	bushies	Byronic	cake-mix	Camenes	cap-à-pie
bucolic	bumpkin	bushily	by sight	calabar	cameral	Cape Cod
buddied	bump off	bushing	byssine	calaber	Camford	Cape fox
buddies	bum-suck	bushman	by steam	calamus	cammock	capelet
budding	Bunbury	Bushman	by the by	calando	camoodi	capelin
budge up	buncher	bushmen	by-thing	calcify	Camorra	caperer
budless	buncoes	bush-pig	by turns	calcine	campana	capfuls
budworm	bundler	bush-rat	by water	calcite	Campari	Caphtor
buffalo	bundook	bush tea	bywater	calcium	camp bed	capital
buffish	bungler	bush-tit	by way of	calculi	camphor	capitan
buffoon	bunjara	busiest	bywoner	caldera	campier	capitao
bugaboo	bunk bed	busking	by wrong	caldron	campily	Capitol
bugbane	bunnies	bus lane	cabaret	calèche	camping	capless
bugbear	Bunraku	bussing	cabbage	calends	campion	caplike
bug-eyed	bunting	bus stop	cabbagy	calfish	campong	capouch
buggery	buoyage	bustard	cabbala	Caliban	camp out	capping
buggier	buoyant	bustier	Cabbala	caliber	camwood	caprate
buggies	burbler	bustler	cabbies	calibre	canakin	caprice
bugging	burdock	busy bee	cabined	caliche	canasta	caprine
bugloss	burdoun	butanol	cabinet	calicle	can bank	cap rock
bug-word	bureaus	butcher	Caboclo	calicos	can-buoy	caproic
bugwort	bureaux	butenyl	caboose	calinda	candela	caproyl
builder	burette	butlery	cabotin	calipee	candent	Capsian
build in	burgage	butment	cab-rank	caliper	candida	capsize
build on	burgeon	butt-end	ca'canny	caliver	candied	capstan
build up	burgess	buttery	ca' canny	callant	candies	capsule
built-in	burghal	but that	cachexy	call box	candiru	captain
built-up	burgher	but then	cacique	call-boy	candler	caption
buirdly	burghul	butties	cackler	call-day	can-dock	captive
bulblet	burglar	buttock	cacodyl	call for	candour	capture
bulbose	Burgund	buttons	cacoepy	calling	canella	capuche
bulbous	Burkitt	buttony	caconym	call off	cane-rat	carabid
bulimia	burlier	butt out	cadaver	callose	canezou	caracal
bulimic	burlily	but what	cad-bait	callous	canions	caracul
bulk-buy	Burmans	butyric	caddice	call out	cankery	caramba
bulkier	Burmese	buvette	caddied	calluna	cannach	caramel
bulkily	burn-bag	buxarry	caddies	calmant	cannery	caratch
bullace	Burnham	buyable	caddish	calomel	cannier	caravan
bull ant	burning	buy a pup	cadence	caloric	cannily	caravel
bullary	burnish	buy-back	cadency	calorie	canning	caraway
bullate	burn low	buy into	cadenza	calotte	cannula	carbene
bull-bat	burn off	buy over	cadgily	caloyer	canonic	carbide
bulldog	burnous	buy time	Cadmean	caltrap	canonry	carbine
bullied	burn out	buzzard	cadmium	caltrop	Canopic	car bomb
bullies	burp gun	buzz off	caducei	calumba	Canopus	carcake
bullion	bur-reed	buzz-saw	cad-worm	calumet	cantata	carcase
bullish	burrito	buzzwig	Caecias	calumny	Cantate	carcass
bullock	bursary	by and by	caesium	Calvary	cant-dog	car coat

carcoon	carry up	cat door	celeste	chalone	chassis	Chicano
cardecu	carsick	catechu	cellist	chaloth	chasten	chic-est
cardiac	cartage	catenae	Cellnet	chamade	chateau	chicken
cardial	cartful	catenas	cellule	chamber	château	chicory
cardies	cartman	cateran	celosia	chambré	chatted	chidden
cardoon	cart off	caterer	celsian	chamfer	chattel	chiding
carduus	cartoon	catfish	Celsius	chamiso	chatter	chiefly
care for	cart-rut	cat flap	cembalo	chamois	chayote	chiefry
careful	cart-way	cat foot	cenacle	champac	chazzan	chiffon
carezza	carvery	Cathari	censual	champer	cheapen	chigger
carfare	carve up	Cathars	censure	chancel	cheapie	chignon
carfuls	carving	cat-haul	centage	chancer	cheaply	chi-hike
cargoes	carvone	cathead	centaur	chancre	cheatee	chikara
cariama	car wash	cathect	centavo	changer	cheater	chikhor
Caribee	cascade	cathode	centile	channel	cheat on	Chilcat
caribou	cascara	cat-hole	centime	channer	chebule	childed
carices	caseate	catlick	céntimo	chanson	Chechen	childly
carinal	case law	catlike	centner	chanter	chechia	Chilean
carioca	case-oil	catling	central	chantey	checked	chiliad
cariole	caseous	catmint	centred	chantry	checker	Chilian
carious	casevac	cat's-ear	centric	chaotic	check in	Chilkat
caritas	cash box	cat's-eye	centrum	chapati	check on	chiller
carjack	cash cow	Catseye	century	chapeau	check-up	chillum
carking	cashier	cat show	cepheid	chaplet	Cheddar	chilver
carline	casinos	cat's-paw	Cepheus	chapman	cheeked	chime in
carling	Caspian	catsuit	ceramic	chapmen	cheeper	chimera
carlish	casquet	cat-tail	cerebra	chappal	cheerer	chimere
Carlism	cassada	cattalo	cereous	chapped	cheerio	chimney
Carlist	cassata	Cattern	ceresin	chappie	cheerly	chinchy
carload	cassava	cattery	cerotic	chappli	cheer up	Chindit
carmine	cassino	catticr	cerotin	chappow	cheetah	Chinese
carnage	cassiri	cattily	certain	chapter	cheetal	chinkle
Carnata	Cassius	catting	certify	charact	chelate	chinned
Carnian	cassock	cattish	cerumen	charade	Chelsea	chinook
carnify	cassone	catwalk	cervine	charged	chemise	Chinook
carnose	Castile	catydid	Cesolfa	chargee	chemism	chintzy
carnous	casting	caubeen	cessile	charger	chemist	chinwag
caroche	castled	caudate	cession	chargés	chequer	chin-wag
caroler	castlet	cauline	cesspit	charier	cherish	chip-axe
Carolin	cast net	caulker	cestode	charily	cheroot	chipped
Carolus	castock	cause of	cestoid	chariot	chervil	chipper
carosse	cast-off	caustic	ceviche	charism	chessel	chippie
carotic	cast out	cautery	Chablis	charity	chested	chirper
carotid	castral	caution	cha-cha'd	Charley	chester	chirrup
carotin	castrum	cavally	chacham	charlie	Chesvan	chitter
carouba	casuist	cavalry	cha-chas	Charlie	chetnik	chizzer
carouse	Catalan	cave art	Chadian	charmed	chevage	chlamys
carozzi	catalpa	caveman	chafery	charmer	chevied	chloral
car park	catapan	cavemen	chaffer	charnel	chevies	chloric
carpent	catarrh	cavetto	chafing	charpie	Cheviot	chobdar
carping	catasta	caviare	chagrin	charpoy	chevron	choc-bar
car pool	catawba	cayenne	chained	charqui	chewier	chochos
carport	catbird	cazerne	chaitya	charred	chewink	choc ice
carrack	catboat	CD video	chalaza	chartae	chew out	chocker
carried	catcall	cecitis	chalcid	charter	Chianti	Choctaw
carrier	catch-22	cedared	Chaldee	chase up	chiasma	choired
carries	catched	cedilla	chalder	chasing	Chibcha	choisya
carrion	catcher	cedrela	chalice	chasmal	chibouk	choke up
carroon	catch it	ceilidh	chalifa	chasmed	chicana	chokeys
carroty	catch on	ceiling	chalk up	chasmic	Chicana	chokier
carry it	catch up	celadon	challah	chasséd	chicane	chokies
carry-on	catchup	celesta	challis	Chassid	chicano	cholate

cholent	ciggies	claries	clogged	coastel	cohabit	comfily
cholera	ciliary	clarify	clogger	coaster	coherer	comfort
choline	ciliate	clarine	cloison	coating	cohibit	comfrey
chookie	cillery	clarion	Clootie	coaxial	coiffed	comical
chooser	Cimbric	clarity	clopped	cobbler	coignye	comital
chopine	cimelia	clarkia	close by	cob coal	coinage	comites
chopped	cindery	clasher	close in	cob-iron	coin box	comitia
chopper	cineast	clasper	closely	cob-loaf	coining	command
chorale	cineole	classer	close on	cob-meal	coition	commend
chordal	cingula	classes	close up	cob-nuts	cojuror	comment
chorded	Cinzano	classic	closing	cob pipe	cokeman	commère
chordee	cipolin	classis	closish	cocaine	cola nut	commish
choreal	Circean	class of	closure	coccoid	Colchic	commode
choregy	circled	clastic	clot-bur	cochlea	coldish	commons
choreic	circler	clatter	clothed	cockade	cold tap	commove
chorine	circlet	clauber	clothes	cockall	cold war	commune
chorion	circlip	claucht	clotted	cock-eye	cole tit	commute
chorist	circuit	claught	clotter	cockier	colibri	compact
chorizo	cirrose	clausal	cloture	cockies	colicin	compand
choroid	cirrous	clavate	clouted	cockily	colicky	company
chorten	cirsoid	clavier	clouter	cocking	colitis	compare
chortle	ciscoes	claw off	clovery	cockish	collage	compart
chouser	cissies	clayish	clubbed	cockler	collard	compass
chowder	cissoid	clay-pan	clubber	cockney	collate	compear
chrisom	cistern	cleaner	club car	cockpit	collect	compeer
Christy	cistron	cleanly	club-law	cockshy	colleen	compend
chromic	citable	cleanse	clubman	cock-shy	college	compère
chromyl	citadel	clean up	club-man	cocobay	collide	compete
chronal	cithara	clearer	clubmen	coconut	collier	compile
chronic	cithern	clearly	clued-up	cocopan	Collins	complex
chrysid	citizen	clear-up	clueing	cocotte	colloid	complot
chubbed	citrate	cleaved	Clumber	cocoyam	collude	componé
chucker	citrine	cleaver	clumper	coctile	colobus	compony
chuckie	citrous	clefted	Cluniac	coction	cologne	comport
chuck in	cittern	clement	clunker	cod-bait	Cologne	compose
chuck it	cityful	clerisy	clupeid	cod-bank	colonel	compost
chuckle	civilly	clerkly	cluster	codding	colonic	compote
chuck up	civvies	cleruch	clutter	coddler	colored	compter
chuddar	clabber	clethra	clypeal	codeine	colosse	compute
chuffed	clachan	cliched	clypeus	codetta	colossi	comrade
chugged	clacker	clichéd	clyster	codexes	coloury	Comtean
Chukchi	clacket	clicker	cnemial	codfish	colrake	Comtian
chumble	cladded	clicket	coachee	codices	colting	Comtism
chunder	cladism	cliency	coacher	codicil	coltish	Comtist
Chunnel	cladist	climate	co-adore	codilla	coluber	conacre
chunner	cladode	climber	coagent	codille	colugos	conatus
chunter	claggum	clinger	coagula	cod-line	colulus	con brio
churchy	claimer	clinker	coal-bed	codling	Columba	concave
churner	clamant	clinoid	coal-box	coehorn	columel	conceal
churrus	clamber	clipped	coal gas	coeliac	columna	concede
chutist	clammed	clipper	coalise	coenoby	comatic	conceit
chutney	clammer	clippie	Coalite	co-equal	combine	concent
chutter	clamour	cliquey	coalize	coequal	combing	concept
chylify	clamper	clitter	coalman	coercer	comb out	concern
chylous	clanger	clivers	coalmen	coexist	combust	concert
chymist	clanism	cloacae	coal oil	coffret	Comecon	conchae
chymous	Clapham	cloacal	coal-pit	cogence	comedic	conched
ciboria	clap-net	clobber	coal tar	cogency	come for	conches
ciboule	clapped	clocher	coal tit	cognate	come off	conchie
cichlid	clapper	clocker	coaming	cognize	come out	concise
cidaris	clarain	clock in	coarsen	cog rail	cometic	concoct
cieling	clarety	clodder	coastal	cog-wood	comfier	concord

Concord	contuse	cork oak	co-tidal	cowbird	crankly	criollo
concuss	convect	Corliss	cotinga	cow-camp	crankum	cripple
condemn	convene	cornage	cotland	cow chip	crank up	crispen
condign	convent	corn cob	cottage	cowfish	crannog	crisper
condole	convert	corneal	cottary	cow-fish	crapaud	Crispin
condone	convict	cornery	cottery	cow-flap	crap out	crisply
conduce	convoke	cornett	cottice	cow-gait	crapped	crissal
conduct	co-occur	corn-fed	cottier	cowgirl	crapper	crissum
conduit	cookery	cornice	cotting	cowhage	crappie	cristae
condyle	cookess	cornier	cottise	cow-hand	crasher	critter
confect	cooking	cornify	cottony	cow-heel	crassly	crizzle
confess	cookout	cornily	cot-town	cowherd	craunch	croaker
confide	cooktop	cornish	couchee	cowhide	craving	crocard
confine	coolant	Cornish	coucher	cow-hunt	crawler	crocean
confirm	cool bag	cornist	Couéism	cowitch	crazier	Crocean
conflab	cool box	corn-oil	Couéist	cow-lady	crazily	crochet
conflow	coolies	corn-row	Couette	cow-lick	creaght	Crocian
conflux	cooling	cornual	cougher	cowling	creamer	crocked
conform	coolish	cornute	cough up	cowpoke	creance	crocket
confuse	coon-can	cornuto	couguar	cow pony	creased	Croesus
confute	coon-dog	corolla	couldn't	cowries	creaser	crofter
congaed	coontie	coronae	couleur	co-write	creator	cro'jack
congeal	coopery	coronal	couloir	co-wrote	credent	crombec
congery	co-optee	coroner	coulomb	cowshed	creedal	Cronian
congest	co-owner	coronet	Coulomb	cow-shot	creeler	cronies
congius	copaiba	coronis	coulter	cow-skin	creeper	croodle
conical	copeman	corozos	council	cowslip	creepie	crooked
conidia	copepod	corpora	co-unite	cow-tail	creeshy	crooken
conifer	coperta	corrade	counsel	cow town	cremate	Crookes
coniine	co-pilot	correct	counter	cow-tree	cremona	crooner
conjoin	copilot	corrida	count on	coxcomb	Cremona	crop out
conjure	copious	corrode	country	coxless	crenate	cropped
conjury	coppery	corrody	count up	coyness	creosol	cropper
con moto	coppice	corrupt	coupled	coyotes	crepine	Cropper
connate	copping	corsage	coupler	cozener	crêping	croppie
connect	cop shop	corsair	couplet	crabbed	cresset	croquet
conning	copsole	corslet	coupure	crabber	crested	crosier
connive	copular	corsned	courage	crab-nut	cretize	crosser
connote	copulas	cortège	courant	crab-oil	crevice	crossly
conquer	copycat	cortina	courida	crab pot	crew-cut	crotala
consarn	copyism	co-ruler	courier	cracked	crewels	crotale
consent	copyist	corvina	courser	cracker	crewman	crottle
consign	coquina	corvine	courter	cracket	crewmen	croupal
consist	coquito	coryzal	courtly	crackle	cribbed	crouton
console	coracle	cosaque	couthie	crackly	cribber	croûton
consols	coranto	cosh boy	couthly	crack up	cribble	crowbar
consort	corbeau	coshery	couture	cradler	cricket	crow-boy
consult	corbeil	cosiest	couvade	cragged	crickey	crowder
consume	corcass	cosmism	couvert	craigie	cricoid	crowdie
contact	corcule	cosmist	covelet	cramble	Crimean	crow-hop
contain	cordage	Cossack	covered	cram-jam	crimine	crownal
contemn	cordate	costard	coverer	crammed	criminy	crowned
contend	cordial	costate	cover in	crammer	crimmer	crowner
content	cording	co-State	cover-up	crammle	crimper	crow-toe
contest	cordite	costean	coveted	cramped	crimple	crozier
context	cordoba	costing	coveter	crampet	crimson	crubeen
contoid	Cordtex	costive	cowardy	crampon	cringer	crucial
contort	corella	costrel	cow-baby	cramp up	cringle	crucian
contour	co-rival	costume	cowbail	cranage	crinite	crucify
contras	corkage	cot-case	cowbane	cranial	crinkle	crudded
control	corkier	coterie	cowbell	cranium	crinkly	cruddle
contund	corking	cothurn	cowbind	crankle	crinoid	crudely

crudify	culchie	curried	cyclian	damp-dry	Davidic	decayer
crudity	Culdean	currier	cycling	dampish	dawdler	decease
crueler	culling	curries	cyclise	damp off	dawning	deceive
cruelly	cullion	currish	cyclist	Danaert	dawn man	decency
cruelty	culotte	curship	cyclize	danaine	daybook	decener
cruiser	culpose	cursive	cycloid	danaite	day care	decibel
cruisie	culprit	cursory	cyclone	Danakil	day-dawn	decided
cruller	culrach	curtail	cyclops	dan buoy	day-girl	decider
crumble	culshie	curtain	Cyclops	dancing	dayless	decidua
crumbly	cultish	curtana	cydippe	dandier	day lily	decimal
crummie	cultism	Curtana	cylices	dandies	day-long	deciner
crumper	cultist	curtate	cymbalo	dandify	daylong	decking
crumpet	culture	curtesy	cymling	dandler	daymare	deckled
crumple	culvert	curtsey	cynical	Dane gun	daypack	declaim
crumply	Cumaean	curucui	Cynthia	Danelaw	day-peep	declare
crunchy	cumbent	curvant	cyperus	dangler	day room	declass
crunkle	Cumbric	curvier	cypraea	Daniell	daysack	decline
crunode	cumdach	curvity	cypress	Dankali	dayside	declive
crupper	cumquat	curvous	Cyprian	dankish	daysman	decoder
crusade	cumshaw	cushier	Cypriot	dannert	day-star	decolor
crusado	cumulet	Cushing	cypsela	danseur	day-tale	decorum
crusher	cumulus	cushion	cystine	Dantean	daytime	decreed
crusily	cuneate	Cushite	cystoid	daphnia	day trip	decreer
crustal	cunette	cusk-eel	cytisus	daphnin	daywork	decrees
crusted	cunning	cuspate	cytosol	dapifer	dazedly	decreet
cruzado	cup-cake	cusping	czardas	dapping	dazibao	decrial
cry-baby	cupcake	custard	czarina	dappled	dazzler	decried
cry back	cupfuls	custock	dabbing	dapsone	dead bat	decrier
cry down	cup hook	custode	dabbler	Darapti	dead end	decries
cryogen	Cupidon	custodi	dab hand	darbies	deadeye	decrown
cryonic	cuplike	custody	Dabitis	dare-all	deadish	decrypt
cryptal	cup-moss	custrel	dabster	dariole	dead man	decuman
cryptic	cupola'd	custron	dacitic	darkful	dead men	decuple
cryptos	cupping	cut a rug	dacoity	darkies	deadpan	decurve
crystal	cuprate	cutaway	dacryon	darkish	dead pay	Dedalic
cry wolf	cuprite	cut-away	Dadaism	darling	Dead Sea	deed-box
csardas	cuprous	cut back	Dadaist	Darling	dead set	deedful
C-shaped	cupular	cutback	daddies	darlint	deaf aid	deedily
C-spring	curable	cut dead	dafadar	darning	deafish	deep end
ctenoid	curaçao	cut down	daffier	dartman	deaf nut	deepest
cubbies	curaçoa	cuticle	daffily	dartoid	dealing	deep-fry
cubbing	curatic	cutikin	daggett	dart-sac	deanery	deeping
cubbish	curator	cut into	daggier	dasheen	deaness	deepish
cubhood	curbash	cutlass	dagging	Dashera	dearest	deep sea
cubical	curb-bit	cutlery	dag-lock	dashiki	deathly	deep-set
cubicle	curbily	cut-line	dago red	dashing	debacle	deep six
cubital	curcuma	cutling	Dagwood	dashpot	débâcle	deer fly
cubitus	curdler	cut loaf	Dahoman	Dassera	debaser	deerlet
cuckold	cure-all	cut moth	dailies	dastard	debater	defacer
cudbear	curette	cut open	dairies	dasturi	debauch	de facto
cuddies	curiara	cut-over	daisies	dasyure	debited	defamed
cudding	curiate	cut-rate	Dakotan	datable	debouch	defamer
cudeigh	curiosa	cutties	dalasis	datival	debride	default
cudweed	curioso	cutting	dallied	dattock	debrief	defease
cudwort	curious	cutwork	dallier	daubery	decadal	defence
cue ball	curlews	cutworm	dallies	daubing	decadic	defense
cue card	curlier	cuvette	damfool	Daulian	decagon	defiant
cuffing	curling	cyanate	dam-head	daunder	decalin	deficit
cui bono	currach	cyanide	damming	daunter	decamer	defiler
cuirass	curragh	cyanine	damn all	daunton	decanal	defined
cuisine	currant	cyanite	damnify	dauphin	decapod	definer
cuittle	current	cyathus	damosel		decarch	deflate

deflect	demulce	despoil	dialyse	digging	dipolar	dismark
defocus	demurer	despond	dialyze	dighter	dippier	dismast
deforce	denarii	dessert	diamide	digital	dipping	dismiss
deframe	dendron	destain	diamine	diglyph	dipshit	dismute
defraud	denizen	De Stijl	diamond	dignify	Diptera	disnest
defrock	Denmark	destine	diandry	dignity	diptote	disobey
defrost	denning	destiny	diapase	digonal	diptych	disomic
defunct	densely	destock	diapasm	digoxin	dipylon	dispark
dégagée	densify	destool	diapery	digraph	diquark	dispart
degauss	density	destour	diapsid	digress	direful	dispend
deglaze	dentary	destroy	diarchy	digynic	dirempt	display
deglute	dentate	detente	diarial	dika fat	dirtier	dispone
degrade	dentine	détente	diarian	dilater	dirtily	dispope
dehisce	dentist	deterge	diaries	dilator	dirt-pie	disport
deicide	denture	determa	diarise	dildoes	disable	dispose
deictic	deodand	detinue	diarist	dilemma	disally	dispost
deified	deontic	detract	diarize	dillies	Disamis	dispute
deifier	de-orbit	detrain	diastem	dilling	disavow	disrank
deifies	depaint	detrude	diaster	dilruba	disband	disrate
deiform	dépaysé	deutzia	diasyrm	dilucid	disbark	disrobe
de-index	depetal	devalue	diaulos	diluent	disbody	disroof
Deipara	deplace	devance	diazine	dilutee	discage	disroot
deistic	deplane	develop	diazoma	diluter	discant	disrump
Deiters	deplete	deviant	dibasic	diluvia	discard	disrupt
deities	deplore	deviate	dibatag	Dimaris	discase	dissava
dekalin	deplume	devilet	dibbing	dimeric	discept	dissave
dekarch	deposal	devilry	dibbler	dimeter	discern	disseat
delaine	deposer	devious	dice-box	dimmest	discerp	dissect
delapse	deposit	devisee	diciest	dimming	discoes	dissent
Delasol	deprave	deviser	dickens	dimmish	discoid	dissert
delator	depress	devisor	dickeys	dimness	discord	dissing
delayed	deprive	devoice	dickier	dimpled	discuss	dissoul
delayer	depside	devolve	dickies	dimpsey	disdain	distaff
deleing	depthen	devoted	dictate	Dinaric	disease	distain
delible	deraign	devotee	diction	din-dins	disedge	distant
delight	derange	dewater	dictums	dine out	diseuse	distend
Delilah	Derbies	dewclaw	didache	dinette	disfame	distent
delimit	de règle	dew-claw	didakai	dingbat	disform	distich
deliver	derider	dewdrop	diddery	dingier	disgown	distort
delouse	derival	dewfall	diddler	dingily	disgulf	distune
Delphic	deriver	dewiest	diddums	dingoes	disgust	disturb
delphin	dermoid	dewless	didicoi	dinki-di	dishelm	distyle
deltaic	derrick	dew-pond	didymis	dinkier	dishful	diswood
deltoid	dertrum	dew-rake	die away	dinkies	dishier	ditcher
deluder	dervish	dew-worm	die-back	dinmont	dishing	dithery
demarch	descale	dextral	die-cast	dinnery	dish-mop	dittany
demency	descant	dextran	die down	dinning	dishome	ditties
démenti	descend	dextrin	die game	dinsome	dishorn	dittoes
demerge	descent	deyship	diehard	diocese	dish out	diurnal
demerit	deserve	dghaisa	die hard	diopter	dish-pan	dive-dap
Demerol	desight	dhrupad	die-link	dioptre	dishrag	dive-dop
demerse	desired	dhurrie	dies non	diorama	disject	diverge
demesne	deskill	diabase	dietary	diorite	disjoin	diverse
demigod	desk job	diabolo	diether	dioxane	disjune	divided
demi-hag	desk-man	diagram	diethyl	dioxide	disleaf	divider
demirep	desktop	diagrid	dietine	dip-head	dislike	diviner
demi-rep	desmans	dialect	dieting	diploid	dislimb	divisor
demi-sec	desmoid	dialing	dietist	diploma	dislimn	divorce
demoded	Desolre	dialist	diffide	diplont	dislink	divorcé
demonic	despair	dialled	diffuse	dipnoan	disload	divulge
demotic	despise	dialler	digamma	dipnoid	dislove	Divvers
demount	despite	diallyl	dig down	dipodia	dismail	divvies

dizzard	dog-tent	dotchin	dragoon	dronage	dualism	dunness
dizzier	dog-town	dottier	drag out	drongos	dualist	dunnies
dizzily	dogtrot	dottily	drag saw	dronish	duality	dunning
djibbah	dog-vane	dotting	drainer	drooler	dualize	dunnish
D-notice	dog-wolf	dottled	drapery	drooper	dualled	dunnock
do about	dogwood	dottrel	draping	drop-fly	duarchy	dunster
do a bunk	doitkin	doubler	drappie	droplet	dub-a-dub	duopoly
do a fade	Dolbyed	doublet	drastic	drop off	dubbing	duotone
do a flit	doldrum	doubter	dratted	drop out	dubiety	dupable
do a mike	doleful	doucely	draught	dropped	dubious	duppies
doatish	dolldom	doughty	drawbar	dropper	ducally	duppion
dobbing	dollied	Douglas	draw bit	drosera	duchess	durable
do brown	dollier	Doulton	draw-boy	droshky	duchies	durably
docetic	dollies	dourine	draw-hoe	drostdy	duck ant	duramen
docible	dolosse	dovecot	drawing	drought	duck egg	durance
dockage	dolphin	dovekie	drawish	droving	duckett	durmast
doddery	doltish	dovelet	drawler	drowner	duckies	duskier
dodecad	domaine	dowable	draw-net	drubbed	ducking	duskily
dodecyl	domelet	dowager	draw off	drubber	duckpin	duskish
dodgast	domical	dowdier	draw out	drucken	ductile	dustbin
dodgery	domicil	dowdily	drayage	drudger	ducting	dust-box
dodgier	dominee	dowfart	drayman	drugged	ductule	dust-cap
dodgily	dominie	dowless	draymen	drugger	duddery	dustier
dodging	domitic	downbow	dreaded	drugget	dudgeon	dustily
doe-eyed	donatee	down-dip	dreader	druggie	dudheen	dusting
doeskin	donator	downier	dreadly	Druidic	due date	dustman
dogbane	doncher	downily	dreamed	Druidry	duelled	dustmen
dogbolt	done for	downish	dreamer	drumble	dueller	dust off
dog cart	Donegal	down-lie	dream up	drum kit	dueness	dustoor
dogcart	dongola	downset	dredger	drumlin	duetted	dustpan
dog days	Dongola	downsun	dreeing	drummed	duffing	dustuck
dogeate	Don Juan	dowries	dreidel	drummer	dugongs	duteous
dogface	donkeys	do wrong	Dresden	drum out	dukedom	dutiful
dog-fall	donnard	doyenne	dresser	drungar	dulcian	duumvir
dogfish	donning	Doyenne	dress up	drunken	dulcify	Duvetyn
doggery	donnish	doyleys	dribble	Drusian	dulcite	dvandva
doggess	donship	doylies	dribbly	druther	dullard	dwarves
doggies	dontcha	dozened	driblet	dryadic	dullify	dwelled
dogging	doodler	dozener	driddle	dry-blow	dullish	dweller
doggish	doomful	dozenth	drier-up	dry-bulb	dulness	dwell on
doggone	doomily	doze off	drifter	dry cell	dulosis	dwindle
doggrel	do or die	doziest	driller	dry cure	dulotic	dyarchy
doghead	doorman	dozzler	drinker	dry dock	dulsome	dybbuks
dog-hole	doormat	drabant	drinkie	dry-eyed	dumbell	dyeable
dog-hook	doormen	drabber	drink in	dry-foot	dummied	dye-line
dog-iron	doorway	drabbet	drink to	dry fuck	dummies	dyester
dogless	doozies	drabble	drink up	dry hole	dummy up	dye-wood
doglike	dope out	drabler	drip-dry	dry land	dumpier	dyingly
dogling	dopiest	drachma	drip-mat	dryland	dumpily	dynamic
dog-meat	Doppler	drackly	drip pan	dry mass	dumpish	dynamos
dog-nail	do proud	dracone	dripped	dry milk	dumpoke	dynasty
dog on it	dorados	Dracula	dripple	dryness	dun-bird	dyslogy
dog-poor	dor-hawk	draftee	drive at	dry-salt	duncery	dysuria
dog-race	Dorking	drafter	drive-by	dry-shod	duncify	dysuric
dog rose	dorlach	drag act	drive-in	dry sink	duncish	each way
dogrose	dormant	drag ass	drive-on	dryster	dungeon	eagerly
dog's age	dormice	dragged	driving	dry suit	dung-fly	eanling
dog's-ear	dornick	dragger	drizzle	drywall	dung-pot	earache
dogskin	dornock	draggle	drizzly	dry-wash	Dunkard	earbash
dog sled	dos-à-dos	draggly	drogher	dry well	Dunkirk	ear-bash
dog-star	do-si-dos	dragnet	droguer	D-shaped	dunnage	ear-clip
dog-tail	dossier	drag-net	dromond	dualise	dunnart	eardrum

ear-flap	écorché	ejector	emblaze	enchase	engross	entrust
earfuls	ecotage	eke-name	emblema	encheer	enguard	entwine
earhole	ecoteur	ekistic	embloom	en clair	enhance	entwist
earldom	ecotone	elaidic	embolia	enclasp	enjewel	E-number
earless	ecotype	Elamite	embolic	enclave	enjoyer	envelop
earlier	ecstasy	elastic	embolus	enclavé	enlarge	envenom
earlike	ectasia	elastin	embosom	enclose	enliven	envious
ear lobe	ectasis	elation	embound	encloud	en masse	environ
ear-lock	ecthyma	elative	embowed	encoder	ennoble	envyful
early on	ectopia	elderly	embowel	encomia	ennuyéd	enweave
earmark	ectopic	eldress	embower	encover	Enochic	enwheel
earmuff	ectypal	Eleatic	embrace	encrini	enolase	enwiden
ear-muff	ecuelle	elector	embrave	encrown	enolate	enwound
earnest	edacity	Electra	embroil	encrust	enology	enzymic
earnful	edaphic	electro	embrown	encrypt	enomoty	epacrid
earning	edenite	eledone	embryon	endarch	enotist	epacris
ear-pick	edestin	elegant	embryos	endemic	enounce	cparchy
earplug	edgiest	elegiac	embused	endgame	enplane	epaxial
earring	edictal	elegies	emender	end-game	enprint	épéeist
earshot	edicule	elegise	emerald	end-gate	enquire	epeiric
ear-stud	edifice	elegist	emerods	end-leaf	enquiry	epergne
earthen	edified	elegize	emersed	endless	enrheum	ephebic
earthly	edifier	element	emetine	end line	enripen	ephedra
earth up	edifies	elenchi	Emilian	endlong	enrober	ephelis
ear-tuft	editing	elevate	eminent	endmost	enrough	ephoral
easeful	edition	elf-bolt	emirate	endnote	enround	epiboly
ease out	edit out	elf-dock	emitted	end-note	en route	epicarp
easiest	educate	elf-lock	emitter	endogen	ensaint	epicene
east end	educrat	elf-shot	emotion	endopod	enshell	epicism
East End	eel-fare	elinvar	emotive	endorse	ensient	epicist
eastern	eel-like	elision	empanel	endower	enslave	epicure
easting	eelpout	elitism	empathy	end-play	ensnare	epiderm
easy all	eelskin	élitism	empearl	endurer	ensnarl	epidote
eatable	eelworm	elitist	emperor	enduros	enstamp	epigeal
eat away	eeriest	élitist	empiric	end-user	enstool	epigean
eat crow	effable	elixate	emplace	endways	enstyle	epigene
eat dirt	effendi	ellagic	emplane	endwise	ensuant	epigone
ebb-tide	efforce	ellipse	employe	end zone	ensuing	epigoni
Eblaite	effulge	ell-wand	employé	enemata	en suite	epigram
ebonies	egality	elm tree	emplume	enemies	ensurer	epigyne
ebonist	egg-case	elmwood	emporia	energic	entases	epigyny
ebonite	egg cell	elocute	empower	energid	entasis	epilate
ebonize	egg cosy	Elohist	empower	enfeoff	entente	epiloia
ebriety	egg-flip	elsehow	empress	enfever	entente	epimera
ebriose	egghead	elusion	emprise	Enfield	enteral	epimere
ebrious	eggiest	elusive	emptier	enflame	enterer	epimyth
ecbatic	eggless	elusory	emptily	enflesh	enteric	epiotic
ecbolic	egg-plum	elution	empting	enforce	enter on	episode
eccrine	egg roll	eluvial	emption	enframe	enteron	episome
ecdysis	egg-yolk	eluvium	empyema	engaged	enthral	epistle
echelle	egoless	Elysian	emu-bush	engagee	enthuse	epitaph
echelon	egotise	Elysium	emulate	engager	enticer	epitaxy
échevin	egotism	elytral	emulous	engined	Entisol	epithem
echidna	egotist	elytron	emu-wren	English	entitle	epithet
echinus	egotize	Elzevir	enabler	englobe	entrail	epitome
echites	ego trip	emacity	enactor	engorge	entrain	epitomy
echoism	eidetic	emanant	enamour	engrace	entrant	epitope
eclipse	eidolon	emanate	enation	engraft	entreat	epizoic
eclogue	eikonal	embargo	enchafe	engrail	entries	epizone
ecocide	einkorn	embassy	enchain	engrain	entrism	epizoon
ecology	eirenic	embathe	enchant	engrasp	entrist	epochal
economy	eis wool	embered	encharm	engrave	entropy	eponymy

epoxide	esquire	evacuee	exition	eyesome	fall-off	fartlek
epsilon	essayer	evangel	exocarp	eyesore	fall out	Far West
epulary	essence	evanish	exoderm	eye-spot	fallout	fasciae
epurate	Essenic	evasion	exogamy	eyespot	falsary	fascial
epyllia	estamin	evasive	exolete	eye view	falsely	fascias
equable	estated	evenest	Exonian	eyewash	falsies	fascine
equably	esthete	evening	exordia	eyewear	falsify	fascism
equally	estival	even now	exotica	eye-wink	falsism	Fascism
equator	estoile	even-odd	exotism	eye-worm	falsity	fascist
equerry	estrade	even out	expanse	fabliau	falutin	Fascist
equiaxe	estrado	eventer	ex parte	fabular	fameful	fashery
equinox	estreat	Everest	expense	face off	familia	fashion
erasion	estrich	evertor	expiate	face out	famille	fast-day
erasive	estrous	eve-star	expiree	faceted	famulus	fast foe
erasure	estuary	evictee	expirer	facient	fanatic	fast ice
erectly	etaerio	evictor	explain	factful	fan belt	fasting
erector	etagere	evident	explant	factice	fancier	fastish
E-region	etamine	evil day	explode	faction	fancies	fast one
erelong	etatism	evil eye	exploit	factive	fancily	fatally
eremite	etatist	Evil One	explore	factoid	fan club	fat-body
erenach	etchant	evirate	exposal	factory	fanfare	fateful
erepsin	etching	evirato	exposer	factual	fanfoot	fat-face
erethic	eternal	evocate	exposit	factums	fanlike	fat farm
ergodic	Etesian	evolute	expound	facture	fan mail	fat-head
ergoism	ethanal	evolver	express	faculae	fannell	fatidic
ergoted	Ethanim	.ewe lamb	expulse	facular	fannies	fatigue
ericoid	ethanol	ewe-neck	expunct	faculty	fanning	Fatihah
erineum	etheric	exacter	expunge	fadable	fan palm	Fatimid
erinnic	ethical	exactly	expurge	faddier	fantail	fatless
erinose	ethmoid	exactor	exscind	faddily	fantast	fatlike
Erinyes	ethoxyl	exalter	exsolve	faddish	fantasy	fatling
eristic	ethylic	examine	exsurge	faddism	fanwise	fatness
erl-king	ethynyl	example	extense	faddist	fanzine	fatsoes
ermelin	Etonian	exarate	externe	fade-out	Fapesmo	fattest
ermined	Euboean	excerpt	extinct	faecula	faraday	fattier
ermines	eucaine	excimer	extract	fagging	Faraday	fatting
erosion	Euchite	excited	extrema	faggoty	faradic	fattish
erosive	euclase	exciter	extreme	fahlerz	faraway	fattism
erotica	eucomis	exciton	extrude	fahlore	far-away	fattist
erotise	eucrasy	excitor	exudate	faience	far-back	fatuity
erotism	eucrite	exclaim	exurban	failing	farceur	fatuoid
erotize	eudemon	exclave	exurbia	failure	farcied	fatuous
errable	eugenia	exclude	exuviae	fainter	farcify	faucial
errancy	eugenic	excreta	exuvial	faintly	far-come	faulter
erratic	eugenol	excrete	ex-votos	fair dos	far-down	faunist
erratum	euglena	excurse	eyeable	fairies	Far East	faunule
errhine	Euglena	excusal	eyeball	fairing	farebox	fauvism
erudite	eulogia	excuser	eye bank	fairish	far from	fauvist
escapee	eulogic	execute	eye-bath	fair sex	far gone	faux pas
escaper	eunomia	exegete	eyebath	fairway	farmery	fawning
escheat	eunomic	exempla	eye-beam	faitour	farming	faxable
escribe	eupathy	exergue	eye bolt	falafel	farmost	fayence
escroll	euphony	ex facie	eye-bree	Falange	farness	fazenda
escuage	eupione	exhaust	eyebrow	Falasha	Faroese	fearful
escudos	euploid	exhibit	eye-drop	falbala	farrago	feaster
eserine	eupnoea	exhumer	eyefuls	falcate	farrant	feather
E-shaped	Euratom	exigent	eyehole	faldage	farrash	feature
esotery	euripus	exilian	eyelash	fallacy	farrier	febrile
espadon	eustasy	exility	eyeless	fall due	farruca	feckful
esparto	eustele	exister	eyelike	fall for	farsakh	federal
esplees	eustyle	exitial	eye mask	fall guy	farsang	feebler
espouse	Eutopia	exiting	eyeshot	falling	farther	feed-bag

feed dog	fervour	filacer	fire-red	flannel	flipped	flybane
feeding	Festino	filaree	firmish	flannen	flipper	fly-bird
feedlot	festive	filaria	firstly	flanque	flip-top	fly-blow
fee-farm	festoon	filbert	first up	flapped	flirter	fly-boat
feeling	fetcher	filcher	fir tree	flapper	fliting	fly-book
feel out	fetch up	filemot	fish-day	flare up	flitted	fly camp
feelthy	fetiche	file off	fishery	flasher	flitter	fly-dope
feering	fetidly	filiate	fish-eye	flashly	flivver	fly-fish
fee tail	fetlock	filibeg	fish-fry	flasket	floatel	fly-flap
Fehling	fettler	filicic	fishful	flasque	floater	fly-flat
feigner	feudary	filicin	fishgig	flat-cap	floccus	fly-half
feirily	feudist	fillies	fishier	flatcar	floe ice	fly high
felafel	feu duty	filling	fishify	flatlet	flogged	fly-hook
fellate	feu-farm	fill out	fishily	flat off	flogger	fly into
fellies	Feulgen	filmdom	fishing	flat out	flookan	fly-kick
felloes	feveret	filmier	fishnet	flat-pea	floorer	flyleaf
felonry	fewness	filmily	fish out	flatted	floozie	fly-line
felsite	feyness	filmset	fishpot	flatten	flopped	flyness
felspar	fiancée	Filofax	fissile	flatter	flopper	flyover
felting	fiascos	fimbria	fission	flattie	Floreal	fly page
felt pen	fibbery	finable	fissive	flat-top	floreat	fly-past
felt tip	fibbing	finagle	fissure	flaucht	Florida	fly-post
felucca	fibroid	finally	fistful	flaught	florist	flyting
felwort	fibroin	finance	fistula	flaunch	floruit	flytrap
feminal	fibroma	fin-back	fitched	flaunty	florula	fly-trap
feminie	fibrose	find for	fitchée	Flavian	flotage	fly upon
femoral	fibrous	find God	fitchet	flavine	flotant	fly-wire
fencing	fibster	finding	fitchew	flavone	flotsam	f-number
Fendant	fibulae	find out	fit fair	flavour	flounce	foamier
fen-fire	fibular	fine art	fitment	fleabag	flouncy	fobbing
fenland	fibulas	fine-cut	fitncss	flea-bug	flouter	focally
fennish	fictile	fineish	fitters	fleapit	flowage	focused
fenster	fiction	finesse	fittest	flea-pit	flowery	focuser
feodary	fictive	finewed	fitting	flebile	flowing	focuses
feoffee	fidalgo	finfoot	fiumara	fledged	flubbed	fodient
feoffer	fiddler	fingery	fixable	fleeced	flubdub	fog bank
feoffor	fiddley	finical	fixed-do	fleecer	flue-gas	foggage
Ferangi	fideism	finicky	fixedly	fleecie	fluence	foggier
feretto	fideist	finikin	fixture	fleerer	fluency	foggily
Ferison	fidgety	finless	fizzier	fleetly	fluidal	fogging
ferling	fidibus	finlike	fizzily	Fleming	fluidic	foghorn
fermail	fiefdom	finnack	flaccid	flemish	fluidly	fog-horn
fermata	fielded	finnied	Flacian	Flemish	flukier	fog lamp
ferment	fielden	finning	flacker	fleshed	flukily	fogless
fermery	fielder	Finnish	flacket	fleshen	flummer	fogydom
fermion	fiendly	finnsko	flag day	flesher	flummox	fogyish
fermium	fiercer	fin-toed	Flag Day	fleshly	flunker	fogyism
fernery	fierier	fin-weed	flagged	fletton	flunkey	foiling
fern-owl	fierily	fiorite	flagger	fleuret	fluoric	foilist
ferrate	fifteen	fipenny	flaglet	fleuron	flusher	folacin
ferrety	fifthly	Firbolg	flagman	flexile	flusker	folding
ferrian	fifties	fir cone	flagmen	flexing	fluster	fold-out
ferried	figbird	firearm	flakier	flexion	fluting	foliage
ferrier	figging	firebox	flakily	flexure	flutist	foliate
ferries	fighter	firebug	flaking	flicker	flutter	foliole
ferrite	fig leaf	fire-bug	flamant	flighty	fluvial	foliose
ferroan	figment	firedog	flambés	flimmer	fluxion	folk art
ferrous	fig tree	firefly	flamfew	flinder	flyable	folkier
ferrule	figural	fireman	flaming	flinger	flyaway	folkish
ferryer	figured	firemen	flâneur	fling to	fly-away	folknik
fertile	figurer	fire-new	flanger	fling up	fly-back	folksay
fervent	figwort	fire-pan	flanker	flip-dog	fly ball	follies

fomites	foreset	foulard	Frelimo	fructan	furioso	gaishen
fondaco	foresty	fouling	fremdly	fructed	furious	gala day
fondant	foretop	foul off	fremmit	fruited	furison	galagos
fondish	for ever	foul out	Frenchy	fruiter	furless	Galahad
fondler	forever	foul tip	frescos	frumper	furlong	galanga
fontful	for fair	foumart	freshen	frumple	furmety	galatea
foodful	forfare	founded	fresher	frustum	furnace	galeate
foodies	forfeit	founder	freshet	F-shaped	furnage	galeeny
food web	forfend	foundry	freshly	FT Index	furnish	galenic
foolery	for free	four-ale	fresnel	fubsier	furrier	galette
fool hen	forgave	fourché	Fresnel	fucated	furring	Galibis
foolish	forgery	Fourier	fretful	fuchsia	furrowy	galilee
footage	forgett	foussie	fretish	fuck all	fur seal	galipot
footbed	forgive	foveate	fretsaw	fucking	further	gallack
foot boy	forgoer	foveola	fretted	fuck off	furtive	gallant
footing	forgone	fovilla	fretter	fucused	fuscous	gallate
footler	for hire	fowling	friable	fuddler	fuse box	galleas
foot-log	forkful	fowl pox	friarly	Fuegian	fusible	Gallego
footman	fork out	fowl-run	fribble	fuehrer	fusidic	galleon
footmen	for life	fox bane	Fridays	fuelled	fusilli	gallery
footpad	for long	fox-fire	Friesic	fueller	fusilly	galleys
foot-rot	forlorn	foxhole	friezer	fuel oil	fusogen	gall-fly
footsie	for love	fox-hunt	frigate	fuel rod	fussier	gallica
Footsie	for luck	foxiest	frigged	fugally	fussify	gallice
footway	formant	foxlike	frigger	fugging	fussily	galliot
foo yong	formate	fox-mark	friggle	fuguing	fussock	gallium
foozler	formful	fox moth	frighty	fuguist	fusspot	gallnut
fopling	formica	foxship	frilled	fulcral	fustian	gall-nut
foppery	Formica	fox skin	fringer	fulcrum	fustier	galloon
foppish	forming	foxtail	frippet	fulgent	fustily	gallous
forager	formose	foxtrot	frisado	full age	futchel	gallows
foramen	formula	foyaite	frisbee	fullery	futhorc	galoped
forayer	formule	fractal	Frisbee	full out	futtock	galopin
forbade	fornent	fracted	Frisian	full pay	futural	galumph
forbear	for nuts	fraenum	frisker	fulmine	fuzzbox	gambade
forbore	for once	fragile	frisket	fulness	fuzzier	gambado
forceps	forpine	frailly	frisson	fulsome	fuzzily	Gambian
for cert	for real	frailty	frisure	fulvous	gabbart	gambier
forcing	for rent	Fraktur	frit-fly	fumaric	gabbier	gambist
fordeal	forsake	frame-up	fritted	fumaryl	gabbing	gambler
fording	for sale	framing	fritter	fumbler	gabbler	gamboge
foreact	for show	franion	frizado	fumette	gabbros	gambrel
forearm	forslow	franker	frizzle	funckia	gabelle	game act
forebay	forsook	frankly	frizzly	functor	gabfest	game all
forebow	for sure	frantic	Froebel	funding	gablock	gamebag
forecar	for that	frapler	frogbit	funeral	gadding	Game Boy
foreday	forth of	frapped	frog-eye	funfair	gadgety	gamelan
foredge	forties	fratery	frogged	funfest	Gaditan	game law
fore-end	fortify	fratter	froglet	fungate	gadling	gametic
foregut	fortlet	fraught	frogman	fungoid	gadroon	gamiest
foreign	Fortran	fraying	frogmen	fungous	gadwall	gammier
forelay	fortune	frazzle	fronded	funicle	Gaekwar	gangdom
foreleg	forward	freckle	frontal	funkier	Gaeldom	ganging
foreman	forwent	freckly	fronted	funkily	gaffled	ganglia
foremen	forworn	freebie	front of	funnier	gaggery	gang-man
forepaw	fossane	freedom	fronton	funnily	gagging	gangrel
foreran	fossick	freeman	froughy	funster	gag-rein	gangsta
forerib	fossula	freemen	frounce	furbery	gagster	gang war
forerun	fouetté	freesia	frousty	furbish	gahnite	gangway
foresaw	fougade	freeway	froward	furcate	gainful	ganosis
foresay	foughty	freezer	frowner	furcula	gaining	gantlet
foresee	foujdar	freight	frowsty	furiant	gainsay	garbage

garbler	gazelle	gesnera	gimlety	gleeful	gnasher	goitred
garboil	gazette	gessoed	gimmick	gleeman	gnathal	go large
garfish	gearbox	gessoes	gingall	glenoid	gnathic	goldarn
garland	gearing	gestalt	gingery	gleying	gnatter	gold bug
garlits	geckoes	Gestapo	gingham	gliadin	gnawing	gold-dig
garment	geebung	gestate	gingili	glibber	gneissy	gold-eye
Garnett	Geechee	gestion	gingkos	glidder	gnocchi	goldish
garnish	geelbek	gesture	gin-mill	gliding	gnomish	golf bag
garotte	gee whiz	get a rat	ginning	glimmer	gnomist	golfdom
garpike	Gehenna	get away	ginseng	glimpse	gnostic	goliard
Gartner	geishas	getaway	giocoso	gliosis	Goa ball	Goliath
gas boat	geladas	get back	gipsies	glirine	Goa bean	gollies
gas coal	gelatin	get down	Gipsify	glissés	go about	gombeen
gaseity	gelding	get even	gipsire	glisten	goadman	gomerel
gaseous	gelidly	get hell	Gipsyfy	glister	go ahead	gonadal
gas fire	gelling	get hers	giraffe	glitchy	go aloft	gondola
gashful	Gemaric	get into	girasol	glitter	go along	gondole
gashion	gemfish	get laid	girding	gloater	Goanese	gongora
gas laws	geminal	get left	girdler	globate	goateed	gonnoff
gasless	Geminid	get lost	girldom	globoid	goat-fig	good and
gas main	gemlike	get on to	girleen	globose	goat-god	good-bad
gas mask	gemmary	get onto	girlies	globous	goatish	good buy
gasohol	gemmate	get over	girlish	globule	goat nut	goodbye
gas oven	gemmery	get sick	Gironde	glochid	goat-rue	good day
gas ring	gemming	get some	gisarme	glomera	gobbing	good-den
gassier	gemmule	getting	gittern	glommed	gobbler	good egg
gassing	gemsbok	get well	give ear	gloomth	Gobelin	good for
gasthof	genappe	get wind	give off	gloppen	gobioid	good God
gastral	general	ghaffir	give out	gloried	go blind	goodhap
gas trap	generic	gharana	give way	glories	go broke	goodies
gastric	genesis	gharial	gizzard	glorify	go close	gooding
gastrin	genetic	ghastly	gjetost	glory be	go crook	goodish
gas well	genette	gheraos	glacial	Glory Be	goddard	good job
gateaus	Genevan	gherkin	glacier	glossal	goddess	good man
gateaux	genever	ghettos	gladded	glosser	goddize	goodman
gateleg	genipap	ghilgai	gladden	glossic	godetia	goodmen
gateman	genista	ghillie	gladder	glottal	go-devil	good now
gatemen	genital	Ghilzai	gladdie	glottic	Godfrey	good oil
gate-net	genitor	ghoster	gladdon	glottis	godhead	good old
gateway	genizah	ghostly	glad eye	glow-fly	Godhead	gooeyly
Gathaic	genning	giantly	gladful	glowing	godhood	go off at
Gatling	Genoese	giantry	gladius	glozing	godless	goofier
gattine	genomic	giardia	gladwin	glucose	godlier	goofily
gauchos	genteel	gibbose	glaikit	glue ear	godlike	gooiest
gaudery	gentian	gibbous	glammed	glueing	godlily	goolies
gaudier	gentile	giblets	glamour	glue-pot	godling	goombah
gaudies	gentler	GI bride	glancer	gluiest	godness	goondie
gaudily	genuant	giddier	glander	glummer	godpapa	goonery
Gaulish	genuine	giddify	glandes	glumose	godsend	goonish
gauntly	geodesy	giddily	glareal	gluonic	godship	goopher
gauntry	geogeny	giddy-up	glaring	glutaei	God slot	goopier
gausses	geogony	gigging	glarney	gluteal	go Dutch	Goorkha
gauzier	geoidal	giggish	glassen	glutean	godward	goosery
gauzily	geology	giggler	glassie	gluteus	Godward	goosish
gavotte	Geordie	gigolos	Glauber	glutted	go Fante	gorcock
gawkier	georgic	gigster	glaucus	glutton	go-fever	gorcrow
gawkily	gerbera	gilbert	glaze in	glycine	go for it	Gordian
gawkish	gerenuk	gilding	glazier	glyoxal	goggled	Gorgios
gayness	germane	gillery	glazily	glyphic	goggler	goriest
gaysome	gertcha	gillion	glazing	glyptal	go hence	gorilla
gazania	gerusia	gill-net	gleaner	glyptic	go in for	go round
gazebos	Gerzean	gimbals	glebous	gnarled	going to	Gorsedd

goshawk	granola	grey eye	grottos	guipure	gutsily	Halacha
go short	grantee	grey fox	grouchy	guisard	guttate	Halakah
gosling	granter	greyhen	grouper	Guisian	guttery	halberd
go snips	Grantha	greyish	groupie	guising	Gut-tide	halbert
go spare	grantor	grey jay	grouser	Gujarat	gutting	halcyon
gossipy	granule	greylag	grousey	Gujerat	guttler	halesia
gossoon	grapery	grey oak	grouter	gulchin	Guyanan	half-cap
Gothick	graphic	grey-out	growbag	Gulf War	guzzler	half-cut
Gothish	grapnel	grey pea	growing	gullery	gwyniad	half-day
Gothism	grapple	grey tin	growler	gulleys	gyle-fat	half-ebb
go to bed	grasper	gribble	grown-up	gullies	gyle-tun	half-god
go to law	grassed	gricing	grow out	gullish	gymnast	half-joe
go to pot	grasser	gridded	grubbed	gumboil	gymnure	half-lap
go to sea	grassum	griddle	grubber	gumboot	gymslip	half-leg
go to war	gratify	grieved	grubble	gumdrop	gypping	half-man
gouache	gratiné	griever	Grubean	gummata	gypsous	half pay
goujons	grating	griffin	grudger	gummier	Gypsyfy	half-pie
Goulard	graunch	griffon	gruelly	gummily	gyrally	halfway
goulash	graupel	grifter	gruffly	gumming	gyrator	halfwit
go under	gravely	griggle	grufted	gummite	gyrinid	halibut
gourami	gravida	griller	grumble	gummous	gyronny	halidom
gourmet	gravies	grimace	grumbly	gumshoe	gytrash	Halifax
gout-fly	graving	grimful	grummel	gum thus	haarder	halitus
goutily	gravity	grimier	grummet	gum tree	habdabs	hall boy
goutish	gravlax	grimily	grumose	gum-wood	habitat	halling
go wrong	gravure	grimmer	grumous	gunboat	habitué	hallion
goyisch	grazier	grimpen	grumphy	gun crew	habitus	hallock
gozzard	grazing	grinder	grunion	gun-deck	habutai	halloes
grab bag	greaser	grindle	grunter	gunfire	hachure	halloos
grabbed	greaten	gringos	gruntle	gunibri	hackbut	hallway
grabber	greater	grinned	grushie	gunless	hackery	halogen
grabble	Greater	grinner	Gruyère	gunlock	hacking	halo hat
grabens	great go	grip car	gryphon	gun moll	hackler	halpace
gracile	greatly	griping	grysbok	gunnera	hacklet	haltere
grackle	greaved	gripman	G-string	gunnery	hackman	halting
gradate	greaves	gripped	guanaco	gunnies	hackney	halyard
gradely	Grecian	gripper	Guanche	gunning	hacksaw	Hamadan
gradine	grecing	gripple	guanido	gunplay	had best	hamated
gradual	Grecise	grisard	guanine	gunroom	haddock	ham-bone
grafter	Grecism	griskin	guanoes	gunship	had need	Hamburg
grained	Grecize	gristle	guarana	gunshot	hadrome	Hamitic
grainer	grecque	gristly	Guarani	gun-site	hafnium	hammada
gramash	Greekly	gritted	guarded	gun slip	Haganah	hammier
grammar	greener	gritter	guardee	gunwale	hag-boat	hammily
grampus	Greener	grizzle	guarder	gunyang	hagfish	hamming
granage	greeney	grizzly	guariba	guppies	haggard	Hamming
granary	greenie	groaner	guayule	gurgler	haggish	hammock
granate	greenly	Grobian	gubbins	gurnard	haggler	hamster
grandad	greenth	grocery	guddler	gurning	hagigah	hamular
grandam	greeter	grockle	gudgeon	gushier	hag-ride	hamulus
grandee	gregale	grogram	guerdon	gushily	hagship	hanaper
grandly	gregory	groined	guereza	gushing	hahnium	Hanbali
grandma	Gregory	Grolier	guesser	gussied	hair bag	hand-axe
grandpa	greisen	gromell	guesten	gussies	haircut	handbag
granfer	greking	grommet	Guianan	gustful	hairdos	handful
granger	gremial	grooved	guichet	gustier	hairier	handgun
granita	gremlin	groover	guiding	gustily	hairily	hand-hot
granite	gremmie	grossen	Guignol	gustoes	hairnet	handier
grannam	grenade	grosser	guilder	gutless	hair net	handily
grannie	grenado	grossly	guildry	gutling	hair oil	hand-jam
grannom	grey box	gross up	guillem	Gutnish	hairpin	handjob
grannum	greyers	Grotian	Guinean	gutsier	Haitian	handled

handler	harrier	haylage	heigh-ho	hereout	Hi-liter	hoecake
hand off	harries	hayloft	heinous	here's to	hillier	hoedown
hand out	harshen	hayrick	heirdom	heretic	hilling	hoe into
handout	harshly	hayride	heiress	heritor	hillman	Hofmann
handsaw	harslet	hayseed	heirmos	herling	hill-man	hogback
handsel	harvest	Haytian	heister	Hermaic	hillmen	hog-deer
handset	has-been	hayward	hei-tiki	herniae	hillock	hog-fish
hands-on	hashish	haywire	helibus	hernial	hilltop	hoggery
hands up	Hasidic	hazeled	helical	hernias	himself	hogging
handy to	Hasidim	hazelly	helices	hernsew	hindgut	hoggish
hangdog	hassock	haziest	helicon	heroify	hinging	hog-head
hanging	hastate	headage	Helicon	heroine	hinnies	hoglike
hangman	hastier	head boy	helipad	heroise	hip bath	hog-line
hangmen	hastily	headier	hell-box	heroism	hip bone	hogling
hang of a	hasting	headily	hell-cat	heroize	hip-hole	hog-mane
hang off	hatable	heading	helldog	heronry	hipless	hog plum
hang out	hatband	headlet	Hellene	herring	hipness	hogskin
hankies	hatchel	headman	hellful	herself	hippest	hogwash
Hansard	hatcher	headmen	hell-hag	hership	hippies	hogweed
hanuman	hatchet	head off	hellier	Heshvan	hippish	hog-wild
Hanuman	hateful	head sea	hellion	hessian	hip roof	hog-yoke
ha'pence	hatfuls	headset	hellish	Hessian	hip-shot	Hohokam
ha'penny	hatless	head tax	hellite	hessite	hipster	hoister
hapless	hats off	head-tie	helluva	hetaera	hip-tile	hokiest
haploid	hattery	headway	hellyon	hetaira	hircine	hokonui
haplont	Hattian	heal-all	helotry	heteros	hire car	Holbein
ha'p'orth	hatting	healing	helpful	heumite	hireman	holdall
happier	hattock	healthy	helping	heurism	hire out	holding
happify	hat-tree	heap big	help out	hexadic	hirsute	hold off
happily	hauberk	heaping	helxine	hexagon	hirudin	hold out
happing	haubitz	hearing	hemiola	hexamer	his nibs	holdout
haptics	haughty	hearken	hemline	hexapla	his-self	hold-out
haratch	haulage	hear out	hemlock	hexapod	hissing	hole-saw
harbour	haul ass	hear say	hemming	hexarch	hiss off	holiday
hard hat	haulier	hearsay	henbane	hexitol	histoid	holiest
hard hit	haul off	hearted	hen-clam	hexogen	histone	hollaed
hardier	haul out	hearten	hen-coop	hexosan	history	holland
hardily	haunchy	heathen	hencote	heyduck	histrio	hollies
hardish	haunted	heather	hen-hawk	hibachi	hit back	holloes
hard nut	haunter	heating	hennaed	hiccupy	hitcher	holmium
hard pad	hautboy	heave-ho	hennery	hickeys	hitch up	holm-oak
hardpan	hauteur	heave to	henpeck	hickory	hit home	holster
hard pan	have a go	heavier	henries	hidalgo	hit list	holy day
hard roe	have fun	heavily	hensure	Hidatsa	hit-mark	holy Joe
hard set	have got	heavy on	henwife	hideous	hitting	Holy Joe
hard-top	havener	Hebraic	hen yard	hide out	Hittite	holy oil
hardtop	have-not	Hebrean	heparin	hideout	hive off	Holy See
harelip	have out	heckler	hepatic	hiemate	hoarder	holy war
haricot	have pat	hectare	heppest	higgler	hoarier	homager
Harijan	haverel	hedging	hepster	highboy	hoarily	Homburg
harmala	have way	hedonic	heptane	high day	hoarsen	home boy
harmful	haviour	heedful	heptode	high-end	hoatzin	homeboy
harmine	hawbuck	heel bar	heptoic	high hat	hobbies	homeish
harmony	hawkbit	heel bug	heptose	high-key	Hobbism	home key
harmost	hawk-eye	heel cup	herbage	high men	Hobbist	home-lot
harness	hawkish	heeling	herbary	high old	hobbler	homelyn
harpies	hawk-owl	heeltap	herbier	high sea	hobnail	Homeric
harping	hay-band	heel-tap	herblet	high-set	hocheur	home run
harpist	hay-barn	heftier	herbose	high tea	Hock-day	homiest
harpoon	haybote	heftily	herbous	highway	hocused	hominid
Harrian	haycock	hegemon	herb tea	Hilaria	hodiern	Homoean
harried	hay-fork	hegumen	herd-boy	hilding	hoe-cake	homolog

homonym	hosiery	hugsome	hydrate	ictuses	imbrued	in a romp
honchos	hospice	Huichol	hydride	Idahoan	imbrues	in a ruck
honesty	hostage	huitain	hydrion	Idalian	imbrute	in a rush
honeyed	hostess	hulking	hydroid	ideally	imbuing	in a snap
Honiton	hostile	humanly	hydrops	identic	imburse	in a snit
honkers	hosting	hum-bird	hydrous	idiotic	imitate	in a sort
honkies	hostler	humbler	hyemate	idiotry	immense	in a spin
honoree	hot bath	humdrum	hygeian	idleman	immerge	in a spot
honorer	hot cake	humeral	hygeist	idlesse	immerse	in a tale
honyock	hotfoot	humerus	hygiene	idolise	immoral	inaugur
hood-end	hothead	humetty	hygroma	idolism	impaint	in a walk
hooding	hotline	humidly	hymenal	idolist	impaler	in a wink
hoodlum	hot line	humidor	hymenia	idolize	impalla	in a wood
hoodman	hotness	humming	hymnary	Idumean	impalsy	in a word
hoodoos	hot seat	hummock	hymnist	idyllic	impanel	in banco
Hookean	hot shoe	humoral	hymnody	iffiest	impasse	in bar of
hooklet	hotshot	humored	Hypalon	I for one	impaste	in being
hook-pin	hot spot	humpier	hyped up	igneous	impasto	in blank
hook-pot	hotspur	humpies	hyperon	igniter	impavid	in blood
hook rug	hot tear	hunched	hypnoid	ignitor	impeach	in bloom
hook-tip	hottest	hundred	hypogea	ignoble	impearl	inboard
hoolock	hotties	Hungary	hypogee	ignobly	imperil	inbound
hooping	hotting	hunkers	hyponym	ignorer	impetus	inbread
Hoosier	hottish	hunkier	hypoxia	iguanid	Impeyan	inbreak
hoot owl	hot tube	Hunnish	hypoxic	ijolite	impiety	inbreed
hop-back	hot well	hunting	hyraces	ikebana	impinge	in brief
hop-bind	hot wind	huntite	I ask you	I knew it	impious	inbring
hop-bine	hot-wire	hunt out	Iberian	ileitis	implant	in-build
hopbush	hot-work	hunt's-up	Icarian	iliacus	implead	inbuilt
hopeful	houbara	hurdler	iceberg	Iliadic	implied	inburst
hophead	Houdini	hurleys	ice-bird	iligant	implies	incense
hoplite	hougher	hurling	ice blue	Illanun	impling	in check
hoppety	houhere	Hurrian	ice-boat	illapse	implode	in chief
hopping	hoummos	hurried	ice-bolt	ill-bred	implore	incipit
hoppity	houngan	hurrier	ice-cold	illegal	implume	incisal
hop-pole	housing	hurries	ice cube	illegit	imposer	incised
hopsack	houting	hurry-up	icefall	ill fame	impound	incisor
hop-sack	hoverer	hurtful	ice-fall	illfare	impregn	inciter
hop-toad	howbeit	husband	ice fish	illicit	impresa	in class
hop tree	how come	hushaby	ice floe	illitic	imprese	inclave
hopyard	however	hushful	ice-foot	I'll live	impress	in clear
horizon	howling	hushion	Iceland	ill luck	imprest	incline
hormone	how many	huskier	iceless	illness	imprint	inclose
horn-bug	how much	huskies	ice milk	illocal	improve	include
hornero	Howship	huskily	Icenian	illogic	impulse	incluse
horn-fly	Hoxnian	husking	ice pack	illoyal	imputer	incomer
hornful	H-shaped	hussies	ice pail	illusor	I myself	Inconel
horn gap	Huastec	Hussite	ice pick	ill will	in a bind	inconnu
hornier	Hubbard	hussive	ice rink	ill wind	in a body	in court
hornify	hubbies	husting	ice show	Ilocano	inadept	incover
hornily	hubless	hustler	ice-wool	ilvaite	in-a-door	incrust
hornist	Hubshee	hut-like	ice-work	imagery	in a drip	incubus
hornito	huddler	hutment	ice-worm	imagine	in a funk	incudes
horn-mad	hueless	hutting	ichabod	imagism	in a glow	incurve
horn-man	huff-cap	Huygens	icicled	imagist	in a huff	indeedy
horn-owl	huffier	hyaenid	iciness	imamate	in aid of	in depth
horrent	huffily	hyaline	icky-boo	imbauba	in a mood	indexer
horrify	huffish	hyalite	iconism	imbiber	in and in	indexes
horsier	huffkin	hyaloid	iconize	imbongi	inanely	indican
horsily	hugeous	hydatid	icosane	imbosom	inanity	indices
hosanna	huggery	hydrant	icteric	imbound	in a oner	indicia
hose-net	hugging	hydrase	icterus	imbower	inaptly	indigos

inditer	infuser	in place	interne	Iranian	isotron	Jahvism
indolic	ingenio	in point	in there	Iranize	isotype	jai alai
indolyl	ingénue	in press	in-thing	Iraqize	isozyme	Jainism
in doors	ingoing	in prest	intimal	irately	Ispahan	Jainist
indoors	ingorge	in print	intoner	ireless	Israeli	Jaipuri
Indo-Pak	ingoted	in proof	in total	irenics	issuant	jalouse
indorse	Ingoush	inquest	in touch	Iricism	issuing	jamadar
in doubt	ingraft	inquiet	intrada	iridial	isthmic	Jamaica
indoxyl	in grain	inquire	in trade	iridian	isthmus	jam-full
indraft	ingrain	inquiry	in train	iridium	Istrian	jammier
indrawn	ingrate	in ruins	intrant	irisate	itacism	jamming
in drink	ingress	in scale	intreat	Irisher	itacist	jam on it
induced	Ingrian	inscape	introit	Irishly	Italian	jam-pack
inducer	in gross	insculp	in troth	Irishry	Italiot	Janeite
indulge	in-group	insecta	intrude	irksome	itchier	jangler
indulto	ingrown	insecty	intruse	iron age	itching	janitor
in dummy	inhabit	inseity	in trust	Iron Age	itemise	jankers
indusia	inhaler	insense	intrust	ironies	itemize	jannock
indwell	in haste	inshell	in truth	ironing	iterant	January
indwelt	inhaust	inshoot	intuent	ironise	iterate	Japlish
Indycar	in heart	in shore	in turns	ironist	itinera	japonic
inearth	inherit	inshore	in twain	ironize	it seems	Jap silk
inedita	inhiate	in short	intwine	iron law	it tells	jarfuls
ineptly	inhibin	insider	intwist	iron man	iulidan	jargoon
inequal	inhibit	in sight	inulase	iron ore	Ivicene	jarkman
inertia	in holes	insight	Inupiaq	iron out	Ivorian	jarldom
inertly	in-house	insigne	Inupiat	iron pan	ivoride	jarless
inesite	inhuman	insipid	in utero	irruent	ivoried	jarring
in evens	in irons	in small	inutile	isagoge	ivories	jasmine
inexact	initial	in smoke	in vacuo	isatoic	ivorine	jaspery
inexist	inition	insofar	invader	ischial	ivy-bush	javaite
in faith	injunct	in sooth	invalid	ischium	ivy-leaf	Java man
infancy	injured	in spate	inveigh	Isfahan	ivy tree	javelin
infanta	injurer	in spawn	inverse	I-shaped	I wonder	jawbone
infante	injuria	inspeak	invigor	Ishmael	jabbers	jaw-hole
infarct	ink ball	inspect	invited	Isiacal	jabbing	jawless
in fault	ink-fish	inspire	invitee	isidial	jacamar	jawline
infauna	inkhorn	inspoke	inviter	isidium	jacinth	jaw-rope
infaust	inkiest	in sport	in vitro	Islamic	jackass	jaws wag
inferno	inkless	in spots	in vogue	isleman	jackdaw	jay-bird
infidel	inkling	install	in voice	isleted	jackeen	jaywalk
infield	in-kneed	instant	invoice	Ismaeli	jackleg	jazz age
in fieri	inkshed	in state	invoker	Ismaili	jackman	jazzier
infight	inkweed	instate	involve	isobath	Jack oak	jazzify
infimum	inkwell	instead	inwards	isocrat	jack off	jazzily
inflame	ink-well	in steam	in way of	isodose	Jack-pin	jazzman
in flank	inky cap	in stock	inweave	isoflor	jackpot	jazzmen
inflate	in large	in-store	in whelp	isogamy	jacksie	jealous
inflect	inlayer	instyle	in whole	isogeny	Jack tar	jeepers
in flesh	inlying	in style	inyanga	isogony	jacobin	jeepney
inflict	innards	insular	iodated	isogram	Jacobin	Jehovah
in focus	innerly	insulin	ion burn	isohyet	Jacobus	jejunal
in folio	innerve	insulse	ionizer	isolate	jaconet	jejunum
infolio	innings	insured	ionogen	isolato	jacuzzi	jellaba
in force	in no way	insurer	ionomer	isoline	Jacuzzi	jellied
inforce	inocula	insurge	ion pair	isonomy	jadedly	jellies
infract	inolith	inswing	ion spot	isopach	jadeite	jellify
inframe	in order	in tears	ion trap	isospin	j'adoube	jemadar
in front	inosate	integer	Io paean	isotely	Jagatai	jenever
in fruit	inosine	intense	ipomoea	isotone	jaggery	jennies
infulae	in pairs	interim	ipseity	isotope	jaggier	jeofail
in funds	in phase	in terms	iracund	isotopy	jagging	jeopard

Jericho	Joe Soap	ju-jutsu	Kannada	kercher	Kikuchi	kitling
jerkier	jogging	jukebox	kantele	Keresan	Kikuyus	kitschy
jerkily	jogtrot	jukskei	Kantian	kernite	kill-cow	kitties
jerk off	jog-trot	jumbuck	Kantism	kerogen	killian	kitting
jerquer	John Doe	jumelle	Karaism	Kerries	killick	kittles
jerries	John hop	jump bid	Karaite	kerseys	killing	Kiwanis
Jerries	Johnson	jump-cut	karakia	keruing	killjoy	Klamath
jerseys	joinant	jumpier	karakul	kerygma	killock	klapper
jessamy	joinder	jumpily	karamat	kestrel	kill off	Kleagle
jessant	joinery	jumping	karanga	Keswick	kill out	Kleenex
Jessean	joining	jump jet	karaoke	ketchup	kiln-dry	kleruch
jestful	jointed	jump-off	karezza	ketolic	kilnful	klezmer
Jesuist	jointer	juncoes	Karnata	ketonic	kilobit	klipbok
jetfoil	jointly	June bug	karstic	ketosis	kiloton	klipdas
Jetfoil	joisted	Jungian	karting	ketotic	kilting	klister
jetties	jokelet	jungled	Kashgai	kettler	kimonos	klompie
jetting	jollier	juniper	Kashgar	key-clog	kinchin	klonkie
jewelly	jollies	junk art	Kashmir	key-cold	kindler	klootch
jewelry	jollify	junkman	Kashrut	key grip	kindred	knacker
jewfish	jollily	Jupiter	Kashube	keyhole	kinesic	knaidel
Jew plum	jollity	jurally	Kassite	keyless	kinesis	knapped
Jewries	jollyer	jurator	kasturi	key move	kinetic	knapper
Jew's ear	jonnick	juridic	Kaszube	keynote	kinetin	knarred
Jew's eye	jonquil	jury box	kathode	keyring	kinfolk	knavery
Jezebel	joss-man	jury-leg	katsura	key-ring	kingcup	knavish
jhuming	jotting	juryman	Kattern	keyster	kingdom	kneader
jibbing	joukery	jurymen	katydid	keyword	king-hit	kneecap
jib-boom	joulean	jury-rig	kayaked	khaddar	Kingite	kneeing
jib-door	journal	jussion	kayaker	khakied	kinglet	kneeled
jiffies	journey	jussive	kaylied	khalasi	King Log	kneeler
jigaboo	journos	justice	Kazakhs	khalifa	king-nut	knee-pan
jig-a-jig	jouster	justify	kazooer	Khalkha	kingpin	kneesie
jig-bore	joyance	justing	kebbuck	khamsin	kinkier	knees-up
jiggety	joyancy	just now	kecksie	khanate	kinkily	kneidel
jigging	Joycean	jutting	kedlock	khanjar	kinkled	Knesset
jiggish	joyless	juvenal	keelage	khanjee	kinless	knicker
jillion	joyride	Juvenal	keeling	Khedive	kinship	knitted
jiltish	joysome	kabaddi	keelman	Khoisan	kinsman	knitter
Jim Crow	J-shaped	kabbala	keelson	kibbler	kinsmen	knittle
jim-jams	jubilee	Kabbala	keep-fit	kibbutz	Kipchak	knobbed
jimmied	Judaean	kaboura	keeping	kibitka	kippage	knobber
jimmies	Judaise	kachina	keepnet	Kichaga	kippeen	knobble
Jimminy	Judaism	Kaddish	keep-net	kick ass	kipping	knobbly
jingall	Judaist	kagoule	keep nit	kicking	kip-shop	knocker
jingler	Judaize	kahawai	keep off	kickish	kipsies	knock on
jingoes	judcock	kainite	keep out	kick off	Kirghiz	knock up
jittery	judgess	kajaten	keertan	kick out	kirkman	knoller
jive-ass	judging	kakapos	keester	kiddier	kirkmen	knopped
Joannes	judoist	kalashy	Keftian	kiddies	Kirlian	knopper
jobbery	jug band	kalends	keg beer	kidding	kirmess	knotted
jobbing	jugfuls	kalimba	keister	kiddish	kirtled	knotter
jobbish	jugging	Kalmuck	keitloa	kiddush	kissage	know-all
job-hunt	juggins	Kalmyks	kelping	kidling	kissing	know how
jobless	juggler	kalpack	ken-mark	kidneys	kiss off	knowing
Jo block	jughead	Kamares	kenning	kidskin	kistful	Knoxian
job shop	juglone	kamassi	kenosis	kid-star	kitchen	knubble
jobster	jugular	kamerad	kenotic	Kieffer	kite bar	knubbly
job-type	jugulum	kampong	Kentish	kierful	kite-man	knuckle
jobwork	juicier	kampung	Kentuck	kiering	kitenge	knuckly
jockeys	juicily	kanchil	kerasin	Kievian	kithara	Knudsen
jocular	ju-jitsu	Kandyan	keratin	kiewiet	kithing	knurled
Joe Blow	jujuism	K'ang-Hsi	kerbing	Kikongo	kitless	Kodaker

koi carp	lacecap	lambast	lap-join	Latvian	leaf-bud	legging
kokanee	Lacerta	lambent	Laplace	Laudian	leafery	leghorn
koklass	laciest	lambert	Lapland	Laudism	leaf-fat	Leghorn
kolkhoz	lacinia	Lambert	lapping	Laudist	leaf-gap	legible
komatik	lack for	Lambeth	Lappish	laugher	leafier	legibly
kombers	lacking	lambkin	lap robe	laugh-in	leaflet	leg-iron
komfoor	lackwit	lamboys	Lapsang	launder	leagued	legitim
kongoni	laconic	lamb-pie	Laputan	laundry	leaguer	legless
koniaku	lacquer	lamella	lap-weld	laurate	leagues	leg-over
Konkani	lacquey	laminae	lapwing	lauroyl	leakage	leg-pull
kookier	lactary	laminal	larceny	Lausitz	leakier	leg-rest
kookily	lactase	laminar	larchen	lavabos	lea-land	leg-ring
kopdoek	lactate	lamming	lard-ass	lave net	leangle	legroom
Koppite	lacteal	lampern	lard oil	lavolta	leaning	leg-room
koradji	lactone	lampers	lardoon	law-book	leanish	leg-rope
Koranic	lactose	lampful	largely	law-hand	lean-tos	leg-show
Koranko	lacunae	lamping	largess	lawless	leap day	leg side
Koranna	lacunal	lampion	largish	lawlike	leaping	leg slip
Koreish	lacunar	lampist	larkish	Law Lord	learned	leg spin
korhaan	lacunas	lamplet	Larnian	lawsuit	learner	leg trap
korowai	Ladakhi	lamplit	larnite	law term	learn up	legumen
Koshare	ladanum	lamp oil	lasagne	lawting	leasing	legumin
kotatsu	laddish	lampoon	lashing	laxness	leather	leg work
kotwali	ladhood	lamprey	lashkar	layaway	leave be	legwork
koumiss	ladinos	lamster	lash out	lay away	leave go	leg-worm
kouprey	Ladinos	land-boc	lassock	lay back	Leavers	Leibniz
K ration	ladrone	land-end	lassoer	lay bare	leaving	leister
kremlin	ladybug	land-ice	lassoes	lay dead	Leboyer	leisure
kriegie	Lady Day	landing	lassy me	lay down	lechery	lemanry
krieker	ladydom	land-law	lastage	lay-edge	Lechish	lemmata
Krilium	lady-fly	ländler	last day	layered	lectern	lemming
krimmer	ladyish	landman	last end	layette	lection	Lemnian
krypton	ladykin	landmen	lasting	lay fast	lectric	lempira
krytron	Laetare	landnam	last lap	layflat	lecture	lemurid
Kuan Yin	lagarto	land-rat	last man	laygear	lecythi	lending
kufiyeh	lag bolt	land tax	last out	lay into	ledging	lengthy
kulchur	lagenar	land-tie	Latakia	laylock	leecher	lenient
kumquat	lagetto	land-war	latania	lay odds	lee helm	lenitic
kunzite	laggard	langite	latchet	lay open	lee-lone	lens cap
kurbash	lagging	langley	latch on	layover	leemost	lensing
Kurdish	lag-last	langsat	late cut	lay over	leerier	lenslet
kursaal	lag time	langued	late fee	lay pipe	leerily	lensman
Kushite	Lagting	languet	lateish	lay wait	leer man	lensmen
kuteera	lah-de-da	languid	latency	lazaret	lee-room	lensoid
Kutenai	laicise	languor	laterad	Lazarus	leervis	lentigo
Kuwaiti	laicism	laniary	lateral	laziest	lee side	lentisk
kwanzas	laicity	laniate	Lateran	lazy arm	leesome	lentoid
kwedini	laicize	lanista	latexes	lazy-bed	leeward	Leonese
kyanise	laidron	lankier	lathery	lazy dog	lee wave	leonine
kyanite	lairage	lankily	lathing	lazy eye	left arm	Leonine
kyanize	lairdie	lanolin	latices	lazyish	lefties	leopard
kylikes	lairdly	lantana	latimer	lazzaro	leftish	leotard
kyoodle	lakelet	lantern	Latiner	L-driver	leftism	leproma
labaria	Lalique	lanyard	Latinic	leacher	leftist	leprose
labarri	lallang	Laocoön	Latinly	lead-ash	legally	leprosy
labarum	Lallans	Laotian	Latinos	leading	legatee	leprous
labella	lalling	lap belt	latitat	leadman	legator	leptome
labiate	lamaism	lap desk	latosol	lead off	legatos	leptons
labored	Lamaism	lapfuls	latrant	lead out	leg bail	lesbian
labroid	lamaist	lap-held	latrine	lead-tin	leg-bone	Lesbian
laccase	Lamaist	lapilli	latteen	leafage	leggero	lessest
lacebug	lambada	lap-iron	lattice	leaf-bed	leggier	lessive

let-down	lie-down	linctus	listful	lockram	loonies	lowerer
let drop	lie over	lindane	listing	lock-saw	loopful	low gear
let fall	lie with	lindorm	lit crit	locoman	loopier	low keep
Lethean	life-day	lineage	literal	Locrian	loosely	lowland
let into	lifeful	Linear A	lithate	locular	loosish	lowlier
let know	life-gun	Linear B	lithely	loculus	lop down	low life
let pass	life net	lineate	lithian	locusta	lop-ears	low-life
let slip	lifeway	lineman	lithify	locutor	loppage	lowlife
let stew	lift-fan	linemen	lithium	lodging	lopping	lowlily
lettiga	lifting	line-out	lithoes	loftier	lopseed	low-loss
letting	lift off	line pin	lithoid	loftily	lop-wood	low mass
Lettish	lift-out	Lingala	lithops	lofting	loquent	low Mass
lettuce	lift-web	lingcod	litotes	logatom	lord-dom	lowmost
let walk	ligancy	lingoes	litster	logbook	lordful	lowness
leucine	ligging	lingual	littery	log-cock	Lord God	low-pass
leucite	lighted	Linguet	littler	logging	lording	low-rise
leucoma	lighten	lingula	littlie	loghead	lordlet	low tech
leucous	lighter	liniest	liturgy	logical	Lorelei	low tide
levancy	lightly	linkage	livable	logiest	Lorentz	lowveld
levator	light on	link-boy	lived-in	log-line	lorgnon	Low Week
leveche	light up	linking	livener	logroll	lorilet	loxodon
leveler	lignify	linkman	live oak	logwood	lorimer	loyally
levelly	lignite	linkmen	live out	log-work	loriner	loyalty
level up	lignose	link off	livered	loiasis	lorisid	lozened
leveret	lignous	link rod	lividly	Lollard	lormery	lozenge
Levitic	ligroin	linnaea	lixivia	lollies	lorries	lozengy
lewisia	ligular	Linnean	llanero	lolling	losable	L-shaped
lew-warm	Lihyani	linocut	lloydia	lollopy	lose bet	lubbard
lexemic	likable	linoxyn	loading	lombard	loselry	lubrify
lex fori	like fun	linsang	loaning	Lombard	lose out	lucanid
lexical	like ice	linseed	loather	Londony	lose way	lucarne
lexicon	like mad	lintern	loathly	loneful	lost wax	lucence
lex loci	like sin	linuron	lobbies	long ago	lot-lead	lucency
ley line	lilacky	lion-ant	lobbing	long arm	lot-mead	lucerne
Lezgian	lily pad	lioncel	lobbyer	longbow	lotment	lucible
liaison	lily-pot	lion dog	lobcock	long-day	lottery	lucidly
liangle	limaces	lioness	lobe-fin	long dog	lotting	lucifee
liassic	limaçon	lionise	lobelia	long ear	loudish	Lucifer
liatris	limbate	lionish	lobopod	longest	lounder	lucific
libbard	limb-bud	lionism	lobster	long-fed	lounger	lucivee
libelee	limbeck	lionize	lob-tail	long hop	louring	luckier
liberal	limbric	lip-deep	lobular	longing	louse up	luckily
liberty	limeade	lipemia	lobulus	long ink	lousier	luculia
Liberty	lime-ash	lipless	lobworm	longish	lousily	Luddism
libidos	limepit	liplike	locable	long leg	loutish	Luddite
library	lime-pot	lip-line	locally	long off	louvred	Luganda
librate	limiest	lipoate	locator	long pig	lovable	Lugbara
Librium	liminal	lippier	lochage	long-pod	lovably	luggage
licence	limited	lipping	lochial	long run	loveful	lugging
license	limiter	lip-read	lockage	long sea	love-lay	lughole
licheny	limites	lip-sync	lock-box	Long Tom	love-pat	lug-mark
lich-owl	limning	lip-work	Lockean	long ton	lovered	lugsail
licitly	Limoges	liquate	lockful	lonning	loverly	lug sole
lickety	limping	liquefy	Lockian	look big	love-tap	Lugwari
licking	limpish	liqueur	locking	looking	lowance	lugworm
lick-log	limpkin	liquidy	Lockist	look out	lowball	Luiseño
lickpot	limulus	liquify	lockjaw	lookout	lowbell	lullaby
licuala	linable	lirella	lockman	look-see	low-born	Lullian
lidgate	linaloe	lisente	locknut	loo mask	low-bred	Lullism
lidless	linalyl	lisping	lock-nut	loomery	lowbrow	Lullist
lie-abed	linaria	lissoir	lock out	looming	low-bush	lumbago
lie back	Lincoln	lissome	lockout	loonier	low-down	lumeter

luminal	machete	mahmudi	malmsey	man-keen	marcato	mascled
Luminal	Machian	Mahomet	malonic	mankier	marcher	masculy
luminol	machila	mahonia	malonyl	mankind	march on	mashlum
lumpers	machine	mahorka	malpais	manless	Marconi	Mashona
lumpier	Machism	Mahound	maltase	manlier	maremma	mash-tub
lumpily	machree	mahseer	Maltese	manlike	maremme	Mas John
lumping	Machzor	maidish	maltier	manlily	Marengo	mask jug
lumpish	maclura	maidkin	malting	manling	margate	masoner
lump sum	macouba	mailbag	maltman	man-made	margent	masonic
lunaria	macramé	mail-box	maltose	manness	margosa	Masonic
lunated	maculae	mailbox	malt-tax	manning	marimba	masonry
lunatic	macular	mail-car	Malvern	mannish	marined	Masorah
luncher	macumba	mail-day	mamaloi	mannite	mariner	masquer
lunette	maddest	mailing	mamboes	mannose	marital	massage
lungful	madding	maillot	mamelle	man o'war	markhor	mass-day
lunulae	maddish	mailman	mamelon	manpack	marking	masseur
lunular	made for	mailmen	mamilla	man-rate	mark man	massify
lunulet	madeira	mail-out	mammary	man-rope	markman	massily
lupanar	Madeira	Mainite	mammies	mansard	mark off	massive
lupulin	made man	ma-in-law	mammock	manship	mark out	mass man
lurcher	madhead	mainour	mammoth	mansion	mark you	massula
lurgies	Madison	main sea	manacle	man-size	marline	mastaba
luridly	mad keen	maintop	managed	man's man	marlion	mastage
lurking	madling	mainway	managee	manteau	marlite	mastery
lushbum	mad mick	maistry	manager	manteca	marloes	mastiff
lustful	madness	maizena	manakin	mantled	marl-pit	mastika
lustier	Madonna	majesty	manatee	mantlet	marmite	masting
lustily	madoqua	makable	manbote	Mantoux	Marmite	mastman
lustral	Madrasi	Makasar	mancala	mantrap	maroela	mastoid
lustred	madroña	make for	manchet	mantric	maroodi	matador
lustrum	madroño	make hay	man cook	Mantuan	Marplan	matcher
luteous	Maduran	make off	mandala	manuary	marplot	matchet
lute-pin	madwort	make out	mandant	manumit	marquee	match up
luthern	maestri	make war	mandate	manurer	marquis	matelot
luthier	maestro	make way	Mandean	manurey	Marrano	mathern
Lutomer	Mae West	Makonde	Manding	manward	married	matiest
lutrine	maffick	Malabar	mandola	man-week	marrier	Matilda
luvvies	Mafiosi	malacca	mandora	manwise	marries	matinal
lychnis	Mafioso	Malacca	mandore	Manx cat	marring	matinee
lycopin	magadis	malacia	Mandrax	Manxman	Marrism	matinée
lycopod	magenta	malacon	mandrel	Manxmen	Marrist	matless
lyddite	maggoty	malagas	maneton	man-year	marrowy	matraca
lye corn	Maghreb	malaise	Manetti	many-one	marry up	matrass
lygaeid	Maghrib	malambo	mangeao	Maori PT	Marsala	matrist
lyingly	Maghzen	malanga	mangier	maormor	marshal	matross
Lyle gun	magical	malaria	mangily	map-fire	Marsian	mattery
lymphad	magmata	Malayan	mangler	mapless	martelé	matting
lyncean	magnate	Malayic	mangoes	mappery	martial	mattins
lyncher	magneto	malcoha	mangold	mapping	Martian	mattock
lynchet	magnify	malease	man-haul	mappist	Martini	mattoid
lyngorm	magnums	maleate	manhole	map-read	martlet	maturer
lynx-eye	magslip	maleesh	manhood	Mapuche	martyry	matweed
Lyonese	magsman	malefic	man-hour	marabou	Marwari	mat-work
lyrated	maguari	malicho	manhunt	Maranao	Marxian	matzoth
lyrical	mahaila	malimbi	manicou	maranta	Marxise	maudlin
macabre	mahaleb	Malines	manihot	marasca	Marxism	Maulana
macadam	Mahamad	Malinke	manikin	Maratha	Marxist	maul oak
macaque	mahatma	malison	manilla	Marathi	Marxite	maunder
macauco	Mahdism	malkoha	Manilla	marbled	Marxize	Maurist
macchia	Mahdist	mallard	manille	marbler	Mary Ann	mauryah
maceral	Mahican	malleus	maniple	marblet	Masarwa	Mauryan
machair	mah-jong	Malling	manitou	Marburg	mascara	mauther

mauvish	medalet	Mennecy	metrete	mileage	minibus	miskick
mavrone	meddler	Mennist	metrify	milfoil	minicab	Miskito
mawkish	medevac	men-only	metrist	miliary	minikin	misknow
mawseed	mediacy	menorah	mettled	milieus	minimal	mislead
mawther	mediant	Men's Lib	me-wards	milieux	minimax	mislear
mawworm	mediate	mens rea	mew gull	militia	minimum	mislike
maxilla	medical	mensual	Mexican	milk bar	minimus	misluck
maximal	medicos	menthol	mezuzah	milk cap	miniver	mismade
maximin	mediety	mention	mezzani	milk-cow	minivet	mismake
maximum	Medinal	meranti	Miaotse	milk dry	Min of Ag	mismark
maxwell	mediums	mercado	miasmal	milkful	Minorca	mismate
Maxwell	medivac	mercery	miasmas	milkier	minster	mismove
May-bird	medleys	merchet	miasmic	milkily	mintage	misname
May-blob	medulla	Mercian	micelle	milking	mintier	misnome
May-bush	medusae	mercies	Michael	milk-leg	mint par	misplay
maycock	medusal	mercury	michery	milkman	mint tea	misrate
mayduke	medusan	mereing	mickery	milkmen	minuend	misread
Mayfair	medusas	merinos	micrify	milk run	minuter	misrule
mayfish	meerkat	merisis	micrite	milksop	minutia	missaid
May game	meeting	merited	microbe	millage	minxish	misseem
May lady	megabit	Merkani	mid-aged	mill-dam	Miocene	missend
May lily	megapod	mermaid	mid-brow	mill-dog	Mipolam	missies
May morn	Megaric	Meroite	mid-calf	Millian	miracle	missile
mayoral	megaron	merrier	midcrop	millime	mirador	missing
maypole	megasea	merrill	midcult	milling	Miranda	mission
May-rose	megaton	merrily	middest	mill-ink	mirbane	missish
maythen	meioses	mersion	middies	million	Mirditë	missive
maythes	meiosis	mesarch	middle C	Millite	mirific	missort
mayweed	meiotic	mesaxon	middler	mill-ken	mirkier	miss out
May Week	mei ping	meseems	Mideast	millman	mirrory	misstay
mazagan	Meissen	meshing	midgern	mill-run	misally	misstep
Mazahua	melaena	meshuga	midibus	milordo	misbode	missuit
Mazatec	melamed	mesityl	midiron	milreis	misborn	mistake
Mazdean	mélange	mesodic	midland	Miltown	miscall	mistbow
mazedly	melanic	mesonic	Midland	Mimamsa	miscast	mistell
mazeful	melanin	mesquit	mid-life	mimesis	mischty	misterm
Mazhabi	melasma	message	midline	mimetic	mis-cite	mistery
maziest	melilot	mess-boy	midmost	mimical	miscode	mistful
mazurka	melisma	Messiah	midnoon	mimicry	miscook	mistico
mazzard	melissa	messier	Midrash	mimness	miscopy	mistier
meacock	melkbos	Messier	midriff	mimulus	misdate	mistily
meadowy	Melkite	messily	midship	minable	misdeal	mistime
mealier	mellite	messing	mid-shot	Minaean	misdeed	mist-net
mealman	mellowy	mess kit	midsole	minaret	misdeem	mistook
meander	melodia	mess tin	midterm	minchen	misdial	mistral
meanies	melodic	mestiza	midtown	mincing	misdoer	mistune
meaning	melonry	mestizo	midward	mindful	misdraw	mistype
mean sun	meltemi	mestome	midweek	mindset	misease	misuser
mearing	melting	metalaw	Midwest	mind-set	miserly	miswent
measled	membral	metaled	midwife	mind you	misfall	misword
measles	memento	metally	mid-wing	mine-car	misfame	misyoke
measure	menacer	metamer	midwive	mine-pig	misfare	Mitanni
meat-ant	menalty	methane	Miesian	mine-pit	misfell	mitchel
meat-axe	menazon	methene	miffish	mineral	misfile	mitella
meat-fly	mendang	methide	might-be	mine tin	misfire	mitered
meatier	mending	Methody	mightn't	minette	misgive	mitogen
meatily	mendong	Methuen	migrant	minever	mishear	mitosis
meatman	mendung	metical	migrate	mingier	Mishnah	mitotic
meat tea	menfolk	Metonic	mikados	mingily	Mishnic	mitring
Meccano	Ménière	metonym	milcher	mingler	mishook	mitzvah
Mechlin	menisci	me-tooer	mildewy	miniate	misjoin	mixable
meconin	menkind	metopic	mildish	minibar	miskeys	mix-down

mixdown	monarch	moorish	mothery	muddler	mumpish	mycelia
mixedly	monarda	Moorish	moth fly	Mudéjar	muncher	mycosis
mixed-up	Mondays	moorlog	mothier	mudfish	munchie	mycotic
mixible	mondial	moorman	Motilon	mudflap	mundane	myeloid
mixture	moneran	Moorman	motivic	mud-flat	muninga	myeloma
mizmaze	moneron	moor-pan	motlier	mudflat	munjeet	myiasis
mizzler	moneyed	mop fair	motored	mud-flow	munnion	mylodon
Moabite	moneyer	mophead	motoric	mudflow	Munsell	mynheer
moanful	mongrel	mopiest	MOT test	mudhead	muntjac	myoball
moaning	moniker	mopping	mottled	mudhole	muntjak	myocoel
mobbing	monilia	moraine	mottler	mudhook	muonium	myocyte
mobbish	monitor	moraled	mottoes	mudlark	muraena	myogram
mobbism	monkdom	morally	moucher	mud-lava	murally	myology
mob rule	monkery	morassy	mouflon	mudless	muramic	myomere
mobsman	monkeys	moratto	mouillé	mud-line	murexes	myoneme
mobster	monkish	morbose	moulage	mud-lump	muriate	myopism
Mochica	monkism	morbous	moulded	mud-mask	murices	myosote
mockage	monocle	morceau	moulder	mud pack	murkily	myotome
mockery	monocot	mordant	moulted	mudpout	murnong	myotomy
mock sun	monodic	mordent	moulter	mud pump	murrain	myotube
modally	monodon	Mordvin	mounted	mud room	murther	myrcene
mod cons	monoecy	moreish	mounter	mud-sill	muscari	myricin
modeler	monofil	morello	Mountie	mud wall	muscled	myricyl
modello	monolog	more meo	mourner	mud wasp	muscose	myronic
moderne	monomer	Moreote	mousaka	mud wing	muscous	myrosin
modesty	mononym	Moresca	mousery	mud-worm	Muscovy	myrrhed
modicum	monoped	Moresco	mousier	mudwort	museful	myrrhic
modiste	monopod	more suo	mousily	muezzin	musette	my stars
modular	monoski	moriche	mouthed	muffish	mush ice	mystery
modulus	monsoon	morille	mouther	muffler	mushier	mystify
moellon	monster	morinda	movable	Muganda	mushily	mytheme
mofette	montage	moringa	movably	mug book	mushlaw	mythify
Mogadon	Montagu	Moriori	move out	mugfuls	mushrat	mythist
mohajir	montane	Morisca	Moviola	muggier	musical	my watch
moharra	montero	Morisco	mowable	mugging	musiker	myxomas
Mohawks	monther	Morlach	mowburn	muggins	musk-bag	nabbing
Mohegan	monthly	morling	mow down	muggish	muskier	nacarat
Mohican	montuno	mormaor	Mozarab	muggler	muskrat	nacelle
moidore	monture	morning	mozetta	mugient	musquaw	nacrite
Moinian	moocher	morocco	mpingos	mug shot	mussuck	nacrous
moisten	moochin	moronic	Mpongwe	mugshot	mustang	naevoid
moistly	moodier	morphew	Mr Clean	mugwort	mustard	naffing
moither	moodily	morphia	Mr Fixit	mugwump	mustier	nagging
mojarra	moolvie	morphic	Mr Right	muhimbi	mustily	nagsman
moko fig	moonack	morphon	Mrs Mopp	mukhtar	mustine	Nahuatl
molasse	mooneas	morpion	mucigel	mulatta	must not	nailery
moldier	moon-eye	mortary	mucigen	mulatto	mutable	nail-rod
molding	moonier	mortice	muckier	mulesed	mutably	Nailsea
mole rat	moonily	mortify	mucking	mullein	mutagen	nail set
molimen	moonish	mortise	mucopus	mullion	mutator	naively
mollify	moonjah	morulae	mucosae	mullite	mutedly	naiveté
mollock	moonlet	morwong	mucosal	mullock	muttony	naivety
mollusc	moonlit	Mosaism	mudbank	mulmull	mutuary	naïvety
mollusk	moon-man	moscato	mud-bath	multure	Muzaked	nakedly
molossi	moon rat	Moselle	mudbath	mumbler	muzzier	nakerer
Molotov	moonset	moseyed	mud-crab	mu-meson	muzzily	nakhoda
Molucca	moorage	Mosotho	muddied	Mumetal	muzzled	Nalline
momenta	Mooress	moss-bag	muddier	mummery	muzzler	Namaqua
mommies	moor-hag	moss-hag	muddify	mummied	myalgia	namaste
monacid	moorhen	mossier	muddily	mummies	myalgic	name-day
monades	moor-ill	moss-oak	muddish	mummify	myalism	name-son
monadic	mooring	mostest	muddled	mumming	myalist	name-tag

nankeen	nebulas	nestler	nibbler	nobbily	noodler	not that
nannies	necking	netball	niblick	nobbins	nookery	not very
naology	necklet	net book	Niblung	nobbler	nooklet	noughty
naperer	neck-oil	net-cord	Nicaean	no-being	noology	noumena
nap hand	necktie	netfuls	niceish	noblest	noonday	nourice
naphtha	necrose	netlike	nice one	no-brand	nooning	nourish
napless	nectary	net-play	nicking	no can do	no other	nouther
nappies	neddies	netsman	nicotia	no class	Nootkan	nouveau
napping	needful	netsuke	nictate	no-'count	nopalry	novator
narcism	needier	netting	niddick	noctuid	no place	novella
narciss	needler	netwise	niduses	noctule	noplace	novelly
nardine	need-not	network	Nielsen	nocturn	Norfolk	novelty
narkier	Ne'erday	Neumann	niffier	nocuous	no-right	novolak
narrate	negater	neumata	niftier	noddies	norimon	nowaday
narthex	negaton	neurine	niftily	nodding	norland	nowcast
nartjie	negator	neurite	nigella	nodical	Norland	nowhere
narwhal	neglect	neuroid	niggard	no doubt	norther	no wight
nasally	négligé	neuroma	niggery	nodular	norward	no wiser
nascent	Negress	neurone	niggler	nodulus	nor'-west	nowness
nash-gab	Negrito	neurula	nighter	no end of	Norwich	now that
Nashiji	Negroes	neuston	nightie	no entry	nose-ape	now then
Naskapi	Negroid	neutral	night in	Noetian	nosebag	nowther
Nasmyth	negroni	neutron	nightly	no-fault	nose cap	noxious
Nasonov	neigher	Nevadan	nigrify	no-fines	no-see-em	N-shaped
Nasrani	neither	never so	nigrous	nogging	no-see-um	nuanced
nastier	nellies	New Ager	Nilotic	no-hoper	nose-fly	nucleal
nastily	nelumbo	new ball	Nimbies	noisier	nosegay	nuclear
nasutus	nematic	newborn	nimbler	noisily	nose job	nucleic
natalid	nemeses	new chum	nimiety	noisome	nose-rag	nuclein
Natchez	nemesia	new-come	nimious	no-knock	nosh bar	nucleon
natrium	nemesis	new deal	Nimonic	nol-pros	noshery	nucleus
nattery	nemmind	newelty	ninepin	nomades	nosiest	nuclide
nattier	nemoral	Newgate	ninnies	nomadic	no siree	nucloid
nattily	Neogene	new girl	ninthly	nomarch	no small	nuggety
natural	neology	new-laid	niobate	nombril	nostril	nullify
natured	neonate	New Left	niobian	nominal	nostrum	nulling
naughty	neo-Nazi	new look	niobium	nominee	no sweat	nullity
nauplii	neoteny	new math	niobous	nomisma	not a bit	numbles
Nauruan	neotype	new moon	Nipmuck	nonagon	notable	numeral
Naussie	Neozoic	newness	nippier	nonamer	notably	numeric
nautili	Nepalis	new poor	nippily	non-bank	not a few	numinal
Navahos	nephric	new rich	nipping	non-drip	not a rap	nummary
navally	nephron	newsboy	nippled	none the	not a sou	nummion
navarch	nepotal	newsful	nirvana	none too	notatin	nunatak
navarin	nepotic	newsier	nitchie	non-flam	notator	nunbird
navette	Neptune	newsily	nithing	non-hero	notched	nun-buoy
navvied	nerdish	newsman	nitinol	non-iron	notcher	nuncios
navvies	nerf-bar	newsmen	Nitinol	non-jury	notedly	nuncius
Navy Cut	neritic	new star	nit-pick	non-life	notelet	nundine
navy rum	nerkish	newtake	nitpick	non-past	notepad	nunhood
nayword	Neronic	new tick	nitrate	nonplus	note-row	nunlike
Nazidom	nervier	new town	nitrene	non-pros	not half	nunnery
Naziism	nervily	new wave	Nitrian	non-sane	nothing	nunnish
Ndebele	nervine	new year	nitride	non-sked	no-throw	nunship
near cut	nervose	New Year	nitrify	non-skid	noticer	nuntius
nearish	nervous	New York	nitrile	non-slip	notitia	nuptial
neatify	nervure	next man	nitrite	non-stop	not much	nursery
neatnik	Nessler	nexuses	nitrous	nonsuch	not once	nursing
nebbich	nest box	Ngbandi	nitweed	nonsuit	no-touch	nurture
nebbish	nest egg	Niagara	niveous	non-user	not over	nut-cake
nebulae	nestful	niaouli	Nizamut	non-word	no trump	nutcase
nebular	nesting	nibbing	Noachic	non-zero	not-self	nutgall

nut-hook	obovoid	odyssey	Ohm's law	old year	one-stop	open out
nutlike	obscene	Oedipal	oil bath	olearia	one-tail	open-pit
nut-meat	obscure	Oedipus	oil-berg	olefine	one-time	open sea
nut-pine	obsequy	oenomel	oil-bird	oligist	one with	open-toe
nutrice	observe	oersted	oilcake	olisbos	on faith	open-top
nutrify	obtrude	oestral	oil-drop	olitory	on-glaze	open war
nuttery	Ob-Ugric	oestrin	oil drum	olivary	onglaze	operand
nuttier	obverse	oestrum	oiled-up	olivine	on-glide	operant
nutting	obviate	oestrus	oiliest	Olmecan	ongoing	operate
nuttish	obvious	of a kind	oil lamp	ologist	on guard	opercle
nut tree	obvolve	of a size	oilless	Olonets	on leave	operose
nut-wood	ocarina	of a sort	oil-meal	oloroso	only not	ophitic
nylghau	occiput	off-axis	oil-mill	Olympic	only too	Ophitic
nyloned	Occitan	off base	oil-palm	Olympus	on offer	opiatic
nymphae	occlude	off beam	oil pool	omalgia	on order	Opimian
nymphal	occluse	off-bear	oil-rich	omander	on paper	opinion
nymphet	Oceania	offbeat	oil-ring	Omarian	on piece	opossum
nymphic	oceanic	off-bore	oil-sand	Omarite	on shore	oppidan
nymphon	Oceanid	offcast	oil-seed	omental	onshore	opposed
nymphos	ocellar	offcome	oilseed	omentum	on sight	opposer
Nyquist	ocellus	off-corn	oil-silk	omicron	onsight	opposit
Nyungar	ochroid	off duty	oilskin	ominous	on space	oppress
oak cist	ochrous	offence	oil-spot	omitted	on-stage	opsonic
oak fern	ockerer	offense	oil trap	omitter	onstead	opsonin
oak-gall	ocreate	offeree	oil well	ommatin	on tally	optable
oak land	octadic	offerer	oily wad	omneity	on terms	optical
oaklike	octagon	offeror	Ojibwas	omniana	on the go	optimal
oakling	octamer	off form	Okazaki	omnibus	ontical	optimum
oak moss	octapla	off from	Okhrana	omnific	on toast	opulent
oak tree	octarch	offhand	okimono	Omnopon	on top of	opuntia
oak wilt	octaval	officer	olation	omomyid	on track	opus Dei
oak-wood	octavic	off-line	old bean	on a bend	on trial	oralism
oak-worm	octavos	offline	Old Bill	on a dime	on trust	oralist
oarfish	octette	offload	old bird	on and on	on-verse	orality
oar-hole	October	off-peak	old boot	onanism	onwards	Oral Law
oarless	octofid	off-ramp	old cock	onanist	on watch	oral sex
oarlock	octonal	off-road	old days	on appro	onychia	oranged
oar-port	octoped	off-sale	old dear	on a roll	onymity	orangey
oarsman	octopic	offscum	old-face	on a wind	onymous	orarion
oarweed	octopod	off side	old firm	Onazote	oof-bird	oration
oatcake	octopus	offside	old fogy	on board	oofless	oratory
oat cell	octuple	off site	old gang	once-off	ooftish	oratrix
oatmeal	oculate	offskip	old girl	oncotic	ooh-la-la	orbicle
Oaxacan	oculism	off spin	old gold	on-drive	oolitic	orbital
Obanian	oculist	offtake	old hand	on earth	oophyte	orbitar
obconic	oddball	off-time	old lady	one-base	ooplasm	orbited
obelion	odd-even	offward	old land	one down	oospore	orbiter
obelise	oddling	off year	Old Left	one-eyed	ootheca	orbless
obelisk	oddment	oficina	old maid	onefold	opacate	orcanet
obelize	oddness	of right	old moon	one-girl	opacify	orchard
obertas	oddside	of sorts	oldness	one-inch	opacity	orcinol
obesely	odd-toed	of state	Old Nick	oneiric	opacous	ordered
obesity	odeling	oftener	Oldowan	one-many	opaline	orderer
obit-day	Odinism	oft-time	old rope	oneness	opalise	orderly
obitual	Odinist	of value	old rose	one of us	opalite	order up
obligee	odonate	of which	old salt	one-pipe	opalize	ordinal
obliger	odorant	of yours	old ship	one-ring	opaquer	ordinar
obligor	odorate	oghamic	old snow	onerous	open air	ordinee
oblique	odorise	o'goblin	oldster	oneself	open day	orebody
Oblomov	odorize	Ogopogo	old-time	one-shot	open-end	orectic
obloquy	odorous	ogreish	old town	one's man	open ice	oregano
obovate	odoured	Ogygian	old wife	one-step	opening	oreweed

organal	Ostmark	outlaid	outstep	overfar	oxalate	paeonic
organic	ostraca	outland	outswim	overfat	oxazine	paganry
organon	ostrich	outlast	out-take	overfit	oxazole	pageant
organum	Ostwald	outleap	out-talk	overfly	ox-berry	page-boy
organza	otalgia	outlier	out-tell	overfur	ox-biter	pageful
orgiast	otariid	outline	out-toil	overget	ox-blood	page-one
orience	otocyst	outlive	out-took	overgot	ox-fence	Pagetic
oriency	otolite	outlook	out-tray	overhie	Oxfordy	paginal
orifice	otolith	out loud	out-trot	overhit	ox-frame	pagurid
origami	otology	outlove	out-turn	overjet	oxhouse	Pahlavi
orignal	ototomy	outlung	outvote	overjoy	oxidant	Pah-utah
Orionid	ottoman	outmode	out-vote	overlap	oxidase	paideia
Orleans	Ottoman	outmost	outwait	overlay	oxidate	pailful
orogeny	ouabain	outness	outwale	overlie	oxidise	painful
orology	oughtn't	out of it	outwalk	overlip	oxidize	pa-in-law
oronoco	ouguiya	out-over	outwall	overlow	Oxonian	painted
Oropesa	Our Lady	outpace	outward	overman	oxonium	painter
orotate	Our Lord	outpart	outwash	overmen	oxyacid	paint-in
orotund	ourself	outpass	outwear	overnet	oxylith	pairing
Orphean	oustiti	outpeep	outweep	overold	oxyntic	pair-oar
Orphism	outback	outpeer	outwell	overpay	oxy-salt	pair off
Orphist	outbawl	outplan	outwent	overply	oxytone	paisano
orphrey	outbear	outplay	out West	overran	oxyuris	Paisley
orra man	outbent	outplot	outwick	overrun	oystery	pajamas
orright	outblot	outport	outwind	oversaw	Ozarker	pakapoo
orsedue	outbrag	outpost	outwing	oversay	ozonide	pak-choi
orterde	outburn	outpour	out with	oversea	ozonify	Pakhtun
orthian	outcamp	outpray	outwith	oversee	ozonise	paktong
orthite	outcant	outrace	outwood	overset	ozonize	palabra
ortolan	outcast	outrage	outwore	oversew	pabouch	palaced
Orvieto	outcome	outrail	outwork	oversow	pabulum	paladin
or worse	outcrop	outrake	outworn	oversum	pacable	palarie
osazone	outdare	outrang	outyell	overtax	pace car	palatal
Osborne	outdate	outrank	ovality	overtip	pace lap	palatic
oscines	outdoes	outrant	ovarial	overtly	paceman	Palauan
oscular	outdoor	outrate	ovarian	overtop	pacemen	Palaung
osculum	outerly	outread	ovaries	overuse	pachisi	palaver
Osetian	outface	outride	ovarium	overwet	pachuco	palazzo
osiered	outfall	outring	ovation	overwin	paciest	paletot
Osirian	outfast	outroar	overact	ovicell	pacific	palette
Osiride	outflew	outrode	over age	ovicide	package	Paleyan
Osmanli	outflow	outroll	overage	Ovidian	pack ice	palfrey
osmiate	outflux	outroom	over all	oviduct	packing	palikar
osmious	outfool	outroot	overall	oviform	packman	palinal
osmolal	outfoot	outrung	overarm	ovistic	packmen	Palissy
osmolar	outfort	outrush	overate	ovocyte	pack off	pallavi
osmosis	outgang	outsail	overawe	ovoidal	pack rat	pallial
osmotic	outgate	outsell	overbid	ovonics	pack-way	pallier
osmunda	outgive	outshew	overbow	ovulary	paction	palling
os penis	outglow	outshop	overbuy	ovulate	paddies	pallion
ospreys	outgoer	outshot	overcup	ovulite	Paddies	pallium
osselet	outgoes	outshow	overcut	Owenism	padding	palmary
osseous	outgone	outshut	overday	Owenist	paddler	palmate
Ossetic	outgrew	outside	overdid	Owenite	paddock	palm cat
ossicle	outgrow	outsing	overdog	owl-like	padlock	palmful
ossific	outgush	outsize	overdot	owl-moth	Padovan	palmier
ossuary	out-half	outsoar	overdry	owney-oh	pad-play	palmiet
osteoid	outhaul	outsold	overdub	own goal	padrone	palmily
osteoma	outhold	outsole	overdue	ownhood	pad room	palmist
osteria	outhowl	outspan	overdye	ownness	Padshah	palmite
ostiary	outjump	outspin	overeat	ownself	paedeia	palmito
ostiole	outkick	outstay	overegg	ownsome	paenula	palm off

palm oil	pantile	parlour	pasties	pay rise	pedlary	pennate
palmtop	pantine	parlous	pastily	payroll	pedocal	pennies
palmula	pantler	Parnate	pastime	paysage	Pedrail	pennill
palm wax	pantoic	parodic	pasting	pay slip	pedrero	pennine
palmyra	pantoyl	parolee	pastose	payslip	ped-xing	penning
palooka	papable	paronym	pasture	pay-tone	peeling	pen-pond
palpate	papally	parotic	patache	P-Celtic	Peelite	Penrose
palship	papaloi	parotid	patagia	pea-bean	peel off	pensile
palsied	papauma	parquet	patamar	Peabody	peeping	pension
palsies	pap-boat	parried	Patarin	pea-bone	peep-toe	pensive
palsify	paperer	parries	patball	pea-bulb	peerage	penster
palting	Paphian	parrock	pat-ball	pea-bush	peerdom	pen-tail
paludal	papilio	parroco	patcher	pea-coat	peeress	pentane
pamment	papilla	parroty	patch-up	pea-comb	peevish	pentene
pampano	papoose	Parsism	patella	pea-crab	pegasse	pentice
pampean	papoosh	parsley	patency	pea-dove	Pegasus	pentode
pampero	pappies	parsnip	patener	peafowl	peg away	pentose
panacea	pappose	Partaga	pat hand	pea-grit	peg doll	pentryl
panache	paprika	partake	pathlet	peak cap	peg down	penuche
Panadol	pap test	partial	pathway	peakier	pegging	penwork
Panagia	Pap test	partied	patient	peaking	peglike	peonage
Panaman	papulae	partier	patinas	peakish	Pehlevi	peopler
pan-Arab	papular	parties	patness	Peakrel	Peierls	pepless
pancake	papulas	partify	patonce	pea-lamp	peladic	peppery
pan-Celt	papyrin	partile	patrial	pelagic	pelagic	peppier
Panchen	papyrus	parting	patrico	pea-meal	pelamyd	pep pill
pandean	parable	partita	patriot	pea-moth	Peléean	pepping
pandect	parader	partite	patrist	pearled	pelican	pep talk
pandoor	parador	partlet	patroon	pearler	pelisse	peptide
pandora	parados	Partlet	patsies	pearlet	pelitic	peptize
pandore	paradox	partner	pattern	Pearson	pellack	peptone
pandour	paragon	part off	patties	peasant	pellety	peracid
pandrop	paralic	partook	patting	peascod	Pellian	percale
paneity	paramos	part-own	paturon	pea-soup	pellock	percase
panfish	parangi	part-way	patwari	peat-ash	peloria	per cent
panfuls	Pará-nut	parvenu	pauchty	peatbog	peloric	percept
Pangaea	parapet	parvise	paucity	peatery	pelorus	perched
pangene	para red	paschal	paughty	peat-hag	peloton	percher
pangful	paraski	pascual	Paulian	peatman	peltast	perches
pangram	parasol	Pashtun	Pauline	pea tree	peltate	percoid
panical	paratha	pasquil	Paulist	pea-vine	Peltier	percuss
panicky	parboil	Pasquin	Paul-Pry	pebbled	pelting	per diem
panicle	parched	passade	paunchy	pébrine	pembina	perdure
panicum	pardner	passado	paviour	peccant	pemphis	pereion
Panjabi	pareira	passage	paviser	peccary	pemphix	perfect
panlike	parerga	passant	pavlova	peccavi	penaeid	perfidy
pan-loaf	pareses	pas seul	Pavulon	pecking	penally	perform
pannage	paresis	passing	pawkier	peckish	penalty	perfume
pannier	Paretan	passion	pawkily	peckled	penance	perfumy
panning	paretic	passive	pawl-rim	pectase	penates	perfuse
panocha	parfait	pass-key	paxilla	pectate	penatin	pergana
panoply	pargana	passkey	Paxolin	pectens	pendant	pergola
panoral	parging	pass law	payable	pectize	pendent	perhaps
panoram	parisis	passman	pay back	pectora	pending	periapt
panorpa	parison	pass off	payback	pectose	pendule	peridia
pan-pipe	parkade	pass out	pay-book	pectous	penfold	peridot
pansala	parkier	passway	pay dirt	pedagog	penguin	perigee
pansied	parking	paste-in	pay down	pedalos	penises	perigon
pansies	parkish	pastern	payload	peddler	penlike	perilla
Panslav	parklet	paste-up	payment	pedicab	pen-mate	periost
panther	parkway	Pasteur	paynize	pedicel	pen-name	perique
panties	parleys	pastier	pay over	pedicle	pennant	peritus

periwig	peytral	pianino	pigging	pine gum	pipping	Pittite
perjure	pfennig	pianism	piggish	pine nut	piquant	pituita
perjury	phaeton	pianist	pig-herd	pine-oil	piquing	pit-wood
perkier	phalanx	piannet	pightle	pinesap	piragua	pitying
perkily	phalera	pianola	pig-iron	pine tag	piranha	pivotal
perlite	phallic	Pianola	pig-jump	pine-top	piratic	pivoted
permain	phallin	Piarist	pig-lead	pinetum	pirogue	pixyish
Permian	phalloi	piaster	piglike	pin-eyed	Pirquet	pizzazz
permsec	phallos	piastre	pig-lily	pin-fire	pisatin	placage
permute	phallus	pibcorn	pigling	pinfold	piscary	placard
peroral	phantom	pibroch	pig meat	pinguid	Piscean	placate
perosis	Pharaoh	picador	pigment	pinguin	piscina	placebo
per pale	pharate	picarel	pigmies	pinhead	piscine	placing
perpend	pharynx	piccolo	pig-root	pin-high	pismire	placita
perplex	phase in	piceous	pig's ear	pinhole	pissant	placket
perrier	phasing	pickage	pigskin	pin-hook	pissing	placode
Perrier	phasmid	pickaxe	pigsney	pinions	piss off	placoid
perries	phellem	pickeer	pigtail	pinkeen	pissoir	placula
persalt	phememe	pickery	pigwash	pinkers	piss-pot	plafond
Perseid	phenate	pickier	pigweed	pink-eye	pisspot	plagium
Perseus	phenoxy	pickily	pikelet	pink gin	pisteur	plagued
Persian	Phidian	picking	pikeman	pinkily	pistole	plaguer
persico	Phillis	pickled	pikemen	pinking	pit-a-pat	plagues
persist	philtre	pickler	pilcher	pinkish	pit-bank	plaguey
persona	phinnoc	pickman	pilcorn	pinkoes	pit-bing	plaided
perspex	phizgig	pickney	pilcrow	pink tea	pit boss	plaidie
Perspex	phlegmy	pick off	pileate	pin-mark	pit-brow	plainer
pertain	phlomis	pick out	pilgrim	pinnace	pit bull	plainly
pertish	Phocian	picotee	pillage	pinnate	pitched	plaited
perturb	phocine	picquet	pill-bag	pinnies	pitcher	plaiter
peruked	Phoebus	picrate	pillbox	pinning	pitch in	planate
perusal	phoenix	picrite	pill-bug	pinnock	pitch on	planche
peruser	phonate	Pictish	pilling	pinnule	pitch up	planful
pervade	phone-in	picture	pillion	pin-pool	pit-coal	planing
pervert	phoneme	piculet	pillock	pin-rack	pit-comb	planish
peskier	phonics	piddler	pillory	pinsapo	piteous	planned
peskily	phonier	piddock	pillowy	pin seal	pitfall	planner
pessary	phonily	piebald	pillule	pinsons	pit-head	planont
petasma	phorate	pie-card	piloted	pin-spot	pithead	plantal
petasus	phorbol	pie-cart	pilotry	pintado	pit-heap	plantar
pet-cock	phoresy	piece on	Pilsner	pintail	pithful	planter
pet-food	Photian	piece up	pilular	pint pot	pith hat	Plantin
pet-form	photino	pie-eyed	pimelea	pin-tuck	pithier	planula
pet hate	photism	pie-face	pimelic	Pintupi	pithily	planxty
petiole	photo CD	pieless	pimento	pinweed	pit-hole	plapper
pet name	photoes	pierage	pi-mesic	pin-work	pith ray	plashet
petrary	photo op	pierced	pi-meson	pinworm	pitiful	plasmal
Petrean	phragma	piercer	pimping	Pinxter	pit-lamp	plasmic
petrify	phrasal	Pierian	pimpish	Pinxton	pitless	plasmid
Petrine	phraser	pierine	pimpled	pioneer	pitmans	plasmin
petroil	phrator	pierrot	pinaces	piosity	Pitman's	plasmon
petrous	phratry	pieties	pinacol	piously	pit-mirk	plaster
pet-shop	phrenic	pietism	pinball	pipe cot	Pitocin	plastic
pettier	phrenzy	pietist	pin-bone	pipeful	pit pair	plastid
pettily	phugoid	piffler	pincers	pipe-gun	pit pony	plateau
petting	physics	pig-boat	pinched	pipe-lay	pit prop	Plateau
pettish	physiog	pig-cote	pincher	pipeman	pit-sawn	platina
petunia	physios	pig-face	pincord	pip emma	pit silo	plating
Petzval	phytane	pigfish	pin-curl	piperic	pit stop	platoon
pewless	phytase	piggery	Pindari	piperly	pitting	platted
pew-rent	phytate	piggier	pin down	pipette	Pittism	platten
pewtery	piaffer	piggies	pin-dust	pipless	pittite	platter

platzel	plounce	podical	polygon	popping	pot-arch	Prakrit
plaudit	plouter	poditic	polyion	poppish	potassa	praline
play-act	plovery	podiums	polymer	pop-shop	potator	prancer
playbox	plowman	Podsnap	polynia	popsies	pot-ball	pranker
playboy	plowmen	podurid	polynya	pop star	pot-bank	prankle
play-day	plucked	podware	polyoma	popster	pot-boil	prasine
playful	plucker	poë-bird	polyped	popular	potcher	prating
play God	pluck up	Poesque	polypod	porched	pot clay	prattle
play hob	plugged	poetast	polypus	porcine	potence	pravity
playing	plugger	poetese	polyrod	porgies	potencé	prawner
playlet	plug-hat	poetess	Polytec	porifer	potency	Praxean
play off	plug off	poetics	polyyne	porkery	potfuls	pray for
play-pen	plugola	poetise	pomatum	porkier	pot-guts	praying
playpen	plug-tap	poetism	pomelos	porkies	pot-head	preachy
play pew	plumach	poetize	Pomerol	porkman	pothead	pre-Aids
play-way	plumage	po-faced	pomeron	pork pie	potheen	prebend
pleaded	plumash	poggled	pomfret	porphin	pot-herb	pre-book
pleader	plumate	poiesis	pommage	porrect	pothery	precary
pleased	plumber	poietic	pommelé	porrigo	pothole	pre-cast
pleaser	plumbet	poinder	Pommies	portage	pot-hook	precast
pleater	plumbic	pointed	pompano	portail	pot-kiln	precede
plebify	plumery	pointel	pompion	portate	pot-lace	precent
plectra	plum-fir	pointer	pomposo	Porteña	pot life	precept
plectre	plumier	point up	pompous	portend	pot-line	precess
pledgee	plummet	poisony	ponchos	portent	pot luck	precise
pledger	plumose	Poisson	pondage	portess	potluck	precoce
pledget	plumous	poitrel	pongelo	portico	pot-mess	pre-cook
pledgor	plumpen	pokable	pongier	porting	potoroo	precook
pleione	plumper	poke-boy	Pongola	portion	pot-oven	pre-cool
plenary	plum-pie	poke-net	ponhaus	portlet	potrero	precool
plenipo	plumply	poke-out	poniard	portman	pot-shot	precure
plenish	plum pox	pokiest	pontage	portray	pottage	predamn
plenist	plumula	polacca	pontiff	posable	pottery	pre-date
pleopod	plumule	polacre	pontile	posaune	pottier	predate
plereme	plunder	Polaris	pontine	poseuse	potties	predial
plerion	plunger	polarly	Pontine	posited	pottily	predict
pleroma	plunket	polaron	pontoon	positon	potting	predoom
plerome	Plunket	poldavy	poodler	possess	pot-work	pre-echo
plessor	pluries	pole-axe	poofter	postage	pouched	pre-edit
pleurae	plusage	poleaxe	Pooh-Bah	postbag	poulard	preemie
pleural	plushed	polecat	pool car	postbox	poulter	pre-empt
pleuric	plushly	poleman	poonask	post-boy	poultry	preener
pleuron	pluteal	polemic	poon oil	post-bus	pounced	preface
plexure	pluteus	polenta	poopsie	post-dam	pouncer	pre-fade
pliable	pluvial	polhode	poor box	post-day	pouncet	prefect
pliably	Pluvius	poligar	poor-cod	postdoc	poundal	pre-fine
pliancy	plywood	politer	poorish	posteen	pounder	prefire
plicate	pneumic	politic	poor law	postern	pouring	preform
Plinian	poacher	polizei	poor man	postfix	poussin	pre-head
plinker	pochard	polizia	popadam	post hoc	poustie	preheat
plodded	Pockels	polkaed	popadom	postica	pouting	prehend
plodder	pocketa	pollack	pop-call	posting	poverty	pre-Inca
ploiter	pockety	pollard	popcorn	postman	powdery	prelacy
plonker	pocosin	pollies	pope-day	postmen	powered	prelate
plopped	poculum	polling	popedom	post-oak	poxiest	prelect
plosion	podagra	pollock	pop-eyed	post-tax	poy-bird	preload
plosive	podalic	poll tax	pop-hole	posture	prabble	prelude
plotful	pod corn	pollute	popinac	post-war	practic	premier
plotted	podding	polo hat	poplexy	postwar	praeses	premise
plotter	poddish	poloist	popover	potable	praetor	premiss
plottie	podgier	polybag	poppied	potager	prairie	premium
plotzed	podgily	polyene	poppies	potamic	praiser	premove

prename	priapic	prodder	prosody	psyllid	pummelo	pussley
prender	Priapus	Proddie	prosoma	ptarmic	pumpage	pussums
prenoun	pribble	prodigy	prosper	pterion	pump gun	pustule
prenova	pribumi	prodrug	prossie	pteroic	pumpion	putamen
pre-oral	price up	produce	prostie	pteroma	pumpkin	put away
pre-pack	pricier	product	prosula	pteryla	pump-log	put back
prepack	pricily	proette	protean	ptyalin	pumpman	putcher
prepaid	pricing	profane	protect	pubbing	pump-rod	put down
prepare	pricked	profert	protégé	pubbish	pumpset	putidly
prepend	pricker	profesh	proteid	puberal	punalua	put it on
pre-plan	pricket	profess	protein	puberty	punched	put it to
preplan	prickle	proffer	protend	publish	puncher	putlock
prepone	prickly	profile	protest	pub rock	punch in	put over
prepose	pridian	pro-form	Proteus	pub-time	punch-up	putrefy
prepped	prigger	profuse	protext	puccoon	punctal	putteed
prepper	primacy	progeny	protide	pucelle	punctum	puttied
preppie	primage	progger	protist	puchero	pungent	putties
prepreg	primary	program	protium	puckaun	puniest	putting
prepuce	primase	project	protoma	puckery	Punjabi	puttock
prepupa	primate	prolate	protome	puckish	punkish	put upon
prequel	primely	pro-life	protyle	pudding	punning	put up to
prerupt	primero	proline	proudly	puddled	punster	putwary
presage	primine	prolong	provand	puddler	punt-gun	puzzler
pre-sell	priming	promise	provant	puddock	pupfish	pyaemia
present	primmed	prommer	provect	pudency	pupilar	pyaemic
preside	primmer	promote	provend	pudenda	puppies	pycnial
presign	primula	pronaoi	proverb	pudgier	pupping	pycnium
pre-soak	pringle	pronaos	prove up	pudgily	pup-tent	pygmean
pre-sold	printed	Pronase	provide	pueblos	pupunha	pygmoid
pressel	printer	pronate	provine	puerile	Puranic	pyjamas
presser	print in	pronely	proviso	puff box	Purbeck	py korry
pressie	priorly	proneur	provoke	puffery	purfled	pyloric
press-on	prior to	pronged	provost	puffick	purging	pylorus
pressor	prisage	pronoun	prowess	puffier	puritan	pyralid
press-up	priscan	pronuba	prowler	puffily	purlieu	pyramid
Prestel	Priscol	propale	proxeny	puffing	purloin	pyretic
prester	prisere	propane	proxies	puff-leg	purpled	pyrexia
prestos	prismal	propend	proximo	pugging	purport	pyrexic
presume	prismed	propene	prozoic	puggish	purpose	pyridyl
pretape	pristaf	prop-fan	prozone	puggled	purpura	pyrites
pre-teen	prithee	propham	prudent	puggree	purpure	pyritic
pretend	privacy	prophet	prudery	pug-mill	pursive	pyrogen
pre-term	private	propine	prudish	pug-nose	pursual	pyronin
preterm	privies	prop-jet	prunase	Pugwash	pursued	pyrosis
pretest	privily	prop-leg	pruning	pukatea	pursuer	pyrrhic
pretext	privity	prop man	prunted	pukekos	pursues	Pyrrhic
pretone	proavis	propone	prurigo	pulaski	pursuit	pyrrole
pretzel	proband	propose	prushun	pullery	purview	pyruvic
prevail	probang	propped	prussic	pulleys	push-car	Pythiad
prevene	probate	propper	prytany	Pullman	push fit	Pythian
prevent	probing	propria	psalmic	pull off	pushful	pyxides
preverb	probity	propyla	psalter	pull out	pushier	pyxidia
preview	problem	propyne	psammic	pull-tab	pushily	Qashgai
previse	pro bono	pro rata	pschent	pulpify	pushing	Q-Celtic
prevost	procain	pro-rate	pseudos	pulpous	push off	Q-switch
prewarn	procarp	prosaic	psionic	pulsant	push-out	qua-bird
pre-wash	proceed	pro shop	p-skhent	pulsate	push-pin	quacker
prewash	process	prosier	psychal	pulsion	push-pit	quackle
prewire	Procion	prosify	psychic	pulsive	pushrod	quadrat
prexies	proctor	prosily	psychon	pulvini	push-tow	quadric
prezzie	procure	prosing	psychos	pulvino	puss-cat	quaffer
Priamel	prodded	prosist	psykter	pumiced	pussies	quahaug

quakier	quilled	radiale	rallier	rasping	realign	rectify
quaking	quillet	radiant	rallies	ratable	realise	rection
qualify	quilter	radiata	ralline	ratafia	realism	rectory
quality	quinary	Radiata	Ramadan	rat-a-tat	realist	rectrix
quamash	quinate	radiate	Ramazan	ratatat	reality	rectums
quangos	Quinean	radical	rambler	ratchet	realize	recurve
quantal	quinine	radicel	ramekin	rate-cap	re-allot	recusal
quantic	quinion	radices	ramenas	ratfink	reallot	recycle
quantum	quinnat	radicle	ram home	rat-fish	realtor	red alga
quarely	quinoid	radioes	ram line	rat flea	reaming	Red Army
quarrel	quinone	radiole	rammies	rat-hare	reannex	red-back
quartal	quintal	radulae	ramming	rathest	reaping	red-bait
quartan	quintan	radular	rammish	rat-hole	re-apply	Red-bait
quarter	quintet	raffish	ramonda	ratlike	reapply	red ball
quartet	quintic	raffler	rampage	ratline	rear end	red-band
quartic	quipped	Raffles	rampant	ratling	reargue	red bark
quartos	quipper	raft-dog	rampart	rat pack	rearing	red bass
quartzy	quiring	rag bolt	rampick	rat race	reassay	red bean
Quashee	quirked	rag book	rampier	rat-tail	Réaumur	red beds
quassia	quirley	rag doll	rampike	ratteen	reawake	red belt
quatern	Quiteño	rageful	rampion	rattier	rebadge	red-bird
quatrin	quitted	rageous	rampire	rattily	rebater	red body
quattie	quitter	raggedy	rampway	ratting	re-beget	redbone
quavery	quittor	ragging	ram-raid	rattish	re-begin	red book
quayage	quivery	rag-head	Ramsden	rattler	Rebekah	red buck
quayful	qui vive	rag-lamp	ramsons	rat-trap	rebelly	red card
queachy	Quixote	rag-shop	ram-stam	raucity	rebirth	red cell
Quechua	quiz kid	ragtail	ramulet	raucous	rebloom	red cent
Queen At	quizzed	ragtime	ramulus	raunchy	reboant	red clay
queenie	quizzee	Ragusan	rancher	rauriki	reboard	redcoat
queen it	quizzer	ragweed	rancour	ravaged	rebound	red core
queenly	quizzes	ragworm	randier	ravager	rebrace	red-cowl
queerer	quoiter	ragwort	randily	ravelin	rebring	red crab
queerie	quomodo	railage	randing	ravelly	rebuild	red deal
queerly	quondam	rail-bus	rangier	ravener	rebuilt	red deer
queller	Quonset	rail-car	rangily	ravined	rebuker	reddest
quelles	quorate	railcar	rangled	ravioli	rebuses	redding
quemely	quotity	rail gun	rangoli	raw deal	recarry	reddish
querent	Quraysh	railing	Rangoon	raw edge	recatch	red drum
queried	rabanna	railman	Rankine	raw feel	receder	red-eyed
querier	rabbit-o	railmen	ranking	rawhide	receipt	red fire
queries	rabbity	rail off	ransack	rawness	receive	redfish
querist	rabidly	railway	ranular	raw silk	recency	red flag
querken	rabinet	raiment	Ranvier	rayless	recense	red gold
quester	rabious	rainbow	rapable	Raynaud	rechase	red hake
questor	raccoon	rain-day	rape-oil	r-colour	recheat	red-hand
quetsch	race man	rain-fly	raphide	reacher	recheck	red hare
quetzal	racemed	rainful	rapider	reach to	recital	redhead
queuing	racemic	rain-god	rapidly	reactor	reciter	red heat
quibble	race off	rain-hat	raploch	readapt	reclaim	red kite
Quichua	raceway	rainier	rapping	readier	reclear	red lamp
quicken	rachial	rainily	Rappist	readily	reclimb	red land
quickie	Rachman	rain off	Rappite	reading	recline	Redland
quickly	raciest	rain-out	rapport	Reading	reclose	red lane
quiddle	rack-bar	rainout	rapture	readmit	reclude	red lead
quidlet	rackett	raising	rarebit	read off	recluse	redlegs
quids in	rackety	raisiny	rare gas	readopt	re-count	red line
quiesce	racking	raisure	rasceta	read-out	recount	red loam
quieten	rackman	Rajpoot	raschel	ready-up	re-cover	red mass
quieter	racloir	rake-off	Raschig	reagent	recover	red meat
quietly	racquet	rake out	rashful	real ale	recross	red mite
quietus	raddled	rallied	rashing	realgar	recruit	red moki

redneck	referee	related	replied	respire	retying	ribible
redness	refined	relater	replier	respite	reunify	ribitol
red-nose	refiner	relator	replies	respond	reunion	ribityl
redoubt	reflate	relatum	replumb	respray	reunite	ribless
redound	reflect	relaxed	repoint	restage	reutter	riblike
red pine	refloat	relaxer	reposal	restain	revalue	ribosyl
redpoll	refocus	relaxin	reposit	restamp	reveler	Ribston
redraft	reforge	relearn	repping	restant	revelry	ribwork
red rain	refound	release	repress	restart	revenge	ribwort
redrawn	refract	relevel	reprice	restate	revenue	ricasso
re-dress	refrain	reliant	reprime	rest day	reverer	rice-rat
redress	reframe	relieve	reprint	resteel	reverie	Richard
red-ripe	refresh	relievo	reprise	restful	reverse	richish
redrive	refroze	relight	reproof	restiff	reversi	Richter
red roan	refugee	reliner	re-prove	resting	reviler	ricinus
red rock	refugia	relleno	reprove	restive	revisal	rickets
red-root	refusal	remains	reptant	restock	reviser	rickety
red rose	refuser	remanet	reptile	restore	revisit	rickeys
redskin	refutal	remarch	repulse	restudy	revisor	ricksha
red snow	refuter	remarry	repunit	restuff	revival	ricotta
red soil	regalia	rematch	repurge	restyle	reviver	ridable
red spot	regally	remicle	reputed	resuing	revivor	ridding
red star	regatta	remiges	request	re-surge	revoice	riddler
Red Star	regauge	remixer	requiem	resurge	revoker	rideman
red-tail	Régence	remnant	require	reswear	revolte	ride-off
red tape	regency	remodel	requite	reswell	revolve	ride out
red-tapy	Reggeon	remorse	requote	retable	revving	rideout
red tide	regimen	remoter	reraise	retablo	rewaken	ridered
red titi	reginal	remould	reredos	retaken	reweave	ridging
reduced	reglaze	remount	re-route	retaker	reweigh	ridglet
reducer	regnant	removal	rescind	retaste	rewound	ridotto
redward	regorge	removed	rescore	reteach	rewrite	rid-work
redware	regosol	remover	rescous	rethink	rewrote	Riemann
red-weed	regrade	renable	rescued	retiary	Reynard	rietbok
red wind	regrant	renably	rescuee	reticle	rhabdom	Riffian
redwing	regrate	reneger	rescuer	retinae	Rhaetic	riffled
red wolf	regreet	renegue	rescues	retinal	rhamnus	riffler
red-wood	regress	renerve	reseize	retinas	rhatany	riflery
redwood	regrind	renewal	re-serve	retinol	Rhemish	rifling
Redwood	regroup	renewer	reserve	retinue	Rhemist	rifting
red worm	regulae	rentage	reshape	retinyl	rhenate	rigaree
reed-bed	regular	rent boy	reshoot	retiral	Rhenish	rigging
reed-cap	regulon	rent car	resiant	retired	rhenium	riggish
reedier	regulus	rentier	resider	retiree	rhizine	righten
re-edify	reheard	rentrée	residua	retirer	rhizoid	righter
reedily	rehouse	reoccur	residue	retitle	rhizome	right-ho
reeding	reified	reoffer	resilia	retouch	Rhodian	rightie
reed-man	reifier	reorder	resilin	re-trace	rhodium	rightly
reef net	reifies	repaint	resined	retrace	Rhodoid	right oh
reek-hen	reigner	repaper	resinic	retrack	rhodora	right on
re-elect	reimpel	repayer	resitol	retract	rhodous	right-up
reel-fed	rein-arm	rephase	reskill	retrain	rhombic	rigidly
reeling	reindue	repiece	reslash	retread	rhombus	Rig-veda
reel off	reinter	repiner	reslush	retreat	rhubarb	Rig-Veda
re-enact	Reisner	repique	resmelt	retrial	rhymist	rikishi
re-endow	reissue	replace	resolve	retrick	rhythmi	rilievo
re-enjoy	reitbok	replant	re-sound	retried	rhytina	Rilkean
re-enter	rejoice	replate	resound	retries	riantly	rilling
re-entry	rejoint	replead	respeak	retsina	ribband	rillock
re-equip	rejudge	replete	respect	rettery	ribbing	rimfire
re-erect	relabel	replevy	respell	retting	ribbony	rimiest
re-exist	relapse	replica	respelt	retwist	ribcage	rimland

rimless	road oil	romancy	Roscius	row crop	rummage	Rydberg
rimming	road tax	Romanes	roseate	rowdier	rummery	ryebuck
rimpled	roadway	Romanic	rosebay	rowdily	rummest	rye-land
rimrock	roanoke	Romanly	rose-bed	row down	rummily	Ryeland
rim-shot	roaring	Romansh	rose bit	Rowland	rummish	ryepeck
ringent	roaster	romaunt	rose box	rowlock	rumness	rye-worm
ringing	robbery	Romayne	rosebud	row over	Rumpish	ryotwar
ringled	robbing	Romberg	rose-bug	row-port	rum ship	Saadian
ringlet	robinet	romneya	rose-cut	royalet	rum shop	saaidam
ring-man	robinia	rompier	rose-hip	royally	run amok	Saalian
ring-net	robotic	romping	roselet	royalty	runanga	Sabaean
ring off	robotry	rompish	rosella	royal we	run away	Sabaism
ring rot	robusta	romulea	roseola	rozella	runaway	Sabaoth
ringway	rock bar	ronchus	rose red	rub-a-dub	run-back	sabatia
rinsing	rock-bed	rondeau	rosette	rubatos	run-boat	sabaton
Riot Act	rock-bun	rondure	rosiest	rub away	runchie	sabayon
riot gun	Rock Day	rongeur	rosined	rubbedy	rundale	sabbath
riotous	rockery	ronquil	rosiner	rubbery	rundlet	sabbing
ripcord	rock fan	röntgen	rosolic	rubbing	run down	sabella
rip cord	rock-hog	Röntgen	rosolio	rubbish	run-down	saboted
ripener	rockier	Rood day	rostral	rubbity	rundown	sabreur
ripieni	rockily	roofage	rostrum	rubbler	rune-row	sacaton
ripieno	rocking	roofing	rota cut	rub down	run-flat	saccade
rip into	rockish	rooflet	rotamer	rubella	run hard	saccate
rip line	Rockism	roof rat	rotator	rubeola	run heel	saccoon
riposte	Rockite	roof tax	rotifer	Rubicon	run high	saccule
rippier	rocklet	rooftop	rotisse	rubious	run idle	sackage
ripping	rockman	rooi-aas	roto-tom	rubisco	run into	sackbut
rippled	rock oak	rooibok	rottack	rub it in	run lace	sackful
rippler	rock-oil	rooibos	rotting	rub over	runless	sacking
ripplet	rockoon	rooi-els	rotular	rub-rail	run mute	sacklet
rip-stop	rock out	rooikat	rotulet	ruby-red	runnage	saclike
ripstop	rodding	rooinek	rotunda	ruching	runnier	sacring
rip tide	rodless	rookcry	rotundo	ruckman	running	sacrist
Ripuary	rodlike	rookish	rouéism	ruction	run over	sacrums
risbank	rod-mill	rook-pie	roughen	ruddier	run riot	saddest
risible	rodster	roomage	rougher	ruddily	run time	saddish
risibly	roebuck	roomful	roughie	ruddock	runting	saddler
riskful	Roedean	roomier	rough it	rude boy	runtish	Sadeian
riskier	roe-deer	roomily	roughly	ruderal	run upon	sad-iron
riskily	roe ring	rooming	rough up	rudesby	run wild	saditty
risotto	Rogallo	roomlet	roulade	ruellia	ruption	sadness
rissala	roguery	roomthy	rouleau	ruffian	rupture	sad sack
rissole	roguish	roosted	rounded	Ruffini	rurally	safaris
Ritalin	Rohilla	rooster	roundel	ruffled	rusbank	Safavid
ritzier	roinish	rootage	rounder	ruffler	rush-nut	safe bet
ritzily	roister	root-cap	round in	ruff out	Russell	safe hit
rivalry	rokelay	rooting	roundle	rufiyaa	russety	safener
rivered	Rolando	rootlet	roundly	rugging	Russian	safe sex
riveret	roll bar	root out	round on	ruinate	Russify	saffian
riveted	rollick	root rot	round to	ruinous	Russkis	saffron
riveter	rolling	ropable	round up	rulable	rustier	safrole
riviera	rollmop	rope-end	rouping	rule off	rustily	saga boy
rivière	roll off	rope-way	rousant	rule out	rusting	saga-man
rivulet	roll-out	ropeway	rousing	rullion	rustler	sagaris
roached	roll-top	ropiest	rouster	Rumansh	rustred	sagathy
roadbed	rollway	rorqual	routine	rum baba	Ruthene	sagbend
road hog	roloway	rortier	routing	rumbler	ruthful	sage hen
road kid	Romaika	rosacea	routous	rumenal	ruttier	sage tea
roadman	romaine	rosaker	rout out	Rumford	rutting	sagging
road map	Romalis	rosalia	rowable	rumices	ruttish	sagitta
roadmen	romance	Roscian	rowboat	ruminal	Rwandan	sag pond

saguaro	salt-tax	sanitar	satchel	scabrid	schemas	scotale
sagwire	salukis	Sankhya	satiate	scaddle	schemer	Scotchy
Saharan	saluter	Santali	satiety	scaffie	schepen	scoters
Sahidic	salvage	Santoor	satined	scaglia	scherzi	Scotify
Sahiwal	salvoes	santour	satinet	scalade	scherzo	Scotism
Sahrawi	samadhi	san ts'ai	satiric	scalded	schisma	Scotist
sahuaro	samango	sanxian	satisfy	scalder	schitzy	Scot Nat
sailage	Samanid	sanyasi	satrapy	scalene	schizos	scotoma
sail-arm	samarra	s-aorist	satsang	scaleni	schizzy	Scottie
sailing	Samarra	saouari	satsuma	scale up	schlepp	scourer
sail-off	sambaed	sapajou	satyral	scalier	schlich	scourge
saimiri	Samboes	saphead	satyric	scaling	schlock	Scouser
sainted	sambuca	saphena	satyrid	scalled	schlong	scouter
saintly	sambuke	sapient	saucery	scallet	schloss	Scouter
Saivism	Samburu	sap lath	saucier	scallom	schlump	scowder
Saivite	Samhain	sapless	saucily	scallop	schmear	scowler
Saktism	Sam Hill	sapling	Saudian	scallot	schmeck	scraggy
salable	Samhita	saponin	saunter	scalped	schmeer	scraich
salamis	samiest	Sapphic	saurian	scalpel	schmelz	scranch
salband	samisen	sappier	sauries	scalper	Schmidt	scranny
salchow	Samnite	sappily	sauroid	scamble	schmuck	scraper
sale day	samogon	sapping	sausage	scammed	schmutz	scrapie
salgram	samolus	sapples	sautéed	scammer	schnook	scrappy
salices	Samorin	saprobe	sautoir	scamper	schnorr	scratch
salicet	samovar	sapsago	savable	scandal	schnozz	Scratch
salicin	Samoyed	sapwood	savanna	scandia	scholar	scraugh
salicyl	sampler	Saracen	savante	Scanian	scholia	scrawly
salient	samsara	sarafan	savarin	scanmag	schooly	scrawny
saligot	samshoo	sarangi	save-all	scanned	schrund	screaky
Salique	samurai	sarazin	saveloy	scanner	schtook	screamy
salival	sanctum	sarcasm	save you	scantle	schtoom	screech
sallied	sanctus	sarcast	saviour	scantly	Schwann	screeve
sallier	Sandawe	sarcina	savoury	scapple	Schwarz	screigh
sallies	sandbag	sarcler	savvied	scapula	sciapod	screwed
Sallies	sand bar	sarcode	savvier	scaredy	sciatic	screwer
sallowy	sandbar	sarcoid	savvies	scare up	science	screw-in
salmiac	sand-bed	sarcoma	sawbill	scarfed	scirrhi	screw up
salmine	sand boa	sarcopt	sawbuck	scarier	scissel	scribal
salmons	sandbox	sarcous	sawdust	scarify	scissel	scriber
salmony	sandboy	Sardian	saw-file	scarily	scissor	scrieve
salpinx	sand-bur	sardine	sawfish	scarlet	sclaffy	scrimmy
salsify	sand cay	sardius	saw-gate	scaroid	scleral	scrimpy
sal soda	sand dab	sardony	sawlike	scarped	scoffer	scrinch
salsola	sand eel	sarinda	sawmill	scarper	scogger	scringe
saltant	sanders	sarissa	sawn-off	scarred	scolder	scritch
saltate	sandesh	Sarkese	saw wood	scarves	Scoline	scriven
salt-box	sandfly	sarkier	saw-wort	scatted	scolion	scroggy
salt-cat	sandhog	sarkily	saxeous	scatter	scollop	scrolly
saltern	sandier	sarking	saxhorn	scauper	scolops	scronch
saltery	sand key	sarment	Saxonic	scavage	scomber	scrooch
saltfat	sandlot	Saronic	Saxonly	sceatta	scooper	Scrooge
salt hay	sandman	sartage	sayable	scenery	scooter	scrotal
saltier	sand pie	sash bar	say over	scenist	scopine	scrotum
saltily	sandpit	sashimi	Say's law	scenite	scoptic	scrouge
saltine	sand rat	sashing	says you	scented	scopula	scroyle
salting	sanfoin	sashoon	say-well	scenter	scoriac	scrubby
saltire	Sangoan	sash saw	say when	scepsis	scoriae	scrub up
saltish	sangoma	sassaby	Sazarac	scepter	scorify	scruffo
Saltoun	sangria	sassier	scabbed	sceptic	scoring	scruffy
salt pan	Sangria	sassily	scabble	sceptre	scorner	scrummy
salt-pit	sanicle	Satanas	scabies	schalet	scorper	scrumpy
salt sea	sanious	satanic	scabish	schappe	Scorpio	scrunch

scrungy	sea-girt	sea-ware	seguing	septate	set shot	shagetz
scrunty	Sea Goat	sea wasp	segundo	septime	setting	shagged
scruple	seagull	seaweed	seismal	septuor	settled	shagger
scrutty	sea hair	sea-wind	seismic	sequela	settler	shagitz
scudded	sea hare	sea-wing	Seistan	sequent	settlor	shag-rag
scudder	sea-hawk	sea-wise	seizing	sequoia	setwall	shahdom
scuddle	sea holm	sea-wolf	seizure	seraphs	sevener	shaheed
scuffer	seajack	sea-worm	selenic	Serbian	seventh	shaheen
scuffle	seakale	sea-worn	selfful	Sercial	seventy	Shaitan
sculler	sea-king	sebacic	selfish	serener	seven-up	shake-up
sculpin	sea lace	sebundy	selfism	serfage	several	shakier
scumbag	sea-lake	seceder	selfist	serfdom	Severan	shakily
scumber	sea lane	seclude	self-set	serfish	severer	shaking
scumble	sealant	secluse	self-sow	serging	seviche	shakudo
scummed	sea-lark	Seconal	selling	seriate	Seville	shallon
scummer	sea legs	seconde	sell off	sericin	sevruga	shallop
scunner	sealery	secondi	sell out	sericon	sewable	shallot
scupper	seal-fur	secondo	seltzer	seriema	sewaged	shallow
scuppet	sealift	secrecy	selvage	serifed	sewster	shallun
scurfer	sealike	secreta	sematic	seringa	sexagon	shalwar
scurred	sea lily	secrete	sememic	serious	sex bomb	shamash
scutage	sealine	sectary	semence	sero-pus	sex cell	shamble
scutate	sealing	sectile	semicha	serosal	sexfoil	shambly
scutter	sea lion	section	semi-det	serovar	sexhood	shambok
scuttle	sea loch	sectism	semigod	Serpens	sexiest	Shammar
scyphus	sea lock	sectist	semi-log	serpent	sexless	shammed
scytale	Sea Lord	secular	seminal	serpigo	sex life	shammel
scythed	sea-luce	securer	seminar	serpula	sexpert	shammer
scyther	sea-maid	sedanca	seminia	Serrano	sex role	shampoo
Scythic	sea-mall	sedated	semi-ped	serrate	sex shop	shandry
sea bass	sea-mark	sedging	semi-pro	serried	sextain	shanked
sea-bean	seamier	sedilia	semi-sub	Sertoli	sextans	shanker
sea-bear	sea mile	seducee	Semitic	servage	sextant	Shannon
sea-beat	seaming	seducer	senarii	servant	sextary	shapely
Seabees	sea-monk	seeable	senator	servery	sextern	shape up
sea beet	sea moss	see-city	senatus	serve up	sextile	shaping
sea belt	seamost	seed-bed	sencion	Servian	sextine	sharded
sea bird	sea-moth	seedbed	send for	service	sextole	shareef
seabird	sea-palm	seed-box	sending	servile	sextula	sharifa
sea-boat	sea-pike	seed fat	send off	serving	sextuor	sharker
sea-born	sea pink	seedful	Senecal	Servite	Seyfert	Shar Pei
sea-calf	seaport	seedier	Senecan	sesamum	sferics	sharpen
sea-clam	searcer	seedily	senecio	Sesotho	sfumato	sharper
sea coal	sea-reed	seeding	senesce	sessile	shabbed	sharpie
seacock	searing	seed-lac	senhora	session	Shabbim	sharply
sea-cook	sea room	seedlet	señores	sestina	shabble	sharrer
sea-coot	sea salt	seed-lip	sensate	sestine	shab-rag	Shastan
sea-crab	sea-sand	seedman	sensify	setaria	shacked	Shastra
sea-crow	seasick	seed set	sensile	set back	shackle	shastri
sea-dace	seaside	see here	sensing	setback	shackly	shatter
sea-duck	sea slug	see into	sensise	set back	shaddup	Shavian
Sea Dyak	sea-song	seeking	sensism	setback	shade of	shaving
sea-dyke	sea-star	seek out	sensist	set down	shad-fly	Shavuot
seafare	sea-time	see life	sensive	set fair	shadier	shawled
sea-fern	seating	seeming	sensize	setfast	shadily	shawlie
sea-fire	sea-toad	see over	sensory	set free	shadine	Shawnee
sea-fish	sea-town	seepage	sensual	Sethian	shading	sheared
seafood	sea turn	seeress	Senussi	Sethite	shadoof	shearer
sea-fowl	sea-view	seerpaw	sepetir	set menu	shadowy	sheathe
sea fret	sea wall	see-safe	sephira	setness	shafted	sheaths
sea-frog	seawant	see to it	seppuku	set over	shafter	sheaved
sea-gate	seaward	segment	septage	set sail	shag-bag	sheaves

shebang	shinner	short on	sibness	silicic	sinuous	sketchy
shebeen	Shinner	shot-bag	sibship	silicle	sinward	skewgee
shedded	shin-oak	shotgun	sice ace	silicon	sipeera	skewing
shedder	Shinola	shotman	Sichuan	siliqua	sipping	skiable
shed-rod	shin-pad	shot-put	sick-bag	silique	siratro	skiapod
sheened	Shinshu	shotted	sickbay	silk hat	siredon	skibbet
sheenly	ship-boy	shotten	sickbed	silkier	sirenic	ski-boat
sheered	shipful	shout at	sickish	silkily	sirenin	skidded
sheerly	Shipibo	shouter	sickled	silking	Sir John	skidder
sheeted	shiplap	shout-up	sickler	sillier	sirloin	skiddoo
shegetz	shipman	showbiz	sicknik	sillily	sirmark	skid-lid
Sheikha	shipmen	show-box	sickout	sillion	sirocco	skid-pan
sheitel	ship off	showery	sick pay	sillock	sirship	skid row
shekere	ship out	show for	sic-like	siltage	sirtaki	skidway
shellac	shipped	showier	Siculan	silumin	sissier	skiffle
shelled	shippen	showily	siddown	silurid	Sistine	ski jump
sheller	shipper	showing	side-arm	silurus	sistrum	skilful
shelter	shippon	showman	side-bar	silvern	sit back	ski lift
sheltie	ship-rat	showmen	side-bet	silvery	sit down	skilled
Sheltie	shipway	show off	side-box	silver Y	sitella	skillet
shelver	shirker	show out	side boy	silvics	sit-fast	ski-mask
shelves	shirred	shreddy	sidecar	simatic	sitient	skimmed
she-male	shirted	shrewly	side-car	simchah	sit over	skimmer
Shemite	Shirvan	shrieky	side cut	similar	sits vac	skimmia
sheogue	shisham	shright	sideman	similor	sit tall	skimped
Sherari	shitbag	shrilly	sideral	simious	sitting	skinful
sherbet	shit-hot	shrimps	sideway	simpkin	situate	skinker
Sherbro	shitted	shrimpy	siemens	simpler	sit-upon	skinkle
Sherden	shitten	shrined	Siemens	simplex	sit well	skinman
shereef	shitter	Shriner	Sienese	simular	sit with	skinned
sheriff	shittim	shritch	sierran	Sinaean	Sivaism	skinner
sherifi	shiveau	shrivel	sievert	sinapic	Sivaite	Skinner
Sherman	shivery	shriven	siftage	sinapyl	sivvens	skin-pop
Sherpas	shmatte	shriver	sifting	sincere	sixfoil	skintle
sherris	shochet	shroudy	sighful	Sindbis	sixfold	ski pole
she-wolf	shocker	shrubby	sighing	sinding	six-four	skipped
shiatsu	shoebox	shrug on	sighted	sine bar	six-inch	skipper
shicker	shoeing	shucker	sighter	sine die	six-pack	skippet
shiften	shoe-tie	shudder	sightly	Sinetic	sixsome	skipple
shifter	shoggle	shuddup	sigmate	sinewed	sixteen	skirlie
shih-tzu	shoneen	shuffle	sigmoid	singara	sixthly	skirret
shikara	shoofly	shuffly	signage	singing	sixties	skirted
shikari	shoo-fly	shuftis	signans	single-o	Sixtine	skirter
shikimi	shoogle	shuggle	signary	singlet	sizable	skitter
shikker	shoot at	shunned	signate	sing out	sizzler	skittle
shilloo	shootee	shunner	sign bit	singult	sjambok	skiving
Shilluk	shooter	shunter	sign for	Sinhala	Sjögren	skookum
shilpit	shoot up	shurrup	signify	sinical	skaldic	Skoptsi
shimada	shop boy	Shuswap	signing	Sinitic	skatist	skreigh
shimmed	shopful	shut-eye	sign off	sinkage	skatole	skulker
shimmer	shoplet	shut-off	signora	sinkful	skedded	skulled
Shin Bet	shopman	shutout	signore	sinking	skeeler	skuttle
shinbin	shopmen	shut out	signori	sinless	skeeter	skybald
shindig	shopped	shutter	signory	sinning	skegger	sky bear
shindle	shopper	shuttle	sign out	sinopia	skeiner	sky blue
shingle	shoppie	Shylock	Sikhism	Sinopic	skelder	sky-clad
shingly	shoring	shyness	Siksika	sinopie	skellum	skydive
Shingon	shorten	shyster	silajit	sinopis	skelper	sky-high
shinier	shortia	siamang	silence	sinople	skelter	sky-hook
shinily	shortie	Siamese	Silenic	sinsyne	skepful	skyhoot
shining	shortly	Siberia	silenus	sinuate	skepsel	skyjack
shinned	short of	sibling	Silesia	sinuose	skeptic	skylark

skyless	sleep in	slumism	snaggle	snouted	softies	songlet
skylike	sleep on	slummed	snaggly	Snovian	softish	songman
skyline	sleep up	slummer	snakily	snowcap	soft roe	sonhood
sky-path	sleeved	slummie	snakish	snowcat	soft rot	Soninke
skyphos	sleever	slumper	snap off	Snowcem	soft-top	sonless
sky-ride	sleight	slurbow	snap out	snow-fly	soft toy	sonlike
skysail	slender	slurper	snapped	snow gum	Sogdian	Sonoran
sky-ship	slewing	slurred	snapper	snow-ice	soggier	sonship
sky-sign	slicken	slusher	snarler	snowier	soggily	sonsier
skytale	slicker	slushie	snarl-up	snowily	soilage	soonish
sky-walk	slickly	slutchy	snatchy	snow job	soil air	soother
skywalk	slidden	slyness	snatter	snowman	soiling	soothly
skyward	slidder	smacker	snavvle	snowmen	soil map	sootier
sky wave	sliding	small ad	sneaked	snow owl	soilure	sootily
slabbed	slifter	smaragd	sneaker	snow pea	sojourn	Sophian
slabber	slighty	smarten	sneak-up	snow-ski	sokeman	Sophies
slab-hut	slimier	smartly	snecked	snozzle	solacer	sophism
slacken	slimily	smashed	snecket	snubbed	Solacet	sophist
slacker	slim jim	smasher	snedder	snubber	solanum	sophora
slackly	slimmed	smash-up	sneerer	snuffer	solaria	soppier
slack up	slimmer	smatter	sneezer	snuff it	solatia	soppily
slagged	slinger	smeared	snekkja	snuffle	soldado	sopping
slagger	slinker	smearer	Snellen	snuffly	soldier	soprani
slainte	slip of a	smectic	snibbed	snugger	sold out	soprano
slammed	slip off	smectis	snibble	snuggle	solebar	sorbate
slammer	slipped	smeddum	snicker	snuggly	Soledon	sorbent
slander	slipper	smelled	snicket	snuzzle	solicit	Sorbian
slanter	slipway	smeller	snickle	soakage	solider	sorbile
slantly	slither	smellie	snick-up	soaking	solidly	Sorbish
slap-dab	slitted	smelter	snidely	soakway	solidus	sorbite
slapped	slitter	smetana	snidery	so-and-so	soliped	sorbose
slapper	sliving	smicket	sniff at	Soanean	soliton	sorcery
slashed	Sloaney	smiddum	sniffer	soapbox	solodic	sordini
slasher	Sloanie	smidgen	sniffle	soapery	soloist	sordino
slather	slobber	smidgin	sniffly	soapier	Solomon	sorghum
slating	slob ice	smiling	snifter	soapily	Solonic	sorites
slatish	sloe-gin	smirker	snigged	soap-lye	solpuga	soritic
slatted	slogged	smitham	snigger	soap-nut	soluble	sororal
slatter	slogger	smither	sniggle	soarage	solunar	soroses
Slavdom	sloping	smiting	snipped	soaring	solvate	sorosis
slavery	slop out	smitten	snipper	sobbing	solvent	sorrier
slaveys	slopped	smocker	snippet	so being	Somalis	sorrily
Slavian	sloshed	smoke-ho	snirtle	soberer	Somasco	sorrowy
Slavise	slot car	smokery	snitter	soberly	somatic	sortied
slavish	slot man	smokier	snittle	socager	some day	sorties
Slavish	slotted	smokily	snobdom	soccage	someday	sorting
Slavism	slotter	smoking	snodger	sociate	some few	sort key
slavist	slouchy	smokish	snogged	society	somehow	sort out
Slavist	sloughi	smolder	snogger	sockeye	someone	so-soish
slavite	sloughy	smoochy	snooded	socking	someway	Sotadic
Slavize	Slovene	smoodge	snoodle	soda ash	somewhy	sotalol
slaying	slowish	smoothe	snooker	soda-pop	somitic	so there
slecken	slubbed	smother	snooper	sod corn	somnial	Sothiac
sledded	slubber	smudger	snoozer	sodding	sonance	so to say
sledder	sludger	smugger	snoozle	sodding	sonancy	sotting
sledger	slugged	smuggle	snoring	soddish	sondage	sottish
sleechy	slugger	smutchy	snorkel	soddite	Soneryl	sot-weed
sleeked	sluicer	smutted	snorker	Sodomic	songful	souffle
sleeken	slumber	smutter	snorter	Sod's law	Songhai	soufflé
sleeker	slumdom	snaffle	snortle	Sod's Law	song-hit	soulful
sleekly	slumgum	snagged	snot-rag	sofa bed	Songish	soulish
sleeper	slum gun	snagger	snotter	so far as	songket	sounder

Soundex	sparsed	spicket	splurgy	spurred	staffer	startle
soundly	Spartan	spicula	spodium	spurrer	stagery	startly
sound on	spartle	spicule	spoiled	spurrey	stagged	start on
soupçon	spasmed	spidery	spoiler	spurter	stagger	start up
soupier	spasmic	spiegel	Spokane	spurtle	staggie	starved
soupily	spastic	spieler	spondee	sputnik	stagier	starven
soup man	spathae	spignel	sponger	sputter	stagily	starver
sour gum	spathic	spikery	spongey	spyhole	staging	statant
souring	spatial	spikier	spongin	spy ring	staidly	statary
sourish	spa town	spikily	sponsal	spy-ship	stained	stately
sourock	spatted	spiking	sponson	spyship	stainer	statera
soursop	spattee	spiling	sponsor	squabby	staired	statice
sousing	spatter	spilite	spoofer	squacco	staithe	statics
souslik	spattle	spilled	spooked	squaddy	stalder	station
soutane	spatula	spiller	spooler	squalid	stalely	statism
southen	spatule	spillet	spooned	squally	stalest	statist
souther	spaulty	spinach	spooner	squalor	staling	stative
sovkhoz	spavied	spindle	spoorer	squalus	stalish	statued
sowable	spawned	spindly	sporont	squamae	stalked	stature
sowarry	spawner	spin-dry	sporran	squarer	stalker	statusy
sowback	speaker	spin-dye	sporter	squashy	stallar	statute
sow-back	speakie	spinier	sportly	squatly	staller	staumer
sowbane	speak of	spinner	sporule	squatty	stall-in	staunch
Sowetan	speak to	spinney	spot map	squawky	stalloy	stave in
Soxhlet	speak up	spinode	spotted	squeaky	stamina	staving
soybean	speared	spin off	spotter	squeamy	stammel	stay-bar
sozzled	spearer	spinone	spousal	squeege	stammer	stay for
spacial	special	spinose	spouted	squeeze	stamnos	stay-law
spacier	species	spinous	spouter	squeezy	stamper	Stayman
spacing	specify	spin out	spraing	squelch	stamp on	stay put
Spackle	specked	spinule	spraint	squench	stand by	stay-rod
spaddle	speckle	spiraea	sprawly	squidge	standby	St Cross
spadger	speckly	spirane	sprayer	squidgy	standee	stead of
spading	specter	spirant	sprayey	squiffy	standel	stealer
spadona	spectra	spirity	spray-on	squilla	stander	stealth
spaeman	spectre	spiroid	sprazer	squinch	stand in	steamed
spag bol	specula	spirtle	spready	squinny	stand on	steamer
spaller	speeded	spirula	spreagh	squinsy	stand to	steamie
spalted	speeder	spit-box	spreath	squinty	stand up	steam in
Spam can	speedos	spite of	sprenge	squiral	staniel	stearic
spancel	speed-up	spitful	spretty	squiret	stanine	stearin
Spandau	speeler	spitish	spriggy	squirmy	Stanley	stearyl
Spandex	spelder	spit-out	spright	squishy	stannel	steddle
spangle	spelled	spittal	springe	squitch	stannic	Stedman
spangly	speller	spitted	springy	squodgy	stanza'd	steeboy
spaniel	spelter	spitter	spritty	sraddha	stapled	steeled
Spanish	spelunk	spittle	sprucer	S-shaped	stapler	steenth
spanker	spencer	spittly	spryest	stabbed	starchy	steepen
spanned	spender	splashy	spud can	stabber	star-cut	steeper
spanner	sperage	splatch	spudded	stabile	stardom	steeple
span-new	sperate	spleeny	spudder	stabler	starful	steeply
sparely	spermal	splenic	spuddle	stabley	staring	steep-to
sparger	spermic	splenii	spulyie	stab-man	starken	steep-up
Sparine	sphagna	splicer	spumoni	stachys	starkly	steerer
sparing	sphecid	splinty	spumose	stacked	starlet	Steiner
sparker	spheges	split-up	spumous	stacker	starlit	stellar
sparkle	spheral	splodge	spunkie	stack up	star-map	stelled
sparkly	spheric	splodgy	spun out	staddle	starnie	Steller
sparoid	spicate	sploshy	spur-bow	staddow	starred	stem-cup
sparred	spicery	splotch	spur-dog	stadial	starrer	stem-fly
sparrer	spicier	splunge	spurion	stadium	starter	stemlet
sparrow	spicily	splurge	spurner	staffed	start in	stemmed

stemmer	stick up	stop-net	striola	stylish	sub-song	sui-mate
stemple	Stiegel	stop off	striped	stylism	subsume	suit bag
stemson	stifado	stop-off	striper	stylist	subtack	suiting
stenchy	stiffen	stopoff	stripey	stylite	sub-teen	sulcate
stencil	stiffly	stop one	strippy	stylize	subtend	sulfide
stengah	stifled	stop out	stritch	styloid	subtest	Suliote
Sten gun	stifler	stopped	strived	stylops	subtext	sulkier
Stensen	stigmal	stopper	striven	stymied	subtile	sulkily
stenter	stigmas	stopple	striver	stymies	subtler	sullage
stenton	stigmat	stop-tap	strobic	styptic	subtone	sullied
stentor	stiller	stopway	stroker	Stypven	subtype	sullies
Stentor	stilted	storage	stromal	styrene	subunit	sulphur
step-cut	stilter	storeys	strophe	Styrian	subvent	sultana
stepdad	Stilton	storial	stroppy	styrone	subvert	Sumatra
stepmum	stimies	storied	strowed	suantly	sub voce	sumless
Stepney	stimuli	storier	strudel	suasion	sub-zero	summage
step off	stinged	stories	strumae	suasive	subzero	summand
step out	stinger	storify	stubbed	suasory	subzone	summary
stepped	stingle	storken	stubber	suavely	succade	summate
stepper	stinker	stormer	stubble	suavity	succeed	summers
stepson	stinted	stotter	stubbly	subacid	succent	summery
stepway	stinter	stourly	stub-end	subadar	success	summing
sterane	stipend	stouten	stub-pen	sub-aqua	succory	Summist
stereos	stipple	stoutly	stuck-up	sub-arch	Succoth	summons
sterile	stipula	stowage	stud-box	subashi	succour	sumpter
sterlet	stipule	stowing	studded	sub-atom	succous	sunbake
sternad	stir-fry	stow-net	studdle	sub-base	succuba	sun-bath
sternal	stirpes	strafer	student	subbing	succubi	sunbeam
sterned	stirred	straint	Student	subcool	succumb	sun bear
sternly	stirrer	straked	studied	subdean	succuss	sunbelt
stern on	stirrup	stramin	studier	subdual	suck dry	sunbird
sternum	St Kilda	strange	studies	subduct	suck-egg	sunburn
steroid	St Leger	strap in	studios	subdued	sucking	sun club
stertor	stocked	strap on	Studite	subduer	suckler	sun-cure
stetson	stocker	strappy	stufato	subdues	suck off	Sundays
Stetson	stock up	stratal	stuffed	sub-edit	sucrase	sun deck
stetted	stodger	stratum	stuffer	subedit	sucrier	sundial
Steuben	stogies	stratus	stuff it	suberic	sucrose	sun-disc
steward	stoical	strawed	stumble	suberin	suction	sundown
stewart	stoiter	strawen	stumbly	subfief	sudamen	sunfall
stew-bum	stomach	strayed	stummed	subform	Sudanic	sunfast
stewing	stomata	strayer	stummer	subfusc	sudaria	sunfish
stewpan	stomate	streaky	stumper	sub-head	Sudeten	sun gear
stewpot	stomion	streale	stumpie	subhead	Sudetic	Sun King
St Faith	stomium	streamy	stump up	subject	sudoral	sun-lamp
sthenia	stomper	streety	stun gas	subjoin	suedene	sunlamp
sthenic	stompie	strepie	stun gun	sublate	suedine	sunless
stibine	stone me	stretch	stunned	sublime	Suevian	sunlike
stibium	stonier	stretta	stunner	submenu	suevite	sunnier
stichic	stonify	stretto	stunted	submiss	suey pow	sunnies
stichoi	stonily	strewed	stunter	suboval	suffect	sunnily
stichos	stonker	strewer	stupefy	suboxic	suffete	sunning
stick at	stooker	strewth	stupent	sub-plot	suffice	Sunnism
stick by	stookie	striata	stupify	sub-rent	sufflue	Sunnite
sticker	stooled	striate	stupose	subring	Suffolk	sunrays
Stickie	stoolie	strider	sturine	sub rosa	suffuse	sunrise
stick in	stooper	stridor	Sturmer	subsalt	Sufiism	sun-roof
stickit	stoopid	striges	stutter	subsere	sufuria	sunroof
stickle	stoothe	strigil	Stygian	subside	sugared	sunroom
stick-on	stop-dog	striked	stylary	subsidy	suggest	sun-rose
stick to	stopgap	striker	styling	subsist	sugging	sunspot
stickum	stop log	stringy	stylise	subsoil	suicide	sunstar

sun-suit	swagger	swinger	syntony	Taffies	tallied	tant pis
sunsuit	swaggie	swing it	syntype	Tagalic	tallier	tantric
suntrap	swagman	swingle	synusia	Tagalog	tallies	tantrum
sunward	swagmen	Swinhoe	Syrette	Tagamet	tallish	tan-yard
sunways	Swahili	swinish	Syriasm	tag axle	tallith	tao-tieh
sunwise	Swakara	swinker	syringa	tagetes	tallowy	taovala
supping	swallow	swipper	syringe	taggant	tally-ho	tap-bolt
suppler	swamper	swipple	syrphid	taggeen	taloned	tapered
support	swanker	switchy	system D	tagging	talonid	taperer
suppose	swankey	swithen	systole	tag line	tal qual	tapetal
suppost	swankie	swither	systyle	tag-lock	taluses	tapetum
suprema	swanned	Switzer	taaibos	tagmeme	talwood	tap-hole
supreme	swanner	swizzes	tabanid	tag sale	tamable	tap-hose
suprême	swannie	swizzle	tabaret	tag-sore	tamarau	tapicer
supremo	Swansea	swollen	Tabasco	tag-tail	tamarin	tapioca
suramin	swapped	swooned	tabbies	tag team	tamasha	tap-kick
suranal	swapper	swooner	tabbing	tag-worm	tambala	tap-lash
surance	swarded	swooper	tabella	tail-bay	tamboti	tapless
surbase	swarmer	swooshy	tabetic	tail-end	tambour	tapping
surcoat	swarthy	sworded	tabific	tail fin	tambuti	taproom
surdity	swasher	sworder	tabinet	tail-fly	tame cat	tap root
surface	swather	swotted	tableau	tail gas	Tammany	tap shoe
surfacy	swathes	swotter	tablier	tail-ill	tammies	tapster
surf-bum	swatted	swy game	tablina	tailing	tampico	tap-tool
surf day	swatter	syconia	tabling	tailism	tamping	tar acid
surfeit	swattle	syconus	tabloid	taillie	tampion	taraire
surfing	sway-bar	sycosis	tabooed	tail off	tanager	Taranji
surfuse	swazzle	syenite	taborer	tailory	Tanagra	tar-baby
surgent	swearer	Sylheti	tab show	tail-pin	tanbark	tar ball
surgeon	swear in	syllabe	tabular	tail-rod	tandava	tar base
surgery	sweated	syllabi	taccada	tail-wag	tandoor	tarbush
surging	sweater	sylloge	tacenda	tainted	tandour	tardier
surlier	sweddle	sylphid	Taceval	Taiping	tangata	tardily
surlily	Swedish	Sylphon	tachism	Tairona	tangelo	tardity
surmise	Sweeney	Sylvian	tachist	takable	tangena	tardive
surname	sweeper	sylvine	ta chuan	take aim	tangent	tardyon
surpass	sweeten	sylvite	tachyon	take air	tanghin	tarheel
surplus	sweetie	Sylvius	tacitly	take-all	tangier	tar kiln
surreal	sweetly	symmory	tackety	take ill	tangily	tarnish
surreys	swelled	symport	tackier	take off	tangled	tarocco
surtout	swelp me	symptom	tackily	take out	tangler	tarried
surveil	swelter	synagog	tacking	taker-in	tangoes	tarrier
surview	sweltry	synapse	tackled	taker-up	tangram	tarries
survive	swept-up	synaxis	tackler	takhaar	tanguin	tarring
suspect	swerver	syncarp	tack rag	Takulli	taniwha	tarrish
suspend	swidden	synchro	tacnode	Talaing	tankage	tarrock
suspire	swiften	syncope	Taconic	talaria	tankard	tar sand
sussing	swifter	syndrum	tacouba	talaric	tank car	tar-seal
suss law	swiftie	synergy	tactful	talayot	tankful	Tarsian
sustain	swiftly	synform	tactics	talcing	tank top	tarsier
sutlery	swigged	synfuel	tactile	talcked	tanling	tartana
suttees	swigger	syngamy	tactily	talcose	tannage	tartane
sutural	swiggle	synnema	taction	talcous	tannaim	tartare
sutured	swigman	synodal	tactoid	talipes	tannase	Tartary
Svanian	swiller	synodic	tactual	talipot	tannate	tartier
svarita	swim-cap	synonym	tadpole	talk big	tannery	tartily
swabbed	swim-fin	synovia	Tadzhik	talking	tanning	tartine
swabber	swimmer	syntagm	taeniae	talk out	tannish	tartish
Swabian	swindle	syntaxy	taenias	tallage	tansies	tartlet
swacked	swinely	synteny	taenite	tallboy	tantara	tar-weed
swaddle	swinery	synthon	taffeta	tallied	tantivy	tar-wood
swagged	swing-by	syntone	taffies	tall hat	tantony	Tasaday

tastier	tear gas	tempery	ternate	Thammuz	theorbo	thinner
tastily	tearing	tempest	ternery	thanage	theorem	Thiokol
tasting	tearlet	tempête	ternion	thankee	theoric	thionic
tattery	tear-off	templar	terpane	thanker	theosis	thionyl
tattier	tearoom	Templar	terpene	thapsia	the outs	thirdly
tattily	tea rose	templed	terrace	thatchy	the Pale	thirsty
tatting	tea shop	templet	terracy	that lot	the pits	this lot
tattler	teashop	tempter	terrage	that one	the Pool	thistle
tattoos	teasing	tempura	terrain	that's it	therapy	thistly
tauhinu	teat-cup	tenable	terrane	that was	thereat	thither
taungya	tea-tent	tenacle	terrene	that way	thereby	thiuram
taunter	teatime	tenancy	terreno	thaught	the Reef	thivish
taupata	tea tray	ten-code	terrier	thawing	therein	tholoid
Taurean	tea-tree	tendant	terries	the arts	thereof	Thomism
taureau	tea-ware	tend bar	terrify	theater	thereon	Thomist
Taurian	techier	tendent	terrine	theatre	thereto	Thomson
taurine	techies	tendenz	tersely	the Axis	theriac	thorian
tavelle	technic	tendril	tersest	Thebaic	therian	thorite
taverna	tectrix	tendron	tertial	Thebaïd	thermae	thorium
tawhine	teddies	teneral	tertian	the Bard	thermal	thornen
tawhiri	tedding	tenfold	tertius	the Bear	thermic	thought
tawnier	Tedesco	ten-foot	tessera	the best	thermit	thratch
taxable	tedious	ten-four	Test Act	the big C	thermos	thraver
taxably	tee-heed	ten-inch	testacy	the bird	Thermos	thready
taxator	tee-hees	tenmoku	testata	the bomb	the Rock	threave
tax bite	teemful	tennies	testate	the bowl	theroid	three Rs
tax-book	teenage	tenoner	test ban	the boys	the ruck	threnoi
tax-cart	teenful	tensely	test bed	the cake	The Rump	threose
tax code	teenier	tense up	test-fly	thecate	the runs	thrifty
tax disc	teer-boy	tensify	testier	the chop	the sack	thrilly
taxemic	teetery	tensile	testify	theccium	Thesean	thrimsa
tax-free	teether	tension	testily	the clod	the Shop	thrinne
taxicab	Tegeate	tensity	testing	the coif	the tomb	thrived
taxi-cab	tegmina	tensive	test out	thecoma	the Turk	thriven
taxiing	tegular	ten-spot	test-pit	the cord	theurgy	thriver
taxiway	Tehrani	tentage	test rig	the cuts	the veil	throaty
taxless	teistie	tent-bed	testudo	the East	the West	thrombi
tax-loss	tektite	tent-fly	tetanal	the evil	the wild	through
taxogen	telamon	tentful	tetanic	the Fens	the Word	throw by
tax year	telecom	tenthly	tetanus	the flat	the Yard	throwed
taxying	telecon	tentily	tetched	the game	they say	thrower
tayassu	telefax	tenting	Tethyan	thegnly	thiamin	throw in
tazetta	Telefax	tentive	tetrode	the hell	thicken	throw on
tchaush	teleost	tent peg	tetrose	the High	thicket	throw to
tea-ball	telesis	tenuity	tetrous	the Hill	thickie	throw up
tea-bowl	teletex	tenuous	tettery	the hole	thickly	thrummy
teacake	Teletex	tenured	teuchat	the Horn	thickos	thruout
tea cart	Telinga	tenutos	tew-iron	the lads	thick 'un	thrutch
teacher	tell-all	ten-year	Texican	the Lamb	thieves	thruway
teach-in	tellies	Teochew	textile	the land	thigger	thrymsa
tea cosy	tellina	tepidly	text-man	the lane	thighed	thudded
tea-dust	telling	tequila	text-pen	the less	thiller	thuggee
tea girl	tell off	terbium	textual	the life	thimble	thujone
tea gown	tell out	terebic	textura	the line	thin air	Thulean
teahead	telogen	terebra	texture	the Mail	thin-cut	thulite
tea lady	telomer	teredos	thacker	the men's	thingly	thulium
tea leaf	telpher	tergite	Thakali	the Moor	thingum	thumbed
tealery	Telugus	Terital	thalami	the most	thinker	thumber
tealess	temblor	term-day	Thalian	The Nine	think-in	thumper
team-man	temenos	termini	thallic	the nuts	think on	thump-up
tear-cat	temmoku	termite	thallus	the Oaks	think up	thunder
tearful	tempera	ternary	thalweg	theolog	thinned	thurify

thus far	timbrel	titmice	toilful	tool-man	torrefy	tow-line
thutter	timeful	Titoism	toiling	too much	torrent	towline
thwaite	time hit	Titoist	toisech	toothed	torsade	town car
thymele	time lag	Titoite	tokamak	tooting	torsion	town-end
thymine	time off	titrant	Tokarev	tootsey	torteau	townful
thymoma	timeous	titrate	told out	tootsie	tortile	town gas
thyroid	time-out	tittery	Toledan	toparch	tortive	townify
thyrsus	time was	titties	Toledos	top-boot	Tortoni	townish
thyself	timider	tittupy	Toletan	topchee	tortrix	townlet
tiaraed	timidly	titular	tollage	topcoat	torture	townman
Tibetan	timolol	Tityrus	toll-bar	top copy	torulae	town-way
tiburon	timothy	tizzies	Tollens	top deck	toruses	towpath
tick-fly	timpani	Tlingit	tollent	top-down	torvity	tow rope
ticking	Timucua	toad bug	tolling	top edge	torvous	toxical
tickler	Timurid	toad-eat	tollman	top-full	Torydom	Toxodon
tick off	tinamou	toadery	tollway	top gear	Toryish	toyless
tidally	tinchel	toadied	toluene	top hand	Toryism	toylike
tiddler	tindery	toadies	to match	top-hole	Toryize	toy-shop
tiddley	tin fish	toadish	tomb bat	topiary	to scale	toyshop
tideful	tinfoil	toadlet	tombola	topical	to spare	toytown
tide-rip	tin foil	to a hair	tombolo	top kick	toss off	trabant
tideway	tingent	toaster	tomelet	topknot	tosspot	trabuch
tidiest	tinging	toastie	tomenta	top-land	tostada	tracery
tidings	tingler	to a turn	tomfool	topless	totally	trachea
tidling	tinhorn	to a wish	Tommies	top-line	to taste	trachle
tidying	tiniest	tobacco	tomming	topmast	tote bag	tracing
tie-back	tinkler	to-burst	tompion	topmost	tote box	tracker
tie-beam	tin-loaf	toby jug	Tompion	topness	totemic	track-in
tie belt	tinnery	tobyman	tom pung	top note	totient	track up
tie-bolt	tinnier	toccata	tonally	to point	Totonac	tractor
tie-clip	tinnies	toc emma	tone arm	toponym	tottery	tractus
tie down	tinnily	tocusso	tonearm	topping	totting	trade in
tie game	tinning	toddies	toneful	toppish	tot up to	trade on
tie into	tin pest	toddler	tonemic	topsail	touch at	trade up
tieless	tin-tack	to death	tonepad	topside	touched	trading
tie line	tinting	tod-hole	tone-row	topsman	toucher	traduce
tierced	tin-type	toe-boot	tonetic	topsoil	touch in	traffic
tiercel	tinware	toe clip	tonette	topspin	touch on	tragedy
tiercet	tipless	toehold	tonging	top view	touch up	traiked
tiering	tip loss	toe-hold	tongman	topwise	toughen	trailer
tiffany	tipping	toe jump	tongued	top-work	toughie	trained
Tiffany	tippler	toeless	tonguer	Toradja	tough it	trainee
tiffler	tipsier	toe loop	tongues	torched	toughly	trainer
tigerly	tipsify	toenail	tonguey	torcher	toughra	train on
tighten	tipsily	toe-puff	tonical	torchon	touladi	traipse
tightly	tipster	toe rake	toniest	tordion	toupeed	traitor
Tigrean	tiptoed	toe-ring	tonight	torenia	touraco	traject
tigress	tiptoes	toering	Tonkawa	tore-out	tourism	tra-la-la
tigrine	tipulid	toe shoe	ton-mile	toreros	tourist	tramcar
tigroid	tiredly	toe-spin	tonnage	torgant	Tournai	trammel
tiki bar	tisicky	toe wall	tonneau	torgoch	Tournay	trammer
tilapia	tissual	toffees	tonnish	torgsin	tournee	trammie
tilbury	tissuey	toffies	tonsure	torment	tourney	tramper
tile-ore	titania	toffish	tontine	tormina	tousing	trample
tillage	titanic	toftman	tool bag	tornada	tou ts'ai	tramway
tilleul	Titanic	togated	tool-bar	tornado	towable	tranced
tillite	tit-bell	toggery	tool-box	torpedo	towards	tranche
tilloid	tithing	togging	toolbox	torpefy	towaway	tranché
tilt cab	titivil	togless	toolies	torpent	tow-boat	traneen
tilt-top	titlark	togt boy	tooling	torqued	towered	trangle
timbale	titling	toheroa	tool kit	torques	towfish	tranked
timbred	titlist	to horse	toolkit	torquey	tow-head	trannie

transit	tribade	trisect	trueing	tucking	Turkdom	twin bed
transom	triblet	triseme	trueish	tuck-net	Turkery	twin-cam
tranter	tribual	trishaw	true rib	tuck-out	turkeys	twindle
trap-bat	tribune	trismus	truffle	Tudesco	Turkify	twingle
trap-cut	tribute	trisome	trugger	Tuesday	Turkish	twin-jet
trapeze	tricast	trisomy	trumeau	tuffite	Turkism	twinkie
trap-gun	triceps	tritaph	trumper	tuftily	Turkize	twinkle
trap-net	tricker	tritely	trumpet	tufting	Turkman	twinkly
trapped	trickle	tritide	trump up	tugboat	Turkmen	twin-law
trapper	trickly	tritish	truncal	tugging	turmoil	twinned
trap-shy	tricksy	tritium	truncus	tuition	turn-cap	twin set
trasher	triclad	tritoma	trundle	tule fog	turn dog	twinset
traumas	tricorn	tritone	trunked	tumbaga	turnery	twinter
travail	trident	triumph	trunker	tumbler	turning	twin-tub
travois	triduan	triunal	trunnel	tumbrel	turnipy	twirler
trawler	triduum	trivial	trusser	tumbril	turnkey	twisted
trayful	triffid	trivium	trustee	Tumbuka	turn off	twister
tray top	trifler	trizzie	truster	tumesce	turn out	twist in
treacle	trifold	Troadic	trustie	tumidly	turnout	twistle
treacly	triform	trochal	trutine	tummied	turn-pin	twistor
treaded	trigamy	trochee	try back	tummies	turn-row	twitchy
treader	trigged	trochus	try it on	tummler	turpeth	twitted
treadle	trigger	trodden	trypsin	tumular	turtler	twitten
treason	triglot	troland	tryptic	tumulus	turtlet	twitter
treatee	trigone	troller	try-sail	tunable	turving	twizzle
treater	trigram	trolley	trysail	tunably	tushery	two-bill
treddle	Trilene	trollop	tryster	tundish	tussive	two-body
tree boa	trilith	tromino	tsaddik	tuned in	tussock	two-cent
tree-cat	triller	trommel	ts'ao shu	tuneful	tussore	two-coat
tree fox	trillet	tronage	tsarate	tune off	tutania	two-eyed
treeful	trilobe	troolie	tsardom	tune out	tutelar	twofold
tree god	trilogy	trooper	tsarian	tung oil	tutenag	two-foot
tree pie	trimmed	troopie	tsarina	tunhoof	tutorer	two-four
tree rat	trimmer	tropane	tsarish	tunicae	tutorly	two-hand
treetop	trim tab	tropary	tsarism	Tunican	tutoyer	two-leaf
trefoil	trinary	tropery	tsarist	tunicin	tutress	two-line
trehala	trindle	trophic	tsarlet	tunicle	tutulus	two-meal
trekbok	tringle	tropine	tsatlee	tunnage	tuxedos	twoness
trekked	trinity	troping	tsatske	tunnery	twaddle	two-part
trekker	trinket	tropism	T-shaped	tunnies	Twaddle	two-pipe
trekkie	trinkle	tropone	tsimmes	tunning	twaddly	two-shot
trek net	trinkum	trot out	T-square	tun-pail	twanger	twosome
trek-tow	triobol	trotted	tsukuri	tupaiid	twangle	two-spot
trellis	triolet	trotter	tsunami	tupelos	Twankay	two-star
tremble	trioxan	trouble	Tswanas	tupping	twanker	two-step
trembly	tripack	troughy	tuatara	turacin	twattle	two-time
tremolo	tripart	trounce	tub-bass	turbary	tweaker	two-tone
trenail	tripery	trouper	tubbier	turbine	tweeded	twybill
trendle	triple-A	trouser	tubbily	turbots	tweedle	twyfold
trental	tripler	trouter	tubbing	turdine	tweeter	tychism
trepang	triplet	Trouton	tubbish	turdish	tweetle	tykhana
tressed	triplex	trowman	tubeful	turdoid	tweezer	Tylenol
tressel	triplum	truancy	tube top	turfdom	twelfth	tylopod
trestle	tripody	truce to	tub-fish	turfier	twelver	tylosin
Trevira	tripoli	trucial	tubfuls	turfing	twibill	tylosis
trey-bit	tripped	trucker	tubifex	turfite	twiddle	tylotic
triable	tripper	truckie	tub-size	turfman	twiddly	tympana
triacid	trippet	truckle	tubster	turfmen	twifold	tympani
triadic	tripple	trudgen	tubular	turgent	twigged	tympany
triarch	tripton	trudger	tubulin	turismo	twiggen	Tyndall
triatic	trireme	true bug	tubulus	turista	twiglet	Tynwald
tri-axle	trisazo	true fly	tuck box	Turkana	twilled	type-bar

typeset	unbeget	undated	un-Greek	unlaced	unpoise	unslate
typhoid	unbegot	undazed	ungreen	unladen	unposed	unslave
typhoon	unbegun	undealt	ungrown	unlamed	unpower	unslept
typhous	unbeing	undeify	unguard	unlatch	unprone	unsling
typical	unbless	underdo	unguent	un-Latin	unproud	unslung
tyranny	unblest	undergo	ungulae	unlawed	unpurse	unsmart
Tyroler	unblind	undevil	unguled	unlearn	unpushy	unsnare
tzarina	unblock	undight	ungyved	unleash	unqueen	unsnarl
Tzeltal	unblown	undinal	unhandy	unleave	unquick	unsneck
tzigane	unboned	undined	unhappy	unlegal	unquiet	unsober
tzimmes	unbonny	undoing	unhardy	unlevel	unquote	unsolid
tzolkin	unbored	undrape	unhaste	unlight	unquoth	unsonsy
Tzotzil	unborne	undrawn	unhasty	unlimed	unraced	unsorry
Tz'u Chou	unbosom	undress	unheard	unlined	unraked	unsound
uberous	unbound	undried	unheart	unlived	unrated	unspell
ubicity	unbowed	undrunk	unheedy	unliver	unravel	unspent
udaller	unbrace	undular	unhinge	unlocal	unready	unspied
uddered	unbraid	undying	unhired	unlodge	unreeve	unspike
ufology	unbrave	undyked	unhitch	unloose	unregal	unspilt
Ugandan	unbrick	uneager	unhoard	unloved	unright	unsplit
ugliest	unbuild	uneared	unhomed	unloyal	unrimed	unspoil
uht-song	unbuilt	unearth	unhoped	unlucid	unrisen	unspool
ukelele	unbulky	uneaten	unhorse	unlucky	unriven	unstack
ukulele	unburnt	unedged	unhosed	unlusty	unrivet	unstagy
ulcered	unburst	unended	unhouse	unmaker	unrobed	unstaid
ulexite	uncaged	unequal	unhuman	unmanly	un-Roman	unstall
ullaged	uncanny	unexact	uniaxal	unmarry	unroost	unstate
ulnager	unchain	unfaded	unibody	unmated	unroped	unsteek
Ultisol	uncharm	unfaith	unicell	unmeant	unrough	unsteel
ululant	unchary	unfamed	unicist	unmerry	unround	unstick
ululate	unchild	unfazed	unicity	unmeted	unroyal	unstill
Ulysses	unchoke	unfiled	unicode	unmined	unruled	unsting
Umayyad	uncinch	unfined	unicorn	unmixed	unsaint	unstock
Umbanda	uncinus	unfired	unidea'd	unmoist	unsated	unstout
umbella	uncited	unfitly	unideal	unmoral	unsaved	unstrap
umbilic	uncivic	unfitty	uniface	unmould	un-Saxon	unstrip
umbonal	uncivil	unfixed	unified	unmount	unscale	unstuck
umbones	unclamp	unflesh	unifier	unmoved	unscrew	unstuff
umbrage	unclasp	unflown	unifies	unmowed	unseely	unstung
Umbrian	unclean	unfound	uniflow	unnamed	unsense	unsunny
umbrose	unclear	unframe	uniform	unneedy	unsewed	unswear
umbrous	uncling	unfreed	unineme	unnerve	unsexed	unsweet
umpteen	uncloak	unfresh	uninemy	unnoble	unshape	unswell
umwhile	unclose	unfrock	unional	unnoted	unsharp	unswept
unacted	uncloud	unfroze	Unionic	unoften	unshawl	unswore
unadept	unclued	unfumed	unipole	unoiled	unshell	unsworn
unaided	uncoded	unfunny	unireme	unorder	unshent	untaken
unaimed	uncomfy	unfused	un-Irish	unowned	unshewn	untamed
unaired	uncoped	unfussy	unitard	unpaced	unshift	untaxed
unalert	uncouch	ungated	unitary	unpagan	unshiny	unteach
unalike	uncouth	ungaudy	unities	unpaged	unshoed	untense
unalism	uncover	ungazed	uniting	unpaint	unshook	untenty
unalist	uncowed	ungiddy	unition	unpaper	unshorn	unthink
unalive	uncramp	ungirth	unitise	unpared	unshout	untight
unanism	uncrest	ungiven	unitive	unpaved	unshown	untiled
unaptly	uncross	unglobe	unitize	unpeace	unshowy	untimed
unarmed	uncrown	unglove	unjaded	unperch	unsight	untired
unasked	uncruel	unglued	unjoint	unplace	unsilly	untitle
unaware	unction	ungodly	unjolly	unplain	unsinew	untoned
unawful	uncured	ungrace	unjuicy	unplait	unsized	untread
unbaked	uncurse	ungrate	unkempt	unplank	unskill	untried
unbated	undared	ungrave	unknown	unplume	unslain	untripe

untrite	uplight	uranium	vagancy	variole	venomed	vetoism
untruly	uplying	uranous	vaginae	various	venomer	vetoist
untruss	upmount	uredial	vaginal	varment	ventage	vetting
untrust	up north	uredium	vaginas	varmint	ventail	vettura
untruth	up-piled	urethra	vagitus	varnish	Ventile	vetusty
untuned	upraise	urgence	vagrant	varsity	venting	vexable
untwine	upright	urgency	vaguely	varying	ventose	vexedly
untwist	uprisal	uricase	vaguish	vascula	Ventose	vexilla
untying	uprisen	uridine	vainful	vaseful	vent-peg	viaduct
unurged	upriser	urinant	vaivode	vastily	ventrad	vialled
unurned	up-river	urinary	valance	vastity	ventral	viatica
unusual	upriver	urinate	Val-A-Pak	VATable	venture	vibrant
unvenom	upscale	urinous	valence	Vatican	venturi	vibrate
unvexed	upshift	urnfuls	valency	vatting	Venturi	vibrato
unvisor	upshoot	urodele	valeric	Vaudese	Venuses	vibrion
unvital	upsides	urogram	valeryl	Vaudois	Vepsian	vibrios
unvocal	upsilon	urology	valeted	vaulted	veranda	vice-god
unvoice	upskill	urotoxy	valetry	vaulter	verbage	viceroy
unvowed	upslope	ursinia	valiant	vaumure	verbena	vicinal
unwaged	upspeak	urucuri	validly	vaunter	verbify	vicious
unwaked	upstage	useable	vallate	vecchio	verbose	Vickers
unwares	upstair	useless	valleys	Vectian	verdant	victory
unwater	upstand	use-life	vallota	vedalia	Verdian	victrix
unwaxed	upstare	ushabti	valonia	Vedanta	verdict	victual
unweary	upstart	U-shaped	valpack	Veddoid	verdite	videnda
unweave	upstate	usherer	valuate	vedette	verdure	vidette
unwiped	upsteer	Usonian	valuing	veeboer	verglas	vidicon
unwitch	upstood	Ustashi	valvate	veering	veridic	vidimus
unwitty	upsurge	usually	valving	veganic	veriest	Vidonia
unwived	upswarm	usucapt	valvula	Veganin	verismo	viduage
unwoman	upsweep	usuress	valvulc	vegetal	vermeil	viduity
unwooed	upswell	usurped	vamoose	vehicle	vermian	Vietnik
unworld	upswept	usurper	vampire	veiling	Vermont	viewing
unworth	upswing	utensil	vampish	veinier	vernage	vigogne
unwound	uptaken	uterine	vampyre	veining	Vernean	vigonia
unwoven	uptaker	utilise	vanadic	veinlet	verneuk	vihuela
unwrite	up-tempo	utility	vanadyl	veinous	vernier	villaed
unwrung	up there	utilize	vandola	veinule	veronal	villafy
unyoked	upthrew	Utopian	vandyke	velamen	verruca	village
unzoned	upthrow	Utopism	Vandyke	velaria	verruga	villain
up a tree	uptight	Utopist	vanessa	velaric	versant	villein
upblown	uptower	Utrecht	vanette	velated	Versene	villose
upbound	uptrend	utricle	vanilla	veldman	versify	villous
upbraid	up until	utterer	vanille	veld pig	versine	Vincent
upbreak	upvalue	utterly	Van John	veld rat	version	vin cuit
upbring	upwards	U-valley	van pool	velella	versute	vincula
upbuild	upwound	uveitis	vantage	veliger	vertant	vinegar
upburst	up yours	uxorial	vanward	velites	vertigo	vine-rod
upcatch	urachal	vaatjie	vapidly	vellumy	vervain	vinewed
upchuck	urachus	vacance	vaporer	velours	vesania	vin gris
upclimb	uraemia	vacancy	vapoury	velouté	vesical	vinnied
upclose	uraemic	vacatur	vaquero	velvety	vesicle	vin rosé
upcoast	Uralian	vaccary	varanid	venally	vespine	vintage
updater	uralite	vaccine	varanus	venatic	vespoid	vintner
upfield	Uralite	vacuist	variant	vendace	vestige	Vinylon
upfloor	uralium	vacuity	variate	Vendean	vesting	violate
upflung	Ural owl	vacuole	varicap	venefic	vestock	violent
up front	uranate	vacuome	varices	veneral	vestral	violine
upfront	Uranian	vacuous	variety	venerer	vesture	violist
upglide	uranism	vacuums	varimax	Venetic	vesuvin	violone
upgrade	uranist	V aerial	Varinas	V-engine	veteran	viperid
upheave	uranite	vagally	variola	venison	vetiver	viragos

virally	voivode	waggler	want for	washier	waygate	weirdie
virelay	volante	wagoner	wanting	washily	waylaid	weirdly
viremia	Volapük	wagonry	want-wit	washing	wayless	weirdos
virgate	volatic	wagtail	wapitis	Washita	waymark	weiring
Virgoan	volcano	Wahhabi	wappato	washman	way-port	welcome
virgula	volleys	waifish	wapping	wash-off	way-post	welding
virgule	voltage	wailful	waratah	wash out	wayside	welfare
viridin	voltaic	wailing	war baby	wash-out	way-stop	well-cut
viroled	Voltaic	wainage	war-bird	washout	wayward	well day
virosis	voluble	wainful	warbled	wash-pan	way-wise	well-fed
virtual	volubly	wainman	warbler	wash-pen	waywode	wellies
virtued	volumed	waipiro	Warburg	wash-pot	way-worn	wellish
visaged	volumen	waisted	Wardian	washrag	wazzock	well-man
visaing	volupty	waister	warding	washtub	weakish	well met
vis-à-vis	voluted	waiting	wardite	wash-way	Wealden	well-off
viscera	volutin	wait out	ward off	Waspdom	wealthy	we'll see
viscoid	vomited	waitron	war-drum	wasp-fly	wearier	well-set
viscose	vomiter	Wakamba	wareful	waspily	wearily	well-way
viscous	vomitus	wakeful	warehou	Waspily	wearing	well-won
visible	voodoos	wakeman	wareshi	waspish	wearish	welsher
visibly	voorbok	wakener	warfare	Waspish	wear off	Welsher
visited	vorlage	Walapai	war game	wassail	wear out	Welshry
visitee	votable	walkies	war-hawk	wassell	weasand	welting
visiter	vote off	walking	warhead	wastage	weather	wemless
visitor	vote out	walkist	war hero	wastery	weazeny	wencher
Visking	votress	Walkman	wariest	wastrel	web-beam	wendigo
visnomy	vouchee	walk off	warless	watcher	Webbian	Wendish
visored	voucher	walk out	warlike	watchet	webbing	Wepsian
vistaed	vouchor	walkout	warling	watch it	web-foot	wergeld
vis viva	Vouvray	walkway	warload	watch up	weblike	wershly
vitally	vowelly	wallaba	war loan	watered	web-nest	werwolf
vitamin	voyager	wallaby	warlock	waterer	webster	west end
vitarum	vriddhi	Wallace	warlord	water in	web-toed	West End
vitelli	vriesia	Wallach	warm-air	water-ox	web-work	western
vitenge	V-shaped	wall bar	warming	wattage	webwork	westing
vitiate	V-thread	wall bed	warmish	Watteau	web-worm	westlin
vitious	vugular	wall-box	warning	wattled	webworm	wetback
vitrain	vulgate	wall-eye	warnish	wave-hop	wedding	wet bulb
vitrify	Vulgate	wallful	warn off	wavelet	wedging	wet dock
vitrine	vulpine	wallies	war-note	wave-off	wedlock	wet fish
vitriol	vulture	walling	warpage	waverer	weedery	wetland
vitrous	Wabenzi	Walloon	warpath	waveson	weedful	wet look
vittate	wackily	wall-rib	warping	wavicle	weedier	wetness
vivaing	wackoes	wall rue	war poet	waviest	weeding	wet pack
vivaria	wadable	wall-tie	war-post	wax bath	Wee Free	wet rent
vivency	waddies	Walther	warrant	wax bean	Weejuns	wet-shod
viverra	wadding	waltzer	warring	waxbill	weekday	wetsuit
vividly	waddler	wambais	warrior	wax doll	weekend	wettest
vivific	wad hook	wameful	war risk	waxiest	weenier	wet time
vixenly	Wafdist	wandery	war road	wax jack	weepier	wetting
Viyella	wafered	wangler	war room	waxlike	weepies	wettish
vizored	waferer	wanhope	warship	wax moth	weepily	wetware
vocable	waffler	wanigan	warthog	wax palm	weeping	wet wing
vocably	waftage	wanluck	wartime	wax shot	weep out	whacked
vocalic	wafting	wannabe	war-torn	wax-tree	weevily	whacker
vocally	wafture	wanness	war-wolf	waxwing	weftage	whack-up
vocoder	wagedom	wannest	war work	waxwork	weigela	whalery
voetsek	Wagener	wannion	war-worn	way back	weighed	whaling
voguish	wagerer	wannish	war zone	waybill	weigher	wham-bam
voicing	waggery	wanrest	washbag	way fare	weigh in	whammed
voidage	wagging	wanruly	washday	wayfare	weighty	whangee
voiture	waggish	wantage	washery	way-gang	weigh up	whanger

wharfie	whippin	wide-cut	wine fly	with pup	Woolpit	wrecker
wharrow	whip-ray	widener	wine-god	witless	woolsey	wren-boy
Wharton	whipsaw	wideout	wine gum	witling	wool wax	Wrenean
wharves	whirled	widgeon	wine-pot	witloof	woomera	Wrenian
whate'er	whirler	widower	wine red	witness	woonerf	wrenlet
what for	whirred	widowly	winesap	wittier	Wooster	wren-tit
what fun	whisker	wielder	wine-vat	wittily	woozier	wrester
Whatman	whiskey	wifedom	wing-bar	witting	woozily	wrestle
whatnot	whisper	wiggery	wing-bow	wit-worm	wordage	wriggle
whatsit	whister	wigging	wing-bud	wizened	wordier	wriggly
what's up	whistle	wiggler	wing-dam	wobbler	wordily	wringer
whatten	whistly	wightly	winglet	woe is me	wording	wrinkle
what way	whitbed	wigless	wingman	woesome	wordman	wrinkly
wheaten	whitely	wig-tree	wingmen	wolf-cry	work-bag	wristed
wheedle	Whiteys	wild cat	wing nut	wolf cub	workbox	wrister
wheeled	whither	wildcat	wing rib	wolf-dog	workday	write in
wheeler	whiting	wild dog	wing-tag	wolfess	workful	write up
wheelie	whitish	Wildean	wing-tip	Wolfian	working	writhed
wheeple	Whitley	wilding	winiest	wolfing	workman	writhen
wheetle	whitlow	wildish	winking	wolfish	workmen	writher
wheezer	whitret	wild man	winkler	wolfkin	work off	writing
wheezle	Whitsun	wild oat	winless	wolf-net	work out	written
whelked	whitten	wild pig	winning	wolfram	workout	writter
whemmel	whitter	wild rye	winnock	wolvish	work-shy	wronger
whene'er	whittle	wiliest	win over	womanly	worktop	wrongly
whereas	whizgig	Wilkism	winsome	wommera	worlded	wrong'un
whereat	whiz-kid	Wilkite	winters	wonkier	worldly	Wrotham
whereby	whizzed	willful	wintery	wonkily	worm-eel	wrought
where'er	whizzer	William	wipe off	wonning	wormery	wrybill
wherein	whoever	willies	wipe-out	wooable	wormian	wryneck
whereof	wholely	willing	wire act	wood ant	wormier	wryness
whereon	wholism	willock	wire bar	wood-axe	worming	wry-tail
whereso	wholist	willowy	wire bcd	woodcut	wormish	W-shaped
whereto	whommel	wilsome	wire-cut	woodeny	worm red	Würmian
wherret	whoness	wimbler	wired-in	wood-god	worn out	wussies
whether	whoofle	wimbrel	wireman	wood-hen	worried	wüstite
whetted	whoompf	wimpily	wiremen	woodier	worrier	Wyandot
whetten	whoopee	wimpish	wire-rim	wooding	worries	wych elm
whetter	whooper	wimpled	wire-tap	woodish	worsest	wyerone
wheyish	whoop-up	wimpler	wireway	woodlet	worship	wysiwyg
which-so	whopped	winceys	wiriest	wood-lot	worsted	WYSIWYG
whicker	whopper	wincher	wised-up	woodman	worth it	xanthan
whiddle	whorage	windage	wise guy	woodmen	wotcher	xanthic
whiffer	whorish	windbag	wise man	wood-oil	would-be	xanthin
whiffet	whorism	wind-egg	wise saw	wood-owl	woulder	Xavante
whiffle	whorled	wind gap	wishful	wood rat	wouldn't	Xenopus
Whiglet	whortle	windier	wishing	wood rot	wouldst	xerarch
while as	whoseso	Windies	wishmay	wood-saw	wounded	xerosis
whilere	who's who	windigo	Wishram	woodsia	wounder	Xiphias
whimper	whuffle	windily	wispier	wood-tar	woundly	xiphoid
whimsey	whummel	winding	wispily	wood-tin	wound up	xograph
whindle	whyever	wind off	wispish	woodwax	wourali	X-shaped
whinger	whyness	windore	wistful	woofits	wrangle	xylenol
whinier	wichert	windowy	wistiti	woofter	wrapped	xylitol
whining	Wichita	windrow	witched	woolder	wrapper	yabbies
whinner	Wickham	Windsor	witchen	wool-fat	wrassle	yachter
whip-hem	wicking	wind-tie	witcher	wool-hat	wrastle	yachtie
whipman	wickiup	wind-way	withers	woolled	wreaker	Yahvist
whip-pan	wickner	wine bar	withery	woollen	wreathe	Yahwism
whipped	wickyup	wine box	with God	woolman	wreaths	Yahwist
whipper	widdrim	wine-dot	withies	woolmen	wreathy	yakking
whippet	wide boy	winefat	without	wool-oil	wrecked	Yamasee

yam-bean	yeasted	yolk-bag	ywroken	zemeism	Zingano	zonular
yandied	yellowy	yolk-sac	zacaton	zemstvo	Zingari	zooidal
yandies	yen hock	yonside	zagging	Zennist	Zingaro	zookers
yangban	Yenisei	York gum	Zairean	Zenonic	zingier	zoology
yang-yin	yenning	Yorkish	Zairese	zeolite	zingily	zooning
Yankton	yen pock	Yorkist	Zairian	zephyry	Zionism	zoonomy
yapness	yen shee	Yoruban	Zairois	zeppole	Zionist	zootaxy
yappier	Yerkish	you hear	Zambian	zeranol	zip code	zootomy
yapping	yes-girl	you know	Zamorin	zero day	ZIP code	zootype
yardage	yeshiva	younger	zanella	zeroing	zipless	zopissa
yardang	yestern	youngly	zaniest	zeroize	zip-lock	zorilla
yard-arm	yetling	young 'un	Zapotec	zero-sum	zippier	zorille
yardarm	yettlin	younker	zappier	zestful	zippily	zorrino
yard-dog	yew tree	youthen	zapping	zestier	zipping	zostera
yardful	Y-fronts	youthly	zarnich	zetetic	zizania	zoukish
yarding	Yiddish	you wait	zealous	Ziebart	zloties	Z-plasty
yard-man	yielder	yperite	zebraed	Ziegler	Zoilean	Z-shaped
yardman	Yi-hsing	Y-shaped	zebrano	zigging	Zoilism	Zulu hat
Yarkand	yin-yang	yttrium	zebrina	zillion	Zoilist	zygaena
yashmak	yipping	Yucatec	zebrine	zinc-air	zoisite	zygosis
Yavapai	yobbery	yukkier	zebroid	zincate	Zolaism	zygotic
yaw axis	yobbish	Yukoner	zebrule	zincian	Zolaist	zymogen
yawnful	yobboes	yule-day	zecchin	zincite	Zöllner	zymosan
yawning	yoghurt	yule log	zedoary	zincode	zomboid	zymosis
year-end	yohimbe	yummier	zelator	zincoes	zonally	zymotic
yearner	yokable	yuppies	zelkova	zinc ore	zonated	zymurgy
year-old	yoke-elm	yuppify	zelotic	zingana	zonking	

EIGHT LETTERS

aandblom	absentee	achillea	actively	adoptive	affright
aardvark	absenter	Achilles	activism	adorable	affronty
aardwolf	absently	Achinese	activist	adorably	affusion
aasvogel	absinthe	achiness	activity	adorally	afghanis
abacuses	absolute	achingly	act of God	Adriatic	aflutter
a bad life	absolver	achromat	actorish	adrogate	Africana
abapical	absonant	achromic	actressy	adroitly	after all
abasedly	absorbed	acicular	actually	adscript	after-wit
abatable	absorber	aciculum	actuator	adularia	after you
abatised	absterge	acid drop	aculeate	adulator	agar-agar
abatises	absterse	acid head	acutance	adultery	agatized
abattoir	abstract	acidness	adamance	aduncity	agedness
a battuta	abstruse	acidosis	Adamical	aduncous	age group
abbacies	absurdly	acidotic	Adam's ale	advanced	agencies
abbatial	abundant	acid rain	adaption	advancer	agenesis
abdicant	abusable	acid rock	adaptive	advisory	agential
abdicate	abutilon	acid salt	addendum	advocaat	agentive
abditory	abutment	acid test	addicted	advocacy	age range
abducens	abutting	acid tide	addition	advocate	ageratum
abducent	academia	aciduria	additive	advowson	ages with
abductor	academic	acorn-cup	additory	aecidial	aggrieve
Aberdeen	acanthus	acorning	addorsed	aecidium	agiotage
aberrant	Accadian	acosmism	adducent	aedicule	agitator
aberrate	accaroid	acosmist	adductor	aegirine	agitprop
abessive	accentor	acoustic	adenitis	aegirite	aglimmer
abetment	accepted	acquaint	adenoids	aegrotat	aglisten
abetting	accepter	acquired	adenoidy	aeration	aglitter
abeyance	acceptor	acquiree	adenomas	aerially	aglycone
abhorred	accident	acquirer	adenylic	aeriform	agnathan
abhorrer	accolade	acreable	adequacy	aerobics	agnation
abidance	accolled	acre-foot	adequate	aerofoil	agnition
a bit much	accollée	acridian	adessive	aerogram	Agnoetae
abjectly	accorder	acridiid	a devil of	aerolite	agnostic
ablation	accoster	acridine	adherend	aerology	Agnus Dei
ablative	accouche	acridity	adherent	aeronaut	agonized
ableness	accoutre	acrimony	adhesion	aeronomy	a good cry
ablution	accredit	acroatic	adhesive	aerostat	a good few
abnegate	accroach	acrobacy	adhocery	Aesopian	a good one
abnormal	accruing	acrodont	adhocism	aesthete	a good sup
abomasum	accuracy	acrolect	Adivasis	aestival	a good way
aborally	accurate	acrolein	adjacent	a fair cop	agraphia
abordage	accursed	acrolith	adjudger	afebrile	agraphic
aborning	accusant	acromial	adjuster	affected	agraphon
abortion	accusing	acromion	adjutage	affecter	agrarian
abortive	accustom	acronych	adjutant	affeeror	agreeing
abounder	Aceldama	acrostic	adjuvant	afferent	agrestal
above all	acentric	acrylate	Adlerian	affiance	agrestic
above par	Acephali	act a part	ad libbed	affinity	agrimony
abrasion	acephaly	actiniae	admire to	affirmer	agrology
abrasive	aceramic	actinian	admiring	afflatus	agronome
abridger	acerbate	actinide	admitted	affluent	agronomy
abrogate	acerbity	actinism	admitter	affodill	ague-tree
abruptly	acervate	actinium	admonish	afforder	aguishly
abscisic	acescent	actinoid	adnation	afforest	a hell of a
abscissa	acetable	actional	adolesce	affrayed	A horizon
abseiler	achiever	activate	adoption	affrayer	aigrette

aiguille	alchemic	alley-oop	alterity	amortise	anechoic
airborne	Alcmanic	alleyway	although	amortize	anestrus
air brake	aldehyde	all-fired	altitude	amperage	anethole
air-brick	alder fly	all flesh	alto clef	amphibia	aneurine
airbrick	alderman	all found	alto horn	amphipod	aneurism
airbrush	aldermen	all fours	altruism	amphorae	aneurysm
air-burst	Alderney	all hands	altruist	amphoral	Angeleno
aircraft	aldoxime	alliable	aluminum	amphoras	angelica
airdrome	aleatico	alliance	alum-rock	amphoric	angelize
Airedale	aleatory	all in all	alum-root	amplexus	angerful
air ferry	ale-bench	all-in-one	alunogen	ampullae	anginoid
airfield	aleberry	allision	alveolar	ampullar	Anglican
air force	alehouse	all-might	alveolus	amputate	angriest
airframe	aleurone	all-night	amacrine	Amratian	angstrom
airified	Aleutian	allocate	amadavat	amuletic	ångström
airiness	alewives	allodial	amandine	amusable	angulate
airliner	alfresco	allodium	Amapondo	amusedly	angulous
Air Miles	Algerian	allogamy	amaracus	amusette	anhedral
airplane	Algerine	allomone	amaranth	amygdala	anhedron
air plant	algicide	allopath	amaretti	amygdale	anhydric
air power	algidity	allotted	amaretto	amygdule	aniconic
air rifle	alginate	allottee	amazedly	anabases	animalic
airscrew	algology	allotter	Amazonic	anabasis	animally
air-shaft	Algonkin	allotype	amberoid	anabatic	animated
airspace	algorism	allotypy	ambiance	anabolic	animater
air speed	alguacil	all-party	ambience	anaconda	animator
airspeed	alguazil	all right	ambition	anaerobe	aniridia
airstrip	alibiing	all round	ambivert	anaglyph	anisated
air-tight	Alicante	all-sorts	ambligon	anagogic	anisette
airtight	alienage	allspice	amblygon	analcime	ankerite
air-to-air	alienate	all the go	Ambonese	analcite	ankylose
air-twist	alienism	all there	ambrette	analecta	annalist
airwaves	alienist	alluring	ambrosia	analects	Annamese
airwoman	alighted	allusion	ambulant	analemma	Annamite
airwomen	alizarin	allusive	ambulate	analogic	annealer
akinesia	alkahest	alluvial	ambusher	analogon	annexion
akinetic	alkalide	alluvian	amelcorn	analogue	annexure
Akkadian	alkalify	alluvion	amenable	analyser	annotate
akosmism	alkaline	alluvium	amenably	analyses	announce
Alabaman	alkalize	allylene	American	analysis	annually
Alabarch	alkaloid	all yours	Amerikan	analytic	annulary
à la carte	alkermes	almagest	amethyst	anapaest	annulate
alacrity	alkoxide	almanack	amiantus	anaphase	annulene
à la daube	alkylate	almeirah	amicable	anaphora	annulled
à la reine	all along	almighty	amicably	anarchal	annulose
alarming	allanite	alms-deed	amidated	anarchic	anodizer
alarmism	allative	almsfolk	amissing	anasarca	anointer
alarmist	all at sea	aloe vera	amitosis	anathema	an old one
à la russe	All Black	alogical	amitotic	anatheme	anomeric
albacore	all-clear	alopecia	ammoniac	Anatolic	Anomoean
Albanian	allegate	alphabet	ammonify	anatomic	anomuran
albiness	allegory	alpha ray	ammonite	ancestor	anoretic
albinism	allegros	Alpinism	ammonium	ancestry	anorexia
albinoid	allelism	Alpinist	ammonoid	anchoret	anorexic
albitite	alleluia	Alsatian	amnesiac	and a half	anorthic
albitize	alleluya	alstonia	amnestic	andesine	Ansafone
alburnum	Allen key	altarage	amniotic	andesite	Anselmic
alcabala	allergen	altar boy	amoebean	Andorran	anserine
alcahest	allergic	altarist	amoeboid	androgen	anserous
alcatras	allerion	alterant	amoretto	anecdota	answerer
alcavala	alley cat	alter ego	amorosos	anecdote	Antabuse

anteater	aperient	apprizer	ardurous	arsedine	asperser
antecede	aperitif	approach	area code	arsehole	aspheric
antedate	aperture	approval	areca nut	arsenate	asphodel
antelope	aphanite	approver	Areopagi	arsenide	asphyxia
antennae	aphasiac	après-ski	argentic	arsenite	aspirant
antennal	aphelion	apricate	argentry	arsenous	aspirate
antennas	aphetism	apronful	arginase	arsonist	aspirins
antepast	aphetize	apterous	arginine	artefact	assailer
ante-post	aphicide	aptitude	Argonaut	arterial	Assamese
anterior	aphorise	apyretic	argosies	arteries	assassin
ante-room	aphorism	apyrexia	arguable	artesian	assemble
antetype	aphorist	aqualung	arguably	artfully	assembly
antevert	aphorize	aquanaut	arguendo	artifact	assenter
anthelia	aphthous	Aquarian	argufied	artifice	assentor
anthelix	apiarian	aquarist	argufier	artiness	asserter
anthemia	apiaries	aquarium	argufies	artistic	assertor
antheral	apiarist	Aquarius	argument	artistly	assessee
anthesis	apically	aquatile	Argus eye	artistry	assessor
antibody	apiculus	aquatint	argutely	art of war	Assidean
antidote	aplastic	aqueduct	Arianism	art paper	assiento
antiform	aplustre	aquiline	Arianize	artsiest	assignee
anti-grav	apoapsis	aquosity	Aridisol	art union	assigner
Antiguan	apocrine	arachide	aridness	arum lily	assignor
anti-hero	apodixis	arachnid	arightly	Aryanism	Assisian
anti-life	apodoses	Araldite	arillate	Aryanize	assister
anti-lock	apodosis	Aramaean	arisings	as a whole	assonant
antilogy	apograph	araneous	aristate	asbestos	assonate
antimere	Apolline	arapaima	Arkansan	ascender	as soon as
antimony	Apollyon	Arawakan	Arkansas	ascetism	assorted
antinode	apologia	a raw deal	ark shell	ascidian	assuager
antinomy	apologue	arbalest	Armagnac	ascocarp	assuming
antiphon	apomixes	arbitral	armament	asconoid	Assyrian
antipode	apomixis	Arbor Day	armature	ascorbic	astatine
antipole	apophony	arboreal	armazine	aseismic	asterion
antipope	apophyge	arboreta	armchair	as ever is	asterisk
antiqued	apoplexy	arborist	Armeniac	as good as	asterism
antiques	aporetic	arborize	Armenian	ash blond	asteroid
anti-self	apospory	arborous	Armenoid	ashimmer	asthenia
antisera	apostasy	arboured	arm in arm	ash-plant	asthenic
anti-tank	apostate	arbuscle	Arminian	ashplant	as though
antithet	apothegm	arcadian	armorial	ashy-grey	as-told-to
antitype	appalled	Arcadian	armories	Asian flu	astonied
antlered	appanage	arcading	armorist	Asianize	astonish
Antonian	apparent	arcanely	armoured	as I see it	astragal
Antonine	appealer	arcanist	armourer	as it were	astrally
antonymy	appear as	Archaean	armozeen	ask after	astringe
ant-plant	appearer	archaise	arms race	ask for it	astucity
antrorse	appeaser	archaism	Army List	askingly	Asturian
ant's eggs	appellee	archaist	army worm	as long as	astutely
anudatta	appellor	archaize	aromatic	Asmonean	as well as
anybody's	appendix	archdean	arpeggio	as one man	asyndeta
anyplace	appetent	archduke	arquebus	asparkle	asystole
anything	appetise	archival	arranger	aspartic	Atabrine
anywhere	appetite	archlute	arrantly	A Special	at a guess
Anzac Day	appetize	arch-mime	arrestee	aspected	at anchor
aoristic	applause	archness	arrester	asperate	at a pinch
Apachean	apple-bee	archwise	arrestor	asperges	at a price
apagogic	apple-pie	arc light	Arretine	asperity	ataraxia
apastron	appliqué	arcology	arrive at	aspermia	ataraxic
apatheia	apposite	arcuated	arrogant	aspermic	at a touch
apathist	appraise	ardently	arrogate	asperous	at bottom

atenolol	audacity	aventail	Babygros	back-word	ballahoo
at hazard	audience	aventure	babyhood	backyard	ballahou
atheling	audit ale	averager	babykins	bacon fat	ball clay
Athenian	auditing	averment	baby-like	Baconian	ballcock
atherine	audition	averring	baby talk	bacteria	balletic
atheroma	auditive	aversely	Bacardis	Bactrian	ball game
athetize	auditory	aversion	baccarat	baculine	ballgirl
athetoid	auditual	aversive	bacchant	Badarian	ball gown
athletic	augelite	aviaries	Bacchant	bad blood	ball hawk
Athonite	au gratin	aviation	bacchiac	bad books	ballista
atlantal	augurate	aviatrix	bacchius	bad break	ball-like
atlantes	augurial	avidious	bachelor	bad faith	ballocks
Atlantic	auguries	avifauna	bacillar	badge-man	ballonet
at length	augurous	avionics	bacillus	badgerer	balloted
at livery	Augustal	avocados	backache	badigeon	balloter
at nights	Augustan	Avogadro	backband	badinage	ballpark
atom bomb	augustly	avoucher	back beat	badlands	ball-peen
atomical	aularian	avowable	backbeat	bad loser	ball-race
atomiser	aulnager	avowedly	backbite	badly off	ballroom
atomizer	auntship	avulsion	back-bond	bad mouth	ballyhoo
atonally	auramine	awakener	backbone	bad penny	ballyrag
atrament	aurelian	awanting	back-cast	bad scran	balmiest
at random	aureolin	away game	backchat	Baedeker	balmoral
at reflux	au revoir	away with	backcomb	baffling	balneary
atremble	auricula	awearied	backdate	baggager	balsamic
atrocity	aurorean	aweather	back door	baggiest	baluster
atrophic	Ausonian	awninged	backdoor	bagpiper	bamboula
atropine	austerer	aw-shucks	back down	baguette	banality
atropism	Austrian	axiality	backdown	Bahamian	banalize
atropous	autarchy	axillant	backdrop	Bahraini	banausic
a truce to	autarkic	axillary	backer-up	bailable	bandanna
at sermon	authorly	axiology	backfall	bail-bond	bandboxy
at source	autistic	axle-tree	backfill	bail-dock	bandeaux
at strain	autobahn	axolemma	backfire	bailiery	bandelet
attacher	autocade	axonemal	backflip	bailment	banderol
attacker	autocode	axoplasm	backhand	bailsman	bandfish
attar-gul	autocrat	axostyle	back-heel	bailsmen	bandiest
attemper	auto-da-fé	aye-green	backland	Bakelite	banditry
attendee	autogamy	Ayrshire	backlash	bake-meat	banditti
attender	autogiro	ayurveda	backless	Baker day	bandlike
attentat	autogyro	azedarac	back-lift	bakeries	bandpass
attercop	autoharp	azotemia	back-line	bakeware	bandsman
attester	autoland	azoturia	backlist	Bakewell	bandsmen
attestor	autology	Aztec hop	backmost	bakingly	bandster
at the bar	autolyse	baasskap	back on to	balanced	banewort
at the end	automacy	Baathism	backpack	balancer	bangalow
at the top	automata	Baathist	back pain	balanoid	bangster
Atticise	automate	babelish	backrest	bald coot	bangstry
atticism	automath	babelism	back room	baldhead	bangtail
Atticist	autonomy	babelize	back-rope	bald ibis	banisher
Atticize	autopsic	babirusa	back seat	baldness	banister
Attic wit	autoptic	babouche	backside	baldpate	banjoist
attiring	autosome	babushka	back-spin	Balearic	banjolin
attitude	autotomy	baby beef	backspin	balefire	bankable
attorney	autotype	baby blue	backstay	baleless	bank-barn
attritor	autumnal	baby boom	back-stop	Balinese	bank bill
at whiles	autunite	baby bust	backstop	balinger	bank book
atwitter	avadavat	baby-doll	back talk	balkiest	bank card
atypical	availing	baby face	backveld	ballader	bankerly
aubretia	avanious	baby-farm	backward	balladic	bank-full
aucupate	Ave Maria	baby food	backwash	balladry	bankless

banknote	baronial	bastardy	bearably	bee-biter	bellower
Bank Rate	baronian	bastille	bear a bob	bee-bread	bell pull
bankroll	baronies	Batavian	bearance	beech-oil	bell push
bankrupt	barostat	bateless	bear arms	bee dance	bell-rope
banksian	barouche	bateleur	bear away	bee-eater	bell tent
bankside	barrable	batement	bearbind	beefcake	bell-wire
banksman	barracan	Batesian	bear date	beefiest	bellwort
bank vole	barragan	Bath chap	beardlet	beef loaf	bellyful
bannered	barragon	bath cube	bear down	beef-wood	belly-god
bannerer	barranca	bathetic	bear hard	beefwood	be lost in
banneret	barrator	bat-horse	bearherd	bee plant	be lost on
bannerol	barratry	bathotic	bearlike	beeregar	be lost to
banterer	Barr body	bathrobe	bear's ear	beer hall	below par
bantling	barrenly	bathroom	bearskin	beeriest	Bel Paese
banxring	barrette	bat-money	bear tack	beerless	belt down
baptizer	barrulet	Batswana	bearward	beer pump	beltless
barathea	bar stool	battalia	bear with	beeswing	belt line
Barbados	barterer	batteler	beastish	beetroot	be mother
barbaric	Barthian	battered	be at abay	beetster	be myself
barbasco	bartizan	batterer	beatable	befallen	bench-end
barbecue	Bartlett	battiest	beat down	befitted	benchlet
barberry	baryonic	batwoman	beaten-up	beflower	bendable
barbette	barytone	batwomen	beatific	befogged	bend over
barbican	basaltic	baudekin	beatster	befriend	bendwise
barbicel	basanite	baudrons	beat time	befringe	beneaped
barbiers	bascinet	bauhinia	beat to it	befuddle	Benedick
barbital	baseball	bauxitic	beauties	begetter	benefact
barbiton	baseband	Bavarian	beautify	beggarly	benefice
barbitos	baseborn	bawdiest	beavered	beginner	Bengalis
Barbizon	baselard	bayadère	be baking	begirdle	benignly
barbless	baseless	bayberry	bebopper	begotten	Beninese
Barbudan	baseline	Bayesian	béchamel	begrease	benjamin
barbwire	base load	Bay State	bechance	begrudge	Benjamin
bar chart	basement	bdellium	Bechuana	beguiler	bent brow
bardling	baseness	bdelloid	beclothe	be hard on	bentwood
bardship	base-pair	beach bum	become of	behave to	benzilic
bareback	base rate	bead-folk	becoming	behavior	benzoate
barefoot	basic dye	beadiest	becudgel	beheadal	benzylic
barehead	basicity	beadlike	be cut out	behemoth	be packed
bareness	basic pay	bead-roll	bedabble	behither	beplumed
baresark	basidium	beadsman	bedarken	beholden	bepommel
barflies	basilary	beadsmen	bedazzle	beholder	bepowder
Bargello	basilect	bead-tree	bed-cover	behovely	bepraise
bargeman	Basilian	bead-work	bedcover	be hung up	bepuzzle
barghest	basilica	beadwork	beddable	be in a wax	bequeath
bar-goose	basilisk	be afraid	be dear of	be in a way	berattle
bar graph	basinful	be agreed	bedeguar	bejabers	berberis
baritone	basketry	be ailing	bedesman	bejesuit	berberry
barkless	basophil	beak-head	bedimmed	belabour	berceuse
bark-tree	basquine	beak-iron	bedlinen	bel canto	berdache
barmiest	Basquish	beakless	bedmaker	belfries	bereaved
barm-skin	bassarid	beaklike	be down on	believer	bergamot
barnacle	bass clef	beam-ends	be down to	belittle	bergenia
Barnardo	bass drum	beamless	bedplate	Belizean	berghaan
barn-ball	bassette	beam-tree	bedrench	bellbird	berg wind
barn door	bassetto	bean ball	bedskirt	bell-buoy	beriberi
barnyard	bass-horn	bean curd	bedstead	bell-cord	Berliner
barogram	bassinet	bean-meal	bedstock	bell-cote	Bermudan
barometz	bass viol	beanpole	bedstraw	belleric	Bermudas
baronage	basswood	bean tree	bedtable	bell-like	berthage
baroness	bastarda	bearable	bedwards	bell lyra	berthing

be rude to	Bible-box	billiard	Bismarck	blandish	blotting
beryllia	biblical	billiken	bistable	blankety	blow away
bescrawl	Biblical	billions	bistoury	blarneys	blow-back
bescreen	bibulous	billycan	bit by bit	blastema	blow-ball
be seated	bickerer	bilobate	bitchery	blast off	blowfish
beseemly	bicolour	bimanous	bitchier	blastoid	blowhard
be served	biconvex	bimanual	bitchily	blastula	blow-hole
beshadow	bicuspid	bimbashi	bite back	blatancy	blowhole
be shot of	bicycler	bimbette	bite-size	blaze out	blowiest
be shut of	bicyclic	binaries	bitingly	blazered	blowlamp
besieger	bid a bead	binaural	bitterly	blazoner	blow over
besilver	biddable	bindi-eye	bittiest	blazonry	blowpipe
beslaver	biddance	bind over	biunique	bleacher	blow upon
besmirch	biddy-bid	bindweed	bivalent	bleakish	blowzier
besmutch	bidental	bingeing	biweekly	blearier	blowzily
be soft on	bidibidi	bin liner	bixbyite	blearily	blubbery
besotted	biennale	binnacle	biyearly	bleeding	blubbing
besought	biennial	binomial	blabbing	bleeping	bluchers
bespoken	biennium	binormal	black ant	blencher	bludge on
bespread	bifacial	bio-assay	black art	Blenheim	bludgeon
besprent	bifidity	bioassay	black ash	blennies	blue baby
Bessemer	bifolium	biocidal	black box	blenniid	blueback
best girl	biforked	biogenic	blackboy	blesbuck	bluebell
bestiary	biformed	biologic	black bun	blessing	blue bice
bestness	bigamies	biometry	black cap	blighted	blue-bill
bestowal	bigamist	biomorph	blackcap	blighter	bluebird
bestower	bigamous	bionomic	black dog	blimbing	blue book
bestreak	Big Apple	biopsies	black eye	blimpery	blue-bush
bestrewn	bigarade	bioscope	blackfly	blimpish	blue-chip
bestride	Big Board	biotical	black fox	blindage	blue-coat
bestrode	big chief	biparous	black gum	blind god	blue crab
bestrown	Big Chief	biparted	black ice	blind gut	blue duck
beta plus	Big Daddy	biphasic	blacking	blinding	blue-eyed
beta test	big eater	biphenyl	black ink	blindish	bluefish
betatron	bigeminy	biplanar	blackish	blind pig	blue funk
betel-nut	biggonet	bi-racial	Black Jew	blinkard	blue gown
Bethesda	big house	biramose	blackleg	blinking	blue-grey
bethwack	big money	biramous	black man	blipping	blue hare
bethwine	big mouth	birching	black neb	blissful	blue hawk
betonies	big noise	birch-rod	black oak	blissout	Blue John
betrayal	bignonia	bird bath	black oil	blistery	blue laws
betrayer	big smoke	birdcage	black out	blithely	blue line
bevatron	big stick	bird call	blackout	blizzard	blue ling
bevelled	big stiff	birdless	black-pot	blockade	blue moon
beveller	big-timer	bird-life	black rat	blockage	blueness
beverage	big wheel	birdlike	Black Rod	blocking	blue-nose
Bevin boy	bijugate	birdlime	black tar	blockish	blue note
bewailer	bilabial	birdseed	black tea	block out	blue pill
bewigged	bilander	bird's-eye	black tie	block tin	blue roan
bewilder	bilberry	bird shot	black til	bloc vote	blue rock
be wise to	bile duct	birdsong	black tin	blondine	blue ruin
bewrayer	biliment	birdying	blacktop	blondish	blue spot
bezantee	bilinear	birretta	bladdery	bloodier	blue-wing
B horizon	billable	birthday	blagging	bloodily	bluff off
biannual	billeted	birthing	blagueur	blood red	bluntish
biassing	billetee	biscacha	blah-blah	blood-tub	blur over
biaswise	billeter	Biscayan	Blakeian	bloomers	blurrier
biathlon	billfish	biscuity	blamable	bloomery	blurring
bibacity	billfold	bisector	blameful	blooming	blushful
bibation	billhead	bisexual	blancoed	blossomy	blustery
bibition	billhook	bishoply	blancoes	blotless	boarding

boar-fish	bolt-hole	book-post	bouldery	brancher	brideman
boastful	boltless	book-rest	bouncier	branchia	bridging
boatable	bolt-rope	bookshop	bouncily	brandies	brief-bag
boat-bill	bombarde	book-wise	bouncing	brandise	briefing
boat-deck	bombilla	bookwork	boundary	brandish	brigalow
boatfuls	bomb-site	bookworm	bounding	brand new	brighten
boat-hook	bombykol	boom town	bounties	brangler	brightly
boatlift	bona fide	boondock	bountith	branlike	brim-full
boatload	bonallie	boongary	bourtree	brassage	brimless
boat neck	bona-roba	bootable	boutique	brassard	brimming
boat race	bonavist	bootakin	bouzouki	brass hat	brim over
boat-tail	bondager	boot camp	bovarism	brassica	brindled
boat-yard	bond-land	Boot Hill	bovarize	brassier	brine-pan
bobachee	bondmaid	boot-hose	bovinely	brassies	bring low
bob-apple	bondsman	bootikin	bowelled	brassily	bring off
bobbinet	bondsmen	bootjack	bowenite	bratchet	bring out
bobby pin	bonc ache	boot-lace	boweries	bratling	brisling
bobolink	bonefire	bootlace	bowlfuls	brat pack	bristols
bobskate	bonefish	bootless	bowl game	brattery	britchel
bobsy-die	bonehead	bootlick	bowl over	brattice	Britonic
bobwhite	bone idle	boot-tree	bowsprit	brattish	broacher
bocconia	bone-lace	boozeroo	box-cloth	braunite	broad-axe
bodement	bone lazy	booziest	box elder	brawnier	broadish
Bode's law	boneless	boracite	box pleat	brazenly	broadway
bode well	bone-meal	borassus	box score	braziery	broccoli
bodeword	bonemeal	Bordeaux	box-thorn	brazilin	brochure
bodiless	bone-seed	bordello	boyishly	bread bin	brodekin
bodingly	bone-yard	borderer	Boy Scout	breakage	broderer
Bodleian	bongrace	bord-land	boy's-love	breaking	broidery
body blow	bonhomie	borecole	boys' play	break off	brokenly
bodyhood	bonhomme	borehole	B-picture	break out	brollies
body shop	Boniface	boresome	brabbler	breakout	bromelia
bodysuit	boniform	boringly	bracelet	breasted	bromelin
body type	boniness	borrower	brachial	breathed	bromidic
body wave	bonitary	borrow of	brachium	breather	Brompton
bodywork	bonneted	boss-eyed	brackeny	breeches	bronchia
body wrap	bonnibel	bossiest	brackish	breeding	bronchus
Boehmist	bonniest	boss-ship	braconid	breed out	bronzite
boehmite	bonsense	boss-shot	bracteal	breeze up	brood-hen
Boeotian	bons mots	bostangi	bractlet	breezier	broodier
boffinry	bonspiel	bosthoon	Bradbury	breezily	broodily
bog berry	bontebok	botanise	braggart	breloque	brookite
bogeyman	bony fish	botanist	braggery	brennage	brooklet
boggiest	boob tube	botanize	bragging	bretelle	brotulid
bog onion	boobyish	botchery	brahminy	bretessy	brougham
Bohairic	boogaloo	boteroll	braiding	brethren	brouhaha
Bohemian	boohooed	botflies	brain-box	breveted	brow-band
bohereen	bookable	both laws	brainbox	breviary	browbeat
boil away	bookcase	both ways	brain-fag	brewster	browless
boil down	book club	botryoid	brainier	Brewster	brown ale
boil over	book-fell	botrytis	brainily	Briarean	brown bag
boistous	book-hand	bottle-oh	brainish	Briareus	brown eye
bold-face	bookkeep	bottomed	brain-pan	bribable	brown fat
boldface	bookland	bottomer	brainpan	brickbat	Brownian
boldness	bookless	bottomry	brakeman	brickish	browning
Bolivian	booklike	bottom up	brakemen	brick-red	Browning
bollocks	bookling	botulism	brake pad	bridally	brownish
bollworm	book-lung	bouffant	brake van	bridalty	Brownism
boloneys	bookmark	bough-pot	brakevan	bride-ale	Brownist
Bolshies	book name	boughten	Bramleys	bride-bed	brown job
bolt-head	book page	bouillon	branched	bride-cup	brown-out

brown owl	bull-dust	burritos	bylander	calabaza	calypsos
brown rat	bulletin	burrower	bylawman	caladium	calyptra
brown top	bullfrog	burr-pump	by my hand	calamari	camalote
browsing	bullgine	bursitis	by myself	calamary	cambiums
brow tine	bullhead	burst out	by nature	calambac	camboose
bruilzie	bull-horn	bushbaby	by-passer	calamine	Cambrian
bruising	bullhorn	bush-bean	by reason	calamint	cameleer
Brumaire	bull huss	bushbuck	by rights	calamite	cameline
brumbies	bull-kelp	bush burn	Byronism	calamity	camellia
Brummies	bull-neck	bushfire	by spurts	calandra	cameloid
bruncher	bull-nose	bushiest	by square	calanoid	camelote
brunette	bullocky	bushless	byssuses	calathus	camerate
brushite	bull-pine	bushline	by starts	calcanea	camerist
brush off	bullring	bushment	by-street	calcanei	camisado
Brussels	bullrout	bush-rope	by the bye	calcific	Camisard
brutally	bullrush	bush-sick	by the way	calciner	camisole
brutedom	bull's-eye	bushveld	by weight	calcitic	camomile
bryology	bullshit	bush-walk	caatinga	calcrete	camoudie
bryonies	bull-weed	business	caballer	calc spar	campagna
bryozoan	bull-whip	buskined	Cabernet	calcspar	campaign
bryozoon	bullwort	bust a gut	cabin boy	calc-tuff	camp-fire
B Special	bully boy	busteous	cabining	calculus	campfire
bubaline	bully off	bustiest	Cabistan	calendar	camphene
bubblier	bullyrag	bustious	cable car	calender	camphine
buccally	buln-buln	bustuous	cable-ese	calfhood	campiest
buccinum	bumbaste	busybody	cableway	calfless	camp it up
bucellas	bum-clock	busyness	caboceer	calflike	camp oven
buckaroo	bum fluff	busywork	caboched	calf love	campshed
buckbean	bummaree	butanoic	cabochon	calfskin	camp-site
buck-bush	bump-ball	butanone	caboodle	calibred	campsite
bucketed	bumpiest	butcher's	caboshed	calicoes	campuses
buck-horn	bump into	butchery	cabotage	caliduct	camshaft
buckhorn	bum's rush	butoxide	cabriole	calipash	camstone
buck-jump	bum steer	butteris	cachalot	caliphal	Canadian
buckle to	buncombe	butter up	cachexia	Calippic	canaille
Buckley's	bundle up	butt-head	cachucha	callable	canalise
buckling	bun fight	buttoned	cacodoxy	callaloo	canalize
buckshee	bungalow	button up	cacology	call away	Canarese
buckshot	bungarra	buttress	cactuses	call back	Canarian
buckskin	bunged up	butt weld	cadastre	call down	canaries
Buddhism	bung-hole	but which	caddying	call-girl	canaster
Buddhist	bungling	butylate	cadenced	call home	cancelli
buddleia	bunny-hug	butylene	caducean	calliard	cancrine
budgeree	bunodont	butyrate	caduceus	calliope	cancroid
budgerow	buntline	butyrous	caducity	calliper	candidly
budgeted	buoyancy	buy money	caducous	call note	candy ass
buff coat	Burberry	buzz-bomb	caecitis	callosal	candy bar
buffeted	burglary	buzz-word	caesious	call-over	candy-man
buggiest	burgonet	buzzword	caesural	callowly	cane toad
bughouse	burgrave	by chance	caesuras	call sign	cane-work
Buginese	burgundy	by choice	café noir	call time	Canfield
bugology	buriable	by-corner	caffeine	call upon	can-hooks
building	Burkinan	by deputy	cafuffle	calmness	canicule
bulberry	burletta	by design	cage bird	Calor gas	caninity
bulblike	burliest	by dint of	cageling	calories	canister
bulfinch	burnable	by-effect	cage-work	calotype	canities
bulkhead	burn away	by George	caginess	calvados	cankered
bulkiest	burn down	by halves	cajolery	calvaria	cannabis
bullated	Burnsian	by heaven	cake-hole	calx vive	cannella
bull-dike	burnside	by inches	cakewalk	calycine	cannelon
bulldoze	burnt-out	by itself	calabash	calycled	cannibal

canniest	caracara	carrozzi	casually	cavalier	cerclage
cannikin	caracole	carry-all	casualty	cavatina	cerebral
cannonry	caragana	carry-cot	catacomb	cavayard	cerebrum
cannulae	carangid	carrycot	catalase	caveatee	cerement
cannulas	carapace	carrying	catalyse	caveator	ceremony
canoeing	carbamic	carry off	catalyst	cave bear	cernuous
canoeist	carbamyl	carry out	catalyze	cave-fish	cerotate
canoness	carbinol	Carshuni	catamite	cavelike	cerulean
canonise	carbolic	carstone	catapult	caverned	cervelat
canonist	carbonic	cart-body	cataract	cavesson	cervical
canonize	carbonyl	cartfuls	catch-all	cavilled	cervices
canon law	carboxyl	cart-load	catchfly	caviller	Cesarean
canoodle	carburet	cartload	catchier	cavitary	Cesarian
canopied	carcajou	cartoony	catchily	cavitate	cessavit
canopies	carcanet	cart-road	catching	cavities	cesspipe
canorous	carceral	cart-shed	catch out	cavy-yard	cesspool
can skill	cardamom	cart tail	catechin	cayenned	Cestrian
canstick	cardamum	cart-whip	catechol	cecidium	cetacean
cantator	card case	carucage	category	cecropia	ceterach
cant-hook	card game	carucate	catenary	Celarent	cetology
canticle	cardigan	caruncle	catenate	celature	chabutra
cantikoy	cardinal	carve out	catenoid	celeriac	cha-chaed
cant-line	cardines	caryatid	cateress	celerity	chaconne
cantonal	cardioid	Casanova	catering	celibacy	chadless
cantoned	carditis	cascabel	Cathayan	celibate	chafe-wax
cantoris	card-room	casebook	cathedra	cellared	chaffron
cantrail	card vote'	case-load	catheter	cellarer	Chagatai
canzonet	carefree	caseload	cathetus	cellaret	chagigah
Caodaism	careless	casemate	cathexes	cellated	chainlet
Caodaist	Carelian	casement	cathexis	cell-like	chainsaw
capacity	caretake	case-shot	cathodal	cellular	chain-saw
capeador	care-worn	case-weed	cathodic	cell wall	chair-bed
Cape cart	careworn	casework	catholic	cembalos	chair-car
capeline	cargador	case-worm	Catholic	cementer	chairman
capeskin	cargoose	cashable	cat-house	cementum	chairmen
Capetian	carillon	cash book	Catiline	cemetery	chalazae
Cape-weed	carinate	cash card	cationic	Cencibel	chalazal
capitana	caritive	cashcard	Catonian	cenobite	Chaldaic
capitano	carmined	cash crop	cat's-foot	cenotaph	Chaldean
capitate	carminic	cash desk	cat's-head	Cenozoic	chaldron
capitula	carnally	cash down	cat's-meat	censurer	chaliced
cap-money	Carnatic	cash flow	cat's-tail	censuses	chalkier
caponier	carnauba	cashless	catstick	centaury	chalk out
caponise	carneous	cashmere	cattiest	centavos	chalk-pit
caponize	carnifex	cash-sale	cattleya	centrale	challahs
capotted	carnival	cassette	Catullan	centring	chaloner
cap-paper	Carolean	Castalie	Caucasic	centrism	chalonic
capriole	Carolina	castanet	caucused	centrist	chaloupe
capriped	Caroline	cast away	caucuses	centrode	Chambéry
caproate	carolled	castaway	caudally	centroid	chambray
caprylic	caroller	cast down	caudated	centuple	champain
caprylyl	carotene	casteism	caudicle	cephalic	champers
capsicum	carousal	casteist	caudillo	cephalin	champion
capsizal	carousel	castelet	caught up	cephalon	chance on
capstone	carouser	castelry	cauldron	ceramics	chancery
capsular	carpeted	cast iron	caulicle	ceramist	chancier
captious	car phone	castling	causable	cerastes	chancily
capturer	carplike	cast lots	causally	ceration	chandler
capuchin	carriage	castrate	causerie	ceratite	change up
Capuchin	carriole	castrati	causeway	Cerberus	chanties
capybara	carritch	castrato	cautious	cercaria	chaology

chapatti	chemosis	chip shot	Christer	cingular	classier
chapbook	chempaka	chirayta	Christie	cingulum	classify
chapeaux	chemurgy	chiretta	Christly	cinnabar	classily
chapelry	chenille	chirpier	chromate	cinnamic	classism
chaperon	chequeen	chirpily	chromite	cinnamon	classist
chapiter	Cherokee	chirping	chromium	cinnamyl	class war
chaplain	cherries	chirrupy	chromone	cinqfoil	clattery
chapless	cherubic	chit-chat	chromous	cipherer	Claudian
chapping	cherubim	chittack	chrysene	Circinus	clausula
characin	Cheshire	chitties	chthonic	circlage	clavated
charcoal	chessman	chivalry	chubbier	circling	clavecin
chariest	chessmen	chloasma	chubbily	circuity	clavicle
charisma	chess set	chlorate	chuckler	circular	claviger
charlady	chestful	chloride	chuck off	circuses	claw back
charlock	chestier	chlorine	chuck out	circussy	claw-back
charmful	chestily	chlorite	chugging	cirriped	clawback
charming	chestnut	chloroma	chummage	Ciskeian	clawless
charring	cheverel	chlorous	chummery	cislunar	clawlike
Chartism	chewable	choanoid	chummier	cisterna	claylike
Chartist	chewiest	Choctaws	chummily	cis-trans	claymore
chase-gun	chew over	choicely	chump end	cistvaen	clay pipe
chasseur	Cheyenne	choirboy	chumship	citation	Clayton's
chastely	Chiantis	choirman	chunkier	citatory	cleading
chastise	chiasmus	choirmen	chupatti	citified	clean-cut
chastity	chiastic	choir nun	chupatty	citruses	cleanish
chastize	Chibchan	choke off	churchly	city desk	clean out
chasuble	chicaner	chokidar	churinga	city farm	clean-run
chatelet	Chicanos	chokiest	churlish	cityfied	cleanser
chatline	chick-pea	choleric	churning	city gent	clearage
chat show	chickpea	choliamb	churn out	city hall	clear-air
chattery	chiefdom	chondrin	churn-owl	cityless	clear-cut
chattier	chiefess	choo-choo	chutneys	city page	clearing
chattily	chiffony	choosier	chutzpah	cityward	clearish
chatting	childbed	choosily	chylific	civet cat	clear off
chauffer	childish	chop-chop	chyluria	civil day	clear-out
chaunter	children	choppier	ciabatta	civilian	clearway
chawdron	chiliasm	choppily	cibarial	civilise	cleavage
cheapish	chiliast	chopping	cibarian	civility	cleavers
cheatery	chillier	chop suey	cibarium	civilize	clecking
chebulic	chillies	chopsuey	ciborium	civil law	cleft lip
checkers	chillily	choragic	cicatrix	civil war	cleidoic
check-nut	chill out	choragus	cicelies	clabbery	clematis
check off	chilopod	chorally	cicerone	clackety	clemency
check out	chimaera	chordate	ciceroni	cladding	clencher
checkout	chimeric	chording	cicisbeo	claimant	clergess
check sum	chimneys	chore-boy	ciderist	clambake	clergies
checksum	China ink	choregus	ciderkin	clammier	clerical
chedarim	Chinaman	choriamb	ci-devant	clammily	clerihew
chee-chee	Chinamen	C horizon	cigarito	clamming	clerkage
cheekier	China tea	chorused	ciliated	clangour	clerkdom
cheekily	chin-chin	choruses	Cilician	clannish	clerkess
cheerful	chinkara	chota peg	Cilicism	clanship	clerkish
cheerier	Chinkies	chouette	cimarron	clansman	cleruchy
cheerily	chinless	choultry	cimbalom	clansmen	cleveite
cheese it	Chinooks	chow-chow	Cimbrian	clap-dish	cleverer
cheesier	chins wag	chow mein	cimmaron	clapping	cleverly
cheewink	chipmunk	Chrisake	cinchona	claptrap	clew-line
chelator	Chippewa	chrismal	cincture	claqueur	cliental
cheliped	chippies	chrismon	cineaste	clarence	clientry
Chellean	chipping	Christed	cinéaste	clarinet	climatal
chemical	chip-shop	christen	cinerary	Clarisse	climatic

clinamen	Club Soda	cockerel	coiffure	colt foal	complect
clincher	clubster	cock-eyed	coigning	colthood	complete
clingier	clueless	cockiest	coinable	colubrid	complice
clinging	clumpier	cock-loft	coincide	Columban	complied
clinical	clumpish	cockneys	co-inhere	columbic	complier
clinkery	clumsier	cock's egg	coistrel	Columbus	complies
clinking	clumsily	cockspur	coke-oven	columnal	compline
clip-clop	clunkier	cocksure	colander	columnar	complish
clipping	clupeoid	cocktail	colation	columned	composal
cliquier	cly-faker	cocoanut	Colchian	Comanche	composed
cliquish	clypeate	cocobolo	cold bath	comatose	composer
cliquism	cnidocil	coco palm	cold call	combated	compotus
clitoral	coach-box	coco-plum	cold cuts	combater	compound
clitoris	coach-dog	cocorite	cold deck	comb-back	compress
cloaking	coachful	code book	cold feet	combined	comprise
clobiosh	coachman	code name	cold lead	combiner	compulse
clock off	coachmen	codiaeum	cold meat	combless	computer
cloddish	coaction	codified	coldness	comblike	computor
clodpate	coactive	codifier	cold-slaw	come away	computus
clodpole	coadjust	codifies	coldslaw	come back	comrogue
clodpoll	coagency	codology	cold snap	comeback	con amore
cloggier	coagment	codomain	cold sore	comedian	conarium
clogging	coagulin	co-domini	cold wave	comedies	conation
cloister	coagulum	codpiece	cold work	comedist	conative
clonally	coal dust	co-driver	colerake	come down	concause
clopping	coalesce	cod seine	coleseed	comedown	conceder
closable	coalface	cod's-head	coleslaw	come home	conceity
closed-in	coal fire	co-editor	colewort	come into	conceive
close off	coalfish	coeffect	coliform	comelier	concerti
close out	coal-hole	coelomic	coliseum	comelily	concerto
close-run	coalizer	coenurus	collagen	comeling	concetto
close-set	coal mine	coenzyme	collapse	come near	conchies
closeted	coalmine	coercion	collards	come over	conchoid
cloth-cap	coal-sack	coercive	collared	cometary	conclave
clothier	coal-seam	co-estate	collator	come true	conclude
clothing	coarsely	coevally	colleger	come upon	concrete
clotpole	coarsish	coextend	collider	comfiest	condense
clotting	coassume	cofactor	colliery	comfreys	condoler
clottish	coatless	coffered	collogue	comingle	condoner
cloudier	coatroom	cofferer	colloque	comitant	conducti
cloudily	coat-tail	cofferet	colloquy	comitial	condylar
cloudlet	coattest	coffined	colluder	comities	conelike
clownery	co-author	cogently	collyria	commando	conferee
clownish	cobaltic	cogitate	colobine	commence	conferva
cloyless	cobwebby	cognatic	colobium	commenda	confetti
cloysome	Coca-Cola	cognizee	coloboma	commerce	confider
clubbier	coccagee	cognizor	colonial	commoner	confined
clubbing	Cocceian	cognomen	colonies	commonly	confiner
clubbish	coccidia	cognosce	colonise	commonty	conflate
clubbism	coccyges	cognovit	colonist	communal	conflict
clubbist	coccyxes	cogueful	colonize	communer	confocal
club foot	cochleae	cog-wheel	colopexy	commuter	confound
club-haul	cochlear	cogwheel	colophon	comozant	confrère
clubland	cochlite	cohelper	colorant	compadre	confront
clublike	cockaded	coherent	coloring	compages	confused
clubmate	cockatoo	cohering	colossal	comparer	confuter
clubmoss	cock-bead	cohesion	colossus	compesce	congaing
club-root	cock-bill	cohesive	colotomy	compiler	congener
clubroot	cockboat	cohobate	coloured	compital	congiary
club-rush	cock crow	coiffeur	colourer	complain	conglobe
club soda	cockcrow	coiffing	colour in	compleat	Congoese

Congo pea	convulse	cordwain	corsetry	courtesy	cram-full
congrats	cony-fish	cordwood	Corsican	courtier	cramming
congress	conynger	core area	cortical	courtlet	cramoisy
Congreve	cony-wool	co-regent	cortices	court-man	crampoon
conicity	cooeeing	coreless	cortisol	couscous	crane-fly
conicoid	cooingly	core loss	corundum	cousinly	craneman
conidial	cookable	core time	corvette	cousinry	craniate
conidium	cookbook	core tool	Corybant	covalent	craniums
coniform	cook-camp	Corfiote	Corycian	covenant	crankier
conjoint	cookless	Coriolis	coryphée	Coventry	crankily
conjugal	cook-maid	corkiest	cosecant	coverage	crankous
conjunct	cookshop	corklike	cosherer	coverall	crankpin
conjurer	cookware	cork lino	cosiness	covercle	crannied
conjuror	coolabah	cork tree	cosmetic	covering	crannies
conniver	coolamon	corkwing	cosmical	coverlet	crap game
conodont	coolibah	corkwood	cosseted	co-versed	crappier
conoidal	cooliman	corn baby	costated	covertly	crapping
conoidic	coolness	corn-ball	costless	coveting	crashing
conquest	coonjine	corn beef	costlier	covetise	crash pad
conserve	coonskin	corn cake	costmary	covetous	crassula
consider	coon song	corn chip	cost-plus	covinous	crateful
consoler	co-optate	corn crib	cost push	cowardly	crateman
consommé	co-option	corneous	costumer	cowberry	crateral
conspire	co-optive	cornered	cosy up to	cow-cocky	cratonic
constant	co-ossify	cornerer	cot death	cow-heart	cravenly
constate	cop a plea	cornetcy	cotectic	cow-hitch	craw-craw
construe	copastor	cornetti	co-tenant	cow-horse	crawfish
consular	cophosis	cornetto	coterell	cow-house	crayfish
consulta	copiable	corn-flag	cot-house	cowl neck	craziest
consumed	coplanar	corn-husk	cotsetla	co-worker	crazy ant
consumer	copperas	corniced	Cotswold	co-writer	creakier
consumpt	copperer	corniche	cottaged	cow shark	creakily
contango	coppiced	cornicle	cottager	cow-wheat	cream bun
contempt	coprosma	corniest	cottagey	coxalgia	creamery
contessa	copulate	Corn Laws	cotterel	coxalgic	cream ice
continua	copyable	corn lily	cottoner	coxiness	creamier
continue	copybook	cornmeal	cotton on	coxswain	creamily
continuo	copydesk	corn-pipe	cotton to	cozenage	cream nut
contline	copy-edit	corn pone	cotton up	crabbier	cream off
contorni	copyhold	corn-rent	cotyloid	crabbily	cream tea
contorno	copyread	corn rose	couchant	crabbing	creatine
contract	coq au vin	cornrows	couching	crab-hole	creation
contrail	coquetry	corn silk	coughing	crablike	creative
contrair	coquette	corn smut	cough out	crabmeat	creatrix
contrary	coquitos	corn snow	could use	crab's-eye	creature
contrast	coracoid	cornuted	coulisse	crab tree	crebrity
contrate	coradgee	corn-worm	coumarin	crabwise	credence
con-trick	coraleta	coronach	countess	crabwood	credenda
contrite	coralled	coronary	counties	crackers	credenza
contrive	corallum	coronate	counting	cracking	credible
convener	coral pea	coronium	countour	crack-jaw	credibly
convenor	coral rag	coronoid	count out	crackled	credited
converge	coral-red	corporal	count ten	cracknel	creditor
converse	Coramine	corporas	coup-cart	crackpot	creeklet
conversi	cordelle	corpsman	coupling	cradling	creelful
convexly	cordiner	corpuses	couponed	craftier	creepage
conveyer	cordless	corridor	couraged	craftily	creepier
conveyor	cordlike	corrival	courante	craggier	creepily
convince	cordoned	corroder	courbash	craggily	creeping
convolve	cordovan	corselet	coursing	cragsman	cremator
convoyer	corduroy	corseted	court-day	cragsmen	crenated

crenelle	crossbar	crutched	cupidone	cutgrass	cytosine
crenellé	crossbow	cruzados	cup of tea	Cuthbert	czarevna
creodont	cross bun	cruzeiro	cupolaed	cuticula	czaritsa
creolian	cross-cut	cry havoc	cupreous	cutinize	dabchick
creolise	cross fox	cryingly	cup shake	cut it out	dactylic
creolism	crossing	cryolite	cupulate	cutlings	dado-rail
creolist	crosslet	cryonics	curacies	cut loose	Daedalic
creolize	cross-ply	cryopump	curaçoas	cut no ice	daemonic
creosote	cross-sea	cryostat	curarine	cut paper	daffiest
crepitus	cross-tie	cryptand	curarize	cut-price	daffodil
crescent	crossway	cryptate	curassow	cutpurse	daftness
crescive	crostini	cry quits	curatage	cut short	dageraad
crespine	crotalum	cry uncle	curation	cuttable	Dagestan
cresting	crotched	C Special	curative	cuttanee	daggered
cresylic	crotchet	cubature	curatory	cut-under	daggiest
cretonne	crottels	cube root	curatrix	cutwater	daimonic
crevasse	croucher	cubiform	curbless	cutwithe	dainteth
creviced	croupade	cubistic	curb roof	cyanelle	daintier
crew neck	croupier	cuboidal	curculio	cyaneous	daintify
cribbage	crousely	Cub Scout	curdlike	cyanidin	daintily
cribbing	crow-bait	cuckoldy	curd soap	cyanogen	daintith
cribrose	crow-bill	cucumber	cureless	cyanosed	daiquiri
cribwork	crowd out	cucurbit	curlicue	cyanosis	dairying
Crichton	crowfoot	cuddikie	curliest	cyanotic	dairyman
crimeful	crown all	cuddlier	curlless	cyanuric	dairymen
criminal	crown cap	cudgerie	curl-pate	cyathium	daker-hen
crimpage	crowning	cuffless	curlycue	cycadean	Dalcroze
crimpily	crownlet	cuff link	currance	Cycladic	dalesman
crimsony	crown rot	cufuffle	currency	cyclamen	dalesmen
cringing	crown saw	culching	curricle	cycleway	dalmatic
crinière	crow step	cul-de-sac	cursedly	cyclical	dal segno
crippler	cruciate	culicide	curseful	cyclitis	Damascus
crispate	crucible	culicine	cursillo	cyclonic	damnable
crispier	crucifer	culinary	cursitor	cyclopes	damnably
crispish	crucifix	culottes	curtness	Cyclopes	damn-fool
cristate	cruddier	culpable	curtseys	cyclopia	damn well
criteria	crude oil	culpably	curtsies	Cyclopic	Damocles
critical	crudités	cultigen	curvated	cyclosis	damp down
critique	cruelest	cultivar	curvedly	cydippid	dampener
crivvens	cruelled	cultrate	curveted	cylinder	dampness
croakier	crueller	cultural	curviest	cymatium	danalite
croakily	cruellie	cultured	cush-cush	cynicism	dancette
Croatian	crumb-bum	culverin	cushiest	cynodont	dancetté
croceate	crumbier	cumacean	cushiony	cynology	dandiest
crockard	crumblet	Cumanian	Cushitic	cynosure	dandilly
crockery	crumhorn	cumarone	cusparia	cyprides	dandling
crocoite	crummier	cumberer	cuspated	cyprinid	dandruff
crocuses	crummily	Cumbrian	cuspidal	Cypriote	dandydom
crofting	crumpled	cumbrous	cuspides	cypselae	dandyish
cromlech	crumpler	cum laude	cuspidor	Cyrenaic	dandyism
cromorne	cruncher	cumulate	cussedly	Cyrenian	Danebrog
Cromnodal	crunodal	cumulous	cuss word	Cyrillic	Danegeld
cronyism	crusader	Cunarder	custardy	cysteine	dane-hole
crookdom	crush bar	cuneated	custodee	cystitis	danewort
crookery	crush-hat	cuneatic	custodes	cystlike	dangling
crookish	crushing	cuniform	customal	cytaster	Danishry
crop-full	crush-pen	cunjevoi	customer	cytidine	dankness
crop-mark	crustate	cupboard	custumal	cytisine	danseuse
crop-over	crustier	cupelled	cut a dash	cytogamy	Danubian
cropping	crustily	Cup Final	cuteness	cytokine	Daphnean
crop-sick	crustose	cupidity	cut glass	cytology	dapperly

Darbyite	dead lift	deceiver	defatted	demersal	depilate
daringly	deadlily	December	defeater	Demetian	depilous
Dark Ages	deadline	decemvir	defecate	demijohn	deplorer
dark blue	dead load	decenary	defector	demi-lion	depolish
dark days	deadlock	decennia	defender	demilune	deponent
darkener	dead loss	decenter	defensor	demister	deportee
darkfall	dead-melt	decently	deferent	demitted	depraver
darkling	deadness	decentre	deferral	demiurge	deprival
darkmans	dead shot	decidual	deferred	demobbed	deprived
darkness	dead time	decigram	deferrer	democrat	depriver
darkroom	dead well	decimate	defiance	demo-disc	depurate
darksome	dead wood	decipher	defilade	demolish	deputies
dark star	dead work	decision	definite	demoness	deputise
Dartmoor	de-aerate	decisive	deflater	demoniac	deputize
dart-moth	deafened	deck-beam	deflator	demonial	deration
dartrous	deaf mute	deck-hand	deflexed	demonian	Derby day
dash down	deafness	deckhand	deflower	demonise	Derby Day
dastardy	dealable	declared	defluent	demonish	derelict
data bank	dealbate	declarer	deforcer	demonism	de-rigged
database	deal-fish	déclassé	deforest	demonist	derision
datacoms	dealings	decliner	deformed	demonize	derisive
data link	deal with	declutch	deformer	De Morgan	derisory
data type	deanship	decohere	defrayal	demotion	derivate
datebook	dearborn	decolour	defrayer	dempster	derogate
dateless	dearie me	decorate	defreeze	demurely	derrière
date line	Dear John	decorous	deftness	demurest	descaler
date-mark	dearness	decouple	defusion	demurity	describe
date palm	deathbed	decrease	degasify	demurral	descried
date-plum	death cap	decrepit	degassed	demurred	descrier
date rape	death cup	decretal	degraded	demurrer	descries
datively	death-day	decuplet	degrader	demyship	descript
datolite	deathful	decurion	degrease	denarius	descrive
daturine	death-ray	decurved	dehorner	denatant	deseeder
daubster	death row	decypher	dehorter	denature	deselect
daughter	death tax	Dedalean	deicidal	denazify	deserted
daunting	deaurate	dedendum	deionise	dendrite	deserter
Davy lamp	debagged	dedicant	deionize	dendroid	desertic
dawn raid	debarred	dedicate	dejected	dene-hole	deserved
daybreak	debility	dedition	delation	de-netted	deserver
day by day	debitage	dedolent	Delaware	deniable	designed
daydream	debiting	deedless	delectus	denizate	designer
daylight	deblazon	deed poll	delegacy	dennebol	desilver
day shift	debonair	deemster	delegant	denotata	desirous
day-to-day	deboshed	deep-down	delegate	denotive	desition
dazzling	debruise	deepener	deletion	denounce	desk lamp
deaconry	debtless	deep-etch	delicacy	Denshire	desolate
dead beat	debugged	deep kiss	delicate	dentalia	despatch
deadbeat	debugger	deep-laid	delirium	dentally	despisal
dead body	debunker	deepmost	delivery	dentaria	despiser
deadbolt	debussed	deepness	Delphian	dentated	despotat
dead-born	debutant	deep-read	delusion	dentelle	despotic
dead cert	débutant	deepsome	delusive	denticle	destinal
dead duck	decadary	deep tank	delusory	dentinal	destrier
deadener	decadent	deer-ball	delustre	denudate	destruct
deadfall	decalage	deer-horn	demagogy	deny bail	desyatin
dead-fire	decanate	deer-lick	demander	departed	detached
dead hand	decanter	deerlike	démarche	departer	detailed
dead-head	decarchy	deer-park	demented	depender	detailer
deadhead	decatize	deerskin	dementia	depeople	detainee
dead heat	deceased	de-excite	demerara	depicter	detainer
deadlier	decedent	defamous	demerger	depictor	detassel

detecter	dial-bird	diecious	dioecism	discless	disponee
detector	diallage	diederik	Diogenes	disclike	disponer
deterred	dialling	diegesis	Diogenic	disclose	disponge
detester	diallist	diegetic	Dionysic	discolor	disposal
dethrone	dialogic	dieldrin	diopside	discount	disposed
detonate	dialogue	dielytra	dioptase	discover	disposer
detoxify	dial tone	dieresis	dioptric	discreet	dispread
detrital	dialyser	Dies irae	dioramic	discrete	disprize
detrited	dialyses	diestrum	dioritic	discrown	disproof
detritic	dialysis	dietetic	diphasic	discuses	disprove
detritus	dialytic	diffract	diphenyl	diseased	dispunct
detrusor	diamanté	diffuser	diplegia	disedify	dispunge
deuce ace	diameter	diffusor	diplexer	disembed	disputer
deucedly	dianetic	digamist	diploidy	disenact	disquiet
deuce set	dianthus	digamous	diploma'd	disendow	disrober
deuteric	diapalma	digenean	diplomat	disenjoy	disseise
deuteron	diapason	digenite	diplopia	disfaith	disseize
devalued	diapause	digester	diplopic	disflesh	disserve
devalues	diapente	diggings	diplopod	disfrock	dissever
devaster	diaphane	digitate	dippiest	disgavel	dissight
deverbal	diaphone	digitise	dip slope	disgorge	dissolve
deviable	diaphony	digitize	dipstick	disgrace	dissuade
deviance	diapiric	dihedral	dipteral	disgrade	distally
deviancy	diarchal	dihybrid	dipteran	disguise	distance
deviator	diarchic	dihydric	Dircaean	dishevel	distancy
devildom	diascope	dikaryon	directee	dishevel	distaste
deviless	Diaspora	diketone	directly	dishfuls	distinct
deviling	diaspore	Dilantin	director	dishiest	distract
devilish	diastase	dilatant	direness	dishoard	distrain
devilism	diastema	dilatate	dirgeful	dishonor	distrait
devilize	diastole	dilation	diriment	dishorse	distress
devilkin	diastral	dilative	dirt bike	dishouse	district
devilled	diastyle	dilatory	dirtiest	disinter	distrust
devil ray	diatomic	diligent	dirtless	disjoint	disunify
deviltry	diatonic	dill weed	dirt road	disjunct	disunion
devolute	diatreme	dillybag	dirty dog	diskette	disunite
Devonian	diatribe	dilution	dirtyish	diskless	disunity
devotion	diazepam	dilutive	disabled	disk pack	disvalue
devourer	diazinon	diluvial	disabuse	disliker	ditement
devoutly	diborane	diluvian	disagree	dislodge	ditheism
dewberry	dicacity	diluvium	disallow	disloyal	ditheist
dewiness	dicastic	dimerise	disannex	dismally	ditherer
dew point	dicentra	dimerize	disannul	dismarry	dithying
dew-snail	dichoree	dimerous	disapply	dismayer	ditty bag
dewy-eyed	dichotic	dimethyl	disarmer	dismoded	ditty box
dextrose	dichroic	Dimetian	disarray	dismount	diuresis
dextrous	Dickensy	diminish	disaster	Disneyfy	diuretic
dey-house	dickerer	diminute	disavail	disorder	divagate
dey-woman	dickhead	dimities	disbench	disowner	divalent
dhu stone	dickiest	diner-out	disboard	dispatch	dive-bomb
diabasic	dicky bow	dingbats	disbound	dispeace	diverger
diabetes	dicrotic	ding-dong	disbowel	dispense	diversly
diabetic	dictamen	ding down	disbrain	dispermy	diverter
diabolic	dictator	dinghies	disburse	disperse	divertor
diabolos	didactic	dingiest	discandy	dispetal	dividant
diacetic	didactyl	dinkiest	discette	dispiece	dividend
diaconal	didapper	Dinky car	discharm	dispirit	divi-divi
diaculum	diddicoy	dinky-die	discinct	displace	dividual
diagnose	didrachm	dinosaur	disciple	displant	divinely
diagonal	didymium	dintless	disclaim	displode	divinest
diagraph	didymous	diocesan	disclass	displume	divinify

divinise	doghouse	donation	doublure	downward	dreadful
divinity	dog-hutch	Donatism	doubtful	downwarp	dreamery
divinize	dog Latin	Donatist	doubting	downwash	dreamful
division	dog-leech	donative	douçaine	downwell	dreamier
divisive	dogmatic	donatory	doughboy	downwind	dreamily
divisory	do-gooder	donatrix	doughier	down with	dreamish
divorcee	dog's-bane	doneness	doughnut	downzone	drearier
divorcée	dogsbody	do no harm	doum-palm	Dowsabel	drearily
divorcer	dog-shore	do no less	douppion	doxology	dreggish
divulger	dogshore	do-nought	dourness	do you see	dreichly
dizygous	dog-sleep	Don Pedro	douzaine	doziness	drencher
dizziest	dog's life	don't-care	douzeper	drabbest	drengage
Dizzyite	dog's meat	don't-know	dovecote	drabbish	dressage
djellaba	dog's-nose	doolally	dove-eyed	drabbler	dressier
DNA virus	dog's-tail	doombook	dove grey	drabness	dressing
do a Melba	dog-stone	doom-ring	dove-hawk	dracaena	dress out
do a mooch	dog-stove	doomsday	dovelike	drachmae	dribbler
do battle	dog-tired	doomsman	doveling	drachmas	dribblet
dobchick	dog-tooth	doomster	dovetail	draconic	driftage
Docetism	dog-trick	doom-tree	dove tree	Draconid	drift-ice
Docetist	dogwatch	doorbell	dowdiest	draftier	drifting
dochmiac	dog-weary	door-case	dowdyish	draggier	drift-net
dochmius	dog-whelk	doorcase	dowdyism	dragging	drift-pin
docilely	dohickey	door head	dowelled	drag-hook	driftway
docility	do homage	door-knob	dowfness	drag-hunt	drilling
docimasy	Doketism	doorknob	Dow–Jones	drag-line	Drinamyl
docketed	doldrums	doorless	downbear	dragline	drinkery
dockland	dolerite	doornail	downbeat	dragoman	drinking
dockside	dolesome	doorpost	downcast	dragomen	drink off
docksman	dolichos	door-sill	downcome	dragonet	drip-drip
dockyard	do-little	doorsman	down east	drag race	drip-drop
doctoral	doll-baby	doorstep	downface	drag-rope	drip-feed
doctorer	dollhood	doorstop	downfall	dragsman	drippier
doctorly	dolliest	doorward	downfold	dragster	drippily
doctress	dolloped	dooryard	downhaul	drainage	dripping
doctrine	dollship	dopamine	down helm	drama-doc	drip tray
document	dolly-bag	dopchick	downhill	dramatic	drisheen
doddered	dolly mop	dope-ring	downhole	Drambuie	drivable
dodderel	dolly peg	dopester	down-home	drammock	drive off
dodderer	dolly pot	dopiness	downiest	dram-shop	drive out
dodecane	dolly-tub	dormancy	downland	dratting	driveway
dodgiest	dolmades	dormered	down lead	draughty	drollery
do dirt to	dolmenic	dormient	downless	Dravidic	drollish
Dodonean	dolomite	dormouse	downlike	drawable	dromical
do duty as	doloroso	dormy one	downlink	draw back	drone-bee
doegling	dolorous	dorsally	download	drawback	drone-fly
dogberry	domainal	do scathe	downmost	drawcard	drongoes
Dogberry	domanial	dosseret	downpipe	drawcord	droopier
dog-cheap	domelike	dotation	downplay	draw down	droopily
dog-daisy	Domesday	do the ton	downpour	drawdown	drop away
dog-eared	domestic	dotiness	downrate	draw-gate	drop back
dogeship	domicile	dotingly	downrush	draw-kiln	drop dead
dog-faced	dominant	dot plant	downside	draw-leaf	drop down
dog fence	dominate	dottable	downsize	draw-loom	drop goal
dogfight	domineer	dottered	Downsman	draw lots	drop-head
doggedly	dominial	dotterel	down time	drawn-out	drophead
doggerel	dominion	dottiest	downtime	draw rein	drop into
dog-goned	dominoed	douanier	down town	drawstop	drop-keel
dog-grass	dominoes	double up	downtown	draw-well	drop kick
dog-grate	Dom Pedro	doubling	downtrod	dray-cart	drop-leaf
doggy bag	donatary	doubloon	downturn	dray-road	dropless

droplike	dubbined	dumpiest	dynamist	eburnean	effluvia
drop-line	duberous	dumpling	dynamite	ecaudate	effusion
drop on to	dubitant	dumpoked	dynamize	Ecce Homo	effusive
dropping	dubitate	dumpster	dynastic	ecclesia	eftsoons
drop-ripe	Dubliner	dump tank	dynatron	ecdysial	egestion
drop-seed	Dubonnet	duncedom	dysgenic	ecdysone	egestive
drop shot	ducatoon	duncical	dyslalia	ecgonine	egg-bound
dropside	Duchenne	dun-diver	dyslexia	echinate	egg-crate
dropsied	duchesse	dungaree	dyslexic	echinite	egg cream
dropsies	duck arse	dung-cart	dyspathy	echinoid	egg-dance
drop-tank	duckbill	dung-fork	dyspepsy	echogram	egg-eater
drop test	duck-dive	dung-heap	dyspnoea	echoless	eggplant
dropwise	duck-hawk	dunghill	dystocia	eclectic	egg sauce
dropwort	duckling	dung-worm	dystonia	eclipser	eggshell
drop zone	duckmeat	dunnakin	dystonic	eclipsis	egg-slice
droughty	duck-mole	dunniken	dystopia	ecliptic	egg-spoon
drown out	duck's-egg	dunstone	dytiscid	eclogite	egg-timer
drowsier	duck-shot	duodecad	dytiscus	eclosion	egg-tooth
drowsily	duck soup	duodenal	Dzongkha	ecocidal	egg-whisk
drubbing	ducktail	duodenum	eagle eye	eco-label	egg white
drudgery	duck-walk	duologue	eagle owl	ecologic	ego-ideal
drug bust	duckweed	dupeable	eagle ray	economic	egoistic
druggery	ductible	duplexer	ear-biter	ecophene	egomania
druggies	ductless	duration	ear drops	Ecotopia	Egyptian
drugging	ductwork	durative	Earl Grey	ecstasis	E horizon
druggist	duelling	duskiest	earliest	ecstatic	eicosane
drugless	duellist	duskness	earlship	Ecthesis	eidently
Druidess	duetting	Dussehra	earlyish	ectoderm	eidolons
Druidism	duettino	dust-bath	earnings	ectoloph	eighteen
drumbeat	duettist	dust bowl	earphone	ecumenic	eighthly
drumfire	duffadar	dustcart	earpiece	edacious	eighties
drum fish	dukeling	dust-coat	ear-shell	eddyless	Einstein
drumhead	dukeship	dust down	earth god	eddy-wind	either-or
drum into	Dukhobor	dustheap	earthier	edentate	ejection
drumming	dulcetly	dustiest	earthily	edgeless	ejective
drum roll	dulciana	dustless	earth-man	edge-rail	ekistics
drunkard	dulcimer	dust-shot	earth-nut	edge-tool	elasipod
drunkery	dulcinea	dust-trap	earth-pig	edgeways	elastane
drunkish	dulcitol	Dutch act	earth-wax	edge well	elastase
drupelet	dull-head	Dutch cap	ease away	edgewise	elatedly
druzhina	dullness	Dutch hoe	easeless	edginess	elbowing
dry-clean	dumb ague	Dutchify	easement	edifying	elbow-pad
dry cough	dumb-bell	Dutchman	easiness	editress	el cheapo
dry death	dumb cane	Dutchmen	easterly	educable	Eldonian
dry-flied	dumb chum	dutiable	Eastlake	educated	Eldonine
dry-flies	dumb down	dutiless	eastland	educator	eldorado
dry goods	dumb-dumb	duty-free	eastmost	educible	El Dorado
dry joint	dumbhead	duty-paid	East Side	eduction	eldritch
dry light	dumb-iron	duxelles	eastward	eductive	election
dry-nurse	dumbness	dwarfish	East—West	eel-grass	elective
dry plate	dumb peal	dwarfism	east wind	eelgrass	electret
dry-point	dumb play	dwelling	easy-care	eel-spear	electric
dry prune	dumb show	dybbukim	easy game	eeriness	electron
dry scall	dumbshow	dye-house	easy meat	effecter	electros
dry shave	dum casta	dye laser	eateries	effector	electrum
dry slope	dumfound	dyer's oak	eat pussy	effendis	elegance
dry spell	dummerer	dyestuff	eau-de-Nil	efferent	elegancy
dry steam	dummkopf	dying god	eau-de-vie	efficacy	elegiast
dry-stone	dummy run	dynamics	Ebenezer	effigial	elenchus
drystone	dummy tit	dynamise	Ebionite	effigies	elenctic
dualling	dumosity	dynamism	ebullism	effluent	eleolite

Eleonora	eminency	encomium	enleague	enuresis	epistasy
elephant	emissary	encrinal	enlistee	enuretic	epistler
eleusine	emissile	encrinus	enlister	envassal	epistoma
elevated	emission	encroach	enmarble	envelope	epistyle
elevator	emissive	encumber	enmities	enviable	epitasis
elevener	emitting	encyclic	enmuffle	enviably	epitaxis
eleventh	emmarble	encypher	enneagon	environs	epitheca
elf-arrow	emmarvel	endamage	ennobler	envisage	epitomic
elf-shoot	Emmental	endanger	Enochian	envision	epitopic
Elgarian	empacket	endarken	enormity	Enzedder	epitrite
elicited	empanada	endemial	enormous	enzootic	epitrope
elicitor	empathic	endemism	enquirer	éolienne	epizooty
eligible	emphases	endermic	enravish	eolithic	eponymic
eligibly	emphasis	end grain	enricher	epanodos	eponymus
eliquate	emphatic	end it all	enrolled	ependyma	epopoeia
elk-hound	empierce	endocarp	enrollee	ephebeum	epsomite
ellipses	employee	endoderm	ensample	ephectic	eptitude
ellipsis	employée	endoderm	ensconce	ephemera	epulotic
elliptic	employer	endogamy	enscroll	Ephesian	epyllion
elongate	empocket	endogeny	ensearch	Ephesine	equaeval
eloquent	empoison	end organ	ensemble	ephorate	equalise
elsewhen	empolder	endorsee	enshadow	epibiont	equalist
elsewise	emporial	endorser	ensheath	epiblast	equality
eludible	emporium	endosome	enshield	epibolic	equalize
eluviate	emptiest	end-paper	enshrine	epically	equalled
emaciate	emptying	endpaper	enshroud	epicalyx	equal pay
embalmer	empty set	end-piece	ensialic	epicedia	equation
embanker	empurple	end-plate	ensiform	epichile	equative
embattle	empyreal	end point	ensigncy	epicotyl	equiaxed
Ember day	empyrean	end to end	ensilage	epicycle	equiform
Ember eve	emu-apple	endurant	enslaver	epidemic	equinely
embetter	emulator	enduring	ensnarer	epidotic	equipage
embezzle	emulgent	energies	ensphere	epidural	equipped
embitter	emulsify	energise	enswathe	epifauna	equipper
emblazer	emulsion	energize	entailer	epifocal	equiseta
emblazon	emulsive	enervate	entangle	epigamic	equitant
embodied	emulsoid	enfeeble	entellus	epigenic	equities
embodier	enaction	enfetter	entemple	epigeous	equivoke
embodies	enactive	enfilade	entering	epigones	equivote
embolden	enactory	enflower	enthalpy	epigraph	Equuleus
embolism	enallage	enfolder	enthrone	epigynum	eradiate
embolium	enanthic	enforcer	enticing	epilepsy	erasable
embolize	enargite	enfrenzy	entirely	epilogue	Erasmian
embossed	enascent	engaging	entirety	epimeral	Erastian
embosser	en brosse	engender	entities	epimeric	erectile
embracer	encaenia	engineer	entoderm	epimeron	erection
embryoid	Encaenia	enginery	entoptic	epinasty	erective
embryoma	encavern	engirdle	entozoal	epinicia	eremitic
embusing	enceinte	Englishy	entozoon	epiphany	eremurus
embussed	encentre	engolden	entr'acte	epiphora	ereption
emendate	encharge	engorger	entrails	epiphyte	erethism
emergent	enchaser	engouled	entrance	epiplasm	erewhile
emerited	encipher	engraven	entreaty	epiploic	ergastic
emeritus	encircle	engraver	entrench	epiploon	ergative
emersion	enclisis	engroove	entrepôt	epipubic	ergogram
emery bag	enclitic	enhancer	entresol	epipubis	ergotism
emetical	enclosed	enhearse	entropic	episcope	ericetal
emiction	encloser	enheaven	entryism	episodal	Eridanus
emigrant	enclothe	enjoiner	entryist	episodic	erigeron
emigrate	encoffin	enkindle	entryman	episomal	Eritrean
eminence	encolour	enlarger	entryway	epispore	erminois

erodable	esthetic	eugenist	eventing	exemplar	exponent
erodible	estimate	euhedral	even-toed	exemplum	exporter
erogenic	estivate	eulachon	eventual	exequial	exposita
erotesis	Estonian	Eulerian	everdamp	exequies	exposure
erotetic	estopped	eulogies	evermore	exercise	expresso
erotical	estoppel	eulogise	eversion	exergual	expulser
errantly	estovers	eulogism	eversive	exertion	expunger
errantry	estrange	eulogist	everyday	exertive	exscribe
erringly	estriche	eulogium	every few	ex gratia	extended
error bar	estridge	eulogize	everyhow	exhalant	extender
error box	estrogen	Eunomian	Everyman	exhibit A	extensor
errorist	esurient	eunuchry	every one	exhorter	exterior
eructate	eta patch	euonymus	everyone	exhumate	external
eruction	eta prime	eupatrid	every way	exigence	extispex
erumpent	et cetera	eupepsia	everyway	exigency	extolled
eruption	etcetera	eupeptic	eviction	exigible	extoller
eruptive	etchable	euphenic	evidence	exiguity	extorter
eryngium	eternise	euphonia	evil days	exiguous	extrados
erythema	eternity	euphonic	evildoer	exilarch	extra dry
erythrol	eternize	euphonon	evil hour	eximious	extra sec
escalade	ethanoic	euphoria	evilness	existent	extremal
escalado	ethanoyl	euphoric	evil will	existing	extremum
escalate	ethenoid	euphotic	evincive	exit line	extrorse
escaline	etherate	euphrasy	evitable	exit poll	extruder
escallop	ethereal	euphuism	evocable	exit visa	extubate
escalope	etherean	euphuist	evocator	ex-libris	exultant
escapade	etherial	euploidy	evolvant	ex nihilo	exundant
escapism	etherify	eupnoeic	evolvent	exocrine	exuviate
escapist	etherise	Eurasian	evulgate	exoergic	ex-votive
escargot	etherism	Eurobond	evulsion	exogamic	eye-black
escarole	etherize	Eurocrat	exacting	exogenic	eyeblack
eschalot	Ethernet	European	exaction	exonumia	eyedness
eschewal	ethician	europium	examinee	exophora	eyeglass
eschewer	ethicise	eurythmy	examiner	exoplasm	eyeleted
escudero	ethicism	eurytope	examplar	exorable	eye level
esculent	ethicist	Eusebian	excamber	exorcise	eye-liner
Eskimoid	ethicize	eusocial	excavate	exorcism	eyeliner
esoteric	ethidium	eustatic	excedent	exorcist	eye of day
espalier	ethionic	eustelic	excelled	exorcize	eye-patch
esparcet	Ethiopic	eutectic	exceptor	exordial	eyepatch
espartos	ethnarch	eutrophy	exchange	exordium	eyepiece
especial	ethnical	euxenite	exciplex	exospore	eye-rhyme
espiegle	ethnonym	evacuant	excision	exossate	eyes down
espousal	ethogram	evacuate	excitant	exoteric	eye-shade
espouser	ethology	evadable	exciting	exotherm	eyesight
espresso	ethoxide	evaluate	excitive	exotoxin	eyes left
Esquimau	ethylate	evanesce	excitory	expanded	eye-stalk
essayism	ethylene	evangile	excitron	expander	eye-tooth
essayist	etiolate	evasible	excluder	expected	eyewater
essaylet	etiology	eve-churr	excretal	expecter	fabliaux
Essenian	Eton crop	evection	excreter	expedite	fabulate
Essenism	Eton suit	even-aged	excursus	expelled	fabulist
essexite	Etrurian	evendown	excuse me	expellee	fabulous
essoinee	Etruscan	even-even	excusive	expeller	faburden
essoiner	eucalypt	evenfall	execrate	expender	façadism
essonite	eucharis	evenings	executer	expertly	façadist
estancia	eucrasia	even just	executor	expiable	face-ache
esteemer	eudaemon	evenness	executry	expiator	face-bone
esterase	eudemony	evensong	exegeses	explicit	face card
esterify	Euganean	eventful	exegesis	exploder	face down
esthesis	eugenics	eventide	exegetic	explorer	faceless

face-lift	fall-pipe	fashious	feebless	fenchone	field pea
facelift	fall-rope	fastback	feeblest	fencible	fiendish
face mask	fall-trap	fastball	feebling	fenestra	fiercely
face pack	fall void	fast-boat	feeblish	feng shui	fiercest
face-play	fall zone	fast buck	feedable	fen sedge	fieriest
facetiae	false god	fastener	feed back	fen tiger	fife-rail
faceting	false key	fast food	feedback	feracity	fifth day
face up to	false leg	fasthold	feed cock	Feraghan	fiftieth
facially	false oat	fast land	feed crop	feretory	fiftyish
facilely	false rib	fast lane	feed high	fermatas	fight for
facility	falsetto	fastness	feed-pipe	fern ally	fighting
factious	faltboat	fast-talk	feed pump	fern-bird	fight off
factotum	falterer	fastuous	feed-room	fernland	fight out
faculous	fameless	fast-wind	feed-tank	Fernleaf	figuline
faddiest	familial	fatalism	feelable	fernless	figurant
fade away	familiar	fatalist	feel free	fernlike	figurate
fadeless	families	fatality	feel-good	fern-seed	figure on
fadingly	Familism	fat-faced	feel like	fernyear	figure up
Faeroese	Familist	fatherly	feel up to	ferocity	figurine
faggoted	famished	fathomer	fees tail	ferreous	figurist
faggoter	famously	fatigate	feetless	ferreted	filagree
fail-dyke	Fanagalo	fatigued	feigning	ferreter	filament
fail-safe	fancical	fatigues	feijoada	ferriage	filander
fainéant	fanciest	Fatimite	feistier	ferritic	filariae
fainness	fanciful	fatmouth	feistily	ferritin	filarial
faintest	fancy man	fatstock	Felapton	ferruled	filature
faintish	fan dance	fattener	feldspar	ferryage	filching
fair copy	fandango	fattiest	felicide	ferryman	file away
fair-face	fanfaron	fatty oil	felicity	ferrymen	file-fish
fair fall	fangless	faubourg	felinely	fervency	filefish
fair game	fanlight	faultful	felinity	fervidly	filially
Fair Isle	fantasia	faultier	fellable	festally	filicide
fairlead	fantigue	faultily	fellahin	festival	filiform
fair maid	faradaic	faulting	fellatio	fetation	filigree
fair name	faradism	faulture	fellator	fetching	Filipina
fairness	faradize	faunally	fellness	fetch out	Filipino
fair play	farcical	Faustian	fellowly	fetch way	filix mas
fair rent	farcy bud	fauterer	fell-wool	feticide	fillable
fairyism	farewell	fauteuil	felonies	fetterer	fill a gap
faithful	far-famed	favonian	felsitic	feudally	filleted
Faithist	far-flung	favoured	felstone	feverfew	filleter
fake book	far forth	favourer	feltlike	feverish	filliped
fakement	farinose	fayalite	feltness	feverous	filmable
Falashas	farmable	fealties	femalely	fewtrils	film buff
falcated	farm-hand	fearless	femality	fibre-tip	film clip
falchion	farmhand	fearsome	femalize	fibrilla	filmfest
falconer	farmhold	feasible	femerell	fibromas	film-goer
falconet	farm land	feasibly	feme sole	fibrosis	filmiest
falconry	farmwife	feast day	femicide	fibrotic	film pack
falderal	farmyard	feastful	feminine	Fichtean	film star
Faliscan	farnesol	feathery	feminise	fiddlier	film unit
fall away	faro bank	featness	feminism	fiddling	filterer
fall-back	farouche	featural	feminist	Fidelism	filthier
fall down	farragos	featured	feminity	Fidelist	filthify
fallfish	farriery	febrific	feminize	fidelity	filthily
fall flat	farthest	February	feminoid	fidgeted	filtrate
fallible	farthing	feckless	fen-berry	fidgeter	finagler
fallibly	fasciate	feculent	fenceful	fiducial	finalise
fall-leaf	fascicle	fedayeen	fence-row	field-bed	finalism
fall-line	fasciola	federacy	fenchane	field day	finalist
fall over	fascitis	federate	fenchene	fieldful	finality

finalize	fire pink	five-leaf	flatland	flimsily	flowerer
findable	fire-plug	fivesome	flatling	flincher	floweret
find a way	fireplug	five-star	flatmate	flinders	flow-line
find-spot	fire-raid	fixation	flatness	Flinders	flow pipe
fineable	fire-risk	fixative	flat-nose	flindosa	flubbing
fine arts	fire-room	fixature	flat-pack	fling mud	flue-cure
fine-draw	fire sale	fixed-doh	flat race	fling off	flue-dust
Fine Gael	fire-ship	fixed oil	flat rate	flintier	flueless
fine-hand	fireship	fixidity	flat spin	flintily	fluellen
fine lady	fireside	fizz-boat	flattery	flip-flap	fluently
fineless	fire-step	fizziest	flattest	flip-flop	flue pipe
fineness	fire trap	flabbier	flatties	flip jump	flue-stop
fineries	fire-tree	flabbily	flatting	flippant	flue-work
fine-spun	fire-walk	flackery	flattish	flipping	fluffier
fine-tune	fire wall	flag-boat	flat tyre	flip side	fluffily
fingered	fireweed	flag down	flatware	flirtier	fluidics
fingerer	firewood	flagella	flatwise	flirtish	fluidify
fingrigo	firework	flag-fall	flatworm	flitchen	fluidise
finicism	firm land	flagging	flaunter	flittern	fluidism
finished	firmness	flagless	flautino	flitters	fluidist
finisher	firmware	flag-list	flautist	flittery	fluidity
finish up	first aid	flag-pole	flavonol	flitting	fluidize
finitary	first day	flagpole	flavoury	flixweed	fluidram
finitely	first off	flag-rank	flawless	floatage	fluigram
finitise	First War	flagrant	flax-blue	float-cut	flukiest
finitism	fiscally	flag-root	flax-bush	floating	flummery
finitist	fishable	flagship	flax-comb	float-ore	flunkeys
finitize	fish-beam	flake out	flax-lily	floccose	flunkies
finitude	fish-bolt	flakiest	flax-seed	floccule	flunk out
finnesko	fish-bowl	flambeau	flaxseed	flocculi	fluorene
finnowed	fishbowl	flambéed	fleabane	flock-bed	fluorian
fin whale	fish cake	flame gun	flea bite	flogging	fluoride
fippence	fish farm	flamelet	flea-dock	flooding	fluorine
fippenny	fish-fork	flamenco	fleasome	floodlit	fluorite
fireable	fish-glue	flame out	fleawort	flood out	flurried
firearms	fish-hawk	flameout	fleckled	floorage	flurries
fire away	fish-hook	flamines	flection	flooring	flushing
fireback	fishiest	flamingo	fleecier	floor-mop	Flushing
fire-ball	fishless	flammant	fleecies	floozies	flush out
fireball	fishlike	flancard	fleecily	floppier	fluttery
fire-bird	fishling	Flanders	fleeting	floppily	flux-line
fire-bomb	fish-meal	flânerie	flesh-fly	flopping	fly a kite
firebomb	fishmeal	flapjack	fleshier	Flora day	fly-blown
fire-boot	fish pond	flapless	fleshing	florally	flyblown
firebrat	fish-pool	flapping	flesh out	Florence	fly-drive
fireclay	fishtail	flare-out	fleshpot	floreted	fly-eater
fire-cure	fish-tank	flash-dry	fletcher	floriate	fly frame
firedamp	fishwife	flash-gun	flexible	florican	fly-mould
fire door	fishworm	flashgun	flexibly	Floridan	fly-paper
fire exit	fissiped	flashier	flextime	floridly	fly-pitch
fire-eyed	fissural	flashily	flexuose	florigen	flysheet
fire-fang	fissured	flashing	flexuous	florikan	fly-speck
firefish	fistfuls	flash out	flexural	floscule	fly-spray
fire-fork	fistiana	flat arch	fleysome	flossied	fly-strip
fire hall	fistical	flat boat	flicflac	flossier	fly-swish
fire hose	fistmele	flatfish	flichter	flotilla	flyunder
fire-iron	fistulae	flat foot	flickery	flounder	flywheel
fireless	fistular	flatfoot	flighted	flourier	fly-whisk
fire-line	fistulas	flat-four	flighter	flourish	foalfoot
firelock	fitfully	flat-head	flimflam	flow-blue	foamback
fire-opal	fivefold	flat iron	flimsier	flowered	foamiest

foamless	foot-drop	foregoes	for keeps	foul play	free-born
fob-chain	footfall	foregone	for kicks	founding	freeborn
fob watch	foot-folk	forehand	forklike	fountain	free city
focaccia	foot-gear	forehead	fork over	fountful	freedman
focalise	foothill	forehear	forktail	four-ball	freedmen
focalize	foothold	forehock	formable	four-eyes	free fall
focusing	footless	forehold	formalin	fourfold	Freefone
focussed	footlike	foreknow	formally	four-foot	free-form
fodderer	footling	forelady	form book	four-four	free gift
fog-bound	footmark	forelaid	form drag	Fournier	free hand
fogbound	foot-muff	foreland	formedon	four-part	freehand
fogeydom	footnote	forelimb	formeret	four-post	freehold
fogeyish	foot pace	forelive	formerly	fourreau	free-kick
foggiest	foot page	forelock	formicid	fourrier	Free Kirk
foglight	footpath	forelook	formless	foursome	freelage
foie gras	foot-race	foremast	form-line	four-star	free list
foldable	footrest	foremean	for money	fourteen	freeload
fold away	foot-rope	foremilk	Formosan	fourthly	free love
foldaway	foot-rule	foremost	form-room	fowl pest	freeness
foldboat	footslog	forename	formulae	foxberry	free pass
folderol	footsore	forenoon	formular	fox-chase	free path
foldless	footstep	forensic	formulas	foxglove	free port
foliated	footsure	foreoath	form word	fox-grape	Freepost
foliator	footwall	forepart	formwork	foxhound	free rein
folivore	footwear	forepeak	forprise	foxiness	free soil
folk-club	footwell	foreplan	forrader	fox shark	free vote
folk epic	footwork	foreplay	forsaken	fox snake	freeware
folkfest	footworn	forerank	forsaker	frabjous	free will
folkiest	foralite	foreroom	for shame	fractile	freeze up
folkland	foramina	foresaid	forshape	fraction	freezing
folklore	for a song	foresail	for short	fracture	fremitus
folkmoot	forborne	foreseat	forsooth	fragment	Frencher
folk rock	force cup	foreseer	forspeak	fragrant	Frenchie
folksier	forcedly	foreshew	forspend	framable	Frenchly
folk song	forceful	foreship	forspoke	frame-saw	frenetic
folk tale	force-out	foreshot	forswear	frampold	frenulum
folk ways	forcible	foreshow	forswore	francisc	frenzied
folkways	forcibly	foreside	forsworn	francise	frenzies
follicle	fordable	foreskin	forthink	francium	frequent
folliful	fordless	foreslow	fortieth	francize	frescade
follower	forebear	forestal	fortress	frank-fee	frescoed
follow-on	forebode	forestay	fortuity	Frankish	frescoes
follow-up	forebody	forested	fortuned	franklin	freshish
fomenter	forecall	forester	fortyish	Franklin	freshman
Fomorian	forecame	forestry	forwards	frapping	freshmen
fondling	forecast	foretack	forweary	frascati	fresh-run
fondness	forecome	foretell	foryield	Frascati	Fresison
font-name	foredawn	foretime	forzando	fraudful	fretless
fontware	foredeck	foretold	fossette	fraughan	fretting
food call	foredoom	forewarn	fossiled	Fräulein	frettish
food-fish	foredoor	forewent	fosterer	fraxetin	fretwork
foodless	foredune	forewing	fostress	freakdom	Freudian
food-pass	fore-edge	foreword	Foucault	freakier	friaries
fool away	foreface	foreyard	fougasse	freakily	fribbler
foolscap	forefeel	forge-man	foughten	freakish	friction
foolship	forefend	forgiven	foul ball	freak-out	friended
football	forefoot	forgiver	foul copy	freckled	friendly
foot-bank	foregame	forinsec	foul-hook	free alms	Friesian
foot bath	foregate	forjudge	foul line	free ball	frigging
footbath	foregift	forkball	foulmart	freebase	frighted
foot-bone	foregoer	forkedly	foulness	freeboot	frighten

frigidly	fructify	full tilt	fusilier	gambades	garbless
frijoles	fructose	full-time	fusional	gambeson	garboard
frillery	frugally	full toss	fussiest	gambling	garcinia
frillier	fruitage	full vent	fustiest	gambroon	gardener
frilling	fruit bar	full word	futilely	game ball	gardenia
Frimaire	fruit-bat	fulminic	futility	game bird	gardyloo
fringing	fruitbat	fumarate	futilize	gamebook	garefowl
frippery	fruitery	fumarole	futurism	gamecock	garganey
frisette	fruit fly	fumaroyl	futurist	game fish	gargoyle
friskier	fruitful	fumed oak	futurity	game-fowl	garishly
friskily	fruit gum	fume hood	futurize	gamefowl	garlicky
frithing	fruitier	fumeless	fuzz-ball	gameless	garreted
frittata	fruitily	fumerole	fuzziest	gameness	garrison
fritting	fruition	fumigant	fuzzword	game park	garrotte
Friulian	fruitist	fumigate	gabbiest	game plan	Garry oak
frizzier	fruitive	fumingly	gabbroic	game show	Garshuni
frog-face	fruitlet	fumishly	gabbroid	gamesman	gartered
frog-fish	fruit set	fumitory	gable-end	gamesmen	gas alarm
frogfish	frumenty	funboard	gadabout	gamesome	gas black
froggery	frumious	function	Gadarene	gamester	gaselier
froggies	frumpier	fundable	gadflies	gaminess	gas field
frogging	frumpily	funerary	gadgetry	gammarid	gas-fired
froggish	frumpish	funereal	Gadhelic	gammiest	gas gland
frogland	frustrum	fungible	gadzooks	gammoner	gas-house
froglike	frustule	fungibly	gainable	Gandhian	gasified
frog-lily	frustums	funguses	gainings	Gandhist	gasifier
frogling	frutices	funiform	gainless	gandoura	gasifies
frog-spit	fubsiest	funk-hole	gainsaid	gang-bang	gasiform
froideur	fuchsine	funkiest	gain time	gang-cask	gaslight
frolicky	fuchsite	funkster	gaitered	gang-days	gas meter
from afar	fucoidal	funniest	galabiya	Gangetic	gasolene
from A to B	fuel cell	funny man	galactan	gang-gang	gasolier
from A to Z	fuel food	furacity	galactic	gangland	gasoline
from home	fuelless	furanose	galangal	ganglial	gaspacho
fromward	fuelling	furbelow	Galatian	gangliar	gas pedal
frondage	fuel tank	furcated	galaxies	ganglier	gas plant
frondent	fugacity	furcraea	galbanum	gangling	gas poker
frondeur	fughetta	furcular	galeated	ganglion	gassiest
frondlet	fugitate	furculum	Galenian	gang rape	gasteral
frondose	fugitive	furfural	Galenism	gangrene	gasthaus
frondous	fugleman	furfuran	Galenist	gang-shag	gas-tight
frontage	fuglemen	furfurol	Galician	gang show	gastraea
front end	fulcrate	furfuryl	Galilean	gangsman	gastrula
frontier	fulcrums	furibund	Gallegan	gangster	gasworks
frontlet	Fulfulde	furlable	galleria	ganister	gate-bill
front man	fulgorid	fur-lined	gall-gnat	gannetry	gate city
frontman	fulgural	furlough	galliard	ganoidal	gatefold
frostier	full-back	furphies	galliass	gantline	gateless
frostily	full beam	furriery	Gallican	gantlope	gatepost
frosting	full butt	furriest	gallipot	gantries	gate-ward
frost-nip	full cock	furriner	gallivat	Ganymede	gatherer
frothier	full face	furrowed	gall-less	gaolbird	gather up
frothily	full hand	furthest	galloped	gape-seed	gauchely
frottage	full lock	furuncle	galloper	gape-worm	gaudiest
frotteur	full moon	fusarium	galloway	gapeworm	gaudy-day
frottola	fullness	fusarole	Galloway	gapingly	Gaullism
frou-frou	full page	fuselage	galluses	garaging	Gaullist
frowsier	full pelt	fuseless	gall wasp	garagist	gaumless
frowster	full sail	fusel oil	galopade	Garamond	gauntlet
frowzily	full stop	fuse wire	galoping	garancin	Gaussian
frozenly	full term	fusiform	galvanic	garbanzo	gauziest

Gavel Act	geologic	ghostily	giveable	gliffing	glycolic
gavelled	geomancy	ghosting	give a fit	glimmery	Glyconic
gaveller	geometer	ghostish	give alms	glissade	glycosyl
gavelock	geometry	ghoulish	give away	glissant	gnashers
gawkiest	geophagy	giantess	giveaway	glistery	gnashing
gay Greek	geophone	giantish	give back	glittery	gnathion
gazeboes	geophyte	giantism	giveback	glitzier	gnatlike
gazement	geoponic	giantize	give best	glitzily	gnatling
gazoomph	Georgian	gibbeted	give down	gloaming	gnat-snap
gazpacho	geotaxis	gibbsite	give fits	globally	gnawable
gazumper	geranial	gibingly	give hell	globated	gneissic
gazunder	geraniol	gib-staff	give it to	globical	gnomical
gear down	geranium	giddiest	give odds	globular	gnomonic
gearless	gerardia	giff-gaff	give on to	globulin	goalball
geelhout	germanic	gift-book	give over	glomming	goal kick
Gelasian	Germanic	giftedly	give skin	gloomful	goalless
gelastic	Germanly	giftless	give suck	gloomier	goal-line
gelatine	germ bomb	gift shop	glabella	gloomily	goalpost
gelation	germ cell	giftware	glabrate	glooming	go around
geldable	germinal	gift-wrap	glabrous	gloriole	go-ashore
gelidity	Germinal	giftwrap	glaciate	glorious	Goa stone
gematria	germless	gigaflop	gladdest	glory-box	go astray
geminate	germ line	gigantic	gladding	glory-pea	goatfish
Geminian	gerocomy	gigglier	glad hand	glossary	goat-foot
geminous	Geronimo	gigglish	gladiate	glosseme	goathair
gemmeous	gerontic	gig-lamps	gladioli	glossier	goatherd
gemshorn	geropiga	gigmanic	gladless	glossily	goatlike
gemstone	gestagen	gildable	gladness	glossist	goatling
gendarme	gestogen	Gilderoy	glad rags	glove box	goat moth
gendered	gestural	gild over	gladsome	glovebox	goatskin
gene bank	gesturer	gill arch	glaistig	glove-fit	goat's-rue
gene flow	get about	gillaroo	glamming	glow-lamp	goat tang
gene pool	get a grip	gillenia	glamoury	glow plug	goat-weed
generant	get ahead	gill slit	glance at	glow-worm	go back on
generate	get a heat	gilt-edge	glanders	gloxinia	goblinry
generous	get along	gilt-head	glandule	glucagon	gobstick
genetics	get a rush	gilt-tail	glareose	glucaric	God-awful
genetrix	get going	giltwood	glareous	glucinum	God bless
Genevese	get ideas	gimcrack	glasnost	gluconic	godchild
Genevize	get in bad	gimmicky	glass eye	glucosan	God-given
genially	get out of	gin and it	glassful	glucosic	God grant
genitive	get rid of	gin berry	glassier	glueball	God knows
genitory	get round	gin-crawl	glassify	glue-like	godliest
geniture	gettable	gingerly	glassily	gluelike	godmamma
geniuses	get taped	gingival	glassine	glühwein	God's Acre
gennemic	get thank	gingkoes	Glassite	glummest	God's book
genoa jib	get there	ginglymi	glass-man	glumness	God's gift
genocide	Getulian	ginned up	glastick	glumpily	Godspeed
genotype	get where	gin rummy	glaucoma	glumpish	God squad
Genovese	get wired	gin sling	glaucose	glutaeus	godwards
gentilic	get wrong	Gioconda	glaucous	glutamic	Godwards
gentlest	gewgawed	giraffes	glaziery	glutaric	Goethean
gentrice	geyseric	giraffid	gleaming	glutenin	Goethian
gentrify	Ghanaian	girasole	gleaning	glutting	goethite
geodesic	ghastful	girlhood	glee club	gluttony	goffered
geodetic	ghawazee	girl-less	gleesome	glyceria	go-getter
geogenic	ghettoes	Girondin	glegness	glyceric	go halves
geognost	Ghiordes	girthing	gletcher	glycerin	Goidelic
geognosy	Ghoorkha	girth-web	glibbest	glycerol	goings-on
geogonic	ghostess	girtline	glibness	glyceryl	goitrous
geologer	ghost gum	gisement	gliddery	glycogen	Golconda

Goldbach	go off pop	graffiti	great pox	grimmest	grubbily
gold bloc	goofiest	graffito	great tit	grimness	grubbing
gold card	googlies	grainage	great toe	grimoire	grubhood
gold disc	gooiness	grainier	Great War	grinagog	grub-kick
gold dust	go on fire	graining	great wen	grindery	grub-worm
goldenly	go on tick	grain-pit	greedier	grinding	grudging
goldfish	goopiest	gralloch	greedily	grinning	grueller
gold foil	goose-cap	gramarye	greegree	griphite	gruesome
gold king	goose egg	gram-atom	Greekdom	gripless	gruffish
gold leaf	goosegog	gramercy	Greekery	gripping	gruiform
goldless	go places	grandada	Greekess	gripsack	grumbler
gold mine	go public	grand air	Greek god	Griselda	grumness
gold-rush	gorbelly	grandame	Greekish	griseous	grumphie
gold salt	gorgeous	grand cru	Greek key	grisette	grumpier
golf ball	gorgeret	granddad	greement	gris-gris	grumpily
golf cart	gorgerin	grandeur	greenery	grislier	grumpish
golf club	gorgonia	grandfer	green eye	grith-man	Grundies
golgotha	goriness	grand mal	green fat	gritless	grunting
golliwog	gormless	grandpop	green fee	grittier	gryphite
golloped	go see-saw	grandson	greenfly	grittily	guacharo
go long on	go soft on	granitic	Greenian	gritting	guaiacol
Gomarian	go sour on	grannies	greening	grizzled	guaiacum
Gomarist	gospeler	grant aid	greenish	grizzler	Guaicuru
gomashta	gossamer	granular	greenlet	groanful	guanacos
gombroon	gossiped	grapelet	green man	groaning	guanylic
gonadial	gossiper	grapheme	green tea	groggery	guarache
go native	gossipry	graphics	greeting	groggier	guaranty
gondolet	gossypol	graphite	greffier	groggily	guardant
Gondwana	go steady	grappier	Grelling	grog-shop	guard dog
gone away	Gothonic	grappler	Grenache	groining	guardful
gone coon	go to bits	grapsoid	Grenadan	gromwell	guardian
goneness	go to hell	grasping	Grenfell	groo-groo	guarding
gonfalon	go too far	grass box	Gretchen	groomish	Guaycuru
gonfanon	go to seed	grassier	grey area	groovier	Guelphic
gong-gong	go to show	grassing	grey-back	groovily	guéridon
gonidial	go to town	grass pea	grey-coat	grope out	guerilla
gonidium	go to work	grass ski	grey crow	grosbeak	Guernsey
gonoduct	gouge-bit	grateful	grey duck	groschen	Guesdism
gonopore	gourdful	gratiola	grey-eyed	gross out	Guesdist
good book	gourmand	grattage	grey fowl	gross sum	Guianese
good Book	goutweed	grattoir	greymail	gross ton	Guianian
goodbyes	governor	gratuity	grey mare	grottier	guidable
good debt	go wallop	gravamen	greyness	grottoed	guidance
good deed	gownsman	gravelly	grey pine	grottoes	guide dog
good doer	Goyesque	Gravette	grey seal	grounded	Guide Law
good-even	Graafian	gravific	grey wolf	grounder	guideway
good form	grabbing	gravitas	grid bias	groupage	guidguid
goodlier	grab-hook	graviton	gridelin	grouping	guileful
good luck	grab rail	grayling	gridiron	groupism	guiltier
good name	grace-cup	grazable	gridlock	groupist	guiltily
goodness	graceful	graziery	griefful	grouplet	guimauve
good show	gracilis	greasier	grievous	group sex	Guinness
good-time	gracioso	greasily	griffaun	grouting	Gujarati
good turn	gracious	great age	griggish	growable	Gujerati
goodwife	gradatim	great ape	Grignard	grow away	gulfweed
good will	gradient	great auk	grillade	grow down	gullable
goodwill	graduand	great big	grillage	growlery	gullible
good word	graduate	great day	grilling	Growmore	gullibly
goodyear	Graecise	Great Dog	grimacer	groyning	gull-like
goodyera	Graecism	great gun	Grimaldi	grubbery	gull-wing
goof-ball	Graecize	greatish	grimiest	grubbier	gulosity

gumbotil	habendum	half-door	handfast	hardball	Hasidism
Gummidge	hability	half-face	handfuls	hard-boil	hassocky
gummiest	habitant	half-hear	handgrip	hard case	hasteful
gummosis	habitate	half-hose	hand-held	hard cash	hastener
gumpheon	habitual	half-hour	handhold	hard clam	hastiest
gumption	habitude	half-inch	handhorn	hard coal	hatchery
gum resin	habs-nabs	half-jack	handicap	hard copy	hatchety
gum-water	hachures	half-life	handiest	hard core	hatching
gunfight	hacienda	half-lift	hand it to	hard-core	hatchway
gunk-hole	hackette	half-line	handless	hardcore	hateable
gun-layer	hackneys	half-mark	handline	hard disk	hateless
gunmaker	hackster	half-mast	handlist	hard doer	hate mail
gun-metal	hackwork	half-mile	handloom	hardener	Hathoric
gunmetal	Hadassah	half-moon	handmade	hard fact	hat-money
gunny bag	hadronic	half-move	handmaid	hard fern	hatstand
gunpoint	haematic	halfness	hand-mill	hardhack	hat-trick
gunpower	haematin	half note	hand over	hard-head	hauerite
gun-range	haere mai	half-pace	handover	hardhead	haulyard
gunsight	Hagarene	half-part	handpass	hardiest	haunched
gunsmith	hagberry	half-pass	hand-pick	hard-laid	haunting
gunstock	Haggadah	half-pike	handpump	hard line	haurient
gunstone	Haggadic	half-pint	handrail	hardline	hausfrau
gurdwara	hag-taper	half-shot	hand-sewn	hard luck	haustral
gurgeons	Hail Mary	half-slip	hands off	hard-meat	haustrum
Gurkhali	hair-ball	half-sole	handsome	hardness	haüynite
Gurmukhi	hairband	half-step	hand tool	hard-nose	have a few
guruship	haircare	half-term	handwork	hard porn	have a fit
gushiest	hair-cell	half-tide	handy for	hard rock	have a job
gusseted	hair clip	half-time	handyman	hard sell	have done
gustable	hair-cord	half-tone	handymen	hardship	have left
gustiest	hair-grip	halftone	hanepoot	hard soap	have legs
gut flora	hairgrip	half-wave	hangable	hard tack	haveless
gut-level	hairiest	half-word	hang a leg	hardtail	havelock
guts-ache	hair lace	half-year	hang back	hard tick	havenage
gut-shoot	hairless	haliotis	hangbird	hardware	have need
gutsiest	hairlike	hall door	hanger-on	hardwood	have pity
guttated	hairline	hallmark	hang fire	hard word	haversin
guttatim	hair-lock	hallmote	hang it up	harebell	have to be
guttered	hair moss	hallooed	hangment	harefoot	have to do
guttural	hair seal	hall tree	hangnail	harelike	havildar
Guyanese	hair-worm	hallucal	hang-nest	haremlik	havocked
guzzling	Halachic	halluces	hangover	hare-pipe	Hawaiian
Gwentian	Halafian	haloform	Hang Seng	hare's-ear	hawfinch
gyle-kier	Halalcor	haltered	hankerer	hare's fur	hawk-eyed
gymkhana	halalled	halteres	hanksite	harewood	hawklike
gymnasia	halation	halt sign	Hannibal	Hargrave	hawkmoth
gymnotus	haleness	halutzim	Hanukkah	hark back	hawk-nose
gynander	halesome	hamartia	haploidy	Harleian	hawkshaw
gynarchy	half-arse	hamerkop	happen-so	harlotry	hawkweed
gynobase	half-back	hammerer	happiest	harmless	hawthorn
gypseous	half-ball	hammiest	happy day	harmonic	hay fever
gypsy cab	half-beak	Hanafite	haptenic	haroseth	hayfield
Gypsydom	half-belt	hanaster	hapteron	harp seal	haymaker
gypsyish	half-blue	handball	haqueton	harridan	haystack
Gypsyish	half-boot	handbell	hara-kiri	harrower	hazarder
Gypsyism	half-bred	handbill	harangue	harrow in	hazardry
gyration	half-butt	handbook	harasser	harrumph	hazelnut
gyratory	half cock	handcart	harbinge	hartwort	haziness
gyrostat	half-dead	handclap	hard at it	haruspex	headache
habanera	half-deck	handcuff	hardback	Harveian	headachy
Habdalah	half-dime	hand down	hardbake	hash sign	head back

headband	heavy mob	hellweed	hereunto	high camp	hired man
head-butt	heavy oil	helmeted	hereupon	high card	hireless
head case	heavy wet	helminth	herewith	higher-up	hireling
headfast	hebdomad	helmless	herisson	high-five	his heels
headgear	hebetate	helmsman	heritage	high gear	Hispanic
head girl	hebetude	helmsmen	heritrix	high-hole	Hisperic
head-hunt	Hebraean	helotage	hermetic	high jump	hiss away
headhunt	Hebraise	helotism	hermitic	high kick	histerid
headiest	Hebraism	helotize	hermitry	highland	histioid
headlamp	Hebraist	helpable	herniary	high life	histogen
headland	Hebraize	helpless	Herodian	high-lone	histomap
headless	hecatomb	helpline	heroical	high-lows	historic
headline	hectical	help-mate	heroship	high mass	Histosol
headlock	hedgehog	helpmate	herpetic	High Mass	histrion
headlong	hedge-hop	helpmeet	herptile	highmost	his watch
headmost	hedge-pig	Helvetic	herseems	highness	hit a blot
head-note	hedgerow	helvolic	herstory	high-risc	hitch pin
headnote	hedonism	hemiopia	Hertzian	high-risk	hitherto
head noun	hedonist	hemiopic	her watch	high road	hit it off
head-race	heedless	hemipode	Hesiodic	high seas	hit squad
head-rail	heelaman	hemisect	hesitant	high sign	hit woman
headrest	heelball	hempland	hesitate	high spot	hit women
headroom	heel-bone	hempseed	hesperid	hightail	hoactzin
head-rope	heel grip	henchman	Hesperus	high-tech	hoarding
head-sail	heelless	henchmen	hetaerae	high tide	hoarhead
headsail	heel-lift	henequen	hetairai	high time	hoariest
headship	heel-post	hen-fruit	heuchera	highveld	hoarsely
headsman	heel-rope	hen house	heuretic	high wine	Hoastman
headsmen	heemraad	hennaing	hexagram	high wire	hobbitry
head-tire	heftiest	hen-party	hexanoic	highwood	hobbyism
headward	hegberry	hen-roost	hexaplar	hijacker	hobbyist
head wind	Hegelian	hepatica	hexapody	hilarity	hob-or-nob
headwind	Hegelism	hepatoma	hexatone	hill-folk	hock-cart
headword	hegemony	hepialid	hey jingo	hill fort	hockelty
headwork	heighten	heptagon	hiatuses	hilliest	hocklety
head-yard	heirless	heptamer	hibernal	hillocky	hock-shop
healable	heirloom	heptarch	hibiscus	hillside	Hocktide
healsome	heir male	heraldic	hiccough	himation	hocusing
hearable	heirship	heraldry	hiccuped	himseems	hocussed
hear hear	HeLa cell	herbaged	hic jacet	Hinayana	hodgepot
hear of it	helenium	herbaria	hickwall	hinderer	Hoffmann
hear tell	heliacal	herb beer	hidalgos	hind-head	hoggerel
heartful	helicity	herbiest	hiddenly	hindmost	hog-Latin
heartier	helicoid	herbless	hide away	hindside	hog louse
heartily	heliodon	herblike	hideaway	Hinduise	hogmanay
heart rot	heliodor	Hercules	hidebind	Hinduism	hog-maned
heat-drop	heliport	herd book	hideland	Hinduize	hog-nosed
heatedly	Helladic	herdsman	hideless	hindward	hog on ice
heathery	hell-bent	herdsmen	hideling	hindwing	hog's back
heath-hen	hell-born	Herdwick	hidlings	hingeing	hog-score
heat lamp	hell-bred	hereaway	hidrosis	hinge-pin	hogshead
heat pump	Hellenic	heredity	hidrotic	hinnible	hog-tight
heat rash	hell-fire	Hereford	hidy-hole	hip-boots	ho-ho bird
heat sink	hellfire	herefrom	hielaman	hip flask	hokiness
heat wave	hell-hole	heregeld	hierarch	hip joint	holdable
heatwave	hellicat	here goes	hieratic	hipparch	hold back
heavenly	hell-kite	herenach	hierurgy	hippuric	holdback
heaviest	hell-like	hereness	higgling	hippydom	hold dear
heavy bag	he'll live	here's how	highball	hiragana	hold down
heavyish	hell-ship	heresies	high-born	hircarra	holdfast
heavy man	hellward	heretoga	highbrow	hireable	hold good

hold hard	homespun	hoop pine	hotbrain	humanise	Hyde Park
hold over	homester	hoop ring	hotchpot	humanism	hydracid
hold pace	home town	hooroosh	hoteldom	humanist	hydranth
hold true	home unit	hoosegow	hotelier	humanity	hydrarch
hold with	homeward	hooshtah	hot flash	humanize	hydrated
holeable	homework	hopeless	hot flush	humanoid	hydrator
hole-card	homicide	hopingly	hothouse	humantin	hydremia
holiness	homilete	hop joint	hot metal	humblest	hydridic
holistic	homilies	hop-plant	hot money	humidify	hydrogel
hollaing	homilise	Horatian	hot pants	humidity	hydrogen
Hollands	homilist	Horlicks	hotplate	humified	hydromel
hollowly	homilite	hormonal	hot-press	humifies	hydronym
holly oak	homilize	hormonic	hot-short	humility	hydropic
holmgang	hominess	horn-band	hot-stove	hummable	hydropot
Holmgren	hominine	hornbeak	hot stuff	hummocky	hydropsy
holm tree	hominoid	hornbeam	hot water	humorise	hydroski
Holocene	homodont	hornbill	hound-dog	humorism	hydrosol
hologamy	homogamy	hornbook	hounding	humorist	hydrotic
hologram	homogene	horn cell	houndish	humorize	hydroxyl
holoptic	homogeny	hornfels	hour hand	humorous	hyena-dog
holotype	homology	horn-fish	hour-long	humoured	hyenaism
holozoic	homonymy	horniest	houseboy	humpback	hygienic
Holstein	homotopy	hornless	house dog	humpiest	hylicist
Holy City	homuncio	hornlike	housefly	humpless	hylology
holy fire	honchoes	hornpipe	houseful	humstrum	hylozoic
Holy Lamb	Honduran	hornpout	house-lot	humulone	hymeneal
Holy Land	honestly	horn-rims	houseman	humusify	hymenean
holy loaf	honewort	horn-ring	housemen	Hunanese	hymenial
Holy Mary	honey ant	horntail	house row	hundreds	hymenium
Holy Name	honey bag	hornwork	house-sit	hungered	hymn book
Holy Rood	honey bee	hornworm	housetop	hungerer	hymnless
holytide	honeybee	hornwort	hoveller	hungerly	hyoidean
Holy Week	honey-bun	horologe	hoverfly	hung-over	hyoscine
Holy Writ	honeybun	horology	how about	hungrier	hypaxial
Holy Year	honeydew	horopter	howdahed	hungrily	hypergol
home base	honeyish	horrible	howgozit	hunkiest	hypernym
home-bird	honey pot	horribly	howitzer	huntable	hyperope
homebody	honey sac	horridly	howl down	hunt away	hyperper
home-bred	honorand	horrific	how's life	huntaway	hyphaema
home-brew	honorary	horse ant	howsoe'er	hunt ball	hypnosis
home farm	honorial	horsebox	how's that	hunt down	hypnotic
home-felt	honourer	horse-car	huarache	huntress	hypocone
homegirl	hoodless	horsefly	hub brake	hunt riot	hypodigm
home help	hoodlike	horse-hoe	hubbuboo	huntsman	hypogamy
homeland	hoodooed	horseman	huck-bone	huntsmen	hypogeal
homeless	hoodwink	horsemen	huckster	Huon pine	hypogean
homelier	hoofless	horse-pox	huet-huet	hurcheon	hypogene
homelike	hoof-pick	horse-way	huff-duff	hurroosh	hypogeum
homelily	hook-bill	horsiest	huffiest	hurtless	hypogyny
homeling	hook-bolt	hortulan	hügelite	hurtsome	hyponome
home loan	hook-bone	hoseless	hugeness	hushabye	hyponymy
home-made	hooked on	hose-pipe	huggable	hushedly	hypopyon
homeobox	hookless	hosepipe	Huguenot	hush-hush	hyposmia
home perm	hooklike	hospital	hula hoop	huskanaw	hypothec
home port	hook-nose	hospitia	hula-hula	huskiest	hypotony
Homerist	hook shop	hospodar	hull down	hustings	hyraceum
Homerite	hook shot	hosteler	hully gee	Huweitat	hysteria
homeroom	hookworm	hostelry	hum and ha	Huxleyan	hysteric
home rule	hooligan	hostessy	humanely	hyacinth	iambical
homesick	hoop-back	hostless	humanics	Hyblaean	iambuses
homesite	hoop-iron	hot blast	humanify	hybodont	I am sorry

Iapygian	idolater	immersed	in accord	indamine	infamize
iatrical	idolatry	imminent	in a creel	indazole	infamous
Ibicenco	idolizer	immingle	in action	Indebele	infantry
ibotenic	idoneity	immobile	inaction	indebted	infaunal
Ibsenish	idoneous	immodest	inactive	indecent	in favour
Ibsenism	idrialin	immolate	in a hurry	in defect	infector
Ibsenist	id ul-fitr	immortal	in and out	in demand	infectum
Ibsenite	idyllian	immotile	in a pause	indented	infecund
iceblink	idyllise	immotive	inarable	indenter	inferior
iceblock	idyllist	immunise	in armour	indentor	infernal
ice-bound	idyllize	immunity	in a sense	indesert	infernos
ice chest	iggerant	immunize	inasmuch	in detail	inferred
ice cream	Ignatian	impacted	in a trice	indevout	infilter
ice field	ignition	impactor	in a whiff	India ink	infinite
ice-front	ignitron	impaired	in a while	Indiaman	infinity
ice house	ignobler	impairer	in a whisk	Indiamen	infirmly
ice lolly	ignominy	impalace	in back of	Indianan	infixion
ice-piton	ignorant	impaling	in-basket	indicant	inflamer
ice plant	iguanian	impanate	inbreath	indicate	in flames
ice sheet	iguanoid	imparity	Inca dove	indicial	inflated
ice shelf	iimbongi	imparter	incalver	indicium	inflater
ice-skate	ijolitic	impedite	in camera	indictee	inflator
ice storm	Iliadist	impelled	in candle	indicter	inflexed
ice-water	illation	impeller	in care of	indigena	in-flight
ice-yacht	illative	impellor	in case of	indigene	inflight
ichoglan	ill blood	imperial	Inca tern	indigent	in flower
ichorous	I'll buy it	imperium	incensed	indigest	influent
ichthyic	ill-deedy	impetigo	incenser	indigoid	infolded
Ichthyol	ill-fated	impierce	incenter	indirect	informal
iconical	illigant	impinger	incentor	inditing	informed
icterine	illinium	impishly	incentre	indocile	informer
id al-adha	Illinois	impleach	inceptor	indolent	infra dig
I dare say	illiquid	impledge	in charge	Indology	infra-red
idealess	I'll say so	implicit	inchmeal	indrawal	infrared
ideal gas	ill-timed	implunge	inchoate	inducive	in fresco
idealise	ill-treat	impocket	in chorus	inductee	infringe
idealism	illumine	impolder	inchworm	inductor	infusion
idealist	illusion	impolicy	incident	indulged	infusive
ideality	illusive	impolite	in-circle	indulger	infusory
idealize	illusory	imponent	incision	induline	in future
ideation	illuvial	imporous	incisive	indument	ingather
idée fixe	Illyrian	importee	incisure	indurate	in grease
identify	Illyrism	importer	incitive	indusial	ingroove
identity	Illyrist	imposing	incitory	indusium	in-ground
ideogram	ilmenite	imposter	incivism	industry	ingrowth
ideology	imaginal	impostor	inclined	inedible	inguinal
idiocies	imaginer	imposure	incliner	inedited	inhalant
idiogram	imagines	impotent	in clover	in effect	inhalent
idiolect	imambara	imprimis	included	in effigy	inhauler
idiosome	imbecile	imprison	incoming	in embryo	inhearse
idiot box	imbolden	improper	in common	inequity	inheaven
idiotish	imbrices	improver	in convoy	inerrant	inherent
idiotism	imbruing	impudent	in course	inert gas	inhesion
idiotize	imitable	impugner	incourse	inertial	inhibine
idiotope	imitator	impunity	increase	inertion	in his way
idiotype	immanely	impurely	increate	in escrow	inhumane
idiozome	immanent	impurify	incubate	inessive	inhumate
idle away	immantle	impurist	incubous	in excess	inimical
idlehood	immarble	impurity	incumber	inexpert	iniquity
idleness	immature	I must say	incurred	in face of	initiand
idocrase	immember	in a blaze	indagate	infamies	initiate

in itself	insanely	interbed	intruder	iridious	Islamize
in its way	insanify	intercom	intubate	Irish elk	islander
injected	insanity	intercut	intuiter	Irishian	isleless
injector	inscient	interest	inturned	Irishism	islesman
injuries	inscribe	interior	in two ups	Irishize	Ismailis
inkberry	inscript	interlap	inundant	Irishman	is no more
ink block	inscroll	interlay	inundate	Irishmen	isobaric
inkiness	in season	intermit	in unison	Irish Sea	isocheim
inkstand	in secret	intermix	inurbane	Irish yew	isochore
in labour	insectan	internal	invalidy	ironbark	isochron
inlander	insecure	internee	invaried	iron blue	isocline
in league	inseeing	Internet	invasion	ironclad	isocolon
inleague	in series	Interpol	invasive	iron-clay	isocracy
in liquor	inserter	interred	invecked	Iron Duke	isocryme
in little	insertor	interrer	invected	iron gang	isogenic
in livery	insetted	interrex	inveigle	iron-grey	isogloss
inlooker	insetter	intersex	in velvet	iron hand	isogonal
inmostly	in sheets	intersow	inventar	iron-hard	isogonic
in motion	in shreds	intertex	inventer	iron hoof	isograft
in muster	in shtook	intertie	inventor	ironical	isograph
in my book	inside of	interval	in verity	iron lace	isohelic
in my mind	insignia	inter-war	inversed	iron lady	isoionic
innately	insignis	interwar	inverted	ironless	isolable
innatism	in sign of	in the air	inverter	iron-like	isolated
in nature	insister	in the bag	invertor	iron loss	isolator
in need of	insist on	in the can	investor	iron lung	isolexic
inner bar	insolate	in the ear	inviable	iron mask	isologue
inner ear	insolent	in the end	in view of	iron mike	isomeric
inner man	insomnia	in the log	invigour	iron-mold	isometry
in no case	insomuch	in theory	inviscid	iron-sand	isomorph
innocent	in spades	in the raw	invitant	iron-shot	isonomic
in no mood	in-sphere	in the red	inviting	Ironside	isophane
in no time	insphere	in the sun	invocant	iron tree	isophene
innovate	inspired	in the way	invocate	iron ware	isophone
in no wise	inspirer	inthrall	involute	ironware	isophote
innuendo	in spirit	inthrust	involved	ironweed	isopleth
inoculum	inspirit	intifada	involver	ironwood	isopodan
in orders	instable	intilted	in wake of	ironwork	isoprene
inornate	instance	intimacy	in want of	Iroquois	isospore
inosinic	instancy	intimate	inwardly	irrelate	isostasy
inositol	instinct	intimism	inwinter	irrigate	isostere
in pastel	institor	intimist	inworker	irrision	isothere
in person	instress	intimity	iodinate	irritant	isotherm
in pickle	in-stroke	intitule	iodoform	irritate	isotonic
in pieces	instruct	into fits	iodophor	irrorate	isotopic
in places	insulary	intonaco	iodyrite	irrumate	isotropy
in pocket	insulate	intonate	ion drive	Isabella	isotypic
in proper	insulter	intoneme	Ionicism	isagogic	isozooid
in public	in sunder	intonico	ionicity	Isaianic	isozymic
inputted	insurant	into play	Ionicize	isangoma	ispaghul
inputter	intaglio	intorted	ionizing	Isaurian	Israelis
inquirer	intaking	intra-day	ionogram	Iscariot	issuable
in quires	in tandem	intrados	iotacism	ischuria	issuably
in reason	intarsia	intrench	ipso jure	is he ever	issuance
in relief	integral	intrepid	irefully	Ishihara	isthmian
in retard	Intelsat	intrigue	irenarch	isidiate	itaconic
in return	intended	intrinse	irenical	isidioid	ITAR-Tass
in review	intender	intromit	irenicon	Islamise	itchiest
in revolt	intenser	intronic	Irgunist	Islamism	itch mite
inrolled	intently	introrse	Irianese	Islamist	itchweed
in room of	interact	intruded	iridesce	Islamite	I tell you

itemizer	Japanesy	Jew's harp	jovially	jury-mast	kedgeree
iterance	Japan ink	jib-sheet	jovialty	justicer	keek-keek
iterancy	Japanise	Jiffy bag	joy-bells	justness	keel-bill
it is said	Japanism	Jiffy pot	joyfully	jut-jawed	keelboat
it is told	Japanize	jig about	joy-house	juvenile	keelhaul
it is true	japanned	jig borer	joy juice	Kababish	keelless
it's a deal	Japanner	jiggerer	joyously	kabassou	keel-like
ivory-nut	Japan wax	jig plate	joyrider	Kabbalah	keenness
ivy-berry	Japhetic	jillaroo	joy-stick	kabeljou	keepable
I warrant	japishly	jim-dandy	joystick	Kabinett	keep away
Ixionian	japonica	jingbang	joy-wheel	Kabistan	keep back
jabberer	jararaca	jingoish	jubilant	kabloona	keep cave
jacitara	jargoner	jingoism	jubilate	kafenion	keep down
jackaroo	jargonic	jingoist	jubilean	kaffiyeh	keep fair
Jack bean	jarlship	jipijapa	jubilize	kailyard	keep from
Jack boat	jarosite	jiu-jitsu	Judahite	kaimakam	keep goal
jackboot	jasmined	jive talk	Judaical	kaka-beak	keep-left
Jack-bowl	jaspered	Joachism	Judaizer	kakariki	keep over
jackeroo	jasponyx	Joachist	judgment	kakemono	keep pace
jacketed	jaundice	jobation	judicial	Kakiemon	keep rank
jackfish	jauntier	job-coach	jugglery	kala-azar	keepsake
Jack-fish	jauntily	job horse	Jugoslav	kale-bell	keep shop
jack-line	Javanese	job house	jugulate	kalendar	keep step
Jack-pine	javanite	job press	juiciest	kale-runt	keep time
jack plug	Java plum	job-print	Julia set	kale-time	keep tune
Jack plug	jaws harp	job-share	julienne	kale-worm	keep with
Jack-roll	jawsmith	jobsheet	jumboism	kaleyard	keeshond
jackshay	jaw-tooth	jockette	jumboize	kalicine	keffiyeh
jackstay	Jaycette	jocosely	jumbo jet	kallidin	kelewang
jackyard	jazerant	jocosity	jumpable	Kalmucks	kelp crab
Jacobaea	jazziest	joctaleg	jump bail	kamacite	kelp-fish
Jacobean	jazz-rock	jocundly	jump ball	Kamakura	Kemalism
Jacobian	jealousy	jodhpurs	jump boot	kamikaze	Kemalist
Jacobite	jeepable	Joe Blake	jumped-up	Kanarese	kennedya
Jacobson	Jehovist	Johannes	jumpiest	Kanesian	kennetic
jacquard	jejunely	John boat	jump lead	kangaroo	kenspeck
jactance	jelloped	John Bull	jump-rock	kantikoy	Kentucky
jactancy	jelly bag	John Crow	jump rope	kaoliang	keratoma
jaculate	jelutong	Johndarm	jump seat	kaolinic	keratose
jacuzzis	jeopardy	John Dory	jump ship	Kapenaar	kerbside
jadeitic	jeremiad	johnnies	jump shot	Karabagh	kerchief
jaggedly	Jeremiah	joinable	jump suit	Karelian	Kermanji
jaggiest	jerepigo	joint box	jumpsuit	Karitane	kermesse
jagirdar	jerkiest	jointing	jump to it	Karnaugh	kernelly
jail-bait	jerk-line	joint-saw	jump turn	Karshuni	kerosene
jailbait	jeroboam	jointure	jump-weld	karstify	kerosine
jailbird	jerrican	joisting	junction	karsting	Kerr cell
jakealoo	jerrycan	jokeless	juncture	karyotin	Kerry cow
jalapeño	jerryism	jokesome	junk bond	Kashmiri	keskidee
jalopies	jerseyed	jokester	junketed	katakana	ketamine
jalousie	jerupiga	jokiness	junketer	katheter	ketazine
Jamaican	jessamin	jokingly	junk food	katonkel	ketimine
jambolan	jest-book	jolliest	junk mail	Katyusha	keto-acid
jamboree	Jesuitic	jolt-head	junk shop	kauri gum	keto-enol
Jamesian	Jesuitry	joltless	junkyard	kawakawa	ketonize
jammiest	jet black	Jonathan	Junonian	kayaking	ketoxime
jam-proof	jettison	jonglery	jurament	kayakist	keurboom
Janglish	jewelled	jongleur	Jurassic	kazachoc	key-block
janitrix	jeweller	Jonkanoo	juratory	kazooist	keyboard
janizary	Jewishly	journeys	juristic	Keating's	key-bugle
Japanese	jew's harp	jousting	jury-list	Keatsian	key money

keynoter	King high	knee-boot	korrigum	lactonic	lamenter
key-plate	kinghood	knee-boss	kourbash	lacunary	laminary
keypunch	kingklip	knee-deep	kouskous	lacunate	laminate
keystone	King Kong	knee-high	kowtower	lacunose	laminose
khaki bos	kingless	knee-hole	krameria	lad-bairn	laminous
khalasis	kinglike	kneehole	kratogen	laddered	lampless
khalassi	kingling	knee-jerk	kraw-kraw	ladified	lamp-post
Khaldian	king lory	kneelike	kreutzer	ladifies	lamppost
Khaskura	king post	kneeling	kromesky	ladleful	lampreys
Khedival	king rail	knee-roof	Kuchaean	ladle out	lampyrid
Khilafat	kin group	knickers	Kulinism	lad of wax	lancegay
Khoikhoi	kingship	knife-bar	Kurilian	lad's love	lancelet
Khurasan	king-side	knife-boy	Kuroshio	ladybird	lanceted
khus-khus	king-size	knifeful	kurtosis	lady-fern	land ahoy
kibitzer	kingsman	knife-man	kurumaya	ladyfied	land army
kickable	king's peg	knightly	kurveyor	ladyfish	land bank
Kickapoo	kingston	knitbone	Kushitic	ladyhood	land-bank
kick back	kingwood	knitchel	kvetcher	ladyless	landbank
kickback	kinkajou	knitting	Kwakiutl	ladylike	land-bred
kick-ball	kinkhost	knitwear	kyanitic	lady-love	land crab
kickball	kinkiest	knitwork	kymogram	Lady Luck	landfall
kick-down	kinkless	knobbing	kyphosis	Lady Muck	land-fast
kickseys	kinsfolk	knobbled	kyphotic	ladyship	landfill
kickshaw	kip house	knobbler	kyrielle	lady's man	land-floe
kicksies	kipperer	knoblike	Labadist	lady ware	land-folk
kickster	Kipsigis	knobwood	labdanum	lady wife	landform
kick-tail	kirkless	knocking	labelled	laen-land	land-fyrd
kick-turn	kirk-town	knock off	labeller	Laetrile	land girl
kidflick	kirkyard	knock out	labellum	lagander	landlady
kid-glove	kirn-baby	knockout	labially	Lag b'Omer	land legs
kidology	Kir-Shehr	knorhaan	labiated	lag fault	landless
Kilkenny	kiskadee	Knossian	lability	lagoonal	land line
killable	kissable	knot-head	labilize	lag phase	landline
killbuck	kissably	knot-hole	Laborism	Lagrange	landlord
killcrop	kiss away	knotless	laborous	laically	landmark
killdeer	kiss-curl	knottier	laboured	laicizer	land mass
kill-lamb	kissless	knottily	labourer	laid-back	land-mine
killogie	kistvaen	knotting	Labrador	laid work	landmine
kill-time	kitcheny	knotweed	laburnum	laitance	land-pike
kill zone	kitefish	knotwork	Lacanian	Lakeland	land-poor
kilobase	kite-mark	knowable	lace-fern	lakeless	landrace
kilobuck	Kitemark	know best	lacelike	lakeside	landrail
kilobyte	kithless	knuckled	lacerate	lake-weed	Landseer
kilogram	Kiwanian	knuckler	lacertid	lallygag	Land's End
kilovolt	Kjeldahl	knurling	lacewing	lamanism	land ship
kilowatt	Klansman	kohekohe	lacewood	lamantin	land-sick
kimonoed	Klansmen	koh-i-noor	lacework	lamasery	landside
Kim's game	Kleinian	kohlrabi	laciness	lambaste	landslip
kindless	klephtic	koinonia	lackaday	lambdoid	landsman
kindlier	kleywang	Kolarian	lackland	lambency	landsmen
kindlily	klipfish	kolinsky	Laconian	lambhood	land-take
kindling	klipkous	Kol Nidre	Laconise	lambkill	landward
kindness	Klondike	komitaji	laconism	lamblike	land-wash
kinesics	klystron	Komsomol	Laconize	lambling	land-wind
kinetics	knackery	kookiest	lacqueys	lamb's fry	land wire
kingbird	knallgas	Kootenai	lacrimal	lambskin	Langhans
kingbolt	knapping	koradjis	lacrosse	lame duck	lang-kale
king-carp	knapsack	korfball	lacrymal	lamellae	langlauf
king crab	knapweed	korimako	lactated	lamellar	Langmuir
king fern	knee-bend	koromiko	lacteous	lameness	langosta
kingfish	knee-bone	korrigan	lactogen	lamented	langrage

langsuir	laterite	lawyerly	leadwort	left bank	lens-work
lang syne	laterize	laxation	leaf beet	left-hand	lenticel
language	late-wake	laxative	leafbird	leftmost	lenticle
languish	late wood	layabout	leaf cast	leftness	Lent lily
lankiest	lathe-bed	lay an egg	leaf curl	leftover	Lent term
lankness	latherer	lay aside	leaf-fall	left turn	Lenz's law
lanneret	lath-nail	laybarge	leaf-flea	leftward	Leonberg
lanosity	lathyrus	lay clerk	leaf-frog	left-wing	lepidote
lanthana	latifund	lay elder	leaf-gold	legacies	leporine
lanthorn	Latinate	layer-cut	leafiest	legal aid	leprolin
lap-board	Latinise	layering	leaf-lard	legal cap	lepromin
lapelled	Latinish	layer-out	leafless	legalese	leptonic
lapicide	Latinism	layer pit	leaflike	legalise	Lesghian
lapidary	Latinist	layer vat	leaf node	legalism	les girls
lapidate	Latinity	lay gauge	leaf-roll	legalist	lessness
lapidify	Latinize	laylight	leaf-scar	legality	less than
lapidist	latitant	lay pipes	leaf-soil	legalize	let alone
lapillus	latitude	layshaft	leaf-spot	legal man	let blood
lap joint	Latonian	laystall	leaguing	legatary	let drive
lappeted	lattener	lay to wed	leaguite	legatine	lethally
Lapponic	latterly	lay vicar	leakance	legation	lethargy
lapsable	latticed	lay waste	leakiest	legative	let loose
lapstone	laudable	laywoman	lean-burn	leg-break	let me see
lap strap	laudably	laywomen	leanness	leg drive	lettable
lap-table	laudanum	lazarets	lean-over	legended	lettered
Laputian	laudator	Lazarist	lean upon	Legendre	letterer
larboard	laudible	Lazarite	leapable	legendry	letteret
larcener	laughful	laziness	leap-frog	legerity	lettrine
larch gum	laughing	lazulite	leapfrog	leggiero	lettrism
larderer	laugh off	lazurite	leap year	leggiest	lettrist
lardiner	laughter	lazy-back	learning	leg-guard	leucitic
largesse	launcher	lazyhood	learn off	legioned	leucoses
lark-heel	Laurasia	lazy-jack	learn out	legitime	leucosin
larksome	laureate	lazy-Jack	leasable	leg stump	leucosis
larkspur	Laurence	leachate	leaseman	legumina	leucotic
larrigan	lava bomb	leadable	leash law	leg woman	leukemia
larrikin	lava flow	lead-acid	leathern	Leibnitz	leukosin
larruped	lava-lava	lead away	leathery	Leishman	leukosis
larvated	lavatera	lead-back	leavable	leisured	levanter
laryngal	lavation	lead-bars	leave for	lemmatic	Levanter
larynges	lavatory	lead-burn	leave off	lemonade	levelism
lashed-up	lava tube	lead cell	leave out	lemonish	levelled
lashings	lava ware	lead comb	leavings	lemon law	leveller
lashless	lave-ears	leadenly	Lebanese	lemon oil	level off
lash rope	lavement	leadered	Lechitic	lemurian	level out
laspring	lavender	leaderly	lecithin	lemurine	leverage
last days	Laverack	lead flat	lectrice	lemuroid	leviable
last gasp	laverock	lead-free	lecturee	lenation	levigate
last home	laver-pot	leadless	lecturer	lendable	levirate
last name	lavishly	lead-line	lecythus	lengthen	levitant
last post	law agent	lead-mill	ledgment	lenience	levitate
last word	law court	lead-nail	leeangle	leniency	levodopa
latanier	lawcourt	lead-rope	lee-board	Leninism	levulose
latching	lawfully	lead shot	leeboard	Leninist	levyable
latchkey	lawgiver	leadsman	leechdom	Leninite	lewdness
latch-pan	law Latin	lead-spar	leechery	lenities	lewdster
lateener	law-maker	lead time	lee gauge	lenition	Lewis gun
late mark	lawmaker	lead-tree	leeriest	lenitive	Lewisian
latemost	lawn meet	lead-wash	leerness	leno loom	lewisite
lateness	lawn sand	lead wool	lee shore	lens hood	Lewisman
latently	Lawrence	leadwork	left-back	lensless	lexigram

liar dice	lifetime	limberly	linesmen	literati	lobbyist
libament	life-tree	limbless	line-wire	literato	lobeless
libation	life-vest	limblike	line-work	literose	lobelike
libatory	lifeward	limb-meal	ling-bird	litharge	lobeline
libeccio	life-work	lime-cast	lingerer	lithemia	loblolly
libelled	liftable	limekiln	lingerie	lithosol	lobotomy
libellee	liftback	limeless	linguine	lithsman	lobstick
libeller	lift down	Limenian	linguist	litigant	lobulate
libelous	lift-gate	limerick	lingular	litigate	local bus
liberate	liftless	Limerick	lingworm	litreage	localise
Liberian	lift-slab	lime-rock	liniment	litterer	localism
libretti	lift wire	lime-sink	linisher	little go	localist
libretto	ligament	lime soap	linking r	littlest	locality
licensed	liganded	lime-soda	link road	littling	localize
licensee	ligation	lime tree	linkspan	littlish	local pub
licenser	ligature	lime-twig	link-verb	littoral	location
licensor	ligeance	limewash	link-word	liturgic	locative
lichanos	lightage	lime-work	link-work	Litz wire	locellus
lichened	light air	limicole	Linnaean	liveable	Loch Fyne
lichenin	light-bob	liminary	linoleic	live bait	Lochlann
lich-gate	light-box	liminess	linolein	live-born	lochside
lich-path	light-day	limitary	linoleum	live coal	lockable
lick-hole	light due	limitate	Linotype	live down	locketed
licorice	lightful	limit bid	linstock	live it up	lockfast
lie about	light-gun	limit dog	lint-head	livelier	lock-knit
lie ahead	lighting	limiting	lion-head	livelily	lockless
lie along	lightish	limit man	lionhood	live load	lock on to
lie close	light-man	limnetic	lionizer	livelong	locksman
lie doggo	light oil	limnoria	lion-like	liveness	locksmen
liegedom	light out	limonene	lion's ear	liveried	lockspit
liegeman	light-pen	limonite	lionship	liveries	lock step
liegemen	light red	limonium	lipaemia	liverish	locofoco
Liégeois	ligneous	Limousin	lipaemic	liver pad	locomote
lie heavy	lignitic	limpidly	lip-brush	liver rot	loco-weed
lie in wed	ligulate	limpness	lip gloss	live up to	locution
lientery	Ligurian	limuloid	lipogram	liveware	locutory
lie to wed	likeable	linalool	lipoidal	live well	lodesman
lie under	likeably	linarite	liposome	live wire	lodestar
lie waste	like a log	linchpin	lippiest	live with	lodgment
lifebelt	like fury	lincture	lipsalve	liveyere	lodicule
lifeboat	like hang	lindworm	lipstick	lividity	loessial
lifebuoy	like hell	lineable	lip-strap	living-in	loftiest
life cord	likelier	lineally	Liptauer	livingly	loftsman
life form	likeness	linearly	liquesce	Livonian	log-board
life-hold	likening	line-boat	liquidly	lixivial	log cabin
lifeless	likesome	line-book	liquidus	lixivium	log canoe
lifelike	like that	line-bred	liration	lizardly	log flume
lifeline	like this	line-camp	liripipe	llaneros	log-house
life list	like well	line drop	lispound	load line	logician
lifelong	like wild	linefeed	lissomly	loadstar	logicise
life peer	likewise	line gale	listable	loaf-cake	logicism
life-raft	lilliput	line haul	listener	loaiasis	logicist
liferent	lily bell	lineless	listen in	loamless	logicize
life-ring	lily feet	line loss	listeria	loanable	logistic
life-save	lily-iron	linen tea	listless	loan-farm	logogram
life-size	lily-like	line pipe	list vote	loanword	logology
lifesome	lily-pond	line-ride	Lisztian	loathful	logotype
life span	lily-turf	line scan	litanies	loathing	log sheet
lifespan	lima bean	line-side	literacy	lobation	log table
life test	limacine	lineside	literary	lobby-gow	loiterer
life-tide	limation	linesman	literate	lobbyism	Lollardy

lollipop	long seas	loquence	love-pass	lumberer	lutidine
lolloped	long ship	loquency	love-play	lumberly	lutulent
lollygag	long shot	loquitur	lover boy	luminant	luxation
lomentum	longsome	lordless	lovering	luminary	luxmeter
Londoner	longspur	lordlier	love seat	luminate	luxuries
lone hand	long-stay	lordlike	lovesick	luminise	luxurist
lonelier	longstop	lordlily	lovesome	luminism	lycaenid
lonelily	long suit	lordling	love-song	luminist	lych-gate
loneness	long-tail	Lord Muck	love-tree	luminize	lycopene
lone pair	long-term	lordosis	love-vine	luminous	Lycurgan
lonesome	long-time	lordotic	lovingly	lump coal	lyke wake
lone star	long togs	lord over	low-alloy	lumpfish	lymphoid
lone wolf	longueur	Lord's day	low-class	lumpiest	lymphoma
long acre	long view	Lord's Day	Low Dutch	lumpless	lymphous
long bill	longwall	lordship	low enema	lump work	lynching
longbill	longward	loreless	lower jaw	lumpy jaw	lynch law
long blow	long wave	loricate	low-flung	lunabase	lynch mob
longboat	longways	lorikeet	low-grade	lunacies	lynchpin
long bone	longwise	lorisoid	low heels	luna moth	lynx-eyed
long card	long-wool	lornness	low-keyed	Luna Park	lynxlike
long cist	long word	Lorraine	Low Latin	lunar day	Lyonnais
long clam	lonicera	lorry-bus	low-level	lunarian	Lyonnese
long clay	look as if	lorry-hop	lowliest	lunarite	Lyonnois
long-coat	look back	loseable	lowlight	lunarium	lyophile
long date	look down	lose face	low-lived	lunation	lyophobe
long-dead	looker-in	lose time	low-lives	lunch box	lyrately
long dung	looker-on	lossless	low-lying	luncheon	lyra viol
long-ells	look good	lostness	low point	lung book	lyre-bird
longeron	look here	lost rock	low water	lungeing	lyre-tail
longeval	look like	lost soul	low-wines	lungeous	lyricise
long face	look over	lote-tree	low-yield	lungfish	lyricism
long firm	look sick	Lothario	loxodont	lungfuls	lyricist
long game	look up to	lotiform	loyalism	lungless	lyricize
longhair	looniest	lotus-eat	loyalist	lungworm	lyriform
longhand	loony-bin	Loucheux	loyalize	lungwort	lysarden
long haul	loop film	loud-hail	Loyolite	lunkhead	lysergic
longhead	loophole	loudness	lozenged	lunulate	lysogeny
long home	loopiest	lousiest	lozenger	Lupercal	lysopine
longhorn	loop jump	loveable	lubberly	lupulone	lysosome
long hour	loop-knit	love-bird	Lubecker	lurement	lysozyme
long john	loop-knot	lovebird	lubrical	Lurgi gas	lyzarden
long John	loop-lace	lovebite	Lucanian	luringly	Macanese
long jump	loop line	love bush	Lucchese	Lusatian	Macaoese
long-legs	loop pile	love-curl	lucently	luscious	macaroni
long lens	loop-work	love-dart	lucernal	lushburg	macaroon
long-life	loop-worm	loved one	Lucianic	lush drum	Macassar
long line	loop yarn	love game	lucidity	lush-head	Maccabee
long live	loose box	love-hate	luciform	lushness	maccoboy
long-lost	loose end	love-knot	luckiest	lustered	macerate
long mark	loose ice	Lovelace	luckless	lustiest	machinal
long-moss	loosener	loveless	lucky-bag	lustless	machiner
longneck	loosen up	lovelier	lucky dip	lustrate	machismo
longness	loo table	love life	lucky him	lustring	macilent
long nine	lootable	lovelify	luculent	lustrous	mackerel
long nose	lop-eared	lovelike	Lucullan	lustrums	Mackinaw
long odds	lop-grass	lovelily	lucumony	lutanist	macropod
long-play	lophioid	loveling	luderick	lutecium	macruran
long pull	lopolith	lovelock	lug-chair	lutenist	maculate
long rape	loppered	lovelorn	luggable	Lutetian	maculose
long room	lopsided	love-mate	luggaged	lutetium	maculous
long rope	lopstick	love nest	lukewarm	Lutheran	macushla

Madagass	mailable	make love	maltwort	mannitol	marginal
mad-apple	mail boat	make over	malvasia	man of God	margined
mad-brain	mailboat	make play	Mameluco	man of law	margrave
made dish	mail cart	make post	Mameluke	man of men	mariachi
Madeiran	mail drop	make room	mamillar	man-of-war	maribout
Madelung	mailgram	make sail	Mamma mia	man of wax	marigold
made mast	mailless	make sure	mammifer	manorial	marikina
maderize	maillots	make time	mammilla	manostat	marinade
made road	mailroom	make up to	mammitis	manpower	marinara
made wine	mailshot	make wing	mammogen	man-shift	marinate
mad Greek	mail-time	make with	Mam'selle	man-sized	marinise
madhouse	maimedly	make-work	managing	mansonia	Marinism
mad money	main beam	Makololo	man alive	mansuete	Marinist
madrigal	main body	makomako	man-child	manswear	marinize
madroños	main crop	maladies	manciple	mantelet	Mariotte
madstone	maincrop	maladive	man-crazy	mantical	mariposa
Madurese	main deck	mala fide	Mandaean	man-tiger	mariscal
madwoman	main dish	Malagash	Mandaite	mantiger	maritime
madwomen	main drag	Malagasy	mandamus	mantilla	marjoram
maeander	Maine Law	malamute	mandarin	mantises	markable
Maecenas	mainland	malapert	mandator	mantissa	mark-boat
maenadic	main line	malaprop	mandelic	mantling	mark down
maestoso	mainline	malarial	mandible	man to man	markdown
maestria	mainmast	malarian	Mandingo	man-trade	markedly
Maffiosa	mainpast	malarkey	Mandinka	manually	marketed
magadize	mainsail	Malawian	mandolin	manucode	marketer
magatama	mainstay	malaxate	mandorla	manumise	markless
magazine	main stem	Malayali	mandrake	manumize	marksman
magaziny	maintain	mal de mer	mandrill	manurial	marksmen
magdalen	main-ward	Malecite	man-eater	man-woman	mark time
Magellan	main yard	maledict	maneless	manyatta	marmoset
maggotry	maiolica	male fern	manerial	many-body	marocain
Maghribi	Maithili	malefice	maneuver	manyfold	Maronite
magic eye	Maitrank	malemute	manfully	many—many	marooner
magician	Maitreya	maleness	mangabey	manyness	marquess
magicked	majestic	malengin	manganic	manzello	marquise
magister	majolica	male pill	manganin	Maori bug	marriage
magmatic	Majorana	malgrace	Manganja	Maori dog	marrowed
magnesia	Majorcan	maligner	mangiest	Maoridom	marrying
magnesic	Majorism	malignly	mango-fly	Maori-hen	marry off
magnetic	Majorist	malihini	mangonel	maple key	marry out
magneton	majority	Malikite	mangrove	maple pea	Marshall
magnetos	major key	malinger	man-hater	map-maker	marsh gas
magnific	make a bag	Maliseet	maniacal	mappable	marsh hay
magnolia	make a bed	malistic	Manichee	maquette	marshier
Magosian	makeable	mallards	manicure	marabout	marshman
maharaja	make a bow	malleate	manifest	maracock	marsh tit
maharana	make a hit	mallecho	manifold	marantic	Marsilid
maharani	make a row	malleoli	maniform	marasmic	Martaban
Mahayana	make as if	malodour	Manipuri	marasmus	martagon
mah-jongg	make away	malonate	manistic	marathon	Martello
mahogany	makebate	Malorian	manitoka	marauder	Martenot
mahoitre	make down	Maloryan	mani wall	maravedi	martinet
Mahratta	make eyes	maltdust	mankiest	marbling	martynia
Mahratti	make fast	Malthoid	manliest	marcella	martyred
maidenly	make-game	maltiest	manna-ash	March fly	martyrly
maid-fish	make good	malt-kiln	manna-gum	marching	Mary Jane
maidhood	make-hawk	maltreat	mannered	march-man	Maryland
maidless	make head	malt shop	mannerly	Margaret	Mary lily
maidling	make it up	maltster	mannikin	margaric	Marymass
maieutic	makeless	maltworm	mannitic	margarin	marzipan

mascotry	maturest	meat-hook	melanite	menseful	messiest
mash note	maturity	meatiest	melanoid	men's room	messmate
mash-roll	matutine	meatless	melanoma	menstrua	mess-room
mason-bee	maumetry	meat loaf	melanose	mensural	messuage
Masonite	maundful	meat rack	melanous	menswear	mesteque
Mason jar	mausolea	meat-rail	Melchite	mentally	mestizos
Masorete	mauveine	meat safe	melilite	menthone	metaboly
Masorite	maverick	meatuses	melinite	menu card	metacism
massacre	maxillae	mechanic	melismas	mephitic	metacone
massager	maximand	mecholyl	melissic	mephitis	metadyne
mass-book	maximise	meconium	melissin	Mercator	metagram
masseter	maximist	medalist	melissyl	merchant	metal age
masseuse	maximize	medalize	melitose	merciful	metalate
massicot	maximums	medalled	melittin	Merckani	metaling
massless	Mayanist	medallic	melktert	mercuric	metalist
mass noun	mayapple	medially	melleous	mereness	metalize
massoola	May-apple	medianly	mellitic	merengue	metalled
Massorah	mayflies	mediated	mellowly	meresman	metallic
mast cell	mayordom	mediator	melodeon	meretrix	metamere
mast coat	mayoress	Medicaid	melodial	mergence	metamict
masterer	mayorlet	Medicare	melodies	mericarp	metanoia
masterly	May queen	medicate	melodion	meridian	metaphor
masthead	mazarine	Medicean	melodise	meringue	metarule
mastitis	Mazdaean	medicine	melodist	meristem	metasoma
mastless	Mazdaism	medieval	melodium	meristic	meta-talk
mastodon	Mazdaist	medimnus	melodize	meriting	metatony
mast-step	Mazdeism	mediocre	melomane	merit pay	Metatron
mast year	mazelike	meditant	melonist	merocele	metazoan
masurium	mazement	meditate	melon-oil	merogamy	metazoic
Matabele	mazer cup	mediumly	meltable	merogony	metazoon
matachin	maziness	medjidie	melt away	Meroitic	meteoric
matadora	M-capture	medullar	melt down	merriest	metewand
Mata Hari	McGuffin	medusoid	meltdown	merryman	meteyard
matamata	McIntosh	meekness	melt-spin	merry men	methanal
matchbox	McKenzie	meeterly	melusine	mersalyl	methanol
match-fit	mea culpa	meetness	membered	Mersenne	methinks
matehood	mead-hall	meet with	membrane	merwoman	methodic
mateless	meadowed	megabuck	mementos	merycism	methoxyl
matelote	meagrely	megabyte	memorate	mescalin	methylal
material	mealable	megacosm	memorial	Mesdames	methylic
matériel	mealiest	megadont	memoried	meshumad	metonymy
maternal	mealless	megaflop	memories	meshwork	me-tooism
mateship	meal moth	megalith	memorise	mesially	metopism
mat-grass	mealtide	megalopa	memorist	mesmeric	metreage
mathemeg	mealtime	megalops	memorize	mesnalty	metrical
mathesis	meal-worm	megapode	Memphian	mesocarp	metritic
mathetic	mealworm	Megarian	memsahib	mesoderm	metritis
Mathurin	mealy bug	megastar	menacing	mesoform	meunière
matiness	me-and-you	megaunit	Menapian	mesolabe	Mexicano
matrical	mean moon	megavolt	menarche	mesolect	mezereon
matrices	meanness	megawatt	mendable	mesomere	mezuzoth
matrixes	mean time	Meg Dorts	mendment	mesosome	mezzroll
matronal	meantime	Megillah	Menevian	mesotron	miasmata
matronly	mean tone	megimide	menhaden	mesozoan	mica flap
mattedly	mean well	meionite	menially	Mesozoic	Micawber
Matthean	measlier	meiosis I	meninges	mesozoon	micellar
mattress	measured	meiotaxy	meningic	mespilus	Michigan
maturant	measurer	Meissner	meniscal	mesquite	micritic
maturase	meatball	melamine	meniscus	Messapic	microamp
maturate	meat cube	Melanian	men-of-war	mess hall	microbic
maturely	meathead	melanism	menology	Messidor	microbus

microdot	Milky Way	minihole	misgiver	mistryst	modistic
micrurgy	millable	minimise	misgrown	misusage	modulate
midas fly	mill band	minimism	misguide	misvalue	mofussil
midbrain	mill bill	minimize	mishmash	miswrite	Mohammed
mid-cycle	mill-dust	mini-moke	Mishnaic	Mithraic	Moharram
middling	mill-hand	minimums	misinfer	miticide	mohonono
mid-earth	millhand	mini pill	misjudge	mitigant	mohoohoo
midfield	mill-head	minipill	miskeyed	mitigate	moieties
midnight	milliamp	minister	Miskitos	mitre box	moirette
mid-ocean	milliard	ministry	mislearn	mitt camp	moistful
midpoint	milliary	minneola	misliker	mittened	moistify
mid-range	millibar	minorate	misliver	mittimus	moistish
midships	millième	Minorcan	mislodge	mitzvoth	moisture
mid-spoon	milliner	Minoress	mismatch	mixed bag	mokaddam
midstead	millions	Minorite	mismated	mixed bed	moki-moki
mid-water	mill-pick	minority	mismetre	mixer tap	moko-moko
midwater	millpond	Minotaur	misnomer	Mixtecan	molality
midwives	mill-pool	minstrel	misogamy	mizen top	molarity
mightest	mill-post	mint-bill	misogyne	mnemonic	molassed
mightful	mill-race	mint cake	misogyny	Mobilian	molasses
mightier	mill-rind	mintiest	misology	mobilise	moldiest
mightily	mill-ring	mint mark	misorder	mobilism	Moldovan
mighty me	mill-sail	minueted	misplace	mobilist	mole-cast
migmatic	mill seat	minutely	misprint	mobility	molecule
mignonne	mill site	minutest	misprize	mobilize	mole-head
migraine	mill tail	minutial	misproud	mobocrat	molehill
migrator	mill town	minyanim	misquote	moccasin	moleskin
mijnheer	mill-weir	Miocenic	misroute	Mochican	molester
miladies	mill-work	miositic	misruler	mockable	molinary
Milanese	miltonia	Miquelet	missable	mock-bird	Molinism
milch cow	Miltonic	mirepoix	Miss Anne	mock croc	Molinist
mild beer	mimester	miriness	missense	mock lead	molleton
mildness	mimetism	mirkiest	misserve	mock moon	mollient
mile-mark	mimetite	mirliton	miss fire	moco-moco	Mollisol
milepost	mimiambi	mirrored	misshape	modalise	moll-shop
Milesian	mimicked	mirthful	missikin	modalism	mollusca
miliaria	mimicker	Mirzapur	missound	modalist	mollycot
militant	minacity	misagree	Missouri	modality	molossid
military	minatory	misalign	misspeak	modalize	molossus
militate	mince pie	misandry	misspell	modeless	Moluccan
milk bank	minchery	misanter	misspend	modeliar	molybdic
milk-bush	mind-cure	misapply	misspent	modeling	molysite
milk drop	mind-game	misaward	misspoke	modelist	momental
milk-duct	mindless	misbeget	miss-stay	modelled	momently
milkfish	mind-read	misbegin	misstate	modeller	momentum
milkiest	mineable	misbirth	misstyle	Modenese	monachal
milkless	mine dump	misbound	missworn	moderacy	monadism
milk line	mine host	miscarry	missyish	moderant	monadist
milk-loaf	mine-hunt	mischief	mistaken	moderate	Mona Lisa
milkmaid	mine-iron	miscible	mistaker	moderato	monamide
milk name	minerval	miscount	misteach	moderner	monamine
milkness	minestra	miscreed	misthink	modernly	monandry
milk-pail	mine-town	misdoing	mistiest	modestly	monarchy
milk room	mine-work	misdoubt	mistimed	modicity	monaster
milk-sick	mingiest	misdrive	mistitle	modified	monastic
milk-tree	minicell	misentry	mistless	modifier	monaural
milk-tube	mini-coat	miserere	mistlike	modifies	monaxial
milk-walk	Mini Disc	miseries	mistreat	modiolar	monazite
milk-warm	minidisk	misery me	mistress	modiolus	mondaine
milkweed	minigene	misfaith	mistrial	modishly	mondongo
milkwort	minigolf	misfield	mistrust	Modistae	Mondrian

monellin	monosemy	moot hall	Mortlake	mounseer	mudirieh
monensin	monosign	moot-hill	mortmain	mountain	mud-laden
monetary	monosome	mootness	mort-skin	mountant	mud pilot
monetise	monosomy	mop-board	mortuary	mounting	mud puppy
monetite	monotint	mopiness	Mosaical	mournful	mudslide
monetize	monotone	mopishly	mosasaur	mourning	mud snail
money-bag	monotony	mopper-up	moshavim	mouse-dun	mud snake
money box	monotype	mopstick	mosquito	mouse-ear	mudstone
money-man	monoxide	moquette	Mosquito	mousekin	mud trout
mongcorn	Monsieur	morainal	moss-back	mouselet	muff cock
Mongolic	monstera	morainic	moss-crop	mouse pox	muffetee
mongoose	Montague	moralise	moss horn	mousiest	muffling
monicker	Montanan	moralism	mossiest	moussaka	muga silk
monilial	monteith	moralist	mosslike	mouthful	muggiest
monistic	monte-jus	morality	moss opal	mouthier	mug-house
monition	Monterey	moralize	moss-peat	mouthily	mug's game
monitory	monticle	moral law	moss pink	mouth off	Muhammad
monitrix	Montilla	moralled	moss rose	mouth rot	Muharram
monk bond	monument	moration	moss-wood	moveable	muishond
monkeyfy	mood drug	moratory	Most High	move a peg	muisvoël
monkfish	moodiest	Moravian	most like	move away	mujtahid
Mon-Khmer	moodooga	morbidly	moteless	move into	mulattos
monkhood	moonball	morbific	motelier	moveless	mulberry
monk seal	moonbeam	morbilli	moteling	movement	mulching
monk-seam	moon boot	mordancy	mothball	move over	mule-bird
monk's gun	moon-cake	more like	mothered	moviedom	mule deer
monkship	mooncalf	morellos	motherer	movieola	mulesing
monk shoe	moon-dial	moreness	motherly	movingly	muleteer
monniker	moon-down	moreover	mothiest	mowburnt	muley cow
monoacid	moon-eyed	morepork	mothlike	moyen-âge	mulishly
monobloc	moon-face	Morescos	motility	mozzetta	mullered
monobuoy	moonfish	Moresque	motional	Mrs Thing	mulligan
monocarp	moongate	moribund	motivate	Mswahili	mullocky
monocled	mooniest	moriform	motivity	muchacha	mulloway
monocrat	moonless	morillon	mot juste	muchacho	multeity
monocule	moonlike	morindin	motliest	much less	multifid
monoculi	moon pool	Morlacco	Motorail	muchness	multimer
monocyst	moonrise	mormyrid	Motorama	mucilage	multiped
monocyte	moonseed	mormyrus	motor bus	mucinous	multiple
monodies	moonshee	mornings	motor car	muck-heap	multi-ply
monodist	moonshot	mornless	motor cop	muckiest	multiply
monodont	moonsiff	morn star	motordom	muckluck	multi-use
monogamy	moonwalk	Moroccan	motorial	muckrake	multi-way
monogeny	moonward	moroccos	motoring	muck soil	multurer
monogerm	moonwort	morology	motor inn	muckworm	mummy bag
monoglot	moon-year	moronism	motorise	mucky pup	muncheel
monogram	moor-bird	moronity	motorism	mucocele	munch out
monogyny	moorburn	morosely	motorist	mucoidal	mung bean
monohull	moor-coal	morosity	motorium	mucoitin	municipy
monokini	moorcock	morosoph	motorize	mucosity	muniment
monolith	moor-evil	Morphean	motorman	mucrones	munition
monology	moorfowl	morpheme	motormen	muculent	munyeroo
monomial	moor game	Morpheus	motorway	mud-brick	muralist
monomino	moor-head	morphine	mottling	mudbrick	muralled
monopody	moorland	morphing	moufflon	muddiest	Muranese
monopole	Moorpark	morphism	mouldery	muddle up	murchana
Monopole	moor-pout	morphoea	mouldily	mud fever	murderee
monopoly	moor-sick	mortally	moulding	mud fluid	murderer
Monoprix	moorsman	mortgage	mould oil	mud flush	murenger
monoptic	moose fly	mortific	moulinet	mudguard	murexide
monorail	mootable	mortiser	mound ant	mudirate	muriatic

muricate	mutinize	nail down	natatory	nearness	nembutsu
Muridism	mutinous	nail file	nathless	near-seal	Nemedian
muriform	mutterer	nail-gall	natiform	nearside	nemesism
muringer	muttoned	nail head	national	near-silk	nenuphar
murkness	mutually	nail-hole	natively	near upon	neoblast
murksome	muzziest	nailless	nativism	neatherd	neo-Latin
murmurer	myatonia	nailsick	nativist	neatness	neolocal
murphies	mycelial	nainsell	nativity	Nebbiolo	neologic
murrelet	mycelium	nainsook	nativize	nebulate	neomorph
murrhine	mycetoma	naissant	natterer	nebulise	neomycin
murrnong	mycetome	naked ape	nattiest	nebulist	neonatal
muscadel	mycology	naked bed	Natufian	nebulium	neo-Nazis
Muscadet	mydas fly	naked eye	naturise	nebulize	neon fish
muscatel	myelitic	nakhlite	naturism	nebulose	neon lamp
muscimol	myelitis	naloxone	naturist	nebulous	neon sign
muscling	myelomas	namaskar	naturize	neckband	neon tube
muscular	myelosis	nameable	naucrary	neck-beef	neophron
museless	mylodont	name-drop	naukrary	neck-bone	neophyte
musellim	mylonite	nameless	nauplial	neck-hole	neoplasm
mush-head	mylonize	name part	naupliar	necklace	neoprene
mushiest	myoblast	namesake	nauplius	neckless	Neorican
mushroom	myocomma	name-tape	nauseant	neckline	neotenic
musicale	myogenic	Namibian	nauseate	neck-lock	neotenin
music box	myograph	nanberry	nauseous	neck-rein	neoteric
musician	myokymia	nancy boy	nautical	neck-roll	Nepalese
musicker	myomeric	nannydom	nautilus	neck-vein	nepenthe
music-mad	myomorph	nannygai	navalism	neckwear	nephrite
musingly	myopathy	nannyish	navalist	neckweed	nephroid
musk-ball	myopical	Nantgarw	navarchy	necropsy	nephrops
musk deer	myoplasm	napellus	Navarran	necrosis	nepionic
musk duck	myositis	naphthol	navel-ill	necrotic	nepotism
muskeggy	myosotis	naphthyl	navicert	nectared	nepotist
musketry	myotatic	napiform	navicula	Ned Kelly	neptunic
muskiest	myotomic	napkined	naviform	needfire	Neronian
musklike	myotonia	napoleon	navigate	neediest	Neronize
Muskogee	myotonic	nappy pin	navy bean	needless	nerve gas
musk-rose	myriadth	narceine	navy blue	needment	nervelet
musk tree	myriapod	narcissi	Navy List	Néel wall	nerve net
musk-wood	myristic	narcosis	navy plug	negation	nerve war
muskwood	myristin	narcotic	navy yard	negative	nerviest
Muslimin	myristyl	narghile	Naxalism	negatory	nescient
muslined	myrmidon	naringin	Naxalite	negatron	neshness
muslinet	myronate	narkiest	nay-sayer	negligee	nestfuls
musquash	Mysoline	Narodnik	naysayer	negligée	nestlike
mustache	Mysorean	narratee	Nazarean	Negretti	nestling
mustardy	mystical	narrator	Nazarene	Negrillo	net-layer
mustelid	mysticly	narrower	Nazarite	Negritic	netmaker
musterer	mystique	narrowly	Nazified	Negritos	netsukes
muster in	mythical	nasalise	Nazifies	Negro dog	nettable
mustiest	mythless	nasalism	Nazirite	Negrodom	nettling
mutation	myxedema	nasality	Ndebeles	Negroish	neumatic
mutative	myxinoid	nasalize	neap tide	Negroism	neurally
mutchkin	myxomata	nascence	near-beer	Negro yam	neuraxis
muteness	naartjie	nascency	nearctic	neighbor	neuritic
mute swan	nabobess	nasiform	Nearctic	nektonic	neuritis
muticous	nacreous	nasology	Near East	Nelsonic	neuromas
mutilate	Naderism	nassella	near gale	nelumbos	neuronal
mutillid	nag's-head	nastiest	near hand	nemacide	neuronic
mutineer	nailable	Natalian	near home	nematode	neuropil
mutinied	nail a lie	natality	near miss	nematoid	neuroses
mutinies	nail bomb	natation	nearmost	Nembutal	neurosis

neurotic	nick-nack	Nixonian	non-licet	notalgia	nucellus
neuterly	nickname	Nixonite	non-metal	notalgic	nuciform
neutrino	nicotian	Noachian	non-moral	notarial	nucleant
Nevadian	nicotina	Noah's ark	non-party	notaries	nucleary
never-was	nicotine	Nobelist	non-polar	notarise	nuclease
new-baked	nicotize	nobelium	non-rigid	notarize	nucleate
new birth	nidation	nobility	non-sched	not at all	nucleoid
new blood	nidering	noble gas	nonsense	notation	nucleole
new-blown	nidicole	nobleman	non-stick	notative	nucleoli
new bread	nidified	noblemen	non-toxic	not-being	nuclidic
new broom	nidifies	noble rot	non-union	notchier	nudeness
newcomer	nidifuge	noblesse	nonuplet	notching	nude pact
New Delhi	nidorous	nobodies	non-usage	notebook	nugacity
newelled	nidulant	no bottle	non-voter	note card	nugation
new entry	niellist	nocturia	non-white	notecase	nugatory
Newlands	nielloed	nocturne	non-White	noteless	nuisance
New Light	nieveful	nodality	non-woven	not go far	nullable
newly-wed	niffiest	nodosity	no object	notified	null cone
Newmania	niff-naff	nodulate	noogenic	notifier	null link
new maths	Niflheim	nodulize	noontide	notifies	nullness
new-model	niftiest	nodulose	noontime	notional	numberer
New Model	Nigerian	nodulous	nopalery	not least	numb-fish
new money	niggling	noematic	nopaline	notornis	numb hand
New Negro	nigh-hand	noetical	no picnic	not quite	numbhead
new order	night bag	no-frills	normalcy	no trumps	numbness
New Right	night-box	no-go area	normally	not so bad	numeracy
newscast	nightcap	no-gooder	Normandy	not so hot	numerary
news desk	night eye	no-hitter	Norseman	not to say	numerate
newsgirl	night-fly	nohowish	Norsemen	noumenal	numerist
newshawk	night-hag	noiseful	northern	noumenon	numerous
newsiest	nightjar	noisette	northing	nounally	Numidian
newsless	nightman	noisiest	Northman	nounless	numinous
Newspeak	night off	no lack of	Northmen	nounness	nummular
newsreel	night out	no little	northpaw	nouveaux	numskull
news room	night owl	no longer	North Sea	nouvelle	nunation
newsroom	Nigritic	nomadise	norwards	Novatian	nunchaku
new-style	Nigrotic	nomadism	Norweyan	novation	nuncheon
New Style	nihilism	nomadize	noseband	noveldom	nunciate
new thing	nihilist	nomarchy	nose-clip	novelese	nundinal
new waver	nihility	no matter	nose-cone	novelise	nuppence
new woman	nil-grade	nominata	nosedive	novelish	nuraghic
New World	nimblest	nominate	nose door	novelism	nursling
New Year's	nimbused	nomistic	nose-down	novelist	nurtural
next-best	nimbuses	nomogram	nosehole	novelize	nurturer
next door	nine-eyed	nomology	nose leaf	novellas	nutation
nextness	ninefold	no mortal	noseless	November	nut brown
Nez Percé	nineteen	nonanoic	noseling	novenary	nut-crack
Nganasan	nineties	nonaries	nosepipe	novercal	nut-grass
Niam-Niam	Ninevite	non-Aryan	nose-ring	novitial	nuthatch
nibbanic	ning-nong	non-being	nosering	Novocain	nut-house
nibble at	ninjutsu	non-black	nose-tube	nowadays	nuthouse
nibbling	ninnyish	non-claim	nose-wipe	nowhence	nutmeggy
Nibelung	nippiest	non-count	nose-worm	nowheres	nutrient
niccolic	nitchevo	non-elect	noshable	no wonder	nutshell
niceling	nit-grass	non-empty	nosiness	nowtherd	nut-steak
niceness	nitrated	non-entry	nosology	n quadrat	nuttiest
niceties	nitriary	nonesuch	no sooner	nubecula	Nyamwezi
nice work	nitrogen	non-event	nostalgy	nubilate	nymphaea
Nichiren	nitrosyl	non-human	not a bean	nubility	nymphean
Nichrome	nitroxyl	non-ionic	nota bene	nubilous	nymphish
nickelic	nivation	nonjuror	not a hope	nucellar	nystatin

oafishly	occurred	of a truth	oil trade	Olympism	one while
oak-apple	oceanful	of course	oinochoe	omadhaun	one-woman
oakiness	Oceanian	of family	ointment	omelette	one-world
oat-grass	Oceanids	off and on	oiticica	omission	onhanger
oathable	oceanite	off-board	okey-doke	omissive	onion-fly
oat-plant	oceanity	off-brand	Okinawan	omitting	onion set
obduracy	ocean sea	off-break	Oklahoma	ommateal	on liking
obdurate	ocellate	offcomed	oknophil	ommateum	onliness
obeahism	ochreate	offcomer	old field	Ommayyad	onlooker
obeahman	ochreish	off-drive	old flame	omniform	only just
obedient	ochreous	offended	old fruit	omnitude	on my word
obeisant	ockerdom	offender	Old Glory	omnivore	on nights
obeyable	ockerism	offering	old guard	omnivory	onolatry
obeyance	ocnophil	off-gauge	Old Harry	omo-hyoid	onomancy
obituary	ocotillo	off-glide	Old Irish	omoplate	onomatop
objectee	octanoic	off-grain	Old Latin	omphalos	Onondaga
objector	octanoyl	off guard	Old Light	on a level	on pain of
oblately	octantal	officese	old-maidy	on and off	on parade
oblation	octapody	official	old money	on a plate	on parole
oblatory	octapole	offishly	Old Norse	on a slant	on points
obligant	octarchy	off-lying	old poker	on broach	on record
obligate	octaroon	off-piste	Old Saxon	on camera	on relief
obligato	octavian	off-pitch	old socks	once-born	on remand
obliging	octobass	off-price	Old South	once more	on screen
obliqued	octofoil	offprint	Oldspeak	onceness	on-screen
obliques	octonary	off-rhyme	old squaw	once-over	onscreen
oblivial	octopean	offscape	old stick	on change	onsetter
oblivion	octopian	offshoot	old story	on charge	on shares
oblongly	octopine	offshore	old-style	oncidium	on shikar
obnounce	octopoid	offsider	Old Style	oncogene	on stilts
obnoxity	octopole	off-stage	old sweat	oncolite	on stream
obrogate	octopush	off-track	old thing	oncology	on-street
obscurer	octoroon	off-verse	old-timer	oncoming	on strike
observer	octuplet	off-white	old times	oncosine	on supply
obsidian	octupole	of no name	old-timey	on course	on-target
obsolete	ocularly	of renown	Old Welsh	on credit	Ontarian
obstacle	oculated	of resort	old woman	on demand	on the air
obstruct	oddities	oftenest	old-world	one-acter	on the bit
obtainal	odd trick	of theirs	Old World	one-armed	on the bow
obtainer	Odinitic	oft-times	oleander	one-baser	on the bum
obtected	odiously	ogee arch	oleaster	one-berry	on the dot
obtemper	odometer	Oghuzian	olefiant	one by one	on the ebb
obtruder	odometry	ohmmeter	olefinic	one flesh	on the fly
obturate	odontoid	oil baron	olibanum	one-horse	on the gad
obtusely	odontome	oil-break	oligarch	one-idea'd	on the hip
obtusity	odourful	oilcloth	oligemia	one in six	on the hop
Ob-Ugrian	Odyssean	oilfield	oligomer	one-liner	on the jar
obvolute	odysseys	oil-fired	oligopod	one-night	on the job
Occamism	oeconomi	oil-gauge	oliguria	one-on-one	on the lam
Occamist	oecumene	oil-gland	oliguric	one or two	on the map
occasion	Oedipean	oiliness	oliphant	one-piece	on the mat
Occident	oenochoe	oil-paint	olive dun	one-place	on the nod
occluder	oenocyte	oil-paper	olive-fly	one's bark	on the pad
occlusal	oenology	oil-plant	olive oil	one's bite	on the pan
occlusor	Oerlikon	oil-press	olive pie	one's game	on the peg
occulter	oestrane	oil-shale	Olivetan	one-sided	on the run
occultly	oestriol	oil-shark	olivette	one's mark	on the sea
occupant	oestrone	oil slick	Olmecoid	one thing	on the sly
occupied	oestrous	oil spill	olorosos	one-to-one	on the tap
occupier	oestrual	oilstone	Olympiad	one-track	on the vag
occupies	of a piece	oil-tight	Olympian	onewhere	on the way

on thirds	operator	ordinant	osculate	outdress	outshove
on thorns	opercula	ordinary	osier bed	outdrink	outsider
on tiptoe	operetta	ordinate	Osmanlis	outdrive	outsight
ontogeny	operette	ordnance	osmicate	outer Bar	outsized
ontology	Ophelian	oreillet	osnaburg	outer ear	outskirt
on ullage	ophidian	ore-shoot	oso-berry	outer man	outsleep
on velvet	Ophitism	orfrayed	ossature	outfence	outsmart
on view of	ophiuran	organdie	Ossetian	outfield	outspeak
on wheels	ophiurid	organ-gun	Ossianic	outfight	outspeed
onymatic	opinicus	organise	ossicula	outflame	outspend
oofiness	opium den	organism	ossified	outflank	outstand
oogamete	Opium War	organist	ossifies	outflash	outstare
oogamous	opopanax	organity	osteitis	outflies	outstart
oogonial	oppilate	organize	ostinati	outfling	outstate
oogonium	opponens	organ-man	ostinato	outflung	outsteal
ookinete	opponent	organoid	ostomate	outflush	outstink
oolichan	opposing	orgasmal	ostracod	out front	outstood
oologist	opposite	orgasmic	ostracon	outfront	outstrip
oomycete	opposive	orgastic	ostreger	outfrown	outswear
oophoron	oppugner	orgonomy	Otaheite	outgases	outswell
oosphere	opsimath	orgulous	otarioid	outglare	outswing
oothecal	opsonize	oribatid	other man	outgoing	out-taken
ooze-calf	optation	orichalc	otiosely	out-group	out there
ooziness	optative	orielled	otiosity	outgrown	out-think
opacious	optic cup	oriental	otolitic	out-guard	out-throw
opacular	optician	oriented	otophone	outguess	out-trade
opal dirt	opticist	origanum	otoscope	out-Herod	out-trick
opalesce	opticity	original	ototoxic	outhouse	out-trump
opal ware	optimacy	orillion	otter-dog	outlaugh	outvalue
opaquely	optimate	orinasal	ottomans	outlawry	outvoice
opaquest	optimise	ormering	Ottomans	outlearn	out-voter
openable	optimism	ornament	Ottonian	outlying	outwards
open-arse	optimist	ornately	ought not	outmarch	outwatch
open bite	optimity	ornation	ouistiti	outmatch	outweary
opon book	optimize	ornature	ouricury	outmoded	outweigh
opencast	optimums	ornithic	outargue	outmouth	outworld
open city	optional	orogenic	outbirth	outnoise	outwrite
open date	optotype	orometry	outblaze	out of bed	outyield
open door	opulence	oronasal	outbloom	out of key	ovalness
open-eyed	opuscula	orphancy	outblush	outpaint	Ovaltine
open file	opuscule	orphreys	outboard	out-place	ovariole
open fire	oracular	orpiment	outbound	outplace	ovaritis
open goal	oraculum	or rather	outbrave	outpoint	ovenbird
open line	oragious	Orrefors	outbreak	outpoise	oven-cook
open loop	orangery	orreries	outbreed	outpower	ovenette
open mind	orangish	orthesis	outbroke	outpsych	ovenware
open-neck	Orangist	orthicon	outbuild	outpunch	overaged
openness	oratoric	orthodox	outburst	outrager	overarch
open-plan	oratorio	orthoepy	outcarry	outrange	overbank
open-reel	oratress	orthopod	outcaste	outreach	overbark
open road	orbicule	orthosis	outcharm	outreign	overbear
open shop	orbitale	orthotic	outclass	outrider	overbeat
open-side	orbiting	orticant	outclimb	outright	overbend
open town	Orcadian	ortstein	outcrier	outrival	overbite
open ward	orchella	Ortygian	outcries	outscold	overblow
openwork	orchilla	Orvietan	outcross	outscore	overbody
operable	orchitis	oryzenin	outcurve	outshame	overboil
opera hat	ordainer	oscinine	outdance	outshine	overbold
operance	order man	oscitant	outdated	outshone	overbook
operancy	order pad	Oscotian	outdoors	outshoot	overboot
operatic	ordinand	osculant	outdream	outshout	overbore

overbrim	overhard	overrise	overwell	pacifico	palesman
overbrow	overhaul	overrode	overwent	pacified	palestra
overbull	overhead	overroll	overwind	pacifier	paleways
overbump	overheap	overroof	overwing	pacifies	palewise
overburn	overhear	overruff	overwise	pacifism	palfreys
overbusy	overheat	overrule	overwood	pacifist	palilogy
overcall	overhigh	oversail	overword	Pacinian	palimony
overcame	overhill	oversalt	overwork	packable	palinode
overcare	overhung	overseas	overworn	packager	palinody
overcast	overhunt	overseen	overwrap	packaway	palisade
overclad	overjump	overseer	overyear	pack-flat	palisado
overcloy	overkeep	overself	overzeal	pack it in	palladia
overcoat	overkill	oversell	ovicidal	pack-road	palladic
overcoil	overkind	over-shoe	ovicular	pack-sack	palliard
overcold	overking	overshoe	oviducal	packshot	palliate
overcome	overknee	overshot	oviposit	pack them	pallidly
overcook	overlade	overside	ovomucin	pad-cloth	palliest
overcool	overlaid	oversize	ovulator	Paddyism	palliums
overcrop	overlain	overslip	owleries	Padishah	pall-mall
overcrow	overland	overslow	owlglass	pad money	palmated
overcure	overlard	oversnow	owlishly	pad-steam	palm-ball
overdamp	overlate	oversoar	owl-light	padstone	palm-bird
overdear	overleaf	oversold	owl midge	paduasoy	palm crab
overdeck	overlean	oversoon	owl train	paeonies	palmella
overdoer	overleap	oversoul	own brand	pagandom	Palmerin
overdoes	overlier	overspan	own-label	paganise	palmette
overdo it	overline	overspin	own woman	paganish	palmetto
overdone	overling	overspun	oxalosis	paganism	palmfuls
overdoor	overlive	overstay	oxaluria	paganity	palm-grub
overdose	overload	overstep	oxathiin	paganize	palmiest
overdraw	overlock	oversway	oxazepam	pagehood	palmiped
overdrew	overlong	overswim	ox-botfly	pageship	palmitic
over ears	overlook	overt act	oxbow key	page-turn	palmitin
overeasy	overlord	overtake	Oxbridge	paginary	palm leaf
overface	overloud	overtalk	ox-fenced	paginate	palmlike
overfall	overloup	overtask	ox-harrow	pahoehoe	palm-lily
overfeed	overlove	overteem	oxidable	pailfuls	palm-play
overfell	over-many	overtell	oxidized	pain-free	palm-room
overfill	overmany	overtilt	oxidizer	painless	palm tree
overfilm	overmark	over time	oximeter	pain spot	palm-wasp
overfine	overmast	overtime	oximetry	paint box	palm wine
overfire	overmitt	overtire	ox-pecker	paintbox	palm-worm
overfish	overmost	overtoil	ox-tongue	paintier	palomino
overflew	overmuch	overtone	oxtongue	painting	palpable
overflow	overname	overtook	ox-warble	paint out	palpably
overfold	overnice	overtrap	oxyanion	paint-pot	palpebra
overfond	overpaid	overtrim	oxygenic	pair-bond	palpifer
overfree	overpark	overtrow	oxymeter	pair-feed	palpiger
overfull	overpass	overture	oxymoron	pair-mate	palstave
overgang	overpeer	overturn	oxyphile	pairment	palterer
overgave	overplay	overveil	oxytocic	pair-toed	palterly
overgaze	overplus	over vert	oxytocin	pairwise	paltrier
overgild	overpole	overview	oxytonic	Palamite	paludina
overgive	overrank	overwalk	oysterer	palander	paludine
overglad	overrash	overward	Ozarkian	palatial	paludism
overglut	overrate	overwarm	ozonizer	palatian	pamaquin
overgrew	overread	overwash	pabulary	palatine	pamperer
overgrow	overrent	overweak	pacation	palative	pamperos
overhair	overrich	overwear	pace-note	paleface	pamphlet
overhand	override	overween	pachalic	pale flax	panacean
overhang	overripe	overweep	pachinko	paleness	panached

panarchy	papalise	parashah	part-bred	pastoral	paxillar
panatela	papalism	parasite	parterre	pastorly	pay a call
pan-broil	papalist	paratomy	part fair	pastrami	pay claim
pancetta	papalize	paratype	part from	pastries	paynimry
panchama	Papal See	paravail	Parthian	pastural	pay phone
pancheon	paparchy	paravane	partiary	pasturer	payphone
Pancoast	papaship	par avion	partible	pat-a-cake	pay sauce
pancreas	paper bag	parawing	particle	patacoon	peaberry
panda car	paper boy	paraxial	partisan	patagial	pea-brain
pandanny	paper cup	parazoan	partitas	patagium	peaceful
pandanus	papering	parbreak	partizan	patch-box	peace-man
pandemic	paper man	parcener	partless	patchery	peacenik
panderer	paper run	parclose	part-load	patch fox	peachery
pandowdy	papillae	pardoner	partners	patchier	pea-chick
panegyry	papillar	pardon me	partness	patchily	peachier
paneless	papillon	parental	part-song	patching	peach-pip
paneling	papirosa	parented	part time	pâte dure	peacocky
panelist	papisher	pareoean	part with	patellae	pea-flour
panelled	papistic	parergon	part-work	patellar	pea green
panel pin	papistly	Paretian	partyism	patentee	peak hour
panel saw	papistry	parfocal	party man	patently	peakiest
panel van	papulose	pargeted	parvenue	patentor	peak load
panforte	papulous	pargeter	parwanah	Paterian	pea-plant
pangeran	papyrosa	pargetry	parylene	paternal	pear drop
pangless	parabema	parhelia	parypate	pathetic	pearl ash
panglima	parabola	parhelic	pasch-egg	pathless	pearl-hen
Pangloss	parachor	parietal	pascuant	pathogen	pearlier
pangolin	paracone	parietes	pashadom	patience	pearling
pan-human	paradigm	parietin	pashalic	patiency	pearlish
panic bar	paradise	Parisian	pasilaly	patinaed	pearlite
panicked	paradors	parkiest	paspalum	patinate	pearmain
panicled	paradoxy	parkland	passable	patootie	pear tree
Paninean	paradrop	parklike	passably	patriate	pearwood
pan juice	paraffin	parlance	passalid	patrices	peasanty
panmixia	paraffle	parlando	pass away	patronal	peasecod
pannikin	parafoil	parlleys	passback	patronee	pea-shell
Pannonic	paraform	Parma ham	passband	patronly	pea-stake
panoptic	paragoge	Parmesan	passbook	patronym	peat-coal
panorama	paragone	parodial	pass door	pattable	peatland
pan pipes	Paraguay	parodied	passer-by	pattamar	peatmoss
panplain	parajump	parodies	Passeres	pattened	peat-reek
pan-Roman	parakeet	parodist	pass—fail	patterer	peatship
pansophy	parakite	parodize	pass-hemp	patterny	pea-viner
panstick	parallax	paroemia	passible	pattress	peccable
pansyish	parallel	parolein	passival	pattypan	peccancy
pantcoat	paralyse	paronymy	pass laws	patulent	peccavis
panterer	paralyze	paroquet	passless	patulous	peck horn
pantheon	parament	parosmia	pass line	pauldron	peck mood
pantiled	paramese	parotoid	pass-mark	Paulista	pecorino
pantiler	par amour	Parousia	passmark	paunched	pectines
pantless	paramour	paroxysm	pass over	pauropod	pectoral
pantoate	paranete	parroted	Passover	pavement	peculate
pantofle	paranjah	parroter	pass play	pavilion	peculiar
pantonal	paranoia	parrotry	passport	pavisade	pedagogy
pantopod	paranoic	Parseval	password	pavisand	pedal bin
Pantopon	paranoid	parsonic	pastance	pavonian	pedal car
pantries	paraoxon	parsonly	pastiche	pavonine	pedalfer
pant suit	parapack	parsonry	pastiest	pawkiest	pedalier
panurgic	paraquat	partaken	pastille	pawl-bitt	pedalled
papabile	parasail	partaker	pastless	pawnable	pedaller
papacies	parasang	part-book	pastness	pawnshop	pedaloes

pedantic	penalize	Percaine	Pershing	Pfeiffer	phthalic
pedantry	penchant	per caput	personae	phacelia	phthises
pedately	pencraft	perceant	personal	phacopid	phthisic
peddling	pendency	perceive	personas	phalaena	phthisis
pederast	pendicle	percepta	perspire	phalange	phulkari
pedestal	pendular	perchery	perspiry	Phalange	phut-phut
pedicate	pendulum	perentie	persuade	phalaris	phylarch
pedicure	Penelope	perester	Pertelot	phallism	phyletic
pediform	penetral	perfecta	perthite	phalloid	phyllary
pedigree	penitent	perfecto	pertness	phantasm	phyllite
pediment	penknife	perflate	Perugian	phantast	phyllode
pedipalp	pen-light	perforce	perukier	phantasy	phyllody
pedology	penlight	perforin	Peruvian	Pharisee	phylloid
pedregal	pennated	perfumed	perverse	pharmacy	phyllome
peduncle	pennoned	perfumer	pervious	phase out	physalis
peekaboo	penn'orth	Pergonal	perylene	pheasant	physeter
peekapoo	penny-fee	periagua	Peshitta	phenagle	physical
peelable	penology	perianal	peskiest	phenetic	physicky
peep-hole	penseful	perianth	pessimal	phengite	physique
peephole	pen shell	periblem	pessimum	phenogam	piacular
peep-show	pensiful	pericarp	pesterer	phenolic	pia mater
peep-toed	penstock	pericope	pest-ship	phenylic	pianette
peerless	pentacle	pericyte	petaline	phialine	pianiste
peership	pentagon	periderm	petalism	philabeg	piassava
peesweep	pentamer	peridial	petalite	Phillips	piazzaed
peetweet	pentanol	peridium	petalled	philobat	piblokto
Pegasean	pentarch	periergy	petalody	philodox	picaroon
pegboard	Pentelic	perifuse	petaloid	Philomel	picayune
peggotty	pentitol	perigean	pétanque	Philonic	piccolos
peggy bag	Pentland	Périgord	petchary	philtrum	Picenian
peggy tub	Pentomic	perigyny	petechia	phimosis	pichurim
peg-house	pentosan	perijove	peterman	phimotic	piciform
peignoir	pent roof	perilled	petermen	phlegmon	pickable
Peircian	penumbra	perilous	Peternet	phloxine	pickerel
pejorate	penuries	perilune	Peter Pan	Phocaean	picker-up
pejorism	Penutian	perineal	Peterson	Phoebean	picketed
pejorist	penwiper	perineum	petiolar	phonemic	picketer
Pekinese	penwoman	periodic	petioled	phonetic	pickfork
pelagian	peonidin	perioral	petition	phoniest	pickiest
Pelagian	peperino	periotic	petitive	phononic	pickings
pelandok	peperite	perisarc	petit mal	phoresis	picklock
Pelasgic	peperoni	perisher	petitory	phoretic	pick-me-up
pelerine	peplumed	peritomy	petrific	phorminx	pick over
peliosis	peppered	perjured	petrolic	phormium	pick-pole
pellagra	pepperer	perjurer	petronel	phoronid	picksome
pelleted	pepper-up	perkiest	petrosal	phosgene	pickwick
pelleter	peppiest	perlitic	pettable	phosphor	picloram
pellicle	pep rally	permeant	pettedly	photoact	picnicky
pell-mell	peptidic	permease	pettiest	photofit	picoline
pellucid	peptidyl	permeate	pettifog	photogen	picritic
peloidal	peptizer	per mille	pettitoe	photo lab	Pictland
pelorism	peptogen	permuter	Petty Bag	photomap	pictural
pelorize	Pepuzian	Permutit	petty pan	Photomat	pictured
pelt-wool	Pepysian	pernancy	petulant	photonic	piddling
pelvises	peracute	peroneal	petuntse	photopic	pie-biter
Pembroke	perahera	peroneus	pew group	photo-set	piece-bag
pemmican	peramble	Peronism	pewterer	photoset	piece-dye
pemoline	per annum	Peronist	Peyerian	phrasing	piecener
penacute	per arsin	perorate	peyotism	phratric	piece out
penalise	perboric	peroxide	peyotist	phreatic	pie chart
penality	Perbunan	perseity	Pfalzian	Phrygian	piecrust

pied crow	pimentos	pinprick	pitchier	planking	playhour
pied duck	pimiento	pinscher	pitching	plankter	playland
Pied Monk	pimpling	pinswell	pitchman	planktic	playless
piedmont	pinacoid	pin-table	pitch-oil	plankton	playlist
piedness	pinacone	pint-size	pitch-ore	plank-way	playmake
pie-eater	pinafore	pin valve	pitch-out	planless	playmate
pie-faced	pinakoid	pin-wheel	pithiest	planning	playroom
pie graph	pinaster	pinwheel	pithless	planosol	play safe
pie-melon	pinboard	pipe away	pithlike	planster	playsome
pie-plant	pince-nez	pipe band	pith-tree	plantain	play-suit
piercing	pincette	pipe bomb	pitiable	plant-bug	playsuit
pier-head	pinch-bar	pipeclay	pitiably	planting	playtime
pierless	pinch-bug	pipe down	pitiless	plantlet	play upon
pie-wagon	pinch-gut	pipefish	Pitmanic	plant out	play up to
piffling	pinch-hit	pipefuls	pitmatic	plantula	pleached
piff-paff	pinching	pipeless	pit organ	plantule	pleading
pig along	pinch-off	pipelike	pittance	plan view	pleasant
pigeonry	pinch-out	pipeline	pit viper	plashily	pleasing
piggiest	pinch-run	pipe-rack	pivoting	plashing	pleasure
piggling	Pindaric	piperade	pivotman	plasmoid	plebania
pig Latin	Pindarry	piperine	pixelate	plasmoma	plebbish
pig louse	pine cone	pipe roll	pixie cap	plasteel	plebeian
pig-metal	pine-knot	pipe-stem	pixie hat	plastery	plectrum
pig-mould	pine land	pipe tree	pixie-led	plastify	Pleiades
pigsties	pineries	pipe-vine	pize-ball	plastome	plein-air
pig's wash	pine tree	pipework	pizzeria	plastral	plenarty
pigswill	pine vole	pipewort	placable	plastron	plentify
pikehead	pineweed	pipkrake	placably	platanna	pleonasm
pike-pole	pine wood	piquable	placater	platanus	pleoptic
pilaster	pinewood	piquance	placcate	platband	plethora
pilchard	ping-pong	piquancy	Placc Act	plateaus	plethory
pile arms	pin-grass	piracies	place-bet	plateaux	plethron
pileated	pinguefy	pirastic	placebos	plateful	pleurisy
pile it on	ping-wing	piratess	placeman	platelet	pleurite
pileless	pin hinge	piriform	place mat	plate pie	plexuses
pilentum	pinioned	piri-piri	placemen	platform	pliantly
pile-shoe	pin joint	piripiri	placenta	platinic	plicated
pile-work	pink-foot	piroshki	placidly	platinum	plimsole
pilewort	pink gold	pirozhki	Placidyl	Platonic	plimsoll
pilferer	pink lady	pis aller	placitum	platting	Pliocene
piliated	pinkness	pisanite	plagiary	platypus	Pliofilm
pilidium	pinkroot	piscator	plaguily	platysma	pliosaur
piliform	pink slip	piscinae	plaguing	plaudite	pliotron
Pilipino	pink spot	piscinas	plaiding	plausive	plip-plop
pillager	Pinkster	pishashi	plain bob	Plautine	plodding
pillaloo	pinkwash	pishogue	plainful	playable	plombage
pillared	pink wine	pish-pash	plaining	play away	plopping
pillaret	pinkwood	pisiform	plainish	play back	plotless
pill head	pinledge	pisolite	plain man	playback	plot-line
pilliver	pin lever	pisolith	plain-saw	play ball	plottage
pillowed	pin money	pissabed	plaister	playbill	plotting
pill slab	pinnacle	piss away	plaiting	playbook	plotwise
pillwort	pinnated	piss down	plancher	play-debt	ploughed
pilosity	pinniped	pisshead	planchet	play down	plougher
pilotage	pinnular	piss-hole	plancier	play face	plough in
piloting	pinochle	piss-take	plane-bit	play fair	plowland
pilotism	pinoleum	pistacia	planeful	Playfair	pluckier
pilot jet	pin-paper	pistolet	planetal	playfere	pluckily
pilot-man	pin-patch	pitahaya	planetic	playgame	plucking
Pilsener	pin plate	pit canal	planform	playgirl	plug back
Piltdown	pinpoint	pitch-cap	plangent	playgoer	plug-cock
pilulous	Pinpoint	pitch for	plank bed	play high	plug flow

plug fuse	podgiest	polisher	polypite	poor show	Portland
plugging	podiatry	polish up	polypody	poortith	port-last
plug-hole	podiform	politely	polypoid	poor-will	portlier
plughole	podocarp	politest	polypore	popehood	portmote
plug-ugly	podocyte	politico	polypose	Pope Joan	portolan
plumaged	Podolian	politics	polypous	popeless	portrait
plumbago	podomere	politied	polyseme	popelike	portress
plumbane	pod razor	polities	polysemy	popeling	portsman
plumbate	pod shell	politize	polysome	pope's eye	port tack
plumb-bob	podzolic	polka dot	polysomy	Pope's eye	portuary
plumbean	Poe-esque	polkaing	polytene	popeship	Portugal
plumbery	poethood	pollable	polyteny	pop group	portulac
plumbian	poetical	poll-book	polytomy	popinjay	portunal
plumbing	poetizer	poll card	polytope	popishly	port wine
plumbism	poetless	poll deed	polytype	poplared	porulose
plumbite	poetling	pollenin	polytypy	poplolly	poseable
plumbous	poetship	poll-evil	polyuria	pop music	poshness
plum cake	pogonion	pollical	polyuric	popocrat	poshteen
plum duff	poignant	pollices	polyzoan	Popovets	positing
plumelet	Poincaré	pollinia	polyzoic	poppadam	position
plumeria	pointage	pollinic	polyzoon	poppadom	positive
plumetis	point bar	polliwog	pomander	Poppy Day	positron
plumetty	pointful	pollster	pomarine	pop-rivet	posology
plumiest	pointier	polluted	pomelled	Popsicle	possible
plumiped	pointing	polluter	pomerium	popskull	possibly
plumlike	pointlet	pollywog	pommellé	populace	postally
plummier	point man	polo coat	pommetty	populate	postbase
plummily	point net	polocyte	pomology	populism	post-boat
plumping	point out	poloidal	pompanos	populist	postcard
plumpish	pointrel	polo neck	Pompeian	populous	post-cart
plum tree	poisoner	Polonian	pompilid	pop-valve	postcode
plumular	Poitevin	polonies	pompless	pop-visit	postcure
plungeon	poke-nook	polonium	pomponed	poquosin	post-date
plunging	pokerish	Polonize	ponchoed	poristic	postdate
plunther	poke-root	polo-pony	ponderal	pork-chop	postdict
plurally	pokeweed	Polovtsy	ponderer	porkfish	post-echo
pluriarc	pokiness	polt-foot	pond-fish	porkiest	post-edit
plushier	Polabian	poltroon	pond life	porkling	postface
plushily	Polabish	Polwarth	pond-lily	porkwood	post-fine
plus sign	Polander	polyacid	pond-pine	porky-pie	postform
plus-twos	polar cap	polyadic	pondweed	porn-shop	post-free
plutonic	Polar cap	polyarch	ponerine	porocyte	post-girl
plutonyl	polarise	polybase	pongiest	porogamy	postgrad
Pluviose	polarity	polyclad	ponticum	poroporo	post-hole
pluvious	polarize	polydrug	pontifex	porosity	post-horn
Plyglass	Polaroid	Polyfoto	pontific	porously	posthuma
plymetal	pole-bean	polygala	pony-tail	porphyry	postical
Plymouth	pole-boat	polygamy	ponytail	porpoise	postiche
pnicogen	pole-jump	polygene	pooh-pooh	porridge	posticum
pnictide	poleless	polygeny	pool-ball	porridgy	post-lady
pochards	pole-mast	polyglot	pool hall	portable	postlude
pochette	polemise	polygram	pool room	portably	postmark
pocketed	polemist	polygyny	poolside	portales	post-mill
pocketer	polemize	polylogy	poonghie	Portaloo	post-note
pock-mark	pole-reed	polymath	poontang	portance	post-obit
pockmark	pole star	polymery	poop deck	port arms	post-oral
pockwood	polestar	polymict	poor-farm	porteous	post-paid
podagral	pole-trap	polyneme	Poor-Jack	portfire	postpone
podagric	poleward	polyopia	Poor John	porthole	postpose
podalgia	policies	polypary	poor man's	porticos	post rank
podargus	policing	polypide	poorness	porticus	post-road
podetium	poliosis	polypier	poor rate	portière	post room

post ship	Powindah	prehuman	prestore	prizable	propanal
post-sync	powwower	pre-ictal	presumer	prizeman	propanol
post-term	Powysian	prejudge	pretence	prizemen	propenal
post town	poxvirus	prelatic	pretense	proavian	propense
postural	Poynting	pre-Latin	pretonic	probable	propenyl
posturer	Pozidriv	prelatry	pretrain	probably	properly
posy ring	practice	prelimit	pretreat	procaine	property
potassic	practise	preluder	pretrial	proceeds	prophage
potation	praecipe	preludia	prettier	procello	prophase
potatoes	praedial	Preludin	prettify	prochain	prophecy
potatory	praefect	preludio	prettily	proclaim	prophesy
pot-au-feu	Praesepe	premerit	previous	Proclian	prophyll
pot-belly	Praguean	premiate	prevotal	procline	propiska
pot-board	Praguian	premiere	priapean	Procline	proplasm
pot-bound	Prairial	première	priapism	proclive	propless
pot-earth	prairied	premisal	Priapist	procural	propofol
potented	praise be	premiums	price-cut	procurer	propolis
potently	Pramnian	premolar	price out	prodding	proposal
potholed	pram-park	pre-moral	price tab	prodelta	proposed
potholer	prandial	premorse	price tag	prodigal	proposer
potholey	prankful	premotor	price war	prodnose	propound
pot-house	prankish	premoult	priciest	prodroma	propoxur
potlatch	praskeen	prenasal	prick-ear	prodrome	proppily
pot-metal	pratfall	prenatal	pricking	producer	propping
pot-paper	pratique	prentice	pricklet	proemial	proprium
pot plant	prat-kick	pre-order	prideful	profaner	prop-root
potreros	prattler	pre-owned	prie-dieu	profiler	prop wash
pot roast	prayable	preparer	priestly	profilin	prop-word
potsheen	prazosin	prep chef	priggery	profited	propylic
potsherd	preacher	prepense	priggish	profiter	propylon
pot-shoot	preach up	preppier	priggism	pro forma	prorogue
pot stand	preadapt	preppies	primally	profound	prosaism
potstick	pre-adult	prepping	primatic	profunda	prosaist
pot still	preamble	pre-print	primeval	profundi	proseman
potstone	pre-axial	preprint	primmest	progeria	prosiest
potterer	preboard	prepubes	primming	progeric	prosodia
pottiest	precaval	prepubic	primness	proggins	prosodic
pot-train	precinct	prepubis	primrose	prognose	prosopon
pot-water	precious	prepulse	primrosy	prograde	prospect
pot-woman	precipit	prepupal	princely	progress	prostate
poulaine	précised	prequark	princeps	prohibit	prostyle
pouldron	précises	pre-rinse	princess	pro-knock	protalus
poulette	preclose	pre-Roman	princock	prolapse	pro tanto
poultice	preclude	presager	printery	pro-lifer	protases
poundage	precurse	prescind	printing	prolific	protasis
pound-fee	predator	presence	print out	Prolixin	protatic
Poundian	predella	preserve	printout	prolixly	protease
pounding	Predmost	presider	print run	prologue	protégée
pound-net	pre-elect	Presidia	priorate	promisee	proteose
pound out	preening	presidio	prioress	promiser	protheca
pourable	pre-entry	presolar	priories	promisor	prothyle
poverish	pre-exist	press bed	priority	promotee	protidic
povidone	prefacer	press box	prisable	promoter	protocol
Povindah	preferee	press day	Priscian	promotor	protomer
power car	prefetch	press fit	prismane	prompter	protonic
power cut	prefixal	pressing	prismoid	promptly	protopod
power-egg	prefocus	pression	prisoned	promulge	protozoa
powerful	preggers	pressive	prisoner	pronator	protract
power law	pregnane	pressman	prissier	prong-hoe	protrude
power-net	pregnant	pressmen	prissily	pronotal	pro-tutor
power set	prehnite	pressure	pristane	pronotum	protypon
Powhatan	pre-human	prestige	pristine	pro or con	proudful

proudish	ptilinal	pulpiter	pupilled	put about	quadrate
provable	ptilinum	pulpitis	pup joint	putanism	quadriga
provably	ptilosis	pulpitry	puppetry	putative	quadroon
provedly	ptomaine	pulpitum	puppy-dog	putchock	quaestor
Provence	ptyalism	pulpless	puppydom	put forth	quagmire
provenly	pubarche	pulpwood	puppy fat	put out of	quagmiry
prove out	pub crawl	pulsator	puppyish	putridly	quailery
Proverbs	pubertal	pulse jet	puppyism	put right	quaintly
proviant	publican	pulsific	purblind	putterer	Quakerly
provided	Publican	pultrude	purchase	put to bed	quakiest
provider	publicly	pulvilio	purdahed	put to sea	qualmish
province	pub lunch	pulvinar	pure-bred	putt-putt	quandary
proviral	pucellas	pulvinus	pure line	put under	quandong
provirus	puckauly	pumicite	pure milk	put-up job	quantify
provisor	puckeroo	pumpable	pureness	put-you-up	quantile
provisos	puckerow	pump-down	pure pute	puzzlist	quantise
provoked	puckfist	pump iron	pure tone	pycnogon	quantity
provoker	pucklike	pumpless	purflewe	pycnosis	quantize
provosty	puckster	pump room	purfling	pyelitic	quaranty
prowl car	puddingy	pump ship	purgator	pyelitis	quarrian
proxemic	puddling	pump-tree	purified	pygidial	quarried
proxenus	pudendal	pump-well	purifier	pygidium	quarrier
proximad	pudendum	punaluan	purifies	pygmaean	quarries
proximal	pudgiest	punch-bag	puriform	pygmy owl	quarrion
proxy war	pudibund	punchbag	puristic	pyinkado	quarrons
prudence	pudicity	puncheon	Purkinje	pyjamaed	quartern
prudency	puebloan	punchery	purlieus	pyknosis	quartile
pruinose	puffball	punchier	purparty	pyknotic	quart-pot
prunable	puffbird	punchily	purplish	pylagore	quatorze
prunasin	puffiest	punching	purposed	pyoderma	quatrain
prunella	puffinry	punch out	purposer	pyranose	quaverer
prunello	puff pipe	punctate	purpuric	pyrazine	quay-punt
prurient	puff port	punctual	purpurin	pyrazole	quayside
pruritic	puff-puff	punctule	purse-bag	Pyrenean	queasier
pruritus	puggaree	puncture	purseful	pyrenoid	queasily
Prussian	pugilant	punditry	purse-net	pyrexial	Quebecer
Prutenic	pugilism	pungence	purse-web	pyridine	Quechuan
pryddest	pugilist	pungency	purslane	pyriform	Quechuas
pryingly	Puginian	Punic War	pursuant	pyritify	queen ant
prytanis	pug-nosed	puniness	pursuing	pyritise	queen bee
psalmist	puissant	punisher	purulent	pyritize	queen cat
psalmody	Pulfrich	punition	purveyor	pyritose	queendom
psaltery	pulicose	punitive	purwanah	pyritous	queening
psammite	pulicous	punitory	Puseyism	pyrology	Queenite
psammoma	pulingly	Punjabis	Puseyist	pyrolyse	queenlet
psellism	Pulitzer	punk chic	Puseyite	pyrolyze	Queen Mum
psephism	pullable	punkette	pushable	pyrosoma	queen-pin
psephite	pull-back	punk rock	push-ball	pyroxene	queerdom
pseudery	pull-bell	punnable	push-bike	pyroxyle	queer for
pseudish	pullbone	Punt e Mes	pushcart	pyrrolic	queerish
psilocin	pull caps	punt-pole	push-down	pyruvate	queerity
psilosis	pull-cord	pupa-case	push hold	pythonic	quencher
psilotic	pull-date	puparial	pushiest	pyx-cloth	quenelle
psionics	pull-down	puparium	pushover	pyxidium	quercine
psoralen	pull foot	pupation	push pass	qaimaqam	querying
psychism	Pullmans	pupiform	push-pull	qindarka	quesited
psychist	pull over	pupilage	push-shot	Quaalude	question
psychoid	pullover	pupil age	puss boot	quackery	questman
psych out	pull rank	pupilage	puss moth	quackish	queueing
psyllium	pulmonic	pupilary	pussy cat	quackism	quibbler
pteropod	pulmotor	pupildom	pustulan	quadplex	Quichean
pterotic	pulperia	pupillar	pustular	quadrant	quick fix

quickish	racegoer	rail-bird	ram-sammy	ratchety	real life
quick one	racemate	rail bond	Ramsauer	rateable	real line
quick-set	racemise	railcard	ramshack	rateably	real live
quickset	racemize	rail-head	ram's head	rate-card	realness
quiddany	racemose	railhead	ram's horn	rat-goose	real time
quiddity	racemous	raillery	ramulose	rat-house	re-anchor
quidnunc	race riot	railless	ramulous	raticide	reanneal
quietest	rachides	rail-line	ranalian	ratified	reanswer
quietish	rachilla	rail link	ranarian	ratifier	reapable
quietism	rachitic	railroad	ranch egg	ratifies	reap-hook
Quietism	rachitis	rail yard	ranchero	rational	reappear
quietist	racially	rain band	ranchito	rationes	rear-arch
Quietist	raciness	rainbird	ranchman	rat-racer	rear lamp
quietude	Racinian	rainbowy	randiest	rat-rhyme	rearmost
quillaja	racistic	rain-cape	Randlord	ratsbane	re-arouse
quilling	rack-deal	raincoat	randomly	rat-snake	rearrest
quill pen	rackcted	rain crow	rangette	rat's tail	rear-view
quilting	racketer	rain date	range war	rattiest	rearward
quincunx	rack-rail	rain-door	rangiest	rattling	reascend
quindene	rack-rent	raindrop	rangiora	rattoner	reascent
quinella	raclette	rainfall	raniform	raurekau	reasoner
quiniela	Racovian	rain-fowl	rankness	rave it up	re-aspire
quinovic	radar map	rain frog	ranksman	Ravelian	reassail
quinsied	radar net	rainiest	ransomer	ravelled	reassert
quintain	radially	rainless	rapacity	raveness	reassess
quintile	radiance	rainsuit	rapakivi	ravening	reassign
quintole	radiancy	rain-tree	rape-cake	ravenous	reassort
quippery	radiated	rain-wash	rape-seed	ravingly	reassume
quipping	radiator	rainwear	rapeseed	ravisher	reassure
quippish	radicand	rain-worm	rap group	raw-boned	reattach
quipster	radicate	rainworm	raphanus	raw humus	reattack
Quirinal	radicule	rainy day	rapidest	Rawlplug	reattain
quirkier	radio cab	raisable	rapidity	raw umber	reawaken
quirkily	radio car	raisedly	rap music	ray fleck	re-become
quirkish	radio fix	raise hob	rapontic	Rayleigh	re-behold
quisling	radio ham	rajaship	rapparee	rayogram	rebeldom
quiteron	radio map	raja yoga	rap sheet	Rayonism	rebelled
quit rate	radio net	rake down	raptness	Rayonist	rebeller
quit-rent	radionic	rakehell	raquette	razor cut	rebellow
quitting	Radio One	rake over	rara avis	razor-man	reboiler
quivered	Radio Two	rakishly	rare bird	reabsorb	reborrow
quixotic	radiused	ralli car	rare book	reaccept	rebottle
quixotry	radiuses	rallying	rarefied	reaccess	rebranch
quiz game	radwaste	rallyist	rarefier	reach for	rebuffal
quiz show	raft-duck	Ramadhan	rareness	reaching	rebunker
quizzery	raftered	ramarama	rarified	reach rod	reburial
quizzing	raftsman	rambling	rarifies	reactant	reburied
quoad hoc	raftsmen	Ramboism	rarities	reaction	reburies
quoddity	ragabash	rambutan	rascally	reactive	rebuttal
quod vide	raga rock	ramentum	rascalry	readable	rebutted
quoining	rageless	Ramessid	rascasse	readably	rebutter
quotable	rag frame	ramicorn	rascette	readerly	rebutton
quotient	raggedly	ramified	rasgulla	readiest	Récamier
rabbeted	raggling	ramifies	rashling	readjust	recanter
rabbinic	ragingly	ramiform	rashness	read-only	recapped
rabbited	Ragnarok	ramillie	rasplike	read over	recapper
rabbiter	rag paper	Ramistic	Rasputin	readvise	recaptor
rabbitry	ragstone	ramosely	Rastaman	ready-mix	recceing
rabidity	ragtimer	rampager	rastered	reaffirm	receival
race card	ragtimey	rampancy	ratanhia	reagency	receiver
racecard	rag trade	rampiked	rataplan	reaginic	re-cement
race game	rag-wheel	rampsman	rat-arsed	realizer	recently

re-centre	redeemer	reed mace	regioned	relaxant	renogram
receptor	redefect	reed-mark	register	relaxing	renounce
recessed	redefine	reed pipe	registry	relaxity	renovate
rechange	redeless	reed-stop	regnancy	relay bid	renovize
recharge	redemand	reed-wren	regolith	relearnt	renowned
recidive	redeploy	reef flat	regrater	releasee	renowner
recision	redesign	reef knot	reground	releaser	rentable
reckless	redesman	reelable	regrowth	releasor	rent-a-car
reckling	red-faced	reel foot	regulate	relegate	rent-free
reckoner	red giant	reel-rall	reguline	relevant	rentless
reckon up	red gland	re-embark	rehallow	relexify	rent roll
recliner	red grass	re-embody	rehandle	reliable	rent-seck
reclothe	red–green	re-emerge	reharden	reliably	renumber
recoiler	Red Guard	re-employ	rehearse	reliance	renversé
Recollet	red-heart	re-enable	reheater	relicary	reobtain
recolour	red horse	re-engage	rehoboam	reliefer	reoccupy
recommit	redirect	re-engine	Rehoboth	relieved	reoffend
reconfer	redistil	re-enlist	Reichert	reliever	reopener
reconvey	redivide	re-excite	Reichian	religate	reordain
Recordak	red judge	re-expand	reigning	religion	reorient
recordal	red light	re-export	reignite	relisher	reovirus
recorder	red maple	refained	reillume	reloader	repairer
recouple	red mavis	refasten	reimbibe	relocate	repartee
recourse	red mulga	refereed	reimport	relucent	repealer
recovery	red noise	referees	reimpose	relumine	repeated
recradle	red-nosed	referend	reincite	remainer	repeater
recreant	red ochre	referent	reindeer	remanent	repelled
recreate	redolent	referral	reindict	remanned	repeller
rectally	red osier	referred	reinduce	remarker	repenter
rectenna	redouble	referrer	Reinecke	remarque	repeople
rectoral	Red Paint	refigure	reinette	remaster	reperuse
rectress	red panda	refinery	reinfect	remedial	repetend
recurred	red perch	refining	reinform	remedied	rephrase
recusant	Red River	refinish	reinfuse	remedies	repiqued
recycler	red route	refitted	reingulf	remember	repiques
redactor	Red Rover	reflexly	reinless	remiform	replacer
red adder	red sable	reflower	reinsert	remigate	repledge
red alder	red scale	refluent	reinsist	reminder	replevin
red alert	redshank	reforest	reinsman	remissly	replicar
redargue	red shift	reformat	reinstil	remittal	replicon
red-beard	redshift	reformed	reinsure	remitted	replight
red beech	red shirt	reformer	reinvade	remittee	replough
red biddy	red-short	refreeze	reinvent	remitter	replunge
red birch	redstart	refrozen	reinvest	remodify	repolish
red-blind	red steer	refugium	reinvite	remolade	reporter
red board	red-stone	refunder	Reissner	remotely	repotted
red bream	red tabby	re-fusion	reissued	remotest	repoussé
red-brick	red-taped	refusion	reissues	remotion	repreach
redbrick	red-tapey	refusnik	Reithian	remotive	reprieve
red cedar	reducing	regainer	rejected	remskoen	reprisal
red chalk	reduviid	regalian	rejectee	remurmur	reproach
Red China	red viper	regalism	rejecter	remuster	reproval
red coral	red-water	regalist	rejector	renature	reprover
red cross	redwater	regality	rejigged	renderer	republic
Red Cross	red wheat	regarder	rejigger	rendzina	repugner
reddenda	re-echoed	regasify	rejoicer	renegade	repulser
reddendo	re-echoes	regather	rejumble	renegado	repurify
red devil	reed-bird	regelate	rekindle	renegate	required
red Devon	reedbuck	regicide	relapser	reneguer	requirer
red dwarf	reediest	regifuge	relation	reniform	requital
red-eared	reedlike	regiment	relative	renitent	requiter
red earth	reedling	regional	relaunch	renminbi	re-reader

rere-arch	ressalah	reusable	rhonchus	rightish	rippling
re-record	rest-balk	revalued	Rhoosian	rightism	rip track
re-refine	rest-cure	revalues	rhopalia	rightist	riroriro
re-reform	rest gown	revealer	rhopalic	right now	rise time
re-relate	rest home	reveille	rho-theta	right off	rishitin
re-repeat	restitch	revelled	rhubarby	right out	riskiest
re-return	restless	reveller	rhymable	righty-ho	riskless
re-reveal	rest mass	revelous	rhymical	rigidify	risoluto
re-revise	restoral	revenant	rhyolite	rigidity	risorius
re-roller	restorer	revenger	rhythmed	rigidize	risottos
re-rubber	re-strain	revenuer	rhythmic	rigorism	riteless
resaddle	restrain	reverber	rhythmus	rigorist	ritenuto
resalute	restrict	reverend	ria coast	rigorous	ritornel
rescreen	restrike	reverent	ribaldry	Rig-vedic	ritratto
rescribe	restring	reverify	ribandry	rigwiddy	ritually
rescript	rest room	reversal	ribboned	rilievos	ritziest
rescuing	restroom	reverser	ribboner	rim-brake	rivaless
research	restruck	reversis	ribbonry	rim drive	rivality
reselect	restrung	reverter	rib-grass	rimeless	rivalize
reseller	resubmit	revestry	rib-joint	rimester	rivalled
resemble	resummon	revetted	ribosome	rim light	riveling
resenter	resupine	reviewal	ribozyme	rimosity	rivelled
reserved	resupply	reviewer	rib-roast	rimstone	riverain
reserver	resurgam	reviling	ribulose	rindless	river-bed
resetter	resurvey	revision	rice-bird	ring back	river-god
resettle	retailer	revisory	rice-bowl	ringbark	river gum
resident	retainer	revivify	rice milk	ringbolt	river hog
Residenz	retarded	revolted	ricercar	ringbone	riverine
residing	retardee	revolter	richesse	ring book	riverlet
residual	retarder	revolute	richness	ring-dial	riverman
residuum	retarget	revolver	richwccd	ring-dove	river oak
resignal	retaught	revuette	ricketed	ring dyke	rivet gun
resigned	retemper	rewarder	ricketic	ringette	riveting
resignee	retender	rewarewa	rickrack	ring-fort	rivulose
resigner	rethatch	re-weight	rickshaw	ring gear	RNA virus
resilium	rethread	rewhiten	rickyard	ringhals	roadable
re-silver	rethrone	rewinder	ricochet	ringlead	road band
resinate	retiarii	reworker	riddance	ringless	road-book
resinify	reticent	rewriter	riddling	ringlety	road fund
resining	reticula	Reynolds	rideable	ringlike	road hand
resinize	reticule	rezoning	ride down	ring main	road-head
resinoid	retiform	rhabdite	ride high	ring-neck	road hump
resinous	retimber	rhabdoid	rideress	ring-pull	road kill
resister	retinene	Rhaetian	ride work	ring road	roadless
resistor	retinoid	rhagades	ridgelet	ring-rope	road show
resmooth	retinula	rhamnose	ridgeway	ringside	roadshow
resoften	retiracy	rhapsode	ridicule	ringspot	roadside
resolder	retiring	rhapsody	rid space	ringster	road sign
resolute	retorted	rheidity	Riesling	ringtail	roadsman
resolved	retorter	rhematic	rifampin	ring true	roadster
resolver	retrally	rheobase	rifeness	ring-walk	road test
resonant	retrench	rheogram	riffling	ring-wall	roadwork
resonate	retrieve	rheology	riff-raff	ringwise	roasting
resorcin	retroact	rheopexy	rifle-gun	ring-work	robeless
resorter	retrofit	rheostat	rifleman	ringworm	roborant
resource	retrorse	rhetoric	riflemen	rinkhals	robotics
respirit	Retrovir	rhinitis	riftless	riometer	robotise
resplend	returned	rhizopod	rift-sawn	riot gear	robotism
responsa	returnee	rhodinal	rigadoon	riparial	robotize
response	returner	rhodinol	rigatoni	riparian	robuster
respread	returnik	rhomboid	right arm	ripeness	robustic
respring	reuniter	rhonchal	rightful	ripienos	robustly

rocaille	roll-call	root-leaf	rosiness	rowdiest	rum booze
Rochelle	roll cast	rootless	rosining	rowdy-dow	rum go run
rocheted	roll feed	rootlike	rosin oil	rowdyish	rum-hound
rock-a-bye	rollicky	rootling	rosoglio	rowdyism	ruminant
rock alum	roll mark	root node	ros solis	rowelled	ruminate
Rockaway	roll-neck	root sign	Ross seal	row house	rummager
rock-bird	rollocks	root-weed	rostrate	rowiness	rumorous
rock bolt	roll over	root-worm	rostrums	royalise	rumoured
rock cake	roll rate	ropeable	rosulate	royalism	rumourer
rock cavy	rolwagen	rope-band	rosybill	royalist	rump-bone
rock coal	roly-poly	rope burn	rosy drop	royalize	rumpless
rock cook	Romagnol	rope down	Rotarian	royal oak	rumption
rock-dove	romancer	rope into	rotaries	rub along	rum start
rock duck	Romanese	ropelike	rotation	rubashka	rumti-too
rock-dust	Romanian	rope-roll	rotative	rubbaboo	run about
rocketed	Romanies	rope's end	rotatory	rubberdy	runabout
rocketer	romanise	rope-walk	rotavate	rubbishy	run after
rocketry	Romanish	rope-work	rotenone	rub-board	runagate
rock face	Romanism	rope-yard	rot-grass	rubby-dub	run along
rockfall	Romanist	rope-yarn	rotor arm	rubeanic	run a mile
rockfest	Romanity	ropiness	rototill	Rubenist	run a risk
rock-fill	romanize	roqueted	rotproof	rubeolar	rune-tree
rockfish	Roman law	roquette	rottener	rubeosis	run for it
rockfoil	romantic	rortiest	rottenly	rubicund	rungless
rock goat	Roman tub	rosalger	rotundly	rubidium	run metal
rock hair	Rome-scot	rosaline	roughage	rub noses	runnable
rock-hewn	Romeward	rosarian	rough cut	rubrical	runnered
rockiest	rompiest	rosaries	rough dab	rubstone	runner-up
rock jock	Romulian	rosarium	rough-dry	ruby-back	runniest
rockless	roncador	rose boss	rough-hew	ruby mine	runology
rocklike	rondache	rosebowl	roughies	ruby port	run out on
rockling	rondavel	rose bush	roughing	ruby-tail	run short
rock pile	rondeaux	rose comb	roughish	ruby zinc	ruralise
rock pool	rondelet	rose-drop	rough log	rucksack	ruralism
rock rose	rondelle	rose-fish	rough mix	ruddered	ruralist
rock-salt	rood-beam	rose-gall	rough-out	ruddiest	rurality
rock star	rood-loft	rose gold	rouleaus	rude joke	ruralize
rockster	roof bolt	rose-grub	rouleaux	rudeness	rush-bush
rock-weed	roofless	rose leaf	roulette	ruderate	rush hour
Rockwell	rooflike	roseless	rouncing	rudiment	rushlike
rock-wool	roofline	roselike	round-arm	rudistid	rush line
rock-work	roof-rack	roselite	roundeye	ruefully	rush-toad
rock worm	roof rail	rosemalt	rounding	rufflike	russeted
rock wren	roof-tile	rosemary	roundish	ruffling	Russniak
rodomont	roof-tree	rose-mole	roundlet	rugately	rust belt
roentgen	rooigras	rose nail	round log	Rugbeian	rustical
Roentgen	rooihout	roseolar	round lot	rug brick	rusticly
roe-stone	rook-worm	rosepath	round off	ruggedly	rustiest
roestone	roomette	rose pink	round out	rugosely	rustless
Rogatian	roomfuls	rose-rash	round pin	rugosity	rustle up
rogation	roomiest	rose rial	round-top	rugulose	rustling
Rogatist	roomless	roseries	roundure	ruinable	rusty dab
rogatory	room-mate	rose-root	rousable	ruinated	rutabaga
Rogerene	roorback	roseroot	rousette	ruinator	ruthenic
roitelet	roosting	rose show	rousting	ruleless	ruthless
Rolandic	root-ball	rose-spot	routeing	rule over	rutilant
role-play	root beer	rose tree	route man	ruleress	rutilous
rollable	rootedly	rosetted	routeman	Rumanian	Ruy Lopez
rollaway	rootfast	rose vine	routiner	rumänite	rye bread
roll axis	root gall	rosewood	rovingly	rum baron	ryegrass
roll back	root-hair	rose-work	row-barge	rumbelow	ryotwary
roll cage	root-knot	rosewort	row-de-dow	rumbling	Ryukyuan

Sabba-day	saginate	salt away	sand flea	saponify	satirism
sabbatia	sagittal	salt bath	sand goby	saponite	satirist
sabbatic	sago palm	salt beef	sand-hill	saponule	satirize
Sabellic	sag wagon	salt-burn	sandhill	saporous	satranji
sabellid	Sahaptin	saltbush	sand-hole	sapphire	satrapal
sabinene	Saharaui	salt-cake	sandiest	sapphism	satrapic
Sabinian	Sahelian	salt dome	sand-iron	sapphist	saturant
sabotage	sahibdom	salt fish	sandiver	sappiest	saturate
saboteur	sahib-log	salt flat	sand lark	saprobic	Saturday
sabre-cut	sahuaros	saltiest	sand leek	sapropel	saturnal
sabre leg	sailable	salt junk	sandlike	sapskull	saturnic
sabre saw	sail-boat	salt lake	sand lily	sap spout	satyress
sabulous	sailboat	saltless	sand-lime	sap-stain	satyrion
sac-à-lait	sailfish	salt lick	sandling	sapucaia	satyrish
sacbrood	sail into	saltlike	sand pear	saraband	saucebox
saccadic	sailless	salt mine	sand-pump	Saraband	saucepan
saccated	sail loft	saltness	sand-reed	Sarabite	sauciest
saccular	sailorly	salt plug	sand-rock	sarangis	saunders
sacculus	sailsman	salt-pond	sand-shoe	sarassin	sauropod
sacellum	sail wing	salt side	sandsoap	Saratoga	sausagey
sackable	sailyard	salt sore	sand sole	sarcelly	savagely
sackfuls	sainfoin	salt-weed	sand-star	sarcenet	savagery
sackless	saintdom	salt well	sand-trap	sarcodic	savagess
sacklike	saintess	saltwort	sand-tray	sarcomas	savagism
sack race	saintish	salutary	sandveld	sardelle	savannah
sack ship	sakabula	salvable	sand-wash	sardonic	saveable
sack suit	salacity	salvager	sand-wasp	sardonyx	save face
sack time	salad bar	salvific	sand wave	sargasso	savingly
sacraria	saladero	salvinia	sandwich	Sargonid	savories
sacredly	saladine	samarium	Sandwich	sarkiest	savorous
sacristy	salading	sambaing	sand-worm	Sar-Major	savourer
saddlery	salad-oil	samcloth	sandwort	saronged	Savoyard
Sadducee	salarian	same here	sandyish	Saronian	savviest
sadhuism	salariat	same like	sandy ray	sarpanch	sawbench
sadistic	salaried	sameness	saneness	sarplier	sawbones
sado-maso	salaries	samizdat	sangaree	sarrazin	sawdusty
Safaitic	saleable	Samnitic	Sangrado	sarsenet	saw-edged
safe area	saleably	samphire	sangrail	Sartrean	sawed-off
safe edge	sale ring	samplery	sanguine	Sarum use	sawflies
Safehand	saleroom	sampling	san-hsien	Sasanian	saw frame
safe-hold	Salesian	samsaric	sanidine	sasanqua	saw-grass
safekeep	salesman	samskara	sanified	sash cord	sawgrass
safe lamp	salesmen	Sam Slick	sanifies	sash-door	saw-horse
safe load	sales tax	samtchoo	sanitary	sashless	sawhorse
safeness	sale-yard	sanative	sanitate	sash tool	saw-shark
safe seat	salicine	sanatory	sanitise	Sassanid	sawtooth
safeties	Salic law	Sancerre	sanitize	Sassella	saw-wrest
safe-tray	salictum	sanctify	sannyasi	sassiest	saxatile
saffraan	salience	sanction	Sanscrit	sastruga	saxboard
saffrony	saliency	sanctity	sanserif	sastrugi	saxe blue
safranin	salinely	sanctums	sans-gêne	Satanise	Saxe blue
sagacity	salinity	sandarac	Sanskrit	Satanism	Saxondom
sagakomi	Salishan	sandbank	sans peur	Satanist	Saxonian
sagamité	salivant	sand-bath	Santa Ana	Satanity	Saxonise
sagamore	salivary	sand blow	santalin	Satanize	Saxonish
saganaki	salivate	sand boil	santalol	sateless	Saxonism
sagebush	sallower	sand-cast	santonin	satiable	Saxonist
sage cock	Sally-man	sand-club	santorin	satining	Saxonize
sage hare	salmonet	sand core	saperavi	satinize	sayonara
sageness	salmonid	sand crab	sap green	satin oil	say uncle
sageship	Salopian	sand dune	sapidity	satin-top	scabbard
sage-wood	salpicon	sand-fish	sapience	satirise	scabbier

scabbing	scentful	sclerose	scraggly	scrupler	sea eagle
scabbler	scenting	sclerous	scramble	scrutiny	seafarer
scabious	scent out	scoffery	scrambly	scuddick	sea-fever
scabland	sceptism	scofflaw	scramjet	scudding	sea-fight
scablike	sceptral	scoinson	scrammed	scuffing	sea-flood
scab-mite	sceptred	scolding	scrannel	scuffler	sea-floor
scabrous	schapska	scoleces	scraping	scuggery	sea front
scabweed	schedule	scolices	scraplet	scuggish	seafront
scacchic	Scheiner	scolytid	scrapped	scullery	seagoing
scaffold	schemata	scombrid	scrapper	scullion	sea-grape
scalable	scheming	scomfish	scrappet	sculptor	sea grass
scalawag	schemist	scone cap	scrapple	scumless	sea green
scald-hot	scherzos	scone-hot	scratchy	scummier	sea gypsy
scalding	Schiedam	scoopful	scrattle	scumming	sea heath
scale-bug	schiffli	scooping	scraunch	scungier	sea holly
scalenus	schiller	scoop-net	scrawler	scurfily	sea horse
scale-pan	schizoid	scoparin	screamer	scurfing	sea-hound
scaliest	schizont	Scophony	screechy	scurried	sea ivory
scallion	schliere	scopolin	screeder	scurrier	sea-jelly
scalprum	schlocky	scopulae	screed in	scurries	sealable
scamming	schmaltz	scorable	screener	scurrile	seal calf
scammony	schmatte	scorcher	screever	scurvied	sea lemon
scamping	schmooze	score-box	screw cap	scurvier	sea level
scampish	schmucky	score off	screw-die	scurvily	seal-hole
scandent	schnapps	score out	screw eye	scutated	sea-light
Scandian	scholard	scores of	screw fly	scutcher	sea-louse
scandium	scholion	scorious	screwier	scutella	seal ring
scanning	scholium	scornful	screwing	scuttled	sealskin
scansion	schooler	scorpene	screwish	scuttler	sea-lungs
scantier	schoolie	Scorpian	screw-pin	scutulum	Sealyham
scantily	schooner	scorpion	screw-tap	scuzzbag	seamanly
scantity	Schottky	Scorpios	screw top	scybalum	seamfree
scaphoid	schradan	Scorpius	scribble	scyphate	seamiest
scapulae	Schrader	scot-free	scribbly	scyphose	seamless
scapular	Schröder	Scotican	scribing	Scythian	sea-morse
scapulas	schryari	scotomas	scribism	scything	seamount
scarabee	sciaenid	scotomia	scriggle	Scythism	sea mouse
scarcely	sciagram	scotopia	scrimish	sea-acorn	seam-rent
scarcity	sciatica	scotopic	scrimped	sea-adder	seamster
scaredly	scienced	Scots fir	scrimply	sea-angel	seam weld
scareful	scienter	Scotsman	scripted	sea-arrow	sea-nymph
scare out	scilicet	Scotsmen	scripter	sea aster	sea onion
scarf pin	scimitar	Scots Nat	scriptor	sea-bathe	sea otter
scariest	scincoid	Scottice	scrofula	sea beach	sea-perch
scariose	sciolism	Scottify	scrogged	sea-beast	sea-piece
scarious	sciolist	Scottish	scroggin	sea-blite	sea-pilot
scarless	sciolous	scourger	scrolled	seaboard	seaplane
scarpine	scioness	Scourian	scroller	seaborne	sea poppy
scarping	scioptic	scouring	scrotums	sea-bound	sea-power
scarring	scirocco	scout bee	scrouger	sea bream	sea price
scatback	scirrhus	scout car	scrounge	sea cadet	sea purse
scathing	scissile	Scoutery	scroungy	sea-chest	seaquake
scattald	scission	scouting	scrubbed	sea-clerk	sea-raven
scattery	scissors	Scoutish	scrubber	sea-cliff	searcher
scattier	sciurine	Scoutism	scrubble	sea-cloth	search me
scattily	sciuroid	Scout Law	scrub jay	sea-coast	searobin
scatting	sclareol	scowbank	scrub oak	seacraft	sea-rover
scavager	sclereid	scrabble	scrub-tit	sea crust	seascape
scavenge	sclerema	Scrabble	scrumble	sea-cunny	Sea Scout
scenario	sclerite	scrag-end	scrum-cap	sea-daisy	sea shell
scenical	scleroid	scragged	scrumple	sea devil	seashell
scent-bag	scleroma	scragger	scrunchy	seadrome	seashore

sea-shrub	sedulous	Selenite	semi-open	septfoil	set of day
seasider	see about	selenium	semiosis	septimal	set piece
sea snail	see after	selenous	semiotic	septoria	set point
sea snake	see a wolf	Seleucid	semi-oval	septuple	set right
sea-snipe	seecatch	self-bias	semi-pros	sequelae	set scene
seasonal	seed ball	self-born	semi-ring	sequence	set screw
seasoner	seed bank	self-bred	Semitise	sequency	set scrum
sea speed	seed-bird	self-care	Semitism	sequined	Setswana
sea-stack	seed bull	self-ease	Semitist	seraglio	settable
sea-state	seed cake	self-good	Semitize	seraphic	settle in
sea-stick	seed-coat	self-hate	semitone	seraphim	settle up
sea stock	seed-corn	self-heal	semolina	seraphin	settling
sea-swine	seedcorn	self-help	semology	serenade	setulose
seat belt	seed down	selfhood	semplice	serenata	seven-day
seat-bone	seed-fish	self-hunt	sempster	serenely	severely
sea-thief	seed-head	selfless	sempstry	serenest	Severian
sea-thong	seediest	self-life	semuncia	serenise	severies
sea tiger	seed-leaf	self-loop	senarian	serenity	severish
seatless	seedless	self-lost	senarius	serenize	severity
seat-mate	seedlike	self-love	senatory	serfhood	Sevillan
seat-mile	seedling	self-made	sendable	serfship	sewaging
sea train	seed-plot	self-mass	send away	sergeant	sewellel
sea trial	seedsman	selfmate	send back	serially	sewerage
sea trout	seedsmen	selfness	send down	seriated	sewer-air
sea-valve	seed-time	self-pity	send word	seriatim	sewer rat
seawards	seed year	self-rule	senecios	sericite	sew-round
sea water	seedy toe	selfsame	sengreen	seriffed	sex-blind
seawater	seek dead	self-seed	Senhouse	serigala	sex crime
sea-weary	seemless	self-sown	senicide	serjeant	sex drive
seaweedy	seemlier	selfward	senilely	sermoner	sexenary
seawoman	seemlily	self-will	senility	sermonic	sexiness
sea wrack	seerlike	self-wise	senilize	serology	sexology
sebesten	seership	sellable	sennight	serosity	sexploit
Sebilian	see stars	sellette	señorita	serotine	sextette
secateur	segolate	selvaged	Senoussi	serotiny	sextolet
secesher	sego lily	selvagee	senseful	serotype	sextuple
Sechuana	segreant	selvedge	sensible	Serpasil	sextuply
secluded	seicento	semantic	sensibly	serpolet	sex-typed
secodont	seiching	semblant	sensific	serpulae	sexually
secondee	Seidlitz	sembling	sensoria	serpulid	sexupara
seconder	seif dune	semester	sensuism	serranid	sforzato
secondly	seigneur	semi-arid	sensuist	serrated	shabbier
secretin	seignior	semi-axis	sensuous	serratic	shabbify
secretly	seignory	semi-beam	sentence	serratus	shabbily
secretor	seine-net	semi-bold	sentient	servable	shabrack
sectator	seismics	semi-cell	sentinel	serve out	shackage
sectoral	seismism	semi-coke	sentries	servicer	shack-job
sectored	sei whale	semidine	sentry-go	servient	shackles
secundly	seizable	semi-dome	Senussia	servitor	shadblow
secundus	seized of	semiflex	sepaline	servo tab	shaddock
securely	sejugate	semi-hoop	sepalled	sesamoid	shades of
secure of	seladang	Sémillon	sepalody	sescuple	shadiest
security	selamlik	semilune	sepaloid	sesterce	shadower
sedately	seldseen	semi-main	separate	sestetto	shadowly
sedation	selected	semi-mute	separist	sestonic	shafting
sedative	selectee	seminary	Sephadex	set about	shagbark
sederunt	selectly	seminate	Sephardi	set a fire	shaggery
sedge-fly	selector	seminium	sepiment	set apart	shaggier
sediment	selenate	Seminole	septagon	set aside	shaggily
sedition	selenian	seminoma	septated	se-tenant	shagging
seducing	selenide	semi-nude	septenar	set forth	shagreen
sedulity	selenite	semi-opal	septette	setiform	shagroon

shahbanu	sheather	shift key	shocking	shotting	siallite
shakable	shedding	shift off	Shockley	should-be	Sibelian
shake-bag	she-devil	shigella	shoddier	shoulder	Siberian
shake off	shedhand	shiitake	shoddily	shouldn't	sibilant
shake out	shed roof	shikasta	shoebill	shout for	sibilate
shake-rag	shed-room	shikimic	shoe-deep	shouting	sibilous
shakiest	sheeling	shilling	shoehorn	shoveler	Sibiriak
shale oil	sheep-bot	shimmery	shoelace	shove-net	sibyllic
shalgram	sheep-bug	shimmied	shoe-last	shove off	Sicanian
shalloon	sheepcot	shimmies	shoeless	showable	sicarius
shamanic	sheep-dip	shimming	shoepack	show a leg	Siceliot
shambles	sheepdog	shim-sham	shoe-tree	showance	Sicilian
sham-damn	sheep-fly	shin bone	shofroth	show band	sick call
shamedly	sheepish	shindies	shogunal	showband	sickener
shameful	sheep-ked	shingled	shonkier	showboat	sickerly
shamiana	sheepman	shingler	shooting	show-card	sick flag
shamisen	sheep-pen	shingles	shootist	showcard	sickless
shammies	sheep pox	shiniest	shoot-off	showcase	sicklied
shamming	sheep-ree	shin-leaf	shoot-out	showdown	sicklier
shammock	sheep-rot	shinnery	shop-book	showerer	sicklily
shampoos	sheep-run	shinnied	shop-gaze	show flat	sickling
shamrock	sheet-fed	shinnies	shop girl	showfolk	sick list
shamyana	sheetful	shinning	shopless	showgirl	sickness
Shandean	sheet ice	shinties	shoplift	show home	sick note
shandies	sheeting	Shinwari	shopping	showiest	sickroom
Shangaan	sheetlet	ship a sea	shoppish	showjump	sidalcea
Shangana	sheikhly	shipless	shop talk	showreel	sida-weed
shanghai	Shekinah	shiplike	shop-worn	showroom	side arms
shanking	shelduck	shipload	shopworn	show tune	side band
shank-net	shelf cod	shipmate	shorebug	show wood	sideband
shannies	shelfful	shipment	shore fly	shrapnel	side bend
shanties	shelf ice	ship over	shore-gun	shredded	side-blow
shantung	shelf sea	shippage	shoreman	shredder	side-bone
shapable	shell-bit	shipping	shortage	shred-pie	sideburn
shapeful	shell egg	shipside	shortall	shrew-ash	side-coat
shape out	shell ice	ship time	short-arc	shrewdie	side-comb
sharable	shelling	ship-work	short-arm	shrewdly	side dish
Shararat	shell out	shipworm	short-ass	shrewish	side door
Shardana	sheltery	shipyard	short con	shrew-run	side drum
shareman	shelties	shiralee	short cut	shrieker	side-face
share-out	sheltron	shireman	short-day	shrieval	side-foot
sharkish	shelving	shire-oak	short dog	shrimped	side-head
shark-ray	Shemitic	shirring	short-eat	shrimper	sidehill
sharn-bud	shending	shirtier	short end	shrinker	side-hold
sharp end	shepherd	shirtily	short for	shrink on	sidekick
sharpish	shepster	shirting	shorties	shrouder	side lamp
sharp-set	Sherarat	shirt-jac	shortish	shrubbed	sidelamp
shashlik	Sheraton	shirt-pin	short leg	shrublet	side-land
shattery	Sherlock	shit-face	short rib	shrub oak	sideless
shauchle	sherries	shithead	short run	shrugged	sideline
shauchly	sherwani	shit-hole	short-set	shrug off	sideling
Shaviana	Shetland	shitless	short ton	shrunken	side lobe
Shavuoth	Shevuoth	shit-list	Shoshone	shuddery	side-lock
shawabti	shey-shey	shittier	shot-bush	shuffler	sidelong
shawling	shickery	shitting	shot-free	shunless	side-look
shawmist	shielded	shitwork	shot gold	shunning	side meat
shay-shay	shielder	shivaree	shot-hole	shunpike	side mill
sheading	shieling	shiverer	shot line	shuriken	side note
shealing	shiftful	Shiv Sena	shot-mark	shut down	side play
shearing	shiftier	shkotsim	Shotokan	shutdown	side pond
shearman	shiftily	shoading	shot-peen	shutting	side-post
sheathed	shifting	shoaling	shot rope	shuttler	sidereal

siderean	silicify	Sindhian	six-eight	skinnery	slangism
siderite	silicone	sinecure	sixpence	skinnier	slanting
side road	silicula	sine tone	sixpenny	skinning	slap bang
side-rope	siliquae	sine wave	sixscore	skin pass	slap-bass
side-scan	siliques	sinewous	sixtieth	skin test	slapdash
side seat	silkbark	sin-flood	sixtyish	skin worm	slaphead
sideshow	silkenly	sinfonia	sixty-six	skiogram	slapjack
side-slip	silk-fowl	sinfully	sizeable	skip bail	slapping
sidesman	silkiest	singable	sizeably	skipjack	slap shot
sidesmen	silklike	singeing	size-bone	ski-plane	slashing
side spin	silk moth	singhara	sizeless	skippery	slat-back
sidestep	silk road	singling	siziness	skipping	slateful
side suit	silk-tail	sing-sing	sizzling	skip-read	slattern
side-sway	silk-tree	singsing	skate key	skip-rope	slatting
side tone	silkweed	sing-song	skean-dhu	skip zone	slave ant
side trip	silkworm	singsong	skedding	skirmish	slavedom
side view	silky oak	singular	Skeeball	skirting	slave jib
sidewalk	sillabub	sinicize	skeelful	ski stick	slaverer
side-wall	silladar	sinigrin	skeeling	skittery	Slavonic
sideward	sillapak	sinister	skeeting	skittish	slayable
sideways	silliest	sinkable	skeletal	skittler	sleazier
side wind	sillikin	sink-hole	skeleton	skivvied	sleazily
sidewind	silly ass	sinnable	skelloch	skivvies	sledding
side-wing	silly-how	Sinn Fein	skelping	skokiaan	sledging
side-wipe	sillyism	sinogram	skerrick	skullcap	sleepery
sidewise	siloxane	sinology	skerries	skullery	sleepful
Sidneian	silphium	Sinology	sketcher	skunkdom	sleepier
Sidonian	silurian	sinuated	skew arch	skunkish	sleepily
siege gun	Silurian	sinumbra	skew-back	sky cloth	sleeping
sierozem	siluroid	sinusoid	skewback	skydiver	sleep-out
sieveful	silverer	Siphnian	skewbald	skylight	sleeveen
sieve map	silverly	siphonal	skew gear	skylined	sleeving
siffleur	silvical	siphoner	skewness	sky pilot	sleigher
Sigalert	silylate	siphonic	skiagram	skyrmion	sleighty
Sigatoka	simazine	sireless	Skiatron	skyscape	slendang
sight bar	simetite	sirename	skid beam	sky shade	slew-foot
sightful	similise	sirenian	skidding	skytrain	slew rate
sight gag	similize	sireship	skid mark	skywards	slew-rope
sighting	simoleon	siriasis	skid road	skywatch	slick ear
sightsee	simoniac	siscowet	skiffler	sky-write	slickens
sigmatic	Simonian	siserary	ski-jorer	slabbery	slidable
signable	simonise	sissiest	skilless	slabbing	slidably
signally	simonist	sissonne	skillful	slab-cake	sliddery
signator	Simonite	sissy bar	skilling	slabline	slide-bar
signatum	simonize	sissyish	skillion	slack-jaw	slideway
sign away	simperer	sisterly	skim milk	slack off	slifting
signifer	simplest	sit about	skimming	slaggier	slighten
signific	simplify	sitarist	skimpier	slagging	slighter
signless	simplism	sithence	skimpily	slag heap	slightly
signoria	simplist	sit-inner	skimping	slag-lead	slim cake
sign over	simpulum	sit loose	skincare	slagless	slime-eel
signpost	simuland	sitology	skin-deep	slag-wool	slimiest
silanize	simulant	sit shiva	skin-dive	slaister	slimline
Silastic	simulate	sittella	skin flap	slalomer	slimmest
silbador	simulfix	sitter-in	skinfold	slambang	slimming
silcrete	simulium	sit tight	skin-food	slam dunk	slimness
silenced	Sinaitic	situlate	skinfuls	slamdunk	sling-bag
silencer	sinapine	sit under	skin game	slamming	sling mud
silently	sinapism	sitz-bath	skinhead	slammock	sling off
Silesian	sin bosun	sitzmark	skinking	slangier	slinkier
silicate	sincerer	six by six	skinless	slangily	slinkily
silicide	sinciput	Six Clerk	skinlike	slangish	slip away

slip-case	slowdown	smellage	snap-brim	snootier	soapless
slip face	slow-drag	smellier	snap head	snootily	soaplike
slip form	slow-foot	smelling	snap-hook	snoozier	soap-rock
slip-hook	slowness	smell out	snap-link	snore-off	soapsuds
slip-horn	slow pass	smeltery	snap-lock	snorting	soap-tree
slip into	slowpoke	smidgeon	snappier	snort out	soapweed
slip-knot	slow-scan	smig bait	snappily	snotnose	soapwort
slip-over	slow time	smileful	snapping	snottier	soarable
slipover	slow-worm	smircher	snappish	snottily	soaraway
slippage	slubbery	smirkily	snap-ring	snoutish	Soberano
slippery	slubbing	smirkish	snapsack	snowball	soberest
slippier	sludging	smithers	snapshot	snow-bank	soberize
slipping	slugabed	smithery	snapweed	snow bear	Sobieski
slip-rail	slug-fest	Smithian	snarkily	snow-belt	Sobranye
slip ring	sluggard	smithier	snarkish	snowbird	sobriety
slip road	slugging	smithies	snarlier	snow boot	sob story
slip-rope	sluggish	smocking	snarling	snow-clad	sob-stuff
slipshod	slug-horn	smoggier	snarlish	snowcock	so-called
slip-shoe	slughorn	smoggily	snatcher	snow-cold	sociable
slip-slap	slug-line	smogless	snatch it	snow-cone	sociably
slip-slop	slumbery	smokable	snazzier	snow crab	socially
slip-ware	slumland	smoke box	snazzily	snowdrop	societal
slipware	slumless	smoke dry	sneak-box	snowfall	Socinian
slit drum	slumlord	smoke-hos	sneakier	snow flea	sockeroo
slit-eyed	slummier	smoke out	sneakily	snow-hole	socketed
slit gong	slumming	smoke pot	sneaking	snowiest	socketer
slithery	slummock	smokiest	sneakish	snowless	sockette
slit lamp	slump sum	smoocher	sneaksby	snowlike	sock it to
slitless	slurries	smoodger	sneerful	snow lily	sock-lamb
slittier	slurrily	smoothen	sneering	snowline	sockless
slitting	slurring	smoother	sneezing	snow-melt	Socratic
slobbery	slushier	smoothie	snibbing	snowpack	soda-acid
slobbish	slushily	smoothly	sniffier	snowshoe	soda alum
slob-land	slushing	smørbrød	sniffily	snow-slip	soda card
sloe-eyed	slush pit	smothery	sniffing	snow-tyre	soda jerk
sloganed	sluttery	smoulder	sniffish	snow vole	soda lake
slogging	sluttish	smudgier	sniffler	snow wolf	soda lime
slope off	slyboots	smudgily	sniff out	snow worm	sodalist
slop-over	smack-dab	smuggery	snifting	snowyish	sodalite
sloppage	smacking	smuggest	sniggery	snowy owl	sodality
slop-pail	smallage	smuggish	snigging	snubbing	sodamide
sloppery	small-arm	smuggler	sniggler	snubbish	soda pulp
sloppier	small cap	smugness	snipe eel	snub cube	soddenly
sloppily	small end	smut-ball	snipe fly	snub nose	soddyite
slopping	small fry	smut-mill	snippety	snuffbox	sod house
slop-shop	smallish	smuttier	snippier	snuffier	sodomise
slop-work	smallpox	smuttily	snippily	snuffing	sodomist
sloshier	smaltine	smutting	snipping	snuffler	sodomite
sloshing	smaltite	smythite	snip-snap	snuffman	sodomize
slot-back	smarmier	snack bar	snitcher	snuff out	sod widow
slothful	smarmily	snackery	snobbery	snuggery	softback
slot hole	smarties	snagging	snobbess	snuggest	softball
slot seam	smarting	snaggled	snobbier	snuggish	soft clam
slotting	smartish	snailery	snobbily	snuggler	soft coal
slouched	smart set	snailish	snobbing	snugness	soft copy
sloucher	smashery	snake-bit	snobbish	soakaway	soft-core
slovenly	smash hit	snake fly	snobbism	soak-hole	soft corn
slovenry	smashing	snake oil	snobling	soak it to	soft crab
slow back	smear-dab	snake-pit	snogging	so-and-sos	softener
slow bell	smearing	snap-back	snooding	soapbark	soft food
slow burn	smectite	snap bean	snoopery	soapiest	soft-foot
slow-down	smeethly	snap-bolt	snootful	soap-lees	soft hail

soft-head	Solignum	soothing	soup-bone	spanglet	specious
soft-land	solitary	soothsay	soupiest	Spaniard	speckled
soft line	solitude	sootiest	soup line	Spanishy	spectate
softling	solleret	sootless	sourball	spanking	spectral
soft loan	solodize	sophical	sour beef	span-long	spectred
softness	solonetz	soporose	sour crop	spanning	spectrin
soft rush	so long as	soporous	sourdine	span roof	spectrum
soft sell	Solonian	soppiest	sour dock	spanspek	specular
soft-shoe	solo stop	sopranos	soured on	spansule	speculum
soft soap	solpugid	Sorabian	sour mash	Spansule	speeched
soft sore	solstice	soralium	sourness	span wire	speecher
soft spot	solution	sora rail	sour plum	spanwise	speed bug
soft tack	solvable	sorbitan	sourpuss	span-worm	speed cop
soft tick	solvency	sorbitic	sour veld	sparable	speedful
software	Somalian	sorbitol	sourwood	sparaxis	speed hog
soft wart	somatism	sorcerer	soutache	spar-buoy	speedier
softwood	somatist	sordidly	southard	spar-deck	speedily
soggiest	somatize	soredial	southern	spare for	speedway
so help me	sombrely	soredium	southing	spare rib	speering
soil bank	sombrero	sorehead	southpaw	spargana	spekboom
soil-less	sombrous	Sorelian	Southron	sparhawk	spelaean
soilless	somebody	soreness	South Sea	spark-gap	spelding
soil mark	somedeal	Sörensen	souvenir	sparkish	spellful
soil pipe	somegate	soricine	souvlaki	sparkled	spelling
soil type	some hope	sororate	Sovietic	sparkler	spell out
soil wash	somerset	sororial	sovranly	sparklet	speltoid
solacing	sometime	sororise	sovranty	spark out	Spencean
solander	somewhat	sorority	sow-belly	sparling	spend-all
solandra	somewhen	sororize	sowbread	sparmate	spending
solanine	somewise	sorption	sow-drunk	sparring	spent tan
solar day	somnific	sorptive	sow-louse	sparrowy	spergula
solarise	so muckle	sorriest	sow-metal	sparsely	spermary
solarism	sonantal	sorrower	sow's-baby	sparsity	spermata
solarist	sonatina	sorryish	soya bean	spartina	spermine
solarium	sonerila	sortable	soya meal	spar tree	sperm oil
solarize	songbird	so soon as	soya milk	spasmous	spermous
solaster	songbook	Sotadean	soy frame	spasm war	Spetsnaz
solation	songfest	souchong	soy sauce	spatfall	sphagnum
solatium	song-form	soul bell	space age	spathose	sphecoid
sola topi	songless	soul-body	space bar	spathula	sphenoid
solderer	songlike	soul-cake	spaceful	spatiate	spherics
soldiery	song-plug	soul-case	space gun	Spätlese	spherify
solecism	song-post	Soul City	space lab	spatting	spheroid
solecist	songster	soul food	spaceman	spatular	spherule
solecize	sonicate	soulhood	spacemen	spavined	sphinges
soleless	Sonifier	soulical	space out	spawling	sphingid
solemnly	son-in-law	Souliote	spaceway	spawning	spianato
soleness	sonneted	soul kiss	spaciest	speak-box	spicated
solenium	sonnetry	soulless	spacious	speak for	spiccato
solenoid	sonny boy	soul-like	spadeful	speaking	spice bag
sole-tree	Sonny Jim	soul-mass	spade lug	speak out	spice-box
solfeggi	sonobuoy	soul mate	spademan	spear gun	spiciest
solidago	Son of God	soulmate	spadices	speargun	spicular
solidary	son of man	soul-scot	spadille	spearing	spiculum
solidate	sonogram	soul-shot	spadroon	spearman	spidered
solidest	sonolyse	soul-sick	spaewife	Spearman	spiderly
solidify	sonorant	sound-bow	spaggers	spearmen	spiffier
solidism	sonority	soundbox	spagyric	spear oak	spiffily
solidist	sonorous	soundful	spalding	speciate	spiffing
solidity	sonsiest	sounding	spalpeen	specific	spigelia
soliform	soonness	sound-law	spandrel	specimen	spiggoty
solifuge	soothful	sound off	spangler	speciose	spikelet

spikiest	splicing	spouting	spurries	squirely	stamp war
spilitic	splinder	sprackle	spurring	squiress	stanchel
spillage	splinter	sprackly	spur road	squirish	stancher
spilling	split end	spraddle	spur-wing	squirism	standage
spillway	split-new	spragger	sputtery	squirmer	standard
spinachy	split pea	sprangle	spyglass	squirrel	stand for
spinally	split pin	sprangly	spy plane	squirter	standing
spindled	split run	spratted	squabash	squitter	standish
spin-down	splitter	spratter	squabbed	squizzed	stand off
spin echo	splotchy	sprattle	squabble	squizzle	stand oil
spine-oak	splutter	sprauncy	squabbly	squopper	stand out
spinette	Spodosol	sprawler	squab pie	stabbing	standout
spin flip	spoffish	spray can	squad car	stablest	stand pad
spiniest	spoilage	spray-dry	squaddie	stabling	stand pat
spinifex	spoliate	spray-gun	squadrol	stablish	stand Sam
spiniken	spondaic	spraying	squadron	staccato	staneraw
spinless	spondean	sprayman	squailer	stackful	stanhope
spinnbar	spondyle	spreader	squalene	stack gas	Stanhope
spinnery	spongier	spreckle	squaller	stadiums	stanitza
spinneys	spongily	spreeish	squaloid	staffage	stank-hen
spinning	sponging	Sprengel	squamate	stag bush	stannary
spinodal	spongoid	spriggan	Squamish	stage box	stannate
Spinozan	sponsion	sprigged	squamose	stage-set	stannite
spin-scan	spontoon	sprigger	squamous	stag film	stannous
spin-spin	spoofery	spriglet	squamule	staggard	stanzaed
spinster	spookery	springal	squander	staggeen	stanzaic
spinstry	spookier	springer	square go	staggers	stapedes
spintext	spookily	springle	squarely	staggery	stapelia
spin wave	spooking	sprinkle	square on	stagging	star-beam
spiny eel	spookish	sprinter	square up	stag head	starched
spiny rat	spookist	spritely	squarish	stag-horn	starcher
spiracle	spooming	sprittle	squarson	stag-hunt	starchly
spirally	spoon bow	spritzer	squasher	stagiary	star drag
spirated	spoonful	sprocket	squashes	stagiest	stardust
spirelet	spoonier	sprosser	squat tag	staglike	stare-cat
spirifer	spoonily	sprottle	squatted	stagnant	starfish
spirilla	spoonish	sprouted	squatter	stagnate	stargaze
spirited	spoonist	sprouter	squattle	Stahlian	stargazy
spirit up	sporadic	sprowsie	squawker	staining	starkers
spiritus	sporonin	sprucely	squaw-man	stair-rod	starless
spirling	sporosac	spruce-up	squeaker	stairway	starlike
spitball	sportful	spruiker	squealer	stake-net	starling
spit-curl	sportier	spruntly	squeamer	stake out	starosta
spiteful	sportily	spryness	squeegee	stalagma	starosty
spitfire	sporting	spudding	squeezer	stalking	starrier
spit-jack	sportive	spumante	squegger	stalklet	starrily
spitlock	sporular	spun gold	squelchy	stallage	starring
spitskop	spot-ball	spunkier	squibbed	stallary	star ruby
spitting	spot kick	spunkily	squibber	stall-fed	starship
spittled	spot lamp	spun silk	squidded	stalling	star-shot
spittoon	spotlamp	spun yarn	squidger	stallion	startful
spivvery	spotless	spunyarn	squid jig	stallite	starting
spivvish	spot-list	spur-gall	squiffed	stall off	startled
splasher	spot news	spur-gear	squiffer	stallout	startler
splatchy	spot test	spurious	squiggle	stalwart	start off
splatted	spottier	spurless	squiggly	Stamford	start out
splatter	spottily	spurlike	squilgee	staminal	star turn
splendid	spotting	spur line	squinacy	Stamp Act	starward
splenial	spot-weld	spurling	squinted	stampage	Star Wars
splenium	spoucher	spur mark	squinter	stampede	starwort
splenius	spousage	spurreys	squirage	stamping	stasimon
splenoid	spout cup	spurrier	squireen	stamp out	statable

statedly	stellify	sticking	stockist	storable	strenkle
statelet	stelline	stick-jaw	stockman	storeman	strepent
statical	stelling	stick-lac	stockmen	storemen	Strepyan
staticky	stellini	stickler	stock-out	store pay	stressed
statolon	stellion	stick-man	stockout	storeyed	stressor
statuary	Stellite	stick out	stockpot	storiate	stretchy
statuefy	stem cell	stick-pin	stodgier	storkish	streusel
statural	stemflow	stickpin	stodgily	stormful	strewage
staumrel	stemless	stiction	stoechas	storm-god	strewing
Staunton	stemlike	stiff-arm	stoicise	stormier	striatal
stay-away	stem-line	stiffish	Stoicism	stormily	striated
stay-down	stemmata	stiff one	stoicize	storming	striatum
stay-hook	stemmery	stifling	stolidly	storm-jib	stricken
staylace	stemming	stigmata	stolones	Stormont	strickle
stayless	stem-post	stigmate	stolonic	Storting	strictly
stay over	stem root	stilbene	stolport	stotinka	stridden
staysail	stem rust	stilbite	Stolypin	stoupful	striddle
stay-ship	stem turn	stiletto	stomachy	stoutish	strident
stay-tape	stemware	stillage	stomapod	stowable	striffen
stay-wire	stenlock	still-air	stomatal	stow away	strigate
steadier	stenosed	stilling	stomatic	stowaway	striggle
steadily	stenosis	stillion	stomping	stow-ball	strigose
steading	stenotic	Stillson	stone-age	stow-boat	strigous
steadite	stenting	stilt bug	Stone Age	strabism	strike in
steady on	stent-net	stimulus	stone axe	straddle	strike up
stealage	step back	stingier	stone-bow	stradiot	striking
stealing	stepdame	stingily	stonecat	strafing	strimmer
stealthy	step down	stingray	stonefly	straggle	Strimmer
steam age	stephane	stinkard	stone-jug	straggly	stringed
steam-car	step into	stink-bug	stoneman	straight	stringer
steam fly	step iron	stink-cat	stone nct	strain at	string up
steamier	stepless	stinkier	stone-pit	strained	strinkle
steamily	steplike	stinking	stone run	strainer	strip cup
steaming	step on it	stink-pot	stonc saw	strain up	stripier
steam tug	step over	stinkpot	stoniest	straiten	striping
steapsin	steppage	stintage	stonking	straitly	striplet
stearate	stepping	stinting	stooling	stramash	strip map
steatite	stepsire	stipites	stooping	strammel	stripped
steatoma	stepwise	stippled	stoop tag	stranded	stripper
Stechkin	stereome	stippler	stop a gap	stranger	striving
steel-bow	stericks	stipular	stop band	strangle	strobila
steelbow	sterigma	stipuled	stopbank	strap-end	strobile
Steel boy	sterling	stirless	stop bath	strapped	strobili
steelier	Sterling	Stirling	stop bead	strapper	strobing
steelify	sternful	stirring	stop-butt	strapple	stroddle
steeling	Sternist	stitchel	stopcock	stratege	stroking
steel pan	sternite	stitcher	stop dead	strategy	stroller
steel pen	sternman	stitch up	stop down	stratify	stromata
steenbok	sternson	St Kildan	stop-gate	stratose	strombus
steening	sternums	St Lucian	stop-knob	straught	stronger
steeping	sternway	St Monday	stop lamp	stravaig	strongly
steepish	stetting	stob-mill	stopless	strawboy	strong of
steepled	stewable	stoccado	stop list	straw-dry	strontia
steepler	stewarty	stocious	stop-lock	straw hat	strophae
steerage	stewpack	stockade	stop-loss	strawish	strophic
steering	stibious	stock-boy	stopover	straw man	stropped
steerman	stibnite	stock car	stoppage	streaked	strouter
steer-oar	sticcado	stock-hut	stopping	streaker	Strowger
steer off	stickage	stockier	stop sign	streamer	struck on
steevely	stickful	stockily	stop time	streeted	struggle
steeving	stickier	stocking	stop word	strelitz	strummed
stellate	stickily	stockish	stop-work	strength	strummer

strumose	sturgeon	subserve	sudorous	sumpitan	supinate
strumous	sturnoid	sub-shell	sudsable	sumption	supinely
strumpet	stylitic	subshrub	suedette	sum total	suppable
strung-up	stymying	subsidia	suet face	sun-baked	supplant
strutted	suasible	subsizar	sufferer	sun-bathe	supplely
strutter	subacute	subsolar	sufficer	sunbathe	supplest
stub-axle	subadary	subsonic	suffixal	sunbeamy	supplial
stubbard	subadult	subspace	sufflate	sun-blind	supplice
stubbier	subagent	substage	suffling	sunblind	supplied
stubbily	subahdar	substant	suffrage	sunblock	supplier
stubbing	Subarian	substorm	suffragi	sunbreak	supplies
stubbled	sub-basal	substyle	suffrago	sunburst	supposal
stubborn	sub-breed	subtalar	sugar-bag	sun-crack	supposed
stub-bred	Subbuteo	subtense	sugar-box	sun cream	supposer
stub-iron	subchela	Subtiaba	sugar-gum	sun-dance	suppress
stub-nail	subclass	subtidal	sugaring	Sundayed	suprafix
stub-tail	subcycle	subtilin	sugarish	sunderer	supremos
stub wing	subduing	subtilly	sugar pea	sun-dress	supremum
stub wire	subduple	subtilty	sugar rag	sundress	surbahar
stuccoer	subdural	subtitle	suggesta	sun-dried	surbased
stuccoes	subdwarf	subtlest	suicidal	sundries	surcease
stud-bolt	subequal	subtlety	sui juris	sundrops	surculus
stud book	suberane	subtlist	suitable	sungates	sure card
studding	suberate	subtonic	suitably	sungazer	sure find
stud farm	suberect	subtopia	suitcase	sunglass	sure-fire
stud-fish	suberize	subtotal	suit-hold	sungrebe	sureness
studious	suberone	subtract	suitlike	sunlight	sureties
stud-mare	suberose	subtribe	suit real	sunn hemp	surfable
stud-wall	suberous	subtrist	suitress	sunniest	surfaced
stud-work	sub-floor	subucula	suit-roll	Sunny Jim	surfacer
stuffage	subfloor	subulate	sukebind	sun-perch	surfbird
stuffbag	sub-frame	suburban	sukiyaki	sun plant	surf-boat
stuffier	subgenus	suburbia	sulcated	sun-print	surf-clam
stuffily	subgiant	sub verbo	sulculus	sun-scald	surf-coot
stuffing	subgrade	subverse	sulfamic	sunsetty	surf-duck
stultify	subgrain	subvital	sulindac	sunshade	surf-fish
stumbler	sub-group	subvocal	sulkiest	sun-shaft	surf-ride
stummick	subgroup	succinct	sullenly	sunshine	surgeful
stumming	subhuman	succinea	sulliage	sunshiny	surgency
stumpage	subimago	succinic	sulphane	sunspecs	surgical
stump bed	subitize	succinum	sulphate	sunstone	surhuman
stump-end	subjoint	succinyl	sulphide	sun visor	suricate
stumpier	subjugal	succubus	sulphite	sunwards	Suriname
stumpily	sub-lease	such a one	sulphone	sun-wheel	surliest
stumping	sublease	suchlike	sulphury	Supadriv	surmisal
stumpish	sublevel	suchness	sultanic	supellex	surmiser
stump leg	sublimer	suchwise	sultanry	superadd	surmount
Stundism	sublunar	suckable	sul tasto	superate	surplice
Stundist	submerge	suckener	sultrier	superbly	surprise
stunkard	submerse	suckered	sultrily	superego	surquidy
stunning	sub-nosed	suckerel	Sumatran	superfix	surrebut
stunpoll	suborder	sucker-up	sumbitch	superfly	surround
stunsail	suborned	suck-fish	sum check	superhet	surroyal
stunt man	suborner	suck-hole	Sumerian	superior	surtitle
stuntman	subovate	suckling	summable	superius	surucucu
stuntmen	suboxide	sucupira	summator	superloo	surveyal
stupeous	subphyla	Sudanese	summerly	superman	surveyor
stupider	subpoena	sudarium	summitry	supermen	survival
stupidly	subpolar	sudation	summoner	supernal	surviver
sturdied	subprior	sudatory	sumotori	super-rat	survivor
sturdier	sub-range	suddenly	sumphish	superset	suspense
sturdily	subsella	suddenty	sump-hole	supertax	Sussex ox

susumber	sweating	sybarite	synochal	tacsonia	take down
susurrus	sweat-rag	sycamine	synochus	tactical	take fire
suttinly	sweat rug	sycamore	synodite	tactless	take five
suzerain	Swede saw	sycomore	synonymy	tactosol	take from
Svedberg	sweenied	syconium	synopses	taeniate	take gate
Svengali	sweepage	syconoid	synopsis	taenioid	take heat
Sverdrup	sweeping	syenitic	synoptic	tafferel	take hold
swabbing	sweep-net	syllabic	synovial	taffrail	take-home
swaddler	sweet-bag	syllable	syntagma	tag along	take life
Swadeshi	sweet bay	syllabub	syntaxes	tagboard	take note
swaggery	sweetful	syllabus	syntaxic	taggable	take odds
swagging	sweet gum	sylphish	syntaxis	Taghairm	take over
swag lamp	sweeting	Sylvaner	syntenic	taglioni	takeover
swagsman	sweetish	sylvanly	syntexis	tagmemic	take part
swainish	sweet man	sylvanry	synthase	tagmosis	take post
Swainson	sweet pea	sylvatic	syntonic	tag strip	taker-off
swamp gas	sweetsop	symbiont	syphilis	tagua-nut	take root
swamphen	swell-box	symbiose	syphonic	Tahitian	take rust
swampier	swelldom	symbiote	Syriarch	Tahunian	take ship
swampish	swelling	symbolic	syringes	taiglach	take sick
swamp-oak	swellish	symmachy	syrinxes	tail-area	take silk
swamp ore	swellism	symmelia	systatic	tail away	take that
swan-dive	swell mob	symmetry	systemed	tail back	take vent
swan-drop	swift fox	sympathy	systemic	tailback	take wind
swanherd	Swiftian	sympatry	systolic	tail-bone	take wine
swankier	swiftlet	symphile	syzygial	tail boom	take wing
swankily	swigging	symphily	syzygies	tailcoat	take-with
swanking	swilling	symphony	syzygium	tail comb	takingly
swankpot	swill-tub	symplasm	Szechuan	tail cone	Taki-Taki
swanlike	swim fair	symplast	Szechwan	taileron	talapoin
swan-mark	swim-hole	symploce	tabarded	tail-flap	talcking
Swanndri	swimming	sympodia	tabby cat	tailgate	talcumed
swan-neck	swimmist	symposia	tableaux	tail-head	talented
swannery	swim-pool	sympotic	table-cut	tail lamp	tale-piet
swanning	swimsuit	synalgia	tableful	tailless	talesman
swan's egg	swimwear	synangic	table-hop	tail-like	talesmen
swan-shot	swindler	synanthy	table mat	tail male	talionic
swanskin	swine flu	synaphea	table top	tailored	talisman
swansong	swine-pox	synapses	tabletop	tailorly	talkable
swap fund	swine-sty	synapsid	tablette	tail-pipe	talk away
swap-hook	swingbin	synapsis	tablinum	tailpipe	talk back
swap meet	swingier	synaptic	tabooism	tail-pole	talkback
swapping	swinging	synarchy	Taborite	tail-race	talk down
swap shop	swing man	synastry	tabouret	tail-rope	talkfest
swartish	swing set	syncarpy	tabulary	tail-skid	talk over
swashing	Swissess	syncline	tabulate	tailspin	talk shop
swash way	switched	syncopal	tac-au-tac	tail unit	talk show
swastika	switchel	syncopic	T account	tail-walk	talk tall
swatchel	switcher	syncrude	tachinid	tailward	Tallensi
swathing	switch in	syncytia	tachisme	tail wind	talliate
swatting	switch-on	syndeses	Tacitean	tailwind	tallness
swayable	swizzled	syndesis	taciturn	tailwise	tallowed
sway-back	swizzler	syndetic	tack coat	tainture	tallower
swear off	swooning	syndeton	tack-duty	takeable	tall ship
swear out	swooping	syndical	tackiest	take a bow	tall talk
sweat-bee	sword-arm	syndrome	tackling	take a low	tallwood
sweat-box	sword-cut	synechia	tack-nail	take away	tally-hos
sweat fly	swording	synectic	tack room	take-away	tallying
sweatful	sword-law	synergic	tacksman	takeaway	tallyman
sweat-hog	sword-mat	synergid	tack weld	take back	tallymen
sweatier	sworn man	syngamic	taco chip	take boat	Talmudic
sweatily	swotting	syngraph	taconite	take care	talukdar

tamandua	tappable	tawdrily	teardown	telsonic	terai hat	tetrical
tamanoir	tap pants	tawniest	tear-drop	temerity	terakihi	tetrobol
tamarack	tap-rivet	tawny owl	teardrop	temerous	teraphim	tetrodon
tamarind	tap stock	taxation	tear duct	tempered	teratoid	tettered
tamarisk	tap water	taxative	tear into	temperer	teratoma	teuchter
tamarugo	taqueria	tax break	tear it up	Templary	terawatt	teucrium
Tamashek	tarakihi	tax-eater	tear-jerk	template	terebene	teuf-teuf
tambouki	Taranchi	taxemics	tearless	templify	Teresian	Teutonic
tamboura	Tarascan	tax exile	tearlike	temporal	teriyaki	textbook
tameable	tarbagan	tax haven	teasable	tempting	terminal	text file
tameless	tarboosh	taxiarch	tea-scrub	temulent	terminer	text-hand
tameness	tar-brush	taxi-boat	teaseler	tenacity	terminus	textless
Tamilian	tardiest	taxi-girl	tease out	tenacula	termitic	textuary
tamperer	targeted	taxinomy	Teasmade	tenaille	termless	textural
tamponed	targetry	taxi rank	teaspoon	tenantry	termoner	textured
Tamworth	Targumic	taxi-ride	tea-table	tendance	term-time	thacking
Tanaiste	tarkashi	taxodium	tea towel	tendence	termwise	Thai silk
tandemer	tarlatan	taxonomy	tea-treat	tendency	terraced	thalamic
tandemly	tarnhelm	taxpayer	tea wagon	tenderer	terrapin	thalamus
tandoori	tarogato	tax point	techiest	tenderly	Terrapin	thalline
tanekaha	tar-paper	tax-taker	tectonic	tendines	terraria	thallium
tangelos	Tarpeian	Tayacian	Teddy boy	tenebrae	terrazzo	thalloid
tangency	tarragon	tayberry	teenaged	tenebrio	terrella	thallose
tang-fish	tarriest	Tay-Sachs	teenager	tenement	terrible	thallous
tangible	tarrying	T-bar lift	teenhood	Tenerife	terribly	Thamudic
tangibly	tarsioid	teaberry	teeniest	tenesmus	terrific	thanadar
tangiest	tarsitis	tea-billy	teensier	ten-gauge	Terry Alt	Thanatos
tanglier	Tarskian	tea-board	teenybop	tenon saw	tertiary	thanedom
tangling	tartanry	tea-bread	tee shirt	tenorino	tertiate	thanewer
tangoist	tartaret	tea break	teething	tenorist	teru-tero	thankful
tan-house	tartaric	tea-brick	teetotal	tenorite	Terylene	thank God
tanistry	Tartaric	tea caddy	teetotum	tenoroon	terzetti	thanking
tankette	tartarin	tea chest	teguexin	tenotomy	terzetto	thanks be
tank farm	Tartarly	teaching	tegument	tenpence	tessella	thanks to
tankfuls	Tartarus	tea cloth	teichoic	tenpenny	tesserae	thank you
tankless	tartiest	tea dance	teiglach	ten-pound	tesseral	thataboy
tank suit	tartness	tea fight	telecast	tensible	tessular	thataway
tank town	tartrate	tea glass	telechir	ten-speed	testable	thatched
tank trap	Tartuffe	tea green	telecine	tentacle	testamur	thatcher
tannable	tar-water	tea house	telecoms	tent city	testator	that gate
tantalic	tarwhine	teal blue	telefilm	tent club	testatum	that'll do
tantalum	task-work	tea-maker	telegony	tent coat	test card	that long
tantalus	tasselly	team-boat	telegram	tent-door	test case	thatness
tantrism	tastable	team game	tele-lens	tentless	test-fire	that once
tantrist	taste bud	team-land	telemark	tentlike	testicle	that said
Taoistic	taste-cup	team-mate	telepath	ten to one	testiest	thaw-lake
tapaculo	tasteful	team race	teleport	ten-to-two	test meal	thawless
tapadero	tastiest	teamsman	teleseme	tent ring	test tube	the Apple
tapas bar	tattered	teamster	telestic	tent-sack	testudos	thearchy
tap-borer	tattiest	team-talk	teletext	tent show	test well	the Ashes
tap-dance	tattling	teamwork	telethon	tent town	tetanise	Theatine
tapeable	tattooed	tea olive	teletype	tentwise	tetanize	theatral
tape deck	tattooer	tea party	Teletype	tentwort	tetanoid	theatric
tape hiss	tau cross	tea place	teleview	tenuious	tetchily	the Backs
tapeless	taunting	tea plant	televise	tenurial	tetchous	thebaine
tape-line	tau-staff	tea plate	telework	Ten Words	tetradic	the Beast
taper tap	tautness	tearable	tellable	teocalli	tetragon	the bends
tapestry	tautomer	tear a cat	tell a lie	teosinte	Tetralin	the Blitz
tape-tied	tautonym	tear-arse	tell away	tephrite	tetramer	the Blues
tapeworm	taut ship	tearaway	tell-tale	tepidity	Tetra Pak	the board
tap-house	taverner	tear bomb	telluric	teraflop	tetrapod	the brink
tapiroid	tawdrier	tear down	telomere	teraglin	tetrarch	the brute

the Buffs	thermics	thinnest	threaten	thwartly	tillable
the bumps	thermion	thinning	three-bar	thwittle	tillered
the Burse	thermite	thinnish	three-day	thyme-oil	tillicum
the chase	thermode	thin seam	three-one	thymitis	till-roll
the cloth	the Rolls	thin-sown	three-ply	thymosin	Tilsiter
the Coast	theropod	thin-spun	three-two	thyrsoid	tiltable
the Craft	the round	thin-worn	three-way	Tia Maria	tilt-boat
the Creed	the rules	thio-acid	threitol	tiarella	tilt-wing
the creep	the Salon	thioctic	threnode	Tiberian	tilt-yard
the Devil	thesauri	thionate	threnody	Tibetian	Timacuan
The Downs	the Shake	thionine	threshel	tibialis	timarchy
the drink	the shits	thiotepa	thresher	Ticinese	timariot
the Duchy	the Skins	thiourea	Thresher	tickameg	timbered
the enemy	the small	third age	thribble	tick-bean	timbrous
theetsee	the Smoke	third ear	thriller	tick-bird	time-ball
the Exile	the solid	third eye	thrimble	ticketed	time base
the faith	The Souls	third man	thrinter	ticketer	time-bill
the first	the South	third sex	thripple	tickling	time bomb
the Flood	the Speck	thirlage	throatal	ticklish	time code
the girls	thespian	thirster	throated	tick over	Timeform
the goods	Thespian	thirteen	throbbed	tick-seed	time-fuse
thegosis	Thetford	thirties	throbber	tick-tack	timeless
the hills	the thing	thisaway	thrombin	tick-tick	timelier
the House	thetical	this baby	thrombus	tick-tock	timelike
the Index	the Tombs	this bout	thronger	tidal air	time lock
the issue	the Tower	this gate	thropple	tiddlier	time-rate
theistic	the trots	this here	throstle	tide-boat	time slot
the jumps	theurgic	this is it	throttle	tideland	time span
the Kavir	the weeps	this life	throwing	tideless	time warp
the knife	the widow	this much	throw mud	tideline	timewise
the Lakes	thewless	thisness	throw off	tidemark	time-work
thelemic	thewness	this once	throw out	tide mill	time-worn
the Lords	the Yards	thistled	throw rug	tide over	time zone
thematic	thiamine	thiswise	thrumble	tidesman	timidest
the McCoy	thiazide	thole-pin	thrum cap	tidewave	timidity
theme pub	thiazine	Thompson	thrummed	tidiness	timoneer
the Mogul	thiazole	thoracal	thrummer	tie-break	Timorese
the mopes	thick-cut	thoraces	thruster	tie clasp	timorous
themself	thick ear	thoracic	thudding	tie match	tin-arsed
the night	thick end	thoraxes	thuggery	Tientsin	tincture
the North	thickety	thornier	thuggish	tie one on	tingeing
theocrat	thickish	thornily	thuggism	tiffined	tingible
theodicy	thickset	thorough	Thuggism	tiger-cat	tin-glass
theogony	thief ant	thoughty	thumbful	tiger-eye	tin-glaze
theology	thiefdom	thousand	thumb nut	tigerine	tinglier
theonomy	Thiersch	thowless	thumb-pad	tigering	tinglish
theorbos	Thiessen	Thracian	thumb-pin	tigerish	ting-tang
theories	thievery	thraldom	thumb-pot	tigerism	ting-ting
theorise	thieving	thralled	thumbs up	tiger-nut	tininess
theorism	thievish	thraneen	thumpety	tight-ass	tinkerer
theorist	thimbled	thranite	thumping	tight end	tinkling
theorize	thin-film	thrapple	thundery	tightish	tin-mouth
theosoph	thingamy	thrasher	thurible	tightwad	tinniest
theowdom	thingies	thraving	thurifer	tigridia	tinnitus
the peace	thingify	thraward	thurrock	Tigrinya	tin-panny
the pools	Thingman	thrawing	Thursday	Tigurine	tin plate
the pouts	think big	thrawnly	thus-gate	Tikopian	tinselly
the ranks	think box	threaded	thusness	tilefish	tinselry
therblig	think fit	threaden	thuswise	tile game	tinsmith
therefor	thinking	threader	thwacker	tile-kiln	tinsnips
theremin	think out	threadle	thwarter	tile-work	tin-stone
thereout	thinness	threaper	thwartle	tile-yard	tinstone

tintable	to a fault	tomatoey	top-graft	total sum	toxodont
tintless	to and fro	tombless	tophaike	total war	toxology
tint-tool	tobaccos	tombolos	top-heavy	tote fair	toymaker
tiny mind	to be sure	tombotie	Tophetic	totemism	trabeate
tippable	toboggan	tomentum	to pieces	totemist	tracheae
tippeter	Tobralco	Tom Jones	top-level	totemite	tracheal
tippy-toe	tochered	Tommy-bag	top light	tote road	trachean
tipsiest	tocology	tommy bar	top-liner	to the bad	tracheas
tip speed	todayish	Tommy-bar	toplofty	to the nth	tracheid
tipstaff	toddy cat	tommy-gun	top-notch	totitive	trachoma
tip-touch	to die for	tommy-rot	topology	totterer	trachyte
tiramisu	tod-tails	tommyrot	top onion	tottling	trackage
tired Tim	toe-board	Tommy-rot	toponium	tottlish	track-bed
tireless	toe brake	Tom-noddy	toponymy	totty-pot	trackbed
tiresome	toe-cover	tomogram	topotaxy	toucanet	tracking
tiringly	toe-crack	tomorrer	topotype	touch box	track-man
Tir-na-nog	toe-piece	tomorrow	top-score	touchier	trackman
Tironian	toe-plate	tom thumb	top-shell	touchily	trackmen
tirrivee	toe-strap	Tom Thumb	Topsider	touching	track rod
Tisha b'Av	toe to toe	to my mind	top-stone	touch off	trackway
tissular	to excess	tonalism	top table	touchous	tractate
titanate	to-flight	tonalist	top-water	touch-pad	tractile
Titaness	Tofranil	tonalite	top whack	tough guy	traction
titanian	together	tonality	top yeast	toughish	tractive
Titanian	Togolese	tone-deaf	toquilla	tough nut	tractlet
Titanism	tohu-bohu	tone down	torchère	touracos	tractrix
titanite	toileted	toneless	torchlit	tourdion	tradable
titanium	toiletry	tone poem	torch-man	tourelle	tradeful
titanous	toilette	tone poet	toreador	Tourette	trade gap
titchier	toilinet	ton-force	toreutic	touristy	trade off
tithable	toilless	tongkang	tor-grass	tour jeté	trade war
titheman	toilsome	tongsman	to rights	tourneys	traditor
tithe-pig	toil-worn	tonguing	Torinese	Tournois	traducer
titihoya	tokening	tonicity	tornadic	tournure	tragical
titivate	tokenism	tonology	tornados	tout seul	tragopan
titmouse	tokenist	tonstein	tornaria	tovarich	tragulid
tit-pipit	tokenize	tonsured	torn-down	tovarish	trailing
titrator	tokonoma	ton tight	tornillo	towardly	trail mix
titterer	Tok Pisin	toodle-oo	toroidal	towelled	trail-net
tittuped	Tokugawa	toolache	tor ouzel	towering	trailway
titty-bag	Tokyoite	tool-crib	torpidly	town ball	trainage
tittymeg	tolbooth	tool head	torquate	town-bull	traineau
titubant	tol-de-rol	toolless	torridly	town hall	trainful
titubate	tolerant	tool-mark	tortelli	town home	training
titulary	tolerate	tool-post	tortilla	townhood	trainman
tjanting	tolerize	toolroom	tortilly	townland	trainmen
tjurunga	tolidine	tool shed	tortious	townless	train-oil
tlachtli	tollable	tooraloo	tortoise	town plan	train set
Tlapanec	toll-bait	too right	Tortolan	Townsend	Trajanic
toadfish	toll call	toothful	tortuose	township	Traminer
toadflax	toll-dish	toothier	tortuous	townsman	tramless
toad-frog	toll-free	toothily	tortured	townsmen	tramline
toadless	toll gate	toothing	torturer	town-talk	trampdom
toadlike	toll-road	toothlet	torulose	townward	tramping
toad-lily	tollroad	tooth-mug	torulous	tow-plane	trampish
toadling	toloache	tootsies	tosafist	towplane	trampled
toad-rush	Toltecan	toparchy	toss oars	tow-start	trampler
toad's cap	toluylic	topazine	tosylate	toxaemia	tram-rail
toadship	tomahawk	top board	totalise	toxaemic	tram road
toad-spit	tomalley	top brass	totality	toxicant	tram silk
toadyish	tomatine	top dress	totalize	toxicity	tranchet
toadyism	tomatoes	top fruit	totalled	toxocara	trancing

trannies	trecento	tribunal	triology	troubler	tubbiest
tranquil	tre corde	tributor	trioxide	trouncer	tub chair
transact	tree-bear	tributyl	tripcock	troupial	tubchair
trans-bay	tree calf	trichina	tripedal	trousers	tube-feed
transect	tree-crab	trichite	triphane	trousies	tube-foot
transept	tree-crow	trichome	triplane	trout-fly	tubeless
transfer	tree cult	trichord	triplice	troutful	tube-lift
transfix	tree duck	trickery	triploid	trouting	tubelike
tranship	tree fern	trickful	tripodal	troutlet	tube line
transire	tree frog	trickier	Tripolye	trouvère	tubercle
transmew	treeless	trickily	trippage	truantly	tuberize
transmit	treelike	tricking	trippant	truantry	tuberose
transoid	tree line	trickish	trippery	truchman	tuberous
transude	tree-moss	tricklet	trippier	truckage	tube sock
transume	treenail	trick out	tripping	truckful	tube-well
trantery	tree ring	tricorne	trippist	trucking	tube worm
trap-ball	tree-rune	Tricouni	trippler	truckler	tubiform
trap boat	tree toad	tric-trac	tripsome	trucklot	tubipore
trap cage	tree wasp	tricycle	triptane	truckman	tubulate
trap-crop	trek Boer	tridacna	triptote	true bill	tubulose
trapdoor	trek-cart	tridecyl	triptych	true blue	tubulous
trapezia	trekking	Tridione	trip-wire	true-born	tubulure
trapezii	trembler	triennia	tripwire	true-bred	tub-wheel
trapfall	tremblor	triethyl	trisomic	true grit	tuckahoe
trap-hook	Tremcard	trifecta	tristeza	true leaf	tuck-away
traplike	tremella	trifling	tristful	true left	tuck-comb
trap-line	tremolos	trifocal	tristich	true love	tucked up
trap-nest	trencher	triforia	tristubh	trueness	tuck into
trappean	trendier	trigenic	trithing	truffled	tuck-mill
trapping	trendify	trigging	tritiate	truistic	tuck-rail
trappist	trendily	triglyph	tritical	trumeaux	tuck shop
Trappist	trending	trigness	tritonal	trumpery	tuco-tuco
trap-play	trendoid	trigonal	Tritonly	trumpety	tucutucu
trappoid	Trentinc	trigonia	trit-trot	truncage	Tudesque
trap-rock	trephine	trigonid	triumvir	truncate	Tudorish
trap-shot	trepidly	trigonon	triunion	trunched	Tudorize
trap-tree	tresaiel	trigonum	triunity	trundler	Tuesdays
trapunto	tresance	trigraph	trizonal	trunkful	tuff-tuff
trap-yard	tresayle	trihedra	trochaic	trunking	tug-of-war
trash can	tresette	trilbied	trochili	trunnion	tug pilot
trashery	trespass	trilbies	trochlea	trussing	tuilette
trash-ice	tressure	trilemma	trochoid	truss-rod	tukutuku
trashier	trevalli	tri-level	troilism	trustful	tule wren
trashily	trevally	trilling	troilist	trustier	tullibee
trashman	triactor	trillion	troilite	trusties	tumandar
Traskite	triadism	trillium	trolleys	trustify	tumble up
trattles	trialism	trilobal	trollius	trustily	tumbling
trauchle	trialist	trilobed	trollopy	trusting	tumefied
traulism	triality	trimaran	trombone	truthful	tumefies
traverse	trialled	trimeric	trombony	truth set	tumidity
traverso	trial run	trimesic	troopial	try a fall	tummy bug
travesty	triangle	trimeter	trophied	tryingly	tumorous
trawl net	triapsal	trimmest	trophies	tryworks	tumoural
trayfuls	triarchy	trimming	tropical	tsarevna	tump-line
treacher	Triassic	trimness	troponin	tsaritsa	tump-tump
treading	triaxial	trimodal	trot-cosy	tsarship	tumulary
tread out	triazine	trimoric	trothful	tsessebi	tumulate
treasure	triazole	trimotor	trotteur	T-shirted	tumulous
treasury	tribally	trim-tram	trotting	tsitsith	tuna fish
treaties	tribasic	Trimurti	trottles	tsunamic	tuneable
treating	tribelet	trinklet	trottoir	tsunamis	tuneless
treatise	tribrach	trinodal	troubled	tubbable	tunesome

tunester	turn-tree	twistify	tyrosine	unarched	unbunged
tungsten	turn Turk	twist-off	Tyrrhene	unargued	unburden
tungstic	turpidly	twist tie	Tyrtaean	unartful	unburied
tung tree	turreted	twitched	Tysonian	unasking	unburies
Tungusic	turrible	twitchel	tzatziki	unatoned	unburned
tunicary	turrited	twitcher	tzitzith	unavowed	unburrow
tunicate	tuskless	twittery	Ubiquist	unawaked	unbutton
tunicked	tusklike	twitting	ubiquity	unawares	uncabled
tuniness	tussocky	twittish	uchimata	unbacked	uncalled
Tuniseen	tutelage	twit-twit	udderful	unbadged	uncandid
Tunisian	tutelary	two by two	uddiyana	unbaited	uncapped
Tunisine	tutorage	two-cycle	udometer	unbanded	uncaring
tunnyman	tutordom	two-eared	Ugaritic	unbanked	uncarved
tun tight	tutoress	two-edged	uglified	unbanned	uncashed
Tupamaro	tutorial	two-ended	uglifier	unbarbed	uncastle
tuppence	tutorize	two-faced	uglifies	unbarded	uncaught
tuppenny	Tuvaluan	two-field	ugliness	unbarked	uncaused
tu quoque	Tuvinian	two-holer	ugsomely	unbarred	unceiled
Turanian	tuxedoed	two hoots	Uigurean	unbarrel	uncellar
turanose	tuxedoes	two-horse	Uigurian	unbarrel	uncement
turbaned	TV dinner	two-lined	uintaite	unbathed	uncenter
turbidly	Twaddell	two parts	ulcerate	unbeaten	uncentre
turbinal	twaddler	twopence	ulcerous	unbecome	unchancy
turbined	twa-grass	twopenny	uliginal	unbedded	uncharge
turbiner	Twainian	two-piece	ulterior	unbegged	unchaste
turbines	twanging	two-rowed	ultimacy	unbeheld	uncheery
turbocar	twangler	two-shear	ultimata	unbelief	unchewed
turbofan	twatchel	two-shoes	ultimate	unbelted	unchoked
turbojet	twattler	two-sided	ultimity	unbended	unchosen
Turcoman	tweedier	two-state	Ultonian	unbenign	unchurch
turfiest	tweedily	two-teeth	ultraism	unbenumb	uncially
turfless	tweedler	two-timer	ultraist	unbereft	unciform
turf-line	tweeness	two times	ultra-red	unbeseem	uncinate
turgency	tweezers	two-tooth	ululance	unbiased	uncipher
turgidly	twelvemo	Tychonic	Ulyssean	unbidden	unclench
Turinese	twenties	Tylorean	umbellar	unbigged	Uncle Ned
Turkmens	twentymo	Tylorian	umbelled	unbishop	Uncle Sam
Turkoman	twiddler	tympanal	umbellet	unbitted	Uncle Tom
Turk's cap	twiffler	tympanic	umbilici	unbitten	unclever
turlough	twiggage	tympanum	umble pie	unblamed	unclinch
Turlupin	twig-gall	type area	umbonate	unbloody	unclosed
turmeric	twiggery	type-ball	umbrella	unbobbed	unclothe
turnable	twigging	typecast	umbrette	unbodied	uncloudy
turn away	twilight	typeface	umpirage	unbodily	uncloven
turnaway	twilling	type-form	umpiress	unboiled	uncloyed
turn back	twin-bill	type-high	umptieth	unbolted	unclutch
turnback	twin-born	type site	umpty-ump	unbonded	uncoated
turn-beam	twin city	type size	umquhile	unbonnet	uncocked
turn-bolt	twinging	type test	unabated	unbooked	uncoined
turncoat	twinhood	typhonic	unabused	unboring	uncombed
turncock	twi-night	Typhonic	unaching	unbottle	uncomely
turn down	twinkler	typified	una corda	unbought	uncommon
turndown	twinleaf	typifier	unactive	unboyish	uncooked
turnkeys	twin-lens	typifies	unadored	unbraced	uncooled
turn-mark	twinling	typology	unaffied	unbreech	uncopied
turn over	twinning	tyramine	unafraid	unbribed	uncorked
turnover	twin-pair	tyrannic	unageing	unbridle	uncosted
turnpike	twinship	tyrannis	unallied	unbright	uncostly
turnsick	twin soul	tyre-iron	unamazed	unbroken	uncouple
turnsole	twin-spot	tyreless	unamused	unbuckle	uncovery
turnspit	twin town	Tyrolean	unanchor	unbudded	uncreate
turn tail	twistier	Tyrolese	unaneled	unbudget	unctuous

unculled	undersow	unfenced	ungutted	unionize	unlooped
uncumber	undertax	unfetter	unhabile	union nut	unloosen
uncurbed	undertie	unfilial	unhacked	unipivot	unlopped
uncurled	undertip	unfilled	unhailed	unipolar	unlorded
uncursed	undertow	unfirmly	unhaired	uniquely	unlordly
undamned	underuse	unfished	unhallow	uniquity	unlovely
undamped	under way	unfitted	unhalter	unironed	unloving
undaring	underway	unflawed	unhamper	unisonal	unmaiden
undarken	underwit	unfluted	unhanged	unissued	unmaimed
undarned	undesert	unfolded	unhappen	unitable	unmalted
undashed	undesire	unfolder	unharden	unit cell	unmanned
undation	undevout	unfooted	unharmed	unit cost	unmantle
undaubed	undieted	unforbid	unhatted	unitedly	unmapped
undazzle	undimmed	unforced	unheaded	unit load	unmarked
undecane	Undinism	unforged	unhealed	univalve	unmarred
undecent	undinted	unforgot	unhealth	universe	unmasked
undecide	undipped	unformal	unhearty	univocal	unmasker
undecked	undivine	unformed	unheated	un-Jewish	unmeetly
undecree	undoable	unfought	unhedged	unjoined	unmelted
undeemed	undocked	unfouled	unheeded	unjolted	unmended
undelete	undoctor	unframed	unhelmed	unjoyful	unmerged
undelved	undoffed	unfreeze	unhelped	unjoyous	unmighty
undenied	undoomed	un-French	unhemmed	unjudged	unmilked
undented	undotted	unfriend	unherded	unjustly	unmilled
underact	undouble	unfrozen	unheroic	unkeeled	unminded
under age	undraped	unfrugal	unhidden	unkenned	unminted
underage	undreamt	unfunded	unhinged	unkennel	unmissed
underarm	undriven	unfurred	unholier	unkilled	unmitred
underbed	undubbed	ungainly	unholily	unkilned	unmixing
underbid	undulant	ungalled	unholpen	unkindly	unmoaned
underbit	undulate	ungarter	unhomely	unkinged	unmocked
undercap	undulled	ungauged	unhonest	unkingly	unmodern
undercup	undulose	ungeared	unhooded	unkissed	unmodish
undercut	undulous	ungelded	unhooked	unknight	unmolten
underdip	undunged	ungenial	unhoping	unkosher	unmoored
underdog	undusted	ungentle	unhopped	unlanded	unmortal
underdot	unearned	ungently	unhorned	unlawful	un-Mosaic
underfed	uneasier	un-German	unhoused	unleaded	unmoving
underfit	uneasily	ungifted	unhulled	unleafed	unmuffle
under fog	unedible	ungilded	unhumble	unleared	unmuzzle
underfug	unedited	ungirded	unhunted	unlearnt	unnailed
underfur	unelated	ungiving	unhusked	unleased	unnapped
under-god	unending	ungladly	unhymned	unlevied	unnature
under God	unendued	unglazed	unialgal	unliable	unneeded
underhew	unenvied	ungloved	Uniatism	unlicked	unnimble
underjaw	unequals	ungnawed	uniaxial	unlidded	unnimbly
underlap	unerotic	ungoaded	unicycle	unlifted	unobeyed
underlay	unerring	ungolden	unifilar	unlikely	unopened
underlet	unespied	ungorged	unilobar	unliking	unordain
underlid	unevenly	ungotten	unimaged	unlimber	unpacked
underlie	unexotic	ungowned	unimbued	unlineal	unpacker
underlip	unfading	ungraced	unimodal	unlinked	unpained
underman	unfairly	ungraded	un-Indian	unliquid	unpaired
under one	unfallen	ungraven	uninemic	unlisted	unpalled
underpan	unfamous	ungrazed	uninfeft	unlively	unparted
underpay	unfanned	ungreasy	uninodal	unlivery	unpassed
underpin	unfarced	ungreedy	uninured	unliving	unpathed
underran	unfasten	unground	uninvite	unloaden	unpawned
underrun	unfather	unguided	union dye	unloader	unpaying
undersea	unfaulty	unguilty	unionise	unlocked	unpeeled
underset	unfeared	ungulate	unionism	unlonely	unpeered
undersky	unfelled	ungummed	unionist	unlooked	unpegged

unpeople	unringed	unsigned	unsurely	unversed	upgather
unperson	unrinsed	unsimple	unsurety	unvetted	upgrader
unphased	unripely	unsinful	unswathe	unviable	upgrowth
unphoney	unripped	unsinged	unswayed	unviewed	upheaval
unpicked	unrobbed	unsiphon	untackle	unvirtue	upheaver
unpinned	unrobust	unslaked	untagged	unvizard	upholder
unpitied	unrocked	unsleeve	untailed	unvoiced	up in arms
unplaced	unroofed	unsliced	untalked	unvulgar	uplander
unplaned	unrooted	unslough	untangle	unwalked	uplifter
unplayed	unrotted	unslowed	untanned	unwalled	uplooker
unpliant	unrotten	unsluice	untapped	unwaning	up-market
unplowed	unrouged	unsmoked	untarred	unwanted	upmarket
unplumed	unroused	unsmooth	untasked	unwanton	upper air
unpocket	unrouted	unsoaped	untasted	unwarded	upper-cut
unpoetic	unrubbed	unsocial	untaught	unwarily	uppercut
unpoised	unruffle	unsocket	untenant	unwarmed	upper dog
unpoison	unruined	unsodden	untended	unwarned	upperest
unpolish	unrulier	unsoiled	untender	unwarped	upper jaw
unpolite	unrusted	unsolder	untented	unwashed	upper ten
unpolled	unsacked	unsolemn	untested	unwashen	uppishly
unposted	unsacred	unsolved	untether	unwasted	uprising
unpraise	unsaddle	unsordid	unthatch	unwatery	uprootal
unprayed	unsafely	unsorted	unthawed	unwaving	uprooter
unpreach	unsafety	unsought	unthread	unwealth	uproused
unpretty	unsailed	unsouled	unthrift	unweaned	upsaddle
unpriced	unsained	unsoured	unthrone	unwebbed	upsetter
unpriest	unsalted	unspared	unthrown	unwedded	upsprang
unprimed	unscaled	unsphere	untidier	unweeded	upspring
unprison	unscared	unspiced	untidily	unweened	upstager
unprized	unschool	unspiked	untilled	unweight	upstairs
unprobed	unscored	unspoilt	untimber	unwelded	upstater
unprofit	unsealed	unspoken	untimely	unwemmed	up sticks
Unprofor	unseared	unsprang	untinged	unwetted	upstream
UNPROFOR	unseason	unspread	untinned	unwieldy	up street
unproper	unseated	unspring	untinted	unwifely	up-stroke
unproved	unsecret	unsprung	untipped	unwigged	upstroke
unproven	unseeded	unsquare	untiring	unwilful	upthrust
unpruned	unseeing	unstable	untithed	unwilled	uptilted
unpublic	unseemly	unstably	untitled	unwinged	up to date
unpulled	unseized	unstaled	untoiled	unwinter	uptowner
unpumped	unseldom	unstated	untombed	unwisdom	upturner
unpurged	unselect	unstayed	untoward	unwisely	upwardly
unquoted	unsensed	unsteady	untraced	unwished	uralitic
unrailed	unserene	unstitch	untraded	unwonted	uranitic
unraised	unserved	unstolen	untragic	unwooded	Urartian
unreally	unsettle	unstored	untrendy	unworded	urbanely
unreaped	unsexier	unstrain	untruism	unworked	urbanise
unreason	unsexual	unstream	untrusty	unwormed	urbanism
unrecked	unshaded	unstress	untucked	unworthy	urbanist
unregard	unshadow	unstrike	unturned	unyeaned	Urbanist
unreined	unshaken	unstring	ununited	unzipped	urbanite
unrepaid	unshamed	unstrong	unurgent	unzipper	urbanity
unrepair	unshaped	unstruck	unusable	up-a-daisy	urbanize
unrepose	unshapen	unstrung	unuseful	up-anchor	urbicide
unrested	unshared	unstuffy	unvalued	upas tree	urceolus
unretted	unshaved	unsubtle	unvamped	up a stump	urchinly
unrhymed	unshaven	unsubtly	unvaried	upbubble	uredines
unribbed	unshelve	unsucked	unveiled	up-choked	uredinia
unridden	unshrine	unsuited	unveiler	upcoming	ureilite
unriddle	unshroud	unsummed	unveined	upcurved	ureteral
unrifled	unsicker	unsunned	unvenged	updoming	ureteric
unrigged	unsifted	unsupped	unvented	upfurled	urethane

urethrae	vaginula	vaporous	veinulet	vergence	vibronic
urethral	vagotomy	vapoured	velamina	vergency	viburnum
urethras	vagotony	vapourer	velarise	verified	vicarage
Urfirnis	vagrance	vapulate	velarity	verifier	vicarate
urgently	vagrancy	varactor	velarium	verifies	vicaress
uric acid	vainness	varanian	velarize	veristic	vicariad
uridylic	Valaisan	vardapet	Velcroed	verities	vicarial
urnfield	valanced	vargueño	veld-kost	verjuice	vicarian
urobilin	vale-lily	variable	veldsman	verligte	vicarish
uroboric	Valencia	variably	velleity	vermetid	vicarism
uroboros	valerate	variance	vellinch	vermicle	vice-king
urochord	valerian	variator	velocity	vermined	viceless
urodaeum	valeting	variceal	velodyne	verminer	vice-like
urodelan	Valhalla	varicose	velveret	Vermoral	vicelike
urologic	valiance	variedly	velveted	vermouth	vicenary
uroscopy	valiancy	varietal	vena cava	vernally	vice ring
urostyle	validate	variform	venality	Vernœuil	Vichyist
urotoxic	validity	varihued	venation	vernicle	Vichyite
uroxanic	valinche	variolar	vendable	Veronese	vicinage
Ursuline	Valiumed	variorum	vendetta	veronica	vicinism
urticant	Valkyrie	Variscan	vendeuse	verrucae	vicinity
urticate	valleyed	varistor	vendible	verrucas	Viconian
urushiol	Vallhund	varletry	venenose	verselet	victoria
usedness	valorise	varminty	venerate	verseman	Victoria
used-to-be	valorize	varnishy	venereal	versical	victorin
usefully	valorous	vartabed	Venerean	versicle	victress
use-money	valproic	vascular	Venerian	vertebra	Victrola
usership	Valsalva	vasculum	venerous	vertexes	videofit
usherdom	Valspeak	vasefuls	Venetian	vertical	video map
ustilago	valuable	Vaseline	vengeful	vertices	videotex
usufruct	valuably	vasiform	venially	verticil	Viennese
usurious	valuator	vasquine	venidium	Vertisol	Viet Cong
usurping	valvelet	vassalic	venogram	very good	Viet Minh
uteritis	valvifer	vassalry	venomous	very well	vieux jeu
Utilidor	valvular	vastness	venosity	vesalian	viewable
utilizer	vambrace	Vatinian	venously	vesicant	view card
Uto-Aztec	vampiric	vaultage	vent-hole	vesicate	viewdata
Utopiast	vamplate	vaulting	ventless	vesicula	viewless
utopiate	vanadate	vauntery	Ventolin	vesperal	viewport
utopical	vanadian	vauntful	ventouse	vespiary	viewsite
utriculi	vanadium	vaunting	venturer	vestiary	Vigenere
utterest	vanadous	vauntlay	venturis	vestless	vigilant
uver hand	vandalic	Vauxhall	Venusian	vestment	vigneron
uvermost	Vandalic	vavasory	venville	vestries	vignette
uvularia	vanessid	vavasour	veracity	vestuary	vignoble
uvularly	vanguard	veal calf	verandah	vestural	vigorish
uvulitis	vanillic	vectigal	veratria	vestured	vigorist
uxorious	vanillin	vectored	veratric	vesturer	vigorous
vaalhaai	vanillon	Vedantic	veratrum	Vesuvian	vildness
Vaalpens	vanillyl	veganism	verbally	Vesuvius	vileness
vacantly	vanisher	Vegemite	verbatim	vexation	vilified
vacation	vanities	vegetant	verbiage	vexatory	vilifier
vaccinal	vanitory	vegetate	verbless	vexillum	vilifies
vaccinee	Vanitory	vegetive	verboten	vexingly	vilipend
vaccinia	vanitous	Vegliote	verdancy	via media	villadom
vacherin	vanquish	vehement	Verdelho	viatical	villager
vacuolar	V antenna	veiledly	verderer	viaticum	villaget
vagabond	van't Hoff	veilless	verditer	vibrance	villagey
vagaries	vapidity	vein-gold	verdured	vibrancy	villainy
vagility	vaporise	veiniest	verdurer	vibrator	villakin
vaginant	vaporish	veinless	verecund	vibrioid	villatic
vaginate	vaporize	veinlike	vergaloo	vibrissa	vin blanc

vinchuca	visceral	voice box	waesucks	wall-hook	war-eagle
vincible	viscount	voiceful	Waffen SS	wall-hung	wareless
vincibly	viscuous	voidable	wafflike	wall-knot	wareness
vinculum	Visigoth	voidance	wage bill	wall-less	Warerite
vindaloo	visional	voidless	wageless	wall-nail	warfarin
vinegary	visioned	voidness	wager-cup	walloped	war fever
vine-hook	visioner	voilette	wage stop	walloper	warfront
vine leaf	visitant	voir dire	waggable	wallower	war-gamer
vineless	visiting	volantly	waggoner	wall pass	war grave
vine moth	vis major	volatile	wagonage	wall plug	war-guilt
vineries	Visqueen	volation	wagon-bed	wall-rock	warhorse
vine tree	visually	volatize	wagon box	Wallsend	War House
vine-wood	vital air	volcanic	wagonful	wall-side	wariness
vineyard	vitalise	volitant	wagon-lit	wall-tent	waringin
vinified	vitalism	volitate	wagon-man	wall-tree	warmable
vinifies	vitalist	volition	wagon-way	wall unit	warm bath
vin jaune	vitality	volitive	Wahabism	wall vase	warm boot
vinolent	Vitalium	volkswil	Wahabite	wall-walk	warm down
vino nero	vitalize	volleyer	wahoo elm	wall-wash	warmed-up
vinosity	vitamin A	volplane	waiflike	wall-work	warmer-up
vinously	vitamin B	Volscian	wailsome	wallwort	warmness
vin rouge	vitamin C	volsella	wainscot	wambling	warmouth
vintager	vitamin D	Volstead	waist-gun	wandered	warm over
vintnery	vitamin E	voltaism	wait-a-bit	wanderer	warm work
Vinylite	vitamin H	Volterra	wait-list	wanderoo	warpaint
vinylogy	vitamin K	volumina	waitress	Wandjina	war-party
violable	vitamin M	volution	waivable	wandsman	warp-beam
violater	vitamin P	volvelle	Wakashan	wangrace	warp-lace
violator	vitellin	volvulus	wakeless	wanhappy	war-plane
violence	vitellus	vomerine	wakerife	wan smile	warplane
violency	vitiator	vomit bag	Waldense	wantable	war-proof
violetta	vitiligo	vomiting	Waldeyer	want in on	warragal
viologen	vitreous	vomition	waldhorn	wantless	warranty
viomycin	vituline	vomitory	waldrapp	want list	warrener
viperine	vivacity	vomitous	wale-knot	wantoner	warrigal
viperish	vivarium	voodooed	walkable	wantonly	warspeak
viperous	viva voce	voorslag	walk-away	wanweird	war-steed
viraemia	viverrid	voracity	walk-back	wanwordy	wartless
viraemic	vividity	vortexes	walker-on	wanworth	wartlike
virement	vivified	vortical	walk good	wappered	war trial
virgated	vivifier	vortices	walk home	warbling	wartweed
virgater	vivifies	votaress	walk hots	war bride	wartwort
virginal	vivipary	votaries	walk into	war chest	war-weary
Virginia	vivisect	votarist	walk-mill	war cloud	war-whoop
virginly	vixenish	votation	walk over	warcraft	war widow
virgular	vizarded	vote bank	walkover	war crime	washable
viricide	vizcacha	vote down	walksman	ward aide	washaway
viridian	vizieral	voteless	walk tall	war dance	wash-ball
viridine	vizyless	voussoir	walk up to	wardatar	wash-bowl
viridity	Vlachian	vowelise	walk with	ward-book	washbrew
virilism	vocalese	vowelist	Walkyric	wardency	wash-coat
virility	vocalion	vowelize	Walkyrie	wardenry	wash-deck
virogene	vocalise	vowelled	Wallabee	warderer	wash-dirt
virology	vocalism	voyageur	Wallacea	war diary	wash-dish
virosome	vocalist	vulcanic	wallaroo	ward maid	wash down
virtuosa	vocality	vulgarly	walled-in	wardmote	washdown
virtuosi	vocalize	vulpinic	walled-up	wardress	washed up
virtuoso	vocation	vulsella	wall-eyed	wardrobe	washer-up
virtuous	vocative	vulvitis	wall-face	ward-room	wash-fast
virucide	Vodafone	Wachagga	wall fern	wardroom	wash-hand
virulent	vogesite	wadeable	wallfish	wardship	washiest
viscacha	Vogulian	wade into	wall game	wardsman	washland

wash-line	wave base	web-wheel	well-read	wheat-fly	whipster
wash-pool	wave down	Wechsler	well-room	wheatish	whip tail
washroom	wave drag	Wedgwood	Wellsian	wheedler	whiptail
wash-sale	waveform	weedhead	well then	wheelage	whipworm
wasplike	waveless	weed-hook	well-to-do	wheel bug	whirling
waste bin	wavelike	weediest	well-tomb	wheel car	whirring
wasteful	wave-line	weedless	well-trap	wheel-dog	whiskery
waste-way	wave-mark	weedling	well-used	wheeling	whiskeys
wastrife	wave-path	wee hours	well-wish	wheelman	whiskied
Wasukuma	wavering	weeklies	well with	wheel-map	whiskies
watch-box	wave trap	week-long	well-worn	wheelmen	whisking
watch cap	waviness	weeklong	Welsbach	wheel-ore	whispery
watchdog	wavingly	week-work	Welshman	wheel-pit	whistled
watch for	Wavy Navy	weeniest	Welshmen	wheel-set	whistler
watchful	wax berry	weep-hole	werewolf	wheel-tax	white ant
watchman	waxberry	weepiest	Wernicke	wheezily	white ash
watchmen	wax borer	weetless	Wesleyan	wheezing	white box
watch out	wax-cloth	weet-weet	West Bank	whelpish	white boy
waterage	waxcloth	weft fork	westerly	whenever	whitecap
water-ash	wax gland	wegotism	West Indy	whereout	white elm
water-bag	wax in age	wehrlite	westland	wherever	white-eye
water bat	waxiness	Weichsel	Westmark	wherries	white fir
water-bed	wax-light	weigh-bar	westmost	whetting	whitefly
waterbed	wax paper	weighing	West Nile	whey-face	white fox
water-boa	wax plant	weighman	west side	Whieldon	white-gum
waterbok	wax print	weigh off	West Side	whiffier	white-hat
water-boy	wayboard	weigh out	westward	whiffled	white-hot
water bug	waybread	weirdies	west wind	whiffler	White Hun
water bus	way-chain	weirdish	wet dream	Whiggery	white leg
water-cow	wayfarer	weirdity	wet-eared	Whiggess	white lie
water-dog	way-going	welcomer	wct lease	Whiggify	White man
water elm	waygoose	weldable	wet meter	Whiggish	whitener
water-fly	waylayer	weldless	wet-nurse	Whiggism	white oak
water gas	way-leave	weldment	wet plate	Whigling	white oil
water gum	wayleave	weldmesh	wet shave	Whigship	white-out
waterhen	way-point	weld pool	wet smack	Whillans	white owl
water ice	waypoint	welladay	wet steam	whimbrel	whitepox
waterily	way train	well-aged	wettable	whimmery	white rat
watering	way-wiser	well away	wet trade	whimpish	white rod
waterish	wazirate	wellaway	wet-white	whimseys	white rot
water jug	weakener	well-baby	Weymouth	whimsies	white rum
waterlog	weakfish	well-boat	whackier	whimsily	white tie
Waterloo	weaklier	well-born	whacking	whim-wham	white tin
waterman	weakling	well-bred	whale-fin	whinchat	whitling
watermen	weak link	well-curb	whaleman	whiniest	whitster
water-net	weakness	well deck	whale oil	whinnied	whittler
water oak	weak side	well-dish	whammies	whinnies	Whit walk
Water Pik	weak spot	well-done	whamming	whinyard	whiz-bang
water-pot	weanable	well-head	wharfage	whipbird	whizzing
water rat	weanling	well-hole	wharfing	whip-club	whizz-kid
water-ret	weaponed	well-hung	wharf-rat	whipcord	whodunit
water-rot	weaponry	well-kept	what else	whip-crop	whole lot
water-ski	wearable	well-kerb	whatever	whip hand	whole sum
waterway	weariest	well-kick	what-like	whip-jack	whomever
watsonia	weariful	well-knit	whatness	whiplash	whooping
watt-hour	wear thin	well-like	what of it	whipless	whoopsie
wattless	wear well	well-lost	what size	whip-like	whopping
wattling	weaselly	well-made	what's new	whiplike	whoredom
Waughian	weathery	well-near	what then	whip line	whoreson
Waughism	Weatings	wellness	what time	whipping	Whorfian
waveband	weavable	well-nigh	what with	whip-roll	whorlbat
	Weberian	well-paid	wheatear	whipship	whosever

whydunit	wind-blow	wink hard	wittiest	woodlark	word-book
wickeder	windburn	winkless	wittolly	woodless	wordbook
wickedly	wind-cone	winnable	wizardly	wood lily	word-deaf
wickered	wind down	winnower	wizardry	wood-meal	word-game
wickless	winder-up	winterer	wobblier	woodmote	wordiest
widdiful	windfall	winterim	wobbling	woodness	wordless
wide ball	wind farm	winterly	woefully	woodnote	wordlore
wide-band	wind gall	wintrier	woe is him	wood-opal	word mark
wide-body	wind-harp	wintrify	wolf call	woodpile	word-pair
wide-eyed	wind-hole	wintrily	wolf clan	wood pulp	wordplay
wideness	windiest	wipeable	wolf coat	wood-rock	word-sign
wide open	windlass	wipe down	Wolffian	woodruff	word size
widow-man	windless	wire-draw	wolf-fish	woodrush	wordsman
wieldier	windlike	wiredraw	wolf-head	wood sage	wordster
Wien's law	windling	wire edge	wolflike	wood-sear	word time
wifehood	wind load	wire-hair	wolfling	wood-sere	word-type
wifeless	windmill	wire into	wolf-moth	woodshed	word wrap
wifelike	windowed	wireless	wolf-note	wood shot	workable
wigglier	windpipe	wireline	wolf-pack	woodside	workably
wig-stand	windrock	wire-mark	wolfskin	woodsman	workaday
Wilcoxon	wind-rose	wire nail	wolf tree	woodsmen	work away
wild arum	wind-sail	wirepull	womandom	woodstar	workaway
wild boar	windsail	wire rope	womanise	wood-tick	work back
wildbore	wind-slab	wire wool	womanish	woodwall	workboat
wild card	windsock	wirework	womanism	woodward	workbook
wild deer	windster	wireworm	womanist	woodware	work camp
wild duck	wind-suck	wire-wove	womanity	woodwasp	work card
wildered	windsurf	wiriness	womanize	woodwind	workfare
wildfire	windward	wirrwarr	woman-man	wood-wing	work-flow
wildfowl	wine book	wiseacre	womb-like	wood wool	workfolk
wild goat	wine buff	wisehead	womblike	woodwork	work-hand
wild leek	wine-dark	wiselike	womenish	woodworm	workhead
wildlife	wine farm	wiseling	wonderer	woodwose	workless
wildling	wine lake	wiseness	wonderly	wood-wren	workload
wild mare	wine-lees	wishable	wondrous	woodyard	workmate
wildness	wineless	wishbone	wonkiest	wooingly	work over
wild oats	wine list	wish book	wontedly	wool-card	workover
wild pine	wine-palm	wishless	won't wash	wool-clip	work rate
wild rape	wine rack	wish-list	wood-acid	wool-comb	workroom
wild rice	wineries	wish-wash	wood-bill	woolding	works bus
wild silk	wineskin	wispiest	woodbind	wool-dyed	workshop
wild type	wine snob	wistaria	woodbine	wool-fell	worksite
wild vine	winesour	wisteria	Woodbury	Woolfian	worksome
wild well	wing-band	witch elm	woodchat	wool-hawk	work-team
Wild West	wing-beat	witchery	woodchip	woolleny	workwear
wild woad	wing-case	witch-hat	wood-chop	woollier	workwise
wildwood	Wing Chun	witching	wood-coal	wool-like	workyday
wilfully	wing-clap	wit-craft	woodcock	woollily	world-all
wiliness	wingding	witeless	Wood Cree	Woolmark	World Cup
wiliwili	wingedly	with calf	wood-dove	wool moth	worldful
willable	wing-fish	withdraw	wood-duck	wool-pack	worldish
will-form	wing-game	withdrew	woodenly	woolpack	worldlet
Williams	wing-half	with ease	wood-fire	woolsack	world-old
williwaw	wingless	withered	wood-free	Woolsack	world war
will-less	winglike	witherer	wood-frog	woolshed	worm-cast
willowed	wing root	withe-rod	wood grub	wool-skin	worm-gear
willsome	wing-sail	withhold	woodhack	wool team	worm-hole
willyart	wing-shot	with luck	wood-heap	Woolwich	wormhole
win again	wing span	withness	wood-hole	wool-work	wormiest
winchman	wingspan	with that	wood-ibis	woop woop	wormless
wind axis	wing-wall	withwind	woodiest	wooziest	wormlike
wind band	wink away	withy-bed	woodland	word-base	wormling

wormseed	wristily	yam-stick	Yogacara	Zenonian	zoogenic
worm-tube	wristlet	yanggona	yoghurty	zeolitic	zoogloea
wormwood	wrist-pin	Yang Shao	yokelish	Zephiran	zoolatry
worn-down	writable	Yank tank	yoke-mate	zephyrus	zoologer
wornness	write off	Yanomami	yoke-skey	Zeppelin	zoologic
worricow	write out	yappiest	yoke-toed	zeroable	zoomancy
worrited	writerly	yardbird	yoke-tree	zero-base	zoometry
worry out	writhing	yardland	Yokohama	zero beat	zoom lens
worse off	writhled	yard-rope	yokozuna	zero hour	zoomorph
worserer	wrizzled	yard sale	yolk duct	zero in on	zoom shot
worthful	wrongful	yardsman	yolkless	zero-rate	zoonosis
worthier	wrongous	yard-wand	yonderly	zero-zero	zoonotic
worthily	wry-faced	Yarkandi	York boat	zerumbet	zoophile
wouldest	wry-mouth	Yarmouth	youngest	zestiest	zoophily
would God	Wundtian	yarmulka	youngish	zetacism	zoophyte
woulding	wurtzite	yarmulke	younglet	zibeline	zooscopy
woundily	xanthate	yarn-beam	young man	Ziegfeld	zoosophy
wounding	xanthene	yarraman	yourself	ziggurat	zoosperm
wrackful	Xanthian	yataghan	youthful	zigzaggy	zoospore
wrangler	xanthine	yawmeter	youthify	zikkurat	zootomic
wrap coat	xanthism	yeanling	youthily	Zimbabwe	zootoxic
wrap it up	xanthoma	year-bird	ytterbia	zimbalom	zootoxin
wrap-over	xanthone	yearbook	yuffrouw	zinc grey	zoot suit
wrappage	xanthous	yearling	Yugoslav	zinc roof	zootypic
wrapping	Xantippe	year-long	Yukaghir	zingiber	zophorus
wrap reel	Xaverian	yearnful	yukiness	zingiest	zopilote
wrathful	xenogamy	yearning	yukkiest	Zionward	zos-grass
wrathily	xenolith	year-ring	yule-clog	Zipf's law	Z-plastic
wreakful	xenology	yea-sayer	yule even	zippered	zubrowka
wreathed	xenotime	yeastier	yule-tide	zippiest	zucchini
wreathen	xerocopy	yeastily	Yuletide	zircaloy	zugzwang
wreather	xerosere	Yeatsian	yummiest	zirconia	Zuricher
wreckage	xiphioid	yellowly	yuppyish	zirconic	zwieback
wreckful	xography	Yemenite	Yusufzai	zirconyl	zygaenid
wrecking	X-ray eyes	yen siang	Yuvaraja	zizyphus	zygodont
wrencher	X-ray tube	yeomanly	yuzbashi	zoanthid	zygology
Wrennery	xylidine	yeomanry	Zadokite	zodiacal	zygomata
wren-tail	xylocarp	yeowoman	zamindar	Zoellner	zygomere
wresting	Xylonite	yersinia	zampogna	zoetrope	zygonema
wrestler	xylotomy	yes and no	zaniness	zombiism	zygosity
wrest-pin	xylulose	Yes and No	zappiest	zonality	zygosome
wretched	yachting	yes siree	zarzuela	zonation	zygotene
wriggled	Yaghnobi	yestreen	zastruga	zoneless	Zylonite
wriggler	yahooism	yes-woman	zealless	zone-melt	zymodeme
wringing	yahrzeit	yield gap	zealotic	zone time	zymogram
wrinkled	yakitori	yielding	zealotry	zoochore	zymology
wrinklie	Yale lock	Yinglish	zebra eel	zoochory	
wrist-bag	yam house	yodelled	zemindar	zooecial	
wrist hit	yammerer	yodeller	zenithal	zooecium	

NINE LETTERS

Aaronical	abscissas	acephalic	aculeated	Admiralty	aerodrome
Aaron's rod	absconder	acerebral	acuminate	admission	aerolitic
abaciscus	absit omen	acervulus	a cut above	admissive	aeromancy
abackward	absorbent	acescence	acuteness	admitting	aerometry
a bad sport	absorbing	acescency	acyclovir	admixtion	aeronomer
a bad taste	abstainer	acetabula	acylation	admixture	aeronomic
abandoned	abstinent	acetamide	adamantly	admonitor	aerophagy
abandonee	abstracta	acetifier	Adamesque	ad nauseam	aerophobe
abandoner	absurdism	acetylate	Adamitism	adnominal	aerophone
abasement	absurdist	acetylene	adaptable	adoptable	aeroplane
abashedly	absurdity	acetylide	adaptably	adoration	aerospace
abashless	abuilding	achalasia	adderbolt	adorative	aerotrain
abashment	abundance	Acheulean	adderwort	adoringly	Aesopical
abatement	abundancy	Acheulian	addicting	adornment	aesthesis
abattises	abusively	Achillean	addiction	adpressed	aesthetic
abbotship	abysmally	achimenes	addictive	adrenalin	aestivate
abdicable	Abyssinia	acholuric	addleness	adrogator	aetheling
abdicator	academese	aciculate	addressed	adsorbate	aethereal
abdominal	academies	acidaemia	addressee	adsorbent	aetiology
abduction	academism	acid house	addresser	adstratum	a fair deal
abductive	Academism	Acid House	addressor	adulation	a fast buck
abearance	Academist	acidified	adducible	adulatory	affecting
abecedary	acalculia	acidifies	adduction	adulterer	affection
Abernethy	acanthine	acidities	adductive	adulthood	affective
aberrance	acanthite	acidulate	ademption	adultness	affectual
aberrancy	a cappella	acidulent	adenoidal	adumbrate	affidavit
abettance	acariasis	acidulous	adenomata	adunation	affiliate
abhorrent	acaricide	aciniform	adenosine	ad valorem	affirmant
abhorring	acarology	a-cock-bill	adeptness	advance on	affixture
abidingly	acathisia	aconitine	adeptship	advantage	afflation
abilities	accedence	a coon's age	a deuce of a	advection	afflicter
abiogenic	accension	acorn worm	adherence	advective	affluence
a bit of fat	accentual	acoustics	adherency	advenient	affluency
a bit thick	acceptant	acquiesce	adhibited	adventism	affluxion
abjection	acception	acquiring	ad hominem	Adventism	affricate
Abkhazian	acceptive	acquittal	adiabatic	adventist	affronted
ablatival	accessary	acquitted	adiaphora	Adventist	affrontee
abnegator	accession	acquitter	Adi Granth	adventive	affronter
abnormity	accessory	acridness	ad interim	adventure	aflatoxin
abnormous	accidence	acritarch	adipocere	adverbial	aforehand
abolisher	accidious	acrobatic	adipocyte	adversary	aforesaid
abolition	accipiter	acronymic	adiposity	adversely	aforetime
abominate	acclaimer	acropetal	adjacence	adversity	a fortiori
abondance	acclimate	acrophobe	adjacency	advertent	Afrikaans
aborigine	acclivity	acropolis	adjection	advertise	Afrikaner
ABO system	acclivous	acrospire	adjective	advisable	after-born
about-face	accompany	activator	adjournal	advisably	after-care
aboutness	accordant	actorship	adjustive	advisedly	aftercare
about time	according	actualise	adjutancy	advocator	afterclap
about-turn	accordion	actualism	adjutator	aedicular	aftercrop
Abrahamic	account of	actualist	ad libbing	aegophony	after-damp
abrogable	account to	actuality	ad libitum	aeolienne	afterdamp
abrogator	accretion	actualize	admeasure	aeolipyle	after dark
abruption	accretive	actual sin	adminicle	aepyornis	after-days
abscessed	accumbent	actuarial	admirable	aerialist	after-game
abscision	accusable	actuaries	admirably	aeriality	afterglow
abscissae	acellular	actuation	admiralty	aerobatic	afterlife

aftermath	airworthy	alignment	all square	amazingly	amphtrack
after meat	airy-fairy	alikeness	all the way	amazon ant	ampleness
aftermost	aisleless	alimental	all-ticket	Amazon ant	amplified
afterness	aitchbone	alimenter	allumette	Amazonian	amplifier
afternoon	aitchless	aliphatic	allurance	Amazonism	amplifies
after-pain	akathisia	aliteracy	alluviate	amazonite	amplitude
afterward	alabaster	aliterate	alluvious	ambagious	amputator
afterword	à la broche	aliveness	alluviums	ambassage	a mug's game
agapemone	alack-a-day	alkalosis	allwheres	amber-fish	amusement
agateware	alarmable	alkekengi	alma mater	ambergris	amusingly
agent noun	alarm-bell	all aboard	Alma Mater	amberjack	amusively
agentship	alarm bird	alla breve	almandine	ambiguity	amygdalin
age of gold	alarm call	allantoic	almandite	ambiguous	amylopsin
aggravate	alarm-post	allantoid	almond eye	ambisonic	anabiosis
aggregate	alaternus	allantoin	almond oil	ambitious	anabiotic
aggressor	albarello	allantois	almsgiver	amblyopia	anabolism
aggrieved	albatross	all-around	almshouse	amblyopic	anabranch
agistment	Albertine	all at once	almswoman	Amboinese	anachoret
agitating	albertite	All Blacks	aloneness	Amboynese	anaclasis
agitation	albescent	all comers	alongside	ambrosial	anacruses
agitative	albespine	allective	along with	ambrosian	anacrusis
aglyphous	albinoism	allegator	aloofness	Ambrosian	anaerobic
agnolotti	albinotic	allegedly	alpargata	ambrotype	Anaglypta
a gone coon	albititic	allegiant	alpenglow	ambulance	anaklasis
agonistes	alburnous	allegoric	alpenhorn	ambulator	analeptic
agonistic	alcarraza	allemande	alpenrose	ambuscade	analgesia
agonizing	alchemies	Allemanic	alpha plus	ambuscado	analgesic
agony aunt	alchemise	allenarly	alpha test	amendable	analogate
a good life	alchemist	all ends up	alpha wave	amendment	analogies
a good many	alchemize	allergies	Alpine fir	Amen glass	analogise
a good step	Alcmanian	allergist	alstonite	amenities	analogist
a good ways	alcoholic	alleviate	altarless	Amerasian	analogize
agreeable	Alcoranic	allicient	altar-tomb	Americana	analogous
agreeably	aldehydic	alligator	altarwise	Americani	analysand
agreeance	alder tree	all kind of	alterable	americium	analysans
agreement	Aldis lamp	all nature	altercate	ametropia	anamneses
agrestial	aleatoric	allocable	alter egos	ametropic	anamnesis
agriology	alecithal	allocator	alternant	amianthus	anandrous
agronomic	aleconner	allodiary	alternate	amidships	anaphoric
a hard case	ale firkin	allogenic	alternity	amino acid	anaplasia
ahistoric	ale gallon	allograft	altimeter	amissible	anaptyxis
à huis clos	Alemannic	allograph	altimetry	ammocoete	anarchial
ahungered	alembroth	allometry	altiplano	ammoniate	anarchism
aid-de-camp	aleph-null	allomorph	altissimo	ammonitic	anarchist
aid-prayer	alertness	allopathy	altricial	amnestied	anarchize
ailanthus	ale-taster	allopatry	aluminate	amnesties	anarthria
aimlessly	Alexander	allophane	aluminise	amniotomy	anastatic
air bridge	alfilaria	allophone	aluminium	amoralism	a nasty one
air-castle	Alfredian	allostery	aluminize	amoralist	anathemas
air-cooled	algarroba	allotment	aluminous	amorality	anatocism
air-filter	algebraic	allotrope	alum-stone	amorosity	Anatolian
air gunner	algebrist	allotropy	alveolate	amorously	anatomies
air letter	algedonic	allotting	amability	amorphism	anatomise
airmobile	Algonkian	allotypic	amanuense	amorphous	anatomist
air piracy	Algonquin	allowable	amaryllid	amourette	anatomize
air pirate	algorithm	allowably	amaryllis	ampersand	anatopism
air pistol	Alice band	allowance	amassment	amphibian	ancestral
air pocket	Alice blue	allowedly	amatorial	amphibium	anchorage
air potato	alicyclic	all-points	a matter of	amphibole	anchoress
airstream	alienable	all-seater	amaurosis	amphiboly	anchorite
air ticket	alienator	all serene	amaurotic	amphilogy	anchorman
air-vessel	alienness	all smiles	amazement	amphioxus	anchormen

anchoveta	animalize	antihelix	apologies	aprosopia	argentine
anchovies	animal oil	antiknock	apologise	apsidiole	Argentine
anchylose	animateur	Antillean	apologist	apyrexial	argentite
anciently	animation	antimeric	apologize	aqua birth	argentous
ancientry	animatism	antimonic	apomictic	Aqua Libra	argillite
ancillary	animistic	antinomic	apophatic	aquaplane	Argus-eyed
Andamaner	animosity	antinovel	apophonic	aqua regia	argy-bargy
andantino	anisogamy	antipasti	apophysis	aquarelle	Arhatship
andesitic	ankle-bone	antipasto	apoptosis	aquariums	arhythmic
and like it	ankle boot	antipathy	apoptotic	aqua vitae	Arianizer
andradite	ankle-ring	antiphony	apostatic	aquilegia	a right one
androecia	ankle sock	antipodal	apostolic	arabesque	Aristarch
androgyne	ankylosis	antipodes	apotheose	Arabicism	Arizonian
androgyny	ankylotic	antiquary	appalling	Arabicize	Arkansian
Andromeda	annectent	antiquate	appalment	arability	armadilla
androsace	annelidan	antiquing	Appaloosa	arabinose	armadillo
and things	annexable	antiquity	appanaged	arachidic	armed camp
anecdotal	annexment	antiscion	apparatus	arachnean	armillary
anecdotic	annotator	antiserum	apparency	arachnoid	armistice
anelastic	announcer	antitoxic	apparitor	Aragonese	Armorican
anemogram	annoyance	antitoxin	appealing	aragonite	armouring
anemology	annoyment	antitrade	appeasive	Arakanese	armstrong
aneuploid	annualize	anti-trust	appellant	araneidan	army corps
angel cake	annuitant	antitrust	appellate	arational	army lorry
angel dust	annuities	antivenin	appendage	araucaria	Arnoldian
angel-fish	annularly	antivenom	appendant	arbitrage	Arnoldism
angelfish	annulated	antiviral	appertain	arbitrary	Arnoldist
angel food	annulling	antivirus	appetence	arbitrate	aromatise
angelhood	annulment	ant-orchid	appetency	arbitress	aromatize
angelical	anodynous	ant-thrush	appetible	arboreous	arousable
angélique	anoestrus	anucleate	appetiser	arboretum	arpeggios
angelship	an old song	a number of	appetizer	arborical	arraigner
angel-skin	anomalies	anxieties	applauder	arbovirus	arrayment
angerless	anomalism	anxiously	apple-cart	archabbey	arrearage
angersome	anomalous	any old how	apple-head	archabbot	arrestive
angiogram	anomalure	à outrance	applejack	archaical	arrhythmy
angiology	anonymity	Apalachee	apple-peru	archaizer	arris-ways
angiomata	anonymous	apart from	apple tree	archangel	arriviste
angle-iron	anopheles	apartheid	appliable	archducal	arrogance
anglesite	anorectic	apartment	appliance	archduchy	arrogancy
angle-wing	anorthite	apartness	applicant	arch-enemy	arrow arum
anglewise	anovulant	apartotel	applicate	archeress	arrow-back
Anglicise	anoxaemia	apathetic	appliquéd	archetype	arrowhead
Anglicism	anschluss	aperiodic	appliqués	arch-fiend	arrowroot
Anglicist	Anselmian	apertness	appointed	archiater	arrow-slit
Anglicize	Antarctic	apertural	appointee	Archibald	arrow-wood
angostura	antefixal	apetalous	appointer	archilute	arrow worm
angriness	antelopes	aphanitic	appointor	archimage	arseniate
Anguillan	antelucan	apheresis	apportion	archimime	arsenical
anguished	antenatal	Aphrodite	appraisal	architect	arsenious
angularly	antennary	aphyllous	appraisee	archivist	arsesmart
angulated	antennule	apiculate	appraiser	archivolt	arsy-versy
angustura	anthelion	apishness	apprehend	archontic	art cinema
anhedonia	anthemion	aplanatic	approbate	archosaur	art editor
anhydride	anthology	apocentre	approve of	arc minute	artemisia
anhydrite	anthozoan	apocopate	April fool	arc second	arteriole
anhydrous	anthropic	Apocrypha	April Fool	Arctic fox	arteritis
anidrosis	anticline	apodictic	apriorism	arcuation	arthritic
animalise	anticodon	apoenzyme	apriorist	arduously	arthritis
animalism	antidoron	apogamous	apriority	arecoline	arthrodia
animalist	antidotal	apolarity	apronfuls	Areopagus	arthrodic
animality	antigenic	Apollonic	aprosexia	aretalogy	arthropod

arthrosis	assiduity	atlas moth	auld thief	auxiliary	baby grand
Arthurian	assiduous	at leisure	au naturel	auxospore	baby house
artichoke	assistant	at liberty	Aunt Sally	auxotroph	babyishly
articular	assistful	at longest	aureation	available	Babylonic
artificer	associate	atmometer	auric acid	availably	bacchanal
artillery	assonance	atomicity	aurichalc	availment	Bacchanal
artisanal	assort ill	atomistic	auricular	avalanche	bacchante
artlessly	assuasive	atonalism	auriscope	avalanchy	Bacchante
art object	assuetude	atonalist	aurorally	avascular	bacchants
arty-farty	assumable	atonality	auspicate	avengeful	baccharis
aryballos	assumedly	at one blow	auspicial	averagely	Bacharach
arytenoid	assumpsit	atonement	austenite	averrable	bacillary
as and when	assurance	at-oneness	austerely	Averroism	back-acter
asbestine	assuredly	at one time	austerest	Averroist	back-along
ascendant	assurgent	at peril of	austerity	avertable	back bench
ascendent	asthmatic	at present	autarchic	avertible	backbench
ascending	astrachan	atrocious	autarkies	avifaunal	backbiter
ascension	astraddle	atrophied	autarkist	avirulent	backboard
ascensive	astragali	atrophies	autecious	avisandum	backboned
ascertain	astrakhan	at seasons	authentic	avizandum	backcloth
ascetical	astrocyte	at soonest	authoress	avocation	back-court
ascitical	astrodome	attainder	authorial	avocatory	back-crawl
asclepiad	astrolabe	attempter	authoring	avoidable	back cross
Asclepiad	astrology	attendant	authorise	avoidably	backfield
asclepias	astronaut	attention	authorism	avoidance	back-flash
ascospore	astronomy	attentive	authority	avoidless	back-front
asexually	Astroturf	attenuate	authorize	avuncular	back-house
ashamedly	AstroTurf	attestant	autoclave	awakening	backlight
Ashantian	astucious	at the helm	autocracy	awardable	back-liner
ash blonde	a sure find	at the last	autocrime	awareness	back-pedal
Ashkenazi	as witness	at the most	autocross	awesomely	backpiece
ashlaring	asyllabic	Attic base	autocycle	awestruck	backplate
aside from	asymbolia	Attic salt	autofocus	awfulness	backsight
asininity	asymmetry	attingent	autogamic	a whale of a	back slang
ask no odds	asymptote	attorneys	autogenic	a whole lot	backslash
as of right	asyndetic	attractor	autograft	awkwardly	backslide
asomatous	asyndeton	attribute	autograph	axe-hammer	back-space
asparagus	as you were	attrition	autogyros	axial flow	backspace
aspartame	atacamite	attritive	autoicous	axiomatic	back stage
aspectful	at a gallop	attritted	autolatry	axle-tooth	backstage
aspectual	at a glance	at unaware	autolysin	axle tramp	backstair
aspergill	at a low ebb	at vantage	autolysis	Axminster	backstone
aspersion	at any cost	at war with	autolytic	axopodium	back-swing
aspersive	at any rate	aubergine	automaker	axotomous	back-sword
aspersoir	at a profit	aubrietia	automatic	ayatollah	backtrack
aspersory	ataractic	au courant	automaton	Aylesbury	backwards
asphalter	at a stroke	auctorial	autonomic	ayurvedic	back water
asphaltic	atavistic	audacious	autophagy	Ayurvedic	backwater
asphaltum	at command	audiogram	autopilot	azeotrope	backwoods
asphyctic	ateliosis	audiology	autopista	azimuthal	bacterial
asphyxial	atemporal	audio tape	Autoplate	azo colour	bacterium
aspirator	atheistic	audiotape	autopsies	azotaemia	bacterize
as regards	athematic	auditoria	autoroute	azotaemic	bacteroid
assailant	athenaeum	auditress	autoscope	Baagandji	bad breath
assaulter	atheology	auger-hole	autoscopy	babacoote	bad cess to
assayable	athetesis	augmented	autos-da-fé	Babbittry	badgeless
assembler	athetosis	augmenter	autosomal	baboonery	bad health
assentant	a thin time	augmentor	autotelic	baboonish	badminton
assertion	athletics	augurship	autotoxic	baby bonus	bafflegab
assertive	at its best	augur well	autotoxin	baby buggy	bagatelle
assertory	Atjehnese	Augustine	autozooid	Baby Buggy	bagginess
assession	Atlantean	aulacogen	autumnity	baby-faced	bag people

bagpiping	bandolero	Barnumese	battering	beatitude	be excused
bag-shaped	bandolier	barograph	battiness	be at pains	befalling
bahuvrihi	bandoline	barometer	battleaxe	beau geste	befitting
bailiwick	bandoneon	barometry	battlebus	beau ideal	befogging
bailliage	band-shell	baronetcy	battle-cry	beau idéal	before God
bain-marie	bandstand	barotropy	battology	beau monde	befortune
bairn-team	bandurria	bar person	baulk line	beauteous	begetting
bakeapple	bandwagon	barracker	bavaroise	beautiful	beggarism
bake blind	bandwidth	barracoon	bawdiness	beaux arts	beggingly
bakehouse	baneberry	barracuda	bay laurel	be avenged	beginning
bakestone	banefully	barrelage	bayoneted	beaver-dam	begin over
baking tin	Bangorian	barrelled	bay-whaler	be awake up	begin upon
baksheesh	banjolele	barretter	bay window	be a wake-up	begin with
Balaamite	banjulele	barricade	be about to	beblister	beglamour
balaclava	bankshall	barricado	beach ball	beblubber	beglerbeg
Balaclava	banner-cry	barrister	beachhead	because of	beg pardon
balalaika	bannerman	barrow-boy	beach plum	beccafico	begrutten
balancing	bannister	barrowful	beach-rock	become man	beguiling
balanitis	banqueted	Barrowist	beachside	be cooking	beguinage
balconied	banqueter	barry wavy	beachwear	becquerel	behaviour
balconies	banquette	bartender	beaconage	becripple	be herself
baldachin	Bantustan	basal body	bead-house	bedangled	be himself
baldaquin	banyan-day	baseboard	beadiness	bed-bottle	Behmenism
bald eagle	baptismal	base-court	beadledom	beddy-byes	beholding
baldicoot	baptistry	base level	bead-plant	be death on	behoveful
baldmoney	barathrum	base metal	bead sedge	bedfellow	be in a flap
Balearian	Barbadian	base-piece	beady-eyed	bediasite	beingness
balection	barbarian	bashfully	be a fool to	bedimming	being that
balefully	barbarise	basically	beak-sedge	bedjacket	be in stays
bale-goods	barbarism	basic salt	be all eyes	Bedlamite	be in touch
Balkanise	barbarity	basic slag	be all over	bedrabble	be in trade
Balkanize	barbarize	basifixed	beaminess	bedraggle	bejabbers
balladeer	barbarous	basifugal	beamingly	bedridden	belatedly
balladize	barbecued	basilical	bean caper	bed-settee	beleaguer
ball-court	barbecues	basilican	beaneries	bedsitter	belemnite
ballerina	barbitone	basipetal	beanfeast	bedspread	belemnoid
ballistae	barbotine	basketful	bean goose	bed-warmer	bel esprit
ballistic	barcarole	basketing	be annoyed	bed-wetter	believe me
ball joint	Barcelona	Basque cap	beanstalk	bedwetter	belittler
ballonnet	bar-coding	bas-relief	be any good	bedworthy	bell curve
ballooner	bare bones	bastinade	bear a hand	beech-fern	bell-glass
ballot box	barefaced	bastinado	bear a part	beechmast	bellhouse
balloting	bargainee	bastioned	bearberry	beech tree	bellicose
ballpoint	bargainer	bastonade	beardless	beechwood	bell metal
ball-proof	bargain on	batch loaf	beardlike	beefeater	bell-miner
ball valve	bargainor	bate an ace	beards wag	beefiness	bell-punch
balm-apple	bargander	Bath brick	bear fruit	beef olive	bell-skirt
balminess	bargepole	bath chair	bear-grass	beefsteak	bell tower
balsam fir	barkcloth	Bath chair	bearishly	bee-keeper	bellyache
balsa wood	barkeeper	bathhouse	Béarnaise	Beelzebub	bellyband
Balthazar	barleymow	Bath metal	bear's foot	bee martin	belly-flop
Baltimore	bar magnet	batholith	bear state	bee-master	bellyflop
Balzacian	barmaster	Bathonian	Bear State	bee orchid	bellyfuls
bamboozle	barmbrack	bath salts	beastings	be equal to	belly-wool
bandaging	barm cloth	Bath stone	beastlier	beer belly	belomancy
bandar-log	Barmecide	bath towel	beastlike	beer glass	belonging
banderole	barminess	bathwater	beat about	beerhouse	below deck
bandicoot	Barnabite	Bath white	be at a loss	beeriness	belt drive
bandiness	barnacled	bathybius	beatenest	beer money	belvedere
banditism	barnbrack	battalion	beatified	Beersheba	be missing
bandobast	barn dance	battening	beatifies	beestings	bemoisten
bandoleer	barnstorm	batteries	beating-up	beet sugar	bemonster

bemusedly	besprenge	bilge keel	birthwort	blackjack	blearness
be my guest	best bower	bilge-pump	bisection	black kite	blemisher
bench-hook	bestially	bilharzia	bishopdom	blacklead	blessedly
benchmark	bestirred	bilingual	bishopess	blacklist	blind coal
bench seat	best-known	biliously	bishopric	black lung	blind date
bench-stop	bestrewed	bilirubin	bismillah	blackmail	blind fish
bench test	be stuck on	biliteral	bismuthic	black mark	blindfold
bendiness	be sweet on	billabong	bismuthyl	black mass	blindless
benedight	beta decay	billander	bismutite	Black Mass	blindling
beneficed	beta waves	billboard	bisontine	black monk	blindness
benefited	betel-palm	bill-clerk	bitchiest	Black Monk	blind side
benempted	bête noire	billeting	biternate	black Moor	blind spot
Bengalese	bethought	billiards	bite-sized	blackness	blindworm
benighted	be through	billiment	bit-player	black pine	blinkered
benignant	be to blame	billionth	bit string	Black Pope	blink-eyed
benignity	betrothal	billycock	bitter end	blackrobe	blissless
benitoite	betrothed	hilly goat	bitterish	black rust	blithcful
be nowhere	better off	bilocular	bitter-nut	black sage	blizzardy
Bensonian	bevel gear	bimonthly	bitter pit	black sand	blockader
Benthamic	bevelling	binderies	bittiness	black soil	block-book
benthonic	bevelment	Binet test	bivalence	black spot	blockhead
bentincks	bewitcher	binocular	bivalency	black swan	blockhole
bentonite	bewritten	binominal	bivallate	blacktail	block move
benzenoid	bez-antler	binturong	bivariate	black tang	block-ship
benzidine	bezesteen	biochemic	biventral	black tern	blockship
be on about	bezoardic	bioethics	bivoltine	black titi	block vote
be one's age	Bhutanese	biofouler	bizarrely	black wash	blonde ray
be oneself	biathlete	biogenous	blab-mouth	blackwood	blondness
be on guard	biaxially	biography	blackback	Blackwood	blood-ally
be on wings	bibacious	biohazard	black ball	blade-bone	blood bank
bepatched	Bible belt	biohermal	blackball	bladeless	blood-bath
bepearled	Bible Belt	biologise	black-band	bladelike	bloodbath
beplaster	Bible oath	biologism	black bass	blade-work	blood cell
berberinc	bicameral	biologist	black bean	blaeberry	blood feud
Berberine	biconcave	biologize	black bear	blameable	blood-heat
be resting	bicyclist	biometric	black belt	blameably	bloodiest
berg adder	bidentate	bionomics	black bent	blameless	blood-knot
bergander	bid fair to	biopoesis	black bile	blandness	bloodless
berkelium	bienniums	biorhythm	blackbird	blank-book	bloodlike
Berkshire	bifarious	biosensor	black body	blanketed	blood-lily
Bermudian	bifilarly	biosocial	black book	blankness	blood-line
Bernician	biformity	biosphere	blackbuck	blank test	bloodline
Bernoulli	bifrontal	biostrome	blackbutt	blank wall	blood-lust
be rolling	bifronted	bipartite	black coal	Blanquism	bloodlust
berry-like	bifurcate	bipedally	blackcock	Blanquist	blood meal
berserker	bigarreau	bipinnate	black damp	blarneyed	bloodroot
berserkly	Big Bertha	bipyramid	black disc	blaspheme	bloodshed
beryllium	big cheese	birch-bark	black drop	blasphemy	bloodshot
bescatter	big dipper	birch beer	blackener	blast bomb	blood test
bescratch	bigeminal	birch tree	black-eyed	blastemal	bloodwite
beseeched	bigeneric	birch-wine	blackface	blast-hole	bloodwood
beseecher	big-headed	birchwood	blackfish	blast-pipe	bloodworm
be set fair	big league	birdbrain	black flag	blastulae	blood-wort
besetment	big-ticket	bird's-foot	blackfoot	blastular	bloomered
besetting	biguanide	bird's nest	Blackfoot	blatantly	bloomless
be shook on	bijection	bird table	black game	blatterer	blossomed
beslobber	bijective	bird-watch	black gold	blaze away	blotchier
beslubber	bike chain	birthmark	black hawk	blazingly	blow a fuse
be soppy on	bilabiate	birth pill	blackhead	bleachery	blow a kiss
bespangle	bilateral	birth rate	black heat	bleakness	blow-drier
bespatter	bilbergia	birth-root	black hole	blear-eyed	blow-dryer
bespeckle	bilboquet	birth-sign	black jack	bleariest	blowflies

blowtorch	body louse	boobyalla	bourgeois	brambling	breasting
blow trade	body odour	booby trap	bouvardia	branchery	breast job
blowziest	body-whorl	boogieing	Bovey coal	branchiae	breast-pin
blubberer	Boeotarch	book-craft	bovrilize	branchial	breathe in
Bluebeard	Bofors gun	bookishly	bovver boy	branching	breathful
blueberry	bog-butter	book-Latin	bow-backed	branchlet	breathier
blue-black	bog cotton	book-louse	bow-bearer	branch out	breathily
blue blood	bog-garden	bookmaker	bow-chaser	brandiron	breathing
blue crane	bogginess	book-plate	bowelless	brandling	brecciate
blue devil	bog myrtle	bookplate	bowerbird	brand-mark	Brechtian
blue-domer	bog orchid	bookshelf	bowhunter	brand name	breeching
bluegrass	bog spavin	bookstack	bowl along	brandreth	breezeway
blue-joint	bogusness	bookstall	bow-legged	brashness	breeziest
blue metal	bog violet	bookstore	bowler hat	brass band	bregmatic
blue mould	boiled egg	book token	Bow Street	brasserie	Brehon law
blue-mouth	boiled oil	book value	bowstring	brassiere	bressumer
blue-nosed	boilingly	boomerang	bow window	brassière	bretessed
Blue Peter	bold-faced	boomingly	Box and Cox	brassiest	Breton hat
blue-plate	boldfaced	boomslang	box camera	brass nail	Breton lai
blue point	bolection	boorishly	box canyon	brass rags	Bretwalda
blueprint	boliviano	bootblack	box clever	brass rule	breveting
blue rinse	Bollinger	boot-faced	box girder	brassware	brevetted
blue shark	Bolognese	bootmaker	Boxing Day	bratwurst	breweries
blue shift	Bolognian	bootstrap	box number	braveness	brewhouse
blue stone	bolometer	booziness	box office	brawniest	bribeable
bluestone	bolometry	borborygm	box spring	brazeless	bric-a-brac
blue water	Bolshevik	bordellos	box-turtle	brazen age	bricabrac
blue whale	bolsterer	bordereau	box-wallah	Brazilian	bric-à-brac
blue-white	Boltzmann	bore rigid	boycotter	Brazil nut	brick-dust
bluffness	bombachas	bore stiff	boyfriend	bread-corn	brick-kiln
blunderer	bombarder	boric acid	Boyle's law	bread-kind	brickwork
bluntness	bombardon	born-again	boy wonder	breadless	brickyard
blurriest	bombasine	Borrovian	brachiate	breadlike	bricolage
blushless	bombastic	borrowing	bracingly	breadline	bricoleur
blusterer	bombazine	borrow pit	brackened	bread roll	bride-cake
blutwurst	bombed-out	Borsalino	bracketed	bread-root	bride-lace
Boanerges	bomb-happy	Borussian	brackmard	breadthen	bridemaid
board foot	bombilate	boss about	bracteate	bread-tree	bridesman
board game	bombinate	bossa nova	bracteole	breakable	bride-to-be
boardroom	bomb-ketch	boss cocky	Brahmanic	break a leg	bridewell
boardwalk	bombproof	bossiness	brahminic	break a set	bridge-man
board-work	bombshell	Bostonese	Brahmoism	break away	bridle-bit
boat-cloak	bomb-sight	Bostonian	Brahmsian	breakaway	bridleway
boat-drill	bombsight	Boston ivy	brain-case	break-back	briefcase
boat-house	bomb squad	botanical	brain-cell	break bulk	briefless
boathouse	bona fides	botanizer	brain-dead	break crop	briefness
boatswain	bond paper	Botswanan	brainiest	break down	brier rose
boat-train	bondslave	bottle-age	brainless	breakdown	brigadier
boatwoman	bondstone	bottle-fed	brain-sand	break even	brigandry
bobarchee	bondwoman	bottle out	brain scan	breakfast	brightish
bobbin-net	bone-black	bottle-tit	brainsick	break in on	brillante
bobbishly	bone china	bottom dog	brainstem	break into	brilliant
bobby calf	bone-earth	bottom out	brainwash	break-line	brimstone
bobby wren	bone-tired	bottoms up	brainwave	breakneck	brimstony
bob-sleigh	bone weary	boudinage	brainwork	break open	bring back
bobsleigh	bonhomous	boulevard	brake disc	break rank	bring down
bobtailed	bonniness	bounciest	brake drum	break ship	bring over
bodacious	bon vivant	boundless	brake-pipe	break step	brininess
body-check	bon viveur	bounteous	brake shoe	break wind	brinjarry
body clock	bon voyage	bountiful	brakesman	breakwind	briquette
body count	boobialla	bouquetin	brakesmen	break with	briskness
bodyguard	booboisie	bourdonné	Bramantip	breast-fed	brislings

bristling	brown-nose	buff-stick	Burnsiana	by my troth	cafeteria
Britannia	brown pink	buffy coat	burnt cork	by no means	cafetière
Britannic	brown rice	bugger all	burrawang	by numbers	cageyness
Briticism	brown spar	bugger off	burrel-fly	by oneself	cailleach
Britisher	brown spot	buggy-ride	bursarial	by parcels	Cainozoic
Britishly	brown-tail	bug-hunter	bursaries	by-product	cairngorm
Britoness	brownwort	bugle-horn	bursiform	by request	cake-bread
brittlely	brow ridge	bugleweed	bur walnut	byrlawman	cake-slice
Brittonic	Brummagem	buildable	bus-driver	by seeming	calaboose
broadband	Brunswick	build down	bush basil	bystander	calabrese
broad bean	brushback	bulbiform	bushcraft	by stealth	Calabrian
broad-bill	brushfire	bulbosity	bushelful	by the book	calamanco
broad-brim	brushless	Bulgarian	bushelman	by the head	calandria
broad-brow	brushlike	Bulgarize	bushiness	by the hour	calavance
broadcast	brush over	bulgingly	bush poppy	by the lump	calcaneal
broad hint	brushware	bulkiness	bush shirt	by the mass	calcanean
broad-jump	brushwood	bullberry	bush vetch	by the rood	calcaneum
broad-leaf	brushwork	bull-diker	bushwhack	by the yard	calcaneus
broadleaf	brusquely	bulldozer	bustiness	bytownite	calcarate
broadloom	brutalise	bullfight	butadiene	Byzantian	calcarine
broadness	brutalism	bullfinch	but and ben	Byzantine	calcedony
broad seal	brutalist	bullimong	butcherer	cabaletta	calcicole
broadside	brutality	bullishly	butcherly	caballada	calcified
broadtail	brutalize	bull-nosed	buteonine	caballero	calcifies
broadwalk	brute fact	bull point	butlerage	caballine	calcifuge
broadways	brutehood	bull-snake	butleress	cabbalism	calcimine
broadwise	bruteness	bull's wool	butsecarl	cabbalist	calculate
brochette	brutishly	bull trout	butter-box	cab driver	calculous
broiderer	Brylcreem	bulltrout	butterbur	cabin crew	calendary
broken man	bryophyte	bully beef	buttercup	cabinetry	calendric
broken tea	Brythonic	bully tree	butterfat	cabin-mate	calendula
brokerage	bubble car	bumble-bee	butterfly	cablegram	calenture
brokeress	bubble gum	bumbledom	butteries	cable-laid	calescent
bromeliad	bubblegum	bum-fodder	butter-nut	cable's end	calf's foot
brominate	bubbliest	bumiputra	butternut	cabriolet	calibogus
bromoform	buccaneer	bumper car	butter-pat	cacao bean	calibrate
bromyrite	buccinoid	bumpiness	buttinsky	cacao tree	calico cat
bronchial	Bucentaur	bumpkinet	butt joint	cachectic	calicular
Bronze Age	buckboard	bumpkinly	buttocked	cacholong	caliphate
brood cell	buck-brush	bumpology	button-boy	caciquism	Calixtine
broodiest	buck dance	bump-start	button day	cacodemon	calla lily
brookable	bucketful	bumptious	button ear	cacodylic	call forth
brook char	bucketing	bum-sucker	buttoning	cacoethes	callidity
brooklime	buck fever	bunchy top	butty-gang	cacophony	Callippic
brookweed	buck-hound	Bundesrat	buxomness	cacuminal	callitrix
broom-corn	bucklered	Bundestag	by a canvas	cadastral	callosity
broomrape	bucko mate	bundobust	by a jugful	cadaveric	calloused
brothelly	Buck's Fizz	bungaloid	by all odds	caddie car	callously
brothelry	buck's horn	bunk-house	by analogy	caddis-fly	call quits
brotherly	buckstall	bunkhouse	by a street	caddishly	call truce
browallia	buckthorn	bunny girl	by default	cadential	calmative
brown alga	buck-tooth	buoyantly	by degrees	cadetship	calmingly
brown bear	buckwheat	burggrave	by force of	cadginess	calorific
brown belt	buckyball	burgh-bote	by herself	caduciary	calumnied
Brown Bess	bucolical	burgherly	by himself	caecilian	calumnies
brown-bill	buddy film	burghmote	by Jupiter	Caenozoic	Calvinian
brown coal	budgetary	burkundaz	by means of	Caen stone	Calvinise
brown-eyed	budgeteer	burlesque	by measure	caerulean	Calvinism
brown hare	budgeting	burliness	by mirrors	Caesarean	Calvinist
brown loaf	buffaloes	burn alive	by mistake	Caesarian	Calvinize
brown malt	buffet car	burningly	by my faith	Caesarism	calycular
brownness	buffeting	burnisher	by my sooth	Caesarist	calyx-tube

camarilla	cannonade	caravette	carolytic	cast about	catechism
Cambodian	cannon bit	carbamate	carpaccio	Castalian	catechist
Cambridge	cannoneer	carbamide	carpenter	cast an eye	catechize
camcorder	cannulate	carbanion	carpentry	cast aside	categorem
camel-back	canoe-like	carbazole	carpet-bag	casteless	categoric
camel-hair	canoe wood	carbolate	carpet-bed	castellan	caterwaul
camel-like	canonical	carbolize	carpeting	castellar	cat-footed
camelries	canonizer	carbonade	carpet-rod	castellet	Catharine
Camembert	canonries	carbonado	carpincho	caste mark	Catharism
cameo part	canonship	Carbonari	carpology	cast forth	Catharist
camera-eye	can-opener	carbonate	car pooler	cast gorge	catharses
cameraman	cantabile	carbonise	carrageen	castigate	catharsis
cameramen	cantaloup	carbonium	carriaged	castilian	cathartic
camera-shy	cantarist	carbonize	carronade	Castilian	cathectic
Camestres	cantation	carbon tax	carrousel	castle-nut	cathedral
camleteen	cantharis	carbuncle	carry away	cast loose	Catherine
campanero	cantharus	carbuncly	carry back	castoreum	catlinite
campanile	cantilena	carburise	carry over	castor oil	cat litter
campanist	cantingly	carburize	carry sail	castrator	catocalid
campanula	Cantonese	carcinoid	cartelise	Castroism	catoptric
campcraft	cantonize	carcinoma	cartelize	cast round	cat-tackle
Campeachy	cantorial	cardboard	Cartesian	cast steel	catteries
camper van	canvassed	cardiacal	carthamin	casualism	cattiness
camp-fever	canvasser	cardialgy	carthamus	casuality	cattishly
camphoric	capacious	card index	cart-horse	casuarina	cattle-dog
campiness	capacitor	cardphone	carthorse	casuistic	cattleman
camp-stool	caparison	card-sharp	cartilage	casuistry	cattlemen
campylite	Cape daisy	card-swipe	cartogram	catabatic	Catullian
Canaanite	Cape Dutch	card table	cartouche	catabolic	cat-witted
Canada Day	capellane	card trick	cartridge	cataclasm	Caucasian
Canada jay	Cape Malay	care-cloth	cart's tail	cataclysm	Caucasoid
Canadiana	Cape smoke	careenage	cart track	catalepsy	caucusing
canal boat	capillary	careerism	cartulary	catalexis	caudillos
canal rays	cap in hand	careerist	cartwheel	catalogue	cauldrife
canceleer	capitally	carefully	carvacrol	catalysed	caulicole
cancelled	capitated	caregiver	carveries	catalyser	causalgia
canceller	capitular	care label	caryatids	catalyses	causality
cancerate	capitulum	care-laden	caryopses	catalysis	causation
Cancerian	capo tasto	car engine	caryopsis	catalytic	causative
cancerous	capotasto	caressive	caseation	catamaran	causeless
candareen	capotting	caretaker	case-bound	catamenia	cautelous
candidacy	capriccio	cargo boat	case knife	catamount	cauteries
candidate	Capricorn	cargo cult	casemated	cat-and-dog	cauterise
candle-end	caprifoil	Caribbean	case study	cataphora	cauterize
candlelit	caprylate	cariosity	cashew nut	cataplasm	cautioner
Candlemas	capsaicin	carjacker	cash nexus	cataplexy	cavalcade
candle-nut	capsicine	Carlylean	cashpoint	catarrhal	cavallard
candy cane	cap sleeve	Carlylese	cash price	catasetum	cavalries
candytuft	capsomere	Carlylism	cash value	catatonia	cavendish
cane-brake	capsulate	Carmelite	Cassandra	catatonic	cavernous
cane chair	capsulise	carnalise	cassareep	catchable	cavewoman
cane-grass	capsulize	carnality	cassation	catch cold	cavewomen
cane-juice	captaincy	carnalize	Casseiver	catch crop	cavilling
canephora	captation	carnation	casserole	catch fire	ceanothus
cane sugar	captivate	carnelian	cassimere	catchiest	cease fire
cane-syrup	captivity	carnivore	Cassinese	catch-line	ceasefire
cane-trash	cap verses	carnivory	cassingle	catchline	ceaseless
canicular	carabidan	carnosity	Cassinian	catchment	cedar-bird
cankerous	carambola	carnotite	cassocked	catchpole	cedar tree
cannelure	carambole	carob tree	cassoulet	catchweed	cedarwood
canneries	carangoid	carolitic	cassowary	catchword	celandine
canniness	carapaced	carolling	Cassubian	catechise	celebrant

celebrate	cereopsis	chancroid	checklist	chieftain	chlorella
celebrity	certainly	chancrous	checkmate	chihuahua	chloritic
celery top	certainty	chandlery	check over	chilblain	chloropal
celestial	certified	changeful	check-rail	childcare	chlorosis
celestine	certifier	change leg	check-rein	childhood	chlorotic
Celestine	certifies	channelly	checkroom	childless	choak-full
celestite	certitude	chantable	check up on	childlike	chock-full
cellarage	cerussite	chanteuse	cheechako	childness	chocolate
cellaress	Cervantic	Chantilly	cheek-bone	childship	chocolaty
cellaring	cervisial	chantress	cheekbone	child-wife	choirgirl
cellarman	Cesolfaut	chantries	cheekiest	Chile pine	choke back
cellarway	cespitose	Chanukkah	cheeriest	chiliagon	choke-coil
cell block	cessation	chaotical	cheerless	chiliarch	choke-damp
celloidin	cetaceous	chaparral	cheese-fly	chilliest	choke down
cellotape	ceylanite	chapeless	cheeselip	chillness	choke-full
cellphone	Ceylonese	chaperone	cheesiest	chillsome	choke-pear
cellulate	ceylonite	chapleted	cheilitis	chime bars	choke-weed
cellulite	chabazite	chaprassi	chelation	chimerism	chokiness
celluloid	chabootra	Chap Stick	chelicera	chiminage	chokingly
cellulose	cha-cha-cha	charabanc	cheliform	china-blue	choleraic
cellulous	cha-chaing	character	chelonian	china clay	Chomskian
celsitude	chaetodon	charbroil	chemisorb	China-root	Chomskyan
Celticism	chafferer	charge cap	chemistry	China rose	chondrify
Celticist	chaffinch	chariness	chemurgic	china shop	chondrite
Celticize	chaffweed	chariotee	cheongsam	China silk	chondroid
Celtic Sea	Chagataic	chariotry	chequered	Chinatown	chondroma
cembalist	chain gang	charities	Cheremiss	China tree	chondrule
cementing	chain gear	charivari	Cherenkov	chinaware	choosiest
cementite	chainless	charlatan	cherimoya	chincapin	chop-house
cenematic	chainlike	charlotte	cherisher	chinch bug	chop logic
censorial	chain link	charmeuse	chernites	chinchona	choppered
censorian	chain-mail	charmless	chernozem	chincough	choppiest
centaurea	chain-pump	Charolais	cherry-bob	chinesery	chopstick
Centaurus	chain-shot	charoseth	cherry pie	chin music	chop sueys
centenary	chain-wale	chartered	cherry red	chinovnik	choragium
centenier	chain-work	charterer	chess-tree	chin-strap	choralism
centering	chairlady	Chartreux	chestiest	chinstrap	choralist
centesimo	chair-lift	charwoman	chevachee	chintzier	choral ode
centésimo	chairlift	charwomen	chevalier	chintzily	Choral Ode
centigram	chalazion	Charybdis	chevaline	chipboard	choriambi
centipede	chalcidid	chaseable	chevrette	Chipewyan	chorionic
centralia	chalcogen	chasséing	chevronel	chipolata	chorister
Centralia	chalkiest	chastener	chevronny	chirality	chorizont
centrally	chalk-line	chastiser	chevrotin	chirimoya	choroidal
centre bit	chalk talk	chatelain	chewiness	chirology	chorology
centreing	challenge	chatoyant	chew-stick	chironomy	chorusing
centrical	Chalybean	chatterer	Chian wine	chiropody	chowkidar
centriole	chalybite	chattiest	chiasmata	chirpiest	Chrissake
centumvir	chambered	chauffeur	chibouque	chirruped	Christian
centurial	chamberer	chaukidar	Chicagoan	chirurgic	Christies
centuried	chameleon	chavender	chicanery	chiselled	Christmas
centuries	chamfrain	chaw-bacon	chickadee	chiseller	chromatic
centurion	chamomile	chaw-stick	chickaree	chisel-toe	chromatid
ceraceous	chamosite	cheapener	Chickasaw	chi-square	chromatin
cerastium	champagne	cheapjack	chickling	chitinize	chromogen
ceratitic	champaign	cheapness	chickweed	chitinoid	chronical
cercarial	champ clos	cheatable	chicories	chitinous	chronicle
cercarian	champerty	checkable	chidingly	chitlings	chronique
cerebella	champlevé	checkered	chidlings	chivalric	chrysalid
cerebrate	chanceful	check into	chief good	chlamydia	chrysalis
cerecloth	chancelry	checkless	chiefless	chloracne	chrysanth
cereology	chanciest	check-list	chiefship	chlordane	chthonian

chubbiest	civically	clearcole	close upon	coat-stand	coenosarc
Chubb lock	civilized	clear-eyed	cloth ears	coaxially	coenzyme A
chuck-full	civilizee	clear grit	cloth-head	coaxingly	co-equally
chuck-hole	civilizer	clearness	cloud base	cobalamin	coequally
chummiest	civil list	clearskin	cloudiest	cobaltite	coercible
chump chop	Civil List	clear soup	cloud-land	cobaltous	coeternal
chunkiest	civilness	clearweed	cloudless	Cobdenism	coevality
chupattis	civil year	clearwing	cloudlike	Cobdenite	coffee bar
chuprassy	clack-dish	cleavable	clout-nail	co-brother	coffee cup
church-ale	cladistic	cleithral	clove pink	cobwebbed	coffee-pot
churchdom	cladogram	clemently	clown fish	cobweb law	coffee urn
churchlet	claimable	clepsydra	clownship	cocainism	coffer-dam
churchman	claimless	clergyman	cloyingly	cocainize	coffering
churchmen	clamantly	clergymen	clozapine	coccidian	coffining
church-owl	clamberer	clerkhood	clubbable	coccidium	co-founder
churingas	clammiest	clerkship	clubbiest	coccolith	cogitable
churnable	clamorous	cleverest	club class	coccygeal	cogitator
churn-milk	clamourer	cleverish	clubhouse	cochineal	cognately
churrasco	clamp down	clianthus	club-money	cochleate	cognation
ciabattas	clamp-down	clientage	clumpiest	cock-a-hoop	cognisant
cibarious	clampdown	clientele	clumsiest	Cockaigne	cognition
cicatrice	clam-shell	clifflike	clunkiest	cockateel	cognitive
cicatrise	clamshell	climactic	clustered	cockatiel	cognizant
cicatrize	clankless	climatize	clutch bag	cocked hat	cohabited
ciclatoun	clansfolk	climbable	cly-faking	cock-fight	cohabitee
cicutoxin	clapboard	climb down	clypeated	cockfight	cohabiter
cigarette	clap-bread	climb-down	cnidarian	cock-horse	cohabitor
cigarillo	clapmatch	climbdown	coachload	cockiness	coheiress
ciguatera	Clarendon	climb into	coach whip	cock-laird	coherence
ciliation	clareteer	cling film	coachwhip	cocklebur	coherency
ciliiform	clarified	clingfish	coachwood	cockle-hat	co-heritor
Cimmerian	clarifier	clingiest	coachwork	cock-light	coiffeuse
cinchonic	clarifies	clinician	coadapted	cockneyfy	coiffured
cincinnus	clarionet	clinquant	coadjutor	cock-penny	coin money
cinderous	classable	clipboard	coadunate	cockroach	Cointreau
cinematic	classical	clip joint	coagulant	cock robin	colcannon
cinephile	classiest	clippable	coagulase	cockscomb	colchicum
cineraria	classless	cliquiest	coagulate	cocksfoot	cold blood
cinereous	class-list	clitellar	coal black	cockshead	cold cream
Cingalese	classmate	clitellum	coalfield	cockshies	cold-finch
cingulate	class-noun	cloakless	coal-fired	cockshoot	cold frame
cinnamate	classroom	cloakroom	coal-heugh	cock-stand	cold front
cinquedea	clathrate	cloche hat	coal-house	cockswain	cold light
cipherdom	clatterer	clock-face	coalhouse	cockyolly	cold-short
circadian	claustral	clock golf	coalition	cocky's joy	cold start
circinate	claustrum	clockwise	coal-meter	cocoa bean	cold steel
circuiter	claviform	clockwork	coal miner	cocoa moth	cold store
circuitor	clay court	clodpated	coalminer	cocoa nibs	cold sweat
circuitry	clay slate	clog dance	coalmouse	cocoa tree	cold table
circulate	claystone	cloggiest	coal-owner	coco-de-mer	cold water
cirrhosis	claytonia	cloisonné	coal-works	coco fibre	colectomy
cirrhotic	cleanable	cloistral	co-aration	coco-grass	colemouse
cirriform	clean-bowl	closeable	coarbiter	cocoonery	colic-root
cirripede	clean down	close a gap	coarctate	code-named	coliphage
cisalpine	cleanlier	close call	coastland	coecilian	collagist
cispadane	cleanlily	closed-end	coastline	coeducate	collapsar
citharist	cleanness	close down	coastward	coelomate	collapsed
citizenly	cleanskin	close-knit	coastways	coelostat	collar day
citizenry	clearable	closeness	coastwise	coemption	collation
cityscape	clearance	close port	coat check	coenobite	collative
city state	clear away	close-reef	coat dress	coenobium	colleague
citywards	clear-cole	closeting	coat-money	coenocyte	collectar

collected	columbite	commonest	concocter	conjobble	continent
collector	columbium	commonise	concoctor	conjoined	continual
collegial	columella	commonish	concordat	conjoiner	continued
collegian	columnist	commonize	concourse	conjugacy	continuer
collegium	coma vigil	common law	concreate	conjugate	continues
Colleries	combatant	commorant	concreter	conjuress	continuos
collidine	combating	commotion	concubine	conjure up	continuum
colligate	combative	communard	concurred	conkering	contorted
collimate	comb-brush	communion	condemned	connately	contourné
collinear	combinate	communise	condenser	connation	contralto
collision	combining	communism	condictio	connected	contrasty
collocate	comb-jelly	communist	condignly	connecter	contrived
collodion	comboloio	community	condiment	connector	contriver
collogued	combretum	communize	condition	Connemara	contrôlée
collogues	comburent	commutate	condolent	connexion	contumacy
colloidal	come about	commutual	conducive	connexity	contumely
colloquia	come again	compactly	conductor	connivent	contusion
collotype	come along	compactor	conductus	connubial	contusive
collusion	come amiss	compactum	condyloid	conqueror	conundrum
collusive	come and go	compadres	condyloma	Conradian	convector
collusory	come apart	compander	cone-sheet	conscient	convenery
colluvial	come clean	companies	cone-shell	conscious	converger
colluvies	comedones	companion	conessine	conscribe	converser
colluvium	comeliest	compasser	Conestoga	conscript	conversus
collyrium	come loose	compelled	cone wheat	consensus	converted
Colly-west	come of age	compeller	confabbed	consenter	converter
colocynth	come off it	compendia	conferral	conserver	convertor
colometry	come-outer	competent	conferred	consignee	convexity
colonelcy	come-o'-will	complaint	conferrer	consigner	convictor
colonizer	come round	completer	confessee	consignor	convinced
colonnade	come short	complexly	confessio	consonant	convincer
colophony	comet-year	complexus	confessor	consonous	convivial
Coloradan	come under	compliant	confidant	consortia	convocate
colorific	comfiness	complicit	confident	conspirer	convolute
colossean	comforter	component	confiding	constable	cony-garth
colosseum	comically	composant	configure	constancy	co-obligor
Colossian	comic book	composite	confinity	constrain	cook-chill
colostomy	Cominform	composure	confirmed	constrict	cookeries
colostrum	Comintern	comprador	confirmee	construal	cookhouse
colourant	comitadji	computist	confirmer	construct	cookie jar
colour bar	commander	comradely	confirmor	construed	cook-shack
colour-box	commandos	comradery	confitent	construes	Cook's tour
colourful	commandry	con and pro	Confiteor	consulage	cook-stove
colouring	commencer	concausal	confiture	consulary	cool-house
colourise	commendam	concavely	confluent	consulate	coolie hat
colourist	commender	concavity	conformal	consuless	cool-store
colourize	commensal	concealer	conformer	consultee	cooperage
colour-man	commenter	conceited	confrater	consulter	cooperant
colour sup	comminate	conceiver	Confucian	consultor	co-operate
colourway	commingle	concenter	confusing	contactor	cooperate
colpotomy	comminute	concentre	confusion	contagion	co-optable
coltishly	commissar	conceptus	conga drum	contagium	copacetic
colt-pixie	committal	concerned	congenial	contained	coparceny
coltsfoot	committed	concerted	conger eel	container	co-partner
colt's tail	committee	concertos	congeries	contangos	copartner
colubrine	committer	concessor	Congolese	contemner	copasetic
columbary	commodate	conchitic	congruent	contemper	copepodan
columbate	commodify	concierge	Congruism	contender	copepodid
columbiad	commodity	conciliar	Congruist	contented	copestone
Columbian	commodore	concisely	congruity	contestee	copiapite
columbine	commonage	concision	congruous	contester	coping saw
Columbine	Common Era	concluder	conically	con thanks	copiously

copolymer	cornfield	costerdom	courtship	cramp-ring	crepitous
Copper Age	cornflake	costering	court shoe	cranberry	crêpoline
copper bit	cornflour	costingly	court week	cranelike	crepuscle
copper-cut	corn-house	costively	courtyard	crane line	crescendi
copperish	cornicing	costliest	cousinage	crane-neck	crescendo
copper-nob	corniness	cost price	cousiness	crank-axle	crestless
copper ore	cornopean	costumery	couturier	crankcase	crest-line
co-present	corn poppy	costumier	covalence	crankiest	cretinise
co-produce	corn-roast	cotangent	covalency	crankness	cretinism
coprolite	corn salad	cote-house	covariant	cranreuch	cretinize
coprolith	corn-shuck	co-tenancy	covellite	crape-fern	cretinoid
coprology	corn snake	cothurnal	coverable	crape hair	cretinous
coprozoic	corn-stalk	cothurned	cover crop	crappiest	crevicing
copsewood	cornstone	cothurnus	cover girl	crapulent	crewelist
copyboard	corn sugar	cotillion	cover note	crapulous	crib-biter
copyright	corn syrup	cotonnade	cover over	crash-dive	cribellum
coral fern	Cornubian	cotter pin	cover slip	crash-halt	cricketed
coral-like	corollary	cottonade	cover-slut	crash-land	cricketer
coralline	corolline	cotton gin	coverture	crash-stop	crimeless
corallita	coronated	Cottonian	covert way	crassness	crime wave
corallite	coroneted	cottonize	covetable	cratefuls	criminate
coralloid	coronilla	cotton-rat	covin-tree	craterlet	criminous
coral-pink	coroplast	cotton-top	cowabunga	craterous	crimplene
coral reef	corozo-nut	cotyledon	cowardice	cravatted	Crimplene
coral-root	corpocrat	couchancy	cowardize	cravingly	crinoidal
coral spot	corporate	couchette	cow-banger	craziness	crinoline
coral tree	corporeal	Couéistic	cow-hocked	crazy bone	crinosity
coral vine	corposant	cough away	cow-keeper	crazy-pave	crippling
coral-wood	corpulent	cough down	cowl-staff	creakiest	crispiest
coralwort	corpuscle	cough drop	Cowperian	cream cake	crispness
corbeille	corralled	coulibiac	co-written	cream-cups	cristated
corbelled	corrasion	coulombic	coxcombic	cream horn	criterial
corbicula	correctly	coumarone	coxcombry	creamiest	criterion
cor blimey	corrector	councilor	crab apple	creamlike	criticise
corchorus	correlate	countable	crabbedly	cream puff	criticism
cord-drill	corrodent	countably	crabbiest	cream soda	criticist
Cordelier	corrosion	countback	crab-grass	cream soup	criticize
cord-grass	corrosive	count down	crabgrass	creamware	critiqued
cordially	corrugate	countdown	crab louse	creatable	critiques
cordiform	corrupter	countless	crab-stick	creatress	croakiest
co-regency	corruptly	count noun	crab-stock	creatural	crocheted
co-regnant	corseting	countries	crack down	crediting	crocheter
coreopsis	corticate	countrify	crackdown	creditrix	crocketed
coriander	corticene	countryfy	crackhead	credulity	crocodile
co-rivalry	corticine	countship	crackless	credulous	croisette
corkiness	corticoid	coup d'état	crackling	creedless	croissant
corkingly	corticole	coup stick	cracksman	creepered	Crokerism
corkscrew	cortisone	courbette	cracksmen	creep-hole	Cro-Magnon
cormorant	coruscant	courgette	cradle-cap	creepiest	Cromerian
corn borer	coruscate	court card	craftiest	creep up on	crook-back
cornbrash	corydalis	courteous	craftless	cremaster	crookback
corn-bread	corymbose	courtesan	craftsman	cremation	crookeder
cornbread	coscoroba	courtezan	craftsmen	crematory	crookedly
corncrake	coseismal	court fool	craftwork	crenation	crookneck
corn dance	cosmogeny	court-hand	crag-bound	crenature	crop-eared
corn dolly	cosmogony	court leet	craggiest	crenelate	croqueted
cornelian	Cosmoline	Court leet	crammable	crenulate	croquette
cornemuse	cosmology	courtlier	cramp-bone	creophagy	crosiered
corner-boy	cosmonaut	courtlike	cramp fish	crêpeline	crossable
corner-hit	cosmorama	courtling	cramp-iron	crêpe sole	cross-beak
corner-man	cosseting	court roll	crampness	crepitant	cross-beam
cornetist	cost clerk	courtroom	cramponny	crepitate	cross-bill

crossbill	crudeness	cunctator	custodiam	cyphonism	damselfly
crossbred	cruellest	cuneiform	custodian	Cyprianic	danburite
cross-date	cruelling	cunicular	custodier	cyprinoid	danceable
cross-eyed	cruelness	cuniculus	customary	cyrtolite	dance band
cross-fade	cruelties	cunninger	custom car	cystalgia	dance-card
crossfire	cruiseway	cunningly	customise	cystidean	dance hall
cross-hair	crumbiest	cupbearer	customize	cystidium	dancehall
cross-head	crumblier	cupelling	custumary	cystiform	danceress
cross-jack	crumbling	cupferron	cut a caper	cystocarp	dancingly
cross-keys	crummiest	cup-fungus	cut across	cystocele	dandelion
cross-kick	crunchier	cup grease	cut and run	cystolith	dandiacal
crossless	crunchily	Cupid's bow	cutaneous	cystotomy	dandified
cross-line	crushable	cup lichen	cut a shine	Cytherean	dandifies
cross-link	crush-room	cup-marked	cut a swath	cytidylic	dandiprat
cross-lots	crustated	cuppiness	cut a tooth	cytocidal	dandruffy
crossness	crustiest	curb-chain	cut capers	cytokinin	dandy-cart
cross over	crustless	curb-plate	cutcherry	cytologic	dandyfunk
crossover	cruzeiros	curbstone	cut didoes	cytolysis	dandy-line
cross-pass	cry craven	curdiness	cuticular	cytolytic	dandyprat
cross-path	cry halves	curettage	cutis laxa	cytoplasm	dandy roll
cross-peen	cry harrow	curetting	cut it fine	cytosolic	danger man
crossroad	cryogenic	curfuffle	cut-out box	cytotoxic	dangerous
cross-ruff	cryoprobe	curialism	cut splice	cytotoxin	Danish axe
crosstalk	cryoscopy	curialist	cutter-bar	czarevich	Danish dog
cross the T	cry out for	curiosity	cut the rug	dachshund	Dannebrog
cross tide	cryptical	curiously	cut-throat	Dadaistic	Dantesque
cross-town	cryptogam	curliness	cutthroat	Daedalian	danthonia
cross-tree	cryptonym	curlingly	cuttingly	daffiness	Dantonist
crosswalk	ctenidial	curl-paper	cut up well	Daghestan	dapatical
crossways	ctenidium	curl-pated	Cuvierian	dailiness	daphnetin
crosswind	Cuba libre	curl the mo	cyanamide	Daily Mail	Dardanian
cross-wire	Cuban heel	curly kale	cyanicide	Daily News	daredevil
crosswise	cubbishly	currajong	cyanolabe	daintiest	dark horse
cross with	cubby hole	currawong	cyanurate	daiquiris	dark lines
crossword	cubically	currently	cybernate	dairy farm	darklings
crosswort	cubic foot	curricula	cyberpunk	dairy-free	dark space
Crostarie	cubicular	currishly	cybotaxis	dairymaid	darnation
crotaline	cubiculum	curry-comb	cycadeoid	daisy-bush	darned net
crotchety	cubic yard	cursillos	cyclamate	daisy-like	dartboard
croton oil	cuckoldom	cursively	cyclamens	daisy tree	Darwinian
crouchant	cuckoldry	cursorial	cycle clip	Dalai Lama	Darwinise
croustade	cuckoo bee	cursorily	cyclicity	dales folk	Darwinism
crowberry	cuckoo-bud	curtailer	cyclogiro	Daliesque	Darwinist
crow-eater	cuckquean	curtain-up	cycloidal	dalliance	Darwinize
crown cork	cucullate	curtal-axe	cyclonite	dally away	dashboard
crown fire	cuddliest	curtation	Cyclopean	Dalmatian	dashingly
crown full	cudgelled	curtilage	Cyclopian	Dalradian	dashlight
crown gall	cudgeller	curvation	cyclopoid	Daltonian	dastardly
crown land	cuirassed	curvature	Cyclopses	daltonism	dasypygal
crown lens	cuisinier	curve ball	cyclorama	Daltonize	data entry
crownless	culicidal	curveless	cyclothem	damascene	dataglove
crown rust	cullender	curvesome	cyclotomy	Damascene	data sheet
crow-quill	culminant	curveting	cyclotron	damaskeen	date-lined
crow's-foot	culminate	curvetted	cylindric	damnation	date stamp
crow's-nest	culs-de-sac	curviform	cymagraph	damnatory	datum-line
crucially	cultistic	curviness	cyma recta	damnified	dauntless
crucified	cultivate	curvingly	cymbalist	damnifies	davenport
crucifier	cultrated	cushiness	cymbidium	damningly	Davenport
crucifies	culturist	cushioned	cymbiform	damoiseau	Davidical
cruciform	cultus-cod	cusimanse	cymophane	dampishly	Davy Jones
cru classé	cumulated	cuspidate	cynegetic	damp-proof	day centre
cruddiest	cunabulum	custodial	cynically	damp squib	day-flower

day labour	debatably	declinate	defection	delineate	dentalise
day letter	debauched	declivity	defective	deliquium	dentality
Day of Doom	debauchee	declivous	defendant	deliriant	dentalium
day of rest	debaucher	decoction	defension	deliriate	dentalize
day return	debenture	decodable	defensist	delirious	dentation
day school	debitable	decoherer	defensive	deliverer	Denticare
day-spring	debit card	decollate	defensory	deliverly	denticule
dazedness	debiteuse	décolleté	deference	Delphinus	dentiform
deaconate	debit side	decomplex	deferment	delta plus	dentistry
deaconess	de Broglie	decompose	deferring	delta rays	dentition
dead-alive	debt-slave	decongest	defiantly	delta wing	denturist
dead broke	debugging	decontrol	deficient	deltidium	denyingly
dead drunk	debussing	decorated	definable	deltoidal	deoculate
dead horse	Debussyan	decorator	definably	demagnify	deodorant
dead house	debutante	découpage	definiens	demagogic	deodorise
deadliest	débutante	decoy-duck	definitor	demagogue	deodorize
deadlight	decachord	decoy ship	definitum	demandant	deoxidate
deadly sin	decadence	decreeing	deflation	demanding	deoxidize
dead march	decadency	decrement	deflector	demand-led	departure
dead point	decagonal	decretion	deflexion	demantoid	depascent
dead's part	decahedra	decretist	deflexure	demarcate	depasture
dead stock	decalcify	decretive	defluence	demeaning	dependant
deadstock	decalitre	decretory	defluvium	demeanour	dependent
dead water	Decalogue	decubital	defluxion	dementate	depiction
dead white	decameric	decubitus	defocused	demersion	depictive
deaf adder	decametre	decumbent	defoliant	demesnial	depicture
deaf-blind	decanally	decuplate	defoliate	demi-devil	depigment
deal board	decaploid	decurrent	deformity	demi-glace	depletion
deaminate	decapodan	decursive	defrauder	demi-gorge	depletive
deaneries	decastyle	decussate	defroster	demi-lance	deplumate
dean's list	decathlon	dedicated	defterdar	demi-monde	depoetize
dear heart	decaudate	dedicatee	degassing	demi-pique	depollute
dear knows	decayable	dedicator	degausser	demisable	deposable
death-bell	deceitful	deducible	degrading	demission	deposited
death-bird	decencies	deduction	degreaser	demitasse	depositee
death blow	decennary	deductive	degree day	demitting	depositor
deathblow	decenniad	deductory	degustate	demiurgic	depot ship
death camp	decennial	deep-drawn	dehiscent	demi-volte	depravity
death cell	decennium	deep field	dehydrase	demnition	deprecate
death duty	decentish	deep-fried	dehydrate	demobbing	depredate
death-fire	deception	deep-fries	Dei gratia	demob suit	depressed
death-head	deceptive	deep-mined	deil a haet	democracy	depressor
deathless	decertify	Deep South	deionizer	demonical	depriment
deathlier	decession	deep space	deiparous	demulcent	depsidone
deathlike	decidable	deep-toned	deistical	demurrage	depth bomb
deathling	decidedly	deerberry	deityship	demurrant	depthless
death mask	deciduate	deer-brush	dejection	demurring	depurator
death rate	deciduoma	deer-grass	Dekabrist	demystify	deputable
death roll	deciduous	deer-hound	Delasolre	dendritic	deputator
death-sick	decilitre	deerhound	delay line	denervate	derealize
deathsman	decillion	deer mouse	delectate	de-netting	derepress
death-song	decimally	deer's hair	delegable	denigrate	de-rigging
death toll	decimator	deer-track	delegatee	denitrate	de rigueur
death trap	decimetre	defaecate	delegator	denitrify	derisible
deathward	deck cargo	defalcate	delftware	den mother	derivable
death wish	deck-chair	defatting	delicious	denominal	dermatome
debagging	deckchair	defaulter	delictual	denotable	dermestid
deballast	deck class	defeatism	delighted	denotatum	derogator
debarment	deck-house	defeatist	delighter	denouncer	derring-do
debarrass	declaimer	defeature	delignify	de nouveau	derringer
debarring	declarant	defecated	delimited	denseness	descanter
debatable	déclassée	defecator	delimiter	densities	descender

describer	detrition	diagnoses	dictatrix	dime novel	disablist
descripta	detrusion	diagnosis	dictature	dimension	disaccept
desecrate	deturpate	dialectal	didactive	dimensive	disaccord
desertify	deuce game	dialectic	diddledum	dime-store	disadvise
desertion	deuterate	dialogise	didelphid	dimidiate	disaffect
desert oak	deuteride	dialogism	diervilla	dimissory	disaffirm
desert rat	deuterium	dialogist	dieselise	dimorphic	disagreed
deserving	deutoxide	dialogize	dieselize	dim-witted	disagreer
desiccant	devaluate	dialoguer	diesel oil	Dinantian	disagrees
desiccate	devaluing	dial-plate	die-sinker	dine out on	disanchor
designata	devastate	dialysate	dietaries	ding-a-ling	disanoint
designate	developed	dialyzate	diet-bread	dinginess	disappear
designful	developer	diamagnet	diet-drink	dining car	disarming
designing	Devensian	diametral	dietetics	dinkum oil	disattire
desinence	devesture	diametric	dietician	dinothere	disavowal
desipient	deviation	diamidine	dietitian	dioecious	disbarred
desirable	deviative	diamonded	diet-sheet	dioestrus	disbelief
desirably	deviatory	diandrous	different	diogenite	disbranch
desireful	deviceful	Dianetics	difficile	Dionysiac	disbudded
desk-bound	devil a bit	dianoetic	difficult	Dionysian	disburden
desk diary	devil a one	diapering	diffident	diopsidic	disbursal
desmosome	devil bird	diaphanie	diffluent	dioptrics	disburser
desolater	devilfish	diaphonic	diffusant	Dioscuric	discalced
desolator	devilhead	diaphragm	diffusate	diosgenin	discarder
desorbent	devilhood	diaphysis	diffusely	dip candle	disc brake
despaired	devil-like	diapirism	diffusion	dip circle	discerner
despairer	devilling	diaristic	diffusive	dipeptide	discharge
desperado	devilment	diarrhoea	Digambara	diphthong	disciform
desperate	devil's bit	diascopic	digastric	diploidal	disclimax
despite of	devilship	diastasic	digenesis	diplomacy	disclosed
despoiler	devil's own	diastasis	digenetic	diplomaed	discloser
desponder	devil-wood	diastatic	digestant	diplomate	discoboli
despotism	deviously	diastolic	digestion	diplonema	discohere
despotist	devisable	diasystem	digestive	diplotene	discoidal
despotize	devitrify	diathermy	digitalin	dip needle	discolour
despumate	devonport	diathesis	digitalis	dipperful	discomfit
destinate	devotedly	diathetic	digitally	dip switch	discommon
destinies	dew-clawed	diatomite	digitated	DIP switch	discouple
destitute	dewlapped	diatonism	digitizer	dipterist	discourse
destroyer	Dexedrine	diazonium	digitoxin	dipterous	discovert
desuetude	dexterity	diazotize	diglossia	dipyramid	discovery
desultory	dexterous	diazotype	diglossic	direct dye	discreate
detailing	dextrally	dibstones	diglottic	direct hit	discredit
detail man	dextrorse	dicastery	dignified	direction	discumber
detection	dezincify	dicentric	dignifier	directive	discusser
detective	dhobi itch	dichasium	dignifies	directory	disdainer
detension	diablerie	dichogamy	dignitary	direct ray	disembark
detention	diablotin	dichoptic	dignities	directrix	disembody
detergent	diabolify	dichotomy	digraphic	direct tax	disemploy
determent	diabolise	dichroism	digresser	direfully	disenable
determine	diabolism	dichroite	diguanide	dirigible	disengage
deterrent	diabolist	dichromat	dihydrate	dirigisme	disentail
deterring	diabolize	dichromic	dika bread	dirigiste	disentomb
detersion	diacetate	dicky bird	dike-grave	dirt cheap	disesteem
detersive	diachrony	dicky seat	dilatable	dirtiness	disfavour
dethroner	diachylon	diclinism	dilatancy	dirt money	disfigure
detonator	diaclinal	diclinous	dilatator	dirt track	disflower
detorsion	diaconate	dicrotism	dilettant	dirt-wagon	disforest
detortion	diacritic	dictamnus	diligence	dirty look	disgorger
detracter	diactinic	dictation	dill-water	dirty pool	disgracer
detractor	diaeresis	dictative	dilutable	dirty word	disguisal
detriment	diaeretic	dictatory	dilutedly	dirty work	disguiser

dishallow	disrepair	diversify	dogmatist	door frame	downfield
dishcloth	disrepute	diversion	dogmatize	doorknock	downglide
dish-clout	disrupter	diversity	dognapper	door plate	downgrade
dish-cover	disruptor	diversive	do-goodery	door-stead	downiness
dish-faced	dissected	diverting	do-gooding	door-stone	downlight
dish it out	dissector	divertive	do-goodism	dope-fiend	downrange
dishonest	disseisee	divesture	dog-paddle	do penance	downright
dishonour	disseisin	dividable	dog-robber	dope-sheet	down-river
dishtowel	disseisor	dividedly	dogs of war	do poo-poos	downriver
dishwater	dissemble	divi-divis	dog's onion	dor-beetle	downscale
disimmure	dissensus	dividuity	dog's tooth	do right by	downshift
disimpale	dissenter	dividuous	dog's trick	dormition	downslope
disinfect	disshadow	divinator	dog trials	dormitive	down south
disinfest	disshroud	divisible	dog tucker	dormitory	downspout
disinform	dissident	divisibly	dog-violet	Dormobile	down-stage
disinhume	dissimile	divulgate	dog-winkle	doronicum	downstage
disinvent	dissipate	divulsion	Dolbyized	dorsality	downstair
disinvest	dissocial	divulsive	dolce vita	dorsiflex	downstart
disinvite	dissogeny	Dixiecrat	dolefully	doryphore	downstate
disjaskit	dissogony	Dixieland	dole queue	dosemeter	down-swept
disk drive	dissolute	dizygotic	doleritic	dosimeter	downswing
dislocate	dissolver	dizziness	dollar day	dosimetry	downthrew
dislustre	dissonant	djellabah	Dollardom	doss-house	downthrow
dismality	dissonate	do a mizzle	dollar gap	dot matrix	downtoner
dismalize	disspread	do any good	dollhouse	do to death	down tools
dismantle	dissuader	do a runner	dolloping	dot-stitch	down under
dismarble	dissunder	do a wee-wee	dolly-bird	dottiness	downwards
dismayful	distantly	Dobermann	dolomitic	double act	downweigh
dismember	distemper	dobsonfly	Dolophine	double axe	do wonders
dismissal	distenant	Dobsonian	dolorific	double bar	do wrong to
dismutase	disthrone	dock brief	dolostone	double bed	dowryless
disnature	distichal	docketing	dolphined	double-dig	do you hear
disobeyer	distilled	dock-glass	doltishly	double dip	do you mind
disoblige	distiller	doctorand	Domdaniel	double dot	dozedness
disoccupy	distingué	doctorate	dome-light	double-dye	draconian
disorient	distinguo	doctoress	domically	double-gee	draffsack
disparage	distraint	doctorial	dominance	doubleton	draftiest
disparate	distraite	doctorism	dominancy	double top	draftsman
disparish	disturbed	doctorize	dominator	doubtable	draftsmen
disparity	disturber	doctrinal	dominical	doubtless	drag-chain
dispauper	disulfide	docudrama	Dominican	douceness	draggiest
dispelled	disusance	doddering	Dominique	doucepere	drag-hound
dispeller	disvisage	doddypoll	domitable	douche-bag	dragomans
dispenser	diswarren	dodecagon	donkeydom	dough-face	dragoness
dispeople	ditchless	dodecamer	donkeyish	doughiest	dragonfly
dispermic	diterpene	dodgem car	donkeyman	doughtier	dragonish
dispersal	dithionic	dodginess	donnishly	doughtily	dragonism
disperser	dithizone	dod-rotted	donor card	Doukhobor	dragonize
displacer	dithyramb	do duty for	donorship	dovehouse	drag queen
displayer	ditrochee	dogaressa	do-nothing	Dover sole	drag-seine
displease	dittander	dog-clutch	doodlebug	dove's-foot	drag-staff
dispondee	dittanies	dog collar	doodle-doo	dowagerly	drag-strut
disponent	dittogram	dog-eat-dog	doohickey	dowdiness	drainable
dispose of	dittology	dog-fennel	doojigger	dowelling	draincock
disposure	diurnally	dogginess	doomfully	dower land	drainless
dispraise	diuturnal	doggishly	doominess	dowerless	drainpipe
disprofit	divalence	dog-headed	doom-laden	dowitcher	Dramamine
disproval	divalency	dog-legged	doomsayer	do without	dramatics
disputant	divellent	dog-lichen	doomwatch	down along	dramatise
disregard	divergent	dogmatics	do one's bit	downcoast	dramatism
disrelate	diverless	dogmatise	do one's nut	downcomer	dramatist
disrelish	diversely	dogmatism	door-cheek	downfault	dramatize

drapeable	driveller	duck's bill	Dutchland	earliness	echovirus
draperies	drive over	duck-shove	Dutch oven	early bird	ECHO virus
drape suit	drive-time	duck's meat	Dutch pink	early days	eclampsia
dratchell	drizzling	duckstone	Dutch roll	early wood	eclamptic
Dravidian	Dr Martens	ducted fan	Dutch rush	earnestly	eclectism
drawbench	droitural	ductility	Dutch tile	earringed	ecologist
drawerful	drollness	dude ranch	Dutch wife	earth-ball	economics
draw forth	dromedary	duffel bag	duteously	earth-born	economies
draw-knife	droningly	duffle bag	dutifully	earthfast	economise
drawlatch	droopiest	dufrenite	duty-bound	earthiest	economism
drawn work	drop a hint	dulcamara	duty cycle	earthlike	economist
draw-plate	drop-black	dulcified	duty visit	earthling	economize
draw-poker	drop-eared	dulcifies	dwarfling	earth-rise	eco-raider
draw-shave	drop-forge	dulcitone	dwarfness	earth-soul	ecosphere
draw-sheet	drop-light	dulcitude	dwarf star	earth-star	écossaise
draw steel	droppable	dulcorous	dwarf wall	earthstar	ecosystem
draw-table	droppings	dulocracy	dyarchies	earthward	ecphrasis
draw-works	drop-press	dumb barge	dyer's weed	earthwork	ecstasies
dray horse	drop scene	dumb blond	dyingness	earthworm	ecstasise
dreadless	drop scone	dumb cluck	dying oath	earwigged	ecstasize
dreadlock	drop short	dumbfound	dyke-grave	easefully	ectoblast
dreadness	dropsical	dumb piano	dyke-reeve	eastabout	ectocrine
dream away	dropstone	dummy teat	dynameter	eastbound	ectogenic
dreamboat	droshkies	dumpiness	dynamical	East Ender	ectomorph
dream-book	drotchell	dumpishly	dynamiter	Easter Day	ectoplasm
dream-hole	droughted	dump truck	dynamotor	Easter egg	ectoproct
dreamiest	drove road	dump valve	dynasties	easterner	ectropion
dreamland	drowsiest	duncehood	dyschezia	East India	ecumaniac
dreamless	drug abuse	dunce's cap	dyscrasia	East Sider	ecumenics
dreamlike	drug squad	duncishly	dyscrasic	eastwards	ecumenism
dream-time	drugstore	Dundonian	dysentery	easy as pie	ecumenist
dreamtime	Druidical	Dundreary	dysgenics	easy chair	edelweiss
dreariest	drum brake	dune buggy	dyslectic	easy-going	edibility
Dresdener	drum major	Dunkirker	dyspepsia	easygoing	edictally
dress coat	drumstick	dunnamany	dyspeptic	easy money	edificial
dress down	drum tower	Dunstable	dysphagia	easy-paced	editorial
dressiest	drunkenly	duodecimo	dysphasia	easy-peasy	education
dressmake	drunk tank	duodenary	dysphasic	easy rider	educative
dribbling	dry as dust	duopolies	dysphemia	easy terms	educatory
driftless	Dryasdust	duopolist	dysphonia	easy touch	Edwardian
drift mine	dry-blower	duplation	dysphoria	eau-de-Luce	Edwardine
driftweed	Drydenian	duple time	dysphoric	eau sucreé	effective
driftwood	Drydenish	duplexity	dysphotic	eavesdrop	effectual
drillable	drying-day	duplicate	dysplasia	Ebionitic	efficient
drill-book	drying oil	duplicity	dyspnoeal	ebriosity	effigiate
drill pipe	drylander	dupondius	dyspnoeic	ebulliate	efflation
drill-ship	dry matter	Dupuytren	dysthymia	ebullient	effluence
drill stem	dry-rotten	Duralumin	dysthymic	eccentric	effluvium
drinkable	dry-salter	dura mater	dystocial	ecchymoma	effluxion
drinkably	dry season	duricrust	dystopian	ecclesial	effortful
drink deep	dry shaver	duskiness	dystrophy	ecdysiasm	effulgent
drink down	dry valley	duskishly	dziggetai	ecdysiast	egg-beater
drink hail	dualistic	dusky titi	each other	echeveria	egg-carton
drinkless	dubbining	dust-cloth	eagerness	echiuroid	eggheaded
drip-dried	dubieties	dust cover	eagle-eyed	echograph	egg-shaped
drip-dries	dubiosity	dust devil	eagle-hawk	echoingly	egg-slicer
drip joint	dubiously	dustiness	eagle-wood	echolalia	eglantine
drippiest	dubitable	dust sheet	ealdorman	echolalic	egomaniac
dripstone	dubitably	dust storm	ear-basher	echometer	egotistic
driveable	duckboard	Dutch barn	earbasher	echo organ	egregious
drive-belt	duck decoy	Dutch doll	ear covert	echo verse	egression
drivelled	duck's arse	Dutch door	eared seal	echo-virus	egressive

egromancy	elocution	emotivism	end or mend	entamoeba	epidermic
eider-down	elocutory	emotivity	endorphin	entangler	epidermis
eiderdown	Elohistic	empathise	endoscope	entelechy	epidosite
eider duck	elongated	empathist	endoscopy	enterable	epifaunal
eidetiker	elopement	empathize	endosperm	enterally	epigramme
Eid ul-Adha	eloquence	empennage	endospore	enter into	epigraphy
Eid ul-Fitr	elsewhere	emphasise	endosteal	enteritis	epigynous
eigentone	Elsterian	emphasize	endosteum	entertain	epiklesis
eight ball	elucidate	emphysema	endostyle	enthymeme	epilation
eight days	elumbated	empicture	endotherm	entoblast	epileptic
eightfold	elusively	Empire Day	endotoxic	entoconid	epilimnia
eightieth	elutriate	empirical	endotoxin	entophyte	epilithic
eightsome	emanation	Empsonian	endowment	entoproct	epilobium
eighty-six	emanatist	emptiness	end result	entourage	epilogise
eirenicon	emanative	empty nest	endsville	entrammel	epilogist
eisegesis	emanatory	empty word	endungeon	entrapped	epilogize
either way	embargoes	empyreuma	endurable	entrapper	epimedium
ejaculate	embarrass	emulation	endurably	entrechat	epimerase
ejectment	embassade	emulative	endurance	entrecôte	epimerise
ekphrasis	embassage	emulgence	energetic	entremets	epimerism
elaborate	embassies	emulously	energizer	entre nous	epimerite
elaeolite	embattled	emunctory	energumen	entropion	epimerize
elastance	embayment	enactable	energy gap	entry form	epinastic
elastomer	embedment	enactment	en famille	enubilate	epineural
elatement	embellish	enamelled	enfeebler	enucleate	epinician
elaterite	Ember days	enameller	enflurane	enumerate	epinicion
elaterium	Embertide	enanthema	enfreedom	enunciate	epiphanic
elbow room	Ember week	encapsule	engarland	enveloped	epiphragm
Elder Edda	embezzler	encaustic	engineman	enverdure	epiphyses
elder hand	emblemize	enchanter	englacial	enviously	epiphysis
elderhood	emblossom	enchilada	Englander	envoyship	epiphytal
eldership	embossing	enchorial	Englisher	enwreathe	epiphytic
elder tree	embosture	encircler	Englishly	enwrought	epipodial
eldorados	embowment	enclosure	Englishry	enzymatic	epipodite
electable	embraceor	encomiast	engrailed	eotechnic	epipodium
electoral	embracery	encomiums	engraving	eparchies	epipteric
electress	embracive	encompass	engrosser	epaulette	epirogeny
Electress	embrangle	encounter	enhancive	ependymal	episcopal
electride	embrasure	encourage	enhearten	epeolatry	episcopic
electrify	embrazure	Encratite	enigmatic	ephedrine	episememe
electrize	embreathe	encrimson	enjealous	ephemerae	epistasis
electrode	embrigade	encrinite	enjoinder	ephemeral	epistatic
electroes	embrittle	encurtain	enjoyable	ephemeras	epistaxis
electuary	embrocado	end-around	enjoyably	ephemerid	epistemic
elegantly	embrocate	end-artery	enjoyment	ephemeris	epistoler
elegiacal	embroider	endearing	enkindler	ephemeron	epitapher
elemental	embroiler	endeavour	enlighten	ephialtes	epitaphic
elenchtic	embryonal	endeictic	enlivener	epibiotic	epitaxial
elephanta	embryonic	endemical	en passant	epicedial	epithelia
elephants	embryo sac	endenizen	en pension	epicedian	epitheted
Elers ware	embryotic	endlessly	enquiries	epicedium	epithetic
elevation	embussing	end-member	enquiring	epicenter	epitomise
elevatory	emendator	endocrine	enragedly	epicentre	epitomist
elevenses	emergence	endoergic	en rapport	epiclesis	epitomize
elfin-tree	emergency	endogamic	enrapture	epicormic	epizeuxis
elfin-wood	eminently	endogenic	enrolling	epicritic	epizootic
elf-locked	Emmenthal	endolymph	enrolment	epicurean	epochally
eliciting	emolliate	endomixis	ensaffron	Epicurean	eponymist
eliminant	emollient	endomorph	ensimatic	epicurish	eponymous
eliminate	emolument	endophora	ensorcell	epicurism	epoxidize
elixation	emotional	endophyte	enstatite	epicyclic	epoxy glue
ellipsoid	emotively	endoplasm	ensulphur	epidermal	epulation

epuration	escheator	etymology	even hands	excisable	existible
equaliser	escopette	eucalypti	even money	excise law	exit wound
equalizer	escortage	eucalypts	eventless	exciseman	ex-librism
equalling	Eskimo dog	eucaryote	eventuate	excisemen	ex-librist
equalness	Eskimo pie	eucentric	eve-of-poll	excitable	exocyclic
equal sign	esophagus	Eucharist	ever-being	excitably	exodermal
equatable	esophoria	Euclidean	everglade	excitancy	exodermis
equerries	esoterica	eudemonic	evergreen	excitedly	exodontia
equifinal	esoterism	eugenesic	ever-ready	excitonic	exoenzyme
equimolar	esotropia	eugenesis	eversible	exclaim at	ex officio
equipment	esperance	euglenoid	ever since	exclaimer	exogamous
equipoise	Esperanto	eukaryote	everybody	exclaim on	exogenous
equipping	espionage	eulogizer	every inch	exclosure	exolution
equirotal	esplanade	Eumenides	every last	excluding	exonerate
equisetum	espringal	eunuchism	everylike	exclusion	exophoria
equitable	Esquimaux	eunuchize	ever yours	exclusive	exophoric
equitably	esquiress	eunuchoid	every time	exclusory	exorcizer
equivalve	essayette	euphemise	everywhen	ex-convict	exordiums
equivocal	essayical	euphemism	every whit	excoriate	exosmosis
equivoque	Essenical	euphemist	evidently	excrement	exosphere
eradicant	essential	euphemize	evildoing	excretion	exostosed
eradicate	essenwood	euphenics	evil-liver	excretive	exostosis
era-making	establish	euphonies	evincible	excretory	exostotic
erasement	estaminet	euphonise	eviration	excubitor	exoticism
erbswurst	estampage	euphonism	evitation	exculpate	exotropia
erectable	estate car	euphonium	evocation	excurrent	expanding
erectness	estate tax	euphonize	evocative	excursion	expansile
ergograph	estimable	euphonous	evocatory	excursive	expansion
ergometer	estimably	euphorbia	evolution	excusable	expansive
ergometry	estimator	euphrasia	evolutive	excusably	expatiate
ergonomic	estoppage	euraquilo	evolvable	excusator	expectant
ergotized	estopping	eurhythmy	ewe-necked	execrable	expecting
eriometer	estradiol	euriballi	exactable	execrably	expective
erminites	estranged	Eurocracy	exactness	execrator	expedient
Ernestine	estranger	Euro-rebel	exactress	executant	expediter
erogenous	estuarial	Eurospeak	exaltedly	execution	expeditor
erosional	estuarian	eurytherm	examinant	executive	expellent
erosivity	estuaries	eurythmic	examinate	executory	expelling
eroticise	estuarine	eurytopic	exanimate	executrix	expensive
eroticism	esurience	Euskarian	exanthema	exegesist	experient
eroticist	esuriency	eusuchian	exaration	exegetics	expertise
eroticize	eternally	eutaxitic	exarchate	exegetist	expertize
erotology	ethanoate	eutectoid	Exarchist	exemplary	expiation
errand-boy	ethanolic	euthanasy	excambion	exemplify	expiatory
erratical	ethereous	euthanize	excarnate	exemptile	expiscate
erroneous	etherical	euthenics	excavator	exemption	explainer
errorless	ethically	eutherian	exceeding	exequatur	explanans
erstwhile	ethionine	euthyroid	excellent	exerciser	explanate
Ertebølle	Ethiopian	eutrophic	excelling	exercitor	expletive
eruciform	ethmoidal	Eutychian	excelsior	Exercycle	expletory
eruditely	ethnarchy	evacuable	excentral	exergonic	explicans
erudition	ethnicism	evacuator	excentric	exfoliate	explicate
erythemal	ethnicist	evadingly	except for	exhalable	explodent
erythrina	ethnicity	evagation	excepting	exhauster	exploitee
erythrine	ethnocide	evaginate	exception	exhibited	exploiter
erythrism	ethnogeny	evaluable	exceptive	exhibiter	explosion
erythrite	ethnology	evaluator	excerptor	exhibitor	explosive
erythroid	ethylenic	evangelic	excessive	exhumator	exponence
erythrose	etiquette	evaporate	exchanger	exigenter	exponency
escalator	Eton fives	evaporite	exchequer	exigently	exponible
escapable	etorphine	evasively	excipient	exilement	exposable
escape key	et sequens	even break	excipulum	existence	expositor

expounder	eyebrowed	faintness	fancy-free	fatuously	fermentum
expresser	eye-glassy	fair's fair	fancy-sick	fat-witted	fernbrake
expressly	eyeleting	fair-trade	fancy-work	faultiest	ferneries
expressor	eye-opener	fairwater	fandangle	faultless	fern-house
expressos	eye pencil	fairy cake	fandangos	fault-line	ferocious
expulsion	eyes front	fairy flax	fan heater	faunistic	ferrament
expulsive	eye-shadow	fairy gold	fan mussel	Faverolle	Ferrarese
expulsory	eyeshadow	fairyland	Fannie Mae	favourite	ferreting
expurgate	eye socket	Fairyland	fanny belt	fawningly	ferrocene
exquisite	eye splice	fairy-like	fanny pack	fearfully	ferryable
exsection	eyes right	fairy moss	fantailed	fearingly	ferryboat
exsertile	eye strain	fairy ring	fantasied	feathered	fertilely
exsertion	eyestripe	fairy rose	fantasise	featurely	fertilise
ex-service	Eyetalian	fairy tale	fantasist	febricula	fertility
exsiccate	Fabianism	fairy tern	fantasize	febrifuge	fertilize
exstrophy	Fabianist	fairy wren	fantasque	febrility	fervently
exsuccous	fabricant	faith cure	fantassin	Febronian	fervorous
exsuction	fabricate	faithless	fantastic	feckfully	fess point
exsurgent	fabulator	Falabella	fantastry	feculence	festilogy
extempore	face-brick	Falangism	faradaism	fecundate	festinate
extensile	face-cloth	Falangist	far afield	fecundify	festively
extension	facecloth	Falcidian	farandole	fecundity	festivity
extensity	face cream	falciform	fare stage	federally	festivous
extensive	face facts	faldstool	farmeress	feed a part	festology
extenuate	face-glass	Falernian	farmhouse	feed-floor	festucine
externate	face-guard	Faliscian	farmstead	feedstock	fetch away
externise	face out of	Falklands	far or near	feed-stuff	fetch down
externity	face paint	fall about	farragoes	feedstuff	fetichism
externize	face-piece	fallacies	farrantly	feed-water	fetidness
extirpate	face-plate	fallacion	far-seeing	fee-farmer	fetisheer
extispicy	faceplate	fallalery	far to seek	fee-faw-fum	fetishise
extolling	face-saver	fall apart	Far Wester	feel cheap	fetishism
extolment	facetious	fall-board	fasciated	feelingly	fetishist
extorsion	face value	fall-front	fascicled	feel small	fetishize
extorsive	faciation	fall in two	fascicule	fee simple	fetlocked
extortion	facsimile	fall money	fasciitis	feet first	fettucini
extortive	facticity	Fallopian	fascinate	feignedly	feudalise
extracted	factional	fall out of	fasciolar	feistiest	feudalism
extractor	factitive	fall short	fascistic	Félibrism	feudalist
extradite	factivity	false card	Fascistic	felicific	feudality
extrapose	factorage	false coin	fashioned	fellaheen	feudalize
extra time	factorial	false dawn	fashioner	fellation	feudatory
extravert	factories	false face	fast break	fellatrix	feu de joie
extremely	factorise	false fire	fastening	fell-field	fever heat
extremism	factorize	falsehood	fastidium	fell hound	fever tree
extremist	factotums	false keel	fastigium	fellowess	fiat money
extremity	fact sheet	false move	fast track	felonious	Fibonacci
extremums	factually	falseness	fast train	femineity	fibrefill
extricate	facultate	false step	fatalness	fenceless	fibreless
extrinsic	facultied	falsettos	fatefully	fence post	fibriform
extrovert	faculties	falsework	fat-headed	fence-shop	fibrillar
extrusile	facundity	falsified	fathogram	fenestrae	fibrinoid
extrusion	faddiness	falsifier	fatidical	fenestral	fibrinous
extrusive	faddishly	falsifies	fatigable	Fenianism	fibrocyte
exuberant	fadeproof	falsities	fatiguing	fenoterol	fibrolite
exuberate	fadmonger	family man	fatiscent	fenugreek	fibromata
exudation	Fadometer	famishing	fat-jowled	feoffment	fibrously
exudative	faggoting	fanatical	fattening	feracious	fictional
exultance	fagmaster	fanciable	fattiness	ferberite	fictively
exultancy	fainaigue	fanciless	fatty acid	Feringhee	fiddle-bow
exululate	faineancy	fanciness	fatuities	fermental	fiddliest
eyebright	faintless	fancy cake	fatuitous	fermenter	fideistic

fidgetily	filter aid	fireplace	fixedness	flat-nosed	flood-lamp
fidgeting	filter-bed	fire-power	fixed odds	flattener	flood-mark
fidget pie	filter out	firepower	fixed star	flatten in	flood tide
fiduciary	filter tip	fireproof	fixed-wing	flatterer	floor lamp
field-book	filthiest	fire-stick	fizziness	flatulent	floorless
field boot	filtrable	fire-stone	fizzle out	flatwoods	floor plan
fieldfare	fimbriate	fire-storm	flabbiest	flaughter	floor show
field goal	finagling	firestorm	flabellum	flaunched	flop-eared
field-grey	financeer	firethorn	flaccidly	flaunting	flop-house
field hand	financial	fire-tongs	flacherie	flavonoid	flophouse
field mark	financier	fire-water	flagellar	flavorous	flopperoo
field rank	financist	firewater	flagellum	flavoured	floppiest
fieldsman	finchlike	firewoman	flageolet	flax-brake	floptical
fieldsmen	find fault	firmament	flagitate	flay-flint	floreated
field-test	find Jesus	first base	flagrance	flea-louse	floriated
field vole	find means	first-born	flagrancy	fléchette	floridean
fieldwork	find-place	first chop	flagstaff	fleckered	Floridian
fiendlike	findrinny	first coat	flagstone	fleckless	floridity
fierasfer	fine-drawn	first cost	flag-waver	fledgling	floristic
fieriness	fine grain	first-foot	flail-tank	fleeciest	floristry
fifteenth	fine print	first gear	flake tool	fleetness	florulent
fifth gear	fine rolls	first good	flakiness	fleshhood	floscular
fifth part	fine tuner	first hand	flambeaus	flesh-hook	flos ferri
fiftyfold	fin-footed	first lady	flambeaux	fleshiest	flossiest
fifty-nine	finger-dry	First Lady	flambéing	fleshings	floss silk
fightable	finger-end	first line	flame-cell	fleshless	flotation
fight back	fingerful	firstling	flameless	fleshlier	flouncing
fightback	fingering	first love	flamelike	flesh-meat	flour-bolt
fight down	fingertip	first mate	flamencos	fleshment	flouriest
fight fair	finialled	first name	flame test	fleshpots	flourishy
fig-leafed	finically	firstness	flame-trap	flesh side	flow chart
figmental	finicking	first oars	flame tree	flesh tint	flowerage
fig-parrot	finishing	first post	flame-ware	flesh-worm	flower bed
fig-pecker	finish off	first-rate	flamingly	fletching	flower-bug
figurable	Finlander	first slip	flamingos	flexility	flower-fly
figurally	Finnicize	fiscality	flammable	flexional	flowerful
figure out	finocchio	fish eagle	flammeous	flexitime	flowerily
figurette	fioritura	fisheries	flanchard	flight bag	flowering
file-shell	fiorition	fisherman	flanching	flightier	flowerpot
file snake	fir balsam	fishermen	Flandrian	flightily	flowingly
filiality	fire alarm	fishgarth	Flandrish	flight net	flow-meter
filiation	fireboard	fishiness	flannelly	flimsiest	flowmeter
filigrane	firebrand	fish-knife	flap-sight	fling down	flow sheet
filigreed	fire-break	fish louse	flap-table	fling open	flowsheet
Filipinos	firebreak	fish-plate	flap-valve	fling wide	flowstone
filler cap	fire-brick	fish-sauce	flareless	flint corn	fluctuant
filleting	firebrick	fish slice	flare-path	flintiest	fluctuate
filliping	fire coral	fish-sound	flare star	flintless	fluctuous
fillister	fire-crack	fissility	flashback	flintlock	flue-brush
filly-foal	firecrest	fist fight	flash bulb	flintwood	fluffiest
film badge	fire cross	fisticuff	flashbulb	flip chart	fluid dram
filmcraft	fire-drake	fistulate	flash burn	flippancy	fluid gram
film-going	fire drill	fistulose	flash card	flirtiest	fluidible
filminess	fire-eater	fistulous	flashcard	floatable	fluidizer
film-maker	fire-fight	fistycuff	flash-cube	float-boat	fluidness
film speed	firefight	fittingly	flashiest	floatsome	fluid vein
film stock	fireflies	fit to drop	flash lamp	flocculus	flukiness
film strip	fire-guard	five-a-side	flashless	flock-book	fluoboric
filmstrip	fireguard	five-lined	flashness	flockless	fluorated
filmy fern	firehouse	fivepence	flash over	flockmeal	fluoresce
filoplume	fire-irons	fivepenny	flash tube	floodable	fluorosis
filoselle	firelight	fixed idea	flash unit	floodgate	fluorspar

flushness	fool's mate	foreshock	formicine	fourpence	freestyle
flustered	footboard	foreshore	formolize	fourpenny	free throw
flustrate	footbrake	foresight	formosity	four-rowed	free trade
flutelike	foot-cloth	foreslack	form sheet	fourscore	free verse
flutterer	foot-fault	forespeak	formulaic	fourth day	free wheel
fluxional	footloose	forespend	formulary	four walls	freewheel
fluxmeter	footplate	forespent	formulate	four wheel	free world
fly agaric	foot-pound	forespoke	formulise	foveolate	freezable
fly-bitten	footprint	forestage	formulism	fox-hunter	freeze-dry
fly bridge	foot's pace	forestall	formulist	fractious	freeze out
fly-by-wire	footstalk	forest-bed	formulize	fraenulum	freighter
fly-cruise	footstall	forest fly	formylate	fragilely	fremdness
fly-fungus	footstone	forestful	for my part	fragility	French bed
flying-fox	footstool	forestial	for naught	fragrance	Frenchery
flying jib	foppishly	forestick	fornicate	fragrancy	French flu
fly orchid	forage cap	forest oak	for nought	frailness	French fry
fly screen	forasmuch	forestone	for-profit	frailties	Frenchify
fly stitch	for a spell	foretaste	forsythia	framboise	Frenchily
fly-strike	for a start	foreteach	fortalice	frameable	Frenchism
fly-tipper	forastero	forethink	Fortescue	frame drum	Frenchman
fly to arms	for a while	foretoken	forthcome	frameless	Frenchmen
flyweight	forbearer	foretooth	for the pot	frame work	French oak
foal-tooth	forbiddal	foreutter	forthfare	framework	French pox
foaminess	forbidden	forewheel	forthward	franchise	frequence
foamingly	forceable	forewoman	forthwith	Francoist	frequency
focaccias	forceably	forewomen	fortified	francolin	freshener
focusable	force down	foreworld	fortifier	frangible	fresh-find
focusless	force-feed	forewrite	fortifies	franglais	freshness
focussing	force-land	for fear of	fortitude	frankable	fretboard
foetation	forceless	forfeited	fortnight	frankfold	fretfully
foeticide	forcemeat	forfeiter	for toffee	frankness	friar-bird
fogginess	force-pump	forficate	fortunate	franticly	fribblish
fog signal	forcipate	forgather	forty acre	frascatis	fricassee
foil-borne	foreboder	forgeable	forty-five	fratchety	fricative
foliation	forebrain	forgeries	fortyfold	fraternal	friending
foliature	forecabin	forgetful	forty-nine	fraudless	frightful
folic acid	fore-cited	forgetive	forwander	fraudsman	fright wig
foliolate	foreclose	forgetter	for want of	fraudster	frigidity
folk-blues	forecourt	forgiving	forwarder	fraughted	frikkadel
folk dance	for effect	forgotten	forwardly	freakiest	frilliest
folkiness	forefield	forjeskit	fossicker	freak show	fringe net
folkloric	forefront	forjudger	fossilate	free agent	fripperer
folk music	foregoing	forkiness	fossildom	free bench	friskiest
folksiest	foreguess	fork lunch	fossilise	freeboard	frit-flies
folkweave	forehorse	for lack of	fossilist	free fight	frithborh
follicule	foreigner	for laughs	fossilize	free float	fritterer
following	foreignly	forlornly	fossorial	free grace	frivolity
follow out	forejudge	formalise	fosterage	free house	frivolled
food chain	fore-kamer	formalism	foul brood	free lance	frivoller
food cycle	foreknown	formalist	foul Fiend	freelance	frivolous
food stamp	forenamed	formality	foul mouth	free-liver	frizziest
foodstuff	forenight	formalize	foul proof	free lunch	frock coat
food value	foreorder	formal sin	foundling	Freemason	frog-eater
fool about	forepiece	formamide	foundress	Freephone	frog-faced
fool along	foreplane	formation	foundries	free place	frogmarch
fooleries	foreprise	formative	foundrous	free-range	frogmouth
foolhardy	forereach	formatted	four-by-two	free sheet	frog-spawn
foolishly	forerider	form-board	Fourcault	free space	frogspawn
foolproof	foreright	form class	four-cycle	free State	frog-stool
fool round	foreseize	form-genus	four-flush	free stock	frolicked
fool's coat	foresheet	formicary	Four-H club	freestone	frolicker
fool's gold	foreshine	formicate	four-oared	free-style	from below

from now on	full blast	fusimotor	Galwegian	gas thread	genicular
from out of	full-blood	fusionist	gama grass	gastritis	geniculum
frondesce	full-blown	fusogenic	gamahuche	gastropod	genistein
frontager	full board	fussation	gambolled	gastrulae	genitalia
frontally	full-cream	fussiness	game-board	gastrular	genitival
front door	full dress	fustianed	game chips	gate array	Genoa cake
frontless	full drive	fustigate	game-piece	gatecrash	genocidal
front line	fullerene	fustilugs	game point	gatehouse	genophore
front page	full-faced	fustiness	game rhyme	gate-lodge	genotoxic
front room	full flood	fuzziness	gammadion	gate money	genotypic
frontsman	full-grown	gabardine	gamma plus	gate pulse	genteelly
frontward	full house	gabbiness	gamma rays	gate-stead	gentilise
frontways	full marks	gaberdine	Gammexane	gate-table	gentilism
frontwise	full pitch	gabionade	gammoning	gate valve	gentility
front yard	full point	gabionage	gandharva	gatewards	gentilize
frostbite	full-scale	gadgeteer	Gandhi cap	gathering	gentiness
frost-fish	full score	gadrooned	Gandhi-ism	gather out	gentle art
frostiest	full speed	Gaelicize	gang agley	gather way	gentleman
frostless	full steam	Gaeltacht	gangboard	gaucherie	gentlemen
frostlike	full-timer	Gaetulian	gang drill	gaudeamus	genuflect
frost-nail	fulminant	gainfully	gangliest	gaudiness	genuinely
frost-work	fulminate	gainsayer	ganglions	gaugeable	genu varum
frothiest	fulminous	gainstand	gangplank	gauleiter	geobotany
frowardly	fulsomely	galactase	gannister	gauntness	geocorona
frowsiest	fumarolic	galactose	gaolbreak	gauzelike	geodesist
frowstier	fumigator	gala dress	garbology	gauziness	geography
Fructidor	funambulo	gala night	gardenage	gavelkind	geologise
fructosan	fundament	galantine	gardenery	gavelling	geologist
fructuous	fundatrix	galenical	gardenful	Gawdelpus	geologize
frugality	fundiform	galingale	gardening	gawkiness	geomancer
frugivore	funebrial	gallabiya	gardenist	gay plague	geomantic
fruit-body	fungation	gallamine	garden pea	gay rights	geometric
fruit cake	fungicide	gallantly	garden-pot	gaze-hound	geometrid
fruitcake	fungiform	gallantry	garderobe	gazetteer	geomorphy
fruit-dove	fungology	gall-apple	garganeys	gazpachos	geoponics
fruiterer	fungosity	gallberry	gargarism	gear lever	georgette
fruit-farm	funicular	gallerian	garibaldi	gear shift	Georgiana
fruitiest	funiculus	galleried	garlandry	gearstick	georgical
fruitless	funkiness	galleries	garnished	gearwheel	geosphere
fruit loaf	funnelled	gallicise	garnishee	gee-string	geotactic
fruit tree	funnel-web	Gallicise	garnisher	Gelalaean	geotropic
fruit-wood	funniment	Gallicism	garniture	gelidness	gerfalcon
fruitwood	funniness	gallicize	garreteer	gelignite	geriatric
frumpiest	funny bone	Gallicize	garreting	gelsemine	germander
frusemide	funny-face	gallinazo	garrotter	gelsemium	germanely
frustrate	funny farm	gallingly	garrulity	gemellion	Germanify
fruticose	funny-ha-ha	gallinule	garrulous	geminally	Germanise
frying pan	furacious	Gallionic	Garryowen	geminated	Germanish
fuck about	furbisher	Gallipoli	gartering	gemmation	Germanism
fuel gauge	furcation	gallivant	gasconade	gemmology	Germanist
fuel-value	furfurous	galliwasp	gas cooker	gemütlich	Germanity
fugacious	furiosity	gallonage	gas-cooled	genealogy	germanium
Fulbright	furiously	gallooned	gas engine	generable	German ivy
fulfilled	furnished	gallopade	gas-fitter	generalia	Germanize
fulfiller	furnisher	galloping	gas helmet	generally	germanous
fulgently	furniture	gallstone	gasholder	generator	germarium
fulgorous	furriness	Galoisian	gas-mantle	generical	germicide
fulgurant	furtherer	Galtonian	gasometer	Genesitic	germinant
fulgurate	furtherly	galvanise	gasometry	genetical	germinate
fulgurite	further to	galvanism	gaspereau	geniality	germ layer
fulgurous	furtively	galvanist	gaspingly	genialize	germ plasm
full and by	fusillade	galvanize	gassiness	genically	gerundial

gerundive	giggliest	gladfully	globulite	go belly up	gonangium
Gesolreut	gigmanity	gladiator	globulous	go berserk	gondolier
gestation	gill cleft	gladiolus	glocalize	go-between	gone goose
gestative	gill cover	Gladstone	glochidia	gobletful	gongerine
gestatory	gill-flirt	glaikitly	glomerate	goblinize	gongorism
get abroad	gill plate	glaireous	glomerule	gobstruck	gongorist
get across	gill pouch	glamorize	glomeruli	Goclenian	goniatite
get around	gill raker	glamorous	gloomiest	go counter	gonococci
get-at-able	gilravage	glance ore	gloriette	go current	gonophore
get back at	Gilsonite	glandered	glorified	God-a-mercy	gonotheca
get better	gilt-edged	glandlike	glorifier	goddamned	go nowhere
get down to	gilt spurs	glandular	glorifies	God defend	gonozooid
get ground	gimballed	glareless	glory-hole	go decimal	go nuclear
get hold of	gimcracky	glariness	glory-tree	godemiche	gonyaulax
get in good	gimlet eye	glaringly	glossator	godfather	good buddy
get theirs	gimmer-hog	glass ball	glossiest	God forbid	good cause
get the nod	gimmickry	glass case	glossitis	God help me	good cheer
get the pip	gingerade	glass crab	gloss over	godliness	good fairy
get the rap	ginger ale	glass-dust	glost-fire	godmother	good faith
get the run	ginger-nob	glassener	glost oven	godparent	good grief
get to know	ginger nut	glassfuls	glottalic	God's blood	goodiness
get wind of	ginger-pop	glass-gall	gloveless	God's earth	goodliest
geyserite	ginglymus	glassiest	gloveress	God's penny	good liver
ghastlier	ginormous	glassless	glowingly	God's truth	good looks
ghastlily	gin-palace	glasslike	glow-light	Godwinian	good loser
ghazeeyeh	gin-soaked	glassware	gloze over	Godwinism	good money
ghettoise	giraffine	glass wool	glozingly	go eyes out	good night
ghettoize	giraffoid	glass work	gluconate	go forward	goodnight
ghost crab	girandole	glasswort	glucoside	goggle-box	good on you
ghosthood	girl guide	glaucodot	glueyness	goggle-eye	good sense
ghostless	Girl Guide	glaziness	glutamate	go haywire	good store
ghostlier	girlishly	gleamless	glutamine	going away	good stuff
ghostlike	girl scout	gleanings	glutinize	going-over	good thing
ghostlily	Girl Scout	glebe-land	glutinous	go it alone	good-timer
ghost moth	Girondism	gleditsia	glyceride	go it blind	good times
ghostship	Girondist	gleefully	glycerine	go-karting	good value
ghost town	Girtonian	glengarry	glycerole	goldarned	goodwives
ghost word	gitterner	Glenlivet	glycocoll	gold brick	good works
giant-cell	give a back	glenoidal	glycollic	goldbrick	goody-good
giant clam	give about	glide bomb	glycolyse	goldcrest	gooeyness
gianthood	give again	glide into	Glyconean	golden age	go off well
giant-like	give a hand	glideless	glycoside	golden boy	goofiness
giantship	give a miss	glide path	glyoxylic	golden-eye	goofy foot
giant toad	give beans	glide-twin	glyptical	goldeneye	go one's way
gibbed cat	give birth	glidingly	gnat-eater	golden key	goopiness
gibberish	give chase	glint-lake	gnathonic	golden rod	goosander
gibberose	give ear to	glint-line	gnat's piss	goldenrod	goose-fair
gibbeting	give forth	glissader	gnawingly	gold-fever	goosefoot
Gibbonian	give guard	glissandi	gneissoid	goldfield	goose-girl
gibbosity	give it a go	glissando	gneissose	goldfinch	gooseherd
gibbously	give law to	glitterer	gnomology	goldfinny	gooselike
Gibeonite	give mouth	glitziest	gnomonics	gold medal	goose-neck
giblet pie	given name	globalise	gnostical	gold plate	goose-skin
Gibraltar	givenness	globalism	Goa butter	goldsinny	goose-step
giddiness	giving-set	globalist	go against	goldsmith	goosiness
gift-horse	glabellae	globalize	goal-mouth	Gold Stick	go over big
gift token	glabellar	globe-fish	goalmouth	golf links	go pillion
gigametre	glacially	globelike	Goa powder	golf widow	gorblimey
gigantean	glaciated	globe-trot	goatishly	Golgi body	gorbuscha
gigantise	glaciered	globosely	goat's foot	goliardic	gorgeaunt
gigantism	glacieret	globoside	go bananas	golloping	gorgonian
gigantize	gladdener	globosity	go begging	gomphosis	gorgonise

gorgonize	granaries	gratingly	green lane	groomship	guard rail
goshawful	grandaddy	gratitude	green leek	groomsman	guard ring
gospelize	grand-aunt	gratulant	greenless	grooviest	guardroom
gospeller	grand coup	gratulate	greenling	gropingly	guardship
gossamery	grand duke	gravadlax	greenmail	grosgrain	guardsman
gossipdom	grandeval	gravamens	green meat	gros point	guardsmen
gossiping	grandiose	gravamina	greenness	grossness	guard's van
gossipred	grand jeté	graveless	green road	grossular	Guernseys
Gothamite	grand jury	gravelish	green room	grotesque	guerrilla
go the pace	grand lama	gravelled	greensand	grottiest	guessable
go the vole	grandmama	graveller	greens fee	grouch bag	guess-rope
Gothicise	grandness	gravel-pit	greensick	grouchier	guess-warp
Gothicism	grandpapa	graveness	green spot	grouchily	guess work
Gothicist	Grand Prix	graveside	greenweed	groundage	guesswork
Gothicize	grandsire	grave-trap	Greenwell	ground ash	guest beer
go through	grand slam	graveward	Greenwich	groundhog	guestless
go to court	grand tour	graveyard	greenwood	ground ice	guest list
go to cuffs	graniform	gravidity	greenyard	grounding	guest-rope
go to earth	granitize	gravitate	greeshoch	ground ivy	guestship
go to glory	granitoid	gravitino	gregarian	groundnut	guestwise
go to grass	granivore	gravy boat	gregarine	groundout	Guevarism
go to press	granny-sit	graybeard	Gregorian	groundsel	Guevarist
go to roost	grantable	graywacke	Grenadian	groupment	guidebook
go to scale	grant bail	grazeable	grenadier	group rate	guideless
go to sleep	granulate	grease cup	grenadine	groupware	guideline
go to smash	granulite	grease gun	gressible	group work	guidepost
go to waste	granuloma	greasiest	grevillea	groveless	guide rope
gourdfuls	granulose	great-aunt	greybeard	grovelled	Guidonian
goutiness	granulous	Great Bear	grey birch	groveller	guildable
gouty-stem	grapelike	greatcoat	grey cells	growingly	guildhall
governess	Grape Nuts	Great Dane	grey drake	grownness	guildship
go walkies	grape-shot	great deal	Grey Friar	grow out of	guildsman
go whistle	grapeshot	Great Fire	grey goose	grubbiest	guildsmen
go without	grape tree	great game	grey groat	grub-screw	guileless
gowpenful	grapevine	great-line	greyhound	grubstake	guillaume
Goyaesque	graphemic	greatness	grey nurse	grudgeful	guillemot
grabbable	graphical	Great Seal	grey scale	gruelling	guilloche
graceless	graphited	great ship	grey trout	gruffness	guiltiest
grace note	graphitic	great skua	greywacke	grumbling	guiltless
grace-wife	grappling	Great Week	grey whale	grumpiest	Guinea-hen
gracility	graspable	great year	griefless	Grundyish	Guineaman
gradation	graspless	greediest	grievance	Grundyism	guinea pig
gradatory	grass bird	Greek fire	grihastha	Grundyite	guitarist
grade line	grass carp	Greek fret	grill room	grunerite	Gujaratis
Gradgrind	grasserie	Greek gift	grimalkin	gruntling	Gulf State
gradience	grass frog	Greekless	griminess	guacamole	gulleries
gradually	grass hook	Greekling	Grimm's Law	guacharos	gulleting
graduated	grassiest	Greekness	grindable	guacomole	gully-hole
graduator	grassland	Greek to me	gripe's egg	Guadalupe	gulpingly
Grahamism	grassless	green alga	gripingly	guanidine	gum acacia
Grahamite	grasslike	greenback	grisaille	guanidino	gum arabic
grain-gold	grass moth	green bean	grisliest	guanosine	gumbo filé
grainiest	grass-plat	green belt	grist-mill	guarantee	gum dragon
grainless	grass poly	green card	grit-blast	guarantor	gum mastic
grain side	grassquit	green crop	gritstone	guardable	gummatous
graithing	grass tree	Greeneian	grittiest	guard band	gumminess
gram-force	grass-wren	green-eyed	grizzlier	guard-boat	gumptious
graminous	graticule	greenfeed	grocerdom	guard-book	gum-shield
grammatic	gratified	greengage	groceries	guard cell	gumshield
grampuses	gratifier	greenhead	grocering	guardedly	gum storax
Gram stain	gratifies	greenhorn	groggiest	guard hair	gumsucker
Granadine	gratinéed	Greenland	groomless	guardless	gun cotton

gun-lascar	haematoid	half-plane	handiwork	hard error	hastiness
Gunn diode	haematoma	half-plate	handlebar	hard graft	hatchback
gunpowder	haemocoel	half-price	hand-organ	hard-grass	hatch-boat
gun-runner	haemogram	half-rhyme	hand-press	hardheads	hatchling
gunrunner	haemolyse	half-round	handprint	hard-heart	hatchment
gunwale to	haemostat	half-sheet	hand round	hardiesse	hatefully
gurgitate	Haflinger	half-shell	hands down	hardihead	hatha yoga
Gurneyite	Haggadist	half-stuff	handshake	hardihood	hatha yogi
gurry sore	haggardly	half-title	handsomer	hardiment	hatted kit
gushiness	haggishly	half-track	handspaik	hardiness	haughtier
gushingly	hagiarchy	half-truth	handspike	hard-liner	haughtily
gustation	hagiology	half-value	handspoke	hardliner	Hau-hauism
gustative	hag-ridden	half-verse	hand-staff	hard lines	haulabout
gustatory	hagridden	half-world	handstand	hardly any	haunching
gustfully	hailstone	halieutic	hand-towel	hard money	haustella
gustiness	hailstorm	halitosis	handwrite	hard-nosed	haut monde
gut-bucket	hairbrush	halituous	handygrip	hard-paste	have a bath
gutlessly	haircloth	hall house	handy-work	hard sauce	have a care
gutsiness	hair crack	hallockit	hang about	hardshell	have a go at
guttation	hairdress	Hallow day	hang a jury	hardstone	have a leak
guttering	hairdrier	Hallowe'en	hang a left	hard stuff	have a mind
guttiform	hairdryer	hall-stand	hangarage	hard to get	have a pull
Guy Fawkes	hair-grass	hallstand	hangers-on	hard wheat	have a want
gymnasial	hairiness	Hallstatt	hang-glide	hard-wired	have a word
gymnasium	hairpiece	hall table	hang heavy	hare-brain	have got to
gymnastic	hair-point	halluciné	hang it all	hare's-foot	have had it
gynaeceum	hair shirt	halobiont	hang loose	hare's-tail	have ideas
gynaecoid	hair-sieve	halogenic	hang one on	hariolate	have in tow
gynobasic	hair-slide	halophile	hankering	Harlemese	have it out
gynocracy	hair-space	halophyte	Hanseatic	Harlemite	havenless
gynoecium	hairspray	halothane	Hanse town	harlequin	haver-cake
gynophore	hairstyle	halter top	hansom cab	harmaline	have right
Gypsyhood	hairy frog	haltingly	ha'pennies	harmattan	haversack
gypsy moth	halalling	hamadryad	haphazard	harmfully	Haversian
gypsy rose	halberded	hamadryas	haphtarah	harmonial	haversine
gypsywort	half-adder	hamamelis	haplessly	harmonica	have shame
gyrectomy	half an eye	hamartoma	haplology	harmonies	have wired
gyrfalcon	half-baked	Hamathite	haplontic	harmonise	have words
gyromancy	half-blood	hamburger	happening	harmonist	havocking
gyro-pilot	half board	hamfatter	happi-coat	harmonium	Hawcubite
gyropilot	half-bound	ham-fisted	happiness	harmonize	hawk-eagle
gyroplane	half-breed	ham-handed	happy days	harmotome	hawk-faced
gyroscope	half-caste	Hamletish	happy dust	harnessed	hawk-nosed
haberdash	half-court	Hamletism	happy hour	harnesser	hawksbill
habergeon	half-crown	Hamletize	happy land	harpooner	hawse-full
habitable	half-dozen	hammering	happy pair	harp-shell	hawse-hole
habitably	half-dress	hammerman	happy pill	harquebus	hawse-pipe
habitacle	half-eagle	hammer out	happy ship	harrateen	hawse-plug
habitancy	half-faced	hammer-toe	haranguer	Harrogate	hay asthma
habituate	half-flood	Hampshire	harbinger	Harrovian	haymaking
hacendado	half-frame	Hampstead	harborage	harrowing	hay-scales
hackamore	half-groat	hamstring	harbourer	harshness	hazardous
hackberry	half-hardy	hamstrung	Hardanger	Hartleian	hazard pay
hackerdom	half-heard	Hanbalite	hardboard	hartshorn	hazelwort
hackneyed	half hitch	handbasin	hard-bound	haruspicy	headboard
hack watch	half-James	handbrake	hard bread	harvester	head-chief
had better	half-light	handclasp	hard chine	harveyize	head-cloth
had rather	half-litre	handcraft	hard cover	Hashemite	headcount
Hadrianic	half-miler	hand cream	hardcover	hash-house	head-court
hadrosaur	half-naked	Handelian	hardening	Hashimoto	head-dress
haecceity	half-noble	handglass	harden off	Hasmonean	headdress
haematite	halfpenny	handiness	Harderian	hastilude	head first

headiness	Hebraical	hemstitch	heroinism	high-class	historify
headlight	Hebrewdom	hen-and-egg	heronries	High Court	historize
headliner	Hebrewess	hendiadys	heronshaw	High Dutch	hit and run
headlongs	Hebrewism	henpecked	heroology	high enema	hit a nerve
head louse	Hebrician	Henrician	herriment	higher-ups	Hitchcock
head-money	Hebridean	Henrietta	hesitance	high-flier	hitch-hike
headphone	heckberry	Henry Clay	hesitancy	high-flown	hitchhike
head-piece	hecogenin	Henry's law	hesitater	high-flyer	hit for six
headpiece	hectarage	hen's fruit	Hesperian	high-grade	Hitlerian
headscarf	hectogram	Hentenian	hesperiid	high heels	Hitlerism
headstall	hedge-bill	hepatical	hessonite	high jinks	Hitlerist
head start	hedge-bird	hepatitis	hesternal	high-keyed	Hitlerite
head-stave	hedgebote	heptaglot	Hesychast	high-level	hit-or-miss
headstock	hedgeless	heptanoic	hetaerism	highlight	hit parade
headstone	hedge-side	heptarchy	hetairism	high point	hit the hay
head voice	hedge-wood	Heracleid	heterodox	high-speed	hit wicket
headwards	hedgingly	heracleum	heteronym	high table	Hizbollah
headwater	hedrumite	heraldist	heteropod	high-toned	hoar frost
healingly	hedychium	herbalism	heterosis	high water	hoarhound
healthful	heedfully	herbalist	heterotic	high words	hoariness
healthier	heel-piece	herbalize	heuristic	hilarious	hoarstone
healthily	heel-plate	herbarise	hexacanth	hill-billy	hob-and-nob
hearkener	heffalump	herbarist	hexachord	hillbilly	Hobbesian
heartache	heftiness	herbarium	hexagonal	hill climb	hobgoblin
heartbeat	hegemonic	herbarize	hexahedra	hilliness	hobnailed
heartburn	heinously	herb-grace	hexameric	Himalayan	hobnobbed
heartfelt	heir-at-law	herbicide	hexameron	Himyarite	hobohemia
hearthrug	heliborne	herbivore	hexameter	hindberry	Hobthrush
hearth-tax	helically	herbivory	hexaploid	hindbrain	hockeyist
heartiest	helictite	herborise	hexastich	hinder end	Hock-money
heartland	heliogram	herborist	hexastyle	Hindooism	hocussing
heartless	heliostat	herborize	Hexateuch	hindrance	hodiernal
heartlike	heliotype	herb Paris	hexatomic	hindsight	hodmandod
heart-lung	heliozoan	herb water	hexatonic	hingeless	hodograph
heart-moth	hell-broth	hercogamy	hexestrol	hingewise	hodometer
heart-root	hell-diver	Herculean	hexuronic	hip girdle	hodoscope
heartsick	hellebore	Hercynian	hey presto	hip-length	hogbacked
heartsome	Hellenian	hercynite	Hezbollah	hippiedom	hog-badger
heartsore	Hellenise	herderite	hibakusha	hippocamp	hoggishly
heartwise	Hellenism	herd-grass	hibernate	hip pocket	hog peanut
heartwood	Hellenist	hereabout	Hibernian	hippocras	hog-sucker
heart-worm	Hellenize	hereafter	Hibernize	hippodame	hog-trough
heat death	hell-fired	here below	hiccuping	hippology	hohlflute
heath-bell	hell-gates	hereright	hiccup-nut	hippurite	hoi polloi
heath-bird	hell-hound	heretical	hickories	hired girl	hoist sail
heath-cock	hellishly	hereunder	hiddenite	hirsutism	hokeyness
heathenly	hell to pay	here we are	hidebound	hirundine	holandric
heathenry	Helmholtz	heritable	hideosity	hispanise	holarctic
heathered	helophyte	heritably	hideously	Hispanism	Holarctic
heath-fowl	helpfully	heritance	hidey-hole	Hispanist	hold aloof
heathland	Helvetian	heritress	Hieracite	hispanize	hold a plea
heathlike	hem and haw	herkogamy	hieracium	hispidity	hold at bay
heatproof	hemicycle	hermeneut	hierarchy	hissingly	hold cheap
heat-treat	hemihedry	hermetism	hieratite	Histadrut	hold court
heave down	hemiopsia	hermetist	hierodule	histamine	holderbat
heaviness	hemipenis	hermitage	hierogamy	histidine	hold forth
heavisome	hemiplegy	hermitess	hierogram	histogeny	hold hands
heavy-duty	Hemiptera	Hermitian	hierology	histogram	hold in fee
heavy spar	hemispasm	hermitish	high altar	histology	hold out on
heavy type	hemistich	hermitism	highboard	historian	hold pleas
hebdomade	hemitrope	herniated	high-brown	historied	hold serve
hebdomary	hemitropy	heroic age	high chair	histories	hold short

hold water	homiliary	hormogone	hot bottle	hugeously	hybridity
hole-in-one	homoclime	hormonize	hot button	hula skirt	hybridize
hole-proof	homocline	horned owl	hot chisel	hum and haw	hybridoma
holidayer	homodimer	horniness	Hotchkiss	humanhood	hybridous
holinight	homoeobox	horn poppy	hot-dipped	humanizer	hybrid tea
Hollander	homoeosis	horn-snake	hotdogged	humankind	hydantoin
Hollerith	homoeotic	hornstone	hotdogger	humanness	hydathode
holloware	homo faber	hornwrack	hot-headed	human race	hydraemia
holly blue	homogamic	horologer	hotheaded	human wave	hydraemic
holly fern	homograft	horologic	hot potato	humble-bee	hydraform
hollyhock	homograph	horometry	hot-rodder	humbugged	hydrangea
Hollywood	homologue	horoscope	hot shower	humbugger	hydrastis
Holmesian	homolysis	horoscopy	hot spring	humdinger	hydratase
holoaxial	homolytic	horridity	Hottentot	humectant	hydration
holocaine	homomorph	horrified	hound-fish	humectate	hydratuba
holocaust	homonymic	horrifies	hour-angle	humective	hydraulic
holocrine	homophile	horseback	hourglass	humic acid	hydraulis
holograph	homophobe	horse-balm	houseboat	humic coal	hydraulus
Holophane	homophone	horsebane	housebote	humidness	hydrazide
holophote	homophony	horsebean	house-burn	humiliate	hydrazine
holophyte	homoplasy	horse-boat	house call	hummeller	hydrazoic
holostean	homopolar	horse-colt	housecarl	hummingly	hydrazone
holotypic	homospory	horse-comb	housecoat	hummocked	hydriform
holy basil	homostyly	horse fair	house-flag	humongous	hydriodic
holy bread	homotherm	horse-fish	housefuls	humorsome	hydrocast
holy cross	homotopic	horse-foal	house-girl	hump bluey	hydrocele
holy Cross	homousian	horse-gear	household	humpiness	hydrocoel
Holy Ghost	homuncule	horsehair	house-hunt	hump speed	hydrocool
Holy Grail	homunculi	horse-head	housekeep	humungous	hydrofoil
holy grass	honey-bear	horsehide	housekept	hunchback	hydroform
holy laugh	honey-bird	horse-hoer	house-lamb	hundredal	hydrofuge
holy place	honeycomb	horse-hoof	houseleek	hundreder	hydrolase
holy souls	honey drop	horseless	houseless	hundredor	hydrolise
holystone	honey-flow	horselike	houseling	hundredth	hydrolith
holy water	honeyless	horse-load	housemaid	Hungarian	hydrology
Holy Write	honeymoon	horse-meat	housemate	hungriest	hydrolube
homacanth	honeysuck	horse-mill	houseroom	hunkerish	hydrolyse
home-baked	honeywort	horsemint	housewife	hunkerism	hydrolyst
homebuyer	honky-tonk	horse-nail	housework	hunky-dory	hydrolyze
homefolks	honorable	horseplay	houstonia	hunterman	hydronium
home-grown	honoraria	horse-plum	houyhnhnm	hurricane	hydronymy
home guard	honorific	horse-pond	hoverport	hurriedly	hydropath
Home Guard	honorless	horse race	howardite	hurry call	hydrophil
home-leave	Hoochinoo	horse's ass	how are you	hurtfully	hydroptic
homeliest	hood-mould	horse shit	how goes it	husbander	hydrosere
home-maker	hoodooism	horse-shoe	howlingly	husbandly	hydrosome
home movie	hoof stick	horseshoe	how's about	husbandom	hydrostat
homeopath	Hooke's law	horsetail	how say you	husbandry	hydrovane
homeostat	hook gauge	horsewhip	howsoever	hushfully	hydrowire
home-owner	hook-nosed	horsiness	howtowdie	hush money	hydroxide
homeowner	hoop skirt	hortation	hoydenish	hush-puppy	hydrozoan
home plate	hoop-snake	hortative	hübnerite	huskiness	hydrozoic
home range	hope chest	hortatory	hubristic	Hussitism	hydrozoon
homestall	hopefully	hortensia	huckaback	hustle-cap	hygiastic
homestead	hop-garden	hospitage	huckstery	hut-circle	hygienics
homestyle	hopper-car	hospitium	Hudson Bay	Hutterian	hygienist
home trade	hop-picker	hosteller	Hudsonian	Hutterite	hygrology
home truth	hop-pillow	hostilely	hue and cry	Huttonian	hygrostat
homewards	hopscotch	hostilise	huegelite	Huygenian	hylobatid
homeyness	hop the wag	hostility	huffiness	hybridise	hylozoism
homicidal	hordeolum	hostilize	huffingly	hybridism	hylozoist
homiletic	horehound	hot and hot	huffishly	hybridist	Hymettian

hymnaries	hypotonus	I know what	immensity	importune	incensory
hymnodies	hypsodont	Ilchester	immersion	imposable	incentive
hymnodist	Hyrcanian	ileectomy	immigrant	impostume	inception
hymnology	hysteroid	ileostomy	immigrate	imposture	inceptive
hyoid arch	iatrogeny	iliac vein	imminence	impotable	incessant
hyoid bone	Ibicencan	I like that	imminency	impotence	incidence
hyolithid	ibotenate	ill at ease	immission	impotency	incipient
hypacusis	ibuprofen	Illawarra	immixture	impounder	inciteful
hypakusis	ice-boater	ill-boding	immodesty	imprecate	inclement
hypallage	ice bucket	ill effect	immolator	imprecise	inclining
hypaspist	iced lolly	illegally	immorally	impressed	inclosure
hyperacid	ice-flower	illegible	immovable	imprinter	include in
hyperbola	ice hockey	illegibly	immovably	improbity	including
hyperbole	Icelander	ill-formed	immundity	impromptu	inclusion
hypercube	Icelandic	ill-gotten	immunizer	improving	inclusive
hyperemia	ice-master	ill health	immunogen	improvise	inclusory
hyperfine	ice-skater	ill humour	immusical	imprudent	incognita
hyperform	ichneumon	illiberal	immutable	impsonite	incognito
hypergamy	ichnology	illicitly	immutably	impudence	in-college
hypericum	ichthyoid	illimited	impaction	impudency	income tax
hyperonic	iconicity	Illinoian	impactite	impulsion	incommode
hyperopia	iconodule	ill-judged	impactive	impulsive	incompact
hyperopic	iconology	ill nature	impanated	impulsory	in company
hypertely	iconostas	illogical	impanator	impunible	incomplex
hypertext	icterical	ill-omened	impartial	impunibly	in concert
hyperweak	idealizer	ill-placed	impartite	impuritan	incondite
hypethral	ideal type	ill repute	impassion	imputable	in context
hyphenate	idée reçue	ill-suited	impassive	in a bad way	in control
hyphenism	identical	ill-taught	impatiens	in a big way	incorpsed
hyphenize	identikit	ill temper	impatient	inability	incorrect
hypinosis	Identikit	ill-thewed	impayable	in a canter	incorrupt
hypnoidal	ideograph	illuminer	impeacher	inactuate	in council
hypnology	ideologue	ill-willer	impeccant	in advance	in-country
hypnotise	ideomotor	ill-wisher	impedance	in a fright	increaser
hypnotism	ideophone	imageable	impedient	in a manner	increment
hypnotist	ideoplasm	imageless	impellent	in a moment	incrimson
hypnotize	idioblast	image tube	impelling	inamorata	incubator
hypobaric	idiograph	imaginary	impendent	inamorate	inculcate
hypoblast	idiolalia	imagining	impending	inamorato	inculpate
hypocaust	idiomatic	imaginist	imperator	inaneness	incumbent
hypoconid	idiopathy	imagistic	imperfect	inanimate	incunable
hypocotyl	idiophone	imbalance	imperious	inanities	incurable
hypocrise	idioplasm	imbecilic	impetrate	inanition	incurably
hypocrisy	idiot card	I'm blessed	impetuous	in any case	incurious
hypocrite	idiotical	imblossom	impicture	in a pelter	incurrent
hypoderma	idioticon	imbrangle	impieties	inaptness	incurring
hypogaeal	idiotypic	imbreathe	impinging	in arrears	incursion
hypogenic	idle wheel	imbricate	impiously	in a swivet	incursive
hypogeous	idolatric	imbroglio	impiteous	inaudible	incurvate
hypomania	idrialite	imbuement	implanter	inaudibly	indagator
hypomanic	if and when	imidazole	implement	inaugural	indecency
hypomorph	if he's a day	imino acid	impletion	in ballast	indecorum
hyponasty	ifs and ans	imitation	impliable	in between	in default
hypoploid	if you like	imitative	implicans	in blossom	in defence
hyporchem	ignitable	imitatrix	implicate	inbreathe	indelible
hyposarca	ignitible	immanacle	implicity	inbringer	indelibly
hypostome	ignoblest	immanence	impliedly	in cahoots	indemnify
hypostyle	ignorable	immanency	implosion	incapable	indemnity
hypotaxis	ignoramus	immediacy	implosive	incapably	indenting
hypotheca	ignorance	immediate	impluvium	incarnate	indention
hypotonia	ignorancy	Immelmann	impolitic	incaution	indenture
hypotonic	iguanodon	immensely	important	incendive	in despair

indexable	inerrable	infuriate	innocence	insetting	integrism
indexible	inerrancy	infusable	innocency	in several	integrist
indexical	inerratic	infusible	innocuity	inshallah	integrity
indexless	inertness	infusoria	innocuous	inshining	intellect
index-link	inerudite	in general	in no sense	in shivers	Intelpost
indialite	in essence	ingenious	innovator	inshore of	intendant
Indian cup	I never did	ingenuity	innoxious	inside job	intending
Indian fig	inevident	ingenuous	innuendos	inside out	intensate
Indianian	inexactly	ingestion	inoculant	insidious	intensely
Indian ink	inexpiate	ingestive	inoculate	insighted	intensest
Indianise	in extenso	inglenook	inoculist	in sight of	intensify
Indianism	inextinct	ingleside	inodorous	in silence	intension
Indianist	in extreme	ingliding	in one word	insincere	intensity
Indianize	infalling	ingluvial	inorderly	insinking	intensive
Indian red	infancies	ingluvies	in order to	insinuant	intention
Indian tea	infanteer	ingot iron	inorganic	insinuate	intentive
indicator	infantile	ingrained	inosinate	insipidly	inter alia
indicavit	infantine	ingrowing	inotropic	insipient	interbank
indicible	infantize	inhabited	in outline	insistent	intercede
indiction	infarcted	inhabiter	in passing	insistive	intercept
indigenal	in fashion	inhalator	in-patient	in so far as	intercity
indigence	infatuate	in harmony	in peril of	insolence	InterCity
indigency	infection	inharmony	in place of	insolency	intercool
indignant	infective	in harness	in point of	insoluble	intercrop
indignity	inferable	inherence	inpouring	insolubly	interdeal
indigotic	inferably	inherency	in private	insolvent	interdict
indigotin	inference	inherited	in process	insomniac	interdine
indirubin	inferible	inheritor	in profile	inspanned	interface
in disgust	inferring	inhibited	inputting	inspector	interfere
indispose	infertile	inhibiter	in quest of	inspirate	interfile
in dispute	infestive	inhibitor	inquietly	inspiring	inter-firm
individua	infidelic	in high gig	inquiline	in spirits	interflow
Indo-Aryan	infielder	inhumanly	inquinate	in spite of	interfold
indolence	in-fighter	in ill part	inquiries	installed	interfuse
Indophile	infighter	initially	inquiring	installer	intergrow
indraught	infigured	initiated	inquorate	instanter	interject
inducible	infilling	initiator	in reality	instantly	interknit
inductile	infinitum	injection	in reserve	instigate	interknot
induction	infirmary	injective	in right of	instilled	interlace
inductive	infirmity	in jig time	inrolling	instiller	interlaid
inductory	inflation	injurious	inrunning	institute	interlard
in due form	inflected	injustice	inruption	insuavity	interleaf
indulgent	inflexion	inland ice	inrushing	insuccess	interline
indulging	inflicter	inlandish	in saltire	insuffice	interlink
indumenta	inflictor	inland sea	insatiate	insularly	interlock
indurable	inflowing	in leaguer	insatiety	insulator	interlope
indusiate	influence	in-leakage	inscience	insulsity	interlude
indweller	influenza	inlet pipe	inscriber	insultant	interlune
in earnest	influxion	in light of	insecable	insulting	intermedi
inebriant	infolding	in line for	in secrecy	in support	interment
inebriate	infomania	in low keep	insectary	insurable	intermesh
inebriety	informant	in measure	insectile	insurance	intermine
inebrious	informity	in-migrant	insection	insurgent	intermont
in echelon	infortune	inner city	insectual	insurrect	in terms of
in eclipse	infractor	innermore	inselberg	in-swinger	internist
ineffable	infradian	innermost	insensate	inswinger	internode
ineffably	in fraud of	innerness	insequent	intaglios	interpage
inelastic	infringer	inner tube	inserting	in tatters	interplay
inelegant	in front of	innervate	insertion	integrand	interpole
in epitome	in full cry	innholder	insertive	integrant	interpose
ineptness	in full rig	inningses	in-service	integraph	interpret
inequable	infuriant	innkeeper	in session	integrate	interring

interrupt	intrinsic	ionogenic	Islamitic	isotypism	jacutinga
interseam	introduce	ionophore	island arc	isoxazole	jadedness
intersect	introject	ionosonde	island-hop	Israelite	jade-green
intersole	in trouble	ionotropy	islandman	issueless	jade-stone
Intertype	introvert	ion rocket	islomania	is the case	jaguarete
intervale	intrusion	ion source	Ismaelism	isthmuses	jailbreak
intervein	intrusive	ipse dixit	Ismaelite	itabirite	jaileress
intervene	intuition	ipso facto	Ismailian	itacistic	jail fever
intervent	intuitive	irascible	Ismailite	itaconate	jailhouse
intervert	intumesce	irascibly	isoallele	Italianly	jalapeños
interview	inturning	irateness	isobathic	italicise	jalousied
interweft	in two twos	iridocyte	isocercal	Italicism	jamabundi
interwind	Inuktitut	iridology	isochrony	italicize	jambalaya
interwork	inunction	iridotomy	isocitric	it beats me	jam-packed
interwove	inundatal	irisation	isoclinal	itchiness	janissary
intestacy	inurement	Irish bull	isoclinic	it depends	janitress
intestate	inurnment	Irish deer	isocratic	iteration	Jansenism
intestine	inusitate	Irish harp	isocrymal	iterative	Jansenist
in that way	inutility	Irish lace	isocyanic	itineracy	Januaries
in the buff	invadable	Irish moss	isoenzyme	itinerant	Japanesey
in the cart	invalided	Irishness	isogamete	itinerary	japanning
in the club	invalidly	Irish stew	isogamous	itinerate	Japan rose
in the dark	invariant	irksomely	isogeneic	itsy-bitsy	jargonaut
in the dice	invective	iron-bound	isogenous	itty-bitty	jargoneer
in the dock	inveigher	iron chink	isohaline	ivory-bill	jargonise
in the dust	inveigler	iron Chink	isohydric	ivory gate	jargonish
in the hole	invention	Iron Cross	isohyetal	ivory gull	jargonist
in the know	inventive	Iron Guard	isoimmune	ivory-like	jargonize
in the leaf	inventory	iron horse	isolating	ivory plum	jarringly
in the lump	inventrix	iron-mould	isolation	ivorytype	jarvey-car
in the main	Inverness	iron paper	isolative	ivorywood	jasperize
in the mass	inversely	Ironsides	isolectic	Ivy League	jasperoid
in the milk	inversion	ironsmith	isologous	ivy-leaved	jaundiced
in the mire	inversive	ironstone	isomerase	izimbongi	jauntiest
in the mood	invertant	ironworks	isomeride	jaborandi	jaw clutch
in the pink	invertase	Iroquoian	isomerise	jacaranda	jaw-fallen
in the rear	invertend	irradiant	isomerism	Jack-a-Lent	jay-hawker
in the road	investure	irradiate	isomerize	Jack-block	jaywalker
in the shit	invidious	irreality	isomerous	jack-chain	jazziness
in the soup	inviolacy	irregular	isometric	jacketing	jealously
in the suds	inviolate	irreption	isoniazid	Jack Frost	jeannette
in the swim	inviscate	irrigable	isooctane	jackfruit	jeeringly
in the team	invisible	irrigator	isopachic	Jack Ketch	Jelalaean
in the vein	invisibly	irriguous	isophenal	jackknife	jellified
in the wild	invitress	irritable	isophonic	Jack-light	jellifies
in the wind	invocable	irritably	isophotal	Jack Napes	jelly baby
in the yolk	involucel	irritancy	isophotic	jack plane	jelly bean
in thought	involucra	irritated	isoplasty	Jack plane	jellyfish
in token of	involucre	irritator	isopodous	Jack-screw	jelly-like
intonable	involuted	irrumator	isopolity	Jack shaft	jelly roll
intonator	in witness	irruption	isopropyl	Jack-sharp	Jennerian
intorsion	inworking	irruptive	isopycnal	jack snipe	jenneting
Intourist	inwreathe	Irvingism	isopycnic	jacksnipe	jenny-wren
in-transit	in writing	Irvingite	isorhythm	jackstaff	jequirity
intra-oral	inwrought	isagogics	isosceles	jackstone	jerboa-rat
in trellis	iodimetry	isallobar	isosmotic	jackstraw	jerkiness
intricacy	iodinized	ischaemia	isostatic	Jack-towel	jerkingly
intricate	iodometry	ischaemic	isosteric	Jacobinic	jerkwater
intrigant	iodophile	ischiadic	isotactic	jacopever	jerry-shop
intrigued	ion engine	ischiatic	isotheral	jacquerie	Jerseyman
intriguer	ionically	Isidorian	isotopism	jactation	Jersey tea
intrigues	ionizable	isinglass	isotropic	jaculator	Jerusalem

jessamine	jointedly	Julianist	Kaiserism	kennelled	killingly
jestingly	jointless	julienned	Kaiserist	Kensitism	kill ratio
Jesuitess	jointress	Juliet cap	kakemonos	Kensitite	kiln-dried
Jesuitise	joint-rule	jumboizer	kakkerlak	Kenticism	kiln-dries
Jesuitism	jointured	jumbo-size	kakotopia	kentledge	Kilner jar
Jesuitize	jointweed	jumby-bead	kalanchoe	Kenyanize	kilocycle
Jesus wept	jointworm	jumby-bean	kallitype	Keplerian	kilohertz
jetavator	joistless	jumby-bird	kalsilite	keratitis	kilojoule
jet engine	jokesmith	jumby-tree	kalsomine	keratosis	kilolitre
jet-lagged	jolleying	jumentous	kamachili	keratotic	kilometre
jet-setter	jollified	jump-about	kamagraph	kerb-crawl	kilotonne
jet stream	jollifies	jump blues	Kama Sutra	kerb drill	Kimeridge
Jew-baiter	jolliment	jumper ant	Kamchadal	kerbstone	kindliest
jewel-fish	jolliness	jumperism	Kamilaroi	kerfuffle	kinematic
jewellery	jollities	jumpiness	kanamycin	Kerguelen	kinescope
jewelling	jollopped	jumpingly	kankerbos	kermes oak	king cobra
jewel-weed	jolly boat	jump salty	kaolinise	kernelled	kingcraft
Jew-lizard	jolly-tail	jump spark	kaolinite	Kerry blue	king-devil
Jew's apple	joltiness	jump-start	kaolinize	ketogenic	kingdomed
Jews' stone	joltingly	junctural	kaparring	ketolysis	king-eider
Jew's trump	Jonsonian	Juneberry	karabiner	ketolytic	kingmaker
jib-headed	Jordanian	June grass	Karankawa	ketonemia	king prawn
jib-header	Jordanite	jungle cat	karanteen	ketonuria	king's blue
Jicarilla	Josephine	jungle gym	Karnataka	kettleful	king's evil
jigamaree	Josephism	jungle hen	karrozzin	key-colour	king's-hood
jig button	Josephite	jungle law	karst land	key-holder	king-sized
jill-flirt	Josephson	jungle rot	karyogamy	keyholder	king-snake
jingle-boy	joshingly	juniorate	karyogram	Keynesian	king's pawn
jitterbug	joss-house	juniority	karyology	keystroke	king's rook
jobcentre	joss stick	junkerdom	karyomere	khaki weed	king's ship
jobholder	Joule's law	junketeer	karyosome	khalifate	king's side
job-hopper	journalet	junketing	karyotype	Kharoshti	King Stork
job-hunter	journeyer	Junoesque	Kashubian	Khedivate	kininogen
jobmaster	joviality	juriballi	katabasis	Khedivial	kinkcough
job-office	jovialize	juridical	katabatic	Khorassan	kinkiness
job-sharer	jowlopped	jury-fixer	katabolic	Khotanese	kinoplasm
Job's tears	joy-flight	jurywoman	Katangese	kibbutzim	kinsmanly
jobsworth	joylessly	jurywomen	Kathakali	kick about	kinswoman
jockey-box	joy-popper	Jussiaean	Katharine	kick-boxer	kinswomen
jockey cap	jubilance	just about	katharsis	kick-pleat	kinzigite
jockeydom	jubilancy	justicial	Katherine	kick-stand	kipper-nut
jockstrap	jucundity	justiciar	Kat stitch	kickstand	kippersol
jockteleg	Judaistic	justified	Kavirondo	kick-start	kipper tie
jocularly	Judas goat	justifier	Keatsiana	kick-wheel	Kirbigrip
joculator	Judas-hole	justifies	keel-block	kiddie car	kirby-grip
jocundity	Judas kiss	juttingly	keel-bully	kiddingly	kirkwards
jodhpured	Judas tree	juvenilia	keelivine	kiddushin	Kissagram
Joe Bloggs	judgelike	juventude	keel-plate	kid-gloved	kiss hands
Joe Miller	judge-made	juxtapose	keelyvine	kidnapped	kissingly
Joe Public	judgement	Kaapenaar	keep a coil	kidnapper	kissogram
Johannean	judgeship	Kabardian	keep cases	kidney ore	kissproof
Johannine	judgingly	Kabardine	keep count	kid sister	kistbandi
Johannite	judgmatic	Kabbalism	keepering	kids' stuff	Kiswahili
Johansson	judicator	Kabbalist	keep faith	kiepersol	kitchener
John-apple	judiciary	kadaitcha	keep guard	kieserite	Kitchener
John Canoe	judicious	Kadhakali	keep house	kilderkin	kite-flyer
Johnny Raw	jug-handle	Kaffir pot	keep order	Killamook	kitschier
Johnny Reb	jug kettle	Kaffir tea	keep quiet	Killarney	kitschily
Johnswort	juice harp	Kafir harp	keep score	kill-crazy	kittenish
join hands	juiceless	kahikatea	keep store	kill-devil	Kittitian
join issue	juiciness	kaikomako	keep under	killer bee	kittiwake
joint bolt	juke-joint	kairomone	Kelly pool	killifish	kiwi fruit

Kizilbash	kraurotic	lady-clock	land cress	larkiness	launching
klapmatch	Krugerism	Ladyships	land drain	lark's heel	launchman
Kleenexes	Krugerite	lady's maid	landdrost	larmoyant	launch pad
klendusic	krummholz	lady-smock	land fever	larruping	launderer
klieg eyes	krummhorn	laevulose	land-flood	larvicide	laundress
klinostat	Kshatriya	lafayette	land force	larviform	laundries
Klondiker	kudzu vine	lager beer	land-gavel	larvikite	Laurasian
knackered	Ku Kluxism	lager lout	land grant	laryngeal	laurelled
knaveries	kundalini	laggardly	landgrave	lascivity	laurel oak
knaveship	kungu cake	laggingly	land-leech	laserdisc	lavaliere
knavishly	Kurdistan	lagniappe	land-loper	laserwort	lave-eared
kneadable	kurrajong	lag of duds	landloper	lashingly	lavendery
knee-board	kusimanse	lag of tide	land of Nod	lassitude	law centre
knee-brace	kymograph	lagomorph	landowner	lasso-cell	law-church
knee-holly	kynurenic	laid paper	landplane	last agony	law French
knee joint	labelling	lairdship	land-right	last-court	lawgiving
knee-piece	label-stop	lake-basin	Landrover	last ditch	law-keeper
knee-plate	labialise	Lake poets	landscape	lastingly	lawlessly
knickered	labialism	Lake Poets	land scrip	last night	law-making
knife-edge	labiality	lake trout	land-shark	last rites	lawn chair
knife-fish	labialize	lallation	landslide	last sleep	lawn edger
knifeless	labilizer	lamb-creep	land speed	last straw	lawnmower
knifelike	laborious	Lambegger	land-swell	last thing	lawn party
knife rest	laborsome	lambently	land-thief	last trump	lawn sieve
knife-work	labourage	lamb fries	land-value	last words	law office
knightage	labour day	lamb's ears	landwards	latch bolt	law of kind
knightess	Labour Day	Lamb shift	land-water	latchkeys	laws of war
kniphofia	labouring	lamb's-wool	land wheel	late comer	law-worthy
knob-nosed	labourism	lambswool	land yacht	latecomer	lay aboard
knobstick	Labourism	lamburger	Langobard	late hours	lay abroad
knock back	Labourist	lame-brain	langouste	late Latin	lay a ghost
knock cold	Labourite	lamebrain	languaged	Late Latin	lay before
knock down	labour spy	lamellate	langue d'oc	late-model	lay bishop
knocker-up	labyrinth	lamellose	languidly	late night	lay deacon
knock over	laccolite	lament for	laniaries	laterally	layer cake
knock wood	laccolith	laminable	lankiness	lateritic	layer tint
knotberry	lace-glass	laminaran	lanterloo	lathe-head	lay eyes on
knotgrass	lacemaker	laminaria	lanthanum	lather-boy	lay figure
knottiest	lacerable	laminarin	Laodicean	lathyrism	lay hold of
know about	lacertian	laminated	lapageria	laticlave	lay open to
knowingly	lacertine	laminator	lapideous	latimeria	layperson
know-it-all	lachrymal	lamington	lapidific	Latinical	lay reader
knowledge	laciniate	laminitis	Laplacian	Latinizer	lay rector
koala bear	lac insect	Lammas Day	Laplander	Latinless	lay sister
kobellite	lackeyism	lampadite	Lapponian	Latin rite	lay to rest
koenenite	lack-Latin	lampblack	Lapponoid	latitancy	lazaretto
koesister	laconicum	lampbrush	lapsarian	latration	lazarlike
Kohs block	lacquerer	lamper-eel	lapse rate	latreutic	lazulitic
kokerboom	lacrimals	lamp-house	lap-strake	latter-day	lazy-board
kok-saghyz	lactamase	lamplight	larbolins	latter end	lazybones
komatiite	lactamide	lampooner	larcenies	latterkin	lazy eight
komitadji	lactarium	lampshade	larcenist	latticing	Lazy Susan
konimeter	lactation	lamp shell	larcenous	laudanine	lazy-tongs
kookiness	lactifuge	lanarkite	larch tree	laudation	lazzarone
kopa Maori	lactocele	Lancaster	larchwood	laudative	leachable
Koreanize	lactonize	lance-jack	lardy-cake	laudatory	leaderene
kornelite	lactulose	lance-oval	Largactil	laughable	leaderess
Korsakoff	ladder way	lancewood	large-eyed	laughably	lead glass
koulibiac	ladies' man	lanciform	largeness	laugh away	lead glaze
kozatchok	ladlefuls	lancinate	large type	laugh down	lead-horse
kopa Maori	Lady altar	land agent	larghetto	laugh-line	leadingly
kraurosis	lady-chair	landaulet	largition	laughsome	lead large

lead light	legalness	lettering	lie around	Lille lace	lion dance
lead ochre	legantine	letter-man	lie fallow	lily liver	lion-heart
lead-paper	leg before	letterset	liegeless	lily white	Lions Club
lead-plant	leg-cutter	Leucadian	liege lord	limaceous	lion's foot
lead ratio	legendary	leucocyte	lienteric	limber-box	lion's leaf
lead-reins	legendist	leucoderm	Liesegang	Limburger	lion's tail
lead-screw	leger line	leuconoid	lifeblood	lime green	lion-tawny
lead sheet	legginess	leucotome	life cycle	Limehouse	lipidosis
lead story	legginged	leucotomy	life-force	lime juice	lip-labour
lead-swing	leg glance	leukaemia	lifefully	limelight	lipolysis
leaf-brown	legionary	leukaemic	life-giver	lime-punch	lipolytic
leaf green	legislate	leukocyte	lifeguard	limestone	lipophile
leafiness	leg-puller	Levallois	life-plant	lime water	lipothymy
leafleted	leg theory	Levantine	life-saver	lime-works	lippitude
leaf-louse	leguleian	level down	life-sized	limitable	lip-reader
leaf miner	leg warmer	level-free	lifestyle	limitedly	lipsticky
leaf mould	Leicester	levelling	life's work	limitless	lip-syncer
leaf-nosed	leiomyoma	levelness	life-table	limnology	liquation
leaf-point	leisurely	level test	life-while	limonitic	liquefied
leaf scald	leitmotif	level tube	life-world	limousine	liquefier
leaf-scale	leitmotiv	leverwood	lift truck	limpidity	liquidate
leaf-spine	lemanless	leviathan	lift valve	limpingly	liquidise
leaf-stalk	lemmatize	levigator	lightable	limp wrist	liquidity
leaf-trace	lemniscus	leviratic	lightboat	linamarin	liquidize
leakiness	lemon balm	levitator	light bulb	linch-hoop	liquified
lean times	lemon curd	Levitical	light-buoy	Lincrusta	liquifies
lean years	lemon drop	levulinic	light cone	linea alba	liquorice
learnable	lemon-game	levulosan	light cord	line ahead	liquorish
learnedly	lemon sole	levy-money	lightener	lineality	liquorist
leaseback	lemon tree	Lewis acid	light-fast	lineament	liquorous
leasehold	lemonwood	Lewis base	lightfast	line angle	lispingly
lease-lend	lend a hand	lexically	lightfoot	linearise	Lissajous
leastways	lend an ear	Leyden jar	light hand	linearity	listen for
leastwise	Lend-Lease	liability	light into	linearize	listening
leathered	lengthful	libellant	lightless	lineation	listen out
leathwake	lengthier	libelling	lightmans	line block	listerial
leave flat	lengthily	libellist	lightness	line-drawn	list price
leave from	lengthman	libellous	lightning	line-drive	literally
leave go of	lengthmen	libellula	lightship	line-fence	literatim
leave over	leniently	liberally	light show	line gauge	literator
leave up to	lenitable	liberator	lightsome	line graph	literatus
Leavisian	lens paper	liberties	lights out	line judge	lithaemia
Leavisite	Lenten pie	libertine	light-time	linenfold	lithaemic
lecherous	lenticule	libidinal	light trap	linen-hall	litheness
Leclanché	lentiform	librarian	light-well	linenless	lithesome
lectorate	lentiscus	libraries	lightwood	lineolate	lithiasis
lectotype	lentitude	libration	light year	line-rider	lithiated
lecturess	leotarded	libratory	lign-aloes	liner note	lithocyst
ledge-door	leprophil	libriform	lignified	line shaft	lithoidal
ledgeless	leprosery	licensure	lignifies	line space	lithology
ledgement	leprously	lichenism	ligniform	line-storm	Lithol red
leechlike	leptocaul	lichenist	ligularia	line-width	lithopone
leech-line	leptonema	lichenoid	ligulated	lingberry	lithosere
leech-rope	leptosome	lichenose	ligustrum	lingering	lithotint
leek-green	leptotene	lichenous	Lihyanite	lingually	lithotomy
leeriness	lespedeza	lich-house	like a shot	lingulate	lithotype
leeringly	Lesser Dog	lich-stone	like as not	linksland	Lithuanic
leewardly	lesser fry	licitness	like crazy	linograph	litigable
left bower	Lestrigon	lickerish	likeliest	linoleate	litigator
left field	lethality	lick-penny	like magic	linolenic	litigious
left flank	lethargic	lick whole	likkewaan	lintelled	litoptern
leftwards	letter box	lidocaine	lilangeni	lintwhite	litterbug

littering	localizer	long dress	loose rein	loving cup	lunar node
little auk	localness	long drink	loose shot	lowballer	lunar year
little-boy	local time	long-eared	loose smut	lowbeller	lunatical
Little Dog	local veto	longevity	lop and top	low-browed	lunch hour
little end	locatable	longevous	lopez-root	lowbrowed	lunchless
little Joe	locellate	long-faced	lophiodon	Low Church	lunch-room
little man	Lochinvar	long field	lophodont	low comedy	lunch-time
little old	locked jaw	long-fours	lop-rabbit	lowerable	lunchtime
little owl	lock horns	long glass	loquacity	lower case	Lundyfoot
little toe	lockjawed	long grass	loquently	lower deck	lung-fever
liturgies	locksmith	longhouse	lorazepam	lowermost	lung fluke
liturgise	locomotor	longicorn	Lord Derby	Lowestoft	lung-power
liturgism	loculated	longingly	lordliest	Low German	lunisolar
liturgist	locuplete	longitude	Lord Mayor	low-headed	lunitidal
liturgize	lodestone	long johns	lordships	low-income	lunulated
live-birth	lodgeable	long knife	Lordships	lowlander	lupinosis
live fence	lodgement	Long Knife	lorgnette	Lowlander	lupulinic
live in sin	lodge-pole	long-liner	loricated	lowlihead	luridness
liveliest	lodgerdom	long-lived	Lorrainer	lowliness	lurkingly
live on air	loftiness	Long March	lorry park	low-loader	lusophone
liverance	logaoedic	long metre	lose an eye	low-minded	lustering
liverleaf	logarithm	long-nosed	lose caste	low-necked	lustfully
liverless	log-basket	Longobard	lose count	low relief	lust-house
live rough	logginess	long price	lose flesh	low season	lustihead
Liverpool	logheaded	long purse	lose heart	Low Sunday	lustihood
liver spot	logically	long rains	lose touch	loxodrome	lustiness
liver-wing	logic bomb	long-range	lose track	loxodromy	lustreful
liverwort	logic gate	longshore	loss-maker	loyalness	lutaceous
liveryman	logistics	long-short	loss-proof	loyalties	luteinize
liverymen	log-normal	long sight	lost cause	lubricant	lutescent
live steam	logograph	long sixes	lost river	lubricate	Lutherism
livestock	logogriph	long straw	Lotharios	lubricity	Lutherist
live tally	logolatry	long-timer	lot-jumper	lubricous	lutulence
lividness	logomachy	long verse	Lotophagi	Lucianist	luxuriant
Livornese	logophile	long views	lotteries	lucidness	luxuriate
lixiviate	logothete	long vowel	lotus-bird	luciferin	luxurious
lixivious	logroller	long waist	lotus-land	luckiness	Lycaonian
load-and-go	logrunner	longwards	loud-mouth	luck-money	Lycurgean
loadberry	loincloth	long whist	loudmouth	lucrative	Lycurgian
loadspace	Lollardry	long-wings	loud pedal	Lucretian	lyme-grass
loadstone	lollingly	long years	lounge bar	lucubrate	lymphatic
loaf-bread	lolloping	look about	loup-garou	Lucullean	lymph node
loaf-eater	Lombardic	look after	louringly	Lucullian	lymphomas
loaferdom	London fog	look-ahead	louse-trap	Ludditism	Lyon Court
loaferism	London gin	look-alike	lousewort	ludicrous	lyophilic
loaf sugar	Londonian	lookalike	lousiness	Luftwaffe	lyophobic
loaminess	Londonish	look alive	loutishly	lullabied	lyotropic
Loamshire	Londonism	look askew	love-apple	lullabies	lyrically
loan-blend	London ivy	looker-out	love beads	lullingly	lysimeter
loan-money	Londonize	look round	love child	lumbering	lysogenic
loan-place	loneliest	look sharp	love feast	lumberman	lysosomal
loan shark	Lone Scout	look small	love-juice	lumbermen	lytically
loan-shift	longaeval	look smart	loveliest	lumbrical	macabrely
loathness	long-beard	looniness	love-light	lumbricus	macadamia
loathsome	longboard	loon pants	lovely and	luminaire	macaronic
lobectomy	long-chain	loose back	love match	luminance	Macartney
lobscouse	long chair	loose-fill	loverless	luminesce	Maccabean
Lob's pound	long cloth	loose fish	loverlike	luminizer	Maccabees
lobulated	long cross	loose head	love-scene	lumpiness	macédoine
local call	long-dated	loose-knit	love-spoon	lumpishly	macerator
localitis	long dozen	loose-leaf	love-story	lump sugar	MacGuffin
localized	long-drawn	looseness	love-token	lunarnaut	Machiavel

machinate	magnetize	make entry	malt-floor	manicotti	maranatha
machinery	magnetoid	make feast	malt-house	manifesto	Marangoni
machinist	magnetron	make fun of	malthouse	maninosay	marbleize
Machmeter	magnifico	make haste	maltiness	manipular	marcasite
macilence	magnified	make hay of	malt-maker	man-killer	marcassin
macilency	magnifier	make merry	malt sugar	manlihood	marcelled
macintosh	magnifies	make money	malvoisie	manlikely	March hare
MacIntosh	magnitude	make or mar	mamillary	manliness	march-land
MacKenzie	Magyarize	make peace	mamillate	manna-tree	March moth
mackerels	maharajah	make ready	mammalian	mannequin	marchpane
Maclaurin	maharanee	makeready	mammalogy	mannerise	march past
macrobian	maharishi	make sense	mammaries	mannerism	Marconist
macrocosm	Mahlerian	make shift	mamma's boy	mannerist	Marcusian
macrocyst	mahlstick	makeshift	mammering	mannerize	Mardi gras
macrocyte	Mahometan	make speed	mammiform	mannishly	Mardi Gras
macro lens	Mahometry	make sport	mammillar	mano a mano	mareogram
macrolide	maidenish	make terms	mammogram	Manoeline	mare's nest
macrology	maieutics	make tired	Mammondom	manoeuvre	mare's tail
macromere	mail coach	make use of	Mammonish	manometer	margarate
macropsia	mail cover	make water	Mammonism	manometry	margarine
macrurous	Mailmerge	make waves	Mammonist	man orchid	margarita
mactation	mail order	Malabaric	Mammonite	manorship	margarite
maculated	mail-rider	malachite	mammy-sick	manoscope	marginate
madam-shop	mail train	maladroit	man and boy	man-riding	margining
madarosis	main brace	mala fides	mananosay	mansarded	marialite
madcapery	mainferre	malagueña	man-at-arms	mansionry	Marianism
maddening	mainframe	Malagueña	Manchegan	manslayer	Marianist
mad-doctor	main guard	malagueta	mancipate	man's woman	Mariavite
madeleine	mainliner	malanders	Mancunian	manticism	marigraph
made-up tie	mainplane	malarious	mandarine	manticore	marihuana
mad-headed	mainprize	malathion	mandatary	Mantinean	marijuana
mad minute	main range	Malayalam	mandative	mantology	marimonda
madrepore	mainsheet	Malay fowl	mandatory	manualism	Mariology
madrilene	Maintenon	Malaysian	mandilion	manualist	maritally
Madrileño	maize-bird	Maldivian	mandoline	manubrial	Maritimer
maelstrom	maize-smut	maldonite	manducate	manubrium	marked man
maenadism	majesties	malebolge	man-eating	Manueline	marker pen
maestosos	major axis	maleffect	maned wolf	manurable	market day
maestrale	major-domo	male gauge	man enough	manurance	marketeer
magalogue	majorette	malegueta	man-for-man	Manxwoman	marketing
magaziner	major part	male organ	man Friday	Manxwomen	market man
maggot-pie	majorship	male rhyme	Man Friday	many a moon	Markovian
maghemite	major suit	male screw	manganate	many a time	marlberry
magianism	major term	malformed	manganese	manyogana	Marlovian
magically	majuscule	malgré lui	manganite	manyplies	marl slate
magic away	make a back	malic acid	manganoan	many-sided	marlstone
magicking	make a book	maliceful	manganous	many-where	marmalade
magic wand	make a face	malicious	mangel-fly	manzanita	marmalady
magistery	make after	malignant	mange mite	Maoriland	marmolite
magistral	make a fuss	malignify	mangerful	Maori oven	marmorate
Maglemose	make a head	malignity	mange-tout	Mapharsen	marmoreal
magmatism	make a mark	malleable	mangetout	maple beer	marmorean
magmatist	make a mess	malleably	manginess	maple bush	marquench
Magnaflux	make a move	mallee hen	mango-bird	maple leaf	Marquesan
magnesian	make a quid	mallemuck	mango-fish	maple tree	marquetry
magnesite	make a rise	malleolar	mango tree	maple-wood	Marranism
magnesium	make a show	malleolus	manhandle	map lichen	marriable
magnetics	make a step	Mallorcan	manhattan	map-making	marrowfat
magnetise	make a time	Malmaison	manhunter	map-reader	marrowsky
magnetism	make a waft	malpraxis	manically	map turtle	Marrucian
magnetist	make a work	maltalent	Manichean	maquisard	Marrucine
magnetite	make doubt	malt-combs	manichord	marabunta	marry into

marry well	mass-point	May-cherry	mediciner	melon-wood	mephitism
marshalcy	mass-ratio	mayflower	meditater	melonworm	merbromin
Marsh Arab	mastalgia	mayhappen	meditator	mélophone	mercaptan
marshbird	masterate	mayoralty	medium dry	melopoeia	mercatory
marshbuck	masterdom	mayorship	mediumism	melopoeic	mercement
marsh fern	masterful	mazedness	medullary	melphalan	mercenary
marsh frog	mastering	Mazzinian	meetinger	meltingly	merceries
marsh hawk	master key	mead-bench	mefenamic	melt water	mercerise
marshiest	master-man	meadowing	megacycle	Melungeon	mercerize
marshland	masticate	meadow rue	megadeath	memberess	merciable
marsh pink	mastigure	meadstead	megafauna	mementoes	merciless
marsh spot	mastoidal	mealberry	megahertz	Memnonian	merciment
marsh tern	matagouri	mealie-cob	megalopod	memoirist	mercurate
marsh worm	matchable	mealiepap	megamouth	memorable	mercurial
marshwort	match ball	mealiness	megaphone	memorably	Mercurian
marsh wren	match-book	mealy tree	megaphyll	memoranda	mercurous
marsquake	matchbook	meandered	megapolis	memorious	mercy-seat
marsupial	match-card	me and mine	megascope	memorizer	mereology
marsupian	matchcoat	meandrine	megashear	Memphitic	mere right
marsupite	match-head	meandrous	megaspore	menaceful	merestead
marsupium	matchless	meaningly	megastore	menadione	merestone
Martellos	matchlock	means—ends	megatonne	menagerie	merganser
martemper	matchmake	means test	meibomian	men-at-arms	merismoid
martially	match-play	mean to say	meiofauna	mendacity	merispore
martin-box	matchplay	meanwhile	meiosis II	Mendelian	meristele
martin bug	match race	mean white	mekometer	Mendelism	meritable
martineta	match-safe	mean White	melaleuca	Mendelist	meritedly
Martinism	match up to	measliest	melanemia	Mendelize	meritless
Martinist	matchwood	measurely	melanized	mendicant	merocrine
Martinmas	matelassé	measure up	melanosis	mendicate	merogonic
martyrdom	materiate	measuring	melanotic	mendicity	meroistic
martyrial	maternity	meat-flies	melanuria	mendipite	merostome
martyries	mateyness	meat-house	melanuric	mend or end	merozoite
martyrion	matfellon	meatiness	melaphyre	mengkuang	merriment
martyrise	matriarch	meat jelly	melastoma	men in blue	merriness
martyrish	matricide	meatotomy	melatonin	meningeal	merry hell
martyrize	matriclan	meat-wagon	melibiase	meningism	merrymake
marvelled	matricula	meat-works	melibiose	Menippean	Mertonian
marveller	matriline	mechanics	Meliboean	meniscate	mesangial
masculate	matriliny	mechanise	meliceris	meniscoid	mesangium
masculine	matrimony	mechanism	meliorate	Mennonist	mesaxonic
masculist	matronage	mechanist	meliorism	Mennonite	mescaline
mashallah	matronism	mechanize	meliorist	menologia	mescalism
masochism	matronize	mechoacan	meliority	Menominee	mesentery
masochist	mattamore	meclozine	melismata	menopause	meshugaas
masonried	matterful	Mec Vannin	melituria	menseless	meshuggah
mason-wasp	matt paint	medallion	mellilite	Menshevik	mesmerian
mason-work	matutinal	medallise	mellitate	menstrual	mesmerise
Masoretic	maudlinly	medallist	mellotron	menstruum	mesmerism
massacrer	Maugrabee	medallize	melocoton	mensurate	mesmerist
massagist	Maugrabin	medal play	melodious	mental age	mesmerize
Massalian	maulstick	mediaeval	melodizer	mentalism	mesne lord
Massaliot	maunderer	median fin	melodrama	mentalist	mesoblast
mass-house	Mauritian	mediately	melodrame	mentality	mesocolic
Massilian	mausolean	mediation	melologue	mentalize	mesocolon
Massiliot	mausoleum	mediative	melomania	mental set	mesoconch
massiness	mawkishly	mediatize	melomanic	mentation	mesocracy
massively	maxillary	mediatory	melongena	menticide	mesogloea
massivity	maximally	mediatrix	melongene	mentioned	mesomeric
mass media	maximizer	medicable	melon-hole	mentioner	mesomorph
Massorete	may as well	medically	melon pink	mentorial	mesonotum
mass-penny	May beetle	medicinal	melon-seed	mepacrine	mesopause

mesophase	methanate	micrology	milk ridge	mindfully	mischarge
mesophile	methanoic	micromere	milk round	minefield	mischieve
mesophyll	metheglin	micromesh	milk shake	minelayer	mischoice
mesophyte	methodise	micromole	milk snake	Minervois	mischoose
mesoscale	Methodism	micronize	milksoppy	mine shaft	mis-cipher
mesospore	Methodist	micro-oven	milkstone	mine-stone	miscolour
mesotherm	methodize	micropore	milk stout	miniature	misconvey
mesotonic	methonium	micropsia	milk sugar	mini-break	miscopied
mess about	methought	micropyle	milk-toast	minidress	miscopies
messagery	methoxide	microsome	milk tooth	minimally	miscreant
Messalian	methylate	microtext	milk train	minimizer	miscreate
Messalina	methylene	microtine	milk-vetch	mining bee	misdecide
messaline	methyl red	microtome	milk white	Minipiano	misdemean
Messapian	metoecism	microtone	millboard	mini-rugby	misderive
messenger	metonymic	microtron	mill-clack	miniscule	misdesert
Messenian	metreless	microunit	millenary	miniskirt	misdirect
Messianic	metricate	microwatt	millenism	ministrer	misemploy
Messieurs	metrician	microwave	millenium	minitrack	miserable
messiness	metricise	microweld	millennia	Minkowski	miserably
mestranol	metricize	micturate	millepede	Minnesong	miserhood
metabasis	metric ton	mid-circle	millepore	Minnesota	misesteem
metabolic	metroland	middle age	Millerian	minor axis	misfeasor
metacarpi	metrology	middle ear	millering	minor suit	misfigure
metaconal	metronome	middle leg	Millerism	minor term	misformed
metaconid	metronymy	middleman	millerite	minoxidil	misgiving
metacryst	metroplex	middlemen	Millerite	mint-green	misgotten
metagnome	metropole	middle rib	mill-horse	mint julep	misgovern
metagnomy	Meursault	middle way	mill-house	mint price	misgrowth
metalaxyl	mevalonic	mid-heaven	milligram	mint sauce	misguided
metalegal	Mezentian	midinette	millinery	mint-sling	misguider
metallide	mezzanine	Midlander	millioned	mint state	mishandle
metalline	mezza voce	Midrashic	millionth	minueting	mishanter
metalling	mezzotint	Midrashim	millipede	minuscule	mishappen
metallise	mianserin	mid-season	millivolt	minus sign	Mishnical
metallist	miasmatic	mid-square	mill-lands	minute-gun	misinform
metallize	micaceous	midstream	millocrat	minuteman	misjudger
metalloid	mica-slate	midsummer	mill-power	Minuteman	misleader
metalmark	mica valve	midwicket	Mills bomb	minutemen	misleared
metalogic	Michelson	midwifely	mill-scale	Minutemen	misliking
metalwork	micky-mick	midwifery	mill-shaft	minuterie	mislippen
metameric	Micoquian	midwinter	millstone	minutiose	misliving
metanotum	microbeam	mightiest	mill-wheel	minutious	mislocate
metaphase	microbial	mightless	milometer	minxishly	mismanage
metaphone	microbian	migmatite	Miltonian	mirabelle	misnumber
metaphony	microbody	migration	Miltonise	miracidia	misoccupy
metaplasm	microbore	migrative	Miltonism	mirligoes	misogynic
metatarsi	microcard	migratory	Miltonist	mirrorize	misoneism
metatonic	Microcard	mild steel	Miltonize	mirthless	misoneist
Metawileh	microchip	mile-eater	miltwaste	mirthsome	misorient
metaxylem	microcode	miles away	mimiambic	misadvice	misosophy
metecious	microcook	milestone	mimically	misadvise	mispickel
meteorise	microcopy	milioline	mimicking	misallied	mispraise
meteorism	microcosm	miliolite	mimicries	misallies	misprisal
meteorite	microcyst	militance	minacious	misassign	misprizer
meteorize	microcyte	militancy	minareted	misaunter	misquoter
meteoroid	microfilm	militaria	minargent	misbecome	misreader
meteorous	microform	milk fever	minarichi	misbehave	misrecite
meterless	microglia	milk float	minced pie	misbelief	misreckon
meter maid	microgram	milk-glass	mincemeat	misbeseem	misrelate
metestrus	microinch	milk-house	minchiate	misbestow	misrender
metformin	microlite	milkiness	mincingly	mischance	misrepeat
methadone	microlith	milk punch	mind-curer	mischancy	misreport

misscript	moderated	moneyless	monoptote	moor-grass	mosaicked
misshaped	moderator	moneywort	monopulse	moor-palms	Mosaic law
misshapen	moderatos	Mongolian	monorchid	moorpunky	Mosaic Law
missilery	modernise	Mongolise	monorchis	moorstone	moschatel
missiness	modernism	mongolism	monorheme	moose-bird	Moses boat
missional	modernist	Mongolize	monorhine	moose bush	moskeneer
missioned	modernity	Mongoloid	monorhyme	moose milk	Mosleyite
missioner	modernize	mongooses	monosemic	moosewood	mosquital
Miss Molly	modiation	mongrelly	monoskier	moose-yard	moss agate
Miss Nancy	modillion	monitress	monosomic	moot court	Mössbauer
misspeech	modularly	monkeyish	monosperm	moralizer	moss-berry
miss plant	modulator	monkeyism	monospore	moralless	moss green
Miss Right	Moeso-Goth	monkey-man	monostich	moralness	moss-grown
miss sahib	Moguntine	monkey-nut	monostome	moral play	moss-house
miss stays	moistener	monkey-pot	monotoned	moratoria	mossiness
mistemper	moistless	monkeypox	monotonic	morbidity	mossy horn
mister man	moistness	monkishly	monotower	morbility	mostlings
misthrive	molarized	Monk-Latin	monotreme	mordacity	mostwhere
mistified	molassied	monkshood	monotropa	mordantly	mot d'ordre
mistigris	Moldavian	monk's-seam	monotropy	mordicant	moth-borer
mistiness	moldavite	monk's shoe	monotypic	Morellian	moth-eaten
mistletoe	molecular	monoamine	monovular	Morescoes	mother hen
Mitannian	mole drain	monobasic	monoxylic	morganise	mothering
mitchella	molehilly	monoblast	monoxylon	Morganism	mother wit
Mithraeum	mole snake	mono-cable	Monroeism	Morganist	mothproof
Mithraism	molestful	monoceros	Monsignor	morganite	motivated
Mithraist	molestive	monochord	monsoonal	morganize	motivator
mitigable	molindone	monocline	mons pubis	morindone	moto-cross
mitigator	moll-heron	monocoque	monstrous	Mormondom	motocross
Mitnagged	mollified	monocracy	Montanian	Mormoness	motorable
mitre gear	mollifier	monocular	Montanism	Mormonish	motor area
mitrewort	mollifies	monoculus	Montanist	Mormonism	motor bike
mitriform	molluscan	monocycle	Montanize	Mormonist	motorbike
mitsumata	molluscum	monocytic	monthlies	Mormonite	motor boat
mitt joint	Mollweide	monodelph	month-long	Mormon war	motorcade
mixedness	mollyhawk	monodrama	month's man	mormoopid	motor camp
Mixmaster	mollymawk	monodromy	monticule	morningly	motor home
mixoploid	Molossian	monoecism	Montonero	morphemic	motorhome
mizen-mast	molossine	monogamic	monzonite	morphined	motorless
mizen-sail	molybdate	monogenic	moodiness	morphogen	motor root
mizen yard	molybdite	monograph	mood swing	morphonic	motor unit
mnemonics	molybdous	monoicous	moon-blind	morphosis	motor wind
mnemonist	mom-and-pop	monolater	moon buggy	Morrisian	mouchette
mnemonize	momentary	monolatry	moon-clock	Morrisite	mouldable
Moabitess	momentous	monolayer	moon-daisy	Morse code	mould-loft
Moabitish	monachise	monologic	moon-faced	morselize	mould-made
moa-hunter	monachism	monologue	moon flask	mortalism	mouldwarp
moanfully	monachize	monomachy	mooniness	mortality	mouldy fig
moaningly	monadical	monomania	mooningly	mortalize	mound-bird
mobbishly	monadnock	monomeric	moonlight	mortal sin	moundsman
mob-handed	monarchal	monometer	moon-month	mortar-bed	mountable
mobiliary	monarchic	monomyary	moon probe	mortarium	mountainy
mobilizer	monastery	mononymic	moonquake	mortcloth	mournival
mobocracy	Monastral	monophagy	moonraker	mortgagee	mousebird
mockeries	monatomic	monophone	moonscape	mortgager	mouse deer
mockernut	Mondayish	monophony	moonshine	mortgagor	mouse-fish
mock goose	monecious	monophyly	moonshiny	mortician	mouse hare
mockingly	money-back	monopitch	moonstomp	mortified	mouse-hawk
mock olive	moneybags	monoplane	moonstone	mortifier	mouse-hole
modelling	money-belt	monoploid	Moon's type	mortifies	mouse-hunt
modellist	money-bill	monopolar	moonwards	mosaicism	mouselike
model-room	money crop	monopsony	Moorcroft	mosaicist	mouseling

mouse moth	mugginses	murder log	mutilator	mystifies	narratory
mouseship	mujahedin	murder-man	mutoscope	mythicise	narratrix
mousetail	mujahidin	murder one	muttering	mythicism	narrow axe
mousetrap	mulattoes	murderous	mutton-fat	mythicist	narrow-cut
mousiness	mulctuary	murder rap	mutualise	mythicize	narrowest
mousseron	mule chest	muricated	mutualism	mythology	narrowish
moustache	mulga tree	murkiness	mutualist	mythomane	narrow way
Moustiers	mulga wire	murmuring	mutuality	myxamoeba	nasal bone
mouthable	muliebral	murmurish	mutualize	myxoedema	nascently
mouthfuls	mulierose	murmurous	mutuation	myxospore	naseberry
mouth glue	Müllerian	Murphy bed	muzziness	myxovirus	Nassanoff
mouth-harp	mullioned	murrained	my cabbage	myzostome	Nasserism
mouthiest	mullipuff	Murray cod	mycelioid	Nabataean	Nasserist
mouthless	mully-grub	musaceous	Mycenaean	Nabeshima	Nasserite
mouthpart	multicore	muscadine	mycobiont	nabobship	nastiness
mouth ring	multifoil	muscarine	mycologic	nache-bone	Natal lily
mouth root	multifold	muscicole	mycophage	nagelfluh	Natal plum
mouthwash	multifont	muscle car	mycophagy	naggingly	Natal sore
move about	multiform	muscle-man	mycophile	Nagualism	Natatores
move along	multigene	muscology	mycotoxin	Nahuatlan	natheless
move house	multigerm	muscovado	mycterism	nail brush	native cat
movie-goer	multihull	muscovite	myctophid	naileress	native dog
movie star	Multilith	Muscovite	mydriasis	nail-maker	native oak
Movietone	multipara	musefully	mydriatic	nail-plate	native son
moving day	multipath	museology	myelocele	nail punch	natrolite
moving-man	multiplet	museumish	myelocyte	naissance	nattiness
moving map	multiplex	mushiness	myelogram	naiveness	naturally
Moygashel	multipole	mushroomy	myelomata	naked boys	nature-god
Mozarabic	multi-role	mushy peas	myenteric	nakedness	naturelle
Mozartian	multi-task	musically	my guess is	nakhlitic	Naugahyde
Mr Charley	multitask	music book	mylohyoid	nalidixic	naughtier
mridangam	multi-tier	music case	mylonitic	namaycush	naughtily
Mr Justice	multitude	music hall	myocardia	name after	naumachia
Mrs Grundy	multi-user	musicless	myoclonic	name-check	nausea gas
Mr Speaker	multiwall	music-roll	myoclonus	name-child	nautilite
muck about	mumbudget	music-room	Myocrisin	name names	nautiloid
muck-a-muck	mumchance	music type	myofibril	name-plate	naval base
muckender	mum-figure	music-wire	myoglobin	nameplate	Navarrese
muckerish	mummeries	musketade	myologist	name-story	Navarrois
muckiness	Mummerset	musketeer	myomatous	Namierian	navelwort
muckraker	mummichog	musketoon	myoneural	Namierite	navicular
muck sweat	mummified	muskiness	myopathic	Namierize	navigable
mucky-muck	mummifies	musk melon	myoseptum	namma hole	navigably
mucolytic	mummiform	Muskogean	myriorama	nancified	navigator
mucronate	mum-mumble	musk plant	myristate	Nandi bear	naya paisa
mudaliyar	mummy-case	musk shrew	myrmecoid	nanny goat	naysasaid
mud-dauber	mummychog	Muslimism	myrmekite	nanometre	naysasays
muddiness	mummy-pits	musselled	myrmeleon	Nanticoke	Nazaritic
muddledly	mummy's boy	mussel mud	myrmicine	naphthene	Naziphile
muddledom	mumpsimus	mussiness	myrobalan	naphthous	nearabout
mud-hopper	mundanely	Mussolini	myrrh tree	Napierian	near money
mudlarker	mundanity	Mussulman	mystacial	napkining	near of kin
mud-logger	mundatory	mussurana	mystagogy	nappy rash	nearshore
mud minnow	mundungus	mustachio	mysterial	narcissus	near sight
mud-sucker	Municheer	mustafina	mysteries	narcolept	near thing
mud-turtle	municipal	mustanger	mysticete	narcotise	neat-house
muff diver	municipia	mustarder	mysticise	narcotism	neat's-foot
muffineer	municipio	musteline	mysticism	narcotist	nebenkern
muffin man	munjistin	muster out	mysticity	narcotize	Nebraskan
muffledly	murder bag	mustiness	mysticize	narratage	nebuliser
mugearite	murderess	must needs	mystified	narration	nebulizer
mugginess	murderish	mutagenic	mystifier	narrative	necessary

necessity	neologism	neurology	nickel bag	night-work	noiseless
neck-break	neologist	neuromast	nickelian	nigricant	noises off
neck-canal	neologize	neuromata	nickeline	Nigritian	noisiness
neckcloth	neo-Nazism	neuromere	nickelite	nigritude	noisomely
neckinger	Neononian	neuropath	nickelled	nigrosine	no kidding
neck-piece	neon tetra	neurotomy	nickelous	Nile perch	nolle-pros
neck-towel	neopentyl	Neustrian	nicknamer	Nilometer	nomadical
neck-verse	neophilia	neuterdom	nickpoint	nilpotent	no-meaning
necrology	neophilic	neutrally	nick-stick	nimbu-pani	nomically
necrotise	neophobia	neutretto	nicotiana	Nimrodian	nominable
necrotize	neophobic	neutrinos	nicotined	nine-holes	nominally
necrotype	neoplasia	neutronic	nicotinic	ninepence	nominator
nectareal	neotenous	never a one	nictation	ninepenny	nominatum
nectarean	neoterism	never ever	nictitant	ninetieth	no mistake
nectarian	neotocite	never-fail	nictitate	ninetyish	nomocanon
nectaries	nepenthes	never fear	niddering	ninhydrin	nomocracy
nectarine	nephalism	never heed	niellated	ninth part	nomograph
nectarium	nepheline	Never Land	niffiness	nip bottle	non-access
nectarous	nepheloid	never mind	niff-naffy	nipcheese	non-action
needfully	nephology	nevermind	niftiness	nipperkin	nonameric
neediness	nephritic	nevermore	Niger seed	nippiness	nonce-word
needle-bug	nephritis	Newcastle	niggardly	nippingly	non-coding
needleful	nephrosis	new-collar	niggerdom	Nipponese	non compos
needle gap	nephrotic	new-create	niggerish	Nirvanist	non-concur
needle-gun	Neptunian	New Critic	niggerism	Nissen hut	non-driver
needle ice	Neptunism	new-fallen	nigger toe	Nissl body	nonentity
needleman	Neptunist	newfangle	night-bell	Nithsdale	none other
needs must	neptunite	new ground	nightbird	nit-picker	non-finite
Néel point	neptunium	New Jersey	night-blue	nitpicker	nongenary
Néel spike	neroli oil	Newmanism	night boat	Nitralloy	non-greasy
nefandous	nervation	Newmanite	night bolt	nitratine	nonillion
nefarious	nervature	Newmanize	night-cart	nitration	non-Jewish
negatival	nerve cell	Newmarket	nightclub	nitrified	nonjurant
neglecter	nerve-cord	newsagent	night-crow	nitrifier	nonjuring
neglector	nerve-knot	newsbreak	nightfall	nitrifies	nonleaded
negligent	nerveless	newsbrief	night-gear	nitro-acid	non-lethal
negotiant	nerve-path	news butch	nightglow	Nitrolime	non-linear
negotiate	nerve-ring	new school	nightgown	nitronium	non liquet
Negrillos	nerviness	newsflash	nighthawk	nitrosate	non-member
negritize	nervosity	news hound	night-herd	nitroxide	non-native
Negritude	nervously	newsiness	night-lamp	nitwitted	non-normal
negro-head	nescience	newspaper	night lark	Nivernois	non-object
Negroidal	nessberry	newsprint	nightless	Nixie tube	no nothing
Negroland	Nestorian	news-sheet	night-life	no-account	nonpareil
Negroness	net-fisher	news-stand	nightlife	Noachical	non-paying
Nehruvian	nether man	newswoman	night-line	nobbiness	non-person
neighbour	netminder	Newtonian	night-long	nobiliary	non placet
neisseria	net-player	Newtonist	nightmare	noble hawk	non-plural
Nelson eye	net profit	new towner	night-rail	nobleness	non-porous
Nelsonian	net system	new wavish	night-robe	Nobodaddy	non-profit
nelumbium	networker	New Yorker	night safe	no chicken	non-racial
nematogen	neuralgia	next of kin	night-side	no comment	non-random
nemertean	neuralgic	next world	night-soil	noctidial	non-reader
nemertine	neural net	Niagarian	nightspot	noctiluca	non-regent
nemophila	neuration	nialamide	night star	nocturnal	non-return
neocortex	neuraxial	nibble-nip	night-stop	noddingly	nonreward
neodamode	neuridine	nibble off	night-tide	noddy-shot	non-sexist
neodymium	neurinoma	niccolite	night-time	node point	non-sexual
neohexane	neuristor	niccolous	night-walk	nodulated	non-smoker
neolithic	neurocyte	nice as pie	nightward	no effects	non-tenure
neologian	neuroglia	nice Nelly	nightwear	no flies on	non-treaty
neologise	neurogram	nick-eared	night-wind	no-fly zone	non-united

non-valent	nose putty	nuisancey	nylon salt	obstinacy	Oddfellow
non-verbal	nose-thirl	nullibist	nymphaeum	obstinate	odd jobber
non-viable	nose trick	nullified	nymphalid	obstruent	odd-job man
non-voting	nose wheel	nullifier	nymphette	obstupefy	odd man out
non-worker	nosheries	nullifies	nymphical	obtention	odd parity
noodledom	nosophile	nullipara	nymphlike	obtrusion	odiferous
noodleism	nostalgia	nulliplex	nystagmic	obtrusive	odorosity
no offence	nostalgic	nullipore	nystagmus	obtundent	odorously
nook-shaft	no starter	nullisome	oak coffin	obturator	odourless
noologist	Nostratic	nullisomy	oak-pruner	obumbrate	oeconomus
noontimes	notabilia	nullities	oarswoman	obvention	oedematic
noosphere	not a cheep	null space	oast house	obversely	oedometer
Nootka fir	notaphily	number one	oat burner	obversion	oenanthic
nootropic	notarikon	number six	oat-celled	obvertend	oenanthol
no problem	not a speck	Number ten	obbligato	obviation	oenomancy
nordcaper	not a thing	Number Ten	obconical	obviative	oenomania
Nordicism	not at home	number two	obcordate	obviously	oenophile
Nordicist	not be in it	numbingly	obduction	occipital	oenothera
norlander	notchback	numbskull	obedience	occludent	oesophagi
normalise	notchiest	numerable	obediency	occlusion	oestrogen
normalism	notepaper	numerably	obeisance	occlusive	of an age to
normality	nothingly	numeraire	O be joyful	occultism	of a sudden
normalize	nothing to	numerator	obeliscal	occultist	of a surety
Normanise	nothosaur	numerical	obeseness	occupance	off-bearer
Normanism	notionary	numero uno	obfuscate	occupancy	off camera
Normanist	notionate	numinosum	objectant	occurrent	off-campus
Normanize	notionist	nummulary	objectify	occurring	off-centre
Normannic	not likely	nummuline	objection	occursion	off chance
normative	not much on	nummulite	objectise	oceanaria	off colour
normocyte	not nearly	nuncupate	objective	Oceanides	off course
Norseland	notochord	nunnation	objectize	ocean pout	off cutter
Norseness	notonecta	nunneries	objet d'art	oceanward	off-design
Northants	notoriety	nun's cloth	objicient	ocean wave	offendant
north-east	notorious	Nuremberg	objurgate	oceanwise	offending
North-East	not proven	nurse cell	obligable	ocellated	offensive
northerly	no-trumper	nurse-crop	obligator	ochlocrat	offerable
northland	nougatine	nurse-fish	obligedly	ocotillos	offertory
Northland	nourisher	nurse-frog	obliquely	octachord	offhanded
northmost	nouvelles	nurseling	obliquing	octagonal	office boy
northness	Novachord	nursemaid	obliquity	octahedra	officeful
north pole	novelette	nurseries	obliviate	octameric	office-man
North Pole	novelness	nurse-tend	oblivious	octameter	officerly
North Star	novelties	nurse-tree	oblongish	octanoate	officiant
northward	Novembery	nursingly	obnoxiety	octaploid	officiary
north-west	novemdial	nurturant	obnoxious	octastich	officiate
North-West	novendial	nutburger	obreption	octastyle	officinal
north wind	novennial	nut-butter	obscenely	Octateuch	officious
Norway rat	noviciate	nut cutlet	obscenity	octave key	off-island
Norwegian	novilunar	nutjobber	obscurant	octennial	off-limits
nor'wester	novitiate	nutmegged	obscurely	octillion	offloader
nor'-wester	novocaine	nutriment	obscurity	Octobrist	off-pricer
nose ahead	Novocaine	nutrition	obsecrate	octocoral	off-putter
nosebleed	nowhither	nutritive	obsequent	octoploid	off ration
nose-candy	noxiously	nutriture	obsequial	octopodan	off-roader
nose drops	no you don't	nut runner	obsequies	octopodes	offsaddle
nose flute	nuclearly	nuts about	observant	octopuses	off-screen
nose-heavy	nucleated	nuts in May	obsession	octostyle	off-season
nose of wax	nucleator	nuttiness	obsessive	Octoteuch	off-shears
nose-paint	nucleolar	nut-weevil	obsidious	ocularist	offspring
nose paste	nucleolus	nux vomica	obsolesce	oculiform	off-street
nose-piece	nucleonic	nuzzerana	obstetric	oculistic	off-target
nose print	nugacious	nyctalope	obstetrix	odalisque	off the air

off the bit	oligomery	one-suiter	on the road	operatize	orchestre
off the map	oligopoly	one-to-many	on the rope	opercular	orchideal
off theory	oliprance	one-upness	on the Rory	operculum	orchidist
off the peg	olive-back	one-valued	on the sick	operosely	orchotomy
offuscate	olive-bark	ongoingly	on the side	operosity	orderable
of its kind	olive drab	on holiday	on the skew	ophiolite	order arms
of one mind	olive-like	oniomania	on the spot	ophiology	order book
of oneself	olivenite	onion dome	on the spur	Ophiuchus	order form
of one's own	olive-plum	onion-like	on the take	ophiuroid	orderless
of purpose	Oliverian	onion-skin	on the tick	ophthalmy	orderlies
oftenness	olive tree	onlooking	on the tilt	opilionid	order mark
oftentime	olive-yard	onomastic	on the town	opiniated	order wire
of that ilk	ololiuqui	onomatopy	on the trot	opinional	ordinaire
of the year	ombrology	on one hand	on the turf	opinioned	ordinance
of treason	ombudsman	on one's arm	on the turn	opodeldoc	ordinator
ogee curve	ombudsmen	on one's day	on the wane	opponency	Oregonian
ogreishly	omegatron	on one's ear	on the wind	opportune	organ-bird
ohmically	ominously	on one side	on the wing	opposable	organdies
oikoumene	omissible	on one's own	on thin ice	oppressed	organelle
oil-beetle	ommatidia	on one's pat	ontically	oppressor	organette
oil burner	omnifocal	on one's tod	ontogenic	oppugnant	organetto
oil colour	omnirange	on one's way	ontologic	opsimathy	organical
oil-cooled	omophagia	on passage	on welfare	optically	organific
oiled-down	omophagic	on purpose	onymously	optic axis	organized
oiled silk	omphaloid	on receive	on your way	optic disc	organizer
oil engine	on a budget	on request	oogenesis	optic lobe	organless
oil heater	on account	onslaught	oogenetic	optimally	organ loft
oil-strike	on a charge	on stand-by	oological	optimific	organosol
oil string	onanistic	on station	ooplasmic	optimizer	organ pipe
oil switch	on a string	on the ball	Oort cloud	optometer	organ stop
oil tanker	on a sudden	on the bash	opacified	optometry	organzine
okey-dokey	on average	on the beam	opacifier	optomotor	orgiastic
Oklahoman	on balance	on the beer	opacifies	optophone	orgillous
Old Bailey	on benefit	on the bias	opal-agate	opulently	orientate
old boy net	onbethink	on the boil	opalesque	opuscular	orienteer
old codger	once again	on the case	opal glass	opuscules	orientite
Old French	oncogenic	on the club	open-armed	opusculum	orifacial
old fustic	oncolitic	on the cuff	open chain	oraculate	orificial
old Indian	oncologic	on the dead	open class	oraculous	oriflamme
old leaven	oncolysis	on the dole	open cover	orangeade	Origenism
old master	oncolytic	on the fang	open cycle	orange bat	Origenist
old school	oncometer	on the feed	open-ended	Orangeism	originant
old sledge	on deposit	on the fret	open-faced	Orangeman	originary
old soaker	on draught	on the game	open field	Orangemen	originate
old stager	one and all	on the hoof	open-heart	orange-oil	Orkneyman
old-wifish	one-design	on the hook	open house	orange-red	Orleanian
oleaceous	one-for-one	on the hour	open newel	orang-utan	Orleanism
olecranal	one-handed	on the jump	open range	orangutan	Orleanist
olecranon	one in five	on the lees	open score	orational	ornithine
oleic acid	one-legged	on the line	open shelf	orationer	ornithoid
olenellid	one-lunger	on the make	open-skies	oratorial	orobanche
oleograph	one moment	on the mark	open space	oratorian	orocratic
oleometer	one nation	on the mend	open stage	oratories	orofacial
oleoresin	one-old-cat	on the move	open-stock	oratorios	orography
olfaction	one-reeler	on the nail	open-tread	oratorize	orologist
olfactive	onerosity	on the nose	open water	orbicular	orometric
olfactory	onerously	on the outs	open woods	orbivirus	orotidine
oligaemia	one-seater	on the pill	operatics	orb-weaver	orphanage
oligaemic	one's Maker	on the piss	operating	orcharded	orphandom
oligarchy	one's needs	on the prod	operation	orchester	orphanise
oligistic	one's scene	on the rack	operatise	orchestic	orphanize
Oligocene	one's spies	on the rise	operative	orchestra	orpharion

Orphic egg	other than	out of play	oven-ready	over-large	overstood
orphreyed	otherways	out of rule	oven timer	overlarge	overstrew
Orpington	otherwise	out of step	over again	overlayer	overstudy
orris root	otoconium	out of sync	overalled	overlearn	overstuff
ortanique	otolithic	out of time	overaward	overlight	overswarm
or the like	otologist	out-of-town	overblown	overlying	oversweep
orthocone	otoplasty	out of true	overboard	overmatch	oversweet
orthodoxy	otorrhoea	out of tune	overborne	overmount	overswell
orthoepic	otoscopic	out of turn	overbound	overnight	overswing
orthoform	otter tail	out of wind	overbrood	overpaint	overtaker
orthology	ottocento	out of work	overbuild	overpedal	overterve
orthopter	oubliette	out-parish	overcarry	overpitch	overthink
orthoptic	oughtness	outplacer	overcatch	overplant	overthrew
orthostat	Ouled Nail	outporter	overcheck	overpoise	overthrow
orthotist	Our Father	outpreach	overcivil	overpower	overtired
orthotone	ouroboros	outputter	overclimb	overpress	overtness
Orwellian	ourselves	outraging	overcloak	overprice	overtower
oscillate	out and out	outreason	overclose	overprint	over to you
oscitancy	outasight	outreckon	overcloud	overprize	overtrace
os frontis	out at feed	out-relief	overcomer	over proof	overtrade
osmanthus	outbacker	outréness	overcount	overproof	overtrain
osmic acid	out-basket	outridden	overcover	overproud	overtrawl
osmically	outbellow	outriding	overcreep	overpunch	overtread
osmometer	outbranch	outrigged	overcroft	overquick	overtrick
osmometry	outbrazen	outrigger	overcross	overrapid	overtrump
osmophile	outcoming	outrunner	overcrowd	overreach	overtrust
osmophore	out-county	outsearch	overcrust	overreact	over-under
osmundine	outcrying	out-sentry	overdated	overready	overvalue
osseously	outcurved	outsetter	overdraft	overrider	overvault
Ossianism	outcurved	outshifts	overdrank	overright	overwatch
ossicular	outdoorsy	outshrill	overdrawn	overrigid	overwater
ossiculum	outermost	outside in	overdress	overripen	overweary
ossifrage	outerwear	outside of	overdried	overrisen	overweigh
osso bucco	outfitter	outskirts	overdrink	overroast	overwhelm
ossuaries	outgallop	outsource	overdrive	overruler	overworld
ostectomy	outgassed	outspoken	overdrove	oversales	overwound
ostension	outgiving	outsprang	overdrunk	overscore	overwrite
ostensive	outgrowth	outspread	overeager	oversexed	ovibovine
ostensory	outhauler	outspring	overearly	overshade	oviductal
ostentate	outhector	outstrain	overerupt	oversharp	oviferous
osteocyte	outhumour	outstream	overexert	overshine	ovigerous
osteoderm	out island	outstride	overfleet	overshoot	oviparity
osteology	outjockey	outstrike	overflies	overshort	oviparous
osteopath	outjuggle	outsucken	overfloat	oversight	ovivorous
osteotome	outlabour	out-thrown	overflood	oversized	ovomucoid
osteotomy	outlander	out-thrust	overflown	overskirt	ovotestis
ostinatos	outlet box	out-tongue	overflush	oversleep	ovulation
ostleress	outlinear	out-travel	overglaze	overslide	ovulatory
ostracion	outlustre	outwardly	overglide	overslung	owdacious
ostracise	outmaster	outwinter	overgloom	oversmoke	owlet-moth
ostracism	outnumber	out with it	overgorge	overspeak	owl monkey
ostracite	out of a hat	outworker	overgraze	overspeed	owl-parrot
ostracize	out of a job	Ovaherero	overgreat	overspend	owl-pigeon
ostringer	out of curl	ovalbumin	overhappy	overspill	ownerless
Ostrogoth	out of date	ovaliform	overhardy	overspoke	ownership
Oswego tea	outoffice	ovational	overharsh	overspray	oxacillin
other half	out of form	ovationed	overhaste	overstaff	oxazolone
otherkins	out of gear	oven-bread	overhasty	overstain	oxbow lake
other life	out of hand	oven-cloth	overhorse	overstand	ox-eye arch
otherness	out of line	oven-glass	overissue	overstate	Oxfordian
other some	out of love	oven glove	overjoyed	oversteer	Oxfordish
other such	out of luck	ovenproof	overladen	overstock	Oxfordism

oxidation	paillette	palmistry	panoramic	parabolic	paratroop
oxidative	painfully	palmitate	panorpoid	parabrake	parbuckle
oximetric	pain perdu	palm-print	pan-sexual	parachute	parcelize
oxybaphon	pain point	palm sugar	pansified	Paraclete	parcelled
oxygenase	pain-proof	palm swift	Panslavic	paraconid	parcenary
oxygenate	paintable	palm viper	pansophic	Pará cress	parc fermé
oxygenise	paintball	Palmyrene	pantagamy	paracrine	parcheesi
oxygenize	paint bomb	palominos	pantaleon	paradeful	parch mark
oxygenous	painterly	paloverde	pantalets	paradisal	parchment
oxy-helium	paintiest	palpation	pantaloon	paradisic	pardalote
oxyphilic	paintless	palpebral	pantdress	paradores	paregoric
oxytropis	paintress	palpiform	pantheism	paradoses	parenesis
oysterage	paint-root	palpitant	pantheist	paradosis	parentage
oyster bed	paint shop	palpitate	pantie leg	paradoxer	parentela
oystering	paintwork	palsgrave	pantihose	paradoxic	parenting
oysterish	pair-horse	Palsgrave	pantiling	parafango	parfilage
oyster-man	pair-oared	paltriest	pantingly	paraffiny	parfleche
oysterous	pair royal	Paludrine	Pantocain	parafovea	pargasite
ozocerite	Pakistani	palustral	pantology	paraglide	pargeting
ozokerite	Pakkawood	Pampangan	pantomime	paragnath	parge-work
ozonation	palace car	pampas cat	pantoufle	paragnost	parhelion
ozone hole	palaeosol	pampas fox	pantropic	paragogic	parhypate
ozoneless	palaestra	pampootie	pantryman	paragraph	pariah dog
pacemaker	palampore	panaceist	pantrymen	Pará grass	pariahdom
pace-stick	palankeen	Panama hat	pantskirt	paragutta	parichnos
pachycaul	palanquin	pan-Arabic	pants suit	paralalia	paring bee
pachyderm	Palantype	panatella	pantyhose	paralegal	pari passu
pachynema	palatable	Panatrope	paparazzi	paralexia	Paris blue
pachytene	palatably	pan-Celtic	paparazzo	paralexic	Paris club
pacifarin	palatally	panchayat	paperback	paralogia	parisonic
pacifical	palaverer	panchrony	paper-bank	paralysed	parity bit
packaging	pale-faced	pancosmic	paper-bark	paralyser	Parkerize
pack-cloth	Paleocene	pancratic	paper clip	paralyses	Parkesine
pack drill	Paleozoic	panderess	paper-coal	paralysis	parkwards
packed out	Palestine	panderism	paper doll	paralytic	parlatory
packet rat	paletoted	pandurate	paper-feed	paramatta	parleyvoo
pack-frame	palilalia	pandurina	paper game	paramedic	parlously
packhorse	Palladian	panegyric	paper girl	parameter	parlyaree
pack-house	palladium	panel-back	paperless	paramorph	parnassia
pack sheep	palladous	panel game	paper mill	paramount	parnassim
packstaff	Pallas cat	panelling	paper pulp	paramylum	Parnassus
pack-track	pallasite	panellist	paper-reed	paranasal	parochial
pack-train	palletise	panel show	paper sack	paranatal	parodical
pactional	palletize	panel wall	paper-spar	paranemic	paroecism
pactolian	palliasse	panel-work	paper tape	paranoiac	paroemiac
paddle-box	palliator	panettone	paper-thin	paranotal	paroicous
paddy-bird	pallidity	pan-German	paper town	paranotum	paromoeon
Paddyland	palmarian	panhandle	paper ware	paranymph	parosteal
Paddy mail	palmarosa	panic bolt	paper-wasp	parapatry	parotitic
pademelon	palmately	panicking	paperwork	parapegma	parotitis
pad mangle	palmation	pan-Ionian	papillary	parapeted	parqueted
pad-saddle	Palm Beach	panlectal	papillate	paraplane	parquetry
pad stitch	palm-borer	panlogism	papilloma	para-rhyme	parrakeet
paedagogy	palm civet	panmictic	papillose	parascend	parrhesia
paedarchy	Palm Court	panniered	papillote	parascene	parricide
paederast	palmellin	panniform	papillous	parasital	parr marks
paedogamy	palmettos	Pannonian	papulated	parasitic	parroting
pageantry	palm-heart	panograph	parabasal	paraskier	parrotism
page-paper	palm honey	panoistic	parabasis	parasoled	parrotize
page-proof	palminess	panoplied	parabiont	para-state	parrot-pea
paillasse	palmipede	panoplies	parabolae	parataxis	Parseeism
pailleted	palmister	panoramal	parabolas	parathion	parse-tree

parsimony	pasticcio	Paul Jones	pearlwort	pegmatite	pennanted
parsleyed	pastiness	paulownia	pear midge	pegmatoid	penniform
parsonage	pastorage	paunchier	peasantry	pegomancy	penniless
parsondom	pastorale	pauperage	pease-meal	pegtopped	penninite
parsoness	pastorali	pauperdom	pea-souper	peirastic	pennoncel
Parsonian	pastorate	pauperise	peat-house	Pekingese	penny ante
parsoning	pastosity	pauperism	peat-spade	Peking man	penny gaff
parsonish	pasturage	pauperize	pea-urchin	Pelasgian	pennyland
partaking	pasturing	pauperous	pea-weevil	pelecypod	penny pies
part hence	patch cord	paupiette	pebble-bed	Pelignian	penny post
parthenic	patchiest	pauseless	peccaries	pellagrin	penny wise
partially	patch lead	Pavlovian	peck order	pellet bow	pennywort
partified	patchouli	pawkiness	peck-right	pelleting	Penobscot
parti pris	patch-plug	pawn chain	Pecksniff	pelletise	pen-pusher
partition	patch reef	pawn storm	pecorinos	pelletize	penseroso
partitive	patch test	paxillose	pectinase	pellicule	pensioner
partogram	patchwork	pax Romana	pectinate	pellitory	pensively
part-owner	patellate	pay a score	pectineal	pellotine	penstemon
partridge	patent log	pay dearly	pectineus	Pelmanise	pentagram
part-timer	paternity	pay freeze	pectinite	Pelmanism	pentagrid
party boat	pathogeny	pay gravel	pectinous	Pelmanist	pen-tailed
party game	pathology	pay its way	pectolite	Pelmanize	pentalogy
party-goer	pathotype	Payloader	peculator	pelobatid	pentalpha
partyless	patiently	paymaster	pecuniary	pelophile	pentamery
party line	patinated	pay-off man	pecunious	peloriate	pentangle
partyness	patio door	pay packet	pedagogal	peltately	pentanoic
party plan	patio rose	paysagist	pedagogic	pelvic fin	pentapody
party-poop	patissier	pay toilet	pedagogue	pemphigus	pentarchy
party wall	patlander	pea-beetle	pedal boat	pempidine	pentarsic
party wire	Pat Malone	peaceable	pedal bone	penalties	pentathol
parvitude	Patmorean	peaceably	pedalling	pen and ink	Pentecost
Pascalian	Patna rice	peace camp	pedal note	Penbritin	penthouse
pas de chat	patriarch	peaceless	pedal pole	penceless	pentomino
pas de deux	patrician	peace pipe	pedantise	pencil box	Pentothal
pas glissé	Patrician	peace sign	pedantism	pencilled	pentoxide
paso doble	patricide	peace talk	pedantize	penciller	pentrough
passament	patriclan	peacetime	pedatifid	pendanted	penultima
pass check	patriline	pea-chafer	pede-cloth	pendently	penumbrae
pass-court	patriliny	peach-blow	pederasty	pendicler	penumbral
passement	patrimony	peacheroo	pediatric	Pendleton	penumbras
passenger	patriotic	peach fuzz	pedicator	pendragon	penurious
passepied	patristic	peachiest	pedicular	Pendragon	peperomia
passerine	patrol car	peach-palm	pedigreed	pendulant	pepperbox
passers-by	patrolled	peach tree	pediplain	pendulate	pepper gas
pass-guard	patroller	peacockly	pediplane	penduline	pepperina
passingly	patrolman	peacockry	pediunker	pendulous	peppering
passional	patrolmen	pea-combed	pedlarism	peneplain	pepperoni
passioned	patrology	pea-flower	pedocalic	penetrant	pepper pot
passivate	patronage	pea gravel	pedogenic	penetrate	Pepsi-Cola
passively	patronate	pea-jacket	pedologic	pen-friend	pepsinate
passivise	patroness	peakiness	pedomancy	penfriend	peptidase
passivism	patronise	pearl bulb	pedometer	pen holder	peptonise
passivist	patronite	pearl-bush	pedophile	penholder	peptonize
passivity	patronize	pearlfish	pedoscope	penicilli	Pepysiana
passivize	patterned	pearliest	pedotribe	penillion	peracarid
pass round	patterner	pearlitic	peduncled	peninsula	peracetic
pass water	patty-cake	pearlized	peel-house	penis-bone	peragrate
paste-down	paucality	pearl-like	peep-sight	penis-envy	perborate
pastelist	Paulician	pearl-opal	peer group	penistone	percaline
paste-over	Paulinism	pear-louse	peeringly	penitence	per capita
pasterned	Paulinist	pearl spar	peevishly	penitency	perceiver
paste-wash	Paulinize	pearlware	peg-legged	penknives	percenter

per centum	perisperm	perverted	phalangid	phlorizin	physicism
perceptum	perispore	perverter	phalanxed	phlyctena	physicist
perchance	peristome	peshmerga	phalanxes	phonation	physicked
perch-bolt	peristyle	peskiness	phalarope	phonatory	physic-nut
percheron	peritonea	pessaries	phalluses	phone bank	physisorb
perciform	peritrack	pessimise	phanariot	phone book	phytocide
percolate	peritreme	pessimism	phanotron	phonecard	phytogeny
per contra	peritrich	pessimist	phansigar	phonemics	phytolith
per curiam	peri-urban	pessimize	phantasma	phonetics	phytology
percussor	perjuries	pesterous	Pharaonic	phonetise	phytosaur
perdition	perkiness	pest-house	Pharisaic	phonetism	phytotomy
Père David	Perkinism	pesticide	pharmacal	phonetist	phytotron
peregrine	perlative	pestilent	Pharsalia	phonetize	Piagetian
pereiopod	perlemoen	pestology	pharyngal	phoney war	pia-matral
perennate	permalloy	Pétainism	pharynges	phoniness	pianistic
perennial	permanent	Pétainist	phase down	phonodisc	pianoless
perfecter	permeable	petalless	phaseless	phonofilm	pianolist
perfectly	permeance	petal-like	phase-lock	phonogram	piano roll
perfector	permeator	petalodic	phaseolin	phonolite	piano trio
perfectos	perminvar	petal ware	phase rule	phonology	piano wire
perfervid	permitted	petardeer	phasitron	phonotype	piazzetta
perfidity	permittee	petaurist	phellogen	phonotypy	Picassian
perfluent	permitter	petechiae	phenacite	phoronomy	Picco pipe
perforant	permutate	petechial	phenakite	phosphate	Picentine
perforate	permutite	peter-boat	phenazine	phosphene	piceworth
performer	pernettya	Peter-fish	Phenergan	phosphide	pickaback
perfumery	perniosis	petersham	phenetics	phosphine	pick a lock
perfusate	perorally	Petertide	phenetole	phosphite	pick-a-tree
perfusion	perorator	pethidine	Phenidone	phosphori	pickeerer
perfusive	perosmate	petillate	phenobarb	phossy jaw	pickerels
Pergamene	perovskia	petiolate	phenocopy	Photinian	picketing
pergunnah	peroxided	petiolule	phenogram	photo call	pickiness
periapsis	peroxidic	petit four	phenolase	photocall	pick-proof
peribolus	perpetual	petit jury	phenolate	photocell	pickpurse
periclase	perplexed	petrefact	phenology	photocopy	pickthank
Periclean	perradial	Petri dish	phenoloid	photoemit	picktooth
pericline	perrhenic	petrified	phenol red	photo-etch	pick-up arm
pericolic	perrotine	petrifies	phenomena	photogram	picnic ham
pericycle	persecute	Petrinism	phenotype	photolyse	picnicked
perifovea	persevere	petrogeny	phenoxide	photolyze	picnicker
Périgueux	persimmon	petrol cap	phenylate	photomask	picolinic
perihelia	persister	petroleum	phenylene	photonics	picrolite
perilling	personage	petrolize	phenytoin	photoplay	pictogram
perilymph	personate	petrology	pheromone	photoscan	pictorial
perimeter	person-day	petticoat	philander	photostat	picturing
perimetry	personify	pettiness	philately	Photostat	picturize
perimorph	personize	pettishly	philippic	phototube	pidginist
perinatal	personnel	petty cash	Philippic	phototype	pidginize
periodate	persuader	petty jury	philister	phrasally	piece down
periodize	Pertelote	petty whin	Philistia	phrenetic	piecemeal
perioecic	perthitic	petulance	phillyrea	phrenitic	piece-rate
periostea	pertinent	petulancy	philogyny	phrenitis	piecewise
peripatos	perturbed	phacoidal	philology	phthalate	piece-work
peripatus	perturber	phacolite	philomath	phthiocol	piecework
periphery	pertussal	phacolith	Philomela	phycology	pied goose
periphony	pertussis	Phaeacian	Philonian	phylarchy	Pied Piper
periplasm	perusable	phaenogam	Philonize	phyletism	pie-funnel
periproct	pervagate	phage type	philosoph	phyllitic	piepowder
perirenal	pervasion	phagocyte	phlebitic	phyllomic	pier glass
Periscian	pervasive	phagosome	phlebitis	phyllopod	pierrette
periscope	perveance	phalanger	phlogosis	phylogeny	pierrotic
perishing	pervenche	phalanges	phloretin	physician	pier-stake

pier-table	pine-mouse	piripiris	pityingly	planeness	Platonist
pietistic	pine-snake	piroplasm	pivotable	planeside	Platonize
pigeoneer	pine straw	pirouette	pivotally	planesman	platytera
pigeonite	piney wood	piscation	pivot foot	planetary	plausible
pigeon-pea	pinheaded	piscatory	pivot-hole	plane time	plausibly
piggeries	pinholder	piscicide	pivot word	planetoid	plaustral
piggishly	pinholing	pisciform	pixie hood	plane tree	play about
piggyback	pin-hooker	piscinity	pixie-like	plangency	play-actor
piggy bank	pinjrapol	pishrogue	pixie-path	planiform	play along
pig-headed	pink coral	Pismo clam	pixie-pear	planigale	play a part
pigheaded	Pinkerton	pisolitic	pixilated	planigram	play booty
Pig Island	pinkiness	piss about	pizotifen	planisher	play by ear
pigmeater	pink noise	piss-house	pizzicati	plankless	play-dough
pigmental	pinko-grey	pissingly	pizzicato	plank-road	played out
pigmented	pink paper	piss-proud	placarder	planktont	play false
pignerate	pink-stern	piss-taker	placating	plankways	playfight
pignorate	pinnacled	pistachio	placation	plankwise	playfully
pigtailed	pinnately	pistacite	placatory	Planorbis	playgoing
piked horn	pinnation	pistareen	placeable	plantable	playgroup
piked shoe	pinnay oil	pistoleer	place-book	plant-cane	play house
pikeperch	pinniform	pistolled	place card	plantless	playhouse
pikestaff	pinnulate	piston pin	place-kick	plantlike	play-lunch
pilau rice	PIN number	piston rod	placeless	plantling	playmaker
pile-drive	pinocytic	pit-bottom	placement	plantmilk	play smash
pilferage	Pinot Noir	pit cavity	place name	plantsman	play-table
pilgarlic	pin pallet	pitch axis	placentae	plantsmen	plaything
pilgrimed	pin-setter	pitch-dark	placental	planuloid	pleadable
pilgrimer	pin-stitch	pitchfork	placentas	plaquette	plea-house
pillar box	pinstripe	pitch-hole	placidity	plasma arc	plea-in-bar
pillarist	pintadera	pitchiest	plackless	plasmagel	plea-in-law
pillicock	pintailed	pitch into	placoderm	plasma jet	pleasable
pilloried	Pinterish	pitch-knot	placodont	plasmasol	pleasance
pillories	pint glass	pitchlike	placulate	plasmatic	pleasedly
pillorize	pint-sized	pitch-line	plague pit	plasmodia	please God
pilomotor	pint stoup	pitch-mark	plague-rat	plastered	pleasured
pilonidal	pin-tucked	pitch-opal	plain card	plasterer	pleasurer
pilot-bird	pious hope	pitch pine	plain cook	plasticky	plectrums
pilot-boat	piousness	pitch-pipe	plain hunt	plasticly	pleiomery
pilot-coat	pipe berth	pitchpole	plain jane	plastigel	pleiotaxy
pilot fish	pipe dream	pitch shot	plain Jane	plastique	plenarily
pilot hole	pipedream	pitch tree	plainness	plastisol	plenarium
pilot lamp	pipe-fiend	piteously	plainsman	plateaued	plenilune
pilotless	pipe-layer	pitfalled	plainsmen	platefuls	plenitude
pilotship	pipe-light	pithecian	plainsong	plateless	plenteous
pilot tone	pipeliner	pithecoid	plain suit	platelike	plentiful
pilot wire	pipe major	pith fleck	plain text	plate line	pleonexia
pilpulist	pipe-metal	pithiatic	plaintful	plate-mark	pleophony
pimientos	pipe organ	pithiness	plaintiff	plate mill	pleoptics
pimpernel	piperonal	pitifully	plaintile	plate rack	plerionic
pinaceous	piperonyl	pitometer	plain time	plate-rail	plethoric
pinafored	piperoxan	pitot head	plaintive	plate-roll	pleuritic
pinarette	pipesnake	pitot tube	plain-work	platinate	pleuritis
pinchable	pipe-still	Pitot tube	plaitless	platinise	plexiform
pinchbeck	pipe-stone	Pitressin	plait-work	platinite	plexiglas
pin-cherry	pipetting	pit-sawyer	planarian	platinize	Plexiglas
pinch-fist	piping hot	pit silage	planarity	platinode	plicately
pinch-roll	pipradrol	pittancer	planation	platinoid	plication
pin clover	pipsqueak	pitticite	planching	platinous	plicature
Pindarism	piquantly	pituicyte	Planckian	platitude	plightful
pinealoma	piquetist	pituitary	Planck law	Platonian	plinthite
pineapple	piratedom	pituitous	plane away	Platonise	plombière
pine-drops	piratical	Pituitrin	planeload	Platonism	ploration

plosional	pocketful	poke-salad	polyester	Pommyland	porphyrio
Plotinian	pocketing	polar bear	polyether	pomoerium	porrected
Plotinism	pocket rot	polar body	polygamic	pompadour	porringer
Plotinist	pockiness	polar hare	polygenic	pompholyx	Porsonian
Plotinize	pockmanty	polariton	polygonal	pompoleon	port-a-beul
plot-ratio	Pocomania	polarized	polygonic	pomposity	Portainer
plottable	podagrous	polarizer	polygonum	pompously	portalled
plough-boy	podginess	polar star	polygraph	ponderate	portatile
ploughman	podiatric	polarward	polygynic	ponderosa	portative
plowshare	podocytic	pole-horse	polyhedra	ponderous	porterage
pluckiest	podoscaph	pole-lathe	polyimide	pond snail	porteress
pluckless	podotheca	polemarch	polyionic	pontianak	portfolio
pluck side	podzolise	polemical	polylogue	pontoneer	portholed
plugboard	podzolize	pole-piece	polymathy	pontooner	porticoed
pluggable	poemscape	pole vault	polymeric	Pontypool	porticoes
plug gauge	poetaster	polewards	polymetre	poodle-cut	portional
plugged-in	poeticise	polianite	polymodal	poodle-dog	portioner
plug horse	poeticism	police box	polymorph	poodledom	portliest
plug riots	poeticize	police dog	polymythy	pool house	portolano
plumbagos	poeticule	policedom	polymyxin	pool shark	portolans
plumbeous	poet's poet	policeman	polyomino	poopnoddy	portrayal
plumbicon	pogey bait	policemen	polyonymy	poop scoop	portrayer
plumbless	pogie bait	Polisario	polyopsia	poop-sheet	portreeve
plumb line	pogo stick	polishing	polyorama	poop-stick	Port Salut
plumb rule	pogromist	polish off	polyphage	poor child	port-sider
plumeless	pohickory	politarch	polyphagy	poorhouse	Portuguee
plumelike	poignance	politburo	polyphant	poor loser	portulaca
plume moth	poignancy	politeful	polyphase	poor mouth	port watch
pluminess	poinciana	politesse	Polypheme	poor snake	port-winer
plummeted	poindable	political	polyphone	poor white	port-winey
plummiest	pointable	politicly	polyphony	poor White	posigrade
plumosite	point duty	politicos	polyphyly	Pooterish	possessed
plumosity	pointedly	poll-clerk	polypidom	pop artist	possessor
plumpness	pointelle	pollen-sac	polypifer	pop-bottle	possident
plunderer	pointiest	pollinary	polyploid	pope's head	poss-stick
plunge bed	point lace	pollinate	polypnoea	pope's nose	postalize
plunge cut	pointless	pollinise	polyporus	Poplarism	post-axial
pluralise	pointlike	pollinium	polyposis	Poplarist	postcaval
pluralism	point mass	pollinize	polyptych	popliteal	postcenal
pluralist	point shoe	poll-taker	polypuses	popocracy	post-coach
plurality	pointsman	pollucite	polysemia	Popperian	post crown
pluralize	pointsmen	pollutant	polysemic	Popperism	post-entry
plurative	pointwise	pollution	polysomal	poppet-leg	posterial
pluriform	point-work	pollutive	polysomic	poppycock	posterior
plurisign	poisonful	Pollyanna	polyspike	poppy-head	posterish
plus fours	poison gas	polonaise	polyspore	poppy-seed	posterist
plushette	poisoning	polo shirt	polyspory	popularly	posterity
plushiest	poison ivy	polo stick	polystely	porbeagle	posterize
plushness	poison oak	polyamide	polytenic	porcelain	post-exist
plutarchy	poisonous	polyamine	polythene	porchless	posthabit
plutocrat	poison pen	polyandry	polytonal	porcupine	post-haste
plutology	poitrinal	polyanion	polytonic	porcupiny	posthitis
Plutonian	poke-berry	polyantha	polytopic	pore water	post-horse
plutonism	poke-check	polyarchy	polytrope	poriferan	post-house
Plutonist	poke fun at	polybasic	polytypic	pork-eater	posticous
plutonium	pokelogan	polyblast	polyvinyl	pornocrat	post-ictal
plutonomy	poker back	polychord	polywater	porogamic	postilion
ply rating	poker chip	polyclone	polyxenic	poromeric	postnasal
pneograph	poker dice	polyconic	pomace-fly	porometer	post-natal
pneumatic	poker-face	polycrase	pomaceous	porphyria	postnatal
pneumonia	poker-work	polycross	pomewater	porphyric	postnatus
pneumonic	pokerwork	polyergus	pommelled	porphyrin	post-paper

postponer	pound sign	pre-action	preferent	presbyope	pretty-boy
postposit	pourboire	pre-adamic	preferred	presbyter	prettyish
post-rider	pour-point	preadvise	pre-feudal	presbytia	prettyism
post-tonic	pourpoint	pre-agonal	prefigure	prescaler	pretypify
postulant	poussette	pre-assign	prefixion	pre-school	prevailer
postulata	poutassou	preassume	prefixoid	preschool	prevail on
postulate	poutingly	preassure	pre-flight	prescient	prevalent
posturing	powder-bag	pre-atomic	preflight	prescreen	preventer
posturist	powder-box	preatomic	preformer	prescribe	preverbal
posturize	powdering	preattune	pregnable	prescript	prevernal
postvelar	powderize	prebendal	pregnance	pre-season	previable
postviral	powder keg	prebender	pregnancy	pre-select	previewer
postwoman	powder-man	prebiotic	prehallux	preselect	prevision
postwomen	powder rag	Preboreal	preheater	presenile	priapulid
potagerie	Powellise	precancel	pre-inform	presenium	priceable
potashery	Powellism	precancer	pre-intone	presentee	priceless
potassium	powellite	precative	prejacent	presenter	price list
potato-bug	Powellite	precatory	prejudger	presently	price-mark
potato-eye	Powellize	precedent	prejudice	presentor	price ring
potato-fly	power base	preceding	prelacies	preserval	price stop
potato pie	powerboat	precentor	prelatess	preserver	priciness
potato pit	power-dive	preceptee	prelatial	presexual	pricklier
potato rot	power game	preceptor	prelation	preshrink	prickling
potato set	powerless	precipice	prelatist	pre-shrunk	prick-mark
pot-boiler	power line	precisely	prelatize	president	prick-post
potboiler	power-load	precisian	prelature	presidial	prick-seam
pot-bunker	power-loom	précising	prelector	presiding	prick-song
pot cheese	power pack	precision	preludial	presidium	prick-spur
potentate	power play	precisive	preludise	Presidium	prickwood
potential	power pole	preclimax	preludium	pressable	prideless
potentize	power tool	precocene	preludise	press book	prie-dieux
pot-garden	power unit	precocial	preludize	press card	priest-cap
pot-gutted	powldoody	precocity	prelusion	press-gang	priestdom
pothecary	pox-doctor	pre-coital	prelusive	press home	priestess
pot holder	pozzolana	precoital	prelusory	press lord	priggable
potholing	practical	preconise	premature	press-mark	primacies
pot-hunter	practicum	preconize	premedial	pressmark	Primacord
pot-licker	practised	precooler	premiumed	press roll	primaeval
pot-likker	practiser	precordia	premodify	press-room	primality
pot-liquor	praenomen	precostal	premonish	press show	primaries
pot of gold	praetexta	precursor	premorbid	press stud	primarily
pot-pourri	praetoria	precystic	premortal	pressured	primarize
potteries	pragmatic	predacity	pre-mortem	press view	primatial
pottiness	Prague ham	predation	premotion	presswork	primavera
pottinger	praisable	predatory	premunise	press-yard	prime cost
pottle-pot	praisably	predefine	premunize	prestable	prime lens
pot-valour	praiseach	predesign	preneural	prestance	primeness
potwaller	praiseful	predicant	pre-notice	prestigey	prime rate
pouchless	pranksome	predicate	prenotion	prestress	primer DNA
pouchlike	prankster	predictor	preoccupy	presuming	prime-sign
poudrette	pratchant	predigest	preocular	pretectal	prime time
Poujadism	pratement	predikant	pre-option	pretectum	prime tone
Poujadist	prattling	predilect	preordain	pretenced	primidone
poulterer	prayerful	predorsal	preparate	pretended	primigene
pound away	prayer mat	pre-echoes	prepartum	pretender	primipara
pound-boat	prayer-nut	pre-editor	prepatent	pretensed	primitial
pound cake	prayer rug	pre-embryo	preponder	preterist	primitive
pound coin	pray in aid	pre-emptor	prepostor	preterite	primordia
pound lock	preachier	pre-engage	prepotent	pretermit	primo uomo
pound-meal	preachify	pre-exilic	preppiest	pretibial	primrosed
pound note	preachily	pre-expose	preputial	pretorian	primstaff
pound open	preaching	prefatory	pre-reader	prettiest	primuline

princedom	procyonid	promising	pro re nata	protostar	pterygote
princekin	prodigies	promissor	prorogate	prototype	Ptolemaic
princelet	prodition	promittor	prorogued	protoxide	ptygmatic
principal	prodromal	promoting	prorogues	protozoal	pubescent
principes	prodromic	promotion	prosaical	protozoan	pubiotomy
principle	producent	promotive	prosateur	protozoic	public act
printable	productor	prompt box	proscenia	protozoon	public bar
print down	proembryo	prompting	proscribe	proudness	publicise
print hand	proenzyme	promptive	proscript	Proustian	publicist
printhead	proestrus	prompture	prosector	proustite	publicity
printless	pro-ethnic	promulger	prosecute	proveable	publicize
print-room	pro-family	pronation	Prose Edda	provedore	public law
print-shop	profanely	proneness	proselyte	Provençal	publisher
priorship	profanity	prongbuck	prose poem	provender	Puccinian
prismatic	professed	pronghorn	proseucha	provident	puckishly
prisonful	professor	pronounal	prosified	providing	puddening
prisoning	profferer	pronounce	prosifies	provision	pudginess
prisonize	profilist	Prontosil	prosimian	provisory	puerilely
prison-van	profilmic	pro-nuncio	prosiness	provocate	puerilism
prissiest	profiteer	prooemium	prosocial	provoking	puerility
privateer	profiting	proofless	prosodeme	provolone	puerperal
privately	profluent	proof load	prosodiac	provostal	puff-adder
privation	profugate	proof-read	prosodial	provostry	puffickly
privatise	profundal	proofread	prosodian	proxemics	puffiness
privatism	profundus	propagand	prosodion	proximate	puff-paste
privative	profusely	propagate	prosodist	proximity	puff piece
privatize	profusion	propagule	prosopyle	proxy vote	puftaloon
privilege	profusive	propanoic	prostatic	Prozymite	pug-engine
privities	progenote	propanone	prosthion	prudelike	pugillary
privy seal	progestin	propargyl	prostrate	prudently	pugnacity
prizeable	prognathy	propelled	protamine	pruderies	puissance
prizeless	prognoses	propeller	protandry	prudishly	pulicious
prize-list	prognosis	propellor	protanope	prune tree	pull about
prize ring	programme	propenoic	protargol	prurience	pull a face
proaction	proguanil	properdin	protarsal	pruriency	pull apart
proactive	projector	prophasic	protarsus	prussiate	pull a rock
pro and con	prolabium	prophetic	proteanly	prytaneum	pull-drive
probation	prolactin	propidium	protectee	psalm-book	pullicate
probative	prolamine	propinque	protector	psalmodic	pull round
probatory	prolapsus	propionic	proteinic	psaltress	pullulant
probeable	prolately	propionyl	protester	psammitic	pullulate
probingly	prolation	propodeum	protestor	psephitic	pull wires
probiotic	prolative	propodium	prothalli	pseudodox	pully-haul
probosces	prolepses	proponent	protheses	pseudoism	pulmonary
proboscis	prolepsis	Propontic	prothesis	pseudonym	pulmonate
procacity	proleptic	proposant	prothetic	pseudopod	pulp-canal
procedure	proletary	proposita	prothorax	pseudosex	pulpiness
proceeder	prolidase	propositi	prothyrum	psoriasis	pulpiteer
procerity	prolixity	propriate	protistan	psoriatic	pulpotomy
processal	prologist	propriety	protistic	psoroptic	pulp-stone
processor	prologize	propshaft	protocone	psychical	pulqueria
prochiral	prologued	proptosed	protocorm	psychonic	pulsatile
pro-choice	prologuer	proptosis	protoderm	psychoses	pulsation
proclisis	prologues	propugner	proto-form	psychosis	pulsative
proclitic	prolonged	propulsor	protogram	psychotic	pulsatory
proconsul	prolonger	propylaea	protogyny	ptarmical	pulse code
procreant	prolusion	propylene	protohaem	ptarmigan	pulseless
procreate	prolusory	propylite	protolith	pteridine	pulse-wave
proctitis	promazine	propylons	protology	pteropine	pulverise
procuracy	promenade	pro-rating	protonate	pterosaur	pulverize
procuress	promethea	proration	protonema	pterygium	pulverous
procurved	prominent	pro-rector	protopope	pterygoid	pulvillus

pulvinate	pursuable	pyorrhoea	quamoclit	quietener	racialist
pumiceous	pursuance	pyramidal	quantally	quietlike	racialize
pummelled	purulence	pyramidic	quantizer	quietness	raciation
pump-brake	purulency	pyramidon	quarryman	quiet-room	racing car
pump drill	push about	Pyramidon	quarrymen	quietsome	raciology
pump-water	push along	pyrethrin	quartered	quiet time	rackarock
punchable	push-and-go	pyrethrum	quarterer	quietuses	rack-block
punchayat	push-chain	pyrexical	quarterly	quillback	rack chain
punchball	pushchair	pyridoxal	quartette	quillwork	rack chase
punch bowl	push-cycle	pyridoxic	quartetto	quillwort	racked-out
punchbowl	pusher set	pyridoxol	quartzite	quinarian	racketeer
punch card	pusher-tug	pyritical	quartzose	quinarius	racketing
punchcard	pushfully	Pyroceram	Quasimodo	quindecim	rack mount
punchiest	pushiness	pyroclast	quaverous	quinidine	rack-punch
punchless	pushingly	pyrogenic	quay crane	quinoidal	rack-wheel
punch-line	push money	pyrograph	queasiest	quinoline	raconteur
punchline	push plate	pyrolatry	Quebecker	quinology	racoon dog
punch-mark	push-start	pyrolysis	Québecois	quinonoid	radar trap
punch-pull	pussyfoot	pyrolytic	quebracho	quinquina	radial-ply
punch tape	pussy hair	pyromancy	Queen-Anne	quintette	radiantly
punctated	pussy palm	pyromania	queen cake	quintuple	radiately
punctilio	pussy-toes	pyromanic	queen-cell	quintuply	radiating
punctuate	pussy-whip	pyrometer	Queen City	quinzaine	radiation
pungently	pustulate	pyrometry	queenfish	quiritary	radiative
puniceous	pustulous	pyromucic	Queen high	quiritian	radiature
punishing	put across	pyrophori	queenhood	quirkiest	radically
punningly	put at risk	pyrothere	queenless	quitclaim	radicchio
punt-about	putidness	pyrotoxin	queenlier	quite a few	radicular
pupariate	put in mind	pyroxenic	queenlike	quite some	radio buoy
pupillage	put paid to	pyroxylin	queen lily	quittance	radiocast
pupillary	put-putted	Pyrrhonic	Queen Mary	quiverful	Radio Five
pupilless	putrefied	pyrroline	queen post	quixotism	Radio Four
pupillize	putrefier	pythoness	queenship	quizzable	radiogram
pupil-room	putrefies	qinghaosu	queen-side	quizzical	radioland
pupilship	putridity	Q-spoiling	queen-size	Qumranite	radioless
puppeteer	putriform	quadrable	queen wasp	quoad hanc	radiology
puppetish	putrilage	quadratic	queer fish	quoad hunc	radionics
puppy foot	putschism	quadratus	queerness	quodlibet	radio star
puppyhood	putschist	quadrifid	quercetin	quotation	radiothon
puppy love	put them up	quadrille	querimony	quotative	radio wave
purchaser	put to rout	quadruped	querulist	quotidian	radiumize
pure-blood	putty-like	quadruple	querulity	rabatment	radius bar
pure quill	putty-root	quadruply	querulous	rabbeting	radiusing
purgation	put up with	quaesitum	queue-jump	rabbinate	radius rod
purgative	put wise to	quaffable	quibbling	rabbinise	radknight
purgatory	puzzle-box	quail-call	quickbeam	rabbinism	radon seed
purgeable	puzzledly	quail-dove	quick-clay	rabbinist	raffinate
puritanic	puzzledom	quail hawk	quickener	rabbinize	raffinose
purloiner	puzzle-peg	quail-pipe	quick-eyed	rabbiship	raffishly
puromycin	puzzolana	quaintish	quick-fire	rabbit-dog	rafflesia
purposely	Pybuthrin	Quakerdom	quickgold	rabbiting	raftering
purposive	pycnidial	Quakeress	quick kill	rabbitish	ragefully
purpurate	pycnidium	quaker gun	quick-knit	Rabelaism	rag picker
purpureal	pyelogram	Quakerish	quicklike	rabidness	ragpicker
purpurean	Pygmalion	Quakerism	quicklime	raceabout	rail fence
purpurite	pygomelus	quakingly	quick-look	racehorse	railinged
purringly	pygopagus	qualified	quickness	race-knife	rain-caped
purse-belt	pygostyle	qualifier	quicksand	race music	rain-charm
purse boat	pyococcal	qualifies	quick step	racetrack	rain check
purseless	pyococcus	qualitied	quickstep	rachidial	rain cloud
purse-pick	pyodermia	qualities	quick time	rachidian	rain dance
pursiness	pyodermic	qualmless	quiescent	racialism	rain gauge

rain-goose	rascality	read-write	reckoning	recumbent	redressal
raininess	Raskolnik	ready-made	reclaimer	recurrent	redresser
rainlight	rasophore	ready room	reclinate	recurring	redressor
rainmaker	raspatory	Reaganaut	reclusely	recursant	red riband
rain print	raspberry	Reaganism	reclusion	recursion	red ribbon
rainproof	rasp-house	Reaganite	reclusive	recursive	red setter
rain-slick	raspingly	realistic	recognise	recurvate	red sorrel
rain-stone	Rastafari	realities	recognize	recurvous	red spider
rainstorm	rasterise	realmless	recoinage	recusance	red squill
rainswept	rasterize	real money	recollate	recusancy	red-streak
rainwater	rat cheese	reanalyse	re-collect	redaction	red-tailed
raise Cain	ratcheted	reanimate	recollect	red anchor	red tangle
raised bog	ratemeter	reapplied	Recollect	red-backed	red-tapery
raised pie	ratepayer	reapplies	recombine	Red-baiter	red-tapish
raise hell	ratheness	reappoint	recomfort	red banner	red-tapism
raise sand	ratherest	rearguard	recommand	red bishop	red-tapist
Rajmahali	rathe-ripe	rear-horse	recommend	Red Branch	Red Terror
rakehelly	ratherish	rear light	recompact	redbreast	redthroat
rakeshame	rationale	rearmouse	recompose	red carpet	red thrush
ralli cart	rationate	rearousal	recompute	red caviar	red tombac
rambootan	rat-racing	rearrange	reconcile	Red Centre	reducible
ramellose	rat-tailed	rear sight	recondite	red clover	reducibly
rammishly	rat-tat-tat	rearsight	reconduct	red darnel	reductant
rampantly	rattening	rearwards	reconfine	reddendum	reductase
ramparted	rattiness	reasoning	reconfirm	reddishly	reduction
ram-raider	rattlebox	reassault	reconjure	reddition	reductive
ramuscule	raucously	reassurer	reconnect	red duster	redundant
rancellor	raunchier	reattempt	reconquer	redeliver	red vision
rancelman	raunchily	rebaptism	reconsign	redemptor	red willow
rancheria	rauwolfia	rebaptize	reconsult	red ensign	red-winged
ranchcros	ravelling	rebatable	recontest	redeposit	red wrasse
ranchette	ravelment	rebbitzin	reconvene	redescend	reed-grass
ranch mink	raven-duck	rebelling	reconvert	redevelop	re-edifier
rancidity	raven-like	rebellion	reconvict	red fescue	reediness
ranciéite	raven-tree	rebel yell	reconvoke	red figure	re-edition
rancorous	ravishing	rebidding	record hop	red-footed	reed-organ
randiness	raw sienna	rebirther	recording	red godwit	reed relay
randkluft	ray blight	reblossom	recordist	red groper	re-educate
randomise	ray-finned	rebounder	Recordite	red grouse	reef heron
randomize	ray floret	rebreathe	recounter	red-handed	reef knoll
rangatira	ray-fungus	rebuilder	recoveree	red-headed	reef-point
rangeland	rayograph	rebukeful	recoverer	red howler	reefpoint
ranginess	Rayonnism	rebutment	recreance	redialled	reek penny
rank order	Ray's bream	rebutting	recreancy	Red Indian	re-embrace
rankshift	razor-back	recapping	recreator	redingote	re-enfeoff
ransacker	razorback	recaption	recrement	redivivus	re-enforce
ransackle	razorbill	recapture	recruital	red-legged	re-engrave
Ranterism	razor clam	recedence	recruiter	red menace	re-enslave
rantingly	razor edge	receiptor	rectangle	red monkey	re-entrant
rantipole	razor-fish	receiving	rectified	red mullet	re-entries
ranunculi	razor gang	recension	rectifier	red myrtle	reevesite
rapacious	razor plug	reception	rectifies	red-necked	re-examine
rap centre	razor wire	receptive	rectional	red nettle	re-express
rapid-fire	razzberry	recession	rectitude	redolence	refashion
rapidness	reachable	recessive	rectocele	redoubler	refection
rappelled	reachless	Rechabite	rectopexy	redoubted	refective
raptorial	reacquire	recharger	rectorate	red-pencil	refectory
rapturous	reactance	recharter	rectoress	red pepper	referable
rare earth	readathon	rechauffe	rectorial	red planet	reference
raree-show	readdress	réchauffé	rectories	Red Prince	referenda
rascaldom	readiness	recherché	rectorite	red rattle	referring
rascalism	readvance	recipient	rectrices	red reflex	refinable

refinance	rehearsal	remarries	replacive	resecrete	reswallow
refinedly	rehearser	Rembrandt	replanned	resection	retaliate
refitment	rehearten	remeasure	replaster	resembler	retardant
refitting	rehydrate	remediate	repleader	resentful	retardate
reflagged	Reichsrat	remigrate	repledger	resequent	retardive
reflation	Reichstag	remindful	replenish	reserpine	retardure
reflecter	reign mark	Remington	repletion	reservist	retentate
reflector	reign name	reminisce	replevied	reservoir	retention
reflex arc	reimburse	remissful	replevies	resetting	retentive
reflexion	reimmerge	remission	replicant	res gestae	retexture
reflexive	reimmerse	remissive	replicase	reshuffle	rethinker
refluence	reimplace	remissory	replicate	residence	rethought
refocused	reimplant	remitment	reply-paid	residency	rethunder
Reform Act	reimpress	remittent	reportage	residuary	retiarian
reformado	reimprint	remitting	reposeful	residuous	retiarius
reformate	reinclose	remixture	repositor	resignant	reticella
reformism	reindeers	remnantal	repossess	resilient	reticello
reformist	re infecta	remontant	repotting	resin-bush	reticence
refortify	reinflame	remontoir	reprehend	resinosis	reticency
refounder	reinflate	rémoulade	re-present	resin-weed	reticular
refractor	reinforce	removable	represent	resistant	reticulin
refreshen	reinhabit	renascent	repressed	resistent	reticulum
refresher	reinherit	rencontre	represser	resistful	retinally
refuelled	reinspect	rendering	repressor	resistive	retinence
refulgent	reinspire	render-set	repricing	resitting	retinitis
refurbish	reinstall	rendition	reprieval	resizable	retinular
refurnish	reinstate	renewable	reprimand	re-soluble	retiredly
refusable	reinsurer	renewedly	reprinter	resoluble	retorsion
refusenik	reissuing	renewment	reprobacy	resolvent	retortion
refutable	reiterant	renguerra	reprobate	resonance	retortive
refutably	reiterate	renitence	reprocess	resonator	retoucher
regal lily	rejection	renitency	reprocure	resorbent	retractor
regal moth	rejective	renneting	reproduce	respecter	retreaded
regardant	rejigging	renouncer	reprofile	respelled	retreader
regardful	rejoicing	renovator	reprogram	respirate	retreatal
regarding	rejoinder	renownful	reptation	responaut	retreater
regencies	relatable	rent party	reptilian	responder	retribute
re-genesis	relatival	rent table	republish	responser	retrieval
regentess	relaxedly	reoxidize	repudiant	responsor	retriever
Reggeized	relay race	repackage	repudiate	responsum	retrocede
reggeonic	relay rack	repairman	repugnant	ressaldar	retrodden
Regge pole	relearned	repairmen	repulsion	rest frame	retrodict
regicidal	relection	reparable	repulsive	restfully	retro-fire
regiminal	relegable	reparably	reputable	rest house	retroflex
regionary	relenting	repassage	reputably	restiform	retroject
regisseur	relevance	repassant	reputedly	restitute	retroussé
registral	relevancy	repayable	requalify	restively	retrovert
registrar	relic area	repayment	requester	rest level	retrusion
registree	relief map	repeat fee	requicken	restraint	return-day
registrer	relighted	repeating	requisite	restringe	returning
regosolic	religiose	repéchage	re-radiate	restudied	return key
regrading	religious	repellent	re-reading	restudies	reunified
regressor	reliquary	repelling	rere-brace	resubject	reunifies
regretful	reliquiae	repentant	re-release	resublime	reunition
regretted	relucence	repercuss	reremouse	resuggest	reutilise
regretter	relucency	reperform	re-resolve	resultant	reutilize
reguerdon	reluctant	reperfume	rerunning	resultful	revaluate
regulable	reluctate	reperible	resalable	resumable	revaluing
regularly	remainder	repertory	rescinder	resummons	revarnish
regulator	remanence	reperusal	rescoring	resurface	revelator
reguluses	remanning	repicture	rescuable	resurgent	revelling
rehearing	remarried	repiquing	rescue bid	resurrect	revelment

revelries	rhizotomy	ridiculer	riskiness	rockburst	Romantsch
reverable	rhizotron	riemskoen	risk money	rock candy	Romany chi
reverence	rhodamine	rifamycin	rissaldar	rock chuck	Romany rye
reversely	rhodanthe	riff-raffy	ritenutos	rock cress	Rome-penny
reversify	Rhodesian	rifle bird	ritodrine	rocker arm	Romewards
reversing	rhodonite	rifle shot	ritualise	rocker box	rommelpot
reversion	rhodopsin	rifomycin	ritualism	rockeries	rompingly
revertant	rhombogen	rift block	ritualist	rocketeer	rood goose
revetment	rhombuses	rigescent	rituality	rocketing	roof-brain
revetting	rhopalial	rightable	ritualize	rocket net	roof-climb
revibrate	rhopalium	right away	ritziness	rocket pad	roof light
revictual	rhotacise	right-back	rivalless	rock-flour	roof prism
revisable	rhotacism	right bank	rivalling	rock hound	roofscape
revisited	rhotacize	right-down	rivalries	rock-house	roof-slate
revivable	rhumb-line	righteous	rivalrous	rock hyrax	roof-water
revocable	rhymeless	right-hand	rivalship	rockiness	rooikrans
revocably	rhymester	rightless	river-bank	rock maple	rookeries
revokable	rhyolitic	right line	riverboat	rock melon	rook rifle
revolting	rhythmise	rightmost	river crab	rock music	room clerk
revoluble	rhythmist	rightness	river duck	rock 'n' roll	roominess
revolving	rhythmite	right side	river fish	rock ouzel	rooming-in
revulsant	rhythmize	right turn	riverless	rock pipit	roomstead
revulsion	rhytidome	rightward	river-like	rock pitch	Roosevelt
revulsive	ribanding	right-wing	riverside	rock plant	roost-cock
revusical	Ribandism	rigidness	riverward	rock-shaft	root-bound
rewardful	Ribandist	rigmarole	river-weed	rock-slide	root canal
rewarding	Ribandman	rigourism	riverwise	rock-solid	root-graft
rewhisper	ribavirin	rillettes	rix-dollar	rock-stone	root-house
rewirable	rib-bender	rime-frost	roach pole	rock tripe	rootiness
rewording	Ribbonism	rimestock	roadblock	rock waste	root-prune
reworking	Ribbonman	rimrocker	road brand	rock-water	rootstock
rewrapped	rib-digger	rind graft	roadcraft	rod and gun	root swell
rewriting	ribosomal	ring a bell	roadfarer	rodential	rooty-toot
rewritten	ribozymal	ring-bound	road-goose	rodentian	rope-a-dope
rhabditic	Ricardian	ring-canal	roadhouse	rodent-run	rope brown
rhabditid	rice-field	ringcraft	road metal	rodgersia	rope horse
rhabditis	rice-grain	ring-cross	roadscape	rodingite	rope-house
rhapontic	rice-grass	ring dance	road sense	rod puppet	rope-maker
rhapsodic	rice-paper	Ringerike	roadstead	Rodriguan	rope-sight
rhatanies	ricercare	ring false	road train	rogan josh	rope-trick
rhematize	ricercata	ring-fence	roaringly	rogueries	Roquefort
rheobasic	rice table	ring flash	roast beef	rogueship	roqueting
rheometer	rice-water	ring-frame	robber-fly	roguishly	Rorschach
rheometry	richardia	ring gland	robberies	roisterer	Rörstrand
rheophile	Richelieu	ringingly	Robertian	role model	rosaceous
rheophobe	rich rhyme	ringleted	Robertine	roller bit	rosary pea
rheophyte	ricketily	ring light	robin-chat	roller-gin	rose aphid
rheoscope	ricky-tick	ring-oiled	Robin Hood	rollicker	rose-apple
rheotaxis	ride again	ring oiler	robin huss	rollingly	rose-a-ruby
rhetorize	riderless	ring ouzel	robin-snow	Romagnese	rose-berry
rheumatic	ridership	ring round	robot bomb	Romagnola	rose-color
rheumatiz	ride rusty	ring shake	robotical	Roman alum	rosefinch
rhinarial	ride short	ringsider	robustest	romancing	rosemaled
rhinarium	ridgeback	ring-snake	rocambole	romancist	rose-noble
Rhineland	ridge-band	rinky-dink	roche alum	Romanesco	Rosenthal
Rhine wine	ridge-bone	rinky-tink	roche lime	Roman foot	roseolous
rhinology	ridgeling	riotously	Roche lobe	Romanizer	rose-point
rhipsalis	ridge pole	riparious	Roche zone	Roman mile	rosetting
rhizobial	ridge tent	rippingly	rock along	roman noir	rose water
rhizobium	ridge tile	Ripuarian	rock-basin	Roman nose	Rosinante
rhizocarp	ridge tree	rise above	rock-bound	romantism	rosin-back
rhizoidal	ridgewise	rising sun	rock brake	romantist	rosinweed

Rosminian	round hand	rubeoloid	rurbanism	sacrifice	saleratus
rosoglios	Roundhead	rubeolous	rurbanist	sacrilege	salesgirl
Rossinian	round heel	rubescent	Ruritania	sacristan	saleslady
Ross River	round meal	rubicelle	rushingly	saddle-ass	salesroom
Ross's gull	roundness	rubricate	rushlight	saddle-bag	sales talk
rostellar	round rape	rubrician	Ruskinese	saddlebag	Salic code
rostellum	round seam	rubricism	Ruskinian	saddle-bar	salicetum
rostrally	round shot	rubricist	Ruskinism	saddle bow	salicylic
rostrated	roundsman	rubricity	Ruskinite	Sadducaic	saliently
rosy cross	roundsmen	ruby glass	russeting	Sadducean	saligenin
rosy finch	round text	rucervine	Russified	Sadducize	salinator
Rotameter	round trip	ruck-rover	Russifies	safari ant	salitrose
rotascope	round turn	rudaceous	rust-brown	safeguard	salivaria
rotatable	roundward	rudbeckia	rusticate	safe house	Sallee-man
Rotavator	roundways	rudder-bar	rusticism	safe light	sallowest
rotavirus	roundwise	ruddiness	rusticity	safety cab	sallowish
rotochute	round wood	ruddleman	rusticize	safety man	sally-hole
rotometer	roundworm	ruddy duck	rustiness	safety net	Sally Lunn
rotor disc	rousement	rue the day	rustproof	safety pin	sally-port
rotor head	rousingly	rufescent	rutaceous	safety rod	sallyport
rotor ship	rout-chair	ruffianly	ruthenate	safflower	salmon fry
Rotovator	route-goer	Rufflette	Ruthenian	saffranon	salmonoid
rottenest	route taxi	rug-cutter	ruthenium	safranine	salmon run
Rotten Row	routinary	rug-headed	ruthfully	sagaciate	Salomonic
rotundate	routineer	ruination	rutilated	sagacious	saloon bar
rotundity	routinely	ruinosity	rye coffee	sagapenum	saloon car
roughback	routinise	ruinously	rye whisky	sagebrush	saloonist
rough bent	routinish	rule-joint	sabadilla	sage Derby	salopette
rough calf	routinism	rule of law	Sabbathly	sage green	salpinges
roughcast	routinist	rule-right	Sabbatian	sagginess	salsifies
rough coal	routinize	rulership	sabbatise	sagittary	salt a mine
rough coat	routously	rum butter	Sabbatism	sagittate	saltation
rough copy	roving eye	rum-cherry	sabbatize	sago-grass	saltative
rough deal	rowan tree	rumenitis	Sabellian	Sahaptian	saltatory
Rough Fell	rowdiness	ruminated	Sabianism	sahibhood	salt cedar
rough file	rowelling	ruminator	sablefish	Saigonese	salt chuck
rough-hewn	row-galley	rumminess	sableness	sailboard	salt-glaze
rough leaf	row matrix	rump steak	sabrewing	sailcloth	salt grass
rough-lock	row vector	rum-runner	saccharic	sail-fluke	salt horse
roughneck	Royal Anne	run across	saccharin	sailmaker	salt-house
roughness	royal blue	run around	saccharum	sailoress	saltiness
rough pâté	royal duke	run at tilt	sacciform	sailor hat	salt marsh
rough ride	royal fern	runcinate	sacculate	sailoring	saltpetre
rough seal	royal fish	rune-staff	sacerdoce	sailor-man	salt spoon
roughshod	royal mast	rune-stave	sacerdocy	sailor top	salt spray
roughsome	Royal Navy	run foul of	sachaline	sailplane	salt water
rough spin	royal road	run holder	sachemdom	sainthood	salt works
rough-tail	royal sail	run-in shed	sack chair	saintless	salubrity
rough-tree	royal stag	run it fine	sackcloth	saintlier	salumeria
rough work	royalties	runners-up	sack dress	saintlike	saluresis
rouletted	royetness	runner-ups	sack drill	saintling	saluretic
Roumanian	rubber boa	runningly	Sack-friar	saint's day	Salvarsan
Roumelian	rubber dam	run ragged	sack lunch	saintship	salvation
rouncival	rubber ice	runrigged	sack paper	sakawinki	salvatory
round-arch	rubberise	run scared	sacrality	salacious	Samaritan
roundball	rubberize	run to meet	sacralize	salad days	Sam Browne
round clam	rubberoid	run to seed	sacrament	salangane	same again
round coal	rubbisher	Runyonese	sacrarium	salaryman	same to you
round down	rubbishly	rupestral	sacred axe	salarymen	sameyness
roundelay	rub elbows	rupicapra	sacred cow	Saldanier	Samoyedic
round fish	rubellite	rural dean	Sacred War	Salempore	sample bag
round game	Rubensian	ruralness	sacred way	sale price	sam-sodden

Samson fox	sapphiric	satisfier	scale-worm	sceptical	scioptric
Samsonian	sappiness	satisfies	scaliness	schapping	sciroccos
samsonite	sapraemia	satrapies	scallawag	schedular	scirrhoid
Samuelite	sapraemic	saturable	scalloped	scheduled	scirrhous
sanatoria	saprobity	saturated	scalloper	scheduler	scissorer
sanbenito	saprolite	saturator	scallywag	scheelite	scleritis
sanctoral	sapsucker	Saturdays	scalogram	schelling	sclerogen
sanctuary	Sarabaite	Saturnian	scalpette	schematic	sclerosed
sandalled	sarabande	saturniid	scalpless	Scherbius	sclerosis
sandarach	Saracenic	saturnine	scalp-lock	Schermuly	sclerotal
sandblast	sarbacane	saturnism	scalpture	scherzino	sclerotia
sand-blind	sarcastic	satyrical	scalp yell	schilling	sclerotic
sand-clock	sarcelled	sauce-boat	scaly dove	Schilling	sclerotin
sand cloud	sarcocarp	sauceless	scaly-foot	schistose	scobiform
sand-crack	sarcocyst	saucer eye	scaly-tail	schistous	scold's bit
sand-devil	sarcoidal	saucerful	scamander	schlemiel	scolecite
sand drown	sarcolite	saucerian	scambling	schlenter	scolecoid
sandflies	sarcomata	saucerize	scammered	schlepped	scoliosis
sand-gaper	sarcomere	saucerman	scamperer	schlepper	scoliotic
sand-glass	sarcoptic	sauciness	scamphood	schlieren	scolopale
sand-grain	sarcoptid	saunterer	scannable	schmaltzy	scolopoid
sand-happy	sarcosine	Sauternes	scantiest	schmecker	scolytoid
sandiness	sarcosome	scantling	scantling	schmutter	scombroid
sand lance	Sardinian	savagedom	scantness	schnapper	scoopfuls
sand-mason	sargassum	savage man	scapegoat	schnauzer	scoop neck
sand-mould	sarkiness	Savile Row	scapement	schnitzel	scoparius
sandpaper	Sarmatian	savonette	scaphopod	schnorkel	scopeless
sand perch	sartorial	savourily	scapolite	schnorrer	scopiform
sandpiper	sartorian	saw-billed	scapulary	schnozzle	scopoline
sand-plain	sartorius	saw-doctor	scarabaei	scholarch	scopperil
sand plant	sarvodaya	saw gourds	scaraboid	scholarly	scopulate
sand-shark	sash cramp	saw-handle	scare-babe	scholiast	scorbutic
sand-smelt	sash frame	sawmiller	scarecrow	Schönlein	scorbutus
sand-spout	saskatoon	saw the air	scare-head	school age	scorching
sandstock	sasquatch	saw-timber	scarf ring	schoolboy	score-book
sandstone	Sasquatch	Saxe paper	scarf-skin	schoolday	scorebook
sandstorm	sassafras	saxifrage	scarf-wise	schooldom	score-card
sand-table	Sassanian	saxitoxin	scarified	schoolery	scorecard
sand wedge	Sassenach	Saxon blue	scarifier	schoolful	score draw
sand yacht	sassiness	saxophone	scarifies	schooling	scoreless
sang-froid	sassolite	scabbiest	scariness	school-ma'm	scoreline
Sanhedrim	satanical	scagliola	scarp-bolt	schoolman	scorified
Sanhedrin	Satanship	scald-crow	scarpetti	schoolmen	scorifier
sanitaria	satedness	scald-fish	Scatchard	schorlite	scorifies
sanitizer	satellise	scald-head	scatheful	Schrammel	scoriform
sanjakate	satellite	scald milk	scatology	Schreiner	scorodite
sanjakbeg	satellize	scale-bark	scattered	Schroeder	scorpaena
sans façon	satelloid	scale-beam	scatterer	schvartze	scorpioid
sans serif	satiation	scale-blue	scattiest	schwartze	Scotch cap
santolina	satin bell	scale carp	scavagery	sciaenoid	Scotch egg
santonica	satin-bird	scale down	scavenage	sciagraph	Scotch elm
sapanwood	satinette	scale-fern	scavenger	sciamachy	Scotchery
sap-beetle	satinized	scale-fish	scazontic	sciatical	Scotch fir
sap-headed	satin-like	scale-leaf	scelerate	sciential	Scotchify
saphenous	satin moth	scaleless	scenarios	scientise	Scotchman
sapiently	satin spar	scalelike	scenarist	scientism	Scotchmen
sapodilla	satin wire	scale-moss	scene-dock	scientist	Scotch peg
sapogenin	satinwood	scalenous	scene-plot	scientize	Scoticise
saponaria	satirical	scale-roof	scene-room	scintilla	Scoticism
saponarin	satirizer	scalesman	scentless	sciomachy	Scoticize
saporific	satisfice	scalewise	scent tuft	sciomancy	scotomata
sapotoxin	satisfied	scale work	scent-wood	sciophyte	scotomize

scotophil	scriptory	seajacker	secretion	selenitic	semilunar
scotophor	scripture	sea jockey	secretive	Seleucian	semi-major
Scots pine	scrivello	sea-kindly	secretory	self-abuse	semi-metal
scoundrel	scrivener	sealapack	sectarial	self-actor	semi-minor
scrabbled	scroddled	sea-lawyer	sectarian	self-aware	seminally
Scrabbler	scroll bar	sea league	sectaries	self-being	semi-nomad
scraggier	scrolling	sealeries	sectarism	self-black	semiology
scraggily	scroll saw	sealer jar	sectility	self-build	semi-opera
scragging	scrounger	seal point	sectional	self-color	semiotics
scramasax	scrubbery	sealpoint	sectorial	self-doubt	semi-plume
scrambled	scrubbing	seal-stone	secularly	self-drive	semi-prone
scrambler	scrub-bird	sea marker	secundine	self-exile	semi-rigid
scramming	scrubbish	seaminess	securable	self-faced	Semi-Saxon
scrapbook	scrub-fowl	sea monkey	securance	self-field	semi-smile
scrap heap	scrubland	sea myrtle	sedentary	self-given	semi-solid
scrapiana	scrub pine	sea-needle	sedge-bird	self-glory	semi-steel
scrap iron	scrub suit	sea-nettle	seditious	self-image	semi-sweet
scrappage	scrub tick	sea-orange	seducible	selfishly	semitonal
scrappier	scrub-wren	sea-parrot	seduction	self-lover	semitonic
scrappily	scruffier	sea-parson	seductive	self-moved	semivowel
scrapping	scruffily	sea-pigeon	seed-eater	self-noise	semi-works
scrapyard	scrum-half	sea-purple	seed-field	self-poise	sempitern
scratched	scrummage	sea radish	seediness	self-pride	senatress
scratcher	scrunchie	searchful	seed money	self-serve	sendaline
scrawling	scrutable	searching	see double	self-study	Sendzimir
scrawnier	scrutator	sea rocket	seed-pearl	self-timer	Seneca oil
screaking	scrutoire	sea-roving	seedpearl	self-trust	senectude
screaming	scuba-dive	sea-salted	seed-plant	self-twist	senescent
screecher	sculpture	sea-scurvy	seedsnipe	selfwards	seneschal
screeding	scummiest	sea seiche	seeing eye	self-worth	senhorita
screed off	scuncheon	sea shanty	seek after	Seljukian	seniority
screenage	scungiest	sea-slater	seekingly	sellathon	sennachie
screenful	scurviest	seasoning	seemingly	Sellotape	senocular
screening	scutation	sea-sorrow	seemliest	sell short	sensation
screwable	scutcheon	sea-spider	see much of	Semainean	sensatory
screw axis	scutellar	sea spurge	see of Rome	semanteme	senseless
screwball	scutellum	sea squirt	See of Rome	semantics	sensillum
screw-bean	scutiform	sea-strand	see reason	semantron	sensitise
screw-bolt	scybalous	sea-sucker	see things	semaphore	sensitive
screw-down	scytheman	Seatainer	Seger cone	semblable	sensitize
screwed-up	sea anchor	sea-tangle	segholate	semblably	sensorial
screw gear	sea-angler	sea thrift	segmental	semblance	sensorily
screw hook	sea-animal	sea turtle	segmented	semeiosis	sensorium
screwiest	sea bamboo	sea urchin	segmenter	semen bank	sensually
screw-jack	sea barley	sea voyage	segregant	semestral	sentencer
screwless	sea battle	sea-walled	segregate	Semi-Arian	sentience
screw-nail	sea-beaten	seawardly	Seguridad	semi-Bantu	sentiency
screw pile	sea beggar	sea-washed	Sehna knot	semibreve	sentiment
screw pine	sea-bottle	seaweeded	Sehnsucht	semi-broch	sentition
screw-pump	sea breeze	seaworthy	seigneury	semicolon	sentry box
screw-rate	sea-canary	sebaceous	seigniory	semi-deity	Senussian
screwsman	sea change	secateurs	seignoral	semi-domed	separable
screw tail	sea-cradle	secernent	seine-boat	semi-feral	separably
screw-wise	sea-crafty	secession	seismical	semi-field	separated
screw worm	sea dingle	seclusion	Seitz disc	semi-final	separator
scribable	sea dragon	seclusive	selachian	semifinal	separatum
scribbler	seafaring	secondary	selection	semi-fluid	Sephardic
scribe-awl	sea-farmer	second cut	selective	semifluid	Sephardim
scrimmage	sea-fisher	second day	selectman	semi-globe	Sepharose
scrimshaw	sea-flower	secondman	selectron	semi-grand	sepiolite
scrippage	sea-insect	Second War	selendang	semi-group	septanose
scription	sea island	secretary	selenious	semi-lunar	septarian

septarium	serrefine	sewerless	shakefork	shaveling	shelf back
septation	serrulate	sexagenae	Shakeress	shavetail	shelffuls
September	servaline	sexagonal	shakerful	shawlless	shelf-life
septemfid	servantry	sex appeal	Shakerism	sheaf oats	shelf-like
septemvir	serveries	sexcapade	shake wave	shear flow	shelflike
septenary	Servetian	sex change	shakiness	shear-head	shelf-list
septenate	serve time	sexennial	Shakspere	shear-hulk	shelf mark
septennia	Servetist	sexennium	shallowly	shear-legs	shelf room
septicity	serviette	sexercise	shamaness	shearling	shell-back
septiform	servilely	sex factor	shamanism	shear mark	shellback
septimole	servilism	sexfoiled	shamanist	shear wave	shell bean
septotomy	servility	sex kitten	shamanize	sheat-fish	shell-bird
septuplet	servitrix	sexlessly	shamateur	sheathing	shell-duck
sepulcher	servitude	sex-linked	shambling	shebeener	Shelleyan
sepulchre	servo flap	sex maniac	shambolic	Shechinah	shellfire
sepulture	sessility	sex object	shambrier	sheddable	shellfish
sepurture	sessional	sex symbol	shameface	sheenless	shell game
sequacity	sessioner	sextoness	shamefast	sheep-back	shell-gold
sequencer	sesterces	sextuplet	shameless	sheep-bell	shell-heap
sequently	sestertii	sextuplex	sham fight	sheep-bush	shell-less
sequester	set abroad	sextupole	shampooed	sheep-camp	shell-like
sequestra	setaceous	sex typing	shampooer	sheepcote	shell-lime
sequinned	set afloat	sexual act	shanachie	sheepfold	shell pink
seraglios	set a lot by	sexualise	Shandyism	sheep-hook	shell rock
seraphine	set at ease	sexualism	shanghais	sheepkill	shell roof
seraskier	set at rest	sexuality	Shangri-La	sheeplike	shell-sand
Serbonian	set battle	sexualize	shank-bone	sheepling	shell suit
serenader	set copper	sexvalent	shantyman	sheep-mark	shell-type
sergeancy	set eyes on	sforzandi	Shaoshing	sheepmeat	shell-work
sergeanty	set fire to	sforzando	shapeable	sheepnose	shelterer
serialise	set foot in	sforzatos	shapeless	sheep-rack	shemozzle
serialism	set foot on	sgraffiti	shapelier	sheep's-bit	shenachie
serialist	set in hand	sgraffito	shape-note	sheep scab	she-oak net
seriality	set much by	shabbiest	sharashka	sheep's eye	shepstare
serialize	set on fire	shabbyish	shard-born	sheep-sick	sheriffry
seriately	set on foot	shackbolt	shareable	sheepskin	sheshbesh
seriation	set phrase	shackling	share-beam	sheep-tick	she's right
sericeous	set square	shad-belly	share-bone	sheepwalk	she's sweet
sericitic	set theory	shadberry	sharecrop	sheep-wash	shevelled
serigraph	setting-up	shade card	share shop	sheepwash	shewbread
serinette	settle bed	shade deck	sharesman	sheer-hulk	Shibayama
seriosity	set to work	shadeless	shareware	sheerlegs	shibuichi
seriously	set up shop	shade tree	sharifate	sheer-line	shickered
serjeancy	seven-bore	shadiness	sharifial	sheerness	shickster
serjeanty	seven days	shadow box	sharifian	sheer-plan	shield arm
sermonise	seven-eyes	shadowily	shark-bait	sheer-pole	shield-bud
sermonist	sevenfold	shadowing	shark-moth	sheer-rail	shield bug
sermonize	seven seas	shadowish	sharkskin	sheet bend	shieldbug
sermonoid	sevensome	shad-trout	sharpbill	sheet film	shielding
serogroup	seventeen	shaft-hole	sharpener	sheet-flow	shiftable
serologic	seventhly	shaftless	sharp-eyed	sheet iron	shiftiest
serositis	seventies	shaftment	sharpling	sheetless	shiftless
serotinal	seven year	shaftsman	sharpness	sheetlike	shift lock
serotonin	severable	shaggiest	sharp rush	sheet-mill	shift work
serotypic	severally	shaggy cap	sharpshin	sheet-pile	shikimate
serpentin	severalth	Shahaptan	sharp-shod	Sheetrock	shillaber
serpently	severalty	shahtoosh	sharpster	sheet-wash	shime-waza
serpentry	severance	shahzadah	sharp-tail	Sheffield	shimiyana
serranoid	Sevillana	shakeable	Shastraic	sheikhdom	shine away
serration	Sevillano	shake a leg	shatterer	sheld-duck	shine down
serrature	Sevillian	shake down	shavecoat	sheldrake	shineless
serrefile	sewee bean	shakedown	shavehook	shelducks	shine upon

shine up to	shogunate	shortstop	shrinkage	siderosis	silential
shin-guard	shonicker	short suit	shrink fit	siderotic	silentish
shininess	shonkiest	short-term	shroffage	siderurgy	silica gel
shiningly	shootable	short time	shroudage	side salad	silicated
Shintoism	shoot away	short-toed	shrouding	side-shoot	siliceous
Shintoist	shoot back	short view	shrubbage	side-split	silicious
shipboard	shoot down	shortwall	shrubbery	side-stick	silicosis
shipborne	shoot-'em-up	shortward	shrubless	side-swipe	silicotic
ship canal	shop-board	short wave	shrublike	sideswipe	siliquose
ship-craft	shop class	short wind	shrub rose	side table	siliquous
ship-fever	shopcraft	short-wool	shrugging	sidetrack	silkaline
ship money	shop floor	shot alloy	shubunkin	side valve	silk-gland
ship-of-war	shopfront	shot-blast	shuffling	sidewards	silk grass
shipowner	shop-house	shot-borer	shunnable	side-wheel	silkiness
shippable	shopocrat	shotcrete	shunt line	side-wiper	silkoline
ship plane	shopwoman	shot-drill	shut-knife	sieva bean	silk waste
shippound	shorebird	shot-firer	shuttance	sieve cell	silliness
ship-royal	shore-boat	shot-glass	shuttling	sievelike	siltation
ship's boat	shore crab	shot-group	sialidase	sieve tube	siltstone
shipshape	shoreface	shotmaker	siallitic	sighfully	silver age
ship's time	shore-fish	shot-metal	sialogram	sighingly	Silverblu
ship-to-air	shore lark	shot noise	sialolith	sightable	silver eel
shipwreck	shoreless	shot-pouch	sibilance	sight bill	silver-eye
shire-hall	shoreline	shotproof	sibilancy	sight feed	silver fir
shire-jury	shore-rope	shot-tower	sibilator	sight-hole	silver fox
shiremoot	shoreside	shout down	siblicide	sightless	silvering
shire-town	shoresman	shovelard	sibylline	sight line	silverish
Shirodkar	shoreward	shovelful	sibyllism	sight-read	silverite
shirtiest	shoreweed	shovel hat	Sibyllist	sightseer	silverize
shirtless	shore zone	shovelled	siccative	sight-sing	silver key
shirt stud	shorn lamb	shoveller	sice-point	sightsman	silver-tip
shirt-tail	short-arse	shovel-man	siciliana	sight tube	silvester
shite-hawk	short ball	showbizzy	siciliano	sigillary	silvicide
shitepoke	short bill	show cause	sick-berth	sigillate	simantron
shit-faced	shortcake	shower box	sickening	sigma-bond	simarouba
shit-house	short-coat	shower-cap	sickishly	sigmatism	Simeonite
shithouse	short date	show fight	sick leave	sigmoidal	similarly
shittiest	short dung	show forth	sicklemia	signal box	Simmental
shivering	shortened	show-glass	sicklemic	signalise	simmering
shlimazel	shortener	show house	sicklepod	signality	simo chart
shmegegge	shorten in	showiness	sickliest	signalize	simonious
shmendrik	shortfall	show-piece	sick nurse	signalled	simon-pure
shoal-mark	short fuse	showpiece	Sicyonian	signaller	Simon Pure
shoalness	short game	show-place	Siddonian	signalman	Simon Says
shockable	short gown	showplace	side-aisle	signalmen	simpatico
shock cone	short-hair	show round	sideboard	signal red	simpering
shock cord	shorthair	show sport	side chain	signaries	simple eye
shockedly	shorthand	show trial	side chair	signatary	simplesse
shock-head	short haul	show-woman	sidedness	signation	simpleton
shock test	short head	Shqipetar	side drift	signatory	simple vow
shock tube	shorthold	shragging	side entry	signature	simulacra
shock wave	shorthorn	shredding	sideguard	signboard	simulacre
shoddiest	short hour	shrewdish	side-horse	sign digit	simulated
shoddyism	short leet	shrewlike	side issue	significs	simulator
shoddyite	short list	shrew-mole	side lever	signified	simulcast
shoeblack	shortlist	shrieking	side-light	signifier	sincerely
shoe-brush	short mark	shriek out	sidelight	signifies	sincerest
shoemaker	shortness	shriek-owl	sidelings	signorial	sincerity
shoe-piece	short odds	shrike-tit	side order	signories	Sindebele
shoeshine	short-punt	shrillish	side-piece	signorina	sine curve
shoesmith	short seas	shrimpish	side plate	Sikkimese	sinewless
shoe-valve	short stop	shrimplet	sideritic	silent cop	sing along

singalong	skateable	sky border	Slavonism	sloganeer	small reed
singed cat	skatepark	sky burial	Slavonize	sloganize	small room
singingly	skate-sail	sky-colour	sleazebag	slop about	small sail
single cut	skedaddle	skydiving	sleaziest	slop basin	small shot
single tax	skeezicks	sky-farmer	sleekness	slope arms	small slam
singleton	skeletony	sky filter	sleep-away	slopehead	small talk
sing small	Skeltonic	sky-flower	sleepered	slope wash	small-time
singsongy	skeptical	skyjacker	sleep fast	slopeways	small-town
singulary	sketchier	skylarker	sleepiest	slopingly	small type
singultus	sketchily	skylounge	sleepless	sloppiest	smalt-blue
Sinhalese	sketching	sky-marker	sleep over	sloppy joe	smaragdus
sinistral	sketchist	sky-rocket	sleepover	sloshiest	smarmiest
sinlessly	sketch map	skyrocket	sleep sofa	sloth bear	smart alec
sinneress	sketch pad	sky screen	sleepwalk	slot-hound	smart-arse
sinningia	skew field	slab bacon	sleeve-cap	slot-meter	smart card
sinologue	skew-whiff	slab-sided	sleeve dog	slot racer	smartcard
Sinologue	skiagraph	slab-stone	sleeve gun	slot wedge	smartness
Sinophile	skiamachy	slackener	sleevelet	slot-wound	smartweed
Sinophobe	skiascope	slack hand	sleeve-nut	slouch hat	smasheroo
sinuately	skiascopy	slack lime	sleigh bed	slouchily	smatterer
sinuation	ski-bobber	slackness	slenderer	slouching	smear-case
sinuosely	skiddooos	slack rein	slenderly	Slovakian	smear test
sinuosity	ski-joring	slack-rope	sleuth-dog	Slovakish	smegmatic
sinuously	ski jumper	slackster	sliceable	Slovenian	smellable
sinusitis	skilfully	slack suit	slickered	Slovenish	smell a rat
siphonage	skill-less	slaggiest	slickness	slow-belly	smelliest
siphonate	skim-board	slag-glass	slickster	slowcoach	smell-less
siphonein	skimobile	slag notch	slideable	slow-hound	smilacina
siphonous	skimpiest	slakeless	slide-rest	slow loris	smileable
siphuncle	skin cream	slalomist	slide-rock	slow march	smileless
sippingly	skin depth	slammakin	slide rule	slow match	Smilesian
sirenical	skin diver	slanderer	slide-wire	slow track	smilingly
siren suit	skin-dried	slangiest	slidingly	slow virus	smith shop
Sir Garnet	skin-flick	slangster	slightish	slow wheel	smock-face
Siryenian	skinflint	slanguage	slime-ball	slug it out	smockless
sisal hemp	skin graft	slant-eyed	slime-flux	slug-nutty	smock-mill
sisserara	skin house	slant-eyes	sliminess	slug-snail	smock-race
sissified	skinniest	slant-line	sling-back	sluice-box	smoggiest
sissiness	skinny-dip	slantways	sling-cart	sluice-way	smokeable
sistering	skinny-rib	slantwise	sling pump	slumberer	smoke-ball
Sisyphean	skin-tight	slap-happy	slingshot	slumbrous	smoke-boat
Sisyphism	skintight	slapstick	slingsman	slummiest	smoke bomb
sitatunga	skin tonic	slash-hook	slinkiest	slummocky	smoke bush
sit-downer	skin trade	slash-pine	slip a disc	slump test	smoke-free
site value	skiograph	slate blue	slip-cased	slung shot	smoke-head
sit-me-down	skiomachy	slate club	slip-catch	slush-cast	smoke-hole
sitomania	skippable	slate grey	slip-coach	slush fund	smoke-jack
sitringee	skirt duty	slat fence	slip cover	slushiest	smokeless
situation	skirt-land	slatiness	slipe wool	slush-lamp	smoke-pole
situtunga	skirtless	slaughter	slip joint	slush pump	smoke ring
sit well on	skirtlike	slave-born	slip-noose	slut's wool	smoke-room
sitzkrieg	skirt soil	slave-fork	slippered	smackeroo	smoke-shop
Six Day War	Skokomish	slaveless	slippiest	smacksman	smoke tree
six-seater	Skoptsism	slavering	slip-plane	small arms	smokiness
sixteenmo	skotophil	slave ship	slip ratio	small beer	smoochier
sixteenth	Skraeling	Slavicist	slip sheet	small-bore	smoochily
sixth form	skrimshaw	Slavicize	slipstone	small-cell	smoothish
sixth part	skull-fish	slavishly	slittiest	small coal	smorzandi
sixtyfold	skull-less	Slavistic	slivovitz	small debt	smorzando
sixty-nine	skunk-bear	slavocrat	slobberer	small deer	smotherer
sizarship	skunk-bird	Slavonian	slob trout	small guts	smudge pot
size-stick	skunkweed	Slavonise	sloe-thorn	smallness	smudgiest

smuggling	snootiest	soap-stock	soil-creep	solvolyse	sorrel-top
smut-grass	snooziest	soapstone	soil group	Somaschan	sorriness
smut-hound	snore away	soap-suddy	soil phase	sombreros	sorrowful
smuttiest	snore-hole	soap-works	soil water	someplace	sorrowing
Smyrnaean	snoreless	soaringly	sojourner	something	sortation
Smyrniote	snoringly	sobbingly	sokemanry	sometimes	sortieing
snack food	snot-nosed	soberness	solaceful	sometimey	sortilege
snag-tooth	snottiest	sobriquet	solar apex	somewhere	sortilegy
snailfish	snout-face	sob sister	solar cell	somewhile	sortition
snail-horn	snoutless	soccer fan	solar hour	sommelier	sostenuto
snail-like	snout-moth	soccerite	solariums	somnolent	Sothiacal
snail mail	snowberry	socialise	solar lamp	Somocista	so to speak
snail-slow	snow-blind	socialism	solar mass	so much for	sottishly
snake bird	snow-blink	socialist	solar myth	so much the	sotto voce
snake eyes	snowboard	socialite	solar pond	Sonagraph	soubrette
snakefish	snowbound	sociality	solar pool	song cycle	soufrière
snake-head	snow-break	socialize	solar salt	songfully	soughless
snake hips	snow-broth	social war	solar time	song-motet	soul-force
snakelike	snow buggy	sociation	solar wind	song-perch	soulfully
snakeroot	snow bunny	sociative	solar year	songsmith	soul-house
snakeship	snow-camel	societary	soldering	sonically	soul music
snakeskin	snow-craft	societies	soldierly	sonicator	soul stuff
snakesman	snow-creep	sociogram	soldier on	sonic bang	sou markee
snakeweed	snow devil	sociolect	solemness	sonic boom	sound bite
snakewise	snowdrift	sociology	solemnify	sonic mine	sound boom
snakewood	snow-eater	sociopath	solemnise	sonneteer	sound card
snakiness	snowfield	socketing	solemnity	sonneting	sound cell
snakishly	snow finch	socket set	solemnize	sonnetize	sound-film
snap gauge	snowflake	Socotrine	solenette	son of a gun	sound gate
snaphance	snow-fleck	Socratean	solenodon	son of toil	sound head
snap out of	snow goose	Socratist	sole-plate	sonograph	sound-hole
snappable	snow grain	Socratize	solfatara	sonolysis	soundhole
snappiest	snow-grass	soda bread	solfeggio	sonolytic	soundless
snap-sound	snowiness	soda glass	solferino	sonometer	soundness
snare drum	snow-maker	soda nitre	solicited	sons-in-law	sound post
snareless	snow mould	soda water	solicitee	soon after	sound wave
snarliest	snow-mouse	sodbuster	solicitor	sooranjee	soup bunch
snazziest	snow plane	sodomitic	solidaire	sooterkin	soupiness
sneak-boat	snow plant	Soerensen	solid body	soothfast	soup plate
sneakered	Snow Queen	soft-board	solid fuel	sootiness	soup spoon
sneakiest	snowscape	soft brome	solidness	sooty tern	soup-stock
sneaksman	snowshoed	soft-cover	soliflual	sophianic	sour bread
sneck-band	snowshoer	soft drink	solifugid	sophister	sour cream
sneck-draw	snow-sleep	softening	soliloquy	sophistic	sour crout
sneeshing	snowstorm	softer sex	soli-lunar	sophistry	sourdough
sneeze gas	snow-water	soft focus	solipsism	sophomore	sour gourd
Snell's law	snow white	soft fruit	solipsist	soporific	sour grass
snelskrif	snub-nosed	soft goods	solipugid	soppiness	sour-sweet
snideness	snuff-dish	soft-grass	solitaire	sopranino	souteneur
sniffable	snuff film	soft maple	sollicker	sopranist	South Bank
sniffiest	snuffiest	soft-nosed	solmizate	sorb-apple	Southdown
sniggerer	snuffless	soft-paste	solodized	sorbitize	south-east
snipe bill	snuffling	soft pedal	soloistic	Sorbonist	South-East
snipe fish	snuff-mill	soft-shell	Solomonic	sorceress	southerly
snipiness	soakingly	soft sugar	solonchak	sorceries	Southeyan
snippiest	Soanesque	soft Tommy	solonized	sorcerize	southland
snivelled	soapberry	soft touch	solo whist	sorcerous	southmost
sniveller	soapboxer	soft wheat	solstitia	sordidity	southness
snobbiest	soap-house	sogginess	solutizer	sorediate	south pole
snob value	soapiness	soi-disant	Solutrean	soredioid	South Seas
snockered	soap opera	soil auger	Solutrian	sore point	south-side
Snohomish	soap-plant	soil class	solvation	soritical	southward

south-west	sparingly	speedboat	spikenard	spiritous	spokeless
South-West	spark ball	speed bump	spike-rush	spiritual	spoken for
south wind	spark coil	speed hump	spike-team	spirituel	spokesman
souvlakia	sparkless	speediest	spikiness	spirogram	spokesmen
souvlakis	sparklike	speed king	spillikin	spirogyra	spokewise
sou'wester	spark line	speedless	spill over	spiroidal	spoliator
sovereign	sparkling	speed-read	spillover	spirulina	spondylus
Sovietise	sparkover	speedster	spinal tap	spissated	sponge bag
Sovietism	spark plug	speed trap	spination	spit blood	spongeful
Sovietist	sparkplug	Speed-walk	spin a yarn	spit chips	spongeing
Sovietize	sparsedly	speedwell	spindlage	spiteless	spongelet
Sovnarkom	spar-stone	speedy cut	spindlier	spitework	spongeous
sow-backed	Spartanly	speldring	spindling	spit image	spongiest
sow-gelder	sparteine	spellable	spin-drier	spit it out	spongiole
soya sauce	Spartiate	spellbind	spindrift	spit-roast	spongiosa
space-ager	spasmatic	spell down	spin-dryer	spit-shine	spongiose
space club	spasm band	spelldown	spinebill	spitstick	spongious
spaceless	spasmodic	spellican	spinefoot	splashier	sponsalia
space lift	spasmogen	speluncar	spineless	splashily	sponsible
spacelike	spathodea	spelunker	spinelike	splash-net	spookiest
space-line	spatially	spendable	spine road	splash out	spoon-back
space mine	Spätleses	spent gnat	spinetail	splat-cool	spoon-bait
spaceport	spattered	spermatia	spin glass	splatting	spoonbill
space race	spatulate	spermatic	spin-house	splay-foot	spoon-feed
spacer gel	spatulose	spermatid	spiniform	spleenful	spoonfeed
spaceship	spatulous	sperm bank	spininess	spleenish	spoonfuls
space shot	speakable	sperm cell	spin label	splendent	spoon-hook
space-sick	speakably	speronara	spinnable	splendour	spooniest
spacesuit	speak-back	spew frost	spinnaker	splenetic	spoonless
space-time	speakeasy	spewiness	spinneret	splenitis	spoon-meat
space walk	speak fair	sphacelia	spinniken	splenosis	spoonwood
space warp	speak past	sphacelus	spin-orbit	spleuchan	spoonworm
space wave	speak with	sphagnose	spinorial	splice-bar	spoonyism
spaciness	spearfish	sphagnous	spinosely	splintage	sporangia
spacistor	spearhead	sphendone	spinosity	splintery	spore-case
spade-bone	spearlike	sphenotic	Spinozism	splinting	sporeling
spade-farm	spearmint	sphere gap	Spinozist	split-arse	sporidium
spadefish	spear-play	spherical	Spinozite	split beam	sporocarp
spade foot	spear side	spherular	spin-rinse	split-dose	sporocyst
spadefuls	spearsman	sphincter	spintrian	split-down	sporocyte
spadelike	spearwood	sphinxian	spinulate	split flap	sporogony
spadesman	spearwort	spicebush	spinulose	split gear	sporozoan
spade-tree	specially	spice-cake	spinulous	split-half	sporozoon
spadewise	specialty	spice mill	spiracles	split jeté	sportance
spadework	specie jar	spice rack	spiracula	split jump	sportfish
spae-craft	specified	spicewood	spiral arm	split mind	sportiest
spaghetti	specifier	spiciness	spirality	split page	sportless
spagyrist	specifies	spick-span	spiralize	split rail	sportling
Spam medal	speckless	spiculate	spiralled	split ring	sports car
spanaemia	speckling	spiderish	spiraloid	split shot	sports day
spanandry	spectacle	spider-leg	spirantal	split time	sportsman
Spanglish	spectator	spiderman	spiration	splitting	sportsmen
Spanishly	spectrous	spidermen	spireless	splittism	sportster
spareable	speculate	spiderweb	spiriform	splittist	sporulate
spareless	speculist	spiffiest	spirillar	splodgily	spot board
spareness	speech act	spigelian	spirillum	spluttery	spot check
spare part	speech day	spike-buck	spiritful	spodumene	spot level
spare time	speechful	spike-fish	spirit gum	spoilable	spotlight
spare tyre	speechify	spike heel	spiriting	spoil-five	spot meter
sparganum	speeching	spike-horn	spiritism	spoilless	spot-nosed
sparge arm	speechlet	spikelike	spiritist	spoilsman	spot plate
spargosis	speedball	spike-nail	spiritize	spoilsmen	spottiest

spousally	squashier	stackless	staminody	start over	steel-iron
spout-bath	squashily	stack-room	staminoid	star tulip	steel mill
spout-fish	squatness	stack-yard	stammerer	starvedly	steel tape
spout-hole	squat rack	stackyard	stampable	star-wheel	steel trap
spoutless	squattage	staddling	stamp book	statehood	steel wool
sprackish	squattest	stadhouse	stamp duty	stateless	steelwork
spratting	squattily	staffette	stampeder	statelily	steelyard
sprayable	squatting	staffless	stamp-mill	State line	steenbras
sprayed-on	squattish	staff-room	stanchion	statement	steenbuck
sprayless	squaw corn	staffroom	stand away	stateroom	steenkirk
spraylike	squaw duck	staff vine	stand back	Stateside	steentjie
spray zone	squawfish	stageable	stand buff	statesman	steep-down
spreading	squawk-box	stage door	stand down	state-wide	steephead
sprechery	squaw-root	stage hand	stand easy	staticize	steepness
spreckled	squaw-weed	stagehand	stander-by	stational	steerable
sprekelia	squeakery	stage hero	stand good	stationer	steerhide
sprigging	squeakier	stage left	stand high	statistic	steerling
sprightly	squeakily	stagelike	stand mute	statively	steersman
sprigtail	squeamish	stage name	stand on me	stativity	steersmen
springald	squeamous	stage play	stand over	statocone	stegomyia
spring bed	squeegeed	staggerer	standpipe	statocyst	stegosaur
springbok	squeegees	staghound	stand upon	statocyte	steinbock
spring-gun	squelcher	staginess	stand up to	statolith	steinkirk
springier	squencher	Stagirite	stand well	statuette	Steinmann
springily	squibbery	stag movie	stanhopea	statusful	Stelazine
springing	squibbing	stagnance	stannator	status quo	stellaria
springlet	squibbish	stagnancy	stapedial	statutory	stellated
sprinkler	squidding	stag-night	stapedius	staunchly	stellerid
spritsail	squid fish	stag-party	stapeliad	stave-wood	stellular
sprouting	squidgier	stag's head	staple gun	stay-awake	stem borer
spruce fir	squidgily	stag's horn	star-anise	Staybrite	stem-glass
spruce hen	squiffier	staidness	star-apple	stay-clean	St Emilion
spruce tea	squillion	stainable	star atlas	St Bernard	stemmatic
spunkiest	squinancy	stainless	starboard	steadfast	stem piece
spunkless	squint-eye	staircase	starburst	steadiest	stenchful
spur-rowel	squiralty	stair-foot	star chart	steadyish	Stenonian
spur royal	squirarch	stairhead	starchier	steady pin	stenosing
spur-wheel	squiredom	stairless	starchily	steak raid	stenotope
sputcheon	squirelet	stairlift	star cloud	stealable	stenotype
sputterer	squirmier	stair-step	star coral	steam bath	stenotypy
spymaster	squirt can	stairwell	star-delta	steam beer	stent-roll
squabbier	squirt gun	stake-boat	stare down	steam-bent	stepbairn
squabbish	squirting	stake-body	star-facet	steamboat	stepchild
squabbler	squishier	stalactic	star fruit	steam-coal	step-dance
squaddies	squitters	stalemate	stargazer	steam-cure	step fault
squadrism	Sri Lankan	staleness	star-grass	steam-heat	step-gable
squadrist	stabilate	staleness	staringly	steamiest	stephanic
squalidly	stabilise	Stalinise	starkness	steam iron	step motor
squalmish	stabilism	Stalinism	starlight	steamless	step-stool
squameous	stabilist	Stalinist	star-proof	steam line	step wedge
squamosal	stability	Stalinite	starquake	steamroll	steradian
squarable	stabilize	Stalinize	starriest	steamship	stercoral
square cap	stable boy	Stalinoid	star route	steatitic	sterculia
square cut	stable-fly	stalkable	starry ray	steatosis	sterilant
square hit	stableful	stalk-eyed	starscape	steedless	sterilely
square law	stable lad	stalkless	star shell	steekgras	sterilise
square leg	stableman	stalklike	star-shine	steel band	sterility
squareman	stablemen	stall-feed	star-stone	steel-clad	sterilize
square off	staccatos	stall seat	start in on	steel drum	stern-boat
square pin	stachyose	stall turn	start-line	steel-face	sternebra
squarrose	stackable	stalworth	startling	steelhead	stern-fast
squash bug	stack arms	staminate	startlish	steeliest	Stern Gang
		staminode			

stern-line	stimulate	stomachal	stop thief	straplike	strikable
sternmost	stingaree	stomached	stop valve	strap-line	strike off
sternness	sting-fish	stomacher	stopwatch	strappado	strike oil
stern-port	stingiest	stomachic	stop-water	strapping	strike out
sternpost	stingless	stomatose	store card	strap-rail	strike pay
stern-rail	stinglike	stomatous	store-farm	strap shoe	string art
stern tube	stink-bird	stompneus	storeroom	strap-work	string bed
stern-walk	stink bomb	stone-bark	storeship	strapwork	string cot
sternward	stinkeroo	stone-bass	storesman	strapwort	stringent
steroidal	stinkhorn	stone-blue	store-wide	Strasburg	stringful
Stetsoned	stinkiest	stone-boat	storey box	stratagem	stringier
stevedore	stinkweed	stonebuck	storiated	strategic	stringily
stewardly	stinkwood	stone-cast	storiette	strategus	stringing
stewardry	stintedly	stone-cell	storkling	stratiote	string man
stewartry	stintless	stonechat	stormable	straw boss	string out
stibophen	stipended	stone-coal	storm-area	strawless	string tie
stichical	stipiform	stone-cold	storm-bird	strawline	striolate
stick at it	stipitate	stone-crab	storm coat	strawneck	strip cell
stick-back	stippling	stonecrop	storm-cock	straw poll	strip club
stickball	stipulate	stone-dead	storm cone	straw ring	strip-down
stick bean	stipulode	stone-deaf	storm cuff	straw tick	stripiest
stick-bomb	stirabout	stone-delf	storm-door	straw vote	stripline
stick down	stir-crazy	stone-dust	storm-drum	straw wine	stripling
stick 'em up	stir-fried	stone-dyke	storm-flap	straw-work	strip-loin
sticker-up	stir-fries	stone face	stormiest	straw-worm	strip mall
stick fast	stirpital	stone-fall	stormless	straw yard	strip mill
stick free	stitchery	stonefish	storm-sail	strayaway	strip mine
stickiest	stitching	stoneless	storm-wave	stray-line	stripping
stick it on	stock-book	stonelike	storm wind	strayling	strip well
stickless	stock-card	stone-lily	stornello	streakier	strobilus
sticklike	stock cube	stone line	story book	streakily	strokable
stickling	stock dove	stone-mint	storyette	streaking	stroke oar
stick pigs	stock duck	stone pine	storyless	streaming	strolling
stick-slip	stockfish	stone ring	story-line	streamlet	stromatic
stick to it	Stockholm	stone-root	storyline	stream-tin	stromboid
stick up to	stockiest	stone-shot	stoss-side	stream-way	strong-arm
stickweed	stockinet	stonewall	stounding	streelish	strongbox
stick with	stockless	stoneware	stourness	street boy	strongers
stickwork	stock line	stoneweed	stoutness	streetcar	strongest
sticky dog	stocklist	stonework	stoveless	street dog	strong eye
sticky end	stock-lock	stonewort	stove-pipe	streetful	strongish
sticky-out	stockpile	stone-yard	stow-blade	street kid	strong man
stiffener	stock rail	stoniness	stow-board	streetlet	strongman
stiff-leaf	stockroom	stonkered	straddler	streetman	strongmen
stiff-neck	stock-size	stony-iron	straggler	street rod	strongyle
stiffness	stocktake	stoolball	straight-A	streetway	strontian
stigmaria	stock unit	stoop ball	strainful	strengite	strontium
stigmatic	stock up on	stoop crop	straining	strengthy	stroppier
stigmergy	stock-whip	stoothing	stranding	strenuity	stroppily
stilettos	stockwork	stop-and-go	strangely	strenuous	stropping
stillborn	stockyard	stop-block	strangled	stressful	structure
stilleite	stodgiest	stop-drill	strangler	stressman	struggler
still-head	stoep-room	stop-hound	strangles	stretcher	strumatic
still hunt	stoically	stop light	strangury	strewment	strumitis
still less	stokehold	stop-order	strap-bolt	striation	strumming
still life	stoke-hole	stoppable	strap-down	striature	strung-out
stillness	stokehole	stoppo car	strap-fork	striction	strutting
still room	Stokes' law	stop press	strap-game	stricture	strychnia
stiltedly	stole-fees	stop-ridge	strap-hang	stridence	strychnic
stilt heel	stolidity	stop-seine	strap iron	stridency	strychnos
stilt-root	stolonate	stop short	strap-laid	strifeful	stubbiest
stimulant	stolonial	stop-start	strapless	strigated	Stubbsian

stub-tenon	subahship	submucous	succourer	sulphamic	sunset law
stub track	subalpine	subnormal	succubous	sulphated	sun-spider
stuccador	subaltern	suboctave	succulent	sulphazin	sun-spring
stuccoist	subapical	subocular	succumber	sulphidic	sun spurge
stuckness	subaquean	subpatent	succursal	sulphinic	sunstroke
studental	subarctic	subphylum	suckening	sulphinyl	sunstruck
studentry	subastral	subpoena'd	sucker-cup	sulphonal	Sun Yat-sen
stud-groom	subatomic	subramose	sucking-up	sulphonic	superable
stud-horse	Sub-Boreal	subregion	suck-teeth	sulphonyl	superacid
stud-house	subbotnik	subrision	suctional	sulphured	superbike
studiable	sub-bottom	subrisive	suctorial	sulphuret	superbity
studiedly	sub-branch	subrogate	suctorian	sulphuric	superbomb
stud poker	subcaudal	subrotund	sudatoria	sulphuryl	Super Bowl
study hall	sub-cheese	subsample	sudoresis	Sulpician	supercede
stuff coat	sub-clause	subscribe	sudorific	sulpiride	supercity
stuff gown	subclause	subscript	suedehead	sultanate	supercoil
stuffiest	subclimax	subsecive	suede shoe	sultaness	supercool
stuffless	subcostal	subsellia	suet crust	sultanism	supercrat
stuffover	subdeacon	subserous	suet-faced	sultanize	superegos
stump-foot	subdivide	subsidies	Suez group	sultriest	superette
stumpiest	subdolous	subsiding	suffering	summaries	superfine
stump-jump	subdorsal	subsidise	suffixoid	summarily	superflow
stump mast	subduable	subsidium	suffixual	summarise	superflux
stumpnose	subduedly	subsidize	suffocate	summarist	superfuse
stump-tail	sub-editor	subsocial	Suffolker	summarize	supergene
stump word	subeditor	subsoiler	suffragan	summation	superglue
stump-work	subentire	substance	suffrutex	summative	supergrid
stuntedly	subereous	substract	suffusion	summer-day	superheat
stunt-head	subfactor	substrata	suffusive	summer egg	superhero
stuntness	subfamily	substrate	sugar beet	summering	superhive
stupefied	subfossil	substruct	sugarbird	summerish	supermale
stupefier	subgenera	substylar	sugar-bush	summerize	supermart
stupefies	subhedral	subsultus	sugar-camp	summing-up	supermind
stupidest	subiculum	subsystem	sugar cane	summiteer	supernate
stupidish	subincise	subtenant	sugar-coat	summonses	supernova
stupidity	subinfeud	subtenure	sugarless	summulist	superpose
stuporose	subjacent	subterete	sugar loaf	sump guard	super-race
stuporous	sub judice	subtilely	sugar-mite	sumptuary	super-real
sturdiest	subjugate	subtilise	sugar palm	sumptuous	supersede
stutterer	sublation	subtilism	sugar-pine	sun awning	supersign
style-book	sub-lessee	subtility	sugar-plum	sun-bathed	superstar
styleless	sub-lessor	subtilize	sugarplum	sunbather	supervene
stylidium	sub-lethal	subtitler	sugar sack	sun-bonnet	supervise
styliform	subletter	subtopian	sugar sand	sun-bright	superweak
stylishly	sublimate	subtribal	sugar snap	Sundanese	supinator
stylistic	sublimely	subtriple	sugar snow	Sundayish	suppering
stylitism	sublimest	subtropic	sugar soap	sundowner	suppliant
stylobata	sublimity	subulated	sugar-sops	sun filter	supply day
stylobate	sublimize	subungual	sugar-teat	sunfisher	supply-led
stylohyal	sublinear	subvassal	sugar-tree	sunflower	supporter
stylolite	sublunary	subversal	sugar vase	sun-grazer	supposing
stymieing	subluxate	subverter	suggester	sun-helmet	suppurate
styptical	submarine	subwarden	suggestor	sunk fence	supremacy
styrofoam	submaster	subwoofer	suggestum	sun-kissed	supremely
Styrofoam	submental	succedent	sugillate	sun-kissed	supremity
styrolene	submerged	succeeder	suicidism	sun lotion	surcharge
suability	submicron	succentor	suikerbos	sun lounge	surcingle
suasively	submissly	successor	suit at law	sunniness	surculose
suaveness	submittal	succinate	suit regal	sunny side	sure thing
suavities	submitted	succinite	suit royal	sunrising	surfacely
subaerial	submitter	succorant	sulciform	sun-scorch	surfacing
subagency	submucosa	succotash	sulkiness	sunscreen	surfboard

surfeited	swampiest	sweet papa	sword-belt	sympodial	syntaxial
surfeiter	swampland	sweet rush	swordbill	sympodium	Syntaxian
surf-grass	swamp lily	sweetshop	sword-cane	symposiac	syntectic
surficial	swamp-pink	sweet-sour	sword-case	symposial	synthalin
surf music	swamp rock	sweet spot	sword-fern	symposium	syntheses
surf-perch	swan goose	sweet talk	swordfish	synagogal	synthesis
surfusion	swanimote	sweet-veld	sword-hand	synagogue	synthetic
surgeless	swankiest	sweet wine	sword knot	synalepha	syntrophy
surgeoncy	swan plant	sweetwood	swordless	synangium	syphilide
surgeries	Swan River	sweet wort	swordlike	synanthic	syphilise
surge tank	swansdown	swellfish	sword lily	syncellus	syphilize
Surinamer	swan-upper	swell-head	swordplay	Synchromy	syphiloid
surliness	swan-white	swept-back	sword-side	synchrony	syphiloma
surmaster	Swarajist	swept-wing	swordsman	synchysis	syphonage
surmullet	swarm cell	Swiderian	swordsmen	syncitium	Syracusan
surpasser	swarthier	swift-foot	swordtail	synclinal	Syriacism
surpliced	swarthily	swiftness	sword-work	syncopate	Syrianize
surplus to	swartness	swimathon	swung dash	syncretic	syringeal
surprisal	swartzite	swimdress	swy school	syncytial	syringing
surprised	swash mark	swimgloat	sybaritic	syncytium	systaltic
surpriser	swash-work	swimmable	sycophant	syndactyl	systemise
surquidry	Swatantra	swimmeret	syllabary	syndicate	systemist
surreally	swatching	swindlery	syllabify	syndromic	systemize
surrejoin	swatchway	swine-back	syllabise	synechism	systoflex
surrender	sway-brace	swine-cote	syllabism	synechist	systrophe
surrendry	swayingly	swine-head	syllabize	synecious	taaffeite
surrogacy	swear pink	swineherd	syllabled	synectics	tabacosis
surrogate	swear word	swinehood	syllepses	synedrian	tabasheer
survivant	sweat-band	swine-hull	syllepsis	synedrion	tabbouleh
suscitate	sweatband	swing-back	sylleptic	synenergy	tabbyhood
Susianian	sweat-bath	swingball	syllogise	syneresis	tab collar
suspected	sweatered	swing-boat	syllogism	synergise	tabellion
suspecter	sweatiest	swingboat	syllogist	synergism	tablature
suspector	sweatless	swing-coat	syllogize	synergist	table bell
suspended	sweat-pore	swing-door	sylphlike	synergize	table-book
suspender	sweatshop	swingeing	sylvanite	syngameon	table desk
suspensor	sweat sock	swing-gate	sylvanity	syngamous	tablefuls
suspicion	sweatsuit	swing hand	sylvester	syngeneic	table game
Sussex cow	sweep away	swingiest	Sylvester	synizesis	table lamp
sustained	sweepback	swing-over	sylvinite	synizetic	tableland
sustainer	sweep hand	swing pass	symbioses	synkaryon	table-maid
sustenant	sweep-wire	swing room	symbiosis	synneusis	tablement
susuhunan	sweerness	swing-rope	symbiotic	synochous	table-plan
susurrant	sweet corn	swingster	symbolise	synodally	table ruby
susurrate	sweetcorn	swing-tail	symbolism	synodical	table salt
susurrous	sweetener	swing-tool	symbolist	synodsman	table talk
sutleress	sweet-eyed	swing-tree	symbolize	synoecism	table tape
sutteeism	sweet fern	swing vote	symbolled	synoecize	table-tomb
suturally	sweet flag	swing-wing	symbology	synoekete	tableware
Svanetian	sweet gale	swinishly	symmelian	synoicous	table wine
Svengalis	sweetikin	swipe card	symmetral	synonymic	tablewise
swaddling	sweet John	swipecard	symmetric	synopsise	tabularly
swag belly	sweetleaf	Swiss bank	sympathic	synopsize	tabulator
swaggerer	sweet life	Swiss file	sympatric	synoptist	tacamahac
Swahilize	sweet lime	Swiss roll	symphilic	synostose	tachylite
swainmote	sweetling	switching	symphonic	synovitis	tacitness
Swaledale	sweetlips	switchman	symphonie	synsacral	tackifier
swallower	sweetmart	switch off	symphylan	synsacrum	tackiness
swamp deer	sweetmeal	swivel eye	symphylid	syntactic	tack-money
swamp fire	sweetmeat	swivel-gun	symphyses	syntagmas	tactfully
swamp hare	sweet milk	swivelled	symphysis	syntagmic	tactician
swamp hook	sweetness	sword-bean	symplasma	syntaxeme	tacticity

tactilely	take aside	tangental	tarsalgia	Taylorism	telematic
tactility	take a step	tangerine	tarsotomy	Taylorize	telemeter
tactually	take a toll	tanginess	Tartarean	Tchambuli	telemetry
tae kwon do	take a toss	tangliest	Tartarian	Tchuktchi	telemotor
taeniasis	take a walk	tank wagon	tartarise	teaboardy	teleology
taffy pull	take a wife	tannaitic	tartarize	tea-broker	teleonomy
taft joint	take cover	tanneries	tartiness	teachable	teleosaur
tag and rag	take guard	tantadlin	tartronic	teachably	telepathy
tagmemics	take hands	tantalate	Tashi Lama	teacherly	telephone
tagnicati	take heart	Tantalean	tasimeter	teacupful	telephony
tag-phrase	take issue	tantalian	task force	tea garden	telephote
tahsildar	take it ill	Tantalian	task group	tea-kettle	telephoto
tail-block	take-leave	tantalise	Tasmanian	tea master	telepoint
tailboard	take place	tantalite	Tasmanoid	team-teach	teleprint
tail-drain	take roost	tantalize	tasselled	team vicar	telerobot
tail-ender	take shape	tantivies	tasseller	teapotful	telesales
tailer-out	take short	tant mieux	tasteable	tear apart	telescope
tailgater	take sides	Tanzanian	tasteless	tear-fault	telescopy
tail-grape	take stock	tanzanite	tastesome	tearfully	teleseism
tail-heavy	take to bed	Taoiseach	taste-test	tear-gland	telestich
tail-hound	take turns	tap-cinder	tastiness	tear sheet	teletyper
tail light	take water	tap-dancer	tastingly	tear-smoke	televisor
tailordom	Talbotype	tape-delay	tasto solo	tear-thumb	tell apart
tailoress	talc light	tape drive	tatami mat	teartness	tell a tale
tailoring	talcuming	tape-grass	tater-trap	teasel-bur	tellingly
tailorism	talegalla	tape punch	Tatianist	teashoppy	tellinite
tailorize	tale of woe	taper-lock	tattiness	teasingly	tell tales
tailpiece	taliation	taperness	tattooing	tea-taster	tell-truth
tailplane	talismans	taperwise	tattooist	tea-things	tellurate
tail-rhyme	talk about	tape-sizer	Tauberian	Tebilized	tellurian
tail rotor	talkathon	tapespond	Tauchnitz	technical	telluride
tail-screw	talkative	taphonomy	taunt-song	technicum	tellurion
tail-shaft	talking of	Tapleyism	tauricide	technique	tellurism
tail-slide	talking-to	tap-rooted	tauriform	tectiform	tellurite
tail-spine	talk round	tapstress	tauroboly	tectogene	tellurium
tailstock	talky-talk	tap wrench	taurodont	tectonics	tellurous
tail-valve	tall drink	tar and tig	tautology	tectonism	teloblast
tailwards	tall-grass	tarantass	tautonymy	tectonite	telomeric
tail-water	talliable	tarantism	Tavastian	tectonize	telophase
tail wheel	tall order	tarantula	tawdriest	tectorial	telotaxis
tailwheel	tallow-cut	taraxacin	tawniness	tectrices	temazepam
tainchell	tallow-dip	taraxacum	tawny port	teddy bear	temperate
taintless	tallowish	tar-barrel	taxaceous	Teddy girl	temperish
tai-otoshi	tallow-nut	tardiness	tax credit	tediously	temper-pin
tai-sabaki	tallow-top	tarentaal	tax-dodger	teenagery	tempietto
Taiwanese	tall poppy	Tarentine	tax dollar	teensiest	temporale
takamakie	tally card	tarentola	tax-eating	teenspeak	temporary
take aback	tally-hoes	targeteer	taxed cart	teeny-tiny	temporise
take a bath	Talmudism	targeting	taxed ward	Teeswater	temporize
take about	Talmudist	target man	tax-evader	tegmental	temptable
take a fall	talmudize	target pin	tax-exempt	tegmentum	tempt fate
take after	talookdar	targetted	taxi dance	tegularly	temptress
take a hint	talus cone	target-tug	taxidermy	Tehuelche	temulence
take a joke	tamarillo	Targumist	taximeter	teknonymy	temulency
take alarm	tambookie	Targumize	taxiplane	telamones	tenacious
take a leak	tambourer	tarmacked	taxi squad	telecomms	tenaculum
take amiss	tambourin	tarnation	taxi strip	teleferic	tenaillon
take apart	tamoxifen	tarpaulin	taxonomer	telegenic	tenancies
take a pull	tamponade	Tarragona	taxonomic	telegonic	ten a penny
take a punt	tamponage	tarriance	tax relief	telegraph	tenderest
take a risk	tamponing	tarriness	tax return	teleguide	tenderise
take a seat	tanalized	tarryhoot	Taylorise	teleiosis	tenderish

tenderize	termagant	test strip	thecodont	therapies	thingness
tenderpad	terminate	tête-à-tête	the common	therapist	thingummy
tendinous	terminism	tête-bêche	thecosome	therapsid	thing-word
tendonous	terminist	tetracene	the Deluge	Theravada	thinkable
tendrilly	termitary	tetractys	the Divine	the Reaper	thinkably
tenebrism	termiting	Tetradite	the dozens	thereaway	think back
tenebrist	term paper	tetragamy	the Eleven	therefore	think long
tenebrity	term-piece	tetraglot	the Empire	therefrom	think over
tenebrose	ternately	tetragram	the Fringe	thereinto	think-tank
tenebrous	terpenoid	tetraktys	theft-boot	there it is	think with
ten-eighty	terpineol	tetralogy	theftuous	thereness	thinnings
ten-finger	terra alba	tetrapody	the Garden	thereover	thin on top
ten-gallon	terracing	tetrarchy	the glassy	Theresian	thin space
Tennessee	terraform	tetrasome	thegnhood	thereunto	thioester
tennis arm	terraglia	tetrasomy	thegnship	thereupon	thio-ether
tennis net	terramara	tetrazole	the hounds	therewith	thionazin
tennis pro	terramare	tetromino	theileria	theriacal	thiophene
ten o'clock	terranean	tetroxide	the ladies	the rise of	third-best
tenonitis	terrarium	tetterous	the Ladies	thermally	third gear
tenor bell	terra rosa	Teutonise	the latest	thermical	third hand
tenor clef	terrazzos	Teutonism	the League	thermidor	third last
ten-seater	terrenely	Teutonist	thelemite	Thermidor	thirdness
tenseless	terrenity	Teutonize	the Litany	thermoset	third part
tenseness	terricole	textology	thelytoky	thermotic	third rail
ten signal	terrified	textorial	them and us	the road to	third-rate
tensility	terrifier	text paper	the man who	therology	third root
tensional	terrifies	textually	the mass of	thesaurus	third slip
tensioner	territory	texturing	thematize	the Scrubs	thirdsman
tensorial	terrorise	texturise	the matter	these days	thirstful
ten-strike	terrorism	texturize	theme park	the shakes	thirstier
tentacled	terrorist	thack-tile	theme song	the size of	thirstily
tentacula	terrorize	Thai stick	theme tune	the smalls	thirtieth
tentacule	terseness	thalamite	the missis	the sooner	thirtyish
tentative	tervalent	thalassic	the moment	the spit of	thirty-one
tent-cloth	Tervueren	thallious	then-a-days	the squits	thirty-six
tent dress	terza rima	Thamudite	the nation	the States	thirty-two
ten tenths	terzettos	thanatoid	theobroma	the sticks	this child
tent-flies	Tesla coil	thanehood	the occult	the Stores	this world
tenth Muse	tessaract	thane-land	theocracy	the street	thitherto
tenth part	tesselate	thaneship	theocrasy	the Sweeps	tholeiite
tenth-rate	tessellar	thankless	theogonic	the Tarmac	Thomistic
Tenthredo	tesseract	than usual	theolatry	thetatron	thong-weed
tenth wave	tesserate	thatching	the old sod	the Terror	Thorazine
tent-maker	tessitura	that's flat	theologal	the Twelve	thoriated
tentorial	testacean	that's that	theologer	theurgist	thornback
tentorium	testacies	that's what	theologic	the Usages	thornbill
tent-stake	testament	that there	theologue	the Virgin	thorn bush
ten-twenty	testation	thaumatin	theomachy	the waters	thorniest
tenuously	testatrix	the absurd	theomancy	they're off	thornless
teocallis	test chart	theandric	theomania	thickener	thornlike
tephigram	test-cross	the animal	theopathy	thick-film	thorn moth
tephritic	test drive	thearchic	theophagy	thickhead	thorntail
tephritid	test-frame	theatrics	theophany	thick-knee	thorn tree
tephroite	testified	theatrize	theorbist	thick-knit	thornveld
tepidness	testifier	the Baltic	theorboed	thickness	thornwood
teporingo	testifies	Thebesian	theoretic	thickskin	thorow-wax
teratogen	testimony	the best of	theorizer	thick-sown	thoughted
terceroon	testiness	the boards	theosophy	thieflike	thoughter
terebinth	test match	the Border	the plains	thigh bone	thousands
terebrant	test paper	the Broads	the Psalms	thigh-boot	thralldom
terebrate	test-piece	the Castle	the queen's	thigh roll	thrashing
Terentian	test pilot	the Circus	the Queens	thinghood	thrash out

thrasonic	thrustful	tiger-like	time study	tizziness	tonalitic
thread bag	thrusting	tiger lily	timetable	T-junction	Tonbridge
threadfin	thumb-band	tiger milk	time train	Tlaxcalan	toneburst
threadier	thumbless	tiger moth	time trial	toad-eater	toned-down
threading	thumbling	tiger's-eye	timidness	to a degree	tone-group
threadlet	thumb-lock	tiger-ware	timocracy	toadstone	tongue-bit
threatful	thumb-mark	tiger-wolf	Timor deer	toadstool	tonguelet
three ages	thumbnail	tiger-wood	Timor pony	to a nicety	tongue-pad
three-axis	thumb pick	tight back	timorsome	toast rack	tongue-tie
three-ball	thumb-ring	tight cask	timpanist	toastrack	tonically
three-body	thumb-rope	tightener	tinder-box	to a tittle	tonic wine
three-card	thumbtack	tight head	tinderbox	to a wonder	tonka bean
three-deck	thundered	tightness	tinder-dry	toccatina	Tonkinese
threefold	thunderer	tightrope	tin-enamel	Tocharian	tonograph
three-foot	thuringer	tight ship	tingliest	Tocharish	tonometer
three-four	Thursdays	tight spot	tin-hatted	today week	tonometry
three-line	Thurstone	tikinagun	tin helmet	toddy-bird	tonoplast
three-mast	thus and so	tiki torch	tinkerdom	toddy palm	tonotaxis
threeness	thwacking	tile-drain	tin-kettle	toddy-tree	to nothing
three-part	thwarting	tile-maker	tin Lizzie	toe-dancer	tonotopic
three-pile	thwart-saw	tile-sherd	tinned air	toe-ragger	tonsillar
threesome	Thyestean	tilestone	tinned dog	toe-rubber	tonsorial
three-spot	thylacine	till-alarm	tinniness	toe-weight	tonsurate
three-star	thylakoid	Tillamook	tin-opener	toftstead	ton weight
three-toed	thymallus	tillering	tinselled	togavirus	Tony award
threnetic	thymidine	tillerman	tin-stream	togidashi	toodle-pip
threnodes	thymocyte	tilt guard	tint-block	toilet bag	tool-house
threnodic	thyratron	tiltmeter	tintinnid	toilet box	tool-maker
threonine	thyristor	tilt rotor	tip-and-run	toileting	toolmaker
threshing	thyrocele	tilt-wheel	tip for tap	toilet set	tool steel
threshold	thyroidal	timber-dog	tipsiness	toilfully	toothache
thresh out	thyroidic	timber due	tipsy-cake	toilingly	toothachy
thriftier	thyronine	timbering	tip-tap-toe	tokenless	toothcarp
thriftily	thyrotomy	timber jam	tip-tilted	token ring	tooth-comb
thrilling	thyroxine	timberman	tiptoeing	token vote	toothcomb
throatful	Tiburtine	timbermen	tip-topper	Tokharian	toothiest
throatier	tick-a-tick	timber-toe	tiredness	tokoloshe	toothless
throatily	tick-borne	Timbuctoo	tiretaine	tolerable	toothlike
throating	ticket-day	time about	tire-woman	tolerably	tooth-mark
throatlet	ticketing	time check	tirshatha	tolerance	toothpick
throbbing	tick fever	time clock	tit and ass	tolerancy	tooth-pulp
throbless	tickicide	time-delay	titchiest	tolerator	toothsome
thrombose	tidal boat	time depth	tit for tat	tolerogen	toothwort
thronedom	tidal bore	time frame	tithe barn	tolguacha	toothy-peg
throppled	tidal flow	timefully	titheless	toll-booth	toot sweet
throttler	tidal wave	time-lapse	titillate	tollbooth	top banana
througher	tiddliest	timeliest	titivator	toll-house	top cutter
throughly	tiddy oggy	time limit	title deed	tol-lol-ish	top cymbal
throwable	tidelands	timenoguy	titleless	toll plaza	top dollar
throw a fit	tide table	time of day	title-page	toll-taker	top drawer
throw away	tidetable	timeously	title-part	Tolstoyan	topectomy
throwaway	tidewater	timepiece	title role	toluidine	top-flight
throw back	tie a can on	time-saver	titleship	tomatillo	top-hamper
throwback	tie and dye	time-scale	title song	tomboyish	top-hatted
throw down	tiercelet	timescale	titration	tomboyism	topiarian
throw-line	tierceron	time-share	tit-tat-toe	tombstone	topiaries
throw open	tiffanies	timeshare	tittivate	tomentose	topiarist
throw over	tiffining	time sheet	tittlebat	tomentous	topically
throwster	tiger barb	time-shift	tittuping	tommyhawk	top-loader
thrum-eyed	tigerfish	time slice	tittupped	tommy ruff	topminnow
thrumming	tigerhood	time–space	titubancy	Tommy-shop	topocline
thrumwort	tiger-iris	time-stamp	titularly	tomograph	topograph

topologic	to the last	townscape	Trafalgar	trapezial	tree onion
toponymic	to the life	townsfolk	tragedian	trapezing	tree peony
toposcope	to the lips	townwards	tragedies	trapezist	tree pipit
toposcopy	tother day	toxaphene	tragedist	trapezium	treescape
top people	to the skin	toxically	tragedize	trapezius	tree shrew
toppingly	to the wide	toxicosis	tragelaph	trapezoid	tree snake
top-sawyer	to this day	toxigenic	Tragerian	trap-hatch	tree swift
top scorer	to this end	toxocaral	traghetto	trap-house	tree trunk
top secret	Totonacan	toxophily	trailable	trap-light	trefoiled
top-stitch	totting-up	toxophore	trail arms	trap-match	tregetour
topstitch	touchable	Toynbeean	trail bike	trappings	trehalase
topsy-turn	touch-back	trabeated	trail boss	trap-point	trehalose
top-timber	touchback	trabecula	trail head	trapshoot	treillage
top twenty	touch base	traceable	trailless	trapskiff	trek chain
top-weight	touch down	traceably	trail-rope	trapstick	trek fever
torbanite	touchdown	traceless	trailside	trash fish	trek wagon
torch-fish	touch-hole	traceried	trainable	trashiest	trellised
torchless	touchiest	traceries	trainband	trash nail	trematode
torch lily	touch-kick	tracheary	train down	trash-rack	tremblant
torch race	touch-last	tracheate	trainless	trash rock	tremblier
torch song	touchless	tracheole	trainload	trashtrie	trembling
torchwood	touch-line	trachytic	train-mile	trattoria	tremissis
toreutics	touchline	track-ball	train-shed	traumatic	tremogram
tormented	touch-mark	trackball	trainsick	travailer	tremolant
tormentil	touch shot	track-boat	trainside	traveling	tremolist
tormentor	Touch Tone	track down	train-spot	travelled	tremolite
tormentry	touch-type	trackless	train-stop	traveller	tremorine
tornadoes	touch wood	track-line	traitress	traversal	tremulant
torpedoes	touchwood	track shoe	Trakehner	traversed	tremulate
torpefied	toughener	trackside	tralucent	traverser	tremulous
torpefies	tough luck	trackster	tramphood	travisher	trenchant
torpidity	toughness	track-suit	tram-plate	trawl-beam	trenchful
torpitude	tough shit	tracksuit	trample on	trawl-buoy	trenchman
torquated	Touretter	track with	trampling	trawl-head	trench-rat
torrefied	Tourettic	track-work	trampoose	trawl line	trendiest
torrefies	touristic	tractable	trancedly	trawl-warp	trendless
torridity	tournasin	tractably	tranceful	tray-buggy	trend line
torsional	tournedos	tractator	transaxle	tray stand	trendyism
tortillon	tournesol	tract home	Transcash	tray table	trepanger
tortrices	tournette	tractless	transcend	treachery	trepanned
tortricid	tourneyer	tradeable	transcode	treadless	trepanner
torturous	Tourte bow	trade book	transduce	treadmill	trepidant
torulosis	tourtière	trade card	transfect	treasurer	trepidate
Toryishly	Toussaint	trade down	transform	treatable	trepidity
to satiety	tout court	trade-last	transfuse	treatably	treponeme
tosheroon	towelette	tradeless	transgene	treatment	tressette
to speak of	towelhead	trade mark	transient	Trebbiano	triagonal
tosticate	towelling	trademark	transited	trebuchet	trial-bred
total heat	towel rail	trade name	translate	trebucket	trial heat
totalizer	towerless	trade-room	transmake	treddling	trial jury
totalling	towerlike	trade-sale	transmiss	tredrille	trialling
totalness	tow-headed	trade show	transmute	tree agate	triallist
totem pole	towing-net	tradesman	transomed	tree civet	trialogue
to the boil	town clerk	tradesmen	transonic	tree daisy	triangled
to the bone	town clown	trade term	transpire	tree deity	triannual
to the dogs	town crier	trade-test	transport	tree-goose	triathlon
to the east	town-guard	trade wind	transpose	tree heath	triatomic
to the echo	town house	tradition	trans-ship	tree house	triatomid
to the fore	towniness	traditive	transship	tree limit	triazolam
to the full	town-major	traditors	transstage	tree-louse	tribadism
to the good	town mayor	traducian	transumpt	tree lupin	tribalism
to the hilt	town mouse	traductor	trap-drums	tree mouse	tribalist

tribalize	trihedral	trochlear	trunk-hose	tumescent	turntable
tribeless	trihedron	trollopee	trunkless	tumidness	turn-under
tribeship	trihybrid	trombenik	trunk line	tummy-ache	turpitude
tribesman	trihydric	tron-pound	trunk main	tumorigen	turquoise
tribesmen	trijugate	troop-ship	trunk road	Tunbridge	turreting
tribology	trilineal	troopship	trunk-work	tunefully	turriform
tribulage	trilinear	troostite	truss-beam	tunesmith	Tuscanism
tribulate	trilithic	troparion	truss-hoop	tungstate	Tuscanize
tribunate	trilithon	trophaeum	trustable	tungstite	Tuscarora
Tribunite	trillions	trophy tax	trust deed	tungstous	tusk shell
tributary	trilobate	tropicana	trust fund	Tungusian	tussilago
tricenary	trilobite	tropistic	trustiest	tunicated	tussocked
trichinae	trilogies	tropology	trustless	tunicless	tussocker
trichinal	trimerous	tropolone	truth drug	tuning-key	tutiorism
trichitic	trimester	tropylium	truth game	tuning peg	tutiorist
trichogen	trimethyl	trothless	truthless	tunnelist	tutorhood
trichroic	trimetric	troubling	truthlike	tunnelled	tutorless
trichrome	Trimphone	troublous	trying-pot	tunneller	tutorship
trichuris	trinality	troughful	try-scorer	tunnel-net	twaa-grass
trickiest	Trinidado	troughing	try-square	tunnel-pit	twaddling
trickless	trinities	trouncing	Tsakonian	Tupamaros	twayblade
trickling	trinitrin	trousered	tsarevich	Tupinamba	tweediest
trickment	trinketry	trousseau	tsaricide	Tupperian	twelfthly
tricksier	trinomial	Trousseau	Tsimshian	Tupperism	twelvemos
tricksily	trionymal	troutless	tsugi ashi	turbaries	twentieth
tricksome	triparted	trout-lily	Tsukahara	turbidite	twentyish
trickster	tripelike	trout-line	tsurikomi	turbidity	twenty-one
triclinia	triplasic	troutling	tubbiness	turbinate	twenty-two
triclinic	triploidy	trowelful	tubectomy	turboprop	twice-born
tricolour	trip-madam	trowelled	tube dress	turbopump	twice-laid
tricosane	tripmeter	troweller	tube-nosed	turbulent	twice-told
Tricotine	tripoline	troxidone	tubercled	turcopole	twiddling
tricresyl	trippiest	truanting	tubercula	tureenful	twifallow
tricrotic	triptyque	truantism	tubercule	Turfanian	twig-borer
tricuspid	tripudist	truceless	tube skirt	turfiness	twilighty
tricycler	tripudium	truck crop	tube steak	turgidity	twin-birth
tricyclic	triquetra	truckload	tube train	turkeyhen	twin float
tridactyl	triradial	truck-shop	tub garden	turkey oak	twingeing
tridecane	triradius	truckster	tubicolar	Turkey red	twiningly
tridental	Trisagion	truck stop	tubificid	Turkey rug	twinkling
tridented	trisector	truckstop	tub-pulpit	Turkicize	twin plate
tridrachm	trisomy-21	truculent	tubularly	Turkishly	twin prime
tridymite	tristesse	true coral	tubulated	Turk's head	twin-screw
triecious	tritanope	true-false	tuckamore	turmoiler	twirligig
triennial	triteness	true lover	tucker-bag	turn about	twistable
triennium	tritheism	true-metal	tucker-box	turnabout	twistedly
trierarch	tritheist	true molar	tuck-plate	turn after	twisteroo
Triestine	tritheite	true north	tuck-point	turn again	twist grip
trieteric	tritiated	truepenny	tuck-seine	turnagain	twistical
trifacial	triticale	true right	Tudor rose	turn-bench	twistiest
trifolium	Tritoness	true topaz	tufaceous	Turnerian	twist knot
triforial	triturate	trump card	tug of love	Turnerism	twist-lock
triforium	triumphal	trumpeted	Tuileries	turnerite	twist pile
triformed	triumpher	trumpeter	tuitional	turnip-fly	twist yarn
trigamist	triumviri	trumpetry	tulip fire	turn loose	twitchety
trigamous	triumvirs	truncated	tulip-like	turn out of	twitchier
trigemini	trivalent	truncheon	tulip-root	turnpiker	twitchily
triggered	trivially	trunkback	tulip tree	turn round	twitterer
trigintal	tri-weekly	trunk-band	tulip-wood	turnround	two and two
trigonous	trocheize	trunk call	tulipwood	turn-screw	two a penny
trig point	trochilus	trunkfish	tumble-bug	turnstile	two-bagger
trigynous	trochleae	trunkfuls	tumble-dry	turnstone	two-bottle

two-by-four	uki-gatame	unannoyed	unbundler	uncongeal	underbear
two cheers	uki-otoshi	unanxious	unburning	uncontent	underbill
two-Chinas	Ukrainian	unapplied	unburthen	uncontrol	underbite
two-decker	ulcerated	unapropos	uncandour	unconvert	underbody
two-figure	uliginose	unaptness	uncannier	uncordial	underbred
two-fisted	uliginous	unarrayed	uncannily	uncorrect	underbrim
twofoldly	ulotrichy	unarrived	uncapping	uncorrupt	underburn
two-footed	Ulsterman	unashamed	uncareful	uncounted	underbush
two-forked	Ulstermen	unaskable	uncarried	uncoupled	undercard
two-handed	ultimatum	unassayed	unceasing	uncoupler	undercart
two-hander	ultracold	unassumed	uncentral	uncoursed	undercast
two-headed	ultradian	unassured	uncentred	uncourted	underclad
two-leaved	ultra-high	unattaint	uncertain	uncourtly	underclay
two-legged	ultrahigh	unattired	uncessant	uncouthie	underclub
two-lipped	ultrathin	unattuned	unchained	uncouthly	undercoat
two-old-cat	ululation	unaudited	unchalked	uncovered	under-cook
two-piecer	ululatory	unavenged	unchanged	uncoveted	undercook
two-seater	umbellate	unaverted	unchanted	uncracked	undercool
two-stroke	umbellule	unavoided	uncharged	uncramped	undercure
two-suiter	umbilical	unbaffled	uncharity	uncreased	underdamp
two-tailed	umbilicar	unbalance	uncharmed	uncreated	underdeck
two-thirds	umbilicus	unbandage	uncharnel	uncrested	underdone
two-valued	umbratile	unbanning	uncharred	uncrinkle	underdose
Tyburnian	umfundisi	unbaptise	uncharted	uncropped	underdraw
Tychonian	umpteenth	unbaptize	unchecked	uncrossed	underdrew
tycoonery	umpty-nine	unbarring	uncheered	uncrowded	underedge
tycoonish	umzimbeet	unbashful	unchidden	uncrowned	underface
tylectomy	unabashed	unbearded	unchilded	uncrumple	underfall
tympanist	unabating	unbearing	unchilled	uncrushed	underfeed
tympanums	unabiding	unbeguile	unchinked	unctional	underfeet
Tynesider	unability	unbeknown	unchipped	unculture	underfelt
type genus	unabraded	unbelieve	unchopped	uncunning	underfill
type-lever	unaccused	unbeloved	uncinated	uncurable	under fire
type metal	unactable	unbending	uncivilly	uncurdled	underflow
type-wheel	unadapted	unbethink	unclaimed	uncurious	under foot
typewrite	unadmired	unbewitch	unclarity	uncurling	underfoot
typhlitic	unadopted	unbiassed	unclasped	uncurrent	underfund
typhlitis	unadoring	unbigoted	unclassed	uncurried	undergang
typhoidal	unadorned	unbinding	unclassic	uncurtain	undergear
Typhonian	unadvised	unblasted	uncleaned	undamaged	undergird
typically	unaerated	unblended	uncleanly	unda maris	undergrad
typograph	unaffable	unblessed	uncleanse	undaunted	undergrip
typophile	unaffixed	unblinded	uncleared	undazzled	underhair
tyranness	unaidable	unblooded	unclearly	undebased	under hand
tyrannies	unaidedly	unbloomed	uncleaved	undebated	underhand
tyrannise	unalarmed	unblotted	unclerkly	undecagon	underhang
tyrannize	unaligned	unblunted	uncleship	undecayed	under-head
tyrannous	unallayed	unblurred	unclimbed	undeceive	underhive
tyrantess	unallowed	unbookish	unclipped	undecency	underhold
tyre chain	unalloyed	unbounded	uncloaked	undecided	underhole
tyre gauge	unaltered	unbraided	unclogged	undefaced	underhung
tyrocidin	unamended	unbranded	unclothed	undefiled	underided
tyromancy	unamiable	unbridged	unclotted	undefined	underived
ubication	unamiably	unbridled	unclouded	undelayed	underkeel
ubiquitin	unamorous	unbriefed	uncloying	undelight	underkill
ude-garami	unamusing	un-British	unclutter	undeluded	under-king
ude-gatame	unangelic	unbrother	uncoerced	undenoted	underlaid
ufologist	unanimism	unbrought	uncombine	underarch	underlain
Uganda kob	unanimist	unbruised	uncomplex	under arms	underland
ugglesome	unanimity	unbrushed	unconcern	under a vow	underlead
ugli fruit	unanimous	unbuckled	unconfine	underback	underleaf
Uitlander	unannexed	unbuilded	unconfirm	underbark	underlier

underlife	undeserve	unexalted	ungodlike	unilineal	unlenited
underlift	undesired	unexcised	ungodlily	unilinear	unlighted
underline	undevious	unexcited	ungrafted	unimpeded	unlikable
underling	undevised	unexerted	ungranted	unincited	unlimited
under load	undignify	unexpired	ungrasped	unindexed	unliteral
underload	undiluted	unexposed	ungrassed	uninhumed	unlivable
underlook	undimpled	unextinct	ungreased	uninjured	unlived-in
under-lord	undivided	unfadable	un-Grecian	uninomial	unlocated
underlout	undivined	unfailing	ungreeted	uninsured	unlogical
undermass	undonnish	unfancied	ungrieved	uninvaded	unlosable
undermine	undoubted	unfarrant	ungritted	uninvited	unlovable
undermost	undowered	unfashion	ungroomed	uninvoked	unluckier
undernote	undrained	unfazable	ungrooved	uniocular	unluckily
under oath	undreaded	unfearful	ungrown-up	union down	unmakable
underpaid	undreamed	unfearing	ungrudged	Union flag	unmanacle
underpart	undressed	unfeather	unguarded	un-ionized	unmanaged
underpass	undresser	unfeeling	unguessed	unionized	unmangled
underpeep	undrilled	unfeigned	unguiform	union jack	unmanlike
underplay	undrowned	unfertile	ungulated	Union Jack	unmanning
under-plot	undrugged	unfestive	unhabited	union list	unmanured
underplot	undrunken	unfigured	unhandily	union pipe	unmarried
underpole	undulancy	unfitness	unhandled	union shop	unmartial
underprop	undulated	unfitting	unhappier	union suit	unmatched
underrate	undulator	unflanked	unhappily	union-wide	unmatured
under-read	undurable	unflecked	unharbour	uniovular	unmeaning
underread	unduteous	unfledged	unharmful	uniparous	unmeasure
underride	undutiful	unfleshed	unharming	uniplanar	unmeddled
underring	undyingly	unfleshly	unharness	unipotent	unmedical
underripe	undynamic	unflooded	unhassled	uniramous	unmelodic
underrobe	unearnest	unfloored	unhasting	uniserial	unmelting
underroof	unearthed	unflushed	unhatched	unisexual	unmenaced
underruff	unearthly	unflyable	unhaunted	un-Islamic	unmerited
under sail	uneaseful	unfocused	unhealthy	unisonant	unmetered
underseal	uneasiest	unfoolish	unheard-of	unisonous	unmindful
undersell	uneatable	unfortune	unhearing	Unitarian	unmingled
undershot	unechoing	unfounded	unheedful	unitarily	unminuted
underside	unedified	unfranked	unheeding	unitarism	unmixable
undersign	uneducate	unfraught	unhelpful	unitarist	unmixedly
undersize	uneffaced	unfreedom	unhelping	unitarity	unmonarch
underskin	unelastic	unfreeman	unheroism	unitively	unmoneyed
undersoil	unelbowed	unfretted	unholiest	unit price	unmorally
undersold	unelected	unfrosted	unholster	unit train	unmotived
undersong	unelegant	unfructed	unhonesty	unit trust	unmoulded
undersort	unemptied	unfuelled	unhopedly	univalent	unmounted
underspin	unenacted	unfunnier	unhopeful	universal	unmourned
undertake	unendowed	unfunnily	unhostile	unjarring	unmovable
undertide	unengaged	unfurnish	unhumanly	unjealous	unmovably
undertint	un-English	unfussily	unhumbled	unjointed	unmovedly
undertone	unenjoyed	ungainful	unhurried	unjustice	unmuddied
undertook	unentered	ungallant	unhurtful	unkedness	unmuscled
undertrod	unenticed	ungarbled	unhurting	unkemptly	unmusical
underturf	unenvious	ungarnish	unicelled	unkindled	unmuzzled
undervest	unequable	ungenteel	uniclinal	unkindred	unnatural
underwave	unequably	ungenuine	unicolour	unknitted	unneedful
underwear	unequally	unghostly	unicursal	unknotted	unnerving
underwent	unerrable	ungirdled	unicuspid	unknowing	unneutral
underwind	unerrancy	ungirthed	unifacial	unknown to	unnotable
underwing	unerupted	ungleaned	unifiable	unlasting	unnotched
underwire	unessayed	unglorify	uniformal	unlatched	unnoticed
underwood	unessence	unglossed	uniformly	unlatined	unobliged
underwool	unethical	unglutted	unignited	unleached	unobvious
underwork	unevolved	ungoddess	unijugate	unlearned	unoffered

unopening	unpuritan	unsavable	unsmelled	unsuiting	unvisored
unopposed	unpursued	unsavoury	unsmelted	unsullied	unvouched
unordered	unquailed	unsayable	unsmiling	unsuspect	unvoyaged
unorderly	unqualify	unscalped	unsmitten	unswaddle	unwakened
unorganic	unqueenly	unscanned	unsmoking	unsweeten	unwalking
unpacific	unquelled	unscarred	unsnapped	unswollen	unwarlike
unpainful	unquietly	unscathed	unsnuffed	untactful	unwarming
unpainted	unrallied	unscented	unsoberly	untainted	unwasting
unpalsied	unrattled	unscepter	unsolaced	untakable	unwatched
unpapered	unravaged	unsceptre	unsoldier	untamable	unwatered
unpartial	unrazored	unscience	unsoluble	untapered	unwealthy
unpassing	unreached	unscorned	unsonlike	untaxable	unwearied
unpatched	unreacted	unscoured	unsoothed	untelling	unweeting
unpatient	unreadily	unscraped	unsounded	untempted	unweighed
unpausing	unreading	unsecular	unsoundly	untenable	unwelcome
unpayable	unrealism	unsecured	unsparing	untenably	unwheeled
unpegging	unrealist	unseduced	unspawned	untenured	unwhipped
unpeopled	unreality	unseeable	unspecked	unthanked	unwillful
unperfect	unrealize	unseeking	unspelled	unthinned	unwilling
unperplex	unrebated	unseeming	unspilled	unthought	unwinding
unpervert	unrebuked	unselfish	unspliced	unthrifty	unwinking
unpetrify	unrecited	unselling	unspoiled	unthriven	unwishful
unphrased	unreduced	unsensual	unsported	unthumbed	unwishing
unpickled	unrefined	unserious	unspotted	untidiest	unwistful
unpierced	unrefuted	unservile	unsprayed	untighten	unwittily
unpiloted	unregular	unsetting	unspringy	untimeous	unwitting
unpinning	unrelated	unsettled	unspurred	untirable	unwomanly
unpiteous	unrelaxed	unsevered	unsquared	untoasted	unworking
unpitiful	unremoved	unsewered	unstabler	untoiling	unworldly
unpitying	unrenewed	unsexiest	unstacked	untongued	unworried
unplagued	unreplied	unshackle	unstaffed	untouched	unwounded
unplaited	unrescued	unshapely	unstained	untracked	unwrapped
unplanked	unreserve	unsheared	unstalked	untrained	unwreaked
unplanned	unresolve	unsheathe	unstamped	untrapped	unwreathe
unplanted	unrestful	unshelled	unstarred	untreated	unwrecked
unplastic	unresting	unshifted	unstarted	untrended	unwrested
unplaying	unretired	unshining	unstately	untressed	unwrinkle
unpleased	unrevised	unshipped	unstaunch	untrilled	unwritten
unpleated	unrevived	unshirted	unstaying	untrimmed	unwronged
unpledged	unrevoked	unshocked	unsteeled	untrodden	unwrought
unpliable	unridable	unshodden	unsteeped	untrusted	unzealous
unpliancy	unriddler	unshrined	unsterile	untumbled	unzipping
unplucked	unrigging	unshrived	unstiffen	untunable	up against
unplugged	unrightly	unshriven	unstifled	untunably	up and down
unplumbed	unripened	unshutter	unstilled	untuneful	up-and-over
unpointed	unripping	unsighing	unstinted	unturning	Upanishad
unpoliced	unrippled	unsighted	unstirred	untutored	uparching
unpolitic	unriveted	unsightly	unstocked	untwinned	upbraider
unpompous	unroasted	unsimilar	unstopped	untwisted	upbreathe
unpopular	unrounded	unsincere	unstopper	untypable	upbrought
unpotable	unroyally	unsinewed	unstoried	untypical	upbrushed
unpowered	unruffled	unsinking	unstrange	ununiform	upbuilder
unpraised	unrulable	unsinning	unstretch	unushered	up-channel
unprecise	unruliest	unskiable	unstriped	unusually	upconvert
unprepare	unrumpled	unskilful	unstudded	unuttered	up-country
unpressed	unsaddled	unskilled	unstudied	unvarying	upcurrent
unpricked	unsainted	unskimmed	unstuffed	unvaulted	updatable
unprickly	unsaintly	unskinned	unstylish	unveiling	updraught
unprinted	unsalable	unslacked	unsubdued	unvenomed	upfilling
unpromise	unsaluted	unsmartly	unsubject	unverdant	up for sale
unpropped	unsampled	unsmashed	unsuccess	unviolent	Uphaliday
unprovide	unsatiate	unsmeared	unsugared	unvisited	uphearted

upheaving	urine mark	vagarious	vaporetto	vein-stuff	vermicule
Up-Helly-Aa	urinology	vaginally	vaporific	veld-craft	vermiform
uphoisted	urkingdom	vaginitis	vaporizer	veldskoen	vermifuge
upholster	urochrome	vagolytic	vapouring	veld sores	vermilion
up Jenkins	urodelous	vagotonia	vapourise	vellicate	verminate
uplandish	urography	vagotonic	vapourish	velocious	verminous
uplift bra	urokinase	vagrantly	vapourize	velodrome	Vermonter
uplifting	urolagnia	vagueness	Varangian	velometer	vernaccia
uplighter	urolagnic	vainglory	variation	velvet ant	vernalise
upmanship	urologist	Vaishnava	variative	velveteen	vernality
upon sight	urophilia	Valaisian	varicella	velveting	vernalize
upon trust	uropygial	Valencian	varicosed	vendition	vernation
upper case	uropygium	valencies	variegate	venditive	verneuker
upper deck	Ursa Major	valentine	varieties	veneering	veronique
upper hand	Ursa Minor	Valentino	varietism	venerable	verrucose
uppermost	urticaria	valet-park	varietist	venerably	verrucous
upperwing	urticated	valiantly	varifocal	venerator	versatile
up-pricked	Uruguayan	validator	variolate	vengeable	verseless
up-putting	usability	validness	variolist	vengeably	versicule
uprightly	use-by date	Valkyrian	variolite	vengeance	versified
uprooting	uselessly	vallation	varioloid	veniality	versifier
ups-a-daisy	use the sea	vallecula	variolous	venireman	versifies
upsetting	usherette	valleyful	variously	venomness	versional
upsidaisy	usherless	valley tan	variphone	venomsome	vers libre
upsitting	ushership	valproate	variscite	venospasm	vertebrae
upstander	usitative	Valsalvan	vari-sized	ventiduct	vertebral
upstartle	usualness	valuation	varletess	ventifact	verticity
upswallow	usucapion	valuative	varnished	ventilate	Very light
upsy-daisy	usucaptor	value-free	varnisher	ventosity	vesicular
up the ante	usurpress	valueless	Varronian	ventrally	vespasian
up the flue	uterotomy	valvassor	varsities	ventricle	vesselful
up the line	utilities	valve head	Varsovian	venturous	vestibula
up the pole	utopianly	valveless	varvelled	Venusberg	vestibule
up the wall	Utraquism	valviform	varyingly	Venus clam	vestigial
up to putty	Utraquist	valvotomy	vasectomy	Venus' hair	vestigium
up to snuff	utricular	vambraced	vasomotor	veracious	Vestinian
uptrained	utriculus	vampiness	vasovagal	verandaed	vestiture
upturning	utterable	vampirine	vassalage	verapamil	vestryman
upwards of	utterance	vampirish	vassaldom	veratrine	vestrymen
upwarping	utterless	vampirism	vassaless	veratrole	vetchling
upwelling	uttermost	vampirize	vassalize	verbalise	vetoistic
upwhirled	utterness	vanadiate	vastation	verbalism	vetturino
uraninite	uvarovite	vanadious	vastidity	verbalist	vexatious
uranology	uvulatomy	vanaspati	vastitude	verbality	vexedness
uranotile	uvulotomy	vance-roof	vatically	verbalize	vexillary
urataemia	uxoricide	vandalise	Vatican II	verballed	viability
urban myth	vaaljapie	vandalish	vaticinal	verbascum	Via Crucis
urceolate	vacancies	vandalism	Veblenian	verberant	viaducted
urchin cut	vacatable	vandalize	vectorial	verberate	Via Lactea
urea cycle	vaccinate	Van der Hum	vectoring	verbicide	viatorial
ureameter	vaccinial	Van Gelder	vectorise	verbosely	vibracula
urea resin	vaccinist	vanillaed	vectorize	verbosity	vibraharp
uredinial	vaccinium	vanity bag	Vedantism	verdantly	vibrantly
uredinium	vaccinoid	vanity-box	Vedantist	verdigris	vibraslap
ure of land	vacillant	vanity set	vee engine	verdurous	vibratile
ureometer	vacillate	Vannetais	vegetable	vergeress	vibration
ureotelic	vacuolate	van-pooler	vegetally	Vergilian	vibrative
Uriah Heep	vacuously	vantbrace	vehemence	vergobret	vibratory
uricaemia	vacuumize	Vanuatuan	vehemency	veridical	vibriones
uricaemic	vacuum wax	vapidness	vehicular	veritable	vibrionic
uridrosis	vade-mecum	vaporable	veininess	veritably	vibriosis
urination	vadiation	vaporetti	veinstone	vermicide	vibrissae

vibrogram	vino dolce	visitress	Volterran	waggishly	wallpaper
vicariant	vinolence	visorless	voltinism	Wagnerian	wall-piece
vicariate	vinolency	vista-dome	voltmeter	Wagnerism	wall-plate
vicariism	vinometer	visual aid	volumetry	wagon boss	wall-sided
vicarious	vino rosso	visualise	voluminal	wagonette	wall space
vicarship	vino santo	visualist	voluntary	wagon-head	wall-stone
vicennial	vino secco	visuality	volunteer	wagon-load	Walpolian
Vicentine	vino tinto	visualize	vomitoria	wagonload	Walpurgis
vice-queen	vinylogue	visual ray	von Gierke	wagon-road	Walrasian
viceregal	violation	vital heat	voodooism	wagon-roof	Walras' law
vicereine	violative	Vitallium	voodooist	wagon-tent	Waltonian
viceroyal	violatory	vitaminic	voorloper	wagon-tree	waltz king
vicesimal	violently	Vitaphone	voracious	wagon-yard	wambenger
vice squad	violet bee	vitellary	vorlaufer	waifishly	Wampanoag
vice versa	violet-ear	vitelline	vorticism	wailfully	wanchance
viciously	violetish	vitiation	vorticist	wailingly	wanchancy
vicontiel	violet ray	vitiosity	vorticity	waistband	wandering
victimage	violet tea	Vitreosil	vorticose	waistcoat	Wanderobo
victimise	violinist	vitrified	vouchsafe	waist-deep	wandought
victimize	viosterol	vitrifies	vowelless	waist-high	wanked-out
Victorian	viperfish	vitriform	vox humana	waistless	wanthrift
victories	viper-like	vitrinite	vox nihili	waistline	wantonize
victorine	viperling	vitriolic	vox populi	wait about	want out of
victrices	viper-wine	Vitrolite	voyeurism	waitering	wapentake
victualer	viragoish	Vitruvian	voyeurist	wait for it	Wapishana
videlicet	virescent	vivacious	Vulcanian	waitingly	Wappinger
videodisc	virgation	Vivaldian	vulcanise	wait on God	war artist
video film	Virgilian	vive le roi	vulcanism	wait state	warble fly
video game	Virginian	viverrine	vulcanist	wakefully	war bonnet
videogram	virginity	vivianite	vulcanite	wake-robin	war damage
video jock	virginium	vividness	vulcanize	wakon-bird	wardrober
videotape	virgin wax	vivifying	vulgar era	Walachian	ward round
videotext	Virgoulee	vivotoxin	vulgarian	Walcheren	ward woman
vie en rose	virialize	vizierate	vulgarise	Waldenses	war effort
vie intime	viricidal	vizierial	vulgarism	waldflute	warehouse
viewgraph	virilized	vocabular	vulgarity	wale-piece	warfaring
viewiness	virilocal	vocal cord	vulgarize	walk about	war gaming
viewphone	virologic	vocalized	vulnerary	walkabout	Warholian
viewpoint	viropexis	vocalizer	vulpanser	walkathon	war-kettle
vigesimal	virtually	vocal line	Vulpecula	walk a turn	warlockry
vigilance	virtuosic	vocalness	vulpicide	walk-clerk	warmblood
vigilante	virucidal	vodkatini	vulpinism	Walkerite	warm front
vignetter	virulence	vo-do-deo-do	vulsellum	walk-march	warmonger
Vikingism	virulency	vogue word	vulturine	walk on air	war museum
villagery	virus-like	voice coil	vulturish	walk out on	warm-water
villaless	visagiste	voiceless	vulturous	walk-round	warningly
Villanova	vis a tergo	voice mail	vulviform	walk short	War Office
villiform	viscerate	voice-over	wackiness	wallabies	war orphan
villosity	viscidity	voice part	wadcutter	Wallacean	warp print
vimineous	viscidium	voice-tube	Wade–Giles	wall-board	warp speed
vinaceous	vis comica	voice vote	Wadhamite	wallboard	warranted
Vincennes	viscosity	voilà tout	wadsetter	wall brown	warrantee
vindemial	viscounty	voiturier	wafer-iron	wall chart	warranter
vindicate	viscously	vol-au-vent	waferlike	wallchart	warrantor
vin du pays	Vishnuism	volcanian	wafer-thin	wall clock	war-saddle
vine black	Vishnuite	volcanism	wage claim	wall cress	wart-biter
vine louse	visionary	volcanist	wage drift	walled-off	wart-cress
vine snake	visioning	volcanity	wagenboom	Wallerian	wart snake
vingerpol	visionist	volcanoes	wager-boat	walletful	warty newt
vingt-et-un	visitable	volkslied	wage scale	wall-fruit	war-worker
vino cotto	visitador	volkspele	wage slave	walloping	wash-basin
vino crudo	visitator	volte-face	waggeries	wallowish	washbasin

washboard	water-cool	Watsonian	web offset	wellstead	wheat-corn
wash-brush	water-crow	wattle-eye	weddinger	well-sweep	wheat-duck
washcloth	water cure	wattmeter	wedgebill	well-taken	wheat germ
washed out	water deer	wave aside	wedge-form	well-timed	wheatgerm
washerman	water down	wave-bread	wedge-heel	well-tried	wheat-land
washers-up	water drum	wave cloud	wedgelike	well water	wheatless
wash-house	water-dust	wavefront	wedge-shoe	well-wheel	wheatmeal
washiness	waterfall	wave group	wedgetail	well-willy	wheedling
washing-up	water fern	wave guide	wedge tent	well woman	wheel-back
washplain	water flag	waveguide	wedgewise	well worth	wheelbase
washstand	water flea	wavellite	Wednesday	Welsh aunt	wheelless
wash-table	Waterford	wavemeter	weed-grown	Welshcomb	wheel-like
wash-water	waterfowl	wave-motor	weedicide	Welsh harp	wheel lock
washwoman	watergall	wave-power	weediness	Welsh main	wheel-made
Waspiness	watergate	waverider	weekender	Welshness	wheel-seat
waspishly	Watergate	waveshape	weeknight	Welsh wave	wheel slip
wasp-paper	water-gilt	wave-siren	weepiness	wenchless	wheelsman
wasp's nest	water-head	wave train	weepingly	wenchlike	wheelsmen
wasp-waist	water-hole	wax-billed	Wehrmacht	wend again	wheel-spin
wassailer	waterhole	wax candle	weighable	Wernerian	wheelspin
waste-book	water jump	wax-colour	weigh a ton	wernerite	wheel well
waste-cock	water-knot	wax flower	weigh-beam	werowance	wheelwise
waste-gate	water-laid	wax-insect	weigh down	Werterean	wheelwork
waste-heap	water-lane	wax-kernel	weigher-in	Werterism	wheely bin
waste heat	water-leaf	wax museum	weigh into	Wesleyism	whelphood
wasteland	waterless	wax myrtle	weighment	westabout	whelpless
wasteless	water lily	wax pocket	weightage	westbound	whelpling
wasteness	water-line	wax resist	weightier	west coast	whencever
waste-pile	waterline	wax tablet	weightily	West-ender	whensoe'er
waste pipe	water main	wayfaring	weighting	westering	whereaway
waste plug	watermark	way letter	weinkraut	westerner	wherefore
waste silk	water mass	waymarker	weird-like	westernly	wherefrom
waste-weir	water mica	way of life	weirdness	West India	whereinto
wastingly	water-mill	way-ticket	weirdsome	West Saxon	whereness
Waswahili	watermill	waywarden	welcomely	West Sider	whereunto
watchable	water-mite	waywardly	welcoming	westwards	whereupon
watchband	water-mole	wayzgoose	weld decay	wether hog	wherewith
watch-bell	water pipe	weakening	welfarism	wet season	wherryman
watch-bill	water polo	weaker sex	welfarist	Weyl group	wherrymen
watch-boat	water-pore	weak grade	wellanear	whackiest	whetstone
watch-care	water pump	weak-kneed	well aware	whakapapa	whey-cream
watch-case	water rail	weakliest	wellawins	whaleback	whey-faced
watch-fire	water rate	weak point	well-being	whale-bird	whichaway
watchfire	water ring	weald-clay	well-brick	whaleboat	whichever
watch hill	water-sail	wealdsman	well-built	whalebone	whichways
watchless	watershed	wealthful	well-cress	whale-feed	whiffiest
watch-list	waterside	wealthier	Wellerism	whale-food	whiffling
watch-mate	water silk	wealthily	well-found	whalehead	whillaloo
watch over	water-spot	wealth tax	well-grate	whalerman	whillywha
watch room	water-stop	weaponeer	well-grown	wharf-boat	whimberry
watchword	water taxi	wear-dated	well-house	wharfless	whimperer
watchwork	water tree	weariable	well-kempt	what about	whimsical
water-bath	water tube	weariless	well known	what a life	whinberry
water bear	water vine	weariness	well-liked	what and if	whingeing
water bird	water vole	wearingly	well-lined	what cheer	whininess
waterbird	water-wave	wearisome	well-loved	what gives	whiningly
waterbody	waterweed	weaselled	well-meant	what price	whinstone
water-buck	water-wolf	weatherly	well-oiled	whatsoe'er	whip-craft
water-bull	waterwork	weaver ant	well-order	what's what	whip-crane
Waterbury	water-worm	weaveress	well-point	what's with	whip-graft
water-butt	waterwort	weavingly	well-saved	wheat belt	whippable
water-cart	wathstead	web-footed	well spent	wheat-bird	whipper-in

whip-round	white monk	wide-scale	windhover	wirephoto	wolf's head
whip snake	White Monk	wide-where	windiness	wirescape	wolf's-milk
whipstaff	white mule	wide world	windingly	wire story	wolf-snake
whipstall	whiteness	widow-bird	winding up	wire wheel	Wollaston
whip-stick	whitening	widowered	windolite	wire-wound	wolverene
whipstock	white note	widowhood	window box	Wisconsin	wolverine
whirl-bone	white pine	widow's men	windowful	wisecrack	woman-body
whirligig	white port	widow-wail	windowing	wise woman	woman-born
whirlpool	White Raja	widthways	window tax	wish-dream	womanhead
whirl-puff	white rent	widthwise	windproof	wishfully	womanhood
whirlwind	white room	wiederkom	windrower	wishingly	woman-hour
whiskered	white rose	wieldable	wind-shake	wishtness	womanizer
whisk tail	white rust	wieldiest	wind shear	wispiness	womankind
whiskyish	white sage	Wiener dog	windstorm	wistfully	womanless
whisky mac	white sale	Wiffle bat	windswept	witch-ball	womanlike
whisperer	white-shoe	wiggliest	windthrow	witch-bowl	womanness
whistling	white-skin	wightness	wind-tight	witchetty	woman's man
White Army	white sock	wig-picker	wind-trunk	witch-hunt	womenfolk
whitebait	white soup	wigwagged	wineberry	witch-knot	womenkind
white bass	white spot	Wilburite	wineglass	witchlike	women's lib
whitebeam	white titi	wild basil	wine-grape	witch-lock	wonder boy
white bear	whitewall	wild beast	wine-house	witch-mark	wonderful
white belt	white ware	wild goose	wine label	witch-post	wondering
white bird	whitewash	wild horse	wine lodge	witchweed	wonkiness
white book	whitewear	wild Irish	winemaker	witchwork	wood apple
white cane	whiteweed	wild pansy	wine-party	witereden	wood avens
white cell	whitewing	wild pitch	winepress	with a bang	woodbined
white clay	whitewood	wildscape	wing chair	with a bump	wood bison
white coal	white work	wild tansy	wing-cover	with a rush	woodblock
white coat	white worm	willemite	winged elm	with a will	wood-borer
whitecoat	whitherso	Willesden	wing-shell	with child	woodchuck
white comb	whittawer	willingly	wing-snail	with costs	woodcraft
white crow	whittling	will needs	wink-a-peep	withdrawn	wood-drake
white-damp	Whitworth	willowily	winkle-pin	withering	wooden cut
white deal	whizz-bang	willowish	Winnebago	witherite	wooden leg
white-eyed	whodunnit	willow oak	winningly	withernam	woodentop
whiteface	wholefood	willow tit	winsomely	withouten	wood fibre
white fish	whole gale	will-power	winterage	withstand	wood-fired
whitefish	whole-life	will to art	winter bud	with usury	wood-flour
white flag	whole meal	wilsomely	winter day	with young	wood-grain
white flux	wholemeal	Wilsonian	winter egg	withywind	woodhenge
white fuel	whole milk	Wilsonism	wintering	witlessly	wood-house
white goat	wholeness	Wilsonite	winterise	witnesser	woodhouse
white gold	whole note	Wiltshire	winterish	witteboom	woodiness
white grub	whole-rock	Wimbledon	winterize	wittering	wood-knife
white hake	wholesale	wimpiness	Winter War	witticism	woodlouse
Whitehall	wholesome	wimpishly	win the day	witticize	wood mouse
whitehead	whole-time	wincingly	wintriest	wittiness	wood nymph
white heat	wholewise	wind a horn	wipe-clean	wittingly	wood-paper
white hole	whoop-de-do	wind-bells	Wiradhuri	woadwaxen	wood-print
white hope	whoop it up	wind-blown	Wiradjuri	wobbegong	wood-pussy
white iron	whoo-whoop	wind-bound	wire birch	wobbliest	woodquest
White Lady	whore-hunt	windbound	wire brush	wobbygong	wood-reeve
white land	whore's egg	wind-brace	wire cable	woebegone	woods boss
white lead	whoreship	wind-break	wire cloth	woe betide	woods colt
whitelike	whore-shop	windbreak	wire-drawn	woe be to us	wood-screw
white lime	whorishly	wind-chest	wire-frame	wolfberry	woodscrew
white line	whosoever	wind-chill	wire gauge	wolfhound	wood-seary
white list	wickedest	wind-crust	wire gauze	wolfishly	woodsmoke
white loaf	wide-angle	wind-drift	wire-glass	wolframic	wood-snail
white meat	wide awake	wind force	wire grass	wolfsbane	wood-spell
white mica	wideawake	wind-gauge	wire house	wolf's claw	woodspite

wood stain	World Bank	wrestling	xylophone	yolk gland	Zetlander
wood-stork	world fair	wretchock	xylorimba	Yom Kippur	Zetlandic
wood-stove	worldhood	wriggling	yacht club	yonderway	zeuglodon
wood sugar	worldless	wrighting	yachtsman	Yorkshire	zeugmatic
woodwards	worldlier	wring-bolt	yachtsmen	Yoshiwara	zeunerite
woodwaxen	world-life	wrinklier	yacht-yard	you bet you	zigzagged
woody pear	worldlily	wrinklies	Yahwistic	you name it	zillionth
wool alien	world-line	wrinkling	yam potato	youngerly	zinc green
wool-blind	worldling	wristband	yamstchik	young-eyed	zincotype
wool-flock	world's end	wrist-bone	Yang–Mills	young fogy	zinc oxide
wool-grass	world-soul	wrist-drop	Yankee bet	young lady	zinc white
wool-house	world-view	wrist jerk	Yankeedom	younglike	Zinfandel
woolliest	worldward	wrist-play	Yankeeish	youngling	zinkenite
woollyish	worldwide	wrist-slap	Yankeeism	young lion	Zionistic
wool-pated	world-wise	wrist-work	Yankeeize	youngness	Zionwards
wool-press	worm-eaten	writative	Yanktonai	youngster	zippiness
wool-scour	wormeaten	write-back	yard-grass	Young Turk	zirconate
wool table	worm-eater	write down	yard of ale	yours ever	zirconian
wool-track	worm-fence	write-once	yardstick	you said it	zirconium
wool-wheel	worm grass	writeress	yarn count	youth camp	zitherist
Woolworth	worm-holed	writ large	yashmaked	youth club	Zolaesque
woomerang	worminess	wrongdoer	Yawelmani	youthhead	Zolaistic
wooziness	worm-shell	wrong-foot	yawniness	youthhood	zombified
Worcester	worm-snake	wronghead	yawningly	youthless	zone-level
word-blind	wormstall	wrongness	yea and nay	yrast line	zone plate
word-bound	worm-wheel	wrong side	year class	ytterbite	zoogamete
word-break	worriedly	wrong-slot	year-round	ytterbium	zoogloeal
word-class	worriment	wrong-wise	year's mind	Yucatecan	zoography
word-field	worrisome	wrought-up	yeast cake	yucca moth	zoo-keeper
word-final	worriting	wry-necked	yeastiest	yucca-palm	zookeeper
word-hoard	worry-guts	wulfenite	yeastless	yuckiness	zoologise
word-index	worry-wart	Wulfilian	yeastlike	Yung Chêng	zoologist
wordiness	worse luck	wunnerful	Yeibichai	Yunnanese	zoologize
word-magic	worsement	wuthering	yellow ant	yuppiedom	zoophilia
word order	worseness	Wyandotte	yellow boa	yuppie flu	zoophilic
word-paint	worst-case	wych hazel	yellow bob	yuppieism	zoophobia
word-salad	worthiest	Wyclifist	yellow box	yuppified	zoophorus
wordsmith	worthless	Wyclifite	yellow-boy	yuppifies	zoophytic
word-stock	wouldn't it	Xanthippe	yellow cat	zamacueca	zoosporic
word-watch	woundable	xanthomas	yellow dog	zamindari	zootechny
workalike	wound cork	xenoblast	yellowfin	Zanzibari	zootheism
workbench	woundedly	xenocracy	Yellow Hat	zapateado	zootomist
workerist	woundless	xenocryst	yellowish	Zapotecan	zoot-shirt
work ethic	wound wood	xenograft	yellow-leg	Zealander	zosterops
workforce	woundwort	xenolalia	yellow oat	zealotism	zucchetto
work group	wove mould	xenomania	yellow ore	zealously	zucchinis
workhorse	wowserish	xenophile	yellow yam	zebra fish	zumbooruk
workhouse	wowserism	xenophobe	yeomaness	zebra-wolf	Zwinglian
workingly	wrain-bolt	xeroderma	yerba maté	zebrawood	zygantrum
workmanly	wrangling	xerograph	yesterday	Zechstein	zygomatic
work of art	wrap party	xeromorph	yestereve	Zeitgeist	zygophore
work out of	wrapperer	xerophagy	Yggdrasil	Zeldovich	zygospore
workpiece	wraparound	xerophile	Yiddisher	Zendicism	zymogenic
workplace	wrathless	xerophily	yieldable	zeolitize	zymolysis
work point	wreakless	xerophyte	yieldless	zephyrean	zymolytic
worksheet	wreathing	xi hyperon	yield sign	zephyrous	zymometer
work-space	wreathlet	xiphoidal	Y junction	zero grade	zymophore
workspace	wreckfish	x-question	yobbishly	zero-graze	
work study	wreckfree	xylocaine	yodelling	zero-point	
work table	wreckling	xylocopid	Yogacarin	zero-power	
workwoman	wreck-wood	xylograph	yo-heave-ho	zero sound	
workwomen	wrenching	xylophage	yohimbine	zestfully	

TEN LETTERS

aardwolves	absorbancy	accredited	acroterion	adjectival
a bang-up job	absorbedly	accrescent	acrylamide	adjudgment
Abbe number	absorbency	accruement	actability	adjudicate
abbreviate	absorption	accubation	act and deed	adjunction
abdication	absorptive	accumulate	acting copy	adjunctive
abdominous	abstemious	accuracies	acting part	adjuration
aberdevine	abstention	accurately	acting play	adjuratory
Aberdonian	abstergent	accursedly	actinolite	adjustable
aberrantly	abstersion	accusation	actionable	adjustment
aberration	abstersive	accusative	actionably	administer
abhorrence	abstinence	accusatory	action-noun	admiration
abhorrible	abstinency	accusingly	action rear	admirative
abiogenist	abstracted	accustomed	action song	admiringly
abjectness	abstracter	acephalous	activation	admissable
abjuration	abstractly	acerbities	active duty	admissible
ablatively	abstractor	acervation	active life	admittable
able-bodied	abstractum	acervuline	active list	admittance
able rating	abstrusely	acetabulum	activeness	admittedly
able seaman	abstrusity	acetic acid	active verb	admonisher
abnegation	abstrusive	acetogenic	activities	admonition
Abney level	absurdness	acetonuria	act of faith	admonitory
abnormally	abundantly	acetylator	act of grace	adolescent
abominable	abusefully	acetylenic	actomyosin	Adonis blue
abominably	Abyssinian	acetyl silk	act one's age	adoptively
abominator	acacia tree	Achaemenid	act the fool	ad personam
aboriginal	academical	Acherontic	act the goat	adrenaline
aborigines	acanthosis	achievable	actualness	adrenergic
abortional	acaricidal	achirality	acute angle	adrogation
abortively	acatalepsy	achondrite	Adam-and-Eve	adroitness
abortorium	acausality	achromatic	adamantane	adsorbable
above board	accelerate	achronical	adamantine	adsorbtion
above-cited	accentuate	acicularly	adamellite	adsorption
above price	acceptable	acidimetry	Adamitical	adsorptive
above proof	acceptably	acidophile	a damn sight	Adullamite
above water	acceptance	a-cock-horse	Adam's apple	adulterant
Abraham-man	acceptancy	acoelomate	adaptation	adulterate
abrasional	acceptedly	acolythist	adaptative	adulteress
abreaction	accessible	acorn shell	adaptitude	adulteries
abreactive	accessibly	acotyledon	adaptively	adulterine
abridgment	access road	acoustical	adder-stone	adulterize
abrogation	access time	acquainted	Addisonian	adulterous
abruptness	accidental	acquirable	additament	advance man
abscission	accidented	acquitment	additional	advantaged
absconsion	accidently	acquitting	additively	adventurer
absent from	accipitral	acrimonies	additivity	advertence
absentness	accomplice	acroamatic	addle-brain	advertency
absinthium	accomplish	acrobatics	addressing	advertiser
absolutely	accordable	acrobatism	adenovirus	advisement
absolution	accordance	acrolithic	adequately	advisories
absolutise	accordancy	acromegaly	adequation	advocatess
absolutism	accordment	acronychal	adequative	advocation
absolutist	accostable	acronymize	adherently	advocatory
absolutize	accoucheur	acrophobia	adhesively	adzuki bean
absolvable	accountant	acrophobic	adhibiting	aeciospore
absolvitor	account day	across lots	adhibition	aedileship
absorbable	account for	acrostical	adiaphoron	aegophonic
absorbance	accounting	acroterial	adipose fin	aeolotropy

aerenchyma	afterpiece	albumenize	alleviator	altar-bread
aeriferous	aftershave	albuminoid	all-firedly	altar-cloth
aerobatics	after-shock	albuminous	All Hallows	altarpiece
aero-engine	aftershock	alchemical	alliaceous	altar-stone
aerogramme	aftersight	alchemilla	allicholly	altazimuth
aerography	aftertaste	alcheringa	alliciency	alteration
aeronautic	after-times	alchymical	alligation	alterative
aeronomist	aftertouch	alcoholate	all in a rush	alternance
aerophobia	afterwards	alcoholise	alliterate	alternator
aerosolize	after-world	alcoholism	all kinds of	altimetric
aerostatic	after-years	alcoholist	all-nighter	altisonant
aero-towing	agallochum	alcoholize	allocation	altivolant
aerotowing	agapanthus	alcoometer	allochthon	altogether
aeruginous	agency shop	Alcoranist	allocution	altruistic
Aeschylean	aggeration	aldermanic	allodially	alum-schist
aestivator	agglutinin	aldermanly	allogeneic	amalgamate
aetiologic	aggrandise	aldermanry	allometric	Amandebele
a fair shake	aggrandize	alderwoman	allopathic	amanuenses
a fair treat	aggravator	alderwomen	allopatric	amanuensis
a fat chance	aggregable	Alemannian	allophonic	amastigote
affability	aggression	Alemannish	allosteric	amateurish
affectable	aggressive	alexanders	allotheism	amateurism
affectedly	aghastness	Alfvén wave	allotropic	amatorious
affectless	agitatedly	algal bloom	allottable	amazedness
affeerment	agnominate	algebraist	all-overish	ambassador
affettuoso	agnostical	algebraize	alloy steel	ambidexter
affinities	agonic line	algolagnia	all-purpose	ambisexual
affinitive	agonizedly	algolagnic	all right by	ambisonics
affirmable	agonothete	algologist	all-rounder	ambivalent
affirmance	agony uncle	Algonquian	all-Russian	ambiverted
affixation	a good field	algorismic	all sorts of	ambosexual
affliction	a good sport	alienation	all the best	ambulacral
afflictive	a good while	alien-enemy	all the mode	ambulacrum
affluently	agoraphobe	alimentary	all the rage	ambulation
affordable	a great loss	alimentive	all the same	ambulative
affordably	agreeingly	a little wee	all the time	ambulatory
affrighted	agrimonies	alkalaemia	allurement	ambuscader
affrighten	agrologist	alkalinity	alluringly	ambushment
affrontive	agronomist	alkalinize	allusively	a measure of
Afghan coat	aguishness	alkaloidal	all-weather	ameliorate
aficionado	a hand's turn	alkylation	almacantar	ameloblast
aforetimes	a heap sight	alla marcia	almond cake	amen corner
afraidness	a-horseback	all-America	almond-eyed	amendatory
Africander	aid and abet	all and each	almond eyes	amenity bed
Africanise	aide-de-camp	all and some	almond milk	amercement
Africanism	aid fatigue	Allan Water	almond pink	amerciable
Africanist	air bladder	allargando	almond tree	Americanly
Africanity	air cushion	all-creator	alms-basket	Amerindian
Africanize	air-freight	all day long	almsgiving	amiability
Afrikander	air hostess	allegation	almucantar	amianthine
afrormosia	airmanship	allegeable	aloha shirt	ammoniacal
after a sort	Air Marshal	allegement	Aloha State	ammoniacum
afterbirth	air officer	allegiance	along about	ammoniated
aftercomer	Air Officer	allegiancy	alongshore	ammunition
aftergrass	akroterion	allegories	alpenstock	amoebiases
after-guard	alabastron	allegorise	alphabetic	amoebiasis
after-hours	alacritous	allegorism	alpha decay	amoebicide
after-image	alarm clock	allegorist	alphametic	amoebiform
after leech	alarmingly	allegorize	alpha minus	amoebocyte
afterlight	alarm watch	allegretto	alpha waves	ampelopsis
afternoons	Albigenses	Allen screw	Alphonsine	ampere-hour
afterpains	albinistic	allergenic	Alpine rose	ampère-hour

ampere-turn	anchorless	anhidrosis	antibiotic	apart-hotel
amphibious	anchor-ring	anhidrotic	antibodies	aphaeresis
amphibolic	anchylosis	anhungered	anti-busing	aphaeretic
amphibrach	and all that	aniline dye	anti-choice	aphorismic
amphictyon	Andalusian	animadvert	Antichrist	aphoristic
amphigouri	andalusite	animalcule	antichthon	apiculture
amphimacer	Andaluzian	animatedly	anticipant	aplanatism
amphimixis	Andamanese	anisocoria	anticipate	apocalypse
Amphitryon	andantinos	anisotropy	anticlimax	Apocalypse
amphoteric	and knows it	ankle-biter	anticlinal	apocalypst
ampicillin	androcracy	ankylosaur	antidromic	apocarpous
ampliation	androecium	annalistic	anti-emetic	apochromat
ampliative	androgenic	annexation	antifreeze	apocryphal
amputation	androgynal	annihilate	antigorite	apodeictic
amygdaline	Andromedid	Anno Domini	anti-heroes	apolaustic
amygdaloid	androspore	annominate	antilogies	apolitical
amylolysis	androstane	annotation	antilogism	Apollinian
amylolytic	and so forth	annotative	antilopine	Apollonian
amyotrophy	and the like	annoyancer	antimasque	apologetic
anabaptise	and welcome	annoyingly	antimatter	apologizer
Anabaptism	anecdotage	annualized	antimonate	apophthegm
Anabaptist	anecdotist	annual ring	antimonial	apophyseal
anabaptize	anemochore	annularity	antimonian	apoplectic
anachronic	anemograph	annulation	antimonide	aposematic
anaclastic	anemometer	annullable	antimonite	aposporous
anacolutha	anemometry	annunciate	antinomian	apostasies
anadromous	anemophily	annuntiate	antinomies	apostatise
anagenesis	anemoscope	anodically	Antiochene	apostatism
anagenetic	anesthesia	anoestrous	Antiochian	apostatize
anaglyphic	aneuploidy	anogenital	antipathic	apostolate
anaglyptic	aneurismal	anointment	antiphonal	apostolize
anagogical	aneurysmal	anopheline	antiphoner	apostrophe
anal-erotic	angelicize	anorexiant	antiphonic	apothecary
analogical	angel-noble	answerable	antipodean	apothecial
analphabet	angelology	answerably	antiproton	apothecium
anal sadism	angel's eyes	answer back	antiquated	apotheoses
analysable	angel-shark	answerless	anti-racism	apotheosis
analyse out	angioblast	antagonise	anti-racist	apotropaic
analytical	angiosperm	antagonism	anti-Semite	Appalachee
anamnestic	angleberry	antagonist	antisepsis	apparelled
anamorphic	angledozer	antagonize	antiseptic	apparently
anapaestic	angle of lag	ante-bellum	antisocial	apparition
anapaestus	anglepoise	antecedent	antistatic	appealable
anaplastic	Anglepoise	antecessor	antitheism	appearance
anaptyctic	angler fish	antechapel	antitheist	appeasable
anarchical	Anglistics	ante-chapel	antitheses	appendaged
anarthrous	Anglo-Irish	antedating	antithesis	appendance
anasarcous	Anglo-Latin	anteflexed	antithetic	appendancy
anastigmat	Anglomania	antelopine	antitrades	appendence
anastomose	Anglophile	ante-mortem	antitragus	appendical
anastrophe	Anglophobe	antepartum	antivenene	appendices
anathemize	anglophone	antepenult	antlerless	appendicle
anatomical	Anglo-Roman	anteriorly	antler-moth	appendixes
anatomizer	Anglo-Saxon	ante-temple	antonymous	apperceive
anatropous	angora goat	antheridia	antorbital	appetition
ancestress	angora wool	anthomania	antrustion	appetitive
ancestrial	anguineous	anthophore	anvil cloud	appetizing
ancestries	angularity	anthracene	anxiolytic	applausive
ancestrula	angulation	anthracite	any time now	apple cider
anchoretic	angwantibo	anthracoid	anywhither	apple-green
anchor-hold	anharmonic	anthropoid	aortic arch	apple sauce
anchoritic	anhelation	antibiosis	apagogical	apple-woman

applianced	arcubalist	ascendable	associater	Athapaskan
applicable	arc welding	ascendance	associator	at high wish
applicably	area bishop	ascendancy	assoilment	athletical
applicator	arenaceous	ascendency	assonantal	at interest
applotment	arena stage	asceticism	assortment	at its worst
appointive	arenavirus	ascidiform	assumingly	at long last
appositely	arenovirus	ascogenous	assumption	atmosphere
apposition	Areopagite	ascogonium	assumptive	atomically
appositive	Argand lamp	ascomycete	assurgency	atomic bomb
appraisive	argonautic	as concerns	astarboard	atomic heat
appreciate	argumental	ascribable	asteriated	atomic mass
apprentice	arguteness	ascription	asteroidal	atomic pile
approacher	argyrodite	ascriptive	asthma herb	at one's best
approvable	Arimaspian	asexuality	astigmatic	at one's ease
approvance	aristocrat	ashen-faced	astonisher	at one sweep
approvedly	aristology	ashipboard	astounding	at one swoop
apron stage	arithmancy	Ashkenazic	astragalar	at outrance
apterygote	arithmetic	Ashkenazim	astragalus	atrabiliar
aqua fortis	arles-penny	ash of roses	astral body	atramental
aquamanile	armadillos	Asiaticism	astral lamp	atraumatic
aquamarine	Armageddon	as it stands	astriction	atrocities
aquarobics	armigerous	aslantwise	astrictive	attachable
aquatinter	armipotent	aspalathus	astringent	attachment
a quick buck	armorially	asparagine	astrobleme	attackable
aquiferous	armour-clad	aspergilla	astrograph	attainable
arable land	armourless	asperities	astrohatch	attainment
arachis oil	arm the lead	as per usual	astrolabic	attendance
arachnidan	arm-wrestle	asphaltene	astrolatry	attenuated
arachnitis	aromatizer	asphaltite	astrologer	attenuator
araneology	arpeggione	aspherical	astrologic	attestable
Araucanian	arrear-band	asphyxiant	astrometry	attestator
araucarian	arrestable	asphyxiate	astronomer	at that rate
arbalester	arrestment	aspidistra	astronomic	at the climb
arbitrable	arrhythmia	aspiration	astrophile	at the least
arbitrager	arrhythmic	aspiringly	astuteness	at the money
arbitrated	arrogantly	Asquithian	asymmetric	at the point
arbitrator	arrogation	assailable	asymptotic	at the ready
arboretums	arrow-grass	assailment	asyntactic	at the trail
arboricide	arrowsmith	assaultive	at all costs	at the wheel
arborvirus	arse-kisser	assemblage	at all hours	at the worst
arbor vitae	arse-licker	assemblies	a tall order	at this rate
arc furnace	arsenolite	assembling	at any price	Attic order
archaicism	art and part	assentator	at a pin's fee	attirement
archaicist	arteriolar	assentient	at a premium	attornment
archaistic	artfulness	assentment	at a sitting	attractant
archbishop	art gallery	assertible	at a squeeze	attraction
archdeacon	arthralgia	assertoric	at a stretch	attractive
archegonia	arthrodial	assessable	at a tangent	attritting
archeology	articulacy	assessment	at a venture	attunement
archer fish	articulate	asseverate	ateleiosis	at unawares
archetypal	artificial	assibilate	ateleiotic	at variance
arch-flamen	artisanate	assientist	at farthest	at what time
Archimedes	artistical	assignable	at full cock	atypically
architrave	artistlike	assignably	at full pelt	auctioneer
archonship	art nouveau	assignment	at full sail	Audenesque
archontate	art therapy	assimilate	at full tilt	audibility
archpriest	arty-crafty	assishness	at furthest	audiogenic
arcologies	asafoetida	assistance	at gunpoint	audiometer
Arctic char	asarabacca	assistancy	Athabascan	audiometry
Arctic hare	as a starter	ass-kissing	at half cock	audiophile
Arctic skua	asbestosis	ass-licking	at half mast	audit-house
Arctic tern	ascariasis	associable	Athanasian	auditorial

auditorily	autostrada	bacitracin	ballistics	barn-gallon
auditorium	autotheism	back-action	ball of fire	baroclinic
audit trail	autotheist	back-berand	balloonist	barometric
auger-shell	autotomize	backbiting	balneology	baron court
augmentive	autotrophe	backblocks	balsam pear	baronetage
auguration	autoxidize	back boiler	balustrade	baronetess
augustness	autumnally	back burner	bamboo-fish	baronetize
Auld Reekie	auxanogram	back-double	bamboozler	barotrauma
Aureomycin	auxochrome	back-fanged	banalities	barotropic
auriculate	auxotrophy	backfriend	banana bird	barracouta
auriferous	avant-garde	backgammon	Bananaland	barracudas
aurigation	avanturine	background	bananaquit	barramundi
aurivorous	avaricious	backhanded	banana skin	barratrous
auscultate	avengement	backhander	banana tree	barrel-fish
auspicious	avengeress	backing dog	banderilla	barrelling
austenitic	aventurine	backmarker	bandleader	barrenness
Australian	average out	back-marker	bandmaster	barrenwort
australite	aversation	back number	Band of Hope	barring-out
Australoid	averseness	backpacker	bandy-bandy	barterable
Australorp	aviculture	backsheesh	bangtailed	bartizaned
Austrasian	avidiously	backslider	banishment	bar tracery
austringer	avirulence	back-spacer	bank charge	barycentre
autarchies	avondbloem	backstairs	bank martin	barysphere
autarkical	avouchable	back-stitch	bankruptcy	baselessly
autecology	avouchment	backstitch	banqueteer	base-minded
authigenic	avunculate	backstreet	banqueting	base relief
authorized	awakenment	backstroke	Bantingism	base-runner
authorizer	award wages	back-to-back	banyan tree	bashawship
authorless	awkwardish	backvelder	Baphometic	basilectal
authorling	axe-breaker	backwardly	baptistery	Basilidian
authorship	axemanship	back-winter	baptizable	basil thyme
autochthon	axenically	bacterioid	Baralipton	basketball
autocratic	axinomancy	bacteruria	barasingha	basket-boat
autocrator	axiologist	bad bargain	Barbary ape	basket case
autodidact	axiomatize	bad company	barbecuing	basket fish
autoecious	Aylesburys	bad feeling	barbed wire	basket hilt
auto-erotic	azeotropic	badger game	barberries	basket meal
autogamous	azomethine	bad weather	barber-shop	basket star
autogenous	azoprotein	bafflement	Barbie doll	basketwork
autography	azygos vein	bafflingly	barbituric	basophilia
autoimmune	babblative	bagassosis	barcarolle	basophilic
autologous	babblement	baggage car	bardee grub	basse dance
autolysate	babblingly	baggage tag	bardolater	basse danse
automation	babe in arms	bag of bones	bardolatry	basset-horn
automatise	babesiasis	bagpudding	bare-backed	bass guitar
automatism	babesiosis	bagstuffer	barefooted	basso buffo
automatist	babiroussa	bail bandit	bare-footed	bassoonist
automatize	baby boomer	bailieship	barehanded	bass-relief
automatons	baby buster	bail-jumper	bareheaded	bastardize
automatous	baby-farmer	bains-marie	bargain for	bastillion
automobile	baby-jumper	bairn's part	bargeboard	bastnäsite
automotive	Babylonian	baked beans	barium meal	Bath Oliver
autonomies	Babylonish	baking soda	bark beetle	bathometer
autonomism	baby-minder	balance due	barkentine	bathometry
autonomist	baby powder	Balbriggan	barley-bird	bathymeter
autonomous	babysitter	balderdash	barley-bree	bathymetry
autophagic	baby walker	bald-headed	barley-corn	bat mitzvah
autoplasty	bacchantes	baldmoneys	barleycorn	batologist
autoptical	bacchantic	balibuntal	barley-hood	baton round
autorotate	Bacchantic	ballasting	barley-wine	batrachian
autoscopic	bachelorly	ball-buster	Barmecidal	battailous
autosexing	bacilluria	ball flower	bar mitzvah	Battenberg

battery hen	bed of roses	belly dance	be taken ill	bilocation
battledore	be done with	belly laugh	beta rhythm	bimanually
battlement	bed-wetting	belongings	be the end of	bimestrial
battleship	bedwetting	below decks	be the limit	bimetallic
baulkiness	beech-drops	below there	be to do with	bimodality
baum marten	beefburger	Belshazzar	be to praise	binary code
bawdy house	beef cattle	be master of	betrayment	binary form
bayberries	beef tomato	bemusement	better days	binary star
bayoneting	beef-witted	bench press	better half	binary tree
bay whaling	beehive-hat	bench-screw	betterment	binational
BBC English	bee-keeping	bench-table	betterness	binaurally
beach buggy	beer bottle	benedicite	better-to-do	Binitarian
beach front	beer cellar	Benedictus	betweenity	binoculars
beachfront	beer engine	benefactor	beudantite	binomially
beach-grass	beer garden	beneficent	be up to trap	binoxalate
beach-la-mar	beetle-back	beneficial	bevel wheel	binucleate
Beach-la-mar	beetle-head	benefiting	bewailable	biocenosis
beachwards	be even with	Beneventan	bewailment	biocentric
beadleship	beforehand	benevolent	be well left	biochemist
be a fool for	before long	Bengal kino	bewildered	biodegrade
be a hit with	before meat	benignancy	bewitchery	biodynamic
Beaker Folk	before time	bent double	bewitching	bioethical
beam engine	beforetime	Benthamism	beyond seas	biofouling
bean sprout	befoulment	Benthamite	be yourself	biogenesis
bearded tit	be free with	bentonitic	biannually	biogenetic
bear down on	befriender	ben trovato	Bible class	biographee
bear garden	be geared up	Benzedrine	Bible clerk	biographer
beargarden	beggarhood	benzhydrol	Bible paper	biographic
bear hard on	be great fun	benzpyrene	biblically	biological
bear in hand	behind bars	be on record	bibliology	biomedical
bear in mind	behindhand	be on the rag	bibliomane	biometrics
bearleader	behind line	be open with	bibliopegy	biomimetic
bear malice	behind time	be prepared	bibliopole	biomorphic
bear market	be hung up on	bequeathal	bibliopoly	bionically
be a skinner	be in hiding	bequeather	bibliothec	bionomical
beastliest	bejewelled	bergerette	bibulosity	bio-organic
be at a stand	be laughing	Bergsonian	bibulously	biophysics
beatifical	be left with	beribboned	bicultural	biopolymer
Beatrician	belemnitic	Berkeleian	bid against	bioscience
beat the air	Belgravian	Berlin blue	bidonville	biospheric
beat the bat	believable	Berlin wool	bid welcome	biotically
beat the gun	be like that	Berlin work	biennially	biparental
beat the rap	belladonna	Berliozian	bifacially	biparietal
Beaujolais	bell-animal	Bermuda rig	bifocalled	bipartisan
beautician	bellarmine	Bernardine	bigamously	bipedalism
beautified	bell-bottom	bescribble	Big Brother	bipedality
beautifier	bell-crater	beseeching	bigeminate	bipolarity
beautifies	belle laide	be set round	big-hearted	birational
beautiless	belletrism	besottedly	big-leaguer	birch-water
beauty spot	belletrist	besprinkle	big-mouthed	bird cherry
beaver lamb	bellflower	best friend	bijouterie	bird of Jove
beaver-tail	bell-hanger	bestialise	bikini line	bird of Juno
bêche-de-mer	bell-pepper	bestiality	bilberries	bird of prey
becomingly	bell-ringer	bestialize	bilge water	bird's-foots
be confined	bell-shaped	bestiaries	bilharzial	bird-strike
bedazement	bell-sleeve	bestirring	biliverdin	bird-witted
bedchamber	Bell's palsy	bestowment	bill and coo	Birmingham
bedclothes	bell-string	bestridden	billbergia	birthnight
be deceived	bell the cat	best-seller	billet-doux	birthplace
bedevilled	bell-topper	be stuck for	bill of fare	birthright
Bedlington	bell-wether	best wishes	bill of sale	birthstone
bed of nails	bellyacher	be sure that	billposter	bishop-bird

bishophood	black plate	block plane	blustering	bookbinder
bishoplike	black power	blond beast	blusterous	bookkeeper
bishop's cap	Black Power	blonde lace	board-wages	bookmaking
bismuthate	black sheep	blood-borne	boastfully	bookmobile
bismuthine	blackshirt	blood count	boastingly	book-muslin
bissextile	blacksmith	blood donor	boat people	book of fate
bistouries	black-snake	blood eagle	boat-shaped	book of life
bisulphate	blacksnake	blood fluke	bobbin lace	bookseller
bitchiness	Black Stone	blood group	bobby socks	book-trough
bite and sup	black stump	blood-guilt	bobby-soxer	boondoggle
biting lice	blackthorn	blood horse	bob-periwig	boosterism
bit of fluff	black tripe	bloodhound	Bob's-a-dying	bootlegger
bit of goods	black vomit	bloodiness	bodiliness	bootlessly
bit of rough	Black Watch	blood money	body colour	bootlicker
bit of skirt	black water	blood royal	body double	borborygmi
bit of spare	black widow	blood serum	body search	borderland
bit of stuff	bladder nut	blood sport	body warmer	borderline
bitonality	blady grass	bloodstain	body weight	boringness
bitten with	blamefully	bloodstock	Boehmenism	borrow-head
bitter bark	blanchfarm	bloodstone	Boehmenist	borrow-hole
bitter beer	blanch over	blood sugar	bog-blitter	borsholder
bitterling	blancmange	blood wagon	bog iron ore	bosselated
bitterness	blandander	bloody flux	bog lemming	bossy-boots
bitter pill	blanket bog	bloody hand	Bogomilian	bossyboots
bitter-root	blanketeer	Bloody Mary	Bogomilism	Boswellian
bitter sage	blanketing	bloomeries	bog-trotter	Boswellism
bitter-weed	blank verse	bloomerism	bogtrotter	Boswellize
bitter-wood	blanquette	bloomingly	boiler room	Botany wool
Bitumastic	blasphemer	Bloomsbury	boiler suit	bothersome
bituminise	blastocyst	blotchiest	boiler-tube	botryoidal
bituminize	blastoderm	blottesque	boiling hot	bottle bank
bituminous	blastodisc	blow a cloud	boil the pot	bottled gas
biuret test	blastomere	blow-by-blow	boisterous	bottle-feed
bivouacked	blastopore	blowziness	boldacious	bottle-head
biweeklies	blazonment	bludgeoner	bolivianos	bottleneck
bizarrerie	bleariness	blue-bonnet	Bollandist	bottlenose
black alder	bleary-eyed	bluebottle	bollocking	bottle tree
blackamoor	bleatingly	blue cheese	boll-weevil	bottom edge
blackberry	bleed white	blue cohosh	bolometric	bottom gear
black birch	blenchfarm	blue-collar	Bolshevism	bottom-land
blackboard	blight-bird	blue dahlia	Bolshevist	bottomless
black bread	blind alley	blue ensign	Bolshevize	bottom line
black cumin	blind drunk	blue groper	bolshiness	bottommost
Black Death	blindingly	blue ground	bolstering	bottomried
black earth	blindlings	blue heeler	bombardier	bottomries
black-faced	blind snake	bluejacket	Bombay duck	bough-house
blackflies	blind tiger	Bluemantle	bomb-vessel	bought deal
Black Friar	blind trust	blue monkey	bondholder	bougienage
black frost	blissfully	blue murder	boneheaded	Boulangism
black grape	blister-fly	blue-pencil	bone marrow	Boulangist
blackguard	blister gas	blue riband	bone-setter	bouleverse
black-heart	blistering	blue ribbon	boneshaker	bounce back
black house	blitheness	blue-rinsed	bone spavin	bounciness
black Irish	blithering	blue runner	bonitarian	bouncingly
black ivory	blithesome	blue streak	bonnethead	boundaries
black level	blitzkrieg	blue tangle	bonsai tree	bountihead
black light	block-board	bluethroat	bonus issue	bouquetier
black magic	blockboard	bluetongue	bon vivants	Bourbonism
Black Maria	block grant	bluff it out	bon viveurs	Bourbonist
black money	blockhouse	bluishness	boobook owl	bourgeoise
black-mouth	blockishly	blurriness	booby-hatch	bournonite
black olive	block party	blushingly	booby prize	bouts rimés

bovver boot	brazenness	bridgeward	brow antler	bulk buying
bow-compass	braziletto	bridgework	browbeater	bulkheaded
bowdlerise	Brazil wood	bridle-hand	brown argus	bullamacow
bowdlerism	breadboard	bridleless	Brown Betty	bull-and-cow
bowdlerize	breadcrumb	bridle path	brown bread	bulldog ant
bower-cable	breadfruit	bridle-rein	brown earth	bullet-head
bowie knife	bread-knife	bridle-road	browned off	bullet-tree
bowl-barrow	bread sauce	bridle-wise	brown goods	bull-fiddle
bow the knee	bread-stick	brigandage	brown hyena	bull-headed
box barrage	bread wheat	brigandine	brown-noser	bullionist
boxing ring	break a blow	brigandish	brown ochre	bull market
box of birds	break a fall	brigandism	brown paper	bull-necked
box spanner	break bread	brigantine	brown sauce	bullroarer
boyishness	break cover	brightener	Brown-shirt	bull thatch
boys in blue	break-dance	brightness	Brownshirt	bum-bailiff
braaivleis	break faith	brightsome	brown snake	bum-freezer
braceleted	break forth	brightwork	brownstone	bump and run
brachialis	break-front	brilliance	brown study	bumpkinish
brachiator	break of day	brilliancy	brown sugar	bump supper
brachiopod	break point	brimborion	brown trout	bum-sucking
brachylogy	break-point	bring about	bruisewort	bunch-berry
brachyuran	breakpoint	bring forth	brunch coat	bunch grass
bracketing	break ranks	bring round	brush aside	bunder-boat
bracteated	break shins	bring to bay	brusquerie	bungee cord
bradykinin	breakstone	bring under	brute force	bungee rope
bradypepsy	break water	Britannian	bryologist	bunglesome
bradyseism	breakwater	Britishism	bryophytic	bunglingly
braggingly	breastbone	broad arrow	bubble bath	bunya bunya
Brahmanism	breastfeed	broad-brush	bubblehead	Burberries
brahminism	breast-high	broadcloth	bubblement	burdensome
brainchild	breast-pump	broad gauge	bubble over	bureaucrat
brain coral	breast-wall	broad-piece	bubble pack	burgessdom
brain death	breastwise	broadscale	bubble wrap	burglaries
brain drain	breastwork	broadsheet	bubbly-jock	burglarise
brain fever	breathable	broadsword	bubonocele	burglarize
braininess	breathe out	Broca's area	buccinator	Burgundian
brainpower	breathiest	brocatelle	Bucephalus	burgundies
brain-stone	breathless	brocatello	Buchmanism	burlesqued
brainstorm	breath test	broken-down	Buchmanite	burlesquer
brain trust	breech baby	broken home	bucketfuls	burlesques
brake block	breechless	broken line	bucket seat	Burmese cat
brake fluid	breezeless	brokenness	bucket shop	burnet-moth
branchiate	breeziness	broken reed	buck-jumper	burnet rose
branchless	brekekekex	broken time	buckle down	burnt cream
branchlike	brent-goose	broken wind	Buddhahood	burnt ochre
branch-line	brevetting	bromic acid	Buddhistic	burnt taste
branch-work	breviaries	bronchiole	buddy movie	burnt umber
brandering	brick-built	bronchitic	budgerigar	bur-parsley
brand image	brick-earth	bronchitis	budget plan	burrow-duck
brandisher	brick-field	brontology	buffalo fly	burrow into
brandy ball	bricklayer	brontosaur	buffalo-nut	bursarship
brandy snap	brickmaker	bronzewing	buff arches	bursectomy
brandy-wine	bridegroom	broodiness	buffer area	burstproof
brassed off	bride price	broodingly	buffer stop	Buscot Park
brassiness	bridesmaid	brood patch	buffer zone	bushbabies
brass plate	bridgeable	brood pouch	buffet meal	bush canary
brass tacks	bridge a gap	brood queen	bufflehead	bush clover
brat packer	bridge-bote	brook trout	buffoonery	bushelfuls
bratticing	bridge-deck	broom-grass	buffoonish	bush-harrow
brave it out	bridgehead	broom-sedge	bufotenine	bush jacket
brawniness	bridgeless	broomstaff	bugologist	bush lawyer
brazen-face	bridge roll	broomstick	build round	bush league

Bushmanoid	cabin fever	calmodulin	cannibalic	capturable
bushmaster	cachinnate	calumniate	cannibally	carabineer
bush-ranger	cack-handed	calumnious	cannon ball	carabinier
bushranger	cacodaemon	calyculate	cannon-bone	caramelise
bush-shrike	cacodorous	cambric tea	cannon-shot	caramelize
bus shelter	cacodylate	camelopard	cannot wait	Carancahua
bus-spotter	cacography	camel's-hair	canoe birch	caravaneer
bus station	cacomistle	camel-thorn	can of worms	caravanned
bustlingly	cacophonic	cameo glass	canonicate	caravanner
busybodied	cactaceous	camera crew	canonicity	carbonados
busybodies	cadaverine	cameralism	canonistic	carbonator
busy Lizzie	cadaverous	cameralist	canophilia	carbon copy
butcheries	caddie cart	camera-work	Canopic jar	carbonizer
butlership	caddis-worm	camerawork	Cantabrian	carbonless
butterball	cadilesker	camerlingo	cantaloupe	carbonnade
butter-bean	caecostomy	Cameronian	cantatrice	carboxylic
butter-bump	Caerphilly	camouflage	canterbury	carbuncled
butter-bush	Caesar baby	campaigner	Canterbury	carcel lamp
butter dish	caespitose	campestral	canti fermi	carcinogen
butterfish	café au lait	campground	cantilever	carcinomas
butterless	caffeinism	camphorate	cantillate	cardboardy
buttermilk	Caffrarian	campimeter	canto fermo	cardholder
butter-tree	ca'ing whale	campimetry	cantonment	cardinally
butterwort	cajolement	camp-on busy	can't seem to	Cardiofunk
buttery-bar	cake of soap	Canaanitic	canvas-back	cardiogram
button-back	calamander	Canada bird	canvassing	cardiology
buttonball	calamaries	canalicule	canzonetta	cardmember
button-bush	calamitean	canary-bird	caoutchouc	card player
button-down	calamities	Canary sack	capability	carelessly
buttoned up	calamitous	canary-seed	capacitate	caressable
buttonhole	calaverite	cancellans	capacities	Care Sunday
buttonhook	calcareous	cancellate	capacitive	caricature
buttonless	calcarious	cancelling	Cape brandy	carination
button-like	calceolate	cancellous	Cape doctor	cariogenic
button-tree	calciferol	cancelment	Cape gannet	carjacking
button-wood	calcinable	cancer bush	Cape pigeon	Carmathian
by accident	calcitonin	cancer-root	Capernaite	carnallite
by all means	calcitrate	cancrinite	Cape salmon	carnassial
by a long way	calc-sinter	cancrizans	capillaire	Carolinian
by and large	calculable	candelabra	capitalise	carotenoid
by any means	calculably	candelilla	capitalism	Carpathian
by courtesy	calculated	candescent	capitalist	carpellary
by-election	calculator	candidness	capitalize	carpet-moth
by eminence	calculuses	candle-beam	capital sum	carpet-tack
by marriage	Caledonian	candle-fish	capitation	carphology
by one's will	caledonite	candle-tree	capitellum	carpopedal
by reason of	calendarer	candlewick	Capitolian	carpophore
by rotation	calenderer	candle-wood	Capitoline	carpospore
by snatches	calescence	candy apple	capitulary	carragheen
byssinosis	calf-length	candy-assed	capitulate	carrier bag
byssinotic	calf's snout	candyfloss	capnomancy	carrying-on
bystanding	calibrator	candy-store	capo tastos	carry it off
by the dozen	caliciform	candy-sugar	cappuccino	Carthusian
by the great	calico-bush	cane-worker	capriccios	cartomancy
by the gross	caliginous	caniniform	capricious	cartonnage
by then that	call a truce	canker-rose	Capri pants	cartoonery
by the piece	calligraph	cankerworm	capsulated	cartoonish
by the stern	call it a day	canker-worm	capsulitis	cartoonist
by virtue of	callithrix	cannabinol	captainess	cartophily
by yourself	callowness	cannel-bone	captiously	cartwright
caballeros	call signal	cannel coal	captivater	caruncular
cabin class	call to mind	cannelloni	captivator	carwitchet

caryatides	catch a crab	censorship	chalcid fly	charismata
cascarilla	catchflies	censurable	Chalcidian	charitable
case-bottle	catchiness	centauries	chalcocite	charitably
case-harden	catchpenny	centennial	chalkboard	charladies
caseinogen	catch-title	centerfold	chalk cliff	Charles' law
caseworker	catch-water	centesimal	chalkiness	Charles' Law
cashew tree	cat cracker	centigrade	chalk-stone	charleston
Caspian Sea	catechesis	centilitre	challenged	Charleston
Cassegrain	catechetic	centillion	challenger	charmingly
cassia tree	catechizer	centimetre	chalybeate	charmonium
cassinette	catechumen	centipedal	Chamaeleon	Charollais
Cassiopeia	categorial	centralise	chamberlet	charophyte
cassolette	categories	centralism	chamber-lye	chartreuse
cassumunar	categorise	centralist	chamber pot	chartulary
cast a clout	categorize	centrality	Chambertin	chasmogamy
cast adrift	catenarian	centralize	chamfering	chastelain
cast anchor	catenaries	centre back	chamositic	chasteness
castaneous	catenation	centrefold	champagney	chaste tree
cast around	catenulate	centre half	champertor	chatelaine
cast ashore	catheretic	centre line	champignon	chatellany
castellany	cathode ray	centremost	chanceable	chattelism
castellate	catholicly	centricity	chancellor	chatterbox
cast-for-age	Catholicly	centrifuge	chanceries	chattermag
castigator	catholicon	centriolar	chanciness	chattiness
casting-net	Catholicos	centromere	chandelier	Chaucerian
castleward	catoptrics	centrosome	changeable	Chaucerism
castor bean	catostomid	centuriate	changeably	chaud-froid
castration	cat's cradle	cephalalgy	change down	chaud-mellé
castrative	cattle cake	cephalitis	change ends	chauffeuse
cast stones	cattle grid	cephalopod	change eyes	chautauqua
casualness	cattle stop	cerambycid	change gear	chauvinism
casual poor	caulescent	ceramicist	changeless	chauvinist
casualties	cauliflory	ceratohyal	changeling	cheapskate
casual ward	cause havoc	cerebellar	changement	checkerman
casus belli	causidical	cerebellum	change note	checkermen
catabolism	causticity	cerebrally	change over	check out of
catabolite	cautionary	ceremonial	changeover	checkpoint
catabolize	cautiously	ceremonies	change step	check-stone
cataclases	cavalierly	Cerinthian	channel cat	check-taker
cataclasis	cavalryman	cerography	channelise	check valve
catafalque	cavalrymen	certiorari	channelize	cheddaring
catagmatic	cavitation	certiorate	channelled	cheekiness
Catalanist	cavity wall	ceruminous	chaologist	cheek-pouch
catalectic	celebrated	cervantite	chaparajos	cheek-tooth
cataleptic	celebrator	cervicitis	chaparejos	cheerfully
catalogued	celebrious	cessionary	chapelries	cheerie-bye
cataloguer	celery pine	cetologist	chaperonin	cheeriness
catalogues	celery salt	Ceylon moss	chap-fallen	cheeringly
Catalonian	cellar-book	chaetodont	chaplaincy	cheesecake
catamenial	cellobiose	chaffingly	chaplainry	cheese-head
catananche	cellophane	Chagataian	chaptalize	cheese-mite
cataphatic	Cellophane	chain drive	chapterman	cheese-pare
cataphoric	cellulated	chain-plate	characeous	cheesewood
cataphract	cellulitic	chain-smoke	charactery	cheesiness
cataractal	cellulitis	chain snake	Chardonnay	cheirology
catarrhine	cellulosic	chain store	chargeable	Chekhovian
catarrhous	Celtic nard	chain wheel	charge-book	cheliceral
catastasis	cemeterial	chair-borne	charge card	Chelsea bun
catatoniac	cemeteries	chair organ	charge-hand	Cheltonian
catawampus	cenematics	chairwoman	chargehand	chemiatric
cat burglar	censorable	chairwomen	chargeless	chemically
catch a cold	censorious	chalcedony	charioteer	chemisette

chemotaxis	chinquapin	chorus girl	cinder-cone	Clark's crow
cheque-book	chintziest	chota hazri	Cinderella	clarschach
chequebook	chionodoxa	chowchilla	cinder path	clasp hands
cheque card	chip basket	christener	cine camera	clasp-knife
cherry-like	chip heater	Christhood	cinema-goer	classicise
cherry-pick	Chippewyan	Christless	cinematize	classicism
cherry plum	chippiness	Christlike	cinerarium	classicist
cherry tree	chirognomy	chromaffin	ciné-vérité	classicize
cherry wood	chirograph	chromatism	cinquefoil	classified
cherrywood	chiromancy	chromatoid	cipherable	classifier
chersonese	chironomic	chrome alum	Circassian	classifies
chess-apple	chironomid	chromosome	circensian	classiness
chessboard	chirpiness	chronicity	circle back	claudicant
chess-clock	chirruping	chronicler	circlewise	clavichord
chessylite	chirurgeon	chronogram	circuiteer	clavicular
chestiness	chirurgery	chronology	circuition	Clavioline
chestnutty	chisel-like	chrysaline	circuitous	clawed toad
chest voice	chiselling	chrysalize	circulable	claw hammer
chevesaile	chi-squared	chrysaloid	circularly	clayeyness
chevisance	chitarrone	chrysolite	circulator	clay pigeon
chevrotain	chit-chatty	chrysotile	circumcise	clean break
Chevy Chase	chitty-face	chrysotype	circumduce	clean hands
chewing gum	chivalrous	chubbiness	circumduct	clean house
chew the cud	chlamydiae	chuck-a-luck	circumflex	cleanliest
chew the fat	chlamydial	chucker-out	circumfuse	cleansable
chew the rag	chloramine	chuck-wagon	circummure	clean sheet
chicharron	chloridize	chuckwagon	circumoral	clean slate
chickenpox	chlorinate	chuckwalla	circumvent	clean sweep
Chief Rabbi	chlorinity	chukka boot	cire perdue	clearstory
chiffchaff	chloritize	chumminess	cismontane	clementine
chiffonier	chloritoid	chunkiness	cispontine	Clementine
chiffon pie	chloritous	chupatties	Cistercian	clerestory
chifforobe	chlorodyne	Church Army	citizeness	clergiable
child abuse	chloroform	church-bell	citizenish	clerically
childbirth	choanocyte	church-book	citric acid	cleromancy
child bride	chocaholic	churchgoer	citronella	clever Dick
Childermas	chockstone	churchless	citrulline	cleverness
childishly	chocoholic	churchlike	city editor	clew-garnet
childproof	chocolatey	church mode	City editor	click-clack
child's play	choiceness	church-rate	city father	clientship
child-woman	choir organ	church-scot	civil court	climatical
Chile hazel	choir stall	church-text	civil death	clinginess
Chile nitre	chokeberry	churchward	civilities	clingingly
chiliarchy	choke-berry	churchwise	civil state	clingstone
chiliastic	choke chain	church work	civil wrong	clinically
chilliness	cholagogue	churchyard	cladistics	clink-clank
chillingly	choliambic	Church year	cladoceran	clinkstone
chimaeroid	chondritic	churlishly	claim a foul	clinometer
chimerical	choose ends	churn-staff	clamminess	cliometric
chimney-bar	choosiness	cicatrices	clangorous	clioquinol
chimney pot	choosingly	cicatrizer	clanjamfry	clippingly
chimney-top	chop-fallen	Ciceronian	clankingly	clish-clash
chimpanzee	chopper-cot	cicisbeism	clannishly	clockmaker
China aster	choppiness	cider apple	clanswoman	clock radio
China berry	Chorasmian	cider press	clanswomen	clock tower
China crêpe	choregraph	cigaresque	clap eyes on	clock-watch
chinagraph	choreiform	cigarillos	clapped out	cloddishly
China grass	choreology	cigar plant	claptrappy	clodhopper
china plate	choriambic	cimeliarch	clarabella	clog-dancer
Chinawoman	choriambus	cimetidine	Clarenceux	clogginess
chinchilla	chorically	cinchonine	claret wine	cloistered
Chinese box	choropleth	cinchonism	clarichord	cloisterer

cloisterly	coat of mail	coffinless	colloquist	comicality
close as wax	cobalt blue	coffin-nail	colloquium	comic opera
closed book	cobalt bomb	coffin-ship	colloquize	comic paper
closed door	cobwebbery	cogitabund	colometric	comic strip
closed loop	cobweb bird	cogitation	colonially	comitative
closed shop	cobweblike	cogitative	colonnaded	commandant
close-range	coccydynia	cognisable	colonnette	commandeer
close ranks	cochleated	cognisance	Coloradian	commandery
close shave	cockabully	cognizable	coloration	commanding
close-stool	cockalorum	cognizably	coloratura	commandite
close thing	cockamamie	cognizance	colorature	commeasure
closet play	cockamaroo	cognominal	colorectal	commentary
cloth-bound	cock-and-hen	cognoscent	colossally	commentate
cloth-eared	cock a snook	co-guardian	colossuses	commercial
clotheless	cockatrice	cohabitant	colotomies	comminator
clothes-bag	cock-beaded	cohabiting	colourable	comminutor
clothes-peg	cockchafer	coheirship	colourably	commissary
clothes-pin	cockernony	coherently	colour code	commission
cloudberry	cockleburr	cohesively	colour fast	commissive
cloudburst	cockmaster	cohibition	colour film	commissure
cloud cover	cockneydom	coincident	colourizer	commitment
cloudiness	cockneyess	co-infinite	colourless	committing
cloudscape	cockneyish	co-inherent	colour line	commixtion
clove-brown	cockneyism	coking coal	colour over	commixture
clove hitch	cockneyize	co-labourer	colour wash	commodatum
cloven foot	cock-paddle	co-latitude	colportage	commodious
cloven hoof	cock-sucker	colchicine	colporteur	commonable
clover leaf	cocksurely	cold chisel	colposcope	commonalty
cloverleaf	cock-tailed	cold fusion	colposcopy	common cold
clownishly	cock-teaser	cold shower	coltsfoots	common form
club-footed	cocky-leeky	cold turkey	colt's tooth	common gull
cluelessly	coconut ice	colemanite	columellar	commonhold
clumsiness	coconut shy	Coleoptera	columnated	common hunt
cluster fly	codability	coleoptile	column-inch	common jury
Clydesdale	coddled egg	coleorhiza	combattant	common land
cnidoblast	code number	collar-beam	combinable	common mica
coacervate	codicology	collar-bone	combinedly	common name
coach-built	codirector	collarbone	comburgess	commonness
coach-horse	codominant	collarette	combustion	common noun
coach house	codswallop	collarless	combustive	common opal
coadjutant	coeducator	collar of SS	come abroad	common room
coadjutrix	coelacanth	collar-stud	come across	common salt
coagulable	coeliotomy	collar-work	come-at-able	common seal
coagulator	coenobitic	collatable	come before	common sole
coal-bunker	coenocytic	collateral	come copper	common suit
coal-cellar	co-equality	collection	comedienne	common tern
coalescent	coequality	collective	comedietta	common time
coal-heaver	coercitive	collegiate	come easy to	common vole
coal-master	coercively	collicular	come-hither	common weal
coal mining	coercivity	colliculus	come home to	commonweal
coalmining	coetaneous	collieries	come it over	common year
coal of fire	coeternity	colligable	comeliness	commorancy
coal-worker	co-executor	colligible	comestible	commorient
coaptation	coexistent	collimator	come to good	communally
coarse fish	coffee bean	colloblast	come to hand	communiqué
coarseness	coffee cake	collocable	come to life	commutable
coassessor	coffee mill	collocutor	come to mind	commutator
coastguard	coffee nibs	colloguing	come to pass	compact car
coat armour	coffee-room	collophane	come to rest	compaction
coat-hanger	coffee shop	colloquial	come to that	company car
coatimundi	coffee tree	colloquies	comfortful	company law
coat of arms	coffin-bone	colloquise	comforting	comparable

comparably	conceive of	confession	consimilar	contraries
comparator	concentric	confidante	consistent	contrarily
comparison	conception	confidence	consistory	contravene
compassion	conceptive	confidency	consociate	contrecoup
compassive	conceptual	confinable	consolable	contre-jour
compass saw	concerning	confinedly	consonance	contribute
compatible	concertina	confirmand	consonancy	contritely
compatibly	concertino	confiscate	con sordino	contrition
compatriot	concertize	conflation	consortion	control key
compelling	concession	confluence	consortism	controlled
compendium	concessive	conformism	consortium	controller
compensate	concettism	conformist	conspectus	control rod
competence	concettist	conformity	conspiracy	controvert
competency	conchiolin	confounded	conspirant	convalesce
competitor	conchoidal	confounder	constantan	convection
compilator	conchology	confronter	Constantia	convective
complacent	conciliate	confusable	constantly	convenable
complainer	concinnate	confusedly	constative	convenance
complain of	concinnity	confusible	constipate	convenient
complanate	concinnous	confutable	constitute	convention
complected	concipient	congeneric	constraint	conventual
complement	conclavist	congenital	constringe	convergent
completely	concludent	congestion	construing	conversant
completion	conclusion	congestive	consuetude	conversely
completist	conclusive	conglobate	consulship	conversion
completive	conclusory	congregant	consultant	conversive
completory	concoction	congregate	consulting	convertend
complexant	concoctive	congruence	consultory	convertism
complexify	concordant	congruency	consumable	convertite
complexion	concrement	conhydrine	consumedly	convertive
complexity	concretely	conicopoly	consummate	convex lens
compliable	concretion	coniferous	contact man	convexness
compliance	concretise	conjecture	contagious	conveyable
compliancy	concretize	conjointly	containing	conveyance
complicacy	concubinal	conjugally	contentful	conviction
complicate	concurrent	conjugated	contention	convictism
complicity	concurring	conjunctly	contentive	convictive
compliment	concursion	conjurator	contentual	convincing
complotter	concussion	connatural	contestant	convoluted
compluvium	concussive	connecting	contextual	convoyance
composable	condensate	connection	contexture	convulsant
composedly	condensery	connective	contiguity	convulsion
composed of	condensity	conniption	contiguous	convulsive
compositor	condescend	connivance	continence	co-obligant
compositum	condignity	connivancy	continency	cooker hood
composture	condolence	connivence	contingent	cooking top
compotator	condonable	conoidical	continuant	cook's knife
compounded	conducible	conqueress	continuing	cool-headed
compounder	conducting	conquering	continuity	cooperancy
compradore	conduction	conscience	continuous	cooperator
comprehend	conductive	consecrate	contortion	Cooper pair
compresent	condurango	consectary	contour map	cooper-shop
compressed	condylarth	consension	contraband	co-optation
compressor	coneflower	consensual	contrabass	co-optative
compromise	cone-in-cone	consentant	contracted	co-ordinate
compulsion	confabbing	consentive	contractee	coordinate
compulsive	confection	consequent	contractor	cop a packet
compulsory	confederal	conservate	contradict	coparcener
computable	conference	considered	contraflow	copartnery
Comstocker	conferment	considerer	contrahent	copepodous
conalbumin	conferring	consignify	contraltos	Copernican
conatively	confessant	consilient	contrapose	copper belt

copperhead	cornerback	cosmic dust	coupleteer	crab nebula
copper-knob	corner flag	cosmic rays	coupon bond	Crab nebula
copper loss	corner-kick	cosmodrome	coupon-free	crab plover
copper-nose	cornerless	cosmogenic	courageous	crab-spider
copperskin	corner shop	cosmogonic	course-book	crack a crib
copper wire	cornerwise	cosmopolis	coursebook	crackajack
co-presence	cornetcies	cosmoramic	course unit	crack-brain
co-producer	cornettist	co-specific	courseware	cracked-pot
coprolalia	corn-factor	Cossack hat	coursework	crack hardy
coprolitic	cornflower	Costa Rican	court-baron	crack house
copromania	corn-ground	costliness	court-craft	crackiness
co-promoter	corn-husker	costmaries	court dress	cradle-roof
coprophagy	Cornishman	cosy corner	courtesies	cradle song
coprophile	Cornishmen	cote-hardie	court-house	craft guild
coprophily	corn-popper	coterminal	courthouse	craftiness
copulation	cornstarch	cothurnate	courtierly	craft-union
copulative	cornucopia	cottage pie	courtliest	cragginess
copulatory	Coromandel	cotton belt	court-metre	craneflies
copy editor	coronalled	cotton-bush	court of law	cranesbill
copyholder	coronaries	cotton cake	court order	craniology
copyreader	coronation	cotton-fish	court party	craniotome
copy-taster	corpocracy	cotton lord	cousinhood	craniotomy
copy-typist	corporally	cotton-mill	Cousin Jack	crankiness
copywriter	corporator	cotton-seed	cousinship	crankshaft
coquelicot	corporeity	cottontail	couturière	crank-wheel
coquetries	corpulence	cotton tree	couverture	crap-artist
coquettish	corpulency	cottonweed	covalently	crapaudine
coquimbite	corpuscule	cottonwood	covariance	crapulence
coracoidal	corpus vile	cotton wool	covariancy	craquelure
coral-berry	corralling	cotton-worm	covenantal	crashingly
coral-plant	correction	couch grass	covenanted	crassitude
coral polyp	corrective	cough candy	covenantee	crater-lake
coral snake	correctory	cough sweet	covenanter	crater-like
coram nobis	corregidor	coulombian	covenantor	cravenness
cor anglais	correption	Coulomb law	coverchief	crawlingly
corbelling	correspond	coulometer	cover drive	crawl space
corbie-step	Corriedale	coulometry	covered way	crazy about
corbin-bone	corrigenda	coulterneb	cover-glass	creakiness
corded ware	corrigible	councillor	cover point	creakingly
cordelière	corrigibly	councilman	cover-shame	creameries
cordialise	corroboree	councilmen	cover story	creaminess
cordiality	corrodable	council tax	covert coat	cream sauce
cordialize	corrodiary	counselled	covertness	creatinine
cordierite	corrodible	counsellee	covetingly	creational
cordillera	corrosible	counsellor	covetously	creatively
cordon bleu	corrugator	counteract	covinously	creativity
corduroyed	corruptful	counterbid	cowardness	creaturely
cordwainer	corruption	counter-ion	cowberries	credential
corelation	corruptive	counterman	cow-catcher	creditable
corelative	corselette	counterspy	cowcatcher	creditably
core memory	corsetière	countertop	cow-creamer	credit card
coriaceous	corsetless	count heads	coweringly	Creditiste
Corinthian	Cortaillod	count noses	cow-hearted	credit note
cork-jacket	corticated	countryman	cow-parsley	creditress
corkscrewy	corybantic	countrymen	cow parsnip	credit sale
cork-tipped	coryneform	country put	Cowperitis	credit side
corn brandy	coryphaeus	count sheep	cowpuncher	credulence
corn circle	coryphodon	county hall	cowslipped	creepiness
corn-cockle	Cosa Nostra	county seat	cow-spanker	creepingly
corncockle	Coslettize	county town	coxopodite	creep-joint
corn dodger	cosmetical	coup de main	crabbiness	creep-mouse
corned beef	cosmically	coupleress	crab-harrow	crematoria

crenellate	cross slide	cuckoo wasp	curtain-rod	cystoscope
crenulated	cross-staff	cuculiform	curvaceous	cystoscopy
crêpe paper	cross the t's	cucullated	curvedness	cystostomy
crépinette	crosstrees	cucumiform	curvetting	cytochrome
crescendos	cross-vault	cuddleable	Cushingoid	cytologist
crescented	cross wires	cuddlesome	cuspidated	cytopathic
crescentic	crotchless	cudgelling	cussedness	cytophilic
crested tit	crouchback	cudgel-play	custard pie	cytotropic
cretaceous	Crouch ware	cuirassier	customable	daffodilly
crèvecoeur	crow-flower	cuir-ciselé	customably	daggerhead
crewel work	crow-footed	culdoscope	customizer	daggle-tail
crib-biting	crow garlic	culdoscopy	custom-made	Daguerrean
cribellate	crownation	culicicide	cut a corner	dahabeeyah
cribriform	crown conch	culicifuge	cut a figure	daily bread
crick-crack	crown court	culinarian	cut-and-fill	daily dozen
cricketana	Crown Court	culinarily	cut a splash	daintihood
cricket bag	Crown Derby	cultically	cut corners	daintiness
cricket-bat	crown ether	cultivable	cut-offness	dairy cream
cricketing	crown glass	cultivator	cut the knot	daisy chain
crime sheet	crown graft	cultriform	cuttle-bone	daisy roots
criminally	crown green	culturable	cuttlefish	daisy wheel
criminator	crown-piece	culturally	cutty grass	Dalton plan
crimpiness	crown roast	culverkeys	cutty-stool	damageable
cringeling	crown vetch	culvertage	cut up rough	damagement
cringingly	crown wheel	Cumberland	cyanic acid	damagingly
crinkle-cut	cruciality	cumberless	cyanine dye	damascener
crinolined	cruciation	cumberment	cyanogenic	damask rose
criosphinx	cruelty man	cumbersome	cyanometer	damask work
crippledom	cruet-stand	cumbrously	cyanometry	dame school
crispation	cruise ship	cummerbund	cyanophyte	damfoolery
crispature	cruisewear	cumulately	cyathiform	damned well
crispbread	crumbiness	cumulation	cybernetic	damn my eyes
crispiness	crumbliest	cumulative	cyberspace	damp course
criss-cross	crumbiness	cumuliform	cybotactic	damselfish
critically	crunchiest	cunctation	cycle track	damson plum
criticizer	crushingly	cunctative	cyclically	damson tree
criticling	crustacean	cunctatory	cyclo-cross	dance-drama
critiquing	crustation	cundurango	cyclograph	dance floor
crocheting	crustiness	cunningest	cyclometer	dance-house
crookedest	cryoconite	cup-and-ball	cyclometry	dancercise
crooningly	cryogenics	cup-and-cone	cyclopedia	dandizette
crop circle	cryonicist	cup-and-ring	cyclopedic	dandy brush
croqueting	cryophorus	Cupid's dart	cycloramic	dandy-horse
cross-bench	cryoscopic	cup of assay	cyclostome	dandyishly
crossbones	cryosphere	cuprea bark	cyclostyle	dandyzette
cross-breed	cryptogram	curability	cyclothyme	Danes' blood
crossbreed	cryptolect	curate's egg	cyclotomic	dangerless
cross-check	cryptology	curatively	cylindered	danger line
cross-court	cryptozoic	curatorial	cylindrite	danger list
cross-dress	cryptozoon	curd cheese	cylindroid	dangersome
cross-grain	cry shame on	curelessly	cylindroma	danglement
cross-guard	crystallic	Curetonian	cymotrichy	Danish blue
cross-hatch	crystallin	curiologic	cynegetics	dapperling
cross-index	crystal set	curled kale	cynophobia	dapperness
crossleted	ctenophore	curly-wurly	Cyrenaican	dapple grey
cross-light	cubby house	curmudgeon	cyrtometer	daringness
crossmatch	cubic nitre	curmurring	cystectomy	Darjeeling
crosspatch	cuboid bone	currencies	cystinosis	dark matter
crosspiece	cuckoo-land	curricular	cystinotic	Darling pea
cross-point	cuckoo pint	curriculum	cystinuria	darning-egg
cross-react	cuckoo scab	curry paste	cystometer	dastardize
cross-refer	cuckoo spit	cursedness	cystometry	dasylirion

data-logger	debateable	decorement	deflowerer	delusively
data stream	debauchery	decorously	defocusing	demagogism
date back to	debentured	decreation	defocussed	demandable
date-cancel	debilitate	decree nisi	defoliator	demand note
datelessly	debonairly	decreolize	deforciant	demand pull
date-letter	debouchure	decrepitly	deformable	demarcator
daubréeite	debriefing	decrescent	deformedly	dementedly
daughterly	decadently	decretally	defrayable	demi-cannon
daunomycin	decagynous	decryption	defrayment	demi-circle
dauntingly	decahedral	decumbence	defunction	demi-lancer
dauphinate	decahedron	decumbency	defunctive	demi-ostage
dauphiness	Decalogist	decurrence	de Gaullism	demiourgos
dawn chorus	decametric	decurrency	degeneracy	demi-piqued
daydreamer	decampment	decussated	degenerate	demissness
day nursery	decandrous	dedecorate	degradable	demobilise
day of truce	decangular	dedication	degreeless	demobilize
day release	decapitate	dedicative	degression	democratic
day tripper	decathlete	dedicatory	degressive	Democritic
dazzlement	Decauville	deductable	dehiscence	demodectic
dazzlingly	deceivable	deductible	dehumanise	demodulate
deaconhood	deceivably	deed of gift	dehumanize	Demogorgon
deacon-seat	decelerate	de-emphasis	dehumidify	demography
deaconship	Decembrist	deep-bodied	dehydrator	demoiselle
deactivate	decempedal	deep-freeze	deiformity	demolisher
dead-beaten	decemviral	deep-frying	deinothere	demolition
dead centre	decentness	deep litter	dejectedly	demonetise
dead colour	deceptible	deep-rooted	delaminate	demonetize
dead-end kid	deceptious	deep-seated	Delawarean	demoniacal
dead letter	decigramme	deep waters	Delawarian	demonology
deadliness	decimalise	deer-culler	del credere	demoralise
deadlocked	decimalism	deer forest	delectable	demoralize
dead nettle	decimalist	de-escalate	delectably	demoticist
deadpanned	decimalize	de-ethicize	delegacies	demotivate
dead ringer	decimation	defaceable	delegation	demureness
dead-tongue	decinormal	defacement	delegatory	demurrable
dead weight	decipherer	defalcator	Delhi belly	denatation
de-aeration	decisional	defamation	deliberant	denaturant
deafferent	decisively	defamatory	deliberate	denaturize
de-afforest	decivilize	defeasance	delicacies	dendriform
deaf-mutism	deckle edge	defeasible	delicately	dendrogram
deaf-nettle	deck quoits	defeasibly	deligation	dendrology
dealbation	deck tennis	defecation	delightful	denegation
dealership	declarable	defectible	delimitate	denegatory
dealkylate	declarator	defeminize	delimiting	denigrator
deambulate	declaredly	defenceman	delineable	denization
dear-bought	declare war	defendable	delineator	denominate
death adder	declassify	defendress	delinquent	de nos jours
death agony	declension	defenseman	deliquesce	denotation
deathfully	declinable	defensible	delirament	denotative
death grant	decollator	defensibly	deliration	denotement
death house	décolletée	deferrable	deliveress	denouement
deathiness	decolonise	deficiency	deliveries	dénouement
death knell	decolonize	defilement	delocalise	densimeter
deathliest	decolorise	definement	delocalize	densometer
death-place	decolorize	definitely	delphinine	denticular
death's head	decomposer	definition	delphinium	dentifrice
death squad	decompound	definitive	delphinoid	dentiscalp
deathwards	decompress	definitory	delta waves	denudation
death-watch	deconvolve	definitude	deltiology	denudative
death-wound	decorament	deflagrate	delucidate	denunciate
deauration	decoration	deflection	deluginous	deobstruct
debasement	decorative	deflective	delusional	deodorizer

Deo gratias	derogatory	detectival	diagrammed	dig a pit for
deontology	derricking	detergency	diagraphic	digestedly
Deo volente	desalinate	determined	diagrydium	digestible
deoxidizer	desalinize	determiner	diakineses	digestibly
department	desaturate	deterrable	diakinesis	digger wasp
dependable	descendant	deterrence	dialectics	digitalise
dependably	descendent	detestable	dialogical	digitalize
dependance	descending	detestably	dialoguist	digitately
dependancy	descension	detonation	dialoguize	digitation
dependence	descensive	detonative	dialysable	digitiform
dependency	descramble	detoxicate	diamantine	digitorium
deperition	descriptor	detoxified	diamond-cut	diglottism
depilation	descriptum	detoxifies	diamondize	digression
depilatory	desecrator	detraction	diapedesis	digressive
deplorable	desert boot	detractive	diaphanous	dijudicate
deplorably	desert lark	detractory	diaphoneme	dikaryotic
deployment	desertless	detruncate	diaphorase	dilacerate
deplumated	desertness	devalorize	diaporesis	dilapidate
depolarise	desert rose	Devanagari	diarrhoeal	dilatation
depolarize	deservedly	devastator	diarrhoeic	dilatative
depopulate	deshabille	developing	diasceuast	dilatorily
deportable	déshabille	deviatoric	diaskeuast	dilemmatic
deportment	déshabillé	deviceless	diastaltic	dilettante
depositary	desiccator	devil dance	diathermal	dilettanti
depositing	desiderata	devil-devil	diathermic	diligently
deposition	desiderate	devilishly	diatribist	dilligrout
depository	designable	devil's club	diazeuctic	dill pickle
depositure	designator	devil's dirt	dibasicity	dilly-dally
depravedly	designatum	devil's dung	dichloride	dilucidate
deprecator	designedly	devil's dust	dichlorvos	diluteness
depreciate	designless	devil's grip	dichotomic	dilutional
depredator	designment	devil's guts	dichroitic	dime a dozen
depressant	desipience	devil's limb	dichromasy	dimetrodon
depressing	desipiency	devil's milk	dichromate	dimication
depression	desireless	deviltries	dickcissel	diminished
depressive	desiringly	devisement	Dickensian	diminisher
deprivable	desirously	devitalise	dicoumarin	diminuendi
depuration	desistance	devitalize	dicoumarol	diminuendo
depurative	desolately	devocalize	Dictaphone	diminution
depuratory	desolation	devolution	dictatress	diminutive
deputation	desolative	Devonshire	dictionary	dimorphism
deputative	desorption	devotement	Dictograph	dimorphous
deputyship	despairful	devotional	dictyosome	dim-sighted
deracinate	desperados	devourable	dicynodont	Ding an sich
derailleur	despicable	devourment	didactical	dingle-bird
derailment	despicably	devoutness	didascalic	dining hall
Derbyshire	despisable	dewberries	didgeridoo	dining room
deregister	despiteful	dewdropped	didjeridoo	dinner-bell
deregulate	despiteous	dextrality	didynamous	dinner-horn
derestrict	despondent	dextrorsal	did you ever	dinner lady
deridingly	desquamate	dhobi's itch	die-casting	dinnerless
derisively	dessiatine	diabetical	die-hardism	dinner-pail
derivately	destructor	diabolical	dielectric	dinner time
derivation	desudation	diacaustic	difference	dioestrous
derivative	detachable	diachronic	difficulty	Diogenical
dermatitis	detachedly	diaconicon	diffidence	dioptrical
dermatogen	detachment	diademated	diffidency	diorthosis
dermatosis	detainable	diagenesis	diffluence	diorthotic
dernier cri	detainment	diagenetic	diffusable	diotically
dernier mot	detectable	diaglyphic	diffusedly	Diotrephes
derogation	detectably	diagnostic	diffusible	diphonemic
derogative	detectible	diagonally	digammated	diphtheria

diphtheric	discomfort	disgarland	disputably	disulphide
diphyletic	discommend	disgarnish	disputator	disuniform
diphyllous	discommode	disglorify	disqualify	disutility
diphyodont	discommons	disgregate	disquieten	disyllabic
diplacusis	discommune	disgruntle	disquieter	disyllable
diplococci	discompose	disguising	disquietly	ditchwater
diplodocus	disco music	disgustful	Disraelian	ditch-water
diplograph	disconcert	disgusting	disrealize	ditheistic
diploidion	disconfirm	dishabille	disrespect	dithematic
diplomatic	disconnect	dish aerial	disruption	dithionate
diplophase	discontent	disharmony	disruptive	dithionite
Dippel's oil	discophile	dishearten	disrupture	dithionous
diprotodon	discordant	disherison	dissatisfy	ditriglyph
dipsomania	discordful	dishonesty	dissceptre	ditrigonal
diptychous	discordous	dishwasher	dissection	ditrochean
directable	discounsel	dishwatery	dissective	dittograph
direct dial	discounter	disimagine	disselboom	ditto marks
direct mail	discourage	disimprove	dissembler	diurnal arc
directness	discourser	disincline	dissension	diurnalist
Directoire	discoverer	disinherit	dissenting	diurnation
directress	discreeter	disinhibit	dissention	diuturnity
directrice	discreetly	disinvolve	dissertate	divagation
direct rule	discrepant	disjection	disservice	divaricate
diremption	discrepate	disjointed	dissheathe	dive-bomber
dirt-eating	discretely	disjointly	dissidence	dive-dapper
dirt farmer	discretion	dislikable	dissightly	divergence
dirty Allan	discretive	disloyally	dissilient	divergency
dirty linen	discretize	disloyalty	dissimilar	divertible
dirty money	disculpate	dismalness	dissipated	divestment
dirty trick	discursion	dismantler	dissipater	dividually
disability	discursive	dismission	dissipator	divination
disamenity	discursory	dismissive	dissociate	divinatory
disanalogy	discussant	dismissory	dissoluble	divineness
disanimate	discussion	Disneyland	dissolubly	divineress
disapparel	discussive	disordered	dissolvent	diving bell
disappoint	discutient	disorderly	dissonance	diving duck
disapprove	disdainful	disorganic	dissonancy	diving suit
disarrange	diseasedly	disownment	dissuasion	divinities
disastrous	diseaseful	disparager	dissuasive	divinitize
disbalance	diseconomy	dispassion	distensile	divisional
disbarment	diseducate	dispatcher	distension	divisively
disbarring	disembogue	dispelling	distichous	divulgence
disbelieve	disembosom	dispensary	distillate	dizzyingly
disbenefit	disembowel	dispensate	distillery	do a swelter
disbudding	disembroil	dispensive	distilling	do away with
disburthen	disempower	dispeopler	distilment	dobby-weave
discarnate	disenamour	dispermous	distinctly	Dobos Torte
disc camera	disenchant	dispersant	distortion	docibility
discectomy	disendower	dispersion	distortive	docimastic
discerning	disengaged	dispersive	distracted	dock-tailed
disc floret	disennoble	dispersoid	distractor	Doc Martens
dischargee	disenslave	disphenoid	distrainee	do credit to
discharger	disenthral	dispiteous	distrainer	doctorally
disc harrow	disentitle	dispondaic	distrainor	doctor bird
discipline	disentrail	disponible	distraught	doctor-fish
discipular	disentwine	disposable	distressed	doctorhood
discission	disenvelop	disposedly	distribute	doctorship
disc jockey	disepalous	dispositor	distringas	doctrinary
disclaimer	disfashion	dispossess	distruster	doctrinate
disclosing	disfeature	dispraiser	disturbant	doctrinism
disclosure	disfigurer	disprovide	disturbing	doctrinist
discobolus	disfurnish	disputable	disulfiram	documental

dodecanoic	doorkeeper	Douglasite	draught-net	drop astern
dodecarchy	door-to-door	doulocracy	draw a blank	drop down to
dog and bone	dope-runner	douzainier	draw breath	drop hammer
dogberries	Dorian mode	dove-colour	drawbridge	drop-handle
dog biscuit	dormer room	dove-flower	draw bridle	drop-letter
dog-bramble	Dorothy bag	dove-marble	Drawcansir	droppingly
dogfighter	dorsalmost	dove orchid	drawerfuls	drop serene
doggedness	Dorset Down	dovetailed	draw-gloves	drop-stroke
dog handler	dorsifixed	dovetailer	drawing-pad	drosometer
dog-leg hole	dosimetric	dovishness	drawing pin	drosophila
dogmatical	do the downy	do well to do	draw it mild	drossiness
dogmatizer	do the trick	dower chest	drawlingly	droughtily
dognapping	do things to	dower house	draw near to	drowningly
dogsbodies	dotishness	down and out	draw straws	drowsihead
dog's dinner	dot product	down at heel	drawstring	drowsiness
dog's letter	dotted line	down cellar	draw stumps	drowsy-head
dog's-tongue	dottrified	downcoming	dreadfully	drudgingly
dog-whipper	Douay Bible	down-coming	dreadingly	drug addict
Dolcelatte	double back	down-curved	dreadlocks	drug buster
dolesomely	double-bank	down-easter	dreamfully	druggister
do less than	double bass	downhiller	dreaminess	drug pusher
dollar area	double bill	down-market	dreamingly	Druid stone
dollarbird	double bind	downmarket	dreamscape	drumlinoid
dollar mark	double bond	downstairs	dream-world	drupaceous
dollar sign	double-book	downstater	dreamworld	druzhinnik
dollar spot	double chin	downstream	drearihead	dry battery
doll's house	double-crop	down-street	drearihood	dry-blowing
dolomitize	double cube	down-stroke	dreariment	dry canteen
dolorifuge	double date	downstroke	dreariness	dry-cleaner
dolorously	double-deck	down the pan	drearisome	dry farming
dolus bonus	double-dink	down timber	dredge-boat	dry Martini
dolus malus	double-dyed	down-to-date	dreikanter	dry measure
dome-headed	double-face	downtowner	dress house	dry monsoon
domestical	double flat	downwardly	dressiness	dry saltery
dominantly	doublefold	downy birch	dressmaker	dry shampoo
domination	double harp	dowsing rod	dress-sense	dual number
dominative	double-head	doxography	dress shirt	dubitation
dominatrix	double life	doxologies	Dreyfusard	dubitative
domineerer	double-lock	doxologize	drift apart	dub-skelper
Dominicker	doubleness	drabbiness	driftingly	duffel coat
Donald Duck	double-park	draconites	drift sight	duffle-coat
Donatistic	double play	dracontine	drill order	duke cherry
doner kebab	double reed	draegerman	drink-drive	dulcetness
Don Juanism	double-reef	drag-anchor	drinking up	dull-headed
donkey deep	double room	drag artist	drink-money	dullsville
donkey drop	double salt	dragginess	drink-taken	dull-witted
donkey-lick	double-shot	draggingly	drip coffee	dumb animal
donkey pump	double star	dragon arum	drippiness	dumb blonde
donkey vote	double stop	dragonfish	drivelling	dumb crambo
donkey work	double take	dragonnade	driven well	dumb friend
Donnybrook	double-talk	dragon root	driverless	dumbledore
Don Quixote	double team	dragon ship	drive shaft	dumb nettle
don't-carish	double time	dragon tree	driveshaft	dumb sheave
don't mind me	doubletree	drag-racing	driving box	dumbstruck
doodle-sack	double-wide	drainboard	drolleries	dumb waiter
doohickeys	doubtfully	drake's tail	dromomania	dumpy level
doomsaying	doubtingly	dramatical	droopiness	Dundee cake
do one's best	douc langur	dramaturge	droopingly	dunderhead
do one's dash	dough-baked	dramaturgy	droop-snoot	dunderpate
do one's duty	doughiness	draught ewe	drop a brick	dung-beetle
do one's face	doughtiest	draughtily	drop anchor	duniwassal
do one's head	Douglas fir	draughtman	drop asleep	dunnage bag

duodecimal	earth-light	ecstatical	eighty-nine	emblem book
duodecimos	earth-mover	ecthlipsis	eisteddfod	emblements
duodenitis	earthquake	ectodermal	ejaculator	embodiment
dupability	earthshine	ectogenous	ekistician	emboldener
duple ratio	earthwards	ectomorphy	elaborator	embolismic
duplicable	earth-woman	ectromelia	elasmosaur	embolismus
duplicator	ear-trumpet	Ecuadorian	elastician	embonpoint
durability	earwigging	ecumenical	elasticise	embossment
durational	ear-witness	eczematous	elasticity	embothrium
duratively	ease nature	edentulous	elasticize	embouchure
durativity	East Africa	edge-runner	elatedness	embowelled
Düreresque	Easter-dues	edge to edge	elbow chair	emboweller
dusky perch	easterlies	edible crab	elbow-joint	embrasured
dustbinman	Easter lily	edible frog	elderberry	embrighten
dust-colour	Easterling	edibleness	eldest hand	embroidery
dust jacket	Easter term	edifyingly	Eleaticism	embryogeny
Dutch feast	Eastertide	editionize	elecampane	embryology
Dutch light	Eastertime	editorship	electional	embryonary
Dutch lunch	Easter Week	educatable	electively	embryonate
Dutch metal	East German	edulcorate	electorate	embryotomy
Dutch treat	East Indian	Edwardiana	electorial	emendation
Dutch uncle	East Indies	effaceable	electrical	emendatory
Dutchwoman	East Riding	effacement	electrojet	emeraldine
Dutchwomen	eastwardly	effectible	electronic	emergently
duumvirate	easy does it	effectless	electrotin	Emersonian
dwarf elder	Easy Street	effectuate	elementary	emery board
dwarfishly	easy virtue	effeminacy	elephantic	emery cloth
dyeability	eat Chinese	effeminate	elephantry	emery paper
dyer's broom	eat dinners	effeminize	Eleusinian	emery wheel
dynamicist	eat one's hat	effervesce	elevatedly	emetically
dynamistic	eat the leek	effeteness	elevenfold	emigration
dynamitard	eaves-board	efficacity	eleven-plus	emigratory
dynastical	ebb and flow	efficience	eleventhly	emissaries
Dyophysite	Ebionitism	efficiency	eliminable	emissivity
Dyothelite	ebracteate	effleurage	eliminator	emmetropia
dypsomania	ebullience	effloresce	eliotropus	emmetropic
dysarthria	ebulliency	effortless	eliquation	emollience
dyscrasite	ebullition	effraction	elliptical	emparadise
dysenteric	eburnation	effrontery	elongation	empathetic
dysgraphia	ecce signum	effulgence	eloquently	empathetic
dysgraphic	ecchymosed	effusively	elsewhence	emphasizer
dyskinesia	ecchymoses	egg-coddler	elucidator	emphatical
dysphemism	ecchymosis	egg custard	elucubrate	emphyteuta
dysplastic	Eccles cake	egg tempera	elutriator	Empire City
dysprosium	ecclesiast	egocentric	eluviation	empire-line
dysprosody	echinoderm	egoistical	Elzevirian	empiricism
dystrophia	echinulate	egurgitate	emaciation	empiricist
dystrophic	echoically	Egypticity	emalangeni	emplastrum
each to each	echolocate	Egyptizing	emancipate	employable
eagle-stone	echopraxia	Egyptology	emancipist	employment
Eames chair	eclaircise	eicosanoic	emarginate	empoisoner
earbashing	eclectical	eicosanoid	emasculate	emulsified
early grave	eclipsable	eicosenoic	embalmment	emulsifier
early hours	ecliptical	eigenstate	embankment	emulsifies
early music	ecoclimate	eigenvalue	embarkment	enablement
early night	ecological	eighteenmo	embattling	enaliosaur
early riser	economical	eighteenth	embeddable	enamelling
ear-stopple	economizer	eighth note	ember-goose	enamellist
earth-board	ecotourism	eighth part	embitterer	enamelware
earthbound	ecotourist	eightpence	emblazoner	enamelwork
earth house	ecphonesis	eightpenny	emblazonry	enantiomer
earthiness	ecstasiate	eightyfold	emblematic	encampment

encasement	enfacement	entombment	epigastric	equanimous
encashable	enfant gâté	entomology	epigenesis	equestrial
encashment	enfleurage	entophytic	epigenetic	equestrian
encephalic	enfoldment	entrancing	epiglottal	equiatomic
encephalin	enforcedly	entrapment	epiglottic	equicrural
encephalon	enforcible	entrapping	epiglottis	equilibria
encephalos	engagement	en travesti	epigrapher	equilibrio
enchanting	engagingly	entreasure	epigraphic	equiparate
enchiridia	engarrison	entreaties	epileptoid	equipotent
encincture	engenderer	entrenched	epilimnion	equiradial
encomienda	engendrure	entryphone	epilogical	equi-signal
encourager	engineless	Entryphone	epimorphic	equitation
encrinital	engine room	enumerable	epineurium	equivalent
encrinitic	English elm	enumerator	epipelagic	equivocacy
encroacher	Englishism	enunciable	epiphanies	equivocate
encrustate	Englishize	enunciator	epiphanize	eradiation
encryption	Englishman	enveloping	epiphanous	eradicable
encyclical	Englishmen	environing	epipharynx	eradicated
encystment	engrossing	enwrapment	epiphonema	eradicator
endangerer	engulfment	enwrapping	epiphyllum	erectility
end by doing	enharmonic	enzymology	epiphyseal	eremitical
endearance	enhungered	eosinophil	epiphytous	Erewhonian
endearment	enigmatise	epagomenal	epipleural	ergastulum
endemicity	enigmatize	epagomenic	epiplocele	ergativity
endergonic	enjambment	epanaphora	episcleral	ergodicity
endingless	enjoinment	eparterial	episcopacy	ergonomics
end in smoke	enjoyingly	epaulement	episcopate	ergonomist
end moraine	enkephalin	epauletted	episcopize	ergonovine
endocarpic	enlacement	epeirogeny	episematic	ergophobia
endocervix	enlistment	epentheses	episiotomy	ergosphere
endocyclic	enlivening	epenthesis	episodical	ergosterol
endocytose	enmeshment	epenthetic	episomally	ergotamine
endodermal	enomotarch	epexegeses	epispastic	ergotoxine
endodermic	enormities	epexegesis	epistemics	eria cocoon
endodermis	enormously	epexegetic	episternal	ericaceous
endodontal	enough said	ephemerist	episternum	erosionist
endodontia	enquirable	ephemerons	epistolary	erotically
endodontic	enragement	ephemerous	epistolise	erotogenic
endoenzyme	enregister	Ephthalite	epistolist	erotomania
end of steel	enrichment	epiblastic	epistolize	errability
endogamous	ensanguine	epicanthic	epistrophe	erraticism
endogenous	enserfment	epicanthus	epitaphial	erubescent
endolithic	ensoulment	epicardiac	epitaphian	eructation
endomorphy	entailable	epicardial	epitaphize	eruptional
endophoric	entailment	epicardium	epithalamy	erysipelas
endophytic	enterclose	epicentral	epithecium	erythrasma
endorsable	enterocele	epichordal	epithelial	erythremia
endorsible	enterocyte	epiclastic	epithelium	erythritol
endoscopic	enterolith	epicondyle	epithetize	erythrosin
endosmosis	enterotomy	epicranial	epitomator	escadrille
endosmotic	enterprise	epicuticle	epitomical	escalation
endosulfan	enthraldom	epicycloid	epitomizer	escalatory
endothermy	enthronize	Epidaurian	epoch angle	escallonia
end product	enthusiasm	epideictic	eponychium	escalloped
end-scraper	enthusiast	epidemical	epoophoron	escape code
end-stopped	enticement	epidendrum	epoxy resin	escapeless
enduringly	enticingly	epidermoid	eprouvette	escapement
eneolithic	entincture	epididymal	Epsom salts	escape road
energetics	entireness	epididymis	equability	escapology
energy band	entireties	epidiorite	equational	escarpment
enervation	entitative	epidotized	equatorial	escartelee
enervative	entodermal	epigastria	equanimity	escharotic

eschatocol	euhemerist	every stick	exhaust gas	explicator
escheatage	euhemerize	everything	exhaustion	explicitly
eschewment	eukaryotic	everywhere	exhaustive	explodable
escritoire	eulogistic	evidential	exheredate	exploitage
escutcheon	eupatorium	evil spirit	exhibitant	exploitive
Eskimo roll	euphausiid	eviscerate	exhibiting	explorator
esoterical	euphemious	eviternity	exhibition	explosible
espacement	euphemizer	evolvement	exhibitive	exportable
espadrille	euphonical	evulgation	exhibitory	exposition
especially	euphonious	exacerbate	exhilarant	expositive
espressivo	euphorbium	exactingly	exhilarate	expository
esprit fort	euphoriant	exactitude	exhumation	expressage
essayistic	Euphratean	exaggerate	exigencies	expression
estanciero	euphuistic	exaltation	exiguously	expressive
estate duty	Eurafrican	examinable	exit permit	expressman
esterified	Eurasiatic	examinator	ex-meridian	expressway
esterifies	eurhythmic	exannulate	exobiology	expunction
esthiomene	Euripidean	exasperate	exocentric	expurgator
estimation	euroaquilo	exaspidean	exocuticle	exsanguine
estimative	Eurobabble	excalceate	exocytosis	exsibilate
estimatory	Eurocheque	ex cathedra	exocytotic	ex silentio
esuriently	euroclydon	excavation	exodontist	exsolution
etch figure	Eurodollar	excavatory	exogenetic	exspuition
Eteocretan	Euromarket	excecation	exoglossic	exsufflate
eternalise	Europeanly	exceedable	exomphalos	extemporal
eternalism	Eurosummit	excellence	exo-narthex	extendable
eternality	Eurovision	excellency	exorbitant	extendedly
eternalize	eurybathic	Excellency	exorbitate	extendible
eternities	euryhaline	exceptable	exorcistic	extensible
ethacrynic	euryhydric	exceptious	exospheric	extenuator
ethambutol	eurypterid	excerption	exoterical	exteriorly
ethanediol	eurythmics	excess fare	exothermal	exterior to
ethereally	Eustachian	excise duty	exothermic	externally
ethicalism	Euston Road	excisional	exotically	extinction
ethicality	euthanasia	excitation	exoticness	extinctive
ethnically	eutrapelia	excitative	expandable	extinguish
ethnologic	evacuation	excitatory	expandible	extirpator
ethologist	evacuative	excitement	expansible	extra cover
ethylamine	evaluation	excitingly	expatiater	extractant
ethyl ether	evaluative	excludable	expatiator	extracting
ethylidene	evanescent	excogitate	expatriate	extraction
etiolation	evangelise	excrescent	expectable	extractive
Eton collar	evangelism	excruciate	expectably	extractory
Eton jacket	evangelist	excursuses	expectance	extradural
etymologer	evangelize	excusatory	expectancy	extralegal
etymologic	evaporable	excuseless	expectedly	extramural
eucalyptic	evaporator	ex dividend	expedience	extraneity
eucalyptol	evaporitic	execration	expediency	extraneous
eucalyptus	even chance	execrative	expeditate	extricable
eucaryotic	even-handed	execratory	expedition	extrudable
euchlorine	evenliness	executable	expellable	extubation
eudaemonic	even parity	executancy	expendable	extuberant
eudaimonia	eventfully	exegetical	expendably	exuberance
eudemonics	even though	exemptible	expenditor	exuberancy
eudemonism	eventually	exenterate	experience	Exucontian
eudemonist	ever-during	exercitant	experiment	exulcerate
eudiometer	ever-living	Exeter hall	expertness	exultantly
eudiometry	every bit as	exfiltrate	expilation	exultation
eugenicist	every other	exhalation	expiration	exultingly
eugeocline	every penny	exhalative	expiratory	exumbrella
euglobulin	everyplace	exhalatory	explicable	exundation
euhemerism	every steek	exhalement	explicably	exurbanite

exuviation	faithfully	fasciation	federalize	feuilleton
eye-catcher	falciparum	fascicular	federation	feverishly
eye contact	Falklander	fasciculus	federative	feverously
eye-dialect	fall aboard	fascinated	fed to death	fever pitch
eyeglassed	fallacious	fascinator	feebleness	fianchetto
eye-legible	fall astern	fascistoid	feeding-cup	Fianna Fáil
eyelet hole	fall back on	fashionist	feed-trough	fiberboard
eye-opening	fall behind	fast asleep	feelingful	fiberglass
eye-service	fallen arch	fast bowler	feel no pain	fible-fable
eyespotted	fallenness	Fastens-een	feet of clay	fibreboard
eyestrings	fall foul of	fast friend	feigningly	fibreglass
eyewitness	falling-out	fastidious	feistiness	fibre-optic
fabricable	fall in love	fastigiate	felicitate	fibrescope
fabricator	fall in with	fasting-day	felicities	fibrillary
Fabry—Pérot	fallow deer	fast-twitch	felicitous	fibrillate
fabulation	fallowness	fastuously	felix culpa	fibrillose
fabulosity	false alarm	fast worker	fellmonger	fibrinogen
fabulously	false brome	fatalistic	fellow-heir	fibroblast
face-fungus	false front	fatalities	fellowless	fibrogenic
facelessly	false issue	fatherhood	fellowlike	fibrositic
face powder	false jalap	fatherland	fellowship	fibrositis
face-saving	false molar	fatherless	fell walker	fickleness
face-symbol	false point	fatherlike	felon-grass	fictionary
face to face	false scent	Father's Day	felony de se	fictioneer
faceworker	false start	fathership	felspathic	fictionist
face-worker	false teeth	Father Time	felt-tip pen	fictionize
facileness	false topaz	fathomable	female fern	fictitious
facilitate	falsettist	fathometer	female hemp	fiddle-back
facilities	false whorl	fathomless	femaleness	fiddle-case
facinorous	famatinite	fatiguable	feme covert	fiddle dock
facsimiled	familiarly	fat-soluble	feminality	fiddle-fish
fact-finder	familistic	fault-block	femininely	fiddle-head
factionary	family name	faultiness	femininist	fiddler ray
factioneer	family room	Fauntleroy	femininity	fiddlewood
factionist	family tree	fautorship	feministic	fidejussor
factiously	famishment	favourable	fence-month	fiducially
factitious	famousness	favourably	fenestella	field event
fact of life	fanaticise	favouredly	fenestrate	field glass
factorable	fanaticism	favourless	fen-runners	field guide
factorship	fanaticize	fawn-colour	fer de lance	field mouse
factor VIII	fancifully	fax machine	feretories	field notes
factualism	fancy bread	fazendeiro	fermentate	fieldstone
factualist	fancy dress	fearlessly	fermentive	fieldwards
factuality	fancy goods	fearnought	ferntickle	fiendishly
Fade-Ometer	fancy-piece	fearsomely	ferocities	fiend's limb
fadingness	fancy woman	feather-bed	ferredoxin	fierceness
faggot-iron	fandangoes	feather-cut	ferric acid	fiery cross
faggot vote	fanglement	featherfew	ferricrete	fifth wheel
Fahrenheit	Fanny Adams	feathering	ferro-alloy	fifty-fifty
faint heart	fantastico	featherlet	fertilizer	fight dirty
faintingly	fan-tracery	featherman	fervidness	fightingly
fair dinkum	far and away	feather ore	Fescennine	fight it out
fair enough	far and near	feat of arms	festerment	fight shy of
fairground	far and wide	featurally	festoonery	figuration
fair-haired	far between	featurette	fetch about	figurative
fair-minded	farcically	febrifugal	fetchingly	figurehead
fair-spoken	Far Eastern	Februaries	fetch-light	figureless
fair-trader	far-fetched	februation	fetch round	filamented
fairy cycle	farmerette	fecklessly	fetiferous	filariases
fairy-floss	farouchely	federalise	fetterless	filariasis
fairy prion	far-sighted	federalism	fetterlock	filariosis
fairy story	Far Western	federalist	fettuccine	file server

filialness	fire-vessel	fivestones	flea-circus	flood-hatch
filibuster	fire-walker	fixed focus	flea collar	floodlight
filler hose	fire warden	fixed point	flea-hopper	flood plain
fillet weld	fireworker	flabbiness	flea market	flood water
film colour	firing line	flabellate	fledgeless	floorboard
filmically	firing-step	flaccidity	fledgeling	floorcloth
film-making	first aider	Flacianist	fleeceable	floppiness
filmsetter	first blood	flagellant	fleecelike	floppy disk
filopodial	first blush	flagellate	fleece-wool	Flora dance
filopodium	first brush	flagellist	fleeciness	floral leaf
filterable	First Cause	flag-flying	fleeringly	Florentine
filter cake	first-class	flagginess	fleetingly	flore pleno
filthiness	first comer	flagitious	Flemish eye	florescent
filtration	first cross	flagrantly	flesh-brush	floriation
fimbriated	First Fleet	flagstoned	flesh-flies	floribunda
final cause	first floor	flag-waving	fleshiness	florideous
final drive	First Folio	flail chest	fleshliest	floridness
finalistic	first-fruit	flail-joint	flesh-quake	florilegia
finalities	first light	flail mower	flesh tints	floristics
final proof	first mover	flake-stand	flesh wound	flosculous
find favour	first night	flake-white	fleur-de-lis	flote-grass
find its way	first of all	flak jacket	fleur-de-lys	flounderer
fine tuning	first paeon	flamboyant	fleurettée	flouriness
finger bowl	first-rater	flamdoodle	flexuosity	flourisher
finger food	First Reich	flameproof	flexuously	floutingly
finger-hole	first sound	flame-proof	flickering	flower girl
finger lake	first table	flamingoes	flicker out	flower head
fingerless	first thing	flanconade	flick knife	flowerless
finger-like	first-timer	Flanderkin	flight call	flower-like
fingerling	first water	flangeless	flight crew	flown cover
finger-mark	First World	flannelled	flight deck	flow of soul
fingermark	fiscal drag	flapdoodle	flightiest	flue-boiler
fingernail	fiscal year	flap-dragon	flightless	fluffiness
finger-pick	fish-basket	flapperdom	flight-line	flugelhorn
fingerpick	fish-carver	flapperish	flight path	fluidified
finger-post	fish-eaters	flash-board	flight plan	fluidifies
finger-ring	fisherfolk	flash flood	flight-shot	fluid ounce
finger-snap	fish-farmer	Flash Harry	flight-test	fluidounce
finger-wave	fish finger	flash-house	flimsiness	fluid ounce
finicality	fishing-fly	flashiness	fling aside	flummeries
finishable	fishing rod	flashlight	flint glass	flunkeydom
finish line	fish kettle	flashpoint	flintiness	flunkeyism
finishment	fish-ladder	flat bottom	flint paper	fluoborate
finish with	fishmonger	flat-footed	flintstone	fluocerite
finiteness	fish poison	flat-headed	flippantly	fluorescer
finitistic	fish supper	flat racing	flirtation	fluoridate
Finlandise	fisticuffs	flattening	flitch beam	fluoridize
Finlandize	fisting cur	flatten out	floatation	fluorinate
Finno-Ugric	fistycuffs	flatteries	floatative	fluoroform
fire blight	fit as a flea	flattering	float-board	flurazepam
fire-eating	fitchet pie	flatulence	float glass	flurriedly
fire engine	fitfulness	flatulency	float-grass	Flushinger
fire escape	fittedness	flatuosity	floatingly	fluttering
fire-hearth	fit the bill	flavescent	float-light	fluvialist
fire-master	FitzGerald	flavourful	floatplane	fluviatile
fire-office	five-corner	flavouring	float-stone	fluviology
fire-plough	five-eighth	flavourist	floccipend	fluxionary
fire-policy	five-finger	flawlessly	flocculate	fluxionist
fire-raiser	five orders	flax-hackle	flocculent	fly-by-night
fire-ranger	fives-court	flax-lilies	flock paper	flycatcher
fire screen	five-seater	flea beetle	flooded box	fly-fishing
fire-shovel	five senses	flea-bitten	flooded gum	fly-flapper

fly in amber	for a change	forest tree	Fortune 500	franchisal
flying boat	forage crop	foresuffer	forty-eight	franchisee
flying bomb	forage-fish	foreteller	forty-fifth	franchiser
flying fish	for a giggle	forewarner	forty-first	franchisor
Flying Fish	for all that	for example	forty hours	Franciscan
flying jump	for all time	forfeiting	forty-niner	Franconian
flying leap	foraminate	forfeiture	forty-ninth	frangipane
flying mare	for a moment	forficated	forty-sixth	frangipani
flying ring	for a season	forge ahead	forty-third	fraternise
flying spot	for a surety	forgetness	forty winks	fraternity
flying suit	for a wonder	forgetting	forwearied	fraternize
flying wing	forbearant	forgettory	fossil fuel	fratricide
fly-pitcher	forbearing	forgivable	fosterable	fraudfully
fly-specked	forbidding	forgivably	fosterling	fraud squad
fly-swatter	force a card	forked head	foudroyant	fraudulent
fly the coop	forced move	forkedness	foul anchor	fraughtage
fly-tipping	forcedness	fork supper	foul befall	Fraunhofer
foamed slag	force field	fork-tailed	foul papers	fraxinella
foam flower	forcefully	forlornity	foul strike	freakiness
foam rubber	for certain	formalness	foundation	freakishly
focal plane	forcing pen	formal wear	founderous	freebooter
focal point	forcipated	formatting	foundryman	Free Church
fodderless	fordrunken	form-critic	fountained	free energy
foetalized	fore and aft	form factor	four-by-four	free-for-all
foeticidal	forebitter	formic acid	fourchette	free grower
foisonless	foreboding	formidable	four-colour	free-handed
fold-course	forebreast	formidably	four-figure	freeholder
foliaceous	forecaddie	formlessly	four-footed	free labour
foliar feed	forecaster	form letter	four-handed	freelancer
folie à deux	forecastle	form-master	Fourierism	free-living
foliferous	fore-elders	formulable	Fourierist	freeloader
folivorous	forefather	formula one	four-in-hand	free market
folk dancer	forefinger	formulator	four-letter	freemartin
folk guitar	foregainst	for my money	four o'clock	free pardon
folklorish	foreganger	for my share	four-parter	free period
folklorist	foregather	fornicator	four-poster	free school
folk memory	foreglance	for nothing	four-seater	free speech
folksiness	foreground	for openers	four-square	free spirit
folk singer	forehammer	forsakenly	four-stroke	free-spoken
follicular	forehanded	forshowing	fourteener	Free Stater
followable	forehander	forspeaker	fourteenth	freestyler
follow-spot	foreheaded	forsterite	fourth gear	free-tailed
follow suit	foreign aid	forswearer	fourth part	free-trader
fontanelle	foreignism	forte forte	fourth wall	free vector
font of type	foreignize	fortepiano	four-vector	free warren
foodaholic	foreintend	forte piano	four-winged	freewiller
foodoholic	foreladies	forthcomer	foveolated	freeze on to
fool around	foreloader	for the best	fowl plague	freeze over
foolometer	foremostly	for the jump	fox-hunting	freeze-thaw
fool's cress	foremother	for the rest	fox sparrow	freezingly
footballer	foreordain	for the ride	fox terrier	freightage
footbridge	forepassed	forthgoing	foxtrotted	freight car
foot-candle	foreperson	for this end	foxtrotter	freight ton
foot guards	forerunner	forthought	frabjously	fremescent
foot-licker	foreshadow	forthright	fractional	French bean
footlights	foresheets	fortissimi	fragmental	French blue
foot-locker	foresleeve	fortissimo	fragmented	French cuff
foot plough	forest fire	fortravail	fragranced	French door
foot-pounds	forest laws	fortuities	fragrantly	French grey
foot to foot	forestless	fortuitism	framboesia	French horn
footwarmer	forest park	fortuitist	frame house	French kiss
footy-footy	forestroke	fortuitous	frame story	French knot

Frenchlike	from on high	fumblingly	gallantize	Gartnerian
French loaf	from thence	fumigation	galleryite	gas bracket
French maid	from the way	fumigatory	galley-west	gas chamber
Frenchness	frondosely	fumishness	galleyworm	gasconader
French pink	frontality	functional	galley-yarn	gas guzzler
French roll	front bench	functorial	galliambic	gasifiable
French roof	frontignac	fund-holder	gallic acid	gas lighter
French seam	front money	fundholder	gallicizer	gasometric
frenziedly	front-pager	fund-raiser	galloglass	Gassendist
frequenter	frontstead	funduscopy	Gallophile	gas station
frequently	frontwards	funebrious	Gallophobe	gasteropod
fresh-baked	frostbound	funeralize	Gallo-Roman	gastralgia
fresh blood	frost crack	funeral urn	Gallup poll	gastralgic
fresh-faced	frost grape	funereally	galvanical	gastric flu
fresh out of	frost heave	fungaceous	galvanizer	gastrocele
freshwater	frostiness	fungicidal	Gambia kino	gastrolith
freshwoman	frothiness	fungitoxic	gambolling	gastrology
frettingly	frowningly	fungus-gnat	gamekeeper	gastronome
fretworked	frowstiest	funksticks	gamesomely	gastronomy
Freudianly	frowziness	funnel-like	gamestress	gastropexy
friability	frozen mitt	funnelling	gametangia	gastrotomy
fricandeau	frozenness	funniosity	game-tenant	gas turbine
fricasseed	fructified	funny money	game theory	gatekeeper
fricassees	fructifies	funny paper	gametocyst	gatelegged
fricatrice	frugalness	furanoside	gametocyte	gate of horn
frictional	fruitarian	furnishing	gametogeny	gatherable
Friedreich	fruitfully	furnish out	game warden	gather head
friendless	fruitiness	furosemide	gaminesque	Gatling gun
friendlier	fruit-juice	furrowless	gamma grass	gaucheness
friendlike	fruit-knife	furrow-like	gangbuster	gaudy-green
friendlily	fruit salad	furuncular	gangliated	gauging-rod
friendship	fruit salts	fusibility	gangliform	gaultheria
friezeless	fruit sugar	fusion bomb	ganglionic	gauntleted
frightened	frumpiness	fusion weld	gangrenous	gaylussite
frightener	frumpishly	fussbudget	gangsta rap	gazunderer
frightment	frustrable	fussocking	gannetries	gear change
Frigidaire	frustrater	fustanella	ganomalite	geiger tree
frigidness	frutescent	futileness	Gantt chart	geikielite
frigid zone	fruticetum	futureless	gap-toothed	geisha girl
frigorific	fuddy-duddy	future life	garage rock	gelatinase
frilliness	fugitation	futureness	garage sale	gelatinate
fringeless	fugitively	futuristic	garbage bin	gelatinise
fringe-tree	fulfilling	futurities	garbage can	gelatinize
fripperies	fulfilment	futurition	garden city	gelatinoid
friskiness	fuliginous	futurology	garden flat	gelatinous
frith-stool	full-bodied	fuzzy logic	gardenless	gemination
fritillary	full-bottom	fuzzy-wuzzy	garden path	geminative
frivolling	full chisel	gabblement	garden seat	genderless
frizziness	full colour	gabbroidal	gargantuan	genealogic
Froebelian	full growth	Gaditanian	gargoylism	genecology
Froebelism	full-length	gadolinite	garibaldis	generalate
froghopper	full nelson	gadolinium	garishness	generaless
frog orchid	full of shit	gadzookery	garlanding	generalise
frog's march	full-rigged	gaff-rigged	garlic pear	generalism
frolicking	full-rigger	gag-toothed	garnierite	generalist
frolicsome	full sister	Gaiety Girl	garnisheed	generality
from abroad	full-summed	gaillardia	garnishees	generalize
from a child	fulminator	gain-giving	garnishing	generation
from choice	fulmineous	gain ground	garnwindle	generative
from day one	fulminuric	galactonic	garrotting	generatrix
from memory	fulvescent	galia melon	garter belt	generosity
from nature	fumadiddle	galimatias	garter-blue	generously

Genesiacal	gesticular	gilt bronze	glasspaper	glyoxaline
genethliac	get a grip on	gimbal-ring	glass paper	glyoxylate
geneticism	get a hump on	gimmer-lamb	glass snail	glyphosate
geneticist	get a line on	gin and lime	glass snake	glyptodont
Geneva gown	get a load of	ginger beer	Glaswegian	gnamma hole
Geneva stop	get a load on	ginger lily	glauberite	gnashingly
genialness	get a move on	ginger-race	glauconite	gnathobase
geniculate	get clear of	ginger snap	gleaminess	gnomically
geniohyoid	get hitched	ginger wine	gleamingly	gnomologic
genius loci	Gethsemane	gingivitis	glebe-house	gnomonical
gentamicin	get in a flap	ginglyform	gleesomely	gnoscopine
genteelish	get in wrong	ginglymoid	gleization	gnosiology
genteelism	get it in one	gin pennant	glendoveer	gnosticise
genteelity	get knotted	Giottesque	gleyzation	Gnosticism
gentiledom	get nowhere	gippy tummy	glide-plane	gnosticize
gentilesse	get one's way	girdle-cake	glider bomb	gnotobiote
gentlefolk	get outside	girl Friday	glimmering	go a-begging
gentlehood	get round to	girlfriend	gliomatous	go-aheadism
gentleness	get stuck in	girly-girly	glitterati	goalkeeper
gentrified	get stuffed	gismondine	glitziness	goal-kicker
gentrifier	get the bird	gismondite	gloatingly	goal-minder
gentrifies	get the boot	give battle	globe daisy	goalminder
genu valgum	get the gate	give best to	globe tulip	go a long way
geobotanic	get the kirn	give change	globularly	goalscorer
geocentric	get the push	give fire to	glochidium	goal-tender
geochemist	get the ring	give ground	glomerular	goaltender
geocoronal	get the sack	give heed to	glomerulus	goat-footed
geocronite	get the swap	give it a fly	gloominess	goat's-beard
geodesical	get through	give or take	gloriation	goat's horns
geodetical	get to sleep	give rein to	gloriously	goat's-thorn
geodynamic	get unstuck	give rise to	glossarial	goatsucker
geognostic	get-up-and-go	give thanks	glossaries	goat willow
geographer	get up steam	give the gun	glossarist	gobemouche
geographic	get weaving	give to know	glossiness	gobsmacked
geological	Ghassulian	give tongue	glossology	gob-stopper
geometrize	ghastliest	give vent to	gloss paint	gobstopper
geomorphic	Ghibelline	glacé icing	glossy ibis	go critical
geophagist	ghost dance	glacialist	glottalize	God bless me
geophysics	ghostiness	glaciarium	glottology	God-fearing
geoponical	ghostliest	glaciation	Gloucester	Godfearing
geoscience	ghostology	glaciology	glove money	God help you
geotechnic	ghost story	glad-hander	glucosidal	go downhill
geotextile	ghost train	gladsomely	glucosidic	go down with
geothermal	ghost-write	Glagolitic	glucuronic	God save you
geothermic	ghoulishly	glamour boy	glucuronyl	God's wounds
geotropism	Giacobinid	glamourise	glumaceous	God willing
geratology	giant brain	glamourize	gluttoness	Godwottery
geriatrics	giant fibre	glance coal	gluttonise	go fly a kite
German band	giant order	glance over	gluttonish	go for broke
Germanical	giant panda	glancingly	gluttonize	goggle-dive
Germanizer	giant racer	glanderous	gluttonous	goggle-eyed
Germantown	giardiasis	glandiform	glycocalyx	go hard with
German wool	Gibson girl	glandulose	glycogenic	going on for
germicidal	gift coupon	glandulous	glycolipid	goings-over
germinable	giftedness	glass cloth	glycollate	going train
germinally	giggliness	glass coach	glycolysis	go it strong
germinator	Gilbertese	glass-faced	glycolytic	gold-beater
germ theory	Gilbertian	glass fibre	glycophyte	gold bridge
Geronomite	Gilbertine	glass-green	glycosidic	gold-digger
gerundival	gilded cage	glasshouse	glycosuria	golden ager
gestaltism	gill maggot	glassiness	glycosuric	golden alga
gestaltist	gilravager	glassmaker	glycuronic	golden calf

golden disc	go platinum	grand-daddy	gratuities	green pound
golden girl	gorbellied	grand-ducal	gratuitous	green salad
Golden Horn	gorblimeys	grand duchy	grave-cloth	green sauce
golden mean	gorgeously	grande dame	grave-goods	greenshank
golden mole	gorgoneion	Grand Fleet	gravelling	greenstick
goldenness	Gorgonzola	Grand Lodge	gravel-rash	greenstone
golden orfe	gormandise	grandmamma	gravel-walk	greenstuff
golden rose	gormandize	grand monde	grave-mound	greensward
golden rule	gormlessly	Grand Mufti	graveolent	green thumb
golden seal	gosh-darned	grand-niece	gravestone	gregarious
gold fringe	gospel oath	grand opera	Gravettian	greisening
goldilocks	Gospel side	grandpappy	gravewards	grenadilla
gold record	gospel-song	grand piano	gravimeter	gressorial
gold thread	gossamered	grand scale	gravimetry	grey market
goldwasser	gossiphood	grand Sophy	gravity-fed	grey matter
Goldwynism	go straight	Grands Prix	gravy train	grey mullet
go lemony at	go the limit	grandstand	grease-ball	grey parrot
golf course	go the round	grand style	grease-band	grey willow
Golgi organ	go the route	grand total	greaseless	gridlocked
Golgi stain	gothically	grand-uncle	grease-trap	grieveship
goliardery	Gothically	grangerism	greasewood	grievingly
goluptious	gothicness	grangerite	greasiness	grievously
gombeen man	go to blazes	grangerize	greasy pole	griffinage
gondola car	go to church	granitical	great Argus	griffiness
go near to do	go together	granny bond	Great Bible	griffinish
gongoozler	go to ground	granny flat	great egret	griffonage
goniatitic	go to market	granny knot	great grief	Grignolino
goniometer	go to pieces	granophyre	great gross	grille-work
goniometry	go to school	grant-aided	great horse	Grimaldian
gonioscope	go to shrift	grant-in-aid	great house	Grimbarian
gonioscopy	go to the bar	granularly	Great Lakes	grimliness
gonococcal	go to the mat	granulated	great-niece	grimthorpe
gonococcus	governable	granulator	great organ	grind an axe
gonorrhoea	governably	granulitic	Great Power	grind house
gonotocont	governance	grapefruit	Great Scott	grindingly
good bearer	governessy	grape-paper	great sheer	grindstone
good fellow	government	grape-stone	great-uncle	grinningly
good for you	grab handle	grape-sugar	Grecianize	gripe water
Good Friday	grab hold of	graphemics	greediness	Gripe Water
good humour	gracefully	graphicacy	greedy-guts	grippingly
good-liking	graciosity	graphicate	Greek cross	grisliness
goodliness	graciously	graphitise	green baize	grittiness
good living	gradualism	graphitize	Green Beret	grizzliest
good-looker	gradualist	graphitoid	green-blind	groaningly
good-morrow	graduality	graphology	green brier	groceteria
good nature	graduation	graphotype	green cloth	groggified
good people	graffitied	graph paper	Green Cloth	grogginess
goody-goody	graffitist	graptolite	green drake	grog-shanty
goofer dust	Graham's law	graspingly	green earth	groove cast
googolplex	grainering	grass-cloth	Greeneland	grooveless
go one's gait	graininess	grasscloth	greenfield	grooviness
go one's ways	gramicidin	grass court	greenfinch	Gros Michel
go on record	gramineous	grass-finch	greenflies	Gros Ventre
go on the hop	grammarian	grass-green	green goose	Grotianism
gooseberry	grammatist	grassiness	greenheart	grottiness
goose bumps	gramophile	grass roots	green heron	grouchiest
goose-flesh	gramophone	grass skirt	greenhouse	ground arms
goosegrass	Gram's stain	grass snake	green light	groundbait
goose quill	gram-weight	grass widow	greenlight	ground-bait
goose-wings	granadilla	grass-wrack	Green Paper	ground ball
gopher-hole	grandchild	gratefully	Green Party	ground bass
gopher wood	Grand Cross	gratifying	green plant	ground crew

ground dove	guide-board	hackmatack	Hall effect	Hansardize
ground down	guided tour	hackneydom	hallelujah	Hanse-house
groundedly	guilefully	Hadley cell	Hall of Fame	haplophase
ground-fish	guillotine	Haeckelian	Hallowmass	happy event
ground game	guiltiness	haemanthus	Hallowtide	haptically
ground itch	Guinea corn	haematinic	halloysite	harassment
groundless	guinea fowl	haematitic	hall porter	harbourage
ground-line	Guinea-fowl	haematomas	halocarbon	hardbitten
groundling	Guinea worm	haematosis	halo effect	hard-boiled
ground loop	guitar-fish	haematuria	halogenate	hard cheese
groundmass	Gulf Stream	haematuric	halophilic	hard-done-by
ground-pine	gulli-gulli	haemocoele	halophytic	hard-earned
ground plan	gully-gully	haemolymph	halter neck	hard-fisted
ground rent	gum benzoin	haemolysin	Haman's ears	hard growan
ground rule	gumbo-limbo	haemolysis	hamber-line	hard-handed
ground-sill	gum juniper	haemolytic	hambro-line	hard-headed
groundsman	gummy shark	Hafflinger	hamesucken	hard-hitter
groundsmen	gum succory	hagiocracy	hammerbeam	hard labour
groundward	gunfighter	hagiolatry	hammer-blow	hardly ever
ground wave	gun-harpoon	hagiologic	hammerhead	hard mother
ground wood	gunkholing	hagioscope	hammer home	hard palate
groundwork	gunpowdery	hail shower	hammerless	hard-pushed
ground zero	gun-running	hair-powder	hammerlock	hard rubber
groupthink	gunrunning	hairspring	hammer-work	hard solder
grouse moor	gun shearer	hairstreak	hand-barrow	hard ticket
groutiness	gunslinger	hair-stroke	handedness	Hardyesque
grovelling	Guomindang	hakenkreuz	hand-gallop	hare-finder
growing bag	gurglingly	halberdier	handgunner	hare-lipped
growlingly	gurry-shark	halberdman	hand-habend	harelipped
growth area	gutterling	hale and how	handicraft	harem skirt
growth ring	gutter-tile	half a crown	handicuffs	harmlessly
growth zone	gutturally	half a dozen	hand in hand	harmonical
grubbiness	guzzle-guts	half an hour	hand-labour	harmonicon
grubstaker	gymnadenia	half-bottle	handleable	harmonious
Grub Street	gymnasiast	half-circle	handleless	harmonizer
grudgement	gymnasiums	half-cocked	handmaiden	Harmon mute
grudgingly	gymnastics	half-dollar	hand-me-down	harness cop
gruesomely	gymnosophy	half-duplex	hand of writ	harpooneer
grumpiness	gymnosperm	halfendeal	handpicked	harpoon gun
grumpishly	gynandrous	half-frames	handselled	harp-string
grunge rock	gyneocracy	half-galley	handshaker	harpy eagle
grunginess	gynocratic	half-guinea	hand signal	Harry groat
gruntingly	gynodioecy	half-headed	handsomely	Harry noble
guaiac test	gynophobia	half-hourly	handsomest	hartebeest
guanophore	gynophobic	half-hunter	handspring	haruspical
guaranteed	gyppy tummy	half-length	hand-to-hand	haruspices
guarantees	gypsophila	half-minute	handworked	Harvardian
guaranties	gypsophile	half-mooned	handworker	harvest-bug
guard-chain	gypsy winch	half nelson	handy-billy	harvestman
guardfully	gyrocopter	half-relief	handycuffs	harvestmen
guardhouse	gyroscopic	half-ringer	handy-dandy	hash browns
guardingly	gyrostatic	half-shaved	handy-sized	hastefully
Guarnerius	gyrotiller	half-sister	hang a right	hatcheller
Guatemalan	habiliment	half-stress	hang around	hatcheries
Guaycuruan	habilitate	half-timber	hanger-back	hatchet job
gubernator	habitation	half-topped	hang-glider	hatchet man
gudgeon pin	habitative	half-uncial	hanging day	haughtiest
guessingly	habit-shirt	half-volley	hanging lie	haunch-bone
guest house	habitually	half-witted	hangworthy	hauntingly
guestimate	hackbuteer	halfwitted	hanky-panky	haustellum
guest-night	hackbutter	half-yearly	Hannibalic	haustorial
Guggenheim	hack-hammer	hallabaloo	Hanoverian	haustorium

hautboyist	heartening	heliograph	heptarchal	heterogony
haute école	heartfully	heliometer	heptarchic	heterology
haut-relief	hear things	heliometry	heptastich	heteronomy
have a fly at	heartiness	helioscope	heptateuch	heterosite
have a heart	heart of oak	heliotrope	Heptateuch	heterotaxy
have a nerve	heartquake	helipterum	heptathlon	heulandite
have a point	heart's-ease	heli-skiing	heptatonic	hew one's way
have a shy at	heartsease	hellacious	Heraclitic	hexadecane
have a smoke	heart-spoon	hellbender	heraldical	hexaemeron
have done it	heart-throb	hell-driver	herbaceous	hexagonous
have in mind	heartthrob	Hellenizer	Herbartian	hexahedral
have in view	heartwater	Hellespont	herb bennet	hexahedron
have it away	heart-whole	hellishing	herb-doctor	hexahydric
have it made	heat engine	hellraiser	herb Gerard	hexamerism
have mind of	heath-berry	hell-raiser	herbicidal	hexamerous
have need of	heathendom	hell's angel	herb mastic	hexametric
have need to	heathenish	Hell's Angel	herb Robert	hexandrous
have no idea	heathenism	hell's bells	hercogamic	hexangular
have no legs	heathenize	helmetless	herdswoman	hexaplaric
have no peer	heath-grass	helmet-like	hereabouts	hexaploidy
have no soul	heath-poult	helminthic	here and now	hexavalent
have off pat	heat-seeker	helmswoman	hereditary	hexoestrol
have scathe	heat shield	helplessly	heresiarch	hexokinase
have the pip	heatstroke	hemelytron	hereticate	hexosamine
have the say	heaven-born	hemi-acetal	heretofore	Hezbollahi
have to burn	heavenless	hemianopia	here you are	hiawaballi
have to wife	heavenlike	hemianopic	her indoors	hibernacle
hawk-cuckoo	heaven-sent	hemibranch	heriotable	hibernator
hawk's-beard	heavenward	hemicircle	herky-jerky	hibiscuses
hawse-piece	heavy-armed	hemicrania	Hermes seal	Hib vaccine
hawser-laid	heavy going	hemidesmus	hermetical	hidden hand
hazard side	heavy metal	hemihedral	hermit crab	hiddenmost
Hazlittian	heavy swell	hemihedron	hermithood	hiddenness
headbanger	heavy water	hemiplegia	hermit ibis	hide and hue
head cheese	hebdomadal	hemiplegic	hermitical	hide beetle
header-tank	hebetation	hemipteran	hermitship	hiding-hole
headhunter	Hebraistic	hemisphere	herniation	hiera picra
head-hunter	hecatomped	hemitropic	herniotomy	hierarchal
heading dog	hectically	hemizygote	Herodotean	hierarchic
headlessly	hectograph	hemizygous	heroically	hieratical
headlinese	hectolitre	hemp-nettle	heroi-comic	hierocracy
headmaster	hectometre	henceforth	heron's-bill	hieroglyph
head office	hedge-fence	henchwoman	herpolhode	hierograph
head of hair	hedgehoggy	hendecagon	Herrenvolk	hierolatry
headspring	hedge maple	hen harrier	Herrnhuter	hierophant
headsquare	hedonistic	hen-hearted	hesitantly	hieroscopy
headstrong	heedlessly	Henle's loop	hesitation	high and dry
head-to-head	heel-and-toe	henotheism	hesitative	high and low
headwaters	hegemonist	henotheist	hesitatory	highbinder
health camp	Heidelberg	henpeckery	Hesperides	highbrowed
health care	heightened	hen-scratch	hesperidia	High Church
health club	heightener	heortology	hesperidin	high colour
health farm	heil Hitler	heparinise	Hessian fly	highermost
health food	heir female	heparinize	hetero-atom	high-flying
healthiest	heir in tail	hepatitis A	heterocosm	high forest
healthless	heirs-at-law	hepatitis B	heterocyst	High German
healthsome	Heisenberg	heptachlor	heterodont	high ground
hearing aid	heliacally	heptachord	heterodoxy	high-handed
hear sermon	helianthus	heptagonal	heterodyne	high-headed
heart-block	helicoidal	heptahedra	heterogamy	high-heeled
heart-blood	Heliconian	heptameric	heterogene	high-income
heartbreak	helicopter	heptameter	heterogeny	high-jumper

highlander	hit the pipe	Holy Father	homuncular	horse daisy
Highlander	hit the road	Holy League	homuncules	horse-drawn
high living	hit the roof	Holy Office	homunculus	horseflesh
high-minded	hit the sack	holy orders	Honest John	horseflies
high-octane	hit the silk	holy roller	honeybunch	horse guard
high places	hit the spot	Holy Spirit	honey chile	horse-laugh
high priest	hitty-missy	holy terror	honey-eater	horseleech
high relief	Hoabinhian	holy Willie	honeyeater	horse opera
high roller	hoar-headed	home and dry	honeyguide	horsepower
high school	hoarseness	homebodies	honey mouse	horse-racer
high season	hobbadehoy	home-brewed	honeystone	horse sense
high-souled	hobblebush	home-coming	honey-sweet	horse-shoer
high spirit	hobblingly	homecoming	honorarium	horse's neck
high street	hobby horse	homeliness	honourable	horse's tail
high-strung	hobnobbing	home-making	honourably	horsewoman
highwayman	hobohemian	Home Office	honourless	horsewomen
highwaymen	hocking ale	homeopathy	hooded crow	hose-in-hose
high yaller	Hock Monday	homeotherm	hooded seal	hospitable
high yellow	hocus-pocus	Homerology	hoodlumism	hospitably
Hilary term	hodden grey	home signal	hook and eye	hospitaler
hillwalker	hoddy-doddy	home thrust	hook-billed	hostelling
Himyaritic	hoddy-noddy	homeworker	hook-ladder	hostelries
hinderling	Hodegetria	homishness	hook stroke	hot-blooded
hindermost	hodgepodge	homme moyen	hootenanny	hot-brained
hindersome	hoernesite	homocercal	hopelessly	hot cathode
Hindustani	Hogan Mogan	homochromy	hop into bed	hotchpotch
hinterland	Hogarthian	homoclinal	Hopkinsian	hot cockles
hip-huggers	hog cholera	homocyclic	hopping mad	hot coppers
hip-hugging	Hogen Mogen	homodesmic	Hoppus foot	hot-desking
hipped roof	hog-killing	homoeomery	hopshackle	hotdogging
hippety-hop	hog's fennel	homoeopath	hop the twig	hot-presser
hippieness	hoity-toity	homo-erotic	Hopton wood	hot pursuit
hippocampi	hokey-cokey	homoerotic	hop trefoil	hotsy-totsy
Hippocrene	hokey-pokey	homogamety	horizontal	Hottentots
hippodrome	hold in play	homogamous	hormonally	hour-circle
hippogriff	hold it good	homogenate	horn beetle	house agent
hippogryph	hold out for	homogeneal	hornblende	housebound
hippomanes	hold the bag	homogenise	horned dace	housebreak
hippophagy	hold to bail	homogenize	horned frog	housebuyer
hippophile	holes-in-one	homogenous	horned lark	housecarle
hipsterism	hollabaloo	homokaryon	horned pout	house-clean
hirdy-girdy	Hollantide	homologate	horned toad	housecraft
hirondelle	hollow-eyed	homologise	hornet moth	house finch
hirudinean	hollow horn	homologize	hörnesite	houseflies
his and hers	hollowness	homologous	horn-rimmed	house guest
histaminic	hollow-ware	homomorphy	horn silver	house mouse
histiocyte	hollowware	homonymity	horography	house music
histogenic	holobranch	homonymous	horologion	house of God
histologic	holocarpic	homoousian	horologist	house party
histolysis	holoenzyme	Homoousion	horologium	house-place
histolytic	hologamete	homoousios	horoscopal	house plant
historical	hologamous	homophobia	horoscoper	house-proud
histrionic	holography	homophobic	horoscopic	house snake
hit-and-miss	holohedral	homophonic	horrendous	house style
hitch-hiker	holohedron	homoplasty	horridness	house-train
hitchhiker	holophrase	homopteran	horrifying	housewares
hithermost	holophytic	homorganic	horse-block	housewives
hitherside	holostylic	homosexual	horse brass	hovercraft
hitherward	holothuria	homostyled	horse-bread	hoverflies
Hitler's war	holus-bolus	homothally	horse-cloth	hoveringly
hit the deck	Holy Church	homozygote	horse-coper	hover-mower
hit the gong	Holy Family	homozygous	horse cubes	hovertrain

how do you do	husbandmen	hymnologic	hypolydian	ideologies
howsomever	Husserlian	hyoscyamia	hypomaniac	ideologist
how's tricks	hustlement	hyoscyamus	hyponastic	ideologize
hubba-hubba	Hutchinson	hypabyssal	hypophoria	ideophonic
Hubble's law	hutch table	hypaethral	hypophyses	idiolectal
huckle-back	hyalinized	hypalgesia	hypophysis	idiopathic
huckle-bone	hyalinosis	hypalgesic	hypoplasia	idiot board
hucksterer	hyaloplasm	hypanthial	hypoploidy	idiot light
huddlement	hyaluronic	hypanthium	hypostases	idiot-proof
huebnerite	hyawaballi	hyperacute	hypostasis	idolatress
hug-me-tight	hybridized	hyperaemia	hypostatic	idolatrize
hullabaloo	hybridizer	hyperaemic	hypotactic	idolatrous
hully gully	hydragogic	hyperalgic	hypotenuse	idoloclast
humanation	hydragogue	hyperbaric	hypothecal	idolothyte
human being	hydramnios	hyperbaton	hypotheses	I don't think
human chain	hydrastine	hyperbolae	hypothesis	if anything
humaneness	hydratable	hyperbolas	hypothetic	if I were you
humanistic	hydraulics	hyperbolic	hypoxaemia	if possible
humanitary	hydrelaeon	hyperdrive	hypsiconch	ifs and ands
humanities	hydrochore	hyperdulia	hypsodonty	ifs and buts
humbleness	hydrocrack	hyperdulic	hypsometer	if so be that
humblingly	hydrogenic	hyperfocal	hypsometry	if you ask me
humbuggery	hydrograph	hypergluon	hysteresis	ignes fatui
humbugging	hydrologic	hypergolic	hysteretic	ignicolist
humdudgeon	hydrolysis	hypermedia	hysterical	igniferous
humidified	hydrolytic	hypermorph	hystericky	ignimbrite
humidifier	hydromancy	hyperoodon	iambically	ignipotent
humidifies	hydromania	hyperplane	iatrogenic	ignivomous
humidistat	hydrometer	hyperploid	ice-breaker	ignobility
humidities	hydrometry	hyperpnoea	ice dancing	ignorantly
humid scall	hydronymic	hypersexed	Icelandish	ignoration
humiliator	hydropathy	hypersonic	ice machine	ilang-ilang
humming-top	hydrophane	hyperspace	icemanship	ileocaecal
humoresque	hydrophile	hypertelic	ice-skating	ill-advised
humoristic	hydrophily	hypertonia	ice station	illaqueate
humorously	hydrophobe	hypertonic	ichthammol	illatinate
humourless	hydrophone	hypertonus	ichthyosis	illatively
humoursome	hydrophyte	hyperurban	ichthyotic	illaudable
humpbacked	hydropical	hyphenated	icing sugar	illaudably
hump bridge	hydroplane	hyphenless	iconically	I'll be bound
humusified	hydroplant	hypnagogic	iconoclasm	ill-behaved
humusifies	hydroponic	hypnogenic	iconoclast	ill-beloved
hundredary	hydropower	hypnogogic	iconolater	ill-defined
hunger-weed	hydroscope	hypnotizer	iconolatry	illegality
hungriness	hydrospire	hypoactive	iconomachy	illegalize
hungry rice	hydrotheca	hypoacusia	iconometry	ill feeling
hunker down	hydrotical	hypoacusis	iconophile	ill-fitting
hunting-box	hydrotreat	hypocapnia	iconoscope	ill-founded
hunting cat	hydrotropy	hypocapnic	icosahedra	illinition
hunting dog	hydroxylic	hypocentre	I dare swear	Illinoisan
Huntington	hydrozoate	hypocorism	iddingsite	illiteracy
huntswoman	hyetograph	hypocrisis	ideal fluid	illiterate
hunt the fox	hygrograph	hypocrital	idealistic	illiterati
hurdle race	hygrometer	hypocritic	idealities	ill-looking
hurdy-gurdy	hygrometry	hypodermal	ideational	ill-matched
hurly-burly	hygrophile	hypodermic	idempotent	ill-natured
hurry along	hygrophyte	hypodermis	idem sonans	illocality
hurrygraph	hygroscope	hypodorian	identified	illocution
hurryingly	hylotheism	hypogamous	identifier	I'll show you
hurtlessly	hymeneally	hypogeusia	identifies	ill-starred
hurtlingly	hymenopter	hypogynous	identities	ill success
husbandman	hymn of hate	hypolimnia	ideography	illucidate

illuminant	immoralize	impresario	incandesce	inculpably
illuminate	immortally	impression	incantator	incumbence
illuminati	immortelle	impressive	incapacity	incumbency
illuminato	immoveable	impressure	Incaparina	incunabula
illuminise	immunities	imprimatur	incasement	incurrable
illuminism	immunology	imprisoner	incautious	incurrence
illuminist	immuration	improbable	incavation	indagation
illuminize	immurement	improbably	incendiary	in danger of
illuminous	impact test	improlific	incendiate	indebtment
illusional	impairment	impromptus	Inceptisol	indecently
illusively	impalement	improperly	incessable	indecision
illusorily	impalpable	improvable	incessably	indecisive
illustrate	impalpably	improvably	incessancy	indecorous
illuviated	impanation	improviser	incestuous	in defect of
ill-willing	imparadise	imprudence	in chancery	indefinite
image-maker	imparlance	imprudence	in charge of	indefinity
imaginable	imparsonee	impudently	inchastity	indelicacy
imaginably	impartable	impudicity	inch by inch	indelicate
imaginally	impartible	impugnable	inchoately	indevotion
imaginator	impartibly	impugnment	inchoation	indevoutly
imaginings	impartment	impuissant	inchoative	indexation
imbecilely	impassable	impulse buy	incidental	India House
imbecility	impassably	impunctate	incidently	in diameter
imbibition	impassible	impunitive	incinerate	Indian club
imbodiment	impassibly	impureness	incipience	Indian corn
imbreviate	impatience	impurities	incipiency	Indian file
imbricated	impatiency	imputation	incisiform	Indian hemp
imbroccata	impeccable	imputative	incisional	Indian lake
imbroglios	impeccably	in absentia	incisively	Indian meal
imbruement	impeccancy	inaccuracy	incitation	Indianness
I'm damned if	impediment	inaccurate	incitement	Indian path
imipramine	impeditive	inactivate	incivility	Indian pear
imitatress	impendence	inactively	inclemency	Indian pink
immaculacy	impendency	inactivity	inclinable	Indian pipe
immaculate	impenitent	inadaptive	includable	Indian poke
immanental	imperative	in addition	include out	Indian rice
immanently	imperatrix	inadequacy	includible	Indian shot
immanifest	imperially	inadequate	incoctible	Indian sign
immaterial	imperilled	inadhesive	incogitant	Indian teak
immaturely	impersonal	in a fashion	incognitos	Indian weed
immaturity	impervious	in a measure	incoherent	India paper
immeasured	impishness	inamoratos	incohesion	India proof
immemorial	implacable	in a morning	incohesive	indication
immergence	implacably	in-and-outer	incomeless	indicative
immersible	implicitly	in any event	incomplete	indicatory
immetrical	impolitely	in a pig's eye	in conclave	indicatrix
imminently	importable	inapparent	inconcrete	indicolite
immiscible	importance	inappetent	in conflict	indictable
immiscibly	importancy	inapposite	inconjunct	indictably
immiserate	importuner	inaptitude	inconstant	indictment
immittance	imposement	inarguable	incoronate	indigenise
immobilise	imposingly	inarguably	in course of	indigenist
immobilism	imposition	in arms with	incrassate	indigenity
immobility	impossible	inartistic	incredible	indigenize
immobilize	impossibly	in a twinkle	incredibly	indigenous
immoderacy	impostress	inaugurate	increscent	indigested
immoderate	impostrous	in bad order	incrustate	indigitate
immodestly	impotently	in bad stead	incubation	indignance
immolation	impoundage	in breach of	incubative	indignancy
immoralism	impoverish	inbreaking	incubatory	indigo-bird
immoralist	impregnant	inbreeding	inculcator	indigo blue
immorality	impregnate	in business	inculpable	indigolite

indirectly	infallibly	infusorial	initiatory	in parallel
indiscreet	infamatory	infusorian	initiatrix	in poor nick
indiscrete	infamously	infusorium	injectable	in position
in disgrace	infanthood	in garrison	injudicial	in practice
in disguise	infantries	ingatherer	injunction	in presence
indisposed	infarction	ingeminate	injunctive	in pretence
indisputed	infatuated	ingenerate	injury time	in progress
indistinct	in favour of	ingle-bench	inkhornism	in prospect
in distress	infeasible	ingle-cheek	inkosikazi	in question
inditement	infectible	inglorious	ink-slinger	inquietude
individual	infectious	in-goal area	inland duty	inquirable
individuum	infeftment	in God's name	inland port	inquirendo
indivision	infelicity	in good case	in line with	inquisitor
Indo-Briton	inferiorly	in good form	in love with	in regard of
indocility	infernally	in good keep	in marriage	in regard to
indolently	inferrable	in good nick	in memoriam	in register
Indologist	inferrible	in good part	in memory of	in response
Indonesian	inferribly	in good time	in mourning	insalivate
inducement	infibulate	ingrateful	in multiple	insalutary
inductance	infidelise	ingratiate	in name only	in samizdat
indulgence	infidelism	ingredient	innateness	ins and outs
indulgency	infidelity	ingression	inner forme	insaneness
indumentum	infidelize	ingressive	inner light	insanitary
induration	in-fighting	Inguaeonic	inner space	insanities
indurative	infighting	inguinally	inner woman	insatiable
industrial	infiltrate	ingustable	innkeeping	insatiably
industries	infinitely	Ingvaeonic	innocently	insatiated
indwelling	infinities	inhabitant	Inn of Court	insculptor
ineducable	infinitise	inhabiting	innominate	in search of
inefficacy	infinitism	inhalation	innovation	insect-like
inelegance	infinitist	in hardback	innovative	insecurely
inelegancy	infinitive	inharmonic	innovatory	insecurity
ineligible	infinitize	inherently	in no want of	inseminate
ineligibly	infinitude	inheritage	innuendoes	insensible
ineloquent	infirmarer	inheriting	innumeracy	insensibly
ineludable	infirmness	inheritrix	innumerate	insentient
ineludible	infixation	inhibiting	innumerous	inseparate
ineptitude	inflatable	inhibition	inoculable	in sequence
inequality	inflatedly	inhibitive	inoculator	insertable
inequities	inflection	inhibitory	inofficial	in set terms
inerasable	inflective	in his pride	in one piece	insightful
inertially	inflexible	in honour of	in one's cups	insinuator
in especial	inflexibly	in hospital	in one's face	insinuendo
inesthetic	infliction	inhumanely	in one's hair	insipidity
inevasible	inflictive	inhumanism	in one's head	insipience
in evidence	influencer	inhumanity	in one's line	insistence
inevidence	influenzal	inhumation	in one's pelt	insistency
inevitable	informally	inhumorous	in one's pots	in snatches
inevitably	informator	inimicable	in one's road	insobriety
in excess of	informedly	inimically	in one's skin	insociable
in exchange	infraclass	inimitable	in one's time	insolation
inexertion	infraction	inimitably	in one's turn	insolently
inexistent	infragrant	iniquities	in one swoop	insolidity
inexorable	infrahuman	iniquitous	inoperable	insolvable
inexorably	infraorder	initialese	inoperably	insolvably
inexpertly	infrarenal	initialise	inordinacy	insolvency
inexpiable	infrasonic	initialism	in ordinary	in some sort
inexpiably	infrasound	initialize	inordinate	insouciant
inexplicit	infrequent	initialled	inosculate	inspanning
inextended	in full face	initial set	inotropism	inspection
in extremis	in full play	initiation	in our midst	inspective
infallible	in full view	initiative	inoxidable	inspeximus

inspirator	inter-class	intervenor	intraneous	invitement
inspiredly	intercross	intervisit	intra-urban	invitingly
inspirited	interested	intervital	intra vires	invocation
inspissate	interfaith	intervocal	intravital	invocative
installant	interferer	intervolve	intrazonal	invocatory
installing	interferon	interweave	intrenched	involatile
instalment	interfluve	interwound	intrepidly	involucral
Instamatic	intergenic	interwoven	in triangle	involucrum
instantial	intergrade	interzonal	intrigante	involution
instantize	intergroup	intestinal	intriguant	involutory
instigator	interictal	in that case	intriguess	involvedly
instilling	interionic	in that view	intriguing	inwardness
instilment	interiorly	in the act of	introduced	in your face
in stitches	interior to	in the black	introducer	iodimetric
instituter	interlayer	in the blade	introgress	iodination
institutor	interleave	in the chips	introscope	iodization
in store for	interlevel	in the clear	introspect	iodometric
in strength	interloper	in the event	intrusive r	iodophilic
instructer	interlunar	in the field	intubation	ion chamber
instructor	intermarry	in the flesh	intuitable	ion etching
instrument	intermedia	in the frame	in two ticks	Ionian mode
insudation	intermedii	in the green	inundation	ionisation
insufflate	intermedin	in the issue	inurbanely	ionization
in suit with	intermewed	in the large	inurbanity	ionography
insularism	intermezzi	in the least	invaginate	ionosphere
insularity	intermezzo	in the money	invalidate	ionotropic
insularize	intermodal	in the night	invalid car	iproniazid
insulation	internally	in the nuddy	invaliding	Ipswichian
insulative	internment	in the pay of	invalidish	iracundity
insultable	internodal	in the pound	invalidism	Iranianist
insurgence	internship	in the pouts	invalidity	irefulness
insurgency	interocean	in the print	invaluable	irenically
insurrecto	interphase	in the right	invaluably	iridaceous
in sympathy	interplait	in the rough	invariable	iridectomy
intabulate	interplane	in the round	invariably	irideremia
intactness	interplant	in the shell	invariance	iridescent
intaglioes	interplead	in the straw	invariancy	iridodesis
intangible	interpoint	in the vague	inventable	iridosmine
intangibly	interpolar	in the way of	inventress	Irish green
integrable	interposal	in the white	inveracity	Irish horse
integrally	interposer	in the whole	inverecund	Irish point
integrated	interpubic	in the wilds	invertedly	Irish pound
integrator	interpulse	in the works	invertible	Irish Sweep
integument	interreges	in the world	invert soap	Irishwoman
intemerate	interregna	in the wrong	in very deed	Irishwomen
intemporal	interreign	inthronize	investable	iron-glance
intendance	interrenal	intimacies	investible	iron-handed
intendancy	interrogee	intimately	investment	iron-headed
intendedly	intershock	intimation	inveteracy	ironically
intendence	intershoot	intimidate	inveterate	iron maiden
intendency	interspace	intinction	invigilate	ironmaster
intendment	interstage	intolerant	invigorant	ironmonger
intenerate	interstate	intonation	invigorate	iron-sponge
intentness	interstice	intonement	invination	ironworker
interactor	intertidal	into pieces	invincible	irradiance
inter-agent	intertonic	intoxicant	invincibly	irradiancy
inter alios	intertrigo	intoxicate	inviolable	irradiated
interblend	intertwine	intractile	inviolably	irradiator
interbrain	intertwist	intragenic	inviolated	irrational
interbreed	interunion	intragroup	invirtuate	irregulate
interceder	interurban	in training	invitation	irrelation
interchain	intervener	intramural	invitatory	irrelative

irrelevant	isoseismal	jam session	jimson weed	judgematic
irreligion	isoseismic	janitorial	jimswinger	judgmental
irremeable	isosporous	Janus green	jingoistic	judication
irremeably	isosterism	Japan cedar	jinricksha	judicative
irresolute	isothermal	Japan earth	JK flip-flop	judicatory
irresolved	isothermic	Japanesery	jnana-marga	judicature
irreticent	isotropous	Japanesque	Joachimism	judicially
irreverend	Israelitic	Japan paper	Joachimist	Jugendstil
irreverent	issue of law	Japhethite	Joachimite	jugged hare
irrigation	I suppose so	japishness	job analyst	juggernaut
irrigative	Italianate	jardinière	jobbernowl	Juggernaut
irrigatory	Italianise	jargonelle	job-control	jugglement
irritament	Italianism	jar ramming	job-hopping	juggleress
irritating	Italianist	jasmine tea	job-sharing	jug-handled
irritation	Italianity	jasper-opal	jockey-boot	jugulation
irritative	Italianize	jasper-ware	jockey club	juice-joint
irroration	Italophile	jauntiness	jockey-coat	Julian Alps
irrumation	itinerancy	Java almond	jockeyship	Julian year
isabelline	it isn't done	Java canvas	jocoseness	jumble-bead
isatogenic	I told you so	Java pepper	jocosities	jumblement
Iscariotic	it's this way	javelineer	jocularity	jumble sale
isentropic	ivory black	javelin man	joe-pye weed	jumbomania
isethionic	ivory board	Javel water	John Dories	jumper stay
Ishmaelite	ivory-paper	jaw-breaker	johnny-cake	jumper suit
Isindebele	ivory tower	jaw-crusher	John Roscoe	jumper-wire
Islamicize	ivory-white	Jazzercise	Johnsonese	jump for joy
island-hill	ivy-garland	jealousies	Johnsonian	jumping rat
islandless	Ivy Leaguer	Jehosaphat	Johnsonism	jump jockey
Ismaelitic	jaborandis	Jehovistic	John Thomas	jump-master
isoallelic	jaboticaba	jejuneness	join action	jump the gun
isoantigen	jack-a-dandy	jelly-belly	join battle	junctional
isocaloric	jackanapes	jellygraph	joiner-work	Jungianism
isocephaly	Jack ashore	jelly paint	join forces	jungle cock
isocheimal	jackassery	jelly-plant	joint-grass	jungle fowl
isochronal	jackbooted	jeopardise	joint mouse	jungle-rice
isochronic	Jack curlew	jeopardize	joint-plane	junior dean
isochroous	jacketless	Jeremianic	joint-snake	junior miss
isocitrate	jackhammer	jerkin-head	joint stock	juniorship
isocyanate	Jack-ladder	jerry-build	joint-stool	juniper oil
isocyanide	jacklegged	jerry-built	jointuress	junk-bottle
isodynamic	Jack-merlin	Jersey blue	jolie laide	junk-dealer
isoenzymic	Jack Mormon	Jersey pine	Jollof rice	jurisprude
isoeugenol	jackrabbit	jestership	Jolly Roger	juristical
isoglossic	Jack's alive	Jesuitical	jolter-head	jury-fixing
isoglottal	Jack salmon	Jesuits' nut	jolt-headed	jury-rigged
isoglottic	Jack-socket	Jesuits' tea	Joshua tree	jury-rudder
isohalsine	jack socket	Jesus freak	jostlement	just as well
isokinetic	Jacksonian	jet-setting	journal-box	justiciary
isolatable	Jack the Lad	jet turbine	journalese	just in case
isoleucine	jackyarder	jeu d'esprit	journalise	just-in-time
isometrics	Jacobethan	Jew-baiting	journalism	just my luck
isomorphic	Jacobinism	jewel-block	journalist	just the job
isonitrile	Jacobinize	Jewishness	journalize	just too bad
iso-osmotic	Jacobitish	Jewish year	journeyman	Juvenalian
isopachous	Jacobitism	Jew's mallow	journeymen	juvenilely
isopachyte	jaculation	jib topsail	jovialness	juvenility
isopiestic	jaggedness	jigger coat	joyfulness	juvenilize
isoplastic	jaguarundi	jigger-mast	joyousness	juvescence
isoplethal	jailership	Jim Crowism	jubilantly	juxtaposit
isoprenoid	jamesonite	Jimmy Ducks	jubilarian	kabaragoya
isorrhythm	James Royal	Jimmy Grant	jubilation	kaempferol
isosbestic	Jamie Green	Jimmy Green	Judaically	kaersutite

kafferboom	kerb market	King's Guide	knight-head	laboursome
Kaffir beer	kerb weight	king's peace	knighthood	labour ward
kaffirboom	kerchiefed	King's Scout	knightlike	laccolitic
Kaffir corn	Kermanshah	king's spear	knightling	lace-border
Kaffir lily	kernelless	king's truce	knightship	lace lizard
Kaffir plum	Kerr effect	King Willow	knobbiness	lacemaking
Kaffir work	kerseymere	kinocilium	knobkerrie	lace-pillow
Kaffrarian	kerygmatic	kinspeople	knock about	laceration
Kafkaesque	ketohexose	Kiplingese	knockabout	lacerative
Kaiser roll	ketonaemia	Kiplingism	knock-kneed	lachenalia
kaisership	ketone body	Kiplingite	knock knees	lachrymary
Kaisership	kettledrum	Kiplingize	knockmeter	lachrymate
Kaiser's war	kettlefuls	Kiriwinian	knock silly	lachrymist
kaleyarder	kettle hole	kirkin-head	knock-stone	lachrymose
kalicinite	kettle lake	kirk-master	knock under	lachrymous
kallikrein	kettle-pins	Kirmanshah	knockwurst	laciniated
Kalmuckian	keyboarder	kiss better	knopkierie	lackadaisy
kamagraphy	key-drawing	kissing bug	knot-garden	lackey moth
Kamchatkan	keyhole saw	kissing kin	knot-stitch	lackeyship
Kampuchean	keypuncher	kiss my arse	knottiness	lacklustre
kangarooer	keystroker	kiss of life	know better	laconicism
Kantianism	khidmutgar	kiss the cup	know by name	lacquering
kaolinitic	khitmutgar	kiss the rod	knowledged	lactam ring
Kara-Kalpak	Khmer Rouge	kitchen-fee	know-little	lactescent
Karamojong	kibbutznik	kitchen tea	knuckle-bow	lactic acid
Karankawan	kick-boxing	kite-flying	knuckle-end	lactogenic
karaoke bar	kickshawed	kith and kin	Knudsen gas	lactometer
karate-chop	kicksorter	kitschiest	Kodiak bear	lactoscope
Karimojong	kick-the-can	kittenhood	koeksister	lactosuria
Karmathian	kick up a row	kittenlike	koettigite	lacustrian
Karrenfeld	kid brother	kittle-pins	kohlrabies	lacustrine
karst tower	kiddie-porn	klaberjass	kolbeckite	ladder-back
karyologic	kiddiewink	Klangfarbe	kolinskies	ladder fern
karyolysis	kidnapping	Klanswoman	kollergang	ladder-stop
karyolytic	kidney bean	Klanswomen	komatiitic	ladder-work
karyoplasm	kidney dish	klebsiella	kookaburra	ladies' room
karyotypic	kidney fern	klendusity	Korean pine	Lady chapel
Kashmirian	kidney worm	kleptocrat	Koreishite	ladyfinger
katabolism	kieselguhr	klieg light	kraft paper	lady-killer
keep a House	kiewietjie	klutziness	kratogenic	ladykiller
keep a tab on	killer cell	knackeries	Krebs cycle	lady orchid
keepership	kill or cure	knackwurst	Krems white	lady's horse
keep in play	Kilmarnock	knapsacked	krennerite	lady's laces
keep in with	kilometric	knave-bairn	kriegspiel	lady's smock
keep tabs on	kimberlite	knave noddy	Krishnaism	lady's waist
keep wicket	Kimmeridge	knee-action	kromeskies	Laestrigon
Kelvin's law	kinchin-lay	knee-braced	krugerrand	laevulinic
Kennel Club	kindliness	knee by knee	Ku Klux Klan	laevulosan
kennelling	kinematics	knee-halter	Kuomintang	lageniform
kennelmaid	kinetic art	knee-length	kurdaitcha	Lagrangian
kenoticism	kineticism	knee-rafter	kymography	lake-crater
kenoticist	kineticist	knee-timber	kynurenine	Lakelander
Kensington	kinetosome	knee to knee	Labarraque	Lake poetry
kenspeckle	King at Arms	knick-knack	labial pipe	lake salmon
Kentish rag	King Caesar	knickpoint	labiomancy	Lake school
Kentuckian	kingfisher	knife-blade	labiovelar	Lamarckian
Kenya Asian	king-hunter	knife-board	laboratory	Lamarckism
Kepler's law	kingliness	knife-edged	labour camp	lamaseries
keratinise	King of Arms	knife-guard	labouredly	lambdacism
keratinize	king parrot	knife-pleat	labour hero	lambdoidal
keratinous	king salmon	knife-point	labourless	lambrequin
keratotomy	King's Bench	knifepoint	labour-only	lamb's-tails

lamb-suckle	lantern-fly	laundermat	leaderless	legatorial
lamellated	lanternist	laundrette	leadership	Legendrian
lamentable	lantern-man	laundromat	leader tape	legibility
lamentably	lanthanide	Laundromat	lead glance	legionaire
laminagram	lanthanite	laundryman	leading dog	legionella
laminarian	lanthanoid	laundrymen	leading man	legislator
laminarize	lanuginose	laureation	lead pencil	legitimacy
lamination	lanuginous	laurelling	lead the van	legitimate
laminboard	laparotomy	Laurentian	lead the way	legitimise
Lammas-land	lapidarian	laurustine	leaf-beetle	legitimism
lamp holder	lapidaries	lautermash	leaf blight	legitimist
lampoonery	lapidarist	lavatorial	leaf blotch	legitimity
lampoonist	lapidation	lavatories	leaf-cutter	legitimize
lamprey-eel	lapidicole	laver bread	leafcutter	leg-pulling
lamp-socket	Laplandish	Laves phase	leaf-folder	legrandite
Lancashire	lappet-moth	lavishment	leafhopper	legs eleven
lanceolate	lap winding	lavishness	leaf insect	leg-spinner
lance-snake	lardaceous	law-abiding	leafleteer	leguleious
lancet arch	lardy-dardy	law-borrows	leafleting	leguminose
lancet-fish	largamente	lawbreaker	leaf monkey	leguminous
land agency	large print	law-burrows	leaf-roller	Leibnizian
landammann	large-scale	lawfulness	leaf scorch	Leichhardt
land-battle	larghettos	lawkadaisy	leaf-shaped	leiotrichy
land breeze	larvicidal	lawkamercy	leaf-sheath	leishmania
land-bridge	laryngitic	lawn tennis	leaf spring	leisurable
land forces	laryngitis	law-officer	leap second	leisurably
landholder	lascivious	Law of Moses	lear-father	leisureful
land-hunger	Lassa fever	Lawrencian	least of all	lemmatical
land-hungry	last but one	lawrencium	leathering	lemniscate
landing net	last but two	Lawrentian	leatheroid	lemon grass
landing pad	last hurrah	Law Society	leave alone	lemon plant
landing run	last minute	lawsoniana	leave a mark	lemon thyme
land-jobber	last moment	law station	leave aside	lemuriform
land-junker	last resort	lawyer cane	leave it out	lengthened
landladies	Last Supper	lawyer-like	leavenless	lengthener
Land League	last things	lawyer's wig	leave out of	lengthiest
land-locked	late blight	lay a charge	leave-taker	length-mark
landlocked	late dinner	lay a ground	Lebensraum	lengthsman
land-looker	lateen sail	lay analyst	leberwurst	lengthways
landloping	latent heat	lay an eye on	lectionary	lengthwise
landlordly	latentness	laybacking	lectorship	lenitively
landlordry	latent root	lay brother	lecturette	lens turret
land-louper	lateral cut	lay claim to	ledeburite	lentamente
landlubber	lateralise	layer cloud	lederhosen	Lenten corn
landocracy	laterality	lay hands on	ledged door	Lenten face
land office	lateralize	lay in ashes	ledger-bait	Lenten fare
landowning	lateritize	laying mash	ledger book	Lenten-kail
landscaper	latest word	Laysan duck	ledger line	Lenten rose
land spring	latex paint	Laysan rail	ledger-pole	lenticular
land-stream	latifundia	Laysan teal	leechcraft	lentigines
landswoman	Latin cross	lay siege to	Lee-Enfield	lentivirus
långbanite	Latinesque	lay store by	Lee-Metford	Leonberger
Langerhans	Latinistic	lay to heart	left centre	leontiasis
langlaufer	latitation	lay to sleep	left-footed	leopard cat
langue d'oïl	lattermath	lazarettos	left-footer	leopardess
languisher	lattermost	lazar-house	left-handed	Leopardian
languorous	latter-will	lead astray	left-hander	leopard-man
laniferous	Laudianism	leadbeater	left-winger	leper-house
lanigerous	Laue method	lead bronze	legal eagle	lepidolite
lanosterol	laughingly	leadenness	legalistic	lepidopter
lansquenet	laugh track	leaden seal	legalities	leprechaun
lantern bug	laumontite	leaderette	legateship	leptocauly

leptomonad	liberty boy	lignoceric	linguister	litholatry
leptomonas	liberty cap	like a charm	linguistic	lithologic
leptoquark	liberty day	like a dream	linguistry	lithomancy
leptosomic	liberty man	like a leech	linkage map	lithomarge
leptospira	libidinous	like billy-o	linked list	lithophane
leptospire	Lib-Labbery	like blazes	linkedness	lithophany
lesbianism	librarious	like enough	lin-lan-lone	lithophile
lesseeship	librettist	likelihead	linnet-hole	lithophone
Lesser Asia	licensable	likelihood	linocutter	lithophyte
Lesser Bear	licentiate	likeliness	linography	lithoprint
lesser evil	licentious	like-minded	linolenate	lithotomic
lesserness	lichenized	liliaceous	linoleumed	lithotrite
Lesser Wain	lichenless	lilli-pilli	linotypist	lithotrity
lethal dose	licitation	lilly-pilly	linseed oil	Lithuanian
lethargize	Lieberkühn	lily flower	lion-hunter	litigation
let's face it	lie heavy on	lily-footed	lion's heart	litmus blue
letter bomb	lie in ruins	limaciform	lion's share	litmus test
letter-card	lie in state	limber hole	Lipizzaner	litterfall
letterform	lie leaguer	limber-neck	lipochrome	litter lout
lettergram	lieutenant	limberness	lipofuscin	Little Bear
letterhead	life-breath	limber pine	lipography	little-ease
letterless	life-estate	limber-rope	lipoidosis	little-girl
letter-wood	life-giving	limburgite	lipophobic	Little Lion
letter-word	Life Guards	lime-burner	lipothymic	Little Mary
let through	life jacket	lime-juicer	lipotropic	little neck
leucoblast	lifelessly	lime-squash	Lippes loop	littleness
leucocidin	life member	limicoline	Lippizaner	little ones
leucocytic	life-office	liminality	lip-service	little slam
leucoderma	life-policy	limitation	lip-syncing	little Turk
leucopenia	lifcrenter	limitative	lip-worship	littorinid
leucophore	life-saving	limited war	liquescent	liturgical
leucoplast	lifesomely	limit gauge	liquidator	live action
leucotaxin	life spring	limit point	liquid drop	livelihood
leucotaxis	life-string	limitrophe	liquid fire	liveliness
leucotoxin	life tenant	limnograph	liquidiser	liver fluke
leukaemoid	life-writer	limnometer	liquidizer	liverishly
leukovirus	lift-bridge	limpet mine	liquidness	liver salts
lever frame	lift the leg	limpidness	liquorless	liverwurst
lever watch	ligamental	Lincolnian	lis pendens	live weight
levigation	light-armed	Lincoln imp	lissomness	living area
levitation	light bread	Lincoln Red	list broker	living dead
levitative	light curve	lincomycin	listenable	livingless
levy in mass	lightening	linearizer	listen good	livingness
lexicalize	lighterage	line astern	listlessly	living room
lexicology	lighterman	linebacker	list system	living wage
lexiconize	lightermen	line by line	litany-desk	living will
lexigraphy	light-grasp	line editor	literalise	lizardfish
Lexiphanes	light guide	line-ending	literalism	lizard-like
Lexiphanic	light horse	line finder	literalist	lizard-skin
ley farming	lighthouse	line-firing	literality	Lloyd's List
liableness	light meter	linen-panel	literalize	loaded down
libationer	light-money	linen-press	literarily	loaded with
libellulid	light of day	line of fire	literarism	load factor
liberalise	light o' love	line of life	literately	loading bay
liberalism	light organ	lineolated	literation	loading rod
liberalist	lightproof	linerboard	literatist	loadmaster
liberality	light-tight	line-riding	literature	loafer wolf
liberalize	light touch	liner train	literosity	loanholder
liberation	light value	line-squall	lithia-mica	loan-monger
liberative	light valve	lingualise	lithoclast	loan-office
liberatory	light water	lingualize	lithoglyph	loathingly
liberty act	lignocaine	linguiform	lithograph	lobe-finned

lobopodial	long corner	Lord Rector	Lubberland	lute-string
lobopodium	long drawer	Lord Warden	lubberlike	lutestring
lobotomies	long family	Lorentzian	lubber line	Lutine Bell
lobotomise	long figure	lorication	lubricator	luxuriance
lobotomize	long finger	lose ground	lubricious	luxuriancy
lobscouser	long-footed	lose height	luciferase	lycoperdon
lobsterish	longhaired	lose no time	Luciferian	lycopodium
lobster pot	long handle	lose the way	luciferous	Lydian mode
lobulation	long-headed	lose weight	lucifugous	lymphedema
local derby	long-horned	losing game	lucklessly	lymph gland
local group	long-jumper	loss-leader	lucubrator	lymphocyte
localistic	long-legged	loss-making	luculently	lymphokine
localities	long-lining	loss of face	ludibrious	lymphomata
local paper	long-living	loss of life	Ludolphian	lynchetted
local radio	long-lugged	lost labour	luff-tackle	lyophilise
local train	long-lunged	lost motion	luggage van	lyophilize
locational	long manure	Lost Tribes	lugubrious	lyre-flower
lock-and-key	long memory	lot and scot	lukewarmly	lyre-shaped
Lockeanism	long mirror	lotos-eater	lukewarmth	lyric drama
locked-coil	long-nebbed	lotus-eater	lumachelle	lyric stage
locker room	long-necked	loud hailer	lumber-camp	Lysenkoism
lock-keeper	long of life	loud-spoken	lumberjack	Lysenkoist
lock stitch	long pepper	loundering	lumber-port	lysigenous
lock-washer	long-player	lounge suit	lumber-raft	lysimachia
locomobile	long primer	louping-ill	lumber-room	lysogenize
locomotion	longshanks	louse-borne	lumbersome	maasbanker
locomotive	long sleeve	lovability	lumber town	macadamise
locomotory	longsomely	lovat green	lumber-yard	macadamize
loculament	long-spined	love affair	lumbricine	macaronies
locust bean	long-splice	lovelessly	lumbricoid	macaronism
locust-bird	long-staple	love letter	lumichrome	mace-bearer
locust tree	long stroke	lovelihead	lumiflavin	Macedonian
locutorium	long-tackle	loveliness	luminaries	maceration
Loddon lily	long-tailed	lovemaking	luminarism	macfarlane
lodemanage	long-termer	love-object	luminarist	Machangana
loganberry	long tongue	love-potion	lumination	machinable
logan-stone	long-winded	lover's knot	luminosity	machinator
loggerhead	look-and-say	lovers' lane	luminously	machine age
logicality	look around	lovers' tiff	lumisterol	machine-gun
logicalize	look babies	loveworthy	lumpectomy	Mach number
logical sum	look down on	lovey-dovey	lump of clay	mackintosh
logic-tight	look lively	lovingness	lumpsucker	Maconochie
logistical	look slippy	lowbrowism	luna cornea	macrocarpa
logography	loom the web	low-calorie	lunar cycle	macrocycle
logomaniac	loop aerial	low-country	lunar month	macrocytic
logophobia	loop-stitch	lower class	lunar orbit	macrofauna
logorrhoea	loop system	lower court	lunarscape	macromeric
logrolling	loose cover	Lower House	lunate bone	macrophage
Lollardism	loose-ended	lower sixth	lungs of oak	macrophyte
löllingite	loose order	lower world	lunkheaded	macropodid
Lombardian	loose scrum	low-melting	lurchingly	macro-scale
Lombardism	lop and crop	low opinion	lusciously	macroseism
Lombrosian	loperamide	low-pitched	Lushington	macrospore
London clay	lophiodont	low-powered	Lusitanian	maculation
lonelihood	lophophore	low profile	lustration	maculature
loneliness	lopolithic	low-residue	lustrative	Madagascan
lone ranger	lopsidedly	Lowryesque	lustratory	Madagascar
lonesomely	loquacious	low spirits	lustreless	madapollam
long-acting	Lord Bishop	low tension	lustreware	mad-brained
long barrow	lord it over	low to paper	lustrously	Madeira nut
long chalks	lordliness	loxodromic	luteolysis	Madonnaish
long chance	lordolatry	loyal toast	luteolytic	madreporic

Madura foot	Makasarese	Malpighian	man of mould	marination
maeandrine	make a House	Malta fever	man of sense	marine band
maeandrous	make a job of	malted milk	man of straw	marine blue
maedi-visna	make a match	Maltese cat	man of virtu	marine glue
magazinery	make amends	Maltese dog	manometric	marineland
magazinish	make a noise	Malthusian	manor house	marine soap
magazinist	make a point	malt liquor	manostatic	marine toad
Magellanic	make a raise	maltreater	manqueller	Mariolater
Magen David	make a shift	malt whisky	manservant	Mariolatry
Maghrebine	make a vaunt	malvaceous	man's estate	marionette
magicality	make-belief	Malvernian	mansionary	mariposite
magic glass	make bold as	malversate	manslaying	maritality
magistracy	make boot of	mamillated	mansuetude	markedness
magistrand	make eyes at	mammal-like	manteltree	marketable
magistrate	make game of	mammillary	mantically	marketably
Magna Carta	make its way	mammillate	mantletree	market-rate
magna opera	make it up to	mammogenic	mantlewise	market town
magnetical	make leeway	mammotroph	manucaptor	marking ink
magnetizer	make meat of	mammy wagon	manumitted	marking-nut
magnifical	make mock of	manageable	manumitter	markswoman
magnificat	make much of	manageably	manumotive	mark-vessel
magniloquy	make noises	management	manure-heap	markworthy
magnolious	make no sign	manageress	manuscript	marmennill
magnum opus	make or mend	managerial	many-headed	marquisate
magpie lark	make report	man and wife	many-valued	marrowbone
magpie moth	makeshifty	manavilins	many valved	marrowless
mahoganies	make the bag	Manchester	manzanilla	Marseilles
maidenhair	make the bed	manchineel	Maoritanga	Marshalate
maidenhead	make tracks	Manchurian	maple candy	marshaless
maidenhood	make up a bed	mancipable	maple-honey	marshalled
maidenlike	makeweight	mandevilla	maple sugar	marshaller
maiden name	malacology	mandibular	maple syrup	marshal-man
maiden over	malapertly	mandragora	mappemonde	marshalsea
maiden pink	malapropos	manducable	maquillage	marsh elder
maidenship	malaxation	manfulness	maraschino	marsh fever
Maid Marian	Malayanize	manganitic	marathoner	marsh grass
mail-armour	Malay apple	mangosteen	marble bone	marshiness
mailed fist	Malay tapir	maniacally	marble cake	marsh quail
maimedness	malconduct	Manichaean	marble gall	marsh tacky
main chance	malcontent	Manicheism	marble-wood	martellato
main clause	maldescent	manicurist	marcelling	martensite
main couple	maledicent	manifester	marcel wave	Martha Gunn
main course	malefactor	manifestly	marcescent	martial art
mainlander	maleficent	manifestos	marchantia	martialism
mainpernor	maleficial	manifolder	March brown	martialist
mainspring	maleic acid	manifoldly	March court	martiality
mainstream	malevolent	manifold to	march stone	martialize
main street	malfeasant	maniformly	Marcionist	martial law
Main Street	malgré tout	Manila hemp	Marcionite	martingale
maintained	maliferous	man-in-space	Marcomanni	martingana
maintainer	malignance	manipulate	marcottage	Martinware
maintainor	malignancy	man-midwife	mareograph	marvelling
maisonette	malingerer	manna-grass	marginalia	marvellous
maize-thief	mallardite	manna sugar	marginally	Marxianism
majestatic	malleation	mannerable	margin call	Marylander
majestical	mallee bird	mannerless	marginless	Mary Stuart
majestuous	mallee fowl	Mannesmann	margravate	Mary Warner
major-domos	malleiform	Mannlicher	margravial	marzacotto
Majoristic	mallenders	manoeuvrer	margravine	mascarpone
majorities	Mallorquin	man of blood	marguerite	masked ball
major piece	malodorous	man of ideas	Marheshvan	maskinonge
majuscular	malolactic	man of means	marigenous	mason's mark

masquerade	maturative	medievally	membranous	merry Greek
mass action	matureness	mediocracy	membranula	merrymaker
Massagetae	maudlinism	mediocrist	memomotion	Merry Widow
massasauga	maundering	mediocrity	memorandum	Mertensian
mass defect	Maundy coin	meditation	memorative	mesenchyme
massecuite	Maundy dish	meditative	memorially	mesenteric
mass effect	mausoleums	medium rare	memory bank	mesenteron
mass energy	mauvais pas	mediumship	memory book	mesethmoid
masseteric	mauvais ton	medium shot	memory drug	meshugener
mass market	mavourneen	medium wave	memory drum	mesitylene
mass medium	maxilliped	medrinaque	memory lane	mesmerical
mass-monger	maximalism	medullated	memoryless	mesmerizer
mass number	maximalist	medusa-fish	memory span	mesocephal
mass-priest	maximality	medusiform	menacement	mesoconchy
mastectomy	Maxwellian	meek mother	menacingly	mesocratic
master card	Maxwell law	meerschaum	menagerist	mesodermal
master hand	Mayfairish	meet in with	menarcheal	mesodorsal
masterhood	mayonnaise	meet the ear	mendacious	mesogaster
masterless	McLuhanism	meet the eye	mendicancy	mesogloeal
mastermind	McNaughten	mefloquine	mengkulang	mesognathy
master race	meadow bird	megagamete	mengovirus	mesokurtic
mastership	meadow foam	megalithic	meningioma	mesolectal
master-work	meadow frog	megalocyte	meningitic	mesolimbic
masterwork	meadowland	megalosaur	meningitis	mesolithic
masterwort	meadowlark	megaphonic	menologies	mesomerism
masticable	meadowless	megaripple	menologist	mesomorphy
masticator	meadow vole	megascopic	menopausal	mesophilic
mastic tree	meagreness	meiofaunal	menopausic	mesophytic
mastiff bat	meal-beetle	meiophylly	menorrhoea	mesopodium
mastodonic	mealie meal	melanaemia	Menshevism	mesorrhine
mastodynia	mealie rice	melanaemic	Menshevist	mesoscaphe
mastopathy	meal ticket	melancholy	menstruant	mesoscopic
masturbate	mealy-mouth	Melanesian	menstruate	mesosphere
mataeology	meandering	Melanesoid	menstruous	mesostasis
matchboard	meaningful	melanistic	mensurable	mesothelia
match-maker	mean-souled	melanocyte	mensurator	mesothorax
matchmaker	mean square	melanoderm	mental note	mesovarium
match-plane	measurable	melanosome	mental test	message-boy
match point	measurably	Melba sauce	mental year	Messianism
match-rifle	measuredly	Melba toast	menu-driven	mess jacket
matchstick	meat-headed	Melburnian	meperidine	metabiosis
materially	meat-market	melezitose	mephenesin	metabiotic
maternally	meat-packer	melianthus	mephitical	metabolise
mathematic	meat ticket	meliorater	mepyramine	metabolism
mating call	mechanical	meliorator	mercantile	metabolite
matriarchy	mechanizer	melismatic	mercaptide	metabolize
matricaria	meconopsis	melizitose	merchandry	metacarpal
matricidal	medal chief	mellophone	merchantry	metacarpus
matriculae	medal round	mellowness	mercifully	metacentre
matricular	meddlesome	melocactus	mercury arc	metacetone
matrifocal	meddlingly	melodially	mercy sakes	metachrome
matrilocal	media event	melomaniac	meretrices	metaconule
matriotism	mediagenic	melon-shell	meridional	metacyclic
matrocliny	mediastina	meloplasty	merismatic	meta-ethics
Matronalia	mediatress	melting pot	meristelic	metagalaxy
matronhood	mediatrice	Melvillean	merit money	metagnomic
matronlike	medicalize	Melvillian	meritocrat	metalation
matronship	medicament	member bank	merogamete	metalepsis
matronymic	medicaster	memberless	merohedral	metaleptic
matterless	medication	membership	meromictic	metalleity
matter wave	medicative	membranate	meromyosin	metallizer
maturation	Medici lace	membranoid	merozygote	metallurgy

metameride	Mezzofanti	midden cock	mill finish	minnarichi
metamerism	mezzo forte	midden fowl	mill-hopper	minnerichi
metamerous	mezzo piano	middle-aged	millilitre	Minnesotan
metanalyse	miargyrite	middle-ager	millimetre	minor canon
metaphonic	miarolitic	Middle Ages	millionary	minorities
metaphoric	mica-schist	middlebrow	millionism	minor piece
metaphrase	Michaelmas	middle deck	millionist	minstrelsy
metaphrast	Mickey Finn	Middle East	milliprobe	mint master
metaphysic	mickey-take	middle game	millocracy	mint parity
metaphysis	micklemote	middle life	millstream	minuscular
metaplasia	microatoll	middlemost	mill-stream	minute bell
metapodial	microbarom	middle name	millworker	minute-book
metapodium	microbiota	middleness	millwright	minute hand
metastable	microblade	middle rail	miltsiekte	minuteness
metastably	microburin	middle-rank	mime artist	mirabilite
metastases	microburst	middle-rate	mimeograph	miracidial
metastasis	microcline	middle-road	mim mouthed	miracidium
metastatic	microcrack	middle term	minatorily	miracle man
metatarsal	microcytic	middle-tone	minauderie	miraculize
metatarsus	microdrama	middleveld	minced meat	miraculous
metatheses	microdrive	Middle West	mind-bender	mirror carp
metathesis	microfauna	middlingly	Mindererus	mirror-like
metathetic	microfiche	mid-engined	mind-healer	mirror-work
metathorax	microflora	mid-feather	mindlessly	mirthfully
metempiric	microglial	midfielder	mind out for	mirthquake
meteoritic	micrograph	midi system	mind-reader	misaddress
methanogen	microgyria	midnightly	mine hunter	misapplied
methanolic	microimage	mid-oceanic	mine-laying	misapplies
methedrine	microlevel	midshipman	mineralise	misbelieve
Methedrine	microlight	midshipmen	mineralist	miscarried
methiocarb	microlitic	midsummery	mineralize	miscarries
methionine	microlitre	Midwestern	mineralogy	miscellany
methodical	micrologic	mightiness	mineraloid	mischanter
methodizer	micromania	migmatitic	mineral oil	misch metal
methodless	micromazia	migmatized	mineral rod	misclosure
methomania	micrometer	mignonette	mineral tar	miscompute
methoprene	micrometre	migraineur	mineral wax	misconceit
Methuselah	micrometry	migrainous	miner's inch	misconduct
methylator	micromolar	milecastle	miner's lung	miscontent
methyldopa	microphage	miliaceous	mine-sinker	miscounsel
meticulous	microphone	militantly	minestrone	miscreance
metoecious	microphony	militarily	mineworker	miscreancy
metoestrus	microphoto	militarise	mingimingi	miscreated
metoprolol	microphyll	militarism	mingle eyes	misdeliver
metre-angle	microphyte	militarist	minglement	misdeserve
metre psalm	microprint	militarize	mingle with	misdevoted
metrically	microprism	militation	Mingrelian	misdrawing
metrisable	microprobe	militiaman	miniaceous	miseducate
metrizable	micropylar	militiamen	mini-budget	misericord
metrocracy	micro-scale	milk-coffee	minikin pin	misery guts
Metroliner	microscope	milk powder	minimalism	misexecute
metrologic	microscopy	milk the ram	minimalist	misexplain
metromania	microseism	milled lead	minimality	misexpress
metronomic	microsleep	millefiore	minimalize	misfeature
metronymic	microslide	millegrain	mining-hole	misfortune
metropolis	microsomal	millennial	mining town	misimprove
mettlesome	microspore	millennian	miniseries	misincline
mevalonate	microstate	millennism	ministrant	misjoinder
Mexicanize	microstrip	millennium	ministrate	misleading
Mexican tea	microtherm	miller-moth	ministress	mismanager
Mexican War	microtonal	millesimal	ministries	mismeasure
mexiletine	Midas touch	millet-seed	mini-summit	misogamist

misogynism	mixty-maxty	Monarchian	monogenist	montelimar
misogynist	mizzen-mast	monarchies	monogenous	Montessori
misogynous	mizzen-sail	monarchise	monography	Montgomery
misologist	mizzen yard	monarchism	monogynist	month clock
misperform	mnemically	monarchist	monogynous	month's mind
misprision	mnemicness	monarchize	monohybrid	Montrealer
misreading	mnemonical	monastical	monohydric	monumental
misrecital	mobile home	monaurally	monoideism	monzonitic
missal book	mobocratic	Monday Club	monokaryon	moon-bounce
miss a trick	moccasined	Monégasque	monolithal	mooncalves
misseeming	mocha brown	monegenism	monolithic	moon-curser
missileman	mock-heroic	Monel metal	monologian	moon-flower
missiology	mock orange	monetarian	monologise	moonraking
missionary	mock privet	monetarily	monologist	moon-rocket
missionate	modacrylic	monetarism	monologize	moon-shaped
missioneer	modalistic	monetarist	monomaniac	moonshiner
missionist	modalities	moneymaker	monomerous	moonstruck
missionize	modal logic	money order	monometric	moonwalker
mission oak	mode-locked	money-power	monomictic	moose berry
Missisauga	modenature	money-saver	monophasic	mopane worm
Missourian	moderately	money-worth	monophonic	mophrodite
missourite	moderation	mongreldom	monoplegia	mopishness
misspender	moderatism	mongrelise	monoplegic	moral fibre
miss the bus	moderatist	mongrelism	monoploidy	moralistic
mistakable	modernizer	mongrelize	monopodial	moralities
mistakably	modern jazz	moniliasis	monopodium	moralizing
mistakenly	modernness	moniliform	monopodous	moral sense
mist-blower	modern side	monishment	monopolies	moral tutor
mist-flower	modifiable	monitorial	monopolise	morass-weed
misthought	modificand	monitories	monopolism	Morasthite
mistress it	modishness	monkey bars	monopolist	moratorium
mistressly	modularity	monkey-boat	monopolize	morbidness
mistruster	modularize	monkey-face	monopteral	morbillous
mistutored	modulation	monkey-rope	monopteros	morcellate
misventure	modulative	monkey suit	monorhinal	mordacious
miswriting	modulatory	monkliness	monorhymed	Mordvinian
mitch-board	Mohammedan	monk's bench	monosexual	more like it
mithridate	moissanite	monk's table	monosodium	more or less
mitigation	moist scall	monocarpic	monospermy	Moreton Bay
mitigatory	moist sugar	monocausal	monostable	morganatic
mitre-bevel	moisturise	monochroic	monostatic	morigerate
mitre block	moisturize	monochrome	monotheism	morigerous
mitre board	molariform	monochromy	monotheist	Morisonian
mitre-cramp	molendinar	monoclinal	monothetic	Mormon City
mitre joint	mole-plough	monoclinic	monotocous	morning-gun
mitre-plane	molinology	monoclonal	monotonely	morning tea
mitre-shell	moll-buzzer	monocormic	monotonize	morologist
mitre wheel	mollescent	monocratic	monotonist	moroseness
mitten crab	mollitious	monocrotic	monotonize	morphemics
mitt-reader	mollrowing	monoculist	monotonous	morphinism
Mittyesque	molluscoid	monoculous	monotropic	morphinist
mixed angle	molluscous	monocyclic	monotypous	morphodite
mixed blood	moll-washer	monocystic	monovalent	morphogeny
mixed bunch	molybdenum	monocystid	monoxenous	morpholine
mixed grill	moment-hand	monodactyl	monozygous	morphology
mixed media	monadiform	monodontal	Monsignori	morphoneme
Mix-Hellene	monadistic	monodromic	monsoonish	morris bell
mixing desk	monadology	monoecious	monstrance	Morris tube
mixohaline	Mona marble	monogamian	Montagnais	morrowless
mixologist	monandrous	monogamist	montagnard	morrow-mass
mixolydian	monarchess	monogamous	montbretia	Morse taper
mixoploidy	monarchial	monogenean	Monte Carlo	mortadella

mortadelle	mountained	muesli belt	muon number	mutilation
mortal mind	mountainet	muffin-face	mural crown	mutilative
mortarless	mountebank	muffle kiln	Muratorian	mutinously
mortifying	mount guard	muff pistol	murderable	mutter over
mortuaries	mournfully	mugearitic	murder book	mutton-bird
mosaically	mourningly	mugwumpery	murder game	mutton chop
mosaic gold	mouse-eared	mugwumpish	murder room	mutton-fish
mosaicking	mouse-lemur	mugwumpism	muriculate	mutton-head
mosaic work	mousseline	Muhammadan	Murphy's Law	mutton quad
mosasaurus	moustached	mujahideen	Murray lily	mutual fund
moscatello	moustachio	mulattress	Murray pine	mutualness
Moscow mule	Mousterian	mulberries	muscardine	myasthenia
mosquitoes	Mousteroid	mule-driver	muscarinic	myasthenic
mosquitoey	mouth guard	mule-headed	muscle cell	mycetocyte
moss-backed	mouthiness	mule-killer	muscleless	mycetozoan
mossbunker	mouthingly	mule rabbit	muscle pull	mycologist
moss stitch	mouth music	muliebrity	muscle scar	mycophilic
mother cell	mouth organ	mulishness	muscovados	mycoplasma
mother-city	mouthpiece	mullein tea	muscularis	mycorrhiza
mother coal	moutonnéed	mullet-head	muscularly	mycotrophy
motherhood	movability	mulligrubs	mushroomer	myelinated
motherkins	movable-doh	multiaxial	musical bow	myeloblast
motherland	movable rib	multifidly	musical box	myelocoele
motherless	move in with	multiflash	musical ear	myelocytic
motherlike	movelessly	multiflora	musicalise	myelogenic
motherling	movie-going	multifocal	musicality	my lady wife
mother lode	movie house	multigrade	musicalize	mylonitize
mother love	movie-maker	Multigraph	musical saw	myoblastic
mother's boy	moving-coil	multilayer	music drama	myocardiac
Mother's Day	moving-iron	multilevel	musicianer	myocardial
mother ship	movingness	multimedia	musicianly	myocardium
mothership	mower's mite	multimeric	musicology	myoelastic
mother's pet	Mozambican	multimeter	music paper	myofibroma
mother's son	mozzarella	multimodal	music-shell	myogenesis
mother-to-be	Mr Chairman	multi-party	music stand	myographic
motherwort	Mr Next-Door	multiphase	music stool	myological
moth orchid	Mrs Justice	multiplane	musk beetle	myomectomy
motionable	mucedinous	multiplied	musket ball	myometrial
motionally	much to seek	multiplier	musket shot	myometrium
motionless	muciferous	multiplies	Muskhogean	myomorphic
motion-work	mucigenous	multipoint	musk mallow	myopically
motitation	muciparous	multipolar	musk orchid	myoplasmic
motivation	mucka-mucka	multisided	musk turtle	myosarcoma
motivative	muckleness	multi-stage	mussel-bank	my pleasure
motiveless	muckraking	multistage	mussel crab	myriadfold
motleyness	mucousness	multi-track	mussel duck	myriapodal
motor coach	mucronated	multivalve	mussel plum	myringitis
motor court	mud and stud	multiverse	mussel rake	myriologue
motor cycle	mud balance	multivious	mustachios	myristicin
motorcycle	muddle-head	multivocal	mustard gas	myrmekitic
motor-drive	muddlement	multocular	mustard oil	myrtaceous
motor hotel	muddliness	mumblement	mustard-pot	myrtle bird
motor lodge	muddlingly	mumblingly	muster-book	myrtle wine
motor mouth	mud-flinger	mumbo-jumbo	muster-roll	mysophobia
motormouth	mudguarded	mummy brown	mutability	mystagogic
motor nerve	mud-logging	mummy-cloth	mutagenize	mystagogue
motor sport	mud-skipper	Munchausen	mutarotate	mysterioso
motor yacht	mudskipper	mundane egg	mutassarif	mysterious
mottramite	mud-slinger	municipium	mutational	mystery-bag
mould-board	mud swallow	munificent	mute button	mystery man
mouldiness	mud-thrower	munitioner	mutessarif	mystically
Moulinette	mud volcano	Muntz metal	muthafucka	mystifying

mythically	natalities	neck-spring	nematocyst	neural tube
mythicizer	natatorial	necrogenic	nematology	neuraminic
mythoclast	natatorium	necrolatry	Nemean lion	neurectomy
mythogenic	nationally	necrologue	nemesistic	neurilemma
mythologem	nationalty	necromance	nemocerous	neuroblast
mythologer	nationhood	necromancy	neo-classic	neurocrine
mythologic	nationwide	necrophile	neoclassic	neurogenic
mythomania	native bear	necrophily	neocyanine	neuroglial
mythopoeia	native-born	necrophobe	neo-fascism	neurolemma
mythopoeic	native bush	necropolis	neo-fascist	neuromotor
myxococcal	nativeness	necroscopy	neogenesis	neuronally
myxococcus	native oven	nectar-bird	neoglacial	neuropathy
myxomatous	native rock	nectareous	neographic	neuroplasm
myxomycete	nativistic	nectarious	neolocally	Neuroptera
myzostomid	nativities	nectocalyx	neological	neurotoxic
nabocklish	natron lake	needle-beam	neomorphic	neurotoxin
Nabokovian	natterjack	needle beer	neonatally	neuterness
nab the rust	natty dread	needle-book	neontology	neutralise
nail-biting	natural day	needle-bush	neopallial	neutralism
nail enamel	natural gas	needle-case	neopallium	neutralist
nail-headed	naturalise	needle-cast	neopentane	neutrality
nail-making	naturalism	needlecord	neophiliac	neutralize
nail polish	naturalist	needlefish	neoplastic	neutrodyne
nail-tailed	naturality	needlefuls	neotechnic	never again
nail violin	naturalize	needle game	neoterical	never-dying
naked force	natural law	needle-lace	nephewship	never-never
naked truth	nature cure	needle-like	nephometer	New Academy
nalbuphine	nature food	needleloom	nephoscope	new arrival
nalorphine	natureless	needle's eye	nephralgia	New Dealish
naltrexone	nature poem	needlessly	nephralgic	New England
namby-pamby	nature poet	needle time	nephridial	New English
namelessly	nature walk	needle-whin	nephridium	newfangled
name the day	naturistic	needle-wood	nephrocyte	New Kingdom
nameworthy	naturopath	needlework	nephrology	New Leftist
nannyishly	naughtiest	need-to-know	nephropexy	New Mexican
nanosecond	nauseating	ne'er-do-well	nephrotome	new nothing
naological	nauseation	negational	nephrotomy	New Orleans
naphthalic	nauseously	negatively	nephsystem	new realism
naphthenic	nautch girl	negativism	nepotistic	new realist
napkin ring	nautically	negativist	nerve agent	news agency
Napoleonic	nautiluses	negativity	nerve block	newscaster
nappy-liner	naval brass	negentropy	nerve fibre	news cinema
narcissine	naval crown	neglectful	nerve-force	newsletter
narcissism	navel-stone	neglecting	nerve storm	newsmonger
narcissist	naviculoid	neglection	Nesselrode	newspapery
narcolepsy	navigation	neglective	nesslerize	newsreader
narcomania	Navy League	negligence	nesting box	news ticker
narcotical	Nazarenism	negligency	net-drifter	news-vendor
nard pistic	Nazaritish	negligible	net-fishing	newsvendor
narratable	Nazaritism	negligibly	nethermore	newsworthy
narratress	Nazca lines	negotiable	nethermost	New Thought
narrowback	Nazi salute	negotiable	nether vert	New Worlder
narrow band	Neapolitan	negotiator	netherward	new wrinkle
narrow boat	near at hand	Negro cloth	net-masonry	New York cut
narrowcast	neat cement	Negrophile	nettle beer	New Yorkese
narrowness	neat-handed	Negrophobe	nettle-like	New Yorkish
narrow seas	neatly shod	Negro's head	nettle-rash	New Zealand
nasal organ	nebulosity	Negro State	nettlesome	next door to
nasologist	nebulously	Nelson cake	nettle-tree	next friend
Nassauvian	neck-collar	Nelsoniana	net tonnage	nibblingly
nasturtium	neckercher	nematicide	networking	Nicaraguan
natal cleft	Necker cube	nematocide	neural arch	nickel-iron

nickelized	night-spell	nodularity	non-utility	noteworthy
nickelling	nightstick	nodulation	non-vintage	not exactly
nickel note	night-stool	noegenesis	non-violent	not go nap on
nick of time	night-sweat	noegenetic	non-working	not half bad
nick-tailed	night-times	noise-maker	noogenesis	no thanks to
Nicobarese	nightwards	noise storm	noological	nothingism
Nicobarian	night watch	noisy miner	noon-flower	nothingist
Nicodemite	night-water	no man's land	noospheric	nothofagus
Nicolaitan	nigrescent	nom de plume	norbergite	nothomorph
nicol prism	nigromance	nomenclate	Norbertine	noticeable
Nicol prism	nihilistic	nomen nudum	Nordenfelt	noticeably
nicotinate	nihilities	nominalise	Nordhausen	notifiable
nicotinian	Nile lechwe	nominalism	normal form	not in order
nicotinise	nilly-willy	nominalist	normalizer	notionally
nicotinism	Nilo-Hamite	nominalize	normalness	notionless
nicotinize	Nilometric	nominately	Normanizer	not much cop
nidamental	nimbleness	nomination	normoblast	not one's day
nidderling	nimble Will	nominative	normocytic	notopodial
niddy-noddy	nincompoop	nomineeism	norsteroid	notopodium
nidicolous	nine-killer	nomography	northabout	not so dusty
nidificate	nine points	nomologist	northbound	not the less
nidifugous	nine-seater	nomothetic	north canoe	Nottingham
nidulation	nineteenth	non-abelian	North Downs	not to worry
nifedipine	nine-tenths	non-ability	northerner	not without
niffy-naffy	nine to five	non-aligned	northernly	noumenally
Niger-Congo	ninetyfold	non-capital	north light	nourishing
niggardize	nip and tuck	non-central	north-south	novaculite
nigger fish	Nipkow disc	nonchalant	Northumber	Novanglian
niggerhead	nippleless	non-citizen	northwards	novelesque
nigger luck	nipple-like	nonconform	Norway pine	novelistic
nigglingly	nipplewort	non-content	nose bot fly	novicehood
night adder	niridazole	noncurance	nose-bridge	noviceship
night-blind	Nissl stain	non-drinker	noselessly	novobiocin
night-bound	nit-picking	non-earning	nose-monkey	now and then
night chain	nitrazepam	non-elastic	nose tackle	nowanights
night-chair	nitric acid	non-essence	nose to nose	nowcasting
night class	Nitrochalk	non-ferrous	nose-to-tail	now or never
night clock	nitrofuran	non-fiction	nosocomial	nubiferous
night coach	nitro group	non-genital	nosography	nuciferous
night cream	nitrometer	nonjoinder	nosologist	nucivorous
nightdress	nitrophile	nonjurancy	nosophobia	nuclearism
night error	nitro-proof	non-logical	nosopoetic	nuclearist
night-glass	nitro-prove	non-morally	nostalgist	nuclearize
night heron	nitwittery	non-natural	Nostratian	nuclear sap
night horse	Nixonomics	non-nuclear	nostrility	nuclear war
night-house	Noah's Flood	nonny-nonny	nostrilled	nucleation
night-latch	no amount of	no-nonsense	no such luck	nucleonics
night light	Nobel prize	non-organic	nosy parker	nucleoside
nightmarey	Nobel Prize	non-patrial	Nosy Parker	nucleosome
night-night	nobilities	non-payment	notability	nucleotide
night nurse	noblemanly	non-playing	not a little	nuculanium
night or day	noble metal	nonplussed	not all that	nudibranch
night-piece	noblewoman	non-smoking	notaphilic	nulla-nulla
night-raven	noblewomen	non-soluble	notarially	nullibiety
night rider	nobody-crab	non-starter	notational	nullisomic
nightscape	nociceptor	non-stellar	not but what	nulliverse
night-scene	nocifensor	non-success	notch-house	numbedness
nightshade	no conjuror	non-summons	notchiness	numberable
night shift	nodal point	non-swimmer	not cricket	number-form
nightshirt	nodosarian	non-trivial	note-broker	numberless
night sight	nodosarine	nontronite	note-holder	number line
night snake	nod through	non-uniform	note-shaver	numbheaded

numeration	objectless	ocean spray	of a morning	old country
numerative	object love	ocean tramp	of even date	old crumpet
numerology	objectness	oceanwards	off balance	Old English
numerosity	object word	ochlocracy	offcasting	olde worlde
numerously	objets d'art	ochraceous	offenceful	old-fangled
numinosity	objuration	ochratoxin	offendable	Old Italian
numinously	oblateness	ochronosis	offendedly	Old Kingdom
numismatic	oblational	ochronotic	offer price	old-maidish
nummulated	obligately	ocnophilic	of few words	old-maidism
nummulitic	obligation	octadrachm	off-flavour	old-man bird
nummulitid	obligative	octaeteric	offhandish	old-mannish
numskulled	obligatory	octaeteris	office girl	Old Pals Act
nunciative	obligement	octagynous	office hymn	Old Pharaoh
nunciature	obligingly	octahedral	officeless	Old Scratch
Nupercaine	obliterate	octahedron	office wife	old soldier
nuptiality	Oblomovism	octamerism	officially	Old Stripes
nuptial pad	oblongness	octamerous	officiator	old-womanly
nurse-child	obnebulate	octandrous	offishness	old-womanry
nurse hound	obnubilate	octangular	off-licence	oleaginous
nurse-plant	oboe d'amore	octavalent	off one's dot	oleandrine
nurseryful	oboi d'amore	octave stop	off one's nut	oleiferous
nurseryman	obrogation	octodecimo	off-putting	oleography
nurserymen	obscurancy	octodrachm	off-roading	oleophilic
nurse shark	obscuredly	octofoiled	offset well	oleophobic
nurses' home	obsequence	octogenary	off-spinner	oleothorax
nursing bra	obsequious	octogynous	off the ball	oleraceous
nurturance	observable	octohedron	off the beam	olfactible
nutational	observably	octomerous	off the boil	oligarchic
nutcracker	observance	octonarian	off the cuff	oligoclase
nut factory	observancy	octonarius	off-the-face	oligoester
nutmeg-bird	obsidional	octopamine	off the hook	oligomeric
nutmeg tree	obsoletely	octoploidy	off the mark	oligomycin
nutritious	obsoletion	octopodous	off the pace	oligophagy
nutty slack	obsoletism	octopusher	off the rack	oligopsony
nyctalopia	obstacular	octovalent	off the reel	olistolith
nyctalopic	obstetrics	oculogyral	off-the-road	olivaceous
nyctinasty	obstinance	oculogyric	off the wall	olive crown
nympholept	obstinancy	oculomotor	off the wind	olive green
nystagmoid	obstructor	oculonasal	of like mind	olive-plant
oafishness	obtainable	odd and even	of no effect	Olonetsian
oak-barrens	obtainment	odditorium	of one piece	Omarianism
oaken towel	obtruncate	odd-pinnate	of one's will	ombrometer
oak-opening	obturation	odiousness	of one's word	ombrophile
oak-spangle	obtuseness	odontalgia	of some size	ombrophobe
oath-helper	obvelation	odontalgic	oftentimes	omega minus
obbligatos	obvolution	odontocete	of the blood	Omega point
obdurately	occasional	odontogeny	of the clock	omentopexy
obduration	occasioner	odontology	oh be joyful	ommatidial
obediently	occidental	odorimeter	oil-clothed	ommatidium
obeisantly	Occitanian	odorimetry	oil company	ommochrome
obeliscoid	occlusally	odoriphore	oil-gilding	omnibus box
obeliskoid	occultness	odynometer	oil of amber	omnificent
obituarial	occupation	oedematose	oil of roses	omnigenous
obituarian	occupative	oedematous	oil of spike	omnilucent
obituaries	occupiable	Oedipodean	oil of thuja	omnipotent
obituarily	occurrence	oenologist	oil of thyme	omniscient
obituarist	occurrency	oenomaniac	oil on water	omnivorous
obituarize	oceanarium	oenophilic	oil-painter	omophagist
objectable	ocean-basin	oesophagal	oilskinned	omphalitis
object-ball	ocean-going	oesophagus	Oireachtas	on a bowline
object code	oceanicity	oestradiol	Old Academy	on all fours
objectival	oceanology	of all loves	Old British	on all hands

on a platter	on the march	opera buffa	orcharding	orological
on approval	on the outer	opera cloak	orchardist	oropendola
on behalf of	on the prowl	opera house	orchardman	oropharynx
on business	on the queer	opera seria	orchardmen	orotundity
on campaign	on the quiet	operatable	orchestral	Oroya fever
once in a way	on the rails	operculate	orchestric	orphan drug
oncologist	on the rocks	operettist	orchideous	orphanhood
on commando	on the ropes	ophicleide	orchiopexy	orpheonist
oncosphere	on the scene	ophiolater	ordainment	Orphically
one and only	on the scent	ophiolatry	ordeal bean	orthoclase
one another	on the scoop	ophiolitic	order about	orthoconic
one at a time	on the shelf	ophiomancy	Order Order	orthodoxal
one fine day	on the skids	ophthalmia	order paper	orthodoxly
one-nighter	on the slate	ophthalmic	ordinaries	orthodrome
one-of-a-kind	on the sneak	opiniative	ordinarily	orthoepist
one or other	on the spree	opinionate	ordination	orthogonal
one-over-one	on the stuff	opinionist	ordinative	orthograde
one-plus-one	on the stump	opisometer	ordonnance	orthometry
one-sidedly	on the table	opisthotic	Ordovician	orthopedic
one-striper	on the tapes	opium dream	Oregon pine	orthophony
one-time pad	on the tapis	opium joint	oreography	orthophoto
one too many	on the tiles	opium poppy	organ clock	orthophyre
one-worlder	on the track	opossuming	organ-coral	orthopnoea
on good form	on the tramp	oppilation	organellar	orthopraxy
onion couch	on the twist	opposeless	organicism	Orthoptera
onion-grass	on the wagon	opposingly	organicist	orthoptere
onisciform	on the watch	oppositely	organicity	orthoptics
onlay graft	on the water	opposition	organic law	orthoptist
on my honour	on the way in	oppositive	organigram	orthotomic
on occasion	on the whole	oppression	organismal	orthotopic
onocentaur	ontogenist	oppressive	organismic	orthotropy
onomastics	ontologism	opprobrium	organistic	or whatever
on one's back	ontologist	oppugnable	organ-metal	or whenever
on one's feet	ontologize	oppugnance	organogeny	or wherever
on one's game	on transmit	oppugnancy	organogram	oryctology
on one's head	onwardness	optatively	organology	oscheocele
on one's jack	on your mark	optical art	organonomy	oscillator
on one's legs	onyx marble	optic angle	organ-point	oscitation
on one's mind	oophoritis	optic nerve	orguinette	osculation
on one's toes	oops-a-daisy	optic tract	orientable	osculatory
on schedule	oozlum bird	optimality	orientalia	Osiandrian
on the alert	opacimeter	optimistic	orientally	osmeterium
on the beach	opalescent	optionally	orientated	osmication
on the bench	opaqueness	option card	originally	osmiridium
on the blink	open access	optionless	originator	osmoceptor
on the block	open cheque	optometric	orimulsion	osmolality
on the books	open dating	opus magnum	Orimulsion	osmolarity
on the booze	open-handed	orache moth	orinasally	osmometric
on the brain	open letter	oracularly	Orion's belt	osmophilic
on the buroo	open market	orange-chip	orismology	osmophoric
on the cards	open-minded	orange dove	Orkney vole	osphradial
on the cheap	open-necked	orange lily	ornamental	osphradium
on the crook	open outcry	orange moth	ornamenter	ossiferous
on the cross	open prison	orange peel	ornateness	ostensible
on the dodge	open sandal	orangequit	orneriness	ostensibly
on the drink	open season	orangeries	ornithopod	osteoblast
on the fritz	open secret	orange-root	ornithosis	osteoclast
on the green	open sesame	orange tree	ornithotic	osteocolla
on the house	Open Sesame	orange-wood	orogenesis	osteologic
on the latch	open system	oratorical	orogenetic	osteolysis
on the level	open-topped	oratorship	orogenital	osteolytic
on the loose	openworked	orbiculate	orographic	osteomancy

osteometry	outmodedly	outwrought	overlavish	overtopple
osteopathy	out of blast	ouvrierism	overlaying	overtravel
osteophyte	out of blood	Oval Office	overlength	overtumble
Ostpolitik	out of court	ovariotomy	overliness	overturner
ostraceous	out of doors	oven-bottom	overlisten	overviewer
ostreiform	out of habit	overabound	overlocker	overwander
ostrichism	out of heart	overaction	overlooker	overweight
Oswego bass	out of joint	overactive	overmantel	overwinder
othergates	out of order	overageing	overmantle	overwinter
otherguess	out of phase	over and out	overmaster	overwisely
other place	out of place	overbelief	overmatter	ovicapsule
other ranks	out of plumb	overbidder	overmickle	oviposited
otherwhere	out of print	overbitter	over-mighty	ovipositor
other woman	out of reach	overbleach	overmodest	ovogenesis
other world	out-of-round	overblouse	overnicely	ovogenetic
otioseness	out of scale	overboldly	overnicety	owlishness
otological	out of score	overbought	overparted	owl monkeys
otomycosis	out of shape	overbridge	overplease	owl-swallow
ottava rima	out of sight	overbright	overpraise	oxalacetic
otter-board	out of sorts	overbudget	overpreach	oxalic acid
otter civet	out-of-state	overburden	overpunish	Oxbridgean
otter-hound	out of stock	overcanopy	overrashly	ox-eye daisy
otter-shell	out of taste	overcharge	overreckon	Oxford bags
otter shrew	out of touch	overchosen	overrecord	Oxford blue
otter-trawl	out of truth	overclothe	over-refine	Oxford clay
Ottomanism	out of twist	overcoated	overrefine	Oxford Down
Ottomanize	out of whack	overcolour	overriding	Oxford grey
ouananiche	out on a limb	overcommit	overrunner	Oxford shoe
oudstryder	out-patient	overcooked	overshadow	Oxford weed
Ouidaesque	outpatient	overcutter	overshroud	oxidizable
Ouija board	out-pension	overdaring	overslaugh	oxosteroid
Our Saviour	outperform	overdeepen	oversleeve	oxprenolol
out and away	outpouring	overdesign	overspeech	oxybromide
out at heels	outpromise	overdesire	overspread	oxycephaly
outbackery	out-quarter	overdilute	overspring	oxygen acid
outbalance	outrageous	overdosage	oversprung	oxygenator
outblossom	outrigging	overdrawer	oversquare	oxygen debt
outbreathe	outrightly	overeasily	overssized	oxygenless
outbreeder	outs and ins	overesteem	overstayer	oxygen mask
outcasting	outscourer	overexcite	overstitch	oxygen tent
out-college	outsetting	overexpand	overstorey	oxymoronic
out-cricket	outsettler	overexpose	overstrain	oxyphilous
out-dooring	outshining	overextend	overstream	oxyproline
outdoorish	outside job	overfavour	overstress	oxy-propane
outdraught	outside man	overflight	overstrict	oxytonical
outdweller	outsiderly	overfondly	overstride	oyster-bank
outer forme	outskirter	overfulfil	overstrike	oyster-boat
Outer House	outsparkle	overgovern	overstring	oyster-farm
outer space	outstander	overgreedy	overstrode	oyster-fish
outer woman	outstation	overground	overstroke	oyster-like
outer world	outstretch	overgrowth	overstrong	oyster loaf
outfielder	outswagger	overhanded	overstruck	ozone layer
outflowing	outsweeten	overhasten	overstrung	ozonolysis
outgassing	out-swinger	overhearer	oversubtle	ozonolytic
outgeneral	outswinger	overhoused	oversupply	ozonometer
outglitter	out-thunder	overinform	overtaking	ozonometry
outgrowing	out to grass	over-insure	overtender	ozonoscope
outhousing	out to lunch	overinsure	over the sea	pace bowler
outjockeys	outvillain	overjacket	over-the-top	pacemaking
outlandish	outward man	overkindly	over the way	pace-setter
outmeasure	outworking	overlabour	overthrust	pachycauly
outmigrant	outwrestle	overlander	overthwart	pacificate

pacificism	Paisleyite	pancratium	paperboard	paragaster
pacificist	palace coup	pancreatic	paperbound	parageusia
Pacific rim	Palaeocene	pancreatin	paper cable	paraglider
Pacific Rim	Palaeogene	pandectist	paper chain	paraglossa
pacifistic	palaeolith	pandemonic	paper-chase	paragneiss
pack animal	palaeopole	panegyrise	paperchase	paragnosis
packet-boat	palaeowind	panegyrist	paper cover	Paraguayan
packet ship	Palaeozoic	panegyrize	paper-faced	parahelium
packet soup	palaestral	panel board	paper guide	parakeelya
packing box	palaestric	panel fence	paper hanky	parakiting
pack-leader	palagonite	panel gauge	paperiness	paralipsis
pack-needle	palatalise	panel-house	paper-knife	paralleled
pack or peel	palatality	panel plane	paperknife	parallelly
pack-pedlar	palatalize	panel stamp	papermaker	paralogise
packsaddle	palateless	panel study	paper money	paralogism
pack-saddle	palatially	panel-thief	paper plate	paralogist
pack-straps	palatinate	panel truck	paper round	paralogize
pack them in	palatogram	Pangasinan	paper route	paralogous
packthread	paleaceous	pangenesis	paper shale	Paralympic
padded cell	Palermitan	pangenetic	paper-shell	paramagnet
paddle ball	palfrenier	panguingue	paper tiger	paramecium
paddle boat	palimpsest	panhandler	paper towel	paramedian
paddle-crab	palindrome	Panhard rod	paper-works	parametral
paddlefish	palisading	panic party	Papiamento	parametric
paddle foot	palisander	paniculate	papilionid	parametron
paddle-like	palladious	Panislamic	papillated	paramnesia
paddle-wood	pallasitic	pani-wallah	papillitis	paramnesic
Paddy Doyle	pall-bearer	panjandrum	papillomas	paramoudra
paddy field	pallbearer	pannier bag	papistical	paramouncy
paddymelon	pallescent	pannierman	papulation	paramyosin
paddy wagon	palliation	panography	papulosity	Parana pine
Paddy wagon	palliative	panophobia	papyrology	paranormal
paddywhack	palliatory	panopticon	para-aortic	parapatric
pad the hoof	pallidness	panoramist	Parabellum	paraphasia
paederasty	palmaceous	panpsychic	parabiosis	paraphasic
paedeutics	palmatifid	pan-pudding	parabiotic	parapherna
paediatric	palm branch	pan-scourer	parablepsy	paraphilia
paedicator	palmchrist	Panslavism	parabolise	paraphilic
paedocracy	palmelloid	Panslavist	parabolist	paraphonia
paedophile	palmer-worm	pansophism	parabolize	paraphonic
paedotribe	palm-kernel	panspermia	paraboloid	paraphrase
Paelignian	Palm Sunday	pantalette	paracasein	paraphrast
paganistic	palm weevil	pantheress	para-church	paraphysis
pageanteer	palo blanco	pantherine	parachuter	paraplegia
page charge	palsy-walsy	pantherish	parade drum	paraplegic
page-galley	paltriness	pantie hose	parade ring	parapodial
page-turner	paludament	pantie raid	paradiddle	parapodium
pagination	palustrine	pantograph	paradingly	parapraxis
pagoda tree	palynology	pantologic	paradisaic	para-rescue
paideutics	pampas deer	pantometer	paradisean	paraselene
pailletted	pampelmoes	pantometry	paradisiac	parasexual
painkiller	pamphleted	pantomimic	paradisial	parasitise
painlessly	pamphletic	pantophagy	paradisian	parasitism
paintbrush	pan-African	pantoscope	paradoctor	parasitize
painted cup	Panamanian	pantothere	paradoxism	parasitoid
paint-frame	pan-and-tilt	pan-washing	paradoxist	parasol ant
paintiness	pan-Arabism	papal court	paradoxure	parastades
paint spray	Pancake Day	papal cross	paraenesis	parastatal
paint stick	pancake-ice	papal vicar	paraenetic	parastichy
paintstick	panchronic	papaverine	paraffinic	paratactic
pair of oars	pancosmism	papaverous	parafiscal	parathesis
Paisleyism	pancratist	paper birch	parafoveal	paratroops

paravisual	parramatta	pastorally	pave the way	pecker-head
paraxially	parricidal	pastorship	paving-tile	peckerwood
paraxylene	parrotbill	pastry-cook	pawnbroker	pectinated
parazonium	parrot-coal	pasturable	pawn-ticket	peculation
parcel bomb	parrot-fish	Patagonian	payability	peculative
parcel-gilt	parrotfish	Patavinian	pay-as-you-go	peculiarly
parcellate	parrot-like	Patavinity	Payne's grey	pedagogics
parcelling	parsley-bed	patch-board	pay-off line	pedagogism
parcel post	parson-bird	patchboard	pay station	pedagogist
parcel-wise	parsonhood	patchiness	pea-brained	pedalboard
parchmenty	parsonical	patch panel	Peace Corps	pedal cycle
pardonable	partakable	patchworky	peacefully	pedalferic
pardonably	parthenian	pâté maison	peacemaker	pedal point
pardon-bell	partialise	patentable	peace prize	pedal power
pardonless	partialism	patent roll	peach aphid	pedal straw
pareiasaur	partialist	Patent Roll	peach-black	pedantical
parenchyma	partiality	Pateresque	peach-bloom	pedanticly
parentally	partialize	paternally	peacherino	pedantries
parent cell	partial sum	pâte tendre	peachiness	pederastic
parentelic	participle	patha patha	peach Melba	pedestrial
parenteral	particular	pathematic	peach-stone	pedestrian
parenthood	partisanly	pathetical	peachy-keen	pede-window
parentless	partnering	pathfinder	peacockery	pediatrics
parents' day	partocracy	path length	peacock-eye	pedication
parent ship	partridges	path-master	Peacockian	pedicatory
parentship	parturiate	pathogenic	peacockish	pedicellar
par exemple	parturient	pathognomy	peacock ore	pedicelled
parfocally	party-liner	pathologic	peakedness	pediculous
pariah brig	party piano	pathotoxin	peak factor	pedicurist
Parian ware	parvenudom	patibulary	peak-to-peak	pedigerous
paribuntal	parvenuism	patibulate	Peano curve	pediluvium
pari-mutuel	parvovirus	patination	peanut worm	pedimental
Paris daisy	pas ciseaux	patisserie	pear-blight	pedimented
Paris green	pas d'action	patriality	pearl-berry	pedologist
parish mass	pasigraphy	patriarchy	pearl-diver	pedomotive
parish poor	Pasionaria	patriation	pearl-fruit	pedosphere
parish pump	pasquinade	patriciate	pearliness	pedotrophy
parish work	passageway	patricidal	pearl onion	peduncular
park course	passed pawn	patrilocal	pearl-perch	peely-wally
parking bay	passiflora	patrioteer	pearl-shell	peeping Tom
parking lot	passimeter	patriotess	pearlsides	peerie folk
parking tag	passionary	patriotism	pearl-stone	peerlessly
park-keeper	passionate	patristics	pearl-white	peer review
park-leaves	passionful	patrocliny	pearly king	pegmatitic
parliament	Passionist	patrolette	Pearly King	peg-tankard
parlour-car	passivator	patrolling	pearmonger	Peirce's Law
parmacetty	pass muster	patronizer	Pearsonian	pejoration
parmigiana	pass the hat	patronless	pear-sucker	pejorative
Parnassian	pasteboard	patronship	peasantess	Peking duck
Parnellism	paste grain	patronymic	peasantism	pelargonic
Parnellite	pastellist	pattawalla	peasantist	pelargonin
parodiable	pasteurise	patten-shoe	pease-brose	Pele's tears
parodistic	Pasteurism	patterning	pea-shooter	pellagrose
paroecious	pasteurize	patternise	peashooter	pellagrous
paronychia	paste-water	patternism	peau-de-soie	pelletable
paronymous	past future	patternist	pebble-dash	pellet bell
parovarian	pasticcios	patternize	pebble lens	pellet bomb
parovarium	pasticheur	patter-song	pebble tool	pelletizer
paroxysmal	pastillage	patulously	pebble-ware	pellet mill
paroxysmic	past master	Paulianist	peccadillo	pellicular
paroxytone	pastorales	Paul Revere	pêche Melba	pellucidly
parqueting	pastoralia	paunchiest	pecked line	peltmonger

pelvic arch	pentatomid	perflation	peritectic	personally
pelvic brim	pentatonic	perfoliate	peritoneal	personalty
pelvimeter	pentimenti	perforable	peritoneum	personator
pelvimetry	pentimento	perforated	periungual	personeity
pelycosaur	pentograph	perforator	periwigged	personhood
pemphigoid	pentosuria	perforce of	periwinkle	personkind
pemphigous	pentosuric	performing	perjurious	per stirpes
penalty box	pentstemon	pergelisol	perlaceous	perstringe
penannular	penumbrous	periapical	perlection	persuading
pencil beam	peoplehood	periastral	permafrost	persuasion
pencil case	people-king	periastron	permanence	persuasive
pencil-line	peopleless	pericardia	permanency	pertinence
pencilling	people's car	pericardic	permansive	pertinency
pencil mark	people's war	pericentre	permeation	perturbant
pendeloque	pepperbush	periclinal	permeative	perturbate
pendentive	peppercorn	periclinia	permethrin	perversely
Penelopean	pepperette	periculous	permillage	perversion
Penelopize	pepperidge	pericyclic	permirific	perversity
penetrable	pepper mill	pericystic	permission	perversive
penetralia	peppermint	peridental	permissive	peshwaship
penetrance	pepper-root	peridermal	permitting	Pestalozzi
penetrator	pepper soup	peridinian	Permo-Trias	pesterment
pen-feather	pepper tree	peridotite	permutable	pestersome
penguinery	pepper-vine	periegesis	Pernambuco	pesticidal
penicillia	pepperwood	perifoveal	pernicious	pestilence
penicillin	pepperwort	perifusate	pernickety	petaloidal
penicillus	pepsinogen	perifusion	pernoctate	petechiate
peninsular	peptizable	perigonial	perofskite	Peter-penny
penitently	peptolysis	perigonium	peroration	Peter's fish
penmanship	peptolytic	perigynium	peroratory	petiteness
pennatulid	peptonizer	perigynous	perovskite	petitional
penny-a-line	peptonuria	perihaemal	peroxidase	petitionee
penny black	peracetate	perihelion	peroxidize	petitioner
penny cress	peralkalic	perikaryal	peroxisome	petit point
penny-grass	percentage	perikaryon	perpension	petits pois
penny plain	percentile	perilla oil	perpetrate	Petrarchan
pennyroyal	percentual	perilously	perpetuana	petrescent
penny Scots	perception	peril point	perpetuate	petrogenic
penny stock	perceptive	perimetral	perpetuity	petroglyph
penny-stone	perceptron	perimetric	perplexing	petrograph
pennyworth	perceptual	perimysium	perplexity	petrolatum
penologist	perchloric	perineural	perquisite	petrol blue
pen-pushing	percipient	periocular	perrhenate	petrol bomb
pensionary	percolator	periodical	perruquier	petroleous
pensioneer	perculsion	periosteal	per saltire	petrol head
pension off	percurrent	periosteum	persecutee	petrolless
pentachord	percursory	peripatize	persecutor	petrologic
pentagonal	percussion	peripeteia	Persian cat	petrol pump
pentahedra	percussive	peripherad	Persianist	Petronella
pentalogue	perdricide	peripheral	Persianize	petrosilex
pentameral	perdurable	peripheric	Persian red	pets' corner
pentameric	perdurably	periphonic	Persian rug	pettedness
pentameter	perdurance	periphrase	persicaria	pettichaps
pentapedal	père et fils	periportal	persiennes	petticoaty
pentaploid	peremptory	peripteral	persiflage	petting zoo
pentapolis	perfect gas	periscopic	persifleur	petty canon
pentaprism	perfection	perishable	persistent	petty morel
pentastich	Perfectist	perishably	persistive	petulantly
pentastome	perfective	perishless	personable	Petzval sum
pentastyle	perfervour	perishment	personably	pewterwort
Pentateuch	perficient	peristomal	personal ad	phagedaena
pentathlon	perfidious	peristylar	personalia	phagocytic

phagosomal	philosophe	photophily	picket line	pilgriming
phalangeal	philosophy	photophore	picking peg	pilgrimise
phalangist	phlebogram	photo-print	pickpocket	pilgrimize
Phalangist	phlebology	photo-recce	pick-up tube	piliferous
phalangite	phlebotomy	photo-shock	picnic area	piligerous
phalangium	phlegmasia	photo shoot	picnickery	pillar-buoy
Phaleucian	phlegmatic	photostory	picnicking	pillar-file
phallicism	phlegmless	phototaxis	picnic meal	pillarless
phallocrat	phlegmonic	phototoxic	picric acid	pillar rose
phalloidin	phlogistic	phototroph	picrotoxin	pill-beetle
phanerogam	phlogiston	phototropy	pictograph	pilliwinks
phantasied	phlogopite	phragmites	pictorical	pillow-bere
phantasies	phocomelia	phrase book	Picts' house	pillow-book
phantasise	phocomelic	phraseless	picturable	pillowcase
phantasize	Phoenician	phrase name	picturedom	pillow lace
phantasmal	pholcodine	phrenology	picture hat	pillow lava
phantasmic	phone booth	phthisical	piece-goods	pillow-sham
phantastry	phonematic	phthisicky	piece-mould	pillowslip
Pharisaean	phone patch	phycobilin	piece-price	pillow sofa
Pharisaism	phoneyness	phycobiont	pie-counter	pillow talk
pharmacies	phonically	phylactery	pied-à-terre	pillow tank
pharmacist	phonogenic	phylarchic	Pied Friars	pillow-word
Pharsalian	phonograph	phyllodial	pie diagram	pill-popper
pharyngeal	phonolitic	phyllosome	piemontite	pill pusher
phascogale	phonologic	phyllotaxy	pierceable	pilocystic
phase angle	phonometer	phylloxera	piercement	pilot-bread
phase-array	phonometry	phylogenic	piercingly	pilot cable
phasemeter	phonotypic	Physeptone	pier-master	pilot chute
phaseollin	phorometer	physiatric	pier-mirror	pilot-cloth
phase space	phoronomic	physically	Piesporter	pilot-flame
phasically	phosgenite	physic-ball	piet-my-vrou	pilot house
pheasantry	phosphagen	physicking	piezometer	pilot light
phelloderm	phosphated	physiocrat	pig-boiling	pilot-major
phenacaine	phosphatic	physiology	pigeon drop	pilot snake
phenacetin	phosphinic	phytocidal	pigeongram	pilot valve
phenelzine	phosphonic	phytogenic	pigeon-hawk	pilot whale
phenformin	phosphoric	phytolacca	pigeon-hole	Piltdowner
phenocryst	phosphorus	phytometer	pigeonitic	pimento red
phenolized	phosphoryl	phytomonad	pigeon-loft	pimpmobile
phenologic	Photianism	phytophagy	pigeon pair	pinacocyte
phenomenal	Photianist	phytotoxic	pigeon-plum	pinacoidal
phenomenon	photically	phytotoxin	pigeon-post	pina colada
phenotypic	photodimer	pianissimi	pigeonries	pinacoline
pheromonal	photodiode	pianissimo	pigeon tick	pinacolone
philatelic	photo-essay	pianoforte	pigeon-toed	pince-nezed
Philippian	photoflash	piano organ	pigeon-weed	pincer-like
philippina	photoflood	piano score	pigeon-wing	pinchingly
Philippine	photogenic	piano stool	pigeon-wood	pinchpenny
Philippini	photograph	piano-tuner	piggy-wiggy	pinch-point
Philippise	photolitho	picaresque	pig-hunting	pinch-waist
Philippist	photolysis	picayunish	pig in a poke	pinch-wheel
Philippize	photolytic	Piccadilly	pigmentary	pincushion
Philistian	Photomaton	piccalilli	pig-sticker	pineal body
Philistine	photomesic	piccaninny	pigsticker	pine-barren
phillumeny	photomeson	piccoloist	pig-washing	pine beauty
philocynic	photometer	pichiciago	piked whale	pine-kernel
philologer	photometry	pichiciego	pilastered	pine lander
philologic	photomixer	pick a fight	pilastrade	pine linnet
philologue	photomural	pickaninny	pile-driver	pine-lizard
philomathy	photonovel	pick a thank	piledriver	pine marten
philopatry	photopathy	pick-cheese	pilgrimage	pine-needle
philopoena	photophile	picket-boat	pilgrimess	piney resin

pin-feather	pitchiness	plank-owner	play-centre	plough back
pinguecula	pitchmeter	plank sheer	play-doctor	plough-beam
pinguicula	pitch-penny	plank steak	playfellow	ploughbote
pinguidity	pitchstone	planktonic	playground	plough-foot
pinguitude	pit-headman	planlessly	play hookey	plough-gate
pin-jointed	pitheciine	planometer	play it cool	plough-gear
pink button	pith helmet	planosolic	playleader	plough-head
pink chaser	pithiatism	planospore	playmonger	plough-iron
pink-collar	Pithiviers	plansifter	play possum	plough-land
pink-footed	pitilessly	plantation	play scales	ploughland
pink salmon	pitot meter	planterdom	play school	plough-line
pink-washed	pityriasis	plant-louse	playsomely	plough-shoe
pinnatifid	pivotalism	plashingly	playstreet	plough-soil
pinnothere	pivotal man	plasma cell	play the ape	plough-stot
pinocytose	pivot class	plasmacyte	play the fox	plough-tail
pinosylvin	pivot-joint	plasmagene	play the hop	pluck a rose
pinpointed	pixelation	Plasmochin	play the man	pluckiness
pinstriped	pixilation	plasmocyte	play the wag	plug-drawer
pinstriper	pixillated	plasmodial	play truant	plug nozzle
Pintsch gas	pizzicatos	plasmodium	playwright	plug-switch
pioneerdom	place brick	plasmogamy	playwriter	plug-uglies
pious fraud	place horse	plasmolyse	pleadingly	plumassier
piped music	place-money	plasmolyte	pleasanter	plum-colour
pipelining	placentary	plasmosome	pleasantly	plummeting
Pipe-Office	place-value	plasmotomy	pleasantry	plumminess
pipe-opener	placidness	plastering	pleasaunce	plum tomato
piperazine	placodioid	plasticate	pleasingly	plunderage
piperidine	plagiarise	plastician	pleasurist	plunderous
pipe wrench	plagiarism	plasticine	plebeiance	plunge bath
piping crow	plagiarist	Plasticine	plebeianly	plunge pool
pipperidge	plagiarize	plasticise	plebiscita	plungingly
pipsissewa	plagiosere	plasticism	plebiscite	pluperfect
Piranesian	plague-flea	plasticity	pledgeable	pluralizer
pirimicarb	plagueless	plasticize	pledge card	plurimodal
pirouetter	plague pipe	plastidome	pleiomazia	plus-foured
piscifauna	plaguesome	plastidule	pleiotropy	plushiness
pisolithic	plague spot	plastifier	plenilunal	pluteiform
piss artist	plainchant	plastogamy	plenilunar	plutocracy
piss-cutter	plain flour	plat du jour	plenishing	plutogogue
piss-taking	Plains Cree	plate count	plentitude	plutolater
pistachios	plain tripe	plated wire	pleochroic	plutolatry
pistillary	plain weave	plate glass	pleomastia	plutomania
pistillate	plait-dance	platelayer	pleomorphy	plutomanic
pistilline	planarioid	platemaker	pleonastic	plutonomic
pistillode	planchette	plate metal	pleonectic	pluviosity
pistillody	Planck's law	plate paper	plerematic	pneumatics
pistilloid	plane chart	platformed	pleromatic	pneumatism
pistolgram	plane crash	platformer	plerophory	pneumatist
pistol grip	planer-tree	Platformer	plesiosaur	pneumatize
pistol-hand	planeshear	Platonical	pleurodont	pneumocele
pistolling	plane stock	platteland	pleurotomy	pneumogram
pistol-shot	plane-table	platterful	pleximeter	pneumotach
pistol-whip	planetaria	platycodon	plexometer	pochade box
piston-head	planet cage	platymeria	pliability	pocketable
piston ring	planetfall	platymeric	pliantness	pocketbook
piston slap	planet-gear	platypuses	plimsolled	pocketfuls
Pitcairner	planet-wide	plauditory	pliosaurus	pocket-hole
pitch-black	plangently	play-acting	ploddingly	pocketless
pitch-brand	plangorous	play around	plonkingly	pocket-like
pitch curve	planholder	playboyish	plottingly	pocket-size
pitcherful	planimeter	playbroker	ploughable	pocket veto
pitch-fibre	planimetry	play-by-play	plough-alms	pock-marked

pocomaniac	Police Motu	polygenous	pomiferous	porrection
podiatrist	police trap	polyglycol	pommelling	portacabin
podothecal	policlinic	polygonize	pomologist	portacaval
poena damni	policy loan	polygonous	Pomoranian	Portakabin
poetastery	policy-slip	polygraphy	pompelmous	portal vein
poetically	polioviral	polygynist	ponce about	portamenti
Poetic Edda	poliovirus	polygynous	pond-barrow	portamento
poeticizer	polishable	polyhalite	ponderable	port-crayon
poeticness	polishedly	polyhedral	ponderance	portcullis
poetry-book	Polishness	polyhedric	ponderancy	portentous
poetryless	politburos	polyhedron	ponderment	porterless
pogamoggan	politeness	polyhistor	pond-skater	porterlike
pogonotomy	politician	polyhybrid	pond slider	portership
pohutukawa	politicise	polyhydric	ponerology	portfolios
poignantly	politicize	polyketide	ponticello	portionary
poikilitic	politicked	polylectal	pontifical	portionist
poinsettia	polkamania	polylithic	pontifices	portliness
point angle	pollen-cell	polymastia	pony-engine	portocaval
point-blank	pollenless	polymastic	pony report	port of call
point block	pollen-tube	polymathic	poodle-fake	port of exit
point break	pollinator	polymerase	pooh-pooher	portolanos
pointed fox	pollinctor	polymeride	Pooh-sticks	Portuguese
point-event	polling day	polymerise	pools panel	positional
point focus	pollinical	polymerism	poor fellow	positioner
point group	poll parrot	polymerize	poor people	positively
pointleted	Poll-parrot	polymerous	poor relief	positivism
point of lay	poll-rating	polymethyl	poorshouse	positivist
point paper	pollutedly	polymetric	pop culture	positivity
pointy-head	polo collar	polymictic	Popemobile	positronic
Poiseuille	polocrosse	polymorphy	popishness	posnjakite
poisonable	polo-necked	Polynesian	poplar grey	possession
poison book	Polovtsian	polynomial	poplar hawk	possessive
poison-bulb	Poltalloch	polyocracy	poplinette	possessory
poison-bush	polyanthus	polyolefin	popocratic	postage due
poison pill	polyarchic	polyparies	poppet-head	postal card
poison-tree	polyatomic	polyphagia	popularise	postal code
poison vine	polybasite	polyphasic	popularish	postal note
poisonwood	polycarpic	Polyphemic	popularism	postal vote
Poissonian	polycation	Polyphemus	popularist	post-and-pan
Poisson law	polychaete	polyphenol	popularity	post-bellum
poke-bonnet	polycholia	polyphonic	popularize	post-chaise
poke-greens	polychoral	polyploidy	population	post-climax
poker-faced	polychrest	polypnoeic	populistic	postclitic
poke-sleeve	polychrome	polypodies	populously	post-coital
polar curve	polychromy	polypoidal	poriferous	post coitum
polarities	polyclimax	polyprotic	porismatic	post-common
polar light	polyclinic	polyrhythm	pork barrel	postcostal
polarogram	polyclonal	polysarcia	pork-pie hat	postcyclic
polar orbit	polycormic	polysemous	pornbroker	postdating
polar plant	polycotton	polysomaty	pornocracy	postdental
polatouche	polycyclic	polyspermy	pornograph	post-editor
pole-jumper	polycystic	polystelic	pornophile	post-exilic
polemicise	polydactyl	polytheism	porogamous	post factum
polemicist	polydipsia	polytheist	porousness	post festum
polemicize	polydymite	polythelia	porpentine	postholder
polemology	polyethene	polythetic	Porphyrian	posthumous
polemonium	polyethnic	polytocous	porphyries	postillate
poles apart	polygamist	polytomous	porphyrise	postillion
pole-screen	polygamize	polytropic	porphyrite	post-larval
policeable	polygamous	polytypism	porphyrize	postliminy
police bail	polygenism	polyvalent	porphyroid	postmaster
police boat	polygenist	Pomeranian	porraceous	postmature

postmedial	powder-like	prayer-bead	predecease	prenuptial
post-modern	powder-mill	prayer-bell	pre-decimal	pre-Oedipal
postmodern	powder-plot	prayer book	predeclare	pre-orbital
post-mortem	powder puff	prayer card	predestine	pre-package
post-ocular	powder room	prayer-desk	predestiny	prepalatal
post office	powder snow	prayer-flag	prediality	preparable
Post Office	power block	prayerless	predicable	preparator
post-partum	power board	prayer-mill	predicator	preparedly
post-runner	power brake	prayer-wall	prediction	prepayable
postscript	power cable	prayerwise	predictive	prepayment
post-season	power-crane	praying mat	predictory	prepensely
postulancy	power-drive	preachable	predispose	pre-planned
postulator	power élite	preach down	prednisone	prepollent
postulatum	powerfully	preacherly	pre-eminent	prepolymer
postverbal	powerhouse	preachiest	pre-emption	prepositor
potability	power level	preachment	pre-emptive	prepossess
potamogale	power plant	pre-adamite	preen gland	prepotence
potamology	powerplant	pre-adjunct	pre-English	prepotency
potash alum	power point	prealbumin	pre-exilian	preppiness
potato-bean	power train	preallable	prefashion	preprimate
potato-cake	pozzolanic	preallably	prefecture	pre-process
potato chip	practicant	preambular	preferable	preprocess
potato fern	practician	preamplify	preferably	pre-program
potato hook	practising	pre-animism	preference	preprogram
potato-ring	praecocial	pre-appoint	preferment	prep school
potato-trap	praecordia	pre-arrange	preferring	prepuberal
potato-vine	Praedesque	prearrange	prefixable	prepuberty
Potawatomi	praefervid	pre-baiting	prefixally	prepunched
pot-bellied	praelector	prebendary	prefixture	pre-qualify
pot bellies	praeludium	prebiology	preformism	prequalify
pot courage	praemunire	precarious	preformist	Pre-Raphael
potentiate	praepositi	precaution	prefrontal	pre-release
potentilla	praepostor	precedence	pregenital	prerequire
potentness	praeputium	precedency	preglacial	presageful
pot-furnace	praesidium	precentral	pregnantly	presbyopia
pot-hunting	Praesidium	precentrix	preharvest	presbyopic
pot-pourris	praetorial	preceptial	prehensile	presbytery
pot-shooter	praetorian	preception	prehension	prescience
pot-shotter	praetorium	preceptive	prehensive	pre-scoring
potter's rot	pragmatica	preceptory	prehistory	prescriber
potter wasp	pragmatics	preceptual	prehominid	presension
potty-chair	pragmatise	precession	pre-imagine	present-day
potty-train	pragmatism	preciosity	pre-incline	presential
pot-valiant	pragmatist	preciously	pre-Islamic	presentism
pot-walling	pragmatize	precipitin	prejudiced	presentist
pouch-mouth	prairie dog	Preclassic	prelatical	presentoir
Poulsen arc	prairie fox	preclusion	prelection	pre-service
pouncet-box	prairie hen	preclusive	prelingual	preserving
pound brush	praiseless	precocious	prelogical	presidence
pound close	praise name	precognise	preludious	presidency
pound-force	praise poem	precognize	premarital	presidiary
pound-house	praise poet	precompose	premaxilla	presignify
pound overt	praise song	preconcert	premedical	press agent
pound Scots	praisingly	precondemn	pre-meiotic	press baron
poundstone	praisseagh	precontour	pre-mention	press-board
powderable	pram-pusher	precordial	premiation	pressboard
powder base	prandially	precordium	pre-milking	press cloth
powder blue	prat digger	precurrent	premixture	press corps
powder-burn	prate-apace	precursive	premonitor	press flesh
powder-down	pratincole	precursory	prenatally	press-house
powder-horn	praxeology	predaceous	prenominal	pressingly
powderless	praxiology	predacious	pre-nuclear	press-money

press proof	primevally	procedendo	proinsulin	propellent
pressurise	primiparae	procedural	projectile	propelling
pressurize	primipilar	proceeding	projection	propendent
prestation	primipilus	process ink	projective	propensely
prestellar	primo buffo	procession	projecture	propension
pre-stretch	primordial	processive	projicient	propensity
presumable	primordian	processual	prokaryote	propeptide
presumably	primordium	prochloraz	prokinesis	proper name
presumedly	primrosing	pro-choicer	prokinetic	properness
presuppose	princehood	proclaimer	proleptics	proper noun
presystole	princelier	proclivity	proletaire	Propertian
pretendant	princelike	procoelous	proletkult	propertied
pretendent	princeling	procreator	prolixness	properties
pretending	princeship	procrypsis	proloculus	prophecies
pre-tension	princessly	procryptic	prolocutor	prophesied
pretension	prince-wood	proctalgia	prologizer	prophesier
pretensive	principate	proctology	prologuing	prophesies
pretenture	principled	proctorial	prologuise	prophetess
prettified	print chain	proctorize	prologuize	prophetism
prettifier	printeries	procumbent	prolongate	prophylaxy
prettifies	printfield	procurable	promenader	propionate
prettiness	printmaker	procurance	Promethean	propitiate
pretty much	print media	pro-curator	promethium	propitious
pretty near	print order	procurator	prometryne	proportion
pretty well	print train	procurrent	prominence	proposable
prevailing	print union	procuticle	prominency	propositum
prevalence	print wheel	prodeltaic	prominenti	propositus
prevalency	printworks	prodigally	promiscous	propounder
prevenance	priorities	prodigious	promiseful	propraetor
prevenient	prioritise	producible	promissive	proprietor
prevention	prioritize	production	promissory	pro-proctor
preventive	Priscoline	productive	promontory	propulsion
previously	prismatoid	profection	promotable	propulsive
prevocalic	prismoidal	profession	promotress	propulsory
prevoyance	prison bars	proficient	prompt book	propylaeum
prezygotic	prison-bird	profile cut	prompt-copy	propylitic
price-fixed	prison camp	profitable	promptness	pro-ratable
price index	prison-crop	profitably	prompt-note	proroguing
price point	prisonment	profitless	prompt side	proruption
prick-eared	prissiness	proflavine	promptuary	prosaicism
prick-hedge	pristinely	profligacy	promulgate	proscenium
pricking-up	private bar	profligate	pronephric	prosciutto
prickliest	private car	profluence	pronephros	proscriber
pricklouse	private eye	profluvium	pronograde	prosecutor
prickly ash	private law	profounder	pronominal	prose idyll
prickly rat	private war	profoundly	pronounced	proseology
prick-madam	privatizer	profulgent	pronouncer	prose sense
prick punch	privet hawk	profundity	pronucleus	prosilient
pridefully	privet-like	progenitor	pro-nuncios	prosimious
priesthood	privileged	proglacial	prooestrus	prosodical
priestless	privy parts	proglottid	proof-glass	prosopylar
priestlike	privy purse	proglottis	proof-plane	prospector
priestling	prize agent	prognathic	proof-sheet	prospectus
priestship	prize court	prognostic	propachlor	prosperity
priggishly	prizefight	programmed	propadiene	prosperous
prima donna	prize money	programmer	propagable	prostanoic
prima facie	probenecid	progressor	propaganda	prostatism
primaquine	problemist	pro hac vice	propagator	prosternal
primatical	procacious	prohibited	propagular	prosternum
primaveral	procambial	prohibiter	propanidid	prostheses
prime mover	procambium	prohibitor	propanoate	prosthesis
primer fine	procaryote	prohormone	propellant	prosthetic

Prostigmin	protrudent	pteromorph	pump-handle	push-towing
prostitute	protrusile	pterylosis	pump island	pussy posse
prostomial	protrusion	Ptolemaean	pumpkin pie	put a mock on
prostomium	protrusive	Ptolemaism	pump-primer	put-and-call
prostrator	proud flesh	Ptolemaist	punch board	put-and-take
protandric	proud-heart	puberulent	punch-drunk	put an end to
protanopia	provection	puberulous	punch graft	put a slur on
protanopic	proveditor	pubescence	punch-house	put a stop to
proteanism	provenance	publically	punchiness	putatively
protectant	proverbial	public bill	punch-press	put forward
protection	providable	public good	punctation	put in force
protective	providence	publicitor	punctiform	put it there
protectory	provincial	public life	punctiliar	putlog-hole
protectrix	provitamin	publicness	punctilios	put on an act
protegulum	provocable	public weal	punctually	put on a show
proteiform	provocator	pub theatre	punctuator	put on flesh
proteinase	provokable	puck-chaser	punctulate	put-putting
proteinoid	prowessful	puck-needle	Punic faith	putrescent
proteinous	proximally	pudding-bag	punishable	putrescine
pro tempore	prudential	pudding-pie	punishably	putridness
protension	pruriently	puddle-duck	punishment	put spurs to
protensity	Prussianly	puerperium	punitively	put store by
protensive	Przewalski	puffed rice	punk rocker	put through
protention	psalmodise	puffer fish	punto banco	putting-off
proteolyse	psalmodist	puffinosis	pupiparous	put to a vote
protervity	psalmodize	puff pastry	puppet-play	put to death
Protestant	psalterial	puff sleeve	puppet-show	put to grass
protestive	psalterian	pugilistic	puppyishly	put to shame
prothallia	psalteries	pugil stick	puppy-tooth	put to sleep
prothallus	psalterion	Puginesque	Purbeckian	putty-knife
prothetely	psalterium	pugnacious	purblindly	putty medal
protobiont	psammosere	puirt-a-beul	Purcellian	puzzlehead
protocolar	psephocrat	puissantly	purchasing	puzzlement
protocolic	psephology	pukka sahib	pure merino	puzzle-pate
protoconch	pseudandry	pulicosity	purging nut	puzzlingly
protoconid	pseudobulb	pull a boner	purinergic	pycnocline
protogenic	pseudocarp	pull a train	puritanise	pycnogonid
protograph	pseudocide	pulled wool	puritanism	pycnometer
protohuman	pseudocode	pull-hitter	puritanize	pycnospore
protologue	pseudocoel	pullovered	Purkinjean	pycnostyle
protolysis	pseudocyst	pull stakes	purlieu-man	pygmy-flint
protolytic	pseudodoxy	pull-stroke	purple haze	pygmy goose
protomeric	pseudogamy	pull-switch	purple lake	pyjama case
protonemal	pseudogene	pull the pin	purpleness	pyknolepsy
protopapas	pseudogley	pully-hauly	purple zone	pyocyanase
protophyll	pseudogout	pulmometer	purposeful	pyocyanine
protophyte	pseudology	pulmonaria	purse-pride	pyogenesis
protoplasm	pseudosoph	pulp-cavity	purse-proud	pyogenetic
protoplast	pseudostem	pulpectomy	purserette	pyracantha
protostele	psilocybin	pulpitical	pursership	pyramidate
protostome	psittacine	pulsatance	purse seine	pyramidion
prototroch	psittacism	pulsatilla	pursuantly	pyramidist
prototroph	Psyche knot	pulse-label	pursuivant	pyramidize
prototropy	psychiater	pulse radar	purtenance	pyranoside
prototypal	psychiatry	pulsimeter	purulently	pyrazoline
prototypic	psychicist	pultaceous	purveyance	pyrazolone
protovirus	psychogeny	pultrusion	puschkinia	pyrenocarp
protoxylem	psychogram	pulverable	push around	pyrethroid
protozoans	psychology	pulverizer	push-button	pyretology
protracted	psychopath	pulvinated	pushmobile	pyridazine
protractor	psychopomp	pummelling	push-stroke	pyridoxine
protreptic	pteranodon	pump-action	push things	pyrimidine

pyrochlore	qualup bell	quick-grass	radarscope	rain-doctor
pyrogallic	quandaries	quickhatch	radar-sonde	rainforest
pyrogallol	quangocrat	quick march	radar-track	rain jungle
pyrogenous	quantified	quick-match	radial axle	rainmaking
pyrography	quantifier	quicksandy	radial-flow	rain shadow
pyrologist	quantifies	quickthorn	radicalise	rain-shower
pyrolusite	quantitate	quick trick	radicalism	raise a dust
pyromaniac	quantities	quick water	radicality	raisedness
pyrometric	quantitive	quiddative	radicalize	raisin tree
pyromucate	quarantine	quiddities	radication	Rajasthani
pyrophoric	quarentene	quid pro quo	radicchios	rajpramukh
pyrophorus	quarkonium	quidsworth	radicellar	Rajya Sabha
pyrosphere	quarrelled	quiescence	radiculose	rakishness
pyrotechny	quarreller	quiescency	radio-assay	rally-cross
pyroxenite	quarrenden	quietistic	radioassay	rallycross
pyroxenoid	quarriable	quill drive	radiogenic	rallyingly
pyrrhichii	quarry tile	quinacrine	radiograph	ramblingly
Pyrrhonian	quartation	quinestrol	radio-label	Ramboesque
Pyrrhonism	quarterage	quingenary	radiolaria	ramfeezled
Pyrrhonist	quarter-boy	quinquefid	radiologic	ramificate
pyrrhonize	quarter day	quinsy-wort	radiolysis	rampacious
pyrrhotine	quarter-ill	quint major	radiolytic	rampageous
pyrrhotite	quartering	quint minor	radiometal	ram-raiding
Pythagoras	quarterman	quintuplet	radiometer	ramshackle
Pythagoric	quarter-saw	quirkiness	radiometry	ramshackly
pythiambic	quart major	quite other	radiopaque	ranch house
pythogenic	quartzitic	quit hold of	radiophare	ranch wagon
pythonical	quartz lamp	quiverfuls	radiophone	rancidness
pythonissa	quaternary	quizmaster	radiophony	randomizer
Qatabanian	quaternate	quiz-master	radiophoto	randomness
quack-quack	quaternion	quizzingly	radio range	random shot
quadrangle	quaternise	quoad sacra	radioscope	random walk
quadrantal	quaternity	rabbinical	radioscopy	range-plate
quadrantic	quaternize	rabbinship	radio shack	range-proof
Quadrantid	quatorzain	rabbit ball	radiosonde	rangership
quadraplex	quatrefoil	rabbit-fish	radiotelex	ranging-rod
quadratrix	queasiness	rabbit food	Radio Three	ranitidine
quadrature	queen conch	rabbit-foot	radiotoxic	ranivorous
quadrennia	queenliest	rabbit-like	radium beam	rank entire
quadriceps	queen olive	rabbit's ear	radium bomb	rannel-tree
quadriform	queenright	rabbit test	radium burn	rannygazoo
quadrilled	queen's head	rabblement	radium dial	ransomable
quadrilogy	queen-sized	rabble rout	raft-bridge	ransom-bill
quadripole	queen's lace	racecourse	rafterless	ransomless
quadrireme	Queensland	race memory	raft spider	ransom note
quadrivial	queen's pawn	race-reader	ragamuffin	ranterpike
quadrivium	queen's rook	race record	rag-chewing	rantle-tree
quadrumane	queen's-ware	race theory	rag content	ranunculin
quadrumvir	quenchable	race walker	raggedness	ranunculus
quadrupler	quenchless	rachiotomy	ragman roll	Raoult's law
quadruplet	quercitrin	Rachmanism	rah-rah girl	rappelling
quadruplex	quercitron	Rachmanite	railleries	rapping bar
quadrupole	quern-stone	racing flag	railroader	rapporteur
quaestuary	queryingly	racing form	rail timber	raptorious
quagginess	questingly	racing-line	railwayana	Rarotongan
quailfinch	questionee	racket-ball	railwaydom	rascallion
quaintness	questioner	racket-tail	railwayman	rasterizer
Quaker City	quick bread	rackleness	railwaymen	rat-catcher
Quaker Oats	quick-break	rack-master	railway rug	ratcheting
qualitated	quick death	rack-renter	rain bonnet	rate-buster
qualminess	quickening	raconteuse	rainbow boa	ratifiable
qualmishly	quick-firer	radar fence	raincoated	rationally

ration book	reasonable	reconsider	redialling	reflective
ration card	reasonably	recontinue	red iron ore	reflexible
rattle-bush	reasonless	recontract	rediscount	reflourish
rattle-head	reason will	recordable	rediscover	refocusing
rattle-jack	reassemble	record club	redissolve	refocussed
rattle-pate	reassembly	recordless	redistrict	reformable
rattletrap	reassertor	record type	redivision	Reform Club
rattle-weed	reassuring	recoupable	red jasmine	refractile
rattlingly	rebaptizer	recoupment	red lattice	refracting
raunchiest	rebatement	recoveries	red meerkat	refraction
raveningly	Rebeccaite	recreantly	Redmondism	refractive
ravenously	rebellious	re-creation	Redmondite	refractory
raven-stone	rebiddable	recreation	red morocco	refreshful
ravinement	rebirthing	recreative	red nucleus	refreshing
ravishment	reboundant	recrudency	redolently	refringent
rawinsonde	rebukeable	recrudesce	redoubling	refuelling
raw lobster	rebukingly	rectangled	red palm oil	refugeedom
ray diagram	rebuttable	rectorship	redressive	refugeeism
ray therapy	recallable	rectoscope	red rock-cod	refulgence
ray-tracing	recallment	rectoscopy	red sanders	refulgency
razor blade	recappable	recumbence	redshifted	refundable
razor-edged	recarriage	recumbency	red snapper	refundment
razor-grass	receivable	recuperate	red spinner	refuse bail
razor's edge	recentness	recurrence	red-spotted	refutation
razor-sharp	receptacle	recurrency	red stopper	refutative
razor-shell	receptible	recusation	reduceless	regainable
razor-slash	recercelée	recyclable	redundance	regainment
razzmatazz	rechristen	redactoral	redundancy	regalement
reablement	recidivate	red admiral	red warning	regalities
reaccustom	recidivism	red arsenic	red zinc ore	regardable
reach truck	recidivist	red atrophy	reed-and-tie	regardless
reacquaint	recidivous	red-bellied	reed dagger	regard ring
reactivate	recipience	red-blooded	reed switch	regelation
reactively	recipiency	red buckeye	reef-tackle	regeneracy
reactivity	reciprocal	red cabbage	re-election	regenerant
readership	recitalist	red campion	re-eligible	regenerate
reading age	recitation	Red Chamber	reel-to-reel	regent-bird
readjuster	recitative	red channel	re-emergent	regentship
readmitted	recivilize	red-cheeked	re-emission	reggaefied
read-mostly	recklessly	red-chested	re-emphasis	regicidism
readoption	reckonable	Red Chinese	re-enaction	regimental
ready-mixed	reclassify	red-cooking	re-enforcer	regionally
ready money	reclinable	red country	re-engineer	registered
reafferent	recogitate	red-crested	re-enlister	registerer
reafforest	recognitor	red-crossed	re-entrance	registrant
Reaganomic	recognizee	redcurrant	re-entrancy	registrary
realizable	recognizer	redecorate	Reeperbahn	registrate
realizably	recognizor	rededicate	re-erection	registries
reallocate	recoil gear	redeemable	re-evaluate	regnal year
reallotted	recoilless	redeemably	re-exchange	regolithic
real school	recoilment	redeemless	re-existent	regratress
real tennis	recolonise	redefector	re-exporter	regression
reanalysis	recolonize	redelivery	refainment	regressive
reappraise	recommence	red emperor	referendum	regretting
re-approach	recompense	redemption	referrible	regular guy
reap-silver	recomplete	redemptive	refillable	regularise
rear-facing	recompound	redemptory	refinement	regularity
reargument	recompress	redescribe	refineries	regularize
rear gunner	reconceive	red flannel	refiningly	regulation
rearmament	reconciler	red grouper	refixation	regulative
rear-vassal	recondense	red gurnard	reflagging	regulatory
rearwardly	reconquest	red herring	reflection	Rehobother

Reichsmark	remediless	repeatable	resarcelée	restenosis
reidentify	rememberer	repeatedly	reschedule	rest-harrow
reignition	remigation	repeatered	rescission	restlessly
reillumine	reminiscer	repeat mark	rescissory	restorable
reimburser	remissible	repeat sign	resealable	restrained
reim-kennar	remissness	repellence	researcher	restrainer
reimprison	remittable	repellency	resectable	restricted
reincrease	remittance	repentance	resediment	restrictee
reineckate	remittence	repersuade	resemblant	restrictor
reinforcer	remittency	repertoire	resembling	resultance
reinitiate	remobilize	répétiteur	resentment	resultless
reinscribe	remodelled	repetition	reservable	resumption
reinspirit	remodeller	repetitive	reservedly	resumptive
reinstator	remodified	repinement	resettable	resupinate
reinstruct	remodifies	repiningly	res extensa	resupplied
reinthrone	remonetise	replanning	Resh Galuta	resupplies
reintrench	remonetize	replicable	reshipment	resurgence
reinvasion	remoralize	replicably	residenter	retailment
reissuable	remorseful	replicator	residually	retainable
reiterance	remortgage	repolarize	resignedly	retainment
rejectable	remoteness	repopulate	resignment	retaliator
rejectment	remotivate	reportable	resilience	retardance
rejoiceful	removalist	report back	resiliency	retardancy
rejunction	removement	reportedly	resin canal	retardment
rejuvenant	remunerate	reposition	res integra	reticently
rejuvenate	Renaissant	repository	resistable	reticulate
rejuvenize	renal colic	repressing	resistance	reticulose
relabelled	renascence	repression	resistible	retinalite
relational	rencounter	repressive	resistless	retinulate
relatively	renderable	repressory	resmethrin	retired pay
relativise	rendezvous	reproacher	res nullius	retirement
relativism	rend the air	reprobance	resolidify	retiringly
relativist	renegadism	reprobater	resolutely	retouching
relativity	renegadoes	reprobator	resolution	retourable
relativize	renegation	reproclaim	re-solution	retractile
relaxation	renewalism	reproducer	resolutive	retraction
relaxative	renewalist	reprovable	resolutory	retractive
relay valve	renography	reptiliary	resolvable	retransfer
releasable	renominate	reptilious	resolvedly	retransmit
relegation	renovation	republican	resolvible	retraverse
relentless	renovative	repudiable	resonantly	retravirus
relentment	renownedly	repudiator	resonatory	retreatant
relevantly	renownless	repugnance	resorbence	retreatism
reliefless	rentalsman	repugnancy	resorcinol	retreatist
relief road	rent-charge	repurchase	resorcylic	retreative
relief roll	Rentenmark	repurified	resorption	retrencher
relief well	rent strike	repurifies	resorptive	retributor
relievable	renunciant	reputation	resounding	retrochoir
relievedly	renunciate	reputative	respectant	retrofocus
religation	reoccupied	requestman	respectful	retrograde
religioner	reoccupies	requiescat	respecting	retrogress
relinquish	reoccurred	requirable	respective	retrorsely
relishable	reorganise	requisitor	respirable	retrospect
relocation	reorganize	re-readable	respirator	retroverse
reluctance	repaganize	rereadable	respondent	retroviral
reluctancy	repaginate	rere-dorter	responsary	retrovirus
remand home	repairable	re-register	responsion	returnable
remarkable	reparation	rere-supper	responsive	return date
remarkably	reparative	re-revision	responsory	return fare
remarriage	reparatory	re-romanize	restaurant	return game
remediable	repatriate	resaleable	restaurate	returnless
remedially	repealable	resanctify	rest energy	return room

reundulate	rheophobic	Richardson	ringletted	robustness
reunionism	rheophytic	ricinoleic	ringmaster	Roche limit
reunionist	rheoscopic	rickettsia	ring-necked	rockabilly
reunitable	rheostatic	ricky-ticky	Ring of Fire	rock badger
revalidate	rheotactic	ricocheted	ring-opener	rock beauty
revalorize	rheotropic	ridability	ring pigeon	rock-bottom
revanchism	rhesus baby	riddlingly	ring plover	rocker foot
revanchist	rhetorical	ride a hobby	ring scaler	rocket-bomb
rev counter	rheumatics	ride and tie	ring-tailed	rocket ship
revealable	rheumatise	ride a tiger	ring-thrush	rocket sled
revealment	rheumatism	ride bodkin	ring velvet	rock garden
revegetate	rheumatize	ride cymbal	riot police	rock grouse
revelation	rheumatoid	ride herd on	rip and tear	rockhopper
revelative	Rhinegrave	ridge piece	rip current	Rockingham
revelatory	rhinestone	ridge stone	ripicolous	rock martin
revengeful	rhinobatid	ridgy-didge	ripping-saw	rock of ages
revenue tax	rhinoceral	ridiculize	rippleless	rock pigeon
reverencer	rhinoceros	ridiculous	ripple mark	rock python
reverendly	rhinocerot	riding boot	ripple sole	rock rabbit
reverently	rhinophore	riding-coat	ripplingly	rock-ribbed
reverse bid	rhinophyma	riding-crop	rip-roaring	rock salmon
reversible	rhinoscope	riding-hood	ripsnorter	rocksteady
reversibly	rhinoscopy	riding lamp	risibility	rock stream
revertible	rhinovirus	riding sail	rising damp	rock-thrush
revestiary	rhizogenic	riebeckite	rising five	Rodinesque
reviewable	rhizomania	Riemannian	rising line	rogational
revigorate	rhizomorph	rifampicin	rising main	roghan josh
revilement	rhizophora	rifle-green	risky shift	roistering
revisiting	rhizophore	rifle range	ritardandi	roisterous
revitalise	rhizoplane	riflescope	ritardando	role player
revitalize	rhizoplast	rift timber	ritornelli	roll-collar
revivalism	rhodamine B	rift valley	ritornello	rolled gold
revivalist	rhodophyte	Riga balsam	Ritschlian	rolled oats
revivement	rhodoplast	rigescence	rittmaster	rollerball
revivified	rhomboidal	right about	ritual bath	roller-coat
revivifies	rhomboidei	right angle	river birch	roller tube
revivingly	rhumbatron	right bower	river-drift	roll-formed
revocation	rhyme royal	right field	river-drive	rollicking
revocatory	rhyme sheet	right flank	river-horse	rolling pin
revokeable	rhyodacite	rightfully	river pearl	roll latten
revolution	rhythmetic	right-lined	riverscape	roll-necked
revolvable	rhythmical	right of way	river-shrew	rollocking
revolvency	rhythmless	right on end	river snail	Rolls-Royce
revolvered	ribaldrous	right-sided	river stone	roll-up fund
rewardable	riband-fish	rightwards	river trout	roly-polies
rewardably	riband wave	right whale	riverwards	Romanaccio
rewardless	ribbon cane	rigidified	river-water	roman-à-clef
rewrapping	ribbon copy	rigidifies	rivetingly	romancical
rewrite man	ribbon-fern	rigoristic	road apples	Romanesque
rhabditoid	ribbonfish	rigorously	road bridge	Roman fever
rhabdocoel	ribbon-like	rijsttafel	road roller	Romanicist
rhabdolith	ribbonwood	Rimbaldian	roadroller	Romanistic
rhabdomere	ribbon worm	rinderpest	roadrunner	Roman-nosed
rhapsodies	rib-digging	ring-armour	road-tester	Romanowsky
rhapsodise	riboflavin	ring-billed	road tunnel	Roman snail
rhapsodist	ribophorin	ring-binder	roadworthy	romantical
rhapsodize	rib-tickler	ring burner	robber crab	Romany chal
Rhenish fan	Riccadonna	ringed dove	robberhood	rombowline
rheologist	rice-flower	ringed seal	robing room	Rome-runner
rheometric	rice powder	Ringelmann	roboticist	Romishness
rheopectic	rice stitch	ring finger	robotology	romper room
rheophilic	Richard Roe	ringleader	robustious	romper suit

rondeletia	rotativism	r selection	rum-running	Sabbath day
rongo-rongo	rotativist	rub-a-dub-dub	runability	Sabbath goy
Ronsardist	Rothschild	rubber band	run afoul of	sabbathize
rood-screen	rotiferous	rubber game	run against	sabbatical
roof garden	rotisserie	rubber heel	run a game on	sabota lark
rooibekkie	Rotissomat	rubberless	run and fell	sabretache
rooibos tea	rotor blade	rubberneck	run-and-read	sabretooth
rooirhebok	rotor cloud	rubber tree	run athwart	saccharase
room-ridden	rotorcraft	rubberware	run a voyage	saccharate
room-to-room	Rototiller	rubberwear	runcinated	saccharide
root-aorist	rottenness	rubbish bin	rune-ribbon	saccharify
root-balled	Rottweiler	rubbishing	Runge–Kutta	saccharine
root cellar	rotundness	rubbity-dub	run greenly	saccharize
root digger	Rouge Croix	rubble-work	runner bean	saccharoid
root doctor	rouge de fer	rubby-dubby	runnerless	saccharose
rootedness	rouge royal	Rubenesque	running dog	sacculated
root-fallen	Rouget cell	rubiaceous	running fit	sacerdotal
root ginger	rough-dried	rubicundly	running fix	sachemship
rootlessly	rough-dries	rubiginous	running ice	sackalever
root nodule	rough hound	Rubik's cube	running off	sack-bearer
rope-barrel	rough house	rubredoxin	running set	sackbutter
rope border	rough music	rubrically	run-of-river	sacred band
rope-dancer	rough-rider	rubricator	runologist	sacred book
rope ladder	rough scuff	ruby blende	run on a rail	sacred ibis
rope of sand	rough shoot	ruby copper	run the foil	sacredness
rope stitch	rough stuff	ruby silver	run the show	Sacred Writ
rope-walker	rough trade	ruby spinel	run through	sacrificer
roping-pole	rouletting	ruby-tailed	run to earth	sacrileger
roquelaure	Roumeliote	rubythroat	run to waste	sacristies
roriferous	round about	rucksacked	run-with-ram	sacroiliac
rosaniline	roundabout	rudder-bird	rupestrian	sacrosanct
roscoelite	round-armed	rudder-fish	rupturable	saddleback
rose acacia	round-armer	rudderless	Ruritanian	saddlebill
rose-beetle	round bilge	ruddy goose	rush candle	saddlebred
rose-chafer	round dance	ruderation	Russellian	saddle-gall
rose colour	round-eared	rudimental	Russellite	saddleless
rose copper	round-faced	Rudolphine	Russenorsk	saddle-like
rose-engine	roundhouse	ruefulness	russet coat	saddle-nose
rose-hopper	round-nosed	rufescence	Russia duck	saddle reef
rose linnet	round robin	ruffianage	Russian egg	saddleries
rose lintie	Round Table	ruffiandom	Russianise	saddle seat
rose madder	round towel	ruffianish	Russianism	saddle shoe
rose-maggot	round tower	ruffianism	Russianist	saddle-sore
rosemaling	rouseabout	ruffianize	Russianize	saddle-tank
rose-mallow	Rousseauan	rufter-hood	Russian tea	saddle tree
rose quartz	Roussillon	Rugby fives	Russonorsk	saddle vein
rose sawfly	roustabout	Rugby Union	Russophile	saddle wire
Rose Sunday	route march	rug-cutting	Russophobe	Sadducaean
rose-temple	route sheet	ruggedized	rust bucket	safari camp
rose-tinted	rove beetle	ruggedness	rust fungus	safari look
rose window	Rover Scout	rugulosity	rustically	safari park
Rosh Hodesh	rowan-berry	ruinatious	rusticater	safari suit
Rossby wave	rowdy-dowdy	rumblement	rusticness	safe-blower
Rossettian	rowing boat	rumble seat	rustic work	safe period
Ross's goose	rowing race	rumbullion	rustlingly	safety belt
rostellate	rowing tank	rumenotomy	rutheniate	safety boat
rostriform	royal burgh	rumfustian	ruthenious	safety bolt
rosy-billed	royal flush	rumination	Rutherford	safety film
Rotary club	royal icing	ruminative	ruthlessly	safety fuse
Rotary Club	royalistic	rumpsprung	rye whiskey	safety lamp
rotary-wing	royal jelly	rumpus room	Saarlander	safety play
rotational	royal paper	rumpy-pumpy	sabbath day	safety vent

safety zone	salt finger	sand plover	satellited	scale house
saffron bun	saltigrade	sand ripple	satellitic	scale of two
sage cheese	salt-making	sand shadow	satin paper	scalloping
sage grouse	salt meadow	sand-sucker	satin weave	scallopini
sage rabbit	salt rising	Sanfedista	satin white	scaloppine
saggar clay	salt shaker	Sanforized	satisficer	scammonies
sagination	salt spring	Sängerfest	satisfying	scandalise
sagittally	salt tablet	Sangiovese	satrapical	scandalize
sagittated	salubrious	sanguinary	saturation	scandalous
sago spleen	salutarily	sanguinely	saturnalia	scandaroon
sail-flying	salutation	sanguinity	Saturnalia	scanningly
sailmaking	salutatory	sanguinous	satyagraha	scansional
sail-needle	Salvadoran	Sanhedrist	satyagrahi	scansorial
sailor-fish	salverform	sanidinite	satyresque	scantiness
sailor knot	Salzburger	sanitarian	satyriasis	scapegrace
sailorless	samarskite	sanitarily	sauce-alone	scarabaeid
sailorship	sameliness	sanitarium	saucer bath	scarabacus
sailor suit	Samian ware	sanitation	saucer-eyed	scaramouch
saintliest	sampaguita	San Luiseño	saucerfuls	scarcement
saintology	sample book	Sanocrysin	saucerless	scarceness
sakes alive	sample card	sans blague	sauerkraut	scarcities
salad cream	sample case	Sanskritic	sausage dog	scaredy-cat
salamander	sample room	sans nombre	Saussurean	scare rigid
salbutamol	Samson-fish	sans pareil	saussurite	scare stiff
sale of work	Samson post	sans phrase	Saut Basque	scarlatina
Salernitan	sanatarium	Santa Claus	savageness	scarlet day
sales clerk	sanatorium	Santa Maria	savageries	scarlet hat
sales drive	sanctified	Santobrite	savagerous	scarlet oak
sales pitch	sanctifier	saouari nut	save the day	scar tissue
saleswoman	sanctifies	sapiential	savingness	scatheless
saleswomen	sanctilogy	saponified	savings-box	scathingly
salicional	sanctimony	saponifier	saviouress	scatologic
salicylate	sanctioned	saponifies	Savonarola	scatomancy
salicylism	sanctioner	saporosity	Savonnerie	scattalder
salientian	sanctities	sappanwood	savourless	scatter-gun
saliferous	sanctitude	sapperment	savoursome	scattering
salifiable	sanctology	sapphirine	Savoy opera	scatter rug
salineness	sanctorale	saprogenic	sawmilling	scattiness
salivarian	sandal-foot	saprolitic	sawtoothed	scaturient
salivarium	sandalling	sapropelic	saw-whet owl	scavengery
saliva test	sandal tree	saprophile	saxicavous	scene-steal
salivation	sandalwood	saprophyte	saxicoline	scenically
sallenders	sandbagger	saproxylic	saxicolous	scent gland
sallowness	sand-barite	Saracenism	Saxon green	scent organ
salmagundi	sand-binder	Sarakatsan	Saxony blue	scent scale
salmanazar	sandcastle	Saramaccan	saxophonic	scepticise
Salmanazar	sand cherry	sarcococca	saxotromba	scepticism
salmon bass	sand dollar	sarcocolla	say a lot for	scepticize
salmonella	sanderling	sarcolemma	say ditto to	sceptredom
salmon-leap	sand filter	sarcophagi	say much for	schalstein
salmon pass	sand garden	sarcophagy	say that for	scheduling
salmon peal	sand goanna	sarcoplasm	say the word	schefflera
salmon pink	sand-groper	sarcopside	scabbarded	schematise
salon music	sandgrouse	sarcotesta	scabbiness	schematism
salonnière	sand-hiller	sarmentose	scabridity	schematist
saloon deck	sand-hopper	sarmentous	scabrously	schematize
saloon girl	Sandinista	sarracenia	scaffolder	schemeless
salopettes	sand lizard	sash weight	scala media	schemingly
saltarelli	sandlotter	sash window	scald-berry	schemozzle
saltarello	sand martin	Satanistic	scald cream	scherzandi
salt bridge	sand myrtle	Satanology	scale-board	scherzando
salt cellar	sandpapery	satchelled	scaledrake	scherzetto

Schiff base	scoria cone	screen dump	sculleries	sea spurrey
Schiff test	scoriation	screen grid	sculptress	sea-swallow
schipperke	scornfully	screenings	sculptural	seat-belted
schismatic	scorpaenid	screenless	sculpturer	sea thistle
schizocarp	scorpionic	screen pass	scumminess	sea trumpet
schizogony	scorpionid	screenplay	scurfiness	sea-unicorn
schizoidal	scortation	screen test	scurrility	sea-walling
schizoidia	scortatory	screen time	scurrilous	seborrhoea
schizotype	scorzalite	screwiness	scurviness	Secchi disc
schizotypy	scorzonera	screw-joint	scutellate	secernment
schlepping	scot and lot	screwmatic	scuttleful	secludedly
Schlieffen	Scotch cart	screw-plate	scuzziness	second Adam
schlimazel	Scotchgard	screw-press	scyphiform	second-best
schmegegge	Scotch kale	screw stock	scyphozoan	second chop
Schmeisser	Scotchlite	screw-stone	scytheless	second-foot
schmendrik	Scotch mist	screw valve	sea anemone	second gear
schnozzola	Scotchness	scribbling	sea-angling	second-hand
scholardom	Scotch rose	scribe-mark	sea-bathing	second home
scholarism	Scotch snap	scribeship	sea-biscuit	second last
scholastic	Scotch spur	scrimmager	sea blubber	second line
schoolable	Scotch tape	scrimshank	seaborgium	secondment
schooldays	Scotch yoke	scrip issue	sea-bristle	second name
school-days	scotometer	script girl	sea campion	secondness
schoolgirl	scotometry	scriptless	sea-captain	second-rate
school land	scotophase	scriptoria	sea-catfish	second self
schoolless	scotophily	script type	sea coconut	second slip
school-marm	scotoscope	scriptural	sea-farming	second wind
schoolmate	Scots-Irish	scriptured	sea-feather	secretaire
school milk	Scotswoman	scritch-owl	sea-fingers	secret life
schoolroom	Scotswomen	scrivenery	seafishery	secret list
school-ship	Scotticise	scrivening	sea-fishing	secretness
school time	Scotticism	scrobicule	sea-gherkin	sectionary
schoolward	Scotticize	scrofulide	sea horizon	sectionise
school year	Scottie dog	scrofulous	sea-keeping	sectionist
schorl rock	Scottishly	scrollable	sea lamprey	sectionize
Schwannoma	Scottishry	scroll back	sealed-beam	sector scan
sciagraphy	scout plane	scroll-bone	sealed book	secular arm
scientific	scovan lode	scroll-copy	sea-leopard	secularise
Scillonian	scowbanker	scroll-gall	sea lettuce	secularism
scimitared	scowdering	scroll-head	sealing wax	secularist
scindapsus	scowlingly	scroll salt	seamanlike	secularity
scintigram	scraggiest	scrollwork	seamanship	secularize
scintiscan	scraggling	scrubbable	seam bowler	secure arms
sciolistic	scraggy end	scrub board	seamlessly	securement
scissor-cut	scrambling	scrub-brush	sea-monster	secureness
scleriasis	scrape a leg	scrub-robin	seamstress	securiform
sclerified	scrap-metal	scrub round	seam welder	securities
scleromata	scrap paper	scruffiest	sea-officer	securitise
sclerosant	scrappiest	scrummager	sea passage	securitize
sclerosing	scratch hit	scrunch-dry	Sea Peoples	sedan chair
sclerotium	scratchier	scrunchies	sea-poacher	sedateness
sclerotize	scratchily	scrupulant	seaquarium	sedge-grass
sclerotome	scratching	scrupulist	searchable	sedimental
sclerotomy	scratch-mix	scrupulous	search coil	seditioner
scoffingly	scratch pad	scrutineer	sea returns	seducement
scoldingly	scratch-wig	scrutinies	seascapist	seducingly
scooterist	scrawniest	scrutinise	sea serpent	seductress
scopoletin	screechier	scrutinize	sea-service	sedulously
score a miss	screeching	scrutinous	seasonable	seed-cotton
scoreboard	screech owl	scuba-diver	seasonably	seed-furrow
score sheet	screenable	scuddiness	seasonally	seed parent
score under	screen door	scull about	seasonless	seed potato

seed stitch	self-rising	send word to	sermonical	severation
seed vessel	self-secure	Senecanism	sermonizer	severeness
seek repose	self-seeded	Senegalese	sermonneer	sewability
seem good to	self-seeder	senescence	serologist	sewage farm
seemlihead	self-seeker	senior year	serotinous	sexagenary
seemliness	self-slayer	sennegrass	serpentary	Sexagesima
see one's way	self-styled	sense datum	serpentile	sexangular
seersucker	self-system	sense organ	serpentine	sexational
see service	self-taught	sensitizer	serpentize	sexavalent
seethingly	self-willed	sensoriums	serpigines	sexduction
see through	self-wisdom	sensualise	serradilla	sex hormone
segmentary	sell-by date	sensualism	serrulated	sexivalent
segregable	Selsdon man	sensualist	sertanista	sex-limited
seguidilla	semantemic	sensuality	serum broth	sex-linkage
seicentist	semaphoric	sensualize	servantdom	sex offence
seignorage	sematology	sensuistic	serventism	sexologist
seignorial	semblative	sensuosity	service bus	sexparlite
seismicity	semeiology	sensuously	service car	sexploiter
seismogram	semeiotics	sentential	serviceman	sex-starved
seismology	semi-annual	sentiently	servicemen	sex therapy
sejunction	semi-chorus	Senussiite	serving-man	sextillion
seldomness	semicircle	senza bassi	servitress	sextonship
selectable	semicirque	separately	servo brake	sexual cell
selectness	semi-closed	separation	servo-motor	sexual role
selenodesy	semi-coking	separatism	servomotor	sexuparous
selenodont	semi-column	separatist	sessile oak	shabbiness
selenology	semi-desert	separative	sessionary	Shabbos-goy
Seleucidan	semi-direct	separatory	sessioneer	shabu-shabu
self-acting	semi-divine	separatrix	session man	shadow-cast
self-action	semi-double	septectomy	sestertium	shadowland
self active	semiferine	septemfoil	sestertius	shadowless
self-binder	semi-fitted	septemviri	set abroach	shadow mask
self-colour	semi-formed	septenarii	set a copy to	shadow play
self-deceit	semi-lethal	septennary	set against	shadow test
self-denial	semi-liquid	septennate	set a stitch	shadow work
self-denied	semilunate	septennial	set forward	shaft-alley
self-denier	semi-mature	septennium	setiferous	shaft-drive
self-driven	seminarial	septically	setigerous	shaft grave
self-energy	seminarian	septicemia	set spurs to	shaft-horse
self-esteem	seminaries	septichord	set store by	shaganappi
self-exiled	seminarist	septicidal	settecento	shagginess
self-feeder	semination	septic tank	setterwort	shag-haired
self-formed	seminative	septillion	set the pace	shagreened
self-giving	seminology	septostomy	setting-dog	Shahanshah
self-hatred	semi-nudity	Septuagint	setting sun	shahbandar
self-helper	semi-opaque	sepulchral	settleable	shake hands
self-insure	semiotical	Sepulchran	settlement	shakuhachi
self-killed	semi-portal	sepultural	settlerdom	shallow end
selflessly	semiquaver	sequacious	settle with	shallow-fry
self-loader	semi-rotary	sequenator	set to music	shamefaced
self-loving	semi-savage	sequential	set up house	shamefully
self-motion	semi-sports	sequestral	seven-hilly	shame on you
self-motive	Semiticize	sequestrum	sevenpence	shandrydan
self-moving	semi-uncial	seralbumin	sevenpenny	shandygaff
self-murder	semi-weekly	Serbo-Croat	Seven Sages	shanghaied
self-opened	semotactic	sereneness	sevenscore	Shanks' mare
self-parody	sempstress	serenities	seven stars	shanty town
self-poised	senatorial	sergeantcy	seventieth	shape forth
self-praise	senatorian	serge denim	seventyish	shapeliest
self-raised	send abroad	serigraphy	Seven Words	Sharawaggi
self-rating	Senderista	serio-comic	severality	shard-borne
self-regard	send off for	sermonette	severalize	sharedness

shark-louse	sherardise	shit-eating	short grain	shrink-ring
sharp cedar	sherardize	shit-kicker	short-grass	shrink-wrap
shattering	sherbet dab	shit-scared	short-hairs	shrivelled
shaughraun	sheriffdom	shittiness	short horse	Shropshire
shavegrass	sheriffing	shiversome	short-lived	shroud-knot
Shavianism	sherry wine	shoaliness	short metre	shroud-laid
shea-butter	she's apples	shockingly	short order	shroudless
shear board	Shetlander	shock-mount	short price	shroudlike
shear force	Shetlandic	shockproof	short-range	shroud line
shear-grass	shewelling	shock stall	short score	Shrovetide
shear plane	shibboleth	shock strut	short sight	shrug aside
shear steel	shield-back	shoddiness	short-stage	Shtokavian
shearwater	shield fern	shoddy-hole	short story	shuddering
sheathbill	shieldless	shoe-buckle	short sword	shunt-wound
sheath cell	shieldlike	shoe-flower	short-timer	shut-out bid
sheath-fish	shield-maid	shoemaking	short title	shutter-bug
sheathless	shieldrake	shoeshiner	short waist	shutter-dam
shed master	shieldtail	shoestring	shortwards	shuttering
shed-roofed	shift dress	shoneenism	short whist	shuttle car
sheepberry	shiftening	shonkinite	Shoshonean	shut up shop
sheep-biter	shiftiness	shoofly pie	shoshonite	Shylockian
sheep-crook	shiftingly	shooldarry	shot effect	shystering
sheep-house	shift-lever	shoot ahead	shot-firing	shysterism
sheepishly	shift-round	shoot a line	shotmaking	sialagogue
sheep-money	shift-stick	shoot craps	shot-peened	sialogogue
sheep's bane	shift valve	shoot it out	shot-putter	sialomucin
sheep's foot	shillelagh	shopaholic	shot-window	Siamese cat
sheepshank	shillibeer	shop around	shouldered	sibilantly
sheep's head	shillooing	shop-bought	shoulder-in	sibilation
sheep-shear	shingle cap	shop-finish	shoutingly	sibilatory
sheet-block	shingle-oak	shop-fitter	shove-groat	sicca rupee
sheet cable	Shinkansen	shopfitter	shovelfuls	sicilianos
sheet-flood	shin-tangle	shopkeeper	shovelhead	sicilienne
sheet glass	ship-broken	shoplifter	shovelling	sick as a dog
sheet metal	shipbroker	shopocracy	shovelnose	sickerness
sheet music	ship-broker	shoppiness	shovel pass	Sickertian
sheldgoose	ship burial	shop-soiled	showboater	sickle-bill
sheldrakes	shipentine	shopwalker	shower-bath	sickle-cell
shelf paper	ship-keeper	shop window	shower head	sickle hock
shellacked	ship-ladder	shopworker	showerless	sickliness
shell beach	ship-lapped	shore-based	shower-room	sick-making
shell-briar	ship-letter	shore break	shower tree	sick parade
shell cocoa	shipmaster	shore-going	shower unit	side-branch
Shelleyana	ship-repair	shore leave	showground	sideburned
Shelleyism	ship-rigged	shore party	showjumper	side by side
Shelleyite	ship's store	shore seine	show-offish	sidecarist
shell-gland	ship-timber	shorewards	show-people	side chapel
shell-money	ship-to-ship	short-arsed	show temper	side effect
shell-mould	shipwright	short-assed	show the way	side glance
shell-mound	shire-horse	shortbread	show-window	side-kicker
shell-plate	shire-house	short cards	shrewd-head	side-ladder
shellproof	shire-reeve	short chain	shrewdness	side-loader
shell-shock	shire-stone	short cloth	shrewishly	side-pocket
shell-snail	shirt-dress	short-comer	shrewmouse	sideration
shell steak	shirt-frill	short cross	Shrewsbury	sidereally
shelly-coat	shirt-front	shortcrust	shrievalty	side-remark
shelterage	shirtiness	short-dated	shrillness	side-result
shelter leg	shirtmaker	short drink	shrimp-boat	siderocyte
shenanigan	shirt-waist	shortening	shrimplike	siderolite
shepherded	shirtwaist	short field	shrimp-pink	siderosome
shepherdly	shish kebab	short focus	shrinkable	siderostat
shepherdry	shit a brick	short-fused	shrink film	side-saddle

side-screen	silverless	singletree	skepticism	slashingly
side-stitch	silverlike	single-wide	sketchable	slate-black
side-stream	silverling	single-wire	sketch-book	slate-stone
side street	silver mail	sing-songed	sketchbook	slattering
side-stroke	silver orfe	singularly	sketchiest	slatternly
sidestroke	silver ring	sinisterly	skeuomorph	slaughtery
sideswiper	silver sand	sinistrous	Skevington	Slave Coast
side-taking	silverside	sinker-ball	skew bridge	slave-drive
sideways on	silvertail	sinkerless	skew chisel	slave-maker
sidewinder	silver thaw	sink or swim	skewer tree	Slave State
siege-piece	silver-tree	sinnership	skew system	slave trade
siege-train	silverware	Sinn Feiner	skiagraphy	slavocracy
Sierpinski	silverweed	sino-atrial	skiascopic	Slavophile
sieve plate	silver-work	sinography	skiddoooed	sleazeball
Sievers' law	silylation	sinologist	ski jumping	sleaziness
sight-board	similarity	Sinologist	skimmer hat	sleekstone
sight draft	similarize	Sinophilia	skimmingly	sleep a wink
sight-glass	similative	Sinophobia	skimpiness	sleepiness
sigillaria	similitude	sinsemilla	skim-plough	sleepingly
signal-book	simillimum	sin-shifter	skin a flint	sleep rough
signalling	simmer down	sinuatrial	skin-beater	sleep sound
signet ring	Simmerstat	sinus gland	skin beetle	sleep tight
sign-manual	simnel cake	sinusoidal	skin diving	sleep-waker
sign-writer	simoniacal	siphoneous	skin-drying	sleepyhead
signwriter	simple lens	sipunculan	skin effect	sleepy-head
silent heat	simpleness	sipunculid	skinflinty	sleepy-time
silentiary	simple time	sis-boom-bah	Skinner box	sleeve-fish
silentious	simplicial	sister cell	Skinnerian	sleeveless
silentness	simplicist	sister city	Skinnerism	sleeve link
silhouette	simplicity	Sister Dora	skinniness	sleeve note
silication	simplified	sisterhood	skin-search	sleigh bell
silicicole	simplifier	sister-hook	skin the cat	sleigh-ride
silicified	simplifies	sisterless	skippingly	slenderest
silicifies	simplistic	sisterlike	skirmisher	slenderise
siliconize	simulacral	sister ship	skirt-board	slenderize
siliculose	simulacrum	sistership	skirt-chase	slick paper
silk cotton	simulation	sister-wife	skirt-dance	slickstone
silk screen	simulative	sisymbrium	skittishly	slide-valve
silly billy	sincipital	sit heavy on	skittle-pot	slightness
silly house	sinecurism	sit loose to	skrimshank	slime mould
Silly putty	sinecurist	sit on brood	skunk works	slim volume
Silly Putty	sine qua non	sitophobia	sky fighter	sling chair
silo buster	sinfulness	sitosterol	skylighted	sling off at
silverback	Singhalese	sit pillion	sky marshal	sling-stone
silver band	singing arc	sit through	sky-parlour	slinkiness
silver bath	singing man	Sitwellian	sky-rockety	slinkingly
silver beet	singing saw	Sitwellism	skyscraper	slipperily
silverbill	single beer	Siwash camp	sky-surfing	slippering
silverbird	single-copy	Siwash duck	sky the wipe	slippiness
silver-bush	single-eyed	six-pounder	sky-writing	slip stitch
silver cord	single file	six-shooter	slacken off	slipstream
silver disc	single-foot	sixteenmos	slack water	slip-string
silver fern	single-hand	sixth sense	slag-hearth	slit-limpet
silverfish	singlehood	sixty-seven	slaked lime	slit pocket
silver foil	single-line	sizzlingly	slake water	slit trench
silver-fork	single malt	sjambokker	slammerkin	slitty-eyed
silver gilt	singleness	skateboard	slanderous	sloop of war
silver-grey	single reed	skate-leech	slanginess	slop bucket
silver king	single-reef	skedaddler	slangishly	sloppiness
silver lace	singles bar	skeletally	slangwhang	slopping-up
silver-lead	single-step	skeletonic	slantingly	slopseller
silver-leaf	single team	Skeltonian	slap-tongue	slop-worker

sloshiness	smell of oil	snappingly	snow-sports	soft-lander
slot aerial	smelteries	snappishly	snow-wreath	soft mother
slothfully	smirchless	snap switch	snowy egret	softnomics
slot-racing	smirkingly	snarkiness	snubbiness	soft option
slovenlike	smithcraft	snarlingly	snubbingly	soft palate
Slovincian	smithereen	snatchable	snubbishly	soft sawder
slow bowler	smitheries	snatch-back	snuff-brown	soft-soaper
slow cooker	Smithfield	snatch crop	snuff-gourd	soft solder
slow motion	smith's coal	snazziness	snuffiness	soft-spoken
slow-twitch	smith's work	sneak-guest	snuffingly	soft target
slow-witted	smock-faced	sneakiness	snuff movie	soft wicket
sluggardly	smock-frock	sneakingly	snuff video	soft-wooded
sluggishly	smoke alarm	sneakishly	snuggeries	soil catena
slug pellet	smoke-black	sneak thief	soaking pit	soil cement
sluice-fork	smoke-dried	sneaky pete	soaking wet	soiled dove
sluice-gate	smoke-house	sneeringly	soap-boiler	soil mantle
sluice-head	smoke-meter	sneezeweed	soap-bubble	soil sample
slumber cap	smoke plant	sneezewood	soap cerate	soil series
slumberful	smoke point	sneezewort	soap flakes	soil stripe
slumbering	smoke shell	snick-snarl	soap powder	soil survey
slumber net	smokestack	sniffer dog	soavemente	sojourning
slumberous	smoke-stick	sniffiness	soberingly	Soka Gakkai
slum burner	smoke-stone	sniffingly	sobersides	solacement
slumminess	smoke-wagon	sniggering	social cost	solan goose
slummocker	Smokey Bear	snipe's-head	social evil	solanidine
slurry seal	smoking gun	snipocracy	social fact	solar flare
slushiness	smoochiest	snippiness	socializer	solar month
slush-money	smoothable	snivelling	socialness	solar panel
slush mould	smooth-bore	snob appeal	social unit	solar power
sluttishly	smooth-head	snobberies	social wage	solar still
smackering	smoothness	snobbiness	social work	soldanella
Smalcaldic	smooth newt	snobbishly	societally	solderable
small bower	smooth talk	snobocracy	sociocracy	solderless
small craft	smooth tare	snob-screen	sociodrama	soldier ant
small fruit	sm rrebr d	snoopiness	socio-legal	soldier-bug
smallgoods	smorzandos	snootiness	sociologic	soldieress
small hours	smother-fly	snooziness	sociometry	soldier-fly
small mercy	smudge-fire	snore-piece	socionomic	soldieries
small-pipes	smudgeless	snorkelled	sociopathy	soldierize
small print	smudginess	snorkeller	sock chorus	solecistic
small-scale	smugglable	snortingly	sock cymbal	solemnizer
small-sword	smut fungus	snottiness	socketless	solemn mass
small-timer	smuttiness	snotty-nose	Socratical	Solemn Mass
smallwares	snaffle-bit	Snovianism	soda bottle	Solenhofen
small world	snail-fever	snowblower	sodalities	solenocyte
small-yield	snailishly	snowcapped	soda syphon	solenoidal
smaragdine	snail-paced	snow-capped	soddenness	solfataric
smaragdite	snail's pace	Snowcemmed	sodium lamp	solicitant
smarminess	snake dance	snow course	sodium pump	soliciting
smart aleck	snake-fence	Snowdonian	Sodom apple	solicitous
smart alick	snake-gourd	snow-grouse	Sodomitish	solicitrix
smart-arsed	snake house	snow-insect	sod webworm	solicitude
smartingly	snake juice	snow-making	soetkoekie	solid angle
smart money	snakeology	snowmaking	soft answer	solidarism
smart-mouth	snake plant	snowmobile	soft-boiled	solidarist
smashingly	snake's head	snow pellet	soft cancer	solidarity
smattering	snake-stone	snow petrel	soft centre	solid-drawn
smear glaze	snake story	snow pigeon	soften down	solidified
smeariness	snap-action	snowplough	soft-footed	solidifier
smeethness	snap-beetle	snow powder	soft ground	solidifies
smell-feast	snapdragon	snow roller	soft-headed	solid newel
smelliness	snappiness	snow-snakes	soft hyphen	solid South

solids pump	sopping wet	spacebound	spattering	spermatize
solid state	sopraninos	space cabin	spatulated	sperm count
solifidian	sops-in-wine	space cadet	speakeress	spermicide
soligenous	sorbetière	spacecraft	speakerine	spermidine
solitaries	sordidness	space curve	speaker-key	spermoderm
solitarily	sore-headed	spacefarer	speak-house	spermogone
solivagant	sore throat	space flyer	speak ill of	spermology
Solochrome	sororicide	space frame	speakingly	sperm whale
Solomonian	sororities	space group	spear-grass	sphacelate
solonetzic	sorrel tree	space opera	spearminty	sphacelial
solstitial	sorrowless	space-order	spear-shaft	sphacelous
solstitium	sorrow song	spaceplane	specialise	sphalerite
solubilise	sortileger	space probe	specialism	sphenoidal
solubility	sostenutos	spacescape	specialist	sphereless
solubilize	Sothic year	space stage	speciality	sphericity
soluble RNA	soubriquet	spacewoman	specialize	spheriform
solutional	soucouyant	spacewomen	speciation	spherocyte
solvolysis	soughfully	spaciously	specie-room	spheroidal
solvolytic	soul-candle	spade beard	speciesism	spherosome
somatalgia	soul-doctor	spade-graft	speciesist	spherulite
somatocoel	soul-friend	spade-money	specifical	spheterize
somatogamy	soullessly	spade-press	speciosity	sphinxlike
somatology	soul-search	spade-wheel	speciously	spice-berry
somatotype	soul sister	spadiceous	spectacled	spice-plate
sombreness	sound-alike	spagyrical	spectacles	spiculated
sombreroed	soundalike	spallation	spectation	spider-band
somebodies	soundboard	spanandric	spectatory	spider-cell
somersault	sound check	spander-new	spectatrix	spider crab
somewhat as	soundcheck	spaniolate	spectrally	spider hole
somewhence	soundingly	spaniolize	spectredom	spider-hoop
somewheres	sound meter	Spanish elm	specularly	spider-like
somnambule	sound mixer	Spanish flu	speculator	spider lily
somnolence	sound print	Spanish fly	speech area	spider-line
somnolency	soundproof	Spanish nut	speech coil	spiderling
son and heir	soundscape	spankingly	speechless	spider mite
sonata form	sound shift	sparagmite	speech-song	spider-rest
Sonderbund	sound stage	sparge pipe	speed clock	spider's web
song-ballet	soundtrack	spark-erode	speed demon	spider-wasp
song-flight	sound truck	spark guard	speed freak	spider-work
songlessly	soup maigre	sparkiness	speediness	spiderwort
song period	soup-ticket	sparkishly	speed limit	spiflicate
song-school	sourcebook	sparmannia	speisesaal	spiked buck
songstress	sourceless	sparrow owl	speleology	spilitized
song thrush	source rock	sparseness	speleothem	spill blood
songwriter	sour cherry	Spartacism	spellbound	spill valve
sonication	sour grapes	Spartacist	spell-check	spinal cord
sonic speed	sour orange	spartakiad	spellingly	spin bowler
soniferous	sousaphone	Spartanism	spelunking	spindleage
sonorities	souterrain	Spartanize	Spencerian	spindleful
sonorosity	southabout	spasm music	Spencerism	spindliest
sonorously	southbound	spasmodism	Spencerite	spin doctor
sons of guns	South Devon	spasmodist	Spenserian	spinel ruby
soon or late	South Downs	spasmoneme	spermaceti	spine point
soon or syne	southerner	spasticity	spermaduct	spinescent
soothingly	southernly	spatangoid	spermagone	spinningly
soothsayer	southwards	spatchcock	spermalege	spinsterly
sooty mould	Sovietizer	spathulate	spermarium	spinstress
sophically	sovnarkhoz	spatialise	sperm-aster	spin tunnel
sophiology	sowthistle	spatialism	spermatise	spin vector
Sophoclean	Soyer stove	spatialist	spermatism	spiny mouse
sophomoric	spacearium	spatiality	spermatist	spiny shark
sophrosyne	space-borne	spatialize	spermatium	spiracular

spiraculum	spoliation	spray tower	square foot	stadthouse
spiral gear	spoliative	spreadable	square-free	staff corps
spiralling	spoliatory	spread head	squarehead	staff nurse
spiramycin	spondulick	spread-over	square John	staff-sling
spirantize	spongeable	spreaghery	square meal	stag beetle
spire-grass	sponge bath	sprightful	Square Mile	stagecoach
spire-shell	sponge cake	spring-back	squareness	stagecraft
spiritedly	sponge crab	spring bolt	square pole	stage right
spirit lamp	spongeless	spring bows	square root	staggering
spiritless	spongelike	springhaas	square sail	stag-headed
spirit-like	sponge tree	springhalt	square-tail	stag-horned
spirituous	spongiform	spring hare	square-toed	stag-hunter
spirit-weed	sponginess	springhead	square-toes	stagnantly
spirograph	spongiosis	springiest	square up to	stagnation
spirometer	spongolite	spring-jack	square wave	stair-tower
spirometry	spongology	springless	squarewise	stake-truck
spissitude	sponsoress	springlike	square yard	stalactite
spitballer	sponsorial	spring line	squashable	Stalag Luft
spitchcock	spookiness	springling	squash bite	stalagmite
spitchered	spool valve	spring lock	squashiest	stalk borer
spit cotton	spoon-bread	spring rate	squatarole	stalkiness
spite fence	spoon canoe	spring roll	squat board	stall-board
spitefully	spoon drain	springtail	squaw-berry	stallenger
spit-insect	spoondrift	spring tide	squeakiest	stall plate
spittle-bug	spoonerism	springtide	squeezable	stalwartly
Spitzflöte	spoonerize	springtime	squeeze-box	stamineous
splacknuck	spooniness	spring-wood	squeeze toy	stamp-album
splanchnic	sporadical	sprinkling	squeteague	stamp and go
splashback	sporangial	spritehood	squidgiest	stamp hinge
splash-dash	sporangium	sprocketed	squid-hound	stamp paper
splash down	spore print	sprout-land	squiffiest	Stancarist
splashdown	Spörer's law	spruce beer	squinch-owl	stanchless
splashiest	sporidiole	spruceness	squint-eyed	stand about
splash pool	sporoblast	spruce pine	squint-eyes	stand-alone
splash-work	sporophore	spud barber	squirarchy	stand aloof
splash zone	sporophyll	spud wrench	squirearch	stand apart
splay fault	sporophyte	spun-golden	squirehood	standardly
spleenless	sporozoite	spunkiness	squireless	stand aside
spleenwort	sportfully	spur blight	squirelike	stand at bay
splendidly	sportiness	spurge hawk	squireling	stand forth
splenetive	sportingly	spuriosity	squireship	stand guard
splenocyte	sportively	spuriously	squirmiest	stand on end
splenology	sportscast	spur-winged	squirrelly	standpoint
splenotomy	sports coat	sputtering	squishiest	standstill
splint-bone	sports page	spycatcher	stabbingly	stand treat
splint-coal	sports team	squabasher	stabilator	stand up for
split-brain	sportswear	squabbiest	stabiliser	stannaries
split-field	spot effect	squabbling	stabilized	stannotype
split graft	spot height	squab-chick	stabilizer	stanza-form
split hairs	spotlessly	squadronal	stable door	stanzaical
split-image	spotted dog	squadroned	Stableford	staphyloma
split-level	spotted gum	squalidity	stablefuls	starbolins
split-phase	spotted ray	squall line	stable girl	star-bright
split shift	spottiness	squamation	stable-lass	starch fish
split stuff	spot-welder	squamiform	stablemate	starchiest
split wheel	spot zoning	squamosity	stableness	starchness
splutterer	spousehood	squamulose	stablisher	star-flower
spodomancy	spouseless	squanderer	stab-stitch	staring mad
spoilsport	sprauncier	square away	stab stroke	stark naked
spokenness	spray-dried	square deal	stackfreed	starriness
spokeshave	spray-dries	square-eyed	stack-garth	starry-eyed
spokeslady	spray-paint	square eyes	stadholder	star stream

star-struck	steam navvy	stereobate	stigmergic	stone-brake
starstruck	steam organ	stereo card	stillatory	stone-brash
star system	steam point	stereogram	stillbirth	stonebreak
start a hare	steam power	stereology	still-house	stone-broke
starter set	steam radio	stereo pair	stillicide	stone canal
startingly	steam table	stereopsis	still lifes	stone-china
starvation	steam-tight	stereoptic	still-stand	stone-coral
starveling	steam train	Stereoscan	still water	stone-craft
stasiology	steel fixer	stereotaxy	stiltified	stone cream
state a case	steel frame	stereotomy	stimulable	stone-field
state-cabin	steeliness	stereotype	stimulancy	stoneflies
statecraft	steelworks	stereotypy	stimulator	stone fruit
stated case	steep-grass	sterically	stinginess	stone guard
State-house	steeple cup	sterilizer	stingingly	stonehatch
state of war	steep-water	sterlingly	stinkblaar	Stonehenge
State-paper	stellardom	sternalgia	stink gland	stone loach
State trial	stellately	sternal rib	stinkingly	stonemason
State visit	stellation	stern-board	stinkstone	stone river
statically	Steller jay	stern-chase	stipellate	stony-broke
staticisor	stelleroid	sterndrive	stipulator	stony coral
static line	stelliform	sterner sex	stirringly	stoopingly
staticness	stem family	stern-gland	stirrup-bar	stop-action
static test	stem ginger	stern-piece	stirrup cup	stop behind
static tube	stemmatics	sternsheet	stishovite	stop button
stationary	stem mother	stern speed	stitchbird	stop chords
station-day	stem sawfly	sternutory	stitchless	stop chorus
stationery	stem stitch	sternwards	stitch weld	stop-handle
stationman	stem-winder	stern-wheel	stitch-work	stop-motion
statistics	stench-pipe	stertorous	stitchwort	stop signal
statoblast	stench trap	stethogram	stob-thatch	stop-thrust
statocracy	stencilled	stevioside	stochastic	stop-volley
statolatry	stenciller	steward boy	stock-blind	store buyer
statoscope	Stengunner	stewardess	stock-board	storefront
statospore	stenograph	stiacciato	stock-brick	storehouse
statuarist	stenopaeic	stibialism	stock-frost	storiation
statueless	Stenorette	stichidium	stockhorse	storiology
statuesque	stenotherm	stichology	stockiness	stork's-bill
statutable	stenotopic	stickadove	stockinged	storm apron
statutably	stenotyper	stick chair	stockinger	storm-beach
statute law	stenotypic	stick dance	stockishly	stormbound
staurolite	stentorial	stick fixed	stock knife	storm choke
staurotide	stentorian	stick force	stockpiler	storm cloud
staverwort	step astray	stickiness	stock-proof	storm drain
stavesacre	step by step	stick it out	stock-purse	storm-finch
stay-at-home	step-dancer	stick one on	stock-rider	stormfully
stay-putter	stepfamily	stick shift	stock-route	storm-glass
stay shtoom	stepfather	sticktight	stock split	storminess
stay-stitch	step-gabled	stick up for	stock-still	storm-light
steadiment	stephanion	stickwater	stocktaker	storm-porch
steadiness	stephanite	sticky-back	stodge-full	stormproof
steady down	stepladder	stickybeak	stodginess	storm sewer
steak Diane	steplessly	sticky bomb	Stokes' line	storm surge
steak-house	step lively	sticky tape	stolen-wise	storm track
steakhouse	stepmother	stiff-arsed	stolidness	storm troop
steak knife	step-parent	stiffening	stomachful	storm-water
stealingly	step rocket	stifle-bone	stomatitic	storyboard
stealthful	stepsister	stiflingly	stomatitis	stout heart
stealthier	stercolith	stigmarian	stomatopod	stout party
stealthily	stercorary	stigmatise	stomochord	stove-grate
steamer rug	stercorate	stigmatist	stomodaeal	stow-master
steam gauge	stercorean	stigmatize	stomodaeum	strabismal
steaminess	stercorous	stigmatose	stomp dance	strabismic

strabismus	streetward	strippeuse	stultifies	subjectile
stracchino	streetwise	strip-poker	stumblebum	subjection
Stracheyan	strelitzia	strip steak	stump fence	subjective
stragglier	strengthen	striptease	stumpiness	subjoinder
straggling	strepitant	strivingly	stump plant	subjugable
straight A's	strepitoso	strobe disc	stump water	subjugator
straighten	strepitous	strobe lamp	stunningly	subkingdom
straightly	stressable	strobiloid	stupefying	sublateral
straight-up	stress-free	strobotron	stupendous	sublattice
strainable	stressless	stroganoff	stupidness	sublexemic
strainedly	stress mark	Stroganoff	sturdiness	sublimable
straitened	stress test	stroke book	stylistics	sublimator
strait-lace	stretching	stroke-haul	stylograph	subliminal
straitness	stretch jet	strokeless	stylohyoid	sublingual
stramonium	stretch out	stroke play	stylolitic	subliteral
strandflat	striaeform	strokeplay	stylometry	subluminal
strand-line	strickenly	stroke-side	stylophone	submariner
Strandveld	strictness	strokesman	stylopized	submarshal
strand-wolf	strictured	stromateid	stypticity	submediant
strap brake	striddling	stromatous	suabe flute	submersion
strap hinge	stridently	strong-back	suaveolent	submission
strappados	stridingly	strong card	subacidity	submissive
Strasbourg	stridulant	strong-eyed	subacutely	submitting
strategian	stridulate	strong gale	sub-almoner	submontane
strategics	stridulent	strong hand	subangular	submucosal
strategies	stridulous	strong head	subaquatic	subnascent
strategise	strifeless	stronghold	subaqueous	sub-nuclear
strategist	strike back	strong meat	subarcuate	subnuclear
strategize	strike call	strongness	subaudible	subodorate
strathspey	strike down	strongroom	subauditur	sub-officer
stratified	strike fire	strong suit	sub-calibre	suboptimal
stratifies	strike home	strophical	sub-carrier	sub-orbital
stratiform	strike-over	strophiole	subcentral	suborbital
stratocrat	strike rate	strophulus	subception	subordinal
stratotype	strike root	stroppiest	subchanter	subpassage
Straussian	strike-slip	structural	subchelate	subpoenaed
stravaiger	strike upon	structured	subclavian	sub-prefect
strawberry	strike wide	struggle on	subclavius	subprogram
straw-blond	strike zone	struggling	subcompact	subreption
strawboard	strikingly	Struldbrug	subconical	subreptive
straw braid	strim-stram	strumatous	subcordate	subroutine
straw-death	string bass	struthioid	subcranial	sub-Saharan
straw paper	string bean	struthious	subculture	subscriber
straw plait	stringency	strychnine	subdeanery	subsection
stray field	stringendo	strychnism	subdialect	subsellium
streakiest	stringhalt	stubbed-out	subdivider	subsensual
stream-flow	stringiest	stubbiness	subduction	subsequent
streamless	stringless	stubble-fed	subduement	subserrate
streamline	stringlike	stubble-rig	subduingly	subsessile
streamside	string-line	stubbornly	sub-element	subshrubby
stream-tide	string vest	stub equity	subequally	subsidence
street arab	strinkling	stub-switch	subfuscous	subsidency
street Arab	striolated	studentess	subgeneric	subsidiary
street cred	strioscopy	studentish	subglacial	subsidizer
street door	stripagram	studentize	subglobose	subsistent
street drug	strip-chart	studio flat	sub-heading	subsolidus
street girl	strip-graze	studiously	subheading	subspecies
street-grid	stripiness	study group	subhumanly	subspinous
street lamp	strip joint	stuffed owl	subinfeoff	substanced
street name	strip light	stuffiness	subintrant	substance P
street tree	stripogram	stultified	subjacency	substantia
	strippable	stultifier	subjectify	sub-station

substation	sufferance	summer teal	superoxide	surf-riding
substellar	suffibulum	summer-tide	superpower	surf scoter
substitute	sufficient	summer time	super-royal	surgeoness
substratal	suffisance	summertime	superseder	surgically
substratum	suffragism	summer-tree	supersonic	Surinamese
subsultive	suffragist	summer wood	supersound	surjection
subsultory	sugarallie	summitless	superspace	surjective
subsumable	sugar-apple	summonable	superstate	surmisable
subsurface	sugar-baker	sumphishly	superstore	surmounted
subtangent	sugar-berry	sun balcony	supertonic	surnominal
subtenancy	sugar-candy	sun bittern	supertunic	surpassing
subterfuge	sugar daddy	sun compass	supervener	surplusage
subterrane	sugar-grass	Sunday best	supervisal	surprising
subterrene	sugar-house	Sunday face	supervisee	surrealism
subtertian	sugariness	Sundayfied	supervisor	surrealist
subtextual	sugar maple	sunderable	superwoman	surreality
subtilisin	sugarollie	sunderancc	superwomen	Surrentine
subtleness	sugar-paper	Sunderland	supination	surreption
subtleties	sugar stick	sunderment	supineness	Surrey fowl
subtracter	sugar-tongs	sundriness	suppedanea	surrounder
subtractor	sugar-works	sun furnace	supper club	surveyable
subtrahend	suggestion	sunglasses	supperless	surveyance
subtropics	suggestive	sun-grazing	supper-time	survivable
subtypical	suicidally	sunk garden	supplanter	survivance
suburbanly	sui generis	sunk storey	supplejack	susception
suburbican	suit length	sun-lighted	supplement	susceptive
subvariety	suitorship	sun-lounger	suppleness	suscipient
subvention	suit-weight	sunlounger	suppletion	suspectful
subversion	sullenness	sun parlour	suppletive	suspension
subversive	sulphamate	sun-picture	suppletory	suspensive
succedanea	sulphamide	sunset home	suppliable	suspensoid
succeeding	sulphatase	sunsetting	suppliance	suspensory
successful	sulphatide	sunshining	suppliancy	suspicable
succession	sulphation	superalloy	supplicant	suspicious
successive	sulphinate	superaltar	supplicate	suspirious
succinctly	sulpho-acid	superbitch	supply base	Sussex fowl
succorance	sulphonate	superbness	supply drop	sustaining
succulence	sulphonium	superbrain	supply-side	sustenance
succussion	sulphosalt	supercargo	supportive	sustentate
succussive	sulphoxide	supercilia	supposable	sustention
such as it is	sulphurate	superclass	supposably	sustentive
suck around	sulphurise	supercross	supposedly	sutlership
suck-bottle	sulphurity	super-duper	suppressal	suturation
sucker-disc	sulphurize	superexalt	suppressed	suzerainty
sucker-fish	sulphurous	superexcel	suppresser	suzuribako
sucker-foot	sulphydric	super-extra	suppressor	Svetambara
sucking-pad	sulphydryl	superfecta	suprahuman	swage-block
sucralfate	sultan pink	superfluid	supralunar	swami-house
suction box	sultanship	supergiant	supraoptic	swamp angel
suction fan	sultriness	supergrass	suprapubic	swamp apple
suction gas	Sumerogram	supergroup	suprarenal	swamp buggy
suctorious	Sumerology	superheavy	supratidal	swamp fever
Sudan grass	summarizer	superhelix	supravital	swampiness
sudatories	summer bird	superhuman	surcharger	swamp quail
sudatorium	summer camp	superindue	sure as a gun	swamp robin
suddenness	summer duck	superionic	sure enough	swan flower
suede brush	summer-heat	superiorly	sure-footed	swan-hopper
suede-cloth	summer-land	superlunar	suretyship	swankiness
suede-shoed	summerless	supermanly	surfaceman	swan-maiden
suet-headed	summer-like	supermodel	surface-rib	swan mussel
sufferable	summer-long	supernally	surfactant	swan-necked
sufferably	summer's day	superorder	surfeiting	swanneries

Swan of Avon	swing Kelly	symphonies	synthetist	tailor-bird
swan-upping	swingle-bar	symphonise	synthetize	tailor-made
swarm-spore	swing-round	symphonism	Syntocinon	tailor-make
swarthiest	swing shift	symphonist	syntrophic	tailor-shad
swashingly	swing-swang	symphonize	syphilitic	tailorship
swash-plate	swing-wheel	symphyseal	syphilosis	tailor-wise
swashplate	swirl skirt	symphysial	syringeful	take a brief
swastikaed	swish-swash	symplasmic	systematic	take a chair
swatch-book	swish-swish	symplastic	systemizer	take a class
swath-board	Swiss chard	symplectic	systemless	take action
swayamvara	Swiss cream	symposiast	tabardillo	take advice
sway-backed	Swiss guard	symposiums	tabby weave	take a flyer
swear blind	Swiss steak	sympotical	tabernacle	take a knock
sweat blood	switchable	symptomize	table-board	take a level
sweat gland	switchback	synaereses	table-clock	take an oath
sweat-house	switch cane	synaeresis	tablecloth	take a smoke
sweatiness	switch deal	synaloepha	table-cover	take as read
sweatingly	switched-on	synanthous	table d'hôte	take breath
sweat it out	switcheroo	synaxarion	table jelly	take care of
sweat lodge	switchfoot	synaxarist	table knife	take charge
sweat pants	switchgear	syncarpous	table linen	take effect
sweatpants	switch gene	synchronal	table-money	take flight
sweatshirt	switch-girl	synchronic	tablemount	take fright
Swedish ivy	switch hook	Synclavier	table-music	take heed of
sweepingly	switch-horn	syncopated	table-plate	take in hand
sweepstake	switch-lamp	syncopator	tablescape	take in sail
sweet Alice	switch over	syncretise	table-shore	take it easy
sweet basil	switch tail	syncretism	tablespoon	take it slow
sweet bread	switchyard	syncretist	table-stone	take kindly
sweetbread	Switzeress	syncretize	table-water	taken aback
sweet-brier	swivel-eyed	syndactyly	tabloidese	take notice
sweet broom	swivel hips	synderesis	tabula rasa	take orders
sweet cumin	swivel-hook	syndicator	tabulation	take pity on
sweetening	swivelling	synecdoche	tabulatory	take refuge
sweet-grass	swooningly	synecology	tachograph	take sights
sweetheart	sword dance	synergetic	tachometer	take the air
sweetie-pie	sword grass	syngenesis	tachometry	take the bun
sweet Jesus	sword-proof	syngenetic	tachygraph	take the rap
sweet lemon	sword-sedge	syngnathid	tachykinin	take the rue
sweet mamma	sword-smith	synkinesis	tachymeter	take the sea
sweetmouth	swordstick	synkinetic	tachypnoea	take the sun
sweet music	sybaritish	synoecious	tachyscope	take the way
sweet Nancy	sybaritism	synonymies	tachyzoite	take to task
sweet olive	sycophancy	synonymise	taciturnly	take to wife
sweet sedge	Sydney-side	synonymist	tack-hammer	take up arms
sweetstuff	syllabuses	synonymity	tackle-fall	take up with
sweet tooth	syllogizer	synonymize	tackle-room	takhtrawan
sweet water	sylvestral	synonymous	tactically	takingness
swell-front	symbolatry	synoptical	tactlessly	Talbot's law
swellingly	symbolical	synostosis	tactuality	talc powder
swell-organ	symbolizer	synostotic	taeniacide	talc schist
swell-shark	symbolling	synovially	taeniafuge	talc window
sweltering	symmetries	syntactics	taeniodont	talebearer
swerveless	symmetrise	syntagmata	taffy apple	talentless
swim-feeder	symmetrize	syntaxemic	tagliarini	talent show
swimmingly	sympathies	syntaxical	tagraggery	talent-spot
swimsuited	sympathise	synteresis	tailcoated	tale of a tub
swine-cress	sympathist	synthesise	tail covert	taleteller
swine fever	sympathize	synthesist	tail female	talismanic
swing-chair	sympelmous	synthesize	tail-flower	talk down to
swing-glass	symphilism	synthetase	tail gunner	talk turkey
swingingly	symphilous	synthetise	tailorable	talkwriter

talky-talky	tariff wall	team spirit	Teller mine	tensometer
tallow-drop	tarmacadam	tea-planter	tellership	tentacular
tallow-face	tarmacking	tear bottle	telligraph	tentaculum
tallow tree	tarocchino	tear-jerker	telling-off	tenterhook
tallow-wood	Tarquinian	tearlessly	tellograph	tenth-value
tall timber	tarsectomy	tea-scented	telophasic	tent-master
tally-board	tarsonemid	tea-seed oil	telpherage	tent-pegger
tally clerk	tartareous	tea-service	temenggong	tent stitch
tally sheet	tartrazine	tea-tasting	temeritous	tenurially
tally-stick	tartronate	tea trolley	temerously	tepidarium
tallywoman	Tartuffian	tea yellows	temperable	teppan-yaki
Talmudical	Tartuffism	teaze-tenon	temperance	teratogeny
tamarillos	taskmaster	technetium	tempersome	teratology
tamboritsa	tassel-bush	technician	tempestive	terebellid
tambourine	tassel fish	technicise	Templardom	tergiverse
tamburitza	tasselling	technicism	templeless	termagancy
tameletjie	tassel-weed	technicist	temporalis	terminable
tame-poison	taste-blind	technicity	temporally	terminably
Tammanyism	taste blood	technicize	temporalty	terminalia
Tammanyite	tastefully	technocrat	temporizer	terminally
tandem axle	tat protein	technofear	temptation	terminator
tangential	tatpurusha	technology	temptingly	terminuses
tanglefoot	tattersall	technonomy	temulently	term-policy
tangle-legs	tattie-trap	tectogenic	tenability	term symbol
tanglement	tattle-tale	tectonical	tenantable	terne metal
tanglingly	tattlingly	teeny-weeny	tenantless	terne-plate
tank-buster	tauntingly	teeter-tail	tenantship	terpolymer
tank engine	tauromachy	teeth ridge	tendencies	terracette
tannic acid	tautologic	teetotaler	tendential	terracotta
tantalizer	tautomeric	teetotally	tenderable	terra firma
tantamount	tautonymic	tegumental	tender-eyed	Terramycin
Tantum ergo	tautophony	teichopsia	tenderfoot	terraneous
tap-changer	tautozonal	Tel Avivian	tenderizer	terrariums
tap-dancing	tawdriness	telecabinc	tenderling	terra rossa
tape player	tawny eagle	telecamera	tenderloin	terreplein
tape reader	tawny pipit	telecaster	tenderness	terre-verte
tape-record	taxability	telechiric	tender spot	terrier-man
taperingly	tax bracket	telecobalt	tendinitis	territoria
tapescript	tax evasion	Telecopier	tendonitis	terrorizer
tapestried	taxflation	telegnosis	tendrillar	terrorless
tapestries	tax holiday	telegraphy	tendrilled	terror raid
taphonomic	taxi dancer	telemarket	tenebresce	Tersanctus
tapotement	taxidermal	telematics	tenebrific	tertiation
tap penalty	taxidermic	telemetric	tenebrious	tessellate
tappety-tap	taxi-driver	teleologic	tenemental	testaceous
tapping-bar	taxonomist	teleonomic	tenemented	test flight
tapping key	taxonomize	teleostean	tenementer	testicular
taradiddle	tax shelter	telepathic	tenmantale	test-market
Tarahumara	tayberries	telephoner	tennantite	test-retest
tarantella	T-bone steak	telephonic	Tennessean	test signal
tarantelle	Tcheremiss	telephotos	tennis ball	testudinal
tarantular	tchinovnik	teleprompt	tennis club	testudines
Tarantulle	T-connected	telepuppet	tennis knee	tetarteron
tarbooshed	teacherage	teleradium	tennis-play	tetchiness
tardigrade	teacheress	telerecord	tennis shoe	tetrabasic
targetable	tea-clipper	telescopic	tenotomies	tetracaine
target area	teacupfuls	telescreen	tenotomize	tetrachord
target cell	tea-drinker	televiewer	ten-pointer	tetracolon
target date	tea infuser	television	ten-pounder	tetracoral
target-rich	tea machine	televisual	tensegrity	tetradecyl
targetting	team player	teleworker	tensimeter	tetraethyl
tariffable	team rector	teliospore	tension bar	tetragnath

tetragonal	the classes	theophoric	think aloud	thread-mill
tetrahedra	the Commune	theopneust	thinkingly	thread vein
tetrameric	the Company	theorician	think-piece	thread-wire
tetrameter	thé complet	theosopher	think scorn	threadwork
tetramorph	the Creator	theosophic	think shame	threadworm
tetraploid	the Curragh	the Prophet	think twice	threatened
tetrapolis	The Customs	thereabout	thiochrome	threatener
tetrapylon	thé dansant	thereabove	thiocyanic	three balls
tetrarchic	the Descent	thereafter	thioindigo	three-eight
tetrasomic	the dickens	thereamong	thioketone	three-field
tetraspore	the dismals	thereanent	thiomersal	Three in One
tetrastich	the Eternal	therehence	thiopental	three parts
tetrastoon	the fair sex	thereright	thiophenol	threepence
tetrastyle	The Fifteen	thereunder	thiouracil	threepenny
tetrateuch	the Flemish	there you go	third-class	three-phase
tetrathlon	the Forties	thermalise	third floor	three-piece
tetratomic	the glad eye	thermalize	third flute	three-piled
tetterworm	the hard way	thermionic	third force	three-point
tetterwort	the heathen	thermistor	third house	threescore
teuthology	the heavens	Thermogene	third order	three-sixty
Teutomania	the icy mitt	thermogram	third party	three-space
Teutophile	the instant	thermology	third power	threnodial
Teutophobe	the insured	the r months	third-rater	threnodist
Texas fever	theistical	thermophil	Third Reich	thresh over
Texas Tower	the jitters	thermopile	third water	thriftiest
text editor	the likes of	thermostat	Third World	thriftless
text-letter	the low toby	thermotics	thirstiest	thrift shop
textualism	the Macedon	theromorph	thirstless	thriveless
textualist	the Mahatma	therophyte	thirteener	thrivingly
textuality	the Marches	the schools	thirteenth	throat-band
texturally	thematical	the shivers	thirty-five	throat-full
text-writer	theme music	thesis-play	thirtyfold	throatiest
T-formation	Themistian	the species	thirty-four	throat-lash
thack-board	themselves	Thessalian	thirty-nine	throatless
thack house	thenabouts	theta meson	this moment	throat-mane
thack-stone	thenardite	theta pinch	this or that	throat-pipe
Thailander	the nations	the Tempter	thistle cup	throat-wash
thalassian	thencefrom	the three R's	thixotropy	throatwort
thale cress	then-clause	thetically	tholeiitic	thromboses
thaliacean	theocrasia	the Tropics	tholos tomb	thrombosis
thalictrum	theocratic	the Twelfth	Thomsonian	thrombotic
thankfully	theodicaea	theurgical	thomsonite	throneless
thanksgive	theodicean	the visible	thorianite	throne room
thatchless	theodicies	the wee folk	thorn apple	throughout
thatch-palm	theodidact	the year dot	thorn-hedge	throughput
that's right	theodolite	the year one	thorniness	throughway
that will do	Theodosian	thiaminase	thorn-proof	throw about
the accused	Theodotian	thickening	thornproof	throw a look
thearchies	theogonies	thick-skull	Thorotrast	throw aside
theatrical	theogonist	thick space	thoroughly	throw-stick
the Balkans	the Old Dart	thick woods	thoughtful	thruppence
the big bird	theologate	thief-taker	thought-out	thruppenny
the big idea	theologian	thieveless	thoughtway	thrushlike
the big pond	theologies	thieveries	thousandth	thrutching
the big time	theologise	thievishly	thrawnness	thuddingly
the black ox	theologism	thill-horse	threadbare	thuggishly
the Borders	theologist	thimble-eye	thread-cell	thumb-cleat
the Borough	theologize	thimbleful	threadiest	thumb-flint
the Bye Plot	theomaniac	thimblerig	thread-lace	thumbikins
the cap fits	theopathic	thinginess	threadless	thumb index
the cassock	theophanic	thingumbob	threadlike	thumb paper
the Channel	theophobia	think again	thread mark	thumb piano

thumbpiece	tiger heron	tinselling	toddy-ladle	tongue-sole
thumbprint	tigerishly	Tinseltown	toddy-stick	tonguester
thumbscrew	tiger maple	tin soldier	toe and heel	tongues wag
thumbs down	tiger prawn	tintamarre	toe-curling	tongue-tied
thumb-stall	tiger shark	Tintometer	toe-dancing	tongue-work
thumb-stick	tiger-snake	tin wedding	toe of Italy	tongue-worm
thumpingly	tight-assed	tin whistle	toe-tapping	tonguiness
thunbergia	tight-laced	tip one's hat	toe the line	tonic major
thunder-axe	tigrolysis	tip-topmost	toffee-like	tonic minor
thunder-box	tillandsia	tirailleur	toffee-nose	tonic sol-fa
thunderbox	tiller-head	tirelessly	Toggenburg	tonic spasm
thunderbug	tillerless	tiresomely	toggle-bolt	tonic water
thunder egg	tiller-rope	tiring-iron	togt-ganger	tonitruant
thunderfly	tiller soup	tirocinium	to hospital	tonitruous
thunderful	Tilley lamp	tirra-lirra	toilenette	ton-mileage
thunder-god	till-tapper	tissue-bank	toilet-case	tonofibril
thundering	tilly-vally	tissue type	toiletries	tonometric
thunder-mug	tilt-hammer	tit and arse	toilet roll	tonotactic
thunderous	timber-head	Titanesque	toilet-room	Tony Curtis
thunder run	timberjack	titanosaur	toilet soap	tool-holder
thuribuler	timberland	tit-babbler	toilet tent	toolmaking
Thuringian	timberless	titbitical	toilsomely	tool-pusher
thwartness	timberline	tithingman	to infinity	too many for
thwart-over	timber tree	titillator	tokay gecko	too much for
thwartship	timber wolf	titivation	token booth	to one's face
thwartways	timber-work	title entry	tokenistic	to one's feet
thwartwise	timber-yard	title fight	token money	to one's hand
thymectomy	timbreless	title-music	tolazamide	to one's head
thymic acid	time-barred	title-piece	tolazoline	to one's will
thymidylic	time-course	titratable	tolerantly	toothbrush
thyrohyoid	time domain	titrimetry	toleration	tooth fairy
thyroideal	time enough	tits and ass	tolfraedic	tooth-glass
thyrotoxic	time factor	tittupping	Tolkienian	toothpaste
thysanuran	time-fellow	titty-totty	toll bridge	tooth-plate
Tiahuanaco	timekeeper	titubation	toll-farmer	tooth shell
Tibetology	time-killer	titularity	toll-keeper	to outrance
tibiotarsi	timelessly	titulature	tomahawker	top and tail
ticker tape	timeliness	tit warbler	tomatillos	topazolite
ticket fine	time-notice	toad-headed	tomato moth	topgallant
ticketless	time of life	to a frazzle	tomato vine	tophaceous
ticket tout	time pencil	to a miracle	tomato worm	top-heavily
tickety-boo	time policy	to and again	Tom Collins	Tophetical
tickle pink	time's arrow	to a proverb	tomfoolery	topicality
ticklesome	time-series	toast Melba	tomfoolish	topicalize
tickle-tail	time-served	to a surfeit	Tom o'Bedlam	topknotted
ticklishly	time-server	tobacco-box	tomography	Töpler pump
tick-tacker	time signal	tobacco fly	tomorrower	top-lighted
tick typhus	time-spirit	tobacco-man	Tom Pudding	top-notcher
ticky-tacky	times table	Tobagonian	tonalities	topogenous
tic-polonga	time switch	Tobin's tube	tonalitive	topography
tidal basin	time-taking	tobogganer	tone-colour	topoisomer
tidal river	time thrust	tobramycin	toned paper	topologist
tidal train	time travel	to capacity	tonelessly	topologize
tiddlypush	time-waster	Tocharian A	tone-on-tone	toponymist
tiddly suit	timocratic	Tocharian B	tone sandhi	toposcopic
tiddlywink	timorously	tocher-band	tongue-bang	topotactic
tidewaiter	tin-canning	tocher-good	tongue-fish	top-slicing
tidingless	tinctorial	tocherless	tongue-lash	top-spinner
tie-breaker	tinder-like	tocologist	tongueless	topsy-turvy
tie in knots	tin disease	tocopherol	tonguelike	topsy-versy
tie the knot	tinker-bird	toco toucan	tongue-shot	torbernite
tiger-finch	tinktinkie	toddlekins	tongue-slip	torchlight

tornado-pit	Tower pound	tragi-farce	transpolar	tree tomato
toroidally	towing hook	trail a pike	transposal	treillaged
torpedoist	towing line	trailerite	transposer	trek farmer
torpedoman	towing-path	trail-hound	transposon	trek netter
torpedo-net	towing-rope	trailingly	transprose	trekschuit
torpidness	Townsville	train crash	transputer	trellising
torporific	townswoman	train ferry	trans-shape	trembleuse
torrential	townswomen	train-guard	trans-sonic	trembliest
torrid zone	toxalbumin	traitoress	transudate	tremelloid
torsion bar	toxication	traitorism	transvalue	tremendous
tortellini	toxicology	traitorous	transvenom	tremograph
tortfeasor	toxiphobia	trajectile	transverse	tremolando
tortiously	toxophoric	trajection	trans-world	tremolitic
tortuosity	toxoplasma	trajectory	trap-cellar	tremolo arm
tortuously	toy library	trammelled	trapeziums	tremor disc
torturable	toy soldier	trammeller	trap-siding	tremorless
tos and fros	toy theatre	tramontana	trash-house	trenbolone
to some tune	trabaccolo	tramontane	trashiness	trenchancy
toss pillow	trabeation	trampoline	traumatise	trench boot
tosylation	trabeculae	tramp-tramp	traumatism	trench coat
totalistic	trabecular	trance-like	traumatize	trench feet
totemistic	trace-chain	trancelike	trautonium	trench foot
to the death	trace-horse	tranchette	travailous	trenchless
to the north	tracheated	tranexamic	travelator	trenchmore
to the point	tracheidal	tranquilli	travel card	trendiness
tother year	tracheitis	tranquillo	travelling	trepanning
to the skies	trachelate	tranquilly	travelogue	treponemal
to the south	tracheolar	transactor	travel-sick	trespasser
to the teeth	track-brake	transboard	traversely	trestle-bed
to the touch	tracker dog	transcribe	travertine	trevallies
to the winds	track event	transcript	travestied	triacetate
totipotent	tracklayer	transducer	travestier	triaconter
touch-and-go	tractarian	transearth	travesties	trial court
touchiness	Tractarian	transeptal	travolator	trial eight
touchingly	tractatule	transepted	trawlerman	triallelic
touch judge	tractility	transeunce	trawlermen	trial-piece
touch-me-not	tractional	transexual	traymobile	triandrous
touch panel	tractoring	transferee	tread-board	triangular
touch-paper	tractotomy	transferer	tread on air	Triangulum
touchpaper	Trade Board	transferor	tread water	triathlete
touch-piece	tradecraft	transgenic	treadwheel	triatomine
touch rugby	trade cycle	transgress	treasonous	triaxially
touchstone	trade paper	transhuman	treasuress	tribometer
tough pitch	trade plate	transience	treasuries	tribrachic
tough stuff	trade price	transiency	treatyless	trichiasis
tough titty	trade-route	transistor	treaty port	trichinous
Toulousain	tradesfolk	transiting	treble bell	trichocyst
Tourettism	trade union	transition	treble clef	trichogyne
touring car	trade waste	transitive	treble hook	trichology
tourmaline	traditores	transit man	trebleness	trichotomy
tournament	traduction	transitory	trecentist	trichroism
tourniquet	traductive	transitron	tree doctor	trichromat
tout simple	traffic cop	Transkeian	tree-feeder	trichromic
towability	traffic jam	translator	tree hoopoe	tricipital
towardness	trafficked	translucid	tree hopper	trickeries
tow-boating	trafficker	translunar	tree mallow	trick-frame
towel-gourd	tragacanth	transmural	tree martin	trickiness
towel-horse	tragedical	transmuted	tree medick	trickishly
tower block	tragedious	transmuter	tree of life	tricksiest
tower-cress	tragically	transocean	tree-oyster	trick wheel
toweringly	tragic flaw	transplace	treerunner	triclinium
tower karst	tragicomic	transplant	tree search	tricoccous

tricrotism	tripleness	trolley-car	trustingly	tundra swan
tricyclist	triple play	trolleyful	trust-stock	tunelessly
tridecylic	triple salt	trolleyman	truthfully	tuner-timer
tridentate	triple-tail	Trollopian	truth serum	tuning-cone
Tridentine	triple time	trollopish	truth squad	tuning fork
trienniums	triple tree	trombonist	truth table	tuning-wire
trierarchy	triplicate	tromometer	truth-value	tunnel-back
trifarious	triplicist	tron weight	try for size	tunnel-head
triflingly	triplicity	troop-horse	tryingness	tunnel-kiln
trifoliate	Tripolitan	troostitic	trypsinize	tunnel-like
trifurcate	tripperish	tropaeolin	tryptamine	tunnelling
trigeminal	trippiness	tropaeolum	tryptophan	Tupperware
trigeminus	trippingly	trophocyte	try-scoring	turbanless
trigesimal	tripsomely	trophogeny	tube curare	turbanwise
trigger man	trip switch	trophology	tube-flower	turbary pig
triglossia	tripudiant	trophonema	tube of flow	turbiditic
triglyphed	tripudiate	Trophonian	tuberation	turbidness
triglyphic	triquetrae	trophosome	tubercular	turbinated
trigonally	triquetral	tropically	tuberculin	turbodrill
trigonitis	triradiate	tropic bird	tuberculum	turbopause
trihedrons	trisection	tropologic	tuberiform	turboshaft
trihydrate	triseptate	tropopause	tuberosity	turbotrain
trilabiate	tri-service	tropophyte	tuberously	turbulence
trilaminar	triskelion	tropotaxis	tub gurnard	turbulency
trilateral	Tristanian	Trotskyism	tubicolous	Turcophile
trilineate	Tristanite	Trotskyist	tuboplasty	Turcophobe
trilingual	tristearin	Trotskyite	tub-thumper	turf-cutter
trilinguar	tristfully	troubadour	tubularian	turgescent
triliteral	tristichic	troubledly	tubularity	turgidness
trillibubs	tristylous	trouble man	tubulation	Turing test
trillingly	trisulcate	troughlike	tubulature	turkey bush
trillionth	tritanopia	trousering	tubuliform	turkey-call
trilobitic	tritanopic	trousseaus	tuckerless	turkeycock
trilocular	triternate	trousseaux	tuck-stitch	turkey-corn
trimestral	triterpane	trout-perch	Tudoresque	turkey-gnat
trimmingly	triterpene	trouvaille	tuffaceous	Turkey hone
trimnasium	tritiation	trowelling	tuftaffeta	turkey-trot
trimonthly	triturable	troy weight	tufted duck	Turkey work
trimorphic	triturator	Trubenized	tuft-hunted	Turkish rug
tri-motored	triumphant	truce of God	tuft-hunter	turn around
Trinacrian	triumviral	truck frame	tug-boating	turnaround
trinacrite	triungulin	truck-house	tuitionary	turn a trick
trinkerman	triunities	truckle-bed	tularaemia	turn-bridge
trinoctial	trivalence	truck-store	tularaemic	turn bridle
trinocular	trivalency	truculence	tulip break	turnbroach
trinominal	trivialise	truculency	tulip-glass	turn-buckle
trioecious	trivialism	true for you	tumatakuru	turn-button
trio-sonata	trivialist	true to form	tumbledown	turn colour
tripartism	triviality	true to life	tumble-dung	turn-furrow
tripartite	trivialize	true to type	tumble home	turning-pin
trip-bucket	trochaical	truffle-dog	tumble-over	turning-saw
tripe-hound	trochanter	truistical	tumbler-cup	turnip-flea
tripeptide	trochiform	trumperies	tumblerful	turnip moth
trip-hammer	trochoidal	trumpeting	tumbleweed	turnip-tops
triphibian	trochotron	trumpet-lug	tumescence	turnip-wood
triphthong	troctolite	truncately	tumour-like	turn-plough
triphylite	troglobion	truncation	tumulation	turn signal
tripinnate	troglodyte	truncature	tumultuary	turns ratio
triplasian	trogloxene	trundle-bed	tumultuate	turn turtle
triple bond	trolley-bar	trunk-maker	tumultuous	turnverein
triple harp	trolley bus	trustfully	tunability	turpentine
triple jump	trolleybus	trustiness	tun-bellied	turpentiny

turtle-back	tympanitis	umbrellaed	unassorted	unborrowed
turtle-deck	tyndallize	umpireship	unassuaged	unbothered
turtle-dove	type basket	unabatable	unassuming	unbottomed
turtlehead	type-holder	unabatedly	unathletic	unbowelled
turtle-neck	typescript	unabridged	unatonable	unbranched
turtleneck	typesetter	unabsolved	unattached	unbreached
Turveydrop	typewriter	unabsorbed	unattacked	unbreathed
tut-mouthed	typhlosole	unacademic	unattained	unbreeched
tutorially	typhogenic	unaccented	unattended	unbribable
tuxedo sofa	typhomania	unaccepted	unattested	unbroached
tuzzy-muzzy	typhoonish	unaccursed	unavailing	unbrokenly
twanginess	typicality	unachieved	unavowable	unburdened
twangingly	typography	unacquaint	unavowedly	unburiable
tweediness	typologist	unacquired	unawakened	unburnable
Tweedledee	typologize	unactorish	unbackable	unbuttered
Tweedledum	typoscript	unactressy	unbailable	unbuttoned
tweet tweet	typothetae	unactuated	unbalanced	uncalcined
twelfth day	tyrannical	unadaptive	unbanished	uncalendar
Twelfth Day	tyrannizer	unaddicted	unbankable	uncandidly
twelfth man	tyrantship	unadjacent	unbaptized	uncanniest
twelve-bore	tyre-cement	unadjusted	unbarbered	uncanonise
twelvefold	tyrocinium	unadmiring	unbattered	uncanonize
twelve noon	tyrosinase	unadmitted	unbearable	uncanopied
twelve-note	Tyrrhenian	unadvanced	unbearably	uncaptious
twelve-tone	ubiquarian	unaffected	unbeatable	uncaptured
twenty-five	ubiquinone	unagitated	unbeatably	uncardinal
twentyfold	ubiquitary	unalarming	unbeautify	uncared-for
twenty-four	Ubiquitism	unalliable	unbecoming	uncaringly
twenty-nine	ubiquitous	unallotted	unbedimmed	uncarpeted
twiddly bit	ufological	unalluring	unbegotten	uncastable
twig-blight	ugsomeness	unaltering	unbeguiled	uncatholic
twigginess	uintathere	unamenable	unbeholden	uncautious
twig-pruner	ulceration	un-American	unbelieved	uncemented
twilighted	ulcerative	unamusable	unbeliever	uncensored
twin-bedded	ulotrichan	unanalysed	unbemoaned	uncensured
twin double	ulteriorly	unanalytic	unbendable	unchanging
twinflower	ultimacies	unanimated	unbeseemly	uncharming
twing-twang	ultimately	unannealed	unbesieged	unchastely
twi-nighter	ultimation	unannulled	unbesought	unchastity
twin sister	ultimative	unanointed	unbespoken	uncheerful
twist-drill	ultimatory	unanswered	unbestowed	uncheering
twistiness	ultimatums	unappalled	unbetrayed	unchildish
twistingly	ultrabasic	unapparent	unbettered	unchivalry
twitchiest	ultrafiche	unappealed	unbevelled	unchoosing
twittingly	ultraistic	unappeased	unbewailed	unchristen
two-address	Ultralente	unapprised	unbiasedly	unchristly
two figures	ultralight	unapproved	unbiblical	unchurched
two fingers	ultramafic	unarguable	unbiddable	unchurchly
two nations	ultra-short	unarguably	unbirthday	unciliated
two natures	ultrasonic	unarmoured	unbishoped	uncircular
two or three	ultrasound	unarranged	unblanched	uncivilise
two-pronged	Ultrasuede	unarrested	unblazoned	uncivility
two-sticker	ultra vires	unartfully	unbleached	uncivilize
two-striper	ultroneous	unartistic	unblenched	unclashing
two-tongued	ulvospinel	unascended	unblighted	uncleansed
two-wheeler	Umbandista	unasked-for	unblinking	unclerical
Tyburn tree	umbellated	unaspiring	unblissful	unclogging
tycoonship	umbellifer	unassailed	unbloodied	uncloister
tykishness	umbilicate	unasserted	unbloodily	unclosable
tylopodous	umboth duty	unassigned	unblushing	uncoffined
tympanites	umbracious	unassisted	unboastful	uncollated
tympanitic	umbrageous	unassoiled	unbonneted	uncoloured

uncombined	under-agent	undersexed	undisarmed	unenviable
uncomelily	underbelly	undersheet	undiseased	unenviably
uncommixed	underboard	undershirt	undisguise	unequalise
uncommonly	underbough	undershoot	undismayed	unequality
uncompared	underbrush	undershore	undisposed	unequalize
uncomposed	underbuild	undershrub	undisputed	unequalled
unconfined	undercarve	undersized	undistinct	unequipped
unconfused	underclass	underskirt	undiverted	unerringly
unconfuted	under-clerk	underslept	undivinely	unescorted
unconjugal	undercliff	underslung	undivorced	unesteemed
unconsoled	undercloak	undersound	undivulged	un-European
unconsumed	undercount	underspend	undoctored	unevenness
uncontrite	under cover	understaff	undogmatic	uneventful
unconveyed	undercover	understand	undomestic	unexacting
unconvince	undercreep	understate	undoneness	unexamined
uncopiable	undercroft	under steam	undoubtful	unexampled
uncorroded	undercrust	understeer	undoubting	unexcelled
uncorseted	under-devil	understock	undramatic	unexcepted
uncovenant	underdrain	understood	undrawable	unexciting
uncovetous	underdrawn	understory	undreading	unexecuted
uncreative	underdress	understudy	undrivable	unexistent
uncredited	underdrift	underswell	undrooping	unexisting
uncriminal	underdrive	undertaker	undubitate	unexpanded
uncrippled	underearth	underthing	undulately	unexpected
uncritical	under-fives	underthink	undulating	unexpended
uncrumbled	under-flame	undertoned	undulation	unexpiated
uncrumpled	underfloor	undertread	undulatory	unexplicit
unctuosity	underfocus	undertreat	undulously	unexploded
unctuously	underframe	undertrial	uneasiness	unexplored
uncultured	underglaze	undertrick	uneclipsed	unextended
uncumbered	undergrass	undertrump	uneconomic	unfaceable
uncustomed	under-grove	undertunic	unedifying	unfadingly
uncuttable	undergrowl	undervalue	uneducable	unfailable
undangered	undergrown	undervoice	uneducated	unfailably
undarkened	underjawed	under water	uneffected	unfainting
undazzling	underlayer	underwater	unegoistic	unfairness
undeadened	underlease	under weigh	unelectric	unfaithful
undebarred	underlever	underwhelm	unelevated	unfallible
undecaying	underlight	underwired	uneloquent	unfallowed
undeceived	underlinen	underworld	unembanked	unfamiliar
undeceiver	underlying	under wraps	unembodied	unfastened
undecipher	undermatch	underwrite	unembraced	unfathered
undecision	underminer	underwrote	unemphatic	unfatherly
undecisive	undernamed	undescried	unemployed	unfathomed
undeclared	underneath	undeserted	unenclosed	unfatigued
undeclined	under night	undeserved	unendeared	unfavorite
undefeated	undern-time	undesigned	unendingly	unfavoured
undefended	underpaint	undesiring	unendorsed	unfeasible
undefinite	underpants	undesirous	unenduring	unfeasibly
undeformed	underpitch	undestined	unenforced	unfeatured
undefrayed	underplant	undetached	unengaging	unfeigning
undegassed	underplate	undetailed	unenhanced	unfellowed
undegraded	underprice	undetected	unenjoying	unfeminine
undejected	underprint	undeterred	unenlarged	unfeminist
undelaying	underprize	undeviated	unennobled	unfettered
undemanded	under proof	undevoured	unenriched	unfighting
undeniable	underproof	undevoutly	unenrolled	unfilially
undeniably	underquote	undextrous	unentailed	unfillable
undeplored	underroast	undictated	unentangle	unfilleted
undepraved	underscore	undigested	unenthused	unfilmable
undeprived	underscrub	undiligent	unenticing	unfiltered
under-actor	underserve	undirected	unentitled	unfindable

unfingered	unhelpless	uninnocent	unleavened	unmonastic
unfinished	unheralded	uninominal	unlectured	unmorality
unfirmness	unheroical	uninquired	unlessened	unmortared
unfishable	unhideable	uninspired	unlessoned	unmothered
unflagging	unhindered	uninsulate	unlettable	unmotherly
unflurried	unhistoric	uninsulted	unlettered	unmoveable
unfocussed	unholiness	unintended	unlevelled	unmovingly
unfoldment	unhollowed	uninterest	unlicensed	unmurdered
unfoliaged	unhomelike	uninterred	unliftable	unmuscular
unfoliated	unhonestly	unintimate	unlikeable	unnameable
unfollowed	unhonoured	uninuclear	unlikelier	unnational
unforcedly	unhouseled	uninvented	unlikeness	unneatness
unforcible	unhumanise	uninverted	unlistened	unnoticing
unforcibly	unhumanize	uninvested	unliterary	unnotified
unfordable	unhumorous	uninviting	unliterate	unnumbered
unforeseen	unhuntable	uninvolved	unlittered	unnurtured
unforetold	unhurrying	Union House	unliveable	unobedient
unforgiven	unhygienic	unionistic	unlockable	unobjected
unforsaken	uniaxially	union joint	unloveable	unobliging
unfoughten	unicameral	union screw	unlovesome	unobscured
unfrequent	unicameral	unipartite	unlovingly	unobserved
unfriended	unicentral	uniplicate	unluckiest	unobtained
unfriendly	unicorn auk	unipolarly	unluminous	unoccupied
unfrighted	unicyclist	uniqueness	unlustrous	unoffended
unfruitful	unidentate	uniseptate	unmagnetic	unofficial
unfunniest	unifilarly	uniseriate	unmaidenly	unopenable
unfurlable	uniflorous	unisonally	unmailable	unoperable
unfurrowed	unifoliate	unisonance	unmakeable	unoperated
ungardened	uniformise	unitedness	unmanacled	unordained
ungartered	uniformity	unit-factor	unmanfully	unordinary
ungathered	uniformize	unit-holder	unmanifest	unoriental
ungenerous	unilabiate	unitholder	unmannered	unoriented
ungenially	unilateral	unit-linked	unmannerly	unoriginal
ungettable	unilingual	unit matrix	unmartyred	unorthodox
ungimmicky	uniliteral	univalence	unmastered	unossified
unglorious	unilobular	univallate	unmatching	unoxidized
ungoverned	unilocular	univariant	unmaterial	unpacified
ungraceful	unimagined	univariate	unmaternal	unpackaged
ungracious	unimitable	university	unmeasured	unpalpable
ungraithed	unimitated	univocalic	unmechanic	unpampered
ungrateful	unimmersed	univocally	unmeddling	unparadise
ungrounded	unimmortal	univoltine	unmediated	unparallel
ungrudging	unimodular	unjacketed	unmeekness	unpardoned
unguentary	unimpaired	unjoyfully	unmeetable	unparented
unguentous	unimparted	unjudicial	unmeetness	unpassable
unguidable	unimplored	unjustness	unmellowed	unpastoral
unguidedly	unimposing	unkillable	unmemoried	unpastured
unguiltily	unimproved	unkindness	unmendable	unpatented
unhabitual	unimpugned	unkinglike	unmerciful	unpathetic
unhallowed	unincensed	unkinkable	unmeriting	unpeaceful
unhaltered	unincisive	unknighted	unmetalled	unpedantic
unhampered	unincluded	unknightly	unmetallic	unpedestal
unhandsome	unindebted	unknitting	unmetrical	unpenitent
unhappiest	unindented	unknotting	unmilitary	unpeppered
unharassed	unindicted	unknowable	unmingling	unperfumed
unhardened	unindulged	unlabelled	unminished	unperilous
unharrowed	uninfected	unlaboured	unmirthful	unperished
unhazarded	uninfested	unladylike	unmiscible	unperjured
unhealable	uninflamed	unlamented	unmissable	unpestered
unhearable	uninformed	unlaudable	unmistaken	unphonetic
unheavenly	uninitiate	unlaunched	unmodified	unphysical
unhelpable	uninjected	unlawfully	unmolested	unpickable

unpillowed	unrealness	unrivalled	unsingable	unsummoned
unpitiable	unreasoned	unriveting	unsinister	unsupplied
unpitiably	unrebutted	unromantic	unsinkable	unsupposed
unplacable	unrecalled	unrousable	unsisterly	unsureness
un-Platonic	unreceived	unruinable	unsizeable	unsurfaced
unplayable	unreckoned	unruliness	unskillful	unsurgical
unplayably	unrecorded	unrummaged	unslakable	unsurmised
unpleasant	unredeemed	unruptured	unsleeping	unsurveyed
unpleasing	unreelable	unsackable	unslippery	unswayable
unpleasure	unreformed	unsafeness	unslipping	unswerving
unploughed	unrefusing	unsalaried	unslothful	unswinging
unplugging	unregarded	unsaleable	unsmirched	unsyllabic
unpoetical	unrejected	unsalutary	unsmokable	unsymbolic
unpoisoned	unrejoiced	unsalvable	unsmoothed	unsympathy
unpolicied	unrelative	unsanctify	unsmutched	untalented
unpolished	unrelaxing	unsanguine	unsnapping	untameable
unpolitely	unreleased	unsanitary	unsociable	untameness
unpolluted	unrelented	unsatiable	unsociably	untampered
unpopulate	unreliable	unsatiated	unsocially	untangible
unpopulous	unreliably	unsaturate	unsocketed	untappable
unportable	unrelieved	unsavoured	unsoftened	untasteful
unpossible	unrelished	unscabbard	unsoldered	untearable
unpowdered	unremarked	unscalable	unsolidity	untellable
unpowerful	unremedied	unsceptred	unsolvable	untellably
unprecious	unremember	unschooled	unsonorous	untempered
unprefaced	unremitted	unscorched	unsoothing	untempting
unpregnant	unrendered	unscottify	unspeaking	untenanted
unprepared	unrenowned	unscourged	unspecific	untendered
unprettily	unrepaired	unscramble	unspeckled	untenderly
unpriestly	unrepealed	unscreened	unspirited	unterraced
unprincely	unrepeated	unscripted	unsporting	unterrific
unprobably	unrepelled	unscrubbed	unsqueezed	untestable
unproduced	unrepented	unsearched	unstablest	untethered
unprofaned	unrepining	unseasonal	unstanched	unthankful
unprofited	unreplaced	unseasoned	unstarched	unthatched
unprolific	unreplying	unseconded	unstartled	unthematic
unpromised	unreported	unseeingly	unstatable	unthinking
unprompted	unreposing	unseemlier	unstayable	unthrashed
unprovable	unreproved	unseizable	unsteadier	unthreaded
unprovided	unrequired	unselected	unsteadily	unthreshed
unprovoked	unrequited	unsellable	unstinting	unthriving
unpuckered	unresented	unsensible	unstirring	unthronged
unpunctual	unreserved	unsensuous	unstitched	unthwarted
unpunished	unresigned	unsentient	unstooping	unticketed
unpurified	unresisted	unshackled	unstopping	untidiness
unpurposed	unresolved	unshadowed	unstraight	untillable
unquailing	unrespited	unshakable	unstrained	untimbered
unquarried	unrestored	unshakenly	unstrapped	untiringly
unquenched	unretarded	unshapable	unstreaked	untithable
unquotable	unreticent	unsheathed	unstreamed	untogether
unransomed	unreturned	unshielded	unstressed	untouching
unraptured	unrevealed	unshingled	unstriated	untouristy
unrateable	unrevenged	unshipping	unstricken	untowardly
unratified	unreverend	unshivered	unstringed	untradable
unrationed	unreverent	unshoulder	unstripped	untrampled
unravelled	unreversed	unshowered	unstudious	untranquil
unraveller	unreviewed	unshrouded	unsublimed	untreasure
unravished	unrewarded	unshuffled	unsuborned	untrenched
unreactive	unrhythmic	unsilenced	unsufficed	untroubled
unreadable	unrideable	unsilvered	unsuffixed	untrueness
unreadably	unrightful	unsimplify	unsuitable	untrustful
unrealized	unripeness	unsinfully	unsuitably	untrusting

untruthful	unwritable	ureteritis	vaginismus	vaticinate
untuneable	unyielding	urethritis	vagrantize	vauclusian
unturbaned	unyouthful	urgentness	vail bonnet	vaudeville
unturnable	unzippered	urgicenter	Valdepeñas	vaultingly
untwisting	up a gum tree	uricosuric	valerianic	vauntingly
ununitable	up and about	uricotelic	validation	vavasories
unuplifted	up-and-comer	urinalyses	valleculae	Vegeburger
unusedness	up and doing	urinalysis	vallecular	vegetarian
unusefully	up-and-under	urinomancy	Valley Girl	vegetation
unusuality	upbraiding	urinometer	valley lily	vegetative
unutilized	upbringing	urinoscopy	valorously	vehemently
unvaluable	upbristled	urodynamic	value added	vehiculate
unvariable	up for grabs	urogenital	value-laden	veiledness
unvariably	upgradable	urographic	valve train	veld-cornet
unvariedly	uphillward	urological	valvulitis	veligerous
unveiledly	upholstery	uropoietic	vampire bat	velitation
unvendible	up in the air	urothelial	vampiredom	velocipede
unvenomous	upliftment	urothelium	vampirical	velocities
unventured	upon my life	urotropine	vanadinite	veltheimia
unveracity	upon my soul	uroxanthin	vancomycin	velutinous
unverified	upon my word	ursine seal	vancourier	velvet bean
unvigilant	upper class	urticarial	vanilla-pod	velvet crab
unvintaged	upper crust	urtication	vanishment	velvet-dock
unviolable	Upper House	usableness	vanitories	velvet duck
unviolated	upper sixth	usageaster	vanitously	velvetfish
unvirtuous	upper-stock	use and wont	vanity case	velvet-leaf
unvitiated	upper works	useful load	Vanity Fair	velvet-pile
unvolatile	uppishness	usefulness	vanity unit	velvet-worm
unvowelled	uppitiness	use the seas	vanquisher	venae cavae
unvulgarly	uproarious	usquebaugh	vapography	venational
unwalkable	upset price	ustulation	vaporiform	venatorial
unwandered	upsettable	usucapient	vaporosity	vendettist
unwareness	upside down	usucaption	vaporously	Venedotian
unwariness	upslope fog	usuriously	vapour-bath	veneration
unwashable	upstanding	usurpation	vapourless	venerative
unwatchful	upstirring	usurpative	vapour lock	venereally
unwavering	upsurgence	usurpatory	vapourware	venesector
unweakened	up the booay	usurpature	vapulation	venetianed
unweaponed	up the creek	usurpingly	varicellar	Venetianly
unwearable	up the river	utero-tubal	variciform	Venezuelan
unwearying	up the spout	utility man	varicocele	vengefully
unweighted	up the stick	utilizable	varicosity	venialness
unwellness	up to a point	Uto-Aztecan	variedness	venison pie
unwettable	up to no good	Utopianism	variegated	Venizelist
unwhitened	up to the bit	Utopianist	variegator	venoclysis
unwieldier	up to the hub	Utopianize	varietally	venography
unwieldily	upwardness	uvula trill	variformed	venomously
unwindowed	Ural-Altaic	uxoriality	variformly	venostasis
unwinnable	uralitized	uxoricidal	variolitic	ventilator
unwinnowed	Uranianism	uxorilocal	variometer	ventral fin
unwipeable	uranometry	uxoriously	varnishing	ventricose
unwiseness	uranophane	vacationer	vascularly	ventricous
unwithered	urban drift	vaccinator	vasculitic	ventricule
unwontedly	urbaneness	vacillancy	vasculitis	ventriculi
unwordable	urbanistic	vacillator	vase carpet	Venus's comb
unworkable	urbanology	vacuolated	vasoactive	Venus shell
unworkably	urceolated	vacuolized	vasomotion	verbalizer
unworthier	urchin fish	vacuum-pack	vassalship	verballing
unworthily	ureaplasma	vacuum pump	vas vasorum	verbal noun
unwrapping	Urecholine	vacuum tube	Vaticanism	verbicidal
unwrathful	uredosorus	Vagabondia	Vaticanist	Verdicchio
unwrinkled	uredospore	vagabondry	Vaticanize	verdictive

verge-board	vice-warden	vinho verde	vital power	voluptuary
vergerless	Vichy water	viniferous	vital spark	voluptuous
vergership	vicinities	vino blanco	vitaminise	volutation
veridicity	victimhood	vino locale	vitaminize	vomitories
verifiable	victimizer	vinologist	vitaminous	vomitorium
verifiably	victimless	vino tierno	vitrectomy	vortex ring
verkrampte	Victoriana	vinousness	vitremanie	vortically
vermicelli	victoriate	vintage car	vitreosity	vorticella
vermicular	victorious	vintneress	vitreously	vorticular
vermifugal	victualage	vinylidene	vitrescent	vortograph
Vermontese	victualled	vinylogous	vitriolize	vortoscope
vernacular	victualler	vinyl resin	vitrophyre	votability
Verner's Law	vicuña wool	violaceous	vituperant	Vote Office
verneukery	Vicwardian	viol d'amore	vituperate	vote-winner
verrucated	vidarabine	violescent	vituperous	votive mass
Versailles	video diary	violet-blue	vivificate	votive Mass
versecraft	videogenic	violet crab	viviparism	voussoired
verse drama	video nasty	violet wood	viviparity	vow-breaker
versed sine	videophile	viper-broth	viviparous	vowel-glide
versemaker	videophone	viperishly	vivisector	vowel-point
versicular	Vienna coup	viperously	vixenishly	vowel shift
versiculus	Vierendeel	viraginian	vizard-mask	voyageable
versifical	Vietnamese	viraginous	viziership	vulcanizer
versionist	Vietnamize	virescence	vlei loerie	vulgarizer
Vertebrata	view camera	virginally	vocabulary	vulgarness
vertebrate	viewership	virgin clay	vocabulist	vulnerable
vertically	viewfinder	virgin comb	vocal cords	vulnerably
verticilli	view halloo	virginhood	vocal folds	vulpicidal
Very pistol	viewlessly	virgin-like	vocalistic	vulvectomy
vesication	vigilantly	Virgin Mary	vocal score	waddlingly
vesicatory	vignetting	virgin wool	vocal tract	wading bird
vesiculate	vignettist	virialized	vocational	wading pool
vesiculose	vigorously	viridarium	vocatively	wafer-paper
vespertine	vigourless	virilizing	voce di gola	wafer-scale
vespiaries	vihuelista	viripotent	vociferant	waffle-iron
vestiarian	vilipender	virologist	vociferate	wage earner
vestiaries	villagedom	virtualism	vociferous	wage freeze
vestibular	villageful	virtualist	voetganger	wager of law
vestibulum	villaindom	virtuality	voicedness	waggonette
vestmental	villainess	virtueless	voice level	Wagner tuba
vestmented	villainies	virtuosity	voice of God	wagons-lits
vest-pocket	villainize	virtuously	voice-print	wagon train
vestry book	villainous	virulently	voiceprint	wagon-vault
vestry-room	villanella	vis a fronte	voice radio	wainscoted
veteran car	villanelle	viscerally	voicespond	wainwright
veterinary	Villanovan	viscometer	voiturette	waist-cloth
vetustness	villarette	viscometry	Volapükist	waist-rails
vexillator	villeinage	viscountcy	volatilise	wait and see
vibracular	Vincentian	Vishnuvite	volatility	wait-a-while
vibraculum	vin compris	visibility	volatilize	waiterlike
vibraphone	vindemiate	Visigothic	volitation	waiting-man
vibrograph	vin de table	visionally	volitional	waitperson
vibrometer	vindicable	visionless	volitorial	wait the day
vibrophone	vindicator	visitation	volleyball	wakerifely
vibroscope	vindictive	visitorial	Voltairean	wake-up call
vicariance	vinegar eel	visna-maedi	Voltairism	wake-up pill
vice-consul	vinegar-fly	visual axis	voltameter	wakey-wakey
vice-county	vinegarish	visualizer	volubility	Waldensian
vicegerent	vine-scroll	visual line	volumeless	walk-around
vice-legate	vine weevil	visuomotor	volumetric	walking day
vice-rector	vineyarded	vital force	volume unit	walking leg
vice-regent	vinho tinto	vitalistic	voluminous	walk in life

walk of life	war veteran	water gauge	wave-motion	weight gain
walk-on part	wash-basket	water glass	wave number	weightiest
Wallachian	wash-bottle	water-gruel	wave packet	weightless
wall-arcade	washerette	water-guard	wave period	weight loss
walla-walla	washer-wife	water-horse	waveringly	Weimaraner
Wallawalla	washeteria	water-house	wave-system	Weisswurst
wallbanger	washing bat	wateriness	wave theory	welcome mat
wall-barley	washing-day	waterishly	wave vector	welding rod
wall-border	washing-pan	water leech	waving base	well-bodied
wallflower	Washington	water lemon	wax and wane	well-bucket
wall garden	wash-kettle	water level	waxberries	well-chosen
wall lizard	wash-primer	waterlined	wax-cluster	well-decked
wall pepper	wash-trough	waterliner	waxed paper	well-decker
wall-pocket	wasp beetle	water-lungs	waxen image	well-earned
wall-poster	wassail-cup	watermelon	wax-pod bean	well enough
wall rocket	Wassermann	water meter	way-freight	well-faring
Wall Street	wastefully	water-mouse	way-outness	well fitted
wall-to-wall	wastel cake	water-mouth	way station	well-formed
wallwasher	waste mould	water nymph	weak ending	well-gotten
walnut tree	waste paper	water-organ	weak-handed	well-heeled
Walpoliana	waste water	water ouzel	weak-headed	well I never
Walt Disney	waste words	water pipit	weakliness	wellington
wambliness	wastreldom	water-plane	weak-minded	Wellington
wamblingly	watch below	water-power	weak moment	well-judged
wampumpeag	watch-chain	waterproof	weak sister	well-marked
wanderable	watch-charm	waterquake	wealthiest	well-meaner
wanderlust	watch-cloak	waterscape	wealthless	well-meated
wander plug	watchfully	water-screw	weanedness	well-padded
wander-year	watch-glass	watershoot	weaponized	well placed
wand flower	watch-guard	water shrew	weaponless	well-rested
wanking-pit	watch-house	watersider	weaponsman	well-shaped
wanrestful	watch-light	water-skier	wear a crown	well-shapen
wantedness	watchmaker	water slide	wearifully	well shrimp
wan-thriven	watch-night	watersmeet	wear motley	well-spaced
wantonness	watch-paper	water snake	wear willow	well-spoken
Wanyamwezi	watch-stand	water sport	wearyingly	wellspring
wapper-eyed	watch strap	waterspout	weaselling	well-spring
warble tone	watch-tower	water stoma	weaselship	well-suited
Warburgian	watchtower	water-stone	weasel word	well-tasted
War Cabinet	watch-wheel	water-table	weather bow	well to live
war college	water avens	water-thief	weather-box	well to pass
wardenship	water-based	water-thyme	weathering	well-turned
wardership	water beech	watertight	weatherize	well-willed
ward-heeler	water-bloom	water tower	weatherman	well-willer
war economy	Water Board	water wagon	weather map	well-wisher
war-hatchet	water-borne	waterwards	weathermen	well-wooded
warlordism	water-bough	water-waved	weaver-bird	well-worked
war machine	water-bound	water-wheel	web-machine	Welsh Black
warmed-over	water-brash	waterwheel	web-spinner	Welsh corgi
warm-headed	waterbrash	water wings	Websterian	Welsh hound
warming-pan	water break	water-witch	websterite	Welsh niece
warm sector	water-chute	waterworks	wedding day	Welsh onion
warmthless	water clerk	watery tomb	wedge shell	Welsh poppy
war of words	water-clock	Watteauish	Wednesdays	Welsh uncle
war pension	watercraft	wattlebird	weedkiller	Welsh Wales
warrandice	water crane	watt-second	week-to-week	Welshwoman
warranties	watercress	wave-action	Wegenerian	Welshwomen
warrantise	water drive	wave-change	weighboard	welt pocket
war refugee	water elder	wave energy	weigh-house	Wemba-wemba
Warrington	water-flood	wave filter	weigh-scale	Wendy house
warrioress	waterfront	wavelength	weigh-shaft	wentletrap
warriorism	Watergater	wavelessly	weight belt	were-jaguar

Wertherian	wheezingly	white house	wickerwork	windfallen
Wertherism	whelk-stall	White House	wicket-gate	wind-fanner
we shall see	whenabouts	white level	wicket-keep	windflower
West Africa	when-issued	white light	Wicliffian	windjammer
West Banker	whensoever	white liver	Wicliffist	windlessly
West Briton	whereabout	white magic	wide-bodied	windmiller
westerlies	whereafter	white metal	wide-screen	windowless
westerling	whereanent	white money	widespread	window-like
westernise	where it's at	white mouse	widow-finch	window pane
Westernise	wheresoe'er	White Negro	widow-maker	window seat
westernism	whereunder	white night	widow's mite	window-shop
westernize	whey-butter	white noise	widow's peak	window sill
Westernize	whickering	white ox-eye	widow's walk	wind player
western man	whiggamore	White Paper	widow woman	windscreen
Western pug	Whiggishly	white perch	wifeliness	wind-shaken
West German	whimpering	white-point	Wife of Bath	windshield
West Indian	whimsiness	white-print	Wiffle ball	wind-sleeve
West Indies	whip aerial	white satin	wiggletail	Windsor Red
westlander	whippers-in	white sauce	wigwagging	Windsor tie
Westphalia	whippeteer	white scour	wild carrot	wind-spider
Westralian	whippiness	white shark	wildcatter	wind sprint
West Riding	whip-socket	white slave	wild cattle	wind-stream
westwardly	whip stitch	White slave	wild-caught	wind-sucker
wet bargain	whip the cat	whitesmith	wild cherry	windsurfer
wet blanket	whirl-about	white staff	wildebeest	wind tunnel
wet canteen	whirl-blast	white stick	wild endive	wind-vanner
wet cupping	whirlicote	white stock	wilderness	windwardly
wether head	whirlingly	white stone	wildflysch	wine-bibber
wether lamb	whirlybird	white stork	wildfowler	winebibber
wet monsoon	whiskerage	white stuff	wild garden	wine bottle
wet process	whiskified	white sugar	wild garlic	wine butler
wet through	whisky jack	whitethorn	wild ginger	wine cellar
wet-weather	whisky john	white trash	wild orange	wine-farmer
Weyl tensor	whisky-soda	white trout	wild radish	wine-gallon
whaleboned	whisky sour	white water	wild talent	wine-grower
whale louse	whispering	white whale	wild teasel	winemaking
whale shark	whist drive	white wheat	wild turkey	wine-porter
wharf crane	whistle for	white witch	Wilfridian	wine taster
wharfinger	white alder	whiting-mop	wilfulness	wine-vaults
whatabouts	whitebeard	Whitleyism	Wilhelmine	wine waiter
what a shame	white birch	Whitmanish	Williamite	wine writer
what is more	whiteboard	Whitmanism	will or nill	wing-bonnet
what matter	white brass	Whitmanite	willowherb	wing collar
whatsoever	white bread	Whitstable	willow leaf	wing covert
what's yours	whitebrick	Whitsun ale	willow-like	winged bean
wheat-grass	white cedar	Whitsun Day	willow tree	wingedness
wheatgrass	white death	Whit Sunday	willow-ware	wing-footed
wheatsheaf	white dwarf	whity-brown	willow weed	wing mirror
Wheat State	white-eared	whizzingly	willow wren	wing oyster
Wheatstone	white earth	whodunitry	will to live	wing-sheath
wheel brace	white egret	whole cloth	willy-nilly	wingspread
wheelchair	whiteflies	wholegrain	willy-willy	wing-stroke
wheel clamp	white friar	wholesaler	win and wear	win in a walk
wheel-cross	White Friar	wholescale	win by a head	Winstonian
wheel-horse	whitefront	whole-timer	winceyette	winter coat
wheel-house	white frost	wholewheat	winchester	winter duck
wheelhouse	white goods	whomsoever	Winchester	winter-feed
wheelie bin	white grape	whore-house	wind-broken	winter gnat
wheel-organ	White Guard	whorehouse	wind-burned	winter kill
wheel-plate	white-heart	whore's bird	wind chimes	winterless
wheel-press	white heron	whorl-grass	windedness	winter-long
wheeziness	white horse	wickedness	wind energy	winter-moth

winter ovum	woefulness	woodworker	world order	xanthation
winterpick	Wöhler test	woodwright	world-point	xanthistic
winter road	wolframate	woody plant	world power	xanthoderm
winter rose	wolframite	wool-bearer	world's fair	xanthomata
winter's day	wolf spider	wool-broker	world-weary	xanthopsia
winter teal	wolf's tooth	wool-carder	worm-burrow	xenarthral
winter-tide	wolf willow	wool cheque	worm-eating	xenobiosis
wintertide	Wolstonian	wool church	worm-killer	xenobiotic
wintertime	woman-child	wool-comber	worm-lizard	xenogamous
winter-weed	womanfully	wool-gather	worm-spring	xenogeneic
winter wren	woman-grown	wool-grower	worry along	xenogenous
win the kirn	womanishly	woollenize	worry beads	xenoglossy
win through	woman-power	woolliness	worryingly	xenolithic
wintriness	woman's page	woolly-bear	worry lines	xenologist
wiper blade	woman's work	woollybutt	worsenment	xenomaniac
wiping head	womb-to-tomb	woolly-head	worserment	xenophilia
wire basket	womenpower	woolly worm	worshipful	xenophobia
wire-cutter	women's page	woolmaster	worshipped	xenophobic
wire-drawer	women's room	wool-needle	worshipper	xenotropic
wiredrawer	women's wear	wool-packer	worthiness	xerography
wire-framed	womenswear	wool-roller	worth while	xeromorphy
wire ground	women's work	wool-shears	worthwhile	xerophilic
wire-guided	wonder-horn	wool-sorter	woundingly	xerophytic
wire-haired	wonderland	wool-staple	wraithlike	xerostomia
wirelessly	wonderment	wool-winder	wraparound	xiphopagus
wirepuller	wonder-work	wool-worker	wrappering	xiphosuran
wire-tapper	wondrously	Woolton pie	wrap-rascal	xiphosurid
wire-walker	wonga-wonga	Woosterish	wrathfully	X-irradiate
wire-worker	wontedness	Woosterism	wreak havoc	X-radiation
wirrasthru	wonton soup	word by word	wreathless	X-ray source
wishing-cap	wood barley	word-centre	wrest-block	X-ray vision
wishy-washy	wood betony	word-ladder	wrestle out	xyloglucan
witch alder	wood-boring	word length	wrest-plank	xylography
witch broom	wood-burner	wordlessly	wretcheder	xylophonic
witchcraft	wood-carpet	word-medial	wretchedly	xylotomist
witch dance	woodcarver	word method	wrinkliest	xylotomous
witch-grass	wood-copper	wordmonger	wrist-plate	yacht basin
witch hazel	woodcutter	wordsearch	wrist-watch	yaffingale
witchiness	wooden-head	word-square	wristwatch	Yagi aerial
witchingly	woodenness	word-symbol	writership	yaketty-yak
witch-mania	wooden pear	workaholic	writhingly	Yankee bond
witch-stone	wooden suit	work a point	writing bed	Yankee-land
withdrawal	woodenware	work-basket	writing-box	yarborough
withdrawer	woodgrouse	workerless	writing ink	yardlander
witherling	wood hoopoe	workfellow	writing pad	yard of land
withershin	woodlanded	work-harden	writing-pen	yardswoman
withholder	woodlander	workhoused	writ of aiel	Yarkand rug
within call	wood laurel	working day	wrongdoing	yarnwindle
within-door	wood millet	working man	wrongfully	yawing axis
within hail	woodmonger	working-out	wrongously	yawl-rigged
within land	woodpecker	working top	wrong scent	year by year
withinside	wood pigeon	work-master	wry-mouthed	yearnfully
with intent	woodpigeon	work-minded	Wulfrunian	yearningly
without end	wood-rabbit	workmonger	wunderkind	year-on-year
with reason	wood-ranger	workpeople	Wyattesque	yeastiness
with the sun	Wood's glass	work permit	Wycliffian	yedda braid
witness box	Wood's light	work scathe	Wycliffism	yellow-back
witnessing	wood sorrel	workshadow	Wycliffist	yellowback
wit-writing	wood spirit	work to rule	Wycliffite	yellow bean
wobbliness	woods-pussy	world-class	Wykehamist	yellow belt
wobbulated	wood-thrush	worldliest	Wykehamite	yellow bile
wobbulator	woodturner	world music	wyomingite	yellowbill

yellowbird	yeoman work	yourselves	Zhdanovist	zoographic
yellowcake	yerba buena	yours truly	zidovudine	zoolatrous
yellow card	yerba plant	youthfully	zigzaggery	zoological
yellow cell	yerba santa	youthiness	zigzagging	zoomelanin
yellow deal	yester-even	ytter earth	Zimbabwean	zoomorphic
yellow-eyed	yestermorn	yucca-borer	zinc blende	zoonomical
yellow-fish	yester-year	Yukon stove	zinc chrome	zoophagous
yellow flag	yesteryear	zabaglione	zinc-coated	zoophilism
yellowhead	Yiddishism	Zaghlulist	zinc finger	zoophilist
yellow jack	Yiddishist	Zambianize	zincograph	zoophilous
yellow Jack	yieldingly	zapateados	zinc yellow	zoosporous
yellow leaf	yield point	zearalanol	zipperhead	zootechnic
yellowlegs	yield table	zebra danio	zircon blue	zoothecium
yellow line	ylang-ylang	zebra finch	zoanthropy	zootomical
yellowness	yodization	zebra-plant	zodiac ring	zoot-suited
yellow pine	yoke-fellow	zemstvoist	zograscope	zoot-suiter
yellow rain	yotization	Zend Avesta	zollverein	Zoroastric
yellow-root	you can talk	Zener cards	zombie-like	zucchettos
yellow rust	you can't win	Zener diode	zombiesque	zwitterion
yellow soap	you-know-who	Zengakuren	zonal index	zygocactus
yellow spot	youngberry	zephyr lily	zone centre	zygodactyl
yellow star	young blood	zero-coupon	zone fossil	zygologist
yellowtail	young entry	zero-energy	zone of fire	zygomycete
yellow ware	young flood	zero growth	zone-refine	zygosphene
yellow-wood	young fogey	zero option	zoocentric	zygosporic
yellow-wort	youngstock	zero rating	zoochorous	zymogenous
yeomanette	young thing	zerovalent	zooculture	zymologist
yeomanhood	young woman	zeuglodont	zoogeology	
yeomanries	your granny	Zhdanovism	zoographer	

ELEVEN LETTERS

Aaron's beard
abandonedly
abandonment
abandon ship
abashedness
Abbevillian
abbreviator
abdominally
abductively
abecedarian
abhorrently
abidingness
abiogenesis
abiological
abiotically
a bit and a sup
ablactation
ablutionary
abnormality
abnormalize
abolishable
abolishment
abomination
abortionist
aboundingly
above ground
aboveground
a box of birds
abracadabra
abridgeable
abridgement
abscondence
absentation
absenteeism
absent voter
absorbingly
absorptance
abstinently
abstraction
abstractive
absurdities
abusiveness
academician
academicism
academicize
acanthodian
acarologist
acatalectic
acataleptic
acaulescent
accelerandi
accelerando
accelerator
accentually
acceptation
acceptingly
accessaries

accessional
accessorial
accessorily
accessorise
accessorize
accipitrine
acclamation
acclamatory
acclimation
acclimatise
acclimatize
acclivities
acclivitous
accommodate
accompanied
accompanier
accompanies
accompanist
accordantly
accordingly
accoucheuse
accountable
accountably
accountancy
account book
accrediting
accrescence
accrescency
acculturate
acculturize
accumulator
accusatival
accustomary
acerbically
a certain age
acetanilide
acetate silk
acetoacetic
acetobacter
acetonaemia
acetylation
Achaemenian
acharnement
achievement
achondritic
achromatism
achromatize
achromatous
acicularity
acidimetric
acidization
acid of sugar
acidophilic
acidophilus
acid radical
acidulation
acidulously

acinaciform
acknowledge
aclinic line
acorn squash
a couple more
acoustician
acquiescent
acquiescing
acquirement
acquisition
acquisitive
acquittance
acraldehyde
acriflavine
acrimonious
acrocarpous
acrocentric
acromegalic
acropetally
a crow to pick
a crow to pull
acrylic acid
actinolitic
actinometer
actinometry
actinomycin
action front
action group
action point
active birth
active layer
active voice
actual grace
actualistic
actualities
actuarially
acumination
acupressure
acupuncture
acute accent
acute-angled
Adam's needle
adaptedness
adder's grass
adder's mouth
addititious
addressable
adenomatous
adhortation
adhortative
adiaphanous
adiaphorism
adiaphorist
adiaphorous
a dime a dozen
ad infinitum
adjectively

adjectivize
adjournment
adjudgement
adjudicator
adminicular
admiralship
Admiralties
admit to bail
adolescence
adolescency
adonization
Adoptionist
adorability
adrenal rest
adrenolytic
Adriatic Sea
adscription
adulterator
adumbration
adumbrative
advance copy
advancement
adventuress
adventurism
adventurist
adventurous
adverbially
adversarial
adversaries
adversative
adverseness
adversities
advertently
advertising
advertorial
advisedness
aeneolithic
aeolian harp
Aeolian harp
Aeolian mode
aeolotropic
aerobically
aerobiology
aerodynamic
aeroelastic
aerographer
aerological
aeronautics
aeroplanist
aerostatics
aerostation
Aesculapian
Aesculapius
aesthetical
aestivation
aeviternity
a fact of life

a far cry from
affectation
affectingly
affectional
affectioned
affectively
affectivity
affectually
affiliation
affiliative
affirmation
affirmative
affirmatory
afforcement
afformative
affranchise
affrication
affricative
affrightful
Afghan hound
aficionados
African hemp
Africanness
African teak
Afro-Asiatic
Afrocentric
afterburner
after-course
after-effect
after-growth
aftermarket
after-school
after sermon
against time
agamospermy
agathodemon
agelessness
Agent Orange
agglomerate
agglutinant
agglutinate
aggradation
aggrandizer
aggravating
aggravation
aggregately
aggregation
aggregative
aggrievance
aggrievedly
aggroupment
agile gibbon
agitatingly
agitational
aglomerular
agnosticism
agnus castus

agonistical	alizarin red	amalgamable	anachronism	anguishment
agonizingly	alkalescent	amalgamater	anachronous	angwantibos
agony column	alkali metal	amalgamator	anacoluthia	animal black
a good stitch	alkalimeter	amaranthine	anacoluthic	animalcular
agoraphobia	alkalimetry	amateurship	anacoluthon	animalistic
agoraphobic	all-American	amativeness	anacreontic	animatronic
agrammatism	allantoides	amazingness	anadiplosis	animosities
agrarianism	allegorical	Amazon-stone	anaesthesia	aniseed tree
agriculture	allegorizer	ambassadrix	anaesthesis	aniseikonia
agriologist	allegrettos	ambiguities	anaesthetic	aniseikonic
agriproduct	all-electric	ambiguously	anagnorisis	anisogamete
agrobiology	allelomorph	ambilingual	analogously	anisogamous
agronomical	alleluiatic	ambitionist	analysandum	anisotropic
ahead of time	all ends over	ambitiously	analysation	annabergite
ahistorical	alleviation	ambivalence	analyticity	annexionist
aide-mémoire	alleviative	ambivalency	anaphylaxis	annihilable
aides-de-camp	alleviatory	ambiversion	anaplerosis	annihilator
aiguillette	All Fools' Day	amblygonite	anaplerotic	anniversary
ailurophile	alliterator	ambrosially	anarchistic	annotatable
ailurophobe	all manner of	amelanchier	anastomoses	annunciator
aimlessness	alloantigen	ameliorator	anastomosis	anomalistic
air corridor	allocentric	amenability	anastomotic	anomalously
aircraftman	allodialism	amenorrhoea	Anaxagorean	anonymously
aircraftmen	allodialist	amentaceous	ancestorial	anoplothere
air-layering	all of a piece	amerciament	ancestrally	anorthosite
airlessness	allogeneity	Amerenglish	anchor plate	anovulatory
air mattress	allogeneous	American bar	anchorwoman	answeringly
airsickness	allographic	American elk	anchorwomen	answerphone
air terminal	allomorphic	American elm	anchovy pear	antecedence
air-to-ground	all one knows	Americanese	ancientness	antecedency
alabastrine	allopathist	Americanise	ancillaries	antechamber
alamodality	allophylian	Americanism	androconial	antecubital
a large order	allopurinol	Americanist	androconium	anteflexion
albert chain	allotropism	Americanize	androcratic	antemundane
Albigensian	all outdoors	American tea	androgynous	antenatally
albugineous	all-overness	amethocaine	androsphinx	antenniform
albuminuria	all-powerful	amethystine	and then some	antenuptial
albuminuric	All Souls' Day	amiableness	anecdotical	ante-orbital
alchemistic	all standing	amicability	an eight days	antepagment
alcohol-free	all the while	amici curiae	anemometric	antependium
alcyonarian	all together	aminoacetic	anemone fish	anteriority
alder kitten	all to pieces	amontillado	anencephaly	anterograde
aldermanity	all-up weight	amorousness	anfractuous	anteversion
alderperson	alluviation	amorphously	angelically	antheridial
aldosterone	all very well	amortisable	angelolatry	antheridium
alembicated	almond paste	amour propre	angelophany	antherozoid
aleuromancy	almonership	amphetamine	angel-sleeve	anthocyanin
Alexandrian	alongside of	amphibolite	angelus bell	anthography
alexandrine	alphabetise	amphibology	angiography	anthologies
Alexandrine	alphabetize	amphictyony	angiomatous	anthologise
alexandrite	alpha rhythm	amphidromic	angioplasty	anthologist
alexithymia	altercation	amphimictic	angiotensin	anthologize
alexithymic	alternately	amphipathic	Anglicanism	anthomaniac
Alfvén speed	alternating	amphiprotic	Anglicanize	Anthony Eden
algebraical	alternation	amphisbaena	Anglo-French	anthracitic
alginic acid	alternative	Amphiscians	Anglo-Gallic	anthracnose
algological	altitudinal	amplexicaul	Anglo-Indian	anthracosis
algorithmic	altocumulus	amusingness	Anglomaniac	anthracotic
Alien Priory	alto-relievo	amusiveness	Anglo-Norman	anthranilic
alimentally	alto-rilievo	amyloidosis	Anglophilia	antibilious
alisphenoid	altostratus	amylopectin	Anglophobia	Antiburgher
a little bird	alveolarity	amyotrophic	Anglophobic	anticathode

anticipator	apostatical	Arabization	arpeggiated	aspheterism
anticodonic	a posteriori	arachidonic	arraignment	asphyxiator
anticyclone	apostle-bird	arachnoidal	arrangeable	aspidistral
anti-gravity	apostlehood	arachnology	arrangement	asportation
antigravity	apostleship	araliaceous	arrear-guard	a sport of wit
anti-heroine	apostolical	arbitrageur	arrentation	a square deal
anti-Jacobin	apostrophic	arbitrament	arrestation	assafoetida
antimasquer	apotheosise	arbitrarily	arrestingly	assassinate
antimoniate	apotheosize	arbitration	arrhenotoky	assassin bug
antimonious	Appalachian	arbitratrix	arrow bamboo	assaultable
antinomical	appallingly	arbitrement	arrow-headed	assay-master
anti-nuclear	apparatchik	arboraceous	arrow of time	assay office
antioxidant	apparelling	arboreality	arse-kissing	assegai tree
antipathies	apparelment	arborescent	arse-licking	assegai wood
antipathist	Appeal Court	arboricidal	arsenic acid	assemblyman
antipathous	appealingly	Arcadianism	arsenicated	assentation
antiphonary	appearingly	archaeology	arse over tip	assentingly
antiphonies	appeasement	Archaeozoic	arse over tit	assertation
antiphrasis	appellation	archaically	artefactual	assertative
antipyretic	appellative	archangelic	artemisinin	assertional
antiquarian	appertinent	arch-chanter	arterialise	assertively
antiquaries	appetencces	archdeanery	arterialize	assertorial
antiquation	appetitious	archdiocese	arteriogram	asses' bridge
antiqueness	apple brandy	archduchess	arteriotomy	assessorial
antiquities	apple-butter	archduchies	arthrodesis	assiduities
antirrhinum	apple of love	archdukedom	arthropathy	assiduously
anti-Semitic	apple of Peru	archegonial	articulable	assignation
antispastic	apple-pie bed	archegonium	articulated	assimilable
antistrophe	application	arch-enemies	articulator	assimilator
antitetanic	applicative	archenteron	artilleries	Assiniboine
antitetanus	applicatory	Archimedean	artillerist	association
antitypical	appliquéing	archipelago	artiodactyl	associative
antonomasia	appointable	architraved	artisanship	associatory
anxiousness	appointment	arch-prelate	artlessness	assortative
any amount of	apportioner	Arctic cisco	artsy-fartsy	assuagement
any more than	appraisable	Arctic Ocean	arundineous	assubjugate
any number of	appreciable	arduousness	arytenoidal	assuredness
any old thing	appreciably	area bombing	asbestiform	Assyriology
anything but	appreciator	area defence	ascensional	assythement
aortography	apprehender	areocentric	ascetically	as they speak
apartmental	apprizement	areopagitic	ascititious	asthmatical
apatosaurus	approaching	argentaffin	as cold as ice	astigmatism
aphasiology	approbation	Argentinian	a screw loose	astonishing
aphetically	approbative	argle-bargle	as dry as dust	as to the rest
aphrodisiac	approbatory	argumentive	as easy as ABC	astoundment
apicultural	appropinque	argy-bargied	aseptically	astringency
apocalyptic	appropriate	argy-bargies	a set of steps	astrocytoma
apocopation	approvement	argyrophile	ashamedness	astrography
apocrisiary	approvingly	aristocracy	ashamed to do	astrologist
apocynthion	approximant	Aristotelic	ash-coloured	astrometric
apodictical	approximate	arithmetize	Asiatically	astronomize
apodyterium	appurtenant	arithmology	as it happens	astroturfed
apogamously	apricot plum	armalcolite	asking price	asyllabical
Apollinaris	apricot tree	armed forces	ask the banns	asymmetries
Apollonicon	aprioristic	armil sphere	as like as not	as you please
apomorphine	apron-string	Arminianism	as many again	at a discount
aponeurosis	aptly enough	Arminianize	as much again	at a distance
aponeurotic	aqua complex	armoured car	as opposed to	a tale of a tub
apopetalous	aquaculture	armour-plate	aspect ratio	at all events
apophyllite	aquarellist	arms control	aspergillum	at all points
aposiopesis	aquiculture	arm-twisting	aspersorium	at a long stay
aposiopetic	Arabian bird	aromaticity	asphericity	at a loose end

atelectasis	auction sale	avocational	bad medicine	barber's pole
atelectatic	audaciously	avoirdupois	bad-tempered	barber's rash
at every turn	audibleness	awelessness	baffle board	barbiturate
at first hand	audio-active	awesomeness	baffle plate	barbola work
at full blast	audiologist	awestricken	baggage room	Bardolphian
at full speed	audiometric	awkwardness	bag of nerves	barefacedly
at handgrips	audio typing	a work of time	bag of tricks	bare-knuckle
atheistical	audio typist	axe-grinding	bailer-shell	bargain away
atheologian	audio-visual	axial vector	bailiffship	barge-couple
athleticism	audiovisual	axiological	bail-jumping	barge-course
Athole brose	auditoriums	axiomatical	Baily's beads	bargemaster
athwartship	auditorship	axisymmetry	baked Alaska	Barisal guns
at intervals	Auger effect	axonometric	baked potato	barkevikite
at its height	augmentable	azeotropism	baker's bread	barking bird
Atlanticism	Augustanism	Azerbaijani	baker's dozen	barking deer
Atlanticist	Augustinian	azimuthally	baking sheet	barley-break
at long range	aurichalcum	azoospermia	balanceable	barley sugar
at loose ends	auricularly	azotobacter	baldachined	barley water
atmospheric	auriculated	babu English	bald cypress	barnstormer
atomic clock	Aurignacian	baby bouncer	baleen whale	barn swallow
atomic power	aurora snake	baby-farming	balefulness	baron-bailie
atomistical	auscultator	babyishness	ballad metre	baronetcies
atomization	austereness	baby's breath	ballast-tank	baron of beef
atom smasher	austerities	Bacchanalia	ball-bearing	barouchette
at one's elbow	Australiana	bacciferous	ball-breaker	barquentine
at one's heels	Australioid	baccivorous	balletomane	barracoutas
at one's peril	autarchical	bachelordom	balloon-fish	barramundis
atrabiliary	authentical	bachelorism	balloon tyre	barred umber
atrabilious	author-craft	bachelorize	balloon vine	barrel-house
atrociously	authorially	bacilliform	ballot paper	barrel-organ
atropinized	authorities	back and edge	balls-aching	barrel vault
attaché case	autocentric	back and fill	balm-cricket	barricading
attachéship	autochthons	back-bencher	balsam apple	barrier reef
attaintment	autochthony	backbencher	balustraded	barrow-wight
attemperate	autocracies	backblocker	bamboo shoot	bar sinister
attemptable	autocratism	back country	banana split	Bartholomew
attemptible	autocratrix	backcountry	Banbury cake	barycentric
attemptless	auto-erotism	back-draught	bandboxical	basaltiform
attentional	autogenesis	back passage	bandoliered	base on balls
attentively	autogenetic	back-payment	bandy-legged	base-running
attenuation	autographic	backroom boy	baneberries	bases-loaded
attestation	autokinesis	back-scatter	Bangladeshi	base-stealer
attestative	autokinetic	backscatter	bang on about	bashfulness
at the back of	autological	backslapper	bankability	bashi-bazouk
at the cost of	automatical	back-stabber	bank balance	basicranial
at the double	automorphic	backswimmer	banker's card	basifugally
at the feet of	autonomical	back to earth	bankers' ramp	basipetally
at the latest	autoplastic	back to front	bank holiday	Baskerville
at the minute	autosoteric	backtracker	bank machine	basket chair
at the moment	auto-suggest	backup light	bank manager	basket-maker
at the outset	autotherapy	bacon beetle	bank of issue	basket weave
at the risk of	autotrophic	bacteraemia	banksia rose	basket-woman
at the wicket	autumn tints	bacteraemic	bank swallow	Basque beret
at the will of	auxanometer	bacterially	banteringly	bastard balm
attitudinal	auxiliaries	bactericide	banyan shirt	bastard wing
attorneydom	auxochromic	bacteriocin	baptismally	bastel-house
attorneyism	auxotrophic	bacteriosis	baptistries	Bastille Day
attractable	averageness	bacteriuria	Barbaresque	bastle-house
attribution	Averroistic	bad business	barbarities	bath essence
attributive	averruncate	baddeleyite	barbarously	bathing suit
attritional	avicularium	Badger State	barbastelle	batholithic
auction room	avocado pear	bad language	barber's itch	bathometric

Bathurst bur	bêches-de-mer	benefaction	beyond a joke	bioengineer
bathymetric	be concerned	benefactive	beyond doubt	bioethicist
bathyscaphe	bed and board	benefactory	beyond price	biofeedback
bathysphere	bedevilling	benefactrix	beyond words	biogenesist
baton charge	bedevilment	beneficence	bhakti-marga	biographies
batsmanship	Bedford cord	beneficency	bias binding	biographist
battalia pie	bedizenment	beneficiary	biauricular	biographize
battle array	bed-moulding	beneficiate	Bible-banger	biologistic
battledress	bedroom eyes	benefit-club	Bible-basher	biomagnetic
battlefield	bedside book	Beneventine	bibliograph	biomedicine
battle it out	bedside lamp	benevolence	biblioklept	biometrical
battle royal	beech marten	Bengal light	bibliolatry	biophysical
battle-wagon	beehive tomb	Bengal tiger	bibliomancy	biorhythmic
battologize	beer-parlour	benightment	bibliomania	bioturbated
Bayesianism	beetle-brain	benignantly	bibliophile	bipartitely
bay-windowed	beetle drive	benignities	bibliophily	bipartition
be able to use	be expecting	be nothing to	bibliopolic	bipyramidal
beachcomber	befittingly	be no trouble	bibliotheca	biquadratic
beach-master	beggar-ticks	be not to know	bicarbonate	bird-banding
be all thumbs	begging bowl	be nuts about	bicentenary	birdbrained
be all up with	begin school	benzene ring	bicephalous	bird-fancier
be a match for	beguilement	benzoic acid	bicuspidate	bird-nesting
beam-compass	beguilingly	be of service	bicycle clip	bird-ringing
bean-counter	be hard put to	be one's speed	bicycle pump	bird-watcher
bean sprouts	behavioural	be on one's way	biddability	birdwatcher
bean trefoil	behemothian	be on the land	bidialectal	birthday boy
bearability	be in the dark	be on your way	biding-place	birth father
bear a faggot	be in the game	be ourselves	Biedermeier	birth mother
bear a stroke	be in the race	be plain with	bifariously	birth parent
bear-baiting	be in the shit	be pushed for	bifurcation	birthweight
bear company	belatedness	be rained off	big business	biscuit-like
bearded iris	belaying-pin	bereavement	bilaterally	bisexuality
beardedness	beleaguerer	Bergamasque	bilberrying	bishopstool
bearded seal	Belgian hare	bergschrund	bile pigment	bishop's weed
bear heavily	believingly	Berkeleyism	bilinearity	bishop's wort
bearing-rein	bell-bottoms	Berlin black	biliousness	Bismarckian
bearishness	bell captain	Berlin glove	billets-doux	bite one's lip
bear's breech	belle époque	Bernoullian	billiardist	bite the dust
bear's garlic	bell-founder	be rolling in	billionaire	bit of muslin
bear's grease	bell-heather	bertrandite	billitonite	bits and bats
bearskinned	bellicosity	berylliosis	bill of costs	bits and bobs
bear the bell	belligerent	beryllonite	bill of goods	bitter aloes
bear witness	bellipotent	beseechment	billposting	bitter-apple
beastliness	bellows-fish	beseemingly	billsticker	bitter-cress
beast of prey	bell-ringing	Bessarabian	bilophodont	bitter-ender
be at college	belly button	bessemerize	bimetallism	bitter-gourd
beat the band	belly dancer	best friends	bimetallist	bitter pecan
beat the gong	belly-timber	best-selling	bimillenary	bitter-sweet
beat the meat	Belorussian	be stuck with	bimolecular	bitter-vetch
beat the wind	below ground	beta blocker	bimonthlies	bivouacking
beat to a pulp	below stairs	be tempted to	bimorphemic	bizarreness
beau gregory	be mates with	betrothment	binary digit	black Africa
beaumontage	be mixed up in	betting shop	binary scale	Black Africa
beauteously	benchership	betting slip	bindle-stiff	black and tan
beautifully	bench-warmer	between-maid	biocentrism	black arches
beauty queen	bend-leather	betweenness	biochemical	blackavised
beauty salon	bend the head	between-time	bioclimatic	black-backed
beauty sleep	bend the knee	bevel square	biocoenosis	black beetle
beaverboard	Benedictine	bewhiskered	biocoenotic	blackbirder
Beaverboard	benediction	Bewick's swan	biodynamics	black bottom
beaver cloth	benedictive	bewildering	bio-electric	black-browed
be beknown of	benedictory	bewitchment	bio-engineer	black bryony

black butter	blind as a bat	body-builder	botanically	brank-ursine
black cattle	blind corner	bodybuilder	botanomancy	brass monkey
black cherry	blindfolded	body-centred	botheration	brattishing
black coffee	blindfolder	body politic	bottle-arsed	brazen-faced
black cohosh	blind hookey	body-popping	bottle-brush	brazen it out
blackfellow	blind nettle	body scanner	bottle-glass	bread basket
black-figure	blind stitch	body-servant	bottle-gourd	breadbasket
black ginger	blister pack	bog asphodel	bottle green	breadstuffs
black grouse	blithefully	bog rosemary	bottle-nosed	breadthless
black-headed	bloatedness	bog standard	bottle party	breadthways
black latten	blockade-man	bohemianism	bottom yeast	breadthwise
black letter	blockbuster	Bohemianism	boulder clay	breadwinner
black locust	block delete	boil a wallop	boulevarded	break a close
blackmailer	blockheaded	boiled shirt	bounce-flash	break a lance
black market	block heater	boiled sweet	boundedness	break-dancer
Black Monday	block system	boilermaker	bounden duty	breakfaster
black Muslim	blood-flower	boiler-plate	boundlessly	break ground
Black Muslim	blood-guilty	bokmakierie	bounteously	break the ice
black pepper	bloodlessly	bolt upright	bountifully	breast-board
black piedra	blood-letter	bombardment	bourgeoisie	breast-drill
black poplar	blood orange	bombastical	bourrée step	breastplate
black powder	blood plasma	bomb factory	boutonnière	breast shell
Black Prince	blood spavin	bombilation	bower-anchor	breast-wheel
black rubric	blood sports	bombination	bower-maiden	breathalyse
black scoter	bloodstream	bombproofer	boxer shorts	breathe upon
black spauld	bloodsucker	Bonapartism	boxing glove	breathiness
black spruce	bloodthirst	Bonapartist	box junction	brecciation
black squall	blood vessel	bonaventure	box-tortoise	bred and born
black velvet	bloody grave	bondmanship	Boys' Brigade	breech birth
black walnut	bloody shirt	bondservice	boysenberry	breech-block
bladder-fern	bloody sweat	bond-washing	brabblement	breeze-block
bladder-like	blossomless	bone breccia	brace and bit	brewsterite
bladder worm	blotting-pad	bone-seeking	brachiation	bribability
bladderwort	blow a gasket	bonne bouche	brachyodont	bricklaying
blaeberries	blow one's top	bonnet laird	brachyurous	brick-stitch
blamelessly	blow sky-high	bonnet-piece	bracingness	bridal suite
blameworthy	blow the gaff	bons vivants	bracteolate	bridge-house
blank cheque	blueberries	bons viveurs	bradycardia	Bridgettine
blanket bath	blue-blooded	bookbindery	braggadocio	bright spark
blanket coat	blue-cheeked	bookbinding	braggartism	brilliantly
blanket roll	blue-eyed boy	booking hall	Brahmanical	brindled gnu
blank flange	bluefin tuna	bookishness	brahmaputra	brine shrimp
blank window	blue-striped	bookkeeping	Brahmaputra	bring home to
blasphemies	blue tangles	book-learned	brahminical	bring to bear
blasphemous	blue vitriol	Book of Kings	brain damage	bring to book
blastematic	blue whiting	book of words	brainlessly	bring to heel
blast freeze	blunder away	bookselling	brainsickly	bring to life
blastocoele	blunderbuss	boom and bust	brains trust	bring to mind
blastogenic	blunderhead	boon service	brain-teaser	bring to pass
blastoporal	blunder upon	boorishness	brain tumour	bristle-bird
blastospore	B-lymphocyte	bootability	brake harrow	bristle-fern
blateration	boardsailer	boots and all	brake lining	bristle-like
blaze abroad	boardsailor	boot-topping	bralessness	bristletail
blaze a trail	board school	boracic acid	bramble-rose	bristle-worm
blazing star	boatbuilder	borborygmic	branchiated	Bristol milk
blearedness	boatmanship	borborygmus	branchiness	British Lion
blemishless	boat the oars	bordered pit	branchiopod	Britishness
blemishment	bob and weave	border print	brand leader	British warm
blepharitis	bob-sledding	born and bred	brand of Cain	brittleness
blessedness	bobsledding	borohydride	brandy punch	brittle-star
bless my soul	bodaciously	borough-town	brandy-toddy	broach spire
bleu celeste	Bodhisattva	bosom friend	branglement	broadcasted

broadcaster	bulk modulus	butteriness	cakes and ale	campaign wig
Broad Church	bull at a gate	butter knife	Calabar bean	campaniform
broad-leaved	bull-baiting	butter-print	calamancoes	campanology
broadleaved	bulldog bond	buttery-book	calamistrum	campanulate
broad-minded	bulldog clip	button-grass	calcarenite	camphor tree
broadside on	bulletproof	buttonholer	calceolaria	camphor-wood
Brobdingnag	bullet train	button-mould	calcicolous	camp-meeting
brochantite	bullfighter	button-nosed	calciferous	Canaanitish
broken chord	bullishness	button-quail	calcigerous	Canada goose
broken field	bull-mastiff	button-stick	calcination	Canadianism
broken heart	bullock-cart	butyl rubber	calculating	Canadianize
bromatology	bull-puncher	butyraceous	calculation	canalicular
bromidrosis	bull session	butyric acid	calculative	canaliculus
bromination	bullshitter	butyrometer	calculatory	canary grass
bronchially	bull terrier	buy gape-seed	calculiform	cancellable
bronchiolar	bull-whacker	buying spree	calefacient	cancellated
bronchocele	bully pulpit	buy up a storm	calefaction	cancerously
bronchogram	bumble-puppy	by an eyelash	calefactive	cancer stick
bronchotomy	bumpologist	by any chance	calefactory	candelabras
brontothere	bumptiously	by mischance	calendarial	candelabrum
bronze medal	bunch-flower	by one's guess	calendrical	candescence
Brooklynese	Bunyanesque	by ourselves	calibration	candidature
brotherhood	buoyancy aid	by piecemeal	Californian	candidiasis
brotherless	buoyantness	byrlaw-court	californite	candied peel
brothership	buphthalmic	Byronically	californium	candleberry
broth of a boy	buphthalmos	by that means	calisthenic	candlelight
brown-bagger	burble point	by the name of	call a halt to	candlepower
brown George	bureaucracy	by the side of	Callanetics	candlestick
brucellosis	burgess oath	by this means	call changes	candy stripe
brush turkey	burgess-ship	by this token	call cousins	candystripe
brusqueness	burghership	by wholesale	calligraphy	canine tooth
brutalities	burglarious	by your leave	calling card	cannabinoid
brutishness	burgomaster	Byzantinism	calling hare	cannibalean
bryological	burlesquely	Byzantinist	callipygian	cannibalise
bryozoology	burlesquing	caa'ing whale	callipygous	cannibalism
bubble-shell	bur-marigold	cabbage-bark	callistemon	cannibalize
buccinatory	burning bush	cabbage-head	call it quits	cannulation
buck-and-wing	burning marl	cabbage-like	callitriche	canonically
bucket-wheel	burnt almond	cabbage moth	call one's own	canophilist
buckler-fern	burn to a chip	cabbage palm	callosities	Canopic vase
buck-passing	burnt sienna	cabbage rose	callousness	cantharides
buck rarebit	burrows-town	cabbage tree	call the roll	cantharidin
buck-toothed	bush-cricket	cabbalistic	call the tune	canting arms
buck-washing	bush-leaguer	cabinet-work	call the turn	capableness
bucolically	bushmanship	cable length	call to order	capaciously
buddy system	bush-ranging	cable stitch	calorically	capacitance
budge-barrel	bushwhacker	cablevision	calorimeter	cap and bells
buffalo bird	bushy-tailed	cacao butter	calorimetry	Cape buffalo
buffalo fish	business end	cachectical	calumniator	Cape cowslip
buffalo robe	businessman	cache memory	Calvinistic	Cape jasmine
buffer state	businessmen	cacodoxical	calycanthus	Capernaitic
buffer State	Butazolidin	cacographer	calyculated	capernoited
buffer stock	butcher-bird	cacographic	calypsonian	caper spurge
buff leather	butcher blue	cacophonies	Camaldolese	Cape sparrow
bugger about	butcher meat	cacophonous	Camaldolite	capillaries
Buggins' turn	but me no buts	caddis-flies	camaraderie	capillarity
building lot	Butskellism	caddishness	camel-spider	capillitium
built on sand	Butskellite	cadmiferous	camera-ready	capital gain
bulbiferous	butter cloth	cadmium cell	camera shake	capital levy
bulimarexia	butter-cream	Caesar salad	camerawoman	capitalling
bulimarexic	butterflies	Caesar's wife	Cameroonian	capital ship
bulk carrier	butter-icing	café society	camomile tea	capitulator

Cappadocian	carnificial	cataclysmal	cavernously	chain bridge
cappuccinos	carnivalite	cataclysmic	cavernulous	chain letter
capriccioso	carnivorous	catadromous	cavillation	chain-smoker
Capricornus	Carnot cycle	catallactic	ceaselessly	chain stitch
caprolactam	Carolingian	cataloguing	cecidiology	chairladies
capsulotomy	carol-singer	cataloguist	celebration	chairoplane
captaincies	carotid body	cataloguize	celebrative	chairperson
captainless	carpet dance	cat-and-mouse	celebratory	chalcedonic
captainship	carpet layer	cataplectic	celebrities	chalcophile
captivation	carpet-shark	cataractous	celestially	chalice vine
captivities	carpet shell	catastrophe	cellularity	chalk-stripe
carabideous	carpet-snake	catavothron	Celtiberian	challenging
carabiniere	carpogonial	catch a few z's	Celtic cross	chamaephyte
caravanette	carpogonium	catch hold of	cementation	chamberlain
caravanning	carrageenan	catch-phrase	cement mixer	chambermaid
caravan park	carriage dog	catchphrase	cenogenesis	chamber-tomb
caravan site	carriageway	catch-points	censureship	chameleonic
caraway seed	carrick bend	catch-stitch	centenarian	champerties
carbocyclic	carrier wave	catch the sun	centenaries	champertous
Carbonarism	carrion crow	catch-weight	centerboard	championess
carbonation	carryings-on	catchweight	centesimate	chancefully
carbonatite	carry the bat	catechetics	centigramme	chancellery
carbon black	carry the can	catechismal	centimetric	change front
carbon cycle	carry the day	catechistic	cent per cent	change hands
carbon fibre	carry weight	categorical	central bank	change-house
carbon paper	carsickness	cater-corner	centralizer	change of air
carbon steel	cartography	catercorner	centralness	channelling
car boot sale	cartophilic	cater-cousin	Central Park	chantarelle
carborundum	carunculate	caterpillar	Central Time	chanterelle
carboxylate	carvel-built	caterwauler	centreboard	chantership
carbuncular	carving-fork	cathartical	centre field	chanticleer
carburation	case grammar	cathedratic	centrepiece	chaos theory
carburetion	case history	catheterise	centre stage	chaotically
carburetted	case in point	catheterism	centrically	chaparreras
carburetter	cash-account	catheterize	centrifugal	chapeau-bras
carburettor	cashew apple	catholicate	centripetal	chapel royal
carbylamine	cashierment	catholicise	centrobaric	chaperonage
carcass meat	cash payment	Catholicism	centromeric	chapmanship
carcinology	cassiterite	catholicity	centumviral	charcuterie
carcinomata	cassowaries	catholicize	Centuriator	charged with
cardan joint	cast a slur on	Catholicize	cephalocele	charge-house
cardan shaft	castellated	catoptrical	cephalothin	charge nurse
Cardan's rule	caster sugar	cat-purchase	cerargyrite	charge sheet
cardinalate	caste-system	cat's pyjamas	cerebellums	charismatic
cardinalism	castigation	cat's whisker	cerebralism	charitarian
cardinalist	castigatory	cattishness	cerebralist	charitative
cardinality	Castile soap	cattle-egret	cerebration	charity ball
cardinalize	casting vote	cattle guard	cerebroside	charity walk
carding wool	castle-guard	cattle-truck	ceremonious	charlatanic
cardiograph	cast light on	cauliflower	cereologist	charlatanry
cardiospasm	castor sugar	causational	ceroplastic	Charles's Law
card-playing	castrensian	causatively	certain sure	charmlessly
card-sharper	cast the lead	causativity	certainties	charm school
carefulness	cast up gorge	caustically	certifiable	charnockite
caressingly	casual water	caustic bush	certifiably	charophytic
caressively	casuistical	caustic soda	certificate	chartaceous
caribou moss	catabaptist	caustic vine	Cesarewitch	chart-buster
caricatural	catabothron	caustic weed	cetological	chartbuster
carminative	catacaustic	cavalierish	chaetognath	charter-land
carnaptious	catachreses	cavalierism	chaff-cutter	charterless
carnationed	catachresis	cave dweller	chafing dish	Charter Mark
carnauba wax	cataclastic	cavernicole	chain armour	chart-topper

chase chorus	chilli sauce	Christendom	circinately	clay mineral
chasmogamic	chillumchee	christening	circination	clean-limbed
chassisless	chimichanga	Christiania	circle dance	cleanliness
chastisable	chimneyless	Christianly	circuitries	clean-living
chaulmoogra	chimney-nook	Christingle	circularise	clean-shaven
check-action	china-closet	Christmases	circularity	clean ticket
check-string	China orange	Christmassy	circularize	clear-headed
Cheddar pink	Chinese burn	Christology	circular saw	clear-starch
cheek by jowl	Chinese copy	Christ's sake	circulation	clear the air
cheer-leader	Chinese jute	chrome green	circulative	clear the way
cheerleader	Chinese leaf	chrome steel	circulatory	clear-voiced
cheerlessly	Chinese wall	chromic acid	circumciser	cleft palate
cheeseboard	chinoiserie	chrominance	circumlunar	cleistogamy
cheesecloth	chintziness	chromogenic	circumpolar	clergy-house
cheese-flies	Chippendale	chromophile	circumsolar	clergywoman
cheese-knife	chirography	chromophobe	circumspect	clergywomen
cheesemaker	chirologist	chromophore	circumvolve	clericalism
cheese pasty	chiromancer	chromosomal	cirl bunting	clericalist
cheese plant	chiromantic	chronically	cirriferous	clericality
cheese press	chiropodist	chronograph	cirrigerous	clericalize
cheese salad	chiropteran	chronologer	cisatlantic	clerkliness
cheese scone	chitterling	chronologic	cistophorus	cleverality
cheese straw	chitty-faced	chronometer	citizenhood	clever-clogs
cheiranthus	chloanthite	chronometry	citizenship	click beetle
chelicerate	chloric acid	chronoscope	citronellal	client state
cheliferous	chlorinator	chrysalides	citronellol	cliff-hanger
Chelsea boot	chlorophyll	chrysalises	citrus fruit	cliffhanger
Chelsea ware	chlorophyte	chrysarobin	City Company	climacteric
chemicalize	chloroplast	chrysoberyl	city council	climatology
chemin de fer	chloroprene	chrysocolla	city fathers	clinochlore
chemistries	chloroquine	chrysoidine	city manager	cliometrics
chemotactic	chock-a-block	chrysomelid	city marshal	clipper ship
chemotropic	chocolatier	chrysoprase	City marshal	clockmaking
chenopodium	choirmaster	chuckawalla	city mission	clodhopping
chequer-wise	choir office	chucklehead	city slicker	clog-almanac
chequer-work	choir school	churchgoing	civic centre	close-carpet
cherishable	choir sister	church-grith	civic-minded	close-fisted
cherishment	choke cherry	church-house	civilianise	close-handed
chernozemic	choke-cymbal	churchiness	civilianize	close-hauled
chestnut oak	choking coil	churchmanly	civilizable	close-lipped
cheval glass	cholangitis	church mouse	civil parish	close season
chiaroscuro	cholera belt	churchwoman	civil rights	closet drama
chiastolite	choler adust	churchwomen	Civvy Street	close to home
chicaneries	cholesterin	chyliferous	cladogenous	closet queen
chickabiddy	cholesterol	chylomicron	claim-jumper	closing time
chicken feed	cholinergic	cicatricial	clairschach	clostridial
chicken-hawk	chondrocyte	cicatricula	clairvoyant	clostridium
chicken Kiev	chondrodite	cicatrizant	clamorously	clothesless
chicken mite	chondroitin	ciconiiform	clandestine	clothes line
chicken-shit	Chopinesque	cigar flower	clapperclaw	clothes-moth
chicken soup	chordophone	cigar-holder	clapper rail	clothes-post
chicken-weed	chordotonal	cigar-shaped	class action	cloth-headed
chicken wire	choreograph	ciliary body	class-fellow	cloth-miller
chieftaincy	chorography	cinchocaine	classically	cloth of gold
chieftainry	choroid coat	cinema organ	classic race	cloth-worker
chiffonnade	choroiditis	cinerariums	classic tutu	cloud-castle
chikungunya	choux pastry	cinerary urn	class-leader	cloudlessly
chilblained	chowderhead	cineritious	clathration	cloud seeder
child labour	chrismation	cinnabarine	clavecinist	cloud street
child-minder	chrismatory	cinnamon oil	clavel-piece	clouted shoe
childminder	Christ-cross	cinquecento	clavicymbal	clover-grass
chill factor	christendie	Cinque Ports	claw-and-ball	cluster bomb

cluster pine	coffee-spoon	colonizable	commandment	compass rose
coadjutress	coffee stall	colonoscope	command post	compearance
coadunation	coffee table	colonoscopy	commandress	compellable
coagulation	coffin-joint	colorimeter	comme il faut	compendiate
coagulative	coffin-plate	colorimetry	commemorate	compendious
coalescence	coffin-stool	colostomies	commendable	compendiums
coalitioner	co-foundress	colouration	commendably	compensable
coal scuttle	cogenerated	colour atlas	commendador	compensator
coal-whipper	cogenerator	colour-blind	commendator	competently
coarctation	cognateness	colourfully	commend me to	competition
coat checker	cognitional	colour guard	commentator	competitive
coatimundis	cognitively	colour-index	commination	competitory
coaxial line	cognitivism	colouristic	comminatory	compilation
cobalt bloom	cognitivist	colour-light	comminution	compilatory
cobbler's wax	cognominate	colour-phase	commiserate	complacence
cobblestone	cognoscence	colour-plate	commissaire	complacency
coccidiosis	cognoscente	coltishness	commissural	complainant
coccinellid	cognoscenti	columbarium	committable	complaisant
coccosphere	cognoscible	columniated	committible	completable
Cochin China	cohortation	columniform	commodified	complexness
cock-a-leekie	coincidence	combat boots	commodifies	compliantly
cock-brained	co-inherence	combat dress	commodities	complicated
cockle-shell	co-inheritor	combatively	commonality	componentry
cockleshell	cold-blooded	combativity	common chord	comportment
cock one's eye	cold cathode	combination	common crier	comport with
cock one's hat	cold comfort	combinative	common field	compositely
cock sparrow	cold harbour	combinatory	common juror	composition
cock the ears	cold-hearted	combing wool	common maple	compositive
cock the nose	cold storage	combustible	common metre	compossible
cocky-leekie	cold warrior	combustibly	common murre	compostable
cocoa butter	coleopteran	come a gutser	commonplace	compost heap
coco matting	Coleridgian	come a purler	common pleas	compost pile
co-conscious	collaborate	come a stumer	common scold	compotation
coconut crab	collagenous	come between	common sense	compotatory
coconut milk	collapsible	come forward	common sewer	compound eye
coconut palm	collational	come in first	common shore	compresence
coconut tree	collectable	come in handy	common situs	compression
code-breaker	collectedly	come one's way	common snipe	compressive
codefendant	collect eyes	come over big	common stock	compressure
codependent	collectible	come short of	communalise	comprisable
codetermine	collegially	comet-finder	communalism	compromiser
codicillary	collegianer	come the acid	communalist	compte rendu
codling moth	collembolan	come through	communality	Comptometer
cod liver oil	collenchyma	come to a head	communalize	comptroller
co-education	colleterial	come to an end	communicant	compulsitor
coeducation	colligation	come to blows	communicate	compunction
coefficient	colligative	come to grief	communistic	compurgator
coelenteron	collimation	come to light	communities	computation
coelurosaur	collinearly	come to terms	commutation	computeracy
coenenchyme	collisional	comet-seeker	commutative	computerate
coercionist	collocation	come unstuck	compact disc	computerese
coessential	collocative	come-uppance	compactedly	computerise
coeternally	collocutory	come what may	compactness	computerist
co-executrix	colloidally	comfortable	compaginate	computerize
coexistence	colloquiums	comfortably	companioned	computistic
coextension	collusively	comfortless	comparatist	comradeship
coextensive	Collyridian	comfortress	comparative	Comstockery
co-favourite	colonelcies	comicalness	compare with	concamerate
coffee-berry	colonelling	comic relief	compartment	concatenate
coffee-break	colonelship	commandable	compassable	concave lens
coffee house	colonialism	Commandaria	compass card	concaveness
coffee-maker	colonialist	Commanderia	compassless	concealable

concealment	confederate	connotation	contact lens	conventical
conceitedly	conferrable	connotative	containable	conventicle
conceitless	conferrence	connubially	containment	convergence
conceivable	confessedly	connumerate	contaminant	convergency
conceivably	confidently	conquerable	contaminate	conversable
concentrate	confidingly	conquerless	contango day	conversably
conceptacle	configurate	consanguine	contemplant	conversance
concernedly	confineless	conscienced	contemplate	conversancy
concernment	confinement	consciously	contenement	conversible
concertante	confirmable	consecrated	contentable	convertible
concertanti	confiscable	consecrator	contentedly	convertibly
concert-goer	confiscator	consecution	contentious	conveyancer
concert hall	conflagrant	consecutive	contentless	conveyorize
concertina'd	conflagrate	consentient	contentment	convictable
concertinas	conflictful	consequence	content word	convincible
concertinos	confliction	conservable	conterminal	convivially
concessible	conflictive	conservancy	contestable	convocation
conciliable	conflictual	conservator	contextless	convolution
conciliarly	confluently	considerate	continental	convolvulus
conciliator	conformable	considering	continently	co-occurrent
conciseness	conformably	consignment	contingence	cookery book
concitation	conformally	consilience	contingency	cook-general
conclusible	conformance	consistence	continuable	cookie sheet
concolorous	confusingly	consistency	continually	cool chamber
concomitant	confusional	consolation	continuance	cooling-pond
concordable	confutation	consolatory	continuator	cool tankard
concordance	confutative	consolatrix	contorniate	co-operation
concordancy	congealable	consolement	contour line	cooperation
concordatum	congealment	consolidate	contrabasso	co-operative
concreative	congé d'élire	consolingly	contractant	cooperative
concrescent	congee-house	consonantal	contractile	Cooper's hawk
concubinage	congelation	consonanted	contraction	coordinator
concubinary	congenerate	consonantic	contractive	Cootamundra
concurrence	congenerous	consonantly	contractual	co-ownership
concurrency	congenially	consortiums	contracture	coparcenary
condemnable	congratters	consortship	contradance	copiability
condemnator	congregated	conspecific	contraposit	coping stone
condensable	congregator	conspicuity	contraption	copiousness
condensator	congression	conspicuous	contrariant	coplanarity
condensedly	congressist	conspirator	contrariety	copper beech
condensible	congressman	constabular	contrarious	copper-belly
condignness	Congressman	constellate	contrastive	copper Maori
condimental	congressmen	consternate	contratenor	copperplate
condisciple	congruently	constipated	contravener	coppersmith
conditional	congruously	constituent	contrayerva	copper's nark
conditioned	conicalness	constituter	contredanse	coppice-wood
conditioner	conjectural	constitutor	contretemps	coprocessor
condolatory	conjecturer	constrained	contribuent	copromaniac
condolement	conjugality	constrainer	contributor	coprophagia
condolingly	conjugation	constricted	contrivable	coprophagic
condominium	conjunction	constrictor	contrivance	coprophilia
condonation	conjunctiva	construable	controlling	coprophilic
condottiere	conjunctive	constructor	controlment	copyability
conducement	conjuncture	consultable	control room	copywriting
conductance	conjuration	consultancy	control unit	coquilla nut
conduct book	connateness	consumerism	controversy	coral insect
conductible	connectable	consumerist	contubernal	coral island
conductress	connectedly	consumingly	contumacity	coralliform
conduit-pipe	connectible	consummator	conurbation	coralloidal
Condy's fluid	connectival	consumption	convalidate	coram judice
confabulate	connexional	consumptive	convenience	coram populo
confederacy	connoisseur	contactable	conveniency	corbel-stone

corbel-table	corymbiform	counter-mart	coxcombries	crêpe rubber
corbie-gable	corymbosely	countermine	coxopoditic	crepitation
corbie-steps	coryphodont	countermove	crabbedness	crepuscular
cordilleran	co-signatory	countermure	crab-catcher	crepusculum
cordwainery	cosmetician	counterpane	crab-fashion	crescentade
cordwaining	cosmeticize	counterpart	crack down on	crescentric
core sampler	cosmetology	counter-plea	cracked corn	crested newt
co-residence	cosmogonies	counterplot	crackedness	crestfallen
cork cambium	cosmogonist	counter-pole	cracker-bush	Creswellian
corn bunting	cosmography	counterpose	crackerjack	cribellated
corn-cob pipe	cosmologist	counter-roll	crack-headed	cricket-frog
corn ear worm	cosmonautic	counter-seal	crackle-ware	cricket-teal
cornerstone	cosmopolite	countersign	crack of dawn	crime-buster
corner throw	cosmothetic	countersink	crack of doom	crime writer
corn-husking	co-sovereign	counter-step	crack on sail	criminalise
corniculate	Cossack boot	countersunk	crack-voiced	criminalism
cornigerous	Cossack post	counter-tide	crack willow	criminalist
corn in Egypt	cost-benefit	counter-turn	cracovienne	criminality
corn parsley	cost-cutting	countertype	cradle-board	criminalize
corn spurrey	costingness	countervail	craftswoman	criminal law
cornucopian	costiveness	countervair	craftswomen	criminaloid
corn whiskey	costume play	counterview	craftworker	crimination
corollaries	cotemporary	counter-walk	crag and tail	criminative
corolla-tube	coterminous	counterwork	craggedness	criminatory
coronagraph	co-tidal line	countrified	cranberries	criminology
coronal bone	cotoneaster	country-bred	crane-colour	criminously
coronership	cottage loaf	country club	crane-driver	crimson lake
coronograph	cotton candy	countryfied	crane-necked	crinigerous
corpocratic	cotton grass	country-folk	craniometry	crinkliness
corporality	cotton plant	country jake	craniopathy	cripplingly
corporately	cotton plush	country road	crape-myrtle	crithomancy
corporation	cotton-sedge	country rock	crappit-head	criticality
corporatism	cotton state	country seat	crapshooter	criticaster
corporatist	cotton twist	countryship	crapulosity	crochet hook
corporative	cotton waste	countryside	crash course	crocidolite
corporatize	couch potato	country town	crash cymbal	crocodilian
corporeally	Couette flow	country-wide	crash helmet	crocodiling
corporosity	coulometric	county court	crash-tackle	Cromwellian
corps d'élite	council-book	coup de grâce	crashworthy	crook-backed
corpse-light	council-fire	couple-close	crateriform	crookbacked
corpuscular	council flat	coupling-pin	crawling peg	crookedness
corpus juris	counselless	coupling-rod	crazy paving	Crookes tube
correctable	counselling	courageless	cream cheese	crop dusting
correctible	count-bishop	courteously	cream colour	cross-accent
correctness	countenance	courtesy cop	creamometer	cross-action
correctress	counter-arch	courtierism	cream sherry	cross-bearer
correlation	counterbass	court jester	creationism	cross-border
correlative	counter-bill	courtliness	creationist	crossbowman
corrigendum	counterblow	courtly love	creative art	crossbowmen
corroborant	counterbond	Court of Rome	creatorship	cross-corner
corroborate	counter-book	court tennis	credibility	cross-cousin
corrosively	counterbore	couscoussou	credit title	cross-cut saw
corrugation	counterbuff	Cousin Betty	credit union	cross-dating
corruptedly	counter-etch	cousin-in-law	credulously	cross-fenced
corruptible	counterfeit	covariation	cremasteric	cross-garnet
corruptibly	counter-fire	cover charge	crematories	cross-handed
corruptless	counterfoil	cover letter	crematorium	cross-legged
corruptness	counterfort	covert-baron	crème brûlée	cross-member
corruptress	counterglow	covert cloth	crenulation	cross-plough
cors anglais	counterlath	cowboy boots	creolistics	cross-rhythm
corticolous	countermand	cowslipping	creophagous	cross-saddle
coruscation	countermark	coxcombical	creosote oil	cross stitch

cross-street	cub engineer	cushion-like	dairy cattle	deathliness
cross swords	cubicalness	cushion star	dairy farmer	death rattle
cross-tongue	cub reporter	cuspidation	daisy-cutter	death throes
cross-voting	cuckoo clock	customaries	dak-bungalow	deattribute
crotcheteer	cuckoo's mate	customarily	dale and down	debamboozle
crouchingly	cuckoo's meat	custom-built	Dalecarlian	debarbarize
crouch start	cucullately	custom-house	damask steel	debarkation
crowberries	cuir-bouilli	customs duty	dame's violet	debasedness
crowdedness	culicicidal	cut-and-cover	damnability	debauchedly
crowd of sail	culmiferous	cut and dried	Damoclesian	debouchment
crowd on sail	culmination	cut-and-paste	damper pedal	debridement
crowd-puller	culpability	cut both ways	dampishness	debs' delight
Crown Agents	cultishness	cutlass-fish	damselflies	decadentism
crown bowler	cultivation	cut the melon	dance in a net	decahedrons
Crown colony	cultureless	cutting-edge	dancing girl	decalcified
Crown Colony	culturology	cutting room	dandy roller	decalcifier
crowned head	culverineer	cut to pieces	danger angle	decalcifies
crown jewels	cum dividend	cyanidation	danger money	decalescent
Crown Office	cumulonimbi	cyanine blue	dangerously	decantation
crown prince	cunctatious	cyanophycin	Daniell cell	decapeptide
Crown prince	cunnilingue	cyanophytic	daphne heath	decapitator
crow's-footed	cunnilingus	cybernation	dappled-grey	decapsulate
crow-stepped	cunningness	cybernetics	daredevilry	decarbonate
crowstepped	cupellation	cycadaceous	dark-adapted	decarbonise
crucialness	cup-mushroom	cycadophyte	dark current	decarbonize
crucian carp	cup of estate	cyclization	dark glasses	decarburize
cruciferous	cupping-test	cycloalkane	dark lantern	decasualize
crucifixion	cuprammonia	cyclohexane	Darling lily	decaudation
cruelty-free	cupriferous	cyclopaedia	darning-ball	deceitfully
cruise liner	cupro-nickel	cycloplegia	darning-wool	deceivingly
crumbliness	curatorship	cycloplegic	Darwinistic	decelerator
crumple zone	curb service	cyclosporin	Darwin tulip	decemvirate
crunchiness	curettement	cyclothymia	dashingness	decennially
crunchingly	curialistic	cyclothymic	data capture	deceptively
crush stroke	curiosities	cylinder oil	daubréelite	decerebrate
crustaceous	curiousness	cylinder saw	dauntlessly	decerniture
cry cupboard	curling iron	cylindrical	Davis Strait	decidedness
cry harrow on	curling pins	cyma reversa	dawn redwood	deciduously
cryobiology	curling rink	cynanthropy	day after day	decillionth
cryonically	curl one's lip	cynological	day and night	decimo-sexto
cryosurgery	curly endive	cyperaceous	day labourer	deckle-edged
cryotherapy	currant-tree	cypress-knee	days of grace	deckle strap
cryptically	currentless	cypress pine	dazzle paint	declamation
cryptogamic	currentness	cypress tree	de-accession	declamatory
cryptogenic	currishness	cypress-vine	deaccession	declaration
cryptograph	curry favour	cypriniform	deactivator	declarative
cryptomeria	curry powder	cyprinodont	dead against	declaratory
cryptophyte	cursiveness	cypripedium	dead and gone	declination
cryptorchid	cursoriness	cysticercus	dead as a dodo	declinatory
crystal axis	curtailment	cystoscopic	deadeningly	declinature
crystal ball	curtail-step	cystotomies	dead-hearted	declivities
crystal form	curtain call	cytogenetic	deadpanning	declivitous
crystal-like	curtain fire	cytological	dead soldier	decollation
crystalline	curtain-hook	cytomegalic	dead to shame	décollement
crystallise	curtainless	cytoplasmic	deaf and dumb	décolletage
crystallite	curtain line	cytotropism	deaf as a post	decolourant
crystallize	curtain-rail	dactylogram	deafeningly	decolourize
crystalloid	curtain-ring	dactylology	deamination	decommunize
ctenophoral	curtain wall	Dagestan rug	de-Anglicize	decomposite
ctenophoran	curvilineal	dagger-board	death duties	decondition
ctenophoric	curvilinear	daggerboard	death-in-life	deconstruct
cubbishness	cushionless	dagger plant	deathlessly	decorticate

decrepitate	degradingly	demon bowler	depravities	desperation
decrepitude	degranulate	demonianism	deprecation	despisement
decrescendo	degustation	demonically	deprecative	despisingly
decretalist	de haut en bas	demonocracy	deprecatory	despoilment
decretorial	dehonestate	demonolatry	depreciator	despondence
decuman gate	dehortation	demonomania	depredation	despondency
decumbiture	dehortative	demonstrate	depredatory	despumation
decurionate	dehortatory	demoralizer	depressedly	dessert fork
decurrently	dehydratase	Demosthenic	depressible	dessert wine
decursively	dehydration	demountable	deprivation	destabilise
decurvature	deictically	demutualize	deprivative	destabilize
decussately	deification	demyelinate	de profundis	de-Stalinize
decussation	deificatory	demystified	deprogramme	destination
dedentition	deistically	demystifies	depth charge	destitutely
dedicatedly	delabialize	demythicize	depth-finder	destitution
deductively	delafossite	denary scale	deracialize	destoolment
deductivism	delectation	dendritical	deraignment	destroyable
deductivist	deleterious	dendrologic	derangement	destructful
Deely-bobber	deliberator	dendrometer	derecognise	destruction
de-emphasise	deliciously	dendrophile	derecognize	destructive
de-emphasize	delightable	denervation	dereliction	destructure
deep-dish pie	delightedly	deniability	dermapteran	desulfurate
deep drawing	delightless	denigration	dermatology	desultorily
deepeningly	delightsome	denigratory	dermatoptic	desuperheat
deep-etching	delineation	denitration	dermoid cyst	detainingly
deep-fetched	delineative	denitrified	dermopteran	detectional
deep-freezer	delinquency	denitrifies	derring-doer	deteriorate
deep-milking	deliriously	denizenship	desacralize	determinacy
deep-mouthed	delitescent	denominable	descendable	determinans
deep therapy	deliverable	denominator	descendance	determinant
deerstalker	deliverance	dental floss	descendancy	determinata
deer-stealer	deliverness	dental nurse	descendence	determinate
defaecation	delivery van	dentary bone	descendible	determinism
defaillance	Della Robbia	dentellated	descloizite	determinist
defalcation	delphically	denticulate	descrambler	detestation
defatigable	delphinidin	dentigerous	describable	detractress
defectively	delphiniums	dentistical	description	detrainment
defence bond	delta rhythm	denumerable	descriptive	detribalise
defenceless	demagnetise	denumerably	desecration	detribalize
defence plea	demagnetize	denunciator	desecrative	detrimental
Defenderism	demagogical	denutrition	desegregate	deturpation
defensively	demagoguery	deny oneself	deselection	deuteranope
deferential	demand curve	deoxidation	desensitise	deuteration
defiantness	demand draft	deoxygenate	desensitize	deuterogamy
defibrinate	demandingly	deoxyribose	desert lemon	deutomerite
deficiently	demarcation	depasturage	deservingly	Deutschmark
definiendum	demarcative	depauperate	deserving of	devaluation
deflagrator	demarkation	depauperize	desexualise	devastating
defloration	dementation	dependently	desexualize	devastation
defocussing	demesmerize	depending on	desiccation	devastative
defoliation	demethylate	deperdition	desiccative	developable
deforcement	demi-bastion	dephlegmate	desiccatory	development
deformation	demigoddess	deploration	desideratum	deverbative
deformities	demi-pension	deploringly	designation	deviability
defraudment	democracies	deplumation	designative	deviational
defunctness	democratise	depoeticize	designatory	devil dancer
deglamorize	democratism	depolarizer	designingly	devil-dodger
deglutinate	democratize	depopulator	desilverize	devil's bones
deglutition	Democritean	deportation	desinential	devil's books
deglutitory	demodulator	depositable	desiredness	devil's dozen
degradation	demographer	depravation	desperadoes	devil's twine
degradative	demographic	depravement	desperately	deviousness

devirginate	dictatorial	diplococcus	discontinue	dismayingly
devitrified	dictatorily	diplohedral	discordance	dismembered
devitrifies	dictyostele	diplohedron	discordancy	dismemberer
devolvement	didacticism	diplomatese	discotheque	dismissable
devotedness	didactylous	diplomatise	discothèque	dismissible
devotionary	diddly-squat	diplomatist	discourager	dismutation
devotionist	die aborning	diplomatize	discourtesy	Disneyesque
devouringly	die like a dog	dip one's wick	discoveries	disobedient
Dewey system	die-stamping	dipper gourd	disc parking	disobliging
dexterously	die the death	diprotodont	discreation	disobstruct
dharmasutra	differentia	dipsomaniac	discredence	disordinate
Diabolonian	differently	dipterocarp	discredited	disorganise
diachronism	difficultly	dipyramidal	discreetest	disorganize
diachronous	diffidation	direct debit	discrepance	disparately
diacoustics	diffidently	direct-drive	discrepancy	disparities
diacritical	diffraction	direct grant	discriminal	disparition
diadelphous	diffractive	directional	discussable	dispartment
diagnosable	diffuseness	directively	discussible	dispatch box
diagnostics	diffusional	directivity	disdainable	dispatchful
diagonalize	diffusively	directorate	disembodied	dispendious
diagramming	diffusivity	directorial	disembodies	dispensable
dialectally	digestively	directories	disembogued	dispensator
dialectical	digital root	directrices	disembogues	dispensible
dialogician	digitigrade	direfulness	disemburden	dispersable
dialogistic	dignifiedly	dirndl skirt	disencumber	dispersedly
dialogue box	dignitaries	dirt-tracker	disentangle	dispersible
diamagnetic	diguanidine	dirty old man	disenthrone	displacency
diametrally	dihexagonal	disablement	disentrance	displayable
diametrical	dihybridism	disableness	disequality	display type
diamondback	dilapidated	disaccustom	disesteemer	displeasant
diamond-bird	dilapidator	disacquaint	disfunction	displeasing
diamond-like	dilatometer	disaffected	disgarrison	displeasure
diamond pane	dilatometry	disafforest	disgraceful	displicency
diamondwise	dilettantes	disagreeing	disgracious	disportment
diamorphine	diluvialist	disappearer	disgruntled	disposition
diaphaneity	diluvianism	disapproval	disguisedly	dispositive
diaphonemic	dimensional	disapprover	disgustedly	dispository
diaphoresis	dimensioned	disarmament	disharmonic	disprovable
diaphoretic	dimidiately	disarmingly	dishevelled	disputation
diapophysis	dimidiation	disassemble	dishonestly	disputative
diapositive	diminuendos	disassembly	dishonourer	disquantity
diarthrosis	diminutival	disavowable	dishumanize	disquieting
diastematic	dimorphemic	disbandment	disillusion	disquietude
diastrophic	dingleberry	disbeliever	disillusive	disquisitor
diasystemic	dining-chair	discalceate	disimprison	disregarder
diatessaron	dining table	discanonize	disinclined	disremember
diathermacy	dinner dance	discardable	disinfecter	disrobement
diathermous	dinner party	discardment	disinfector	dissectible
diatonicism	dinner-table	discernible	disinterest	disseminate
dicasterion	dinner wagon	discernibly	disinterred	disseminule
dichogamous	dinosaurian	discernment	disjointure	dissentient
dichotomies	dioeciously	discerption	disjunction	dissentious
dichotomise	Dionysiacal	discigerous	disjunctive	dissentment
dichotomist	Diophantine	disciplinal	disjuncture	dissepiment
dichotomize	dipeptidase	discipliner	dislikeable	dissertator
dichotomous	diphosphate	disclaimant	dislocation	dissimilate
dichromatic	diphtherial	discloister	dislocative	dissimulate
dichroscope	diphtheroid	discography	dislocatory	dissipation
Dickensiana	diphthongal	discolorate	dislodgment	dissipative
dicondylian	diphthongic	discomfited	disloyalist	dissociable
dicotyledon	diphycercal	discomfiter	dismal Jimmy	dissolutely
dictatorate	diplococcal	disconsider	dismayfully	dissolution

dissolutive   divining rod   donkey-stone   douroucouli   dressmaking
dissolvable   divisionary   donkey stool   do well out of   dress parade
dissolvible   divisionism   donnishness   do whoopsies   dress shield
dissonantal   divisionist   do not seem to   down-calving   dress weight
dissonantly   divorceable   do not want to   down-channel   driblet cone
dissyllabic   divorce case   Donovan body   downconvert   drift-anchor
dissyllable   divorceless   donovanosis   down-country   drift-bottle
dissymmetry   divorcement   don't I know it   downcurrent   drift mining
dissympathy   divulgation   don't you know   down draught   drift-netter
distaff side   divulgement   doodly-squat   downhearted   drilling mud
Distalgesic   do a line with   doomwatcher   downlooking   drilling rig
distantiate   do a number on   do one's block   down payment   drill string
distantness   dobsonflies   do one's scone   downrightly   drink-driver
distasteful   docetically   do one's stuff   down-the-line   drinker moth
distempered   doch an doris   do one's thing   down the road   drinks party
distemperer   dockominium   door knocker   down-to-earth   drip culture
distendedly   dock-warrant   doorstepper   downtrodden   dripping-pan
distensible   dockyard man   dormant tree   downwarping   dripping wet
distillable   doctor-blade   dormitories   downwelling   drivability
distinction   doctorially   dorsiferous   downy mildew   drive a quill
distinctive   doctrinaire   dorsiflexor   doxographer   driver's test
distinguish   doctrinally   dos and don'ts   doxographic   drive system
distomiasis   documentary   dot and go one   doxological   driving axle
distortedly   documentize   double agent   doxorubicin   driving band
distraction   dodder-grass   double album   doxycycline   driving belt
distractive   dodderiness   double blank   do your worst   driving iron
distressful   dodecahedra   double-blind   dracunculus   driving rain
distress-gun   dodecameric   double bluff   draft dodger   driving seat
distributee   dodecaphony   double-bogey   draggle-tail   driving test
distributor   dodecastyle   double-check   drag-hunting   dromedaries
distrustful   dodge Pompey   double cream   dragon china   dromomaniac
disturbance   dogfighting   double-cross   dragonflies   drone-beetle
disturbancy   doggerelize   double-digit   dragon's head   drop a curtsy
disturbedly   doggishness   double doors   dragon's tail   drop a stitch .
disturnpike   doggy-paddle   double dummy   drama critic   drop curtain
disunionism   dog-handling   double Dutch   dramaticism   drop-forging
disunionist   dogmatician   double eagle   dramaticule   drop initial
disvaluable   dog's-cabbage   double-edged   dramatistic   dropsically
disyllabize   dog's disease   double-ender   dramaturgic   drop-testing
diterpenoid   dog's mercury   double entry   dram-drinker   drug peddler
dithyrambic   doily napkin   double event   drape jacket   drug traffic
dittography   do justice to   double-faced   drastically   drumbledore
divaricator   dolabriform   double fault   draught beer   drumlinized
divellicate   dole-bludger   double feast   draughtsman   drum machine
divergement   dolefulness   double first   draughtsmen   drum printer
divergently   Dolly Varden   double fugue   draught-tree   drunkenness
divergingly   dolorimeter   double helix   draw a bead on   drunkometer
diverseness   dolphinfish   double image   drawing-book   dry diggings
diversified   doltishness   double quick   drawing card   dry gangrene
diversifier   domesticate   double rhyme   drawing room   dry mounting
diversifies   domesticism   double sharp   drawn butter   dry straight
diversiform   domesticity   double-sided   dreadlessly   dual control
diversional   domesticize   double-space   dreadlocked   dual-purpose
diversities   domiciliary   double-speak   dreadnought   dubiousness
diverticula   domiciliate   doublespeak   dreamlessly   Dublin prawn
divertingly   domineering   double steal   dream ticket   duchesse set
divestitive   Dominion day   doublethink   dream vision   ducking-pond
divestiture   domino paper   double tides   dredging-box   dugout canoe
dividedness   done to a turn   doubtlessly   dress agency   Duke of Yorks
dividuality   Donizettian   doughtiness   dress circle   dulcifluous
divine spark   donkey derby   dough-trough   dressing-box   dull emitter
diving board   donkey Derby   Douglas pine   dress length   dumb animals

dumbfounder	easternmost	Egyptianise	electron gun	emmenagogue
dumper truck	Eastern Time	Egyptianism	electronics	emotionally
dumpishness	eating apple	Egyptianize	electroplax	emotionless
duncishness	eating-house	eidetically	electro-slag	emotiveness
dunducketty	eating irons	eigenvector	electrotype	empanelment
duopolistic	eat one's tutu	eighteenmos	electroweak	emperor moth
duple rhythm	eat salt with	eight-seater	electuaries	emperorship
duplication	eaves-trough	eight-square	elegiacally	emphyteusis
duplicative	ebulliently	Einsteinian	elementally	emphyteutic
duplicature	eccentrical	einsteinium	elephant hut	empiecement
duplicitous	ecchondroma	eisegetical	elephantine	Empire State
durableness	ecclesiarch	eisteddfods	elephantoid	empirically
durante vita	echo chamber	ejaculation	eleutherian	emplacement
Durkheimian	echopractic	ejaculative	elevational	empleomania
duskishness	echo sounder	ejaculatory	elevenpence	empowerment
dust disease	eclecticism	ejectamenta	elevenpenny	empty-handed
dust-wrapper	eco-friendly	eject button	elicitation	empty-headed
dusty answer	econometric	ejector seat	eligibility	empty-nester
dusty miller	economic man	elaborately	elimination	emulatively
Dutch cheese	economy-size	elaboration	eliminative	emulsionise
Dutch clover	ectoblastic	elaborative	eliminatory	emulsionize
duteousness	ectogenesis	elaboratory	Elizabethan	enabling act
dutifulness	ectogenetic	elastically	ellipsoidal	enamel paint
duty officer	ectomorphic	elasticated	ellipticity	enamourment
dwarf mallow	ectopically	elastic band	elocutional	enarthroses
dyer's rocket	ectopic beat	elasticized	eloquential	enarthrosis
dynamically	ectoplasmic	elastic-side	elsewhither	encapsidate
dynamometer	ectoplastic	elastomeric	elucidation	encapsulate
dynamometry	ectoproctan	Elastoplast	elucidative	encaptivate
dynasticism	ectothermic	elbow grease	elucidatory	encarnadine
dyscalculia	ectotrophic	elbow-length	elusiveness	encarnalize
dysesthesia	ecumenicity	elbow-sleeve	elutriation	encased knot
dysfunction	edaphically	elderflower	emanational	encephaloid
dyslogistic	eddy current	elderliness	emancipator	enchainment
dyspareunia	edible snail	election bun	emasculator	enchantedly
dyspeptical	edification	electioneer	embarcadero	enchantment
dysrhythmia	edificatory	electorally	embarcation	enchantress
dysrhythmic	editorially	electorship	embarkation	enchiridion
eager beaver	educability	electricals	embarrassed	enchondroma
ear for music	educational	electric arc	embellisher	encomendero
Earl Marshal	edutainment	electric eel	emblematise	encomiastic
early leaver	eff and blind	electric eye	emblematist	encouraging
earn a living	effectively	electrician	emblematize	encrustment
earnestness	effectivity	electricise	embolectomy	enculturate
ear-piercing	effectually	electricity	embowelling	encumbrance
earth almond	efficacious	electricize	embowerment	encystation
earth closet	efficiently	electric ray	embraceable	endaspidean
earth colour	effigiation	electrified	embracement	endearingly
earthenware	effigy mound	electrifier	embracingly	endeavourer
earth hunger	effortfully	electrifies	embracively	endemically
earthliness	effulgently	electrocoat	embrocation	endlessness
earth mother	egalitarian	electrocute	embroiderer	endocardial
earth-moving	egg and bacon	electrocyte	embroilment	endocardium
earth pillar	egg-drop soup	electrofish	embryogenic	endocentric
earth tremor	Egg Saturday	electroform	embryologic	endocranial
easefulness	eggshell-ful	electroglow	embryonated	endocuticle
ease the helm	egocentrism	electroless	embryotoxic	endocytosis
East African	ego-identity	electrolier	Emerald Isle	endocytotic
east and west	egolessness	electrology	emerald moth	endodontics
east-by-north	egomaniacal	electrolyse	emergencies	endodontist
East Coaster	egotistical	electrolyte	emery powder	endogenesis
Easter bunny	egregiously	electrolyze	emmenagogic	endogenetic

endoglossic	enterocoely	epistolizer	erythraemic	eugenically
endometrial	enterocytic	epitaxially	erythristic	eugeoclinal
endometrium	enteropathy	epithalamia	erythrocyte	eulogically
endomitosis	enterostomy	epithalamic	erythronium	eunuch flute
endomitotic	enterotoxin	epithalamus	erythropsia	eunuchoidal
endomorphic	enteroviral	epithelioid	escape hatch	eupepticity
end one's days	enterovirus	epithelioma	escape shaft	euphemistic
endoplasmic	enterpriser	epitheliums	escape speed	euphonistic
endopsychic	entertainer	epithetical	escape valve	eurhythmics
endorsation	enthralment	epithymetic	escape wheel	eurhythmist
endorsement	entitlement	epitrichial	escarbuncle	Euro-African
endoscopist	entomologic	epitrichium	eschatology	Euro-Asiatic
endospermic	entomophagy	epitrochoid	escheatable	Eurocentric
endosteally	entoproctan	epoch-making	escheatment	Euromissile
endothelial	entrainment	eponymously	esemplastic	Europeanise
endothelium	entrance fee	epoxidation	Eskimo-Aleut	Europeanism
endothermic	entreatment	equableness	esotericism	Europeanist
endotrophic	entrustment	equal rights	esotericist	Europeanize
end standard	entry permit	equatorward	Esperantist	Euro-sceptic
enemy action	entwinement	equerryship	espieglerie	euryphagous
energetical	enucleation	equiangular	esquireship	eurythermic
energy level	enumeration	equicaloric	essentially	euthanasiac
enfeoffment	enumerative	equidistant	establisher	euthanasian
enfleshment	enunciation	equiformity	estate agent	euthanatize
enforceable	enunciative	equilateral	estate in fee	evagination
enforcement	envelopment	equilibrant	estate wagon	evanescence
enforcingly	enviability	equilibrate	estrepement	Evangeliary
enfranchise	enviousness	equilibrial	estropiated	evangelical
engaged tone	environment	equilibrise	eteostichon	evangelican
engineering	enzymically	equilibrist	Eternal City	evangelizer
engine house	epanalepsis	equilibrium	eternal life	evanishment
englacially	epanaleptic	equilibrize	eternalness	Evans gambit
English bond	epanaphoral	equinoctial	ethereality	evaporation
English horn	epeirogenic	equipollent	etherealize	evaporative
English Miss	epenthesize	equivalence	ethereal oil	evasiveness
Englishness	ephemerally	equivalency	etheromania	evening star
English rose	ephemerides	equivocally	ethicalness	evening suit
engorgement	epicheirema	equivocator	ethionamide	eventlessly
engraftment	epicondylar	eradication	ethisterone	eventration
engrammatic	epicyclical	eradicative	ethmoid bone	eventuality
engrossedly	epidemicity	erasability	ethnobotany	eventuation
engrossment	epidermical	Erasmianism	ethnography	ever-blessed
enhancement	epidiascope	Erastianism	ethnologist	everlasting
enigmatical	epigastrium	eremacausis	ethological	evertebrate
enjambement	epigenetics	eremejevite	ethoxylated	every stitch
enlargement	epigrammist	ergatocracy	Eton College	everywheres
enlightener	epigraphist	ergographic	Etruscology	evidentiary
enlisted man	epileptical	ergometrine	et sequentes	evidentness
enlivenment	epilogistic	eristically	etymologies	evil-looking
ennoblement	epimorphism	erosiveness	etymologise	eviscerator
enolization	epinephrine	erotogenous	etymologist	evocatively
enorm lesion	epipetalous	erotomaniac	etymologize	evolutional
enouncement	epiphyllous	erratically	eubacterial	exaggerator
enquiringly	epiphysitis	erraticness	eubacterium	exaltedness
enragedness	epiphytical	erroneously	eucalyptian	examination
enrichingly	epiphytotic	error circle	Eucharistic	examiningly
ensepulchre	epiplankton	erubescence	Euchologion	exasperated
enslavement	episcopable	eruditeness	euchromatic	exasperater
ensnarement	episcopalia	eruditional	euchromatin	exasperator
entablature	episcopally	erysipeloid	eudaemonism	excarnation
entablement	episodicity	erythematic	eudaimonism	exceedingly
enterocoele	Epistle side	erythraemia	eudiometric	excellently

exceptional	exorbitance	exquisitely	factor eight	farinaceous
excerptible	exorbitancy	exquisitism	factor group	farkleberry
excessively	exoskeletal	exsangueous	factorially	farmer's lung
excitedness	exoskeleton	exsanguious	Factory Acts	farraginous
excitomotor	exostracize	exsiccation	factory farm	far-reaching
exclamation	exotericism	exsiccative	factory ship	fartherance
exclamative	exotericist	exstipulate	factory shop	farthermost
exclamatory	expansional	extemporary	facts of life	farthingale
exclusioner	expansively	extemporise	factualness	fasciculate
exclusively	expansivity	extemporize	facultative	fascinating
exclusivism	expatiation	extensional	faddishness	fascination
exclusivist	expatiative	extensively	fainéantism	fascinative
exclusivity	expatiatory	extenuation	fainting fit	fashionable
excogitator	expectantly	extenuative	fair-weather	fashionably
excommunion	expectation	extenuatory	fairy lights	fashionless
exconjugant	expectative	exteriorise	fairy martin	fast bowling
excoriation	expectingly	exteriority	faith healer	fast breeder
excorticate	expectorant	exteriorize	faithlessly	fast forward
excremental	expectorate	exterminate	faithworthy	fast neutron
excrescence	expediently	external ear	fall afoul of	fast reactor
excrescency	expeditious	externalise	fall-breaker	fata morgana
exculpation	expenditure	externalism	fallen angel	fat dormouse
exculpatory	expensively	externalist	fallen woman	fatefulness
excursional	experienced	externality	fall herring	father-in-law
excursively	experiencer	externalize	fallibilism	father right
excurvation	expiscation	externation	fallibilist	fatigueless
excystation	explainable	extirpation	fallibility	fatiguesome
ex-directory	explain away	extirpative	falling band	fatiguingly
executioner	explain into	extortioner	falling leaf	fatiloquent
executively	explanandum	extractable	falling star	fatuousness
executorial	explanation	extradition	fall short of	Faulknerian
exemplarily	explanative	extrapolate	fall through	fault-finder
exemplarism	explanatory	extravagant	false acacia	faultlessly
exemplarist	expletively	extravagate	false arrest	faunistical
exemplarity	explicandum	extravasate	false bottom	faussebraie
exemplified	explication	extremeness	false colour	favouritism
exemplifier	explicative	extremities	false gallop	fawningness
exemplifies	explicatory	extrication	false indigo	fearfulness
exencephaly	exploitable	extrinsical	false killer	fearnothing
exercisable	exploration	extroverted	false muster	feasibility
exfoliation	explorative	exuberantly	falsifiable	feather edge
exfoliative	exploratory	exululation	Falstaffian	feather-foil
exhaustedly	explorement	exumbrellar	falteringly	feather-head
exhaustible	exploringly	eyebrowless	familiarise	featherless
exhaustless	explosively	eye-catching	familiarism	feather-like
exhaust pipe	exponential	eye language	familiarity	feather palm
exhibitable	exportation	fabrication	familiarize	feather-pate
exhilarator	exposedness	fabricative	familistery	feathertail
exhorbitant	ex post facto	face-centred	family bible	featherwife
exhortation	expostulant	face flannel	family hotel	feather-work
exhortative	expostulate	face-lifting	fanatically	feature film
exhortatory	expoundable	face-painter	fanfaronade	featureless
ex hypothesi	expressedly	facetiously	fantabulous	febricitant
exinanition	expressible	facial angle	fantastical	Fechner's law
existential	expressless	facial nerve	fan the flame	fecundation
exoculation	express lift	facial sauna	fan vaulting	feed crusher
exoelectron	expressness	facilitator	Faraday cage	feed-forward
exogenously	expromissor	facing brick	Faraday's law	feeding-time
exoneration	expropriate	facioplegic	far-awayness	feeler gauge
exonerative	expulsatory	facsimilize	farcicality	feelingless
exonuclease	expurgation	fact-finding	farcy button	feel oneself
exorability	expurgatory	factionally	fare-you-well	feel one's way

feel strange	fiddlestick	finickiness	fittingness	flinchingly
feignedness	fidejussory	finickingly	fitting-room	flip one's lid
feldspathic	fidgetiness	Finno-Ugrian	fitting shop	flip one's wig
feller-me-lad	fidgetingly	fippenny bit	fit to be tied	flip through
fellow-me-lad	fiduciaries	fipple flute	five-corners	flirtatious
fell walking	fiduciarily	fir clubmoss	five hundred	flitch-plate
feloniously	field-cornet	fire and flet	fixed income	floating rib
female child	field events	fire-balloon	flabbergast	flocculence
female rhyme	field hockey	fire-blanket	flaccidness	flock-master
female screw	field madder	fire brigade	flag-captain	flock pigeon
femme fatale	field magnet	fire company	flagellated	flog to death
fence lizard	field sports	fire-control	flagellator	floor leader
fence-sitter	field system	firecracker	flag-feather	floor-length
fender-stool	field theory	fire-curtain	flagitation	floor polish
fenestrated	fieldworker	fire-fighter	flag-officer	floor-timber
fennel-giant	fieri facias	firefighter	flag of truce	floor-walker
feral pigeon	fifteenthly	fire-flaught	flag-station	floorwalker
fer de lances	fifth column	fire-hunting	flag-wagging	floral dance
fergusonite	fifty-fourth	fire hydrant	flak-catcher	floral whorl
fermentable	fighting fit	fire-lighter	flaky pastry	Florence oil
Fermi energy	fighting mad	firelighter	flamboyance	florescence
ferociously	fighting-top	fire-raising	flamboyancy	Florida moss
ferricyanic	fig-marigold	fire station	flame nettle	Florida room
ferriferous	figure-dance	fire-walking	flammulated	floriferous
ferrimagnet	figured bass	fire-watcher	flannel-cake	florilegium
Ferris wheel	figure of fun	fire-worship	flannelette	floripondio
ferrocyanic	filamentary	firing party	flannelling	flour beetle
ferromagnet	filamentose	firing-point	flapmouthed	flourishing
ferruginous	filamentous	firing squad	flapper vote	flow diagram
ferruminate	filet design	firmamental	flash-freeze	flower-fence
ferry-bridge	filet mignon	First Consul	flash memory	floweriness
fers de lance	fille de joie	first cousin	flash powder	flower-piece
fertileness	fillet steak	first-degree	flat-chested	flower power
ferulaceous	fill the bill	first finger	flat-tummied	flower-spike
ferventness	filmography	first-footer	flatulently	flowery dell
festinately	filmsetting	first-fruits	Flaubertian	flowingness
festination	filter-paper	first lesson	flauntingly	flowing sail
festival-day	filthy lucre	first matter	flavourless	fluctuation
festiveness	fimbriation	first moment	flavoursome	fluid clutch
festivities	final clause	first or last	flecklessly	fluid drachm
festschrift	final demand	first person	Fleet Air Arm	flunkeyiana
Festschrift	financeable	first school	fleet-footed	fluorescein
fetch around	financially	first-sprung	Fleet parson	fluorescent
fête galante	find against	first storey	Fleet Street	fluorimeter
fetishistic	fin de siècle	first strike	Flemish bond	fluorimetry
feudalistic	finding-list	first string	Flemish coil	fluorometer
feudalities	find oneself	fiscal agent	flesh colour	fluorometry
feudatories	find one's way	fiscalities	fleshliness	fluoroscope
fibre optics	find the lady	fishability	fleshmonger	fluoroscopy
fibre-tipped	fine-grained	fish-eye lens	Fletcherian	fluosilicic
fibrillated	fines herbes	fish-farming	Fletcherism	flush-decker
fibrinosity	fine-weather	fishing boat	Fletcherite	flustration
fibro-cement	finger-board	fishing frog	fletcherize	flute player
fibrocystic	fingerboard	fishing line	flexibility	flutter-mill
fibroplasia	finger glass	fissibility	flexionless	fluviometer
fibrousness	finger-paint	fissionable	flexography	flux density
fictionally	finger-plate	fission bomb	flickertail	flying corps
fictiveness	fingerprint	fissiparity	flight-arrow	flying field
fiddle-de-dee	finger-stall	fissiparous	flightiness	flying horse
fiddededee	finger-stone	fissuration	flight-shaft	Flying Horse
fiddler-back	finger-tight	fissure vein	flimflammed	flying jenny
fiddler crab	finicalness	fitted sheet	flimflammer	flying-kites

flying lemur	foreseeable	for the birds	Franklinian	frictionize
flying mouse	foreseeably	for the money	franklinite	friendliest
flying shear	foreshorten	for the nonce	frank-pledge	frigate bird
flying shore	foresighted	for the use of	frantically	frightening
flying speed	foresignify	for the worse	franticness	frightfully
flying squad	forespeaker	fortifiable	fraternally	frigidarium
flying squid	forestaller	fortissimos	fraternizer	frill lizard
flying start	forestation	fortnightly	fratricidal	fringilline
fly in pieces	forest devil	fortunately	fraudulence	fritillaria
fly-pitching	forest floor	fortuneless	fraudulency	fritiniency
fly the track	forest-green	for twopence	free and easy	fritto misto
foam plastic	forethinker	forty-eighth	free company	frivolities
focal length	forethought	forty-footer	free country	frivolously
foetiferous	fore-topmast	forty-seater	freedom ride	frock-coated
folding door	fore-topsail	forty-second	free-hearted	frock of mail
foliage leaf	for evermore	forwardness	free library	from nowhere
foliicolous	forevermore	Fosbury flop	Freemasonic	from scratch
foliiferous	foreverness	fossilation	Freemasonry	from the dead
folk dancing	forewarning	fossil ivory	free on board	from way back
folliculate	forfeitable	foster-child	free-quarter	frondescent
folliculose	forfeit bail	foster-nurse	free radical	frontal bone
fomentation	forficulate	foul-mouthed	free skating	frontal lobe
fons et origo	forfoughten	foundership	freethinker	front burner
foolhardier	forge-master	founder's kin	free thought	front-fanged
foolhardily	forgetfully	fountaineer	freeze-dried	frontierism
foolishment	forget-me-not	fountainous	freeze-dries	frontlessly
foolishness	forgettable	fountain pen	freeze-frame	front-loader
fool's errand	forgiveness	four-channel	freibergite	front matter
football kit	forgivingly	Fourdrinier	French brace	front office
foot breadth	for God's sake	four figures	French bread	frontolysis
foot-lambert	for instance	four-flusher	French chalk	frontolytic
footmanship	forlorn hope	four hundred	French clock	front runner
footslogger	forlornness	four pounder	French crown	frost-flower
foot soldier	formability	Fourth World	French curve	frost pocket
foot-washing	formal cause	four-wheeled	French drain	froth-blower
foppishness	formalinize	four wheeler	French fries	frotteurism
for a full due	formalistic	fowl cholera	Frenchified	frowardness
for a kick-off	formalities	fox and geese	Frenchifies	frowstiness
for all I care	formational	fox-coloured	Frenchiness	frozen limit
for all I know	formatively	fox squirrel	French leave	fructuously
foraminifer	form-history	foxtail lily	French pleat	frugivorous
forasmuch as	formication	foxtrotting	French sixth	fruit-bodies
forbearance	form quality	fractionary	French stick	fruit-grower
forbiddance	form-species	fractionate	French toast	fruitlessly
forbiddenly	formularies	fractionise	French twist	fruit-picker
force a smile	formularise	fractionize	French whisk	frustrating
forced march	formularism	fractiously	Frenchwoman	frustration
force stroke	formularist	fracturable	Frenchwomen	frustrative
forcibility	formularize	fragileness	frenzy-fever	frutescence
for dear life	formulation	fragmentary	frequencies	fucoxanthin
fore-against	formulistic	fragmentise	frequentist	fuel element
fore-appoint	formylation	fragmentize	fresco secco	fugaciously
foreclosure	fornication	fragrancies	fresh breeze	fulfillable
foredestine	fornicatrix	frame aerial	fresnel lens	fulgentness
foredestiny	for one's life	frame of mind	Fresnel lens	fulgurantly
forefeeling	for one's part	Francomania	Fresnel unit	fulgurating
forefighter	for one's sins	Francophile	fretfulness	fulguration
foreign body	for one thing	Francophobe	Freudianism	full as a bull
foreignness	for starters	francophone	friableness	full as a goog
foremanship	Forstner bit	frangipanis	Friars Major	full as a tick
forepurpose	fortepianos	Frankenthal	fricandeaus	full-blooded
forequarter	forthcoming	frankfurter	fricandeaux	full brother

full-fledged	gallanilide	garden stuff	Geneva cross	get in a twist
full-frontal	gallantness	Garibaldian	Geneva watch	get one's blue
full-hearted	gallantries	garlic bread	geniculated	get one's call
fulling-mill	gall bladder	garlic press	genitivally	get one's step
full measure	gallery play	garmentless	genotypical	get religion
full-mouthed	gallery tray	garnishment	genteelness	get the spike
full of beans	galley proof	Garrisonian	gentianella	get together
fulminating	galley slave	garrulously	gentian root	get worked up
fulmination	galliardize	garter snake	gentilician	ghastliness
fulminatory	Gallicanism	gas constant	gentilitial	ghostbuster
fulminurate	Gallicanist	gaseousness	gentilitian	ghostliness
fulsomeness	gallimaufry	gas equation	gentle craft	ghost-writer
fume chamber	gallinacean	gas fittings	gentlemanly	giant fennel
fummadiddle	gallinipper	gas gangrene	gentlewoman	giant hyssop
funambulism	Gallomaniac	gas kinetics	gentlewomen	giant-killer
funambulist	Gallophobia	gas producer	genuflector	giant petrel
fun and games	gallotannin	gastrectomy	genuflexion	giant-powder
functionary	gallousness	gastric mill	genuineness	giant slalom
functionate	Gallovidian	gastrocolic	geobotanist	gibberellic
function key	Gallowegian	gastrologer	geocentrism	gibberellin
fundamental	gallowglass	gastromancy	geochemical	gibber-plain
fundholding	gallows-bird	gastronomer	geodynamics	gibbousness
fund-raising	gallows-tree	gastronomic	geomagnetic	Gideon bible
funduscopic	gally-beggar	gastropathy	geomantical	gift voucher
funeral home	Galois field	gastropodan	geomembrane	gigantesque
funeral pile	gambrel roof	gastroscope	geometrical	giganticide
funeral pyre	gamekeeping	gastroscopy	geophysical	gigantology
fungibility	game licence	gastrostomy	geopolitics	giggle-house
fungistasis	game of goose	gastrotomic	George Cross	giggle-water
fungistatic	game-playing	gastrotrich	George Medal	gigot sleeve
fungivorous	game reserve	gastrozooid	George-noble	gilded youth
fungologist	games master	gatecrasher	geostrategy	gild the lily
fungus-midge	games theory	gauge theory	geostrophic	gild the pill
funny column	gametangium	gavelkinder	geosyncline	gillyflower
furaldehyde	gametically	gay deceiver	geotechnics	gimcrackery
furciferous	gametogenic	gazing-stock	geotectonic	gin and tonic
furiousness	gametophore	geanticline	German clock	gingerbeery
furnishings	gametophyte	gefilte fish	germaneness	gingerbread
furnishment	gaming house	gegenschein	Germanicism	ginger group
furrow-slice	gaming table	geitonogamy	German ocean	girdlestead
furthcoming	gamogenesis	gemmiferous	German sixth	girlishness
furtherance	gamogenetic	gemmiparity	German-Swiss	Giuoco Piano
furthermore	gander-month	gemmiparous	germination	give a lead to
furthermost	Gandhiesque	gemmologist	germinative	give and take
furthersome	gandy dancer	gendarmerie	germ warfare	give a stop to
furtiveness	ganglioside	genealogies	gerontocrat	give a tumble
furunculous	gang of three	genealogise	gerontology	give birth to
fusible plug	gangsterdom	genealogist	gerrymander	give chase to
fustigation	gangsterish	genealogize	gerundially	give faith to
future shock	gangsterism	genecologic	gerundively	give it a name
future state	gang warfare	generalized	gestational	give it hot to
gaberlunzie	gangway seat	generalizer	gestatorial	give leg bail
gable-topped	garam masala	generalness	gesticulant	give lessons
gable-window	garbologist	general post	gesticulate	give loose to
Gaboon viper	garden chair	generalship	gestureless	give offence
gaff topsail	garden cress	generically	get around to	give oneself
gainfulness	gardenesque	genericness	get a shift on	give pause to
gainstander	garden gnome	gene therapy	get a sight of	give place to
galactocele	garden-house	genetically	get a spark up	give the boot
galactoside	garden party	genetic code	get cracking	give what for
galanty show	garden snail	Geneva bands	get done with	give wings to
galenically	Garden State	Geneva Bible	get even with	glabrescent

glacier mill	glutinosity	golden oldie	grade school	gratulatory
glacier snow	glutinously	golden perch	grade up with	grave accent
glade mallow	glycerinate	golden potto	gradiometer	gravedigger
gladfulness	glycocholic	golden share	gradualness	gravel-blind
gladioluses	glycophorin	Golden State	Graecomania	gravel court
Gladstonian	glycophytic	golden syrup	Graecophile	gravel voice
Gladstonism	glycosamine	gold reserve	Graeco-Roman	graven image
Gladstonite	glycosylate	Golgi method	grafting wax	Gravenstein
glaikitness	glycotropic	Goliath frog	grain colour	gravimetric
glamorously	glyphograph	gonadectomy	grain-cradle	graving dock
glamour girl	glyptically	go near doing	grain whisky	graving tool
glamour puss	gnat-catcher	gone gosling	graminology	gravitation
glance pitch	gnathobasic	gone to earth	grammalogue	gravitative
glaringness	gnathostome	gonfalonier	grammarless	gravity feed
glass-blower	gneissosity	gongoristic	grammatical	gravity wave
glass cutter	gnomologist	goniometric	gramophonic	greasepaint
glass-gazing	gnostically	gonioscopic	grandeeship	greaseproof
glassichord	gnotobiotic	gonorrhoeal	grandfather	greasy heels
glass lizard	go a bundle on	good company	grandfilial	great circle
glass-making	goal average	good evening	grandiflora	greatcoated
glass sponge	goalkeeping	good feeling	grandiosely	Great Dipper
Glastonbury	goal-kicking	good-hearted	grandiosity	great divide
glaucescent	go all the way	good heavens	grand manner	Great Divide
glaucomatic	go along with	good-looking	grand master	greaterness
glauconitic	goalscoring	good morning	grandmother	great laurel
glaucophane	goaltending	good-natured	grand-nephew	great-nephew
glazed frost	goatee beard	good success	grand old man	great primer
glazy humour	goatherdess	Good Templar	grandparent	Great Spirit
gleefulness	goatishness	go one better	grand siècle	great vassal
glengarries	go ballistic	goosefleshy	grangerizer	Grecian bend
glimmerless	Gobelin blue	goose-winged	graniferous	Grecian gift
glitter dust	gobemouches	goosishness	Granite City	Grecian knot
glitterless	goblinesque	go overboard	graniteware	Grecian nose
glitter rock	gobsmacking	gopher snake	granivorous	Greek chorus
globe-flower	go by default	Gopher State	granny's knot	Greek Church
globeflower	go by the book	Gordian knot	Granny Smith	greenbottle
globigerina	God Almighty	gormandizer	granny woman	green carder
globigerine	God bless you	gory details	granolithic	green cheese
globoseness	god-daughter	go somewhere	granophyric	green dragon
globularity	goddesshood	gospel music	Granth Sahib	green fallow
glochidiate	goddesslike	gospel-sharp	grants-in-aid	green ginger
Gloger's rule	goddess-ship	gospel truth	gran turismo	greengrocer
glomeration	godforsaken	gossipingly	granularity	greenkeeper
glomerulose	God-forsaken	Gothic novel	granulation	Greenlander
glossalalia	godlessness	go to college	granuliform	Greenlandic
glossematic	godlikeness	go-to-meeting	granulocyte	green linnet
glossolalia	go down a bomb	go to the dogs	grape-brandy	green magpie
glossolalic	God's country	go to the pack	graphematic	greenmailer
glossopetra	God's sonties	go to the wall	graphically	green manure
glottal stop	go end for end	go to the wars	graphic arts	green mealie
glottogonic	go great guns	go up in smoke	graphicness	green monkey
Glou-morceau	go in couples	go up the wall	graphomania	greenockite
glove puppet	going for one	gourmandise	graphometer	green oyster
gloweringly	going strong	gourmandism	graph theory	green pepper
glucosamine	go into orbit	gouvernante	grapple with	green plover
glucosidase	gold amalgam	governorate	graptolitic	green shoots
glucostatic	golden balls	go walkabout	grass-comber	green turtle
glucuronate	golden chain	go with a bang	grass-eating	Gresham's law
glucuronide	golden eagle	go with a roar	grass hockey	Gretna Green
glue-sniffer	golden goose	go with child	grasshopper	Grevy's zebra
glutathione	golden hello	gracelessly	grass skiing	greybearded
gluten bread	Golden Horde	gradational	gratulation	grey economy

grey gurnard	guest artist	haemocyanin	hammer drill	harmfulness
grey meerkat	guest-master	haemoglobin	hammer price	harmonistic
grey snapper	guest worker	haemophilia	hammer-smith	harmonogram
grey wethers	guide fossil	haemophilic	Hamming code	harness bull
griddle cake	Guide Guider	haemoptysis	hamstringed	harness cask
griffinhood	guildswoman	haemorrhage	hand and foot	harpsichord
grimgribber	guildswomen	haemorrhoid	hand-baggage	harrier-hawk
gripingness	guilelessly	haemostasis	handbagging	Harriet Lane
grippleness	guillotiner	haemostatic	hand-breadth	Harris tweed
grithbreach	guiltlessly	haemothorax	handfasting	Harrow drive
grizzly bear	Guinea grass	Haggadistic	hand grenade	harrowingly
grocer's itch	Guinea Negro	haggardness	handicapped	hart's tongue
grocer's port	Guinea peach	haggishness	handicapper	harum-scarum
Groenendael	Gulf Country	Hagiographa	hand in glove	harvestable
groom-porter	gullibility	hagiography	handkercher	harvest home
grooved ware	gum ammoniac	hagiologist	hand-knitted	harvestless
grotesquely	gum benjamin	hail the dool	hand of glory	harvest mite
grottoesque	gum sandarac	hairbreadth	handrunning	harvest moon
grouchiness	gun carriage	hairdresser	handselling	harzburgite
ground-cedar	gunslinging	hair lacquer	handshaking	hat-check boy
ground cover	gurgitation	hairpin bend	handsomeish	hatcheck boy
ground elder	gushingness	hair-raising	hand to mouth	hatchet-face
ground floor	gustatorial	hairstyling	handwriting	hatchet fish
ground frost	gustfulness	hairstylist	handwritten	hatchettine
ground glass	gut instinct	hair-trigger	hang by a hair	hatchettite
ground level	gutlessness	hairy-heeled	hang-gliding	hatchet work
ground-plate	gutta-percha	halcyon days	hang heavily	hatefulness
ground robin	gutter-blood	half a chance	hanging bird	hatlessness
groundsheet	gutter press	half a minute	hanging bowl	hatti-sherif
ground sloth	guttersnipe	half-and-half	hanging drop	haughtiness
ground speed	gutter-stick	half baptize	hanging pawn	haughtonite
ground staff	gutturalism	half-binding	hanging wall	hauntedness
ground state	gutturality	half-blooded	hangmanlike	hausmannite
ground-swell	gutturalize	half-brother	hangmanship	haustellate
groundswell	gymnasiarch	half-century	hapaxanthic	have a bash at
groundwards	gymnastical	half-crowner	haphazardly	have a case on
groundwater	gynaecology	half-hearted	haphazardry	have a dash at
group theory	gynecologic	half holiday	haplessness	have a down on
groupuscule	gynogenesis	half-integer	haplography	have a hand in
growing zone	gynogenetic	half-landing	happy couple	have a lash at
grow into one	gynomonoecy	half measure	happy ending	have a lead on
grown-upness	gynostegium	half-sibling	happy family	have a look of
grow on trees	gypsiferous	half-starved	happy medium	have an eye to
growth curve	Gypsologist	half the time	haptoglobin	have a record
growth point	gyre-carline	half-volleys	harassingly	have a shower
growth stock	gyrocompass	halfway line	harbour-dues	have a show of
grozing-iron	gyro-horizon	hall bedroom	harbourless	have at heart
grudge fight	haberdasher	hallucinant	harbour seal	have eyes for
gruellingly	habituality	hallucinate	hard and fast	have heard of
grumblesome	habitualize	halobiontic	hard as nails	have it in for
grumblingly	habituation	halo-brimmed	hard-hearted	have it in one
gryllotalpa	habitudinal	halogenated	hard-hitting	have kittens
Guadeloupan	hackberries	halomethane	hard landing	have mercy on
guardedness	hacking coat	halomorphic	hard-mouthed	have pride in
guardianess	hadrosaurid	haloperidol	hard-pressed	have sex with
gubernation	haemangioma	halophilous	hardshelled	have the face
gubernative	haematocele	halter-break	hard-wearing	have the time
guelder rose	haematocrit	haltingness	hard-working	hawkishness
guerdonless	haematocyst	ham-fistedly	hardy annual	hazard light
Guernsey cow	haematoidin	ham-handedly	hare-brained	hazardously
guerrillero	haematology	Hamiltonian	Hare Krishna	hazel-grouse
guesstimate	haematomata	hammer-cloth	haricot bean	headbanding

headbanging	Hegelianize	heptavalent	hexametrize	high treason
headborough	hegemonical	Heracleidan	hexapeptide	high voltage
head-dresser	heightening	Heraclitean	hibernation	Highway Code
head-hunting	heinousness	herald-snake	Hibernicise	hilariously
headhunting	heiress-ship	herbiferous	Hibernicism	hill and dale
head of state	heir-general	herbivorous	Hibernicize	hill-billies
head of State	Heldentenor	herb of grace	hide-and-coop	hill of beans
headquarter	helichrysum	herb tobacco	hide-and-seek	hill station
head teacher	helicograph	herb Trinity	hideosities	hillwalking
healthfully	heliography	hereditable	hideousness	hip and thigh
healthiness	heliolithic	hereditably	hiding place	hippeastrum
health salts	heliometric	hereinafter	hiding power	hippiatrics
hearse-cloth	helioscopic	heresiology	hierarchies	hippishness
heart attack	heliostatic	heretically	hierarchise	hippoboscid
heartbroken	heliotroper	Her Majesty's	hierarchism	hippocampal
heart-cherry	heliotropic	hermeneutic	hierarchist	hippocampus
heart cockle	heliotropin	hermeticism	hierarchize	Hippocratic
hearth-money	helleborine	hermodactyl	hierocratic	hippologist
hearth-penny	helleborism	heroic verse	hierography	hippomobile
hearthstead	Hellenicize	heroineship	hieromonach	hippophobia
hearthstone	Hellenistic	heroization	Hieronymian	hippopotami
heartlessly	hellishness	hero-worship	hieronymite	hippotomist
heart of gold	hellraising	herpesvirus	High Admiral	hircocervus
heart's-blood	helmet-crest	herpetology	high as a kite	hire and fire
heart-shaped	helmet shell	herring-bone	highbrowish	hirsuteness
heart sounds	helminthoid	herringbone	highbrowism	Hispanicise
heart-struck	helpfulness	herring gull	high command	Hispanicism
heart-urchin	helping hand	herring-like	high country	Hispanicist
heat barrier	help oneself	herring-pond	higher court	Hispanicize
heathenesse	hemeralopia	Herschelian	higher plant	histiocytic
heather-bell	hemeralopic	hesperidium	highest good	histologist
heath-thrush	hemerythrin	Hessian boot	highfalutin	historiated
heat-seeking	hemianopsia	hetaerolite	high farming	historicise
Heaven knows	hemihydrate	heteracanth	high fashion	historicism
heavens hard	hemimorphic	heteroauxin	high finance	historicist
heavenwards	Hemingwayan	heteroclite	high-hearted	historicity
heave the log	hemiparesis	heterocycle	high holiday	historicize
heaving line	hemiparetic	heterodimer	high incomer	historiette
heavy-footed	hemiplegiac	heteroecism	high-jumping	histrionism
heavy-handed	hemipterous	heterogamic	high-kicking	hitherwards
heavy-headed	hemisection	heterogonic	highlandish	Hitleristic
heavyweight	hemispheral	heterograft	Highlandman	hit the booze
hebdomadary	hemisphered	heterolysis	Highlandmen	hit the skids
hebephrenia	hemispheric	heterolytic	highlighter	hit the trail
hebephrenic	hemitropism	heteromorph	high-melting	Hittitology
Hebraically	hendecarchy	heterophile	high old time	hoary marmot
heckelphone	heneicosane	heterophony	high opinion	hobble chain
hectic fever	Henle's layer	heteroploid	high-pitched	hobbledehoy
hectic flush	hepatectomy	heteropolar	high polymer	hobble skirt
hectogramme	hepatoscopy	heterospory	high-powered	hockey-stick
hectoringly	hepatotoxic	heterostyly	high profile	Hock Tuesday
hedge-doctor	hepatotoxin	heterotherm	high-quality	hoggishness
hedge-garlic	Hephaestian	heterotopia	high-ranking	hog in armour
hedge-hyssop	Hepplewhite	heterotopic	high sheriff	hog's pudding
hedge-priest	heptacosane	heterotroph	High Sheriff	hold against
hedge-school	heptadecane	heterousian	high spirits	hold hostage
hedging-bill	heptahedral	heuristical	high-stepper	hold one's own
hedonic tone	heptahedron	hexadecimal	high steward	hold one's way
hedonometer	heptamerous	hexagonally	High Steward	hold the baby
heedfulness	heptangular	hexahedrons	highstrikes	hold the fort
heel of Italy	heptarchies	hexahydrate	high-tensile	hold the line
Hegelianism	heptathlete	hexametrist	high tension	hold the ring

hold the sack	homothermic	horse-litter	human rights	hydrologist
hold to a draw	homozygotic	horse manure	human shield	hydrolysate
hold wedlock	Honduranean	horse-marine	Humboldtian	hydromantic
holey dollar	honest Injun	horse-master	humboldtine	hydromedusa
holiday camp	honest-to-God	horse mussel	humbuggable	hydrometeor
holiday home	honey badger	horse-pistol	humdrummery	hydrometric
hollandaise	honey bucket	horse racing	humdrumness	hydropathic
holler uncle	honeycombed	horseradish	humectation	hydrophilic
hollow heart	honey-flower	horse-walker	humeral veil	hydrophobia
holobenthic	honey-fuggle	horsfordite	humiliating	hydrophobic
holoblastic	honey fungus	Horst Wessel	humiliation	hydrophytic
holocaustal	honey-lipped	hose company	hummingbird	hydroponics
holocaustic	honey-locust	hospital bed	hunchbacked	hydroscopic
holoendemic	honeymooner	hospitalise	hundredfold	hydrosphere
holographic	honey-myrtle	hospitalism	hunger march	hydrostatic
holomorphic	honey possum	hospitality	hunt counter	hydrothorax
holophrasis	honeysucker	hospitalize	hunter's moon	hydrotropic
holothurian	honeysuckle	hospitaller	hunting-case	hydroxonium
Holsteinian	honorariums	hostageship	hunting crop	hydroxylase
Holy Rood Day	honour point	hostilities	hunting horn	hydroxylate
Holy Trinity	honours list	hot cross bun	hunting pink	hydroxyurea
home cooking	honour-trick	hot cupboard	hunt the hare	hydroxyzine
home-keeping	hooliganism	hotel-keeper	hunt the lady	hygrometric
homeostasis	Hooray Henry	hot-headedly	hurriedness	hygrophytic
homeostatic	Hooverville	hotheadedly	hurry-scurry	hygroscopic
homeothermy	hopefulness	hot-tempered	hurtfulness	hylomorphic
Homerically	hope I may die	houndstooth	hurtleberry	hylophagous
home science	hop hornbeam	houppelande	husbandhood	hylozoistic
Home Service	hop-o'-my-thumb	house arrest	husbandland	Hymenoptera
homesteader	hopper-barge	house-broken	husbandless	hymnography
home stretch	hopperdozer	house-buying	husbandlike	hymnologies
homicidally	hoppergrass	house church	husbandship	hymnologist
homiletical	Hopping Dick	house-father	hyacinthian	hyoscyamine
homiliaries	hopping john	householder	hyacinthine	hyparterial
homocentric	hop the perch	householdry	hyaluronate	hyperactive
homoeomorph	hop the stick	house-hunter	hybrid swarm	hyperacusis
homoeopathy	horizon-blue	housekeeper	hydatidosis	hyperakusis
homoeotherm	horizonless	house lights	hydnocarpic	hyperbolism
homo-erotism	hormogonium	house martin	hydnocarpus	hyperbolist
homogametic	hormonology	housemaster	hydraelaeon	hyperbolize
homogeneate	horn antenna	house-mother	hydra-headed	hyperboloid
homogeneity	hornblendic	house of call	hydralazine	hyperborean
homogeneous	horned adder	House of Keys	hydrapulper	Hyperborean
homogenetic	horned cairn	house-parent	hydrargyria	hypercapnia
homogenized	horned grebe	house-sitter	hydrargyrum	hypercapnic
homogenizer	horned poppy	housesitter	hydrazinium	hypercharge
homographic	horned snake	housewifely	hydrazonium	hypercolour
homoiotherm	horned viper	housewifery	hydroborate	hypercolumn
homoiousian	hornswoggle	housewifish	hydrobromic	hypercritic
Homoiousion	horny-handed	housewright	hydrocarbon	hyperemesis
homolateral	horological	housing list	hydrochoric	hyperextend
homological	horribility	how-do-you-dos	hydrocooler	hypergamous
homologizer	horrifiedly	huckleberry	hydrocyanic	hypergelast
homomorphic	horripilant	hucksterdom	hydrofining	hypergeusia
homonuclear	horripilate	hucksteress	hydroformer	hyperinosis
homophonous	horrisonant	hucksterism	hydrogenase	hyperinotic
homoplastic	horror comic	hudibrastic	hydrogenate	hypermarket
homopterous	hors d'oeuvre	huffishness	hydrogen ion	hypermetric
Homo sapiens	horse-collar	Huguenotism	hydrogenite	hypermnesia
homosporous	horse-doctor	hullabaloos	hydrogenize	hypermnesic
homostylous	Horse Guards	human animal	hydrogenous	hypermobile
homothallic	horse-jockey	human nature	hydrography	hypermodern

hyperphagia	hypotenusal	if and only if	immediately	impignorate
hyperphagic	hypothallus	if you please	immediatism	impingement
hyperphoria	hypothecary	ignis fatuus	immediatist	impiousness
hyperphoric	hypothecate	ignition key	immedicable	implacental
hyperplasia	hypothecium	ignoble hawk	immedicably	implantable
hyperploidy	hypothermia	ignobleness	immelodious	implausible
hyperpnoeic	hypothermic	ignominious	immemorable	implausibly
hypersaline	hypothesise	ignoramuses	immenseness	implemental
hypersexual	hypothesist	ileocolitis	immensikoff	implementer
hypersomnia	hypothesize	ileostomies	immigration	implication
hypersomnic	hypothyroid	iliac artery	immigratory	implicative
hypersonics	hypotyposis	ill-affected	immitigable	imploration
hypersphere	hypsiconchy	illaqueable	immitigably	imploringly
hyperstatic	hypsochrome	ill-assorted	immobilizer	implosively
hypersthene	hypsography	I'll be damned	immodulated	impolitical
hypertensin	hypsometric	ill breeding	immomentous	impoliticly
hypertrophy	hysteresial	ill-disposed	immortalise	imponderous
hypertropia	hystericism	ill-equipped	immortalism	importantly
hyphenation	hysterotome	ill-favoured	immortalist	importation
hyphomycete	hysterotomy	ill-humoured	immortality	importunacy
hypnologist	hythergraph	illiberally	immortalize	importunate
hypnopaedia	iatraliptic	illicitness	immortified	importunely
hypnopaedic	Ibizan hound	illimitable	immunoassay	importunity
hypnopompic	Iceland gull	illimitably	immunogenic	impostorous
hypoacidity	Iceland moss	illimitedly	immunologic	imposturous
hypoalgesia	Iceland spar	ill-informed	impartation	impoundable
hypoblastic	ichneumoned	illiquidity	impartially	impoundment
hypobromite	ichnofossil	I'll learn you	impassioned	impractical
hypobromous	ichnography	ill-mannered	impassively	imprecation
hypocausted	ichthyolite	illogically	impassivity	imprecatory
hypocentral	ichthyology	ill-prepared	impatiently	imprecisely
hypochonder	ichthyornis	ill-tempered	impeachable	imprecision
hypochromia	ichthyosaur	illuminable	impeachment	impregnable
hypochromic	iconodulist	illuminance	impecuniary	impregnably
hypocrisies	iconography	illuminated	impecunious	impregnator
hypocycloid	iconometric	illuminator	impedimenta	impresarios
hypodiploid	iconophobia	illusionary	impenetrate	impressible
hypogastria	iconostases	illusionism	impenitence	impressment
hypogastric	iconostasis	illusionist	impenitency	imprimatura
hypoglossal	icosahedral	illustrated	imperatival	imprimitive
hypoglossus	icosahedron	illustrator	imperfectly	improbation
hypogonadal	icteritious	illustrious	imperforate	improbative
hypokinesis	icterogenic	illuviation	imperialise	improbities
hypokinetic	idempotence	illywhacker	imperialism	improperium
hypolimnial	identically	ilsemannite	imperialist	impropriate
hypolimnion	identic note	I'm a Dutchman	imperiality	impropriety
hypomorphic	ideogrammic	imaginarily	imperialize	improveable
hyponitrite	ideographic	imagination	imperilling	improvement
hyponitrous	ideokinetic	imaginative	imperiously	improvident
hypopharynx	ideological	Imam Bayildi	impermanent	improvingly
hypophyseal	ideoplastic	imbrication	impermeable	imprudently
hypoplastic	idioblastic	imbricative	impermeated	impugnation
hyposcenium	idioglossia	imbrutement	impersonate	impuissance
hypospadiac	idiographic	imbursement	impersonify	impulsively
hypospadial	idiomatical	imitability	impertinent	impulsivity
hypospadias	idiomorphic	imitational	imperturbed	inaccordant
hyposplenic	idiophoneme	imitatively	imperviable	inactivator
hypostasise	idiotically	immalleable	impetration	inadaptable
hypostasize	idiot savant	immanentism	impetrative	in advance of
hypostatize	idling speed	immanentist	impetratory	inadvertent
hypotension	idolization	immantation	impetuosity	inadvisable
hypotensive	idyllically	immarginate	impetuously	inadvisedly

inaesthetic	incoherence	independent	indulgingly	infinitival
in aggregate	incoherency	indesignate	in duplicate	infirmarian
in a great way	in cold blood	index finger	induplicate	infirmaries
inalienable	income group	index fossil	industrious	infirmation
inalienably	in command of	indexically	inebriation	infirmative
inalterable	incommodate	index-linked	in ecstasies	infirmities
inalterably	incommodity	index number	inedibility	in flagrante
inambitious	incompactly	Indian cedar	ineffective	inflammable
in a minor key	incompetent	Indian clubs	ineffectual	inflammably
inamissible	incompleted	Indian cress	inefficient	inflectable
inamoration	incompliant	Indian devil	inelaborate	inflictable
in-and-out boy	incomposite	Indianesque	inelegantly	influencive
in-and-out man	inconditely	Indian giver	ineloquence	influential
inanimately	in condition	Indian grass	ineluctable	infomercial
inanimation	inconfident	Indian Ocean	ineluctably	informality
in an instant	incongenial	Indian paint	inenarrable	informatics
in a nutshell	incongruent	India Office	inequitable	in formation
inappetence	incongruity	indiarubber	inequitably	information
inappetency	incongruous	India rubber	inequivalve	informative
in a small way	inconnected	indicanuria	inertialess	informatory
inattention	inconscient	indictional	inertia reel	informosome
inattentive	inconscious	indifferent	inescapable	infracostal
in at the kill	inconsonant	indigestion	inescapably	infrangible
inaugurator	inconstancy	indigestive	inessential	infrangibly
inauthentic	incontinent	indignantly	inestimable	infrequence
in authority	incorporate	indignation	inestimably	infrequency
in bad repair	incorporeal	indignatory	inevictable	infrigidate
in-betweener	incorrectly	indignities	inexactness	infructuose
incalescent	incorruptly	indigo finch	inexcitable	infructuous
incantation	incrassated	indigo plant	inexcusable	in full flood
incantatory	increasable	indigo snake	inexcusably	in full swing
incapacious	incredulity	indigo white	inexecution	infuriately
incapsulate	incredulous	indirection	inexhausted	infuriating
incarcerate	incremation	indirect tax	in existence	infuriation
incardinate	incremental	individuate	inexistence	ingathering
incarnadine	increpation	indivisible	inexpectant	ingenerable
incarnalize	incriminate	indivisibly	inexpedient	ingeniosity
incarnation	incrispated	Indo-African	inexpensive	ingeniously
incendivity	inculcation	Indo-Anglian	inexpertise	ingenuously
incensation	inculcatory	indoaniline	inexplosive	in good faith
incensement	inculpation	Indo-British	in facsimile	in good heart
incense tree	inculpative	Indo-Chinese	infangthief	in good store
incense-wood	inculpatory	indochinite	infanticide	in good voice
incensories	incunabular	Indo-Hittite	infantilise	ingrainedly
incentivize	incunabulum	Indo-Iranian	infantilism	ingratitude
incertitude	incuriosity	Indological	infantility	ingravidate
incessantly	incuriously	Indo-Malayan	infantilize	ingredience
in character	incurvation	indomitable	infantryman	Ingres paper
incinerator	incurvature	indomitably	infantrymen	ingurgitate
incipiently	Indanthrene	Indo-Pacific	infatuation	inhabitable
inclemently	indanthrone	indorsation	infectivity	inhabitance
inclination	indecencies	indorsement	infecundity	inhabitancy
inclinatory	indeciduous	indubitable	inferential	inhabitress
includingly	in deep water	indubitably	inferiority	inheritable
inclusively	indefinable	induced drag	infernality	inheritably
inclusivism	indefinably	inductional	infernalize	inheritance
inclusivist	indehiscent	inductively	infernalize	inheritress
inclusivity	indemnified	inductivism	infertility	in her wisdom
incoercible	indemnifier	inductivist	infestation	in his wisdom
incogitable	indemnifies	inductivity	infestivity	inhumanness
incognisant	indemnities	in due course	infeudation	inimicality
incognizant	indentation	indulgently	infieldsman	inirritable

in isolation	inquisitive	instigative	intercooler	interrogate
initial line	inquisitory	instigatrix	intercostal	interrupted
initialling	in receipt of	instinctive	inter-county	interrupter
initiatress	in rehearsal	instinctual	intercourse	interruptor
injucundity	in rejoinder	institorial	intercrural	interseptal
injudicious	in residence	institorian	interdealer	intersertal
injuriously	in respect of	institution	interdental	intersexual
in justice to	in reversion	institutive	interdepend	intersocial
ink-blot test	insalubrity	institutrix	interdictor	intersperse
in measure as	insaturable	instreaming	interesting	intersphere
in medias res	inscenation	instruction	inter-ethnic	interspinal
in midstream	inscribable	instructive	interfacial	interstitia
in-migration	inscription	in substance	interfacing	inter-strain
in mimicry of	inscriptive	in such a wise	interfering	intersystem
in miniature	inscrutable	insufflator	interfinger	intertangle
in mothballs	inscrutably	insulin coma	interfluent	intertilled
innavigable	insculpture	insultation	interfluous	intertribal
inner circle	insectaries	insultingly	interfoliar	intervallic
inner planet	insectarium	insuperable	interfusion	interveinal
inner speech	insecticide	insuperably	intergrowth	interventor
inner-spring	insectivore	in support of	interiorise	interviewee
Inner Temple	insectivory	intagliated	interiority	interviewer
innervation	insectology	integralism	interiorize	interxylary
innocuously	in semblance	integralist	inter-island	intestation
innominable	inseminator	integrality	interjacent	in the basket
innoxiously	insensately	integration	interjector	in the case of
innumerable	insensitive	integrative	interleukin	in the clouds
innumerably	insentience	intellected	interlineal	in the face of
innutrition	inseparable	intelligent	interlinear	in the gift of
innutritive	inseparably	intelligize	interlingua	in the grease
inobnoxious	insertional	intemperate	interlining	in the grip of
inobservant	insertioned	intensation	interlobate	in the groove
inobtrusive	insessorial	intensative	interlocker	in the line of
inoculation	inseverable	intenseness	interlucent	in the making
inoculative	inseverably	intensified	interludial	in the middle
inodorously	in severalty	intensifier	intermeddle	in the name of
inoffensive	inside track	intensifies	intermedial	in the offing
inofficious	insidiously	intensional	intermedium	in the rattle
in one's blood	insincerely	intensities	interminate	in the saddle
in one's glory	insincerity	intensitive	intermingle	in the secret
in one's heart	insinuation	intensively	intermitted	in the sequel
in one's shirt	insinuative	intentional	internal ear	in the stream
in one's sleep	insinuatory	intentioned	internalise	in the street
in one's socks	insipidness	intentively	internality	in the upshot
in open court	insistently	interactant	internalize	in the wake of
inoperative	insistingly	interaction	internecine	intimidator
inopportune	insititious	interactive	internecive	intolerable
in order that	insomnolent	inter-agency	interneural	intolerably
inordinancy	insouciance	inter-allied	interneuron	intolerance
inorganized	inspectoral	interamnian	internuncio	into the wind
in paperback	inspectress	interannual	interplanar	intoxicator
in principal	inspiration	interatomic	interpolant	intoximeter
in principle	inspiratory	intercalary	interpolate	intra-atomic
in process of	inspiringly	intercalate	interpreted	intractable
in pursuit of	inspiriting	intercensal	interpreter	intractably
input-output	inspissator	interceptor	interracial	intradermal
inquilinism	instability	intercessor	interradial	intradermic
inquilinous	installment	interchange	interradius	intransient
inquination	instantiate	interchurch	interregnal	intra-ocular
inquiration	instatement	intercities	interregnum	intrapolate
inquiringly	instaurator	intercolumn	interrelate	intraracial
inquisition	instigation	intercommon	interrogant	intraspinal

intrathecal	I promise you	isenthalpic	Jacobinical	joint family
intravenous	ipsilateral	isethionate	Jacobitical	joint patent
intraverbal	Iraqization	isidiferous	Jacob's staff	joint-tenant
intrepidity	iridescence	Island Carib	Jacqueminot	jolly fellow
intricacies	iridologist	isoantibody	jactitation	jolt ramming
intricately	iridoplegia	isochimenal	jaggery palm	jolt-squeeze
intrinsical	Irish bridge	isochronism	jaguarundis	Josephinism
intro-active	Irish coffee	isochronous	Jamaicanism	josephinite
introductor	Irish Gaelic	isoclinally	jam tomorrow	Joule effect
introessive	Irish mantle	isodiabatic	janissaries	Joule–Kelvin
introflexed	Irish potato	isodiaphere	Jansenistic	journal-book
intromitted	Irish setter	isoelectric	Japan clover	journalizer
intromitter	irksomeness	isogeotherm	Japanese ape	journey-work
introverted	iron-binding	isolability	Japanese wax	jovicentric
intrudingly	iron curtain	isolecithal	Japan laurel	Jovinianist
intrusively	Iron Curtain	isomagnetic	Japanolatry	joylessness
intuitional	iron-hearted	isometrical	Japanophile	Jubilee clip
intuitively	iron jubilee	isometropia	Japan pepper	Judaeophobe
intuitivism	ironmongery	isomorphism	Japan quince	Judaization
intuitivist	iron pyrites	isomorphous	jargonesque	Judas-colour
intumescent	iron rations	isopropanol	jargonistic	Judas priest
in two shakes	irradiation	isorhythmic	jarringness	Judas window
inusitation	irradiative	isotonicity	jaunting car	judgemental
inutterable	irradicable	Israelitish	Java sparrow	judgemented
invaccinate	irreceptive	issue of fact	javelin fish	Judges' Rules
invaginated	irreclaimed	itacolumite	jaw-breaking	Judge's Rules
invalidness	irrecusable	Italian hand	jealousness	judiciality
invasionist	irrecusably	Italian iron	Jeffrey pine	judicialize
invectively	irredentism	Italianizer	Jehoshaphat	judiciaries
inventively	irredentist	Italian pink	jejunoileum	judiciously
inventorial	irreducible	Italian roof	jejunostomy	jugular vein
inventoried	irreducibly	Italo-Celtic	jellied eels	jumper cable
inventories	irredundant	Italophobia	jelly powder	jumper dress
inventorize	irreferable	itatartaric	jerboa-mouse	jumper strut
inveracious	irreflexion	itatartrate	jerrymander	jumping bean
invertebral	irreflexive	it blows hard	Jersey wagon	jumping deer
invert sugar	irrefutable	itching ears	Jesuits' bark	jumping hare
in very sooth	irrefutably	itching palm	jet aircraft	jumping jack
investigate	irregularly	itemization	jimber-jawed	jumping-pole
investitive	irregulated	iteratively	Jimmy Riddle	jumping seed
investiture	irrelevance	iteroparity	Jimmy the One	jumping-wire
inviability	irrelevancy	iteroparous	jingle shell	jump Jim Crow
invidiously	irreligious	ithyphallic	jitteriness	jump take-off
invigilator	irreluctant	ithyphallus	job analysis	junction box
invigorator	irremissive	itineraries	job creation	juncturally
inviolately	irremovable	itinerarium	joblessness	jungle bunny
inviscation	irremovably	itineration	jockey-wheel	jungle fever
involucrate	irreparable	it's your baby	jocoserious	jungle green
involuntary	irreparably	it will serve	jocundities	jungle juice
involutedly	irresoluble	ivory-billed	jodhpur boot	jungle music
involvement	irretention	ivy geranium	John-a-dreams	juridically
iodargyrite	irretentive	I want to know	John-Bullish	jurimetrics
iodinatable	irreticence	jabberwocky	John-Bullism	just a minute
iodine value	irreverence	Jack and Jill	John Citizen	justice-seat
iodomethane	irrevocable	jackass brig	John Collins	justiceship
iodoprotein	irrevocably	jackass-fish	John Company	justiciable
ion exchange	irrevoluble	jacket crown	John Hancock	justifiable
Ionic school	irritatedly	Jack-fishing	Johnsoniana	justifiably
ionographic	isadelphous	Jack-hunting	joie de vivre	justify bail
ionophorous	isallobaric	Jack-pudding	join company	just quietly
ionospheric	isapostolic	Jack Russell	joint denial	just-so story
ipecacuanha	Iscariotism	Jacky Winter	jointedness	just the same

juvenescent	kerb-crawler	king's ransom	knucklehead	ladder-proof
juxta-marine	kerb service	king's silver	knucklesome	ladder shell
juxta-spinal	kern counter	King's speech	Knudsen flow	ladder-truck
Kabardinian	kernicteric	king's yellow	kob antelope	laddishness
Kabbalistic	kernicterus	king vulture	koechlinite	ladies' cabin
kachina doll	Kernig's sign	kinsmanship	koilonychia	ladies' chain
Kaffir bread	ketogenesis	Kiowa Apache	Kondratieff	ladies' night
Kaffir crane	ketone group	Kirk-session	Koplik's spot	la dolce vita
Kaffir finch	ketopentose	kissability	koringkriek	Lady Macbeth
Kaffir melon	ketosteroid	kiss and tell	kornerupine	lady's finger
Kaffir piano	Kevenhuller	kissing-ball	kreophagous	lady's mantle
Kalashnikov	keyboardist	kissing gate	kulturkampf	Laffer curve
kalkoentjie	key industry	kissing kind	Kulturkampf	laggardness
kameeldoorn	key of the sea	kissing time	kulturkreis	laicization
kämmererite	Keystone Kop	kiss-me-quick	kulturstaat	lairdocracy
kangaroo-dog	kick-and-rush	kiss of death	Kupffer cell	Lake Country
kangaroo-fly	kick-starter	kiss of peace	kutnahorite	lake-dweller
kangaroo paw	kick the beam	kiss the book	kwashiorkor	lake herring
kangaroo rat	kidney graft	kiss the dirt	kymographic	lake village
Kara-Kirghiz	kidney-piece	kiss the dust	labefaction	lalapaloosa
Karoo series	kidney punch	kitchenable	labia majora	lalapalooza
Kashmir goat	kidney-stone	kitchenette	labia minora	lallygagged
katabothron	kidney table	kitchen-maid	labiodental	lambda point
katavothron	kidney vetch	kitchen-plot	laboriosity	lamb's tongue
kedge anchor	Kikuyu grass	kitchen roll	laboriously	lamb succory
kedgeree-pot	Kilkenny cat	kitchen-sink	labour force	lamebrained
keelboatman	killer whale	kitchenware	labouringly	lamellicorn
keepability	killingness	kite balloon	labour pains	lamelliform
keep abreast	killing-time	kitschiness	Labour Party	lamentation
keep a corner	killing zone	kittenishly	labour union	lamentingly
keep an eye on	kilocalorie	Klamath weed	Labrador dog	laminagraph
keep a school	kilometrage	Klein bottle	Labradorian	laminectomy
keep a secret	kilovoltage	kleptocracy	labradorite	Lammas shoot
keep bad time	kilowattage	kleptomania	Labrador tea	Lammas wheat
keep company	kinderspiel	Klinefelter	labretifery	lammergeier
keep counsel	kind-hearted	knapsacking	labyrinthal	lammergeyer
keeping-room	kind payment	knavishness	labyrinthic	lamp-chimney
keep in shape	kindredness	kneecapping	Lacanianism	lamplighter
keep in touch	kindredship	knee-slapper	laccolithic	lamprophyre
keep measure	kinematical	knee-strings	lace curtain	Lancastrian
keep one's bed	kinesically	knicker yarn	laced valley	lance-knight
keep one's way	kinesiology	knick-knacky	lacertilian	lanceolated
keep silence	kinesthesia	knife switch	lacewing fly	lancepesade
keep track of	kinetically	knock for six	lachrymator	lancet light
kefir grains	kinetochore	knock-me-down	laciniation	lancinating
Kelvin scale	kinetodesma	knock on wood	laconically	land-grabber
Kendal green	kinetograph	knock rating	lacquer disc	landgravate
kenogenesis	kinetoplast	knock rotten	lacquer tree	landgravine
Kentish crow	kinetoscope	Knoevenagel	lacquerware	landholding
Kentish fire	King Charles	knottedness	lacquer-work	landing-beam
Kentish tern	King Country	knowability	lacrimation	landing card
Kenya coffee	kingdom come	know asunder	lacrymation	landing-flap
Kenyan Asian	king of birds	know by sight	lactalbumin	landing gear
Kepler's laws	king of kings	knowingness	lactational	landing-wire
keratectomy	King of Kings	know-nothing	lactescence	Land-leaguer
keratoconus	king penguin	know too much	lactiferous	landlordism
keratoderma	king's bishop	know who's who	lactobionic	land-marshal
keratolysis	King's bounty	knuckleball	lactochrome	land-measure
keratolytic	King's colour	knuckle-bone	lactoferrin	land of cakes
keratometer	king's gambit	knuckle-deep	lactoflavin	landscapist
keratometry	King's gambit	knuckle down	lactophenol	land-service
keratophyre	king's knight	knuckledust	ladder point	landsknecht

land-steward	latrinogram	leading tone	leftishness	less and less
langbeinite	lattice beam	leading wind	left-leaning	lesser breed
Langobardic	lattice site	lead-papered	left luggage	lesser-known
langoustine	lattice wave	lead-plaster	left-wingery	lesser light
language lab	latticewise	lead-swinger	left-wingism	lesson-piece
languidness	lattice-work	lead the ring	legal beagle	lestobiosis
languish for	latus rectum	lead through	legal memory	lestobiotic
languishing	laubmannite	lead-vitriol	legal person	lethargical
laniariform	laudability	leaf blister	legal tender	lethiferous
lansfordite	laudanosine	leaf-cutting	legationary	let off steam
lantern fish	laudatorily	leaf gelatin	legendarily	let's-pretend
lantern jaws	laughing gas	leaflet raid	legerdemain	letter-paper
laparoscope	laughing owl	leaf-opposed	legibleness	letter-plate
laparoscopy	laughworthy	leaf protein	legionaries	letterpress
lap-dissolve	launderette	leaf shutter	legionnaire	letter-scale
lapidescent	Laura Ashley	leaf-tendril	legislation	letter-space
lapis lazuli	laurel-green	leaf-tobacco	legislative	lettuce-like
lap of honour	laurel-water	leaf warbler	legislatrix	leucocratic
Laporte rule	laurustinus	leafy spurge	legislature	leucodermic
lap portable	lavender bag	leaguer-lady	leglessness	leucomatous
larch sawfly	lavender oil	league table	leg-of-mutton	leucoplakia
lard-bladder	laver cutter	leal-hearted	Leidenfrost	leucopterin
large as life	lavishingly	lean against	leishmanial	leucorrhoea
large-handed	law and order	leaning-note	leishmanoid	leucotactic
large-minded	lawbreaking	lean mixture	Leisler's bat	leucotomies
large-souled	lawlessness	leap forward	leisureless	leucotomize
lark bunting	law merchant	leaping ague	leisurewear	leucotriene
lark sparrow	lawn-sleeved	leaping-head	lemming-like	leukaemogen
larrikinism	lawn sleeves	leaping time	lemon cheese	leukotriene
larviparous	law of effect	learnedness	lemon-colour	Levantinism
larvivorous	law of honour	learning set	lemon squash	levantinize
laryngismus	law of nature	leaseholder	lemon yellow	level-dyeing
laryngology	law of sewers	leatherback	lend wings to	level-headed
laryngotomy	Lawrentiana	leather-carp	lengthiness	leviathanic
LaserVision	lawrightman	leather-coat	lens coating	leviratical
lasiocampid	lay about one	leatherette	lentiginous	Levitically
last assizes	lay analysis	leather-head	Leonine City	lexigraphic
last evening	lay down arms	leatherleaf	leopard frog	lexotactics
last honours	layer colour	leather-like	leopard lily	lex talionis
lastingness	layer system	leatherneck	leopard moth	leycesteria
last morning	laying house	leatherwear	leopard seal	liabilities
last offices	lay in pledge	leatherwood	leopard-skin	libationary
last quarter	lay preacher	leave behind	leopard-tree	libellously
last the pace	Laysan finch	leave hold of	leopard-wood	liberal arts
latchkey kid	lay stress on	leave school	Lepidoptera	liberalizer
latch-string	lay together	leave-taking	lepidoptery	liberalness
late licence	lay weight on	leave to stew	lepidosiren	liberatress
latent image	lead balloon	leaving-shop	lepospondyl	libertarian
latent virus	lead bullion	lecanomancy	leprologist	liberticide
lateral line	lead-burning	Le Chatelier	lepromatous	libertinage
lateralward	lead captive	lecheguilla	leprophilia	libertinism
latera recta	lead chamber	lecherously	leprophobia	libertinous
lateritious	lead counsel	lechuguilla	leprosarium	Liberty Bell
latifundist	lead crystal	lecithinase	leprousness	liberty boat
latifundium	leader board	lectureship	leptodactyl	liberty bond
Latin Church	leadhillite	ledge-handle	leptokurtic	liberty hall
Latin letter	leading case	ledger space	leptomeninx	Liberty loan
Latin rights	leading edge	ledger-stone	leptorrhine	liberty-pole
Latin school	leading lady	leewardmost	leptospiral	Liberty ship
Latin square	leading mark	left-brained	Lesbian rule	liberty tree
latitudinal	leading note	left-fielder	lèse-majesté	liberum veto
latreutical	leading-rein	left for dead	lese-majesty	libidinally

librational	lime and hair	liquidation	loading dose	lonely heart
licenceless	lime-rubbish	liquidities	loaf of bread	longanimity
lichenology	lime-sulphur	liquid lunch	loan capital	longanimous
lickerishly	limitedness	liquid paper	lo and behold	long-awaited
lickspittle	limitlessly	liquorishly	loathliness	long clothes
liederabend	limit switch	lirelliform	loathsomely	longimanous
Liederkranz	limnologist	lisle thread	lobectomies	longingness
lie detector	limpingness	list-broking	loblolly bay	longinquity
lie like a log	limp-wristed	listeriosis	loblolly boy	long-keeping
lieutenancy	linch-drawer	literalizer	lobotomized	long-lasting
life and limb	Lincolniana	literalness	lobster-boat	long measure
lifeboatman	Lincoln wool	literaryism	lobsterling	Longobardic
lifeboatmen	Lindabrides	lithia water	lobster moth	long-playing
lifefulness	line abreast	lithochrome	lobster-tail	long purples
life history	linear motor	lithochromy	local colour	long-running
life-in-death	linebacking	lithodipyra	localisable	long service
lifemanship	line-casting	lithodomous	localizable	longshoring
life-or-death	line drawing	lithofacies	local motion	long-sighted
life peerage	line-filling	lithogenous	local option	long-sleeved
liferentrix	line-fishing	lithography	local talent	long-sleever
life science	line manager	lithologist	Lochaber-axe	long-tongued
life-support	linen basket	lithophagic	lock forward	long twelves
life tenancy	linen-draper	lithophanic	loco disease	long-waisted
life-writing	linen duster	lithophytic	locofocoism	long weekend
lift a finger	linen shower	lithosphere	Locrian mode	long-woolled
lifting beam	line officer	lithostatic	loculicidal	look asquint
lifting body	line of force	lithotomies	locum tenens	look daggers
lifting tape	line of march	lithotomise	locus standi	looker-upper
lift the roof	line of metal	lithotomist	locust-berry	looking-over
ligamentary	line of sight	lithotomize	locust-eater	look one's age
ligamentous	line printer	lithotripsy	locust years	look oneself
ligand field	line-soldier	lithotritic	locutionary	look the part
light a shuck	line-spacing	lithotritor	lodging-room	look through
light-footed	lingenberry	litigiosity	lodging turn	loony-doctor
light-handed	lingeringly	litigiously	loellingite	loop-the-loop
light-headed	lingoa geral	litmus paper	lofting-iron	loose-bodied
light-heeled	lingonberry	littérateur	lofting pole	loose cannon
light-limbed	linguacious	little bitty	logarithmal	loose change
light-minded	lingua geral	little death	logarithmic	loose-footed
light-minute	Linguaphone	little grebe	logging-rock	loose-housed
Lightmonger	linguatulid	Little Horse	logical atom	loose-limbed
light-second	linguistics	little house	logical form	loose-lipped
light-skirts	link buttons	little sheer	logicalness	loosestrife
lightsomely	linocutting	little skate	logical word	lophobranch
Light Sussex	linseed cake	little woman	logistician	lophophoral
lightweight	linseed meal	little-worth	log-normally	lord and lady
lignicolous	lint-scraper	liveability	logocentric	Lord bless me
lignivorous	Linzertorte	live-bearing	logodaedaly	Lord Justice
lignum aloes	lion-hearted	live-for-ever	log of claims	Lord love you
lignum vitae	lionization	liver colour	logographer	Lord Marcher
likeability	lion's turnip	live through	logographic	Lord of hosts
like another	lion tamarin	living chess	logogriphic	Lord Provost
like a streak	lipogenesis	living death	logomachies	Lord's Prayer
like it or not	lipomatosis	living floor	logomachist	Lord's Supper
Likert scale	lipoprotein	living image	logopaedics	Lords triers
like the wind	liposarcoma	living space	logorrhoeic	Los Angeleno
like winking	liposuction	lixiviation	loiteringly	lose courage
lilliputian	lipotropism	lizard-green	lollipop man	lose leather
lily-livered	liquefiable	lizard's tail	Lombard band	lose one's rag
lily-trotter	liquescence	loadability	London broil	lose one's way
limber-chain	liquescency	load draught	London plane	lose sight of
limb of Satan	liquidambar	loading coil	London pride	lose track of

lost weekend	Lydian stone	maggotiness	make and mend	mamelonated
lotophagous	Lyman series	magic bullet	make an end of	mamillation
loud-mouthed	Lyme disease	magic carpet	make a pass at	mammalogist
loudspeaker	lymphoblast	magic circle	make a puddle	mammaplasty
Louisianian	lymphocytic	Magic Marker	make a search	mammiferous
loutishness	lymphoedema	magic mirror	make a shot at	mammillated
louvre-board	lymphogenic	magic square	make a show of	mammography
lovableness	lymphopenia	magic stitch	make a splash	Mammonistic
love handles	lyonization	Maginot Line	make believe	Mammonitish
love-in-a-mist	lyricalness	magisterial	make certain	mammoplasty
low comedian	macadamizer	magisterium	make default	mammoth tree
lower fourth	Macassarese	Maglemosian	make friends	managership
lower orders	Macassar oil	Magna Charta	make history	man-bites-dog
lower school	machaerdont	magnanimity	make holiday	mancipation
lower second	machairodus	magnanimous	make light of	mancipatory
lowest terms	machicolate	magnateship	make off with	mandarinate
low fidelity	machicoulis	magnetician	make one's bow	mandarinism
low pressure	machinating	magnetotail	make one's way	mandataries
low-spirited	machination	magnifiable	make or break	mandatories
loxodromism	machine code	magnificent	make request	mandatorily
lozengewise	machine-head	magnificoes	make room for	mandibulary
lubber fiend	machineless	magnipotent	make scruple	mandibulate
lubber's hole	machine-like	magnoperate	make sense of	mandolinist
lubrication	machineries	magnum bonum	make sport of	manducation
lubricative	machine room	magpie diver	make strange	manducatory
lubritorium	machine shop	magpie goose	make the race	manganesian
Lucanian cow	machine tool	magpie-robin	make welcome	manganolite
lucratively	machine-wash	Maharashtri	make whoopee	mango-ginger
lucubration	machine word	maidservant	Malabar plum	mangrove fly
lucubratory	mackerel-fly	mailability	malabathrum	mangrove-hen
ludicrosity	mackereling	mail carrier	malacca cane	Manichaeism
ludicrously	mackerel sky	mailing list	Malacca cane	manifestant
lues venerea	macrobiotic	mailing shot	maladaptive	manifestive
luggageless	macrocosmic	maille noble	maladjusted	manifolding
lumbaginous	macrocyclic	Maimonidean	maladroitly	Manila cigar
lumber baron	macrofossil	main breadth	malapropian	manila paper
lumberingly	macrogamete	main chancer	malapropism	man in motion
lumber trade	macrophagic	main squeeze	malariology	manipulable
lumber-wagon	macrophytic	maintenance	malediction	manipulator
lumbricalis	macroscopic	maintopmast	maledictive	manlessness
lumbriculus	macrosmatic	maintopsail	maledictory	manlikeness
luminescent	macula lutea	maison close	malefaction	man-milliner
luminophore	maddeningly	maisonnette	malefically	man-mountain
lump-account	madder brown	maize-yellow	maleficence	manna-lichen
lumpishness	madefaction	major circle	male incense	manneristic
lunar module	Madeira cake	major league	malevolence	mannishness
lunatically	Madeira wine	major planet	malevolency	Mann–Whitney
lunch-dinner	made of money	make a bid for	malfeasance	manoeuvring
luncheon-car	made to order	make a figure	malfunction	man of action
lunette-shoe	Madonna blue	make a fist at	maliciously	man of honour
Lupercalian	madonna lily	make a fool of	malignantly	ma non troppo
lustfulness	Madonna lily	make a fuss of	malignation	manorialize
Lutheranise	Madras curry	make against	malignities	mansard roof
Lutheranism	madreporite	make a hash of	mallet-shoot	man-tailored
Lutheranize	madrigalian	make a hole in	malmsey wine	mantel clock
Lutyenesque	madrigalism	make a market	Malo-Russian	mantelletta
luxuriantly	madrigalist	make a meal of	malposition	mantelpiece
luxuriation	Madrilenian	make a mess of	malpractice	mantelplace
luxuriously	Maecenatism	make a mock of	Maltese lace	mantelshelf
lycanthrope	magazinedom	make a motion	malt extract	mantle fibre
lycanthropy	Magdalenian	make a muck of	malt spirits	mantlepiece
lychnoscope	magdalenism	make an ass of	malt vinegar	mantleshelf

mantua-maker	Marrucinian	materialize	meditullium	memorizable
manucaption	marry come up	material man	medium-dated	memory board
manuduction	Marseillais	maternalism	mediumistic	memory cycle
manuductory	Marshallese	mathematics	medium-pacer	memory trace
manufactory	Marshallian	mathematize	medium-range	menaccanite
manufacture	marshalling	matinée coat	medium-sized	menaphthone
manumission	marshalship	matinée idol	medley relay	menaquinone
manumitting	marshlander	matriarchal	Medusa's head	mendacities
Maorilander	marsh mallow	matriculant	meet halfway	mendelevium
Maori wrasse	marshmallow	matriculate	meet the case	mendication
map-measurer	marsh orchid	matrilineal	megaloblast	mend matters
maprotiline	marsh violet	matrilinear	megalomania	meneghinite
maraschinos	martensitic	matrimonial	megalomanic	meningocele
Marathonian	martial arts	matrimonies	megalopolis	meniscoidal
marbled newt	martialness	matter of law	megamachine	menorrhagia
marble-paper	martinetish	maudlin tide	meganucleus	menorrhagic
marble-stone	martinetism	Maundy money	megaphonist	menservants
marcescence	martin-house	Maundy purse	megastardom	mensuralist
marchership	Martiniquan	Mauretanian	megatherial	mensuration
march in a net	martyrology	Mauritanian	megatherian	mensurative
marchioness	marzipanned	mavrodaphne	megatherium	mental block
marconigram	masculinely	mawkishness	megatonnage	mentalistic
mare clausum	masculinise	mayonnaised	megavitamin	mentalities
mare liberum	masculinism	mayoralties	meiobenthic	mental nurse
marginalise	masculinist	McCarthyism	meiobenthos	mental ratio
marginalism	masculinity	McCarthyite	meiotically	mentholated
marginalist	masculinize	meadow brown	Mekhitarist	mentionable
marginality	masculinoid	meadow crake	melancholia	mentri besar
marginalize	maskelynite	meadow grass	melancholic	meprobamate
margination	masking tape	meadow mouse	melanoblast	mercapturic
margraviate	masochistic	meadow pipit	melanoderma	mercatorial
maria clausa	Masoretical	meadowsweet	melanophore	Mercatorial
maria libera	masquerader	meal-pennant	melanterite	mercenarian
mariculture	massiveness	mean anomaly	melioidosis	mercenaries
Marie Louise	mass meeting	meaningless	melioration	mercenarily
marinescape	mass-produce	meaningness	meliorative	mercenarism
marine store	mass society	mean streets	meliphagine	merchandise
marital rape	mastaba tomb	measureless	meliphagous	merchant-bar
marked price	masterbatch	measurement	mellaginous	merchantman
marker crude	master-class	meat-grinder	melliferous	merchantmen
market cross	masterclass	meat-packing	mellifluent	mercilessly
market-house	master clock	mechanician	mellifluous	mercuration
market maker	masterfully	mechanicism	mellisonant	mercurially
market mammy	master mason	mechanicist	mellivorous	mercury lamp
market overt	masterpiece	mechanistic	mellowspeak	mercury pool
market-peace	master's mate	mechanology	melodically	mercy flight
market place	master touch	Mechlin lace	melodiously	merdivorous
market price	mastication	medal ribbon	melon-cactus	Meredithian
market stall	masticatory	median strip	meloplastic	meretrician
marketstead	mastigoneme	mediastinal	melo-tragedy	merino sheep
market value	mastodontic	mediastinum	melpomenish	merit monger
market woman	mastoid bone	mediateness	meltability	meritocracy
Markov chain	mastoiditis	mediational	meltingness	meritorious
marlinspike	masturbator	mediatorial	membranella	merit rating
marmoreally	Matabele ant	medical hall	membraneous	merit system
maroon party	matchlessly	medicinable	memento mori	meroblastic
marquessate	matchmaking	medicinally	memorabilia	merocyanine
marqueterie	match-winner	medicine man	memorandums	merodiploid
marquisette	materialise	medievalise	Memorial Day	meromorphic
Marriage Act	materialism	medievalism	memorialise	Merovingian
marriage-bed	materialist	medievalist	memorialist	merry andrew
marron glacé	materiality	medievalize	memorialize	merry Andrew

merrymaking	metanephric	Micawberish	middle guard	mind one's eye
Merthiolate	metanephros	Micawberism	middle piece	mind the shop
mésalliance	metaphorist	Michelsberg	middle price	mineral blue
mesaortitis	metaphorize	Michigander	middlescent	mineral coal
mesencephal	metaphyseal	Michiganian	middle-sized	mineral grey
mesenchymal	metaphysial	Michurinism	middlestead	mineralizer
mesenterial	metaphysics	Michurinist	middle watch	mineralogic
mesenteries	metaplastic	Mickey Mouse	middle-water	mineral soil
meshuggenah	metapsychic	microampere	Middle White	mineral wool
mesoblastic	metascience	microbially	middle world	miner's right
mesocephali	metasequoia	microbicide	middle years	minesweeper
mesocyclone	metasomatic	micrococcal	middy blouse	miniaturise
mesogastric	Metastasian	micrococcus	mid-European	miniaturist
mesognathic	metastasise	microcolony	midlittoral	miniaturize
mesometrium	metastasize	microcopied	midnight sun	minifundism
mesomorphic	metasternal	microcopies	midsagittal	minifundist
mesonephric	metasternum	microcosmic	midship beam	minifundium
mesonephros	metatherian	microcyclic	midshipmite	minimal pair
mesopelagic	metathesize	microdegree	midwife toad	minimum wage
mesophyllic	metatrophic	microfaunal	might as well	ministerial
Mesopotamia	meteoristic	microfibril	migrational	ministrable
mesosalpinx	meteoritics	microfiches	migratorial	ministrator
mesosaprobe	meteorogram	microfilmer	mild-hearted	minnesinger
mesoseismal	meteoroidal	microfloppy	military age	Minnesinger
mesospheric	meteorolite	microfungus	militaryism	minor league
mesosternal	meteorology	microgamete	military law	minor orders
mesosternum	meteor swarm	micrography	milk-blooded	minor planet
mesosuchian	meteor trail	microgroove	milk-livered	minute-glass
mesothelial	meter-feeder	microinject	milk-parsley	minute steak
mesothelium	meter-reader	microlithic	milk pudding	minute-wheel
mesothermal	metethereal	micrologist	milk the bull	miogeocline
mesothermic	methacrylic	micromaniac	milk-thistle	miracle cure
mesothorium	methanation	micromastia	milkweed bug	miracle drug
message card	methenamine	micrometeor	milled board	miracle play
messageless	methicillin	micrometric	millenarian	mirifically
Messiahship	methimazole	micromodule	millenaries	mirror fugue
mesterolone	methisazone	micromotion	millenarism	mirror-glass
metabiology	Methodistic	Micronesian	millenarist	mirror image
metabolizer	methodology	micro-opaque	millenniums	mirror-plate
metacentric	method study	microphoned	Miller index	mirror scale
metachronal	methylation	microphonic	miller's soul	mirror stage
metachrosis	methyl green	microphytal	millet-grass	mirthlessly
meta-ethical	metoestrous	microporous	milliampere	misalliance
metafiction	metonymical	microreader	milligramme	misanthrope
metagenesis	metoposcopy	microrecord	millimetric	misanthropy
metagenetic	metre-candle	microscopic	millinerial	misarranged
metakinesis	metrication	microscreen	millionaire	misbecoming
metakinetic	metric psalm	microsecond	millionfold	misbegotten
metaldehyde	metric space	microsmatic	milliosmole	misbeholden
metalimnion	metric tonne	microsphere	millisecond	misbeliever
metalingual	metrisation	microswitch	Millon's test	miscarriage
metallicity	metrization	microtubule	milpa system	miscasualty
metallocene	metrolander	microvillar	Milquetoast	miscellanea
metallogeny	metrologist	microvillus	mimetically	mischiefful
metalloidal	metromaniac	micrurgical	mimographer	mischievous
metallurgic	metropolite	micturition	minaciously	mischristen
metalogical	metrostaxis	mid-Atlantic	mincingness	miscibility
metal thread	Mexican wave	middenstead	mind-bending	mis-citation
metalworker	mezzofantic	middle class	mind-blowing	misclassify
metamessage	Mezzogiorno	middle earth	mindfulness	misconceive
metamorphic	mezzotinter	middle eight	mind-healing	misconstrue
metanalysis	miasmically	middle genus	mind-numbing	miscreation

miscreative	mixed school	money-jobber	monophthong	moronically
misdecision	mixing valve	moneylender	Monophysite	morosophist
misdelivery	mixolimnion	moneymaking	monopolizer	morphically
misdescribe	mixotrophic	money market	monopsonist	morphinated
misdiagnose	mixtilinear	money-monger	monopterous	morphogenic
misdivision	mnemonician	money spider	monorhinous	morphologic
mise en scène	mnemotechny	money supply	monospermal	morphometry
misemphasis	mobbishness	money's-worth	monospermic	morphonemic
miserliness	mobile phone	monitorship	monosporous	morphophone
misestimate	mobilizable	monkey-apple	monostylous	morphotropy
misfeasance	Möbius strip	monkey-board	monotechnic	Morris chair
misfortuned	mobocracies	monkey bread	Monothelism	morris dance
misfortuner	mock auction	monkey-faced	Monothelite	mortal drunk
misfunction	mockingbird	monkey gland	monotically	mortalities
misgoverned	mode-locking	monkey-house	monotonical	mortarboard
misgovernor	model theory	monkeyishly	monotremate	mortar-piece
misgrounded	moderantism	monkey's fist	monotrochal	mortiferous
misguidance	modern dance	monkeyshine	monotrophic	mortifiedly
misguidedly	modern Greek	monkey trial	monotropism	mortise lock
misidentify	modernistic	monkey trick	monovalence	mortmain act
misinclined	modern Latin	monkishness	monozygotic	Morton's foot
misinformer	modificable	Monmouth cap	Monseigneur	Morton's fork
misinstruct	modificator	monoblastic	monstrosity	mosasaurian
misjudgment	modillioned	monocarpous	monstrously	Moses basket
mislocation	modi vivendi	monocentric	mons Veneris	mosquito-bar
mismarriage	modus ponens	monochasial	Montanistic	mosquito bee
misperceive	Moeso-Gothic	monochasium	Montenegrin	mosquito net
mispersuade	Mohini-attam	monochromat	montes pubis	moss campion
mispleading	moisturizer	monochromic	Montgolfier	moss-cheeper
mispointing	moko disease	monochronic	monthly rose	moss-trooper
misregister	mole-catcher	monoclinous	monticulose	mosstrooper
misremember	mole cricket	monocracies	Montpellier	mossy-backed
misreporter	molecularly	monocrystal	moonlighter	mossy-cup oak
Miss America	molendinary	monocularly	moon-madness	motherboard
misshapenly	molestation	monoculture	moor-band pan	Mother Bunch
missing link	mollescence	monocytosis	mooring-mast	mother-clove
missing mass	mollifiable	monodactyly	mooring-post	mothercraft
missishness	mollycoddle	monodentate	Moorish idol	mother earth
mississippi	molly-dooker	monodically	Moor macaque	mother-house
miss one's tip	Molucca balm	monogastric	mops and mows	mother image
misspelling	Molucca bean	monogeneous	moralizable	mother-in-law
miss the boat	Molucca crab	monogenesis	moratoriums	mother mould
mistakingly	molybdenite	monogenetic	Moravianism	mother-naked
mister wight	momentarily	monoglacial	mordication	Mother of God
mistressing	momentously	monogrammed	more and more	mother plane
mistrustful	monadically	monographer	more by token	mother plant
mistrusting	monarchally	monographic	more majorum	mother queen
mite society	monarchical	monohydrate	morgenstern	mother right
Mithraicism	monasterial	monolatrous	moribundity	mother's help
Mithraistic	monasteries	monolingual	Morlacchian	mother's mark
mithridatic	monasticise	monolithism	Mormon Bible	mother's milk
Mithridatic	monasticism	monolobular	Mormon State	mother's ruin
mitogenetic	monasticize	monological	Mormon trail	mother stone
mitotically	Monbazillac	monologuise	morning call	mother water
mitral valve	monchiquite	monologuist	morning coat	moth mullein
mitred abbey	money broker	monologuize	morning-gift	mothproofer
mitred abbot	money centre	monomorphic	morningless	motion study
mitre-square	money-clause	monomyarian	morning line	motive power
mix and match	money cowrie	Monongahela	morning room	motoneurone
mixed border	money-dealer	mononuclear	morning star	motor cortex
mixed-manned	money flower	monophagous	morningtide	motoring cap
mixed number	money for jam	monophonous	morological	motor racing

motor-sailer	multi-ethnic	muscularity	Myrmidonian	nasal concha
mottled calf	multifactor	muscularize	myrrhophore	nasalizable
mottled iron	multifidous	musculation	myrtle-berry	nasal meatus
mould-candle	multifloral	musculature	myrtle green	naseberries
mould-runner	multigravid	museography	mysteriarch	nasociliary
mountain air	multihulled	museologist	mystery play	nasogastric
mountain ash	multijugate	museum piece	mystery ship	nasopharynx
mountain bat	multilineal	mushroom hat	mystery tour	nasospinale
mountain cat	multilinear	musical film	mysticality	nationalise
mountain dew	multilithed	musicalness	mythography	nationalism
mountaineer	multilobate	musical ride	mythoheroic	nationalist
mountain man	multinomial	music centre	mythologian	nationality
mountainous	multi-occupy	musicianess	mythologies	nationalize
mountain rat	multiparity	musicogenic	mythologise	nation state
mountain tea	multiparous	musico-mania	mythologist	native heath
mouse and man	multipedous	musicophile	mythologize	native peach
mouse-colour	multiphased	music volute	mythomaniac	Native State
moustachial	multiphasic	muskellunge	mythopoeism	natriuresis
Moustierian	multiplanar	musket-arrow	mythopoeist	natriuretic
movableness	multiplaned	musketproof	mythopoesis	nattier blue
movable type	multiple-use	musk thistle	mythopoetic	Nattier blue
move a finger	multiplexer	mussel scalp	Mytilenaean	natural-born
movie camera	multiplexor	mussel-shell	myxamoeboid	natural food
movie-making	multipotent	mussitation	myxofibroma	natural fool
movie palace	multiracial	Mussolinian	myxomatized	natural horn
moving plant	multiserial	Mussolinism	myxomatosis	naturalizer
moving stair	multisonant	Mussulmanic	myxomycetan	natural life
moxibustion	multisonous	Mussulwoman	myxophycean	naturalness
Mozambiquer	multispiral	mustachioed	myxosarcoma	natural note
Mozartianly	multistable	mustard bush	naggingness	natural-sign
Mrs Next-Door	multi-storey	mustard seed	nail varnish	natural sine
much obliged	multistorey	mutableness	naked ladies	natural year
much the same	multivalent	mutagenesis	Namaqua dove	nature-faker
mucicarmine	multivalved	mutationist	nameability	nature-notes
muckle wheel	mumbo-jumbos	Mutt and Jeff	name-calling	nature print
mucociliary	mum's the word	mutteringly	name-dropper	nature strip
mucopeptide	mundaneness	mutualistic	name no names	nature study
mucoprotein	mundanities	mycological	Nancy Dawson	nature trail
mucoraceous	mundivagant	mycophagist	nannofossil	naturopathy
mucronulate	municipally	mycophagous	nanomachine	naughtiness
muddle along	munificence	mycoplasmal	Nantucketer	naughty bits
mud engineer	munitioneer	mycoplasmas	naphthacene	naupliiform
mud-slinging	murderously	mycoprotein	naphthalene	nauticality
mud-throwing	murder squad	mycorrhizae	naphthalize	naval stores
mud-wrestler	murmuration	mycorrhizal	naphthenate	navel-gazing
muffin-fight	murmuringly	mycotrophic	naplessness	navel orange
muffin-worry	murmurously	myelination	Napoleonism	navel string
muffishness	murmur vowel	myelogenous	Napoleonist	n-declension
muffling-box	muscardined	myelography	Napoleonize	Neanderthal
mule-driving	Muschelkalk	mygalomorph	narcissuses	neanthropic
mule-skinner	muscicapine	myocarditis	narcoleptic	near and near
mule-whacker	muscicolous	Myochrysine	narcomaniac	Near Eastern
mulga parrot	muscle-bound	myoelectric	narcoticism	near-sighted
mulierosity	muscle curve	myofilament	Narodnikism	near the bone
mullein moth	muscle fibre	myo-inositol	narrational	near the wind
mullein pink	muscle force	myriametric	narratively	neatherdess
mullein wave	muscle power	myriapodous	narrativity	neat's tongue
multangular	muscle sense	myringotome	narratology	necessarian
multi-access	muscle shirt	myringotomy	narratorial	necessaries
multicolour	muscologist	myriologist	narrow gauge	necessarily
multicuspid	Muscovy duck	myrmecobius	narrow goods	necessarium
multicyclic	Muscovy talc	myrmecology	nasal artery	necessitate

necessities	neonatology	neutral-gear	night-office	nomen dubium
necessitous	Neoplatonic	neutralizer	night parrot	nominatival
necessitude	neostigmine	neutron bomb	night riding	nomogenesis
neck and crop	neostriatal	neutron star	night school	nomographer
neck and neck	neostriatum	neutropenia	night-season	nomographic
neckerchief	neotechnics	neutrophile	night-singer	nomological
necking-cord	neotectonic	never-ending	night vision	noms de plume
necrobiosis	neotenously	never-fading	night-walker	nonagesimal
necrobiotic	neothalamic	never say die	night-worker	non-allergic
necrologies	neothalamus	New Age music	nighty-night	non-American
necrologist	neotropical	newbuilding	nigrescence	nonapeptide
necromancer	nephelinite	New Canadian	nihilianism	non-apparent
necromantic	nephelinize	new Covenant	nihil obstat	non-attached
necrophilia	nephologist	New Covenant	nikethamide	non-believer
necrophilic	nephrectomy	New Critical	Nikkei index	non-Catholic
necrophobia	nephroblast	new frontier	Nile monitor	nonchalance
necrophobic	nephrogenic	Newgate bird	Nilo-Hamitic	non-clerical
necroscopic	nephropathy	New Humanism	Nilo-Saharan	non-clinical
nectar-guide	nephrostome	New Humanist	Nimzo-Indian	non-delivery
nectarivore	nephrostomy	New Jerseyan	Nimzowitsch	nondescript
needcessity	nephrotoxic	new learning	nine-to-fiver	non-election
needfulness	nephrotoxin	Newman-Keuls	ninety-three	non-elective
needlecraft	ne plus ultra	new potatoes	Ningre Tongo	non-electric
needle fight	Neptune's cup	New Rightist	ninny-hammer	nonentities
needle furze	nerve centre	news butcher	nipfarthing	nonentitous
needle-grass	nerve-doctor	newspapered	nip in the bud	none the less
needle match	nerve-ending	news theatre	nirosatable	nonetheless
needle paper	nervelessly	New Year's Day	nitrate bath	non-European
needlepoint	nervousness	New Year's Eve	nitric oxide	non-existent
needle valve	nestle-chick	niacinamide	nitridation	non-existing
needlewoman	nestle-tripe	nice-looking	nitrifiable	nonfeasance
needlewomen	Netherlands	Nicene Creed	nitro-aerial	non-invasive
need not have	netherstock	nickel-bloom	nitro-cotton	non-linearly
ne'er the less	netherwards	nickel brass	nitrogenase	non-literary
nefariously	nether world	nickelodeon	nitrogenate	non-literate
negationist	netherworld	nickel steel	nitrogenize	non-magnetic
neglectable	net-practice	nictitating	nitrogenous	non-material
neglectedly	neural crest	nictitation	nitro-powder	non-metallic
negligeable	neural plate	Niderviller	nitrosamine	non-militant
negligently	neural spine	Niersteiner	nitrosation	non-military
negotiation	neuraminate	Nietzschean	nitrous acid	non-negative
negotiatory	neurapraxia	Nigerianize	nitty-gritty	non-partisan
negotiatrix	neurenteric	niggardness	noble liquid	non-periodic
Negrophobia	neurilemmal	niggerality	noble-minded	non-personal
neighbourer	neurocytoma	nigger brown	noble savage	non-physical
neighbourly	neurofibril	nigger cloth	nobody's fool	nonplussing
Nelson knife	neurohaemal	nigger goose	nocardiosis	non-positive
Nelson touch	neurohumour	nigger-stick	nociceptive	non possumus
nemathecial	neuroleptic	night and day	noctilucent	non-pressure
nemathecium	neurologist	night-attire	noctilucous	non-printing
nematicidal	neuromatous	night bomber	noctivagant	non-provided
nematoblast	neuropathic	nightcapped	noctivagous	non-randomly
nematocidal	neurophysin	night-cellar	nocturnally	non-rational
nematodirus	neuropodial	nightclubby	no fewer than	non-reducing
nematophore	neuropodium	night effect	noise factor	non-resident
nematozooid	neuropteran	night-flower	noise filter	non-secretor
neo-colonial	neuroticism	night flying	noiselessly	non-sensible
neocortical	neurotomies	nightgowned	noisomeness	nonsensical
neo-Georgian	neurotropic	night-herder	nolle-prosse	non-sequence
neo-Hellenic	neurotubule	nightingale	nomadically	non sequitur
neo-linguist	neurulation	nightmarish	nom de guerre	non-sexually
neologistic	neutral axis	night monkey	nomenclator	non-solvency

non-specific	nothing like	nuncupative	obscenities	odorousness
non-standard	nothingness	nuncupatory	obscuration	ods bodikins
non-syllabic	nothing to it	nundination	obscurement	odynophagia
non-thematic	nothosaurus	nun's veiling	obscureness	oecumenical
non-tropical	notice-board	nuptial mass	obscurities	oenological
non-unionist	noticeboard	Nuremberger	obsecration	oenophilist
non-unionize	notice paper	nurse-mother	observantly	oesophageal
non-vascular	notionalist	nursery word	observation	oestrogenic
non-verbally	not miss much	nurse-tender	observative	oestruation
non-violence	not much chop	nursing home	observatory	of a lifetime
non-volatile	not much in it	nurtureless	observingly	of all others
nook-shotten	notochordal	nutmeg-apple	obsessional	of all people
Nootka lupin	not one's line	nutmeg liver	obsessively	of all things
nordmarkite	notoriously	nutmeg melon	obsidianite	of an age with
Norfolk pine	not quite her	Nutmeg State	obsignation	of an evening
Norfolk reed	not up to much	nutrimental	obsignatory	of a suit with
normal fault	nought worth	nutritional	obsolescent	offbeatness
normalizing	noumenalism	nutritively	obstetrical	off-Broadway
Normanesque	noumenalist	nychthemera	obstinately	off-diagonal
Norman Saxon	noumenality	nyctinastic	obstination	offenceless
normatively	nourishable	nyctitropic	obstipation	offensively
normativism	nourishment	nyctophobia	obstriction	offertories
normativist	nouveau poor	nyctophonia	obstruction	offhandedly
normativity	nouvellette	Nymphenburg	obstructive	office block
North Africa	Nova Scotian	nympholepsy	obtemperate	office found
North Briton	Novatianism	nymphomania	obtenebrate	office hours
north by east	Novationist	nymphomanic	obtestation	office-house
north-easter	novelettish	oarsmanship	obtrusively	office party
northeaster	novelettist	oatmeal mush	obumbration	officerless
northerlies	Novemberish	oatmeal soap	obviousness	officerlike
northernism	now and again	obediential	Occam's razor	officership
northernize	nowhere near	obedientiar	occultation	officialdom
Northern Spy	nowhereness	obfuscation	occult blood	officialese
northlander	noxiousness	obfuscatory	occupancies	officialise
North Riding	noxious weed	object-glass	oceanariums	officialism
northwardly	nuclear atom	objectified	ocean stream	officiality
north-wester	nuclear bomb	objectifier	ochlocratic	officialize
northwester	nuclear club	objectifies	ochlophobia	officiation
Norway maple	nuclear-free	objectional	ochlophobic	officinally
no-score draw	nuclear fuel	objectivate	octadecanol	officiously
nose-glasses	nuclear pile	objectively	octagonally	off-islander
nose-nippers	nucleic acid	objectivise	octahedrite	off-licensed
nosographic	nucleolated	objectivism	octahedrons	off-licensee
nosological	nucleolinus	objectivist	octapeptide	off one's base
Nostradamic	nucleophile	objectivity	octave flute	off one's feed
Nostradamus	nucleoplasm	objectivize	octennially	off one's feet
no such thing	nucleosomal	object of art	octillionth	off one's game
not a bit of it	nuée ardente	object-world	octodecimos	off one's head
notableness	null and void	objet de luxe	octopartite	off one's oats
notaphilist	nullibicity	objet trouvé	octuplicate	offscouring
not a sausage	nullifidian	objurgation	oculogravic	offset litho
notationist	nulliparity	objurgative	odds and bobs	off the hooks
not bat an eye	nulliparous	objurgatory	odds and ends	off the latch
not care a fig	number board	oblationary	odds and sods	off the point
notch effect	number-cloth	obligedness	odontoblast	off the press
notch filter	number opera	obliqueness	odontogenic	off the rails
not counting	number plate	obliquitous	odontophore	off-the-shelf
note-cluster	numbers game	obliterator	odoriferant	off the track
note-shaving	numerically	oblivionize	odoriferous	off the watch
not give a sod	numismatics	obliviously	odorimetric	offuscation
nothing in it	numismatist	obnoxiously	odoriphoric	of good cheer
	nuncupation	obsceneness	odorivector	of many words

of necessity	omnipatient	on the square	opto-coupler	Origenistic
of no account	omnipotence	on the stocks	optokinetic	originality
of the moment	omnipresent	on the street	optometrist	original sin
of the name of	omniscience	on the stroke	oracle bones	origination
oillessness	omnisciency	on the view of	oracularity	originative
oil of cloves	omphalocele	on the volley	oraculously	Orion's hound
oil painting	omphalotomy	on the wamble	oral history	Orkney sheep
oil platform	on account of	on the way out	oral society	Orleanistic
oil province	onagraceous	on this score	orange grass	ornamentist
Old Believer	on a sixpence	ontogenesis	orange juice	ornithology
Old Catholic	once or twice	ontogenetic	Orange Lodge	ornithopter
Old Covenant	onchocercal	ontological	orange pekoe	ornithosaur
old identity	on cloud nine	onychomancy	orange stick	orofacially
old-maidenly	oncogenesis	o'nyong-nyong	orange-tawny	or otherwise
Old Man River	oncological	opalescence	orange thorn	orphan virus
old offender	one argument	open-and-shut	orang-outang	orris-powder
Old Prussian	one-coloured	open circuit	oratorially	or something
old religion	one-downness	open cluster	orbicularis	orthocentre
old retainer	onefoldness	open college	orbicularly	ortho-cousin
old-spelling	one-handedly	open harmony	orbiculated	orthodigita
old-standing	one in the eye	open-hearted	Orcagnesque	orthodontia
old Thirteen	oneirocracy	open housing	orchestrate	orthodontic
old-womanish	oneiromancy	opening time	orchestrina	orthodoxian
old-womanism	onerousness	open-mouthed	orchestrion	orthodoxies
old-worldish	one's own kind	open slather	orchidacity	orthodoxism
oleographic	one-storeyed	open society	orchid house	orthodoxist
olfactorily	one's wits' end	open texture	orchidology	orthodromic
olfactorium	on every hand	open the ball	orchidopexy	orthoepical
olfactronic	ongoingness	open verdict	orchidotomy	orthogneiss
oligandrous	on horseback	operability	orchiectomy	orthography
oligarchies	onion-maggot	operas buffa	orderedness	orthohelium
oligarchist	onion-twitch	operational	ordered pair	orthologous
oligarchize	on its merits	operatively	orderliness	orthometric
oligochaete	on no account	operculated	orderly book	orthonormal
oligohaline	onomasticon	operoseness	orderly room	orthopaedic
oligolectic	onomatology	ophicalcite	order to view	orthophonic
oligomerize	on one's guard	ophiologist	ordinary ray	orthophoria
oligomerous	on one's hands	ophitically	ordnance map	orthophoric
oligomictic	on one's heels	opinionated	Ordnance map	orthophyric
oligopolies	on one's plate	opinionator	Oregon cedar	orthopnoeic
oligopolist	on one's way in	opinionless	Oregon grape	orthopraxis
oligotrophy	on penalty of	opinion poll	organ-blower	orthopteran
oligotropic	on principle	opobalsamum	organ-cactus	Orthopteron
olivary body	on probation	opossum wood	organically	orthoscopic
olive branch	on shipboard	opportunely	organic soil	orthostatic
olive button	on that score	opportunism	organisable	orthostichy
olive-shaped	on the back of	opportunist	organistrum	orthotropal
olive thrush	on the batter	opportunity	organizable	orthotropic
olla podrida	on the bottle	opposedness	organogenic	Osage orange
Olympianism	on the bounce	opposite sex	organonomic	oscillating
Olympic-size	on the button	opprobriate	organoscopy	oscillation
ombrogenous	on the carpet	opprobrious	organ-screen	oscillatory
ombudswoman	on the chance	oppugnation	orgiastical	oscillogram
ominousness	on the edge of	optical axis	oriel window	osmiophilic
ommatophore	on the face of	optical disc	orientalise	osmotically
omni-antenna	on the fiddle	optical disk	orientalism	osmund royal
omnibus book	on the fuddle	optical flat	orientalist	ostensively
omnifarious	on the ground	optical path	orientality	ostensories
omnificence	on the moment	optic pencil	orientalize	ostentation
omniformity	on the parish	optic tectum	Oriental Jew	osteoclasia
omnilateral	on the part of	optionality	oriental rug	osteologist
omnilingual	on the pounce	optionalize	orientation	osteopathic

osteophytic	outwardness	overpayment	oyster-grass	pair of steps
ostracoderm	ovariectomy	overpeopled	oyster-knife	pair of tongs
ostreaceous	oven-to-table	overpicture	oyster-piece	pair-skating
ostrich farm	over a barrel	overprecise	oyster-plant	palace guard
ostrich-fern	over a bottle	overproduce	oyster roast	palace hotel
ostrich-like	overachieve	overprotect	oyster-shell	palace style
Ostrogothic	over against	overreacher	oyster-tongs	palacewards
otherwheres	over and over	oversailing	oyster white	palaearctic
otherwhiles	overanxiety	oversparred	oyster-woman	Palaearctic
otitis media	overanxious	overspecify	ozoniferous	palaeofield
ototoxicity	overarching	oversteepen	ozonization	palaeoplain
out and about	overbalance	overstretch	ozonometric	palaeoslope
out-and-outer	overballast	overstudied	ozonoscopic	palaeosolic
out at elbows	overbearing	overstudies	ozonosphere	palaeothere
outbreathed	overblanket	overstuffed	Pacchionian	palagonitic
outbreeding	overbreathe	overtakable	pace-setting	palais glide
outbuilding	overburthen	overtedious	pachymeninx	Palais Royal
outcropping	overcareful	over the hill	pachysandra	palantypist
outdistance	overcasting	over the hump	pacifically	palato-velar
outdoorness	overcaution	over the moon	pacificator	palefrenier
outdoorsman	overchecked	over the odds	Pacific Time	Palestinian
outer planet	overclamour	overthought	pacifyingly	palindromic
outer suburb	overclosely	overthrowal	packability	palingenesy
outfighting	overclosure	overthrower	packageable	palmate newt
outflourish	overcoating	overtime ban	package deal	palmatiform
outjockeyed	overcomable	overtorture	package show	palmatisect
outline plan	overconcern	overtrample	package tour	palm-cabbage
out of action	overcorrect	overviolent	pack and peel	palmiferous
out of bounds	overcunning	overvoltage	packed cells	palm warbler
out of breath	over-curious	overweening	packed lunch	palpability
out of danger	overcurious	overwhelmer	packetarian	palpiferous
out of favour	overcurrent	overwilling	packing case	palpigerous
out of humour	overdevelop	overwrought	paddle board	palpitation
out of livery	overdraught	overzealous	paddle wheel	Palsgravine
out of period	overdryness	oviparously	paddock-hair	palynomorph
out of pocket	overeagerly	ovipositing	paddock-pipe	pampas grass
out of repair	overearnest	oviposition	Paddy Wester	pamphletary
out of season	overeducate	ovuliferous	paediatrics	pamphleteer
out of square	overexploit	oxalacetate	paediatrist	pamphleting
out-of-Stater	overfatigue	oxaloacetic	paedication	pamphletize
out of temper	overflowing	oxamniquine	paedodontic	pampiniform
out of the ark	overforward	oxazolidine	paedogamous	panagraphic
out of the red	overfraught	ox-eye tarpon	paedophilia	pan-American
out of the way	overfreight	Oxford cloth	paedophilic	pan-Anglican
out-of-towner	overgarment	Oxford frame	paedotrophy	Panathenaea
outposition	overglazing	Oxford Group	pageant-play	Panathenaic
outquencher	overgrazing	Oxford ochre	pageantries	pancake-bell
outriggered	overhanging	Oxford shirt	page printer	pancake coil
outside edge	overhastily	oxidability	pagoda stone	pancake race
outside lane	over-indulge	oxidational	pain barrier	pancake roll
outside line	overindulge	oxidatively	painfulness	Panchen Lama
outside loop	overknowing	oxidization	painkilling	pancratiast
outsideness	overlap nail	oxycephalic	painstaking	pancreatize
outsiderdom	overlapping	oxychloride	paintballer	pancultural
outsiderish	overlargely	oxygenation	paint-bridge	pancuronium
outsiderism	overlenient	oxygen lance	painted lady	pandean pipe
outside seat	overliberal	oxy-hydrogen	paint roller	pandemoniac
outsizeness	overlightly	oxyrhynchus	pair bonding	pandemonium
outsourcing	overmastery	oxysulphide	pairing-call	pandiagonal
outspokenly	overmeasure	oxytocinase	pair of cards	pandiatonic
outstanding	overnighter	oyster-brood	pair of hands	Pandora's box
outward form	overpartial	oyster drill	pair of stays	panduriform

panegyrical	papermaking	paraparesis	parlourmaid	pas de cheval
panel beater	paper napkin	parapet line	parlour palm	pasigraphic
panel doctor	paper-pusher	parapet wall	parlousness	passacaglia
panel heater	paper ribbon	paraphernal	Parma violet	passacaille
panentheism	paperweight	paraphiliac	Parmenidean	passage-bird
panentheist	paper window	paraphraser	parochially	passage-boat
pan-European	papier mâché	paraphrasis	parodically	passage-hawk
pangeometry	papilledema	paraphrenia	parole board	passage-room
pan-Germanic	papilliform	paraphrenic	paromomycin	passage tomb
Panglossian	papillomata	paraprotein	paronomasia	passage-work
Panglossism	papillosity	parapsychic	paroophoron	pass a remark
Panhellenic	papoose-root	parasailing	parotid duct	pass current
panic attack	papovavirus	parascender	parotiditis	passecaille
panic button	papyraceous	parascience	paroxytonic	Passe Colmar
panic buying	papyrograph	paraselenae	parquet work	passengered
panic-monger	parabolanus	parasitical	parrot fever	possibility
panicmonger	parabolical	parasol pine	parrot-finch	passing-bell
panic-struck	Paracelsian	parasternal	parrot-house	passingness
paniculated	Paracelsist	parasuicide	parrot mouth	passing note
Panislamism	paracentral	parathecium	parrot's bill	passing shot
panne velvet	paracentric	parathyroid	parrot snake	passing show
pannier tank	paracetamol	para-transit	parrot tulip	passion-dock
panographic	parachordal	paratrooper	parsley fern	passionless
Panomphaean	parachutage	paratrophic	parsley frog	passion play
pan-Orthodox	parachutist	paratyphoid	parsleyworm	Passiontide
panpsychism	paracrystal	parcel paper	parson's nose	Passion-tide
panpsychist	paradidymal	parcel shelf	parson's-week	passion vine
Panslavonic	paradidymis	parchedness	part company	Passion Week
pansophical	paradisical	parchmenter	parthenogen	passivation
panspermism	paradoxical	pare and burn	partialness	passiveness
pantaletted	paraffin oil	par éminence	partial tone	pass the buck
pantalettes	paraffin wax	parenchymal	partial veil	pass through
pantalooned	paragastric	parentalism	partibility	paste-bodied
Panthalassa	paragenesis	parentality	participant	pasteurella
pantheistic	paragenetic	parent—child	participate	pasteurizer
pantheology	paragliding	parentcraft	participial	past oneself
panther-lily	paragogical	parentheses	particolour	pastophorus
panther piss	paragrapher	parenthesis	particulate	pastoralism
pantie-waist	paragraphia	parenthetic	parting shot	pastoralist
pantile-lath	paragraphic	parenticide	parting tool	pastorality
pantisocrat	parahormone	parent-in-law	partitional	pastoralize
Pantocrator	paraldehyde	paresthesia	partitioned	past perfect
pantography	paraleipsis	paretically	partitioner	past redress
pantologist	parallactic	parfocality	partitively	pastureland
pantometric	paralleling	parfocalize	partnerless	pataphysics
pantomimist	parallelise	parheliacal	partnership	patchoulied
pantomogram	parallelism	parietal eye	part-payment	patch pocket
pantoscopic	parallelist	paripinnate	part-playing	patchworker
pantothenic	parallelity	parish altar	part-singing	pâte de verre
pan-tropical	parallelize	parish clerk	parturiency	patelliform
pants rabbit	paralogical	parishioner	parturition	patent house
pan-Turanian	Paralympics	Parisianism	part-writing	patent-right
panty girdle	paramedical	Parisianize	party-pooper	patent still
Papal States	parametrial	parity check	party popper	paternalism
papal system	parametrise	parity digit	party spirit	paternalist
Papal Zouave	parametrium	park-and-ride	party ticket	paternality
paperbacked	parametrize	parking deck	parvalbumin	paternoster
paper-cutter	paramoecium	parking disc	parvanimity	pâte-sur-pâte
paper flower	paramorphic	parking lamp	paschal lamb	path-breaker
paper-hanger	paramountcy	park oneself	Paschaltide	pathogenesy
paperhanger	paramountly	parlour game	Paschen body	pathogenous
paperknives	paranucleus	parlour-maid	pas de basque	pathognomic

pathography	pearl millet	penalty goal	penteconter	pericarpium
pathologist	pearl mussel	penalty kick	pentecostal	pericentric
patienthood	pearl-oyster	penalty line	Pentecostal	perichaetia
patientless	pearl-powder	penalty pass	pentecostys	periclinium
patient Lucy	pearl-sinter	penalty rate	penthemimer	pericranium
patientness	Pearly Gates	penalty spot	pentlandite	peridotitic
Patjitanian	pearly queen	pencil cedar	penultimate	perigenital
patriarchal	Pearly Queen	pencil skirt	penuriously	periglacial
patriarchic	peasantries	pencil-stone	people power	Périgordian
patricianly	pebble grain	pending tray	people's army	Perigordine
patrilineal	pebble stone	pendulosity	people's park	Périgord pie
patrilinear	pebble weave	pendulously	pepper dulse	perinatally
patrimonial	peccability	pendulum saw	pepper-grass	perinephric
patrimonies	peccadillos	penetralium	pepperiness	perineurium
patriotical	peccaminous	penetrating	pepperminty	perinuclear
Patriots' Day	peckishness	penetration	pepper-sauce	periodicity
patristical	Peck's bad boy	penetrative	pepper steak	periodic law
patrologies	pectinately	penguin suit	peptic gland	periodogram
patrologist	pectination	penicillate	peptic ulcer	periodontal
patrol wagon	pectization	penicillium	peptide bond	periodontia
patronizing	pectoral fin	penicilloic	peptidergic	periodontic
patron saint	peculiarism	peninsulate	peptization	period piece
patroonship	peculiarity	penitential	peracaridan	perionychia
patter flash	peculiarize	penniferous	perambulate	periostitis
pattern-bomb	pecuniarily	pennilessly	perceivable	peripatetic
pattern book	pecuniosity	penninerved	perceivance	peripherial
pattern card	pedagogical	penniveined	perceptible	peripheries
patternless	pedagoguery	penny-a-liner	perceptibly	periphrases
pattern room	pedagoguish	penny arcade	perchlorate	periphrasis
patteroller	pedagoguism	penny loafer	perchloride	periplasmic
paucispiral	pedal origin	pennyweight	percipience	periscopism
Paul-Bunnell	pedal-pusher	penny-wisdom	percipiency	perishingly
Paulinistic	pedanticism	penological	percolation	peristalith
Paul's betony	pedantocrat	pen recorder	percolative	peristalsis
paunchiness	pedestalled	Penrose tile	perduellion	peristaltic
pauselessly	pedestal mat	pensionable	perduration	perisystole
paving stone	pedicellate	pensionably	peregrinate	peritectoid
pawnbrokery	pediculated	pension book	peregrinity	perithecium
pawnbroking	pediculosis	pension fund	perennation	peritoneums
paxilliform	pediocratic	pensionless	perennially	peritonitic
pay envelope	pedogenesis	pension plan	perequation	peritonitis
paying guest	pedogenetic	pensiveness	perequitate	peritrophic
paymistress	pedological	pentacyclic	perestroika	peritubular
pay one's dues	pedunculate	pentadactyl	perfectedly	perlocution
pay one's scot	peelability	pentadecane	perfectible	perlustrate
peace-keeper	peevishness	pentagamist	perfectness	permanently
peacekeeper	Pekingology	Pentagonese	perfervidly	permanganic
peacemaking	Peking opera	Pentagonian	perfoliated	permeameter
peacemonger	Peking robin	pentagonoid	perforation	permissible
peace pledge	Pelagianism	pentagynous	perforative	permissibly
peach brandy	Pelagianize	pentahedral	performable	permutation
peacock blue	pelagically	pentahedron	performance	pernavigate
peacock-iris	pelargonium	pentahydric	perfumeless	peroxidatic
peacock moth	Pelican flag	pentamerism	perfumeries	peroxide ion
pea-flowered	pellucidity	pentamerous	perfunction	peroxisomal
peak shaving	pelmatozoan	pentamidine	perfunctory	perpetrator
Peano axioms	pelophilous	pentandrous	Pergamenian	perpetually
peanut valve	pelotherapy	pentangular	perhexiline	perpetuance
pearl barley	Pelton wheel	pentastomid	pericardiac	perpetuator
pearl button	pelvic floor	pentathlete	pericardial	perplexedly
pearlescent	penalty area	pentavalent	pericardium	persecution
pearl-fisher	penalty card	pentazocine	pericarpial	persecutive

persecutory	petrescence	philologise	photomatrix	pianissimos
persecutrix	petrodollar	philologist	photometric	piano-action
perseverant	petrofabric	philologize	photomosaic	piano nobile
perseverate	petrography	philomathic	photo-offset	piano player
Persian blue	petrol gauge	philopatric	photopathic	Piastraccia
Persian lamb	petrologist	philosemite	photoperiod	piccalillis
Persian silk	pettability	philosopher	photophilic	pichiciegos
persistence	petticoated	philosophic	photophobia	pickelhaube
persistency	pettifogged	phlebograph	photophobic	picket-house
persnickety	pettifogger	phlegmatism	photoproton	pick holes in
personal bar	pettishness	phlegmonoid	photoreduce	picking-belt
personalise	petty-minded	phlegmonous	photoresist	picking-fork
personalism	petty school	phlorrhizin	photosensor	picking-hole
personalist	petty spurge	phoenix-like	photosetter	pick-up truck
personality	Petzval lens	phonational	photosphere	Pickwickian
personalize	Peyer's patch	phonematics	photostable	pick-your-own
personal law	Pfund series	phonemicist	photostatic	picnic chair
personation	phaenogamic	phonemicity	photosystem	picnic lunch
personative	phaeochrome	phonemicize	phototactic	picnic plate
personified	phaeophytin	phone number	phototrophy	picnic races
personifier	phaethontic	phone phreak	phototropic	picnic table
personifies	phagedaenic	phonestheme	photovisual	pictography
personology	phagocytise	phonetician	phragmosome	pictorially
persorption	phagocytize	phoneticise	phrasal verb	picture book
perspective	phagocytose	phoneticism	phrase-maker	picture card
perspicuity	phainopepla	phoneticist	phraseogram	picture-goer
perspicuous	phalangitis	phoneticize	phraseology	pictureless
perspirable	phalanstery	phonic motor	Phrygian cap	picture rail
persuadable	phallically	phonic wheel	phthalazine	picture show
persuasible	phallocracy	phonofiddle	phthiriasis	picturesque
persulphate	phallotoxin	phonography	phycocyanin	picture tube
pertainings	phanerozoic	phonologist	phycologist	picture-wire
pertainment	Phantasiast	phonometric	phycomycete	piebaldness
pertinacity	phantasmata	phonophobia	phyllocarid	piece-broker
pertinently	phantastica	phonotactic	phylloclade	piece of arse
perturbable	phantom limb	phosphatase	phyllomania	piece of cake
perturbancy	phantom pain	phosphatide	phylloplane	piece of gold
perturbator	phantomship	phosphatize	phyllotaxis	piece of meat
perturbedly	Pharaoh's ant	phosphazene	physiatrist	piece of tail
pervadingly	Pharaoh's rat	phosphonate	physicalism	piece of work
pervagation	Pharisaical	phosphonium	physicalist	piece-worker
pervaporate	Phariseeism	phosphorane	physicality	Piedmontese
pervasively	pharyngitis	phosphorate	physicalize	piedmontite
pervertedly	phase change	phosphoreal	physicianer	pieds-à-terre
pervertible	phellogenic	phosphorial	physicianly	pied wagtail
pervicacity	pheneticist	phosphorise	physiocracy	pie in the sky
pessimistic	phenetidine	phosphorite	physiognomy	Pierced Nose
pestiferous	phenindione	phosphorize	physiognosy	pietistical
pestilently	phenol resin	phosphorous	physiolater	piezometric
pest officer	phenomenism	photoaction	physiolatry	pigeon-berry
pestologist	phenomenist	photoactive	physiologer	pigeon-chest
petal collar	phenotyping	photocopied	physiologic	pigeon grass
pet aversion	phenoxazine	photocopier	physogastry	pigeon-holer
Peter's pence	philanderer	photocopies	physostegia	pigeon-house
Peter's penny	philatelism	photoeffect	physostigma	pigeon's milk
petiolulate	philatelist	photoenzyme	phytoalexin	piggishness
petitionary	philhellene	photo finish	phytobezoar	pig-headedly
petit-maitre	phillipsite	photography	phytochrome	pig-ignorant
petits fours	philodendra	photoinduce	phytography	Pig Islander
Petrarchism	philodespot	photoionize	phytologist	pigmentless
Petrarchist	philogynist	photoisomer	phytosterol	pignoration
Petrarchize	philologian	photolabile	piacularity	pigsticking

pig's whisper	pirouettist	plane-tabler	plastogamic	pleiomerous
piledriving	piscatology	planetarian	plastometer	pleiophylly
pilfer-proof	piscatorial	planetarium	plastometry	pleiotropic
pilgrim city	piscivorous	Planet Earth	plate armour	Pleistocene
pill and poll	pisha paysha	plane the way	plate camera	plenilunary
pillar clock	piss and wind	planetismal	plate-clutch	plenipotent
pillar drill	pissasphalt	planetoidal	plate girder	plenteously
pillar plate	piss-elegant	planetology	platen press	plentifully
pillar-stone	pistolgraph	planet-wheel	plate number	plenum space
pillow-block	piston corer	planigraphy	plate pewter	pleochroism
pillow cover	piston drill	planimetric	plate-powder	pleocytosis
pillow-fight	pistonphone	planisphere	plateresque	pleomorphic
pillow mound	piston-valve	planispiral	plateworker	plerematics
pill peddler	pit aperture	planktology	platformate	plessimeter
pill-popping	pit-bottomer	plankton net	Platforming	plessimetry
pilocarpine	Pitcairnese	planoconvex	platinotype	pleurodynia
piloerector	pitch accent	planogamete	Platonicism	pleurolysis
pilotaxitic	pitch and pay	planography	Platonistic	pliableness
pilot burner	pitch-and-run	plano-miller	platter-face	plinth block
pilot driver	pitchblende	planospiral	platykurtic	pliosaurian
pilot engine	pitch-circle	Plantagenet	platymerism	ploshchadka
pilot-jacket	pitched roof	plant-animal	platypellic	plotting rod
pilpulistic	pitcherfuls	plant-beetle	platyrrhine	plough-point
pimento dram	pitcher-like	plant-cutter	platyrrhiny	plough-press
pimento tree	pitch-kettle	plantership	platyscopic	ploughshare
pinacotheca	pitch length	plant-feeder	playability	plough-staff
pinch-bottle	pitch the woo	planthopper	play-actress	plough-stilt
pinch effect	piteousness	plantigrade	play clothes	plough-stock
pinch-hitter	pitifulness	plantocracy	player-coach	plough under
pinch-roller	pit membrane	plantswoman	player-piano	plucked wool
pinch-runner	piton hammer	plantswomen	play for time	plug bayonet
pin-dropping	pitot-static	plasmablast	play forward	plug tobacco
pineal gland	pit-planting	plasmacytic	playfulness	plumb a track
pinealocyte	pittosporum	plasmalemma	playing card	plumb jordan
pine-bud moth	pituitaries	plasmalogen	play it by ear	plumigerous
pine warbler	placability	plasmapause	play of words	plummetless
piney tallow	placatingly	plasma probe	play on a word	plum-pockets
pinguescent	place-holder	plasma sheet	play one's ace	plumptitude
pink disease	place-hunter	plasma torch	play on words	plum pudding
pink gilding	place-kicker	plasminogen	play-reading	plumularian
pinking-iron	placelessly	plasmoblast	play-the-ball	plunderbund
pink-sterned	placentitis	plasmodesma	play the fool	plunge basin
pinnatisect	place of arms	plasmolysis	play the game	plunge-churn
pinnywinkle	placer sheep	plasmolytic	play the jack	plunger mute
pinocytosis	placket-hole	Plasmoquine	play the Jack	plunger-pump
pinocytotic	plagal close	plasmotomic	play therapy	pluralistic
Pinteresque	plage region	plaster cast	play the wild	pluralities
pin the rap on	plagiarizer	plasterless	play through	pluriparity
pioneership	plagioclase	plaster-like	playwriting	pluriparous
pionization	plagiostome	plasterwork	plea bargain	pluripotent
pipe-cleaner	plagiotropy	plastically	plead guilty	pluriserial
pipe of peace	plague-house	plastic arts	pleasantest	plurivalent
piperaceous	plain dealer	plasticator	pleasedness	pluri-valued
piperitious	plain-headed	plastic bomb	pleasurable	plush-copper
pipe-stapple	plain people	plastic clay	pleasurably	plush-stitch
pipe the side	Plain People	plasticized	pleasureful	plush-velvet
pipe tobacco	plain sawing	plasticizer	plebeianism	Plutarchian
pipistrelle	plain sewing	plasticware	plebeianize	plutarchies
piquantness	plain-spoken	plastic wood	plebiscitum	plutocratic
Pirani gauge	plaintively	plastimeter	plecopteran	plutography
pirate-perch	plain turkey	plastiqueur	plectognath	plutologist
piratically	plait-stitch	plastochron	plectonemic	plutonomist

pluviograph	polarimetry	polygenetic	pons Varolii	posological
pluviometer	polarisable	polyglacial	pontificate	possessible
Plymouth gin	polariscope	polyglottal	pontificial	possibilism
Plymouth Hoe	polarizable	polyglottic	pony express	possibilist
pneumatical	polar lights	polygonally	pony service	possibility
pneumatique	polarograph	polygrapher	pony-trekker	postabdomen
pneumatosis	polar vector	polygraphic	Ponzi scheme	post-abortal
pneumaturia	pole-finding	polyhaploid	poodle cloth	post-abortum
pneumectomy	polemically	polyhedroid	poodle-faker	postal meter
pneumococci	polemoscope	polyhedrons	pool cathode	postal order
pneumograph	pole-vaulter	polyhedrous	pool-measure	Postal Union
pneumolysis	police court	polyhistory	pools coupon	post-and-beam
pneumonitic	police force	polylingual	poor priests	post and pair
pneumonitis	police judge	polyloquent	pop festival	post-and-rail
pocket beach	policemanly	polymastism	pop in and out	post-axially
pocket knife	police novel	polymerizer	poplar-borer	post captain
pocket money	police state	polymicrian	poppet-valve	postcentral
pocket-mouse	police State	polymignite	poppy-colour	post-chariot
pocket-piece	police wagon	polymitosis	poppy mallow	postclassic
pocket-plums	policewoman	polymitotic	popularizer	post-clypeus
pocket Venus	policewomen	polymodally	popularness	postcranial
pocket-watch	policy wheel	polymorphic .	population I	postdiction
pococurante	poliorcetic	polynuclear	porcelainic	post-entries
poddy-dodger	Polish manna	polyonymous	porcellanic	posteriorly
podophyllin	Politbureau	polypectomy	porcupinish	poster paint
podophyllum	politically	polypeptide	pork butcher	poster paper
Podsnappery	politicking	polyphagous	pork-chopper	post eventum
Podsnappian	polka-dotted	polyphonies	pork-knocker	post-exilian
poena sensus	pollen brush	polyphonist	pornography	postfrontal
poeticality	pollen count	polyphonous	pornophobic	postglacial
poetization	pollen fever	polypropene	poroplastic	post-meiotic
Poets' Corner	pollen grain	polysomatic	porosimeter	post-mineral
pogonophore	pollen index	polyspermic	porosimetry	postmitotic
poikilocyte	pollen-plate	polysporous	porphobilin	post-natally
Poincaré map	pollinarium	polystyrene	porphyritic	postnatally
point-action	pollination	polytechnic	porridge ice	postnominal
point charge	polling card	polyterpene	porriginous	post-nuclear
point defect	pollutional	polythionic	portability	post-nuptial
point-device	Polovetsian	polytonally	portal crane	postorbital
pointed arch	poltergeist	polytopical	portal frame	postpalatal
pointedness	poltroonery	polytrichum	portal strut	postponable
point ground	poltroonish	polytrophic	portamentos	postponence
pointillism	polyacrylic	polyvalence	Portastudio	post-primary
pointillist	polyallomer	polyversity	Port du Salut	post-puberal
pointlessly	polyandrian	polyvoltine	porterhouse	post-tension
point number	polyandrist	poly-wrapped	porter's beer	Post Toastie
point of sale	polyandrium	pomatorhine	porter's knot	postulation
point of view	polyandrous	pomegranate	portiforium	postulatory
point source	polyangular	Pomeranchuk	portionable	post-village
point spread	polyblastic	pomfret-cake	portionally	postvocalic
poison elder	polycarpous	pomiculture	portionless	potableness
poison-green	polycentric	pommel horse	Port Jackson	potamogeton
poisonously	polychaetan	pomological	Portlandian	potato-apple
poison-plant	polychromic	Pompeian red	portlandite	potato-balls
poison sumac	polycratism	pomposities	portmanteau	potato-bogle
pokahickory	polycrystal	pompousness	port of entry	potato bread
poke pudding	polyculture	ponasterone	portraitist	potato crisp
poker school	polydactyly	pond-culture	portraiture	potato-eater
poker-worked	polydentate	pond dogwood	portrayable	potato flour
Poland water	polyenergid	ponderation	portrayment	potato mould
polar circle	polygamical	ponderosity	positive ray	potato onion
polarimeter	polygenesis	ponderously	positronium	potato patch

potato-plant	prairie coal	preconceive	prematurely	presphenoid
potato-salad	prairie cock	preconquest	prematurity	press agency
potato scone	prairie dock	preconsider	premedicant	press-button
potato straw	prairie hawk	pre-contract	premedicate	press-forged
pot cupboard	prairie rose	precoracoid	premeditate	press number
potentially	prairie soil	pre-critical	premenstrua	press office
potentiator	prairie wolf	predatorily	premiership	press of sail
potestative	prairie wool	predecessor	premium bond	press revise
pot-layering	praisefully	prediabetes	Premium Bond	pressure-jet
pot marigold	praise-house	prediabetic	premodifier	pressure pad
potteringly	pralidoxime	predicament	premonition	Prester John
potter's clay	prat-digging	predication	premonitory	prestigeful
potter's lead	prattlement	predicative	premultiply	prestigious
pottery clay	Praxitelean	predicatory	premunition	prestissimo
pottery tree	prayer bones	predictable	premunitory	prestressed
potting shed	prayerfully	predictably	preoccupant	presumingly
potwalloper	prayer-group	predilected	preoccupied	presumption
pot-washings	prayer niche	prediluvian	preoccupies	presumptive
pot-wrestler	prayer plant	prediscover	pre-ordinate	presupposal
poule de luxe	prayer shawl	predoctoral	preparation	presynaptic
poult-de-soie	prayer-stick	predominant	preparative	presystolic
poultryless	prayer wheel	predominate	preparatory	prêt-à-porter
pound-breach	pray in aid of	predynastic	prepatellar	pretaxation
pound covert	praying band	pre-election	pre-planning	pre-teenager
pounded meat	praying-desk	pre-electric	prepollency	pretencedly
pound-keeper	preacheress	pre-eminence	pre-position	pretendedly
poundmaster	preacher-man	pre-eminency	preposition	pretentious
pound-weight	preachified	pre-emphasis	prepositive	pretergress
pour scorn on	preachifies	pre-emptible	prepotently	preterhuman
poverty line	preachiness	pre-existent	pre-prandial	preterition
poverty trap	prc acquaint	pre-existing	preprandial	preteritive
powder-chest	pre-adamitic	pre-exposure	pre-pubertal	preterlegal
powder flask	preadaptive	prefatorial	prepubertal	preterminal
powder-house	preadmonish	prefatorily	prepunctual	pretty penny
powderiness	preambulary	prefectoral	pre-rational	prettyprint
powder paint	preambulate	prefectship	pre-register	prevalently
powder slope	pre-announce	prefectural	prerogative	prevaricate
power-broker	preaspirate	prefigurate	pre-Romantic	preventable
power centre	pre-assemble	prefinished	presagingly	preventible
power factor	pre-assembly	prefixation	presanctify	previsional
Powerformer	preaudience	pre-Freudian	presbycusis	price buster
power hitter	pre-bookable	pregalactic	presbyteral	price-fixing
powerlessly	Precambrian	pregnancies	prescapular	price leader
powerlifter	precatively	pre-graduate	pre-schooler	pricelessly
power-loader	precautious	prehensible	preschooler	price system
power outage	precedented	prehistoric	presciently	prickle-back
power-rating	precedently	pre-ignition	pre-selector	prickle-cell
power series	precellence	pre-indicate	preselector	prickliness
power shovel	precellular	pre-intimate	presenility	prickly heat
power stroke	preceptoral	pre-invasive	presentable	prickly pear
power supply	preceptress	preiotation	presentably	prick-stitch
Poynings' Law	precinctual	prejudicate	present arms	prick-sucker
practicable	precipitant	pre-judicial	pre-sentence	prick-teaser
practicably	precipitate	prejudicial	presentiate	pride and joy
practically	precipitous	prelanguage	presentient	pride of life
practice bar	preciseness	prelateship	presentment	Pride's Purge
Praenestine	precisional	prelibation	presentness	priestcraft
praepositor	preclinical	preliminary	preservable	priest-shire
praepositus	precognosce	prelimitate	preserve jar	priest's hole
praetorship	pre-coitally	preliteracy	presettable	prima donnas
pragmatical	precoitally	preliterate	presocratic	primal horde
pragmatizer	precompress	prelusively	pre-Socratic	primal scene

primariness	probational	prognathism	proper psalm	protandrous
primary coil	probationer	prognathous	property man	protanomaly
primary wave	probatively	programming	property tax	proteaceous
primateship	probingness	progression	prop forward	protectable
primatology	problematic	progressist	prophesying	protectible
primigenial	problemless	progressive	prophethood	protectoral
primigravid	proboscidal	prohibiting	prophetical	protectress
priming-hole	proboscides	prohibition	prophetless	protectrice
priming-iron	procaryotic	prohibitive	prophetship	proteinosis
priming pump	processable	prohibitory	prophylaxis	proteinuria
priming-wire	process heat	projectable	propinquant	proteinuric
primiparity	process lens	projectress	propinquate	proteolipid
primiparous	process-paid	projicience	propinquity	proteolysis
primitively	process shot	prokaryotic	propinquous	proteolytic
primitivism	prochain ami	prolateness	propitiable	proterandry
primitivist	prochronism	prolegomena	propitiator	proterogyny
primitivity	procidentia	proleptical	propneustic	Proterozoic
primitivize	proclaim war	proletarian	proposition	protestator
primogenial	proconsular	proletariat	propranolol	protest flag
primo tenore	procreation	proliferate	propriation	protest vote
Primrose Day	procreative	proliferous	proprietage	Protevangel
primus motor	Procrustean	prolificacy	proprietary	prothalamia
princeliest	proctodaeal	prolificate	proprieties	prothallial
prince royal	proctodaeum	prolificity	proprietory	prothallium
Prince Royal	proctologic	proligerous	proprietous	prothalloid
prince's pine	proctorship	prolocution	proprietrix	prothetelic
princessdom	proctoscope	prologuizer	propugnator	prothetical
principally	proctoscopy	prolongable	propylidene	prothoracic
printergram	procuration	prolongedly	proquaestor	prothrombin
printer's pie	procurative	prolongment	prorogation	protocercal
printing out	procuratory	promeristem	prosaically	protocolist
printmaking	procuratrix	prominently	prosaicness	protocolize
print-script	procurement	promiscuity	pros and cons	protocolled
print-seller	procyclical	promiscuous	prosauropod	protodeacon
prior charge	prodelision	promise well	prosceniums	protofibril
Priscillian	prodigality	promisingly	prosecution	protogalaxy
prismatical	prodigalize	promotional	prosecutive	protogynous
prison-fever	prodigal son	promptitude	prosecutrix	protolithic
prison-house	prodigiosin	prompt table	proselytess	protomartyr
private army	prodromatic	promulgator	proselytise	protomerite
private bank	produceable	promycelial	proselytism	protonation
private bill	producer gas	promycelium	proselytist	protonotary
private life	productress	pronatalism	proselytize	protopathic
private line	pro-European	pronatalist	proseminary	protopectin
privateness	profanation	prooestrous	prosenchyma	protophilic
private room	profaneness	proof-reader	prose poetry	protoplanet
private view	profanities	proofreader	prosiliency	protopodite
private wire	professedly	proof spirit	prosiopesis	protopterus
privatistic	proficiency	proof strain	prosobranch	protoscolex
privatively	profile drag	proof stress	prosodiacal	protostelic
prize-giving	profile shot	proof theory	prosopalgia	protothetic
prize-master	profiterole	propafenone	prospection	prototrophy
prizewinner	profoundest	propagandic	prospective	prototropic
prizeworthy	profuseness	propagation	prostatitis	prototyping
proactively	progenerate	propagative	prosthetics	protractile
proactivity	progenitive	propagatrix	prosthetist	protraction
pro-attitude	progenitrix	propamidine	prostitutor	protrusible
probabilify	progeniture	propargylic	prostration	protuberant
probabilism	progeny test	propatagial	prostrative	protuberate
probabilist	progestagen	propatagium	protagonism	provability
probability	progestogen	propellable	protagonist	provenanced
probasidium	proglottids	proper pride	Protagorean	provenience

providently
provinciate
Provins rose
provisional
provisioner
provisorily
provocation
provocative
provocatory
provokement
provokingly
provostship
proximately
proximation
prudentness
prudishness
Prufrockian
pruniferous
pruning hook
pruriginous
Prussianism
Prussianist
Prussianize
prussic acid
psalm-singer
psammophile
psammophyte
psephocracy
pseudergate
pseudocidal
pseudo-cleft
pseudocroup
pseudocubic
pseudo-event
pseudofovea
pseudograph
pseudokarst
pseudologer
pseudologia
pseudomonad
pseudomonas
pseudomorph
pseudonymic
pseudopodia
pseudoprime
pseudoscope
pseudoscopy
pseudostome
psilomelane
psionically
psittacosis
psittacotic
psophometer
psychagogic
psychagogue
psychedelia
psychedelic
psyche-glass
psychiatric
psychically
psychodrama
psychogenic

psychograph
psychologic
psycholytic
psychomancy
psychometer
psychometry
psychomotor
psychopathy
psychoplasm
psychostasy
psychotogen
pteridology
pterobranch
pterodactyl
pteropodous
ptilopaedic
ptochocracy
publicanism
publication
publicatory
public baths
public enemy
public house
publicistic
public libel
public order
public purse
public woman
public works
public wrong
publishable
publishment
puck carrier
puckishness
pudding face
pudding-head
pudding-time
pudding-wife
pudibundery
puerileness
puerilities
Puerto Rican
puff and blow
pulchritude
pull a stroke
pulley-block
pulley-wheel
pull leather
pull one's pud
pull strings
pull the plug
pull through
pullulation
pull up short
pulp-capping
pulpitarian
pulpousness
pulsatility
pulsational
pulveration
pulverulent
pumice stone

pumpability
pumpkin-head
pumpkin pine
pumpkinseed
pump-priming
pump-turbine
punch biopsy
punched card
punched tape
Punchinello
punching bag
punch-marked
punctilious
punctuality
punctuation
punctuative
punctulated
punishingly
punto in aria
pupariation
pupillarity
pupillogram
pupil-master
puppet-maker
puppet state
puppet-valve
puppy walker
Purbeck beds
purchasable
purchase tax
purdah glass
purdah party
purdah woman
pure and pute
pure-blooded
pure culture
pure science
purgatorial
purgatorian
purgatories
purging flax
purificator
puritanical
purple finch
purple gland
purple heart
purpleheart
purple heron
purple laver
purple osier
purple patch
purple prose
purple-shell
purportedly
purportless
purposeless
purpose-like
purpose-made
purposively
purposivism
purposivist
purpresture

purse-bearer
purse-cutter
purse-seiner
purse-string
pursiveness
pursuit race
Puseyitical
pushability
push-and-pull
push-bicycle
push-cyclist
pushfulness
pushingness
push moraine
push one's way
pushover try
push-process
push through
pussy-cat bow
pussy-footed
pussyfooter
pussy willow
pustulation
put a crimp in
put a match to
put in charge
put in motion
put in pledge
put in the pin
put it across
put on notice
put on the dog
put on weight
putrefiable
putrescence
putrescency
putrescible
putteringly
put the bee in
put the lid on
put the low to
put to flight
put to rights
put to school
putty-colour
putty powder
put up a black
puzzle-pated
pyarthrosis
pycniospore
pycnometric
pyelography
pyeloplasty
pygmy glider
pygmy possum
pyjama party
pyknoleptic
pylorectomy
pylorospasm
pyramidally
pyramidated

pyramidical
pyramid-like
pyramid-rest
pyramid-spot
pyramid-text
pyramidwise
pyranometer
pyrargyrite
pyrobitumen
pyroclastic
pyrogallate
pyrogenetic
pyrographic
pyrogravure
pyrological
pyrophanite
pyrophorous
pyrotechnic
pyroxenitic
pyrrole ring
pyrrolidine
pyrrolidone
pyruvic acid
Pythagorean
pythagorise
pythagorize
Pythonesque
quacksalver
quadrangled
quadraphony
quadrathlon
quadratical
quadrennial
quadrennium
quadricycle
quadrillion
quadrumanal
quadrupedal
quadruplane
quadrupolar
quaestorial
quaestorian
quail-thrush
quaiss kitir
Quaker brown
Quakerishly
Quaker State
qualifiable
qualifiedly
qualitative
qualityless
quality mark
quality time
quantal part
quantum jump
quantum leap
quarrelling
quarrelsome
quarterback
quarter-bell
quarter-boat
quarter-boot

quarter-bred	quinquereme	radio beacon	Ranger Guide	read through
quarterdeck	quinquesect	radiocarbon	ranging-pole	re-advertise
quarter-evil	quinternion	radio-dating	Rangoon bean	readvertise
quarter-hour	quintillion	radio energy	rank and file	ready-to-wear
quarter-jack	quiritarian	radio galaxy	ransom money	ready-witted
quarter-Jack	quislingism	radiography	rant and rave	reafference
quarterland	quislingist	radio-iodine	rapaciously	Reaganesque
quarterlies	quislingite	radiolarian	rapier dance	Reaganomics
quarter-line	quitch-grass	radiolarite	rapping iron	reaggregate
quarter-moon	quit claim to	radioligand	rapscallion	real account
quarter note	quiveringly	radiolocate	rapturously	real essence
quarter peal	quizzically	radiologist	rarefaction	realignment
quarter pole	quodlibetal	radiolucent	rarefactive	realisation
quarter-race	quodlibetic	radiometric	rascalities	realization
quarter-tone	quotability	radio-opaque	Raschig ring	realizingly
quarter-wave	quota method	radiopacity	raspberries	re-allotment
quarter-wind	quota sample	radiophonic	Rasputinism	reallotment
quarto paper	quota system	radioscopic	Rastafarian	reallotting
quartz clock	quotational	radiovision	Rastafarism	really truly
quartz glass	quotidianly	raffishness	rataplanned	real of eight
quartz watch	rabbet plane	raggamuffin	ratatouille	realpolitik
quaveringly	rabbinistic	ragged right	rateability	reanimation
queen closer	rabbit berry	ragged robin	rate-capping	reapportion
queen hornet	rabbit brush	ragged staff	rathskeller	reappraisal
queenliness	rabbit drive	rag-merchant	ratiocinate	rear admiral
queen mother	rabbit fever	rah-rah skirt	rationalise	rear echelon
Queen's bench	rabbit-proof	railing-line	rationalism	rear its head
Queen's Bench	rabbit punch	railroad tie	rationalist	reascension
queen's conch	rabbit's foot	railwayless	rationality	reassertion
Queen's Guide	rabbit tooth	railway time	rationalize	reassociate
Queen's Scout	Rabelaisian	railway yard	rationative	reassurance
queen-stitch	race glasses	rainbow-bird	ration sheep	rebarbarize
queer-basher	race meeting	rainbow fish	rat kangaroo	rebarbative
queer screen	race suicide	rainbow-like	rat-tail-file	rebate plane
Queer Street	race walking	rain or shine	rattle-brain	reborrowing
querulously	racialistic	rainproofer	rattle-mouse	rebroadcast
questionary	racing demon	rain slicker	rattle-pated	rebuildable
questionist	raciologist	rainy season	rattlesnake	rebukefully
queue-jumper	rackan-crook	raise a ghost	raucousness	recalculate
queue theory	racket-court	raise a laugh	raunchiness	recalescent
quibblingly	racketiness	raised beach	ravanastron	recantation
quick-change	racket-press	raise up seed	Ravenscroft	recarbonate
quick-firing	racket sport	raison d'être	ravishingly	receive silk
quick-freeze	rack-jobbing	raking light	raw material	receptively
quick-loader	rack of bones	rallentandi	razor-backed	receptivity
quick-return	rack railway	rallentando	razor-billed	recessional
quicksilver	racquetball	ramanas rose	razzamatazz	recessively
quick-sticks	radar beacon	Raman effect	reaccession	recipiangle
quick-witted	radar picket	Rambouillet	reach-me-down	reciprocate
quid pro quos	radar screen	ramekin case	reactionary	reciprocity
quiescently	Radcliffian	ramgunshoch	reactionism	recirculate
quiet number	radiant flux	ramisection	reactionist	reclaimable
quill-driver	radiant heat	rammishness	reaction jet	reclamation
quilting bee	radiational	ramshackled	readability	reclination
quinazoline	radiatively	ranchslider	reader-aloud	recluseness
quincuncial	radical chic	rancorously	Reading beds	reclusively
quindecagon	radicalness	random error	reading-book	recognisant
quinhydrone	radical sign	randomicity	reading copy	recognition
quinine-tree	radical word	Raney nickel	reading-desk	recognitive
quinologist	radicellose	range beacon	reading room	recognitory
quinoxaline	radiculitis	range-change	readmission	recognizant
quinquennia	radioactive	rangefinder	readmitting	re-collected

recombinant	redoubtable	refrainment	relationary	repertorium
recombinase	redoubtably	refrangible	relationism	repetitious
recommencer	Red Republic	refreshener	relationist	replaceable
recommender	redressable	refreshment	relativizer	replacement
recommittal	redressment	refrigerant	relaxedness	replenisher
recommitted	red river hog	refrigerate	releasement	repleteness
reconditely	Red River jig	refringence	release note	repleviable
recondition	red rockfish	refringency	relentingly	replication
reconfigure	red sea bream	refulgently	reliability	replicative
reconnoitre	red squirrel	regardfully	Relic Sunday	replicatory
reconstruct	red tapeworm	regenerable	relief valve	reply coupon
record album	red-throated	regenerator	religionary	reportative
recordation	reductional	regerminate	religionism	reportorial
recordative	reductively	regimentary	religionist	report stage
record token	reductivism	regionalise	religionize	reposedness
recountable	reductivist	regionalism	religiosity	reposefully
recountless	reductorial	regionalist	religiously	repossessed
recoverable	redundantee	regionality	reliquaries	repossessor
recoverance	redundantly	regionalize	relishingly	representee
recoverless	reduplicate	register ton	relocatable	representer
recremental	red valerian	registrable	reluctantly	representor
recriminate	reed bunting	regium donum	reluctation	repressible
recruitable	reed-sparrow	regretfully	reluctivity	reprimander
recruitment	re-education	regrettable	remancipate	reprivatize
rectangular	reed warbler	regrettably	remediation	reproachful
rectifiable	reef-builder	regroupment	remembrance	reprobation
rectilineal	re-embroider	regular army	remigration	reprobative
rectilinear	re-emergence	regularizer	reminiscent	reprobatory
recultivate	re-emphasise	regulatable	remissively	reprogramme
recumbently	re-emphasize	regurgitant	remodelling	reprography
recuperable	re-enactment	regurgitate	remonstrant	reprovingly
recuperator	re-encounter	reharmonize	remonstrate	reptiliform
recurrently	re-endowment	Rehobothian	remorseless	Republic Day
recurringly	re-enjoyment	rehydration	removedness	Republicrat
recursively	re-equipment	reification	remunerable	republisher
recurvation	re-establish	reificatory	remunerator	repudiation
recurvature	re-existence	reincarnate	Renaissance	repudiative
redactional	re-expansion	reindeer-fly	renal cortex	repudiatory
redactorial	refashioner	reinfection	renal pelvis	repugnantly
redargution	refectioner	reinforcing	renegotiate	repullulate
red bandfish	refectorian	reingestion	renewedness	repulsively
red-breasted	refectories	reinoculate	Renoiresque	repurchaser
Red Brigades	referendary	reinsertion	renormalize	request stop
red children	referendums	reinstation	renosterbos	requirement
Red Crescent	referential	reinstitute	Renshaw cell	requisitely
redding-comb	refinedness	reinsurance	rentability	requisition
reddishness	reflectance	reintegrate	rent-charger	requisitory
redefection	reflexively	reinterment	rent-service	requotation
redetermine	reflexivity	reinterpret	reoccurring	re-radiation
redeveloper	reflexivize	reintroduce	reorganizer	re-recording
red-eye gravy	reflexology	reinvention	reorientate	resale price
red hardness	reflux valve	Reis Effendi	reoxidation	resarcelled
redhibition	refocillate	reiteration	reoxygenate	rescindable
redhibitory	refocussing	reiterative	repackaging	res cogitans
red-hot poker	re-formation	rejectament	repartition	res communis
rediffusion	reformation	rejectingly	repeat order	researchful
redirection	reformative	rejoicement	repellently	researchist
red ironbark	reformatory	rejoicingly	repellingly	resecretion
rediscovery	Reformatsky	rejuvenator	repentantly	resectional
red kangaroo	reformatted	rejuvenesce	repentingly	resegregate
red mangrove	reformeress	relabelling	repertorial	reselection
red orpiment	reformulate	relatedness	repertories	resemblance

resensitize	reticularly	revisionism	ricocheting	ritornellos
resentfully	reticulated	revisionist	ricochetted	ritournelle
resentingly	reticulitis	reviviscent	riddle-me-ree	Rittmeister
reservation	reticulosis	revoltingly	ride on a rail	ritual abuse
reserve bank	retinacular	rewardingly	ride pillion	ritual choir
reserve cell	retinaculum	rewrite rule	ride shotgun	ritualistic
residencies	retinispora	rhabarbarum	ride the fade	river-driver
residential	retinopathy	rhabdomancy	ride the gain	river gravel
resignalled	retinoscope	rhabdomeric	ride the line	river limpet
resignation	retinoscopy	rhabdomyoma	ride the rods	river mussel
resiliently	retinospora	rhabdovirus	ride to scale	river pirate
resinaceous	retinotopic	Rhaeto-Roman	ridge runner	river runner
resistantly	retired list	rhapidosome	riding habit	river salmon
resistively	retiredness	rhapsodical	riding-house	roach-backed
resistivity	retiring age	Rhenish wine	riding light	roadability
res judicata	retort pouch	rheological	riding rhyme	road breaker
res non verba	retort stand	rheomorphic	rifacimento	road company
resourceful	retractable	rheotropism	rigging-loft	road-hoggery
respectable	retractible	rhetorician	right-angled	road-hoggish
respectably	retransform	rhetoricize	right centre	road-holding
respectless	retranslate	rheumatical	right enough	road manager
respectuous	retransmute	rheumaticky	righteously	roadmanship
respiration	retransport	rhexigenous	right-footed	road-pricing
respiratory	retreatment	Rhinelander	right-handed	road sweeper
respite care	retribalize	Rhine maiden	right-hander	roaring game
resplendent	retribution	rhinestoned	right-minded	robber baron
respondence	retributive	rhinocerine	right of user	robe de style
respondency	retributory	rhinologist	rights issue	Robinocracy
responsible	retrievable	rhinoplasty	rights of man	Robinsonade
responsibly	retroaction	rhinorrhoea	right sphere	robotically
rest assured	retroactive	rhinoscopic	right-to-life	roboticized
restatement	retro-bulbar	rhipiphorid	right-to-work	robusticity
restfulness	retrocedent	rhizobially	right-winger	Roche's limit
rest his soul	retro-engine	rhizocarpic	right you are	rockaboogie
restiffness	retroflexed	Rhizoctonia	rigmarolery	rockahominy
restimulate	retrolental	rhizomatous	rigmarolish	rock and roll
restipulate	retro-rocket	rhizopodium	rigor mortis	rock-climber
restitution	retroverted	rhizopodous	rinforzando	rock-crusher
restitutive	return empty	rhizosphere	ring binding	rock crystal
restitutory	return match	Rhode Island	ring circuit	Rockefeller
restiveness	reupholster	rhodologist	ring complex	rocker panel
restoration	reusability	rhombohedra	ring counter	rocket plane
restorative	revaccinate	rhomboideus	ring culture	rocket range
restriction	revaluation	rhyme scheme	ringed perch	rocketsonde
restrictive	revealingly	rhynchosaur	ringed snake	rock glacier
restructure	revengeless	rhythmicise	ringingness	rock lobster
resubjugate	revengement	rhythmicity	ringing tone	rock 'n' roller
resultantly	revengingly	rhythmicize	ring of truth	rock pebbler
resultative	revenue bond	ribaudequin	ring spanner	rock-skipper
resurrector	reverbatory	ribbon chute	ring-straked	rock sparrow
resurrender	reverberant	ribbon grain	ring the bell	rock the boat
resuscitate	reverberate	ribbon-grass	ring the shed	rock wallaby
retaliation	reverential	ribbon plant	ring winding	rock warbler
retaliative	reverse arms	ribbon snake	riotousness	rock whiting
retaliatory	reverse fire	riboflavine	ripping cord	rodenticide
retardation	reverse gear	ribonucleic	ripple cloth	rodomontade
retardative	reversement	rib-roasting	ripple-fired	Rogation day
retardatory	reversional	rib-tickling	ripple-grass	Roger's blast
retelegraph	reversioner	Ricci tensor	riproarious	rogue's badge
retentional	revindicate	rice-bunting	ripsnorting	roguishness
retentively	revirescent	ricketiness	risk capital	role-playing
retentivity	revisionary	rickettsial	ritardandos	rollability

roller arena	rotary table	rucksackful	Russianness	sailboarder
rollerblade	rotator cuff	ruddervator	Russian pony	sailing boat
Rollerblade	rotogravure	ruddy plover	Russian vine	sailing rule
roller blind	rotten apple	Rudesheimer	Russophobia	sailing ship
roller-board	rotten-stone	rudimentary	rust disease	sailorizing
roller-coast	Rouge Dragon	ruffed lemur	rustication	sailor pants
roller derby	rouge-et-noir	ruffian-like	ruthfulness	sailor's knot
roller Derby	rouge flambé	ruffle shirt	Sabbatarian	sailplaning
roller disco	rough as bags	Rugby League	Sabbath lamp	saintliness
roller drier	rough bounds	rugby tackle	Sabbathless	Saint Monday
roller skate	roughcaster	ruinousness	Sabbath loaf	saintpaulia
roller towel	rough-coated	rule of court	Sabine's gull	salaciously
roll-forming	rough collie	rule of three	saccharated	salad basket
rolling boil	rough-footed	rule of thumb	saccharined	salad burnet
rolling mill	rough-handle	Ruling Elder	sacculation	salamandrid
roll-top desk	rough-legged	rumble strip	sacerdotage	sal ammoniac
roll-your-own	roughometer	rumbustical	sackclothed	saleability
Roman candle	rough-scaled	rumbustious	sacramental	salesladies
Roman cement	rough scruff	rum cocktail	sacramentum	salesperson
Roman Empire	rough timber	rum customer	Sacred Blood	salicaceous
Romanensian	rough tongue	rumgumption	Sacred Heart	salient pole
Roman father	round barrow	rummage sale	sacred music	salinometer
roman-fleuve	round-celled	rumour has it	sacred order	salinometry
Roman nettle	roundedness	run away with	sacrificant	Salk vaccine
romanticise	round-headed	run-downness	sacrificial	salmagundis
romanticism	round-heeled	run-in groove	sacrilegist	salmonberry
romanticist	Round Tabler	runnability	sacring bell	salmonellae
romanticity	round timber	running back	saddle block	salmoniform
romanticize	round-winged	running fire	saddle brown	salmon louse
Roman uncial	Rousseauian	running gear	saddle-cloth	salmon stair
rompishness	Rousseauish	running hand	saddle-horse	salmon trout
roof pendant	Rousseauism	running head	saddle-house	saloon rifle
rooibaadjie	Rousseauist	running iron	saddle-joint	salpingitis
rookus-juice	Rousseauite	running jump	saddle point	sal-prunella
room-divider	roust around	running knot	saddle quern	salsuginous
room service	rover ticket	running mate	saddle-shell	saltarellos
rooster comb	Rowland ring	running moss	saddle tramp	Saltash luck
rooster tail	Rowton house	running rope	Sadduceeism	saltational
root-climber	royal assent	running shoe	Saengerfest	saltatorial
root cutting	royal family	running sore	safe-breaker	salt-glazing
rope-dancing	Royal Marine	running toad	safe conduct	saltimbanco
ropemanship	Royal Maundy	runological	safe deposit	saltimbocca
rope-walking	royal octavo	run the pikes	safe keeping	saltireways
roseate tern	royal plural	run to ground	safety-catch	saltirewise
rose blossom	royal quarto	runway light	safety chain	saltishness
rose-campion	royal road to	run-with-bull	safety first	salt of lemon
rose-crystal	royal tennis	Runyonesque	safety glass	salt of steel
rose diagram	Royston crow	rupicaprine	safety match	salvability
rose diamond	rubber goods	rupture a gut	safety paper	Salvadorean
rose du Barry	rubberiness	rupturewort	safety razor	Salvadorian
rose gall-fly	rubber plant	rural school	safety valve	salvageable
Rosenmüller	rubber snake	ruridecanal	saffron cake	salvational
rose-watered	rubber stamp	rush-bearing	saffron plum	Salvationer
Rosh Chodesh	rubble-stone	rush-release	saffron rice	Salvatorian
Rosh Hashana	rubefacient	Ruskinesque	saffron-wood	Salve Regina
Rosicrucian	rubefaction	Russell body	sagaciously	sal volatile
Rossettiana	rubelliform	Russia braid	sage sparrow	Samian earth
rosso antico	Rubensesque	Russian Bank	sagittal ray	Samson's post
Rotarianism	rubicundity	Russian bath	Sagittarian	sanatoriums
rotary blade	rubrication	Russian Blue	Sagittarius	Sancho Pedro
rotary press	ruby-dazzler	Russian boot	sagittiform	sanctionary
rotary quern	ruby wedding	Russian doll	sago pudding	sanctioneer

sanctionism	satin stitch	Scamperdale	schoolchild	scoring-card
sanctionist	satin-walnut	scandalized	schoolcraft	scorpaenoid
sanctuaried	satirically	scandalizer	schoolgirly	scorpioidal
sanctuaries	satisfiable	scansionist	schoolhouse	scorpion fly
sanctuarize	satisfiedly	scapegoater	school-marmy	Scotch argus
sanctus bell	Satsuma ware	scapethrift	schoolroomy	Scotch broth
sandblaster	saturnalian	scapigerous	school shark	Scotch catch
sandbox tree	Saturnalian	scapolitize	schoolwards	Scotch cuddy
sand-casting	saturnalias	scapularies	schottische	Scotchiness
sand culture	saturninely	scarabaeoid	Schrödinger	Scotch-Irish
Sandemanian	satyrically	scarabidoid	Schubertiad	Scotchprint
sand glacier	satyromania	Scarborough	Schubertian	Scotchwoman
sandpaperer	saucepanful	scare-buying	Schwabacher	Scotchwomen
sand-picture	saucepan lid	scaremonger	sciagrapher	scotomatous
sand-skipper	sauerbraten	scare-quotes	sciagraphic	scotometric
sand spurrey	saurischian	scare tactic	sciatically	scotophilic
sand-verbena	Sauromatian	scarlatinal	science book	scotophobia
sandwich box	sausage curl	scarlet-bean	science park	Scotophobia
sandwich-man	sausage meat	scarlet ibis	scientistic	scotophobic
sandwich-men	sausage roll	scarlet lady	Scientology	Scottishman
sandy blight	sausage-tree	scarlet rash	scincoidian	scoundrelly
san fairy ann	save oneself	scatterable	scintigraph	scouring pad
sanguinaria	save the mark	scatter bomb	scintillant	scoutmaster
sanguineous	save the tide	scatteredly	scintillate	Scoutmaster
sanguine red	saving grace	scattergood	scintillous	scragginess
sanitariums	savings bank	scattergram	sciophilous	scramble net
sanitary pad	savings book	scatterling	scire facias	scraper ring
sans-culotte	saviourhood	scatter plot	scirrhosity	scrappiness
sansculotte	saviourship	scattershot	scissor-bill	scrap screen
sansevieria	savoir faire	scelidosaur	scissorbill	scratchable
Sanskritist	Savonarolan	scenarioize	scissor-bird	scratch-back
Sanskritize	savouriness	scenography	scissor-kick	scratch blue
sans recours	savouringly	scent-bottle	scissor-lift	scratch-coat
saplessness	saw palmetto	sceptically	scissor-tail	scratch dial
saplinghood	Saxonically	sceptreless	scissorwise	scratch hole
saponaceous	saxophonist	schaalstein	scleroblast	scratchiest
saponaretin	say the truth	scherzandos	scleroderma	scratchings
sapotaceous	scabby mouth	schiacciato	sclerometer	scratchless
saprobicity	scabby sheep	schillerize	sclerophyll	scratch-weed
saprobiotic	scaberulous	schismatist	Scleroscope	scratch-work
saprolegnia	scaffoldage	schismatize	sclerotesta	scrawliness
saprophytic	scaffolding	schism-house	sclerotinia	scrawniness
Saracen corn	scagliolist	schistosity	sclerotioid	screak of day
Saracenical	scalability	schistosome	sclerotised	screaminess
sarcastical	scalar field	schizanthus	sclerotitis	screamingly
sarcoidosis	scalariform	schizocoele	sclerotized	screechiest
sarcolactic	scald-headed	schizocoely	sclerotomal	screen actor
sarcolemmal	scale armour	schizogenic	sclerotomic	screen-perch
sarcomatous	scale-blight	schizogonic	scolecodont	screen plate
sarcophagal	scale effect	schizotaxia	scolopender	screen porch
sarcophagus	scale factor	schizotaxic	scolopendra	screen-print
sardonicism	scale height	schizothyme	scolopidium	screen saver
Sargasso Sea	scale insect	schizotypal	scoop bonnet	screw around
sartorially	scalene cone	schizotypic	scoop-necked	screw-capped
satanically	scalenotomy	schmaltzier	scopolamine	screwdriver
Satan monkey	scale-stairs	schnockered	scopophilia	screwing die
Satanophany	scale-tailed	Schoenflies	scopophilic	screw-thread
satellitism	scale-winged	scholarhood	scorchingly	scribacious
satin beauté	scalpriform	scholarlike	score points	Scriblerian
satin beauty	scaly lizard	scholarship	score-reader	scrimpiness
satin finish	scaly-tailed	scholiastic	scoriaceous	scrimshoner
satinflower	scamblingly	school board	scoring-book	scripophile

scripophily	secessional	seicentoist	selffulness	semi-ellipse
scriptorial	seclusively	seigneuress	self-gravity	semi-evening
scriptorium	secondaries	seigneurial	self-heating	semi-invalid
scripturism	secondarily	seigniorage	self-imposed	semi-lunated
scripturist	second cause	seigniorial	self-induced	semi-monthly
scrive-board	second-class	seigniories	self-invited	semi-nomadic
scrobicular	second floor	seine-netter	selfishness	semiologist
scrofulitic	second front	seismically	self-knowing	semi-opacity
scroll-lathe	second-guess	seismic wave	self-limited	semiotician
scrub-cutter	second-liner	seismograph	self-loading	semioticist
scrub turkey	second pedal	seismologic	self-locking	semi-palmate
scrub typhus	second rater	seismometer	self-mastery	semiquinone
scruffiness	Second Reich	seismometry	self-mockery	semi-retired
scrumminess	second sight	seismonasty	self-mocking	semi-skilled
scrumptious	second sound	seismoscope	self-neglect	semi-skimmed
scrutinizer	second speed	seize hold of	self-opening	semispecies
scuba-diving	second table	selaginella	self-opinion	semi-sterile
scufflingly	second teeth	selectional	self-pitying	semitonally
sculduddery	second thigh	selectively	self-pleased	semi-trailer
sculduggery	second tooth	selectivism	self-raising	semi-tropics
sculpturing	second water	selectivist	self-reliant	semolexemic
scuppernong	Second World	selectivity	self-relying	semological
scurvy grass	secret agent	selectorate	self-renewal	sempervivum
scutcheoned	secretarial	selectorial	self-reproof	sempiternal
scutellated	secretariat	selenodetic	self-respect	senate house
scuttle-bone	secretaries	selenoscope	self-sealing	senatorship
scuttlebutt	secretional	self-abandon	self-seeding	send away for
scyphistoma	secretively	self-abasing	self-seeking	send packing
scyphostoma	sectile leek	self-accused	self-service	send to grass
Scythianism	sectionally	self-adjoint	self-serving	send to press
sea bindweed	section head	self-admired	self-similar	send to table
sea-blessing	section-line	self-analyst	self-starter	Seneca grass
sea-crawfish	section-mark	self-assured	self-sterile	senectitude
sea cucumber	sectorially	self-blimped	self-support	Senegambian
sea-daffodil	sector-piece	self-builder	self-tapping	seneschalsy
sea defences	secularizer	self-centred	self-torment	seneschalty
sea elephant	secundipara	self-certify	self-torture	senior class
sea-hedgehog	sedentarily	self-closing	self-winding	senior tutor
seakale beet	sede vacante	self-cocking	self-wrought	sensational
sea lavender	sedimentary	self-command	selling race	sense aerial
seal rookery	seditionary	self-conceit	sell oneself	sense-finder
sea lungwort	seditionist	self-concern	sell the pass	senselessly
seam bowling	seditiously	self-content	sell-through	sensibilise
sea milkwort	seductively	self-control	semantician	sensibility
seamstering	seeableness	self-created	semanticism	sensibilize
seam welding	see and serve	self-culture	semanticist	sensiferous
sea-pheasant	see daylight	self-defence	semanticity	sensigenous
sea purslane	seed crystal	self-delight	semanticize	sensitively
searchingly	seed orchard	self-deluded	semaphorist	sensitivity
searchlight	see eye to eye	self-deluder	semasiology	sensiveness
search party	seeing-glass	self-denying	semelparity	sensorially
sea sandwort	see it coming	self-despair	semelparous	Sensurround
sea scorpion	see little of	self-devoted	sememically	sententiary
seasickness	seemingness	self-disgust	semi-animate	sententious
seasonality	seepage lake	self-elected	semi-annular	sentimental
season crack	see the light	self-evident	semi-antique	sentinelled
sea starwort	see the world	self-excited	semi-aquatic	separate off
sea-tortoise	segmentable	self-feeding	semiaquatic	separate out
sea-voyaging	segmentally	self-feeling	semicircled	sephirothic
sea wormwood	segregation	self-fertile	semi-cursive	sepiostaire
seborrhoeic	segregative	self-finance	semi-display	Sepoy Mutiny
sebotrophic	seicentismo	self-fluxing	semi-diurnal	septangular

septanoside	servileness	shake dancer	shelf appeal	shirt of hair
septavalent	servile work	shake free of	shellacking	shirt of mail
septembrise	serving cart	Shakespeare	shelled corn	shirtsleeve
Septembrist	serving dish	shakuhachis	shell-flower	shit-stirrer
septembrize	servitorial	shale shaker	shell-jacket	shittim wood
septenaries	servo system	shallowness	shell midden	shiveringly
septenarius	sesquialter	shallow-pate	shell-silver	shockedness
septenniums	sesquioxide	sham Abraham	shell-stitch	shock-headed
Septentrion	sesquipedal	shamanistic	shelter belt	shock troops
septicaemia	sesquiplane	shamblingly	shelterdeck	shock-worker
septicaemic	sessionally	shamefastly	shelter foot	shoeing-horn
septiferous	setaceously	shamelessly	shelter half	shoe leather
septifragal	set an edge on	shameworthy	shelterless	shonkinitic
Septinsular	set a price on	sham-operate	shelter life	shoot flying
septivalent	set at naught	shanghaiing	shelter tent	shooting box
Sepulchrine	set at nought	shanks's mare	shelter tree	shooting war
sequentiary	set little by	Shanks's mare	shelter wood	shoot the cat
sequestrant	set stocking	shanks's pony	shepherd dog	shoot the sun
sequestrate	set the scene	Shanks's pony	shepherdess	shoot to kill
Sequestrene	set the stage	shanty Irish	shepherdize	shop-breaker
serendipity	set the watch	shape factor	sheriffalty	shop-fitting
serfishness	setting coat	shapelessly	sheriffhood	shopfitting
sergeancies	setting-pole	shapeliness	sheriffship	shopkeeping
sericitized	settledness	shape memory	sheriffwick	shoplifting
sericulture	settling day	shape up well	sheristadar	shopping-bag
series-wound	set to school	shard-beetle	Sherlockian	shop steward
serigrapher	set well with	share-farmer	sherry glass	shore dinner
serigraphic	sevenfolded	shareholder	sherry party	shore-gunner
serio-comedy	seven-hilled	share-milker	shield-board	shore-hopper
seriousness	seven-league	share-pusher	shield-money	shore patrol
serishtadar	seven-seater	share tenant	shiftlessly	short-acting
sermonesque	seventeenth	shark's teeth	shift system	short ballot
sermonology	seventh part	shark's tooth	shigellosis	short change
seroconvert	seventh wave	shark-sucker	shin-cracker	shortcoming
serological	seventy-five	sharon fruit	shingle bank	short corner
serotherapy	seventyfold	sharp-tailed	shingle-nail	short-haired
serotine bat	seventy-four	sharp-witted	shiningness	short-handed
serous gland	seventy-nine	Shasta daisy	shining path	shorthander
serpentaria	severalfold	shatter belt	shin-plaster	short-headed
serpentinic	sewage grass	shatter cone	shin-splints	short-horned
serpent-like	sewage works	shatter-pate	Shintoistic	short manure
serpent-star	sexadecimal	shaver point	ship a stripe	short notice
serpent-wand	sexagesimal	shaving foam	ship biscuit	short octave
serpiginous	sex criminal	shawl collar	ship-breaker	short-period
serradillas	sexdigitism	shear centre	shipbuilder	short shorts
serrulation	sexennially	shear stress	ship of fools	short shrift
servantless	sex instinct	sheath dress	ship of State	short sleeve
servantship	sexlessness	sheath knife	shipping ore	short-spined
serve and sue	sex offender	sheath skirt	ship's papers	short-spoken
serviceable	sexological	shed light on	ship's writer	short square
serviceably	sex-reversal	Sheela-na-gig	shipton moth	short staple
service area	sexsational	sheep-herder	ship-to-shore	Short Street
service book	sextillions	sheep laurel	shipyard eye	short-suited
service club	sextodecimo	sheep-master	Shirburnian	short temper
service flat	sexual organ	sheep-shears	shire-bishop	short tennis
service game	Seychellois	sheep's heart	shire county	short-termer
serviceless	shackle-bolt	sheep-silver	shire-ground	short weight
service line	shackle-bone	sheep sorrel	shirt blouse	short-winded
service mark	shad-bellied	sheer-strake	shirt-button	shoshonitic
service-pipe	shadowgraph	sheet anchor	shirt-cutter	shot-blaster
service road	shadowiness	sheet feeder	shirt-jacket	shot-peening
service tree	shaft pillar	sheet-piling	shirtlifter	shot-putting

shot through	side-partner	silver medal	sinuousness	slate-pencil
shoulder bag	sidereal day	silver paper	sinus rhythm	slate-writer
shouldering	sideroblast	silver perch	siphonogamy	slatternish
shoulder pad	siderocytic	silver plate	siphuncular	slaughterer
shoulder pod	siderograph	silver-point	sipper-sauce	slaunchways
shoulder tab	sideropenia	silver print	sipunculoid	slaunchwise
shovelboard	sideropenic	silversides	sirocco oven	slave-bangle
shovel-penny	siderophile	silversmith	sister-block	slave-driver
show-and-tell	siderophore	silver spoon	sister-in-law	slave labour
showboating	side scraper	Silver State	sister tutor	slave market
shower-cloud	sidestepper	Silver Stick	Sitka spruce	slaveocracy
showeriness	side-wheeler	silversword	sitting duck	slaveringly
showerproof	Sierra Leone	silver tabby	sitting room	slave trader
shower stall	sift through	silver table	situational	slave worker
showjumping	sight cheque	silver trout	situationer	slavishness
showmanship	sight-holder	silver-white	sivatherium	Slavonicize
show of force	sightlessly	silvery pout	Six Counties	sledge-meter
show of hands	sightliness	Simonianism	sixteensome	sleep around
show oneself	sight-player	simperingly	sixteenthly	Sleeperette
show-stopper	sight-reader	simple feast	sixth-former	sleeper seat
show the flag	sight record	Simple Simon	sixty-fourmo	sleeper wall
show through	sight-screen	sincereness	skaapsteker	sleeping bag
show willing	sightseeing	sindonology	skate-barrow	sleeping car
shrew-stroke	sight-setter	sinews of war	skating rink	sleeplessly
shrew-struck	sight unseen	sinfonietta	skeletonian	sleep-shorts
shrew-tenrec	sightworthy	singability	skeletonise	sleep-talker
shrift-shire	sigillarian	Singaporean	skeletonize	sleep-waking
shrike vireo	sigillation	singer's node	skeleton key	sleepwalker
shrimp plant	sigmatropic	singing bird	Skeltonical	sleeve board
shrinkingly	sigmoidally	singing game	sketch-block	sleeve-valve
shrink-proof	signal plate	singing sand	sketchiness	sleigh-rider
shrivelling	signal tower	singing tree	skiagrapher	slenderness
shroud-brass	signatories	single-blind	skiagraphic	sleuth-hound
shrubberies	signaturist	single cream	skid-mounted	slice of life
shrubbiness	signifiable	single entry	skilfulness	slickenside
shrub mallow	significans	Single Grave	skilligalee	slick-licker
shruggingly	significant	single-horse	skim-coulter	slide guitar
shuddersome	significate	single-soled	skimmed milk	sliding door
shuffle beat	sign-painter	single-start	skimmer-cake	sliding keel
shufflewing	sign-vehicle	single stick	skimmington	sliding roof
shufflingly	signwriting	single-taxer	skin and bone	sliding rule
shut one's pan	silica glass	single track	skip-bombing	sliding seat
shutterless	silicic acid	single-tuned	skippership	slightingly
shutter weir	silicon chip	singularise	skirmishing	slim disease
shuttlecock	silicon iron	singularism	skirt-chaser	slimnastics
shuttleless	siliquiform	singularist	skirt-dancer	sling the bat
shuttle-race	silk snapper	singularity	skirt of beef	slip casting
sialectasis	silkworm gut	singularize	skirt patrol	slip edition
sialography	sillimanite	singulative	skulduggery	slipped disc
sialorrhoea	silly season	singultient	skull-buster	slipper bath
Siamese twin	silt-snapper	sinisterity	skullcapped	slipperette
Siberian jay	silverballi	sinistrally	sky-blue pink	slipper sock
Siberian tit	silver beech	sinistrorse	sky-coloured	slipperwort
siblingship	silverberry	sinking fund	Skye terrier	slippery dip
sibyllistic	silver birch	sinking sand	sky-scraping	slippery elm
sick benefit	silver blond	sink the wind	sky-shouting	slit sampler
sick cookery	silver bream	sinlessness	slant height	slit spirant
sickeningly	silver grain	sin-offering	slapdashery	sloop-rigged
sickishness	silveriness	sinological	slap-happily	sloothering
side-flowing	silver Latin	Sinological	slasher film	slope filter
side gallery	silver-lines	Sino-Tibetan	slash pocket	slopping-out
side-looking	silver maple	sinuosities	slate colour	sloth-monkey

slot machine	smooth snake	societarian	solid system	soubrettish
slotted line	smorgasbord	Socinianism	soliflucted	sought after
slot winding	smotherable	Socinianize	soliloquies	soul brother
slouch-eared	smother crop	sociography	soliloquise	soul-catcher
slouchiness	smother-kiln	sociolectal	soliloquist	soulfulness
slouchingly	snail darter	sociologese	soliloquize	sound as a nut
slough grass	snail-flower	sociologism	solipsismal	sound asleep
sloven-wagon	snake-doctor	sociologist	solipsistic	sound camera
slow and sure	snake feeder	sociologize	solmisation	sound effect
slow bowling	snakes alive	sociometric	solmization	Soundex-code
slow but sure	snakishness	sociopathic	solo climber	sounding fit
slow neutron	snap-brimmed	sockdolager	solubilizer	sounding rod
slow reactor	snapper-back	soda biscuit	Soluble blue	soundlessly
sluggardize	snapper fish	soda counter	solutionist	sound-on-film
slug-setting	snapper grab	soda cracker	solution set	sound-ranger
sluice-valve	snap-shooter	soda process	solvability	sound stripe
slumber away	snapshotter	soddishness	solventless	sound system
slumberland	snatch-block	sodomitical	somasteroid	soup and fish
slumberless	snatch squad	sod planting	somatically	soup kitchen
slumber room	sneck-drawer	so far so good	somatic cell	south-by-east
slumbersome	sneezing gas	soft-centred	somatogenic	south-easter
slumberwear	snickersnee	soft chancre	somatomedin	southeaster
slumgullion	sniperscope	soft-focused	somatoplasm	southerlies
smack-bottom	snob-cricket	soft-hearted	somatotonic	southermost
smack-smooth	snobocratic	soft landing	somatotopic	southernism
Smalcaldian	snobography	soft-shelled	somesthetic	southernize
small change	snooze alarm	soft-skinned	something of	southlander
small circle	snorkelling	soft tissues	somewhere in	southwardly
smallholder	snotty-nosed	so help me God	somewhither	south-wester
small letter	snout-beetle	soil climate	somnambular	southwester
small-minded	snowberries	soil colloid	somnambulic	sovereignly
small stores	snow-blinded	soil extract	somniculous	sovereignty
small wonder	snowboarder	soil polygon	somniferous	Sovietology
smart-alecky	snow bunting	soil profile	somnolently	sow one's oats
smarty-boots	snow cruiser	soil release	Somogyi unit	space charge
smarty-pants	Snowdon lily	soil sampler	songfulness	spacefaring
Smectymnuan	snow-dropper	soil science	Song of Songs	space flight
smellfungus	snow leopard	sojournment	song-plugger	space heater
smilelessly	snow machine	solanaceous	song sparrow	space helmet
smilingness	snowmobiler	solar energy	song stylist	spacelessly
smithereens	snow panther	solar-heated	songwriting	space myopia
smithiantha	snow sparrow	solarimeter	son of a bitch	space needle
Smithsonian	snowy petrel	solar plexus	Son of Heaven	space rocket
smithsonite	snowy plover	solar system	soopolallie	spacer-plate
Smith Square	snuffliness	soldatesque	soothfastly	space-saving
Smith-Trager	snufflingly	soldier bird	soothsaying	space travel
smoke candle	soak-the-rich	soldier-crab	sooty blotch	spaceworthy
smoked glass	soapberries	soldier-fish	sophistical	spade guinea
smoked sheet	soapbox cart	soldierhood	sophistries	spade-shaped
smoke helmet	soap of glass	soldierlike	soporifical	spaghettini
smoke-jumper	soapolallie	soldiership	soprano clef	span-counter
smokelessly	soarability	sole-leather	Sorbo rubber	spandrelled
smoke rocket	sober-minded	solemncholy	soroptimist	spangle gall
smokescreen	sociability	solemnities	Soroptimist	Spaniardize
smoke-signal	social climb	solemnsides	sororicidal	Spanish comb
smoke-tunnel	social élite	solenoglyph	sorrowfully	Spanish foot
smoking room	social ethic	solicitancy	sorrowingly	Spanish goat
smoky quartz	socialistic	solicitress	sort program	Spanish ibex
smoochiness	social order	solid-bodied	sort routine	Spanish iris
smooth-faced	social scale	solid colour	SOS redouble	Spanish lime
smooth hound	social space	solid-hoofed	soteriology	Spanish Main
smoothingly	social whale	solid sender	sottishness	Spanish moss

Spanishness	speculative	spifflicate	splash party	spray region
Spanish plum	speculatory	spiflicated	splashplate	spread-adder
Spanish tile	speculatrix	spike-bozzle	splash-proof	spread-eagle
Spanish wood	speech chain	spike Celtic	splat-quench	spreadeagle
spanker-boom	speech-house	spike-fiddle	splay-footed	spreadingly
span loading	speechified	spiking curb	splay-legged	spreadsheet
sparganosis	speechifier	spill burner	spleen index	sprightlily
sparingness	speechifies	spina bifida	splendorous	sprig-tailed
sparklessly	speech sound	spinach beet	splenectomy	spring a leak
sparklingly	speed-bowler	spinach jade	spleniculus	spring a luff
sparrow-bill	speedometer	spinach moth	splenorenal	springboard
sparrow-fart	speed-reader	spinal block	splice-piece	spring-clean
sparrowhawk	speedwriter	spinal canal	splinter-bar	spring fever
sparrow-like	speedy trial	spin-allowed	splinter bid	Springfield
sparrow-tail	spelaeology	spinal nerve	split beaver	spring grass
spasmatical	spellbinder	spinal shock	split-minded	spring green
spasmodical	spelling-bee	spin-bowling	split pulley	spring-house
spasmogenic	spend a penny	spindle-back	split-screen	springiness
spasmolysis	spendthrift	spindle cell	split second	springingly
spasmolytic	Spenglerian	spindleless	split stitch	spring onion
spasmophile	Spenglerism	spindle side	split stroke	spring usher
spastically	spermacetic	spindle tree	split ticket	spring water
spathaceous	spermatheca	spindle-wood	spokeswoman	sprinkingly
spathulated	spermatidal	spine-basher	spokeswomen	sprinklered
spatterdash	spermatozoa	spinelessly	spondulicks	spritellier
spatterdock	sperm candle	spinescence	spondylitic	spritualise
spatterware	spermicidal	spine-tailed	spondylitis	spud-bashing
spatulation	sperm morula	spiniferous	spondylosis	spumescence
spatuliform	spermophile	spinigerous	spondylotic	spurge olive
speakeasies	spessartine	spin-lattice	sponge-cakey	spur-leather
speakership	spessartite	spinning top	sponge cloth	spying-glass
Speakership	sphacelated	spinousness	sponge gourd	spy in the cab
speak evil of	sphaeridium	Spinozistic	sponge-swamp	spy in the sky
speak well of	sphaerocone	spinsterdom	spongiology	squail-board
spear tackle	sphagnum bog	spinsterial	sponsorship	squalidness
special area	sphairistic	spinsterian	spontaneity	squander-bug
special case	sphenochasm	spinsterish	spontaneous	squandering
special jury	sphenocrast	spinsterism	spoon-backed	square-built
specialness	spherically	spinulation	spoon-bender	square dance
specialogue	spherocytic	spiny lizard	spoon-billed	square drive
specialties	spherograph	spiraculate	sporidesmin	square perch
special vert	spheroidism	spiral-bound	sporidiolum	square piano
specieshood	spheroidize	spiraliform	sporiferous	square serif
species pair	spherometer	spirillosis	sporogenous	squarrosely
species-poor	spheroplast	spiritistic	sporogonium	squarrulose
species-rich	spherosomal	spirit level	sporophytic	squash-berry
species rose	spherulitic	spiritually	sportsmanly	squashiness
specifiable	sphincteral	spiritualty	sports shirt	squatterdom
specificate	sphinctered	spirituelle	sportswoman	squat thrust
specificity	sphincteric	spirit world	sportswomen	squaw winter
specimen-box	sphingosine	spirketting	sporulation	squeakiness
specklessly	sphragistes	spirochaete	spotlighter	squeamishly
spectacular	sphygmogram	spirography	spotted deer	squeeze bunt
spectatress	sphygmology	spirometric	spotted dick	squeeze lens
spectrality	sphyrelaton	spiroplasma	Spotted Dick	squeeze play
spectrogram	spic and span	spitfire-jib	spottedness	squeeze tube
spectrology	spiculation	spitsticker	spotted wilt	squinny-eyed
spectrotype	spider conch	spittle-ball	spot-welding	squintingly
specularite	spider plant	Spitzenberg	sprat-barley	squirearchy
specular orb	spider-table	splashboard	spraunciest	Squirearchy
speculation	spider veins	splashguard	sprawlingly	squirocracy
speculatist	spiderwebby	splashiness	spray brooch	squirrel-dog

squirrelish	stand at stud	statutorily	stenography	stimulation
squirrelled	stand camera	statuvolent	stenohaline	stimulative
squishiness	stand in line	statuvolism	stenohydric	stimulatory
stab-and-drag	stand in with	staunchness	stenopodium	sting-tailed
Stabat Mater	stand neuter	staurolitic	stenotyping	stink beetle
stab-culture	stand of arms	stauroscope	stenotypist	stinking bug
stabilitate	stand-offish	stave church	stentmaster	stinking gum
stable block	standoffish	stay-stomach	stentorious	stinking yew
stacked head	stand sentry	stay the pace	step-bearing	stipendiary
stacked heel	stand surety	St Bruno lily	stepbrother	stipendless
stactometer	stand-to-arms	steadfastly	step flaking	stipitiform
stadiometer	staphylinid	steady-going	step forward	stipulation
stadtholder	Star Chamber	steady state	stephanotis	stipulative
staff of life	starchiness	steakburger	step-pyramid	stipulatory
staff system	starch-water	steak hammer	step this way	stir a finger
staff writer	star-crossed	steal a match	stercobilin	stirrup bone
stage centre	Stark effect	stealthiest	stereoblock	stirrup iron
stage design	stark naught	steam boiler	stereograph	stirrupless
stage effect	star-lighted	steam-distil	stereometer	stirrup pump
stage fright	star network	steam engine	stereometry	stirrup-vase
stage-manage	Star of David	steamfitter	stereophony	St John's wort
stage-player	star-studded	steam hammer	stereophoto	St Kilda wren
stage rights	start button	steam-heater	stereoscope	stock bowler
stage school	starter home	steam-jacket	stereoscopy	stockbroker
stage-struck	star-thistle	steam-launch	stereotaxic	stock-father
stageworthy	starting-off	steam-packet	stereotaxis	stockholder
stagflation	startlement	steam plough	stereotyped	Stockholmer
stagger-bush	startlingly	steam-raiser	stereotyper	stockinette
staggerment	star-tracker	steamroller	stereotypic	stocking cap
staggerwort	start school	steam shovel	sterigmatic	stocking-net
stag-hunting	star vehicle	steam-vessel	sterile-male	stockjobber
staging area	stasipatric	stearic acid	stern-chaser	stockkeeper
staging post	State-church	steatopygia	sternohyoid	stock market
stainlessly	statelihood	steatopygic	sternutator	stocktaking
stake a claim	stateliness	steel-bender	stethograph	stoepsitter
stake-bodies	stately home	steel driver	stethometer	stoicalness
stake-driver	statemental	steel-framed	stethometry	Stokes–Adams
stakeholder	state-monger	steel guitar	stethophone	Stokes' aster
Stake of Zion	state of life	steelheader	stethoscope	Stolichnaya
staktometer	state of play	steelworker	stethoscopy	stomach-ache
stalactical	State-prison	steeple-bush	stevedorage	stomachfuls
stalactitae	State rights	steeplejack	stevedoring	stomachical
stalactital	State school	steeplewise	stevengraph	stomachless
stalactited	state secret	steerage-way	Stevengraph	stomach pump
stalactites	statesmanly	steering box	stewardship	stomach tube
stalactitic	stateswoman	steering-oar	stewing beef	stomach-worm
stalagmitic	state vector	steerswoman	stichometry	stomatology
Stalinesque	static water	stegosaurid	stick around	stomp ground
Stalin organ	station-bill	stegosaurus	stick-figure	stone circle
stalk switch	station hand	Stella Maris	stick-handle	stone-colour
stall-holder	station head	stellarator	stick insect	stone curlew
stallholder	station-line	Steller's jay	stickleback	stonecutter
stall-keeper	station pole	stellionate	stick out for	stone-getter
stall-reader	statistical	stellularly	stick-shaker	stone-ginger
stall shower	statoconium	St Elmo's fire	stiff-necked	stoneground
stalwartism	stator blade	stem-rooting	stifle-joint	Stone Indian
Stambouline	statuomania	stem-winding	stilbestrol	stone marten
stamp office	status group	stencilling	still and all	stone-plover
standardise	statute-book	Stender dish	stiltedness	stoneroller
standardize	statute fair	Stendhalian	stilt-heeled	stone stripe
stand at abay	statute mile	stenobathic	stilt-plover	stonewaller
stand at ease	statute-roll	stenocardia	stimulating	stonewashed

stone-weight	strap handle	strike hands	stultiloquy	subjectable
stoneworker	straphanger	strike lucky	stumblingly	subjectedly
stool-pigeon	strap-shaped	strike short	stump jumper	subjecthood
stoop labour	strata-bound	string along	stump-orator	subjectible
stop a packet	strata title	stringboard	stump-tailed	subjectless
stop-netting	strategetic	stringently	stun grenade	subjectship
Stoppardian	strategical	stringiness	stuntedness	subject-term
stop payment	stratocracy	string-piece	stupidities	subjugation
stopperless	stratopause	stringy-bark	stupor mundi	subjunction
stop short at	straw ballot	strionigral	Sturge—Weber	subjunctive
stop the show	straw basher	strioscopic	style critic	sublanguage
stop the tide	straw colour	striped bass	style-setter	sublethally
stop your gab	strawflower	striped tuna	styliferous	sublettable
storability	straw-hatter	strip-mining	stylishness	sublimation
storage cell	straw-needle	strip-search	stylization	sublimatory
storage life	straw-yellow	stripteaser	stylography	sublimeness
storage ring	streakiness	strobe light	stylometric	sublimified
storage unit	streak plate	strobe pulse	stylopodium	sublittoral
storage wall	streamingly	stroboscope	Stymphalian	subluminous
store-bought	streamlined	stroboscopy	stypticness	subluxation
store church	streamliner	strobotorch	Stypven time	submarginal
storekeeper	stream-works	Stroh violin	suasiveness	submergence
store the kin	street child	stroke-maker	subaerially	submergible
storm cellar	street cries	stromateoid	subagencies	submersible
storm centre	street fight	Strombolian	subarcuated	subminister
storm-collar	street floor	strong drink	sub-assembly	submissible
storm petrel	street-legal	strong force	Sub-Atlantic	submittable
storm-signal	street level	strongfully	subaudition	submultiple
storm-stayed	street light	strong grade	subaxillary	submunition
storm-system	street price	strong house	sub-basement	subordinacy
storm troops	streetproof	strong joint	subcategory	subordinary
storm window	streetscape	strong point	subcellarer	subordinate
story editor	street-smart	strong water	subcellular	subornation
storyteller	street style	strong woman	subclinical	subornative
stout fellow	street value	strong woods	subcontract	subpectoral
stove-enamel	strengthful	strongyloid	subcontrary	subpetiolar
stove lifter	strengthily	strontium-90	subcortical	subphonemic
stow-boating	strenuosity	stroppiness	subcritical	subprioress
straddle-bob	strenuously	struck joint	subcultural	subrational
straddle-bug	strep throat	structurate	subdeaconry	subregional
straggliest	stressed out	structurism	subdelegate	subrogation
straight-arm	stressfully	structurist	subdelirium	subscapular
straight-cut	stress grade	structurize	subdiaconal	subscribe to
straight eye	stress-group	struthonian	subdistrict	subscripted
straightish	stress-timed	struttingly	subdivision	subsemitone
straight job	stretchable	stubble-fire	subdivisive	subsensible
straight leg	stretch mark	stub-feather	subdolously	subsensuous
straight man	stretchneck	stub-mortise	subdominant	sub-sequence
straight off	strewn field	stub station	subduedness	subsequence
straight-out	strictarian	student card	sub-economic	subsequence
straight-run	strict tempo	studenthood	subfamilies	subserviate
straight tip	stride level	student lamp	subfraction	subservient
straightway	stridulator	studentless	subglabrous	subsistence
strain gauge	strigillate	student-like	subglobular	subspecific
strainingly	strike a blow	studentship	subgovernor	sub-standard
strainmeter	strike a line	studiedness	subgrouping	substandard
strait-laced	strike a path	studio couch	subharmonic	substantial
Straits-born	strike-bound	studio party	subhumanity	substantive
stramineous	strikebound	stud welding	subincision	substituend
Strangelove	strike-break	study circle	subirrigate	substituent
strangeness	strikebreak	stuffing box	subitaneous	substituted
strangulate	strike force	stultifying	subjacently	substituter

substration	sugar-fungus	sunlighting	suppeditate	survivalism
substrative	sugar glider	sunny side up	supper dance	survivalist
subsumption	sugar-loafed	sun-painting	suppliantly	survival kit
subsumptive	sugar of lead	sun-scorpion	supplicator	susceptance
subtabulate	sugar of milk	sunshine law	supply house	susceptible
subtacksman	sugar trough	sun-stricken	supply-teach	susceptibly
sub-teenager	suggestable	suntan cream	supportable	suscitation
subterminal	suggestible	superabound	supportably	suspectable
subthalamic	sugillation	superaerial	supportasse	suspectuous
subthalamus	suicidality	supercargos	support band	suspendible
subtraction	suicide pact	super-charge	support cost	suspenseful
subtractive	suicidology	supercharge	supportless	suspensible
subtreasury	suitability	supercilium	support line	suspiration
subtropical	suitcaseful	supercooled	supportress	sustainable
subtruncate	suit of court	super-de-luxe	supposition	sustainably
subumbrella	suit oneself	superessive	suppositive	sustainedly
suburbanise	suit-service	superfamily	suppository	sustainment
suburbanism	suits my book	superfatted	suppressant	susurration
suburbanite	sulphanilic	superfemale	suppression	svarabhakti
suburbanity	sulphate ion	superficial	suppressive	swag-bellied
suburbanize	Sulphatriad	superficies	suppuration	swagger cane
suburbicary	sulpholipid	superfinely	suppurative	swagger coat
subvertible	sulphurator	superfluent	suprafacial	swallowable
subvertical	sulphur bath	superfluity	supralethal	swallow-dive
subvocalize	sulphureous	superfluous	supralineal	swallow fork
succedaneum	sulphuretum	superfusate	supralinear	swallow-hole
successless	sulphur-tree	superfusion	supralunary	swallow-kite
succinctory	sulphur tuft	supergalaxy	suprameatal	swallow-like
succinimide	sulphurweed	superheated	suprascript	swallowtail
succourable	sulphydrate	superheater	suprasellar	swallow-tick
succourless	sultanesque	superheroes	supraspinal	swallowwort
succulently	summability	superimpose	suprasterol	swamp laurel
succumbency	summariness	superinduce	supremacism	swamp plough
such-and-such	summational	superinfect	supremacist	swamp privet
such another	summatively	superintend	Suprematism	swamp rabbit
sucking-disc	summer apple	superinvest	suprematist	swan-hopping
sucking-fish	summer cloud	superioress	supremeness	swan-marking
suction lift	summer-dream	superiority	surface blow	sward-cutter
suction pipe	summer-field	superjacent	surface film	swarmer cell
suction pump	summer grape	superlative	surfaceless	swarthiness
suction stop	summer house	superlunary	surface mail	swartrutter
sudden death	summeriness	supermarine	surface-road	swashbuckle
suede-footed	summer lodge	supermarket	surface wave	swath-turner
Suess effect	summer-prune	supermundal	surf-casting	swear an oath
Suess wiggle	summersault	supernatant	surficially	sweat equity
suet-brained	summer snipe	supernature	surgeon-bird	sweater girl
suet pudding	summer stock	supernormal	surgeonfish	sweating pen
sufferingly	summer-tilth	superoctave	surgeonship	sweating-tub
sufficience	summerwards	superscribe	Surgicenter	Swede-basher
sufficiency	summit level	superscript	surpassable	swede turnip
sufficingly	summonsable	supersedure	surprisable	Swede turnip
suffixation	summum bonum	supersexual	surprisedly	sweet alison
suffocating	sumptuosity	supersonics	surrebuttal	sweet as a nut
suffocation	sumptuously	superstrata	surrebutter	sweet cherry
suffocative	sum-totalize	superstrate	surrenderee	sweet cicely
Suffolk bang	Sunday child	superstring	surrenderor	sweet clover
suffraganal	Sunday joint	superstruct	surrogation	sweet dreams
suffragette	Sunday lunch	supersubtle	surrounding	sweet fennel
suffumigate	Sunday punch	supertanker	Sursum corda	sweet orange
sugar-almond	sun-drenched	supervision	surturbrand	sweet pepper
sugar-baking	sunken fence	supervisory	surveillant	sweet potato
sugar-coated	sunlessness	suppedaneum	survival bag	sweet rocket

sweet singer	Sylvestrian	systematise	take-home pay	tank-farming
sweet sultan	symbolistic	systematism	take in a reef	tantalizing
sweet violet	symmetallic	systematist	take it on one	tap-changing
sweet yarrow	symmetrical	systematize	take it out of	tape guipure
swee waxbill	sympathetic	Szechuanese	take it out on	tape machine
swelled head	sympathizer	Szechwanese	take its toll	tape-measure
swell-headed	sympetalous	tabernacled	take leave of	taphonomist
swept valley	symphonious	table-centre	take leave to	taphrogenic
swept volume	symphyllous	table-decker	take lessons	tapping coil
swift-footed	symplectite	table-moving	take lightly	tapping-hole
Swiftianism	sympodially	table napkin	take offence	taradiddler
swift-winged	symposiarch	Table Office	take on board	tarantulate
swim-bladder	symptomatic	table-rapper	take one's way	tarantulous
Swinburnian	symptomless	table-screen	take on trust	taratantara
swine-backed	synagogical	table stakes	takeover bid	Tarbuck knot
swine's cress	synapticula	table talker	take pride in	tare and tret
swine's grass	synaptology	table tennis	take service	target organ
swing bowler	synaptosome	tabletopped	take station	tarnishable
swing-bridge	synchromesh	tablet paper	take stock in	tar-pavement
swingeingly	Synchromism	table-turner	take stock of	tarradiddle
swingle-hand	Synchromist	taboparesis	take tea with	tarry-breeks
swingletree	synchronise	tabular berg	take the bent	tarsoplasty
swing mirror	synchronism	tabular spar	take the cake	tartar sauce
swing needle	synchronist	tacheometer	take the helm	Tartufferie
swingometer	synchronize	tacheometry	take the piss	Tarzanesque
swing-ticket	synchronous	tachometric	take the road	tassel grass
swinishness	synchro-swim	tachycardia	take the veil	tastelessly
Swiss banker	synchrotron	tachygraphy	take the word	tattie-bogle
Swiss cheese	synclinally	tachypnoeic	take thought	tau particle
Swiss-German	syncopation	tachysterol	take to heart	taurocholic
Swiss muslin	syncyanosis	taciturnity	take trial of	tautochrone
switch-blade	syndesmosis	tacking iron	take trouble	tautologies
switchblade	syndesmotic	tackle-block	take warning	tautologise
switchboard	syndicalism	tackle-house	talebearing	tautologism
switch-grass	syndicalist	tackling bag	talent scout	tautologist
switch-knife	syndicateer	tactfulness	tale-telling	tautologize
switch-plant	syndication	tadpole-fish	Taliacotian	tautologous
switch-tower	syndiploidy	taeniae coli	talkatively	tautomerism
swivel chair	synecdochic	tagliatelle	talking book	tautomerize
swollen head	synechthran	tagmemicist	talking cure	tautousian
swollenness	synergistic	tag question	talking drum	taxableness
sword-bearer	synesthesia	t'ai chi ch'uan	talking film	tax gatherer
sword-cutler	syngnathous	tail-bandage	talking head	taxidermist
sword dancer	synodically	tail-dragger	talking shop	taxi service
sword-in-hand	synonymical	tail feather	talk through	taxonomical
swordplayer	synorogenic	tail general	tallow-faced	Tchekhovian
sybaritical	synovectomy	tailor's tack	tallow shrub	tea-canister
sycamore-fig	synsemantic	tail special	tally system	tea ceremony
sycophantic	synsepalous	tail-spindle	Talmudistic	teachership
sycophantly	syntactical	tail-walking	Talmud Torah	teacher's pet
Sydneysider	syntagmatic	taintlessly	tambour desk	teaching aid
syllabaries	syntaxially	take a chance	tambour hook	teach school
syllabarium	syntectonic	take a flight	tambour-lace	tea district
syllabation	synthesiser	take against	tameability	tea-drinking
syllabicate	synthesizer	take a header	Tamla Motown	tea interval
syllabicity	synthetical	take a powder	Tammany Hall	tear and wear
syllabified	syntrophism	take a tumble	tammie norie	tearfulness
syllabifies	syphilology	take a view of	tam-o'-shanter	tear-jerking
sylleptical	syrup of figs	take a wicket	tamper-proof	tear off a bit
syllogistic	syssarcoses	take by storm	Tanganyikan	tear-stained
sylvestrene	syssarcosis	take chances	tangibility	teaspoonful
sylvestrian	systematics	take counsel	tank circuit	tea-strainer

technically	telopeptide	tergeminous	tetrarchate	the Die-hards
Technicolor	temerarious	termination	tetrarchies	the Divinity
technocracy	temperament	terminative	tetravalent	the Dominion
technofreak	temperately	terminatory	tetrazolium	The Elements
technologic	temperative	terministic	tetrazotize	the five wits
technophile	temperature	terminology	tetter-berry	the flower of
technophobe	temper-screw	termitaries	tettigoniid	theftuously
techno-speak	tempestuous	termitarium	Teutonicism	the game is up
tectibranch	temple block	termite-hill	Teutophobia	the glad hand
tectonician	temple mould	term of years	Texas Ranger	the glad mitt
tectosphere	tempo giusto	ternary form	textbookish	the greatest
tectospinal	temporalism	terpeneless	textile cone	the great wen
tediousness	temporalist	Terpsichore	text-picture	the hale ware
teeny-bopper	temporality	terra ignota	textureless	the half of it
teetotalish	temporalize	terraqueous	Thackerayan	the height of
teetotalism	temporaries	Terra Sienna	thalamotomy	the high toby
teetotalist	temporarily	terreneness	thalidomide	the infinite
teetotaller	tempo rubato	terrestrial	thallophyte	theirselves
tegestology	Tempranillo	terre-tenant	thanatology	the last rose
tegumentary	temptatious	terribility	thanatopsis	the length of
Tehuelchian	tenableness	terricoline	thank kindly	the long robe
Teilhardian	tenaciously	terricolous	thanklessly	the Lord's day
teknonymous	tenant right	terrigenous	thanksgiver	thelytokous
tektosphere	tendentious	territorial	thankworthy	the Main Plot
telebanking	tender-dying	Territorian	Thatcherism	the majority
telebetting	tender-eared	territories	Thatcherite	the man for me
telebroking	tender plant	territorium	that depends	the mind's eye
telecentric	tendon organ	terroristic	that is to say	the miseries
telecommand	tenebrionid	tertianship	that's an idea	the Missouri
telecommute	tenebrosity	tertium quid	that's the lot	the moon's age
telecontrol	tenementary	tessaraglot	that's torn it	more part
telecottage	ten feet tall	tessellated	that was that	the Most High
telediphone	tennis court	testability	thaumatrope	the Mountain
telegrapher	tennis dress	testamental	thaumaturge	the Movement
telegraphic	tennis elbow	test batsman	thaumaturgy	the naked ape
telekinesis	Tennysonian	test-furnace	the Almighty	thenceafter
telekinetic	Tenon's space	testiculate	the ancients	thenceforth
telemeeting	tenorrhaphy	testimonial	theanthropy	the noble art
telemessage	ten out of ten	testimonies	the Atlantic	theobromine
teleologies	tenselessly	testimonium	theatre club	theocentric
teleologism	tensile test	testudinate	theatre-goer	theocracies
teleologist	tensiometer	tetanically	theatregoer	Theocritean
telepathise	tensiometry	tetanolysin	theatre-land	theodolitic
telepathist	tensionally	tetrachoric	theatreless	theogonical
telepathize	tensionless	tetracyclic	theatre-list	the old enemy
telephonist	tension wood	tetradactyl	theatre seat	the old story
teleprinter	tensor field	tetradecane	the Big Apple	theological
telerobotic	tensor force	tetradrachm	the Big Drink	theologizer
telescopist	tentability	tetragonous	the big smoke	the Olympics
Telescopium	tentaculate	tetragynous	the Big Three	theomachies
teleseismic	tentaculite	tetrahedral	the biter bit	theomachist
teleshopper	tentatively	tetrahedron	the Brethren	theomorphic
telesthesia	tent-pegging	tetrahydric	the bum's rush	theophagous
teletherapy	tent-trailer	tetralogies	the business	theophanies
televiewing	tent village	tetramerism	the Caudillo	theophanism
televisable	tenuousness	tetramerous	the Cenotaph	theophorous
tellings-off	tenure track	tetrandrous	the Chisholm	theorematic
tell the time	teonanacatl	tetraphonic	the cloister	theoretical
tell volumes	tephramancy	tetraplegia	the Corsican	theory-laden
telmatology	teratogenic	tetraplegic	the Creation	theosophies
telocentric	terbutaline	tetraploidy	the creature	theosophism
telodendron	terebration	tetrapodous	the Crescent	theosophist

theosophize	the wrong way	Thoreauvian	thrust-plane	tiller-chain
the other day	thickheaded	thorium-lead	thrust-shaft	tiller-lines
the other man	thick-leaved	thorny devil	thrust stage	tiller shoot
the outer bar	thick-lipped	thorough-pin	Thucydidean	timber beast
the Prophets	thicknesser	thorough-wax	thujaplicin	timber berth
the Psalmist	thick-witted	those kind of	thumb-bottle	timber drive
therapeusis	thieves' hole	those sort of	thumb-finger	timber-frame
Therapeutae	thigh-length	thoughtless	thumb-lancet	timber hitch
therapeutic	thigmotaxis	thoughtness	thumb-piston	timber-limit
theraphosid	thimblefuls	thought-read	thumb-sucker	time and tide
thereabouts	thimble-like	thought-wave	thunder-ball	time average
therebeside	thingamabob	thowthistle	thunder-bird	time-bargain
the Redeemer	thingamajig	thrasonical	thunderbird	time capsule
theretofore	thingliness	thread belay	thunderboat	time charter
theretoward	thingumabob	thread-board	thunderbolt	time deposit
therewithal	thingumajig	thread-guide	thunderclap	time-expired
therewithin	thingummies	threadiness	thunder-dint	timefulness
there you are	think back to	thread-paper	thunder-drop	timekeeping
theriolatry	think bubble	threatening	thunder-drum	time machine
theriomorph	thinking-box	threatfully	thunder-gust	time-payment
thermalling	Thinking Day	three-banded	thunderhead	time-serving
thermal unit	think it long	three cheers	thunderless	time-sharing
thermically	think it much	three-colour	thunder-pump	time-slicing
thermionics	think much of	three-corner	thuriferous	time-wasting
thermocline	think-tanker	three-decker	thus and thus	timocracies
thermoduric	thin red line	three-double	thwartingly	tin-bounding
thermograph	thin section	three-figure	thwart-ships	tinker's cuss
thermokarst	thin-skinned	threefoldly	thyme-leaved	tin-pan alley
thermolysin	thio-alcohol	three-footed	thymoleptic	Tin Pan Alley
thermolysis	thiocyanate	three-gaited	thymus gland	tinsmithing
thermolytic	thioguanine	three-handed	thyroiditis	tiny garment
thermometer	thiopentone	three-in-hand	thyrotropin	tip of the hat
thermometry	thiophanate	three-legged	thysanurous	tip one's mitt
thermonasty	thioredoxin	three-master	tibiotarsal	Tironensian
thermophile	third cousin	three-piecer	tibiotarsus	Tirthankara
thermophone	third-degree	three-seater	ticket-agent	tissue fluid
thermopower	Third Estate	three-square	ticket booth	tissue-lymph
Thermopylae	third eyelid	three-valued	ticking bomb	tissue paper
thermoscope	third finger	thriftiness	tickled pink	titanaugite
thermotaxic	third market	thrift store	tickle-grass	titanically
thermotaxis	third person	thrillingly	tickler coil	Titanically
thermotical	third stream	throatiness	tick pyaemia	titanothere
theropodous	thirstiness	throat-pouch	tick-tack-toe	Titianesque
Thersitical	thirty-eight	throat-strap	tick-trefoil	titillation
the same very	thirty-seven	throbbingly	tiddlywinky	titillatory
thesaurosis	thirty-three	thrombocyte	tie-breaking	title-holder
thesauruses	thirty-two-mo	thrombolite	Tiepolesque	tit magazine
these kind of	this and that	thromboxane	tierce major	titrimetric
these sort of	this evening	through-ball	tierce minor	tits and bums
the shoe fits	this instant	through-band	tie the rap on	titteringly
thesis-novel	this morning	through-bolt	tiger beetle	titty-bottle
the size of it	thistle-bird	through-deck	tiger-flower	T-lymphocyte
thesmothete	thistledown	throughfall	tiger-hunter	toad's cheese
Thespianism	thistle-head	throughflow	tiger-stripe	toad's eye tin
theta rhythm	thistle-like	through-gang	tight barrel	toad-stabber
the third sex	this-worldly	through-pass	tight corner	to advantage
the Troubles	thitherward	through-toll	tight-fisted	toast-colour
the unco guid	thixotropic	throw a punch	tight-lacing	toaster-oven
the very idea	thole amends	throw stones	tight-lipped	toastmaster
the very same	Thomistical	throw weight	tigroid body	tobacco dove
the wonder is	thoracotomy	thrust block	tile-hanging	tobacco-fish
the Writings	thoreaulite	thrust fault	till and frae	tobacco-leaf

tobaccoless	to one's shame	Totten trust	trades union	transfigure
tobacco lord	tooth-billed	totter-grass	tradeswoman	transfinite
tobacco moth	toothlessly	totteringly	tradeswomen	transfixion
tobacconist	tooth-marked	touch a nerve	trading post	transfluent
tobacco pipe	tooth powder	touch bottom	traditional	transformer
tobacco-root	toothsomely	touched gold	traditioned	transform up
tobacco-shop	top dressing	touch-finder	traditioner	transfusion
tobacco worm	topinambour	touch-in-goal	traducement	transfusive
to begin with	toplessness	touch-needle	trafficable	transglobal
Tobias night	toploftical	touch screen	trafficator	transhumant
Tobin bronze	topocentric	touch tablet	traffic cone	transiently
toboggan-cap	topographer	touch the ark	trafficking	transilient
tobogganing	topographic	touch-typing	traffic lane	transitable
tobogganist	topological	touch-typist	trafficless	transit camp
tocological	top one's part	tough-minded	traffic sign	transit-duty
toddlerhood	topping-lift	toujours gai	tragedienne	transitival
toddy-lifter	toppingness	tourbillion	tragédienne	transit-pass
toddy-tapper	top sergeant	tour de force	tragedietta	transit visa
toenadering	torch-bearer	touristical	trageremics	translatese
Toepler pump	torch-flower	tourist trap	Trager–Smith	translation
toffee apple	torch-holder	tous-les-mois	tragicality	translative
toffee-brown	torchon lace	tout compris	tragic irony	translatory
toffee-nosed	torch singer	tout de suite	tragicomedy	translatrix
toga virilis	tormentedly	tout le monde	trailbaston	translocase
toggle joint	tormentress	tow-coloured	trail-blazer	translocate
togt licence	tormentuous	Tower weight	trailblazer	translucent
toile de Jouy	tornado-lamp	to what avail	trailerable	translunary
toilet brush	Torontonian	towing light	trailer camp	transmarine
toilet-cover	torpedo boat	town council	trailer home	transmittal
toilet-glass	torpedo-body	townishness	trailer park	transmitted
toilet paper	torpedo-like	town marshal	trailer tent	transmitter
toilet table	torpedo tube	town meeting	trail-riding	transmortal
toilet-train	torque motor	town planner	train-bearer	transnature
toilet water	torrent-duck	townscaping	trained band	transnormal
tolbutamide	torrentuous	townspeople	traineeship	transocular
tolerablish	Torridonian	townsperson	training-day	transom-knee
tolerogenic	torsibility	toxicogenic	train-jumper	transpadane
toll and team	torsiograph	toxophilite	trainmaster	transparent
toll an entry	torsionally	toxoplasmic	train ticket	transphasor
Tom-and-Jerry	torsionless	toxoplasmin	traitorhood	transpierce
tomato juice	torsion test	trabeculate	traitorship	transponder
tomboyishly	torso-tosser	tracasserie	trammelling	transportal
tomentulose	torticollis	trace fossil	tranquility	transportee
Tommy-cooker	torturesome	tracelessly	tranquilize	transporter
tommy-gunner	torturously	tracheotomy	transaction	transposase
Tommy system	to shipboard	tracker ball	transalpine	transracial
Tommy talker	to start with	track events	trans-border	transsexual
tomographer	totalisator	track-laying	transcalent	transuranic
tomographic	totalizator	tracklement	transceiver	Transvaaler
tone cluster	total recall	tracklessly	transcreate	transversal
tone control	totemically	track record	transcriber	Transverter
tonemically	to the east of	track-suited	transdermal	transvestic
tonetically	to the height	track system	transductor	trap and ball
tongue thrum	to the letter	track-walker	transection	trap-drummer
tonic accent	to the marrow	tractorcade	transferase	trapeze-line
tonic-clonic	to the moment	tractor feed	transfer fee	trapeziform
tonological	tothersider	tradability	transfer ink	trapezoidal
to no purpose	to the tune of	trade-master	transferral	Trappistine
tonquin bean	to the west of	trade places	transferred	trap-shooter
tonsillitic	totipalmate	trade plates	transferrer	trascinando
tonsillitis	totipotence	trade school	transferrin	travel agent
tool-dresser	totipotency	trade secret	transfer RNA	travellable

traversable	tribulation	triplet code	trouser-clip	tub-thumpery
traverse-map	tribuneship	triple tiara	trouser-cuff	tub-thumping
traverse rod	tribunitial	triplet lily	trouserless	tubular tyre
Traxcavator	tribunitian	triquetrous	trouser suit	tucking-comb
treacheries	tributaries	trisepalous	trucidation	tucking-mill
treacherous	tributarily	tristichous	truck camper	Tudorbethan
tread on eggs	triceratops	tristimulus	trucklingly	tuft-hunting
tread-softly	trichinosis	trisyllabic	truck-master	tug aircraft
treasonable	trichomonad	trisyllable	truck system	tug at the oar
treasonably	trichomonal	tritagonist	truculently	tulipomania
treasurable	trichomonas	tritanomaly	true as steel	tulip poplar
treasury tag	trichopathy	tritheistic	true-hearted	tumble-dried
treble agent	trichophagy	Trito-Isaiah	true horizon	tumble-drier
treble rhyme	Trichoptera	tritonality	Trumanesque	tumble-dries
treckschuit	trichotomic	trituration	trumpet-bird	tumble-dryer
tree babbler	trichromasy	triumphally	trumpet call	tumbler-cart
treecreeper	trickle-down	triumphancy	trumpet-fish	tumblerfuls
tree cricket	tricksiness	triumphator	trumpet-leaf	tumbling-bay
tree diagram	tricoloured	triumph-gate	trumpetless	tumbling-box
tree network	tricolumnar	triumvirate	trumpet-lily	tumefacient
tree of Diana	triconodont	trivet table	trumpet-pipe	tumefaction
tree of Jesse	tricornered	trivializer	trumpet stop	tumescently
tree sparrow	tridecanoic	trivialness	trumpet-tree	tummelberry
tree surgeon	tri-dominium	Trobriander	trumpet-vine	tummy button
tree surgery	triennially	trochal disc	trumpet-weed	tumoricidal
tree swallow	trierarchal	trochophore	trump marine	tumorigenic
tree warbler	trifluralin	troglobiont	trump signal	tumour virus
tree-worship	trifoliated	troglodytic	truncheoned	tunableness
trefoliated	trifurcated	troglophile	trundle-head	tunefulness
trellis-work	triggerable	Trojan horse	trundle-tail	tungstenite
tremblement	trigger area	Trojan Horse	trunk-engine	tunica media
tremblingly	trigger fish	trolley-head	trunk murder	tuning meter
tremolo stop	triggerfish	trolley-pole	trunk-turtle	tuning-slide
tremulation	trigger-hair	trolley shop	trunnel-head	tunnel diode
tremulously	triggerless	trolley-wire	trunnel-hole	tunnel house
trenchantly	trigger tube	trolly-lolly	trust-buster	tunnel-vault
trencher cap	trihydrated	trombiculid	trustbuster	Tupi-Guarani
trencherful	trilobation	tropaeolin D	trustee bank	turban gourd
trencherman	trimellitic	trophobiont	trusteeship	turban shell
trenchermen	trimestrial	trophoblast	trustworthy	turbination
trench fever	trimetrical	trophogenic	truth to tell	turbiniform
trench-knife	Trimetrogen	tropholytic	trying-plane	turbocharge
trench mouth	trimming tab	trophophore	try it on with	turbo-diesel
trend-setter	trimorphism	trophoplasm	try one's hand	turboramjet
trendsetter	trimorphous	trophotaxis	try one's luck	turbosphere
trepanation	Trinidadian	trophozoite	trypanocide	turbulently
trepidation	Trinitarian	trophozooid	trypanosoma	Turcologist
trepidatory	Trinity term	trophy-money	trypanosome	turcopolier
trestle-tree	trinklement	tropicality	trypsinogen	Turgenevian
trestle-work	trinomially	tropicalize	T-shirt dress	turgescence
triadically	tripalmitin	tropomyosin	tubectomies	turgescency
trial lawyer	triparental	troposphere	tube-feeding	turkey-beard
trial trench	tripartisan	tropotactic	tuberculate	turkey-berry
triangulate	tri-personal	troth-plight	tuberculize	turkey-shoot
triantelope	tripetalous	trouble lamp	tuberculoid	Turkey stone
triaxiality	tripe velvet	troubleless	tuberculoma	Turkey wheat
triazine dye	triphibious	troublement	tuberculose	Turkish bath
tribalistic	triphyletic	troublesome	tuberculous	Turkishness
tribeswoman	triple agent	trouble spot	tube shelter	Turk's turban
tribeswomen	triple crown	troublously	tubiflorous	turn-and-bank
tribologist	triple point	trough fault	tubocornual	turn a profit
tribrachial	triple rhyme	trough shell	tub-preacher	turn-crowned

Turneresque	typewriting	unalienable	unblinkable	uncompanied
turning-mill	typewritten	unalienably	unblossomed	uncompelled
turnip-ghost	Typhoid Mary	unalienated	unbonneting	uncompleted
turnipology	typicalness	unallocated	unboundable	uncomplexed
turn of speed	typographer	unallowable	unboundedly	uncompliant
turn the cock	typographic	unalterable	unbreakable	uncomplying
turn the tide	typological	unalterably	unbreathing	unconcealed
turn to ashes	tyrannicide	unambiguity	unbrookable	unconceited
turpeth root	tyrannosaur	unambiguous	unbrotherly	unconceived
turret lathe	tyrannously	unambitious	unbudgeable	unconcerned
turret shell	tyroglyphid	unamendable	unbumptious	unconcerted
turtle-crawl	Tyrolean hat	unamplified	unburnished	unconcluded
turtle-grass	tyrosinemia	unanalogous	unburstable	unconcocted
turtle shell	tyrosinosis	unanimously	uncalcified	uncondemned
turtleshell	tyrothricin	unannotated	uncalled for	uncondensed
turtle-stone	tyuyamunite	unannounced	uncancelled	unconducive
Tuscan straw	Uganda Asian	unanswering	uncanniness	unconfessed
tussock land	uillean pipe	unanxiously	uncanonical	unconfident
tussock moth	ulcerogenic	unapostolic	uncanonized	unconfirmed
tussore moth	ulnar artery	unappealing	uncanvassed	unconformed
tussore-silk	ulotrichous	unapplauded	uncapacious	uncongealed
tutti-frutti	Ulsterwoman	unappointed	uncastrated	uncongenial
twaddlesome	Ulsterwomen	unarraigned	uncatalysed	unconnected
twaddle-toed	ulteriority	unarresting	uncatchable	unconquered
Twelfth-cake	ultima Thule	unashamedly	unceasingly	unconscious
twelfth part	ultrafidian	unaspirated	unceilinged	unconsented
twelve-gauge	ultrafilter	unassaulted	uncelestial	unconsigned
twelvemonth	ultramarine	unassertive	uncertainly	unconsonant
twelvepence	ultrametric	unattainted	uncertainty	unconstancy
twelvepenny	ultrasonics	unattempted	uncertified	unconsulted
twelve-toner	ultrastable	unattracted	uncertitude	unconsuming
twenty-eight	ultraviolet	unaugmented	unchainable	uncontained
twig-girdler	umbellately	unauthentic	unchambered	uncontented
twin brother	umbelliform	unavailable	unchartered	uncontested
twin crystal	umbilically	unavailably	unchastened	uncontrived
twin-engined	umbilicated	unavertable	unchastised	unconverted
twinkle roll	umbilicuses	unavertible	uncheckable	unconvicted
twinkle-toed	umboth tithe	unavoidable	uncheckered	unconvinced
twinklingly	umbriferous	unavoidably	unchequered	uncoroneted
twin paradox	unabashable	unawareness	uncherished	uncorrected
twin species	unabashedly	unballasted	unchildlike	uncorrupted
twist barrel	unabolished	unbarbarize	unchiselled	uncorruptly
twisted pair	unabrogated	unbarrelled	unchivalric	uncountable
twitch grass	unacclaimed	unbashfully	unchristian	uncountably
twitchiness	unaccordant	unbeauteous	uncinctured	uncount noun
two-and-eight	unaccounted	unbeautiful	uncivilised	uncourteous
two cultures	unaccusable	unbeclouded	uncivilized	uncourtlike
twofoldness	unadaptable	unbefitting	unclarified	uncouthness
two-handedly	unaddressed	unbeginning	unclassical	uncouthsome
twopenn'orth	unadjourned	unbeknownst	uncleanness	uncrackable
twopenny ale	unadmirable	unbelieving	unclearness	uncreatable
two-yearling	unadoptable	unbendingly	uncleavable	uncrossable
tympaniform	unadvisable	unbeneficed	unclimbable	uncrushable
tympanogram	unadvisably	unbenefited	uncloudedly	uncuckolded
tympanotomy	unadvisedly	unbeseeming	unclubbable	uncunningly
tympan sheet	unaesthetic	unbethought	uncluttered	uncuriously
Tyndall blue	unaffecting	unbetrothed	uncollected	uncurtailed
type-fallacy	unaffianced	unblameable	uncolonized	uncurtained
type founder	unafflicted	unblameably	uncomforted	uncushioned
type foundry	unaffronted	unblemished	uncommanded	uncustomary
typesetting	unagreeable	unblenching	uncommitted	undamnified
type species	unagreeably	unblindfold	uncompacted	undangerous

undauntable
undauntedly
undebauched
undecayable
undeceitful
undeception
undeceptive
undecidable
undecidedly
undecorated
undecylenic
undedicated
undefending
undefiledly
undefinable
undefinably
undefinedly
undeflected
undelayable
undelighted
undelivered
undemanding
undenatured
undenizened
undenounced
undeparting
undepending
undepressed
under a cloud
under-action
underactive
under a curse
under arrest
under a spell
underbearer
underbidder
underbitted
underbodice
underbodies
underbonnet
underbreath
underbridge
under-butler
under canvas
undercharge
underchosen
underclothe
undercolour
undercovert
undercutter
underdamper
underdogger
underemploy
underexpose
under-farmer
under favour
underground
undergrowth
underhammer
underhanded
underheaven
underhonest

underhorsed
underinsure
underinvest
underivable
underivedly
under-keeper
underlessee
underlimbed
underlining
underloaded
under-looker
undermanned
undermasted
under-master
under notice
underoccupy
underparted
underpraise
underreamer
underreckon
underrecord
under-report
underreport
underrun bar
underrunner
under-school
underseller
undersettle
under-sexton
undershorts
undersigned
undersleeve
underspread
understairs
understated
understater
understorey
understream
understrike
undertaking
undertenant
under the sod
under the sun
underthings
under threat
underthrust
undervaluer
under-vassal
under-viewer
under-warden
underweight
underwitted
under-worker
underwriter
undescended
undescribed
undeserving
undesigning
undesirable
undesirably
undespoiled
undestroyed

undeveloped
undeviating
undiagnosed
undignified
undilutedly
undisbanded
undiscerned
undisclosed
undiscussed
undisgraced
undisguised
undislodged
undispelled
undispensed
undispersed
undisplaced
undisproved
undissected
undissolved
undistilled
undistorted
undisturbed
undividable
undividably
undividedly
undivinable
undivisible
undoubtable
undoubtably
undoubtedly
undrainable
undraperied
undreamable
undressable
undrinkable
undrinkably
undubitable
undubitably
undutifully
undyingness
unegotistic
unelaborate
unelectable
unembattled
unembezzled
unembroiled
unemotional
unempirical
unemptiable
unenamoured
unenchanted
unendearing
unendurable
unendurably
unenergetic
unenfeebled
unenjoyable
unenlivened
unentangled
unenterable
unenviously

unepiscopal
unequalable
unequal hour
unequalized
unequalness
unequitable
unequivocal
unescapable
unessential
unethically
unevidenced
unexamining
unexcavated
unexcitable
unexclusive
unexemplary
unexercised
unexhausted
unexhibited
unexistence
unexorcised
unexpanding
unexpansive
unexpectant
unexpensive
unexplained
unexploited
unexplosive
unexpounded
unexpressed
unextracted
unfailingly
unfalsified
unfaltering
unfanatical
unfantastic
unfashioned
unfatiguing
unfavorable
unfavourite
unfeathered
unfeelingly
unfeignedly
unfermented
unfittingly
unfixedness
unflappable
unflappably
unflattened
unflattered
unflavoured
unflinching
unforbidden
unforeknown
unforfeited
unforgeable
unforgetful
unforgiving
unforgotten
unformatted
unfortified
unfortunate

unfoundedly
unfractured
unfrenchify
unfreshness
unfructuous
unfulfilled
unfunniness
unfurnished
ungainfully
ungallantly
ungallantry
ungarmented
ungarnished
ungenerated
ungenteelly
ungentleman
unget-at-able
unglaciated
unglamorous
unglorified
ungodliness
ungospelled
ungraduated
ungraspable
ungratified
unguardedly
unguerdoned
unguessable
unguiculate
unguligrade
unhabitable
unhackneyed
unhandiness
unhappiness
unharboured
unhardiness
unharmfully
unharnessed
unharvested
unhazardous
unhealthful
unhealthier
unhealthily
unheartsome
unheedfully
unheedingly
unhelpfully
unheritable
unhingement
unhopefully
unhumanized
unhurriedly
unhusbanded
unicapsular
unicellular
unicolorate
unicolorous
unicoloured
unicorn bird
unicorn-fish
unicorn-root
unidiomatic

unification	unity of time	unmomentous	unperturbed	unreceptive
unificatory	universally	unmoralized	unperverted	unreclaimed
uniformally	univocality	unmoralness	unpetrified	unrecounted
uniformless	unjaundiced	unmortgaged	unpigmented	unrecovered
uniformness	unjudicious	unmortified	unpiteously	unrecruited
unigeniture	unjustified	unmotivated	unpitifully	unrectified
unignorable	unkemptness	unmountable	unpityingly	unredressed
unignorably	unkingdomed	unmurmuring	unplaceable	unreducible
unijunction	unknowingly	unmusically	unplantable	unreflected
unilamellar	unknownness	unmutilated	unplastered	unrefracted
unilineally	unlaborious	unnaturally	unplausible	unrefrained
unillumined	unlabouring	unnavigable	unplausibly	unrefreshed
unimaginary	unlacquered	unnavigated	unpleadable	unrefusable
unimitative	unlanguaged	unnecessary	unpleasable	unrefutable
unimmediate	unlaundered	unneedfully	unplumbable	unregardful
unimodality	unlearnable	unnervingly	unplumbable	unregarding
unimpeached	unlearnedly	unnourished	unplundered	unregretted
unimpededly	unlevelness	unnutritive	unpolarized	unregulated
unimperious	unliberated	unobjective	unpolemical	unrehearsed
unimportant	unlightened	unobnoxious	unpolitical	unrejoicing
unimpressed	unlightsome	unobservant	unpollarded	unrelatable
unimproving	unlikeliest	unobserving	unpopularly	unrelenting
unimpulsive	unlimitable	unobstinate	unpopulated	unreligious
unincarnate	unlimitedly	unobtrusive	unportioned	unreluctant
unincreased	unliquefied	unobviously	unpossessed	unremaining
unincubated	unlistening	unoccupancy	unpractical	unremittent
unindicated	unliterally	unoffending	unpractised	unremitting
unindulgent	unlocalized	unofficered	unpraisable	unremovable
unindurable	unlocatable	unofficious	unpreaching	unrenewable
uninflected	unlooked-for	unoperating	unpredicted	unrenounced
uninforming	unloverlike	unopposable	unpreferred	unrepayable
uninfringed	unluckiness	unoppressed	unprescient	unrepentant
uningenious	unlucrative	unorganized	unpresented	unrepenting
uninhabited	unluxuriant	unoriginate	unpreserved	unrepressed
uninhibited	unluxurious	unorthodoxy	unpresuming	unreprieved
uninitiated	unmalicious	unpadlocked	unprevented	unreprinted
uninjurious	unmalignant	unpaintable	unprimitive	unrepugnant
uninnocence	unmalleable	unpalatable	unprintable	unrepulsive
uninquiring	unmanliness	unpalatably	unprintably	unreputable
uninscribed	unmasculine	unpalliated	unprocessed	unrequested
uninspected	unmatchable	unparagoned	unprofessed	unrequisite
uninspiring	unmatchably	unparalyzed	unprofiting	unrescinded
uninstalled	unmeaningly	unparcelled	unprojected	unresentful
uninsulated	unmeditated	unpardoning	unpromising	unresenting
uninsurable	unmelodious	unparriable	unprophetic	unresilient
unintuitive	unmemorable	unpassioned	unprotected	unresisting
uninucleate	unmemorably	unpatriotic	unprovoking	unrespected
uninventive	unmentioned	unpatterned	unpublished	unrestfully
uninvitedly	unmercenary	unpausingly	unpurchased	unrestingly
union-basher	unmeritable	unpeaceable	unputrefied	unrestraint
union rustic	unmeritedly	unpeaceably	unqualified	unretentive
uniparental	unmindfully	unpedigreed	unquickened	unretouched
unipersonal	unmisgiving	unpensioned	unquietness	unretracted
unipolarity	unmitigable	unperceived	unquivering	unretrieved
unirrigated	unmitigably	unperfected	unransacked	unreturning
unirritated	unmitigated	unperfectly	unravelling	unrevealing
uniselector	unmixedness	unperformed	unravelment	unrevenging
uniserially	unmockingly	unperishing	unreachable	unreverence
unisexually	unmodulated	unpermanent	unreachably	unrevivable
unitive life	unmoistened	unpermitted	unreadiness	unrewarding
unitiveness	unmolesting	unperplexed	unrealistic	unrighteous
unitization	unmollified	unpersuaded	unreasoning	unromanized

unroughened	unspareable	unthickened	unwithdrawn	uriniferous
unrufflable	unsparingly	unthinkable	unwithering	urinologist
unsaintlike	unsparkling	unthinkably	unwithstood	urochordate
unsandalled	unspeakable	unthriftily	unwitnessed	urodynamics
unsatisfied	unspeakably	untimeously	unwittingly	urogastrone
unsaturable	unspecified	untinctured	unwomanlike	ursine sloth
unsaturated	unspillable	unto oneself	unworkmanly	urticaceous
unsavourily	unspiritual	untoothsome	unworthiest	urticarious
unscannable	unspoilable	untormented	unwoundable	use immunity
unscattered	unsponsored	untouchable	up against it	uselessness
unsceptical	unspottable	untouchably	up-and-coming	user-defined
unscheduled	unspottedly	untraceable	up-and-downer	user-hostile
unscholarly	unsprinkled	untraceably	Upanishadic	usucaptable
unscissored	unsqueamish	untractable	upconverter	uterine tube
unscrambler	unsquelched	untrainable	upgradation	utero-sacral
unscratched	unstability	untravelled	upgradeable	utilitarian
unscribbled	unstaidness	untraversed	upheavement	utility area
unscrutable	unstainable	untreatable	upholstered	utility pole
unseaworthy	unsteadfast	untrembling	upholsterer	utility room
unsectarian	unsteadiest	untremulous	upholstress	utilization
unseductive	unstiffened	untrimmable	up one's alley	Utopianizer
unseemingly	unstillness	untrumpeted	upon the tilt	utraquistic
unseemliest	unstintedly	untrustable	upper circle	utricularia
unsegmented	unstirrable	untunefully	upper-crusty	uveoparotid
unselective	unstoppable	untwistable	upper fourth	vacationist
unselfishly	unstoppably	untypically	upper-middle	vacation job
unsensitive	unstoppered	ununiformed	upper school	vaccination
unsentenced	unstrapping	ununiformly	upper second	vacillation
unseparated	unstrategic	ununionized	upper storey	vacillatory
unseriously	unstrenuous	unupbraided	upper-tendom	vacuolating
unsettledly	unstressful	unusualness	Upper Voltan	vacuolation
unseverable	unstretched	unutterable	upping-block	vacuousness
unshakeable	unstudiedly	unutterably	upright bass	vacuum brake
unshakeably	unstylishly	unvarnished	uprightness	vacuum-clean
unshapeable	unsubduable	unvaryingly	ups and downs	vacuum flask
unsharpened	unsubjected	unvenerable	upsettingly	vacuum gauge
unsharpness	unsubmerged	unventurous	up shit creek	vacuum-tight
unshattered	unsubverted	unveracious	upstretched	vagabondage
unsheltered	unsucceeded	unversified	upthrusting	vagabondish
unshiftable	unsuccoured	unviability	uptightness	vagabondism
unshockable	unsuffering	unvisitable	up to scratch	vagabondize
unshockably	unsulliable	unvitrified	up to the chin	vaginal plug
unshortened	unsupported	unvocalized	up to the ears	vagotomized
unshovelled	unsurpassed	unvoluntary	up to the hilt	Vaishnavism
unshrinking	unsurprised	unwandering	up to the mark	Vaishnavite
unshunnable	unsuspected	unwarranted	upvaluation	valediction
unshuttered	unsuspended	unwatchable	uraniferous	valedictory
unsightable	unsuspicion	unweariable	uranium bomb	valence band
unskilfully	unsustained	unweariably	uranium lead	valence bond
unslackened	unswallowed	unweariedly	uranography	Valentinian
unslakeable	unsweepable	unweariness	uranometria	vale of tears
unsmilingly	unsweetened	unweathered	uranoplasty	valerianate
unsmothered	unsyllabled	unwedgeable	uranoscopus	valeric acid
unsnubbable	untaintable	unweetingly	urban blight	valinomycin
unsoberness	untalkative	unweighable	urban sprawl	valleculate
unsocialist	untarnished	unwelcomely	urbiculture	valley-board
unsociality	unteachable	unwelcoming	urediospore	valley fever
unsoldiered	untechnical	unwhispered	ureterocele	Valleyspeak
unsoldierly	untemptable	unwholesome	ureterotomy	valley train
unsolicited	Untermensch	unwieldiest	urethrogram	vallisneria
unsoundable	unterrified	unwillingly	urethrotome	valuational
unsoundness	untheorized	unwinkingly	urethrotomy	value-system

value theory	velocimeter	versicolour	Vienna white	virtual work
valvulotomy	velocimetry	versuteness	vie romancée	visceralize
vampire trap	velt-marshal	vertebrated	viewability	viscerotome
vampishness	velvet glove	vertical fin	vigesimally	viscerotomy
Vanbrughian	velvet grass	verticalise	vigilantism	viscometric
vandalistic	velvetiness	verticalism	vigogne yarn	viscosities
van de Graaff	velvet sauce	verticality	vilifyingly	viscountess
Vandemonian	velvet sumac	verticalize	vilipensive	viscounties
van der Waals	venatically	verticillus	villagehood	viscous flow
vanguardism	Vendemiaire	vertiginous	villageless	viscousness
vanguardist	vendibility	vesiculated	village-like	visibleness
vanilla bean	venditation	vesiculitis	village pump	vis inertiae
vanishingly	veneer crown	vesper mouse	villageress	visionaries
vanity basin	veneficious	vespertinal	villainizer	vision mixer
vanity press	venereology	vestigially	Villonesque	vision quest
vanity table	venesection	vestimental	vinaigrette	Visitandine
vaporimeter	Venetian red	vesuvianite	vinblastine	visiting ant
vaporizable	Venice glass	vetoistical	vincibility	visitorship
vaporograph	Venn diagram	vexatiously	vincristine	visive organ
vapour-proof	venographic	vexillation	vin de paille	visor-bearer
vapour trail	ventilation	vexillology	vin d'honneur	Vistavision
variability	ventilative	Via Dolorosa	vindication	visual angle
variational	ventilatory	viaggiatory	vindicative	visual field
varicellous	ventoseness	via negativa	vindicatory	visual point
variegation	ventricular	vibratility	vine-dresser	visual range
variety shop	ventriculus	vibrational	vine-fretter	viticulture
variformity	ventriloque	vibratoless	vinegarroon	vitraillist
variolation	ventriloquy	vibriocidal	vinegar worm	vitrescence
variousness	venturesome	vicar choral	vineyarding	vitrescency
varnish-tree	venturously	vicariously	vineyardist	vitrescible
varsovienne	Venus figure	Vicar of Bray	vinho branco	vitrifiable
vascularise	Venus's basin	vice admiral	vinho da casa	vitriolated
vascularity	Venus's pride	vice-comital	viniculture	vitrophyric
vascularize	veraciously	vicegerence	vin mousseux	vituperable
vasculature	veratridine	vicegerency	vino de color	vituperator
vas deferens	verbalistic	viceregally	vino de pasto	vivaciously
vasectomies	verberation	viceroyalty	vino maestro	vivisection
vasectomise	verbigerate	viceroyship	vintage port	vivisective
vasectomize	verboseness	vicey-versey	vintnership	voce di petto
vasodilator	verd-antique	vichyssoise	viola d'amore	voce di testa
vasopressin	verdantness	viciousness	violational	vociferance
vasopressor	verdigrised	vicissitude	viol da gamba	vociferator
Vatican City	verdureless	victimology	violentness	vodka gimlet
vaticinator	verecundity	Victorianly	violet cream	voice-figure
vectitation	veridically	victory bond	violet shift	voicelessly
vector-borne	verisimilar	victoryless	violet snail	voidability
vector boson	vermiculate	victory roll	violinistic	void and redd
vector field	vermiculite	victory sign	violoncello	voivodeship
vectorially	vermiculose	victualless	viper's grass	volatile oil
vectorscope	vermiculous	victualling	virginalist	volatilizer
vector space	vermination	vicuña cloth	virginality	volcanic ash
veer and haul	verminicide	video arcade	virgin birth	volcanicity
vegeculture	vermiparous	video camera	virgin honey	volcanology
vegetablize	vermivorous	videography	virgin metal	volitionary
vehicle-mile	vernal glass	video piracy	virgin queen	Volsteadism
vehicle mine	vernal grass	video pirate	virgin widow	voltaically
vehicularly	verruciform	video-player	Virgouleuse	voltaic pile
Vehmgericht	verruculose	videorecord	viridescent	voltammetry
vein-banding	versatilely	video signal	virilocally	volubleness
veitchberry	versatility	vie de Bohème	virogenesis	volume table
velamentous	verse anthem	Vienna paste	virogenetic	voluntaries
vellication	versemonger	Vienna steak	virological	voluntarily

voluntarism	walking leaf	washer-drier	water-pepper	weather side
voluntarist	walking shoe	washer-dryer	water pistol	weather-tile
voluntative	walking tour	washer-upper	water pumper	weather-vane
Voortrekker	walk Matilda	washerwoman	water-shield	weathervane
voraciously	walk off with	washerwomen	water skater	weatherward
vortex sheet	walk out with	washing-bowl	water-souchy	weatherwise
vorticellid	walk Spanish	washing-line	water spider	weather-worn
vorticosely	walk through	washing soda	water-spirit	weaver finch
vortiginous	walk with God	wash its face	water-splash	weaver's knot
vote-catcher	wallaby-bush	wash-leather	water-stream	Webernesque
voting paper	Wallace line	Washo canary	water supply	Weber number
voting stock	wall-bearing	Washo zephyr	waterthrush	web-fingered
vowel colour	wall-bracket	waspishness	water tunnel	Weddell seal
vowel height	wallcreeper	wasp-waisted	water vapour	wedding band
vowel-laxing	wall hanging	wassail-bowl	water vessel	wedding-bush
vox angelica	wall-mounted	waste-basket	water violet	wedding cake
voyage royal	Wall of Death	wastebasket	water-waving	wedding-card
voyeuristic	wallowingly	waste breath	water-willow	wedding-knot
vulcanicity	walnut-shell	waste ground	water-worker	wedding list
vulcanizate	Walschaerts	wastel-bread	water yarrow	wedding ring
vulcanology	Waltonizing	wastethrift	watery grave	wedge-shaped
vulgarities	waltz-length	watch-keeper	Wathawurung	wedge-tailed
vulgar Latin	wampum snake	watchkeeper	Watteau back	weeding-hook
Vulgar Latin	wanderingly	watchmaking	Watteaulike	Wee Free Kirk
vulneraries	wand of peace	watch spring	wattled crow	weeknightly
vulpicidism	wanker's doom	water-bailie	wave changer	weeny-bopper
wage-earning	wantingness	water-bearer	wave machine	weeping-hole
wage economy	wappenschaw	Water-bearer	wave pattern	weequashing
wage one's law	war cemetery	water beetle	wave picture	Weichselian
wager-policy	war criminal	water betony	wave-surface	Weierstrass
wage slavery	ward-heeling	water-blinks	wave winding	weigh anchor
waggishness	ward-holding	water-bomber	wax-chandler	weighbridge
waggle dance	Ward-Leonard	water bottle	waxed jacket	weigh in with
wagon-master	ward of court	water bouget	wax-painting	weighmaster
wagon-wright	ward orderly	water budget	waywardness	weight-clock
Wailing Wall	war hospital	water-cannon	waywodeship	weight cloth
wainscoting	war hysteria	water-caster	weakest link	weightiness
wainscotted	warlessness	water closet	weak-hearted	weight-train
waistcoated	warm-blooded	watercolour	weak mixture	Weismannian
waist-gunner	war medicine	water-cooled	weak-sighted	Weismannism
waist-length	war memorial	water-cooler	wealthiness	Weissenberg
wait a minute	warm-hearted	watercourse	weapon-salve	welcome home
wait at table	war minister	water engine	weaponschaw	welcomeness
waiting game	warm the bell	water finder	weapon-smith	welcomingly
waiting list	warning bell	waterfowler	wearability	weldability
waiting-maid	warning-pipe	water garden	wear and tear	welding heat
waiting move	war of detail	water-gilder	wearilessly	welfare roll
waiting race	war of nerves	water hammer	wearisomely	welfare work
waiting room	warping-buoy	water heater	wear two hats	well advised
waiting time	warping-post	water hyssop	weary Willie	well and good
waitressing	warrantable	watering can	weasel-faced	well-behaved
wait the hour	warrantably	watering-pot	weasel-lemur	well-beloved
wakefulness	warrant card	water-jacket	weatherable	well-blooded
waking dream	warrantless	water-kelpie	weatherbitt	well-cistern
Waldenström	war reporter	Waterlander	weathercoat	well content
walk all over	war resister	water lizard	weathercock	well covered
walking bass	warriorship	waterlogged	weather deck	well-defined
walking dead	wart disease	waterlogger	weather-fend	well-dressed
walking doll	warts and all	Waterloo Cup	weather-gall	well-dresser
walking fern	washability	water-meadow	weathergirl	well-endowed
walking fish	wash-and-wear	water-miller	weather helm	well-fitting
walking lady	wash-drawing	water of life	weathermost	well-founded

well-groomed	what you will	White Kaffir	widow's weeds	wingmanship
well-looking	wheatflakes	white kerria	Wiener Kreis	wing-walking
well-managed	wheedlingly	white knight	wiener roast	winnability
well-matched	wheelbarrow	white letter	wienerwurst	winningness
well-meaning	wheel-plough	white-lipped	wife-swapper	winning post
well-ordered	wheel-window	white matter	wigeon-grass	Winnipegger
well-planned	wheel wobble	white-necked	wildcatting	winnow-cloth
well pleased	wheelwright	White nigger	wildebeests	win on points
well-plucked	whelk-tingle	white nutmeg	wildfowling	winsomeness
well-rounded	whensomever	white pepper	wild mustard	winterberry
well-stacked	whereabouts	white plague	wild parsley	winter count
well-stocked	wheresoever	white poplar	wild parsnip	winter-crack
well-studied	wherewithal	white potato	wild tobacco	winter cress
well-thumbed	whether or no	White racism	wild western	winter grape
well-trodden	wheyishness	White racist	will and nill	wintergreen
well-willing	whichsoever	white scours	williamsite	winter-house
well-wishing	whiffle-ball	White Sister	willingness	winter midge
well-wrought	whiffletree	white spirit	willow borer	winter-proof
Welsh cotton	Whig history	white spruce	willow-green	winter-proud
Welsh dragon	whigmaleery	white squall	willowiness	Winter's bark
Welsh Office	whimsically	white squill	will-worship	winter sleep
Welsh rabbit	whingeingly	white-tailed	wilsomeness	winter snipe
Weltschmerz	whippersnap	White Terror	wily beguile	winter-sport
welwitschia	whipping boy	whitethroat	wimpishness	wintersweet
wend one's way	whipping-top	white tombac	windbaggery	winterwards
Wensleydale	whippletree	white-walled	windbagging	win the peace
werewolfery	whipsy-derry	white walnut	wind-bracing	wipe one's eye
werewolfish	whiptail ray	whitewasher	windbreaker	wire-drawing
werewolfism	whiskerando	white willow	windcharger	wiredrawing
Wesleyanism	whiskerless	white window	windcheater	wireless set
West African	whiskey jack	white-winged	wind-furnace	wire netting
west-by-north	whisk-tailed	Whitgiftian	winding-hole	wirepulling
West Coaster	whisky money	whitherward	windingness	wire service
west country	whisky voice	whiting pout	windjamming	wire-tapping
West Country	whisperless	whitishness	windlestraw	wire-walking
Western blot	whistleable	whitleather	wind machine	Wisconsinan
Western boat	whistle punk	whitlockite	window-dress	wisdom tooth
westernizer	Whistlerian	Whitsuntide	window frame	wisecracker
westernmost	Whistlerism	Whittington	window ledge	wisenheimer
westernness	whistle-stop	who-does-what	window plant	wishfulness
western roll	whistle-wood	whole-colour	window scrim	wish I may die
Western roll	whistlingly	whole-hoofed	window table	wishing-well
Westminster	White Africa	whole-length	Windsor bean	wishtonwish
Westphalian	white-backed	whole number	Windsor blue	wish welcome
West-Pointer	Whiteboyism	wholesomely	Windsor knot	wistfulness
wet diggings	white bronze	whole-souled	Windsor soap	witch bottle
wether sheep	white bryony	whole-stitch	windsurfing	witch doctor
wet one's clay	whitecapper	wholly-owned	wind turbine	witches' brew
wet one's line	Whitechapel	whooper swan	wine and dine	witchetties
wet strength	white clover	whoremaster	wineberries	witch-finder
wettability	white coffee	whoremonger	winebibbing	witch-hopple
whalebacked	white cohosh	whorishness	wine-growing	witch-hunter
whale-fisher	white-collar	whorl-flower	wine steward	witchmonger
whaler shark	white ensign	whosesoever	wine tasting	witenagemot
whalesucker	White Father	wichuraiana	wine vinegar	with abandon
whangdoodle	whitefisher	Wicked Bible	wing-and-wing	with an eye to
wharf-lumper	white-footed	widdendream	winged words	with a rattle
Wharncliffe	white ginger	widdershins	wing-feather	with a view of
what have you	white-haired	wide-ranging	wing flutter	with a view to
whatsomever	white-headed	widowerhood	wing formula	with damages
what's trumph	white horses	widowership	wing forward	withdraught
what the hell	White hunter	widow's cruse	wing loading	withdrawing

witheringly	woodworking	wranglesome	xylophonist	youth credit
withershins	woody tongue	wrapped up in	yacht broker	youth hostel
witherwrung	wool-bearing	wrapper leaf	yachtswoman	youth leader
withholding	woolclasser	wreathingly	yachtswomen	yttriferous
within board	wool-clipper	wrecking bar	yackety-yack	Yugoslavian
within cry of	wool-combing	wrecking car	Yagi antenna	Yuwaalaraay
within doors	woolly aphid	wreck-master	Yankee State	zealousness
withinsides	woolly indri	wren-babbler	yard-arm iron	zearalenone
within sight	woolly lemur	wrench fault	yard-measure	zebra mussel
within touch	wool-packing	wren-warbler	Yarkand deer	zebra spider
with justice	wool-pulling	wrestle down	yarn-spinner	Zend-Avestan
with knobs on	wool-stapler	wretchedest	Yarra-banker	Zener effect
with mirrors	word-catcher	wriggle-work	Y chromosome	zenith sweep
without book	word-finally	wrigglingly	year of grace	zenithwards
without door	word for word	wringing wet	yeas and nays	zenocentric
without fail	word-initial	wrinkleless	yeast powder	zenographic
withoutside	wordmanship	wrist clonus	Yeddo spruce	zero-balance
with-profits	word of mouth	wrist-length	yellow alert	zero gravity
with respect	word-painter	writing-book	yellow badge	zero tillage
withstander	word-perfect	writing-case	yellow belle	zerovalency
with the wind	word-picture	writing desk	yellow-belly	zestfulness
witlessness	word problem	writing-lark	yellow birch	zetetically
witnessable	word-process	writ of error	yellow cedar	zigzag fence
wobble-board	words fail me	wrong-headed	yellow-cress	zigzaggedly
wobble plate	word-watcher	wronglessly	yellow earth	zillionaire
wobbulation	word-writing	wrought iron	yellow elder	Zimmer frame
Wodehousian	workability	wunderkinds	yellow fever	zincography
wolfishness	workaholism	Wurtz–Fittig	yellow fibre	zip fastener
wolf-madness	workfulness	wyerone acid	yellow light	zoantharian
wolf whistle	working copy	Wykehamical	yellow metal	zoanthropic
wolvishness	working girl	xanthelasma	yellow ochre	zoidogamous
woman doctor	working load	xanthic acid	yellow ox-eye	zomotherapy
womanliness	working plan	xanthinuria	Yellow Pages	zonal fossil
woman's woman	workmanlike	xanthophore	yellow perch	zona radiata
womanthrope	workmanship	xanthophyll	yellow peril	zone defence
women's group	work of mercy	X chromosome	yellow robin	zone refiner
wonderfully	work release	xenoantigen	yellow sally	zone therapy
wonderingly	work-sharing	xenobiology	yellowshank	zoocultural
wonder rabbi	workstation	xenoblastic	yellow shell	zoodynamics
wonderstone	work surface	xenocrystal	yellow snake	zoomorphism
wood alcohol	work the tubs	xenocrystic	yellow topaz	zoomorphize
wood anemone	work wonders	xenodochium	yellow trout	zooplankter
wood buffalo	world-beater	xenogenesis	yeoman bedel	zooplankton
wood-burning	world-famous	xenoglossia	Yeoman Usher	zootechnics
wood-butcher	world-ground	xenomorphic	yersiniosis	zootheistic
woodcarving	worldliness	xenophiliac	yesternight	Zoroastrian
wood-chopper	worldly-wise	Xenophontic	Yiddishkeit	Zuckerkandl
woodcreeper	worlds apart	xenotropism	yield stress	Zurich gnome
woodcutting	World Series	xeranthemum	yobbishness	zygogenesis
wooden cross	world-spirit	xerocopying	you and yours	zygogenetic
wooden horse	worm-fishing	xerographic	you can't lose	zygological
wooden spoon	worried sick	xeromorphic	you-know-what	zygomorphic
wooden walls	worrisomely	xerophilous	Younger Edda	zygotically
wood-leopard	worshipable	xerophytism	younger hand	zymological
woodmanship	worshipless	xerothermic	youngership	zymoplastic
Woodruff key	worshipping	xiphopagous	young fustic	zymosimeter
wood sanicle	worsted work	X-radiograph	young master	zymotechnic
wood-swallow	worst-seller	X-ray burster	young person	zymotically
wood-turning	worthlessly	xylocarpous	your servant	
woodturning	wortle plate	xylographer	Your Worship	
wood vinegar	woundedness	xylographic	Youth Aliyah	
wood warbler	wound-stripe	xylophagous	youth centre	

TWELVE LETTERS

abaft the beam
a barrel of fun
abbreviation
abbreviatory
abbreviature
abdominal leg
aberrational
abiding-place
a bite and a sup
a bit of no good
abnormalness
abolitionism
abolitionist
aboriginally
abortiveness
abortus fever
above measure
above oneself
above the line
above the salt
Abraham's barm
abscisic acid
absenteeship
absent-minded
absoluteness
absolute term
absolute unit
absolute zero
absolutistic
absorbedness
absorptivity
absquatulate
abstemiously
abstractable
abstractedly
abstractness
abstract noun
abstruseness
a button short
academically
academic year
acanthaceous
accelerandos
acceleration
accelerative
accelerogram
accentuation
access course
accessible to
acciaccatura
accidentally
acclimatizer
accommodable
accommodator
accompanable
accompanyist
accomplished

accomplisher
accordionist
accouchement
accouplement
accoutrement
accretionary
accroachment
accumulation
accumulative
accurateness
accursedness
accusatively
accusatorial
accustomedly
accustomed to
acetaldehyde
acetate fibre
acetoacetate
acetonitrile
Achilles heel
achlamydeous
achlorhydria
achlorhydric
acknowledged
acknowledger
acoustically
acoustic hood
acoustic lens
acoustic mine
acquaintance
acquiescence
acquiescency
acroamatical
acronychally
across the way
acrostically
a crow to pluck
acrylic resin
act counter to
actinometric
actinomycete
action-packed
action replay
active carbon
active matrix
actor-manager
adaptability
adaptational
adaptiveness
adder's tongue
addictedness
additionally
adequateness
Adessenarian
adhesiveness
adhesive tape
adjectitious

adjectivally
adjective dye
adjudication
adjudicative
adjudicature
adjunctively
adjutant bird
adminiculate
administrant
administrate
admonishment
admonitorial
admonitorily
adolescently
adorableness
a dose of salts
adrenal gland
adscititious
adsorptional
adsorptively
adulteration
adulterously
advance guard
advantageous
adventitious
Advent Sunday
adverbialize
advertise for
advisability
advocateship
aecidiospore
aero-allergen
aerodynamics
aeromagnetic
aeronautical
aerostatical
aesthetician
aestheticism
aestheticist
aestheticize
aetiological
affamishment
affectedness
affectionate
affinity card
afflictingly
afflictively
afforestable
affrightedly
affrightment
affrontingly
aforethought
African daisy
African peach
Afrikanerdom
Afrikanerism
Afrikanerize

Afro-American
afterburning
afternoon tea
afterthought
after you with
agalmatolite
agamogenesis
agamogenetic
age-hardening
agent-general
age of consent
age of puberty
ageostrophic
agglutinable
agglutinogen
aggregometer
aggressively
aggressivity
aggrievement
agnomination
agnostically
a good innings
a great one for
agreeability
agribusiness
agrichemical
agricultural
agrobusiness
agrochemical
agro-climatic
agroforestry
agro-industry
a high old time
aides-mémoire
ailurophobia
ailurophobic
air commodore
Air Commodore
air-cushioned
air-freshener
airmail paper
air-sea rescue
air-to-surface
alacritously
Aladdin's cave
Aladdin's lamp
albitization
alcaptonuria
alchemically
aldermanlike
aldermanship
alembication
alexipharmic
algebraicize
Alhambresque
alienability
a likely story

alimentation
alimentative
alive and well
alkalescence
alkalimetric
alkaline tide
alkalization
alkaptonuria
alkaptonuric
all-absorbing
alla cappella
all-alikeness
all and sundry
all-beauteous
all-embracing
All Hallow Eve
alligator gar
alligatoring
all-important
all-inclusive
alliteration
alliterative
all night long
alloantibody
all of a dither
all of a doodah
all of a sudden
all-or-none law
allotmenteer
allotropical
all-pervading
all-pervasive
all-roundness
All Saints' Day
all systems go
all to nothing
all to the good
alluringness
allusiveness
allyl plastic
Almain rivets
almightiness
alphabetical
alphabet soup
alphanumeric
Alpine chough
alstroemeria
alterability
altered chord
altitudinous
alto-rilievos
amalgamation
amalgamative
amateurishly
a matter of law
Amazon parrot
ambassadress
ambassadrice
ambidextrous
ambient music
ambisextrous
ambitionless

ambivalently
ambulance man
ambulatories
amelioration
ameliorative
amenableness
amenorrhoeal
amenorrhoeic
American aloe
American crow
American jute
Americanness
American plan
amicableness
amicus curiae
aminobenzoic
amino-plastic
amissibility
amitotically
ammonium alum
amontillados
amortisation
amortisement
amortization
a mouth to feed
amphibiously
amphibolitic
amphibrachic
amphicoelous
amphictyonic
amphidiploid
amphisbaenid
amphitheatre
amygdaloidal
Anabaptistic
anaerobiosis
anaesthetise
anaesthetist
anaesthetize
anagogically
anagrammatic
analogically
analphabetic
anal sadistic
analytically
anamorphosis
anaphylactic
anaplasmosis
anarchically
an arm and a leg
anastigmatic
anathematise
anathematism
anathematize
anatomically
an axe to grind
anchoritical
anchorpeople
anchorperson
anchovy-paste
anchovy toast
ancien régime

ancient Greek
ancient world
Andean condor
and no mistake
and otherwise
androcentric
androgenesis
androgenetic
androsterone
anecdotalism
anecdotalist
an ecstasy woe
anelasticity
anemographic
anemophilous
anencephalic
angelica tree
angiogenesis
angiographic
angiospermal
angle bracket
angle of pitch
Anglocentric
Anglo-Frisian
anguilliform
anhypostasia
anhypostasis
anhypostatic
aniline black
animadverter
animal rights
animatronics
anisaldehyde
anisocytosis
ankylosaurus
annihilation
annihilative
announcement
annunciation
annunciative
annunciatory
anonymuncule
anorexigenic
anorthoclase
anorthositic
anotherguess
another place
another story
antagonistic
antanaclasis
antebrachial
antecedental
antecedently
antediluvial
antediluvian
antemeridian
anteposition
anteprandial
anteriormost
anthelmintic
anthological
anthophilous

anthoxanthin
anthranilate
anthropogeny
anthropoidal
anthropolite
anthropology
anthroponymy
anthropotomy
anti-abortion
anti-aircraft
anticatholic
anticipation
anticipative
anticipatory
anticlerical
anticlinally
anticyclonic
antidiuretic
antifebrific
antifriction
anti-Gallican
antigenicity
antihysteric
antimacassar
antimalarial
antimoniated
anti-national
antiparallel
antiparticle
antipathetic
antiphonally
antipruritic
antirachitic
anti-Semitism
antisocially
antistrophic
antistrophon
antisymmetry
antitheistic
antithetical
anybody's game
anything like
Anzac biscuit
aoristically
Apache Indian
a painful lack
aperiodicity
apfelstrudel
aphidivorous
aphorismatic
aphoristical
apiculturist
a piece of cake
apocalyptist
apochromatic
apocryphally
Apollinarian
Apollinarist
apologetical
aposporously
apostle spoon
apostolicity

Apostolic See	archesporium	artist's proof	at all hazards
apostrophise	archetypical	Aryanization	at all weapons
apostrophize	Archilochian	as best one can	atamasco lily
apothecaries	archinephric	as black as jet	at an easy rate
apparatchiki	archinephros	as busy as a bee	at arm's length
apparatchiks	archipelagic	Ascension Day	at a short stay
apparentness	archipelagos	as clear as day	at close range
apparent time	archiphoneme	as clear as mud	at death's door
apparitional	architective	Asclepiadean	at discretion
appassionate	architecture	ascomycetous	at first blush
appendectomy	archosaurian	ascorbic acid	at first brush
appendicitis	Arctic Circle	as dead as a nit	at first sight
appendicular	arcubalister	as dry as a chip	at full length
apperception	arcus senilis	as good as gold	at full strain
apperceptive	arena theatre	a show of hands	atheological
appetenccies	aretalogical	Ash Wednesday	atheromatous
appetizingly	arfvedsonite	ask a blessing	athlete's foot
applaudingly	Argand burner	ask me another	athletically
applausively	Argentine ant	a small matter	athletic club
apple-cheeked	argentophile	as often as not	athwart-hawse
apple of Sodom	argillaceous	aspartic acid	at knife-point
apple parings	argue the toss	asphyxiation	at knifepoint
apple strudel	argue well for	aspirational	Atlantic seal
appoggiatura	argumentator	aspiringness	Atlantic Time
apportionate	argyrophilia	assassinator	atmospherics
appositeness	argyrophilic	assault craft	at nought feet
appositional	aristocratic	assembly line	atomic energy
appositively	aristolochia	assembly room	atomic number
appraisement	aristologist	assembly shop	atomic theory
appraisingly	Aristophanic	assertorical	atomic volume
appreciation	Aristotelean	asseveration	atomic weight
appreciative	Aristotelian	asseverative	at one stretch
appreciatory	arithmetical	assibilation	atrabilarian
apprehension	arithmomania	assification	at second hand
apprehensive	arithmometer	assigneeship	at short range
appressorium	armamentaria	assimilation	attemperator
approachable	Armenian bole	assimilative	at the hands of
approachless	Armistice Day	assimilatory	at the heels of
approachment	armour-bearer	assuefaction	at the mercy of
approach road	armour-plated	as sure as a gun	at the outside
appropriable	arm-wrestling	as sure as fate	at the point of
appropriator	a rod in pickle	Asti spumante	Attic dialect
approximator	aromatherapy	a stone's throw	attitudinise
appurtenance	aromatically	astonishable	attitudinize
a pretty penny	aromaticness	astonishedly	attorneyship
aptitude test	arpeggiation	astonishment	attractively
aquacultural	arrhythmical	astoundingly	attributable
Arabian camel	arrière-guard	astringently	at university
Arabian horse	arsenopyrite	astrobiology	auction house
arachnophobe	arsphenamine	astrocompass	audio-lingual
araneologist	art-and-crafty	astrographic	audiological
arbalestrier	artesian well	a stroke above	auditorially
arborescence	arthrography	astrolabical	augmentation
arborisation	arthroplasty	astrological	augmentative
arborization	articulately	astronautics	auld lang syne
archaeologic	articulation	astronomical	Aulic Council
archaeologue	articulative	astrophysics	aurichalcite
archaeometry	articulatory	asymmetrical	auriferously
archdeaconry	artificially	asymptomatic	auscultation
archdiocesan	artilleryman	asymptotical	auscultative
archegoniate	artillerymen	asynchronous	auscultatory
archesporial	artistically	at adventures	auspiciously

Austin Friars	babingtonite	balsam poplar	be after doing
Australasian	baby-blue-eyes	Balsam poplar	beam-splitter
Australopith	baby carriage	balustrading	bean-bag chair
Austrian pine	baby-snatcher	Bananalander	be apprised of
Austronesian	baccalaurean	bandersnatch	bearableness
authenticate	Bacchanalian	bandicoot rat	bear-covering
authenticity	bacchanalize	Bangladeshis	bear evidence
authigenesis	bachelorette	bang to rights	be a ringer for
authorizable	bachelor girl	banker's order	bearing metal
auto-analysis	bachelorhood	banking-house	beast of ravin
auto-antibody	bachelorship	bankruptcies	be astute to do
autocatalyst	back and forth	bantamweight	beat a retreat
autochthonal	backboneless	Barbados lily	beat creation
autochthones	back-breaking	barbarically	beatifically
autochthonic	backgrounder	Barbary sheep	beat into fits
autocritical	backhandedly	bar billiards	beat the clock
auto-destruct	backing store	Barcoo buster	beat the drums
autodidactic	backing track	bardolatrous	beat the Dutch
autofocusing	back-lighting	bare-knuckled	beaver meadow
autogenously	back of Bourke	bargain price	becomingness
autohypnosis	back-pressure	baritone horn	bedazzlement
autohypnotic	backslapping	barnstorming	bedding plane
autoimmunity	back-straight	barometrical	bedding plant
automaticity	back the field	baroque music	be destined to
automobilism	back-to-nature	baroreceptor	be determined
automobilist	backwardness	barratrously	Bedfordshire
automobility	backwoodsman	barrier cream	be displeased
automorphism	backwoodsmen	barristerial	bed of justice
autonomously	bacteriaemia	Bartlett pear	bedroom farce
autoptically	bactericidal	baselessness	bedtime story
autorotation	bacteriology	base-stealing	beef mountain
autosemantic	bacteriostat	Basic English	beer-swilling
autotheistic	bad conductor	basidiospore	bees and honey
autotoxaemia	baggage check	basisphenoid	Beethovenian
autotrophism	baggage claim	basket clause	Beethovenish
autoxidation	bag of mystery	basket-hilted	beetle-backed
autumn crocus	bail bondsman	basking shark	beetle-browed
auxanography	Bailey bridge	bass-baritone	before Christ
availability	Bakewell tart	basso-relievo	be for the best
avant-courier	baking powder	bastard title	befuddlement
avant-gardism	Balaam basket	bastard trout	beggarliness
avant-gardist	balance sheet	batch process	beg one's bread
avariciously	balance wheel	bathing belle	begrudgingly
avascularity	balancing act	bathochromic	behaviourism
a vengeance on	ballade royal	bathroom tile	behaviourist
average out at	ballad-monger	bathypelagic	be here to stay
aviculturist	ball and chain	battered baby	be in derision
avitaminoses	Ballan wrasse	battered wife	be in raptures
avitaminosis	ballet dancer	battering ram	be in the chair
avocado green	balletically	batting order	be in the right
Avogadro's law	ballet-master	battleground	be in the way of
award the palm	balletomania	battlemented	be in two minds
award-winning	ballistician	battles royal	Belgian block
awe-inspiring	ballon d'essai	battleworthy	believe you me
a wink of sleep	balloon frame	Baudelairean	belittlement
awkward squad	balloon glass	baulk-cushion	belittlingly
axisymmetric	ballottement	Bayes' theorem	bell-bottomed
a year and a day	ball-point pen	bayonet-grass	belletristic
Azerbaijanis	ballpoint pen	be a big boy now	bell-founding
babbitt metal	Balmer series	be able to wait	belligerence
babe in Christ	balm of Gilead	be absorbed by	belligerency
babe of clouts	balneologist	beachcombing	belly dancing

belly landing	Bible-thumper	birthday suit	blockheadism
below the belt	bibliography	birthing pool	blockishness
below the line	bibliomaniac	Bishops' Bible	block letters
below the salt	bibliometric	bishop sleeve	block release
belt conveyor	bibliophilic	bismuthinite	blood and iron
bench-warrant	bibliopolist	bismuth ochre	blood-and-soil
bend sinister	bibliothecal	bitch goddess	blood brother
bend the brows	bibliothetic	bit of crumpet	blood-letting
bend the rules	bibulousness	bit on the side	bloodletting
benefactress	bicameralism	bitter orange	blood pudding
beneficently	bicentennial	biuniqueness	blood sausage
beneficiaire	bicycle chain	blabbermouth	bloodshedder
beneficially	bide one's time	black and blue	bloodshotten
benefit match	bikini briefs	Black and Tans	bloodstained
benevolently	bilateralism	blackberried	bloodsucking
Bengal quince	bilaterality	blackberries	bloodthirsty
benjamin bush	bilharziasis	blackbirding	bloody-minded
benjamin-tree	bilharziosis	Blackburnian	Bloody Monday
be no relation	bilification	Black Country	bloody murder
benzaldehyde	bilingualism	blackcurrant	blow one's cool
benzoquinone	bilinguality	black diamond	blubberingly
be of no matter	billiard-ball	black disease	blue asbestos
be one's own man	billingsgate	black draught	bluestocking
be on the mooch	bill of health	black economy	blue titmouse
be poles apart	bill of lading	black English	blunderingly
be pressed for	bill of review	Black English	blusteringly
bepuzzlement	Bill of Rights	black-eye bean	blusterously
bequeathable	binary number	blackguardly	board of trade
bequeathment	binary system	black leopard	boardsailing
bergamot mint	binary weapon	black mustard	boastfulness
Berkeley hunt	binocularity	black panther	boat-building
Bermuda cedar	biochemistry	Black Panther	bobby-dazzler
Bermuda grass	biocoenology	black pudding	bob-sleighing
Bermudian rig	biodiversity	black quarter	bobsleighing
beseechingly	bio-energetic	black salsify	bodice-ripper
beseemliness	bioflavonoid	black-sterned	body-building
besetting sin	biogenically	black tracker	body language
be so good as to	biogeography	black treacle	body of Christ
besottedness	biographical	black truffle	body piercing
bespectacled	biohazardous	black vulture	body-snatcher
bestialities	biologically	bladder senna	body stocking
beta particle	biomagnetism	bladderwrack	bog pimpernel
be the death of	biomechanics	blandishment	Bohr magneton
be themselves	biometrician	blank charter	boiling point
bet one's shirt	biophysicist	blanket-piece	boil the billy
bet on the nose	biorhythmics	blanket stiff	boisterously
be too many for	bioscientist	blast furnace	bomb disposal
between-decks	biosynthesis	blastocoelic	bomber jacket
between times	biosynthetic	blastulation	bona vacantia
be upstanding	bioturbation	blatherskite	bone-charcoal
be up the flume	bipinnatifid	bless my heart	Bonfire Night
be well served	birationally	bless the mark	bonne fortune
bewilderedly	bird's-eye view	bletherskate	bonnet monkey
bewilderment	bird's-nesting	blind tooling	bonny-clabber
bewitchingly	bird-watching	blissfulness	boogie-woogie
beyond a doubt	birdwatching	blisteringly	booking clerk
beyond belief	birefringent	blister pearl	book learning
bibble-babble	birth control	blister steel	book-scorpion
Bible-banging	birthday book	blithesomely	Boolean logic
Bible-bashing	birthday cake	block booking	boor's mustard
Bible-pounder	birthday card	blockbusting	bootblacking
Bible-puncher	birthday girl	block diagram	boot-stocking

Border ballad	breakfasting	bronchophony	burton-tackle
border collie	break silence	bronchoscope	burying place
Border collie	break the bank	bronchoscopy	bus-conductor
boresomeness	break the pack	bronchospasm	bush-fighting
borosilicate	break through	bronco-buster	Bushman grass
borough-reeve	breakthrough	broncobuster	bush sickness
borrowed days	breast collar	brontophobia	business card
borrowed time	breast-plough	brontosaurus	businesslike
Botticellian	breast-pocket	bronze powder	business park
bottle-holder	breast-stroke	broom hickory	business suit
bottle-opener	breaststroke	brothel-house	busybodyness
bottle-washer	breastsummer	brother-in-law	butcher-boots
bottom dollar	breathalyser	brought to bed	butcher's bill
bottom drawer	breathe again	brown creeper	butcher's hook
bouillon cube	breathe short	brown holland	butcher's meat
boulangerite	breathlessly	Brownie Guide	butch haircut
boulderstone	breath of life	brownie point	butter-cooler
bounty hunter	breathtaking	Brownistical	buttercupped
bounty-jumper	breech action	brown mustard	butterfly bow
bouquet garni	breeches-buoy	brush wallaby	butterfly net
bourgeoisdom	breeches part	Brussels lace	butterfly nut
bourgeoisify	breech-loader	bubble memory	butterfly pea
bow and scrape	breed in and in	buccaneering	butter muslin
bow-compasses	breitschwanz	buccaneerish	butterscotch
bowhead whale	Brewster's law	buccolingual	buttery-hatch
bowler-hatted	brickfielder	Buckeye State	button-holder
bowling alley	brick-nogging	buck the tiger	buttress-root
bowling green	bridal wreath	Buddhistical	buyer's market
bow of promise	bride-chamber	budget buster	buyers' market
boxing weight	bridging loan	buffalo berry	buy the rabbit
boy-meets-girl	brigade-major	buffalo chips	by a long chalk
brachycephal	brigadier wig	buffalo grass	by contraries
brachygraphy	bright lights	buffle-headed	by courtesy of
brachylogies	brilliantine	build a sconce	by definition
brachypellic	bring forward	building line	Byelorussian
bracken-clock	bring through	building site	by entireties
bracket clock	bring to a head	building-term	by succession
brackishness	bring to grief	bulldog breed	by themselves
bradyseismic	bring to light	bulldog issue	by yourselves
Brahminy bull	bring to terms	bullen-bullen	cabbage white
Brahminy duck	bring up short	bullet-headed	cabin cruiser
Brahminy kite	brinkmanship	bullfighting	cabinet-maker
brain-damaged	bristle-grass	bull-headedly	cabinetmaker
brain scanner	Bristol board	bull-of-the-bog	cabinet organ
brain-twister	Bristol cream	bunch of fives	cabinet piano
brainwashing	Bristol glass	bunco-steerer	cabin-steward
bramble-berry	Bristol stone	bundle-sheath	cable pattern
brandenburgs	Britannicize	bungarotoxin	cable railway
brandy-bottle	British crown	bungee jumper	cable release
brandy butter	British Isles	bun in the oven	cachinnation
brandy-cherry	Britocentric	Bunsen burner	cachinnatory
brandy-pawnee	broadcasting	Buonapartist	cack-handedly
brass-monkeys	broad pennant	burdensomely	caco-magician
brass rubbing	broiler house	bureaucratic	cactus dahlia
brass section	broken-backed	burglar alarm	cadaverously
Braxton Hicks	broken colour	burial ground	caenogenesis
bread and milk	broken-winded	burn daylight	caenogenetic
bread and wine	broker-dealer	burn in effigy	cainogenesis
bread of trete	bromargyrite	burning-glass	cairn terrier
bread pudding	bromide paper	burn to a crisp	calabash tree
break contact	Bromo-Seltzer	burrowing owl	calamitously
break-dancing	bronchogenic	bursectomize	Calamity Jane

calcalkaline
calcitration
calcium oxide
calculatedly
calendar year
caliginosity
calisthenics
calligrapher
calligraphic
call into play
callisthenic
call of nature
call one's shot
call the shots
call to the bar
calorimetric
calumniation
calumniatory
calumniously
Calvary cross
cameralistic
camera lucida
camiknickers
campanologer
campanulated
camp fire girl
camp follower
campshedding
Canada balsam
canaliculate
canalization
canary yellow
cancellandum
cancellarian
cancellation
cancericidal
candid camera
candleholder
candle-waster
candy-striped
candystriped
candystriper
cane-coloured
cannon fodder
cannot choose
cannot resist
canonisation
canonization
canon regular
Cantabrigian
cantankerous
canterburies
cantharidean
cantharidize
cantilevered
cantillation
cantus firmus
can you beat it
capabilities
capacitation
capacitative
Cape anteater

Cape chestnut
Cape Coloured
Cape hyacinth
Cape marigold
Cape pondweed
Cape primrose
capercaillie
capercailzie
capillaceous
capital goods
capitalistic
Capitan Pasha
capitularies
capitulation
capitulatory
cap of liberty
capriciously
Capricornian
capstan lathe
captiousness
caput mortuum
caravanserai
carbohydrate
carbolic acid
carbolic soap
carbonaceous
carbon dating
carbonic acid
carbunculous
carburetting
carcinogenic
card-carrying
cardinal's hat
cardinalship
cardinal vein
cardinal wind
cardiography
cardiologist
carefreeness
carelessness
caricaturist
carillonneur
Carlovingian
Carlsbad plum
carnal member
Carolina duck
Carolina pink
Carolina rice
carol service
carol-singing
carpenter ant
carpenter bee
carpet-bagger
carpet-beater
carpet beetle
carpet knight
carpet square
Carpocratian
carpological
carriageable
carriage paid
carriwitchet

carry forward
carry one's bat
carry the baby
carry through
carry with one
carte blanche
Cartesianism
Carthaginian
cartographer
cartographic
cartoonishly
cartoon strip
cartophilist
cartouche-box
cartridge-box
cartridge-pen
carunculated
carving knife
case the joint
cash and carry
cash register
cassette deck
cassette tape
cast accounts
cast a stone at
castellation
casting couch
cast in the eye
castor action
cast stones at
cast the glove
casual pauper
casualty ward
catachrestic
catacoustics
catadioptric
catamountain
cataphoresis
cataphoretic
catastrophic
catch a packet
catch a Tartar
catch bending
catchingness
catch napping
catch sight of
catechetical
cathetometer
cathodically
catholically
Catholically
Catholic King
Catilinarian
cat o' mountain
cattle-lifter
cattle-plague
cattle-trough
caulking iron
cause célèbre
caustic plant
caution money
cautiousness

cavalier cuff
cavalry sword
cavalry twill
caveat emptor
cave painting
cedar waxwing
celestiality
celibatarian
cellar beetle
cell membrane
Celsius scale
Celtic fringe
cementitious
censoriously
centesimally
centillionth
central force
central lobby
centre circle
centre of mass
centre-second
centre spread
centrifugate
centrosphere
centumvirate
centuplicate
centuriation
century plant
cephalic vein
cephalometry
cephalopodal
cerebrotonic
ceremonially
cespititious
cessionaries
cestui que vie
cetane number
cetyl alcohol
chacma baboon
chaetigerous
chaffer words
chain printer
chairmanship
chaise longue
chaise lounge
chalcanthite
Chalcedonian
chalcedonies
chalcenteric
chalcogenide
chalcography
chalcolithic
chalcopyrite
chalicothere
chalk and talk
chalk drawing
chalk-striped
chamber music
chamber organ
championship
chance-medley
change-bowler

change colour	cherry-bounce	chokeberries	cinematheque
changelessly	cherry brandy	cholerically	cinéma-vérité
change of gear	cherry laurel	chondrophore	cinnamon bear
change of life	cherry picker	chondrostean	cinnamon fern
change of mind	cherry tomato	choreography	cinnamon rose
change-ringer	cherubically	choreologist	cinquefoiled
changing room	cherubimical	chorographer	circuit board
Channel Fleet	cherubinical	chorographic	circuit court
channel-stone	Cheshire acre	chorological	circuit judge
chapel-master	chesterfield	chorus-master	circuitously
chapel of ease	chest freezer	chosen people	circular loom
chapel of rest	chestnutting	chou moellier	circularness
chapelwarden	chestnut tree	chrematistic	circular tour
chaperonless	chestnut wood	chrestomathy	circumcircle
chaplaincies	chest of viols	chrisom-cloth	circumcision
chaplainship	Cheviot sheep	Christian era	circumfluent
Chaplinesque	Cheyne-Stokes	Christianise	circumfluous
chapter house	chicken brick	Christianism	circumfusion
characterful	chicken gumbo	Christianity	circumgyrate
characterise	chicken-heart	Christianize	circumjacent
characterize	chicken korma	Christmas box	circumjovial
charcoal grey	chicken-liver	Christmas Day	circumjovian
charlatanism	Chief Justice	Christmas Eve	circumnutate
Charles's Wain	Chief of Staff	Christophany	circumscribe
charley horse	chieftainess	Christ's thorn	circumscript
charmingness	child-bearing	chromaticism	circumsphere
charnel house	childbearing	chromaticity	circumstance
charnockitic	child benefit	chromatogram	circumvolute
Charterhouse	child-centred	chromatology	cirrocumulus
charter-party	childishness	chromatopsia	cirrostratus
chart-topping	childminding	chrome yellow	citification
chassé croisé	chiliahedron	chromic oxide	citizens' band
chastisement	chilli pepper	chromophilic	city of refuge
chastity belt	chilli powder	chromophobic	civil defence
château in air	chimerically	chromophoric	civilisation
chattel slave	chimney-board	chromosphere	civilization
chattels real	chimney-money	chronography	civil liberty
chatteration	chimney piece	chronologies	civil servant
chatteringly	chimney stack	chronologise	civil service
chaulmoogric	chimney sweep	chronologist	Civil Service
chauvinistic	chimney swift	chronologize	cladogenesis
checkerberry	chimonanthus	chronometric	cladogenetic
checkerboard	China-watcher	chronotropic	cladosporium
check through	Chinese anise	chrysophanic	clairaudient
cheek to cheek	Chinese block	chrysopoetic	clair-obscure
cheerfulness	Chinese olive	churchianity	clairvoyance
cheeseburger	Chinese white	Churchillian	clairvoyante
cheese-cutter	chirognomist	church-litten	clamjamphrie
cheesemaking	chirographer	church-living	clangorously
cheesemonger	chirological	church parade	clannishness
cheese-paring	chiromantist	church school	clapboarding
cheiloplasty	chiropractic	churchwarden	clapperboard
chemical bond	chiropractor	churlishness	claret colour
chemiosmotic	chiropterous	churnability	clarinettist
chemokinesis	chivalresque	churrascaria	classicalism
chemokinetic	chivalrously	chylifactive	classicalist
chemotherapy	chlorapatite	chymotrypsin	classicality
chemotropism	chlorination	cigarette end	classicistic
chequer-board	chloroformic	cigar-lighter	classic races
chequerboard	chloropicrin	cilioretinal	classifiable
cherishingly	chlorous acid	cinchona bark	claudication
Cherokee rose	chocolate box	cinchonicine	claustration

clavicembalo
clean and jerk
clean fingers
clear as a bell
clearing bank
clear-obscure
clear-sighted
clearstories
cleistogamic
clerk of works
clerodendrum
Cleveland bay
clever-clever
client-server
cliff-hanging
cliffhanging
cliff swallow
climatically
climbing-iron
clinker-built
clinographic
clipper-built
clippety-clop
cliquishness
clock-watcher
cloddishness
cloisterless
close borough
close-coupled
close-cropped
closed season
close-fitting
close-grained
close harmony
close-mouthed
close-quarter
cloth-binding
clothes-brush
clothes-drier
clothes horse
clothing-book
clothing-club
cloth of state
clotted cream
cloudberries
cloud chamber
cloud-hopping
cloud seeding
cloven-footed
cloven-hoofed
clover weevil
clownishness
club armchair
clubbability
club sandwich
cluelessness
coacervation
coachbuilder
coachmanship
coach station
coadaptation
coadventurer

coagulometer
coalitionism
coalitionist
coal measures
coal-merchant
coal-titmouse
coarse-fibred
coarticulate
coast disease
coast to coast
co-authorship
coaxial cable
cobalt glance
cobbler's awls
cobbler's pegs
cobweb spider
cocarcinogen
coccidiostat
cockeye pilot
cock-fighting
cockfighting
cock one's ears
cock one's nose
cock-shut time
cocksureness
cock-throwing
code-breaking
code of honour
codependency
codification
coelacanthid
coelenterate
coenobitical
coerciveness
coetaneously
coffin corner
cogeneration
cogitatively
cognoscitive
cohabitation
cohesiveness
coincidental
coincidently
coindication
co-inhabitant
coin-operated
cold compress
cold shoulder
coleopterist
coleopteroid
coleopterous
collaborator
collared dove
collaterally
collaudation
collectarium
collectively
collectivise
collectivism
collectivist
collectivity
collectivize

collectorate
collegiality
collegiately
collinearity
colliquative
collision-mat
collodionize
colloidality
collophanite
Collop Monday
colloquially
colluctation
collywobbles
cologne water
colombophile
colometrical
Colonel Blimp
colonisation
colonization
coloquintida
colorimetric
colour camera
colour-change
colour-filter
colourlessly
colour scheme
columbaceous
columbic acid
columniation
combat jacket
combinedness
combined pill
come a cropper
come across as
come a long way
come-by-chance
come into line
come into play
come it strong
come one's ways
come on strong
come tardy off
come to a point
come to naught
come to no good
come to nought
come to pieces
come to the top
comfortingly
Cominformist
commandingly
Command Paper
commemorator
commenceable
commencement
commendatary
commendation
commendatore
commendatory
commensalism
commensality
commensurate

commentaries
commentation
commercially
commiserable
commissarial
commissariat
commissaries
commissional
commissioned
commissioner
commit mayhem
committee man
commodiously
commonalties
Common Celtic
commonership
common factor
common ground
commonholder
common jackal
common laurel
common lawyer
common lizard
Common Market
commonplacer
common prayer
Common Prayer
common privet
common roller
common shrimp
common violet
commonwealth
communicable
communicably
communicator
Communion-cup
communionist
community tax
companionage
companionate
companion set
companion-way
companionway
compare notes
compartition
compass plane
compass-plant
compaternity
compatriotic
compellation
compellingly
compenetrate
compensation
compensative
compensatory
competitress
complacently
complainable
complaintive
complaisance
complanation
complemental

complementer
completeness
complete with
complexional
complexioned
complexities
complication
complicative
complimental
complimenter
componential
compo rations
composedness
compos mentis
compoundable
compound leaf
compoundness
compound time
compound word
comprecation
compressible
compulsative
compulsively
compulsorily
compunctious
compurgation
compurgatory
computer game
conceivement
concelebrant
concelebrate
concentrated
concentrator
concentrical
conceptional
conceptively
conceptually
concert grand
concertinaed
concertinist
concert party
concert pitch
concessional
concessioner
concessively
conchiferous
conchoidally
conchologist
conciliabule
conciliarism
conciliarist
conciliation
conciliative
conciliatory
conclamation
conclusively
concomitance
concomitancy
concordancer
concordantly
concordatory
concorporate

concremation
concrescence
concreteness
concupiscent
concurrently
condemnation
condemnatory
condemningly
condensation
condescender
conditionate
conductively
conductivity
conduct-money
conductorial
conduct sheet
conduplicate
confabulator
confectioner
confederator
conferential
confessional
confessorial
confidential
confinedness
confirmation
confirmative
confirmatory
confiscation
confiscatory
conflagrator
conformation
confoundable
confoundedly
confrontment
Confucianism
Confucianist
confusedness
confusticate
congeniality
congenitally
conglobation
conglobulate
conglomerate
conglutinate
congratulant
congratulate
congregation
congregative
congress boot
conic section
conidiophore
conjunctival
conjunctivas
conjure woman
conjurorship
connaturally
connectional
connectively
connectivity
conning tower
connubiality

conqueringly
conquistador
conscionable
conscionably
conscription
conscriptive
consecration
consecratory
consensually
consentience
consentingly
consequently
conservation
conservatism
conservatist
conservative
conservatize
conservatory
conservatrix
considerable
considerably
consignation
consistently
consistorial
consistorian
consistories
consociation
console table
consolidator
consonantism
conspiracies
conspiration
conspirative
conspiratory
constabulary
constatation
constipation
constituency
constitution
constitutive
constriction
constrictive
constringent
construction
constructive
consultation
consultative
consultatory
consummately
consummation
consummative
consummatory
contabescent
contact print
contact sheet
contact sport
contagionist
contagiously
containerise
containerize
contaminator
contemningly

contemplable
contemplator
contemporary
contemporize
contemptible
contemptibly
contemptuous
contentation
contentional
conterminate
conterminous
contestation
contextually
contignation
contiguously
contingently
continuality
continuation
continuative
continuities
continuously
contractable
contractedly
contractible
contractural
contractured
contract work
contradictor
contranatant
contrapuntal
contrariness
contrariwise
contribution
contributive
contributory
contriteness
contrivement
control board
control group
controllable
controllably
control panel
control tower
controverter
contumacious
contumelious
convalescent
convectional
convectively
convenership
conveniently
conventicler
conventional
conventioner
conventually
conversation
conversative
conveyancing
conveyor belt
convictively
convincement
convincingly

convivialist
conviviality
convolutedly
convulsional
convulsively
co-occurrence
cookie-cutter
cookie-pusher
cooking apple
cooking range
cooking-stove
cook the books
cooling tower
co-omnipotent
coordinately
coordination
coordinative
copolymerise
copolymerize
copper-fasten
copper glance
copper-headed
copper-nickel
co-production
coprophagous
coprophilous
co-proprietor
co-prosperity
copulatively
copy of verses
coquettishly
corduroy road
corelatively
core-sampling
co-respondent
corn chandler
corn crowfoot
corn exchange
corniche road
Cornish cream
Cornish pasty
corn marigold
corno inglese
corn on the cob
corn-shucking
corollaceous
coronal plane
coronary gold
coroner's jury
corporal oath
corporalship
corporealism
corporeality
corporealize
corpse-candle
cor pulmonale
corpusculous
corpus luteum
correctional
correctitude
correctively
correlatable

corresponder
corroborator
corruptively
Corsican pine
corticifugal
corticipetal
corticofugal
corticopetal
coscinomancy
cosmetically
cosmic string
cosmocentric
cosmogenetic
cosmogonical
cosmographer
cosmographic
cosmological
cosmonautics
cosmopolitan
costal pleura
costermonger
costing clerk
costlessness
cost of living
costume drama
costume piece
Cotswold lion
cottage ornée
cottage piano
cotton famine
cottonocracy
Cottonopolis
cotton-powder
cotton thread
cotton-woolly
cotyledonary
cotyledonous
cough mixture
Coulomb force
council-board
council-house
councilmanic
council of war
council-table
councilwoman
councilwomen
counsellable
countability
count against
countenanced
countenancer
counter-agent
counter-argue
counterblast
counter-charm
countercharm
countercheck
counter-claim
countercross
countercycle
counter-earth
counter-élite

counterforce
counterguard
counter lunch
countermarch
countermatch
counterminer
counter-offer
counter-order
counterpoint
counterpoise
counterproof
counterprove
counterpunch
counter-scale
counterscarp
countersense
countershaft
counterslope
counter-spell
counterstain
counter-tenor
counter-title
counter-trade
countervalue
counterweigh
countess-ship
counting-room
country dance
country house
country mouse
country music
country party
countrywoman
countrywomen
count the cost
count the days
county family
county school
coup de foudre
coupé de ville
coup the crans
courageously
courtesy call
courtiership
court-martial
court of guard
court plaster
cousin german
cousinliness
covalent bond
covering note
cover version
covetousness
cowardliness
Cowper's gland
coxswainless
coxswainship
crack a bottle
crack-brained
cracked wheat
crack the whip
cradle-rocker

cradle-scythe
cradle-snatch
craft-brother
craftsmaster
craftspeople
craftsperson
cranial index
cranial nerve
cranio-facial
craniologist
craniometric
cranioplasty
cranio-spinal
craniotomies
crapshooting
crash barrier
crash landing
crash the gate
creaking gate
cream cracker
creativeness
creaturehood
creatureship
credibleness
credit rating
creditworthy
creeping bent
creepy-crawly
cremationist
crematoriums
crème brûlées
crème caramel
crème de cacao
crème de noyau
crème fraiche
cremnophobia
crenellation
creolization
creosote bush
crêpe de Chine
crêpe Suzette
crepusculine
crepusculous
crescent moon
crescent roll
crested argus
cretaceously
crico-thyroid
Crimean shirt
crime-busting
crime fighter
criminal code
criminalness
cringingness
crise de nerfs
cristobalite
criteriology
critical mass
criticalness
critical path
critical size
criticizable

Cro-Magnon man
cromoglycate
Crookes glass
Crookes space
cross a cheque
cross and pile
cross-bedding
cross-bencher
cross-buttock
cross-channel
cross-connect
cross-country
cross-dresser
cross-examine
cross-grained
cross-handled
cross-heading
crossing over
cross-linkage
cross-posting
cross product
cross purpose
cross-reading
cross-section
cross-subsidy
crown bowling
crowned crane
Crown Gardens
crown-wearing
crucialities
crush barrier
cryoglobulin
cryopreserve
cry over spilt
cryptanalyst
cryptobiosis
cryptobiotic
cryptococcal
cryptogamist
cryptogamous
cryptography
cryptologist
cryptonymous
cry roast meat
crystal class
crystal clear
crystal-gazer
crystal glass
crystallitic
crystallizer
cubic content
cubistically
cucking-stool
cuckoo flower
cuckoo roller
cuckoo shrike
cuckoo wrasse
cucumber tree
cue and review
Culm Measures
culpableness
cultivatable

culture-bound
culture pearl
culture shock
cumber-ground
cumbersomely
cumbrousness
cumulatively
cumulonimbus
cunctipotent
cuneiformist
cunnilinctus
cupboard love
cupping-glass
cuprammonium
curarization
curativeness
curiological
curled mallow
curlie-wurlie
curling-stone
curling tongs
curl of the lip
curmudgeonly
currant borer
currant jelly
currency note
current asset
curve-fitting
curvifoliate
curvirostral
cushion-dance
custard apple
customizable
customs house
customs union
cut and thrust
cuticularize
cutinization
cut one's lucky
cut one's stick
cut on the bias
cut the cackle
cut the comb of
cutting grass
cutting horse
cyanochroite
cyanogenesis
cyanogenetic
cyanophilous
cyclodextrin
cyclonically
cyclopropane
cyclostomate
cylinder bore
cylinder head
cylinder lock
cylinder seal
cylindricity
cylindriform
cylindroidal
cymotrichous
cynocephalus

cystic artery
cysticercoid
cytochalasin
cytochemical
cytogenetics
cytoskeletal
cytoskeleton
cytotaxonomy
Czechoslovak
dabbling duck
dactylically
dactyloscopy
dactylozooid
daft as a brush
daggle-tailed
dairy factory
dairy-farming
Dalmatian dog
damaged goods
damask violet
damn your eyes
damson cheese
dance hostess
dance macabre
dance of death
Dance of Death
dance the hays
danger signal
Danish modern
Danish pastry
danse macabre
danseur noble
Darby and Joan
dariole mould
Dartmoor pony
Darwinianism
dassievanger
data terminal
datelessness
daughter atom
daughter cell
daughterhood
daughterless
daunorubicin
day blindness
daylight time
day of the week
deactivation
dead-and-alive
dead as mutton
dead-ball line
dead giveaway
de-adjectival
dead language
dead man's hand
Dead Sea apple
dead to rights
deaf-dumbness
de-alcoholize
dealkylation
deambulation
deambulatory

deanery synod
death-dealing
deathfulness
death-or-glory
death penalty
death warrant
debating club
debilitation
debilitative
debonairness
debt of honour
debt of nature
Debussyesque
decaffeinate
decalcomania
decalescence
decapacitate
decaphyllous
decapitalize
decapitation
decasyllabic
decasyllable
deceleration
December moth
decentralise
decentralist
decentralize
decentration
decidability
decimal place
decimal point
decimal scale
decipherable
decipherment
decisiveness
deckled-edged
declassified
declassifies
declensional
declinometer
decoloration
decommission
decomplement
decomposable
decomposible
decompressor
decongestant
decongestion
decongestive
deconsecrate
decontrolled
decoratively
decorousness
decorticator
decreasingly
decrescendos
dedicatorily
dedolomitize
deducibility
deep mourning
deer-coloured
de-escalation

de-excitation	democratical	depreciative	destructible
defatigation	democratizer	depreciatory	desulphurate
defenestrate	demodulation	depressingly	desulphurise
defensive end	demographics	depressively	desulphurize
defibrillate	demolishable	depressurise	desultorious
deficiencies	demolishment	depressurize	desynonymize
definability	demoniacally	deproteinize	detachedness
definiteness	demonization	Deptford pink	deteriorator
definitional	demonologist	depth of field	determinable
definitively	demonomaniac	depth of focus	determinably
deflagration	demonopolise	deputatively	determinator
deflationary	demonopolize	deracination	determinatum
deflationist	demonstrable	deratization	determinedly
deflocculant	demonstrably	deregulation	dethronement
deflocculate	demonstrator	deregulatory	detoxication
defraudation	demoralizing	derelict land	detractation
degenerately	Demosthenean	derepression	detractingly
degeneration	demotivation	derestricted	detractively
degenerative	denaturalise	derisiveness	detruncation
deglaciation	denaturalize	derivability	detumescence
deglutitious	denaturation	derivational	deuteranomal
degree Kelvin	dendrologist	derivatively	deuteranopia
dehumidified	Denmark satin	dermabrasion	deuteranopic
dehumidifier	den of thieves	dermapterous	deuterostome
dehumidifies	denomination	dermatophyte	Deutsche Mark
de-indexation	denominative	dermographia	developement
deionization	denotational	derogatively	deviationism
dejectedness	denotatively	derogatorily	deviationist
delamination	denouncement	desalination	devil-in-a-bush
delayed shock	densitometer	desaturation	devilishness
delegateship	densitometry	descendental	devil-may-care
delegitimize	denticulated	descensional	devil's matins
Delian League	dentilingual	descent group	devil's needle
deliberately	denuclearise	desensitizer	devil's tattoo
deliberation	denuclearize	desertedness	devil-worship
deliberative	denudational	desert island	devolatilize
delicateness	denumeration	deservedness	devotionally
delicatessen	denunciation	desideration	dextrocardia
delightfully	denunciative	desiderative	diabetogenic
delightingly	denunciatory	designer drug	diabolically
delimitation	deoch an doris	desirability	diadem monkey
delimitative	deontologist	desirousness	diadem spider
delinquently	deoperculate	desk sergeant	diageotropic
deliquescent	deordination	desolateness	diagrammatic
delitescence	departmental	desolatingly	dialectician
delitescency	depauperated	despairfully	dialecticism
deliver a jail	dependencies	despairingly	dialectology
delivery room	depend upon it	despecialize	dialling code
Della Cruscan	dephlegmator	desperadoism	dialling tone
deltiologist	depilatories	despitefully	dialogically
delusiveness	depoliticise	despiteously	diamagnetism
demagnetizer	depoliticize	despoliation	diamond-drill
demand-driven	depolymerise	despondently	diamond-field
demembration	depolymerize	despondingly	diamond frame
dementedness	depopularize	despotically	diamond-point
demi-culverin	depopulation	desquamation	diamond snake
demilitarise	depositaries	desquamative	Diamond State
demilitarize	depos: tation	desquamatory	diaphanously
demi-mondaine	depositional	dessert apple	diapirically
demineralise	depositories	dessert-plate	diarthrodial
demineralize	depravedness	dessertspoon	diastrophism
demi-toilette	depreciation	destroyingly	diathermancy

diatomaceous
diatonically
diazomethane
diazotizable
dibranchiate
dicarboxylic
dicatalectic
dichotomized
dichroiscope
dichromatism
Dickensianly
dictatorship
dictionaries
dictyostelic
didactically
diddle-diddle
die in harness
die in one's bed
diencephalic
diencephalon
die of illness
die on someone
diesel engine
dietetically
diethylamide
diethyl ether
Dietl's crisis
differentiae
differential
difficulties
diffusedness
diffusionism
diffusionist
digging-stick
digital clock
digitization
digladiation
dig oneself in
digressingly
digressional
digressively
Dijon mustard
dijudication
dilaceration
dilambdodont
dilapidation
dilatability
dilatational
dilatometric
dilatoriness
dilatory plea
dilettantish
dilettantism
dilettantist
dilly-dallied
dilly-dallier
dilly-dallies
dimensurator
dimerization
diminishable
diminishment
diminutively

dimmer switch
dingle-dangle
dingy skipper
dining saloon
dinner jacket
dioctahedral
Diogenes-crab
dioptrically
diphtheritic
diphtheritis
diphthongise
diphthongize
diploblastic
diplographic
diplomatical
diplostemony
dipole moment
dipyridamole
direct access
direct action
directedness
direct labour
direct method
direct object
directorship
direct speech
dirigibility
dirty weekend
disabilities
disaccharase
disaccharide
disaccordant
disadvantage
disaffection
disaffiliate
disaggregate
disagreeable
disagreeably
disagreement
disallowable
disallowance
disambiguate
disamenities
disanimation
disannulment
disapproving
disassembler
disassociate
disaster area
disastrously
disauthorize
disbursement
discarnation
disceptation
discerningly
discerptible
disciplehood
discipleship
disciplinant
disciplinary
disclamation
discographer

discolourate
discomfiting
discomfiture
discomforter
discommodate
discommodity
discommonize
discomposure
discongruity
disconnected
disconnecter
disconnexion
disconsolate
discontinued
discontinuee
discontinuer
discontinues
discontinuor
discordantly
discountable
discount rate
discount shop
discourteous
discoverable
discoverably
discoverture
discrediting
discreetness
discrepation
discreteness
discretional
discretively
discriminant
discriminate
disculpation
discursively
discursivity
discussional
discussively
disdainfully
diseasedness
disembarrass
disembellish
disemboguing
disenactment
disenchanter
disencourage
disendowment
disentrammel
disestablish
disfranchise
disgorgement
disgradation
disgregation
disguiseless
disguisement
disgustfully
disgustingly
dishabituate
disharmonise
disharmonize
dishevelling

dishevelment
dish of the day
dishonesties
disincarnate
disincentive
disinfectant
disinfection
disinflation
disingenuity
disingenuous
disinherison
disinherited
disinsectize
disintegrant
disintegrate
disintegrity
disinterment
disinterring
disintricate
disjointedly
disk emulator
dislodgement
dismayedness
dismissively
dismountable
disobedience
disorganizer
disorientate
dispatch-boat
dispatch case
dispauperize
dispensaries
dispensation
dispensative
dispensatory
dispensatrix
dispersivity
dispersonate
dispersonify
dispiritedly
dispiritment
dispiteously
displaceable
displacement
displeasance
displeasedly
disposedness
dispossessed
dispossessor
disprivilege
disprovement
disputatious
disqualified
disqualifies
disquietedly
disquietness
disquisition
disquisitive
disrecommend
disregardant
disregardful
disreputable

disreputably
disrespecter
disreverence
disruptively
dissatisfied
dissatisfies
dissected map
disseisoress
dissemblable
dissemblance
disseminator
dissenterism
dissentience
dissentingly
dissertation
dissertative
disseverance
disseverment
dissimilarly
dissimulator
dissociality
dissocialize
dissociation
dissociative
dissolve away
dissolvingly
dissuasively
dissymmetric
distance post
distemperate
distichously
distillation
distillatory
distilleries
distinctness
distomatosis
distortional
distractedly
distractible
distrainable
distrainment
distraughtly
distressedly
distributary
distribution
distributism
distributist
distributive
disturbative
disturbingly
disutilities
disvaluation
ditetragonal
ditheistical
dithyrambist
ditransitive
ditriglyphic
ditrigonally
dittographic
diuretically
divaricately
divarication

diversionary
diversionism
diversionist
diverticular
diverticulum
divertimenti
divertimento
divided skirt
dividendless
divine office
diving beetle
diving petrel
divinity calf
divinityship
divinization
divisibility
divisionally
division-bell
division sign
divisiveness
do a hand's turn
doch an dorris
doctor's stuff
doctrinalism
doctrinalist
doctrinarian
doctrinarity
documentable
documentably
document case
docutainment
dodecahedral
dodecahedric
dodecahedron
dodecandrous
dodecaphonic
doggerelizer
dogmatically
dog-tooth spar
do-it-yourself
dolesomeness
doll hospital
dolly mixture
dolman sleeve
dolorousness
dolphinarium
Domain orator
dome fastener
Domesday Book
domesticable
domestically
domesticator
domestic fowl
dominatrices
dominical day
Dominicaness
domino effect
domino theory
donkey engine
donkey jacket
donkey's years
donor country

do nothing for
donothingism
doodlebugger
do one's utmost
dopaminergic
doppelgänger
Doppler radar
Doppler shift
Doppler width
Dorcas basket
dormer window
dorsiflexion
dorsiventral
dorsolateral
dorsoventral
Dostoevskian
do the dirty on
do the honours
do the naughty
dotted rhythm
Douay version
double-acting
double-banked
double-barrel
double-bitted
double boiler
double bridle
double-clutch
double dagger
double-dealer
double-decked
double-decker
double digits
double-dipper
double-figure
double fleece
double-ganger
double-glazed
double-handed
double-headed
double header
double hyphen
double-minded
double nelson
double obelus
double paddle
double-ported
double-queued
double-spaced
double vision
double walled
double whammy
double yellow
double-yolked
doubtful card
doubtfulness
doubtingness
douceur de vie
doughnutting
douroucoulis
Dover's powder
do violence to

down-and-outer
downloadable
Down syndrome
down the drain
down the hatch
down the river
down the track
down the tubes
downwardness
draconically
dracontiasis
draft dodging
drag one's feet
dragon's blood
dragon's teeth
drag the chain
drainage tube
drain the lees
dramatically
dramaturgist
drapeability
draughtboard
draught horse
draught-house
draughtiness
draught-proof
drawback lock
drawing-block
drawing board
drawing-knife
drawing of tea
drawing paper
drawing-roomy
draw the cloth
dreadfulness
dreamfulness
drenching-gun
Dresden china
dressing case
dressing-comb
dressing down
dressing gown
dressing room
drift-netting
drinkability
drink-driving
drinking-bout
drinking-horn
drinking song
drip-moulding
drip painting
drivellingly
drive-through
driving force
driving range
driving wheel
droopingness
drop a clanger
drop back into
drop-in centre
dropped scone
dropping-well

dropping-zone	Easter Parade	Egyptologist	elliptically
drop the pilot	Easter Sunday	Eidophusikon	elocutionary
drosophilist	East Germanic	eighteenthly	elocutionist
drosophyllum	East Indiaman	eight-pounder	elocutionize
droughtiness	easy of access	eisteddfodau	elongational
drumbledrone	easy on the eye	eisteddfodic	elucubration
drunk as a lord	eat humble pie	Eisteddfodic	email ombrant
drunk-driving	eat one's terms	ejection seat	emanationism
drunken Helot	eat one's words	elasmobranch	emanationist
drying-closet	eau de Cologne	elasmosaurus	emancipation
Dryopithecus	eau de Javelle	elastic fibre	emancipative
dual-standard	eavesdropper	elastic limit	emancipatory
dubitatively	ebulliometer	elderberries	emargination
duchesse lace	ebullioscope	elder brother	emasculation
ducking-stool	ebullioscopy	Elder Brother	emasculative
duck's disease	eccentricity	electability	emasculatory
dufrenoysite	ecclesiastic	electiveness	embattlement
dulciloquent	ecclesiology	electrically	embeddedness
dumbstricken	echinococcus	electric blue	embezzlement
dumdum bullet	echinodermal	electric fire	embitterment
dumortierite	echolocation	electric hare	emblazonment
dunderheaded	echo-sounding	electrogenic	emblematical
dunghill cock	eclectically	electrolyser	embolisation
Dunmow flitch	eco-labelling	electrolysis	embolization
Dunstable way	ecologically	electrolytic	embouchement
duodecennial	econometrics	electromatic	embranchment
duodecimally	econometrist	electromeric	embroideress
duodenectomy	economically	electrometer	embroideries
duodenostomy	economic rent	electrometry	embroidering
durationless	economy class	electromotor	embryoid body
dust and ashes	economy drive	electron beam	embryologist
Dutch auction	eco-terrorism	electron lens	emerald green
Dutch bargain	eco-terrorist	electron pair	Emergicenter
Dutch courage	ecstatically	electron tube	emetic tartar
Dutch defence	ectoparasite	electronvolt	emigrant road
duty-free shop	ectoproctous	electro-optic	emolumentary
dwarfishness	ectrodactyly	electropaint	emotionalise
dynamic range	ecumenically	electrophile	emotionalism
dynamization	edging shears	electrophone	emotionalist
dynamometric	editorialise	electroplate	emotionality
dynastically	editorialist	electroplexy	emotionalize
dysaesthesia	editorialize	electroscope	empathically
dysgenically	educationese	electro-shock	emperor goose
dysphemistic	educationist	electrotonic	emphatically
dysteleology	edulcoration	electrotonus	emphaticness
each and every	Edwardianism	electrotyper	empoisonment
ear-defenders	effectuality	eleemosynary	Empty Quarter
earl palatine	effectuation	elementalism	empyreumatic
Earl Palatine	effeminately	elementarily	emulsifiable
early and late	effervescent	elementarity	enantiomeric
early closing	efficiencies	elephant-bird	enantiomorph
Early English	efflorescent	elephant fish	enantiopathy
early warning	effortlessly	elephant joke	enantiotropy
earned income	effronteries	elephant seal	enarthrodial
earnest money	effusiveness	elephant's ear	encephalitic
earn one's keep	egg and anchor	elevatedness	encephalitis
ear-splitting	eggs and bacon	eleventh part	enchantingly
earth-shaking	eggs Benedict	eligibleness	enchiridions
earth station	egoistically	elixir of life	enchondrosis
easel-picture	Egyptian bean	ellagitannin	encipherment
easterliness	Egyptian days	Ellingtonian	encirclement
Easter Monday	Egyptian lily	ellipsograph	enclitically

encloistered
encroachment
encrustation
encumberment
encumbrancer
encyclopedia
encyclopedic
endamagement
endangerment
endarteritis
endenization
endermically
en déshabillé
endless screw
endocarditic
endocarditis
endocervical
end of the line
end of the road
endogenously
endometritis
endomorphism
endonuclease
endoparasite
endoskeletal
endoskeleton
endosymbiont
endothelioma
endotracheal
endurability
enduringness
energization
enervatingly
enfeeblement
Enfield rifle
enfranchiser
engagingness
engenderment
engine driver
engineership
English flute
Englishwoman
Englishwomen
engrossingly
enharmonical
enhypostasia
enhypostatic
enjoyability
enjoy oneself
enliveningly
enophthalmos
enormousness
enshrinement
enspherement
enswathement
entablatured
entanglement
enter a caveat
enteric fever
enterobiasis
enterococcus
enterocoelic

enterokinase
enteropneust
enterotomies
enterprising
entertaining
enthronement
enthusiastic
enthymematic
entitatively
entomogenous
entomologist
entomologize
entoparasite
entoproctous
entoptically
entotympanic
entrammelled
entrance form
entrancement
entrancingly
entreatingly
entrenchment
entrepreneur
entropically
enviableness
envisagement
enzymologist
eosinophilia
eosinophilic
epexegetical
ephebiatrics
ephemeralism
ephemerality
epicureanism
Epicureanism
epicuticular
epicycloidal
epidemically
epidemiology
epididymides
epididymitis
epiglottitis
epigrammatic
epigraphical
epileptiform
epimorphosis
Epiphanytide
epiphenomena
epipterygoid
episcopacies
episcopalian
episcopalism
episcopality
episcopicide
episcotister
episiotomies
episodically
epistemology
epistolatory
episyllogism
epithalamial
epithalamium

epitheliosis
epitrochlear
eponymically
epoxide resin
equalitarian
equalization
equanimously
equatability
equationally
equatorially
equatorwards
equestrienne
equidistance
equifinality
equilibrator
equilibriate
equilibrious
equilibriums
equimultiple
equinumerous
equiparation
equipendency
equipollence
equipollency
equiprobable
equitability
equivalently
equivocality
equivocation
equivocatory
ergastoplasm
erratic block
erythematous
erythroblast
erythrocytic
erythrogenic
erythromycin
erythrophore
escape clause
escapologist
escutcheoned
Eskimo curlew
esoterically
espagnolette
esparto grass
especialness
essentialism
essentialist
essentiality
essentialize
essential oil
estrangement
eternity ring
eternization
ethanoic acid
ethanolamine
etherealness
etherization
etheromaniac
Ethiopianism
ethnocentred
ethnocentric

ethnogenesis
ethnographer
ethnographic
ethnohistory
ethnological
ethnoscience
ethosuximide
ethoxyethane
ethyl acetate
ethyl alcohol
ethylbenzene
etiquettical
etymological
etymologicon
Euboic talent
eucalyptuses
eucharistize
eudemonistic
eufunctional
euhemeristic
eunuchoidism
eupeptically
euphemiously
euphonically
euphoniously
euphorically
eurhythmical
Euro-American
Eurocentrism
Euro-currency
Euro-election
European plan
eurythermous
eustatically
euthyroidism
eutrophicate
Eutychianism
evanescently
evangelicity
evangelistic
evaporimeter
even-handedly
evening class
evening dress
evening paper
even Stephens
even-tempered
eventfulness
event horizon
eventide home
ever and again
ever-blooming
evergreen oak
everydayness
every man jack
every man Jack
everyone else
every so often
everywhither
evidentially
evil-speaking
evisceration

evolute curve	exobiologist	extended-play	faintishness
evolutionary	exoergically	extensometer	fair-mindedly
evolutionise	exomologesis	exterminable	fairy penguin
evolutionism	exonormative	exterminator	fait accompli
evolutionist	exopeptidase	exteroceptor	faithfulness
evolutionize	exophthalmia	extinguisher	faith healing
exacerbation	exophthalmic	extortionary	falcated teal
exactingness	exophthalmos	extortionate	falcon-gentle
exact science	exophthalmus	extortionist	fallaciously
exaggeration	exopterygote	extracranial	falling short
exaggerative	exorbitantly	extractor fan	fall into line
exaggeratory	exorbitation	extraditable	fall like a log
exalbuminous	exorcistical	extrahepatic	fall together
examinership	exorcization	extralegally	fall to pieces
exanthematic	exorcizement	extralimital	false bedding
exasperation	exoterically	extralogical	false ceiling
excalceation	exothermally	extramarital	false colours
excavational	exotic dancer	extramission	false concord
Excellencies	expansionary	extramundane	false cypress
excel oneself	expansion bit	extramurally	false economy
excentricity	expansion box	extra-musical	false gharial
exceptionary	expansionism	extraneously	false quarter
exchangeable	expansionist	extrapolable	false vampire
exchange rate	expatriation	extrapolator	false witness
excitability	expatriatism	extrasensory	falsificator
excited state	expectancies	extrasomatic	familiarizer
excitingness	expectorator	extra-special	familiarness
excitomotory	expediential	extrasystole	family circle
exclaustrate	expeditation	extra-uterine	family credit
exclusionary	expeditioner	extravagance	family doctor
exclusionism	experiential	extravagancy	family living
exclusionist	experimental	extravaganza	Family of Love
excogitation	experimented	extraversion	famine prices
excogitative	experimenter	extraversive	fancifulness
excruciating	expert system	extrinsicate	fanglomerate
excruciation	explantation	extrinsicism	fantasticate
excursionary	explicitness	extroversion	faradization
excursionist	exploitation	extroversive	fare thee well
excursionize	exploitative	extrovertish	far-sightedly
excusability	exponentiate	exulceration	Farther India
executionary	export reject	eye of a needle	Far Westerner
executorship	expositional	eyes on stalks	fasciculated
exegetically	expositorily	fabulousness	fascinatedly
exencephalic	expostulator	facelessness	fascioliasis
exenteration	express clerk	face-painting	fashion house
exercise bike	expressional	face the facts	fashion-paper
exercise book	expressively	face the music	fashion piece
exercise yard	expressivity	facilitation	fashion plate
exercitation	express rifle	facilitative	fast and loose
exercitorian	express train	facilitatory	fastidiously
exfiltration	exprobration	facsimileing	fastuousness
exflagellate	expromission	factionalise	father figure
exhaustingly	expropriator	factionalism	father-lasher
exhaustively	expulsionist	factionalist	fatherliness
exheredation	exsanguinate	factionalize	Father of lies
exhibitional	ex-serviceman	factiousness	fathers-in-law
exhibitioner	ex-servicemen	factitiously	fathomlessly
exhibitively	exsibilation	factorizable	fatigability
exhilaration	exsufflation	factory floor	fatigue-dress
exhilarative	exsufflicate	faggot-stitch	fatigue-party
exiguousness	extemporizer	fail and divot	fault breccia
existibility	extendedness	faint-hearted	fault-finding

faute de mieux	fibrinolytic	fireproofing	flippantness
favouredness	fibroadenoma	fireside chat	flirtational
favourite son	fibroblastic	fire-watching	flitter-mouse
fawn-coloured	fibrogenesis	first-aid post	floatability
fearlessness	fibrosarcoma	first and last	float-chamber
fearsomeness	fictionalise	first cellist	floating debt
feasibleness	fictionality	first century	floating dock
Feast of Fools	fictionalize	first edition	floating mill
feast of weeks	fictitiously	first-nighter	float process
feather-brain	fiddle-faddle	first officer	flocculation
feather-grass	fiddle-headed	first quarter	floor manager
featheriness	fiddle-string	first reading	Florence wine
feather-light	fidelity bond	first refusal	floriculture
feather-pated	fidus Achates	First Sea Lord	Florida water
febrifacient	field battery	fish and chips	florilegiums
Febronianism	field general	fishing story	flouring mill
fecklessness	field glasses	fit as a fiddle	flourishment
federalistic	field marshal	fitted carpet	floury miller
feeble-minded	Field Marshal	five-spice mix	flower-de-luce
feeing market	field-meeting	five-year plan	flower garden
feel one's feet	field mustard	fixed capital	flowering age
feel one's legs	field officer	flabelliform	flower of Jove
feel one's oats	field spaniel	flagellation	flower of wine
feel the pinch	fiendishness	flagellative	flower-pecker
feel wretched	fiftieth part	flagellatory	flower people
feet foremost	fighter cover	flagelliform	flowers of tan
feldspathoid	fighting cock	flagitiously	flowing sheet
felicitation	fighting fish	flagrantness	fluid extract
felicitously	fighting fund	flake culture	fluidization
fellow-travel	fighting talk	flamboyantly	fluidized bed
felon-setting	fighting trim	flamen dialis	flummadiddle
female condom	figurability	flame-thrower	fluoranthene
feminineness	figuratively	flammability	fluorapatite
femininistic	figure-caster	flammiferous	fluorescence
feminization	figure-dancer	flammivomous	fluoridation
fence-mending	figure skater	flammulation	fluorimetric
fence-sitting	filbert brush	flank forward	fluorination
fend and prove	filet de boeuf	flannelboard	fluorocarbon
fender bender	filibusterer	flannelgraph	fluorometric
fenestration	filter-feeder	flannel-mouth	fluoroscopic
fennel-flower	filter-tipped	flat-footedly	fluosilicate
Fermat number	finalization	flatteringly	fluphenazine
fermentation	final process	flavanthrone	flutteration
fermentative	finance house	flavoprotein	flutteringly
Fermi surface	financialist	flawlessness	flutter-wheel
fern crushing	find an office	fleece-picker	flying bridge
ferricyanide	finding-store	Fleet Admiral	flying change
ferrocyanide	find its level	fleet in being	flying circus
ferrugineous	find one's feet	fleetingness	flying coffin
fers-de-moline	find the means	Flemish horse	flying column
fertilizable	fine and dandy	flesh and fell	flying doctor
fetalisation	fine feathers	flexibleness	flying dragon
fetch a gutser	finely-strung	flexographic	flying façade
feudal system	finger-lickin'	flexor muscle	flying lizard
fever and ague	finger millet	flickeringly	flying picket
feverishness	finger puppet	flickermouse	flying saucer
fever therapy	fingle-fangle	flick through	flying school
fianchettoes	Finnish spitz	flight-number	flying tackle
fibrillation	fire and sword	flimflammery	fly into a rage
fibrilliform	fire-fighting	flimflamming	fly on the wall
fibrinolysin	fire-position	flindermouse	fly-the-garter
fibrinolysis	fire practice	flint-hearted	focalization

fodder-cheese	for Pete's sake	freethinking	fructivorous
folding doors	for pity's sake	freezing cold	fruitfulness
folding money	for reference	freezing rain	fruiting body
fold one's arms	forsakenness	freezing tool	fruit machine
foliage plant	for shortness	Freightliner	frumentation
folie du doute	forswornness	freight train	frumpishness
folkloristic	for the asking	French cotton	frustratedly
folk medicine	for the future	French endive	fuchsinophil
folliculated	for the life of	French letter	fuddy-duddies
folliculitis	for the love of	French polish	fuel-injected
follow-me-lads	for the moment	French sorrel	fugie-warrant
follow the sea	for the record	French turnip	fugitiveness
fondant icing	for the sake of	French window	fuliginosity
food additive	forthputting	frenetically	fuliginously
food for worms	forthrightly	frequentable	full-bottomed
foolhardiest	forthsetting	frequentness	fuller's earth
fool's parsley	fortieth part	fresh as paint	full throttle
football boot	fortuitously	freshmanship	fully-fledged
football pool	forty-seventh	Fresnel rhomb	fulminic acid
for account of	fossilizable	Freudian slip	fume cupboard
forbiddingly	foster-father	friar's balsam	funambulator
forced-choice	foster-mother	friars' balsam	functionally
forced labour	fouled anchor	fricandeaued	functionless
forcefulness	foul one's nest	frictionally	function word
force majeure	foundational	friction-ball	fungological
force the game	foundationer	frictionless	fungus-garden
force the pace	fountain-head	friendliness	funnel beaker
forcibleness	fountainhead	friendly fire	funniosities
forcing frame	fountainless	frigate-built	furfuraceous
fore-and after	four freedoms	frightenable	furnish forth
forebodement	Fourieristic	frightenedly	furniture van
forebodingly	fourpenny one	fringing reef	Further India
forecarriage	fourteenthly	Frisesomorum	furunculosis
forecastable	fourth estate	fritillaries	futilitarian
foreconceive	fourth finger	frolicsomely	futtock plate
forefatherly	Fourth of July	fromage blanc	futurologist
foreheadless	four-went-ways	fromage frais	fuzzy-wuzzies
foreign devil	fowling piece	from day to day	Gaelic coffee
foreign-going	fowl leucosis	from end to end	Gaelic League
foreign trade	fox and hounds	from out to out	gain a march on
forelock bolt	foxtail-grass	from overseas	gain ground on
forelock hook	fractionally	from strength	gain the ear of
forensically	fragmentally	from the first	galactagogue
forepleasure	fragmentizer	from the floor	galactosemia
forequarters	frame-breaker	from the heart	galacturonic
foresightful	francization	from tip to toe	Galbraithian
forestalment	Franck-Condon	from top to toe	Galilean moon
forest falcon	Francophilia	frondescence	gallery grave
forest marble	Francophobia	frondiferous	galley-packet
forest ranger	frangibility	frondoseness	galligaskins
forest red gum	frankalmoign	frontage road	gallinaceous
foretellable	Frankenstein	frontal crest	gallocyanine
for Gawd's sake	frankincense	front-bencher	Gallo-Romance
forgeability	fraternalism	frontbencher	gall-sickness
forked tongue	fraternities	frontierless	Galois theory
for lagniappe	fraudulently	frontiersman	Galsworthian
formaldehyde	freakishness	frontiersmen	galvanically
formalizable	freckle-faced	frontispiece	galvanic pile
formicarioid	free electron	front of house	galvanometer
formlessness	free-handedly	front passage	galvanometry
fornicatress	free of charge	front to front	galvanoscope
for one's pains	free-standing	fructiferous	galvanotaxis

game of chance
gamesmanship
gamesomeness
gametophoric
gametophytic
gamopetalous
gamophyllous
gamosepalous
gangliectomy
ganglionated
gang one's gate
ganophyllite
garden balsam
garden carpet
garden centre
gardener-bird
gardenership
Garden of Eden
garden privet
garden roller
garden suburb
garlic butter
garrison town
garter stitch
gasification
gas-permeable
Gastarbeiter
gastric fever
gastric juice
gastronomist
gastroplasty
gastropodous
gastroscopic
gastrulation
gateleg table
gate receipts
gathering cry
gather straws
Gavelkind Act
geanticlinal
Geissler tube
gelatigenous
gelatination
gelatiniform
gelatinously
gelatin paper
gemmological
genealogical
generability
general court
General Court
generalities
general staff
general store
General Synod
generational
generatively
generativism
generativist
generousness
gene splicing
genethliacal

genethliacon
genetic drift
geniculation
genioglossus
gennemically
genotoxicity
gentilitious
gentle falcon
gentle people
genuflection
genuflectory
geobotanical
geochemistry
geodesic dome
geodesic line
geodetically
geographical
geologically
geomagnetism
geomagnetist
geometrician
geophysicist
geoplanarian
geopolitical
geopotential
geoscientist
geosynclinal
geotechnical
Geraldton wax
geriatrician
Germanically
Germanomania
Germanophile
Germanophobe
German silver
germinal cell
gerontocracy
gerontophile
gerontophily
gesticulator
get a guernsey
get a Guernsey
get a handle on
get a hustle on
get a snitch on
get a wiggle on
get credit for
get hitched up
get one's eye in
get one's leave
get outside of
get-rich-quick
get rough with
get somewhere
get the best of
get the feel of
get the hang of
get the jump on
get the mitten
get the name of
get the needle
get the wind up

get with child
Ghibellinism
ghoulishness
giant noctule
giant sequoia
giant's stride
gibber gunyah
gibble-gabble
Gibraltarian
gift of the gab
gigantically
gigantomachy
gilding metal
gill filament
gin and orange
gingerliness
gingivectomy
Giorgi system
girder bridge
girting-place
give an edge to
give audience
give colour to
give credit to
give effect to
give in charge
give it the gas
give one's hand
give one's life
give one's word
give the elbow
give the guy to
give the lie to
give weight to
gizzard trout
glacial epoch
glacier burst
glaciologist
gladiatorial
gladiatorism
gladsomeness
Gladstone bag
glandiferous
glandulation
glass-blowing
glass ceiling
glass furnace
glass slipper
glassy humour
Glauber's salt
glaucescence
glaucomatous
glaucous gull
gleesomeness
gleification
glenohumeral
Glenurquhart
gliding-plane
glimmeringly
glioblastoma
glisteningly
glisteringly

glitteringly
gloaming-shot
global search
globe-thistle
globe-trotter
globigerinae
globigerinal
globigerinas
globularness
glockenspiel
glomerulitis
gloom and doom
gloriousness
glory be to God
glossatorial
glossography
glossolalist
glossologist
glossoplegia
glossopteris
glottal catch
glucoprotein
glue-sniffing
glutamic acid
glutethimide
gluttonously
glyceric acid
glycobiology
glycogenesis
glycogenetic
glycoprotein
glycyrrhizin
glyphography
glyptography
gnomonically
gnotobiology
gnotobiotics
go-aheadative
go and eat coke
goat-antelope
gobbledegook
gobbledygook
go by the board
go by the worse
go by the worst
God be thanked
God of the gaps
go down a storm
God's bodikins
God-surrogate
go for a burton
go glimmering
go hot and cold
going concern
go into action
go into detail
goitrigenous
gold blocking
Golden Fleece
Golden Friday
golden jackal
Golden Legend

golden number	grafting clay	Greenlandish	guilefulness
golden oriole	grain leather	greenskeeper	guilt complex
golden plover	grallatorial	green tobacco	Guinea flower
golden tettix	graminaceous	green vitriol	Guinea pepper
golden wattle	grammaticise	gregariously	gumptionless
goldfish bowl	grammaticism	Grenzbegriff	gunmetal blue
gold standard	grammaticize	grey antimony	gunmetal grey
Goliath crane	gram-molecule	grey eminence	gunpowder tea
Goliath heron	Gram-negative	grey kangaroo	Gunter's chain
gonadotropic	Gram-positive	greylag goose	Gunter's scale
Gondwanaland	Granary bread	grey squirrel	gurjun balsam
gone a million	grand duchess	grievousness	gutter-splint
good breeding	Grand Guignol	griffinesque	Guy Fawkes day
good clean fun	grand inquest	grindability	gymnasiarchy
good creature	grandisonant	grindle stone	gymnosophist
good-humoured	Grandisonian	grind to a halt	gynaecocracy
good riddance	grandisonous	griseofulvin	gynaecologic
Good Shepherd	grand larceny	grope one's way	gynaecomazia
good-tempered	Grand Ole Opry	gross tonnage	gynodioecism
good thinking	grandpappies	grossularite	gypsophilous
goody-goodies	grand passion	grotesquerie	Gypsyologist
go off at score	grandstander	ground-cherry	gyromagnetic
go one's own way	Granite State	ground-colour	habeas corpus
go one's rounds	granny annexe	groundedness	haberdashery
go on the stage	granny bonnet	ground effect	habilimented
go on the stump	granny-sitter	Groundhog Day	habilitation
gooseberries	granodiorite	groundkeeper	habitability
goose pimples	granulocytic	ground-laurel	habit-forming
go out of style	grapeseed oil	groundlessly	habitualness
Gorbachevian	graphic novel	ground parrot	hack-and-slash
Gordon setter	graphitoidal	ground roller	hacking cough
gorgeousness	graphologist	ground stroke	hackney coach
gormlessness	graphomaniac	ground tackle	hackney horse
go shares with	graspingness	ground thrush	hadrosaurian
gosling-green	grasshoppery	group captain	hadrosaurine
gospel-singer	grass warbler	group dialect	haematemesis
gossip column	grass widower	group therapy	haematologic
gossip monger	gratefulness	grovellingly	haematoxylin
go the knuckle	gratifyingly	growing pains	haemerythrin
go to extremes	gratuitously	growing point	haemodynamic
go to one's head	grave-clothes	growing stock	haemophilia B
go to one's rest	gravel-voiced	growth factor	haemophiliac
go to the devil	grease monkey	grow together	haemopoiesis
go to the Devil	Great Britain	grow whiskers	haemopoietic
go to the front	Great Charter	grudgingness	haemorrhagic
go up in flames	Great Council	gruesomeness	haemosiderin
go up the flume	great-hearted	Guadeloupean	hagiographal
go up the steps	great hundred	Guadeloupian	hagiographer
governmental	great inquest	guaiacum test	hagiographic
governorship	Great Malvern	guanethidine	hagiolatrous
go with a swing	great mullein	guardianless	hagiological
gracefulness	Great Pyramid	guardianship	haidingerite
graciousness	Great red spot	gubernacular	haikal screen
gradeability	Great Russian	gubernaculum	hairdressing
grade cricket	great thought	Guernsey lily	hair follicle
graded school	Grecian plait	guerrilla war	hairlessness
Gradgrindery	Greek Cypriot	guessing game	hair mattress
gradient post	Greek Fathers	guest-chamber	hair of the dog
gradient wind	green alkanet	guest speaker	hair-restorer
gradualistic	green channel	Guide's honour	hair's breadth
graduateship	green fingers	guignolesque	hair-splitter
Graecotrojan	greengrocery	guild-brother	half-integral

half-marathon
half measures
half-mourning
half-seas-over
half-timbered
halfway house
half-wittedly
hallowedness
hallucinator
hallucinogen
hallucinosis
halogenation
halotrichite
hamartiology
hammer-action
hammer-harden
hammerheaded
hammochrysos
hammock chair
Hammond organ
Hampshire hog
handclapping
handicapping
handie-talkie
handkerchief
hand over fist
hand over hand
hand's-breadth
handsomeness
hanging guard
hanging judge
hanging shelf
hang one's head
hang out to dry
hang the rap on
hang together
hapaxanthous
happenchance
happenstance
happy as a clam
happy-go-lucky
happy release
happy warrior
haptotropism
hard currency
hard-favoured
hard-featured
hard feelings
hard-headedly
hard-scrabble
hard shoulder
hard standing
hardstanding
hard swearing
Hare Krishnas
harlequinade
harlequin bug
harlequin cup
harlequinism
Harley Street
harmlessness
harmonically

harmoniously
harmonograph
harmonometer
harquebusade
harquebusier
harrier-eagle
harvest field
harvest mouse
harvest queen
hasenpfeffer
hasty pudding
hatchability
hatchet-faced
hate campaign
Haussmannize
haute couture
haute cuisine
have a crack at
have a crush on
have a derry on
have a feel for
have a fling at
have a good arm
have a good war
have a gust for
have an eye for
have a nice day
have a share in
have a smack at
have a snout on
have a way with
have a whack at
have done with
have got it bad
have it in mind
have no brow of
have no choice
have no use for
have no will of
have one's will
have regard to
have the ear of
have the heart
have the law on
have the nerve
have the right
have the sense
have to do with
have whiskers
Hawaian shirt
head and front
headkerchief
headlongness
headmasterly
headmistress
head over ears
headquarters
head-shrinker
headshrinker
heads of state
headstrongly
health centre

health resort
hear a pin drop
heart and dart
heart and soul
heartbreaker
heart-burning
heart-disease
hearteningly
heart failure
heartfulness
heart of stone
heart-rending
heart-strings
heartstrings
heart to heart
heart-warming
heat capacity
heater-shaped
heath-cropper
heathenishly
heather-bleat
heather honey
heave in sight
Heaven defend
Heaven forbid
heavenliness
heavenly body
heavenly host
Heavens above
Heavens alive
heavy-hearted
heavy petting
heavy sleeper
hebdomadally
hebephreniac
hecatompedon
hectocotylus
hectographic
hedenbergite
hedge-creeper
hedge-mustard
hedge-parsley
hedge sparrow
hedge trimmer
heebie-jeebie
heedlessness
height of land
heir apparent
hekistotherm
helianthemum
helicoidally
heliocentric
Heliogabalus
heliographer
heliographic
heliogravure
heliotherapy
heliotropism
hellaciously
hell and Tommy
Hellenophile
hellgrammite

hell on wheels
hell's delight
hell's kitchen
helmsmanship
helplessness
help-yourself
hemerocallis
hemichordate
hemimorphism
hemimorphite
hemiparasite
hemispheroid
hemp agrimony
henceforward
henotheistic
heortologist
hepatisation
hepatization
hepatomegaly
hephthemimer
heptahedrons
heptahydrate
heptarchical
Heracleitean
Heracleonite
heraldically
herb twopence
Hercules' club
herd instinct
herdsmanship
here and there
hereditament
hereditarian
hereditarily
hereinbefore
heretication
heritability
hermeneutics
hermetically
hermetic seal
hermit thrush
heroicalness
heroi-comical
hero sandwich
hero's welcome
herpes zoster
herpetologic
Hertzian wave
hesitatingly
hesitatively
heterauxesis
heterocercal
heteroclitic
heterocyclic
heterodesmic
heteroduplex
heteroecious
heterogamete
heterogamety
heterogamous
heterogeneal
heterogenist

heterogenous	high-reaching	holoparasite	honour system
heterogonous	high-security	holophrastic	hood-moulding
heterography	high-sounding	holophyletic	Hooker's green
hetero-immune	high-spirited	holoplankton	hootenannies
heterokaryon	high-stepping	holopneustic	hopelessness
heterologous	high thinking	Holy Alliance	hopper-dredge
heteromerous	highty-tighty	Holy Cross Day	horizon glass
heteronomous	highwaywoman	holy mackerel	horizontally
heteronymous	highwaywomen	holy of holies	horn arrester
heteroousian	Hilbert space	Holy Saturday	hornblendite
heteropathic	Hindoostanee	Holy Thursday	horned helmet
heterophasia	hindquarters	home comforts	horned lizard
heterophilic	hippocentaur	Home Counties	horned sungem
heterophonic	Hippocratian	home from home	hornlessness
heterophoria	hippopotamic	home industry	Horn of Africa
heterophoric	hippopotamid	home language	horn of plenty
heterophylly	hippopotamus	homelessness	horometrical
heteroplasia	hire purchase	homeobox gene	horoscopical
heteroplasty	Hispanically	homeothermal	horrendously
heteroploidy	hispaniolize	homeothermic	horribleness
heteropteran	Hispanophile	Homerologist	horrifically
heterosexism	hissing adder	home shopping	horrifyingly
heterosexist	histogenesis	homesickness	horror-struck
heterosexual	histogenetic	homesteading	hors concours
heterosporic	histological	home straight	hors de combat
heterostyled	histoplasmin	homing device	hors d'oeuvres
heterothally	historically	hominisation	horse-breaker
heterothermy	historicizer	hominivorous	horsebreaker
heterotrophy	historiology	hominization	horse-eye bean
heterozygote	histrionical	homocaryotic	horsemanship
heterozygous	hitch and kick	homochromous	horseshoe bat
he won't eat you	Hitchcockian	homoeomerous	horse-soldier
hexadecapole	hitching-post	homoeomorphy	horse-trading
hexahydrated	hither and yon	homoeopathic	horsiculture
hexametrical	Hitler salute	homoeostasis	horticulture
hexamitiasis	hit the bottle	homogentisic	hortus siccus
hexapetalous	hit the breeze	homoiomerous	hospital ball
hexasepalous	hit the bricks	homoiosmosis	hospital gown
hexasyllabic	hobnail liver	homoiosmotic	hospital pass
hexobarbital	Hobson-Jobson	homoiothermy	hospital ship
hiatus hernia	hodometrical	homokaryosis	hostess apron
hibernaculum	hognose snake	homokaryotic	host of heaven
Hibernically	hoist the flag	homolecithal	hot gospeller
Hib infection	Holbeinesque	homologation	hot-shortness
hidden agenda	hold harmless	homomorphism	Hottentot fig
hide one's face	hold one's hand	homomorphous	Hottentot god
hide one's head	hold one's nose	homonymously	hound's-tongue
hierarchical	hold the field	homosexually	house and home
hieratically	hold the stage	homothallism	housebreaker
hierocracies	hold together	homozygosity	housebuilder
hieroglyphed	hold to ransom	honest broker	house colours
hieroglyphic	holiday-maker	honey buzzard	house-heating
hierophantic	holidaymaker	honeycombing	householding
higher animal	holistically	honeycreeper	house-hunting
higher orders	hollow-ground	honey gilding	house-husband
highfaluting	hollow square	honey stomach	housekeeping
high fidelity	Hollywoodean	honeysuckled	house-manager
high-handedly	Hollywoodish	honey-tongued	housemanship
highly strung	Hollywoodism	honnête homme	house of cards
high-mindedly	Hollywoodize	honoris causa	house officer
highmindedly	holmquistite	honour bright	House of Lords
high pressure	holocephalan	honours of war	house-raising

house sparrow	hydrogenator	hyperrealism	hysteroscope
house-surgeon	hydrogen bomb	hyperrealist	hysteroscopy
house-to-house	hydrogen bond	hypersecrete	iambographer
house-trained	hydrogen-like	hyperspatial	iatrochemist
house-warming	hydrogeology	hypersplenic	iatrophysics
housey-housey	hydrographer	hypersthenia	Iceland poppy
housie-housie	hydrographic	hypersthenic	ichnographic
how about that	hydrokineter	hypertension	ichnological
how's yourself	hydrokinetic	hypertensive	ichthyocolla
hubble-bubble	hydrological	hypertextual	ichthyologic
hucker-mucker	hydrolysable	hyperthermia	ichthyophagi
huckle-backed	hydromedusan	hyperthermic	ichthyophagy
hugger-mugger	hydronium ion	hyperthyroid	iconoclastic
human ecology	hydropathist	hypertrophic	iconographer
humane killer	hydropathize	hypnoanalyst	iconographic
humanistical	hydroperoxyl	hypnogenesis	iconological
humanitarian	hydrophanous	hypnological	icosahedrons
humanization	hydrophilous	hypnotherapy	idealization
humble-jumble	hydrophobial	hypnotically	ideationally
humicubation	hydrophobist	hypnotizable	identifiable
humification	hydrophobous	hypoactivity	identifiably
humorousness	hydroponicum	hypocellular	identity card
humourlessly	hydroquinone	hypochlorite	idiomaticity
humoursomely	hydrosalpinx	hypochlorous	Idiom Neutral
humpty-dumpty	hydrostatics	hypochondria	idiomorphism
Humpty-Dumpty	hydrotherapy	hypochondric	idiopathetic
Hungarian cap	hydrothermal	hypocoristic	idiophonemic
Hungary water	hydrotreater	hypocritical	idiosyncrasy
hunger-bitten	hydrotropism	hypodermatic	idiot savants
hunger strike	hydroxide ion	hypodiploidy	idolatrously
hunter-killer	hydrozincite	hypoeutectic	idoneousness
hunter's green	hyetographic	hypofunction	ignitability
hunter trials	hygienically	hypogastrium	ignitibility
hunting-lodge	hygrophilous	hypognathous	ignition tube
hunting-shirt	hylomorphism	hypogonadism	iliac passion
hunting-watch	hymenopteran	hypokalaemia	ill-advisedly
hunt saboteur	hymnographer	hypokalaemic	ill-concealed
huntsman's cup	hypaesthesia	hypolimnetic	ill-conceived
huntsmanship	hypaesthetic	hypomochlion	illegalities
hurdle racing	hyperacidity	hypophrygian	illegibility
hurdy-gurdies	hyperacousis	hypophyllous	illegitimacy
hurtlessness	hyperalgesia	hyposplenism	illegitimate
hyacinth bean	hyperalgesic	hypostatical	illiberalism
hyalopilitic	hyperbolical	hyposulphite	illiberality
hybridizable	hyperchromia	hypothalamic	illiberalize
hybrid vigour	hyperchromic	hypothalamus	illimitation
hydatidiform	hypercomplex	hypothecator	illiterately
hydnocarpate	hypercorrect	hypothesizer	illiterature
hydraulician	hyperdiploid	hypothetical	ill-naturedly
hydraulicity	hyperdulical	hypotonicity	illogicality
hydraulic ram	hyperendemic	hypotrichous	ill-treatment
hydrobiology	hyperkinesia	hypotrochoid	illuminating
hydrocephaly	hyperkinesis	hypovolaemia	illumination
hydrochloric	hyperkinetic	hypovolaemic	illuminatism
hydrochorous	hypermetrope	hypoxanthine	illuminatist
hydrocolloid	hypermorphic	Hypsistarian	illuminative
hydrocracker	hyperosmolar	hypsithermal	illuminatory
hydrodictyon	hyperostosis	hypsochromic	illuministic
hydrodynamic	hyperostotic	hypsographic	illusiveness
hydro-extract	hyperplastic	hysterectomy	illusoriness
hydrofluoric	hyperpyretic	hysterically	illustration
hydroformate	hyperpyrexia	hysterogenic	illustrative

illustratory	impetiginous	in attendance	inconclusive
ilmenorutile	implantation	in at the death	in conference
image-breaker	implicitness	inaudibility	in confidence
image-worship	impoliteness	inauguration	inconfidence
imaginal disc	imponderable	inaugurative	inconformity
imbecilitate	imponderably	inauguratory	incongruence
imbecilities	importunator	inauspicious	inconscience
imbibitional	imposingness	in blanchfarm	inconsequent
imitableness	impostorship	incalculable	inconsidered
immaculately	impoverisher	incalculably	inconsistent
immaterially	impredicable	incalescence	inconsolable
immature soil	impregnation	incandescent	inconsolably
immeasurable	impressional	incapability	inconsonance
immeasurably	impressively	incapacitant	inconsonancy
immemorially	imprevisible	incapacitate	inconstantly
immensurable	imprisonable	incapacities	inconsumable
immersionism	imprisonment	incarcerated	in contention
immersionist	improperness	incarcerator	incontinence
immethodical	impropriator	incatenation	incontinency
immetrically	improsperous	incautiously	incontinuity
immiseration	improvership	incendiaries	incontinuous
immoderately	improvidence	incendiarism	inconvenient
immoderation	improvisator	incense-cedar	incoronation
immoralities	impudentness	incestuously	incorporable
immortalizer	impulse clock	inchoateness	incorporator
immovability	impunitively	incidentally	incorporeity
immune system	impuritanism	incident room	incorrigible
immunization	impurity atom	incineration	incorrigibly
immunologist	imputability	incisiveness	incorrodible
immutability	imputatively	incivilities	incorruption
impact crater	in a bad temper	inclemencies	incrassation
impact wrench	inabstinence	inclinometer	increasement
impartialist	inacceptable	incoagulable	increasingly
impartiality	inaccessible	incogitantly	increditable
impassionate	inaccessibly	incogitative	incriminator
impedimental	inaccuracies	incognisable	incrustation
impenetrable	inaccurately	incognizable	incubational
impenetrably	inactivation	incognizance	incumbencies
impenitently	in a dead faint	incoherently	incunabulist
imperatively	inadequacies	incoincident	incurability
imperativism	inadequately	in commission	indebtedness
imperativist	inadequation	incommodious	indecentness
imperatorial	inadmissible	in common with	indecisively
imperception	inadmissibly	incommutable	indeclinable
imperceptive	inadvertence	incommutably	indeclinably
impercipient	inadvertency	incomparable	indecorously
imperfection	in a fair way to	incomparably	indefeasible
imperfective	in a family way	incompatible	indefeasibly
imperforable	in a good light	incompatibly	indefectible
imperforated	in all but name	incompetence	indefectibly
imperialness	in all seeming	incompetency	indefensible
imperial pint	in-and-out work	incompletely	indefensibly
imperishable	inappeasable	incompletion	in defiance of
imperishably	inappellable	incompletive	indefinitely
impermanence	inapplicable	incompliance	indefinition
impermanency	inapplicably	incompliancy	indefinitive
impersistent	inappositely	incomputable	indefinitude
impersonally	in arrearages	incomunicado	indeformable
impersonator	inarticulacy	inconcinnity	indehiscence
impertinence	inarticulate	inconcludent	indelectable
impertinency	inartificial	in conclusion	indeliberate
imperviously	in a sort of way	inconclusion	indelibility

indelicacies
indelicately
independable
independence
independency
indeprivable
indetectable
indetectible
indetermined
indevoutness
index-linking
Indian almond
Indian madder
Indian mallow
Indian millet
Indian Mutiny
Indian physic
Indian potato
Indian runner
Indian summer
Indian turnip
Indian yellow
indicatively
indifference
indifferency
indigenously
indigestible
indigestibly
indigitation
indigoferous
indirect fire
indirectness
indirect rule
indiscipline
indiscreetly
indiscretion
indisputable
indisputably
indissoluble
indissolubly
indistinctly
indivertible
indivertibly
individually
individuated
indoctrinate
Indo-European
Indo-Gangetic
Indo-Germanic
indoleacetic
Indo-Pakistan
Indo-Scythian
inducibility
inductomeric
industrially
industry-wide
ineffability
ineffaceable
ineffaceably
inefficacity
inefficiency
inelasticity

ineliminable
ineloquently
inenubilable
inequal hours
inequalities
inequivalent
inequivalved
ineradicable
ineradicably
inerrability
inescutcheon
ineuphonious
inexactitude
inexecutable
inexhaustive
inexpectancy
inexpedience
inexpediency
inexperience
inexpertness
inexplicable
inexplicably
inexplorable
inexpressive
inexpugnable
inexpugnably
inexpungible
inextensible
inextirpable
inextricable
inextricably
infamousness
infanticidal
infant school
infatuatedly
infectiously
infelicities
infelicitous
inferability
infibulation
infidelities
infiltration
infiltrative
infinitation
infiniteness
infinitively
inflammation
inflammatory
inflatedness
inflationary
inflationism
inflationist
inflectional
informal vote
informedness
informercial
informidable
infotainment
infra-orbital
infrequently
infringement
infrustrable

infrustrably
infundibular
infundibulum
infusibility
infusoriform
ingemination
ingeneration
ingloriously
in good repair
ingratiating
ingratiation
ingratiatory
ingravescent
ingressively
inhabitation
inhalational
inhalatorium
inharmonious
inhibitingly
in holy orders
inhospitable
inhospitably
inhumanities
inhumorously
iniencephaly
inimicalness
iniquitously
initiatively
injudicially
injunctively
in league with
in like manner
in mistake for
in moderation
inner cabinet
inner Cabinet
inner reserve
Inniskilling
Innocents' Day
innovational
innovatively
innutritious
inobservable
inobservance
inobservancy
inoccupation
in one's favour
in one's regard
in one's senses
in one's sights
in one's sphere
in one's tracks
inoperculate
in opposition
inoppressive
inoppugnable
inordinately
inordination
inosculation
inostensible
inostensibly
in other words

inoxidizable
in particular
in perpetuity
in possession
in proper form
in proportion
inquartation
inquietation
inquire after
inquiry agent
inquisitress
in relation to
in retrospect
in revenge for
insalivation
insalubrious
insanitation
inscriptible
insectariums
insecticidal
insect-powder
insecureness
insemination
inseparately
in severality
in short order
insightfully
in silhouette
insimplicity
insolubilise
insolubility
insolubilize
insomnolence
insomnolency
insouciantly
inspectional
inspectorate
inspectorial
inspissation
installation
instauration
instillation
instinctless
institutress
instructible
instructress
instrumental
insubjection
insubmissive
in succession
insufferable
insufferably
insufficient
insufflation
insulin shock
insupposable
insurability
insurgencies
insurrection
in suspension
intabulation
intarissable

integral sign	intermeddler	interversion	intravitally
integumental	intermediacy	intervocalic	intrepidness
intellection	intermediary	interwovenly	intriguingly
intellective	intermediate	interwreathe	in triplicate
intellectual	interminable	interwrought	introducible
intelligence	interminably	in the balance	introduction
intelligency	intermission	in the bygoing	introductive
intelligible	intermissive	in the cause of	introductory
intelligibly	intermitotic	in the country	introflexion
intemperance	intermittent	in the event of	introgressed
intempestive	intermitting	in the extreme	introjection
inteneration	intermixable	in the general	introjective
interanimate	intermixedly	in the habit of	intromission
intercalator	intermixture	in the highest	intromittent
intercameral	intermontane	in the light of	intromitting
interception	internecinal	in the long run	intropulsive
interceptive	interneurone	in the mainour	introsuction
intercession	internuclear	in the midst of	introversion
intercessive	internuncial	in the morning	introversive
intercessory	internuncius	in the order of	introvertive
interchanger	internuptial	in the picture	intuitionism
interchapter	interoceanic	in the power of	intuitionist
intercoastal	interoceptor	in the running	intumescence
intercollege	interorbital	in the same box	invagination
intercommune	interosseous	in the shape of	invalidation
intercompany	interpellant	in the stead of	invasiveness
interconnect	interpellate	in the streets	inveiglement
interconvert	interpleader	in the teeth of	inverse ratio
intercranial	interplicate	in the thick of	invertebracy
intercurrent	interpluvial	in the train of	Invertebrata
interdiction	interpolable	in the weather	invertebrate
interdictive	interpolator	in this galley	inverted snob
interdictory	interpolymer	intimidating	investigable
interdiffuse	interpretant	intimidation	investigator
interdigital	interpretate	intimidatory	inveterately
interestedly	interpreting	intitulation	invigilation
interfemoral	interpretive	intolerantly	invigorating
interference	interregnums	intoleration	invigoration
interfertile	interrogatee	intonational	invigorative
interfluence	interrogator	intoxicating	invisibility
interfluvial	interruption	intoxication	invisible ink
interfulgent	interruptive	intoxicative	invisible man
intergeneric	interruptory	intracardiac	invitational
interglacial	intersectant	intracoastal	invitingness
interhalogen	intersection	intracranial	involutional
interimistic	intersegment	intragastric	involvedness
interinsular	intersensory	intraglacial	invulnerable
interjacency	inter-service	intrahepatic	invulnerably
interjection	interspersal	intralingual	invultuation
interjectory	interspinous	intralobular	in with a shout
interkinesis	interstadial	intramontane	iodine number
interlacedly	inter-station	intramundane	ion-exchanger
interlaminar	interstellar	intramurally	Ionic dialect
interlibrary	interstitial	intransigent	ionophoresis
interlineary	interstitium	intransitive	ionophoretic
interlineate	intertexture	intranuclear	ionospherist
interlingual	intertillage	intrapluvial	irascibility
interlinkage	intertissued	intrapreneur	iridectomize
interlobular	intertubular	intrapsychic	iridescently
interlocutor	intervallary	intraspecies	iridodonesis
intermarried	intervenient	intrauterine	Irish apricot
intermarries	intervention	intravaginal	Irish pennant

Irish terrier	I should think	javelin-snake	justiciaries
Irish whiskey	I should worry	Javelle water	justifyingly
ironicalness	Islamization	Jeffersonian	Justinianian
ironing board	isoantigenic	jelly-bellied	Justinianist
ironing cloth	isobarically	je ne sais quoi	juvenescence
iron mountain	isobaric spin	jenny spinner	juvenile lead
irrationable	isobilateral	jeremejevite	juvenile leaf
irrationally	isochromatic	jerry-builder	juvenileness
irrealisable	isochronally	Jesuitically	kachina dance
irrealizable	isochronical	Jesus psalter	kaemmererite
irrebuttable	isodiametric	jet-propelled	Kaffirboetie
irreciprocal	isodynamical	jettisonable	Kaffir orange
irredeemable	isolated pawn	jibber-jabber	kainogenesis
irredeemably	isolationism	jigger-tackle	kakistocracy
irreductible	isolationist	jigsaw puzzle	kaleidoscope
irredundance	isomerically	Jimmy O'Goblin	kanban system
irredundancy	isoperimeter	Jimmy Skinner	kangaroo vine
irreflection	isoperimetry	Jimmy Woodser	karaoke music
irreflective	isoprenaline	Jindyworobak	Karitane baby
irreformable	isoprene rule	jingle-jangle	karyokinesis
irrefragable	isoprene unit	job backwards	karyokinetic
irrefragably	isotacticity	jockey pulley	karyological
irregardless	isothermally	jockey-sleeve	karyomitosis
irregenerate	isotonically	jockey spider	karyomitotic
irregularity	isotope shift	jocularities	karyorrhexis
irrelatively	isotopically	John Crow nose	katharevousa
irrelevantly	isotopic spin	Johnny-jump-up	katharometer
irrelievable	Italian earth	Johnson noise	katzenjammer
irremediable	Italianesque	joined patent	keeking-glass
irremediably	Italian paste	joint account	Keene's cement
irremissible	I tell you what	join the flats	keep accounts
irremissibly	it is news to me	joint-tenancy	keep an eye out
irrepairable	ivory-nut palm	joint venture	keep good time
irrepassable	I wouldn't know	jolter-headed	keep one's feet
irrepealable	Jack-a-lantern	jordan almond	keep one's head
irrepealably	jacket potato	Joule heating	keep one's legs
irrepentance	jack-in-office	Joule–Thomson	keep one's seat
irreprovable	Jack-in-office	journalistic	keep one's word
irreptitious	jack-in-the-box	journey-pride	keep the field
irresistable	Jack-in-the-box	journey-proud	keep the house
irresistably	Jack mackerel	journeywoman	keep the peace
irresistance	jack-o'-lantern	joy of a planet	keep together
irresistible	Jack-o'-lantern	Judaeo-German	Kelvin bridge
irresistibly	Jack-spaniard	Judaeophobia	Kendal cotton
irresolutely	Jacobean lily	judgematical	kentallenite
irresolution	Jacobitishly	Judgement Day	Kentish glory
irresolvable	Jacob's ladder	judicial duel	keratectasia
irrespectful	jacquard loom	jug-and-bottle	keratinocyte
irrespective	jail-delivery	jumping-board	keratodermia
irrespirable	Jamaica ebony	jumping louse	keratogenous
irresponsive	Jamaican kino	jumping mouse	keratometric
irreverently	James's powder	jumping shrew	keratoplasty
irreversible	Japan current	jump the queue	kerb-crawling
irreversibly	Japanese deer	junior school	ketoacidosis
irrigational	Japanese iris	jurisconsult	keto-compound
irritability	Japanese rose	jurisdiction	ketonization
irritatingly	Japanese silk	jurisdictive	kettle-bottom
irrotational	Japanization	jurisprudent	kettle-holder
Iscariotical	Japan lacquer	juristically	kettle of fish
Ishmaelitish	Japanologist	Justice Clerk	kettle-stitch
Ishmaelitism	Japan varnish	Justicialism	Keynesianism
I should smile	jarovization	Justicialist	keypunchable

key signature	knee-trembler	ladder stitch	lantern-wheel
Khevenhuller	knick-knacket	ladylikeness	Laodiceanism
Khirbet Kerak	knife-grinder	Lady Mayoress	laparoscopic
kicking plate	knife machine	lady's cushion	laparotomies
kicking-strap	knife-pleated	lady's delight	laparotomize
kick the habit	knife-thrower	lady's slipper	lapidary-mill
kick up a stour	knight errant	lady's thistle	lapidicolous
kick upstairs	knightlihood	lady's tresses	lapis Armenus
kiddie sister	knightliness	Lady Superior	lapis ollaris
kidney potato	knitting-case	lag of the tide	lapsus calami
kidney-shaped	knitting-wire	laisser-aller	larch blister
kidney tubule	knob-cone pine	laissez-aller	larder beetle
killer-diller	knock against	laissez-faire	larderellite
killikinnick	knocking shop	Lake District	large calorie
kilowatt-hour	knowableness	lake-dwelling	large-hearted
Kimmeridgian	knowledgable	lallapaloosa	Larmor radius
kinaesthesia	knowledge box	lallygagging	laryngealist
kinaesthesis	know the ropes	lamb's lettuce	laryngectomy
kinaesthetic	know the score	Lamentations	laryngophone
kindergarten	knuckle-joint	laminability	laryngoscope
kindling-wood	knuckle under	laminagraphy	laryngoscopy
kinesiologic	Knudsen gauge	Lammas growth	laryngospasm
kinglessness	Köchel number	lammervanger	lasagne verdi
king mackerel	koelreuteria	lampadedromy	lasciviously
king of beasts	Kommandatura	lampadomancy	laser printer
king or Kaiser	Komodo dragon	lamprophyric	lasso-harness
King's Counsel	Kremlinology	lamp standard	lasting power
king's cushion	Kriss Kringle	Lancasterian	latch circuit
King's English	Kromayer lamp	lancet window	latchings key
King's Friends	kukumakranka	land-carriage	lateen mizzen
King's highway	kulturträger	land district	late in the day
King's Proctor	kupfernickel	land drainage	latent energy
King's Scholar	kurchatovium	landgraviate	latent period
kinnikinnick	Kyrie eleison	landing craft	lateral plate
kin selection	Labanotation	landing-light	lateralwards
kinship group	labilization	landing place	laterisation
Kiplingesque	labiopalatal	landing stage	laterization
kirk-assembly	laboratorial	landing strip	late tackling
kirschwasser	laboratories	Land-leaguism	laticiferous
kitchen-diner	labouredness	landlessness	Latin America
kitchen Dutch	labouring oar	landlordship	Latinization
Kitchener bun	labour in vain	landlubberly	Latin Quarter
kitchen-knave	labour market	land-measurer	latitudinary
kitchen-Latin	labour of love	Land Registry	latitudinous
kitchen paper	labour-saving	land-surveyor	latter Lammas
kitchen stove	laboursomely	landward-bred	lattice frame
kitchen-stuff	Labrador duck	Langmuir cell	lattice plane
kitchen-wench	Labrador spar	Langobardian	lattice point
kit furniture	labyrinthian	language area	laudableness
kittle-cattle	labyrinthine	language arts	laughing crow
Klaas's cuckoo	lacebark tree	language-game	laughing dove
Klebs–Löffler	Lachmann's law	languageless	laughing-game
kleptolagnia	lachrymation	langue de chat	laughing gull
kleptomaniac	lachrymatory	Languedocian	laughterless
kletterschuh	lachrymosely	languishment	laughter-line
klinokinesis	lachrymosity	languorously	laugh to scorn
klinokinetic	lacing course	lantern clock	launching pad
klipspringer	lacrimal bone	lantern-flies	launch window
klydonograph	lactobionate	lantern-jawed	laundrywoman
knapsack pump	lactogenesis	lantern-light	laundrywomen
knee-breeched	lactonitrile	lantern-shell	laureateship
knee-breeches	lactoprotein	lantern slide	laurel-bottle

laurel-cherry	legendary age	licence plate	line of beauty
lavender-blue	legislatress	license plate	line of credit
lavender soap	legitimately	licentiation	line of vision
law of nations	legitimation	licentiously	line regiment
Law of Octaves	legitimatise	lichenometry	line spectrum
law of the land	legitimatize	lichen planus	line standard
law stationer	leiophyllous	lichen-starch	lingua franca
laxativeness	leiotrichous	lick creation	lingual nerve
lay a finger on	Lemnian earth	lickety-split	linguistical
lay communion	lemon-scented	lick into fits	linguodental
layer-pudding	lemon verbena	lick one's lips	linoleic acid
layer shading	lend colour to	lie down under	lion-huntress
lay it on thick	lend itself to	lie in one's way	liquefacient
lay one's bones	lend one's ears	lie in the dust	liquefaction
lay on the line	lenticellate	lie of the land	liquefactive
leachability	lenticulated	life-and-death	liqueur glass
leadableness	Leonardesque	lifeguardman	liquid manure
leader stroke	leopard's bane	life interest	liquid storax
leading-block	leopard snake	lifelessness	liriodendron
leading light	lepidomelane	lifelikeness	listenership
leading shoot	lepidopteral	life sciences	listlessness
leading-staff	lepidopteran	life sentence	litaneutical
lead in prayer	leptocaulous	lifesomeness	literalistic
leads and lags	lepton number	lifting plate	literariness
lead the dance	Lesser Bairam	lifting screw	lithifaction
leaflessness	lesser diesis	lift one's eyes	lithogenesis
leafless tree	Lestrigonian	lift one's game	lithographer
leaning-stock	let 'em all come	lift one's hand	lithographic
leap to the eye	let oneself go	lift up the leg	litholatrous
learnability	let oneself in	light barrier	lithological
learn by heart	let-out clause	light-fixture	lithophagous
learner plate	Letterer–Siwe	lightfulness	lithophilous
least squares	letter-office	light-hearted	lithospermum
leather-bound	letter-spaced	lighting plot	lithospheric
leathercloth	letter-weight	lightning box	lithotomical
leatheriness	letter-writer	lightning bug	lithotripter
leather medal	lettuce green	lightning-rod	lithotriptic
leave a card on	let well alone	light quantum	lithotriptor
leave-breaker	leucoblastic	light railway	litter-basket
leave for dead	leucocytosis	light station	Little Africa
leave the room	leucopoiesis	light-trapped	Little Dipper
lechenaultia	leucopoietic	likeableness	little finger
lectionaries	leucorrhoeal	like anything	little Hitler
lecturership	Levalloisian	like-mindedly	little ice age
ledger-tackle	levallorphan	like old boots	Little League
leech-extract	Levant storax	like sardines	little master
Leech lattice	levelling rod	like the devil	little people
left and right	level one's aim	like wildfire	Littler's blue
left defender	level pegging	limbic system	little season
left half-back	levitational	limb of the law	little tin god
left-handedly	Leviticalism	limited train	littoral zone
left-hand rope	levorotatory	limnological	liturgically
left-hand rule	lex domicilii	Lincolnesque	liturgiology
left midfield	lexicography	Lincoln green	liveableness
leftwardness	lexicologist	Lincolnshire	liveable with
legacy-hunter	liberalistic	linear search	live and learn
legal charity	Liberal Party	line blanking	liver-hearted
legal fiction	liberticidal	line-breeding	liverishness
legal holiday	liberty horse	line-engraved	Liverpudlian
legalitarian	libidinously	line-engraver	liver sausage
legalization	librarianess	line-integral	liver-spotted
legal opinion	library steps	line of battle	livery stable

live together
living fossil
living memory
lizard canary
lizard cuckoo
lizard orchid
loading gauge
load-shedding
load the bases
loan-sharking
lobeliaceous
loblolly pine
loblolly tree
lobster shift
lobster trick
local cluster
local content
localization
loci classici
locked groove
locking plate
locksmithery
locomotively
locum tenency
lodging house
loganberries
loggerheaded
logical truth
logic circuit
logic element
logistically
logocentrism
lollapaloosa
lollapalooza
lollipop lady
lomentaceous
London bridge
London purple
London rocket
London-shrunk
lonesomeness
long-and-short
long-distance
long division
long-drawn-out
longipennate
longitudinal
long-leaf pine
Longobardian
long rough dab
longshoreman
longshoremen
longsomeness
long-standing
long-tail pair
long trousers
long vacation
long-windedly
Lonsdale belt
looking-glass
look sideways
look who's here

loose-housing
loose-mouthed
loose-skinned
loose-tongued
lophophorate
lopsidedness
loquaciously
Lord Advocate
Lord bless you
Lord Ordinary
Lorentz force
Los Angelenos
lose interest
lose one's cool
lose one's grip
lose one's hair
lose one's head
lose one's life
lose one's mind
lose one's seat
lose one's wool
lose patience
lose the scent
losing battle
losing hazard
loss adjuster
lost property
lot attendant
lotaustralin
Lotharingian
lottery-wheel
lotus capital
loud and clear
loud and still
lounge lizard
loutrophoros
love-begotten
love-interest
lovelessness
love paramour
lovesickness
lovesomeness
love to pieces
Low-Churchism
Low Churchman
Low Countries
Lower Chamber
Lower Chinook
lower classes
lower pastern
lower regions
lower the boom
lower the tone
low frequency
low latitudes
low-molecular
low water mark
lubberliness
luce of the sea
Lucianically
lucklessness
Lucky Country

ludification
luffing crane
luggage check
lugubriosity
lugubriously
lukewarmness
lumber-jacket
lumbriciform
luminescence
luminiferous
luminousness
lumpectomies
lunar caustic
lunar-diurnal
lunar eclipse
lunar regular
luncheonette
luncheonless
luncheon meat
lungeing-ring
lurking-place
lusciousness
lustrousness
luteofulvous
luteotrophic
luteotrophin
Luxembourger
Luxemburgish
luxullyanite
lycanthropic
lychnoscopic
lying-in-state
lymphangioma
lymphangitis
lymphogenous
lymphography
lymphomatous
lymphotropic
lysergic acid
lysogenicity
Macaronesian
macaroni tool
macca-fat tree
machairodont
machiavellic
Machtpolitik
mackerel-back
mackerel-boat
mackerel gale
mackerel gull
mackintoshed
macrauchenia
macrobenthic
macrobenthos
macrobiotics
macrocephaly
macroclimate
macrocytosis
macroglossia
macrognathic
macronodular
macronucleus

macrophagous
macrophallic
macrophysics
macropterous
macrosegment
macroseismic
maculopapule
mad as a hatter
Madeira sauce
Mademoiselle
maderisation
maderization
Madonna braid
mad scientist
magic lantern
magic realism
magic realist
magistracies
magistrature
magma-chamber
magmatically
magnetically
magnetic disk
magnetic drum
magnetic flux
magnetic lens
magnetic mine
magnetic pole
magnetic tape
magnetisable
magnetizable
magnetograph
magnetogyric
magneto-ionic
magnetometer
magnetometry
magnetopause
magnetophone
magnifically
magnificence
magnificency
magniloquent
magnipotence
magnum opuses
Magnus effect
Mahometanism
maidening pot
maidening tub
maidenliness
maiden's blush
maiden speech
maid of honour
mainmortable
main sequence
maintainable
maintainment
maître d'hôtel
majestically
major general
majoritarian
majority rule
major prophet

Major Prophet
make a bad shot
make a bargain
make a dash for
make a day of it
make a fortune
make a habit of
make a merit of
make-and-break
make an impact
make a pig's ear
make a play for
make a point of
make a study of
make a thing of
make away with
make ends meet
make free with
make good time
make it snappy
make little of
make mischief
make muckle of
make no matter
make old bones
make one's gree
make one's mark
make one's soul
make play with
make pleasant
make semblant
make slight of
make the arber
make the grade
make the scene
make up leeway
make wise to do
malacologist
malalignment
malapertness
malaria fever
Malayan tapir
malaysianite
Malaysianize
malbehaviour
malcontented
maldescended
maleducation
malefactress
malevolently
malexecution
malformation
malignancies
malinfluence
Malinowskian
malleability
malleableize
mallet finger
malnourished
malnutrition
malocclusion
malodorously

maloperation
Maltese cross
maltodextrin
maltreatment
Malvern water
malversation
mamenchisaur
mammalogical
mammary gland
mammillation
mammilliform
mammogenesis
mammographic
mammotrophic
mammotrophin
man about town
managemental
managerially
manatee-grass
Manchu-Tungus
mandarin coat
mandarin duck
mandarinship
mandarin vase
mandibulated
maneuverable
manganic acid
mangel beetle
mangel-wurzel
mangrove crab
mangrove jack
Manhattanese
Manhattanite
manifestable
manifestness
manifoldness
man in the moon
manipulandum
manipulation
manipulative
manipulatory
man-midwifery
mannerliness
manoeuvrable
man-of-all-work
man of destiny
man of feeling
man of fortune
man of leisure
man of letters
man of science
man-of-war fish
manometrical
mansion house
Mansion House
manslaughter
manteau-maker
mantis shrimp
mantle-cavity
mantua-making
manufactural
manufacturer

manuscriptal
many moons ago
many's the time
map butterfly
map reference
marbled green
marbled white
marcasitical
marching band
marching girl
March meeting
Marcionitism
marconigraph
Maréchal Niel
mareographic
marginal cost
maricultural
Marie Celeste
marimbaphone
marine iguana
marine stores
Mariolatrous
Mariological
marionettish
marionettist
maritime pine
marked cheque
market basket
market garden
market hunter
market square
marking board
marksmanship
marline-spike
marmalade box
marmalade cat
marmoraceous
marriageable
marriage-ring
marriage-song
married bliss
married print
marrowskying
marrow squash
Marseillaise
marsh harrier
marshmallowy
marsh treader
marsh trefoil
marsh warbler
marsupialize
martagon lily
martial eagle
martinettish
Martiniquais
martyrolatry
marvellingly
marvellously
marvel of Peru
marzipanning
masslessness
mass spectrum

mastectomies
master-at-arms
Master Gunner
masterliness
masterly lode
Master of Arts
master-singer
mastersinger
master-spring
master stroke
master switch
mastigophore
masturbation
masturbatory
matador pants
matchbox bean
match-winning
materializer
materialness
material noun
mathematical
mating season
matriarchate
matriarchies
matricentred
matrilateral
matrilineage
matrilocally
matrix number
matroclinous
matronliness
matter of fact
matter of form
maturational
maudlin-drunk
maunderingly
Mauser action
mauvais sujet
maximization
maximum price
Maxwell demon
McLuhanesque
meadow beauty
meadow fescue
meadow ground
mealy-mouthed
mealy pudding
mealy redpoll
mean business
mean free path
meaningfully
mean mischief
means and ways
mean sea level
means of grace
mean solar day
measured mile
measuredness
measuring-cup
measuring jug
meat and drink
meatlessness

meat-offering	memorization	mesognathism	meteorologic
Mebyon Kernow	memory-belief	mesognathous	meteoroscopy
mecamylamine	memory effect	meso-inositol	meteor shower
mechanically	ménage à trois	mesokurtosis	methacholine
mechatronics	mendaciously	mesometritis	methacrylate
medallionist	Mendelianism	mesomorphism	methanogenic
medallion man	mend one's pace	mesomorphous	methanometer
meddlesomely	mend one's ways	meson factory	methanotroph
mediatorship	men in buckram	mesoplankton	methaqualone
medical board	meningococci	Mesopotamian	methodically
medicamental	meniscectomy	mesosiderite	methohexital
Medici collar	menstruation	mesothelioma	methotrexate
medicine ball	mental asylum	mesothoracic	methoxychlor
medicine line	mental healer	mesquite bean	methyl orange
medicine seal	mental health	message stick	methyl rubber
medicine show	menticulture	Messeigneurs	methyl violet
medicine tree	mercantilely	messenger RNA	methysergide
medicine wolf	mercantilism	metacercaria	meticulosity
mediocrities	mercantilist	metachromasy	meticulously
mediocritize	merchandiser	metachromism	Metonic cycle
mediopalatal	merchantable	metachronism	metoposcopic
mediopassive	merchant bank	metacinnabar	metrological
meditatingly	merchanthood	metacontrast	metropolitan
meditatively	merchant iron	metagalactic	metrorrhagia
medium bowler	merchantlike	metageometry	metrorrhagic
medullary ray	merchant navy	metagnathism	Mexican brown
meeting house	merchant ship	metagnathous	Mexican poppy
meeting-place	mercifulness	metalanguage	Meyerbeerian
megacephalic	mercurialism	metal fatigue	mezzo-relievo
megalocardia	mercurialist	metalimnetic	mezzo-rilievo
megalomaniac	mercuriality	metalinguist	mezzo-soprano
megalomartyr	mercurialize	metallically	mickey-taking
megalosaurus	meretricious	metallic bond	microammeter
megalosphere	meridian line	metallic soap	microanalyst
megaphyllous	meridian-mark	metallic yarn	microanatomy
megatherioid	meridionally	metallogenic	microbalance
Meissen china	meristematic	metallophone	Microballoon
melancholiac	meristically	metallurgist	microbenthic
melancholies	meritocratic	metalogician	microbenthos
melancholily	meroplankton	metalworking	microbicidal
melancholise	merosymmetry	metamictness	microbiology
melancholist	merry as a grig	metamorphise	microcapsule
melancholize	merry dancers	metamorphism	microcephaly
melanization	merry England	metamorphize	microchemist
melanocomous	merry-go-round	metamorphose	microcircuit
melanocratic	merry-meeting	metaphonized	microclastic
melanodermia	merry thought	metaphorical	microclimate
melanodermic	mesarteritic	metaphrastic	microcrystal
mellifluence	mesarteritis	metaphysical	microcytosis
melodic minor	mesatipellic	metapolitics	microdiorite
melodramatic	mescal button	metapsychics	micro-element
melon-thistle	mesenteritis	metapsychist	microfilaria
melted butter	mesityl oxide	metasomatism	microgranite
melting-house	mesmerically	metasomatize	micrographer
melting point	mesmerizable	metathetical	micrographic
melt spinning	mesne process	metathoracic	microgravity
membrane-bone	mesne profits	metavolcanic	microhabitat
membraneless	Meso-American	metempirical	micrological
membraniform	meso-appendix	meteorically	micronodular
membranology	mesocephalic	meteoritical	micronuclear
memorability	mesoconchous	meteorograph	micronucleus
memorializer	mesogastrium	meteorolitic	microphagous

microphonism	Mill's Methods	misexecution	modification
microphysics	Miltonically	misfit stream	modificative
micropipette	miminy-piminy	misformation	modificatory
microprogram	minatoriness	misfortunate	modi operandi
micropterous	mince matters	misinformant	modus tollens
micropublish	mind-boggling	misinterpret	modus vivendi
microscopist	mindlessness	misjudgement	moeritherium
Microscopium	mind one's hits	misknowledge	moire antique
microsection	mind one's step	mislabelling	moistureless
microsegment	mind your back	misleadingly	molarization
microseismic	mine-detector	misogynistic	mole-coloured
microspecies	mineragraphy	misorientate	molecularity
microspheric	mineral black	misplacement	mole fraction
microsporous	mineral brown	mispronounce	molinologist
microstylous	mineral green	mispunctuate	mollifyingly
microsurgery	mineral jelly	misquotation	molluscicide
microtonally	mineralogist	misrecollect	mollycoddler
microtubular	mineral pitch	misrepresent	Molly Maguire
microvillous	mineral water	missel thrush	moloch gibbon
microwavable	mine-sweeping	missiologist	molybdomancy
middle-ageing	mingle-mangle	missionaries	momentaneity
middle course	minicomputer	missionarize	momentaneous
middle finger	minification	mission house	monadelphous
middle ground	minimalistic	mission stiff	monastically
middle-income	minimization	Miss Milligan	mondo bizarro
middle-length	ministership	misstatement	monepiscopal
middle period	ministration	mistakenness	monetaristic
middle-relief	ministrative	mistle thrush	monetization
middlescence	minnow-fisher	mistranslate	money changer
middle school	minority debt	mistreatment	money-grubber
Middle States	minor prophet	mistresshood	moneylending
Middle Temple	Minor Prophet	mistressless	money matters
middleweight	minstrelsies	mistress-ship	money-spinner
middle wicket	miogeoclinal	mistrustless	Mongolian eye
middlingness	Miquelet lock	mithridatise	monistically
midnight blue	miracle fruit	mithridatism	monkey bridge
midnight mass	miraculously	mithridatize	monkey-chaser
midship frame	mirror finish	mitochondria	monkey engine
Midsummer Day	mirror-writer	mixed bathing	monkey flower
mid-Victorian	mirthfulness	mixed company	monkey island
Midwesterner	misadventure	mixed crystal	monkey-jacket
Milanese silk	misaffection	mixed doubles	monkey orchid
mild-mannered	misalignment	mixed economy	monkey parade
militariness	misanthropic	mixed farming	monkey-puzzle
militaristic	misapprehend	mixed-traffic	monkey tricks
military band	misattribute	mixtie-maxtie	monkey wrench
military drum	misbehaviour	mizen topmast	monkeywrench
militiawoman	miscalculate	mizen topsail	monk's rhubarb
milk and honey	miscegenated	mnemonically	monocellular
milk and water	miscellanies	mnemotechnic	monochloride
milk for babes	miscellanist	Moabite stone	monochromasy
milk purslane	mischanceful	mobilisation	monochromate
milk-sickness	misconceiver	mobilization	monochromist
milkwood tree	misconstruct	modalization	monochromous
millefeuille	misdemeanant	model-drawing	monoclinally
Miller effect	misdemeanour	moderateness	mono-coloured
miller's thumb	misdiagnosis	moderatorial	monocularity
millesimally	misdirection	modern Greats	monocultural
milliammeter	miseducation	modernizable	monodelphian
milliardaire	miserabilism	modern school	monodisperse
millions fish	miserabilist	modesty piece	monodramatic
mill-mountain	miserability	modesty skirt	monoeciously

monofilament	moralizingly	motor cyclist	mulberry tree
monogamistic	moral science	motorcyclist	mule-skinning
monogamously	moral support	motorization	mullein shark
monogenistic	moral victory	motor neurone	mullet-headed
monographist	morbilliform	motor scooter	mulligatawny
monohydrated	morcellation	motor vehicle	multi-angular
monoideistic	Morellianism	mottled umber	multicentral
monokaryotic	more's the pity	mouldability	multicentric
monolinguist	morigeration	mould-blowing	multichannel
monomaniacal	Mormon Church	mound-builder	multicircuit
monometallic	morning after	mound of Venus	multicostate
monomorphism	morning dress	mountain bike	multidentate
monomorphous	morning glory	mountain blue	multifaceted
mononucleate	morning paper	mountain cock	multifarious
monopetalous	morning watch	mountain duck	multiflorous
monophonemic	morphallaxis	mountain fern	multifoliate
monophyletic	morphiomania	mountain flax	multiformity
monophyllous	morphography	mountain goat	multiformous
monophyodont	morphologist	mountain hare	multigeneric
monophysitic	morphologize	mountain-high	multigravida
monopodially	morphomaniac	mountain land	multilaminar
monopolistic	morphometric	mountain lion	multilateral
monopsychism	morphonology	mountain mint	multilayered
monoptically	morphophonic	mountain plum	multilingual
monorchidism	morphosyntax	mountain rice	multilobular
monosemantic	morphotactic	mountainside	multilocular
monosepalous	morphotropic	mountain snow	multiloquent
monosiphonic	morris dancer	Mountain Time	multimammate
monospecific	morrow-speech	mountainward	multimillion
monospermous	mortgageable	mountain wine	multinominal
monostichous	mortgage rate	Mount Everest	multinuclear
monostrophic	mortifyingly	Mountmellick	multiovulate
monosyllabic	mosquito-boat	mount of piety	multi-partism
monosyllable	mosquito boot	mount of Venus	multi-partist
monosymmetry	mosquito coil	mournfulness	multipartite
monosynaptic	mosquito fish	mourning-band	multipinnate
monosystemic	mosquito hawk	mourning dove	multiple-disc
monotessaron	moss-trooping	mourning iris	multiple shop
monothalamic	most and least	mourning ring	multiple star
monotheistic	Most Reverend	mouse opossum	multiple twin
Monothelitic	Mother Church	mousquetaire	multiple-unit
monothematic	mother figure	moustache cup	multiplexing
monotonicity	mother-fucker	mouth-breeder	multiplexity
monotonously	motherfucker	mouthbrooder	multipliable
monotriglyph	mother-in-babe	mouth-filling	multiplicand
monozygosity	motherliness	mouth-to-mouth	multiplicate
Montagu shell	mother liquid	movable feast	multiplicity
Montbazillac	mother liquor	movable sheva	multiprogram
Montessorian	mother-loving	movelessness	multi-purpose
Monteverdian	Mother Nature	movie theatre	multiradiate
month by month	mothers-in-law	moving-target	multisection
monthly nurse	Mothers' Union	mucification	multiseptate
monticellite	mother tongue	mucilaginous	multi-tasking
monumentally	motionlessly	muck-spreader	multitasking
mood-altering	motivational	mucopurulent	multi-tracked
Moon Festival	motivelessly	mucormycosis	multi-tracker
Moorish gecko	moto perpetuo	muddle-headed	multivalence
moor-sickness	motor bicycle	mud in your eye	multivalency
moose pasture	motor-boating	mud-wrestling	multivallate
moral courage	motor caravan	muff coupling	multivariant
morality play	motor-coaster	Muggletonian	multivariate
moralization	motorcycling	mulberry-bird	multivarious

multiversity	mutton-birder	nasolacrimal	necroscopies
multivoltine	mutton candle	natalid organ	nectareously
multungulate	mutton-fisted	national bank	needle-and-pin
mumble-the-peg	mutton-headed	national debt	needle biopsy
mummy disease	mutuatitious	National Debt	needle roller
mundane house	muzzle-loader	national grid	needle shower
municipalise	mycetomatous	nationalizer	needlessness
municipalism	mycetophilid	nationalness	needleworker
municipalist	mycoplasmata	national park	neencephalic
municipality	my dear fellow	native orange	neencephalon
municipalize	myelin sheath	native poplar	negation-sign
munificently	myeloblastic	native potato	negative glow
muniment deed	myelogenesis	native quince	negativeness
munitionette	myelographic	native turkey	negative pole
munitionment	myelomatosis	native willow	negative sign
murdermonger	my godfathers	nativity play	negativistic
muriatic acid	mylohyoidean	nativization	neglectfully
murine typhus	mylonization	Natterer's bat	neglectively
muscovitized	myochemistry	natural death	negotiatress
museographer	myofibrillar	naturalesque	Negro English
museological	myrmecochore	naturalistic	Negrophilism
mushroom city	myrmecophile	natural magic	Negrophilist
mushroom loaf	myrmecophily	natural order	Negro tamarin
mushroom-ring	myrmecophyte	natural parts	neighbouress
mushroom town	myrobalan nut	natural right	neighbouring
musical bumps	my sow's pigged	nature-faking	Nelson's blood
musical chime	mystagogical	nature poetry	nematocerous
musical clock	mystagoguery	nature ramble	nematologist
musical drive	mysteriously	nature-spirit	nembutalized
musical sound	mystery novel	naturopathic	neoclassical
musicassette	mystery story	nauseatingly	Neo-Darwinian
music gallery	mystery woman	nauseousness	Neo-Darwinism
music-grinder	mysticalness	nautical mile	Neo-Darwinist
music-hallish	mystificator	naval academy	neo-Hellenism
musicianship	mystifyingly	naval brigade	neon lighting
music licence	mythoclastic	naval officer	Neononmianism
musicography	mythogenesis	naval reserve	neontologist
musicologist	mythographer	naval station	Neoplatonism
musico-phobia	mythographic	navigability	Neoplatonist
music theatre	mythological	navigational	neosalvarsan
music therapy	mythologizer	navy register	neotectonics
musket powder	nail scissors	navy revolver	nephanalysis
musk kangaroo	naive painter	Nazariteship	nephelinitic
musk lorikeet	naive realism	Nazification	nephelometer
muskrat house	naive realist	near infrared	nephelometry
musk tortoise	namby-pambies	near the heart	nephrologist
Muslim League	name-dropping	neat's-foot oil	nephromixium
musquash-root	namelessness	neat's-leather	nephropathic
mussel digger	nankeen cloth	nebulization	nephroptosis
mussel picker	nankeen heron	nebulousness	Neptunianism
Mussorgskian	nanoplankton	nebulous star	nerve impulse
Mussulmanism	Napier's bones	neck and heels	nerve-patient
mustang grape	nap selection	necklace-tree	nerve-racking
muster-master	narcissistic	necktie party	nervous Nelly
mutagenicity	narcissus fly	necrological	nervous wreck
mutarotation	narcotically	necromantist	Nessler's tube
mutationally	Narragansett	necrophagous	Nestorianism
mutation mink	narrowcasted	necrophiliac	Netherlander
mutation rank	narrowcaster	necrophilism	Netherlandic
mutation rate	narrow-minded	necrophilist	nether person
mutation stop	narrow squeak	necrophilous	neurasthenia
mutinousness	nasalization	necropolitan	neurasthenic

neurilemmoma	nicotinamide	non-breakable	Norfolk capon
neuroanatomy	niddle-noddle	nonchalantly	normal forest
neurobiology	nidification	non-Christian	normalizable
neuroblastic	Nigerian teak	non-combatant	normal saline
neurocranium	Niger morocco	non-committal	normal school
neurofibroma	nigger heaven	non-communist	Norman French
neurogenesis	night-adapted	non-Communist	Norman thrush
neurogenetic	nightclothes	non-conductor	normlessness
neurohormone	nightclubber	non-contagion	normoblastic
neurohumoral	night-commode	non-cooperate	normochromic
neurological	night crawler	non-crossover	normotensive
neuropathist	night fighter	noncurantist	normothermic
neuropeptide	night-herding	non-effective	North African
neuropterous	nightie-night	non-efficient	North Britain
neuroscience	night jasmine	non-emptiness	north country
neurosensory	night paddock	nonentitious	North Country
neurosurgeon	night-scented	none-so-pretty	north-eastern
neurosurgery	night terrors	non-essential	Northern blot
neurotically	night-walking	none the worse	northernmost
neurotrophic	night-watcher	non-Euclidean	northernness
neurotropism	nimble-footed	non-execution	northern star
neurypnology	nimble-witted	non-executive	northern wren
neutralistic	nimbostratus	non-existence	Northumbrian
neutral vowel	niminy-piminy	non-explosive	north-western
neutrophilic	nine-nine-nine	non-fattening	Norway spruce
never-ceasing	nineteenthly	non-fictional	noselessness
never-failing	Nippon vellum	non-flammable	no such animal
nevertheless	Nissl granule	non-inflected	notabilities
never you fear	nitrobenzene	non-intervene	not an earthly
never you mind	nitromethane	non-intrusion	notarization
New Criticism	nitromuriate	non-knowledge	notary public
new departure	nitrophilous	non-linearity	notationally
New Englander	nitrous oxide	non-logically	not care a cent
newfangledly	no better than	non-malignant	not care a chip
new-fashioned	noble science	non-migratory	not care a hang
Newfoundland	nocking point	non-necessity	not care a snap
Newgate frill	no-claim bonus	non-Newtonian	notch-bar test
Newgate novel	noctambulant	non-normality	notch-brittle
New Jersey tea	noctambulism	non-obedience	noteworthily
new of the moon	noctambulist	non-objective	not give a damn
New Orleanian	noctambulous	non-poisonous	not give a hang
news bulletin	nocturnal arc	non-political	not give a shit
news-gatherer	nodulization	non-reflexive	not have a clue
newslessness	no fixed abode	non-residence	not having any
newspaperdom	noise contour	non-resistant	nothingarian
newspaperese	noise limiter	non-resisting	nothing doing
newspaperish	nolens volens	non-scheduled	nothing for it
newspaperism	nomadization	non-scientist	nothing loath
newspaperman	nomen agentis	non-sectarian	nothosaurian
newspapermen	nomenclative	non-segmental	notification
newsworthily	nomenclature	non-selective	not if I know it
New Testament	nominalistic	nonsense word	not in the book
New Thoughter	nominal value	non-sensitive	not in the race
Newtonianism	nomothetical	non-technical	not much wiser
Newtonically	non-abstainer	non-trivially	not one's scene
New Zealander	non-addictive	non-vanishing	notoungulate
next the heart	non-admission	non-violently	not to mention
nice-nellyism	nonagenarian	Noogoora burr	not to speak of
nichemanship	non-alcoholic	no question of	not turn a hair
nickel nurser	non-alignment	noradrenalin	not worth a fig
nickel-plated	non-ambiguous	nordmarkitic	nourishingly
nickel silver	non assumpsit	norephedrine	nouveau riche

novelization	oboi da caccia	of good family	on an even keel
Novocastrian	obreptitious	of obligation	on bended knee
nubbing-cheat	obscurantism	of the essence	once and again
nuclear force	obscurantist	of the order of	once in a while
nuclear power	obscure vowel	oidiomycosis	once too often
nuclear waste	obsequiously	oil of juniper	on cloud seven
nucleocapsid	Observantine	oil of vitriol	oncogenicity
nucleolonema	obsessionist	oil on the fire	on commission
nucleophilic	obsolescence	oil pollution	oncornavirus
nucleosidase	obsoleteness	oil the wheels	one-and-thirty
nucleotidase	obstacle race	oil to the fire	one-arm bandit
nude contract	obstetrician	old-fashioned	one had best do
nugatoriness	obstreperous	old-field lark	one-horse race
nuisance raid	obstructedly	old-field pine	oneirocritic
number-crunch	occasionally	Old Gentleman	oneiromancer
number theory	occasonalist	Old Icelandic	one jump ahead
numerability	occidentally	old-maidenism	one of the best
numerologist	occult spavin	old-maidishly	one of the boys
numerousness	occupational	old-man cactus	one's born days
numinousness	oceanic crust	old man's beard	one's cup of tea
numismatical	oceanisation	old moustache	one's ears burn
Nunc Dimittis	oceanization	Old Pretender	one's good lady
nursery class	oceanography	Old Ritualist	one-sidedness
nursery nurse	oceanologist	old school tie	one's luck is in
nursery rhyme	ochlocracies	Old Testament	one's mind's eye
nursery slope	ochlophobist	old wives' tale	one's sun is set
nut chocolate	ochlospecies	oleaginosity	one's writ runs
nutritionist	octahedrally	oleaginously	one-track mind
nutritiously	octahedrical	oleander hawk	one-upmanship
nuts and bolts	octane number	oleandomycin	on firm ground
nychthemeral	octane rating	oleoresinous	on first blush
nychthemeron	octave stanza	oleyl alcohol	only-begotten
nyctitropism	octogenarian	olfactometer	on occasion of
nyctohemeral	octopetalous	olfactometry	onomasiology
nympholeptic	octosepalous	olfactronics	onomastician
nymphomaniac	octosyllabic	oligarchical	onomatomania
obambulation	octosyllable	oligocarpous	onomatopoeia
obdurateness	oculo-agravic	oligodynamic	onomatopoeic
obedientiary	odd-come-short	oligopeptide	on one's honour
obedientness	odontologist	oligophagous	on one's mettle
Oberleutnant	odontophoral	oligophrenia	on one's pulses
obiter dictum	oedematously	oligopsonist	on one's uppers
object choice	oesophagitis	oligosaprobe	on one's way out
object-finder	of easy virtue	oligospermia	on security of
objectionist	off at the nail	oligotrophic	on sufferance
objectlessly	Offenbachian	olistostrome	on the basis of
object lesson	offendedness	Olympic games	on the brink of
object libido	office-bearer	Olympic Games	on the decline
object-matter	office junior	ombrological	on the faith of
objet de virtu	office of arms	ombrophilous	on the high gig
oblanceolate	office-seeker	ombrophobous	on the horizon
obligational	office worker	ombrotrophic	on the kibes of
obligatorily	officious lie	omissibility	on the knocker
obligingness	off one's block	omnibus train	on the one hand
oblique pedal	off one's chump	omnipotently	on the order of
obliteration	off one's guard	omnipresence	on the outlook
obliterative	off one's hands	omnisciently	on the point of
oblivescence	off one's onion	omnitemporal	on the pretext
obliviscence	off-puttingly	omnitolerant	on the qui vive
obmutescence	off-reckoning	omnivorously	on the rampage
obnubilation	off-the-course	omphaloscopy	on the rebound
oboe da caccia	off the record	on a level with	on the schnozz

on the score of	optic chiasma	Orphan's Court	out in the cold
on the streets	optic measure	orphenadrine	outlandishly
on the track of	optic papilla	orthocephaly	outlaw strike
on the up and up	optic vesicle	orthoclastic	outmanoeuvre
on the up grade	optimization	orthodiagram	outmigration
on the upgrade	optoacoustic	orthodigital	outmodedness
on the wallaby	optometrical	orthodontics	out of conceit
on the warpath	oracularness	orthodontist	out of context
on this side of	orange-brandy	orthodoxical	out of control
ontotheology	orange-colour	orthodoxness	out of drawing
onus probandi	orange flower	orthoepistic	out of my sight
onychophagia	orange squash	orthoferrite	out of one's way
onychophoran	orange-yellow	orthogenesis	out of service
oophorectomy	Oratorianism	orthogenetic	out of spirits
open a door for	Oratorianize	orthognathic	out of the blue
open a gate for	oratorically	orthogonally	out of the milk
open-breasted	orbicularity	orthographer	out of the road
Open Brethren	orbiculately	orthographic	out of the swim
open compound	orbital index	orthokinesis	out of the true
open fracture	orchard grass	orthokinetic	out of the wood
open-handedly	orchard-house	orthomorphic	out of the wool
opening night	orchestrally	orthopaedics	out of winding
open interest	orchestra pit	orthopaedist	out on one's ear
open interval	orchestrator	orthopterist	out-pensioner
open juncture	orchestrelle	orthopteroid	outplacement
open learning	orchidaceous	orthopterous	outpocketing
open marriage	orchid cactus	orthorhombic	outrageously
open-mindedly	orchidectomy	orthotropous	outrightness
open one's ears	Order of Merit	orthovoltage	outscourings
open one's face	ordinariness	oryctologist	outside and in
open question	ordinary wine	Oscar-winning	outside cabin
open sandwich	organ-grinder	oscillatoria	outsidedness
open syllable	organicistic	oscillograph	outside track
opéra comique	organisation	oscillometer	outward bound
opera glasses	organistship	oscillometry	ovariotomies
opera recital	organization	oscilloscope	over-abundant
operatically	organizatory	osmoregulate	overabundant
operationism	organ of Corti	osmotic shock	overachiever
operationist	organogenist	ossification	overactivity
operatorship	organogenous	osteichthyan	overambition
ophiomorphic	organography	ostentatious	over and above
ophiophagous	organoleptic	osteoblastic	over-and-under
ophthalmitis	organologist	osteoclastic	overbearance
opinionation	orgasmically	osteogenesis	overbitterly
opinionative	orgastically	osteogenetic	overboldness
opinionnaire	orgiasticism	osteological	overcapacity
opisthodomos	oriental sore	osteomalacia	overcautious
opisthoglyph	orienteering	osteomalacic	overcoatless
opisthograph	original writ	osteopathist	overcomingly
opisthotonic	Orkney cheese	osteoporosis	overcompound
opisthotonos	ornamentally	osteoporotic	overcritical
opposability	ornithogalum	osteosarcoma	overcrowding
oppositeness	ornithologer	ostrich plume	over-delicacy
oppositional	ornithologic	other-worldly	overdelicacy
oppressingly	ornithomancy	otherworldly	over-delicate
oppressively	ornithophile	otosclerosis	overdelicate
opsonization	ornithophily	otosclerotic	overdramatic
optative mood	ornithoscopy	Ottoman Porte	overeasiness
optical bench	orogenically	ouster-le-main	overeffusive
optical fibre	orographical	outdatedness	overemphasis
optical glass	oro-rotundity	outfangthief	overengineer
optical sound	orphan asylum	outgoingness	overeruption

overestimate	Oxford Tracts	palato-dental	pantomograph
over-exercise	oxotremorine	palatography	pantophagist
overexercise	oxyacetylene	palatoplasty	pantothenate
overexertion	oxycellulose	Palestrinian	Papanicolaou
overexposure	oxyluciferin	palette knife	paper-folding
overfamiliar	oxymyoglobin	palimbacchic	paper-hanging
overflourish	oxyphosphate	palimpsestic	paper-machine
overflow pipe	oyster blenny	palindromist	paper pattern
overfondness	oyster-cellar	palingenesia	paper-pushing
overfullness	oyster-farmer	palingenesis	paper-shelled
overgenerous	oyster-plover	palingenetic	paper-stainer
overhand knot	oyster-shaped	palinspastic	paper-taffeta
overhydrated	oyster-veneer	palisade cell	Paphlagonian
over-inflated	pachycaulous	palisade-worm	papillectomy
overkindness	pachydermoid	Palladianism	papilloedema
overlavishly	pacification	Palladianize	papistically
overlook bean	pacificatory	palladiumize	papyriferous
overlordship	Pacific Ocean	palliatively	papyrography
overmodestly	Pacific slope	palma Christi	papyrologist
overmodulate	packing-sheet	palmetto flag	paraboliform
overmuchness	pack one's bags	palm-greasing	paraboloidal
overniceness	paddle tennis	palmitic acid	parabronchus
over one's head	paddling pool	palm squirrel	paracellular
over one's name	paddock-stone	palo de hierro	paracentesis
over-optimism	paddock-stool	palpableness	paracervical
overoptimism	paedobaptism	palsie-walsie	parachronism
overpainting	paedobaptist	palynologist	paraclinical
overpersuade	paedodontics	pamperedness	parade ground
overpopulate	paedodontist	Panathenaean	paradigmatic
overpowering	paedogenesis	pan-Britannic	paradigm case
overpressure	paedogenetic	pan-Christian	paradisaical
overquantity	paedomorphic	panchromatic	paradise-bird
overreaction	paedophiliac	pancreatitis	paradise duck
overridingly	paganization	pancreozymin	paradise-fish
overrigorous	pagoda sleeve	pancytopenia	paradise-tree
overripeness	paid holidays	pandialectal	paradisiacal
oversampling	paid-up member	panel heating	paradoxology
overseership	painlessness	panel painter	paraenetical
oversimplify	paintability	panel patient	paraesthesia
overspeaking	painted cloth	pan-Germanism	paraesthetic
overspecific	painted finch	pan-Germanist	paraffinized
oversprinkle	painted grass	pangrammatic	paraffin test
overstepping	painted quail	Panhellenism	parafoveally
overstrictly	paint the lily	Panhellenist	paraganglion
oversubtlety	pair of arrows	paniculately	paragraphism
oversupplied	pair of gloves	panification	paragraphist
oversupplies	pair of horses	pannikin-boss	parahydrogen
over-the-board	pair of knives	panpharmacon	paralanguage
over the fence	pair of scales	panplanation	paralipomena
over the limit	pair of shears	pan-sexualism	parallel bars
over the rails	pair of stairs	pan-sexuality	parallel-park
overthrowing	pair of wheels	Panslavistic	parallel text
overtrousers	palaeobotany	pantaloonery	parallel turn
overwatching	palaeocortex	pantechnicon	paralogistic
overwhelming	palaeography	pantellerite	paralogously
owl-butterfly	Palaeo-Indian	panther juice	paralysation
oxaloacetate	palaeolithic	pantie-girdle	paralysingly
oxbow stirrup	palaeoniscid	pantisocracy	paramagnetic
Oxford chrome	palaeoradius	pantographer	parameterize
Oxford Circus	palatability	pantographic	parametritic
Oxford hollow	palatine bone	pantological	parametritis
Oxford School	Palatine Hill	pantomimical	paramilitary

paramorphism	Parsonianism	pathographer	pedantocracy
paranatellon	parsonically	pathological	pedestal desk
paranoically	parson's table	patholopolis	pedestalling
paranormally	part exchange	patience-dock	pedestrianly
Paranthropus	Parthenopean	patio process	pedicellaria
paraphimosis	Parthian shot	pat on the back	pedicellated
paraphrastic	partial order	patriarchate	pediculicide
paraphyletic	partial umbel	patriarchess	Pedro Ximenez
paraphysical	participable	patriarchies	pedunculated
parapophysis	participator	patriarchism	peel one's eyes
parasagittal	particularly	Patriarchist	peerie pinkie
parascending	partisanship	patricentric	peerlessness
parasitaemia	partitioning	patricianism	peer pressure
parasite drag	partitionism	patrilateral	pejoratively
parasiticide	partitionist	patrilineage	pelargonidin
parasitology	partners desk	patrilocally	pelecypodous
parasphenoid	part of speech	Patripassian	pelican's foot
parasymbiont	partridge pea	patristicism	Pelican State
paratectonic	partycolored	patroclinous	pellucidness
paraterminal	party manners	patrological	pellucid zone
parathormone	party per bend	patronymical	pelvic girdle
parcellation	party per pale	patternation	pelvic thrust
parcel tanker	party per pile	pattern-paper	penalization
parchmentize	party-pooping	pattinsonize	penalty bench
pareiasaurus	pas de bourrée	patulousness	penalty bully
parenchymous	pas de ciseaux	Paulicianism	Penang lawyer
parenterally	pasque flower	pavor diurnus	pencil flower
parent-figure	passableness	pawn skeleton	pencil pusher
parenthesise	passage grave	pay-as-you-earn	pendente lite
parenthesize	passage-money	pay-off matrix	pendulum-ball
Parfait Amour	passed-master	pay on the line	pendulum-wire
Parian cement	passe-partout	peaceability	penetrameter
Parian marble	passepartout	peace-breaker	penetrometer
parietal bone	passibleness	peace economy	pen-feathered
parietal cell	passing place	peacefulness	penicillanic
parietal lobe	passionately	peace-keeping	penicilloate
paring-chisel	Passion cross	peacekeeping	penitent-form
Paris commune	passion fruit	peace-officer	penitentiary
parish church	passivizable	peach-blossom	penitentness
parish priest	pass one's lips	peach yellows	Pennsylvania
parish-rigged	passportless	Peacock Alley	penny-pincher
paristhmitis	pass the pikes	peacockishly	penny-postage
parisyllabic	past definite	peacock's tail	penny whistle
parking brake	pastern-joint	peanut butter	pen recording
parking light	Pasteur flask	pearlescence	pensifulness
parking meter	past historic	pearlessence	pensionaries
parking orbit	past mistress	pearl-fishery	pentagastrin
Parkinsonian	pastophorium	pearl-fishing	pentagonally
Parkinsonism	pastoralness	pearly whites	pentahedrons
parlour-house	past-pointing	peasant class	pentahydrate
paroccipital	past the chair	pease pudding	pentametrize
parochialism	pataphysical	pebble-dashed	pentapeptide
parochiality	pâté en croûte	pebble-lensed	pentapolitan
parochialize	patellectomy	peccadilloes	Pentateuchal
paroemiology	patent office	pecking order	pentose cycle
paronomastic	Patent Safety	Pecksniffery	People's Court
parotid gland	path-breaking	Pecksniffian	People's front
parquet floor	pathetically	Peclet number	People's Power
parrot's-perch	pathlessness	pectinaceous	pepper-caster
parsimonious	pathobiology	pectoral arch	peppered moth
parsley-piert	pathogenesis	pectoriloquy	pepper shaker
parsley sauce	pathogenetic	pedantically	peptide chain

peptidolysis
peptidolytic
peradventure
peraluminous
perambulator
perceptional
perceptively
perceptivity
perceptually
percipiently
percontation
percussively
percutaneous
peregrinator
peremptorily
perenniality
perestroikan
perfectation
perfect crime
perfectively
perfectivity
perfectivize
perfect pitch
perfidiously
perfoliation
performative
performatory
perfrication
pergameneous
periarterial
pericarditis
pericellular
pericemental
pericementum
perichaetial
perichaetium
perichaetous
perichoresis
periclinally
pericynthion
peridiastole
perigonadial
Perigourdine
perilousness
perimetrical
perinatology
periodic acid
periodically
periodograph
periodontics
periodontist
periodontium
periostracum
peripediment
peripherally
peripherical
periphrastic
perispomenon
peristrephic
perisystolic
peritrichate
peritrichous

periureteric
periurethral
perivascular
perivisceral
perjuriously
permaculture
permanentise
permanentize
permanent set
permanent way
permanganate
permeabilise
permeability
permeabilize
permissively
permissivism
permissivist
permittivity
perniciously
pernoctation
peroperative
perorational
peroxidation
peroxide bond
perpetration
perpetualism
perpetualist
perpetuality
perpetuation
perpetuative
perpetuities
perphenazine
perplexingly
perplexities
perquisition
persecutress
perseverance
perseverator
Persian berry
Persian green
Persian lilac
Persian sheep
Persian wheel
persistently
persistingly
persona grata
personalness
personalties
person-object
perspectival
perspicacity
perspiration
perspirative
perspiratory
persuadingly
persuasively
persulphuric
pertechnetic
pertinacious
perturbation
perturbative
perturbingly

Peruginesque
Peruvian bark
Peruvian lily
perverseness
perversities
pervicacious
perviousness
Pestalozzian
pestilential
pestological
petaliferous
Peterborough
Peter Pannish
Petersen grab
petitionable
petit treason
petrifaction
petrifactive
Petrobrusian
petrofabrics
petrogenesis
petrogenetic
petrographer
petrographic
petrol coupon
petrological
petrophysics
pettifoggery
pettifogging
petty average
petty officer
petty treason
Peutingerian
peyote button
phagedaenous
phagocytable
phagocytosis
phalaenopsid
phallocratic
phallophoria
phallophoric
phallophorus
phalloplasty
phanerogamic
phanerophyte
phantasmally
phantastical
Pharaoh hound
pharmaceutic
pharmacology
pharyngotomy
phase diagram
pheasantries
pheasant's eye
phellodermal
phenanthrene
phenetically
phenological
phenomenally
phenotypical
phentolamine
phenylacetic

Pherecratean
Pherecratian
Phi Beta Kappa
Philadelphia
philadelphus
philanthrope
philanthropy
philatelical
philathletic
philharmonic
philhellenic
philippinite
Philistinian
philistinish
philistinism
Philistinize
phillumenist
philobiblian
philobiblist
philodendron
philological
philosopheme
philosophess
philosophies
philosophise
philosophism
philosophist
philosophize
philotechnic
philotherian
phlebectasia
phlebography
phlebotomise
phlebotomist
phlebotomize
phlegmagogue
phlorizinize
phlyctenular
phoenicopter
phonaestheme
phonemically
phonetically
phonocamptic
phonographer
phonographic
phonological
phonometrics
phonotactics
phosphatemia
phosphatidic
phosphatidyl
phosphaturia
phosphaturic
phospholipid
phosphoresce
phosphoritic
Photinianism
photoallergy
photobiology
photocathode
photochemist
photochromic

photocollage
photocompose
photocontrol
photoconvert
photocurrent
photodimeric
photodynamic
photoelastic
photoemitter
photo-engrave
photofission
photogeology
photographee
photographer
photographic
photogravure
photokinesis
photokinetic
photometrist
photomontage
photoneutron
photonuclear
photo-oxidize
photopigment
photopolymer
photoprocess
photoproduct
photoprotein
photorealism
photorealist
photorespire
photoscanner
photosensory
photo session
photosetting
photospheric
photosurface
phototherapy
phototrophic
phototropism
phototypeset
photovoltaic
phragmoplast
phrase-marker
phraseograph
phreatophyte
phrenic nerve
phrenicotomy
phrenologist
phrenologize
phrontistery
Phrygian mode
phthalic acid
phthisiology
phycological
phycomycosis
phylacteries
phylarchical
phyletically
phyllodinous
phyllopodium
phyllosphere

phyllotactic
phylogenesis
phylogenetic
physicalness
physic garden
physicianess
physiocratic
physiognomic
physiography
physiologist
physiologize
physogastric
physostomous
phytobenthos
phytochemist
phytogenesis
phytographic
phytohormone
phytological
phytophagous
phytophthora
phytosaurian
pia-arachnoid
pianofortist
piano quartet
piano quintet
pibble-pabble
Picassoesque
pickaninnies
pick a quarrel
pickerel frog
pickerel-weed
Pick's disease
pick to pieces
pick up stakes
pick up the tab
picnic basket
picnic ground
picoplankton
picornavirus
pictographic
pictorialism
pictorialist
pictorialize
picture black
picturedrome
picture frame
picturegraph
Picturephone
picture-plane
picture-space
picture stage
piece by piece
piece of eight
piece of flesh
piece of goods
piece of water
piece-payment
pied hornbill
piercingness
pier-head jump
piezo-crystal

pigeon-breast
pigeon's blood
pigmentation
pigs might fly
piked dogfish
Pilate's voice
pile-building
pile dwelling
pillar-box red
pillion cloth
piloerection
pilot balloon
pilot biscuit
pilot carrier
pilot episode
pilot officer
Pilsner glass
pinchpennies
pinealectomy
pineapple rum
pine grosbeak
pine hawkmoth
pine overcoat
piney varnish
pinguedinous
pinguescence
pinhole borer
pink bollworm
pink cockatoo
pink-coloured
pink elephant
pink purslane
pinnatifidly
pinpointable
pip at the post
pipedreaming
pipe one's eyes
piping plover
piping shrike
Pirandellian
Pirandellism
pirate-stream
piscicapture
pisciculture
Piscis Volans
pisiform bone
pistachio nut
pistol-packer
pistol shrimp
piston engine
pitch-and-putt
pitch-and-toss
pitch contour
pitch control
pitcher plant
pitching axis
pitch phoneme
pitch-plaster
pitch wickets
pitiableness
pitilessness
pitter-patter

pivotability
pivot bearing
pivot grammar
placableness
place-betting
placentation
placentogram
placentology
place setting
plagiaristic
plagioclimax
plagiotropic
plain bearing
plain buffalo
plain clothes
plain cooking
plain dealing
plain English
plain-hearted
plain hunting
plain sailing
Plains Indian
plain Spanish
plains turkey
plain weaving
plane sailing
planetariums
planetesimal
planetologic
planet pinion
planigraphic
planispheric
planlessness
planning gain
planoconcave
planogametic
planographic
planorbiform
plantain lily
plant hormone
plant kingdom
plasmacytoid
plasmacytoma
plasma engine
plasmalemmal
plasma sheath
plasmasphere
plasmatocyte
plasmocytoma
plasterboard
plaster saint
plastication
plastic lymph
plastic money
plastic paint
plastocyanin
plate-printer
plates of meat
plate tracery
platform body
platform shoe
platform sole

platinum-blue	plumbaginous	poke one's head	polyneuritic
platinum disc	plumbiferous	poker-machine	polyneuritis
platitudinal	plum-coloured	polar diagram	polyoestrous
platonically	plume-bearing	polarimetric	polyommatous
Platonically	plume-thistle	polariscopic	polypetalous
Platonic body	plummer-block	polarization	polypharmacy
Platonic year	plumpishness	polarography	polyphonical
Plattdeutsch	plum-porridge	polemologist	polyphylesis
plattelander	plumulaceous	pole position	polyphyletic
platter-faced	plunger-valve	pole strength	polyphyllous
platycephaly	plural voting	police action	polyphyodont
platypussary	pluriformity	policeman fly	polypiferous
plausibility	plurilingual	policemanish	polyploidize
play at see-saw	pluriliteral	police matron	polypneustic
play ball with	plurilocular	police office	polyreaction
playfighting	pluripotence	policeperson	polyrhythmic
play for a fool	pluripotency	police record	polyribosome
play hell with	pluriseriate	policyholder	polysaprobic
playing field	plus ça change	policy-making	polysemantic
play-material	plus juncture	poliorcetics	polysensuous
play one's part	plutocracies	polishedness	polysepalous
play opposite	plutological	Polish marmot	polyspermous
play politics	pluviculture	politicalize	polysulphide
playsomeness	pluviometric	politicaster	polysulphone
play straight	Plymouth Rock	pollakanthic	polysyllabic
play the field	pneumaticity	pollen basket	polysyllable
play the whore	pneumatocele	pollen parent	polysymmetry
play with fire	pneumatocyst	polling booth	polysynaptic
plea of tender	pneumatology	polling clerk	polysyndeton
pleasantness	pneumococcal	pollutedness	polysystemic
pleasantries	pneumococcus	Pollyannaish	polytheistic
pleasingness	pneumocystis	Pollyannaism	polytonalist
pleasureless	pneumography	polrumptious	polytonality
pleasure-pain	pneumothorax	polyacrylate	polyurethane
plebbishness	pocket gopher	polyadically	pomacentroid
plebeianness	pocket passer	polyanthuses	pommes frites
plebiscitary	pocket-picker	polyarchical	pompholygous
plecopterous	pocket valley	polybasicity	pons asinorum
pleiochasium	poddy-dodging	polycentrism	Ponsonby rule
pleiomorphic	poeticalness	polychaetous	Pontiac fever
pleiotropism	poeticizable	polychromism	pontifically
plenipotence	poet laureate	polychromous	pontificator
plenipotency	Poet Laureate	polydisperse	pony-trekking
pleomorphism	pogonophoran	polyembryony	poodle-faking
plerocercoid	pogonotrophy	polyethylene	poop-ornament
plesiosaurus	poikiloblast	polygamistic	poor relation
plessimetric	poikiloderma	polygamously	poor-spirited
pleurisy-root	poikilotherm	polygenistic	poperyphobia
pleuronectid	poil de chèvre	polyglottism	poplar beetle
Plimsoll line	point blanket	polyglottous	poplar kitten
Plimsoll mark	point contact	polyhedrical	pop one's clogs
plinth course	point d'esprit	polyhedrosis	poppet-valved
ploddingness	pointfulness	polyhistoric	poppy anemone
plotlessness	pointing-bone	polyisoprene	popular front
plotting-book	point-instant	polymetallic	popular music
plough-driver	point of appui	polymetrical	popular press
plough-ground	point of order	polymodality	populational
plough-handle	point of sight	polymolecule	population II
plough-jogger	point the bone	polymorphean	populousness
Plough Monday	point-to-point	polymorphism	porcelainist
plough-pattle	pointy-headed	polymorphous	Porcelainite
plough-wright	poison oracle	polymyositis	porcelainize

porcelainous	postliminary	powerlifting	precisionist
porcellanite	postmaturely	power loading	precivilized
porcellanous	postmaturity	power package	pre-classical
porencephaly	postmeridian	power-sharing	preclassical
pore pressure	postmistress	power station	preclusively
pornographer	post-modifier	powers-that-be	precociously
pornographic	postmultiply	power take-off	precognition
porphyropsin	postneonatal	practicalism	precognitive
portableness	post-obit bond	practicality	pre-Columbian
portal system	post-obituary	practicalize	pre-Communist
portcullised	postponement	practice game	precondition
porte-bouquet	postposition	practitional	preconfigure
porte cochère	postpositive	practitioner	preconscious
porte-monnaie	postprandial	pragmaticism	predamnation
portentously	post-pubertal	pragmatistic	predecession
porteous roll	postscriptal	Prague circle	predesignate
porter's chair	postscriptum	Prague school	predestinate
porter's lodge	postsynaptic	Prague Spring	predetermine
portmanteaus	post-tectonic	prairie smoke	predial tithe
portmanteaux	posture-maker	Prairie State	predicatival
portrait-bust	Posturepedic	prairie wagon	predictively
portrait-lens	potamologist	praiseworthy	predictivity
Port-Royalist	potato-beetle	pralltriller	predigestion
port-wine mark	potato blight	prankishness	predilection
positionally	Potato Famine	pranksterism	prediscovery
position line	potato masher	praseodymium	predisponent
positiveness	potato peeler	prawn cracker	prednisolone
positive pole	pot-companion	praxeologist	predominance
positive rays	potentialise	praxinoscope	predominancy
positive sign	potentiality	prayer-carpet	pre-eclampsia
positivistic	potentialize	prayerlessly	pre-eclamptic
possessional	potentiation	praying-shawl	pre-embryonic
possessioned	potentiostat	preachership	pre-emergence
possessioner	potichomania	pre-adamitism	pre-eminently
possessively	potter's field	preadmission	pre-emphasize
possessorial	potter's lathe	preamplified	pre-emptioner
postage meter	potter's wheel	preamplifier	pre-emptively
postage stamp	pottery mould	pre-animistic	pre-establish
postal ballot	potwalloping	preassurance	pre-excellent
post-alveolar	pouched mouse	pre-auricular	pre-existence
post-boarding	poulard wheat	prebendaries	prefabricate
post-coitally	poultice-wise	prebiologist	prefectorial
post-colonial	pound and pint	precalculate	prefecturate
post-conquest	pound-noteish	precancerous	preferential
post-diluvial	pound of flesh	precantation	prefloration
post-diluvian	pound one's ear	precariously	prefoliation
post-doctoral	pouring cream	precautional	preformation
postdoctoral	Poussinesque	precedential	preformative
poster colour	poverty-grass	preceptorate	preglacially
posteriority	poverty level	preceptorial	pregnability
post exchange	poverty-plant	precessional	pregnanediol
post-existent	powder closet	pre-Christian	prehensility
post-feminism	powder colour	preciousness	prehistorian
post-feminist	powdering-tub	precious opal	pre-incarnate
postfixation	powder monkey	precipitable	pre-interpret
post-Freudian	power alcohol	precipitance	prejudgement
post-genitive	power-broking	precipitancy	prejudicious
postgraduate	power-centred	precipitated	prelapsarian
post-historic	power density	precipitator	prelingually
posthumously	power failure	precisianism	pre-makeready
post-hypnotic	Powerforming	precisianist	premaritally
postillation	powerfulness	precisionism	premaxillary

premeditated	preshrinkage	pride of China	problematist
premenarchal	presidencies	pride of India	problematize
premenopause	presidentess	pride of place	problem child
premenstrual	presidential	priestianity	proboscidean
premenstruum	press attaché	priestliness	proboscidian
Premonstrant	Press Council	priestly code	probouleutic
premonstrate	press cutting	priest-ridden	procainamide
premyelocyte	pressed steel	priggishness	procarbazine
prenasalized	press gallery	primal father	pro-cathedral
prentice hand	pressingness	primal scream	procedurally
prenticeship	press officer	primary cause	process black
preoccupancy	press release	primary group	process chart
pre-operation	press to death	primary radar	processional
preoperative	pressure-cook	primer seisin	processioner
pre-opercular	pressure drag	prime the pump	process steam
pre-operculum	pressure-feed	primevalness	process water
pre-ovulatory	pressure head	primeval soup	procès-verbal
preparedness	pressure hold	primigravida	prochirality
preplanetary	pressure hull	primogenital	proclamation
preponderant	pressure lamp	primogenitor	proclamatory
preponderate	pressure mine	primordially	proclivities
preponderous	pressure sore	primrose path	procoagulant
preposterous	pressure suit	primulaceous	proconsulate
pre-processor	pressure tank	primuline red	proctologist
preprocessor	pressure-test	primum mobile	proctorially
prepsychotic	pressure tube	Prince Albert	proctoscopic
pre-pubescent	press-warrant	prince-bishop	proctotrupid
prepubescent	prestigiator	princeliness	procyclidine
prepyramidal	prestissimos	Prince Regent	prodigiosity
prereduction	presumptious	prince's metal	prodigiously
pre-reflexive	presumptuous	Prince's metal	producership
prerequisite	pretenceless	princess-ship	productional
prerogatived	Pretenderism	Princetonian	productively
presagefully	pretendingly	principal boy	productivity
presbyterate	pretensively	principality	proembryonic
presbyteress	preterlabent	principal ray	professional
presbyterial	pretermitted	printability	professorate
presbyterian	pretonically	printer's mark	professordom
Presbyterian	pretreatment	printer's ream	professoress
presbyteries	pretty fellow	print spooler	professorial
presbyterion	pretty packet	print-through	professoriat
presbyterism	pretty please	prison editor	proficiently
presbyterium	pretty-pretty	privateering	profilograph
prescribable	prevailingly	private hotel	profilometer
prescription	prevaricator	private house	profilometry
prescriptive	preveniently	private means	profit centre
pre-selection	preventative	private parts	profitlessly
preselection	preventional	private press	profit margin
pre-selective	preventively	private wrong	profit motive
preselective	preventorium	privy chamber	profit-taking
presensation	previousness	privy council	profligately
presensitize	previsionary	Privy Council	profligation
presentation	price control	privy members	profoundness
presentative	price-current	prizefighter	profundities
presenteeism	price-cutting	prizewinning	progenitress
presentiment	price shading	proactivator	progesterone
present value	price support	pro-anaphoral	proglottides
present worth	pricking-iron	pro and contra	prognostical
preservation	prickle-layer	probableness	progradation
preservative	prickly Moses	probate court	programmable
preservatory	prickly poppy	probationary	programmatic
preserveress	prickly withe	problematise	projectional

projectively
projectivity
prolegomenal
prolegomenon
proletairism
proletariate
proliferator
prolifically
prolificness
prolongation
promastigote
prometaphase
promethazine
promised land
promontorial
promontoried
promontories
promontorium
prompt-script
promulgation
promyelocyte
pronominally
pronouncedly
pronunciable
pronunciator
proof-reading
propaedeutic
propagandise
propagandism
propagandist
propagandize
propagatress
propenseness
propensities
proper lesson
proper motion
propertyless
propheticism
prophylactic
propitiation
propitiative
propitiatory
propitiously
proportional
proportioned
proportioner
propoundment
propoundress
propoxyphene
proprietress
prop up the bar
proscribable
proscription
proscriptive
prose account
prosectorium
prosecutable
prose fiction
proselytizer
prosenchymal
prosiphonate
prosodically

prosopolepsy
prosopopoeia
prosopopoeic
prospectless
prospectuses
prospect well
prosperation
prosperously
prospicience
prostacyclin
prostitution
prosyllogism
protactinium
protatically
protectingly
protectional
protectively
protectorate
protectorial
protein shock
protensively
proteoglycan
proteroglyph
protestation
protestatory
protestingly
protest march
prothalamion
prothalamium
prothonotary
protistology
protocolling
proto-history
Proto-Hittite
protological
protomorphic
protonematal
protonmotive
protoplasmal
protoplasmic
protoplastic
Proto-Romance
protostellar
prototherian
protothetics
prototrophic
prototypical
protozoology
protractedly
protreptical
protrusively
protuberance
protuberancy
proud as Punch
proud-hearted
provableness
Provençalism
Provençalist
Provence rose
prove oneself
proverbially
prove too much

providential
province-wide
provincially
provisionary
provost guard
proxy sitting
prudentially
prunella salt
pruning-knife
Prussian blue
Prussian carp
Prussianizer
psammomatous
psammophilic
psephologist
pseudishness
pseudoallele
pseudo-Christ
pseudocrisis
pseudocumene
pseudocyesis
pseudo-entity
pseudofaeces
pseudogamous
pseudo-Gothic
pseudography
pseudohalide
pseudologist
pseudonymity
pseudonymous
pseudopodial
pseudopodium
pseudorabies
pseudorandom
pseudoscalar
pseudoscopic
pseudosexual
pseudouracil
pseudovector
psophometric
psychiatrics
psychiatrise
psychiatrist
psychiatrize
psychoactive
psychobabble
psychography
psycholeptic
psychologese
psychologies
psychologise
psychologism
psychologist
psychologize
psychomachia
psychometric
psychoneural
psychopathic
psychophysic
psychosexual
psychosocial
psychosphere

psychoticism
psychotropic
psychrometer
psychrometry
psychrophile
psychrotroph
pteridomania
pteridophyte
pteridosperm
pteropod ooze
pterosaurian
public figure
public health
public menace
public notary
public office
public orator
public school
public sector
public spirit
publish a will
Pucciniesque
pudding basin
pudding cloth
pudding-faced
pudding-grass
pudding-stone
puddle-jumper
puericulture
pugnaciously
puissantness
pull a fast one
pull-down menu
pull one's rank
pull one's wire
pull the wires
pull together
pull to pieces
pulpitically
pulque brandy
pulsed column
pulverizable
pulverizator
pulverulence
pumpernickel
punch forceps
Punchinellos
punching-ball
punctualness
punctulation
puncturation
punctureless
punitiveness
punkah-wallah
pupillograph
pupillometer
pupillometry
pupil teacher
puppeteering
puppet-master
puppet-player
puppyishness

Purbeck stone	pyritization	quarter-clock	quinquennial
purblindness	pyritohedral	quarter-final	quinquennium
purchaseable	pyritohedron	quarter-grain	quintangular
pure-breeding	pyroelectric	quarter-guard	quintessence
purification	pyrogenicity	quarter-horse	quintillions
purificatory	pyroligneous	quarter-light	quite another
Puritan spoon	pyromagnetic	quarter-miler	quit the scene
Purkinje cell	pyromaniacal	quartern loaf	quitting-time
purple airway	pyromorphite	quarter-piece	quixotically
purple martin	pyrophyllite	quarter-plate	quizzicality
purple urchin	pyrosulphate	quarter-point	quota quickie
purple wreath	pyrotartaric	quarter-round	quotationist
purpose-built	pyrotartrate	quarterstaff	rabbinically
purposefully	pyrotechnics	quarter-tonal	rabbit warren
Puseyistical	pyrotechnist	quarter-watch	rabble-rouser
pushmi-pullyu	pyroxmangite	quartz-locked	racemiferous
push one's luck	Pyrrhonistic	quasicrystal	racemization
pussyfootism	Pythian games	quasi-stellar	race theorist
put a damper on	pythonomorph	quaternarian	race-thinking
put a finger on	Quadragesima	quaternaries	rachischisis
put a jerk in it	quadraminium	quaternionic	rachitogenic
put a sock in it	quadrangular	quatrefoiled	racing driver
put behind one	quadraphonic	quattrocento	racing pigeon
put down roots	quadraplegia	Quebec heater	racketeering
put in the nips	quadrate-bone	Queen Anneish	racket-tailed
put into shape	quadrenniums	queen consort	Rackhamesque
put into words	quadriennium	queen dowager	rack mounting
put it on thick	quadrigamist	Queen Mary hat	radappertize
put money into	quadrillions	Queen of glory	radar plotter
put on a charge	quadrinomial	queen of night	radar scanner
put one across	quadriplegia	queen of tides	radial engine
put one's oar in	quadriplegic	queen pudding	radiant point
put on the line	quadrivalent	queen's bishop	radiant power
put on the spot	quadrominium	Queen's bounty	radiated mole
putrefacient	quadrophonic	queen scallop	radiation fog
putrefaction	quadrumanous	Queen's colour	radical right
putrefactive	quadrupedism	queen's flower	radicidation
put the acid on	quadruplegia	queen's gambit	radiesthesia
put the bite on	quaestorship	queen's knight	radiesthesic
put the boot in	Quaker collar	Queenslander	radiesthetic
put the make on	quaker-ladies	queen's pigeon	radio amateur
put the wind up	quaking aspen	Queen's Speech	radiobiology
put through it	quaking-grass	queen termite	radiochemist
putting green	qualificator	queer-bashing	radio contact
put to expense	quality paper	queerishness	radiodensity
put to silence	qualmishness	quench ageing	radio-element
put to the horn	quantifiable	querimonious	radiographer
put to the rout	quantitation	questionable	radiographic
put to the test	quantitative	questionably	radio horizon
put to the vote	quantitively	questionless	radioisotope
puzzle-headed	quantity mark	question mark	radio licence
puzzlingness	quantization	question time	radiological
Pygmalionism	quantum yield	question word	radiolucency
pyjama bottom	quaquaversal	quick-release	radio network
pyloroplasty	quarter-block	quick-sighted	radionuclide
pyonephrosis	quarter-bloke	quicksilvery	radio-opacity
pyramidology	quarter-blood	quill-coverts	radiophonics
pyramid shell	quarter-board	quill-feather	radio silence
pyrazinamide	quartar-bound	quilting hoop	radiosondage
pyrenomycete	quarter-breed	quinacridone	radio station
pyridoxamine	quarter-caste	quindecemvir	radiotherapy
pyritiferous	quarter-cleft	quinquenniad	radium needle

radius vector	rattle-headed	rechargeable	redemptional
radurization	rauschpfeife	recharge area	redemptioner
ragamuffinly	Ravenna grass	recharge well	Redemptorist
ragged-hipped	ravenousness	recidivistic	redeployment
ragged school	Rayleigh wave	recipiendary	redeposition
raggle-taggle	ray treatment	reciprocally	red eyebright
raglan sleeve	razor-grinder	reciprocator	red-eyed vireo
rags-to-riches	razzle-dazzle	reciting note	red-eye flight
raiding party	reabsorption	Reckitt's blue	redintegrate
railroad bull	reabsorptive	recklessness	red ironstone
railroad flat	reacceptance	reclassified	rediscoverer
railroadiana	reaccumulate	reclassifies	redissoluble
railroad worm	reachability	recognisance	redistribute
rail-splitter	reaction coil	recognizable	Red Leicester
railway guide	reaction shot	recognizably	red-letter day
railway hotel	reaction time	recognizance	redoublement
railway novel	reaction wood	re-collection	red phalarope
railway spine	reactivation	recollection	Red River cart
rainbow smelt	readableness	recollective	Red Sandstone
rainbow snake	readaptation	recombinable	red-shortness
rainbow trout	reading chair	recommission	reducibility
raise a finger	reading clerk	recommitment	reductionism
raise its head	reading-glass	recommitting	reductionist
raise one's hat	readjustment	recompensive	redundancies
raise the roof	readminister	recomplicate	red underwing
raise the wind	readmittance	reconception	re-embarkment
raising-piece	reaffirmance	reconcilable	re-embodiment
raising-plate	reagent grade	reconciliate	re-employment
rallentandos	reagent paper	reconnection	re-engagement
Ramapithecus	reallocation	reconnoitrer	re-enlistment
ramblingness	real presence	reconsecrate	re-evaluation
rambunctious	reannexation	reconstitute	re-excitation
ramentaceous	reapparition	reconvention	re-expression
ramification	reappearance	reconversion	refcrability
rampageously	rearing-house	reconveyance	referred pain
ramshackling	re-articulate	reconviction	reflationary
random-access	reasonlessly	recordership	reflationist
random number	reassemblage	record holder	reflectingly
random sample	reassessment	record player	reflectional
rangefinding	reassignment	record sleeve	reflectively
rank-and-filer	reassimilate	recovery room	reflectivity
Rankine cycle	reassortment	recovery time	reflectorize
Rankine scale	reassumption	recovery ward	reflex camera
rank outsider	reassuringly	recreantness	reflexogenic
ranunculuses	reattachment	recreational	reformatting
Raphaelesque	reattainment	recredential	reform school
rapid transit	rebelliously	recrudescent	refoundation
rapping plate	recalcitrant	rectosigmoid	refractility
rarefication	recalcitrate	recto-uterine	refractively
raspberry jam	recalescence	rectovaginal	refractivity
rataplanning	recapacitate	recuperation	refractories
rat-bite fever	recapitalise	recuperative	refractorily
ratchet-wheel	recapitalize	Red Astrachan	refreshfully
rate constant	recapitulate	red-blindness	refreshingly
ratification	recategorize	red blood cell	refrigerated
ratihabition	receivership	red cobalt ore	refrigerator
ratiocinator	recensionist	red copper ore	refutability
ratio essendi	receptacular	red corpuscle	regardlessly
rationalizer	receptionism	Red Delicious	regeneration
rationalness	receptionist	redecoration	regenerative
rat-tail-grass	receptitious	rededication	regeneratory
rat-tail spoon	recessionary	redefinition	regent oriole

regent parrot
Reggeization
regimentally
register book
register mark
register-ship
registraries
registration
reglementary
regressively
regressivity
regular canon
regulatively
rehabilitate
rehalogenize
rehydratable
Reichsthaler
reilluminate
reimbursable
reimposition
reimpregnate
reimpression
reinaugurate
reindeer moss
reingratiate
reinspection
reinstalment
reinvestment
reinvigorate
reiteratedly
rejectamenta
rejectionism
rejectionist
rejuvenation
rejuvenatory
relatability
relationally
relationless
relationship
relativeness
relativistic
relativitist
relay station
release agent
relentlessly
reliableness
relief agency
Relief Church
relieve guard
religionless
remainder man
remand centre
Rembrandtian
Rembrandtish
Rembrandtism
remedilessly
rememberable
rememberably
remembrancer
rememoration
remilitarize
remineralize

reminiscence
remonstrance
remonstrator
remorsefully
remote sensor
removability
remuneration
remunerative
remuneratory
Renaissancer
renal pyramid
renaturation
render homage
rendezvoused
rendezvouses
renegotiable
renewability
renomination
renounceable
renouncement
renovascular
Renshaw smash
rent of assise
renunciation
renunciative
renunciatory
reoccupation
reoccurrence
reordination
repagination
reparability
repatriation
repeat buying
repeat itself
repercussion
repercussive
reperforator
repetitional
repetitively
replantation
replevisable
replica plate
repopulation
repositories
repossession
repple depple
reprehension
reprehensive
reprehensory
representant
repressively
re-pressuring
repressurize
repristinate
reproachable
reproachless
reproducible
reproducibly
reproduction
reproductive
reproductory
reprogrammed

reprographer
reprographic
repromulgate
reptile house
republicanly
reputability
reputational
reputatively
reputed quart
requiem shark
requiescence
requiredness
rescuability
researchable
réseau rosacé
resectionist
resectoscope
Reserved List
reservedness
reserve grade
reserve price
resettlement
residentiary
residentship
residue class
resignalling
resignedness
resiniferous
resinography
resipiscence
resistlessly
resolubility
resoluteness
resolutioner
resolvedness
resoundingly
resourceless
respectfully
respectively
respirometer
respirometry
resplendence
resplendency
respondentia
responseless
response time
responsively
Responsivist
responsivity
responsorial
responsories
restauranter
restaurateur
restauration
resting place
restlessness
rest one's case
restrainable
restrainedly
restrengthen
restrictable
restrictedly

resubjection
resubmission
resumptively
resupination
resurrection
resurrective
resuscitable
resuscitator
retainership
retaining fee
retentionist
reticulately
reticulation
reticulocyte
retinopathic
retinoscopic
retired flank
retiringness
retort carbon
retractation
retractility
retranscribe
retransplant
retrenchment
retrieveless
retrievement
retrocedence
retrocession
retrocessive
retrodiction
retrodictive
retroduction
retroductive
retroflected
retroflexion
retrogradely
retrogradism
retrogradist
retrojection
retromingent
retropulsion
retropulsive
retrospectus
retrosternal
retroversion
return crease
return flight
return thanks
return ticket
reunionistic
reupholstery
revanchistic
revegetation
revelational
revengefully
reverberator
reverendship
reversal film
reverse angle
reverse fault
reverse lever
reverse plate

reverse video	ride the stang	robustiously	rose of Sharon
reversionary	ride to hounds	rock-climbing	rose plantain
reversionist	ridiculosity	rocker switch	Rosetta stone
revert to type	ridiculously	rocketeering	Rosetta Stone
revirescence	riding-master	rock festival	rosette gauge
revisitation	riding school	rock-hounding	rosette plant
revivability	riempiestoel	rocking chair	Rosh Hashanah
revivalistic	riffle beetle	rocking horse	rostriferous
revivication	rigging lines	rocking-stone	rotary beater
reviviscence	right and left	rock kangaroo	rotary camera
reviviscency	right-fielder	rock samphire	rotary cutter
revocability	rightfulness	Rock scorpion	rotary engine
revolubility	right-hand man	rockumentary	rotary switch
revolutional	right of abode	rococo stitch	rotationally
revolutioner	right of visit	rodenticidal	rote learning
revulsionary	right side out	rodomontader	rotten excuse
rhabdomancer	right the helm	roebuck-berry	roughcasting
Rhadamanthus	right-to-lifer	roentgen rays	rough diamond
rhamphotheca	right-wingery	Roentgen rays	rough grazing
rhenosterbos	right-wingism	Rogation Days	roughing pump
rheomorphism	rigorousness	Rogationtide	rough justice
rheoreceptor	rig the market	Rogation week	rough passage
rhesus factor	rimming steel	roisteringly	roundaboutly
rhesus monkey	ring armature	role reversal	round bracket
rhetorically	ring-building	rollerblader	round herring
rheumatology	ring dotterel	roller hockey	round-mouthed
rhinoceroses	ringed plover	roller skater	round seizing
rhinocerotic	ringed thrush	roller steady	round-sheered
rhinocerotid	ring fracture	rolling drunk	round the bend
rhinological	ringing floor	rolling paper	round-tripper
rhinopharynx	ring-junction	rolling-press	rouse oneself
rhinoplastic	ring pheasant	rolling stock	Rousseauvian
rhipidistian	ringside seat	rolling stone	roving sailor
rhizophagous	ringworm bush	roll in the hay	Rowland ghost
rhododendron	ripple effect	roll of honour	royal binding
rhodomontade	ripple-marked	roll the bones	royal demesne
rhombohedral	rip-roaringly	romaine crêpe	Royal Society
rhombohedric	Rip Van Winkle	Roman balance	royal warrant
rhombohedron	rise and shine	Roman holiday	rubber bridge
rhomboidally	risk analysis	romanization	rubber bullet
rhopaloceral	risk one's neck	Roman numeral	rubber cement
rhyming slang	Risorgimento	romantically	rubber cheque
rhynchocoele	river-bottoms	romanticness	rubber-heeler
rhynchodaeum	river capture	Roman vitriol	rubber johnny
rhynchostome	river dolphin	roof of heaven	rubber Johnny
rhythmetical	river-driving	room at the top	rubbernecker
rhythm guitar	river herring	rooming house	rubber-tapper
rhythmically	river lamprey	Roorkee chair	rubbing stone
rhythm method	river of white	Rooseveltian	Rube Goldberg
rhythmometer	river running	rootfastness	Rubens madder
rhythmopoeia	roan antelope	rootin' tootin'	rubification
rhytidectomy	roaring drunk	rootlessness	rubinglimmer
ribble-rabble	roaring trade	root position	rub one's hands
ribbon figure	roasting-jack	root pressure	rub shoulders
ribonuclease	roasting-spit	rope-moulding	ruby-throated
Ricardianism	robber trench	Rosary-Sunday	ruffed grouse
Richter scale	Robertsonian	rose-breasted	rugose mosaic
ricochetting	Robin-Hoodish	rose cockatoo	rulelessness
ride cushions	Robin-Hoodism	rose-coloured	rule the roast
ride for a fall	Robin ruddock	rose geranium	rule the roost
ride one's luck	robotisation	rose mahogany	rumble-tumble
ride the rails	robotization	rose of heaven	ruminatingly

ruminatively
rummage goods
rump and dozen
rumplessness
run a blockade
run an eye over
run counter to
run its course
running belay
running-board
running brand
running fight
running light
running mould
running noose
running title
running water
run-of-the-mill
run one's mouth
run up against
ruptured duck
ruralization
rush election
Russell fence
Russell lupin
russet-coated
Russian olive
Russian sable
Russian salad
rust-coloured
rustproofing
ruthenium red
ruthlessness
Sabbatianism
sabbatically
Sabellianism
Sabin vaccine
sabre-bayonet
sabre-rattler
sabre-toothed
saccadically
saccharinity
saccharinize
saccharoidal
sacerdotally
sacramentary
sacrament day
sacred circle
sacred egoism
sacred number
sacred orders
sacred poetry
sacred scarab
sacrificable
sacrificator
sacrifice bid
sacrilegious
sacristaness
sacro-iliitis
sac-winged bat
saddlebacked
saddle bronco

saddle-galled
saddle oyster
saddle-shaped
saddle-skirts
saddle stitch
Sadie Hawkins
sadistically
safe and sound
safe as houses
safety factor
safety island
sage and onion
sage thrasher
sailboarding
sail by the log
sailor collar
sailor-suited
Sakellaridis
salad servers
salamandrian
salamandrine
salamandroid
salamandrous
saleableness
sale or return
salesmanship
salicologist
salient point
salification
salinisation
salinization
sal mirabilis
salmon-ladder
saloon-keeper
saloon pistol
Salpausselkä
salpiglossis
salpingogram
salpingotomy
salsolaceous
saltationism
saltationist
salt of sorrel
salt of tartar
salt-spreader
salt the books
salubriously
salutariness
salutational
salutatorian
salutatories
salutatorily
salutiferous
salvationism
salvationist
salvationize
salver-shaped
Samaritanism
Samian letter
Samosatenian
Samothracian
sample bottle

samprasarana
sanctanimity
sanctifiable
sanctificate
sanctimonial
sanctionable
sanctionless
sanctionment
sanding plate
sand-moulding
sand-painting
sandwich-boat
sandwich cake
Sandwich tern
sand-yachting
sanguiferous
sanguinarily
sanguinarine
sanguineness
sanguinolent
sanguivorous
sanification
sanitariness
sanitary belt
sanitary ware
sanitization
sansculottic
sansculottid
sans reproche
santalaceous
sapientially
sapindaceous
saponifiable
sapphire blue
sapphire mink
saprobiology
saprophagous
saprophilous
saprophytism
Saracen's corn
Saracen's head
sarcolactate
sarcomatosis
sarcophagous
sarcoplasmic
sardar-bearer
sardonically
Sardoodledom
sarong kebaya
sarrusophone
sarsaparilla
satanic abuse
Satanophobia
satellitosis
satin de chine
satin leather
satirization
satisfaction
satisfactory
satisfyingly
satispassion
saturability

satyagrahist
satyric drama
satyromaniac
saucepanfuls
saucer-burial
sauce tartare
Saudi Arabian
Saudiization
saunteringly
sausage board
Sauveterrian
save one's face
save one's hide
save one's neck
save one's skin
save one's wind
saving clause
Savi's warbler
saw-sharpener
say a mouthful
say little for
say one's beads
say one's piece
say something
scabbard-fish
scabbardless
scabrousness
scaff and raff
scaffold pole
scala tympani
scale drawing
scale-pattern
scale-reading
scallop shell
scandalously
scandal sheet
Scandinavian
scanning coil
scanning disc
scanning line
scanning spot
scapegoating
scapegoatism
scaphocerite
scaphoid bone
scapular arch
scapulimancy
scapulodynia
scarfed joint
scarificator
scarlet fever
scarlet macaw
scarlet snake
scarlet whore
scarlet woman
scathelessly
scatological
scatophagous
scatteration
scatterbrain
scatteringly
scene-of-crime

scene-painter	scoring board	scyphiferous	secular abbot
scene-shifter	scoring-booth	scyphomedusa	secular canon
scene-stealer	scoring-paper	Scythian lamb	secular games
scenic artist	scornfulness	sea buckthorn	secularistic
Scenicruiser	scorpion fish	sea butterfly	secular plays
scenographer	scorpion-like	sea commander	secundum idem
scenographic	Scotch boiler	seafardinger	security risk
scent marking	Scotch coffee	sea-fisherman	sedge warbler
Scheherazade	Scotch cousin	sea hard-grass	sedimentable
Schellingian	Scotch pebble	sealed orders	seductionist
Schellingism	Scotch whisky	sealed source	sedulousness
schiller spar	Scotland Yard	seam-squirrel	seed dressing
schindylesis	Scotsmanship	sea-porcupine	seedling leaf
schismatical	Scottishness	search engine	seed metering
schistosomal	scoundreldom	searchership	see the back of
schizocarpic	scoundrelism	seaside finch	see what I mean
schizocoelic	scouring-rush	seaside grape	segmentalise
schizomycete	Scout's honour	season ticket	segmentalize
schizophrene	scrambled egg	secessionism	segmentation
schizorhinal	scramblingly	secessionist	seismography
schizostylis	scraperboard	secludedness	seismologist
schizothymia	scrap of paper	seclusionist	seismometric
schizothymic	scratch along	secobarbital	seismonastic
schmaltziest	scratchboard	seconda donna	seismoscopic
scholarchate	scratch-brush	second advent	selectionism
scholar's mate	scratch-build	secondary bow	selectionist
schoolboyish	scratch-grass	second ballot	seleniferous
school-divine	scratchiness	second banana	selenium cell
schoolfellow	scratchingly	second bottom	selenography
schoolkeeper	scratch paper	second coming	selenologist
school leaver	scratch sheet	second cousin	selensulphur
schoolmaster	scratch stock	second-degree	self-absorbed
school report	scratch video	Second Empire	self-accusing
schooner yawl	screechingly	second fiddle	self-activity
schorlaceous	screen editor	second finger	self-adhesive
Schottky line	screen-memory	second-handed	self-admiring
Schottky plot	screen-washer	second-hander	self-aligning
Schreinerize	screenwriter	Second Isaiah	self-analysis
Schroedinger	screw-steamer	second lesson	self-applause
sciatic nerve	screw-worm fly	second master	self-approval
sciatic notch	scribblative	second moment	self-assembly
scientifical	scribblement	second nature	self-begotten
scintigraphy	scribblingly	second person	self-betrayal
scintillator	scrimshander	second storey	self-boasting
scissiparity	scrimshanker	second strike	self-catering
scissiparous	scriptoriums	second string	self-centring
scissors hold	scripturally	second to none	self-changing
scissors-kick	scripturient	secretagogue	self-cleaning
scissor-tooth	scriptwriter	secret ballot	self-coloured
scitamineous	scrobiculate	secret police	self-conquest
sclerenchyma	scrophularia	secret weapon	self-contempt
sclerodermia	scrub wallaby	sectarianise	self-creation
sclerogenous	scrum machine	sectarianism	self-creative
sclerophylly	scrupulosity	sectarianize	self-critical
sclerotomies	scrupulously	sectionalise	self-deceived
scolopaceous	scrutinously	sectionalism	self-deceiver
scolopophore	sculpturally	sectionalist	self-deluding
scombrotoxic	scurrilities	sectionalize	self-delusion
scopophiliac	scurrilously	section-eight	self-destruct
scoptophilia	scutellation	Section Eight	self-devotion
score-reading	scutelliform	section house	self-distrust
scoring block	scuttled butt	sectoral horn	self-educated

self-effacing	semi-detached	septicidally	sesquitertia
self-election	semidiameter	septilateral	session clerk
self-elective	semi-finalist	septipartite	set an example
self-employed	semifinalist	septuagenary	set by the ears
self-enclosed	semi-finished	Septuagesima	set one's cap at
self-estimate	semifluidity	Septuagintal	set one's teeth
self-evidence	semi-globular	sepulchrally	set scrummage
self-exciting	semi-indirect	sequaciously	set-theoretic
self-existent	semi-infinite	sequence book	set the seal to
self-exposure	semi-literacy	sequence date	setting-stick
self-financed	semi-literate	sequence shot	setting stuff
self-flattery	semi-metallic	sequentially	settling time
self-glorious	seminal fluid	sequestrable	set to partner
self-governed	seminiferous	sequestrator	Seven Sisters
self-homicide	seminivorous	seraphically	seven-sleeper
self-hypnosis	semi-official	seraphicness	severability
self-identity	semiological	sergeant-fish	severance pay
self-interest	semiotically	sergeantship	sewage lagoon
self-involved	semi-palmated	serializable	sewing cotton
selflessness	semipalmated	serial killer	sexagenarian
self-limiting	semiparabola	serial number	sexcentenary
self-loathing	semi-Pelagian	serial rights	sex chromatin
self-luminous	semi-precious	sericultural	sex surrogate
self-managing	semiprecious	serio-comical	sex therapist
self-movement	semi-rotatory	serjeantship	sextillionth
self-murderer	semi-sentence	sermonically	sextodecimos
self-oriented	semispheroid	sero-immunity	sexton beetle
self-policing	Semitization	seronegative	sextumvirate
self-portrait	semi-tropical	seropositive	sextuplicate
self-referral	semi-vitreous	seropurulent	sexual system
self-reliance	sempervirent	serotaxonomy	Sezessionist
self-reproach	sempiternity	serotonergic	shade-bearing
self-revealed	senatorially	serpentarium	shade maximum
self-reversal	senior school	Serpentarius	shade-reading
self-righting	sensationism	serpent eagle	shadow-boxing
selfsameness	sensationist	serpent-green	shadowgraphy
self-scrutiny	sense-content	serpenticide	shadow puppet
self-security	sense-finding	serpenticone	shadow-stitch
self-selected	sensibilizer	serpentiform	shadow stripe
self-shielded	sensible heat	serpentinely	shaft turbine
self-starting	sensibleness	serpentinise	shaggy ink-cap
self-steering	sensifacient	serpentinite	shaking palsy
self-violence	sensitometer	serpentinize	shallow-pated
sell a dummy to	sensitometry	serpentinous	shamateurism
selling plate	sensorimotor	serpent-stone	shamble-stave
selling point	sensualistic	serum disease	shame culture
selling price	sensuousness	servants' hall	shamefacedly
sell the dummy	sensu stricto	serve at table	shamefulness
seltzer water	sentencehood	serve a writ on	Shanghainese
semantically	sentence-word	serve the turn	shank-painter
semeiologist	sententially	service alley	shape-changer
semelfactive	sentinelling	service-berry	shaped charge
semi-annually	sentinel pile	service court	shape elastic
Semi-Arianism	sentinelship	service dress	shaping knife
semi-attached	senza sordini	service plate	shareability
semi-basement	separability	servicewoman	share capital
semi-chemical	separateness	servicewomen	sharecropper
semicircular	separatistic	serving-woman	share economy
semicylinder	Septembriser	servitorship	share-farming
semi-darkness	Septembrizer	servo control	shareholding
semi-deponent	septemvirate	sesqualtera	share-milking
semi-derelict	septennially	sesquioxidic	share-pushing

shark-toothed	shine through	short-waisted	siege economy
sharp eyespot	shingle house	short-woolled	sieve element
sharp-shinned	shingle slide	shot-blasting	sighting shot
sharpshooter	shining light	shot in the arm	sigmoid colon
sharp-sighted	ship-breaking	shoulder arms	sigmoidicity
sharp-tongued	shipbuilding	shoulder-belt	signal-caller
shatter-brain	ship chandler	shoulder-bone	significance
shatter crack	ship decanter	shoulder-high	significancy
shatteringly	ship of burden	shoulder-knot	significator
shatter-pated	shipping-bill	shoulderless	significatum
shatter-proof	shipping-note	shoulder line	significavit
shatterproof	ship-repairer	shoulder loop	sign language
shatteryness	ship's biscuit	shoulder mark	signpostless
shauchliness	ship's company	shoulder moth	sign stimulus
shaven latten	ship's husband	shoulder note	silage cutter
shaving brush	Shirley poppy	shoulder-tuft	silanization
shaving cream	shirtwaister	shoulder wing	Silesian stem
shaving horse	shockability	shout the odds	silhouettist
shaving stick	shock-brigade	shovel-hatted	silicicolous
Shawnee salad	shock-excited	shovel-plough	siliciferous
shebeen queen	shockingness	show business	silicon wafer
sheep blowfly	shocking pink	show one's face	silk stocking
sheep-dipping	shock tactics	show one's hand	silk-throwing
sheepishness	shock-testing	show one's head	silkworm moth
sheep-nose-bot	shock therapy	show-stopping	silver bridge
sheep's fescue	shock-workers	shrewishness	silver doctor
sheep-shearer	shoeing-smith	shrievalties	silver-glance
sheepskinned	shoelessness	shrift-father	silver lining
sheep-sleight	shoofly plant	shrike-thrush	Silver Office
sheep's sorrel	shooting coat	shrike tyrant	silver poplar
sheep's tongue	shooting iron	shrinkage fit	silver salmon
sheet-almanac	shooting star	shroud hawser	silver screen
sheet erosion	shoot one's wad	Shrove Monday	silver solder
shelf company	shoot the moon	shrub trefoil	silver string
shell company	shoot through	shudderingly	silver thatch
shellcracker	shopping cart	shuffle-board	silver tongue
shell-gritted	shopping list	shuffleboard	silver wattle
shell program	shopping mall	shunt circuit	silviculture
shell-shocked	shopping tray	shunt machine	Simchat Torah
shepherd king	shoppishness	shut one's face	similarities
shepherdless	shore-shooter	shutter-blind	simoniacally
shepherd's dog	shore station	shutter speed	simple family
shepherdship	shore-whaling	shuttle shell	simple-minded
shepherd's pie	short circuit	shut your trap	simplicistic
Sheridaniana	short-circuit	sialographic	Simpson's rule
sheriff clerk	short clothes	Siamese twins	simulatively
sheriff court	short-coating	Siberian crab	Simultaneism
sheriff's sale	short commons	Siberian ibex	simultaneist
Sherlockiana	shorten sails	sick headache	simultaneity
Shetland lace	short fielder	sickle medick	simultaneous
Shetland pony	short-grained	sickle scaler	Sinanthropic
Shetland wool	short measure	side reaction	Sinanthropus
shield-bearer	short-pitched	sidereal time	singableness
shiftability	short-running	sidereal year	singing hinny
shiftfulness	short service	siderochrome	singing point
shiftingness	short-sighted	siderography	single-acting
shillingless	short-sleeved	siderophilin	single combat
shilling-mark	short-snorter	siderostatic	single-decker
shilly-shally	short-staffed	siderurgical	single-handed
shimmeriness	short-termism	side-splitter	single-hander
shimmeringly	short-termist	side-wall tyre	single market
shimmy damper	short-tongued	side-whiskers	single-minded

single parent	skookum chuck	slop-moulding	snicker-snack
single-seater	skookum house	slothfulness	sniff the wind
single-source	skoptophilia	slot radiator	snifter-valve
single-valued	Skraup method	slotted spoon	sniggeringly
single-vision	skrimshander	slovenliness	snippetiness
single-wicket	skull-busting	slow handclap	snivellingly
singsong girl	skullduggery	slow puncture	snobbishness
singularness	skull session	sluggardness	snobographer
sinicization	skunk cabbage	sluggishness	snollygoster
sinification	skunk currant	slumbercoach	snook-cocking
sinister bend	skutterudite	slumberously	snooperscope
sinisterness	sky-scrapered	slumber party	snooze button
sinistrality	slabber-sauce	slum landlord	snowball tree
sinistrorsal	slack-twisted	slumpflation	snowboarding
sinistrously	slanderously	slush casting	snow-dropping
sinusoidally	slangwhanger	sluttishness	snowdrop tree
sinus venosus	slantingways	small calorie	snow-in-summer
siphonaceous	slapdashness	small capital	snowmobiling
siphonoglyph	slash-and-burn	small-clothes	snow pheasant
siphonophore	slash-burning	smallest room	snowshoe hare
siphonostele	slasher movie	small fortune	snubbishness
siphonozooid	slate-writing	smallholding	snuff-dipping
siphunculate	slatternness	small-mouthed	soap-operatic
sir-reverence	slaughterdom	small pastern	soboliferous
sister german	slaughtering	small-townish	sociableness
sisterliness	slaughterman	smart-aleckry	social action
sisters-in-law	slaughterous	smash-and-grab	social centre
sisyrinchium	Slavonianize	smatteringly	social change
site assembly	Slavophilism	smell of roses	social column
Sitka cypress	sledgehammer	smoke concert	social credit
sit loosely on	sleeper agent	smoke goggles	social gospel
situationism	sleeper shark	smoke grenade	social ladder
situationist	sleepfulness	smoke-jumping	social status
six feet under	sleeping-pill	smoke Persian	social survey
six of the best	sleeping suit	smoker's cough	social system
sixty-fourmos	sleep-talking	smoker's heart	social weaver
sixty per cent	sleep through	smoking point	social worker
sizzle cymbal	sleepy-headed	smoking stand	sociobiology
skateboarder	Sleepy Hollow	smooth blenny	sociocentric
skeletal soil	sleepy lizard	smooth muscle	sociodynamic
skeleton army	sleeve-button	smooth-spoken	socioecology
skeleton crew	sleeve-garter	smooth tingle	sociological
skeleton form	slender loris	smotheration	socio-medical
skeletonized	slickensided	smotheringly	sociometrist
skeletonless	sliding scale	snaffle-mouth	socket outlet
skeleton suit	slip-carriage	snaggle-teeth	Socratically
skeleton weed	slip of the pen	snaggle-tooth	soda fountain
skeuomorphic	slip one's wind	snailishness	sodipotassic
skew-symmetry	slipper chair	snail's gallop	sodium-cooled
Skiddaw slate	slipperiness	snake charmer	sodopotassic
skillion roof	slipper plant	snallygaster	soft as a brush
skin friction	slipper satin	snap-fastener	soft currency
skin-grafting	slipper shell	snappishness	softly-softly
skin magazine	slippery pole	snap-shooting	soft-shoulder
skinnymalink	slipshodness	snap short off	soil separate
skipjack tuna	slit-planting	snarling iron	soil sickness
skipping rope	slitting-mill	sneak-current	soil solution
skip straight	Sloane Ranger	sneak-hunting	soixante-neuf
skirt-dancing	slobber-chops	sneakingness	solar battery
skitteriness	slop-clothing	sneak preview	solar eclipse
skittishness	slope circuit	sneck-drawing	solar furnace
skittle-alley	slope current	snickeringly	solar heating

solarisation
solarization
solar-powered
solar regular
soldier's wind
solecistical
solemniously
solicitation
solicitorial
solicitously
solidaristic
solid circuit
solid geology
solidifiable
solids-not-fat
solid stowing
solidungular
solidus curve
solifluction
soliloquizer
solitariness
solitary dodo
solitary wave
solitudinous
solo climbing
solodization
Solomon's seal
solonization
solstitially
soluble glass
solutionized
solvent abuse
somaesthesis
somaesthetic
somatisation
somatization
somatologist
somatopleure
somatostatin
somatotropic
somatotropin
somebody else
somersaulter
Somervillian
somnambulant
somnambulate
somnambulism
somnambulist
somniloquent
somniloquism
somniloquist
somnolescent
son et lumière
song and dance
song-grosbeak
songlessness
sonic barrier
sonochemical
son of the soil
sonorescence
sonorousness
soogee-moogee

soothingness
sophiologist
sophisticate
sophomorical
soporiferous
sorbefacient
sorediferous
soreheadedly
sorosilicate
sorry-go-round
sortilegious
Sothic period
soullessness
soul-sickness
sound archive
sound as a bell
sound barrier
sound channel
sounding-lead
sounding line
soundingness
sounding sand
sound picture
sound-ranging
Soundscriber
soupfin shark
soup-strainer
sousaphonist
South African
South America
Southcottian
south country
south-eastern
Southern Alps
Southern blot
Southern Cone
Southern Fish
southern hake
southernmost
southernness
southernwood
south sea rose
South Spainer
South Suffolk
Southumbrian
south-western
Sovietophile
Sovietophobe
sow the seed of
space blanket
space capsule
space chamber
space density
space fiction
space lattice
spacemanship
space physics
space shuttle
space station
space vehicle
spaciousness
spandrel wall

span-farthing
Spanish beard
Spanish broom
Spanish brown
Spanish cedar
Spanish dance
Spanish onion
Spanish sheep
Spanish topaz
Spanish tummy
Spanish white
spanner tight
spark chamber
spark counter
sparking coil
sparking plug
sparkishness
sparkleberry
sparrow-brain
sparrow-grass
sparrow's-fart
spasmophilia
spasmophilic
spatiography
spatteration
spatulamancy
speak daggers
speakerphone
speakingness
speaking stop
speaking-tube
speak volumes
spear-carrier
spear-running
spear thistle
special buyer
specialistic
specialities
specifically
specific heat
specific name
specificness
specimen-book
specimen page
speciousness
speck and span
speckled wood
specksioneer
spectatordom
spectatorial
spectatorism
spectral term
spectral type
spectre-lemur
spectrograph
spectrometer
spectrometry
spectrophone
spectroscope
spectroscopy
speech-centre
speechifying

speech island
speechlessly
speech-writer
Speedwriting
Speenhamland
speiss-cobalt
speleologist
spellbinding
spell-checker
spelling-book
spermathecal
spermaticide
spermatocide
spermatocyte
spermatology
spermatozoal
spermatozoan
spermatozoid
spermatozoon
spermogonium
spermologist
spew one's ring
sphacelation
sphagnum moss
sphairistike
sphenoid bone
sphericality
spheroidally
spheroidical
spherulitize
sphincterial
sphingolipid
sphygmograph
sphygmometer
sphygmometry
sphygmophone
sphygmoscope
spice-islands
spick and span
spider beetle
spider flower
spider-hunter
spider monkey
spider-naevus
spider orchid
spider-stitch
spiegeleisen
spiflication
spinach-green
spinal column
spinal marrow
spinal reflex
spina ventosa
spindle-berry
spindle cross
spindle fibre
spindle-shank
spindle-shell
spindle-whorl
spine-bashing
spine-chiller
spine-freezer

spine-tingler	sportfishing	square thread	standardness
spinnability	sportfulness	square wheels	standard time
spinnbarkeit	sporting girl	squash tennis	standardwing
spinning mule	sportiveness	squattocracy	stand between
spinsterhood	sport of kings	squeaky clean	standing army
spinulescent	sport one's oak	squeegee band	standing crop
spiny dogfish	sportscaster	squid-jigging	standing dish
spiny lobster	sports centre	squirarchies	standing iron
spiral galaxy	sports finder	squirearchal	standing joke
spiral nebula	sports ground	squirrel cage	standing part
spiritedness	sports jacket	squirrel-corn	standing post
spirit fresco	sportsperson	squirrel-fish	standing room
spiritlessly	sports writer	squirrel hake	standing salt
spirit of salt	spotlessness	squirrel-like	standing wave
spirit of wine	spotted crake	squirrelling	stand in stead
spirit-rapper	spotted fever	squirrel-tail	stand-off half
spiritualise	spotted hyena	squish-squash	stand of pikes
spiritualism	spouse-breach	stabilimeter	stand the pace
spiritualist	Sprechgesang	stablishment	Stanhope lens
spirituality	Sprechstimme	staccato mark	Stanislavsky
spiritualize	sprightfully	stackability	Stanley crane
spirituosity	spring barley	stacken-cloud	Stanley knife
spirochaetal	spring beauty	stacker crane	stanniferous
spirographic	spring-beetle	stack the deck	stanzaically
spirolactone	spring collet	staddle-stone	stapedectomy
Spitalfields	spring garden	staff college	starchedness
spit and image	spring greens	staff officer	star-cucumber
spitefulness	spring-loaded	Stafford knot	star prisoner
spittle-staff	spring peeper	stageability	Stars and Bars
splash cymbal	spring salmon	stage manager	star sapphire
splatterdash	spring squill	stage-playing	star-spangled
splatterdock	spring to mind	stage-setting	startability
splay-mouthed	spriteliness	stage thunder	start a family
splendacious	spritelliest	stage whisper	starting gate
splendidness	sprocket hole	staggeringly	starting grid
splenic fever	sprocketless	stagger-juice	starting line
splenisation	spruce grouse	stagger-tuned	starting post
splenization	sprung rhythm	stag-horn fern	stasigenesis
splenomegaly	Spud Islander	stag-horn moss	stasigenetic
splenotomies	spurge laurel	stainability	State Council
splenunculus	spurge nettle	stained glass	statementing
splinter-deck	spuriousness	Stakhanovism	state of grace
splish-splash	spur valerian	Stakhanovist	state pension
split bearing	sputteringly	Stakhanovite	State pension
split the atom	spy satellite	stalactiform	states-monger
split the vote	spy strangers	stalled cairn	statesperson
split tin loaf	squabblement	stall for time	States rights
spoils system	squab cushion	stalwartness	State trooper
spokespeople	squacco heron	stammeringly	static thrust
spokesperson	squamiferous	stamp booklet	station agent
sponge-finger	squamigerous	stamping tube	stationarily
sponge rubber	squanderlust	stamp machine	stationarity
spongiferous	square dinkum	stamp mealies	station break
spongioblast	squared paper	stanchion-gun	station house
spongologist	square engine	stand a chance	stationnaire
spoon-bending	square-headed	standard-bred	station-point
spoon-fashion	square Hebrew	Standardbred	station-staff
sporadically	square number	standard cell	station-wagon
sporangiolum	square-rigged	standardizer	statistician
sporodochium	square-rigger	standard lamp	statisticize
sporogenesis	square-rooter	standard lens	statogenesis
sportability	Squaresville	standardless	statuary vein

statuesquely	stercoration	stockbreeder	Straffordian
status-seeker	stereo-acuity	stockbroking	stragglingly
status symbol	stereo-camera	stock company	straight arch
status system	stereochrome	stock control	straight away
stave and tail	stereochromy	stock culture	straightaway
staying power	stereocilium	stockholding	straight-bred
stay-in strike	stereognosis	Stockholm tar	straight-edge
stay one's hand	stereography	stocking-foot	straightener
stay the night	stereoisomer	stockingless	straight face
St Bernard dog	stereologist	stocking mask	straight-line
steady-stater	stereometric	stocking-yarn	straight mute
steak tartare	stereophonic	stock-in-trade	straightness
steal the show	stereopticon	stockishness	straight peen
stealthfully	stereoscopic	stockjobbery	straight talk
stealthiness	stereotactic	stockjobbing	straight time
steamboating	stereotropic	stockmanship	straightways
steamboatman	sterilizable	stoechiology	straight wire
steamer-chair	sterling area	stoichometry	straightwise
steam turbine	sterlingness	stomach-achey	strain ageing
steam-whistle	sternocostal	stomach-tooth	strain a point
steatisation	stern-trawler	stomach upset	strainedness
steatization	sternutation	stoma patient	strain energy
steatopygial	sternutative	stomatodaeum	strainer arch
steatopygous	sternutatory	stone bramble	strainer post
steatorrhoea	sternwheeler	stone-crusher	strain-harden
steel drummer	stertorously	stone-dresser	strainlessly
steel furnace	stethography	stone-dusting	strainometer
steeplechase	stethometric	stone frigate	strait-jacket
steeple clock	stethoscoped	stone garland	straitjacket
steeple-house	stethoscopic	stone-heading	Strandlooper
steerability	Stevensonian	stonemasonry	strangerhood
steer clear of	St George's day	stone parsley	strangership
steering lock	stibocaptate	stone polygon	strange to say
steering post	stichometric	stonewalling	strange woman
steering sail	stichomythia	stony-hearted	stranglehold
stegosaurian	stichomythic	stoop and roop	strangle-weed
stellacyanin	stickability	stoop-gallant	strangulated
stellate hair	stick country	stop-and-frisk	strangullion
Stellenbosch	stick-fighter	stop-and-start	strangurious
Steller's duck	stick grenade	stop-cylinder	strap-handled
stelliferous	sticky wicket	stop one's ears	Stratfordian
stem analysis	stigmasterol	stop one's nose	straticulate
stem-christie	stigmatiform	stoppability	stratigraphy
stemmatology	stilboestrol	stopping rule	stratocirrus
stencil-plate	stiletto heel	stop the cable	stratocratic
stenocranial	still-fishing	stop the press	stratosphere
stenographer	stillicidium	store bullock	Stratovision
stenographic	stills camera	storiologist	Stravinskian
stenophagous	stillwellite	storm lantern	strawberries
stenothermic	stinging tree	storm shutter	straw-breadth
Stensen's duct	stinking bird	storm trooper	strawchopper
stentorianly	stinking fish	storm-warning	streak camera
step aerobics	stinking iris	stormy petrel	stream-anchor
stepdaughter	stinkingness	storytelling	streamlining
stepfamilies	stinking smut	stout-hearted	stream the log
step function	stinking weed	stove-pipe hat	street hockey
stepmotherly	stirrup pants	St Peter's fish	street-keeper
step on the gas	stirrup-strap	St Peter's keys	street people
step response	stir the blood	St Peter's wort	street person
Stercoranism	stitch in time	strabismally	street-porter
Stercoranist	stitch welder	strabismical	streets ahead
stercorarian	St John's bread	Stradivarius	street trader

street urchin	strongylosis	subdivisible	subtopianize
streetwalker	strontianite	subduplicate	subtreasurer
street warden	strophanthin	sub-editorial	subumbrellar
street worker	strophanthus	subeditorial	subvassalage
strengthener	strophiolate	suberization	subversively
strengthless	structurally	subfeudation	subvertebral
strepitation	strudel dough	subfeudatory	subvocalizer
strepsirhine	strugglingly	subglacially	subway alumni
streptococci	strychninize	subinfeudate	subway series
streptolysin	stubble-field	subintellect	succedaneous
streptomycin	stubble-goose	subintroduce	successfully
streptosolen	stubble-quail	subinvoluted	successional
Streptothrix	stubbornness	subjectional	successively
stressed skin	studding-sail	subjectively	successivity
stress raiser	student grant	subjectivise	success story
stress relief	student nurse	subjectivism	succinctness
stress-strain	Student's test	subjectivist	succinic acid
stretcher fly	studio potter	subjectivity	suck an orange
stretchiness	studiousness	subjectivize	sucking louse
stretch marks	study-bedroom	sublapsarian	suck-it-and-see
stricken hour	stuffed olive	Sublime Porte	suction plant
stride accent	stuffed shirt	subliminally	suction valve
stridulation	stump and rump	sublingually	Sudanization
stridulatory	stump cricket	submarine net	sudanophilia
stridulously	stump-grubber	submaxillary	sudanophilic
strike a chord	stump-machine	submergement	sudoriferous
strike a light	stupefacient	subminiature	sudoriparous
strike ground	stupefaction	submissively	sufficiently
strike it rich	stupefactive	subnormality	sufflaminate
strike me pink	stupefyingly	suboccipital	Suffolk latch
striker-plate	stupendously	subopercular	Suffolk punch
striking-line	sturdy beggar	suboperculum	Suffolk Punch
strikingness	sturgeon scow	suborbicular	Suffolk sheep
string-course	stutteringly	subordinator	suffraganate
string figure	stylistician	subpetiolate	suffraganean
stringhalted	stylographic	sub-preceptor	suffragistic
string of tide	stylometrics	subprincipal	suffruticose
string-puller	stylometrist	subsatellite	sugar-boilery
string theory	subabdominal	subscribable	sugar-candied
strip cartoon	subacuminate	subscribe for	sugar-candies
striped hyena	subalternate	subscription	sugar daddies
striped maple	subalternity	subscriptive	sugar nippers
striped mouse	subantarctic	subsectioned	sugar-orchard
striped pants	subapostolic	subsequently	sugar snap pea
strip farming	subarachnoid	subsequent to	sugar the pill
strip-grazing	subarcuation	subservience	sugar-weather
strip lynchet	subarrhation	subserviency	suggestively
stripped-down	sub-brigadier	subsidiaries	suggestivity
strippergram	subcelestial	subsidiarily	suicide blond
stripteasing	subcentrally	subsidiarity	suitableness
strobilation	subcollector	subsizarship	suitcasefuls
strobiliform	subcommittee	subsonically	suit of dittos
stroboscopic	subconscious	substantiate	suit one's book
stroke-stitch	subconstable	substantival	sullied white
stromatolite	subcontinent	substantive	sulphidation
stromatolith	subcutaneous	substitution	sulphocyanic
stromeyerite	subdeaconate	substitutive	sulphonamide
strong-docked	sub-débutante	substitutory	sulphonation
strong-handed	subdelirious	substraction	sulphonylate
strongheaded	subdiaconate	substruction	sulphuration
strong-minded	subdialectal	substructure	sulphur cycle
strong stress	subdividable	subterranean	sulphuretted

sulphur match   superhighway   supranuclear   sweepingness
sulphurously   superhumanly   supraorbital   Sweet Adeline
sulphur print   superhumeral   suprarenalin   sweet alyssum
sulphur vivum   superiorship   suprascapula   sweet and sour
sultana grape   superlattice   suprasensual   sweetback man
sultana queen   superluminal   supraspecies   sweet calamus
Sumatran hare   supermanhood   supraspinous   sweet cassava
Sumerologist   supermassive   suprathermal   sweethearter
summarizable   supermullion   supravaginal   sweetishness
summary punch   supermundane   Supreme Being   sweet maudlin
summer-fallow   supernacular   Supreme Court   sweet-mouthed
summer master   supernaculum   sure-footedly   sweet pinesap
summer savory   supernatural   surface noise   sweet-scented
summer school   superorbital   surface paper   sweet sixteen
summer season   superordinal   surface-plate   sweet sorghum
summer squash   superorganic   surface speed   sweet-toothed
summer-weight   superovulate   surface-to-air   sweet trolley
summiteering   superplastic   surface water   sweet william
sumo wrestler   superposable   surge chamber   swellishness
sumphishness   superradiant   surgeon's knot   swelteringly
sun and planet   super-realism   surge voltage   swimmer's itch
Sunday dinner   super-realist   Suriname toad   swimming bath
Sunday driver   super-reality   surmountable   swimming-bell
Sunday letter   super-refined   surpassingly   swimming crab
Sunday's child   supersedable   surplice fees   swimming hole
Sunday school   supersedence   surplus value   swimmingness
sunken garden   supersensory   surprisingly   swimming pool
sunken storey   supersensual   surrealistic   swindle sheet
sunray pleats   supersession   surrejoinder   swine-chopped
sunshineless   supersessive   surroundings   swine's grease
sunshine roof   superspecies   surveillance   swing bowling
sunspot cycle   superstardom   survey course   swing Douglas
Sun Yat-senism   superstition   surveyorship   swinging boom
supellectile   superstratum   survivorship   swing the gate
superability   superterrene   susceptivity   swing the lead
superacidity   Super Tuesday   suspensively   Swiss cottage
superallowed   supervenient   suspensorial   switch-around
superambient   supervention   suspensorium   switch dealer
superannuate   supervoltage   suspiciously   switch dollar
superaqueous   superworldly   Sussex marble   switch-engine
superaudible   supplemental   sustainingly   switch-hitter
superaverage   supplementer   sustentacula   switch-tender
supercargoes   supplicantly   sustentation   swivel-bridge
supercarrier   supplication   sustentative   swizzle-stick
supercharged   supplicatory   svarabhaktic   swollen shoot
supercharger   supply-driven   swaggeringly   sword-bayonet
superciliary   supportative   swagger stick   sword dancing
supercilious   support group   swallow bobby   swordfishing
supercluster   supportingly   swallow's-nest   Sword of State
superconduct   supportively   swamp cabbage   sworn brother
supercurrent   support price   swamp cypress   sycamore moth
superelevate   suppositious   swamp sparrow   sycamore tree
supereminent   suppressedly   swamp wallaby   sycophantish
supererogant   suppressible   swamp warbler   sycophantize
supererogate   suprachoroid   swashbuckler   syenodiorite
superessence   supraciliary   sweat bullets   Sykes's monkey
superfluence   supracrustal   sweat cooling   syllabically
superfrontal   supraglacial   sweater-shirt   syllabicness
superglottal   supraliminal   sweating-room   Sylvester-eve
supergravity   supramaximal   Swedish drill   sylviculture
superhelical   supramundane   sweep-chimney   symblepharon
super-highway   supranatural   sweep-forward   symbolically

symbological	tabulae rasae	talking point	team-teaching
symbololatry	tacheometric	tall oat-grass	tearlessness
symmetallism	tachycardiac	tallow candle	tear one's hair
symmetallist	tachygenesis	tallow-topped	tear to shreds
symmetrodont	tachygrapher	tamboo-bamboo	teaspoonfuls
sympathy card	tachygraphic	tambour-frame	technetronic
symplasmatic	tackle-porter	tambourinist	technicalism
symposiastic	tactile value	tameableness	technicalist
symptomatize	tactlessness	tamelessness	technicality
symptomology	taedium vitae	tandem garage	technicology
synaesthesia	Tagliacotian	tangentially	technicolour
synaesthesis	tail assembly	tangent point	technobabble
synaesthetic	taillessness	tangent screw	technocratic
synanthropic	tail of the eye	tangibleness	technography
synapomorphy	tailor's chair	tangle-footed	technologies
synaptically	tailor's chalk	tantalic acid	technologism
synapticular	tailor's dummy	tape cassette	technologist
synaptonemal	tailor's twist	tape recorder	technologize
synaptosomal	tail-twisting	tape streamer	technophilia
synarthroses	Taka-diastase	tapestry moth	technophilic
synarthrosis	take a fancy to	tapestry-work	technophobia
synchroflash	take a holiday	taphonomical	technophobic
synchroneity	take a liberty	Tappertitian	technostress
synchronical	take a share in	tapsalteerie	tectocuticle
synchronizer	take a shine to	taramasalata	tectogenesis
synchroscope	take a sight at	Taranaki gate	tectogenetic
synclinorium	take a whack at	Tardenoisian	tectonically
syncretistic	take farewell	tardigradous	tectospheric
syndactylism	take for a ride	target pistol	teddy-bearish
syndactylous	take it from me	target theory	teeing-ground
syndesmology	take it on a lam	target tissue	teensy-weensy
syndiotactic	take kindly to	tariff-reform	teeter-totter
syndyotactic	take no notice	tarnowitzite	teething ring
synecdochism	take notice of	tarsorrhaphy	Teflon-coated
synecologist	take occasion	tartar emetic	tektite field
synergetical	take one's dick	tartare sauce	telaesthesia
synergically	take one's ease	tartaric acid	telaesthetic
syngenesious	take one's pick	taskmistress	telautograph
synkinematic	take one's rest	tassel-flower	telecommuter
synodic month	take one's seat	tassel-stitch	telecomputer
synonymously	take one's time	tastefulness	telegraph boy
synoptically	take one's will	tauntingness	telegraphese
synoptophore	take prisoner	taurocholate	telegraphist
syntactician	take shipping	taurodontism	telegraph key
syntacticist	take the count	tauromachies	telegraphone
synthesis gas	take the field	tautological	teleguidance
syntonically	take the fifth	Tavastlander	telemarketer
syphiloderma	take the floor	tavern-keeper	teleological
systematical	take the knock	tax allowance	teleoperator
systematizer	take the law of	tax avoidance	telepathetic
systemically	take the stage	tax collector	telepherique
tabernacular	take the water	tax deduction	telephonable
table diamond	take together	tax exemption	telephone box
table licence	take to pieces	taxing-master	telephone pad
table manners	take unawares	tax inspector	telephone set
table-rapping	talcum powder	tax-sheltered	telephone tag
table-service	tale of terror	tax threshold	telephone tap
table-setting	talipes varus	Taylor system	telephonitis
table-tilting	talismanical	teachability	telepolitics
table-top sale	talkee-talkee	teachers' aide	telepresence
table-turning	talking blues	team handball	teleprompter
tabloidesque	talking clock	team ministry	telerobotics

telescopical	terminus a quo	thaumaturgic	theologician
teleshopping	termitophile	thaumaturgus	theomorphism
telesoftware	termolecular	the Admiralty	Theopaschite
teleteaching	terms of trade	the Adversary	theopathetic
teleutosorus	terraced roof	theanthropic	theophylline
teleutospore	terrace house	the Architect	theopneustic
televisually	terra cognita	the Argentine	theopolitics
telharmonium	terraculture	the Atonement	theoretician
tell the truth	terribleness	theatregoing	theoreticism
tell the world	terrifically	theatre nurse	theoreticist
telluric acid	terrificness	theatre of war	theorization
Tellurometer	terrifyingly	theatre organ	theosophical
telodendrion	terror-struck	theatre party	the other side
telolecithal	tertiary road	theatrically	the other week
temerousness	tessellation	theatrocracy	the Peninsula
temnospondyl	testamentary	theatrophone	the Potteries
temperatured	testiculated	the bee's knees	the provinces
tempestively	testosterone	the big screen	the pure quill
temple dancer	test specimen	theca externa	therapeutics
temporal bone	test the water	theca interna	therapeutist
temporal lobe	test-tube baby	the Captivity	thereagainst
temporalness	testudinated	the City of God	the real McCoy
temporaneous	testudineous	the clear grit	the real thing
temptability	tetanization	thecodontian	there and then
temptational	tetanus toxin	the Comforter	thereinafter
tempt fortune	tetrachotomy	the Devil's job	there's a thing
temptingness	tetracycline	the devil to do	therethrough
temulentness	tetragonally	the die is cast	thermal cycle
tenant at will	tetrahedrite	the early bird	thermal lance
tenant farmer	tetrahedrons	the fairer sex	thermal noise
tendenzroman	tetrahydrate	the Fall of Man	thermal paper
tender annual	tetramorphic	the following	thermal shock
tender an oath	tetraparesis	the Forty-five	thermal speed
tender-footed	tetraparetic	the gentle art	thermic lance
tender-minded	tetrapolitan	the genus Homo	Thermidorian
tenderometer	tetrapterous	the Grand Turk	thermochromy
tenebrescent	tetrapyrrole	the hard stuff	thermocouple
ten-gallon hat	tetrarchical	the heroic age	thermography
Tengmalm's owl	tetrastichic	the holy table	thermohaline
tennis-ground	tetrathionic	the Household	thermolabile
tennis player	tetrodotoxin	theileriasis	Thermolactyl
tennis racket	teuthologist	the invisible	thermometric
Tennysoniana	Teutonically	theistically	thermonastic
ten per center	Texas leaguer	the jury is out	thermophilic
tensiometric	textological	the king's evil	thermoscopic
tentaculated	texture brick	the Lamb of God	thermos flask
tenuifolious	textured yarn	the land knows	thermo-siphon
tenuirostral	thack and rape	the land of nod	thermosphere
ten-week stock	Thackerayana	the land of Nod	thermostable
tequila plant	thalassaemia	the left bower	thermostatic
Tequistlatec	thalassaemic	the long green	thermotactic
teratologist	thalassocrat	thematically	thermotropic
teratomatous	thallic oxide	the Met Office	the same story
tercentenary	thallophytic	the multitude	the same to you
terebenthene	thankfulness	then and there	the second sex
terebinthina	thank heavens	Thénard's blue	the short robe
terebinthine	thanksgiving	the necessary	Thesmophoric
terebratulid	thank-you-ma'am	theocentrism	the softer sex
terephthalic	that's the idea	theocratical	Thessalonian
tergiversate	that's the shot	the Old Reaper	the story goes
term for years	that's your lot	the old regime	the Ten Tribes
terminalized	thaumatology	theologaster	the three Magi

the time of day
the tother day
theurgically
the very devil
the very thing
the ways of God
the weaker sex
the Windy City
the world over
the world's end
the worst kind
the young idea
thiacetazone
thiazolidine
thick and fast
thick and thin
thick-sighted
thick-skinned
thick-skulled
thick-tongued
thief-catcher
thieves' Latin
thievishness
thigh-slapper
thigmotactic
thigmotropic
thimbleberry
thimble-glass
thin blue line
think balloon
thinkingness
thinking part
think it scorn
think scorn of
think through
thiodiglycol
thioindigoid
thioridazine
thiosulphate
thirdborough
third country
third reading
Third Worlder
thirteenthly
thirty-two-mos
this long time
thistle crown
thistle-finch
thistle glass
thitherwards
thomsenolite
thoracically
thoracic cage
thoracic duct
thoracoscopy
thoracostomy
thorny oyster
thorogummite
thorough bass
thorough-bind
thoroughbred
thoroughfare

thoroughness
thorough post
thorough-sped
thoroughwort
thortveitite
thoughtcrime
thought-forms
thoughtfully
thought model
thought-saver
thought-world
thousandfold
thousand-legs
thowlessness
thread-cutter
thread-needle
threap-ground
three-address
three-cushion
three day week
three figures
three fourths
three monkeys
three-pounder
three-pronged
three-quarter
three-striper
three-tongued
three-wheeler
three wise men
thriftlessly
thrivingness
thrombectomy
thrombogenic
thrombolysis
thrombolytic
thrombopenia
thrombopenic
Throne Speech
throstle-cock
throttleable
throttle back
throughgoing
through-other
through-stone
throw a glance
throw a slur on
throw a wobbly
throw cushion
throw-forward
throwing-mill
throw light on
throw money at
throw one's eye
thrush-fungus
thrust vector
thrust washer
thuggishness
thumb-indexed
thunderation
thunder-blast
thundercloud

thunder-crack
thunder-flash
thunderflash
thunderingly
thunderlight
thunderously
thunder-plant
thunder-plump
thunder-sheet
thunder-snake
thunder stick
thunder-stone
thunderstorm
Thurberesque
thymectomize
thymiaterion
thymopoietin
thyroid gland
thyrotrophic
Tibeto-Burman
Tibetologist
ticket-holder
ticket office
ticket-porter
Ticklenburgs
ticklishness
tidal harbour
tiddledy-wink
tiddledywink
tiddlywinker
tidelessness
tide-surveyor
tiger bittern
tigerishness
tiger-striped
tight as a tick
tight-fitting
tile-drainage
till all hours
till doomsday
tilting rotor
timber-beetle
timber cruise
timber-doodle
timber-framed
timber-getter
timber-grouse
timber-jumper
timber-topper
time and again
time and a half
time constant
time-division
time exposure
time-honoured
timelessness
time-of-flight
time-resolved
time reversal
timocratical
timorousness
timothy grass

tinctorially
tingle-tangle
tinhorn sport
tinkle-tankle
tinmen's snips
tintinnabula
tip one's hands
tip the scales
tip the wink to
tiptoe around
tirelessness
tiresomeness
tirl at the pin
tissue typing
titaniferous
tithe-proctor
Titian-haired
titter-totter
tittle-tattle
titular abbot
titular saint
to admiration
toad-snatcher
toasting-fork
tobacco heart
tobacco house
tobacco plant
tobacco-pouch
tobacco-water
toddy-tapping
toe in the door
toffee hammer
toft and croft
togetherness
together with
toggle switch
to hell with it
toilet humour
toilet tissue
toilsomeness
to-infinitive
token economy
token payment
tolerability
toleratingly
tolerization
Tolkienesque
Tolstoyanism
tomfooleries
tomorrow week
tompot blenny
tone-deafness
tone dialling
tone language
tonelessness
tone-painting
tone-syllable
tongue-tacked
tonification
tonneau cover
tonofibrilla
tonofilament

tonsillotomy	tourmalinize	tragicalness	transitivize
tonsorialist	tournamental	tragic-comedy	transitorily
too late a week	tour operator	tragicomical	transit-trade
to one's credit	tours de force	trail-blazing	translatable
to one's liking	tousle-haired	trailblazing	translatress
tooth and nail	towardliness	trailer-truck	translucence
toothed whale	tower mustard	trailing edge	translucency
to perfection	Tower of Babel	trainability	transmigrant
top-fermented	town and tower	training ship	transmigrate
top-heaviness	town planning	training shoe	transmission
toploftiness	town twinning	train-spotter	transmissive
topochemical	toxicologist	traitorously	transmitting
top of the heap	toxigenicity	trajectories	transmogrify
top of the milk	toxocariasis	tralatitious	transmontane
top of the pops	toxophilitic	trampolinist	transmundane
topographist	to your health	tranche de vie	transmutable
topographize	trabeculated	tranquillise	transnatural
toponomastic	traceability	tranquillity	transoceanic
topotactical	trace element	tranquillize	transom-stern
top-stitching	trace program	tranquilness	transorbital
topstitching	tracheophone	transaminase	trans-Pacific
topsy-turvily	tracheoscopy	transaminate	transpacific
toque macaque	tracheostomy	transannular	transparence
torch-fishing	trachomatous	transcalency	transparency
torch singing	tracing paper	transcendent	transpeciate
torch-thistle	tracing table	transcension	transpicuous
tormentingly	tracing-wheel	trans-channel	transpirable
torpedo beard	trackability	transcribble	transplanter
torpedo juice	track athlete	transcriptor	transpontine
torque wrench	track circuit	transcurrent	transportive
torrefaction	track-clearer	transdialect	transposable
torrentially	tracking shot	transductant	transqualify
Torricellian	tractability	transduction	transrhenane
torsionmeter	traction-load	transelement	trans-species
tortilla chip	tractoration	transfashion	trans-stellar
tortoise core	trade barrier	transfection	transudation
tortoise-like	trade deficit	transferable	transudatory
tortoise-pace	trade dispute	transfer-book	transumption
tortoise race	traded option	transfer case	transumptive
tortuosities	trade-edition	transference	transuranian
tortuousness	trade-English	transfer line	Transvaalian
Tory democrat	trade journal	transfer list	transversary
toss a pancake	trade mission	transferring	transversely
toss one's head	tradescantia	transfixedly	transversion
total eclipse	tradespeople	transfixture	transversive
totalitarian	tradesperson	transfluence	transvestism
totalization	trade surplus	transfluvial	transvestist
to that effect	trading floor	transformant	transvestite
to the north of	trading-house	transformism	Trapezuntine
to the point of	trading-place	transformist	trap-shooting
to the purpose	trading stamp	transfusible	traumatology
tother school	traditionary	transgenosis	traumatropic
to the south of	traditionism	transgressor	travel agency
to this effect	traditionist	transhumance	travel bureau
touchability	traducianism	transilience	travel folder
touch-dancing	traducianist	transinsular	travelleress
touched proof	Trafalgar Day	transitation	traverse-book
touchingness	traffic court	transitional	traverse jury
touch one's hat	traffic light	transitively	travestiment
touch the spot	traffic-proof	transitivise	travesty role
tourist class	traffic snarl	transitivism	treacle sleep
tourist track	tragelaphine	transitivity	treadmilling

treason felon	trick cyclist	troglobiotic	tulipomaniac
treasonously	trickeration	troglodytish	tumble-action
treasure hunt	trickishness	troglodytism	tumbler-drier
treasureless	trick or treat	trolley-wheel	tumbler-dryer
treasury bill	trickstering	trolling pole	tumbler-glass
treasury-bond	tricliniarch	tromba marina	tumbling home
treasury note	tridactylous	troop carrier	tumbling-mill
treasuryship	trident curve	trophallaxis	tumbu disease
treatability	tried and true	trophic level	tumultuation
treaty Indian	trienniality	trophotropic	tumultuously
treble chance	Trifid Nebula	tropical year	tunelessness
tree kangaroo	triflingness	tropological	tunica intima
treelessness	trifoliolate	troposcatter	tuning-hammer
tree of heaven	trifurcation	tropospheric	tunnel effect
tree squirrel	trigger-happy	troubledness	tunnel of love
trembler bell	trigger-plant	troublemaker	tunnel vision
tremendously	trigger-point	troubleshoot	Tupi-Guaranis
tremorlessly	trigger price	trough garden	turban squash
trench-coated	trigger pulse	trouserettes	turban tumour
trench mortar	triglyceride	trouser-press	turbellarian
trench-plough	triglyphical	Trubetzkoyan	turbidimeter
trend-setting	trigonelline	truck tractor	turbidimetry
trendsetting	trigonometer	truck trailer	turbidometer
trend-spotter	trigonometry	true-love knot	turbinectomy
trend surface	trigrammatic	trumpet hypha	turbocharger
trephination	trihemimeral	trumpet major	turbostratic
trestle-board	trihemimeris	trumpet-mouth	Turcocentric
trestle-table	trilaterally	trumpet-shell	Turcophilism
triadelphous	trillionaire	trumpet-snail	Turkey carpet
trial balance	trimeprazine	trumpet style	turkey-fat ore
trial balloon	trimethoprim	trundle-wheel	Turkey red oil
trial per pais	trimethylene	trussing hoop	Turkey sponge
triangle moth	trimming gear	trust-busting	Turkish music
triangulable	trimming-tank	trust company	Turkish towel
triangularly	Trinity House	trustfulness	turn a deaf ear
triangulated	trinomialism	trustingness	turn cat in pan
triangulator	triode-hexode	trust officer	turning-lathe
tribespeople	trioeciously	truthfulness	turning point
tribological	tripartitely	try a fall with	turnip greens
tribophysics	tripartition	try masteries	turnip sawfly
tribosphenic	triphthongal	try one's wings	turn of phrase
Tribune group	triple-decker	trypaflavine	turn one's coat
tribute-money	triple-headed	trypanocidal	turnpike gate
tricentenary	triple-header	trypanolysis	turnpike road
trichiniasis	triple-spaced	trypanolytic	turn the trick
Trichinopoli	triplication	trypanosomal	turn up trumps
trichobezoar	triplicities	trypanosomic	turtle-backed
trichogenous	tripos verses	trypanosomid	turtle-necked
trichologist	trippingness	tryparsamide	tussie-mussie
trichopathic	tripudiation	tschermakite	tussock grass
trichophagia	trismegistic	tube-dwelling	tu-whit tu-whoo
trichophobia	Tristanesque	tubercularly	Twelfth Night
trichophytic	tristfulness	tuberculated	twelve-seater
trichophyton	triterpenoid	tuberculosed	Twelve Tribes
trichopteran	triumphalism	tuberculosis	twentyfourmo
trichothecin	triumphalist	tuberiferous	twenty-seater
trichotomies	triumphantly	tuberization	twenty-twenty
trichotomize	triumvirship	tuberousness	twilight area
trichotomous	trivialities	tuberous root	twilight home
trichromatic	trochanteral	tubocurarine	twilightless
trichuriasis	trochanteric	tubular bells	twilight zone
trick-cycling	trochosphere	tuck position	twine-spinner

twisted-stalk   unaffectedly   unbloodiness   unconforming
twitteration   unaffiliated   unblushingly   unconformity
twitteringly   unaffordable   unbreachable   unconfounded
two-facedness   unaffrighted   unbreathable   unconfronted
twopenny post   unaggravated   unbridgeable   unconfusable
two-way mirror   unaggregated   unbrokenness   unconfusedly
two-way street   unaggressive   unbuttressed   unconfutable
Tyburn ticket   unagitatedly   uncalculated   unconjugated
tychopotamic   unalleviable   uncalendared   unconnection
tympanic bone   unalleviated   uncandidness   unconsecrate
tympanometry   unalphabetic   uncaringness   unconsenting
Tyndall meter   unambivalent   uncastigated   unconsidered
type approval   unamiability   uncatalogued   unconsolable
type-cylinder   unanalogical   uncatechized   unconsolably
type locality   unanalysable   uncelebrated   unconstraint
type specimen   unanalytical   uncensorious   unconsulting
typhoid fever   unanswerable   uncensurable   unconsumable
typhoid state   unanswerably   unchallenged   unconsummate
typification   unapologetic   unchangeable   uncontracted
typographica   unapparelled   unchangeably   uncontrolled
typographist   unappealable   unchangingly   unconvenient
tyrannically   unappealably   unchannelled   unconversant
tyrannicidal   unappeasable   unchaperoned   unconversion
Tyrian purple   unappeasably   uncharitable   unconvincing
tyrosinaemia   unappetising   uncharitably   uncorrelated
ubiquitarian   unappetizing   unchasteness   uncorrigible
ubiquitinate   unapproached   uncheerfully   uncorruption
ubiquitously   unarithmetic   unchivalrous   uncounselled
Ugandan Asian   unarticulate   unchristened   uncourageous
uglification   unartificial   un-Christlike   uncovenanted
Ugly American   unascendable   unchronicled   uncreaturely
ugly customer   unassailable   unchurchlike   uncreditable
ugly duckling   unassailably   uncicatrized   uncritically
ullage rocket   unassignable   uncinariasis   uncriticized
ultimateness   unassociable   uncirculated   unctuousness
ultramontane   unassociated   unclassified   uncultivable
ultramundane   unassumingly   Uncle Tommery   uncultivated
ultraviolate   unastonished   Uncle Tommish   unculturable
ultroneously   unattackable   Uncle Tommism   uncustomable
umbilication   unattainable   uncloistered   undamageable
umbrageously   unattainably   uncoagulable   undeceivable
umbrella bird   unattenuated   uncoagulated   undeciphered
umbrella body   unattractive   uncognizable   undecisively
umbrella fund   unattributed   uncollegiate   undeclarable
umbrellaless   unauspicious   uncombinable   undeclinable
umbrella-like   unauthorised   uncome-at-able   undecomposed
umbrella pine   unauthorized   uncomeliness   undecorative
umbrella tree   unavailingly   uncommenting   undefeatable
unabsorbable   unbeautified   uncommercial   undefendable
unacceptable   unbecomingly   uncommonness   undefensible
unacceptably   unbefriended   uncomparable   undeflowered
unacclimated   unbegottenly   uncompelling   undeformable
unaccredited   unbelievable   uncomplained   undegenerate
unaccustomed   unbelievably   uncompounded   undeliberate
unachievable   unbeneficial   uncomprehend   undelightful
unacquainted   unbenevolent   uncompressed   undelighting
unacquirable   unbequeathed   uncomputable   undemocratic
unactability   unbetterable   unconceiving   undemolished
unadjectived   unbewildered   unconcerning   undependable
unadmonished   unbiasedness   unconfidence   underachieve
unadulterate   unbiological   unconfinable   under-and-over
unadvertised   unblinkingly   unconfinedly   underbearing

underbellies	under the skin	unembittered	unfruitfully
underblanket	under the wind	unemployable	unfrustrable
under-builder	under the wire	unemployment	unfulfilling
underclothed	underthought	unencouraged	unfulfilment
underclothes	undertrained	unencumbered	unfunctional
undercoating	underutilise	unendangered	ungainliness
under control	underutilize	unendingness	ungarrisoned
undercorrect	undervoltage	unenthralled	ungenerosity
under cover to	underworking	unenumerated	ungenerously
undercurrent	under-workman	uneradicated	ungentleness
underdoggery	underworldly	unerringness	ungerminated
underdrawing	underwriting	uneschewable	unglittering
undereducate	underwritten	uneuphonious	ungovernable
underfeature	undesecrated	unevaporated	ungovernably
underfilling	undeservedly	uneventfully	ungracefully
underfitness	undesignated	unexaminable	ungraciously
underfooting	undesignedly	unexecutable	ungratefully
underframing	undespairing	unexpectable	ungregarious
underfunding	undetachable	unexpectedly	ungrudgingly
undergarment	undetectable	unexplicable	unguaranteed
underhanging	undetectably	unexplicitly	unguentarian
under-hangman	undetermined	unexportable	unguentarium
under hatches	undigestible	unexpressive	unguiculated
underivative	undiligently	unexpugnable	unhabituated
under-kingdom	undiminished	unexpurgated	unhandsomely
underlayment	undiplomatic	unextenuated	unharmonious
underleather	undiscerning	unextirpated	unharmonized
underlyingly	undischarged	unextricable	unhealthiest
under-manager	undiscipline	unfadingness	unhealthsome
under-marshal	undiscording	unfaithfully	un-Hellenized
undermeaning	undiscovered	unfamiliarly	unheroically
undermeasure	undiscursive	unfastidious	unhesitating
under-officer	undisfigured	unfathomable	unhinderable
under one roof	undislocated	unfathomably	unhistorical
under one's arm	undismantled	unfatiguable	unhomeliness
underpayment	undismayable	unfavourable	unhoodwinked
underpeopled	undispatched	unfavourably	unhospitable
underperform	undisputable	unfecundated	unhumorously
underpinning	undisputably	unfelicitous	unhydrolysed
underpitched	undisputedly	unfemininity	unhyphenated
underpowered	undisquieted	unfertilised	unhysterical
underproduce	undissembled	unfertilized	unicamerally
underpropper	undissipated	unfinishable	unicorn-plant
under protest	undissolving	unfittedness	unicorn shell
under-servant	undistracted	unflaggingly	unicorn's horn
under-service	undistraught	unflattering	unicorn whale
undersetting	undistressed	unflickering	unidentified
under-sheriff	undisturbing	unforeboding	unidolatrous
under-skinker	undivertible	unforeseeing	unifoliolate
understaffed	undivertibly	unforewarned	uniformalize
understander	undocumented	unforgivable	uniformation
under-steward	undogmatical	unforgivably	uniformities
understoreys	undoubtfully	unformalized	unilaterally
understories	undoubtingly	unformidable	unilinealism
understratum	undramatical	unformulated	unilingually
understudied	undulatingly	unfossilized	unillusioned
understudies	uneconomical	unfranchised	unimaginable
undersucking	unedifyingly	unfrequented	unimaginably
undersurface	uneducatable	unfrequently	unimmergible
under-teacher	uneffaceable	unfriendlier	unimolecular
undertenancy	unelaborated	unfriendship	unimplicated
under the rose	uneloquently	unfrightened	unimportance

unimportuned	unmarkedness	unpatronized	unquenchably
unimposingly	unmarketable	unpavilioned	unquestioned
unimpressive	unmasterable	unpenetrable	unravellable
unimprisoned	unmasticated	unpenetrated	unreactivity
unimprovable	unmeasurable	unperceiving	unrealisable
unincidental	unmeasurably	unperceptive	unrealizable
unindividual	unmechanical	unperforated	unreasonable
uninfectious	unmechanized	unperforming	unreasonably
uninfluenced	unmeddlesome	unperishable	unrebellious
uninitiation	unmeditative	unpermanency	unrebukeable
uninjectable	unmercifully	unpersuasive	unrecallable
uninoculated	unmethodical	unphysically	unreceivable
uninstructed	unmethodized	unpickupable	unreckonable
unintegrated	unmilitarily	unpicturable	unrecognized
unintendedly	unmiraculous	unpierceable	unreconciled
uninterested	unmirthfully	unpleasantly	unrecordable
unintermixed	unmistakable	unpleasantry	unredeemable
unintroduced	unmistakably	unpleasingly	unredeemably
uninvitingly	unmodernized	unpoetically	unreferenced
union-bashing	unmodifiable	unpoliceable	unreflecting
unionization	unmolestedly	unpolishable	unreflective
uniprocessor	unmusicality	unpoliteness	unreformable
unirradiated	unmyelinated	unpopularity	unrefreshing
unirritating	unmysterious	unpopularize	unregainable
unisegmental	unnaturalise	unportentous	unregeneracy
unisexuality	unnaturalism	unprecarious	unregenerate
unison string	unnaturality	unprejudiced	unregimented
unison-tuning	unnaturalize	unprelatical	unregistered
unitalicized	unnoteworthy	unpreparedly	unrejectable
Unitarianism	unnoticeable	unprescribed	unrelievable
unitary group	unnoticeably	unpretending	unrelievedly
United States	unnourishing	unprettiness	unremarkable
unit membrane	unnumberable	unprevailing	unremarkably
unity of place	unnutritious	unprincipled	unremembered
universalian	unobjectible	unprivileged	unremittedly
universalise	unobligingly	unproclaimed	unremorseful
universalism	unobsequious	unprocurable	unrepairable
universalist	unobservable	unproducible	unrepassable
universality	unobservance	unproductive	unrepealable
universalize	unobservedly	unprofitable	unrepeatable
universal set	unobstructed	unprofitably	unrepentance
universities	unobtainable	unprogrammed	unrepiningly
unjudicially	unoffendable	unpronounced	unreportable
unkerchiefed	unoffendedly	unpropertied	unreproached
unkindliness	unofficially	unpropitious	unreprovable
unlawfulness	unoppressive	unprosecuted	unrepublican
unlawyer-like	unoriginally	unprosperity	unrequitable
unlikelihood	unoriginated	unprosperous	unrequitedly
unlikeliness	unornamental	unprotestant	unresembling
unliquidated	unornamented	unprotesting	unreservedly
unlistenable	unorthodoxly	unprovidedly	unresistable
unliturgical	unoverlooked	unprovokable	unresistance
unlocomotive	unoverthrown	unprovokedly	unresistedly
unloveliness	unoxygenated	unprudential	unresistible
unlovingness	unpacifiedly	unpublicized	unresolvable
unlubricated	unparalleled	unpugnacious	unresolvedly
unmagnetized	unpardonable	unpulverized	unrespectful
unmaintained	unpardonably	unpunctuated	unrespecting
unmanageable	unpassionate	unpunishable	unrespective
unmanageably	unpasturable	unpunishably	unrespirable
unmanifested	unpatentable	unquantified	unresponsive
unmanumitted	unpatriotism	unquenchable	unrestrained

unrestricted	unsterilized	unverbalized	urinary tract
unretaliated	unstimulated	unverifiable	urinogenital
unreturnable	unstintingly	unvictorious	urobilinogen
unreturnably	unstockinged	unvindicated	urobilinuria
unrevealable	unstraitened	unvindictive	urochloralic
unreverenced	unstratified	unvirtuously	urolithiasis
unreverently	unstrengthen	unvouchsafed	uroporphyrin
unreviewable	unstructured	unvoyageable	ursine baboon
unrhetorical	unstruggling	unvulcanized	ursine howler
unrhythmical	unsubjugated	unvulnerable	user-friendly
unrightfully	unsublimated	unwantedness	ustilaginous
unroadworthy	unsubmissive	unwashedness	usucapionary
unruly member	unsubmitting	unwatchfully	usufructuary
unsacerdotal	unsubscribed	unwaveringly	usuriousness
unsacrificed	unsubsidized	unwearyingly	uterovaginal
unsalubrious	unsubstanced	unweddedness	uterovesical
unsanctified	unsuccessful	unwieldiness	utility actor
unsanctioned	unsuccessive	unwontedness	utility curve
unsatisfying	unsufferable	unworshipful	utility knife
unsaturation	unsufficient	unworshipped	utility truck
unscandalous	unsuggestive	unworthiness	utterability
unscholastic	unsuperseded	unyieldingly	uxorilocally
unscientific	unsupervised	up and running	uxoriousness
unscriptural	unsuppliable	upbraidingly	vacation home
unscrupulous	unsupportive	upconversion	vacation land
unsculptured	unsupposable	upland cotton	vacationland
unseamanlike	unsuppressed	Upland cotton	vaccine lymph
unsearchable	unsurprising	upland plover	vacuum bottle
unsearchably	unsurrounded	up one's sleeve	vacuum-fitted
unseasonable	unsuspecting	up one's street	vacuum grease
unseasonably	unsuspicious	upon my honour	vacuum-packed
unseasonally	unsustaining	upon occasion	vagabondical
unsecularize	unswervingly	upon straight	vainglorious
unseemliness	unsyncopated	upon the books	valence quark
unsegregated	unsystematic	Upper Chamber	valence shell
unsensitized	untemptingly	Upper Chinook	Valenciennes
unsensualize	untenability	upper classes	valent clause
unsepulchred	untenantable	upper leather	valet parking
unsepultured	untenderness	upper regions	valetudinary
unsettlement	unterminated	uproariously	Vallombrosan
unsheltering	unterrifying	uprootedness	valorisation
unshrinkable	unthankfully	upset stomach	valorization
unsignatured	untheatrical	up the Straits	valorousness
unsignifying	unthinkingly	up-to-dateness	Valpolicella
unsignposted	unthoughtful	up to one's ears	valuableness
unsilicified	unthreatened	up to one's eyes	valuation law
unslackening	untimeliness	up to one's neck	value analyst
unsleepingly	untouchingly	up to the teeth	value calling
unslumbering	untowardness	uranographer	valued policy
unsmoothable	untrammelled	uranographic	value-neutral
unsocialized	untranslated	uranological	vampirically
unsolicitous	untransmuted	uranoplastic	Van Allen belt
unspectacled	untruthfully	uranothorite	Vandiemonian
unsplittable	untumultuous	urbanization	Vandyke beard
unsportingly	ununderstood	urbanologist	Vandyke brown
unsquandered	ununiformity	urban renewal	vanilla plant
unstabilized	unupbraiding	ureterectomy	vanilla sugar
unstableness	unusefulness	ureterostomy	vanity mirror
unstanchable	unvaccinated	urethrometer	vanquishable
unstatutable	unvanquished	urethroscope	vanquishment
unstatutably	unveiledness	urethroscopy	vantage-point
unsteadiness	unventilated	Uriah Heepish	vaporability

vaporization	ventripotent	villainously	visual cortex
vaporousness	ventromedial	vincibleness	visualizable
variable name	Venture Scout	vindemiation	visual purple
variableness	Venusbergian	vindicatress	visuopsychic
variationist	Venus fly-trap	vindictively	visuosensory
varicoloured	Venus flytrap	vinegar Bible	visuospatial
varied thrush	Venus's girdle	Vinegar Bible	visuotactual
variety meats	verbal action	vinegarishly	vitalization
variety store	verbalizable	vinegar stick	vital spirits
variola major	verbenaceous	vinicultural	vitativeness
variola minor	verderership	vinification	vitellogenin
varnish sumac	verecundness	vinolentness	vitellophage
varsity match	veridicality	vin ordinaire	viticultural
vasculotoxic	verification	vinous liquor	vitilitigate
vasoactivity	verificatory	vinyl acetate	vitreous body
vasodilating	verisimilous	viola da gamba	vitreousness
vasodilation	Verlainesque	viola pomposa	vitrifaction
vasodilatory	vermiculated	violaxanthin	Vitruvianism
vasomotorial	vermiculture	violin spider	vituperation
Vaticanology	vermilionize	violoncellos	vituperative
vaticination	vernacularly	viperousness	vituperatory
vaticinatory	vernis martin	Virgilianism	vituperously
vaudevillian	versificator	virgin forest	vivification
vaudevillist	vertebration	Virginia deer	viviparously
vaunt-courier	vertical keel	Virginian sea	vixenishness
veduta ideata	verticillate	Virginia poke	vocabularian
vegecultural	verticillium	Virginia rail	vocabularies
vegetabilise	verumontanum	Virginia reel	vocabularize
vegetability	Very Reverend	virgin's bower	vocalization
vegetabilize	vesicularity	Virgin's spike	vocationally
vegetable dye	vesiculation	viridescence	vocationless
vegetable oil	vespertilian	virile member	vociferation
vegetable wax	vestal virgin	virilescence	vociferative
vegetational	vestimentary	virilisation	vociferosity
vegetatively	veterinarian	virilization	vociferously
vegetivorous	veterinaries	virilocality	vodka martini
veggie burger	vibraharpist	virtual focus	voice channel
vehiculation	vibraphonist	virtual image	voicefulness
vehiculatory	vibratiuncle	virtuosoship	voice leading
velarization	vibronically	virtuousness	voice-printer
veld sickness	vibrotactile	virulentness	voidableness
veldt-marshal	vicar-general	viruliferous	volatileness
Velikovskian	vice-consular	visceral arch	volatile salt
velocipedist	vice-governor	visceral hump	volcanically
velociraptor	vicious cycle	viscerotonia	volcanic bomb
velocity head	Victorianism	viscerotonic	volcanologic
velvet carpet	Victorianist	viscoelastic	volitionally
velvet scoter	Victorianize	viscose rayon	volitionless
velvet sponge	Victoria plum	viscosimeter	Volksdeutsch
venepuncture	victoriously	viscosimetry	Volkspolizei
venerability	victory point	viscountcies	volley-firing
Venetian blue	videographer	viscountship	voltage clamp
Venetian door	videographic	visible index	voltammetric
Venetian lace	video mapping	visible light	volumetrical
vengefulness	vie de château	vision mixing	voluminosity
venipuncture	Vienna Circle	visitatorial	voluminously
venire de novo	vigintennial	visiting-book	voluntariate
venomousness	vigintillion	visiting card	voluntaryism
venous system	vigorousness	visitors' book	voluntaryist
ventre à terre	vilification	visitors' list	volunteerism
ventricosity	village idiot	visual acuity	voluptuaries
ventriculite	villagewards	visual binary	voluptuously

vortex street	warping-frame	water strider	well-attended
vote-catching	warp knitting	water-swallow	well-balanced
vote of credit	warrant chief	water-tabling	well-becoming
votive tablet	warranty deed	water torture	well-breathed
vowel diagram	war to end wars	water-wagtail	well-breeched
vowel harmony	war-weariness	Watteauesque	well-deserved
vowel-quality	washer bottle	Watteau pleat	well-designed
vow of poverty	washing-house	wattled crane	well disposed
voyage policy	washing-place	waulking song	well-dressing
vulcanizable	washing-stand	wave analyser	well-educated
vulgarianism	washing-stock	wave equation	well-equipped
vulgar tongue	washing-stuff	wave function	well-favoured
wag-at-the-wall	Washingtonia	wave-offering	well-grounded
wagelessness	wash one's eyes	wave-particle	well I'm damned
wages council	wash one's head	waveringness	well-informed
Wagnerianism	wastefulness	wave velocity	wellingtonia
wagon-ceiling	wasting asset	way-going crop	well-intended
wagtail dance	watchability	way passenger	well-mannered
wah-wah effect	watch and ward	ways and means	well-ordering
wainscotting	watchfulness	weaponeering	well-pleasing
waistcoateer	watch-keeping	weapons-grade	well-prepared
waistcoating	watch-officer	wearifulness	well received
waiting-woman	watch-setting	wear the horns	well-tempered
wait one's turn	water bailiff	wear the pants	well-timbered
wakerifeness	water balance	weasel's snout	Welsh dresser
Waldorf salad	water-ballast	weasel-worded	Welsh rarebit
walk away from	water biscuit	weather-blate	Welsh terrier
walk away with	water blister	weatherboard	welterweight
walkie-talkie	water-boatman	weather-bound	Wernerianism
walk-in closet	water buffalo	weather chart	Wesleyanized
walking frame	Water-carrier	weather cycle	westerliness
walking party	water company	weather-glass	Western Front
walking-staff	water cracker	weather-house	Western Isles
walking stick	water-cricket	weatherology	Western Ocean
walking-sword	water cushion	weatherproof	Western Union
walking-wheel	water-diviner	weather-strip	West Germanic
walk the chalk	water-drinker	weatherstrip	West Highland
walk the plank	water figwort	weathertight	West-Indiaman
walk the wards	water-finding	weather-tiled	Westinghouse
wallaby-grass	waterfowling	weather-tiles	westwardmost
wallah-wallah	water-gilding	weather woman	Wetmore order
wallcovering	water hemlock	wedding-chest	wet one's pants
wall-eyed pike	watering hole	wedding group	wetting agent
wall painting	waterishness	wedding march	wet to the skin
Wall Streeter	Waterlandian	wedding night	whale-fishery
waltz Matilda	water lentils	wedding-party	whale-fishing
waltz off with	water lettuce	wedding-sheet	Wharton's duct
wandering Jew	Waterloo ball	Weeping Cross	whatever next
wanderluster	Waterloo blue	weeping myall	what is he like
wander-witted	watermanship	weightedness	what's cooking
Wankel engine	water-measure	weightlessly	what serves it
wantlessness	water milfoil	weightlifter	what's-her-face
warbler finch	water monitor	Weil's disease	what's-her-name
war communism	water opossum	weird sisters	what's in a name
wardrobe-room	water-parsnip	welcome wagon	what's the game
warehouseman	water-parting	welding steel	what's the odds
warehousemen	waterproofed	welding torch	wheat bulb fly
warmongering	waterproofer	welfare hotel	wheel and axle
warningfully	water-serpent	welfare state	wheel and deal
warning-piece	water soldier	well-adjusted	wheel balance
warning track	water-soluble	well-affected	wheelchaired
warning-wheel	water spaniel	well and truly	wheel landing

whencesoever	whitlow-grass	wing-shooting	womanishness
wheresomever	Whitmanesque	win in a canter	woman of ideas
wherethrough	who goes there	winkle-picker	woman of means
which is which	whole-earther	winning-chair	woman of sense
Whiggishness	wholehearted	win one's spurs	woman's estate
while-you-wait	whole holiday	winter annual	woman's rights
whimperingly	whoops-a-daisy	winter barley	woman trouble
whimsicality	whortleberry	winterbourne	women's libber
whimsy-whamsy	wibbly-wobbly	winter cherry	women's rights
whip creation	wicket-keeper	winter-fallow	wonder-monger
whipperginny	wicketkeeper	winter-flying	wonder-struck
whipping-girl	wide-reaching	winter garden	wonder-worker
whipping post	wide receiver	Winterhalter	wondrousness
whippoorwill	wifelessness	winterliness	Woodburytype
whip scorpion	wife-swapping	winter packet	wooden dagger
whip-tom-kelly	wiggle-waggle	winter savory	wood engraver
whirly-whirly	wiggly-waggly	winter sports	wooden-headed
whiskered bat	wild angelica	winter squash	wooden nutmeg
whiskey-water	wild bergamot	winter-weight	wooden tongue
whisky priest	wild chestnut	wire mattress	wood hyacinth
whisperingly	wild cinnamon	wire recorder	woodmancraft
white admiral	wild hyacinth	wire-stitched	wood-pheasant
white arsenic	wild Irishman	wire-stitcher	wool-classing
white balance	wildlife park	wire-strainer	woolly-headed
white-bellied	wild marjoram	wire stripper	woolly monkey
white-burning	wild valerian	Wisconsinite	Woolworthian
white campion	Wild West show	wish-thinking	word-category
white-crowned	wild Williams	witches' broom	word-deafness
white currant	Wilhelminian	witch-hunting	word division
white feather	Williamsburg	witching hour	wordlessness
white fingers	will-o'-the-wisp	with a witness	word-medially
whitefishing	willow beauty	withdrawable	word of honour
white-fronted	willow beetle	withdrawment	word-painting
Whitehallese	willow grouse	witheredness	wordsmanship
Whitehallism	willow-leaved	withholdable	workableness
Whiteheadian	willow myrtle	withholdment	worker priest
white-knuckle	willy wagtail	with impunity	work function
white-livered	willy-willies	within limits	work furlough
white mustard	Wilson's snipe	within reason	working class
white-on-white	wimble-wamble	withinside of	working hours
whitepainter	wimbly-wambly	with interest	working lunch
white pelican	win by a canvas	with one eye on	working model
white pointer	winding-sheet	with one mouth	working order
white pomfret	windlessness	with one's will	working party
white pudding	Windmill Hill	with one voice	working space
White Russian	windmill-like	with open arms	working title
white sanicle	wind of change	without a name	working woman
white scourge	window-screen	without avail	worklessness
white slavery	window-washer	without cease	work-mistress
White slavery	wind-scorpion	without delay	work one's will
White's thrush	Windsor brick	without doors	works council
white stopper	Windsor chair	without doubt	World English
white tea-tree	wind-splitter	without limit	world history
white-toothed	wind-stocking	without price	world of words
white truffle	windwardmost	without shame	world-ranking
white vitriol	windwardness	without tears	world-shaking
white wagtail	wine fountain	with pleasure	worm charming
whitewash gum	wineglassful	with this view	worm-conveyor
white wedding	wing-adjutant	witness-stand	worm pipefish
white whiskey	wing-clapping	Wolffian body	worm's-eye view
Whitfieldian	winged oyster	Wolffian duct	wormwood-beer
whitherwards	winglessness	wollastonite	worry oneself

worry through
worshipfully
worthfulness
Woulfe bottle
wound hormone
wranglership
wrathfulness
wreck-fishing
wrecking ball
Wrenaissance
wretchedness
wriggle out of
wrinkledness
wrinkle ridge
write out fair
write-protect
writer's block
writer's cramp
writing block
writing-board
writing paper
writing speed
writing-table
wrongfulness
wrong side out
wunderkinder
xanthelasmic
xanthic oxide
xanthochroic
xanthochroid
xanthomatous
xanthopterin
xanthorrhoea
xenoantibody

Xenophontean
xiphisternal
xiphisternum
X-irradiation
X-radiography
X-ray analysis
X-ray spectrum
xylobalsamum
xylographica
xylographist
Yankee Doodle
yellow baboon
yellow-billed
yellow George
yellow ground
yellowhammer
yellow-headed
yellow horned
yellow jacket
yellow jersey
yellow Monday
Yellow Monday
yellow pepper
yellow poplar
yellow rattle
yellow rocket
yellow-rumped
yellow streak
yellowthroat
yellow tissue
Yeoman Ushers
yeoman waiter
Yeoman Warder
yieldingness

Yindjibarndi
yo-heave-hoing
Yokohama fowl
Yom Kippur War
York shilling
Yorkshire fog
Yorkshireism
Yorkshireman
Yorkshiremen
Yorkshire pud
you don't say so
you never know
Young America
Young England
young-girlish
young hopeful
young-ladydom
young-ladyish
young manhood
young-mannish
you're another
your good self
you should see
youthfulness
yttrium metal
zamindarship
Zeeman effect
Zend-Avestaic
Zener voltage
zenith sector
zeolitically
zero-crossing
zeta function
zeugmatogram

Ziegfeld girl
Ziehl–Neelsen
zinc chloride
zinc chromate
zincographer
zincographic
zinc ointment
zinc sulphide
zonal defence
zone leveller
zone refining
zonule of Zinn
zoochemistry
zoochlorella
zoogeography
zoographical
zoologically
zoomagnetism
zoomechanics
zoomorphosed
zoopathology
zoophytology
zoosemiotics
zootomically
zooxanthella
zuppa di pesce
zuppa inglese
Zwinglianism
zwitterionic
zygapophysis
zygomorphism
zygomorphous
zygomycetous
zymotechnics

THIRTEEN LETTERS

Abbe condenser
Aberdeen Angus
abiogenically
abiologically
a bit of crumpet
abnormalities
aboriginality
abortifacient
about one's ears
above one's bend
above one's head
above reproach
Abraham's bosom
absence of mind
absolute music
absolute pitch
absolute value
absorbability
abstentionism
abstentionist
abstractional
abstractively
Abyssinian cat
Academy figure
accelerograph
accelerometer
acceptability
acceptilation
accessibility
accidentality
accident-prone
acclimatation
acclimatement
accommodating
accommodation
accommodative
accommodatory
accompaniment
accordingly as
account holder
accreditation
accretion disc
acculturation
acculturative
accustomation
acetaminophen
acetification
acetylcholine
aches and pains
achievability
achromaticity
achromatopsia
achromatopsic
acidification
acorn barnacle
acotyledonous
acquiescently

acquiescingly
acquired taste
acquisitional
acquisitively
acrimoniously
acrobatically
acronymically
across country
acrylonitrile
acting version
actinomorphic
actinomycosis
actinomycotic
actinotherapy
actino-uranium
actionability
action of a verb
active citizen
active service
active volcano
act of oblivion
Act of Sederunt
actual cautery
actualization
acupuncturist
adaptableness
Addressograph
a demon for work
adenoidectomy
adiabatically
adjustability
adjutant stork
admeasurement
admensuration
administrable
administrator
admirableness
admiralissimo
admissibility
admonishingly
Adnyamathanha
adrenal cortex
adrenalectomy
adsorbability
adult suffrage
advanced guard
advanced level
advantage game
adventuresome
adventurously
adversatively
advertisement
advisableness
aerial torpedo
aerobiologist
aerodynamical
aerogenerator

aesthetically
affectability
affenpinscher
affinity group
affirmatively
afflicted with
affordability
afforestation
affreightment
African pepper
African violet
African walnut
Afro-Caribbean
after a fashion
after the event
again and again
against nature
against the sun
agents-general
Age of Aquarius
agglomeration
agglomerative
agglutinating
agglutination
agglutinative
aggradational
aggravatingly
agonistically
a good day's work
a good question
agranulocytic
agreeableness
agree to differ
agriculturist
agrimensorial
agrobiologist
agronomically
aha experience
a hard row to hoe
a hundred to one
aides-mémoires
aircraftwoman
aircraftwomen
airs and graces
airworthiness
à la bonne femme
à la Florentine
à la fourchette
à la Portugaise
a laugh a minute
alchemistical
alcoholically
alcoholometer
alcoholometry
aldosteronism
alectryomancy
algebraically

a lion in the way
alisphenoidal
alkaline earth
alkaline metal
allegorically
allelomorphic
Allhallowmass
All Hallows' Day
Allhallowtide
alligator clip
alligator pear
alligator weed
all in a tremble
all in good time
allochthonous
all of a tremble
allowableness
all the day long
all-wheel drive
a long row to hoe
a losing streak
alpha and omega
Alpha and Omega
alphabetarian
alphabetiform
alpha globulin
alpha particle
alterableness
alternatingly
alternatively
altiplanation
aluminium foil
aluminization
aluminothermy
alveolar ridge
a matter of fact
a matter of form
ambassadorial
ambidexterity
ambiguousness
ambisexuality
ambisonically
ambitiousness
American cloth
American dream
American olive
American organ
American robin
American tiger
amitriptyline
amniocenteses
amniocentesis
amniotic fluid
amorphousness
amphibologies
amphidiploidy
amphiprostyle

amphisbaenian	anthelminthic	appellatively	armamentarium
amphitheatric	anthocyanidin	appendiculate	armed bullhead
amplification	anthophyllite	apple-pie order	armed services
amplificatory	anthracothere	apple-polisher	armour-plating
amplitudinous	anthraquinone	Appleton layer	army of reserve
amusement park	anthropically	applicability	a roll in the hay
anachronistic	anthropogenic	apportionable	aromatization
anaerobically	anthropoid ape	apportionment	arrhenotokous
anagrammatise	anthropolatry	apprehensible	arrière-pensée
anagrammatism	anthropologic	apprehensibly	arsenious acid
anagrammatist	anthropometer	appropinquate	arseniuretted
anagrammatize	anthropometry	appropinquity	art and mystery
anal retention	anthropomorph	appropriately	artefactually
anal-retentive	anthropopathy	appropriation	arteriography
analysability	anthropophagi	appropriative	arteriovenous
anaphorically	anthropophagy	approximately	articled clerk
anaphrodisiac	anthroposophy	approximation	artificialism
anaphylactoid	anti-apartheid	approximative	artificiality
anathematical	anti-attrition	April Fool's Day	artificialize
anathematizer	antibacterial	April Fools' Day	arts and crafts
anatomization	antichristian	apron conveyor	arty-and-crafty
anchorpersons	anticlimactic	aqueous humour	arundinaceous
ancient Briton	anticlinorium	arabic numeral	as a last resort
Ancient Church	anticlockwise	Arabic numeral	as bald as a coot
ancient lights	anticoagulant	arachnoiditis	as bold as brass
and all the rest	anticoagulate	arachnologist	ascending node
androdioecism	anti-communist	arachnophobia	Ascensiontide
anecdotically	antigenically	arachnophobic	ascertainable
anencephalous	antihistamine	arbitrariness	ascertainably
an eye for an eye	antilogarithm	arboriculture	ascertainment
anfractuosity	antimonic acid	archaeography	as deaf as a post
angel food cake	antimony ochre	archaeologian	as far as it goes
angelicalness	antinomianism	archaeologise	as good as a play
angioneurotic	anti-personnel	archaeologist	as hard as nails
angiospermous	antiphonaries	archaeologize	as heavy as lead
angle brackets	antipsychotic	archaeometric	a shingle short
angle of attack	antique-dealer	archaeopteryx	Ashkenazic Jew
angle of repose	antiquitarian	archangelical	a shot in the arm
Anglicization	antiresonance	archbishopric	ask for trouble
Anglo-American	antiscorbutic	archdeaconess	as large as life
Anglo-Catholic	antisocialism	archidiaconal	as likely as not
Anglo-Normanic	antisociality	archimandrite	as long as my arm
Anglo-Saxondom	antispasmodic	archipelagoes	a small fortune
Anglo-Saxonism	antisymmetric	archiphonemic	as meek as a lamb
angostura bark	anybody's guess	architectonic	asparagus fern
angry young man	anythingarian	architectress	aspergillosis
anharmonicity	apathetically	architectural	a sport of terms
animadversion	aperiodically	archpresbyter	a sport of words
animalization	aphrodisiacal	Arctic skipper	as right as rain
animal kingdom	apocalyptical	Ardington Wick	assassination
animal spirits	apocatastasis	areolar tissue	assault-at-arms
anisometropia	apodictically	areopagitical	assault course
anisometropic	apokatastasis	argentiferous	assembly rooms
annexationist	apolausticism	argumentation	assertibility
anniversaries	apomictically	argumentative	assertiveness
anniversarily	apoplectic fit	aristocracies	assertorially
anomalousness	apoplectiform	aristocratism	assertory oath
anonymousness	Apostles' Creed	aristocratize	assessionable
answerability	apostolically	aristological	asset-stripper
antenniferous	apotelesmatic	arithmantical	assiduousness
antepenultima	appealability	arithmetician	assistantship
anterolateral	appear in print	arithmomaniac	assisted place

associability
associateship
associational
associatively
associativity
as sure as death
Assyriologist
astereognosia
astereognosis
asthenosphere
as thin as a rail
as thin as a rake
as things stand
asthmatically
astonishingly
astral spirits
astrometrical
astronautical
astrophysical
astrotheology
at a full gallop
at a single heat
atavistically
at full stretch
atheistically
a tight squeeze
Atlantic Ocean
atlas vertebra
at loggerheads
atmospherical
at no allowance
atomic physics
atomic warfare
atomistically
at one's leisure
at one's own risk
at one's wits' end
atrabilarious
at right angles
atrociousness
at short notice
attainability
attemperament
attemperation
attention span
attentiveness
at the earliest
at the furthest
at the long last
at the same time
attitudinizer
attributively
a tub for a whale
auction bridge
auctioneering
audaciousness
audio cassette
Auger electron
aurora polaris
aurum mosaicum
Australianism
Australianize

Austrian brier
autecological
authentically
authenticator
authenticness
authoritarian
authoritative
authorization
autobiography
autocatalysis
autocatalytic
autocephalous
autochthonous
autodigestion
auto-eroticism
autographical
autohypnotism
auto-infection
auto-infective
automatically
autonomically
autoradiogram
autoxidizable
autumn equinox
autumn gentian
auxanographic
auxiliary verb
availableness
avalanche lily
Averroistical
a wipe in the eye
a woman's reason
a word and a blow
a worm will turn
axiologically
axiomata media
axiomatically
babbling brook
baby-snatching
baccalaureate
bachelor party
bachelor's hall
bachelor's wife
back-formation
back-scratcher
backwardation
backward point
bacteriocidal
bacteriologic
bacteriolysin
bacteriolysis
bacteriolytic
bacteriophage
bacterization
Bactrian camel
bad conscience
badger-baiting
bad-temperedly
Baedeker raids
bag and baggage
balance of mind
balance spring

Balkanization
ballistically
ball lightning
balloon-flower
balloon sleeve
ballroom dance
balneological
balneotherapy
balsamiferous
Balto-Slavonic
bamboo curtain
bamboozlement
Bank of England
bank statement
baptismal name
baptismal vows
baptism of fire
Barbados pride
barbarization
barbarousness
Barbary falcon
barbecue sauce
Barbour jacket
barefacedness
barfly jumping
bargain-hunter
barnacle goose
barnyard grass
baroclinicity
barrack square
barrel chested
barrier method
bartonellosis
basal ganglion
bascule bridge
basibranchial
basic industry
basidiomycete
basioccipital
basso cantante
basso continuo
basso ostinato
basso profundo
bastard indigo
bastard-trench
bastardy order
bateleur eagle
bathing beauty
baton sinister
batrachotoxin
battle-cruiser
battlecruiser
battle fatigue
batwing sleeve
Bavarian cream
be a big girl now
beaked parsley
Beaker Culture
beam-compasses
beam in one's eye
bearded collie
bear repeating

bear suspicion
bear testimony
bear the stroke
bear witness to
beast of burden
be a stranger to
beat frequency
beat hell out of
beatification
beat the bounds
beat the pistol
beat the record
Beaufort scale
beauteousness
beautifulness
beauty contest
beauty parlour
be booked solid
be bound up with
be caught short
bed of sickness
bedside manner
beetle-crusher
before the beam
before the fact
before the mast
before the wind
be friends with
begging letter
beginner's luck
beginningless
begin the dance
begin the world
be hard put to do
be hard put to it
behave towards
behaviourally
behind the veil
behind the wire
be in a mood with
being-in-itself
be in the secret
believability
Belisha beacon
belles-lettres
belligerently
bellows-blower
bellows pocket
bellows to mend
belongingness
be lost without
below the chair
belt and braces
belt the bottle
benchmark test
benday process
bend one's elbow
beneath the sun
benedictional
beneficential
beneficiaries
beneficiation

benightedness
benign neglect
be nothing like
be off one's oats
be on the market
be possessed of
be quartered by
Berenice's Hair
Berkeleianism
Berlin pattern
Bermuda shorts
be rolling in it
beseemingness
beside oneself
beside the mark
be skin and bone
be snowed under
be spoiling for
be spoons about
best end of neck
be that as it may
be the making of
Beth Hamidrash
be through with
be torn between
betting office
between-whiles
bewilderingly
be with a person
beyond dispute
beyond example
beyond measure
beyond the pale
beyond the seas
beyond the veil
Bible-punching
Bible-thumping
bibliographer
bibliographic
bibliometrics
bibliothecary
bibliotherapy
bicentenaries
bidding prayer
bidimensional
bidirectional
big-headedness
big white chief
Bildungsroman
bimillenaries
binary fission
binary measure
binding energy
Binitarianism
biochemically
biocompatible
biodegradable
bio-electrical
bio-energetics
bioenergetics
biogeographer
biogeographic

biomechanical
biometrically
biophysically
biospeleology
biostatistics
biosynthesize
biosystematic
biotechnology
bipinnatisect
Bird of Freedom
bird of passage
bird sanctuary
bird's nest soup
birefringence
birthday party
biscuit barrel
bismuth glance
bite by the nose
bite one's nails
bite on granite
bite the bullet
bite the ground
bit of all right
bit-part player
bits and pieces
bitter cassava
black and white
black antimony
blackberrying
black bindweed
black-eyed bean
blackguardism
black mangrove
black mulberry
blacksmithery
blacksmithing
black-throated
bladder of lard
blamelessness
blanket finish
blanket flower
blanket stitch
blasphemously
blast freezing
blastogenesis
blastomycosis
blaze the trail
blear-eyedness
blear the eye of
bleeding heart
bleed like a pig
blended whisky
blennorrhagia
blepharoplast
blepharospasm
bless her heart
blind man's buff
blind stamping
blister-beetle
blister blight
blister copper
block capitals

block-faulting
block mountain
blood-curdling
blood-grouping
bloodlessness
blood pressure
blood relation
blood relative
bloodshedding
blood-vein moth
bloody warrior
Bloomfieldian
Bloomsburyite
Bloomsbury set
blotting paper
blow great guns
blow one's stack
blue beat music
blue-green alga
blue in the face
blunderheaded
board and board
boarding house
boatswain bird
bob's your uncle
Bob's your uncle
bodice-ripping
body corporate
body-snatching
boiled lobster
boil the kettle
bombastically
Bomber Command
bone turquoise
bony labyrinth
booking office
boon companion
booster rocket
boot and saddle
boraginaceous
bord and pillar
Border terrier
born in wedlock
boroughmonger
borrowed light
borrow trouble
botanographer
bougainvillea
bouillabaisse
boundary layer
boundary rider
boundary value
boundlessness
bounteousness
bountifulness
boustrophedon
bowel movement
bowler's wicket
bowling crease
bowstring hemp
box the compass
boysenberries

brachiosaurus
brachycephaly
brachydactyly
brachypterous
bracket fungus
brainlessness
brainstorming
braising steak
brake-cylinder
branchial arch
branchial tuft
branchiomeric
branch library
branch officer
brass farthing
brassicaceous
brave new world
brazen-facedly
breach of faith
bread and water
break and enter
breakfastless
breaking point
break one's duck
break one's fast
break one's head
break one's wind
break one's word
break short off
break the habit
break the mould
break to pieces
breast the tape
breathe freely
breathing-room
bred in the bone
Breeches Bible
breech-loading
breithauptite
brevet captain
breviloquence
Brewster angle
bridge-builder
bridge circuit
bridge of asses
bridge of boats
bridge passage
brilliantined
brimstone moth
brimstone-wort
bring into line
bring into play
bring to anchor
bring to effect
bring to market
bring to naught
bring to nought
bring to reason
bring up to date
Britannically
Briticisation
Briticization

British Empire	burying beetle	campaign trail	carrion-beetle
British Legion	burying ground	campanologist	carrion flower
broad ligament	bush carpenter	campanularian	carrying-place
broad-mindedly	bush cranberry	Campeachy wood	carrying trade
broad spectrum	bush telegraph	camphor laurel	carte-de-visite
Broca's aphasia	business cycle	campylobacter	cartelization
Brock's benefit	business hours	Canada thistle	cartilaginoid
broken-hearted	business lunch	canaliculated	cartilaginous
bromeliaceous	business widow	canary creeper	cartridge belt
Brompton stock	businesswoman	cancerousness	cartridge-case
bronchial tree	businesswomen	candidateship	car washeteria
bronchiolitis	business world	candle-snuffer	casement cloth
bronchography	butcher's broom	Canes Venatici	cash dispenser
bronchophonic	butcher's knife	canicular days	Cassegrainian
bronchorrhoea	butobarbitone	canicular year	Cassinian oval
bronchoscopic	butter-and-eggs	canine madness	cast a veil over
brontosaurian	butter-fingers	cannabis resin	casting-bottle
brother german	butterfly bush	cannibalistic	castle-builder
brother-in-arms	butterfly fish	canonical hour	castle in Spain
brotherliness	butterfly kiss	canonicalness	castle pudding
brotherly love	butterfly nose	Canterbury hoe	castor oil bean
brothers-in-law	butterfly weed	cantonization	casuistically
Brownie Guider	button one's lip	can you tie that	catalytically
Browningesque	button-through	capaciousness	catastrophism
brown thrasher	butyrophenone	Cape buffaloes	catastrophist
brushed fabric	buy oneself out	Capernaitical	catch at a straw
brush kangaroo	buy on the stump	capitation fee	catchment area
brutalitarian	by acclamation	caprification	catch on the hop
brutalization	by all accounts	Captain Cooker	catch-question
brute creation	by analogy with	captivatingly	catch the eye of
brutification	by appointment	carbon dioxide	catch unawares
bryologically	by implication	carboniferous	catechistical
bryozoologist	by night and day	carbonization	catecholamine
bubble chamber	by rule and line	carbonylation	catechumenate
bubonic plague	by word of mouth	carboxylation	categorematic
budget account	cabbalistical	carburization	categorically
buffalo clover	Cabernet Franc	carcinologist	cater-cornered
buffalo runner	cabinet-making	carcinomatous	cathartically
building-block	cabinetmaking	cardboard city	cathedral city
building-brick	cable moulding	cardiac arrest	cat-o'-nine-tails
building-lease	cacographical	cardinalatial	catoptromancy
bulbo-urethral	cacophonously	cardinalitial	cattle-rustler
bulletin board	cadmium yellow	cardinal point	catty-cornered
bullock's heart	Caesaro-papism	cardinal vicar	cattycornered
bulrush millet	caespititious	cardinal vowel	caustic potash
bumper sticker	calcification	cardiographer	cauterization
bumptiousness	calculability	cardiographic	cavernicolous
bungee jumping	calculatingly	cardiological	cayenne pepper
burden of proof	calculational	careers master	ceaselessness
bureaucracies	calendar month	cariogenicity	celebrational
bureaucratise	calico-printer	Carnaby Street	celery-top pine
bureaucratize	calligraphist	carnal members	celestial body
burghermaster	call into being	carnification	celestial pole
burglariously	callisthenics	carnivalesque	cellular phone
Burgundy pitch	callithumpian	carnivorously	cellular plant
burial service	call to account	carpenter-work	cellular radio
burn one's boats	call to witness	carpet bombing	centesimation
burn one's ships	calorifically	carpet slipper	Central Powers
burn to a cinder	Calvinistical	carpet sweeper	centre fielder
burnt offering	Cambridge blue	carriage clock	centre forward
bursting point	camera lucidas	carriage trade	centrifugally
burst its banks	camera obscura	carrier pigeon	centripetally

cephalic index
cephalization
cephalometric
cephalopelvic
cephalopodous
cephalosporin
cephalothorax
cerebral palsy
cerebrospinal
ceremonialism
ceremonialist
ceremonialize
ceremonial law
ceremoniously
certification
certificatory
certified mail
certified milk
cervical smear
cervicofacial
Cetti's warbler
Chagas' disease
chain reaction
chair of estate
chaise longues
chalcenterous
chalcographer
chalcographic
chalcophanite
chalkhill blue
challengeable
challengingly
chamber-deacon
chamber-fellow
chamber of dais
chameleon-like
champ at the bit
chancelleries
chancel-screen
chance-medleys
chance one's arm
chancery court
changeability
changefulness
change of front
change of heart
change of scene
change-ringing
Channel Tunnel
chaparral cock
characterizer
characterless
character part
charge account
charge-capping
charge carrier
charge density
charity school
charity walker
charlatanical
charm bracelet
charmlessness

charter flight
charter member
Charter School
chartographer
chase one's tail
chasseur sauce
chateaubriand
Chattertonian
cheap and nasty
cheat the widdy
checkweighman
cheerlessness
cheese-skipper
cheiloplastic
chemical shift
chemisorption
chemoreceptor
chequered flag
Cherokee Strip
Chestertonian
chest-expander
chestnut brown
chevaleresque
chiaroscurist
Chickasaw plum
chicken-and-egg
chicken-breast
chickenburger
chieftaincies
chieftainship
child guidance
childlessness
childlikeness
child molester
children's hour
chilli relleno
chimney breast
chimney-corner
china-mark moth
China syndrome
Chinese puzzle
chinkerinchee
Chinook jargon
Chinook Jargon
chinook salmon
Chinook salmon
chiromantical
chi-square test
chitinization
chlamydomonas
chlamydospore
chlorocruorin
Chloromycetin
chocolate-boxy
chocolate chip
chocolate drop
chocolate-tree
choir practice
cholecystitis
cholera morbus
choo-choo train
chop and change

chopping-block
chopping-board
choral service
choral society
choreographer
choreographic
chorepiscopal
chorepiscopus
choripetalous
choristership
choroid plexus
choropleth map
chose in action
chowderheaded
chrestomathic
Christianable
Christianlike
Christian name
Christian year
Christmas bush
Christmas cake
Christmas card
Christmas rose
Christmas-tide
Christmas tree
Christologist
chromatically
chromatograph
chromatolysis
chromatophore
chrome leather
chrome tanning
chromium-plate
chromium steel
chromoprotein
chromosomally
chromosome map
chromospheric
chronobiology
chronographer
chronographic
chronological
chrysanthemum
chuck-farthing
chuckleheaded
Church Fathers
Churchilliana
churchmanlike
churchmanship
church service
chylification
cicatrization
Ciceronianism
cigarette card
cigarette-case
ciliary muscle
cinematically
cinematograph
cinnamon stone
cinnamon toast
cinquecentist
circumambages

circumambient
Circumcellion
circumduction
circumference
circumfluence
circumjacence
circumjacency
circumscriber
circumspectly
circumstanced
circumtabular
circumvallate
circumvention
civet de lièvre
civil aviation
civil engineer
civil marriage
cladistically
clairaudience
clairschacher
clairvoyantly
clamorousness
clandestinely
clandestinity
clankety-clank
clap on the back
clarification
clarificatory
classed growth
classlessness
claustrophobe
clavicembalos
claw the back of
clay ironstone
cleansing milk
clearance sale
clearing house
clear the coast
clear the decks
cleavage plane
cleavelandite
cleft sentence
clerical error
click language
climacterical
climactically
climatologist
climbing frame
climbing perch
clincher-built
cling together
clinical death
clinopinacoid
clinopyroxene
cliometrician
clish-ma-claver
cliticization
cloak-and-sword
clock-watching
cloister-garth
closed-circuit
closed society

close mourning	collaboration	commercialist	compound fruit
close one's ears	collaborative	commerciality	compound order
close one's eyes	collard greens	commercialize	compound umbel
close quarters	collar of esses	commiseration	comprehension
close the books	collateralise	commiserative	comprehensive
clothes-hanger	collaterality	commit suicide	compressed air
cloth of estate	collateralize	commit to paper	compressional
cloth of silver	colleagueship	commonalities	compromission
clouded yellow	collectedness	common carrier	comprovincial
cloudlessness	collectorship	common council	Compton effect
clubbableness	college living	Common Council	computability
coach-building	College of Arms	common hamster	computational
coadjutorship	collieshangie	commonization	computer-aided
coagulability	colligability	common-law wife	computer virus
coalification	collisionally	common opinion	comrade-in-arms
coarse fishing	collisionless	common pompano	comradeliness
coarse-grained	collocability	common sensory	concameration
coast of the sea	collocational	common soldier	concatenation
coast sickness	colloquialism	communalistic	concavo-convex
cobaltiferous	colloquialist	communication	concealed land
co-belligerent	colloquiality	communicative	conceitedness
cocainization	colonial goose	communicatory	concentration
cochleariform	colonoscopies	Communion-rail	concentrative
cock an eyebrow	colourability	communitarian	concentricity
cockatoo fence	colourfulness	communitorium	conceptionist
cocker spaniel	colour hearing	community home	conceptualise
Cockney School	colouring book	communization	conceptualism
cock-of-the-rock	colourization	commutability	conceptualist
cock-of-the-walk	column of route	commutatively	conceptualize
cock-of-the-wood	Coma Berenices	commutativity	concernedness
cockspur grass	combat fatigue	compactedness	concertinaing
cockspur thorn	combativeness	compagination	concert master
cocktail dress	combinability	companionable	concessionary
cocktail-mixer	combinational	companionably	concessionist
cocktail onion	combinatorial	companion-cell	conchological
cocktail party	combinatorics	companionhood	concomitantly
cocktail stick	combining form	companionless	concordantial
cock-throppled	combretaceous	companionship	concrete mixer
co-consciously	come in one's way	companion star	concrete music
coconut butter	come into force	comparability	concrete verse
codeterminant	come near doing	comparatively	concretionary
codicological	come out strong	comparativist	concupiscence
co-educational	come short home	compartmental	concupiscible
coeducational	come to a bad end	compass course	condemned cell
coelacanthine	come to nothing	compassionate	condensed milk
coenaesthesia	come to the fore	compass timber	condescending
coenaesthesis	come up against	compass window	condescension
coercive force	come up smiling	compatibility	conditionally
coessentially	comfortlessly	compatriotism	conduciveness
coextensively	comma bacillus	compendiously	conducted tour
coffee essence	commandership	competitioner	conductitious
coffee grinder	command module	competitively	conductometer
coffee grounds	commeasurable	competitivity	conductometry
coffee morning	commemoration	complainingly	conductor rail
cognate object	commemorative	complementary	conductorship
cognizability	commensurable	complex number	condylomatous
cognomination	commensurably	complicatedly	confabulation
co-inheritance	commentitious	complimentary	confabulatory
cold as charity	commercial art	Complutensian	confarreation
cold-bloodedly	commercialese	compositeness	confectionary
cold-heartedly	commercialise	compositional	confectionery
cold in the head	commercialism	compositorial	confederacies

confederation
confederative
confessionary
confessionist
confessorship
confidence man
confidingness
configuration
configurative
confiscatable
conflagration
conflagrative
confraternity
confrontation
confusability
conglomeratic
conglomerator
conglomeritic
congratulator
congressional
Congress Party
congresswoman
congresswomen
Congreve match
congruousness
conjecturable
conjecturally
conjugal rites
conjugate acid
conjugate axis
conjugate base
conjugational
conjunctional
conjunctively
conjunct proof
conjure doctor
connaturality
connaturalize
connectedness
connecting rod
Connemara pony
connotational
connotatively
connumeration
conquistadors
consanguineal
consanguinean
consanguinity
conscientious
consciousness
consecutively
consenescence
consentaneity
consentaneous
consequential
conservancies
conservatoire
conservatoria
conservatorio
considerately
consideration
consideringly

consimilarity
consistometer
consolamentum
consolidation
consolidatory
conspicuously
conspiratress
constableship
constablewick
Constantinian
constellation
constellatory
consternation
constituently
constrainable
constrainedly
constringency
constructible
consuetudinal
consul general
consultancies
consumer goods
consumeristic
consumptively
contabescence
contact flight
contact screen
container port
container ship
contamination
contaminative
contemplation
contemplative
contentedness
contentiously
contextualise
contextualism
contextualist
contextualize
continentally
contingencies
contingential
continualness
continuity man
contortionist
contrabandist
contrabassist
contra-bassoon
contraception
contraceptive
contractility
contractional
contractually
contradiction
contradictive
contradictory
contrafactual
contrafagotto
contrafissure
contraflexure
contralateral
contranatural

contrapuntist
contrariantly
contrariously
contrary terms
contrastingly
contrastively
contrate wheel
contravariant
contravention
contrectation
contributable
controversial
controversies
controversion
controvertist
convalescence
convalescency
convalidation
conventionary
conventioneer
conventionist
convent school
conversazione
conversionism
conversionist
convertiplane
convexo-convex
convocational
convolutional
convolvuluses
convulsionary
convulsionist
cool one's heels
cooperatively
cooperativity
co-partnership
copartnership
Copernicanism
copia verborum
copper-captain
copper pyrites
copper vitriol
co-precipitate
copying-pencil
copyrightable
coralligenous
core implement
co-religionist
coriander seed
Corinthianism
Corinthianize
corkscrew rule
corn buttercup
corner-forward
cornification
Cornish boiler
Cornish chough
Cornish engine
corno da caccia
coronagraphic
coronal suture
coronation mug

coronoid fossa
corporalities
corporate name
corporate town
corporational
corporativism
corps de ballet
corpse-reviver
Corpus Christi
corpusculated
corpus delicti
Correggiesque
correlational
correlatively
correlativity
correspondent
corresponding
corresponsive
corridor train
corrigibility
corroboration
corroborative
corroboratory
corrodability
corrodibility
corrosibility
corrosiveness
corruptedness
corruptionist
corticotropin
corymbiferous
cosignatories
cosmetologist
cosmochemical
cosmographies
cosmographist
cosmopolitism
co-sovereignty
cost-conscious
cost-effective
cost-efficient
costermongery
costly colours
co-trimoxazole
Cotswold sheep
cottage-bonnet
cottage cheese
cottage garden
cottier tenure
cotton batting
cotton flannel
cotton-picking
cotton-spinner
cotton-stainer
cotton-thistle
cough medicine
council estate
council school
countable noun
counteractant
counteraction
counteractive

counter-agency	cranberry bush	crown imperial	cyanotrichite
counter-attack	cranberry tree	crowning glory	cybernetician
counter-caster	crane-coloured	crown of thorns	cyberneticist
counterchange	craniological	crown princess	cycling lizard
countercharge	crapulousness	Crown princess	cyclo-addition
counter-enamel	crash-helmeted	crudification	cyclodialysis
counter-extend	crazy like a fox	cruise control	cyclone cellar
counter-faller	cream-coloured	cruise missile	cycloparaffin
counterfeiter	cream of tartar	cruiserweight	cyclostrophic
counterfeitly	credence table	cruising speed	cylinder-bored
counterfleury	credentialled	crustaceology	cylinder press
counter-gobony	creditability	crusta petrosa	cylindraceous
counter-jumper	credit account	cry for the moon	cylindrically
countermander	credit squeeze	cryobiologist	cynocephalous
counter-marque	credulousness	cryogenically	cypress spurge
countermelody	creedlessness	cryoturbation	cytochemistry
counter-motion	creeping Jenny	cryptanalysis	cytogenetical
counterpoison	creeping Jesus	cryptanalytic	cytologically
counter-potent	creeping palsy	cryptogrammic	cytomorphosis
counter-rhythm	crème caramels	cryptographer	cytopathology
counterrotate	crème de cassis	cryptographic	dactyliomancy
counter-secure	crème de menthe	cryptological	dactylopodite
counter-stroke	crèmes brûlées	cryptozoology	daddy-long-legs
counterstroke	crèmes caramel	crystal-gazing	daguerreotype
counterweight	Cremnitz white	crystalliform	dairy products
counterworker	crêpes Suzette	crystallinity	damage control
counting-frame	cribbage board	crystallogeny	damage-feasant
counting house	cribbage-faced	crystalloidal	damnification
Count Palatine	cricket ground	crystal system	Damocles sword
country cousin	Crimean Gothic	crystal violet	dance barefoot
country-people	crime-fighting	cuboctahedral	dancing-master
county borough	criminal court	cuboctahedron	dancing-school
county council	criminalistic	Cuisenaire rod	Dandie Dinmont
county cricket	criminal libel	cultivability	dandification
county library	criminologist	cultured pearl	dangerous drug
coupling-reins	criminousness	culturologist	dangerousness
coupon-clipper	crimson clover	Cumberland ham	Dano-Norwegian
coup the creels	critical angle	Cumberland pig	Dark Continent
court bouillon	critical point	cum grano salis	dark of the moon
court circular	crocodile bird	cummingtonite	Darling clover
court cupboard	crocodile clip	cumulostratus	Darling shower
courteousness	Crohn's disease	cuneiform bone	darning-cotton
courtesanship	crop husbandry	cupola furnace	darning needle
courtesy light	cross-bearings	curate's friend	darning-stitch
courtesy title	cross crosslet	curious-minded	dastardliness
Court of Appeal	cross-cultural	currant tomato	data processor
Court of Arches	cross-division	Cursitor Baron	data retrieval
Court of Claims	cross-dressing	curtain-raiser	data structure
court of record	cross-examiner	curvilinearly	Daubenton's bat
court of review	cross-gartered	cushion stitch	daughterboard
courts martial	crossmatching	cushla-machree	daughter-in-law
cousins german	cross one's face	custard marrow	daughter of Eve
covered bridge	cross one's mind	custard powder	dauntlessness
cover one's feet	cross one's path	custodianship	day care centre
covert coating	crossover vote	customariness	dazzle-painted
covert feather	cross-question	custom clothes	dead and buried
coxcombically	cross-reaction	customization	dead as the dodo
crab-apple tree	cross-springer	cut a wide swath	dead man's bells
cracked up to be	cross the floor	cut one's losses	dead man's pedal
cracker-barrel	crotchetiness	cut the mustard	dead man's thumb
cradle to grave	crow-blackbird	cut the painter	dead men's bells
craftsmanship	crowned pigeon	cyanoacrylate	dead men's shoes

dead reckoning	deforestation	dependability	deuteromerite
dead to the wide	deformability	depersonalise	devastatingly
deaf as an adder	deformational	depersonalize	developmental
Dean of Faculty	deglutination	dephlegmation	devil's own luck
deathlessness	degradability	dephosphorize	devirgination
death sentence	degradational	depicturement	devolutionary
death-stricken	degranulation	deplorability	devolutionist
deattribution	degree Rankine	deprecatingly	devotionalism
debating point	degrees of cold	deprecatively	devotionalist
debauchedness	dehonestation	deprecatorily	dexamethasone
debenture bond	dehydroacetic	depressed area	dexterousness
debt collector	dehydrogenase	depth-recorder	dharmashastra
decapsulation	dehydrogenate	derationalize	diabolization
decarboxylate	dehydrogenize	derecognition	diacatholicon
deceitfulness	deipnosophist	derequisition	diachronistic
decelerometer	delayed action	derestriction	diacritically
decentralizer	delectability	derivationist	diageotropism
deceptibility	deleteriously	dermatologist	diagnosticate
deceptiveness	Delian problem	dermatophytic	diagnostician
decerebration	deliciousness	dermatoplasty	diagonal cloth
deciduousness	delightsomely	dermographism	diagrammatize
decimal system	delinquencies	descriptively	dialectically
deck passenger	deliquescence	descriptivism	dialogistical
declamatorily	deliquescency	descriptivist	dial telephone
declaratively	deliriousness	desegregation	diametrically
declericalize	deltoid muscle	desertization	diamondbacked
declinational	demand deposit	desert the diet	diamond-cement
declivitously	demand feeding	desert varnish	diamond-shaped
decolouration	dematerialise	deserve well of	diamond stitch
decompensated	dematerialize	deservingness	diamond willow
decomposition	demerara sugar	desirableness	dianoetically
decompression	demeritorious	desmognathous	diaphonically
decompressive	demethylation	desperateness	diaphragmatic
deconcentrate	demi-caractère	despicability	diaphragm down
deconstructor	demineralizer	destituteness	diaphragm pump
decontaminate	demiurgically	destructional	diaphthoresis
decontrolling	demographical	destructively	diastatically
deconvolution	demolitionist	desulphurizer	diathermanous
Decoration day	demonographer	desultoriness	diathetically
Decoration Day	demonolatrous	desuperheater	diazo compound
decortication	demonological	desynchronize	diazotization
decrepitation	demon patience	detachability	dice with death
decriminalise	demonstration	detail drawing	dichlamydeous
decriminalize	demonstrative	detectability	dichoptically
dedecahedrons	demonstratory	detectibility	dichotomously
deducibleness	demyelination	detemporalize	dictatorially
deductibility	demythologise	deterioration	dieffenbachia
deep breathing	demythologize	deteriorative	dieselization
deep structure	denationalise	determinandum	diffarreation
defamiliarize	denationalize	determinantal	differentiate
defeasibility	denaturalizer	determinantia	differentness
defectibility	dendritically	determinately	difficileness
defectiveness	dendrological	determination	difficultness
defencelessly	densitometric	determinative	diffractively
defensibility	dental formula	deterministic	diffractogram
defensiveness	dentalization	detestability	diffusibility
deferentially	dental surgeon	detrimentally	diffusiveness
deferred share	denticulation	deus ex machina	digestibility
defervescence	deodorization	deuteragonist	digestiveness
defibrillator	deontological	deuteranomaly	dig in one's toes
defibrination	deoxygenation	deuterogamist	dig one's feet in
deflectometer	depauperation	Deutero-Isaiah	digressionary

dig the grave of
dihedral angle
dimensionally
dimensionless
dimension line
diminishingly
dimorphotheca
dim-wittedness
dinner service
dinner theatre
dioeciousness
Dionysiacally
Diotrephesian
diphenoxylate
diphenylamine
diphthongally
dipleidoscope
diplobacillus
diploid number
diplomatic bag
dipping-needle
dipsomaniacal
dipterologist
direct address
direct current
directionally
directionless
directiveness
direct mailing
direct oration
directorially
disaccordance
disadvantaged
disaffectedly
disaffirmance
disallegiance
disannexation
disappearance
disappointing
disapprovable
disarticulate
disassemblage
disaster movie
disburdenment
discapacitate
dischargeable
discharge lamp
discharge tube
disciplinable
discographies
discoloration
discolourment
discomforture
discommodious
discomposedly
disconcerting
disconcertion
disconformity
disconnection
discontentful
discontinuing
discontinuity

discontinuous
disconvenient
discount house
discount store
discourtesies
discovery well
discreditable
discreditably
discrepancies
discretionary
discriminable
discriminably
discriminator
discussionist
disembodiment
disembowelled
disemployment
disengagement
disentailment
disentombment
disestimation
disfavourable
disfavourably
disfellowship
disfiguration
disfigurement
disfiguringly
disfranchiser
disgracefully
disguisedness
dishabilitate
disharmonious
dishonourable
dishonourably
dish up the dirt
disillusioner
disinheriting
disinhibition
disinhibitory
disintegrable
disintegrator
disinterested
disintoxicate
disinvestment
disinvitation
disjunctively
dislikelihood
dismal Desmond
dismal science
dismantlement
dismemberment
disnaturalize
disobediently
disobligement
disobligingly
disoccupation
disordinately
disordination
disparagement
disparagingly
disparateness
dispassionate

dispatch rider
dispersedness
dispiritingly
displeasingly
disponibility
disposability
dispositional
dispositioned
dispositively
dispossession
dispraisingly
disproportion
dispunishable
disputatively
disquietingly
disregardable
disreputation
disrespectful
disruptionist
dissemblingly
dissemination
dissentaneous
dissepimental
dissepulchred
dissettlement
disseveration
dissimilarity
dissimilation
dissimilatory
dissimilitude
dissimulation
dissipativity
dissolubility
dissoluteness
dissymmetries
distantiation
distant signal
distastefully
distemperedly
disthronement
distinctively
distinguished
distinguisher
distortedness
distortionist
distractingly
distractively
distressfully
distressingly
distributable
distributress
district court
district nurse
distrustfully
disubstituted
disuniformity
dittographies
diurnal circle
diverging lens
divertibility
diverticulate
divertingness

divertisement
divide and rule
dividend yield
divide the hoof
divine service
divinity fudge
divisibleness
divisionalise
divisionalize
division lobby
DNA polymerase
do a mischief to
do an ill turn to
do a person dirt
do a person good
Doctor Martens
doctor's orders
doctrinairism
documentalist
documentarian
documentaries
documentarily
documentarist
documentation
documentative
dodderingness
dodecahedrane
dodecaphonist
dogmatization
dog's breakfast
dolichocephal
dolichopellic
dollarization
doll's hospital
dolphinariums
Dome of Silence
domestication
domestic trade
domiciliation
domineeringly
dominical year
dominium utile
done to the wide
donothingness
don't mention it
do oneself well
do one's manners
Doppler effect
do reverence to
dormitory town
do the business
double-banking
double bassoon
double century
double-chinned
double coconut
double-crosser
double-dealing
double density
double digging
double-dipping
double feature

double figures	drill-sergeant	edge connector	electropolish
double-fronted	drink and drive	Edict of Nantes	electroscopic
double glazing	drinking water	editor-in-chief	electro-silver
double harness	drink-offering	educatability	electrostatic
double-hearted	drink one's fill	educated guess	electrovalent
double-jointed	dripping crust	educationally	elegiac stanza
double meaning	dripping toast	effectiveness	elephant grass
double obelisk	drive the green	effectualness	elephantiasis
double or quits	drive-yourself	effervescence	elephant paper
double shuffle	driving gloves	effervescency	elephant's foot
double spacing	droopy drawers	efficaciously	elephant shrew
double tertian	dropping-field	efficiency bar	eliminability
double-tongued	drowned valley	efflorescence	ellipsoidally
double wedding	drug addiction	egg flower soup	elocutionally
doubtlessness	drum majorette	eggheadedness	Elysian fields
Douglas's pouch	Drummond light	egg on one's face	Elysian Fields
Douglas spruce	drumstick tree	eggshell china	embarrassedly
dovetail joint	dryopithecine	egocentricity	embarrassment
Dow–Jones index	dualistically	ego-psychology	embellishment
downconverter	duchesse satin	egotistically	embracingness
downheartedly	duchesse-table	egregiousness	embranglement
Downing Street	duchess sleeve	Egyptian black	embrittlement
downrightness	ductless gland	Egyptian goose	embryogenesis
Down's syndrome	dulcification	Egyptian lotus	embryogenetic
down the course	dull the edge of	Egyptian onion	embryological
down to the wire	Dunkirk spirit	Egyptian wheel	embryonically
doxographical	duplicability	Egyptological	emerald cuckoo
doxologically	Durham mustard	eigenfunction	emergency exit
do you happen to	dusting powder	eight-day clock	Emersonianism
dracocephalum	Dutch interior	eightsome reel	éminence grise
draconic month	Dutchman's pipe	elaborateness	eminent domain
dracunculosis	dwelling house	elanguescence	emotionlessly
draftsmanship	dwelling place	elasmotherium	emotive theory
draggle-tailed	dyed in the wool	elastic tissue	emphysematous
drainage basin	dynamogenesis	elder brethren	empire builder
draining board	dysfunctional	elder-sisterly	employability
dramatic irony	dysmenorrhoea	electioneerer	empty calories
dramatization	dyspeptically	electoral roll	emulativeness
dramaturgical	early musician	electric chair	emulsion paint
drapery artist	earth sciences	electric fence	enaliosaurian
draught-bridge	Eastern Church	electric field	enamouredness
draught-screen	Eastern Empire	electric organ	enantiodromia
draughtswoman	east-north-east	electric razor	enantiomerism
draw a veil over	east-south-east	electric shock	enantiopathic
drawing-master	easy listening	electric storm	enantiotropic
drawing-string	easy on the eyes	electric torch	encapsidation
draw level with	eat its head off	electrization	encapsulation
draw one's steel	eat like a horse	electrocution	encephalitis C
draw pig on pork	eat the bread of	electrodeless	encephalocele
draw the badger	eau de toilette	electrodermal	encephalogram
draw the line at	ebullioscopic	electrologist	encomiastical
draw the stumps	eccentrically	electromagnet	encompassment
dreadlessness	ecclesiolatry	electrometric	encoppicement
dreamlessness	ecclesiologic	electromotive	encouragement
dree one's weird	echinopluteus	electronic tag	encouragingly
dress-carriage	eco-geographic	electron shell	enculturation
dress-designer	econometrical	electro-optics	enculturative
dressed to kill	economization	electrophilic	encyclopaedia
dress-improver	ectopterygoid	electrophonic	encyclopaedic
dressing-chest	ectrodactylia	electrophorus	encyclopedian
dressing table	ecumenicalism	electroplaque	encyclopedise
dribs and drabs	ecumenicality	electroplater	encyclopedism

encyclopedist	epigrammatist	ethnomedicine	exclamatorily
encyclopedize	epigrammatize	ethnophaulism	Exclusion Bill
endocrinology	epileptically	ethnosemantic	exclusion zone
end of the world	epileptogenic	ethyl chloride	exclusiveness
endolymphatic	epimerization	ethylene oxide	exclusivistic
endometriosis	epiphenomenal	ethylenically	excommunicant
endometriotic	epiphenomenon	Etruscologist	excommunicate
endonormative	epiphytically	eucalyptus oil	excortication
endoparasitic	epiplanktonic	eucatastrophe	excrescential
endopeptidase	epistemically	Eucharistical	excursion fare
endopolyploid	epithalamiums	eudiometrical	excursiveness
endopterygote	epithetically	eugeosyncline	excusableness
endosymbiosis	epitomization	Euler's formula	excuse oneself
endosymbiotic	epitrochoidal	euphausiacean	exemplariness
endurableness	epizootiology	euphemistical	exemplifiable
energetically	epoxy-compound	euphonization	exhaustedness
energumenical	Equality State	Eurocommunism	exhaust stroke
enforcibility	equestrianism	Eurocommunist	exhibitionism
engaged signal	equianalgesic	European Court	exhibitionist
engine-turning	equidifferent	Europocentric	exhortational
English muffin	equidistantly	Eurostrategic	existentially
English setter	equilibration	eutectic point	exobiological
English walnut	equilibristic	eutectiferous	ex-officio oath
enhypostatize	equimolecular	evangelically	exothermicity
enigmatically	equipartition	evangelistary	expandability
enjoyableness	equipollently	evaporability	expanded metal
enlightenment	equiponderant	evaporatively	expansibility
ensorcellment	equiponderate	evasive action	expansion bolt
enteric-coated	equipotential	evening breeze	expansion card
enterocolitis	equitableness	evening prayer	expansion slot
enterohepatic	equity capital	evening school	expansiveness
enter one's head	equivocalness	eventlessness	expectant heir
enter one's mind	equivoluminal	eventualities	expectoration
enterostomies	erase facility	everlastingly	expectorative
Entero-Vioform	ergonomically	Everton toffee	expedientness
entertainable	eroticization	everybody else	expeditionary
entertainment	errand of mercy	every which way	expeditionist
enter the lists	erroneousness	evocativeness	expeditiously
entomological	erysipelatose	evolutionally	expendability
entomophagous	erysipelatous	exaggeratedly	expensiveness
entomophilous	erythrophobia	examinability	explanatorily
entomostracan	escallop-shell	examinational	explicatively
entoparasitic	escapological	examinatorial	explicit faith
entrammelling	eschatologist	exanthematous	exploding wire
entrance wound	eschatologize	exasperatedly	explorational
enumerability	escheatorship	excandescence	exploratively
enumeratively	eschscholtzia	exceedingness	exploratorium
environmental	esprit de corps	exceptionable	exploring coil
enzymatically	essentialness	exceptionably	explosibility
enzymological	establishable	exceptionally	explosive bolt
eosinophilous	establishment	exceptionless	explosiveness
epeirogenesis	estate-bottled	excess baggage	exponentially
epeirogenetic	estates bursar	excessiveness	exportability
ephemeralness	estimableness	excess luggage	export surplus
ephemeris time	estrangedness	excess postage	expose oneself
epicondylitis	etching ground	exchange blows	expositionary
epidemiologic	ethchlorvynol	exchange force	expostulation
epidermically	ethnobotanist	exchange paper	expostulative
epidermolysis	ethnocentrism	exchange value	expostulatory
epidotization	ethnocultural	exchequer bill	exposure meter
epigrammatise	ethnohistoric	excisemanship	expressionism
epigrammatism	ethnolinguist	excitableness	expressionist

expropriation	false position	fetch a compass	fire insurance
expunctuation	false quantity	fetch and carry	fires of heaven
expurgatorial	false relation	fête champêtre	fire-swallower
exquisiteness	false scorpion	fetishization	first-classman
exquisitively	falsification	feudalization	first-day cover
exsanguineous	familiar angel	feuilletonist	first language
extemporarily	familiarities	fibrous tissue	first offender
extendability	family butcher	fibrovascular	first position
extendibility	fanaticalness	fiddle pattern	first sergeant
extensibility	fantastically	Fiddler's Green	First World War
extensionally	fantasticness	fidepromissor	fisherman's rib
extensionless	Faraday effect	field bindweed	fishing vessel
extensiveness	far be it from me	field-dressing	fissiparously
extenuatingly	fare indicator	field emission	fit like a glove
exterior angle	farmer-general	field equation	five o'clock tea
extermination	farmhouse loaf	field fleawort	five positions
exterminative	fasciculation	field hospital	flagellantism
exterminatory	fascinatingly	field mushroom	flagellomania
externalities	Fascistically	field of honour	flame shoulder
external world	fashion-monger	field of vision	Flanders brick
externization	fashion victim	field-preacher	Flanders poppy
exteroceptive	fat-headedness	field scabious	flannel flower
exterritorial	fatiguability	field strength	flashing point
extinguishant	faultlessness	fifteenth part	flash in the pan
extortionable	faunistically	fifteen-tonner	flatulentness
extracellular	feast of reason	Fifth Monarchy	flauto piccolo
extra-European	feather duster	fifth position	fleet marriage
extragalactic	feather-footed	fifty-year rule	Fleet marriage
extrajudicial	feather-headed	fighter-bomber	flesh and blood
extraliterary	feather stitch	fighting chair	flesh-coloured
extra-metrical	feather-tailed	fighting conch	fleshing-knife
extraordinary	feather-tongue	fighting drunk	flight control
extrapolation	feather-topped	fighting-sails	flight feather
extrapolative	featherweight	fighting words	flight officer
extrapolatory	feature-length	figure-casting	flinty-hearted
extraposition	featureliness	figure-flinger	flirtatiously
extrapunitive	feature writer	figure of eight	flitter-winged
extratropical	fecundability	figure of merit	floating light
extravagantly	federationist	figure skating	floating point
extravagation	fed to the teeth	figure weaving	floating voter
extravasation	feeding bottle	file in the foot	floccillation
extravascular	feed the fishes	filibusterism	flood and field
extrinsically	feel one's wings	filing cabinet	floral diagram
extrospective	fellow-citizen	filmographies	floral formula
eyebrow pencil	fellow-feeling	filterability	floral tribute
fabricability	fellow soldier	filter-feeding	Florence flask
facetiousness	fellow subject	filter-passing	Florentine pie
factorization	feloniousness	final solution	floricultural
factor theorem	felt-tipped pen	financial year	floristically
factory outlet	feminine rhyme	find fault with	flounderingly
facultatively	femmes fatales	find one's level	flourishingly
faculty theory	femoral artery	find one's match	flowering fern
fair and square	Fennoscandian	find one's way to	flowering rush
Fairlight Clay	ferociousness	fine champagne	flowers of zinc
fairy thimbles	ferrimagnetic	fine chemicals	flow of spirits
faithlessness	ferroconcrete	fine gentleman	flow structure
fall from grace	ferroelectric	fineness ratio	fluctuational
fall into place	ferromagnetic	fine-tooth comb	flummerdiddle
fall off a lorry	ferrosoferric	finger-breadth	fluophosphate
fall of the leaf	ferrumination	finger-pillory	fluorescently
Fallopian tube	fertilisation	finishing-line	flush lavatory
false asphodel	fertilization	finnan haddock	flutter-tongue

fluvioglacial	formulaically	friendly match	gallows humour
flying gurnard	formulization	frighteningly	galvanization
flying machine	for once and all	frightfulness	galvanometric
flying officer	for perpetuity	frilled lizard	galvanoplasty
Flying Officer	for preference	fringe benefit	galvanoscopic
flying trapeze	for that matter	frivolousness	galvanotactic
fly on the wheel	forthbringing	Froebel system	galvanotropic
fly-up-the-creek	for the account	from head to toe	gamboge yellow
focal distance	for the present	from here on out	game-preserver
foetalization	fortification	from one's heart	gametogenesis
fold one's hands	fortitudinous	from shipboard	gamma globulin
folk etymology	fortnightlies	from the cradle	garden lettuce
folkloristics	fortunateness	from the word go	garden produce
follow the drum	fortune cookie	from wig to wall	garden village
follow-through	fortune hunter	frondescently	garden warbler
food chemistry	Fortune's wheel	frontlessness	garlic-mustard
food poisoning	fortune-teller	frontogenesis	garnetiferous
food processor	forum shopping	frontogenetic	garrulousness
foolhardiness	fossiliferous	fructuousness	garter-webbing
fool's paradise	fossilization	fruitarianism	gas centrifuge
football pools	foundationary	fruit cocktail	gasteromycete
foot in the door	founder member	fruitlessness	gastrectomies
foot passenger	Fourier series	frumentaceous	gastrocnemial
for a certainty	four-poster bed	frumentarious	gastrocnemian
for a constancy	fowl-paralysis	frustratingly	gastrocnemius
for all seasons	foxtail millet	fuddle one's cap	gastro-enteric
for a long while	fractionalise	fuel injection	gastroenteric
foramen magnum	fractionalism	fugaciousness	gastronomical
foraminiferal	fractionalist	fulfil oneself	gathering coal
foraminiferan	fractionalize	full-bloodedly	gathering peat
forbiddenness	fractionation	fuller's teasel	gauge function
forced landing	fractiousness	full-fashioned	gauge pressure
force the issue	fragmentarily	full-heartedly	gay liberation
fore-and-aft cap	fragmentation	full professor	Gay Liberation
forecastingly	frame dwelling	fumble one's way	gee whillikins
foreconscious	Franciscanism	funambulation	Geiger counter
fore-end loader	frankmarriage	funambulatory	gelatinizable
foregrounding	fraternal twin	functionalise	gemmiparously
foreign legion	freak of nature	functionalism	gemmuliferous
Foreign Office	free Communion	functionalist	genecological
forejudgement	free companion	functionality	general dealer
foreknowledge	free selection	functionalize	generalissima
foreordinance	free to confess	functionaries	generalissimo
foresightedly	freezing point	functionarism	generalizable
forest wallaby	freezing works	function space	general pardon
forget about it	French cricket	fundamentally	general public
forgetfulness	French defence	fungitoxicity	general reader
forget oneself	French disease	funipendulous	general strike
forgivingness	French kissing	funny business	generation gap
for good and all	French morocco	funny-peculiar	generationism
fork-lift truck	French mustard	fur and feather	genericalness
formal concept	French tickler	furnitureless	genethlialogy
formalization	frequency band	fussification	genito-urinary
formationally	frequentation	futtock shroud	Genoese sponge
formation-rule	frequentative	future perfect	genotypically
formativeness	fresh as a daisy	futurological	genre painting
form catalogue	freshen the nip	gain the wind of	gentian bitter
form criticism	fricandeauing	galactorrhoea	gentian brandy
for mercy's sake	friction-brake	galactosaemia	gentian spirit
form-historian	friction match	gallery forest	gentian violet
formidability	fridge-freezer	gallimaufries	gentlemanhood
form of address	friend at court	Gallithumpian	gentlemanlike

gentlewomanly
geocentricity
geochemically
geochronology
geodesic curve
geological map
geometrically
geometric mean
geometrideous
geomorphogeny
geomorphology
geophysically
geopolitician
Georgian green
geostationary
geotechnology
geotropically
gephyrocercal
Germanization
German measles
Germanophobia
German sausage
germinability
gerontocratic
gerontologist
gerontophilia
gerontophilic
gerrymanderer
gerund-grinder
gesticulation
gesticulative
gesticulatory
get a person off
get a person out
get a person wet
get a rise out of
get a thing over
get in on the act
get it over with
get off lightly
get off the mark
get off to sleep
get one's hand in
get one's own way
get one's rag out
get on the brain
get on your bike
get square with
get the laugh on
get the message
get the picture
get the pricker
get the start of
ghetto blaster
ghettoization
ghostly father
giant anteater
giant kangaroo
gibber country
gift of tongues
Giorgionesque
gird one's loins

girl about town
girls together
give a free hand
give an example
give her the gun
give offence to
give of oneself
give one's arm to
give one's heart
give the gate to
give the mitten
give the sack to
give thought to
glacial period
glacio-eustasy
glaciofluvial
glaciological
gladiatorship
glamorization
glance one's eye
Glauber's salts
glenoid cavity
glide-twinning
gloaming sight
globalization
global village
global warming
globe amaranth
globe-trotting
glocalization
glorification
glossographer
glossological
glossophagine
glottological
glow discharge
glucosinolate
glucuronidase
glutinousness
glycerination
glycerine tear
glycerokinase
glycosylation
glyphographer
glyphographic
gnosiological
go a person's way
go-as-you-please
goat and bee jug
Gobelin stitch
go by the name of
godfatherhood
godfathership
God forbid that
godless florin
godmothership
goffering iron
go gangbusters
goggle-eye Jack
go into a huddle
golden-crested
golden hamster

golden jubilee
golden-mouthed
golden section
golden wedding
Goliath beetle
gonadotrophic
gonadotrophin
goniometrical
good afternoon
good for a laugh
good-for-nought
Good King Henry
good-naturedly
good neighbour
good Samaritan
goody two-shoes
go one's own gait
goose barnacle
go over the wall
go over the wire
Gordon Bennett
go the distance
go the whole hog
go the whole way
go the wrong way
Gothic revival
go through with
go to one's heart
governability
governess cart
governing body
governmentese
government man
go with the flow
go with the tide
gracelessness
gradationally
grade crossing
gradual psalms
graduate nurse
grain-elevator
graminivorous
grammar school
grammatically
grammatolatry
granddaughter
grandfatherly
grandiloquent
grandiloquous
grandmasterly
grandmaternal
grandmotherly
Grand National
Grand Old Party
grandparental
grandpaternal
grand seigneur
Grand Seignior
granger shares
granitization
granny bashing
granny glasses

granny's bonnet
granulomatous
granulometric
grape hyacinth
grape-scissors
graphemically
graphicalness
graphic artist
graphological
grappling hook
grappling iron
grasp at a straw
Grassmann's Law
grass parakeet
grass sickness
grass staggers
graticulation
gratification
gratulatorily
gravel culture
Graves' disease
Gravette point
gravimetrical
gravitational
great and small
greatcoatless
Great Entrance
Greater Bairam
greater diesis
great-grandson
great kangaroo
great majority
great omission
great sessions
great sturgeon
great unwashed
Great White Way
Greek valerian
green amaranth
green copperas
green-fingered
greenhouse gas
Greenland dove
green porphyry
greensickness
Greenwich Time
greetings card
gregarization
Gregory powder
grey manganese
grey marketeer
grey partridge
grey phalarope
grieflessness
grief-stricken
grin and bear it
grinding pains
grinding-stone
grinding-wheel
groan inwardly
grody to the max
grotesqueness

ground control	hallucinative	have the wind up	hemicolectomy
ground-hemlock	hallucinatory	have the wood on	hemiparasitic
groundhog case	halophosphate	Hawaiian goose	hemispherical
ground moraine	ham-fistedness	Hawaiian shirt	hemlock spruce
groundsel tree	ham-handedness	hawthorn china	henceforwards
groundskeeper	Hamito-Semitic	hay-home supper	hepaticostomy
group dynamics	hammer-dressed	hazardousness	hepatomegalia
group genitive	handcraftsman	heading-course	heptadecanoic
group language	handkerchiefs	head over heels	heptahydrated
group marriage	handleability	head restraint	heptametrical
group practice	hand-telescope	heads will roll	heptasyllabic
group velocity	hang by a thread	healthfulness	hepthemimeral
growing season	hanging basket	health officer	heraldic tyger
growth hormone	hanging matter	health physics	Heralds' Office
Grumbletonian	hanging sleeve	health service	herbarization
G-strophanthin	hanging valley	health visitor	herborization
Guadalupe palm	Hang Seng index	heap praises on	Hercegovinian
guarantee fund	hang up one's hat	hear a bird sing	Hercules braid
guardian angel	hapax legomena	heartbreaking	heresiography
guard of honour	haphazardness	heartbrokenly	heresiologist
gubernatorial	happy dispatch	hearth and home	hereticalness
guest of honour	happy families	hear the last of	here we go again
guided missile	happy landings	heartlessness	heritage coast
Guignet's green	harbour master	heart-piercing	heritage group
guilelessness	hardenability	heartsickness	heritage trail
guiltlessness	hard-heartedly	heart-stricken	hermaphrodism
gum turpentine	hard of hearing	heat-exchanger	hermaphrodite
gun microphone	hare and hounds	Heath Robinson	hermeneutical
Gunpowder Plot	harlequin duck	heat-resistant	herniorrhaphy
gymnastically	harlequin fish	heat treatment	heroic couplet
gymnospermous	harlequin ring	Heaven forfend	herpes simplex
gynaecocratic	harmonic minor	Heaven help you	herpetologist
gynaecologist	harmonisation	heavenly fires	herring-choker
gynaecomastia	harmonization	heave of the sea	herring-gutted
gynandromorph	harness-racing	heave the gorge	Herzegovinian
gynodioecious	harrowingness	heavy-handedly	heteroblastic
gynomonoecism	Harry-long-legs	heavy hydrogen	heterocarpous
Gypsy's warning	haruspication	heavy industry	heterochromia
gyrofrequency	harvest maiden	hebdomadarian	heterochromic
habeas corpora	harvest-spider	Heberden's node	heterochronic
habitableness	hauling-ground	hecatontarchy	heterogametic
habit-training	have a free hand	hectocotylize	heterogeneity
haemarthrosis	have a good mind	hedge bindweed	heterogeneous
haematidrosis	have a good time	hedge-clippers	heterogenesis
haematogenous	have a regard to	hedgehog holly	heterogenetic
haematologist	have a time of it	heebie-jeebies	heterographic
haematomyelia	have a word with	heel of the hand	heterological
haematothorax	have by the ears	heels over head	heteromorphic
haemodialyser	have designs on	height to paper	heteronuclear
haemodialysis	have eyes to see	heir designate	heteroplastic
haemodynamics	have good sport	heir-portioner	heteropterous
haemorrhoidal	have half a mind	heirs apparent	heterostylism
hairline crack	have in a string	held in demesne	heterostylous
hair-splitting	have itchy feet	Heliogabalian	heterothallic
hair-triggered	have nothing on	Hellenistical	heterothermic
Haitian creole	have no time for	Hellenization	heterotrophic
hale and hearty	have one's eye on	Hellespontine	heterozygotic
half-heartedly	have the care of	helminthiasis	heuristically
half-sovereign	have the drop on	helminthology	hexadactylism
half the battle	have the edge on	helter-skelter	hexadecimally
half-timbering	have the legs of	hemerobaptist	hexamethonium
hallucination	have the rags on	hemicellulose	hexamethylene

hexobarbitone
hey cockalorum
hide-and-go-seek
hieratic paper
hieroglyphist
hierogrammate
hierosolymite
high and mighty
High-Churchism
High Churchman
High Churchmen
High Constable
high explosive
high frequency
Highgate resin
Highland dress
Highland fling
Highland games
high latitudes
high-muck-a-muck
high opinion of
high priestess
high-thoughted
high water mark
hilariousness
Hildebrandine
Hippocratical
hippopotamian
hippopotamine
hispanization
histiocytosis
histochemical
histrionicism
hit a false note
hit the ceiling
hit the jackpot
Hittitologist
hobby-horsical
Hobson's choice
hoist one's flag
hold a brief for
hold aloof from
hold a torch for
hold in demesne
holding ground
hold it against
hold one's peace
hold one's serve
hold one's state
hole-and-corner
hole in the wall
holiday centre
hollow-cheeked
hollow-hearted
hollow-trunked
holluschickie
holoparasitic
holosericeous
Holy Communion
Holy Sacrament
Holy Scripture
Holy Sepulchre

homalographic
home economics
home economist
Home Secretary
homeward-bound
homiletically
homoeoblastic
homoeogeneous
homoeomorphic
homoeopathist
homo-eroticism
homogeneously
homoiothermic
homologically
homolographic
homoscedastic
homosexualist
homosexuality
honeycomb wall
honeydew melon
honorary canon
honorifically
honourability
honours course
honours degree
honours school
hook-and-ladder
Hooke coupling
hoop petticoat
Hopkinsianism
horizon mining
horizontal bar
horizontalism
horizontality
horizontalize
horrification
horripilation
horse-and-buggy
horse chestnut
horsefeathers
horse-foot crab
horsehair worm
horse mackerel
horse mushroom
horseshoe crab
horse sickness
horse traction
horticultural
Hosanna Sunday
hospital blues
hospital fever
hospital train
hospital trust
hot-air balloon
hot dark matter
hot-headedness
hotheadedness
hot laboratory
Hottentot fish
Hottentot's god
Hottentot's tea
houghmagandie

housebreaking
housebuilding
household book
household gods
household name
household word
houselessness
house longhorn
house magazine
housemistress
house of office
house of prayer
House of prayer
housewifeship
housing estate
housing scheme
howling baboon
howling monkey
hubristically
huckleberries
human equation
human interest
humiliatingly
humpback whale
hundredth part
hundredweight
hunger marcher
hunger striker
hungry forties
Huntingdonian
hunting ground
hunting spider
hurricane-bird
hurricane deck
hurricane lamp
hurricane wind
hush one's mouth
Hutchinsonian
hyalinization
hyaloclastite
hyaluronidase
hybridization
hydraulically
hydriodic acid
hydro-aromatic
hydrobiologic
hydroboration
hydrocephalic
hydrocephalus
hydrochloride
hydrodynamics
hydroelectric
hydrofracture
hydrogasifier
hydrogenation
hydrogenosome
hydrogenously
hydromagnetic
hydrometrical
hydroperoxide
hydrophobical
hydroponicist

hydrostatical
hydrosulphide
hydrosulphite
hydrotherapic
hydroxylamine
hydroxylation
hydroxylysine
hygrometrical
hygroscopical
hymenopterous
hyomandibular
hyperactivity
hyperbolicity
hyperboloidal
hypercellular
hypercritical
hyperdiploidy
hyperesthesia
hypereutectic
hyperfunction
hyperhidrosis
hyperkalaemia
hyperkalaemic
hyperlipaemia
hyperlipaemic
hypermetrical
hypermetropia
hypermetropic
hypermobility
hyperparasite
hyperphysical
hyperpolarize
hyperpyrexial
hypersalinity
hypersplenism
hypersthenite
hypertelorism
hypertonicity
hypertrophied
hypertrophous
hyperurbanism
hypervelocity
hyphenization
hyphomycetous
hypnoanalysis
hypnoanalytic
hypnotization
hypoaesthesia
hypobranchial
hypocalcaemia
hypocalcaemic
hypochondriac
hypochondrial
hypochondrium
hypochoristic
hypochromasia
hypochromatic
hypocycloidal
hypoeutectoid
hypoglycaemia
hypoglycaemic
hypolemniscus

hyponatraemia	illuminometer	impersuadable	inappreciable
hyponatraemic	illusionistic	impertinently	inappreciably
hypophosphate	illustratable	imperturbable	inappropriate
hypophosphite	illustriously	imperturbably	inarticulated
hypopituitary	illustrissimo	impetuousness	inattentively
hyposecretion	image orthicon	impignoration	incandescence
hyposensitize	imaginability	implacability	incantational
hypothecation	imaginariness	implicational	incapableness
hypotheticate	imaginatively	implicatively	incarceration
hypothyroidic	imagistically	implicit faith	incarnational
hypotonically	imbalsamation	imploringness	incessantness
hypotrichosis	imitative arts	implosiveness	incidentalist
hypsicephalic	imitativeness	impolitically	in circulation
hypsiconchous	imitative word	impoliticness	incircumspect
hypsometrical	immarcescible	importunately	inclinational
hyracotherium	immaterialise	impossibilism	inclined plane
hysteroscopic	immaterialism	impossibilist	inclusion body
hystricomorph	immaterialist	impossibility	inclusiveness
I am afraid that	immateriality	impostumation	incognoscible
I am yet to learn	immaterialize	impracticable	incoherencies
iatrochemical	immatriculate	impracticably	incoincidence
iatrogenicity	immediateness	impractically	incombustible
iatromechanic	immersion foot	imprecatorily	incomes policy
iatrophysical	immersion suit	impreciseness	income support
Ibero-American	immiscibility	impredicative	incommiscible
ice-cream float	immovableness	impregnatable	incommodation
Iceland falcon	immunochemist	impreparation	incommunicado
Iceland lichen	immunogenetic	impressionary	incompactness
ichneumon wasp	immunological	impressionism	in company with
ichnographies	immunotherapy	Impressionism	incompetently
ichthyologist	impact printer	impressionist	incompletable
ichthyosaurus	impalpability	imprest system	incomposible
iconographies	imparipinnate	improbability	inconceivable
iconographist	impartibility	improficiency	inconceivably
iconometrical	impassability	improgressive	inconclusible
icosahedrally	impassibility	impropriation	incondensable
identicalness	impassionedly	impropriatrix	incondensible
identical twin	impassionment	improprieties	inconformable
ideographical	impassiveness	improvability	incongruently
ideologically	impatientness	improvidently	incongruities
idiomatically	impeccability	improvisation	incongruously
idiorrhythmic	impecuniosity	improvisatory	in conjunction
idiosyncratic	impenetration	imprudentness	inconquerable
idiots savants	impenetrative	imp the wings of	inconsciently
if the shoe fits	imperatorship	impulse buying	inconsciously
if you must know	imperceivable	impulse killer	inconsecutive
Ignatius's bean	imperceivably	impulsiveness	in consequence
ignominiously	imperceptible	impurity level	inconsequence
ileocolostomy	imperceptibly	imputation tax	inconsiderate
illachrymable	impercipience	imputrescence	inconsistence
Illawarra pine	imperfectible	imputrescible	inconsistency
I'll be jiggered	imperfectness	in a brown study	inconsonantly
I'll be switched	imperforation	in a cleft stick	inconspicuous
ill-considered	imperformable	inadventurous	inconstancies
ill-favouredly	imperial eagle	inadvertently	inconstruable
ill-formedness	imperialistic	in a fit state to	incontaminate
ill-humouredly	imperiousness	in a general way	incontestable
illimitedness	impermanently	in a good temper	incontestably
illocutionary	impermissible	inanimateness	incontestible
illogicalness	impersonality	in a person's lap	incontinently
ill-temperedly	impersonation	in a position to	in contumaciam
ill-thought-out	imperspirable	inapplication	inconvenience

inconveniency	individuality	influenceable	inopportunity
inconvertible	individualize	influence line	inorganically
inconvertibly	individuation	influentially	in parenthesis
inconvincible	individuative	informalities	in perspective
incorporating	indoctrinator	informational	in point of fact
incorporation	Indo-Germanist	informatively	in possibility
incorporative	indoor cricket	informatorily	in Queer Street
incorporeally	Indo-Saracenic	infralittoral	inquiry office
incorrectness	induction coil	inframarginal	inquisitional
incorruptible	induction loop	infraspecific	inquisitively
incorruptibly	inductiveness	infrigidation	inquisitorial
incorruptness	induplication	infructuously	in reference to
incredibility	in durance vile	in full feather	in respect that
incredulously	industrialise	infuriatingly	in restraint of
incrementally	industrialism	ingeniousness	insatiability
incriminating	industrialist	ingenuousness	inscriptional
incrimination	industrialize	ingrain carpet	insectiferous
incriminatory	industriously	ingravescence	insectivorous
incubator bird	ineducability	ingravidation	insensateness
inculpability	ineffableness	ingurgitation	insensibility
incurableness	ineffectively	in Heaven's name	insensitively
incuriousness	ineffectually	inhibitedness	insensitivity
indefatigable	inefficacious	in high dudgeon	insertion gain
indefatigably	inefficiently	in high feather	in short supply
in deference to	inegalitarian	in high spirits	inside country
indentureship	inelaborately	inhomogeneity	inside forward
independently	inelastically	inhomogeneous	insidiousness
indescribable	ineligibility	in honour bound	insignificant
indescribably	inequilateral	inhospitality	insincerities
indeterminacy	inequivalence	iniencephalic	insinuatingly
indeterminate	inevitability	iniencephalus	insinuatively
indeterminism	inexclusively	inimitability	in smooth water
indeterminist	inexhaustible	initial letter	insociability
index register	inexhaustibly	in its entirety	insolubleness
Indian currant	inexorability	injection well	insoluble soap
Indian defence	inexpensively	injudiciously	insolvability
Indian English	inexperienced	injuriousness	in so many words
Indian fig tree	in expiation of	ink-jet printer	in some measure
Indianization	inexplainable	inland revenue	inspection-car
Indianologist	inexpressible	inlet manifold	inspectorship
Indian problem	inexpressibly	in-maintenance	inspirational
Indian pudding	infallibilism	innascibility	inspiritingly
Indian saffron	infallibilist	inner-directed	instabilities
Indian tobacco	infallibility	Inniskilliner	Instance Court
indicator lamp	infamous crime	innocent party	instantaneity
indifferently	infanticipate	in no condition	instantaneous
indigo bunting	infantilistic	innocuousness	instantiation
indiscernible	infantilities	innovationist	instant replay
indiscernibly	infant prodigy	innoxiousness	instinctively
indispensable	infant teacher	in obedience to	instinctually
indispensably	infeasibility	inobservation	institutional
indisposition	infectiveness	inoculability	instructional
indissociable	inferentially	inoffensively	instructively
indissuadable	inferior ovary	in one's element	instrumentary
indissuadably	inferribility	in one's hearing	insubmergible
indistinction	infiltrometer	in one's opinion	insubmersible
indistinctive	in fine feather	in one's own name	insubordinate
indisturbable	infinitesimal	in one's own time	insubstantial
indisturbance	infinitivally	inoperability	insufficience
individualise	inflectedness	inopportunely	insufficiency
individualism	inflexibility	inopportunism	insupportable
individualist	inflorescence	inopportunist	insupportably

insuppressive	interlocation	in the middle of	inusitateness
insurpassable	interlocution	in the movement	invaccination
insusceptible	interlocutory	in the nature of	invariability
intangibility	interlocutrix	in the negative	invectiveness
integrability	interlopation	in the person of	inventiveness
integrational	interlucation	in the pipeline	inventorially
integumentary	interlunation	in the recovery	invermination
intellectible	intermarriage	in the region of	Inverness cape
intelligenced	intermediator	in the same boat	inverse square
intelligencer	intermetallic	in the same ship	inverted comma
intelligently	intermittedly	in the shadow of	inverted pleat
intemperately	intermittence	in the short run	invertibility
intensionally	intermittency	in the smallest	investigation
intensive care	intermodalism	in the spud line	investigative
intensiveness	intermountain	in the swim with	investigatory
intentionally	internal clock	in the throes of	invidiousness
intentiveness	internal exile	in the vicinity	invincibility
interactional	internal organ	in the wind's eye	inviolability
interactively	internal rhyme	in the wrong box	inviolateness
interactivity	international	in this context	invisibleness
interalveolar	interneuronal	into matchwood	invita Minerva
inter-American	interoceptive	into the ground	involucellate
interarterial	interoperable	intoxicatedly	involuntarily
intercalarium	interosculate	intra-arterial	involutionary
intercalation	interparietal	intracapsular	inward-looking
intercalative	interpellator	intracellular	iodine scarlet
intercalatory	interpersonal	intracerebral	ion propulsion
intercellular	interpolation	intracultural	iontophoresis
interceptable	interpolative	intradermally	iontophoretic
interceptible	interpolatory	intra-European	iota subscript
interclavicle	interposition	intramuscular	ipsilaterally
intercolonial	interpretable	intranational	iridencleisis
intercolumnar	interpretress	intransigence	iridocyclitis
intercommoner	interproximal	intransigency	iridodialysis
intercommunal	interpunction	intransitable	iris diaphragm
intercommuner	interquartile	intransparent	Irish American
intercostally	interracially	intrapetiolar	Irishman's rise
intercropping	interrelation	intrapolation	iron bacterium
intercultural	interrogation	intraregional	iron in the fire
intercurrence	interrogative	intraspecific	ironmongeries
interdentally	interrogatory	intratelluric	irrationalise
interdigitate	interruptable	intrathecally	irrationalism
inter-dominion	interruptedly	intrathoracic	irrationalist
interesterify	interruptible	intratropical	irrationality
interest group	interscapular	intravarietal	irrationalize
interestingly	intersidereal	intravasation	irreciprocity
interfacially	interspecific	intravascular	irreclaimable
interfamilial	interspersion	intravenously	irreclaimably
interferingly	interstratify	intraversable	irrecognition
interferogram	intersyllabic	intricateness	irrecoverable
intergalactic	intertropical	intrinsically	irrecoverably
intergranular	intervarietal	introduceable	irrecuperable
interindustry	intervolution	introductress	irreflexivity
interior angle	in the abstract	introgression	irrefrangible
interjectural	in the concrete	introgressive	irrefrangibly
interlacement	in the course of	intropunitive	irrelevancies
interlamellar	in the doghouse	introspection	irreligionism
interlaminate	in the employ of	introspective	irreligionist
interlanguage	in the extremes	introversible	irreligiously
interlardment	in the majority	intrusiveness	irremunerable
interlinearly	in the manner of	intuitionally	irreplaceable
interlinguist	in the matter of	intuitiveness	irreplaceably

irrepleviable
irrepressible
irrepressibly
irresponsible
irresponsibly
irrestrictive
irretraceable
irretractable
irretrievable
irretrievably
irreverential
irrigationist
ischaemically
ischiorrhogic
isoagglutinin
isobarometric
isobathytherm
isocarboxazid
isochronously
isodimorphism
isodimorphous
isoelectronic
isogeothermal
isoionic point
isolatability
isolation camp
isomerization
isometrically
isomorphously
isophenomenal
isoproterenol
isostatically
isostructural
isothermobath
isotope effect
isotransplant
isotropically
Istrian marble
Italian garden
Italian millet
Italian stitch
italicization
itching powder
iterativeness
it is equal to me
it is whispered
it makes no odds
it remembers me
itsy-bitsiness
I will thank you
Ixionian wheel
jabberwockies
jackass barque
jackass-rigged
Jack cross-tree
Jack-in-a-bottle
Jack-in-the-bush
Jack-jump-about
Jacksonianism
Jack the Ripper
Jacob Evertsen
jakkalsbessie

Jamaica ginger
Jamaica pepper
Jamaica sorrel
janizary music
Jansenistical
Japanese anise
Japanese cedar
Japanese maple
Japanese paper
Japanese print
jargonization
jazzification
Jekyll and Hyde
jellification
jenny-long-legs
jerry-building
Jersey justice
Jerusalem pony
Jerusalem sage
jet propulsion
jeunesse dorée
jiggery-pokery
jingling match
Job's comforter
Johnny Crapaud
Johnny Newcome
Johnny penguin
Johnsonianism
jollification
Joseph and Mary
journal-letter
journey-weight
Judaeo-Spanish
judge advocate
judgementally
judgement debt
judgement-hall
judgement note
judgement-seat
Judge Ordinary
judge's marshal
judiciousness
Juggernautish
July high-flyer
July highflyer
jumping spider
jump in the lake
jump to the eyes
junction canal
junction diode
jungle-bashing
junior college
junior partner
junk jewellery
junk sculpture
Jupiter's beard
jurimetrician
jurisprudence
jury of inquiry
jury of matrons
justice in eyre
justiciarship

justification
justificative
justificatory
juvenile court
juxtaposition
juxtapositive
kachina dancer
kaleidoscopic
kangaroo apple
kangaroo court
kangaroo-grass
kangaroo mouse
kangaroo thorn
kaolinization
kapellmeister
Kate Greenaway
kathenotheism
katjiepiering
keeled scraper
keen as mustard
keep account of
keep an eye open
keep one's end up
keep one's peace
keep one's state
keep open house
keep the pledge
keep to oneself
Kelvin balance
Kenilworth ivy
Kennelly layer
Kensingtonian
Kentish plover
Kentucky Derby
Kentucky rifle
Kenyanization
Kepler problem
keratinolysis
keratinolytic
keratohyaline
keratomalacia
kermes mineral
kettledrummer
kettle moraine
keyhole limpet
Keystone State
khaki election
Khrushchevian
Khrushchevism
kick one's heels
kick the bucket
kick up a shindy
Kidderminster
kiddie brother
kidney machine
Killarney fern
killing bottle
killing-circle
Kilmarnock cap
kilogram-force
kilogram-metre
kind-heartedly

kindred spirit
kinematically
kinematograph
kinesiologist
kinetic energy
kinetic theory
kinetogenesis
kinetonucleus
King in Council
king of terrors
King's Attorney
King's Champion
King's evidence
King's Serjeant
King's shilling
Kingston valve
Kirchhoff's law
kiss goodbye to
kissing-comfit
kissing cousin
kiss-in-the-ring
kiss the ground
kist o' whistles
kitchen garden
Kitchen Kaffir
kitchen midden
kitchen police
Kitchen rudder
kitchen shower
kittenishness
kitty-cornered
Kjeldahl flask
knickerbocker
knick-knackery
knick-knackish
knife-throwing
knight marshal
knight-service
Knight Templar
knit one's brows
knock-on effect
knockout drops
knock sideways
knock spots off
knock together
know backwards
know inside out
knowledgeable
knowledgeably
knowledge base
knowledgeless
knowledgement
know like a book
know one's place
know one's stuff
know to speak to
know what's what
knuckleduster
knuckle timber
knuckle-walker
Knudsen number
Koch's bacillus

Komodo monitor	lappet-weaving	leap in the dark	letter-perfect
Krag Ørgensen	lapsus linguae	learner driver	letter-quality
Kremnitz white	larch leaf cast	learning curve	letters patent
Ku Klux Klanner	larding needle	learn the ropes	lettre bâtarde
Kundalini yoga	larviposition	least chipmunk	lettre de forme
labialization	laryngealized	leather beetle	lettre de somme
laboriousness	laryngectomee	leather-flower	Letzeburgesch
labour brigade	laryngologist	leather-headed	leukaemogenic
Labour Weekend	laryngoscopic	leather-jacket	Levant morocco
labyrinth fish	laryngotomies	leatherjacket	level crossing
labyrinthical	Last Judgement	leather-turtle	level-headedly
labyrinthitis	latchkey child	leave away from	levelling pole
Lacedaemonian	latent partner	leave it at that	lexicographer
lace-leaf plant	lateroflexion	leave standing	lexicographic
lachrymal vase	lateroversion	leave word with	lexicological
lachrymogenic	Latin American	lecherousness	lexigraphical
lackadaisical	Latin language	lectisternium	Lexiphanicism
lacrosse-stick	latitudinally	left at the post	Liberal-Labour
lactobacillus	latrine rumour	left-hand drive	liberationism
lactoglobulin	lattice energy	left-hand screw	liberationist
lactonization	lattice filter	legal capacity	liberty bodice
ladder polymer	lattice girder	legate a latere	Liberty bodice
ladies' fingers	lattice window	Legion disease	librarianship
Ladies' Gallery	laughableness	legislational	library school
Lady Bountiful	laughing death	legislatively	lichenicolous
lady-in-waiting	laughing goose	legislatorial	lichenivorous
lady of leisure	laughing hyena	leishmaniasis	lichenologist
lady's bedstraw	laughing stock	leishmaniosis	lichenometric
lady's ear-drops	launching-ways	Leishman stain	lickerishness
laevorotation	Launder-Ometer	leisure centre	lick into shape
laevorotatory	lauryl alcohol	leisureliness	lick one's chops
laevotartaric	lavatory paper	lemmatization	Lieberkühnian
laevotartrate	lavatory style	lemon-coloured	Liebfraumilch
lagophthalmia	lavender-water	lemon geranium	lie down and die
lagophthalmic	Law Commission	lemon-squeezer	lie on the gavel
lagophthalmos	law of averages	lend oneself to	lie on the table
laissez-passer	Lawson cypress	lenticularity	lieutenancies
Lamarckianism	Laxton's Superb	lenticulation	life assurance
Lambeth degree	lay by the heels	lepidocrocite	Life Guardsman
lambing season	lay down the law	lepidodendron	life insurance
lamb's quarters	lay emphasis on	lepidopterist	life-preserver
lamellibranch	layer dressing	lepidopterous	life scientist
lamellipodium	lay in the earth	lepidosaurian	lifting-bridge
laminagraphic	lay on one's oars	leptocephalic	lift one's elbow
lampadephoria	lay on the table	leptocephalus	lift one's hands
lance corporal	lay the blame on	leptokurtosis	lift up the horn
lance-sergeant	lazuli bunting	leptoprosopic	light-demander
land-community	lead by the ears	leptospirosis	light-fastness
landed plunger	lead by the nose	leschenaultia	lightfastness
landgraveship	lead guitarist	lesser noctule	light-fingered
landing ticket	leading-in wire	lesser omentum	light-footedly
land-measuring	leading rating	let a thing ride	light-headedly
land of promise	leading seaman	let down gently	light horseman
Land of the Free	leading-string	let George do it	light industry
landownership	leading wheels	lethal chamber	light infantry
land-surveying	lead-pipe cinch	lethargically	lighting tower
language shift	lead poisoning	let it go at that	lightlessness
langue de boeuf	leaf-arrowhead	letter-balance	lightsomeness
languishingly	leaf-butterfly	letter-carrier	lignification
languish under	leafcutter ant	letter-founder	lignitiferous
laparoscopies	leafcutter bee	letter-heading	like a bad penny
laparoscopist	lean to one side	letter missive	like a millpond

like clockwork	little theatre	Lord Treasurer	macro-economic
like grim death	liturgistical	lose one's block	macroeconomic
like lightning	live extempore	lose one's heart	macroglobulin
like one o'clock	live in oneself	lose one's nerve	macromolecule
lily of the vale	live like a lord	lose one's shirt	macronutrient
limb-darkening	liver chestnut	lose one's touch	macrophysical
lime-marmalade	liver-coloured	lose one's voice	macroscopical
limestone fern	livery company	lose sleep over	macrotrichium
limitlessness	livery servant	lose touch with	maculopapular
limnoplankton	live to oneself	lost in thought	Madagascarian
Lincoln rocker	living image of	Lotka-Volterra	mad cow disease
linear algebra	living picture	lotus position	made to measure
linearization	living theatre	Louis-Philippe	Madison Avenue
linear measure	Lloyd-Georgian	lovers' quarrel	madreporarian
line engraving	loaded for bear	low-definition	madrigalesque
line-finishing	loading shovel	lower one's eyes	maduromycosis
line-fisherman	load-water-line	lower one's flag	magazine cover
line frequency	loathsomeness	low-mindedness	magazine story
linen-armourer	loath-to-depart	low side window	magic mushroom
linen-cupboard	Lobachevskian	low technology	magisterially
line of country	lobster bisque	lubricational	magistratical
line of defence	local exchange	luck of the draw	magnanimously
line of fortune	local preacher	lucrativeness	magnetic field
line one's purse	loculicidally	ludicrousness	magnetic north
lingua francas	locum tenentes	Ludwig's angina	magnetic storm
lingual ribbon	locus ceruleus	luggage locker	magnetization
lingue franche	lodge-pole pine	lumirhodopsin	magnetometric
linguistician	logarithmical	lunar distance	magnetomotive
linolenic acid	logical syntax	lunatic asylum	magneto-optics
linsey-woolsey	logistic curve	lunatic fringe	magnetosphere
lip microphone	logit analysis	lunisolar year	magnetostatic
lipodystrophy	logodaedalist	lupus vulgaris	magnification
lipogrammatic	logodiarrhoea	luteinization	magnificently
lipolytically	logographical	luxuriousness	magniloquence
liqueur brandy	lollipop woman	lycanthropist	magnitudinous
liqueur whisky	Lombard Street	lymphadenitis	Magnolia State
liquid compass	Londonization	lymphoblastic	Magyarization
liquid crystal	long-acuminate	lymphocytosis	Maharashtrian
liquid measure	long-case clock	lymphomatosis	mahogany birch
liquid starter	long-continued	lymphopoiesis	maiden-servant
liquorice-root	longiloquence	lymphopoietic	maiden's wreath
liquorishness	longlivedness	lymphorrhagia	maiden thought
listenability	long-sightedly	lymphosarcoma	maid of all work
listening post	long-suffering	macaronically	Mainland China
list processor	long-tailed mag	Macassar ebony	mainstreeting
literal-minded	long-tailed tit	Macaulayesque	Maintenon chop
literary agent	long time no see	machiavellian	maison de passe
lithia-emerald	look askance at	machiavellism	maison de santé
lithification	look daggers at	machiavellist	maison tolérée
lithiophilite	look forward to	machicolation	maitres d'hôtel
lithontriptic	look into space	machinability	Majorana force
lithotripsies	loose coupling	machine finish	major-domoship
litigiousness	lophotrichous	machine-gunner	Major Mitchell
little bittern	lord and master	machine-minder	make account of
little-boy-lost	lord-in-waiting	machine-pistol	make a fine hand
little Masters	Lord love a duck	machine-tooled	make a fuss over
Little Masters	Lord of Misrule	mackerel shark	make a good fist
little mastery	Lord of Sabaoth	macroanalysis	make a market of
Little Red Book	lord of the soil	macrocephalia	make a martyr of
Little Russian	lord paramount	macrocephalic	make a monkey of
little scarlet	Lord Privy Seal	macroclimatic	make a muddle of
little science	Lords temporal	macrodiagonal	make an attempt

make an issue of	manneristical	mastoidectomy	medicine chest
make a secret of	man of his hands	Matara diamond	medicine glass
make a wry mouth	man of pleasure	matchableness	medicine lodge
make expiation	man of the cloth	matchboarding	medicine stamp
make good cheer	man of the house	match dissolve	medicine woman
make good speed	man of the match	matched orders	Medieval Greek
make in one's way	man of the world	Mater Dolorosa	Medieval Latin
make mention of	manufactories	materfamilias	Mediterranean
make merry over	many-sidedness	material cause	medium bowling
make no mistake	maple molasses	material clerk	medium close-up
make nothing of	map projection	materialistic	meet one's Maker
make one's début	maraging steel	material thing	meet one's match
make one's peace	marbled beauty	materia medica	meet-the-people
make reprisals	marble orchard	maternalistic	megacephalous
make residence	march fracture	mathematician	megakaryocyte
make semblance	marching order	mathematicise	megaloblastic
make the best of	marconigraphy	mathematicism	megalocephaly
make the domino	Marek's disease	mathematicize	megalopolitan
make the fur fly	margin of error	matinée jacket	megalosaurian
make the most of	margin release	matriculation	megalospheric
make the papers	mariculturist	matriculatory	megastructure
make the riffle	marigold apple	matrilineally	meibomian cyst
make the rounds	marine biology	matrilocality	Meistersinger
make to measure	marine railway	matrimonially	melamine resin
make tracks for	marine science	matrimony vine	melancholious
malabsorption	marine trumpet	matrix printer	melanogenesis
malacological	mariposa tulip	matter subject	mellifluously
malacostracan	marketability	Matthew Walker	melodiousness
maladaptation	market economy	Matura diamond	melodramatics
maladaptively	market shooter	mature economy	melodramatise
maladjustment	marking cotton	mature student	melodramatist
maladminister	marking stitch	mauvaise honte	melodramatize
maladroitness	marmalade plum	Maxwell's demon	member country
malapropistic	marmalade tree	May and January	membranaceous
malariologist	marquois scale	meadow parsnip	membranogenic
male menopause	mar resistance	meadow saffron	membranophone
malgovernment	marriage lines	meals on wheels	membrum virile
maliciousness	marrons glacés	mean deviation	memorableness
Mallaby-Deeley	marrow pudding	meaninglessly	memory mapping
malleableness	marry a fortune	mean solar time	Mendelssohnic
malleo-incudal	marsh marigold	means-testable	meningococcal
malobservance	marsh samphire	measurability	meningococcus
malt-distiller	marsipobranch	measurelessly	mensurability
Malthusianism	marsupial bone	measure swords	mensurational
mammaliferous	marsupial mole	measuring cast	mental cruelty
manageability	Martello tower	measuring tape	mental healing
managerialism	martyrization	measuring worm	mental hygiene
managerialist	martyrologies	meat-and-potato	mental illness
Manchesterian	martyrologist	meat breakfast	mental patient
Manchesterism	Marxistically	meat poisoning	menticultural
Manchesterize	masculineness	mechanicalism	mento-vertical
Mandelbrot set	mashie-niblick	mechanicalist	Mercalli scale
manganapatite	massification	mechanicality	mercenariness
manganese spar	mass of requiem	mechanicalize	mercerization
manganiferous	Master Aircrew	mechanization	merchant fleet
mangold-wurzel	master-builder	medial cadence	merchant guild
Manichaeistic	masterfulness	median section	mercilessness
manifestation	master mariner	mediastinitis	mercurialness
manifestative	masters-at-arms	mediatization	Mercurochrome
manifold paper	master's degree	medical garden	mercury vapour
Manila cheroot	masticability	medical school	meridionality
manipulatable	mastigophoric	medicamentary	merit increase

meritocracies	methodologist	Middle Eastern	misanthropise
meritoriously	methohexitone	Middle England	misanthropist
mermaid's purse	methyl alcohol	Middle English	misanthropize
mescal buttons	methylbenzene	Middle Kingdom	misappreciate
mesencephalic	methylene blue	middle lamella	misascription
mesencephalon	metonymically	middle manager	misbecomingly
mesmerization	metoposcopist	middlemanship	miscalculator
mesmerizingly	metrification	middle passage	miscatalogued
mesocephalism	metrizability	Middle Pointed	miscegenation
mesquite-grass	metronidazole	Middle Western	miscellaneous
messengership	Mexican dollar	mid-life crisis	mischief-maker
messenger wire	Mexican-Indian	midnight feast	mischief night
Messianically	Mexican orange	Midsummer's Day	mischievously
mess of pottage	mezza-majolica	might-have-been	miscomprehend
metabolically	mezzo-rilievos	migmatization	misconception
metabolizable	mezzo-sopranos	Mikimoto pearl	misconjecture
metachromasia	micellization	milieu therapy	misconnection
metachromatic	Mickey-mousing	military braid	misdoubtfully
metachronally	micrencephaly	military brush	misemployment
metafictional	microanalyser	military chest	miserableness
metagrobolize	microanalysis	Military Cross	misestimation
metal detector	microaneurysm	Military Medal	misexpression
metalliferous	microbiologic	milk chocolate	misexpressive
metallization	microcellular	milk of almonds	misfunctional
metallochrome	microcephalic	milk of sulphur	misgovernance
metallochromy	microcephalus	milk the market	misgovernment
metalloenzyme	microchemical	millennialism	misguidedness
metallography	microclimatic	millennialist	misidentified
metallurgical	microcomputer	milliamperage	misidentifies
metalogically	microcosmical	millionaires	misimpression
metamerically	microcracking	millionairish	mismanagement
metamorphoser	micro-economic	million-dollar	misobservance
metamorphoses	microeconomic	million-seller	misperception
metamorphosic	microfelsitic	millionth part	mispersuasion
metamorphosis	microfilament	mill privilege	misproportion
metamorphotic	microfloppies	millstone grit	misshapenness
metaphosphate	microfracture	millwrighting	missiological
metaphysician	microgranitic	minaciousness	missionary box
metaphysicise	micrographics	mind-bendingly	Mississippian
metaphysicize	microhardness	mind-blowingly	missive letter
metapolitical	microlighting	mind-expanding	miss one's guess
metapsychosis	micrometeoric	mind-numbingly	mistletoe bird
metarhodopsin	micrometrical	mineragraphic	mistresspiece
metastability	micronization	mineralizable	mistrustfully
metasyncrisis	micronutrient	mineralogical	mistrustingly
metasyncritic	micro-organism	mineral purple	misunderstand
metatarsalgia	microperthite	mineral tallow	misunderstood
metempiricism	microphyllous	mineral violet	Mitchell grass
metempiricist	microphysical	mineral yellow	mitochondrial
metempsychose	microplankton	miner's disease	mitochondrion
metencephalic	microporosity	miner's lettuce	mixed blessing
metencephalon	microprinting	miniature golf	mixed feelings
met-enkephalin	microscopical	minikin string	mixed language
meteoric stone	microsurgical	ministerially	mixed marriage
meteoriticist	microteaching	minster church	mixed metaphor
meteorologist	microtonality	mint condition	mixed-pressure
methanoic acid	microvascular	mirror nucleus	mix one's drinks
methapyrilene	microwaveable	mirror nuclide	M'Naghten rules
methemoglobin	microwave oven	mirror writing	mnemotechnics
Methodistical	Middle Academy	mirthlessness	moaning minnie
methodization	Middle America	misadjustment	moaning Minnie
methodologies	Middle Britain	misallocation	moccasin snake

model dwelling	monomolecular	morphonologic	mourning-piece
moderate a call	monomorphemic	morphophoneme	mourning widow
moderationist	mononucleated	morphophonics	mouse-coloured
moderatorship	mononucleosis	morphopoiesis	Moussorgskian
modern English	monophasicity	morphopoietic	moustacheless
modern history	monophthalmic	morphotactics	moustache tern
modernization	monophthongal	morphotropism	mouth-watering
modifiability	monophysitism	morris dancing	movable kidney
modus operandi	monopolizable	morselization	move mountains
moist gangrene	monopolylogue	mortality rate	moving average
moisture cream	Monopoly money	mort d'ancestor	moving picture
moisture meter	monopoly value	mortification	mowing-machine
molecular heat	monopsonistic	mortifiedness	muckle-mouthed
molinological	monosexuality	mosaic disease	muck-spreading
mollification	monosignative	mosquito fleet	mucocutaneous
mollificative	monosiphonous	mother-and-babe	muddle through
molluscicidal	monosyllabism	mother complex	Muhammadanism
molluscum body	monosymmetric	mother country	mulberry molar
momentariness	monothalamous	mother-fucking	mule-ear rabbit
moment of truth	Monothelitism	motherfucking	Müller-Thurgau
momentousness	monotocardian	Mother Hubbard	Mull of Kintyre
momentum space	monotonically	mother-of-pearl	multicellular
monachization	monotrematous	mother of thyme	multicoloured
monadological	monsoon forest	Mother Shipton	multicultural
Monarchianism	monstriferous	motion picture	multifilament
monarchically	monstrosities	motor accident	multifunction
Monday-clubber	monstrousness	motosensitive	multilamellar
Mondayishness	Montefiascone	mottled beauty	multilevelled
Monday morning	Montepulciano	mouldableness	multilinguist
monepiscopacy	montes Veneris	moulding-board	multilocation
money-grubbing	Montserratian	moulding-plane	multiloquence
money illusion	monumentalise	mountain avens	multimodalism
money-spinning	monumentalism	mountain chain	multinational
Mongolian fold	monumentality	mountain daisy	multi-negative
Mongolian spot	monumentalize	mountain devil	multi-partyism
Mongolization	mood-elevating	mountain ebony	multipersonal
monimolimnion	moon-blindness	mountain fever	multiple birth
monkeyishness	moonlight flit	mountain finch	multiple fruit
monkey-pod tree	mooring swivel	mountain green	multiple image
monoaminergic	mops and brooms	mountain heath	multiple ratio
monocarbonate	morale-booster	mountain maple	multiple shift
monocephalous	morality squad	mountainously	multiple store
monochromatic	moral majority	mountain pansy	multiplicable
monochromator	moral pressure	mountain pride	multiplicator
monocistronic	moral sciences	mountain quail	multiplicious
monocondylian	morbid anatomy	mountain range	multipolarity
monocotyledon	morbillivirus	mountain sheep	multi-position
monoculturist	more hispanico	mountains high	multi-positive
monodactylous	Moreton Bay fig	mountain slide	multipresence
monodialectal	Mormon cricket	mountain tiger	multiracially
monodramatist	morning coffee	mountain trout	multiserially
monoenergetic	morning prayer	mountainwards	multispectral
monogamically	morphallactic	mountain witch	multi-threaded
monogenically	morphemically	mountain zebra	multi-tracking
monoglyceride	morphinomania	mountebankery	multitudinism
monogrammatic	morphiomaniac	mountebankism	multitudinous
monographical	morphogenesis	mounting block	multivibrator
monohybridism	morphogenetic	mournful widow	multivocality
monomeniscous	morphographer	mourning bride	mumbo-jumboism
monometallism	morpholexical	mourning cloak	mummification
monometallist	morphological	mourning coach	Munchausenism
monomineralic	morphometrics	mourning-paper	municipal bond

municipalizer
Munsterlander
murder inquiry
murder mystery
murderousness
murder will out
murmurousness
murrhine glass
muscle current
muscle-flexing
muscle spindle
museographist
mushroom cloud
mushroom-coral
mushroom-faker
mushroom spawn
mushroom-stone
mushroom valve
musical chairs
musical comedy
music cassette
musicological
musquash house
mussel-cracker
mussel-crusher
mustard colour
mustard weevil
mutton quadrat
mutton snapper
mutualization
muzzle-loading
mycetophagous
mycobacterial
mycobacterium
mycologically
mycoplasmosis
mycotoxicosis
my grandmother
my noble friend
myoepithelial
myoepithelium
myringoplasty
myrmecologist
myrmecophagid
myrobalan plum
myrtle warbler
my sainted aunt
mysteriosophy
mystery writer
mystification
mystificatory
mythicization
mythification
mythopoetical
mytho-theology
myxobacterial
myxobacterium
myxoedematous
naked flooring
Namaqua grouse
namby-pambyism
name of the game

Namierization
naming of parts
nankeen cotton
nannoplankton
nape of the neck
Napoleonistic
narcomaniacal
narcotization
narrative line
narratologist
narrowcasting
narrow fabrics
Natal mahogany
national flour
National Front
national guard
National Guard
nationalistic
nationalities
National Party
National Trust
native fuchsia
native kumquat
native speaker
natural cosine
natural number
natural person
natural spirit
natural virtue
nature reserve
navicular bone
navigableness
navigation act
navigation law
Neanderthaler
Neapolitan ice
near one's heart
near-sightedly
nebular theory
necessariness
necessitarian
necessitation
necessitously
necklace shell
neck or nothing
necrotization
nectariferous
nectarivorous
nectocalycine
needle bearing
needle contest
needle-pointed
needless to say
nefariousness
negative-going
negative pedal
neglectedness
negligibility
negotiability
negrification
Negro minstrel
neighbourhead

neighbourhood
neighbourless
neighbour-like
neighbourship
nemathelminth
nematological
neocerebellar
neocerebellum
neoclassicism
neoclassicist
neoglaciation
neogrammarian
neo-linguistic
neolithically
neologization
neo-Malthusian
Neo-Melanesian
neonatologist
neontological
neo-plasticism
Neo-Synephrine
nephelometric
nephrectomize
nephridiopore
nephritic wood
nephrorrhaphy
nerve-deafness
nervelessness
nervous system
Netherlandian
Netherlandish
nether regions
network former
neuralgically
neural network
neuraminidase
neurapophysis
neurobiotaxis
neuroblastoma
neuro-effector
neuroelectric
neuroethology
neurofibrilla
neurofilament
neurohormonal
neuromuscular
neurone theory
neuronophagia
neurosurgical
neurosyphilis
neurotoxicity
neuter passive
neutral corner
neutral monism
neutral monist
neutron excess
neutron number
new Australian
New Australian
New Caledonian
New Englandish
New Englandism

newfanglement
newfangleness
Newgate school
New Journalism
New Journalist
new psychology
news-gathering
newsmongering
newspaperland
newspaperless
new technology
Newtown pippin
new world order
New Zealand ash
New Zealandism
New Zealand rug
New Zealand tit
Nicaragua wood
Nicene Council
nickel-and-dime
nickeliferous
nickelization
Nicolaitanism
nicotinic acid
niggardliness
nigger-shooter
night-blooming
nightclubbing
nightmarishly
night-primrose
night-wanderer
night-watching
night-watchman
nightwatchman
Nikkei average
Nile crocodile
nincompoopery
nincompoopish
Nine Days' Queen
nitrification
nitrile rubber
nitro compound
nitrofurazone
nitrogenation
nitrogen cycle
nitrogen fixer
nitroglycerin
nitromuriatic
nitroprusside
nitwittedness
nivellization
Nobel laureate
no-claims bonus
noctivagation
no great shakes
no great things
no holds barred
noiselessness
nolle prosequi
nomen actionis
nomenclatural
nominalizable

nominal ledger	noradrenaline	nucleoprotein	occipital bone
nomologically	noradrenergic	nuisance value	occipital lobe
non-acceptance	Norfolk Howard	null character	occluded front
non-advertence	Norfolk jacket	nullification	occupationist
non-aggression	Norfolk plover	null indicator	oceanographer
non-allergenic	normalization	number-average	oceanographic
non-appearance	Norman English	numbers racket	oceanological
non-attachment	Normanization	numerological	ocean pipefish
non-attendance	normativeness	Numidian crane	ochlocratical
non-biological	normovolaemia	numismatology	octave coupler
non-centrality	normovolaemic	nuncupatively	octocentenary
non-classified	North American	Nuremberg Laws	octocorallian
non-collegiate	north and south	nursery cannon	oculist's stamp
non-compliance	north-easterly	nursery garden	Oddfellowship
non-compounder	north-eastward	nursery school	odontoblastic
non-condensing	northerliness	nursery slopes	odontoglossum
non-conducting	northern canoe	nursery stakes	odontological
nonconformism	Northern Crown	nursing-father	odontophorous
Nonconformism	Northern Irish	nursing-mother	odoriferously
nonconformist	North Germanic	Nusselt number	odourlessness
nonconformity	North Islander	nutmeg hickory	odynometrical
non-contagious	north-westerly	nutritionally	oesophagocele
non-contingent	north-westward	nutritiveness	oesophagotomy
non-cooperator	nortriptyline	obedience test	oestrogenized
nondescriptly	Norway haddock	obedientially	oestrous cycle
non-disclosure	Norway lemming	obedient plant	of all the cheek
non-evaluative	Norway lobster	objectifiable	of all the nerve
non-figurative	Norwich school	objectionable	of a parcel with
non-fulfilment	nose-suspended	objectionably	of a set purpose
non-functional	nosologically	objectivation	of consequence
non-homologous	nostalgically	objective lens	of evil presage
non-infectious	not before time	objectiveness	off and running
non-intervener	not care a whoop	objectivistic	offencelessly
non-membership	notch-planting	object of virtu	offensiveness
non-naturalism	not come to much	object program	offhandedness
non-naturalist	not for a moment	objects clause	officer of arms
non-negotiable	not give a stuff	objurgatorily	officiousness
non-observance	not go anywhere	obliquangular	off microphone
non-occurrence	not good enough	oblique motion	off one's own bat
non-orientable	nothing to lose	oblique speech	off one's rocker
non-parametric	no through road	oblique sphere	off one's rocket
non-perception	noticeability	oblique stroke	off one's stroke
non-performing	not made of salt	obliviousness	of little avail
non-persistent	not miss a trick	obnoxiousness	of one's own head
non-physically	not one's idea of	observability	of some account
nonplussation	not on your life	observational	of the nature of
non-productive	notoriousness	observatories	of unsound mind
non-randomness	not sufficient	obsessionally	oil and vinegar
non-regulation	not want to know	obsessiveness	oil of lavender
non-residenter	noun adjective	obstetrically	oil one's tongue
non-resistance	nouvelle vague	obstructingly	oil the knocker
non-returnable	novel of terror	obstructively	Olbers' paradox
non-scientific	noviciateship	obtainability	old-age pension
nonsense verse	nuclear energy	obtenebration	old as the hills
nonsensically	nuclear family	obtrusiveness	old boy network
non-specialist	nuclear fusion	occasionalism	old clothes man
non-subscriber	nuclear isomer	occasionality	old-field birch
non-successful	nuclear weapon	occidentalise	old-field mouse
non-uniformity	nuclear winter	occidentalism	old gooseberry
non-verbalized	nucleogenesis	occidentalist	Old High German
non-volatility	nucleohistone	occidentality	old-maidenhood
Nootka cypress	nucleoplasmic	occidentalize	old witch-grass

oleomargarine	on the downside	order of battle	oscilloscopic
oleo-pneumatic	on the face of it	order of the day	os intermedium
olfactometric	on the forehand	ordinal number	Osiride column
oligarticular	on the gridiron	ordinary grade	Oslo breakfast
oligochaetous	on the increase	ordinary level	osmoregulator
oligopolistic	on the pavement	ordinary scale	ossiculectomy
oligosaprobic	on the pig's back	ordinary share	ostensibility
oligosyllabic	on the port tack	ordinary table	ostensiveness
olive-coloured	on the premises	ordnance datum	osteoclastoma
olive crescent	on the safe side	organicalness	osteomyelitis
olive whistler	on the scrounge	organogenesis	osteopetrosis
olivine basalt	on the straight	organogenetic	osteopetrotic
Ollendorffian	on the strength	organographic	ostracization
Olympia oyster	ontogenetical	organological	ostreiculture
ombudsmanship	ontogenically	organoplastic	ostreoculture
omnibus volume	ontologically	organotherapy	ostreophagous
omnicompetent	onychomycosis	orgiastically	ostrobogulous
omnipresently	onychophagist	orientability	Ostyak Samoyed
omniprevalent	opacification	orientalizing	Oswego biscuit
omnisubjugant	open admission	oriental plane	Otaheite apple
on a good wicket	open-bill stork	oriental poppy	other-directed
on a person's top	open-circuited	oriental topaz	otitis externa
on approbation	open classroom	orientational	otitis interna
on bended knees	open Communion	Orient Express	otter-trawling
once and for all	open community	orient oneself	outblossoming
once upon a time	open-endedness	originalities	outdoor relief
onchocercosis	open enrolment	original print	outdoor things
ondes martenot	open occupancy	or I'm a Dutchman	outer garments
one and another	open the door to	orismological	outing flannel
one and the same	operating room	ornamentalism	out like a light
one for the book	operationally	ornamentalist	outline stitch
one for the road	operativeness	ornamentality	out of a bandbox
one-handedness	ophthalmology	ornamentalize	out of all sight
one in a million	ophthalmotomy	ornamentation	out of harm's way
oneiroscopist	opinionatedly	ornithischian	out of love with
one man one vote	opisthobranch	ornithologist	out of one's hair
one never knows	opossum-shrimp	ornithologize	out of one's head
one-night stand	opportuneness	ornithopodous	out of one's line
one's blood is up	opportunistic	oropharyngeal	out of one's mind
one's level best	opportunities	orthocephalic	out of one's road
one's little all	oppositionary	orthoepically	out of one's time
one's name is mud	oppositionist	orthogenetics	out of one's tree
one's worse half	opprobriously	orthognathism	out of one's wits
one-time-cipher	optical centre	orthognathous	out of position
one way or other	optical double	orthogonality	out of practice
on its own roots	optical isomer	orthogonalize	out of register
onlie begetter	optical square	orthographies	out of straight
on oiled wheels	optic neuritis	orthographist	out of the woods
onomatologist	opticokinetic	orthographize	out of training
onomatopoeian	optic thalamus	orthohydrogen	outrecuidance
onomatopoeics	optional extra	orthologously	outriggerless
onomatopoesis	oral-formulaic	orthomorphism	outsettlement
onomatopoetic	orange blossom	orthophotomap	outspokenness
on one's account	orange-quarter	orthopinacoid	outstandingly
on one's hunkers	orbital sander	orthopoxvirus	outward things
on one's own hook	orchard oriole	orthoptically	ovariectomies
on pain of death	orchesography	orthopyroxene	ovariectomize
on solid ground	orchestralist	orthosilicate	ovariotomized
on tenterhooks	orchestra seat	orthotectonic	over-abundance
on the backhand	orchestration	oryctological	overabundance
on the beam-ends	orchidologist	oscillography	overambitious
on the contrary	orciprenaline	oscillometric	over-anxiously

overanxiously	over the sticks	palaeocrystic	Pantagruelist
overattention	overvaluation	palaeocurrent	pantheistical
overbearingly	overventilate	palaeoecology	pantisocratic
overcarefully	overvulcanize	palaeo-equator	pantomography
overcivilized	overweeningly	palaeogeology	papaveraceous
overcloseness	overwhelmment	palaeographer	paper carriage
overcommitted	ovipositional	palaeographic	paper-fastener
overconcerned	ovi-viviparous	palaeogravity	paper mulberry
overconfident	ovoviviparity	palaeoniscoid	paper nautilus
overcredulity	ovoviviparous	palaeontology	paper shredder
overcredulous	owlet-nightjar	palaeopallial	paper streamer
over-curiosity	own-categories	palaeopallium	papilliferous
overcuriosity	owner-occupied	palaeospecies	papillomatous
overcuriously	owner-occupier	palaeotechnic	papulo-vesicle
overdecorated	oxalosuccinic	palaeotherian	papyrographic
overdetermine	Oxford corners	palaeozoology	papyrological
overdischarge	Oxford marbles	palagonitized	parabolically
overdispersed	Oxford mixture	palais de danse	paracaseinate
overdramatise	Oxford ragwort	palatableness	paradigm shift
overdramatize	Oxford sausage	palatine uvula	paradise apple
overdraw check	Oxford scholar	palatographic	paradise crane
overeagerness	Oxford Scholar	palatorrhaphy	paradise stock
overearnestly	ox-heart cherry	paleanthropic	paradisically
over-elaborate	oxidizability	palimbacchius	paradoxically
overelaborate	oystercatcher	palingenesian	paraganglioma
over-emotional	oyster-farming	palinspastics	paragrammatic
overemotional	ozone-friendly	palisade layer	paragraphical
overemphasise	ozonification	palletization	para-influenza
overemphasize	pace tanti viri	Palmerstonian	parakeratosis
overexcitable	packet network	Palmerstonism	parakeratotic
overextension	packing needle	Palmetto State	paraleipomena
overflowingly	pack on all sail	palpitatingly	paralipomenon
overforwardly	padding stitch	palynological	parallax error
overfurnished	paddle steamer	palynomorphic	parallelistic
overhastiness	paddle-wheeler	pampas flicker	parallelogram
overhead valve	Paddy's lantern	pan-Africander	paralytically
overhydration	Paddy's lucerne	pan-Africanism	paramagnetism
overinclusion	pad in the straw	pan Africanist	paramenstruum
over-indulgent	paediatrician	Panama disease	paramountship
overindulgent	paedomorphism	panatela cigar	paramyoclonus
over-insurance	pageant master	pancake batter	paramyxovirus
overinsurance	page reference	panchromatize	paranoiacally
overmasterful	page three girl	panchronistic	paranormality
overmastering	pain in the arse	pancratiastic	paraphernalia
overofficious	pain in the neck	pandemoniacal	paraphrasable
overpopulated	painstakingly	pandiculation	parapolitical
overpotential	painted beauty	panegyrically	parapophysial
overprecision	painterliness	panel analysis	parapsoriasis
over-prescribe	painter's brush	panel painting	parareligious
overprescribe	painter's colic	panentheistic	parascientist
overpublicize	Painter's Easel	pangrammatist	parasexuality
overqualified	pain threshold	panharmonicon	parasitically
overreadiness	paint stripper	panic stations	parasiticidal
overrunningly	pair-formation	panic-stricken	parasitopolis
oversaturated	pairing-season	panic-striking	parasymbiosis
oversensitive	pair of bellows	pannier pocket	parasymbiotic
oversharpness	pair of colours	panoramically	parasynthesis
overshot wheel	pair of pincers	pan-Protestant	parasynthetic
overstatement	Palaeo-Asiatic	panpsychistic	parasyntheton
overstimulate	palaeobiology	pansporoblast	paratragoedia
overstitching	palaeobotanic	Pantagruelian	paravertebral
oversubscribe	palaeoclimate	Pantagruelism	parcel-gilding

parcelization	Passion Sunday	pedal keyboard	penuriousness
parchment glue	passive smoker	pedal wireless	Penzance brier
parchment-lace	passivization	pedantocratic	People's Bureau
parchment-skin	passport photo	pedestal basin	people's choice
pareiasaurian	Pasteur effect	pedestal table	People's Palace
parencephalon	pastoral lease	pedestrianate	pepper-and-salt
parent company	pastoral staff	pedestrianise	peppered steak
parenthetical	patentability	pedestrianism	peppermint gum
parent–teacher	patent insides	pedestrianize	peppermint oil
parepididymal	patent leather	pediculicidal	peppermint-tea
parepididymis	patent theatre	pedimentation	peptidoglycan
Pareto-optimal	paterfamilias	pediplanation	peptizability
pare to the bone	paternalistic	pedlar's French	peptonization
par excellence	paternity suit	pedogenetical	peralkalinity
parish council	paternity test	pedogenically	perambulation
parish lantern	pathogenicity	pedologically	perambulatory
parish pumpery	pathognomical	pedunculation	perceivedness
Parisian cloth	pathognomonic	pelican-flower	perceptualize
Parker's cement	patriarchally	pellagragenic	percussion cap
parking ticket	patriarchical	pelletization	percussion gun
Parkinson's law	patricianship	Peloponnesian	percussionist
parlementaire	patrilineally	pelycosaurian	perdurability
parliamentary	patrilocality	penalty clause	perdu sentinel
parliamenteer	patrimonially	penalty double	peregrination
parliament man	patriotically	penalty killer	peregrinatory
Parnassianism	patripotestal	pending basket	peregrine tone
par of exchange	patronization	Pendragonship	perennibranch
parotidectomy	patronizingly	pendulousness	perfectionate
par parenthèse	patte de velour	pendulum-clock	perfectionism
parrot disease	pattern-welded	pendulum swing	perfectionist
parrot-fashion	pauperization	pendulum-wheel	perfectionize
part and parcel	pavement-tooth	peneplanation	perfect square
part brass rags	paxilliferous	penetrability	perfervidness
parthenocarpy	pay-and-display	penetratingly	perforant path
parthenogenic	payback period	penetratively	perfunctorily
parthenospore	pay scot and lot	penicillamine	periarteritis
participation	pay-television	penicillately	periarticular
participative	peaceableness	penicillation	peribronchial
participatory	peace dividend	penicilliform	pericapillary
participially	peacelessness	penicillinase	pericardotomy
particle board	peace-offering	peninsularity	perichondrial
particoloured	peach leaf curl	peninsulation	perichondrium
particularise	peacock copper	penitentially	peridiastolic
particularism	peacock-flower	pennatulacean	periglacially
particularist	peacock throne	pennilessness	perilymphatic
particularity	peak voltmeter	Pennsylvanian	perimenopause
particularize	peanut brittle	penny dreadful	periodic table
partitionment	peanut gallery	penny-farthing	periodisation
partition wall	pearl-bordered	penny-pinching	periodization
partridge shot	pearl of orient	pennyweighter	periodontally
partridge-wood	peasant blouse	Penrose tiling	periodontitis
party politics	pebble-beached	pentachloride	periodontosis
paschal candle	pebble chopper	pentadelphous	perioperative
Paschen series	pebble culture	pentahydrated	peripapillary
passage at arms	pebble-dashing	pentanoic acid	peripatetical
passage of arms	pebble glasses	pentapetalous	peripherality
Passamaquoddy	pebble-grained	pentasepalous	peripheralize
passementerie	pebble hook-tip	pentasyllabic	perisaturnium
passenger-mile	pectoral quail	pentatonicism	perishability
passion flower	peculiarities	penthemimeral	perisplenitis
passion killer	pedagogically	Pentland Crown	perissodactyl
passionlessly	pedal clarinet	pentobarbital	peritendineum

perityphlitis	phalansterian	phosphataemia	phycoerythrin
perivitelline	phallocentric	phosphate bond	phyllocladous
Perkin's purple	phanerogamous	phosphate rock	phyllophagous
perlustration	phantasmality	phosphogypsum	phylloquinone
permanent blue	Pharisaically	phosphokinase	phylogenetics
permanent wave	pharmaceutics	phospholipase	physical force
permeableness	pharmaceutist	phosphoretted	physicalistic
permineralize	pharmacognosy	phosphorylase	physical jerks
Permo-Triassic	pharmacologic	phosphorylate	physicianship
permselective	pharmacopoeia	phosphuretted	physiocracies
permutability	pharyngalized	photoacoustic	physiognomies
permutational	pharyngectomy	photoactivate	physiognomist
peroxide blond	pharyngoscope	photoactivity	physiognomize
peroxide group	phase contrast	photoaffinity	physiographer
perpendicular	phase inverter	photoallergic	physiographic
perpetualness	phase-splitter	photocatalyse	physiological
perplexedness	phase velocity	photocatalyst	physioplastic
perscrutation	phencyclidine	photochemical	physiotherapy
persecutional	phenmetrazine	photochromism	physisorption
perseverantly	phenobarbital	photocomposer	physoclistous
perseveration	phenolization	photocopiable	physostigmine
perseverative	phenol oxidase	photodetector	phytochemical
perseveringly	phenomenalise	photodimerize	phytoecdysone
Persian blinds	phenomenalism	photoejection	phytopathogen
Persian carpet	phenomenalist	photoelectric	phytoplankter
Persian walnut	phenomenality	photoelectron	phytoplankton
personalistic	phenomenalize	photoemission	phytosanitary
personalities	phenomenistic	photoemissive	phytotoxicant
personal space	phenomenology	photo-engraver	phytotoxicity
personal touch	phenothiazine	photofinisher	pianistically
personologist	phenoxyacetic	photogalvanic	piano concerto
perspectively	phenylalanine	photogeologic	pick and choose
perspectivism	phenylarsonic	photographica	picked dogfish
perspectivist	phenylene blue	photographist	pickle-herring
perspectivity	phenylephrine	photoisomeric	pick out of a hat
perspicacious	phenylmercury	photolability	pickpocketing
perspicuously	phenylpyruvic	photomagnetic	Pickwickianly
pertechnetate	Philadelphian	photonegative	picnic blanket
perthitically	philanthropic	photoperiodic	Picnic Society
pervaporation	philhellenism	photophoresis	picrochromite
pervasiveness	philhellenist	photophoretic	picrolichenic
pervertedness	Phillips curve	photophysical	picrolichenin
pestiferously	philobiblical	photopositive	picturability
pest of society	philodendrons	photoproduced	picture palace
Peter Grievous	philomathical	photoreaction	picture search
Petersen graph	philosophical	photoreceptor	picture signal
petite marmite	philosophizer	photorecovery	picturesquely
petrification	phlebographic	photoregulate	picture window
petrochemical	Phlegethontic	photoresistor	picturization
petro-currency	phlogisticate	photoresponse	pidgin English
petroleum coke	phonaesthesia	photoreversal	pidginization
petroliferous	phonaesthetic	photoscanning	piece of silver
petrolization	phonautograph	photosynthate	piece together
petrol lighter	phonematology	phototelegram	piecrust table
petrol station	phonemization	phototoxicity	pietistically
petrophysical	phonendoscope	photovoltaics	piezoelectric
petrotectonic	phonetization	phraseography	piezomagnetic
petticoatless	phoney-boloney	phraseologies	pigeon-chested
petticoat tail	phonocentrism	phraseologist	pigeon fancier
petty sessions	phonographist	phrenicectomy	pigeon-hearted
phaeophorbide	phonoreceptor	phrenological	pigging string
phagolysosome	phonus-bolonus	phycobilisome	pig-headedness

pigheadedness
pig in a blanket
pigmentocracy
pignut hickory
pig's breakfast
pilgrim-bottle
Pilgrim Father
pilgrim's shell
pillar-and-claw
pillar and room
pillar apostle
pill-millipede
pill-woodlouse
pilosebaceous
pinafore dress
pin connection
pineapple bomb
pineapple lily
pineapple weed
pinheadedness
pinhole camera
pink champagne
pink elephants
pinking shears
piroplasmosis
piscatorially
piscicultural
piss in the wind
pistol-packing
piston-engined
pit and gallows
pitch-accented
pitch-darkness
pitched battle
pitch-farthing
pitching-yeast
pitch it strong
pituitary body
placebo effect
place in the sun
placelessness
placentophagy
plagal cadence
plagiocephaly
plagioclastic
plagiogranite
plagiostomous
plagiotropism
plagiotropous
plain language
plain-speaking
plaintiveness
plain-wanderer
plaited stitch
plane-parallel
planetary gear
planetary hour
planetary year
planet carrier
planetography
planetologist
planification

planimetrical
plank-buttress
planktologist
planktonology
plantain-eater
planter's punch
plantsmanship
plasmacytosis
plasma-dynamic
plasmalogenic
plasmaspheric
plasmoblastic
plasmodesmata
plasmolysable
plasmolyticum
plaster-bronze
plaster jacket
plasterworker
plastic bronze
plastic bullet
plastochronic
plastoquinone
plateau basalt
plateau gravel
plate cylinder
platelet count
plate of silver
plate tectonic
platform party
platform plank
platform scale
platform-soled
platform stage
platform truck
platiniferous
platiniridium
platinization
platinum-black
platinum blond
platinum group
platinum metal
platitudinary
platitudinise
platitudinize
platitudinous
Platonic solid
platycephalic
platyhelminth
platykurtosis
plausibleness
player-manager
play for laughs
play for safety
play games with
play hard to get
play havoc with
playing-marble
play oneself in
play propriety
play the market
play the part of
play therapist

playwrighting
plead innocent
please oneself
please the pigs
pleasuredrome
pleasure-house
plebification
plectognathic
pleiophyllous
plenitudinous
plenteousness
plentifulness
plenum chamber
plerocephalic
plesiosaurian
plesiosauroid
plethorically
plethysmogram
pleurocarpous
pleurotyphoid
plotting board
plotting table
plough-bullock
ploughmanship
plumber's snake
plumbosolvent
plumed serpent
plumification
plum-puddinger
plunge cutting
plunkety-plunk
pluralization
plural society
pluripresence
plurisyllabic
plurisyllable
plutocratical
Plymouth china
Plymouth cloak
pneumatically
pneumatic duct
pneumatic tube
pneumatic tyre
pneumatolysis
pneumatolytic
pneumatometer
pneumatophore
pneumogastric
pneumographic
pneumonectomy
pneumonolysis
pocketability
pocket borough
pocket-picking
podzolization
poetical works
poeticization
poetic justice
poetic licence
poetry reading
poetry recital
Poets Laureate

pogonophorous
poikilosmosis
poikilosmotic
poikilothermy
Poincaré cycle
pointillistic
pointing-stick
pointlessness
point mutation
point of honour
points victory
poison-hemlock
poisonousness
Poisson's ratio
poke mullock at
poker patience
polar distance
polari-locular
polarographic
polecat ferret
polemological
policeman-bird
policemanlike
policemanship
police message
police officer
police science
police station
police-witness
policy science
poliomyelitic
poliomyelitis
politicalness
politicianism
pollakanthous
pollen analyst
pollen-chamber
pollen diagram
pollen profile
pollicitation
polliniferous
pollinigerous
pollinivorous
pollinization
polyacetylene
polyadelphous
polyarteritis
polyarthritic
polyarthritis
polyarticular
polybutadiene
polycarbonate
polycephalous
polychotomous
polychromasia
polychromasic
polychromatic
polycistronic
polycythaemia
polycythaemic
polydactylism
polydactylous

polydaemonism	porphyroclast	potential well	precious metal
polydispersed	portal bracing	potentiometer	precious stone
polyembryonic	Portland Place	potentiometry	precipitantly
polyendocrine	Portland stone	potentization	precipitately
polyethylenic	portosystemic	Pott's fracture	precipitation
polygamically	portrait-stone	pound for pound	precipitously
polygenically	position angle	pound sterling	precogitation
polygonaceous	position paper	poverty-struck	preconception
polyhistorian	positive-going	powder and shot	preconization
polykaryocyte	positive logic	powder compact	precursorship
polymeniscous	positive organ	powdering-gown	predatoriness
polymerizable	possessionary	powdering-room	pre-delinquent
polymethylene	possessorship	powder pattern	predestinator
polymolecular	possibilistic	powdery mildew	predeterminer
polymorphemic	possibilities	power-assisted	predicability
Polynesian rat	postabdominal	power dressing	predicamental
polynucleated	postalization	power industry	predicational
polypharmacal	post-apostolic	powerlessness	predicatively
polyphenylene	post-auricular	power-operated	predicativity
polyphosphate	post-Christian	power politics	predictionism
polyphyletism	post-classical	power spectrum	predominantly
polypragmatic	post-Communion	power steering	predominately
polypropylene	post-disseisin	pozzolanicity	predominating
polyprotodont	post-emergence	practical joke	pre-engagement
polyribosomal	poste restante	practicalness	prefabricator
polyserositis	posteriormost	practice-curve	prefatorially
polysomnogram	posterization	praemunientes	preferability
polysyllabism	poster session	praetorianism	preference bid
polysynthesis	post-existence	pragmatically	preferredness
polysynthetic	postglacially	prairie bottom	prefiguration
polytechnical	postlapsarian	prairie buster	prefigurative
polythalamous	postliminious	prairie clover	prefigurement
Pomeranchukon	postman's knock	prairie crocus	preganglionic
Pomeranian dog	post-monarchal	prairie falcon	pregenitality
pomiculturist	postmenstrual	prairie marmot	pregeological
pomologically	postmenstruum	prairie oyster	pregerminated
Pompe's disease	post-modernism	prairie turnip	pregnancy test
pompier ladder	postmodernism	praisefulness	prehistorical
ponderability	post-modernist	Prandtl number	pre-impregnate
ponderomotive	postmodernist	praxeological	pre-industrial
ponderousness	postmodernity	prayerfulness	pre-intimation
pontificality	postnuptially	prayer-meeting	preiotization
pontification	post office box	pray extempore	prejudication
pontoon bridge	post-office red	praying mantis	prejudicially
Ponzo illusion	post-operative	preadaptation	prelectorship
Poona painting	postoperative	preadmonition	preliminaries
pooper scooper	post-ovulative	pre-adolescent	preliminarily
poorly stocked	post-ovulatory	preadolescent	pre-linguistic
popping crease	postreduction	preambulation	prelinguistic
poppy-coloured	postscutellum	preambulatory	prematuration
population III	post-traumatic	preanticipate	prematureness
populationist	post-treatment	pre-aspiration	pre-medication
porcelain clay	postulational	prebiological	premedication
porcellaneous	postwar credit	precalculable	premeditation
porcupine fish	potamological	precarcinogen	premeditative
porcupine-wood	potato creeper	precautionary	premenopausal
porencephalic	potato disease	precautiously	premillennial
porokeratosis	potato pancake	precentorship	premonitorily
porokeratotic	pot-belly stove	preceptorship	premunization
porphyrinogen	potential flow	precinct house	preneoplastic
porphyrinuria	potentialness	precious blood	preoccupation
porphyroblast	potential wall	precious coral	preoccupiedly

preordainment	prick one's ears	private treaty	promorphology
pre-ordination	prick-shooting	privativeness	promotability
preparatively	priest's pintle	privatization	promotiveness
preparatorily	prima donna-ish	prizefighting	pronator teres
prepare the way	primal therapy	probabilistic	pronominalise
preperception	primary colour	probabilities	pronominalize
prepolymerize	primary oocyte	probable cause	pronounceable
preponderance	primary planet	probable error	pronouncement
preponderancy	primary school	probationship	pronunciation
prepositional	primatologist	probativeness	proof positive
prepositively	prime meridian	problematical	proof strength
prepositorial	prime minister	problematique	propagability
prepossessing	Prime Minister	problem column	propagational
prepossession	prime ministry	procarcinogen	propanoic acid
pre-preference	prime vertical	process camera	propantheline
pre-production	primigravidae	process cheese	proparoxytone
preproduction	priming powder	processionary	propellerless
preprohormone	primitive cell	processionist	proper preface
prepubescence	primitiveness	processionize	prophetically
Pre-Raphaelism	primitivistic	process server	propinquitous
Pre-Raphaelite	primogenitary	procès-verbaux	propiolactone
pre-reflective	primogenitive	proclitically	propionic acid
presbytership	primogeniture	proconsulship	proportionate
prescientific	primordialism	procrastinate	propositional
prescriptible	primordiality	proctological	propraetorial
presentiality	primuline base	procuratorial	propraetorian
preserving jar	prince consort	producibility	proprietorial
presidentship	Prince Consort	productionize	proprietously
press coverage	prince-elector	product moment	proprioceptor
press-fastener	princely State	profecticious	proprio-spinal
pressing board	Prince of Peace	profectitious	propugnaculum
press one's luck	Prince of Wales	professoriate	propulsion gun
press the flesh	princess royal	professorship	propyl alcohol
press the point	Princess Royal	profile cutter	propylenimine
pressure cabin	principal axis	profilometric	prosaicalness
pressure gauge	principal girl	profitability	prosecutorial
pressure group	principalness	profit and loss	prosification
pressure plate	principalship	profit-sharing	prosopagnosia
pressure point	printed matter	progenitorial	prosopography
pressure ridge	printer buffer	progestogenic	prospect-glass
pressure-treat	Printers' Bible	prognathously	prospectively
prestigiation	printer's devil	prognosticate	prostaglandin
prestigiously	printing-frame	programmatist	prostatectomy
presumingness	printing-house	programme note	prostate gland
presumptively	printing press	progressional	prosthodontia
pretendership	printing-sheet	progressively	protanomalous
pretentiously	printing union	progressivism	protectionism
preteriteness	print spooling	progressivist	protectionist
pretermission	prismatically	progressivity	protectorless
pretermitting	prisoner of war	prohibitively	protectorship
preternatural	prisoners' bars	projectionist	proteinaceous
pretty-by-night	prisoner's base	prolegomenary	proteoclastic
prettyprinter	prisoners' base	prolegomenous	proterandrous
prevarication	prison haircut	proleptically	proterogynous
prevaricatory	prisonization	proliferation	Protestantdom
preventionism	privateersman	proliferative	Protestantise
preventionist	privateersmen	proliferously	Protestantish
prevocational	private income	prolification	Protestantism
prevotal court	private member	promenade deck	Protestantize
pricelessness	private number	Prometheanism	protest voting
price movement	private school	prominent moth	prothetically
prick-me-dainty	private sector	promiscuously	protoactinium

protochordate	psychasthenia	pulverization	pyramidically
protocultural	psychasthenic	pump attendant	pyrenocarpous
protodynastic	psychiatrical	pumped storage	pyrheliometer
protofilament	psychic income	pumpkin-headed	Pyribenzamine
protogalactic	psychoanalyse	punching press	pyriform fossa
Proto-Germanic	psychoanalyst	punch the clock	pyrimethamine
proto-historic	psychobabbler	punctiliously	pyrocellulose
proto-language	psychobiology	punctuational	pyrolytically
proto-literate	psychocentric	punctus versus	pyromagnetism
proton donator	psychodynamic	punishability	pyrophosphate
protonosphere	psychogenesis	punto a rilievo	pyrosulphuric
protriptyline	psychogenetic	pupillography	pyrosynthesis
protruberance	psychographer	pupillometric	pyrosynthetic
protuberantly	psychographic	puppet-showman	pyrotechnical
proverbialism	psychohistory	Purbeck marble	pyroxferroite
proverbialist	psychokinesis	purchase a writ	pyrrolizidine
proverbiality	psychokinetic	purchase-money	Pythagorician
proverbialize	psychological	purchase price	quadragesimal
Provident Club	psychologizer	pure and simple	quadraphonics
providentness	psychometrics	puritanically	quadratically
provincialate	psychometrist	Purkinje fibre	quadratojugal
provincialise	psychometrize	purple emperor	quadrennially
provincialism	psychopathist	purple grackle	quadridentate
provincialist	psychophysics	purple passage	quadrifoliate
provinciality	psychosomatic	purposelessly	quadrilateral
provincialize	psychostatics	purposiveness	quadrilingual
provisionally	psychosurgeon	purpurogallin	quadriliteral
provisionless	psychosurgery	push-button war	quadrillionth
provisionment	psychotechnic	pusillanimity	quadrilocular
provocatively	psychotherapy	pusillanimous	quadripartite
provokingness	psychotically	put a new face on	quadripinnate
proximateness	psychotogenic	put a premium on	quadrivalence
proximity fuse	psychotrophic	put a stopper on	quadrivalency
prudentialism	psychrometric	put au fait with	quadrivoltine
prudentialist	psychrophilic	put in the fangs	quadrumvirate
prudentiality	psychrosphere	put in the shade	quadrupartite
psammophilous	pteridologist	put in the wrong	quadrupedally
psephological	pteridophytic	put into effect	quadruple time
pseudisodomon	pterygoid bone	put one's face on	quadruplicate
pseudoallelic	pterylography	put one's feet up	quadruplicity
pseudo-archaic	ptygmatically	put one's hand to	Quaker meeting
pseudobedding	public analyst	put one's mind to	qualification
pseudobreccia	public company	put out of sight	qualificative
pseudobulbous	public holiday	put out to grass	qualificatory
pseudo-concept	public inquiry	put out to nurse	qualifiedness
pseudodiploid	publicization	put pen to paper	qualitatively
pseudohalogen	public library	put pressure on	qualitiedness
pseudoleucite	public opinion	putrilaginous	quality circle
pseudological	public servant	put the black on	quality factor
pseudomorphic	public service	put the flag out	qualmlessness
pseudopatient	public utility	put the hooks in	quantophrenia
pseudoplastic	publish a libel	put to the blush	quantum number
pseudo-problem	pudding course	put to the sword	quantum theory
pseudoprophet	pudding-headed	put to the torch	quarantinable
pseudoracemic	pudding-sleeve	putty-coloured	quarrelsomely
pseudo-science	Pulitzer Prize	put up one's hair	quarter-finals
pseudoseizure	pullet disease	put up or shut up	quarter-gunner
pseudosematic	pulmonary vein	put up the spout	quartermaster
pseudosuchian	pulse dialling	pycnidiospore	quarter-racing
pseudouridine	pulselessness	pycnochlorite	Quartier Latin
psychagogical	pulse pressure	pycnoconidium	Quartodeciman
psychanalysis	pulse repeater	pyelocystitis	quartz-halogen

quartziferous
quasi-contract
quasiparticle
quaternionist
quatre-couleur
queen excluder
Queen of the May
Queen's counsel
Queen's Counsel
queen's cushion
Queen's English
Queen's highway
Queensland nut
queen's pattern
Queen's Proctor
queen's pudding
queen staysail
queen's weather
querulousness
questionaries
questioningly
questionnaire
queue fourchée
quick-and-dirty
quick-tempered
quiet American
quiet as a mouse
quilting frame
quilting party
quincentenary
quincuncially
quingentenary
quinquagenary
Quinquagesima
quinquangular
quinquelobate
quinquenniums
quinquevalent
quinquevirate
quintillionth
quintuplicate
quizzicalness
quizzing-glass
quodlibetical
quota sampling
quotation mark
quotativeness
quotient group
rabbit-and-pork
rabbit tobacco
rabble-rousing
race condition
race relations
racialization
racing colours
rack and manger
rack-and-pinion
racy of the soil
radiant energy
radiant heater
radiant region
radiationally

radiation belt
radiation burn
radiationless
radical humour
radiesthesist
radiesthetist
radioactivate
radioactively
radioactivity
radiobiologic
radiochemical
radioisotopic
radiolocation
radio spectrum
radio-telegram
radioteletype
radiotoxicity
radium therapy
Raffaelle ware
Rafferty rules
rag-and-bone man
railroad guide
railway letter
rainbow cactus
rainbow runner
rainbow wrasse
raise one's eyes
raise the Devil
rake's progress
Raman spectrum
ramapithecine
ramentiferous
ramshackledom
ram's-horn snail
ranch bungalow
randomization
Rankine degree
rapaciousness
rapprochement
rapscallionly
rapturousness
rarefactional
raspberry cane
raspberry tart
rasterization
rateable value
ratiocination
ratiocinative
rational dress
rationalistic
rat-tail cactus
rattle-brained
Rayleigh limit
ray of sunshine
reaccommodate
reacquisition
reactionaries
reactionarily
reactive power
reader-printer
read one's shirt
ready reckoner

reaffirmation
reaggravation
reaggregation
realistically
realizability
realizational
realpolitiker
re-application
reapplication
reappointment
rear commodore
rearrangement
reasonability
reason of State
reassociation
Réaumur's scale
rebarbatively
rebroadcasted
rebroadcaster
rebukefulness
recalcitrance
recalcitrancy
recalculation
receiving barn
receiving line
receiving ship
receptibility
reception room
receptiveness
recessiveness
recess-printed
recharge basin
reciprocality
reciprocating
reciprocation
reciprocatory
recirculation
recirculatory
reclusiveness
recoil starter
recollectable
recombination
recommendable
recommunicate
recompensable
recomposition
recompression
recomputation
reconcentrado
reconcentrate
reconcilement
reconciliator
reconditeness
reconditioned
reconditioner
reconsignment
reconsolidate
reconstructed
reconstructor
record changer
recording head
record linkage

recoup oneself
recreationist
recrimination
recriminative
recriminatory
recrudescence
recrudescency
recrystallise
recrystallize
rectangularly
rectification
rectilinearly
rectitudinous
rectus in curia
recultivation
recursiveness
recyclability
recycling time
red-backed vole
red-back spider
red bishop bird
red dead-nettle
redding-stroke
redeemability
redeliverance
redescription
redevelopment
red hartebeest
red-headed smew
rediscoveries
redissolution
redissolvable
red jungle fowl
red phosphorus
red rag to a bull
Red Republican
Red Riding Hood
Red River fever
red sandalwood
red-shouldered
red spider mite
reducibleness
reducing agent
reductionally
reduction gear
reductiveness
reduplication
reduplicative
reduplicature
redwater fever
Redwood second
re-edification
reefing-jacket
re-eligibility
re-embarkation
re-enfeoffment
re-enforcement
re-entry permit
re-examination
re-exportation
refashionment
reference book

reference room
reference tube
referentially
refer to drawer
reflectometer
reflectometry
reflex copying
reflexibility
reflexiveness
reflexogenous
reflexologist
reflorescence
refocillation
reforestation
reformability
reformational
Reformational
reformatively
reformatories
Reform Judaism
reformulation
refractionist
refractometer
refractometry
refrigeration
refrigerative
refrigeratory
refurbishment
refurnishment
regardfulness
regermination
regimentation
regionalistic
regiospecific
register board
Register House
register plate
registrarship
regretfulness
regular clergy
regular fellow
regulator gene
regurgitation
reign of terror
reimbursement
reimmigration
reimportation
reincarnation
reincorporate
reinfestation
reinforcement
reinforce ring
reinoculation
reinstatement
reinstitution
reintegration
reintegrative
reinterpreted
reinterrogate
reinvestigate
reiteratively
rejection slip

rejuvenescent
relationality
relative pitch
relief pitcher
relieving arch
religiousness
remainder over
remancipation
remanufacture
remarkability
rematerialize
remeasurement
reminiscently
remissibility
remittance man
remonstrantly
remonstration
remonstrative
remonstratory
remorselessly
remote control
remote sensing
remythologize
renal dialysis
renationalise
renationalize
rendezvousing
renegotiation
renewal theory
renovationist
rental library
rent of ability
reorientation
reoxygenation
repairability
repealability
repeatability
repeating back
repeating coil
repeat oneself
repeat pattern
repetitionary
repetitiously
replenishment
replicability
replica method
replicatively
reportability
reportorially
reposefulness
reprecipitate
reprehensible
reprehensibly
representable
representment
repressionist
reproachfully
reproachingly
reproduceable
reprogramming
reprographics
reptiliferous

reptilivorous
republicanism
republicanize
republication
repugnatorial
repullulation
repulsiveness
requisiteness
requisitioner
rescue mission
resectability
resegregation
resentfulness
reserved seats
reservoir rock
resettability
residence city
residence time
residentially
resinographer
resinographic
resistibility
resistiveness
resolutionist
resolvability
resourcefully
respirability
respirometric
resplendently
restaurant car
restauranteur
restiform body
restimulation
restipulation
restoratively
restrainingly
restrictively
restrictivist
resublimation
resultant tone
resuscitation
resuscitative
retainability
retaining wall
retentiveness
retiary spider
reticular cell
reticulum cell
retinaldehyde
retirement age
retranslation
retransmitted
retributively
retributivism
retributivist
retroactively
retroactivity
retroanalysis
retrodictable
retrogression
retrogressive
retrospection

retrospective
returnability
return the lead
reunification
reutilization
revaccination
revelationist
revendication
reverberantly
reverberation
reverberative
reverberatory
reverentially
reversal speed
reverse-charge
reverse Polish
reverse thrust
reversibility
reversing mill
reviewability
revindication
revocableness
revoltingness
revolutionary
revolutionise
revolutionism
revolutionist
revolutionize
revolving door
revolving fund
rewardingness
Reye's syndrome
Rhadamanthine
Rhaeto-Liassic
Rhaeto-Romance
Rhaeto-Romanic
rhapsodically
rhematization
rheologically
rheoreceptive
rhesus macaque
rheumatically
Rhine daughter
rhizocephalan
rhizomorphous
Rhodes Scholar
rhodochrosite
rhombohedrons
Rhomboidal Net
rhopalocerous
rhotacization
rhyparography
rhythmicality
rhythmization
rhythm section
Ribbon Society
ribosenucleic
rice Christian
Richardsonian
Richard's pipit
rickety rosary
ride the blinds

ride the clutch
ridge cucumber
riffle-shuffle
rifle regiment
Riga rhine hemp
Riggs's disease
right defender
righteousness
right half-back
right-handedly
rightlessness
right midfield
right of common
right of search
Right Reverend
right-thinking
right triangle
ring blackbird
ring modulator
ripping-chisel
ripple control
ripple counter
ripple-flaking
riproariously
ripsnortingly
Risso's dolphin
rite of passage
Ritschlianism
ritualisation
ritualization
river bullhead
river-diggings
road allowance
robe de chambre
Robespierrist
robin's egg blue
robotomorphic
rob the spittle
rocambolesque
rock and roller
rocket chamber
rock mechanics
rock phosphate
Rocky Mountain
rodent officer
roentgenogram
roentgenology
rogue's gallery
rogues' gallery
rolled into one
roller bandage
roller bearing
roller coaster
rolling moment
rolling strike
roll-on roll-off
Roman Catholic
Roman hyacinth
romanticality
Roman wormwood
root and branch
root vegetable

Rorschach test
rose of Jericho
rose Pompadour
rose-water pipe
rotary cutting
rotary machine
rotary shutter
rotten borough
rotten-hearted
rough-and-ready
rough and round
rough-tonguing
round and round
round brackets
round the clock
round the twist
round-tripping
Rousseauesque
Rousseauistic
routinization
rowing machine
Rowland circle
Roxbury russet
Royal Air Force
royal antelope
royal peculiar
royal standard
royal straight
rubber-proofed
rubber-tapping
rub elbows with
rub of the green
rub on the green
rub resistance
ruddy shelduck
rude awakening
rudimentarily
ruffed bustard
rufous hornero
rugby football
ruggedization
Ruhmkorff coil
rule of the road
ruling passion
rumbustiously
runcible spoon
running battle
running stitch
run out of steam
run rings round
run the gamut of
rural delivery
rural district
rurbanization
Russell's viper
Russia leather
Russian ballet
Russian dinner
Russian stitch
russification
Russification
rustic bunting

rust-resistant
rustyback fern
rutherfordium
rye brome-grass
Sabba-day house
Sabbath candle
Sabbath school
sabbatization
sable antelope
sabre-rattling
saccharic acid
saccharimeter
saccharimetry
saccharolytic
saccharometer
saccharometry
sacerdotalism
sacerdotalist
sacerdotalize
sacralization
sacramentally
Sacred College
sacred concert
sacred history
sacred writing
sacrificially
sacring of mass
sacrosanctity
saddleback pig
saddle-blanket
saddle embolus
saddle feather
saddle-hackled
sado-masochism
sadomasochism
sado-masochist
sadomasochist
safety bicycle
safety curtain
safety deposit
safety-firster
safety harness
safety officer
saffron crocus
saffron-yellow
sagaciousness
sagittal crest
sailing course
sailing master
sailing orders
sailor's choice
Saint-Simonian
Saint-Simonist
salaciousness
salad dressing
salami tactics
Salam—Weinberg
sale-leaseback
sales engineer
salicylic acid
saliva ejector
salmon disease

salmonellosis
saloon theatre
salpingectomy
salpingolysis
salpingostomy
salt an account
salt-and-pepper
salted almonds
salt fingering
Salvation Army
Salvation Jane
Sam Browne belt
sample-and-hold
sampling error
sampling frame
sanctiloquent
sanctimonious
sanctionative
sandalwood oil
sand and canvas
sand-blindness
sand-hill crane
sandpaper tree
sand stargazer
sandwich-board
sandwich panel
sandy laverock
San Franciscan
sanitarianism
sanitary towel
sanitationist
sanitation man
Sankaracharya
San Pellegrino
sans cérémonie
sansculottish
sans-culottism
sansculottism
sansculottist
sansculottize
Santo Domingan
sapodilla plum
sarcastically
Sardanapalian
sargassum fish
Satanic school
satchel charge
satellite cell
satellite dish
satellite town
satellite vein
satellization
satiety centre
satin duchesse
satin sycamore
satiricalness
satisfiedness
Saturday night
Saturday penny
saucerization
Saussureanism
saussuritized

savannah grass
save-as-you-earn
save one's bacon
Savonius rotor
Savoy operetta
say for oneself
scalar product
scalding-house
scalene muscle
scalenohedral
scalenohedron
scaling-ladder
scallywaggery
scalping-knife
scaly anteater
scandalmonger
Scandihoovian
scanning field
scaphocephaly
scarabaeidoid
scarabaeiform
scarcity value
scarification
scarlet letter
scarlet runner
scatterometer
scavenger cell
scavenger hunt
scene shifting
scenic railway
schadenfreude
Schadenfreude
Scheele's green
Scheiner's halo
schematically
Schiff reagent
Schilling test
schinkenwurst
schistosomule
schizocarpous
schizocoelous
schizonticide
schizontocide
schizophrenia
schizophrenic
Schmidt camera
Schmidt number
Schoenbergian
scholarliness
scholasticate
scholasticism
schoolboyhood
school colours
schoolgirlish
school-marming
school-marmish
schoolmastery
school section
schoolteacher
schooner barge
Schottky diode
Schottky slope

Schrammel band
schreibersite
Schumannesque
Schumpeterian
Schwarzschild
Schwenkfelder
sciagraphical
scientificity
scientization
Scientologist
scientometric
scintigraphic
scintillantly
scintillating
scintillation
scintillogram
scintiscanner
scleractinian
scleroprotein
sclerotherapy
sclerotic bone
sclerotic ring
scolopendrine
scolopendrium
scoop the kitty
scorbutically
scorchingness
scorification
scorpion grass
scorpion senna
scorpion shell
Scotch bonnets
Scotch collops
Scotch pancake
Scotch terrier
Scotch thistle
scotomization
scouring paper
scouring-stone
scoutmasterly
scrambled eggs
scrambler bike
scrambling net
scrap merchant
scratched blue
scratch filter
scratch-mixing
screen current
screen editing
screen printer
screen voltage
screenwriting
screw-coupling
scrimmage line
scriptorially
scripturalism
scripturalist
scripturality
scripturalize
scriptureless
script-writing
scriptwriting

scrobiculated
scrofuloderma
scrumptiously
sculpturesque
scyphomedusan
scyphophorous
sea arrow-grass
sea breeziness
sea gooseberry
sea-kindliness
sealed verdict
seals of office
seam allowance
searchingness
search warrant
seaworthiness
sebaceous duct
seclusiveness
secondariness
secondary road
secondary wave
secondary wife
second chamber
second channel
second-guesser
second officer
second reading
second Redwood
Second Sea Lord
second service
second-sighted
secretary bird
secretaryship
secretiveness
secret members
secret service
secret society
sectorization
secular clergy
secundum artem
security check
security guard
sedentariness
sedge reedling
sedimentation
sedimentology
sedoheptulose
seductiveness
Seebeck effect
seek-no-further
segmentalizer
segregational
Seignette salt
seismic survey
seismographer
seismographic
seismological
selectionally
selection rule
selectiveness
selenocentric
selenographer

selenographic
selenological
self-abandoned
self-abasement
self-actualize
self-addressed
self-adjusting
self-adulation
self-analysing
self-appointed
self-asserting
self-assertion
self-assertive
self-assurance
self-assuredly
self-awareness
self-balancing
self-biography
self-centredly
self-cleansing
self-collected
self-communion
self-conceited
self-concerned
self-condemned
self-confessed
self-confident
self-confiding
self-conscious
self-contained
self-contented
self-convicted
self-criticism
self-deceitful
self-deceiving
self-deception
self-deceptive
self-defeating
self-defensive
self-denyingly
self-dependent
self-destroyer
self-diffusion
self-discovery
self-education
self-evidently
self-evolution
self-executing
self-existence
self-explained
self-fertility
self-fertilize
self-financing
self-flatterer
self-forgetful
self-governing
self-hypnotism
self-identical
self-important
self-improving
self-induction
self-inductive

self-indulgent	Seminole horse	sericiculture	Shaking Quaker
self-indulging	seminological	sericulturist	shalwar-kameez
self-inflicted	semiochemical	serjeant-at-law	shamefastness
self-insurance	semi-palmation	serodiagnosis	shamelessness
self-judgement	semi-permanent	serofibrinous	shammy leather
self-knowledge	semi-permeable	serologically	sham operation
self-motivated	semipermeable	serotaxonomic	shape an answer
self-opiniated	semi-porcelain	Serpent-bearer	shape-changing
self-opinioned	semi-sterility	serpenticidal	shapelessness
self-oscillate	semi-synthetic	serpentinitic	sharp-featured
self-parodying	semisynthetic	serpiginously	sharp practice
self-pityingly	Semito-Hamitic	serum reaction	sharpshooting
self-pollinate	semitonically	serum sickness	sharp-wittedly
self-pollution	semi-vitrified	serve one's time	shear strength
self-possessed	semologically	serve one's turn	sheep-shearing
self-propelled	sempiternally	serve-yourself	sheep-smearing
self-quenching	send to the wall	service charge	Sheer Thursday
self-recording	seneschalship	service module	Sheikh-ul-Islam
self-reference	senior citizen	service record	shell concrete
self-referring	senior classic	sesquialteral	shell-moulding
self-reflexive	senior college	sesquiterpene	shepherd plaid
self-regarding	senior officer	sesquitertian	shepherd's club
self-regulated	senior partner	set by the heels	shepherd's pipe
self-reliantly	senior service	set measures to	sherbet powder
self-repugnant	sensationally	set of bagpipes	Sheridanesque
self-restraint	sensationless	set one's face to	sheriffalties
self-revealing	senselessness	set one's hand to	sheriff-depute
self-righteous	sense of beauty	set one's seal to	sheriff's clerk
self-sacrifice	sense of humour	set one's wits to	sheriff's court
self-satisfied	sensibilities	setting lotion	sherry cobbler
self-selecting	sensitive fern	settlement day	sherryvallies
self-selection	sensitiveness	settler's clock	Shetland sheep
self-shielding	sensitivities	settler's twine	shield-budding
self-slaughter	sensitization	Seven Sleepers	shield of brawn
self-sterility	sensitometric	seventeenthly	shield volcano
self-sufficing	sensorineural	seventh heaven	shifting pedal
self-surrender	sententiosity	seven year itch	shiftlessness
self-sustained	sententiously	seven-year-vine	shift register
seller's market	sentimentally	Seville orange	shimmy-foxtrot
selling plater	sentimentless	sewing machine	shine and shade
semantic field	senza ritenuto	sexagesimally	shining armour
semasiologist	separableness	sexationalism	shining cuckoo
sematological	separationism	sex attractant	ship-brokerage
semi-automatic	separationist	sex chromosome	ship carpenter
semi-barbarian	septcentenary	sexploitation	ship in a bottle
semi-barbarism	septemfoliate	sexploitative	ship of the line
semi-barbarous	septentrional	sexualization	shipping agent
semicarbazide	septentrionic	shabby-genteel	shipping clerk
semicarbazone	septifragally	shadelessness	shipping fever
semi-civilized	sequence space	shade-tolerant	ship-repairing
semi-classical	sequentiality	shadow cabinet	ship's articles
semiconductor	sequesterment	shadow-casting	ship's chandler
semicylindric	sequestration	shadowgraphic	ship's corporal
semi-conscious	sequestrotomy	shadow picture	ship's decanter
semi-displayed	Serbo-Croatian	shadow-striped	Shirley Temple
semi-empirical	serendipitist	shadow theatre	shockableness
semi-evergreen	serendipitous	Shaftesburian	shock absorber
semi-intensive	sergeant-at-law	shaggy parasol	Shockley diode
semi-invariant	Sergeant Baker	shake one's head	shock-mounting
semi-lunar bone	sergeant major	Shakespearean	shockproofing
semi-monocoque	serialization	Shakespearian	shoddy dropper
semi-nocturnal	serial section	shake together	shoebill stork

shoemaker's end	Siberian tiger	sintered glass	slick magazine
shoestring tie	sicca syndrome	siphonapteran	slide fastener
shoofly rocker	sick as a parrot	siphonophoran	slide trombone
shoot a profile	sickle-feather	siphonostelic	sliding hernia
shooting brake	sick to death of	siphunculated	sling one's hook
shooting break	side frequency	sissification	slip one's cable
shooting-glove	sidereal clock	sister keelson	slipper limpet
shooting-lodge	sideroblastic	sister nucleus	slipper-orchid
shooting match	siderographic	Sister of Mercy	slippery hitch
shooting range	side-splitting	sisters thread	slippery slope
shooting stick	Siegfried Line	sister uterine	slip the clutch
shoot one's bolt	Sierra Leonean	Sistine Chapel	slit fricative
shoot-the-chute	Sierra Leonian	sit at the stern	slobberhannes
shoot the works	sieve analysis	sit on the fence	sluice one's gob
shop assistant	sight distance	sitting member	slum clearance
shop committee	sightlessness	sitting pretty	slummockiness
shopkeeperish	sigillography	sitting target	slush moulding
shopkeeperism	sigmoid cavity	sitting tenant	smack one's lips
shore platform	sigmoidectomy	situationally	small capitals
shore-shooting	sigmoidoscope	situation room	small-for-dates
short and sweet	sigmoidoscopy	situs inversus	small-mindedly
short-breathed	signalisation	sixteenth note	small potatoes
short covering	signalization	sixteenth part	small seraphim
short delivery	signature dish	sixteen-tonner	small thanks to
short division	signatureless	skeletogenous	smart-aleckism
short-eared owl	signature tune	skeleton brass	smear campaign
short of breath	significantly	skeleton clock	smelling salts
short-tempered	signification	skeleton forme	smoke canister
short trousers	significative	skelpie-limmer	smoked chicken
shot-hole borer	significatory	sketchability	smoke detector
shot in the dark	significatrix	skew-symmetric	smoke-farthing
shoulder blade	sign the pledge	skinny-dipping	smokelessness
shoulder board	silent partner	skin potential	smokeless zone
shoulder flash	silent whistle	Skire Thursday	smoking jacket
shoulder joint	siliciclastic	skirmishingly	smoking pistol
shoulder patch	Silicon Valley	skirting board	smoothing iron
shoulder-piece	silly as a wheel	skunk porpoise	smooth-tongued
shoulder plane	silver amalgam	slab avalanche	smothered mate
shoulder stand	silver jubilee	slack adjuster	smother-tackle
shoulder strap	silver nitrate	Slack-ma-girdle	smoulderingly
shouting match	silver plating	slack variable	snaffle-bridle
shovel-stirrup	silver-pointed	slanging match	snail-creeping
shove the queer	silver service	slap and tickle	snake pipefish
showdown poker	silver-tongued	slap-happiness	snapper ending
shower-bouquet	silver wedding	slap in the face	snapping-point
shower cubicle	silvery arches	slap on the back	sneak-thievery
shower curtain	silvery gibbon	slate-coloured	snifting valve
show one's cards	silvichemical	slaughterable	snigging chain
show one's teeth	silvicultural	slave-bracelet	snow-blindness
shredded wheat	similar motion	Slavification	snow partridge
shrew-hedgehog	simple-hearted	Slavonization	snowy mespilus
shrike babbler	simple machine	sleeping giant	snuff-coloured
shrimp cracker	simplex method	sleep-learning	sober as a judge
shrinkability	simulfixation	sleeplessness	sociable coach
Shrove Tuesday	Sinanthropoid	sleep like a log	social benefit
shuffle rhythm	sindonologist	sleep like a top	social climber
shut one's mouth	single harness	sleep movement	social comment
shut the door on	single-hearted	sleep-teaching	social compact
shutting joint	single spacing	sleeve bearing	social control
sialoadenitis	single-tasking	sleight of hand	social dialect
Siberian crane	singularities	slender-billed	social disease
Siberian husky	sin of omission	slender-bodied	social drinker

social evening
social fascist
social history
socialisation
socialization
social process
social realism
social reality
social science
social service
social studies
socio-cultural
sociocultural
sociodramatic
socio-economic
sociolinguist
sociologistic
sock and buskin
socket spanner
Socratic irony
soda cellulose
soda-lime glass
sodium-amalgam
sodium nitrate
sodomitically
soft detergent
soft in the head
soft sculpture
soft-shell clam
soft-shell crab
software house
soil amendment
soil mechanics
soil scientist
solar constant
solderability
soldering iron
soldier beetle
soldier course
soldierliness
soldier orchid
soldier palmer
soldier's heart
solemnisation
solemnization
solenoid brake
solicitorship
solid geometry
solid solution
solidungulate
solidungulous
solifidianism
soliloquacity
solitary vireo
solubilizable
solutionizing
solution-treat
somatological
somatopleuric
somatopsychic
somatosensory
somatotrophic

somatotrophin
something else
something is up
something like
somethingness
somewhere else
somnambulance
somniferously
somnolescence
son Afro-Cubano
Song of Ascents
Song of Degrees
Song of Solomon
sonochemistry
son of the house
son of the manse
sonolytically
sons of bitches
sooner or later
soothfastness
soothsayeress
sooty mangabey
sophiological
sophistically
sophisticated
sophisticator
soporifically
sorbitization
sorrowfulness
sorting office
soul-searching
soul-sickening
sound and light
sound-boarding
sound engineer
sounding board
soundlessness
sound pressure
sound-symbolic
source program
South American
south and north
south-easterly
south-eastward
southerliness
southern beech
Southern Cross
Southern Crown
southern-fried
Southern Irish
Southern Ocean
South Islander
south-westerly
south-westward
sovereign good
sovereignship
sovereignties
Sovietization
sovietologist
Sovietologist
Sovietophobia
space-averaged

space industry
Space Invaders
space launcher
spacelessness
space medicine
space platform
space-reddened
space-sickness
space velocity
spade terminal
spaghetti bowl
spalding-knife
Spanish Armada
Spanish burton
Spanish dagger
Spanish garlic
Spanish guitar
Spanish squill
Spanish stitch
spanner wrench
span of control
spark-arrester
spark spectrum
sparks will fly
sparry iron ore
spasmodically
spatterdashed
speaker-hearer
speaking clock
speaking front
speak one's mind
speak the truth
speak together
Special Branch
special school
specificality
specification
specific cause
specimen shrub
speckled belly
speckled diver
speckled trout
specklessness
spectacle-case
spectacle clew
spectacled owl
spectacularly
spectatorship
spectinomycin
spectral class
spectral index
spectre-insect
spectrography
spectrometric
spectrophonic
spectroscopic
specular stone
speculatively
speculativism
speculum-metal
speechfulness
speech-reading

speech therapy
speed merchant
speleological
spelter solder
Spencerianism
spending money
spend the night
spermatically
spermatic cord
spermaticidal
spermatocidal
spermatogonia
spermatophore
spermatophyte
speromagnetic
sphericalness
spherical wave
spherocytosis
spheroidicity
sphingomyelin
sphygmography
sphygmometric
spider angioma
spider-catcher
spike lavender
spilitization
spill the beans
spindle-legged
spindle-shanks
spindle-shaped
spine-chilling
spine-freezing
spinelessness
spine-tingling
spinning-frame
spinning-house
spinning jenny
spinning wheel
spin-polarized
spinuliferous
spiny anteater
spiral balance
spiral binding
spiralization
spirit-rapping
spirits of salt
spirits of wine
spiritual home
spiritualized
spiritualizer
spiritualness
spirit varnish
spit and polish
spitting cobra
spitting image
spitting snake
splanchnology
splatter-faced
splendiferous
splenectomies
splenectomize
splenetically

splinter group
splinter party
splinter-proof
split decision
split one's vote
splutteringly
spokesmanship
spondylolysis
spondylolytic
sponge biscuit
sponge mixture
sponge pudding
spongiculture
spongiologist
spongiopiline
spontaneously
spoonbill duck
Spörer minimum
sporidiferous
sporonticidal
sporopollenin
sporting house
sporting woman
sport of nature
sportsmanlike
sportsmanship
sports section
spotted orchid
spray refining
spreadability
spreadingness
spread oneself
Sprengel's tube
sprightliness
spring balance
spring cabbage
spring chicken
spring equinox
spring fashion
spring herring
spritsail yard
sprocket-wheel
spruce budworm
squandermania
square-bashing
square bracket
square flipper
square measure
square-pushing
square-shooter
squashability
squash blossom
squash rackets
squeaking sand
squeamishness
squeezability
squeeze bottle
squeeze-pidgin
squinancy-wort
squirarchical
squire of dames
squirrel grass

stabilimentum
stabilization
stab in the back
stacking fault
stack the cards
staff notation
Staffordshire
staff sergeant
stagecoachman
stage director
stage-entrance
stage lighting
stage presence
staggering bob
stagger tuning
stag-horn coral
stag-horn sumac
stagnationist
stainlessness
stain painting
staircase lock
stakebuilding
stalactitical
stalagmitical
stalagmometer
Stalinization
stalking-horse
staminiferous
standard cable
standard error
standard grade
Standard Grade
stand in a sheet
standing order
standing-place
standing point
standing ropes
standing stone
stand-offishly
standoffishly
stand sentinel
Stanford–Binet
stanhope horse
Stanhope press
stannary court
Stanton number
staphylococci
starboard tack
star catalogue
starch blocker
starch-reduced
starfish plant
star-nosed mole
starting block
starting-place
starting point
starting price
starting stall
start to school
stated account
statelessness
state of nature

state of the art
state of things
state prisoner
State prisoner
States General
statesmanlike
statesmanship
States-righter
stationary air
stationmaster
statistically
stato-acoustic
status anxiety
status quo ante
statute-barred
statute labour
statute staple
statutory rape
stay-stitching
stay the course
St Bernard lily
St Distaff's day
steadfastness
steak au poivre
steal a march on
steal the scene
steam carriage
steam cracking
steaming light
Stedman caters
steel bandsman
steeplechaser
steering wheel
steersmanship
steganography
Steiner system
Stellwag's sign
stem succulent
stenocephalic
stenocrotaphy
stenographist
Stensen's canal
stentoriously
step-and-repeat
step out of line
steppe lemming
steppe polecat
stepping-stile
stepping stone
stercoraceous
stercorarious
stereochemist
stereocontrol
stereodiagram
stereognostic
stereographic
stereological
stereophonics
stereoplotter
stereoregular
stereostatics
stereotropism

stereotypical
stereoviewing
sterilisation
sterilization
stern foremost
sternomastoid
sternopleural
sternopleuron
sternothyroid
steroidogenic
stethographic
stethoscopist
stet processus
St Germain pear
stickfast flea
stick-fighting
stick-handling
sticking place
sticking point
stick-in-the-mud
stick out a mile
stick together
stiff as a poker
stiff-tail duck
stiff upper lip
stigmatically
Still's disease
stilpnomelane
stimulability
stimulatingly
stinking cedar
stinking Roger
stipendiaries
stirpiculture
stir the possum
stitch welding
St Lucie cherry
St Luke's summer
stochasticity
stockbreeding
stock exchange
Stock Exchange
stocking cloth
stocking-frame
stoicheiology
stoichiometry
Stokes' formula
Stokes' theorem
stoloniferous
stolonization
stomachically
stomach muscle
stomatiferous
stomatologist
stomatoplasty
stomatoporoid
stomp one's feet
stone-coloured
stone pavement
stone the crows
stop at nothing
stop consonant

stopping house	streetwalking	stroud blanket	subordinaries
stopping-knife	strengthening	structuralise	subordinately
stopping-place	strenuousness	structuralism	subordination
stopping train	strepsipteran	structuralist	subordinative
storage heater	streptocarpus	structurality	subpopulation
storiological	streptococcal	structuralize	sub-postmaster
storming-party	streptococcic	structuration	sub-post office
Stow-on-the-Wold	streptococcus	structureless	subprefecture
stracciatella	streptokinase	structure plan	subreptitious
straight-ahead	streptomycete	Struwwelpeter	subsequential
straight angle	stressability	stubble-jumper	subserviently
straight-armed	stress analyst	studio theatre	subsidization
straight arrow	stress-breaker	stud-partition	subsistential
straight chain	stress contour	stuffed monkey	subsoil plough
straight drive	stress diagram	stuffed pepper	subspeciation
straight-eight	stress disease	stultifyingly	substanceless
straight-faced	stressfulness	stultiloquent	substantially
straight fight	stress mineral	stump-grubbing	substantiator
straight flush	stress-neutral	Sturm und Drang	substantively
straight forth	stress phoneme	St Vitus's dance	substantivism
straight goods	stress-relieve	stylagalmatic	substantivist
straight-grain	stretch a point	style analysis	substantivity
straight-laced	stretcher bond	stylelessness	substantivize
straight-lined	stretcher case	stylistically	substitutable
straight on end	stretch reflex	stylopization	substructural
straight razor	stria albicans	styptic pencil	substructured
straightwards	striatonigral	suaviloquence	subtabulation
strain at a gnat	stricken field	subadolescent	subterraneity
straining-post	strike a docket	subastringent	subterraneous
strain oneself	strike-breaker	sub-bituminous	subtilisation
strain rosette	strikebreaker	subcategories	subtilization
strandlooping	strike-measure	subcategorise	subtriangular
Strangelovean	strike me blind	subcategorize	subtriplicate
strange matter	strike the beam	subclavicular	sub-underwrite
strangler tree	strike through	subcontractor	suburbicarian
strangulation	striking force	subcontraries	subventionary
strap railroad	striking-plate	subcontrarily	subventionize
Strasbourg pie	striking price	subdeaconship	subversionary
stratagemical	striking-tache	subdelegation	subversionist
strategetical	Strindbergian	subdividingly	succentorship
strategically	stringentness	subdivisional	succenturiate
stratigrapher	string of tools	subdolousness	successionist
stratigraphic	string-pulling	subeditorship	successlessly
stratocracies	striopallidal	sub-elementary	successorship
stratocumulus	strip cropping	subinhibitory	sucker-bashing
stratospheric	striped muscle	subinvolution	sucking reflex
stratovolcano	striped possum	subirrigation	suckling-house
Stravinskyite	striped squill	subjectedness	suck the monkey
strawberry pot	strip lighting	subject matter	suction dredge
strawberry red	stripping film	subject-object	suction stroke
straw-coloured	striptease act	subjunctively	suffering cats
straw potatoes	strobe-lighted	subjunctivity	sufficiencies
straw's breadth	strobilaceous	sublacustrine	suffocatingly
streak culture	strobilanthes	sub-lieutenant	suffraganeous
streak disease	stroke-oarsman	sublimational	suffraganship
streaming cold	stroke of state	sub-linguistic	suffragettism
stream the buoy	stroke of State	sublittorally	suffrutescent
street chemist	stromatolitic	sub-machine gun	suffumigation
street culture	strong stomach	submandibular	sugar and honey
street-orderly	strong-wristed	submarine mine	sugar aquatint
street-sweeper	strongyloides	submillimetre	sugar-candyish
street village	strontia water	submissionist	sugar squirrel

suggestionize	superencipher	Supreme Soviet	sword-rattling
suggest itself	supererogator	sure of oneself	swordsmanship
suicide clause	superexchange	surety of peace	sybaritically
suicidologist	superfamilies	surface-active	sycamore maple
sulfamerizine	superfetation	surface casing	Sydney bluegum
sulfanilamide	superficially	surface-coated	syllabication
sulphadiazine	superfineness	surface-colour	syllabization
sulphamic acid	superfluidity	surface effect	syllable-count
sulpharsenide	superfluities	surprisedness	syllable-timed
sulphocyanate	superfluously	surprise-party	syllabub glass
sulphonylurea	supergalactic	surreptitious	sylleptically
sulphur candle	superhelicity	Surrey chicken	syllogistical
sulphureously	superhumanity	surrogate baby	syllogization
sulphuric acid	superhumanize	surrogateship	Sylow's theorem
sulphur shower	superintender	surround sound	Sylow subgroup
sulphur spring	superior court	sursumduction	symbiotically
sulphur-yellow	superior ovary	sursumversion	symbiotrophic
sul ponticello	superlatively	survivability	symbolic logic
sultana mother	supernational	survival curve	symbolisation
sultana raisin	supernormally	survival value	symbolization
sultan's flower	supernumerary	suspender belt	symbolography
summa cum laude	supernumerous	suspense novel	symmetrically
summarization	superordinary	suspension dot	symmetry group
summation tone	superordinate	suspicionless	sympathectomy
summer boarder	superorganism	Susquehannock	sympathetical
summer cholera	superparasite	Sussex spaniel	sympathoblast
summer country	superpersonal	sustentacular	sympathogonia
summer cypress	superphysical	sustentaculum	sympatholytic
summer-herring	superposition	suttling-house	sympatrically
summer kitchen	superradiance	suxamethonium	symphalangism
summer pruning	superrational	Swainson's hawk	symphonically
summer pudding	supersaturate	swallow a camel	symphonic jazz
summer red-bird	superscripted	swallow pigeon	symphonic pocm
summer sausage	supersensible	swallow-tailed	symphoniously
summer tanager	supersensuous	swallow-winged	symphysiotomy
summit meeting	superstitious	swamp mahogany	sympiesometer
sumptuousness	superstructor	swamp pheasant	symptomatical
Sunday closing	supersubtlety	Swanee whistle	sympto-thermal
Sunday painter	supersymmetry	swashbuckling	synallagmatic
sundown doctor	supertemporal	sweating-house	synaposematic
Sunshine State	supervenience	Swedenborgian	synapticulate
superabundant	suppeditation	Swedish modern	synarthrodial
super-achiever	supplantation	Swedish turnip	synchondroses
superaddition	supplementary	sweep the board	synchondrosis
superannuable	supply teacher	sweet chestnut	synchronicity
superannuated	support buying	sweet marjoram	synchronistic
super-calender	support trench	sweet nothings	synchronology
supercalender	suppositional	sweet scabious	synchronously
supercautious	suppositories	sweet-tempered	syncretically
supercavitate	suppressively	sweet-throated	syndesmophyte
supercollider	supra-axillary	sweetwood bark	syndicalistic
supercolossal	suprachorioid	swineherdship	synecdochical
supercolumnar	supracondylar	swine's feather	synecological
supercomputer	supralittoral	swine's succory	synergistical
supercontract	supranational	swing both ways	synodic period
supercrescent	suprapersonal	swinge-buckler	synonymically
supercritical	suprascapular	switch dealing	synovial joint
superdominant	suprasensible	switch-hitting	syntactically
superelevated	suprasensuous	switching yard	syntactic foam
supereloquent	supraspecific	switch selling	synthetically
supereminence	supraspinatus	swivel shuttle	syphilization
supereminency	supratemporal	swollen-headed	syphilophobia

syringobulbia	talk out of turn	telencephalic	tergiversator
syringomyelia	talk poor-mouth	telencephalon	term-catalogue
systematician	talk to oneself	teleoperation	terminability
systematicity	tally-business	telephone bill	terminational
systemization	Talmudistical	telephone book	terminatively
system program	talmudization	telephone call	terminologies
systems design	tamarind water	telephone dial	terminologist
tabes dorsalis	tambour-needle	telephone girl	termitologist
tableau vivant	tambour-stitch	telephone pole	Terpsichorean
table-mountain	tamper-evident	telephone poll	terraced house
table skittles	tangata whenua	telephoto lens	Terra Japonica
tablespoonful	tangentiality	teleportation	terrestrially
tablet-weaving	tangoreceptor	telerecording	terrible twins
taboparalysis	tantalization	telescope word	terrification
tachistoscope	tantalizingly	televangelism	territorially
tachyphylaxis	tape cartridge	televangelist	terror-bombing
tacking-cotton	tape recording	televisionary	terrorization
tackling dummy	tape recordist	television set	Tertullianism
tail-heaviness	tape transport	televisuality	Tertullianist
tailor-fashion	taphrogenesis	Telinga potato	testification
tailor-herring	tar and feather	teller machine	testificatory
tailor's muscle	tarantula-hawk	tell me another	testing ground
tail parachute	target dialect	tell one's beads	tetanospasmin
taintlessness	target program	telluric ochre	tetartohedral
take a back seat	tariff barrier	tellurous acid	tetartohedron
take account of	Tartarian lamb	temerariously	tetrachloride
take a chance on	Tartarian oats	temperamental	tetradynamous
take a pleasure	Tasmanian wolf	temperateness	tetrahedrally
take a thing ill	tastelessness	temperate zone	tetraparental
take exception	Taunton turkey	temper-brittle	tetrapetalous
take in the rear	tautologously	tempest-tossed	tetraquetrous
take it in turns	tautosyllabic	tempestuously	tetrasepalous
take its course	tax-deductible	temporalities	tetraspermous
take liberties	taxonomically	temporal power	tetrastichous
take lying down	taxonomic name	temporariness	tetrasyllabic
take one's leave	Taylorization	temporization	tetrasyllable
take one's lumps	Tchaikovskian	temporizingly	tetrathionate
take one's place	teachableness	temptableness	Teutonic cross
take on the chin	teach yourself	tenaciousness	Teutonization
take-out double	teapot tempest	tenancy at will	Texas longhorn
take sanctuary	tear to tatters	tenant-righter	text processor
take seriously	technical foul	Tenby daffodil	thalassocracy
take soundings	technicalness	tendentiously	thallium glass
take suspicion	technicolored	tender-hearted	thallous oxide
take the flings	technocomplex	tender mercies	thanatologist
take the ground	technocracies	tendo Achilles	thanatophilia
take the lid off	technographic	tenebrescence	thanatophobia
take the mickey	technological	tenebrousness	thanatophoric
take the part of	tectocephalic	tenement house	thank goodness
take the pledge	tectonisation	ten-minute rule	thanklessness
take the plunge	tectonization	Tennysonianly	thank-offering
take the salute	tectonosphere	Tenon's capsule	thankworthily
take the strain	tectosilicate	tenor clarinet	Thatcheresque
take the waters	tegestologist	tenore robusto	Thathanabaing
take to one's bed	tektosilicate	tenosynovitis	that is as may be
take to the road	telautography	tenpin bowling	that little lot
talent spotter	teleconverter	tentaculiform	that's the stuff
talipes valgus	telediagnosis	tentativeness	thaumatolatry
talk a good game	telefacsimile	teratogenesis	thaumaturgist
talkativeness	telegrammatic	teratological	theanthropism
talk of the town	telegraph pole	tercentennial	theanthropist
talk one's way in	telemarketing	terephthalate	Theatre of Fact

theatre sister
theatricalise
theatricalism
theatricality
theatricalize
the Authentics
the awkward age
the ayes have it
Thebaic marble
the Bard of Avon
Thebesian vein
the best part of
the blood royal
the city of Rome
the clean thing
the Crimean War
the daily grind
the dead ring of
the Depression
the deuce to pay
the devil to pay
the Disruption
the elements of
the five senses
the Five Wounds
the frozen mitt
the fur will fly
the gay science
the gentler sex
the good people
the great enemy
the Great Mogul
the Grim Reaper
the hell you say
the King's peace
the kiss of life
The Life Guards
the likelihood
the lion's mouth
the lion's share
the Lord's house
the Lord's table
the Lost Tribes
the main chance
thematization
the minute that
the Morasthite
the naked truth
thenceforward
the nick of time
the noes have it
the old country
theologically
Theophrastian
theoretically
theosophistic
the other night
the other place
the other thing
the other woman
the other world
the outer world

the penny drops
The Queen's Bays
therapeutical
thereinbefore
the right bower
theriomorphic
thermal motion
thermantidote
thermochemist
thermochromic
thermodynamic
thermo-elastic
thermoforming
thermogenesis
thermogenetic
thermographic
thermological
thermoneutral
thermonuclear
thermophilous
thermophysics
thermoplastic
thermos bottle
thermosetting
thermospheric
thermostatics
thermo-therapy
thermotropism
the rougher sex
the scene opens
these presents
the Shaky Isles
the social evil
the Soviet Zone
the spoken word
the sterner sex
the strength of
the Swan of Avon
theta activity
theta-function
The Temptation
the three kings
the tother year
the voice of God
the whole shoot
the whole story
thiabendazole
thickback sole
thick register
thick sandwich
Thiersch graft
thieves' market
thigmokinesis
thigmotropism
thimblerigger
thing in itself
thinkableness
think better of
think highly of
thinking-aloud
think little of
think straight

thiobacterium
thiocarbamate
thiocarbamide
thioglycollic
thiosulphuric
third position
Third Worldism
Third World War
thirst-country
thirtieth part
thirty-pounder
this afternoon
this day and age
this is the life
this little lot
thistle dollar
thistle funnel
thoracentesis
thoracolumbar
thoracoplasty
thorium series
thorough-brace
thorough-drain
thoroughgoing
thorough-paced
thorough-stone
thoughtlessly
thought police
thought-reader
thought reform
thought-stream
thousand-miler
thrasonically
thread-drawing
threat display
threateningly
three-cornered
three-day fever
three-line whip
threepenny bit
three per cents
three-quarters
thremmatology
threshing-mill
thrillingness
throat-cutting
throat halyard
thrombokinase
Throne of Grace
throstle frame
throttle-lever
throttle-valve
through-lounge
through-valley
throw a stone at
throwing-knife
throwing power
throwing-stick
throwing-table
throw stones at
throw together
thrush babbler

thrust bearing
thrust chamber
thrustfulness
thrust spoiler
thumb-fingered
thumb one's nose
thumb's breadth
thump a cushion
thunder-bearer
thunder-shower
thunderstormy
thunderstrike
thunderstroke
thunderstruck
thurification
thyroglobulin
thyroidectomy
thysanopteran
Tibetan cherry
Tibeto-Burmese
Tibeto-Chinese
tic douloureux
ticket barrier
ticket benefit
ticket chopper
ticket of leave
ticket-scalper
tickling stick
tick paralysis
tidal friction
tiddlywinking
tie the hands of
tight junction
tilting fillet
tilt mechanism
Tilt Yard guard
timber-cruiser
timber licence
timber rattler
time adverbial
time after time
time-and-motion
time-consuming
time out of mind
time ownership
time signature
time traveller
ting-a-ling-ling
ting-tang clock
tinman's solder
tintinnabular
tintinnabulum
tipitiwitchet
tippling-house
tip the balance
tirlie-whirlie
tissue culture
titanium oxide
titanium white
titillatingly
Titius–Bode law
tittle-tattler

titular bishop
toad-in-the-hole
toad-strangler
toast-and-water
toasting glass
toastmistress
tobacco beetle
tobacco-cutter
tobacconalian
tobacco streak
toboggan-chute
to coin a phrase
to distraction
toe-in-the-water
toga praetexta
toggle circuit
toggle-harpoon
to good purpose
to hell and gone
token estimate
token stoppage
tolerableness
tolerance dose
Toleration Act
tolerationism
tolerationist
toluidine blue
tomato pinworm
tomboyishness
to my knowledge
tone generator
tongue-in-cheek
tongue-lashing
tongue-twister
tonotopically
tonsillectomy
toothache tree
toothing-plane
toothlessness
toothsomeness
top dead centre
topknot pigeon
topochemistry
topographical
topoisomerase
topologically
topsy-turvydom
to put it mildly
torch-carrying
toreador pants
tornado-cellar
torpedo-bomber
Torrens system
tortoiseshell
Tory democracy
to say the least
to the backbone
to the contrary
to the eyeballs
totipotential
touchableness
touch football

touch of nature
touch of the sun
touch on the raw
touristically
town-traveller
toxicodendron
toxicological
toxoplasmosis
trabeculation
track and field
tracking error
track lighting
tractableness
Tractarianism
traction motor
traction wheel
trade discount
trade effluent
trade-language
trade magazine
tradesmanlike
tradesmanship
trade unionism
trade unionist
trade-weighted
trading estate
trading profit
traditionally
traditionless
traffic artery
traffic circle
traffic island
traffic-jammed
traffic lights
traffic police
traffic signal
traffic ticket
traffic warden
tragicomedies
trailer-sailer
trailing wheel
trail one's coat
trainsickness
train-spotting
trajectitious
tranquilliser
tranquillizer
transactional
transatlantic
transboundary
transcendence
transcendency
transcendible
transcortical
transcribable
transcribbler
transcriptase
transcription
transcriptive
transcultural
transcurrence
transfeminate

transfer mould
transfer orbit
transfer-paper
transferrable
transfigurate
transformable
transformance
transform down
trans-frontier
transfusional
transgredient
transgression
transgressive
transhumanate
transhumanize
transientness
trans-isthmian
transistorise
transistorize
transistor set
transit-circle
transitionary
transition fit
transitivizer
transit lounge
transketolase
translational
translatorese
transliterate
translocation
translucently
translucidity
transmarginal
transmaterial
transmembrane
transmigrator
transmissible
transmittable
transmittance
transmittancy
transmutation
transmutative
transnational
transom window
transparently
transpersonal
transpiration
transplendent
transportable
transportance
transport café
transport-ship
transposition
transpositive
transreceiver
transriverine
trans-shipment
transshipment
trans-Siberian
trans-specific
trans-synaptic
transthoracic

transurethral
transversally
transvestitic
Transylvanian
trapeze artist
trapezohedral
trapezohedron
traumatic acid
traumatically
traumatropism
traveller's joy
travelling bag
travelling rug
travel trailer
traverse-board
traverse-table
treacherously
tread a measure
tread the stage
treason felony
treasure chest
treasure-house
treasurership
Treasure State
treasure trove
Treasury bench
treatableness
treat like dirt
tree cranberry
tree of liberty
tree partridge
tree porcupine
tree structure
trellis stitch
trellis window
tremblingness
tremulousness
trencherwoman
trench warfare
trend analysis
Trendelenburg
trestle-bridge
trial and error
trial by battle
trial by combat
trial of the pyx
triamcinolone
triangularity
triangulately
triangulation
tribalization
triboelectric
tributariness
tricarboxylic
tricarpellary
tricentennial
trichological
trichopterous
trichothallic
trichothecene
trichromatism
trickle-charge

triconodontid	trunk-breeches	twilight shift	unapprehended
triethylamine	trunk dialling	twilight sleep	unappropriate
trifunctional	trunk murderer	twilight world	unarmed combat
trigger finger	trustlessness	twine-spinning	unarrestingly
trigonal quoin	trustworthily	twist and twirl	unarticulated
trigonometric	truth-function	twisted pillar	unascertained
trilateralism	truthlessness	twister's cramp	unashamedness
trilateralist	truthlikeness	twist the knife	unassaultable
trilaterality	try it on the dog	two-handedness	unassertively
trilateration	try one's hand at	two jumps ahead	unassimilable
trilingualism	tsutsugamushi	twopenny piece	unassimilated
triliteralism	tubal ligation	twopennyworth	unassuageable
triliterality	tuber cinereum	two-revolution	unatmospheric
trimerization	tubercularize	twos and threes	unattemptable
trimming-joist	tuberculation	two times table	unaugmentable
trimming wheel	tuberculiform	two-way stretch	unbashfulness
Trinity Sunday	tubular bridge	tympanometric	unbeautifully
trinucleotide	tubular vision	tympanoplasty	unbefittingly
tripersonally	tubulidentate	type facsimile	unbeginningly
triphibiously	tumbler pigeon	typographical	unbelievingly
tripinnatifid	tumbling stone	typologically	unbendingness
triple century	tumorigenesis	tyrannosaurus	unbeseemingly
triple spacing	turbidimetric	tyrannousness	unblemishable
triple vaccine	turbo-compound	Tyrrhenian Sea	unblessedness
triploblastic	turbo-electric	Ulsterization	unboundedness
tripoli polish	Turing machine	ultimate ratio	unbowdlerized
Tripolitanian	turkey-blossom	ultrafiltrate	unbreakfasted
trisaccharide	turkey buzzard	ultra-marathon	unbrotherlike
trisyllabical	Turkey leather	ultra-royalist	uncalculating
tritanomalous	turkey vulture	ultrasonicate	uncancellable
tritheistical	Turkicization	ultrasonogram	uncanonically
tritocerebral	Turkification	umbelliferous	uncatholicize
tritocerebrum	Turkish carpet	umbilical cord	unceasingness
tritubercular	Turkish coffee	umbrella field	unceremonious
triumfeminate	turmeric paper	umbrella plant	uncertainness
triumphal arch	turn end for end	umbrella stand	uncertainties
troglodytical	turn indicator	Umbrian school	uncertifiable
trolling motor	turning circle	Umbrian School	unchallenging
troop-carrying	turning radius	unabashedness	uncharismatic
trophallactic	turn inside out	unabbreviated	unchristianly
trophectoderm	turnip-cabbage	unabridgeable	uncinate gyrus
trophoblastic	turnip-lantern	unaccelerated	uncircumcised
trophonucleus	turn one's steps	unaccentuated	uncircumspect
trophotropism	turn on the heat	unaccompanied	uncivilizable
tropical month	turnover board	unaccountable	unclassically
tropical storm	turnpike trust	unaccountably	uncleanliness
tropocollagen	turn the corner	unadulterated	unclean spirit
troubadourish	turn the heat on	unadventurous	uncloudedness
trouble-making	turn the scales	unadvisedness	uncognoscible
troublemaking	turn the screws	unalcoholized	uncollectable
troublesomely	turn the tables	unamalgamated	uncomfortable
troublousness	turn to account	unambiguously	uncomfortably
trough battery	turpentine gum	unambitiously	uncommendable
trouser-suited	turpentine oil	un-Americanism	uncommendably
trumpeter swan	turpitudinous	unamiableness	uncommonplace
trumpet-flower	Turveydropian	unanimousness	uncompanioned
trumpet marine	twelvemonthly	unannihilated	uncompensated
trumpet medium	twelve-pounder	unanticipated	uncompetitive
trumpet seance	twentieth part	unappealingly	uncomplaining
trumpet-shaped	twenty-firster	unappointable	uncomplaisant
trumpet spiral	twilight house	unappreciable	uncomplicated
trumpet-tongue	twilight night	unappreciated	uncompromised

unconcealable	underachiever	undiscernibly	unexplainably
unconceitedly	underactivity	undisciplined	unexplanatory
unconceivable	under a mistake	undiscoloured	unexploitable
unconceivably	underbreeding	undiscomfited	unexpoundable
unconcernedly	undercarriage	undiscouraged	unexpressible
unconcernment	underclassman	undiscussable	unfailingness
unconcludable	underclothing	undisguisable	unfalsifiable
uncondensable	under colour of	undisguisedly	unfalteringly
unconditional	under contract	undishonoured	unfamiliarity
unconditioned	undercovering	undispellable	unfashionable
unconflicting	underdiagnose	undispensable	unfashionably
unconformable	underdoctored	undissembling	unfeasibility
unconformably	underdrainage	undissociated	unfeelingness
uncongealable	undereducated	undissolvable	unfeignedness
unconjectured	underemphasis	undistempered	unfermentable
unconnectedly	underemployed	undistinctive	unflinchingly
unconquerable	underestimate	undistributed	unflourishing
unconquerably	underexposure	undistrustful	unfluctuating
unconsciously	under-falconer	undisturbable	unforeseeable
unconsecrated	underfunction	undisturbedly	unforethought
unconsecutive	under-gardener	undiversified	unforfeitable
unconsidering	undergraduacy	undividedness	unforgettable
unconspicuous	undergraduate	undivorceable	unforgettably
unconstrained	undergrounder	undoctrinaire	unforgiveness
unconstricted	underhandedly	undogmaticism	unforgivingly
unconstruable	underivedness	undomesticate	unforthcoming
unconstructed	under-labourer	undulant fever	unfortunately
unconsultable	under-lordship	undulationist	unfoundedness
unconsummated	underminingly	undutifulness	unfriendliest
uncontactable	undermodulate	unearthliness	unfulfillable
uncontainable	under one's belt	uneasefulness	ungainsayable
uncontaminate	under one's feet	uneatableness	ungainsayably
uncontentious	under one's hand	unelectrified	ungenteelness
uncontestable	under one's seal	unemancipated	ungentlemanly
uncontestedly	underpainting	unemasculated	ungenuineness
unconversable	underplanting	unembarrassed	ungeometrical
unconvertible	under-prepared	unembellished	ungrammatical
unconvincible	underpropping	unembroidered	ungual phalanx
uncooperative	underresource	unemotionally	unguardedness
uncoordinated	under-shepherd	unencompassed	unhealthfully
uncopyrighted	understaffing	unencountered	unhealthiness
uncorrectable	understanding	unencouraging	unheedfulness
uncorruptedly	understatedly	unencumbering	unhelpfulness
uncorruptible	understrapper	unenforceable	unhomogeneity
uncorruptness	understrength	un-Englishness	unhomogeneous
uncounterfeit	under the eye of	unenlightened	unhomogenized
uncourteously	under the lee of	unentertained	unicameralism
uncourtliness	under the table	unequivocable	unicameralist
uncreatedness	undescendable	unequivocably	unicorn beetle
uncultivation	undescribable	unequivocally	uniflagellate
uncustomarily	undescribably	unessentially	unilateralism
undauntedness	undescriptive	unestablished	unilateralist
undecapeptide	undeservingly	unevangelical	unilaterality
undecidedness	undestroyable	unevangelized	unilluminated
undefiledness	undeterminate	unexaggerated	unillustrated
undefinedness	undeviatingly	unexceptional	unimaginative
undegenerated	undiagnosable	unexclusively	unimmediately
undeliberated	undifferenced	unexemplified	unimpassioned
undeliverable	undignifiedly	unexhaustible	unimpeachable
undenominated	undiminishing	unexpeditated	unimpeachably
undepreciated	undiscernedly	unexperienced	unimportunate
underabundant	undiscernible	unexplainable	unimpregnated

unimpressible
unincorporate
unincreasable
unindifferent
unindustrious
uninflammable
uninfluential
uninformative
uninhabitable
uninheritable
uninhibitedly
uninquisitive
uninspiringly
uninstructing
uninstructive
unintelligent
unintentional
unintercepted
uninteresting
unintermitted
uninterpreted
uninterrupted
unintimidated
unintuitively
uninventively
uniparentally
unitary matrix
unit character
United Kingdom
United Nations
unit of account
unity of action
Universal Aunt
universalizer
universal maid
universalness
universal time
Universal Time
universal veil
unjustifiable
unjustifiably
unkillability
unknowability
unknowingness
unladen weight
unlearnedness
unlimitedness
unlocalizable
unlovableness
unmacadamized
unmaliciously
unmarriedness
unmeaningness
unmelodiously
unmentionable
unmentionably
unmeritorious
unmindfulness
unmineralized
unministerial
unmisgivingly
unmistakeable

unmistrusting
unmitigatedly
unmixableness
unmonopolized
unmovableness
unmurmuringly
unmusicalness
unnameability
unnaturalized
unnaturalness
unnecessaries
unnecessarily
unneighboured
unneighbourly
unneutralized
unnourishable
unobliterable
unobliterated
unobservantly
unobstructive
unobtrusively
unobviousness
unofficerlike
unorganizable
unoriginality
unoriginately
unpasteurised
unpasteurized
unpatronizing
unpenetrating
unperceivable
unperceivably
unperceivedly
unperceptible
unperfectness
unperformable
unpermissible
unpersonified
unperspicuous
unpersuadable
unpersuadably
unperturbedly
unpetticoated
unphilosophic
unphysiologic
unpicturesque
un-pin-downable
unpitifulness
unplasticized
unpleasantish
unpleasurable
unpleasurably
unpliableness
unpolitically
unpolymerized
unpossibility
unpracticable
unpractically
unprecedented
unpredictable
unpredictably
unpremeditate

unpreoccupied
unpreparation
unpresentable
unpressurized
unpretentious
unpreventable
unpreventably
unpreventible
unproblematic
unproduceable
unprogressive
unproletarian
unpromisingly
unpromulgated
unprostituted
unprotectedly
unprovability
unprovisioned
unprovocative
unpublishable
unpublishably
unpunctuality
unpuncturable
unpurchasable
unpuritanical
unputdownable
unqualifiable
unqualifiedly
unquarrelsome
unquestioning
unquotability
unreadability
unreasoningly
unreceptivity
unreclaimable
unrecognition
unrecognizing
unrecollected
unrecommended
unrecompensed
unrecoverable
unrecruitable
unredressable
unregenerable
unregenerated
unrelatedness
unrelentingly
unreliability
unreligiously
unreluctantly
unremembrance
unremittingly
unremunerated
unrepentantly
unreplaceable
unreplenished
unrepresented
unreprievable
unreproachful
unreproaching
unresentfully
unresistingly

unrespectable
unresponsible
unrestingness
unretractable
unrighteously
unritualistic
unruffledness
unsacramental
unsaleability
unsalvageable
unsatisfiable
unsavouriness
unscandalized
unscholarlike
unscratchable
unscrutinized
unselectively
unselfishness
unself-knowing
unself-seeking
unsensational
unsententious
unsentimental
unsentinelled
unsequestered
unseriousness
unserviceable
unsettledness
unsewn binding
unshapeliness
unshatterable
unshrinkingly
unsightliness
unsight unseen
unsilenceable
unsinkability
unskilfulness
unslaughtered
unsmilingness
unsmotherable
unsociability
unsocial hours
unsoldierlike
unsolicitedly
unsolvability
unsophistical
unsparingness
unspecialized
unspectacular
unspeculative
unspiritually
unspontaneous
unspottedness
unstaunchable
unstereotyped
unstigmatized
unstimulating
unstreamlined
unstylishness
unsubduedness
unsubscribing
unsubstantial

unsubstituted	upon the back of	Vater's ampulla	vertical point
unsuitability	upperclassman	Vater's papilla	verticillated
unsuperfluous	upsettingness	vaulting horse	vertiginously
unsupportable	up to the elbows	Vauxhall light	vesicouterine
unsupportably	up to the eyes in	vector address	vesicovaginal
unsupportedly	up to the handle	vectorization	vesper sparrow
unsurpassable	up-to-the-minute	vector product	vessel element
unsurpassably	uralitization	vegetarianism	vessel of paper
unsurrendered	uranium series	Velikovskyism	vexatiousness
unsusceptible	urban district	Velikovskyite	vexillologist
unsuspectable	urediniospore	vendor placing	vibrationally
unsuspectedly	ureterography	venerableness	vibrationless
unsustainable	urethrography	venereologist	vicariousness
unsustainably	urethroscopic	venetian blind	Vicar of Christ
unswallowable	uricacidaemia	Venetian blind	vicars-general
unsymmetrical	urinary meatus	Venetian chalk	vice-admiralty
unsympathetic	urinary system	Venetian cloth	vice-consulate
untaintedness	ursine dasyure	Venetian glass	vicegerencies
untarnishable	user-definable	Venetian sumac	vice-president
untechnically	user interface	Venetian swell	vice-treasurer
untenableness	ustilagineous	Venetian whisk	vicious circle
unterminating	uterine sister	veno-occlusive	vicious spiral
untheological	utilitarianly	ventriculitis	victimization
untheoretical	utility player	ventriloquial	victimologist
unthreatening	Utrecht velvet	ventriloquise	Victoria Cross
unthriftiness	uveoparotitis	ventriloquism	victor ludorum
untouchedness	vaccine damage	ventriloquist	video cassette
untraditional	vacuolization	ventriloquize	videographics
untransformed	vacuum chamber	ventriloquous	video recorder
untransmitted	vacuum cleaner	ventrolateral	video terminal
untransparent	vacuum forming	venturesomely	vie d'intérieur
untransported	vagabond's skin	venturousness	vie intérieure
untravellable	vagina dentata	Venus's fly-trap	Vienna sausage
untraversable	valedictorian	Venus's flytrap	Viennese waltz
untremblingly	valedictories	veraciousness	vigintivirate
untrimmedness	valedictorily	verbalization	village burrow
untroublesome	valeraldehyde	verbification	villagisation
untrustworthy	valiant beggar	verbigeration	villagization
untunableness	validity check	verdurousness	Villar y Villar
untunefulness	valley of tears	vergence angle	villein socage
ununiformness	Valliscaulian	veridicalness	vinca alkaloid
unutilitarian	value added tax	verifiability	vindicability
unvarnishedly	value analysis	verisimilarly	vindicatingly
unvaryingness	value-for-money	veritableness	vindicatorily
unveraciously	valuelessness	vermiculation	vinegar mother
unvitrifiable	value received	vermilionette	vinho corrente
unwarlikeness	valvuloplasty	vernacularise	viniculturist
unwarrantable	Van Allen layer	vernacularism	vino corriente
unwarrantably	vandalization	vernacularist	vinyl chloride
unwarrantedly	Vansittartism	vernacularity	viola bastarda
unweariedness	Vansittartite	vernacularize	violoncellist
unwelcomeness	vantage-ground	vernal equinox	viperine snake
unwhitewashed	vapour barrier	vernalisation	viper's bugloss
unwholesomely	vapour density	vernalization	Virgilian lots
unwillingness	vapourishness	vernier engine	Virginia fence
unwittingness	vapour tension	verre églomisé	virginiamycin
unwomanliness	variationally	versatileness	Virginian deer
unworkability	varicose veins	versicoloured	Virginian poke
unworkmanlike	variety artist	versification	Virginia stock
unworldliness	vascular plant	versificatory	virialization
upgradability	vasodepressor	vertical angle	virial theorem
upon one's heels	vasovasostomy	vertical plane	virologically

virtual height	wager of battle	water-jacketed	well-knownness
virtual memory	wainscot chair	waterlessness	well languaged
visceral brain	waistcoatless	water measurer	well-meaningly
visceral cleft	wake-up service	water moccasin	well-nourished
visceral layer	Waldeyer's ring	water mongoose	well on one's way
visceral nerve	walking corpse	water-pheasant	well-organized
visceroptosis	walking-on part	water plantain	well-preserved
viscerotropic	walking-orders	water pressure	well-qualified
viscosimetric	walking papers	waterproofing	well-staircase
visible speech	walking-rapier	water purslane	well-supported
visionariness	walking-ticket	water sapphire	well thought of
visiting hours	walk the boards	water scorpion	well-travelled
visitor centre	Wallace effect	water softener	well-turned-out
visual agnosia	walling hammer	water starwort	Wernicke's area
visual display	wall newspaper	water tortoise	Wessex culture
visualization	wall pennywort	water-vascular	Western Church
vital capacity	walls have ears	water-witching	Western Empire
vitelligenous	Wall Streetish	Watteau bodice	Western saddle
vitelline duct	Walsingham way	Watteau mantle	west-north-west
viticulturist	waltzing mouse	wattle and daub	West-of-England
vitrification	wamble-cropped	wattled jacana	west-south-west
vitrified fort	wandering cell	wave mechanics	wet-and-dry bulb
vitriolic acid	wandering fire	waw conversive	whaling-master
vitriolically	wandering star	wayfaring tree	Wharton's jelly
vivaciousness	wanderlusting	way of business	what's your will
vivisectional	warbling vireo	way of the world	what the blazes
vocal ensemble	Warburgianism	way of thinking	wheel-carriage
vocationalise	war department	wayside pulpit	wheel-dwelling
vocationalism	Wardour Street	weak-kneedness	wheel-engraved
vocationalize	wardrobe trunk	weapon-carrier	wheeler-dealer
vodka and tonic	war generation	weaponization	whenceforward
voicelessness	warm-heartedly	weapons system	whereinsoever
voice-printing	warm reception	wearisomeness	where one lives
voicespondent	war resistance	wear the purple	where's the fire
volatilizable	wash-hand basin	wear the willow	Whig historian
volcanic glass	wash-hand stand	weather-beaten	whimsicalness
volcanologist	washing powder	weather bureau	whip into shape
volcano rabbit	Washingtonian	weather centre	whipping-bench
volitionality	Washington pie	weatherliness	whipping cream
Voltaireanism	wash one's brain	Weatherometer	whipping-stock
volume control	wash one's hands	weather-tiling	whirling plant
volume-density	waste disposal	weather window	whirling-table
volumenometer	waste-disposer	wedding canopy	whiskered tern
voluntariness	waste material	wedding-favour	whistle-blower
voluntaristic	waste moulding	wedding-finger	whistle-speech
von Willebrand	waste products	wedding knives	whistling duck
voraciousness	watch and watch	weed inspector	whistling kite
vortex turbine	watching brief	weekly boarder	whistling moth
vote of censure	watchlessness	week of Sundays	whistling-shop
vote on account	watch one's back	weeping willow	whistling swan
voting machine	watch one's step	weighing-house	white antimony
vouchsafement	watch the clock	weightlifting	White backlash
vowel mutation	water-breather	weight-watcher	white-bark pine
vowel-quantity	water caltrops	Weight Watcher	white-breasted
vulcanisation	water chestnut	Weinberg–Salam	white cast iron
vulcanization	watercoloured	welcome aboard	white-collared
vulcanologist	water-crowfoot	well-appointed	white elephant
vulgarisation	water-drinking	well-conducted	Whitefieldian
vulgarization	water-dropwort	well-connected	Whitefieldism
vulnerability	water-flooding	well-developed	Whitefieldite
Wacker process	water hyacinth	well-foundedly	white-knuckled
waffle stomper	watering place	Wellingtonian	white magnesia

white mahogany
white mangrove
white mulberry
whitepainting
white pipe tree
white ribboner
white sapphire
whitesmithery
whitesmithing
whitetail deer
white-throated
whitetip shark
whithersoever
wholesomeness
wholistically
whooping cough
whooping crane
whoremistress
wicket-keeping
wicketkeeping
widdy-widdy-way
wide-awakeness
wide brown land
wide of the mark
Widmanstätten
wife and mother
wild and woolly
wild gardening
wild liquorice
Wild Westerner
William Morris
will not hear of
willow gentian
willow-pattern
willow warbler
Wilson's petrel
Wiltshire Horn
winding engine
windmill grass
windmill plane
windmill plant
window cleaner
window display
window-dresser
window-shopper
window-trimmer
Windsor herald
wineglassfuls
wing-back chair
wing commander
winged thistle
winner-take-all
winning hazard
winning stroke
Winnipeg couch
winter aconite
winter bunting
winter country

winterization
winter jasmine
winter sleeper
wipe off the map
wire recording
wire-stitching
wire-stretcher
wiring diagram
witches' butter
witchetty bush
witchetty grub
witch flounder
witch of Agnesi
witch-smelling
with a bad grace
with a high hand
with all faults
with a siserary
with both hands
withdrawnness
with good grace
within an ace of
within cooee of
within earshot
within oneself
within reach of
with nothing on
with one accord
with open mouth
without a doubt
without gloves
without number
without reason
without result
withoutside of
with the stream
with the view of
with your leave
Wolffian ridge
Wolf—Rayet star
woman-movement
woman question
woman's righter
women's college
women's studies
wonderfulness
wonder-working
woodchip paper
wood engraving
wooden wedding
wood germander
wood-partridge
wood pimpernel
woodskin canoe
wool-blindness
wool-gathering
woollen-draper
woollen-witted

woolly mammoth
word a person up
word-blindness
word frequency
word geography
word-initially
wordmongering
word of command
word processor
Wordsworthian
worked to death
workhouse test
working dinner
work on tribute
work the oracle
world language
worldly-minded
worldly wisdom
wormwood water
worshippingly
worsification
worthlessness
worth one's salt
would-have-been
wound parasite
wraggle-taggle
wrapping paper
wreck of the sea
wrestling bout
wrist-slapping
writer's writer
writing-master
writing slider
writing-tablet
writ of besaiel
writ of inquiry
writ of summons
wrong-headedly
wrong way round
Württemberger
xanthochroism
xanthochromia
xanthochromic
xanthomatosis
xanthophyllic
xenoantigenic
xenobiologist
xenodiagnosis
xerodermatous
xerophthalmia
xerophthalmic
xiphiplastral
xiphiplastron
X-ray astronomy
xylographical
yachtsmanship
Yankee notions
Yarkand carpet

year after year
Yearly Meeting
year of Our Lord
year of the hare
Yeddo hawthorn
yellow admiral
yellow arsenic
yellow atrophy
yellow-bellied
yellow bunting
yellowfin sole
yellowfin tuna
yellow Geordie
yellowishness
yellow wagtail
yellow warbler
yellow warning
Yenisei-Ostyak
yeoman pricker
yeoman service
Yeoman Warders
yesterday's man
yield strength
yield the ghost
Yorkshire tyke
you and who else
you are welcome
young offender
Young's modulus
you should hear
yuppification
Zarathustrian
zebra crossing
zebra firefish
zenana mission
zenographical
zeolitization
zephyr gingham
zeta potential
zeugmatically
zigzag machine
zincification
Zinjanthropus
zinnober green
zodiacal light
Zöllner's lines
zona pellucida
zone levelling
zooflagellate
zoogeographer
zoogeographic
zooidiogamous
zooplanktonic
zoosporangium
zygapophyseal
zygodactylous
zygomatic arch
zygomatic bone

FOURTEEN LETTERS

a beam in one's eye
aberrationally
a bird in the hand
a bit of all right
abjuration oath
abjure the realm
abominableness
above and beyond
above suspicion
abrenunciation
absent-mindedly
absolutization
absorptiometer
absquatulation
abstemiousness
abstersiveness
abstractedness
abstractionism
abstractionist
acceptableness
accessibleness
accessory nerve
accidentalness
accompliceship
accomplishable
accomplishment
accordion pleat
accountability
accountantship
accumulatively
accusatorially
accustomedness
Achilles tendon
achondroplasia
achondroplasic
achromatically
achronological
acknowledgedly
acknowledgment
acquaintedness
across one's knee
across the board
actinide series
actinometrical
actio in distans
action painting
action research
action stations
active charcoal
active driveway
act of attainder
act of indemnity
Act of Supremacy
acupuncttuation
adductor muscle

adenocarcinoma
adjacent angles
administration
administrative
administratrix
Admiralty Board
adoption agency
adrenal medulla
adrenocortical
adult education
advance booking
advanced degree
advantageously
Advent calendar
adventitiously
adverb of manner
Advocate-Depute
aerenchymatous
aerial cableway
aerial ping-pong
aerobiological
aerodynamicist
aeroelasticity
aerosolization
aesthesiometer
aetiologically
affair of honour
affectionately
affectlessness
a flea in one's ear
African cypress
Africanization
African pompano
after-knowledge
after-reckoning
after-sensation
against the hair
against the wall
aggrandization
aggrandizement
aggregate fruit
aggressiveness
agriculturally
agrobiological
agro-ecological
agro-industrial
agrotechnology
air-conditioned
air-conditioner
airing cupboard
Air Vice-Marshal
alcoholization
alcoholometric
alder buckthorn
Alexandrianism

alexipharmacon
Alfred the Great
alignment chart
alimentiveness
a lion in the path
alkalinization
all and singular
allegorization
allelomorphism
all in a day's work
all-in wrestling
alliterational
alliteratively
allodification
all one knows how
allopathically
allopatrically
allosterically
allotetraploid
all-overishness
all over the shop
all over the show
all there is to it
all-too-familiar
alphabetically
alphanumerical
alteration hand
altogetherness
altruistically
aluminium oxide
aluminothermic
amateurishness
ambassadorship
ambidextrously
ambrosia beetle
Ambrosian chant
ambulance woman
American Indian
American Legion
American marten
American plaice
American turtle
ammonification
ammonitiferous
amniotic cavity
amphiarthrosis
amphiarthrotic
amphibological
amylobarbitone
Anabaptistical
anachronically
anagrammatical
analogicalness
anamorphoscope
ancient demesne

ancient history
androdioecious
andromonoecism
angle of weather
Anglo-Gallicism
anhypostatical
annalistically
annular eclipse
annus mirabilis
answerableness
antagonistical
antagonization
antaphrodisiac
Antarctic Ocean
anthropologist
anthropologize
anthropometric
anthropopathic
anthropotomist
Anti-Birmingham
anticipatingly
anticipatively
anticipatorily
anticonvulsant
antidepressant
antidromically
anti-government
antihistaminic
antihysterical
antimacassared
antimetabolite
antimonarchist
antimony glance
antineoplastic
anti-odontalgic
antipathetical
antiperistasis
antiperspirant
antiphlogistic
antiphonically
antiquarianism
antiquarianize
antiscriptural
antiseptically
antisymmetrize
antisyphilitic
antithetically
anxiety complex
apartment block
apartment hotel
apartment house
aphoristically
apocalypticism
apologetically
apophthegmatic
apoplectically
appeal to Caesar
appendicectomy
apple of discord
apple of one's eye
apples and pears

applicableness
apply the brakes
appositionally
appreciatingly
appreciatively
apprehensively
apprenticehood
apprenticement
apprenticeship
approvableness
approved school
Arabian jasmine
Arabic numerals
arachnological
arbitratorship
arboricultural
archaeological
archaistically
archbishophood
archbishopship
archdeaconries
archdeaconship
archidiaconate
archiepiscopal
archipresbyter
archpriesthood
arenaceous rock
argentaffinoma
aristocratical
arithmetically
arithmetic mean
Ark of Testimony
armour-piercing
aromatherapist
arrhythmically
arrondissement
arterial system
article of faith
article of virtu
articulateness
artificialness
artificial silk
artillery plant
arty-craftiness
as a general rule
as clear as a bell
as crazy as a loon
a second opinion
as far as I can see
as fit as a fiddle
as God is my judge
as happy as a clam
as happy as Larry
Asiatic cholera
a smack in the eye
as mad as a hatter
as near as dammit
a sop to Cerberus
asparagus stone
as safe as houses
assertorically

asset-stripping
assimilability
as smart as paint
associationism
associationist
as the case may be
as the crow flies
asthenospheric
as the story goes
astragalomancy
astrochemistry
astrologically
astronomically
astrophysicist
as who should say
asymmetrically
asymptotically
asynchronously
a tap on the wrist
at a rate of knots
at daggers drawn
at equidistance
at full throttle
a thing of nought
Atlantic States
atomic mass unit
atomic particle
atomic spectrum
at one fell swoop
at one's disposal
at one's last gasp
at one's pleasure
atraumatically
atropinization
at swords' points
attainableness
attested cattle
attitude of mind
attitudinarian
attorn tenant to
attractiveness
audio frequency
audiometrician
audio secretary
auditory meatus
Augustinianism
aurora borealis
aurothiomalate
auspiciousness
Australian bear
Australianness
Australian teak
authentication
autobiographer
autobiographic
autocorrelator
autocratically
auto-erotically
autograph album
autolithograph
automatic pilot

automatization
autoradiograph
auto-suggestion
auto-suggestive
autotransplant
aux fines herbes
avariciousness
a will of one's own
a winning streak
a word to the wise
axiomatization
axis of symmetry
axisymmetrical
azidothymidine
babes in the wood
bachelor of arts
Bachelor of Arts
back-projection
backscattering
back-scratching
back-seat driver
bactericidally
bacteriologist
bacteriophobia
bacteriostasis
bacteriostatic
badminton court
baggage reclaim
balance of power
balance of trade
balloon barrage
ballpark figure
Balmoral tartan
banana republic
banded anteater
banged to rights
bangtail muster
banking parlour
banner headline
banqueting-hall
baptism of blood
Barbados cherry
barbituric acid
Bardfield oxlip
barefoot doctor
bargain and sale
bargain-hunting
bargaining chip
baroclinically
barometrically
barotropically
barrage balloon
barrel of laughs
barrister-at-law
baseball league
bastardization
bastard saffron
Batavian endive
bate one's breath
bathing costume
bathing-machine

bathorhodopsin
batsman's wicket
battering-train
batting average
be-all and end-all
be all the same to
bear and forbear
bear animalcule
bear comparison
bearded vulture
bear great state
Béarnaise sauce
beat generation
beatific vision
beat one's brains
beat one's breast
beat the drum for
beat to quarters
beat to the punch
beautification
bedroom slipper
bed-sitting room
beef to the heels
before one's eyes
before one's nose
before one's time
beg the question
behaviouralism
behaviouralist
behaviouristic
behind one's back
behind schedule
behind the times
being-for-itself
believe it or not
belladonna lily
belletristical
bells of Ireland
belted galloway
belt-tightening
benedictionary
beneficialness
benefit society
benzodiazepine
bergamot-orange
beside the point
Bessel function
best before date
better feelings
beyond question
beyond reproach
Bible Christian
bibliographies
bibliographise
bibliographize
bibliomaniacal
bid a person base
bidialectalism
big-heartedness
bilirubinaemia
billiard-marker

billiard saloon
bill of exchange
binary compound
Binet–Simon test
bioclimatology
biodegradation
bio-electricity
bio-engineering
bioengineering
biogenetically
biogeochemical
biographically
bioluminescent
biomathematics
biorhythmicist
biostatistical
biosystematics
biosystematist
bipartisanship
birch partridge
bird of paradise
Bismarckianism
bite the thumb at
bit of crackling
bitter-cucumber
bituminiferous
bituminization
bituminous coal
biuret reaction
black chameleon
black eyed Susan
black guillemot
black horehound
black in the face
black manganese
black marketeer
black raspberry
black snakeroot
black stinkwood
black swallower
black turnstone
bladder-campion
blade-consonant
blank cartridge
blasting powder
blastomylonite
blaxploitation
bleaching-green
bleary-eyedness
Blenheim Orange
blepharoplasty
blessed thistle
blind as a beetle
blockade-runner
block and tackle
blocked letters
blond bombshell
blood poisoning
bloodthirstier
bloodthirstily
bloody-mindedly

blow hot and cold	bright and early	cack-handedness
blue marguerite	Bright's disease	cadaverousness
Blues and Royals	brightsomeness	cadence braking
blue sowthistle	brindled beauty	caisson disease
blue wildebeest	bring into being	calabash nutmeg
boa constrictor	bring up the rear	calamitousness
boarding kennel	Bristol diamond	calamity-howler
boarding school	Bristol fashion	calcaneocuboid
board of control	Britannia metal	California Jack
boatswain's mate	British disease	call in evidence
boisterousness	British English	call in question
Bologna sausage	Britticisation	calliper splint
bolometrically	Brobdingnagian	call to the lot of
boneless wonder	Brocken spectre	calorific value
Book of Proverbs	broiler chicken	calorimetrical
borough council	bronchiectasis	camera obscuras
borough-English	bronchodilator	campanological
boroughmongery	bronze diabetes	campylotropous
borrowed plumes	brother uterine	Canadian French
bottom-dwelling	brown haematite	canary-coloured
bottom falls out	Brownian motion	cannon-ball tree
botulinum toxin	brownish-yellow	canonical hours
bougainvillaea	Brunswick green	cantaloup melon
bouncing castle	brush discharge	cantankerously
boundary umpire	Brussels carpet	can't be bothered
bouquets garnis	Brussels sprout	Canterbury bell
Bourbon biscuit	buccolingually	Canterbury tale
bowdlerization	Buckley's chance	capacitatively
bowling average	buffer solution	Cape gooseberry
Bowman's capsule	bulimia nervosa	Cape hartebeest
brachycephales	bull-headedness	Cape hunting dog
brachycephalic	bullock-puncher	capitalist road
Brackett series	bumper-to-bumper	capitalization
bradymetabolic	bump of locality	capriciousness
brain-fever bird	bundle of nerves	captain-general
brake parachute	Burchell's zebra	captive balloon
branchial cleft	burdensomeness	capuchin monkey
branchiomerism	bur in the throat	caramelization
branchiostegal	burnt to a cinder	carbon monoxide
Bravais lattice	burst in shivers	carboxylic acid
Brazilian tapir	burst one's sides	carcinogenesis
bread and butter	bury the hatchet	carcinological
bread and scrape	bus-conductress	carcinomatosis
breadfruit tree	business person	Cardan's formula
break-bone fever	busman's holiday	cardiac passion
break in shivers	butter-fingered	cardinal bishop
break new ground	butterfly valve	cardinal deacon
break one's heart	buttonball tree	cardinal flower
break the back of	button mushroom	cardinal humour
break the ground	buttonwood tree	cardinal number
break the record	buy a pig in a poke	cardinal spider
break the wicket	by one's lonesome	cardinal virtue
breathing-space	by return of post	cardiomyopathy
breathlessness	by the Lord Harry	cardiovascular
breathtakingly	by the same token	carriage return
breech delivery	by the truckload	carry a torch for
breeder reactor	cabbage lettuce	cartes blanches
breeding ground	cabbage-looking	Cartesian devil
breeding season	Cabinet Council	Cartesian diver
bremsstrahlung	cabinet pudding	cartographical
bridge-building	cabinet scraper	cartoonishness

cartridge paper
cascara sagrada
case conference
casement window
cash on delivery
cassette player
castle-building
castle in the air
cast one's garter
castor oil plant
castrametation
cast the gorge at
casual labourer
catachrestical
catadioptrical
catastrophical
catch a likeness
catechetically
catechumenical
categorization
catenary bridge
cathedral glass
Catherine wheel
cathode ray tube
Catholic Herald
Cauchy sequence
Cauchy's theorem
caudal vertebra
caudate nucleus
cauliflower ear
cause and effect
causes célèbres
causewayed camp
caustic creeper
cedar of Lebanon
celestial globe
Celtic twilight
censoriousness
censurableness
centenarianism
Central America
central heating
centralisation
centralization
central locking
central reserve
centrifugality
centrifugalize
centrifugation
centrolecithal
centuplication
cercopithecoid
cerebral cortex
cerebrocentric
cestui que trust
ceteris paribus
Chagas's disease
chaises longues
chamber concert
chamber foreign
chamois leather

chancellorship
chances are that
Chandler wobble
changeableness
changelessness
change one's feet
change one's mind
change one's mood
change one's note
change one's skin
change one's tune
Channel Islands
channelization
chanson de geste
chaptalization
character actor
characterfully
characteristic
characterology
charcoal-burner
charcoal filter
charioteership
charitableness
charlotte russe
charm offensive
charter parties
Charter Society
chase the dragon
château-bottled
chattel slavery
checkerberries
cheese sandwich
chemical weapon
chemoautotroph
chemoreception
chemosynthesis
chemosynthetic
chemotherapist
chest of drawers
chest-protector
Chewings fescue
chicken à la King
chicken cholera
chicken-hearted
chicken-livered
Chief Constable
child allowance
child of the soil
child-resistant
Chilean jasmine
Chile saltpetre
chilli con carne
chimney swallow
chincherinchee
Chinese cabbage
Chinese lantern
Chinese laundry
Chinese New Year
chinless wonder
chitter-chatter
chivalrousness

chloral hydrate
chloridization
chloritization
chloromelanite
chlorophyllous
chloroplatinic
chlorothiazide
chlorpromazine
chocolate brown
chocolate-house
cholecystotomy
choledochotomy
cholelithiasis
cholinesterase
chondrocranium
chondrogenesis
chondrosarcoma
chorale prelude
chorda tendinea
choreographist
chorographical
chrestomathies
Christlikeness
Christmas carol
Christocentric
Christological
chromatic scale
chromatography
chromatophoric
chromodynamics
chronicle drama
chronobiologic
chronometrical
Church and State
church assembly
Church Congress
Church Covenant
Church Militant
Church Slavonic
churchwardenly
chute-the-chutes
cigarette-paper
cinematography
cineradiograph
cinnamaldehyde
circle of Willis
circuit-breaker
circuitousness
circular letter
circumadjacent
circumambience
circumambiency
circumambulate
circumbendibus
circumferentor
circumgyration
circumgyratory
circumlittoral
circumlocution
circumlocutory
circum-meridian

circumnavigate
circumnutation
circumposition
circumrotation
circumscissile
circumspection
circumspective
circumstantial
circumvolution
citizen's arrest
city missionary
civil commotion
civilizational
clapperdudgeon
claret-coloured
clasp one's hands
class-conscious
classical Latin
classification
classificatory
claustrophilia
claustrophobia
claustrophobic
clavicytherium
cleansing cream
clearance order
cleptoparasite
clerical collar
climatological
climb the ladder
clip the wings of
clitoridectomy
clitter-clatter
cloak-and-dagger
close communion
close Communion
closed interval
closed syllable
close the door on
close the door to
close to the bone
close to the wind
clothing coupon
cloth-yard shaft
clouded leopard
clove carnation
clutch at a straw
coarticulation
coasting vessel
cobalticyanide
co-belligerence
co-belligerency
cocarcinogenic
cochineal plant
cock-a-doodle-doo
cockatoo farmer
cock-of-the-north
cocksfoot grass
cocktail beetle
cocktail-shaker
coconut matting

coeliac disease
coessentiality
coetaneousness
coffee-coloured
cogitativeness
cognizableness
cognoscibility
co-guardianship
cohabitational
coign of vantage
coincidentally
cold dark matter
collapsibility
collectability
collective farm
collectiveness
collective noun
collectivistic
collector's item
college pudding
Colles' fracture
colometrically
colonel-general
Colonel-in-Chief
Colonial Office
Colorado beetle
colour fastness
colourlessness
colour-sergeant
combustibility
combustion-tube
come across with
come from behind
come full circle
come off the pill
come on the scene
come to the front
comfort station
comma butterfly
commandantship
command economy
commandingness
commensurately
commensuration
commentatorial
commissaryship
commissionaire
commit adultery
committee stage
committee woman
commit to memory
commit to prison
commodiousness
common alehouse
common caracara
common centaury
common criminal
common informer
common nuisance
common or garden
common property

common recovery
common ryegrass
commonsensible
commonsensibly
commonsensical
Common Sergeant
Common Serjeant
common shoveler
common toadfish
common valerian
Communion-cloth
Communion table
community chest
companion hatch
companion piece
company officer
comparableness
compassionable
compatibleness
compellability
compenetration
compensatingly
compensational
competitorship
complementally
complementizer
complexionally
complexionless
complimentally
compliment slip
composing-stick
compossibility
compound engine
compound raceme
comprehensible
comprehensibly
compromisingly
compulsatively
compulsiveness
compulsoriness
compunctiously
computer dating
concaulescence
concavo-concave
conceivability
concelebration
concentratedly
concentrically
conceptiveness
conceptualizer
concerti grossi
concerto grosso
concert pianist
concessionaire
concessiveness
conciliatorily
conclusiveness
concorporation
concrete poetry
concretization
concupiscently

condensability
condescendence
condescendency
conditionalism
conditionalist
conditionality
conductibility
conductimetric
conduction band
conductometric
conduplication
confessionless
confidence game
confidentially
confirmability
confirmatively
conformability
conformational
confoundedness
conglobulation
conglomeration
conglutination
congratulation
congratulative
congratulatory
congregational
congregationer
Congresspeople
Congreve rocket
conidiophorous
coniferization
conjecturality
conjugal rights
conjugate angle
conjugate focus
conjunctivitis
conjunct person
conjuring trick
connaturalness
connectibility
Connecticutter
conquistadores
consanguineous
consarcination
conscienceless
conservational
conservatively
conservativism
conservatories
conservatorium
consignificant
consistorially
consociational
consonant shift
conspiratorial
constabularies
constituencies
constitutional
constitutioned
constitutively
constitutivity

construability
constructional
constructively
constructivism
constructivist
consubstantial
consuetudinary
consulting room
consumer-driven
consummateness
consummatively
contact breaker
contact healing
contact process
contagiousness
container-grown
container-lorry
contemperature
contemporaries
contemporarily
contemptuously
conterminously
contiguousness
continental day
Continental day
continentalist
continentality
continentalize
continued story
continuity girl
continuousness
continuous wave
contour-chasing
contour feather
contrabandista
contract bridge
contractedness
contract killer
contradictable
contradictious
contradistinct
contragredient
contra-indicant
contra-indicate
contraindicate
contranatation
contraposition
contrapositive
contrapuntally
contra-rotating
contra-rotation
contrary-minded
contrary-to-fact
contra-seasonal
contrast medium
controlled drug
controllership
control surface
controvertible
contumaciously
contumeliously

convection cell
convection oven
conventionally
converging lens
conversational
convertibility
convexo-concave
convictiveness
convincingness
convolutionary
convulsiveness
Cooley's anaemia
Coolgardie safe
cooperationist
copper-bottomed
copper-fastened
copper sulphate
coproporphyrin
cops and robbers
Coptic Orthodox
coquettishness
coral-limestone
cord-ornamented
core curriculum
core vocabulary
Coriolis effect
corner cupboard
Corona Borealis
coronary artery
coronation oath
corporate image
corporate State
corporation tax
corpus callosum
corpuscularian
corpus striatum
Correggiescity
correspondence
correspondency
corrugated iron
corruptibility
corticosteroid
corticosterone
corticotrophic
corticotrophin
cosmochemistry
cosmographical
cosmologically
cosmopolitanly
cosmopolitical
cost accountant
cost accounting
cost-efficiency
cotemporaneity
cotemporaneous
Cotswold cheese
cotton-leaf worm
coumarone resin
council chamber
council-general
councillorship

counselor-at-law
counterbalance
counter-battery
counter-compony
counter-culture
counterculture
countercurrent
counterfactual
counterlathing
countermeasure
countermissile
counter-opening
counter-passant
counter-passion
counter-penalty
counterpuncher
counter-salient
countershading
countersubject
counting number
count one's beads
country dancing
county palatine
County Palatine
coupled columns
courageousness
course of nature
Court Christian
Court of Appeals
court of inquiry
Court of session
Court of Session
covering letter
cover the ground
cowardy custard
coxcombicality
Coxsackie virus
coyote diggings
cradle Catholic
cradle-snatcher
craft-conscious
cranberry jelly
creamery butter
creatureliness
credibility gap
creditableness
credit transfer
creepy-crawlies
crème Chantilly
crème de la crème
crème renversée
crickle-crackle
crime of passion
criminalistics
criminal lawyer
criminal record
criminological
criminous clerk
crinkle-crankle
crinkum-crankum
critical volume

crocodile tears
crook in one's lot
crook one's elbow
cross-buttocker
cross-countries
cross-fertilise
cross-fertilize
cross-fingering
cross-gartering
cross-infection
cross one's heart
cross-pollinate
cross-reference
cross-sectional
cross-subsidise
cross-subsidize
cross the path of
crouched burial
crown and anchor
Crown privilege
cruciverbalist
cruising radius
crumb structure
crushing stroke
cryobiological
cry one's eyes out
cryoprotectant
cryoprotection
cryoscopically
cryptococcosis
cryptogrammist
cryptographist
cryptoporticus
cryptorchidism
cryptovolcanic
crystal lattice
crystallizable
crystallize out
crystallogenic
crystallomancy
cucumber beetle
cucumber mosaic
cucurbitaceous
culture vulture
culturological
cumbersomeness
cumulativeness
cumulative vote
cumulonimbuses
curate-in-charge
curate's comfort
curiologically
current account
current affairs
current bedding
curricula vitae
curtain lecture
curvilinearity
cushion capital
cushion-thumper
cuss a person out

customary court
customs service
cut a person dead
cut one's teeth on
cut the throat of
cut-throat razor
cutthroat razor
cyanobacterium
cyanocobalamin
cyclomorphosis
cyclorrhaphous
cyclostomatous
cystic fibrosis
cytocentrifuge
cytogeneticist
cytophotometer
cytophotometry
dacryoadenitis
dacryocystitis
dactylographer
daffadowndilly
daffodil yellow
damfoolishness
dance of macabre
dance programme
dancing dervish
dancing-partner
dandelion clock
dark-adaptation
dark arches moth
darkling beetle
darning-machine
data processing
data protection
dative absolute
daughterliness
daughters-in-law
daylight saving
Day of Atonement
day of expiation
Day of Judgement
day of reckoning
dead man's handle
Dead Sea Scrolls
dead to the world
Dear John letter
death's head moth
debenture stock
debilitatingly
decapacitation
deceivableness
deceive oneself
de-Christianize
deciduous tooth
decimal coinage
decimalization
decivilization
declare oneself
declassifiable
declining years
decolonization

decolorization	Derby porcelain	dielectrically
decompensation	Derbyshire spar	diesel-electric
deconsecration	deregistration	differentiable
deconstruction	derivationally	differentially
deconstructive	derivativeness	differentiator
Decorated style	derived fossils	different-sized
decorative arts	dermatoglyphic	diffractometer
decorativeness	dermatographia	diffractometry
decree absolute	dermatological	digestibleness
decreolization	dermatomycosis	digestive gland
deed of covenant	dernier ressort	digestive tract
defeasibleness	derogatoriness	digger's delight
defeminization	desalinization	dig in one's heels
defence in depth	descending node	digitalization
defenestration	descriptionist	digressiveness
defensibleness	desert ironwood	dilemmatically
deferentiality	desert pavement	diluvial theory
defibrillation	desirelessness	dimensionality
definitionally	desk dictionary	diminutiveness
definitive host	desophisticate	dingo on a person
definitiveness	despairingness	dinoflagellate
deflocculation	despicableness	diplographical
degasification	despiritualize	diplomatically
degenerate code	despitefulness	diplomatic copy
degenerateness	destructionist	diplostemonous
degenerescence	desulphuration	dipterocarpous
degree absolute	detached retina	dipterological
degrees of frost	determinedness	direct dialling
dehumanization	detestableness	direct drilling
delaying action	detoxification	directionality
delectableness	detractiveness	direct opposite
deliberateness	devalorization	direct question
deliberatively	devaluationist	direct taxation
delightfulness	devil's advocate	disaccommodate
delocalization	devitalization	disacknowledge
demisemiquaver	dexamphetamine	disaffiliation
demobilization	dextrorotation	disaffirmation
democratically	dextrorotatory	disaggregation
demolition ball	dextrotartaric	disambiguation
demonetization	dextrotartrate	disapplication
demoralization	diabolicalness	disappointedly
demoralizingly	diachronically	disappointment
demountability	diademed monkey	disapprobation
denaturization	diagenetically	disapprobative
denazification	diagnostically	disapprobatory
dendroclimatic	diagonalizable	disappropriate
denominational	diagonal matrix	disapprovingly
denominatively	diaheliotropic	disarrangement
dental mechanic	dialectologist	disassociation
denumerability	diamantiferous	disbelievingly
depart from life	diamondiferous	disciplinarian
departmentally	diamond jubilee	disciplinarily
dependableness	diamond wedding	disciplinatory
depigmentation	diaphototropic	discographical
deplorableness	diathermaneity	discolouration
depolarization	diathermically	discombobulate
deposit account	dichotomically	discomfortable
depot battalion	dicotyledonous	discomfortably
depreciatingly	dictation speed	discommendable
depressingness	die in one's boots	discomposingly
depressiveness	die in one's shoes	disconcertedly

disconcertment
disconfirmable
disconformable
disconnectable
disconnectedly
disconsolately
disconsolation
discontentedly
discontentment
discontinuance
disconvenience
discount-broker
discountenance
discouragement
discouragingly
discourteously
discredibility
discretionally
discretiveness
discretization
discriminately
discriminating
discrimination
discriminative
discriminatory
discursiveness
disdainfulness
disedification
disembarkation
disemboguement
disembowelling
disembowelment
disempowerment
disenchantment
disencumbrance
disenfranchise
disengagedness
disenthralment
disentitlement
disequilibrate
disequilibrium
disestablisher
disforestation
disfurnishment
disgruntlement
disgustfulness
disgustingness
dishcloth gourd
disheartenment
disillusionary
disillusionise
disillusionize
disimpassioned
disimperialism
disimprovement
disincarcerate
disinclination
disincommodate
disincorporate
disinfestation
disinformation

disingenuously
disinheritance
disintegration
disintegrative
disinteresting
disjecta membra
disjointedness
dismissiveness
Disneyfication
disorderliness
disorientation
dispensability
dispensational
dispensatively
dispensatorily
dispersability
dispersibility
dispersiveness
dispersonalize
dispiritedness
dispiteousness
display cabinet
displeasurable
displeasurably
disputableness
disputatiously
disquietedness
disquisitional
disregardfully
disrespectable
disruptiveness
dissatisfiedly
dissertational
disserviceable
dissociability
dissuasiveness
dissymmetrical
distance runner
distemperature
distensibility
distortionless
distractedness
distraughtness
distressed area
distressedness
distress-rocket
distress signal
distributaries
distributional
distributively
distributivity
disulphide bond
disyllabically
dittany of Crete
divaricatingly
divergenceless
diverticulitis
diverticulosis
divertissement
divided highway
do a dishonour to

do a person out of
do a person proud
do a person stead
do a person wrong
Doctors' Commons
doctor's mandate
dodecasyllabic
dodecasyllable
dodge the column
dog in the manger
dogmaticalness
dog-tooth violet
do-it-yourselfer
dolce far niente
dolichocephali
dolichocephaly
dolomitization
dolphin-striker
domaine-bottled
domestic bursar
done to the world
don't-carishness
do one's business
do one's own thing
do one's possible
dormant partner
dormer bungalow
dorsoventrally
dor the dotterel
do something for
dot and carry one
double acrostic
double-breasted
double concerto
double cropping
double-declutch
double entendre
double exposure
double jeopardy
double knitting
double napoleon
double negative
double saucepan
double standard
double-stopping
double-stranded
doublet and hose
double-tonguing
doubting Thomas
downconversion
downhill of life
down in the dumps
down in the mouth
down one's street
down on one's luck
dracunculiasis
Drang nach Osten
draughtmanship
draughtsperson
drawing account
draw the longbow

dress-conscious	eiusdem generis	encephalopathy
dress preserver	elder-brotherly	encounter group
dress rehearsal	elder statesman	encyclopaedism
drift-indicator	Electra complex	encyclopaedist
drilling string	electric charge	encyclopedical
drinking-up time	electric cooker	endarterectomy
drinking-vessel	electric guitar	endocrinologic
drink like a fish	electric kettle	endodontically
drink the waters	electric shaver	endopolyploidy
driver's license	electrobiology	endoscopically
drive the centre	electrocautery	endosmotically
drive to the wall	electrochemist	endotracheally
drive up the wall	electrochromic	enfant terrible
driving licence	electrodeposit	enforceability
drop-handlebars	electrodynamic	enfranchisable
drop one's bundle	electrogenesis	engagement ring
dropping-bottle	electrokinetic	English disease
drunken driving	electrolytical	English English
Dublin Bay prawn	electromedical	Englishization
duchesse sleeve	electromyogram	English mustard
ducks and drakes	electroneutral	English opening
duelling pistol	electronically	English Psalter
duodeno-jejunal	electronic mail	engrossingness
duplicate ratio	electronograph	enharmonically
duplicate whist	electron optics	enregistration
Dutch reckoning	electro-optical	ensemble acting
dyed-in-the-grain	electro-osmosis	ens realissimum
dyer's greenweed	electro-osmotic	entepicondylar
dynamo-electric	electrophorese	enterogastrone
dynamometer car	electrostatics	enterotoxaemia
dysmenorrhoeal	electrosurgery	enterprise zone
dysmenorrhoeic	electrotechnic	enterprisingly
earn one's tucker	electrotherapy	entertainingly
East Coast fever	electrothermal	enter the Church
Easter sittings	electrovalence	enthronization
easy come easy go	electrovalency	enthusiastical
eat oneself sick	electroviscous	entomopathogen
eccentricities	elegiac couplet	epexegetically
ecclesiastical	elementariness	ephebiatrician
ecclesiologist	elephant dugout	epichlorhydrin
echinococcosis	elephant's teeth	epicontinental
echocardiogram	eleutheromania	epidemic typhus
ecocatastrophe	Elizabethanism	epidemiologist
econometrician	ellipticalness	epididymectomy
economic growth	embankment wall	epigenetically
economy of scale	embarrassingly	epiglottiditis
ectrodactylism	emblematically	epigrammatical
edible dormouse	embryoniferous	epigrammatizer
editio princeps	embryotoxicity	epigraphically
educationalist	emission nebula	epistemologist
effectual grace	emission theory	epistolography
effeminateness	empathetically	epistolophobia
efficient cause	emperor penguin	episyllogistic
effortlessness	empire building	epithelization
egalitarianism	emprosthotonos	epizootiologic
eggbutt snaffle	empyreumatical	equanimousness
egocentrically	emulsification	equation of time
Egyptian plover	enamel painting	equiangularity
eigenfrequency	enantiomorphic	equinoctial day
eighteen-tonner	encephalitogen	equiponderance
eight-leaf twill	encephalograph	equiponderancy

equivocatingly
ergastoplasmic
ergocalciferol
err on the side of
erythroblastic
erythrocytosis
erythropoiesis
erythropoietic
erythropoietin
escape velocity
eschatological
essence-peddler
establish a suit
esterification
estoppel in pais
eternalization
etherification
Ethiops martial
Ethiops mineral
ethnic minority
ethnobotanical
ethnographical
ethnohistorian
ethnologically
ethnosemantics
ethylene glycol
etymologically
Euclidean space
eugeosynclinal
Euler's constant
eulogistically
euphorbiaceous
euphuistically
Eurocentricity
Europarliament
Eusebian canons
Eustachian tube
eutrophication
evangelicalism
evangelicanism
evangelistical
evangelization
evaporated milk
evapotranspire
even-handedness
evening lychnis
evergreen hazel
everlasting pea
everywhere else
everywhereness
evolutionarily
evolutionistic
exacerbatingly
exaggeratingly
exaggeratively
exasperatingly
exceptionalism
exceptionality
exceptiousness
exclaim against
exclaustration

excluded middle
exclusion order
exclusive voice
excommunicable
excommunicator
excrementitial
excruciatingly
executioneress
executor dative
exflagellation
exhaustibility
exhaustiveness
exhereditation
exhilaratingly
existentialism
existentialist
exoatmospheric
exonucleolytic
exothermically
expansion board
expansionistic
expansion joint
expedientially
expense account
expergefaction
experienceable
experientalist
experientially
experimentally
explain oneself
exploitability
explosive rivet
exponentiation
expositionally
expressionless
expression-mark
expression-stop
expressiveness
express oneself
exsanguination
ex-servicewoman
ex-servicewomen
extemporaneous
extended burial
extended family
extensibleness
extensionality
extensor muscle
extinct volcano
extinguishable
extinguishment
extortionately
extracorporeal
extractability
extra-essential
extra-foraneous
extramaritally
extraneousness
extraordinaire
extra-parochial
extrapyramidal

extravagancies
extravehicular
extreme unction
face to faceness
face to face with
facinorousness
factitiousness
factor analysis
factor of safety
factory farming
factory trawler
faint-heartedly
fair-mindedness
fair-to-middling
fairy armadillo
fairy godmother
faits accomplis
fallaciousness
falling weather
fall into disuse
fall on deaf ears
fall on one's face
fall on one's feet
fall to the lot of
false hellebore
false pretences
false thorow-wax
falsifiability
fame and fortune
familiar spirit
Family Division
family likeness
family planning
family portrait
family skeleton
fancy franchise
fantasticality
fantastication
fantasy cricket
far-fetchedness
far-sightedness
farthingsworth
fashionability
fast and furious
fast friendship
fastidiousness
fatalistically
fatherlessness
father-long-legs
father of chapel
Father Superior
favourableness
feather-bedding
feather-brained
federalization
Federal Reserve
feeble-mindedly
feed check valve
feel the draught
feel the pulse of
feldspathoidal

felicitousness
fellow-commoner
fellow creature
fen-berrberries
fenestra ovalis
Fermat's theorem
fermentability
fermentescible
ferrimagnetism
ferromagnesian
ferromagnetism
ferroprussiate
Feynman diagram
fibrocartilage
fibrous protein
fictitiousness
fidei-commissum
field-artillery
field character
field-preaching
field telegraph
fifteen-pounder
fifth columnist
fighting chance
fighting-weight
fight up against
fight windmills
figurativeness
figure-floating
figure four trap
figure of speech
filio-pietistic
filling station
fill the stead of
finance company
finders keepers
find one's tongue
fine de la maison
finger alphabet
finger language
finger-pointing
finger's-breadth
finger spelling
finishing touch
Finlandisation
Finlandization
fire department
fire-discipline
fireless cooker
fire-worshipper
first intention
first principle
First Secretary
first-time buyer
fiscal engineer
Fischer–Tropsch
fisherman's bend
fisherman's knit
fisherman's knot
fisherman's tale
fish for oneself

fish out of water
fishtail burner
fissionability
fivepin bowling
flagellomaniac
flagitiousness
flag-lieutenant
flail harvester
flame-projector
flame-retardant
flat as a pancake
flat-footedness
flat-tail mullet
flauto traverso
flax-flower blue
flight envelope
flight recorder
flight sergeant
flight-shooting
flimflammeries
floating anchor
floating bridge
floating island
floating kidney
flocks and herds
flock wallpaper
flog a dead horse
floor exercises
floral envelope
Florence fennel
Florentine iris
floriculturist
flower children
flowering plant
flowerlessness
flow production
fluid amplifier
fluidification
fluid mechanics
fluoridization
fly honeysuckle
flying buttress
Flying Dutchman
Flying Fortress
Flying Scotsman
flying squadron
flying squirrel
fly in the face of
foam at the mouth
foetal distress
folk psychology
follow-my-leader
follow one's nose
follow the crowd
football coupon
for all one cares
for all the world
for a long season
foraminiferous
forbidden fruit
forbiddingness

forbid the banns
force one's voice
for Christ's sake
forcible-feeble
Forefathers' Day
forehandedness
foreign affairs
foreign service
foreordination
foreseeability
forest kangaroo
forest mahogany
forethoughtful
fore-topgallant
forgivableness
for good measure
for heaven's sake
forisfamiliate
Former Prophets
formidableness
for one's own hand
for the duration
for the hell of it
for the life of me
for the most part
for the soul of me
forthrightness
fortuitousness
fortune-hunting
fortune-telling
forward-looking
forward scatter
foundationless
foundation stop
founder's shares
founding father
founding member
four last things
four-leaf clover
four-letter word
four-on-the-floor
fourteenth part
fourteen-tonner
fourth position
four-wheel drive
fovea centralis
fractional note
fragrant orchid
fraternal order
fraternization
freedom fighter
free enterprise
free expression
free-handedness
freestone peach
freieslebenite
French Canadian
French dressing
French knickers
French lavender
French lungwort

French marigold
French mistress
French-polisher
French vermouth
frequency curve
freshwater flea
Fresnel biprism
frictionlessly
friction-murmur
friendlessness
friendly action
fringe medicine
frolicsomeness
from bad to worse
from head to foot
from side to side
from soup to nuts
from time to time
from wire to wire
from year to year
frontal assault
frontierswoman
frontierswomen
froth flotation
frozen shoulder
fructiferously
fructification
fuchsinophilia
fuchsinophilic
fuliginousness
full complement
full employment
full speed ahead
full steam ahead
fully-fashioned
functional food
fundamentalism
fundamentalist
fundamentality
funeral honours
funeral parlour
furfuraldehyde
furnished house
futuristically
futurity stakes
Gaelic football
gain the garland
galactocentric
galactophorous
galactopoiesis
galactopoietic
gall of the earth
galvanocautery
galvanoplastic
galvanotropism
game as Ned Kelly
gamma radiation
ganglionectomy
garboard strake
garden valerian
garnishee order

gastrovascular
gathering sound
gelatification
gelatinization
gelatinousness
geminate leaves
genealogically
general average
generalisation
generalissimos
generalization
general meeting
general-purpose
general service
general warrant
generativeness
generification
genethliacally
genetic profile
Geneva Protocol
geniculate body
gentleman-usher
gentrification
genuine article
geocentrically
geochronometry
geognostically
geographically
geological time
geomagnetician
geometrization
geomorphically
geomorphogenic
geopolitically
geosynchronous
geothermometer
German-American
German Catholic
Germanophilist
German shepherd
gerontological
gerontomorphic
get a person down
get a thing out of
get into trouble
get in touch with
get in wrong with
get it in the neck
get off one's bike
get oneself gone
get one's feet wet
get one's hands on
get one's leg over
get one's own back
get the best of it
get the better of
get the breeze up
get to first base
get to grips with
Gewürztraminer
gingerbread man

gingerbread nut
give a hare a turn
give credence to
give free rein to
give in marriage
give me strength
give occasion to
give one's love to
give one's mind to
give up the ghost
give us your fist
glacierization
glacio-eustatic
Gladstonianism
glandular fever
glanduliferous
glassification
global variable
globe artichoke
globe lightning
globus pallidus
Glorious Fourth
glory-of-the-snow
glossematician
glottalization
glucocorticoid
glucosidically
glyceraldehyde
glycogenolysis
glycogenolytic
glycolytically
glycosidically
goal difference
God bless my soul
God save the mark
God's own country
go for the doctor
go for the gloves
go into raptures
go into training
golden opinions
golden pheasant
golden samphire
golden triangle
gold of pleasure
Golgi apparatus
go like hot cakes
good conscience
good-fellowship
good-for-nothing
good-humouredly
good-temperedly
go off the handle
go on the streets
gooseberry eyes
gooseberry fool
go out of one's way
gopher tortoise
go separate ways
go to one's reward
go to the country

go to the trouble
governableness
governmentally
go with the times
grace and favour
gracious living
graduate school
gram-equivalent
grammaticality
grammaticalize
grammaticaster
grand battement
grandiloquence
grand inquistor
grandparentage
grand serjeanty
grandstand play
grandstand view
grangerization
granulocytosis
granulomatosis
graphic granite
graphitization
grappier cement
grasp the nettle
grass-widowhood
gratuitousness
graveyard cough
graveyard shift
graveyard watch
great attractor
great barracuda
great blue heron
Great Deliverer
greater omentum
great insertion
Grecian slipper
green-blindness
Green Cross code
greengroceries
green in one's eye
Greenland shark
Greenland whale
green sandpiper
gregariousness
Gregorian chant
Gregorian tones
griffon vulture
Grim the Collier
grist to the mill
ground-breaking
ground-fielding
ground-landlord
groundlessness
ground spearing
ground squirrel
group assurance
group insurance
growth industry
guild socialism
gull-billed tern

gurgeon stopper
gutter-crawling
gynaecological
gynomonoecious
gyroscopically
gyrostabilizer
gyro-stabilizer
gyrostatically
gyro-theodolite
haberdasheries
habitation site
haemagglutinin
haematological
haematophagous
haematopoiesis
haematopoietic
hacmatosalpinx
haemocytometer
haemolytically
haemosiderosis
hagiographical
halfpennyworth
half-wittedness
halfwittedness
hallelujah lass
hallucinogenic
hammer and tongs
handicraftsman
hand on the torch
hanging glacier
Hansen's disease
hapax legomenon
harassing agent
hard-headedness
hard-lying money
hardy perennial
harlequinesque
harlequin quail
harmonic motion
harmonic series
harmoniousness
harpsichordist
hate literature
have a concern in
have a soul above
have a thick skin
have a tile loose
have been around
have everything
have got it badly
have got it wired
have in contempt
have in derision
have it both ways
have no guts in it
have no words for
have one's hand in
have one's own way
have one's will of
have one too many
have on one's mind

have recourse to
have relation to
have the bulge on
have the goods on
have the grace to
have the guns for
have the hots for
have the laugh on
have the worse of
have to one's name
Hawaiian guitar
hawkbill turtle
hawk one's mutton
head for heights
head like a sieve
headmastership
head of the river
headstrongness
hear a person out
hearsay account
hearsay witness
heart-rendingly
hearts and minds
heart-searching
heat exhaustion
heathenishness
heather mixture
heath speedwell
heavenly-minded
heavens to Betsy
heavier-than-air
Heaviside layer
heavy breathing
heavy chemicals
hedonistically
heir of one's body
heliacal rising
Heligoland trap
hell for leather
helminthologic
help a person out
hemagglutinate
hemimetabolous
Hemingwayesque
hemispheroidal
hen and chickens
hentriacontane
heparinization
hepar sulphuris
hepaticologist
hepatocellular
hepatopancreas
hepatotoxicity
Heracliteanism
Heralds' College
Hercules beetle
Hercules powder
hereditability
hereditariness
here lies our way
heretoforetime

heritage centre
hermaphroditic
heroine-worship
hero-worshipper
herpetological
hesitation-form
hesitation-step
heteroaromatic
heterocaryotic
heterochromous
heterokaryosis
heterokaryotic
heteromorphism
heteromorphous
heteronomously
heterophyllous
heteropycnosis
heteropycnotic
heterosexually
heterospecific
heterosyllabic
heterothallism
heterotrophism
heterozygosity
hiccius doccius
hickery-pickery
hidden reserves
hierarchically
hieroglyphical
hierogrammatic
Hierosolymitan
High Commission
high-definition
high-handedness
Highland bonnet
Highland cattle
high-mindedness
highmindedness
high technology
Hindenburg line
hippopotamuses
histochemistry
histologically
histopathology
histoplasmosis
historicalness
historiography
histrionically
hit one in the eye
hobbledehoydom
hobbledehoyish
hobbledehoyism
hobnailed liver
Hofmann's violet
hoity-toityness
hold everything
hold in contempt
hold in derision
holding company
holding paddock
holding pattern

hold one's breath
hold one's ground
hold one's horses
hold one's tongue
hold on the slack
hold the clock on
hold the stirrup
hold up one's head
hole in the heart
holiday loading
holiday village
holier-than-thou
holo-alphabetic
holometabolous
holoparasitism
holoplanktonic
home missionary
homing instinct
homicidal mania
homme d'affaires
homoeomorphism
homoeomorphous
homoeoteleuton
homogenization
homoioteleuton
homophonically
homotransplant
honeycomb quilt
honeycomb tripe
honorary degree
honourableness
honours are even
hootchy-kootchy
horary question
horizontal dial
horizontalness
horned pondweed
horned screamer
horn spectacles
horrendousness
horror-stricken
horse-godmother
horse latitudes
horseshoe-vetch
horsewomanship
horticulturist
hospitableness
hostess trolley
hostile witness
hot and bothered
Hottentot bread
hot-water bottle
house detective
household bread
household stuff
housemaid's knee
House of Commons
House of Hanover
house of ill fame
House of Windsor
house physician

house-rent party
housing project
howling dervish
how the land lies
how the wind lies
Hubble constant
human geography
humanification
humanistically
human relations
human resources
humidification
humourlessness
humoursomeness
humpback bridge
humpback salmon
humpback sucker
hump-shouldered
humpty-dumpties
hundred-pounder
hung parliament
hunter-gatherer
hunting leopard
huntsman spider
hunt the slipper
hunt the thimble
hunt the whistle
hurdy-gurdy girl
hurricane force
hurricane-house
hyacinth of Peru
hyaluronic acid
hydatid disease
hydraulic brake
hydraulic organ
hydraulic press
hydrobiologist
hydrocarbonate
hydrocarbonous
hydrocephaloid
hydrocephalous
hydrocolloidal
hydrocortisone
hydrodynamical
hydro-explosion
hydro-extractor
hydrogenolysis
hydrogenolytic
hydrogeologist
hydrographical
hydrologically
hydrolytically
hydromagnetics
hydromechanics
hydronephrosis
hydronephrotic
hydrophilicity
hydrophobicity
hydropneumatic
hydroponically
hydrostatician

hydrotherapist	hypofunctional	illustratively
hydrothermally	hypomixolydian	image converter
hydrotreatment	hypophalangism	image dissector
hydroxonium ion	hypopharyngeal	image processor
hydroxyapatite	hypophosphoric	imaginableness
hydroxybenzoic	hypophysectomy	Immaculate Lamb
hydroxyproline	hypostatically	immaculateness
hyetographical	hyposulphurous	immemorialness
hygroscopicity	hypothetically	immethodically
hymnologically	hypothyroidism	immetricalness
hyperaesthesia	hypotrachelium	immiserization
hyperaesthetic	hypsarrhythmia	immobilization
hyperbolically	hypsarrhythmic	immoderateness
hyperbolic sine	hypsilophodont	immovable feast
hypercalcaemia	hypsographical	immune globulin
hypercalcaemic	hysterectomies	immune response
hyper-Calvinism	hysterectomise	immunochemical
hyper-Calvinist	hysterectomize	immunogenetics
hypercatharsis	hysteresis loss	immunoglobulin
hyperchromasia	hysteretically	impact strength
hyperchromatic	iatrochemistry	imparisyllabic
hyperconscious	iatrogenically	imparticipable
hypercriticism	iatromechanics	impassableness
hypercriticize	iatromechanist	impassibleness
hypereutectoid	iatrophysicist	impassionately
hyperexcitable	I beg your pardon	impeccableness
hyperextension	Ibero-Caucasian	imperative mood
hypergeometric	Ibicencan hound	imperativeness
hyperglycaemia	iceberg lettuce	imperatorially
hyperglycaemic	ichnographical	imperfect rhyme
hyperinflation	ichthyological	imperial gallon
hyperirritable	ichthyophagian	impermeability
hyperkeratosis	ichthyophagist	impersonalness
hyperkeratotic	ichthyophagous	imperturbation
hypermetabolic	ichthyosaurian	imperviousness
hypernatraemia	icing on the cake	implacableness
hypernatraemic	iconographical	implausibility
hyperoxygenate	I dare undertake	implementation
hyperparasitic	idealistically	imponderabilia
hyperphalangia	identification	impossibleness
hyperpituitary	identificatory	impoverishment
hypersecretion	identity crisis	impracticality
hypersensitise	identity matrix	impregnability
hypersensitive	identity parade	impressibility
hypersensitize	idiosyncrasies	impressionable
hypersexuality	idolatrousness	impressionably
hypersomnolent	idols of the cave	impressionless
hypersonically	if peradventure	impressiveness
hyperspherical	I'll be seeing you	improbableness
hyperthyroidic	ill-conditioned	improvableness
hypertrichosis	illegitimately	impulse turbine
hyperuricaemia	illegitimation	inaccentuation
hyperuricaemic	illegitimatize	inaccurateness
hyperventilate	illiberalities	inacquaintance
hypidiomorphic	illicit process	inadaptability
hypnotherapist	illimitability	inadequateness
hypo-allergenic	illiterateness	inadvisability
hypochondrical	illogicalities	inagglutinable
hypochromicity	I'll tell you what	inalienability
hypocritically	illuminatingly	inalterability
hypodermically	illustrational	inamissibility

in a person's arms
in a person's debt
in a person's name
inappositeness
inappreciation
inappreciative
inapprehension
inapprehensive
inapproachable
inarticulately
inarticulation
inartificially
inartistically
in a state of flux
in a thing's stead
inauspiciously
inauthenticity
incandescently
incapacitation
incarnationist
incautiousness
incendiary bomb
incestuousness
incivilization
incline one's ear
incommensurate
incommodiously
incommunicable
incommunicably
incompleteness
incomprehended
incompressible
inconclusively
inconditionate
inconsequently
inconsiderable
inconsiderably
inconsistently
incontrollable
incontrollably
inconveniently
incoordination
incorporeality
incorrectitude
incredibleness
incrementalism
incrementalist
inculpableness
indecipherable
indecisiveness
indecomposable
indecorousness
indefinability
indefiniteness
indeliberately
indeliberation
indemonstrable
indemonstrably
independencies
independentism
indestructible

indestructibly
indeterminable
indeterminably
Indian elephant
Indian plantain
indifferentism
indifferentist
indigenisation
indigenization
indigenousness
indirect object
indirect speech
indiscerptible
indiscoverable
indiscriminate
indisseverable
indisseverably
indissolublist
indistinctness
individualizer
indivisibility
Indo-Abyssinian
indoctrination
indoctrinatory
indomitability
Indo-Portuguese
indubitability
indubitatively
induction motor
industrial park
ineffectuality
ineluctability
inequalitarian
inertial system
inertia selling
inescapability
inessentiality
inevitableness
inexcitability
inexhaustively
inexorableness
inexplicitness
inexpressively
inextinguished
infallibleness
infant mistress
infectiousness
infelicitously
inflammability
inflammatorily
inflation-proof
inflectionally
inflectionless
infralapsarian
inframaxillary
infrangibility
infrasonically
infrastructure
infructescence
ingenerability
ingenerateness

ingloriousness
in good set terms
ingratiatingly
inhabitability
inhabitiveness
inharmoniously
inheritability
inheritance tax
inhumanitarian
inimitableness
iniquitousness
inirritability
initialization
inland ice sheet
in large measure
in loco parentis
in multiplicate
in my conception
innominate bone
innominate vein
innovativeness
Inns of Chancery
innumerability
in one fell swoop
in one's extremes
in one's mind's eye
in one's own right
inordinateness
inorganisation
inorganization
in peril of doing
in possession of
in preference to
inquisitorship
in receivership
insanitariness
insatiableness
inscrutability
inseparability
in sextuplicate
in shirtsleeves
insider dealing
insider trading
inside straight
insightfulness
insignificance
insignificancy
inspirationist
instalment plan
institutionary
instructorship
instrumentally
in succession to
insufficiently
insulating tape
insuperability
insuppressible
insurance agent
insurance stamp
insurmountable
insurmountably

insurrectional
intake manifold
intangibleness
integrationist
intellectively
intellectually
intelligential
intelligentsia
intempestively
intensionalist
intensionality
intentionalism
intentionalist
intentionality
interactionism
interactionist
interanimation
interarticular
interavailable
intercapillary
intercessional
intercessorial
intercommonage
intercommunion
intercommunity
interconnector
intercorrelate
interdefinable
interdependent
interdialectal
interdiffusion
interdigitally
inter-electrode
interestedness
interferential
interferometer
interferometry
interfertility
interfibrillar
interglandular
intergradation
interinfluence
interior design
interior-sprung
interjectional
interlineation
interlocutress
intermaxillary
intermediaries
intermediately
intermediation
intermigration
intermittently
intermittingly
intermolecular
internal energy
internal market
internal object
internal stress
Internationale
internment camp

interpalpebral
interpellation
interpenetrate
interplanetary
interpretation
interpretative
interpretively
interpunctuate
interpupillary
interruptingly
intersectional
intersegmental
intersexuality
interspersedly
interstitialcy
interstitially
intertrochlear
intertwinement
intertwiningly
intervalometer
interval signal
interventional
intervertebral
in the aggregate
in the ascendant
in the event that
in the family way
in the meanwhile
in the old school
in the process of
in the public eye
in the reckoning
in the short term
in this instance
intolerability
intonationally
into the bargain
into the discard
intoxicatingly
intra-abdominal
intracardially
intracisternal
intracranially
intractability
intracutaneous
intrafallopian
intramedullary
intramercurial
intramolecular
intransferable
intransigeance
intransigently
intransitively
intransitivity
intransitivize
intransparency
intrapulmonary
intrinsicality
introductorily
intromolecular
introspectable

introspectible
introsuscepted
intuitionalism
intuitionalist
intuitionistic
intussuscepted
intussusceptum
invaluableness
invariableness
Inverness cloak
inversion layer
investment bond
inveterateness
invigoratingly
invincibleness
inviolableness
invisible green
invitation card
iodimetrically
iodometrically
ionosphericist
ipsissima verba
Irish hurricane
Irish promotion
Irish wolfhound
Iron Chancellor
ironing blanket
ironstone china
irrecognisable
irrecognizable
irrecognizably
irrecollection
irreconcilable
irreconcilably
irreducibility
irreflectively
irrefutability
irregularities
irrelativeness
irrememberable
irremovability
irreparability
irreplevisable
irreproachable
irreproachably
irreproducible
irresoluteness
irrespectively
irresponsively
irrestrainable
irrestrainably
irrevocability
irrotationally
ischiatic notch
isentropically
Islamicization
island-mountain
island platform
island universe
isoagglutinate
isocalorically

isokinetically
isomorphically
isotopic number
Italian cypress
Italianization
Italian opening
it is my pleasure
jackass frigate
jackass penguin
Jack-by-the-hedge
Jack-in-the-green
Jack-in-the-hedge
Jack of the clock
Jacob's membrane
japaleño pepper
Japanese beetle
Japanese cherry
Japanese flower
Japanese garden
Japanese laurel
Japanese medlar
Japanese monkey
Japanese oyster
Japanese privet
Japanese quince
Japanese screen
Japanese vellum
jaune brilliant
jejuno-duodenal
jerboa kangaroo
Jerusalem cross
Jerusalem thorn
jeté en tournant
jeweller's putty
jeweller's rouge
jingling Johnny
jobbing builder
jobs for the boys
Johannisberger
John Barleycorn
joint adventure
joint committee
joint-stock bank
joker in the pack
joukery-pawkery
journal-bearing
judgematically
Judges' lodgings
Judicature Acts
judicial combat
judicial factor
judicial murder
judicial review
Julian calendar
junk playground
jurisdictional
Justice General
justiciability
justiciaryship
justifiability
juxta-articular

kaleyard school
kangaroo-beetle
Kaposi's sarcoma
karaoke machine
karstification
karyologically
karyotypically
Katyusha rocket
Kavirondo crane
keep a calm sough
keep a place warm
keep early hours
keep in suspense
keep one's chin up
keep one's figure
keep one's hair on
keep one's hand in
keep one's temper
keep one's wool on
keep on trucking
keep steeks with
keep to the house
Kepler's problem
keratinisation
keratinization
keratinophilic
kernel sentence
kerygmatically
keyhole surgery
keynote address
keystone effect
kick in the pants
Kierkegaardian
Kilkenny marble
killer instinct
Kimmeridge clay
Kimmeridge coal
kindergartener
kinetheodolite
kinetic heating
king and country
kingfisher blue
King James Bible
King's messenger
King's Messenger
Kiplingesquely
Kipp's apparatus
Kirk of Scotland
kirschenwasser
Kirschner value
kiss impression
kissing gourami
kit-cat portrait
kitchen cabinet
kitchen evening
kitchen-parlour
kite-photograph
kleptoparasite
knight bachelor
knight banneret
knight-errantry

knitting needle
knitting sheath
knock hell out of
knock into shape
knock on the head
know better than
knowledge-based
know-nothingism
know one's onions
know to one's cost
knuckle-walking
Koch postulates
Kohlrausch's law
kraak porselein
Kremlinologist
Ku Klux Klansman
Kupferschiefer
kyphoscoliosis
kyphoscoliotic
labour exchange
Labour Exchange
labour movement
laboursomeness
labyrinthiform
labyrinthodont
lachrymatories
ladies' carriage
Lady Chatterley
lady of pleasure
lady of the house
lady of the manor
lady of the night
lady's companion
lake settlement
lamellirostral
lamentableness
laminarization
lamprophyllite
Lancaster cloth
land-connection
landed interest
land on one's feet
lantern-flflies
lapidification
Lapland bunting
large intestine
large-mouth bass
larger than life
large-stomached
laryngofissure
laryngological
laryngopharynx
laryngoscopist
lasciviousness
last sacraments
Latakia tobacco
latent learning
lateralization
lateral moraine
lateritization
lath and plaster

latitudinarian
Latter-day Saint
Latter Prophets
lattice network
laughing matter
laughing-muscle
laughing thrush
Laura Ashleyish
laurel magnolia
lavatory humour
lavender cotton
law-abidingness
law of parsimony
law of the jungle
Lawson's cypress
lay at the door of
lay it on a person
lay it on the line
lay one's hands on
lay one's leg over
lead apes in hell
leading article
leading counsel
lead tetraethyl
lead to the altar
leaf-cutting ant
league football
lean-to building
learned journal
leather-hunting
leathery turtle
leave no effects
leave of absence
leave well alone
lechatelierite
lecithotrophic
lecture circuit
lecture-recital
lecture theatre
left-handedness
left high and dry
legalistically
legerdemainist
leghaemoglobin
Legion of Honour
legislatorship
legitimateness
legitimization
leiomyosarcoma
leisure complex
lending library
leopard society
lepidotrichium
lepospondylous
leptocephalous
Lesser Antilles
lesser doxology
Lesser Doxology
Lesser Entrance
let a person know
let or hindrance

let out the links
letter by letter
lettering piece
letter of advice
letter of credit
letter of intent
letter of marque
letter of slains
letters missive
let the side down
let things slide
lettre de cachet
Levant wormseed
levelling-screw
levelling staff
lexicalization
lexical meaning
lex loci delicti
Leyland cypress
liaison officer
liberalization
Liberal Judaism
libertarianism
liberty cabbage
libidinousness
library binding
library edition
library science
licentiateship
licentiousness
lichenological
lick one's wounds
lie in one's teeth
lieutenantship
life expectancy
life membership
lift up one's eyes
lift up one's head
light-demanding
lighter-than-air
light flyweight
light-heartedly
lighting bridge
lighting-up time
light knotgrass
lightning chess
lightning-proof
lightning-stone
light pollution
lignocellulose
lignosulphonic
like it or lump it
like-mindedness
lilliputianize
limb of the Devil
limited company
limited edition
limited partner
limnologically
linear equation
line of business

line one's pocket
line-sequential
linguistically
lipogrammatist
liquidity ratio
liquid paraffin
liquid rheostat
liquorice-stick
liquorice vetch
listen to reason
list processing
literalization
literary agency
literary critic
literary editor
lithochromatic
lithographical
lithologically
little boys' room
little by little
Little Entrance
little-girl-lost
little green man
little magazine
little neck clam
Little's disease
little stranger
liturgiologist
live and let live
live by one's wits
live off the land
live on one's hump
liver of sulphur
livery cupboard
livery of seisin
living skeleton
living standard
Lloyd's Register
loan-collection
Lobel's catchfly
lobotomization
lobster Newburg
local authority
localizability
locomotiveness
locus classicus
locus of control
loft conversion
logical atomism
logical grammar
logical paradox
logical product
logical subject
Lombardy poplar
long-headedness
long in the tooth
longitudinally
Long Parliament
longs and shorts
longshore drift
long short story

long sufferance	macrosociology	Malayanization
long sweetening	macrostructure	Malay peninsula
long-tailed duck	madrigalianism	malcontentedly
long-tailed pair	Maeterlinckian	maldevelopment
long-tailed skua	magazine rights	maldistributed
long-windedness	magical realism	male chauvinism
look for trouble	magical realist	male chauvinist
looking-forward	magic-lanterned	male prostitute
look kindly upon	magistrateship	malice prepense
look to one's hits	magnesium flare	malintegration
loose-endedness	magnesium light	malmsey madeira
loquaciousness	magnetic bottle	malnourishment
Lord Chancellor	magnetic bubble	malobservation
Lord God of hosts	magnetic memory	malodorousness
Lord Lieutenant	magnetic mirror	malperformance
Lord Mayor's Show	magnetic moment	Malpighian body
lord of regality	magnetic needle	malt-distillery
Lord of the Flies	magnetic stripe	Maltese terrier
lord of the manor	magnetocaloric	mamenchisaurus
lord proprietor	magnetographic	mammillary body
lords and ladies	magneto-optical	mammilliferous
Lords of Session	magnetospheric	manageableness
Lords spiritual	magnetostatics	managed economy
Lord Woolton pie	magniloquently	mandarin collar
Lorentz triplet	maidenhair fern	mandarin jacket
lose interest in	maidenhair tree	mandarin orange
lose one's bottle	maiden plum tree	mandarin sleeve
lose one's market	mails and duties	mandelonitrile
lose one's temper	main-topgallant	manganese oxide
lose one's tongue	maitre de ballet	manganese steel
lost generation	majesticalness	mangrove cuckoo
love in a cottage	Majorana effect	mangrove oyster
love-in-idleness	major-generalcy	manifold writer
loveworthiness	make a bonfire of	Manila tamarind
lovey-doveyness	make a commotion	man in the street
loving kindness	make a dead set at	manipulability
lower criticism	make a fight of it	manipulatively
lower intestine	make a good job of	mannerlessness
lower one's guard	make allowances	man of the moment
loxodromic line	make a mystery of	man of the people
Ludolph's number	make a night of it	manometrically
lugubriousness	make a pig's ear of	man on the street
lumbar puncture	make a poor mouth	man's best friend
lumps of delight	make a present of	manslaughterer
Luxembourgeois	make a statement	manual alphabet
lycopodiaceous	make one's choice	manual exercise
lymphangiogram	make one's rounds	manufacturable
lyophilization	make relation to	manuscriptural
lysogenization	make rings round	Manx shearwater
macadamization	make so bold as to	marching orders
macaroni cheese	make sweet music	margaritaceous
machinofacture	make the round of	margin of safety
mackerel breeze	make the running	marigold window
mackerel clouds	make the worst of	marine barracks
macrocephalous	make up one's mind	mariner portage
macro-economics	Malabar spinach	marketableness
macroeconomics	malachite-green	market gardener
macro-economist	malacostracous	market research
macro-evolution	malapportioned	marriage broker
macroevolution	malappropriate	marriage bureau
macromolecular	malarrangement	marriage market

marrow-stem kale	megasporophyll	metensomatosis
marry into money	megastructural	meteoritically
marsh blackbird	Meissner effect	meteorological
marsh pennywort	Melanchthonian	meteoroscopist
marsupial mouse	melanophlogite	methaemoglobin
martingale-stay	melanovanadite	methanogenesis
martyrological	melt in the mouth	methodicalness
marvellousness	membra disjecta	methodological
masculine rhyme	membrane filter	meticulousness
Mason–Dixon Line	membrification	metoclopramide
Mason–Dixon line	mendaciousness	metoposcopical
massage parlour	Mendelssohnian	metronomically
masseter muscle	mend one's fences	metropolitical
mass production	Men's Liberation	Mexicanization
Master in Lunacy	menstrual cycle	Mexican Spanish
masterlessness	mensurableness	Mexican thistle
mastigophorous	mental handicap	Michaelmas term
mastoid process	mento-Meckelian	Michaelmas tide
material object	Mephistopheles	microaerophile
maternity dress	mercantilistic	microanatomist
mathematically	mercaptopurine	microbarograph
matriarchalism	merchandisable	microbiologist
matrilineality	merchant banker	microcephalism
matrix sentence	merchant marine	microcephalous
matron of honour	merchant prince	microchemistry
matter of course	merchant seaman	microcircuitry
matter-of-factly	merchant-tailor	microcomputing
matter of record	mercury gilding	microcontinent
Maunder minimum	meretriciously	micro-economics
Maundy Thursday	meridian circle	microeconomics
mauvaise langue	meroplanktonic	micro-economist
Maxwell's duiker	merosystematic	micro-electrode
may it please you	merry Christmas	micro-evolution
McBurney's point	mesaticephalic	microevolution
meadow cat's-tail	Mesdemoiselles	microfibrillar
meadow mushroom	mesoplanktonic	microinjection
meal-worm beetle	messenger cable	micro-machining
mealy-mouthedly	metabiological	micrometeorite
meaningfulness	metachromatism	micrometeoroid
measurableness	metalinguistic	microminiature
mechanicalness	metallic thread	microperthitic
mechanical pulp	metallogenesis	microphthalmia
mechanical twin	metallogenetic	microphthalmic
mechanical zero	metallographer	microphthalmos
mechanocaloric	metallographic	microprocessor
mechanomorphic	metallo-organic	microprojector
mechanotherapy	metalloprotein	micropulsation
meddlesomeness	metamorphopsia	microradiogram
medicalization	metamorphosize	microsporidian
medical officer	metanephridial	microsporocyte
medicamentally	metanephridium	microstructure
medicinal leech	metaphase plate	microtechnique
medicine murder	metaphorically	microtrabecula
meditativeness	metaphosphoric	Middle American
medullary plate	metaphysically	middle-classdom
megakaryoblast	metapolitician	middle distance
megakaryocytic	metapsychology	Middle-European
megalocephalic	metascientific	middle-statured
megalomaniacal	metempirically	midshipmanship
megascopically	metempsychosic	militarization
megasporangium	metempsychosis	military orchid

military police
military school
military tenure
milking machine
milking-parlour
Milk of Magnesia
milkweed beetle
millenarianism
milling machine
millionairedom
millivoltmeter
Milroy's disease
mince the matter
mind-bogglingly
mind over matter
mineralization
mineralography
miniature score
minifloppy disk
mini-roundabout
ministerialism
ministerialist
minority report
miogeosyncline
miraculousness
mirror symmetry
misadventurous
misanthropical
misappellation
misapplication
misappropriate
misarrangement
misattribution
miscalculation
mischief-making
miscommunicate
miscomputation
misconjunction
misconsecrated
miscontentment
misdeclaration
misdescription
misdescriptive
misimprovement
misinformation
misinformative
misinstruction
misinterpreter
misleadingness
mismeasurement
misorientation
misperformance
mispunctuation
misremembrance
misrepresenter
misresemblance
missed abortion
missed approach
missionaryship
mission control
missive of lease

mistake one's man
mist propagator
mistranslation
Mittel-European
mixed technique
mobilizational
moccasin flower
mock auctioneer
mock turtle soup
modifiableness
modificability
modificational
modularization
modus decimandi
molecular layer
molecular sieve
molybdenum blue
momentaneously
moment-to-moment
money-mongering
money of account
money scrivener
mongrelization
monkey business
monkey on a stick
monobrominated
monocarpellary
monochromatise
monochromatism
monochromatist
monochromatize
monofunctional
monogamousness
monoglacialism
monoglacialist
monolingualism
monolithically
monomaniacally
mononucleotide
monophasically
monophonematic
monophonically
monophthongize
monopolization
monopropellant
monorail camera
monosaccharide
monosaccharose
monothetically
monotonousness
monotriglyphic
Monroe doctrine
Montagu's blenny
month of Sundays
Monumental City
moral certainty
moral cowardice
moralistically
morally certain
moral turpitude
morceau de salon

more power to you
more than enough
Moreton Bay pine
morganatically
morocco leather
morphinomaniac
morphometrical
morphophonemic
morphotectonic
mossy saxifrage
Most Honourable
mother-grabbing
mother language
motherlessness
mother of months
mothers' meeting
Mother Superior
mother tincture
motionlessness
motion sickness
motivationally
motivelessness
motor-ambulance
motor generator
motte-and-bailey
moulded breadth
mountain azalea
mountain beaver
mountaineering
mountain laurel
mountain linnet
mountain oyster
mountain parrot
mountain plover
mountain rescue
mountain sorrel
mountain system
mountain thrush
mount the ladder
mourning-brooch
mover and shaker
moving pavement
moving sidewalk
mucilaginously
mucomembranous
mucoperiosteum
mucous membrane
mucoviscidosis
muddleheadedly
Muhammadan blue
mulberry colour
Müllerian mimic
multarticulate
multi-articular
multidialectal
multi-electrode
multifactorial
multifariously
multifoetation
multilamellate
multilaterally

multilingually	narcoterrorism	network theorem
multiple-access	narcoterrorist	neurapophyseal
multiple allele	narratological	neuroanatomist
multiple-aspect	narrow-mindedly	neurobiologist
multiple-choice	nasopharyngeal	neurobiotactic
multiplication	national anthem	neuroendocrine
multiplicative	National Health	neurofibrillar
multiplicities	national income	neurogenically
multipotential	national school	neuroglandular
multiprocessor	Native American	neurologically
multiracialism	native tamarind	neuropathology
multiracialist	natural history	neuroretinitis
multistability	naturalization	neuroscientist
multi-threading	natural liberty	neurosecretion
multivallation	natural numbers	neurosecretory
multiversities	natural pravity	neurotendinous
municipal baths	natural science	neutral-density
municipalities	natural spirits	neutralization
munificentness	natural tangent	neutron capture
munitions of war	natural trumpet	neutron therapy
muscatel raisin	natural uranium	never-failingly
musculofascial	natural virtues	never-never land
museographical	natural wastage	Never Never Land
mushroom anchor	nature printing	Newcastle Brown
mushroom colour	naturistically	Newcastle glass
mushroom growth	naval architect	newfangledness
musical glasses	navigation coal	Newfoundlander
musicalization	Navy Department	new lease of life
musico-dramatic	Neanderthaloid	new mathematics
musk stork's-bill	near-hysterical	new off the irons
mustard plaster	near the knuckle	news conference
mutarotational	neat-handedness	newspaperishly
mutation theory	Nebuchadnezzar	newspaperwoman
muzzle velocity	necessarianism	newsworthiness
myelencephalic	necessary house	New York dressed
myelencephalon	necessary woman	New Zealand flax
myeloblastosis	necklace poplar	nickel carbonyl
myelomonocytic	neck of the woods	nicotinization
mylonitization	necrologically	Nietzscheanism
myohaemoglobin	nectareousness	nigger minstrel
myricyl alcohol	needle-threader	night-blindness
myrmecochorous	negative equity	night-flowering
myrmecological	negative growth	night-wandering
myrmecophagous	negative virtue	nil desperandum
myrmecophilous	neglectfulness	Nilotic monitor
my service to you	negligibleness	nimble-fingered
mystagogically	negro-head beech	nincompoopiana
mysteriousness	Negro spiritual	nine days' wonder
mystery of State	nematodiriasis	nine men's morris
mythographical	Nemean festival	nineteenth hole
mythologically	neoclassically	Nissl substance
naked as a needle	neo-colonialism	nitrobacterium
name one's poison	neocolonialism	nitrocellulose
nankeen kestrel	neo-colonialist	nitrofurantoin
nanotechnology	neocolonialist	nitrogen-fixing
Nansen passport	nephritic stone	nitroglycerine
naphthaquinone	nephroblastoma	noctambulation
naphthenic acid	nephrotoxicity	noise pollution
naphthoquinone	nervous tension	noisy scrub-bird
Napoleonically	nesslerization	no leg to stand on
Napoleonic Wars	nether garments	nomenclatorial

nomenclaturist
nominal account
nominal essence
nominalization
non-associative
non-barbiturate
non-belligerent
non-committally
non-communicant
non-compearance
non-competitive
nonconformance
non-conjunction
non-consequence
non-consumption
non-contentious
non-cooperation
non-destructive
non-dimensional
non-directional
non-disjunction
non-distinctive
non-electrified
non-exportation
non-importation
non-intelligent
non-intercourse
non-judgemental
non-ministerial
non-operational
non-participant
non-penetrative
non-performance
non-proficiency
non-proprietary
non-radioactive
non-rationality
non-referential
non-residential
non-restrictive
nonsensicality
non-significant
non-subscribing
non-substantial
norepinephrine
norethisterone
Norfolk spaniel
Norfolk terrier
Norman Conquest
Normandy butter
Normandy vellum
normoglycaemia
normoglycaemic
north-easterner
north-eastwards
northern lights
Northern Paiute
Northern States
north-north-east
north-north-west
north-westerner

north-westwards
Norwegian steam
Norwich terrier
nose suspension
not a blind bit of
not a dog's chance
not a hope in hell
not a pennyworth
notaries public
not ashamed to do
not bat an eyelid
not by a long shot
not care a bugger
not care a fig for
notch-sensitive
notch-toughness
note of addition
noteworthiness
not for the world
not get anywhere
not have a prayer
no thoroughfare
not if you paid me
not know from Eve
not move a muscle
not once or twice
not on your nelly
not the full quid
Nottingham lace
Nottingham reel
nouveaux riches
novel disseisin
novelistically
nuchal ligament
nuclear battery
nuclear fission
nuclearization
nuclear physics
nuclear-powered
nuclear reactor
nuclear warfare
nudibranchiate
nuisance ground
null hypothesis
null instrument
number-cruncher
numismatically
nundinal letter
Nuremberg rally
nursing officer
nutmeg-coloured
nutritionalist
nutritiousness
nymphomaniacal
Nyquist diagram
nystagmography
oak of Jerusalem
obdiplostemony
obedience class
obedience-train
obedience trial

Oberstleutnant
objective point
object language
objectlessness
oblate spheroid
obligativeness
obligatoriness
oblique oration
obliteratingly
obreptitiously
obsequiousness
observation car
obsessionalism
obsidional coin
obstacle course
obstreperously
obstructionary
obstructionism
obstructionist
occulting light
occupationally
occupation army
occupationless
occupation road
occurrence book
oceanic feeling
octocentennial
ocular spectrum
odd-come-shortly
odour-blindness
Oedipus complex
oenanthic ether
oesophagectomy
oesophagoscope
oesophagostomy
oestrogenicity
offer one's arm to
off-off-Broadway
off one's trolley
offset purchase
offshore island
off-the-shoulder
of public resort
of the essence of
of the first head
of the old school
oil on the flames
old-fashionedly
old-maidishness
old-man kangaroo
old man of the sea
old man saltbush
old woman's tooth
olfactory nerve
oligarchically
oligopsonistic
olivary nucleus
omnibus edition
omnicompetence
omnipercipient
omnium gatherum

omnivorousness
omphaloskepsis
on a full stomach
on a person's tail
onchocerciasis
one-armed bandit
one-dimensional
one-directional
one-downmanship
one had better do
oneirocritical
one of these days
one of the truest
one of the wisest
one of those days
one out of the box
one's better half
one's better self
one's blood boils
one's collocutor
one's finest hour
one's former self
one's number is up
one's Sunday best
one's teeth water
one with another
onomasiologist
onomatological
on one's beam-ends
on one's doorstep
on one's hind legs
on one's last legs
on one's occasion
on one's own terms
on the defensive
on the downgrade
on the down grade
on the high ropes
on the other hand
on the other part
on the pretext of
on the right foot
on the scrap heap
on the sidelines
on the subject of
on the telephone
on the wrong foot
oophorectomies
oophorectomize
Oort comet cloud
open-handedness
open-mindedness
open one's budget
open one's mind to
open subroutine
open university
Open University
open window unit
operating table
operationalise
operationalism

operationalist
operationality
operationalize
operations room
ophthalmic acid
ophthalmologic
ophthalmometer
ophthalmometry
ophthalmoscope
ophthalmoscopy
opiniativeness
opinionatively
opisthocoelian
opisthocoelous
opisthographic
opponent muscle
opposite number
opposite prompt
oppositionless
oppositiveness
oppressiveness
optical density
optical printer
optical scanner
optimalization
optimistically
optoelectronic
optometrically
orange-coloured
orange-strainer
orbitosphenoid
orchidectomize
Order in Council
orderly corpora
orderly officer
Order of the Bath
ordinal numeral
ordinary of arms
ordinary seaman
Ordnance Survey
organification
organismically
organizability
organizational
organized games
organometallic
organ-pipe coral
oriental carpet
oriental medlar
oriental stitch
ornithological
ornithomorphic
ornithophilist
ornithophilous
ornithosaurian
orogenetically
orographically
orohydrography
Orphean warbler
orthocephalous
orthochromatic

orthodiagraphy
Orthodox Church
orthoepistical
orthographical
orthomolecular
orthonormality
orthonormalize
orthophosphate
orthorrhaphous
orthoselection
orthotopically
ortolan bunting
oscillographic
osmometrically
osmoregulation
osmoregulatory
ostentatiously
osteoarthritic
osteoarthritis
osteoarthrosis
osteoarthrotic
osteochondroma
osteologically
osteosclerosis
ostreocultural
ostrich-feather
Otaheite orange
other fish to fry
otolaryngology
Ottomanization
outcountenance
out for the count
outlandishness
out of a clear sky
out of character
out of condition
out of one's depth
out of one's gourd
out of one's shell
out of one's sight
out of one's skull
out-of-roundness
out of the common
out of the window
out of this world
outperformance
outrageousness
outside forward
outward-bounder
outwash deposit
over-abundantly
overabundantly
overarticulate
overbitterness
overburdensome
overcapitalise
overcapitalize
overcautiously
overcommitment
overcommitting
overcompensate

overconfidence
overcorrection
overdispersion
overemployment
overenthusiasm
overestimation
overexcitement
overfamiliarly
overfavourable
overfulfilment
overgeneralise
overgeneralize
overgenerously
overgovernment
over-indulgence
overindulgence
overmodulation
over my dead body
over-optimistic
overoptimistic
over-particular
overparticular
overpersuasion
overpopulation
overpoweringly
overprivileged
overproduction
overprotection
overprotective
over-refinement
overrefinement
overrun oneself
oversaturation
overscrupulous
oversimplified
oversimplifier
oversimplifies
oversolicitous
oversolicitude
overspecialise
overspecialize
overstrictness
over the counter
overthoughtful
overwhelmingly
owe it to oneself
owlet-frogmouth
owl-faced monkey
oxalosuccinate
Oxford Movement
Oxford shirting
Oxford trousers
oxidation state
oxidizing agent
oxidoreductase
oxidoreduction
oxidoreductive
oxidulated iron
oxyhaemoglobin
oxymoronically
oyster mushroom

oyster toadfish
oyster-veneered
pachydermatous
Pacific halibut
Pacific pompano
pacifistically
package holiday
packet-switched
packing density
packing station
paddock-grazing
paedomorphosis
paint by numbers
painted bunting
painter's mussel
pair of bagpipes
pair of breeches
pair of knickers
pair of scissors
pair of trousers
pair production
palaeanthropic
palaeobiologic
palaeobotanist
palaeochemical
palaeoclimatic
palaeocortical
palaeoecologic
palaeogeologic
palaeographist
palaeolatitude
palaeomagnetic
palaeontologic
palaeopedology
palaeosalinity
Palaeo-Siberian
palaeostriatal
palaeostriatum
palaeotectonic
palaeothalamus
palaeotropical
palatalization
palato-alveolar
palato-quadrate
paleoanthropic
palmatipartite
palmetto thatch
pan-Americanism
pancake landing
Pancake Tuesday
panchronically
pancreatectomy
pan-diatonicism
panel technique
pan-Europeanism
panidiomorphic
pantisocratist
pantographical
pantomimically
pantomographic
pantopragmatic

pantoyltaurine
pan-Turanianism
papilionaceous
papillomatosis
papulo-erythema
papulo-pustular
papulo-squamous
parabiotically
Paracelsianism
parachute flare
paraconformity
paradiplomatic
paradisaically
paradisiacally
paradoxicality
parafollicular
paraganglionic
paragonimiasis
paragrammatism
parajournalism
parajournalist
paraleipomenon
paralinguistic
paraliturgical
parallel cousin
parallelepiped
parallel market
parallel-medium
parallelopiped
parallel rulers
parametrically
paramilitaries
paramount chief
parapatrically
paraphrastical
parapsychology
pararosaniline
parascientific
parasitization
parasitologist
paratactically
parcel delivery
parchment paper
pardonableness
parenchymatous
Parent's Charter
parents' meeting
pareschatology
pare to the quick
parietal pleura
parish magazine
parish register
Parisian matins
Parisian stitch
parity checking
parity of esteem
parliament-cake
parliament heel
parlour-boarder
Parmesan cheese
parodistically

paroemiography
paroemiologist
parole of honour
parsimoniously
pars intermedia
parthenocarpic
parthenogenone
partial counsel
partial denture
partial eclipse
partial product
partial valency
partial verdict
particularness
particular rule
partridge-berry
party political
passage-migrant
pass as sterling
pass in one's ally
passionateness
passive smoking
pasteurellosis
pasteurization
Pasteur pipette
pastille-burner
pastoral letter
past participle
past redemption
Patagonian cavy
Patau's syndrome
pâté de campagne
pâté de foie gras
patellofemoral
patent medicine
Paterson's curse
path difference
pathogenically
pathologically
patresfamilias
patriarchalism
patrilineality
patrimonialism
patriotic front
patronymically
patte de velours
pattern bombing
pattern darning
patternization
pattern-welding
pauciarthritis
pauciarticular
paucibacillary
pavement artist
pavor nocturnus
pay a compliment
pay for one's scot
pay reverence to
peacockishness
peak experience
pearly nautilus

peasant economy
pectinesterase
pectoral girdle
pectoral muscle
peculiar people
pedunculate oak
peeping Tommery
peer of the realm
Peltier cooling
penal servitude
penalty killing
pencil-and-paper
pendulum-spring
Penelope canvas
penetration aid
penicillin unit
penitentiaries
penny for the guy
penny-in-the-slot
Penrose diagram
Penrose process
pensionability
pentamethylene
pentatonically
Pentecostalism
Pentecostalist
pentobarbitone
People's Charter
people's theatre
peppercorn hair
peppercorn rent
peppercorn tree
peppermint-drop
peppermint lump
peppermint-tree
peptide linkage
percentage-wise
perceptibility
perceptiveness
perceptuo-motor
perchloric acid
percontatorial
percussion lock
percussiveness
percutaneously
perdurableness
Père David's deer
peremptoriness
perfect binding
perfect cadence
perfectibilian
perfectibilism
perfectibilist
perfectibility
perfectionment
perfectivation
perfectiveness
perfidiousness
perforated tape
performability
performance art

performance car
performatively
performatories
performing arts
perfunctionary
pericardectomy
pericardiotomy
pericementitis
perichondritis
periglaciation
perimenopausal
perimeter track
perimetrically
perinatologist
periodic system
periodontology
peripateticism
peripherically
periphrastical
periscope depth
periscopically
periscopic lens
perishableness
peristrephical
peritectically
peritelevision
peritoneoscopy
peritrichously
perlocutionary
permanent press
permanent tooth
permanent white
permissibility
permissiveness
perniciousness
pernicketiness
peroxosulphate
perpetual check
Persianization
Persian morocco
personableness
personal action
personal column
personal estate
personal injury
personal stereo
personificator
person of colour
personological
person-to-person
perspirability
persuadability
persuasibility
persuasiveness
Perthes disease
pertinaciously
perturbational
perturbatively
pervicaciously
pestilentially
Peter Pan collar

Peter principle
Peter Principle
petit battement
petit bourgeois
petite noblesse
petrochemistry
petrographical
petrol-electric
petroleum ether
petroleum jelly
petrologically
petrophysicist
petrosiliceous
petrotectonics
petty apartheid
petty bourgeois
petty constable
petty serjeanty
phagocytically
phagocytizable
phagolysosomal
phallocentrism
phantasmagoria
phantasmagoric
phantom circuit
pharmaceutical
pharmacologist
pharmacopoeial
pharmacopoeian
pharmacopolist
pharyngealized
pharyngotomies
phase converter
pheasant coucal
phenanthridine
phenanthroline
phenethicillin
phenobarbitone
phenosafranine
phenotypically
phenylbutazone
phenylene brown
phenylpyruvate
phenylthiourea
philanthropine
philanthropise
philanthropism
philanthropist
philanthropize
philanthropoid
philatelically
philologically
philosophaster
philosopheress
philosophistic
phlegmatically
phlegmaticness
phloroglucinol
phonematically
phonologically
phonoreception

phoronomically
phosphate glass
phosphodiester
phosphonitrile
phosphoprotein
phosphor bronze
phosphorescent
phosphoric acid
phosphorolysis
phosphorolytic
phosphoroscope
photoabsorbing
photoautotroph
photobiologist
photobleaching
photoblepharon
photocatalysis
photocatalytic
photochemistry
photocoagulate
photoconductor
photodecompose
photodetection
photoduplicate
photo-engraving
photoenzymatic
photofacsimile
photogenically
photogeologist
photogrammetry
photographable
photoinducible
photoinduction
photoinductive
photoinitiated
photoisomerism
photoisomerize
photolytically
photometrician
photonymograph
photo-oxidation
photo-oxidative
photoperiodism
photophthalmia
photophthalmic
photo-potential
photoradiogram
photorealistic
photoreception
photoreceptive
photoreduction
photoregulator
photo-reportage
photoreproduce
photoresistive
photosensitise
photosensitive
photosensitize
photostability
photostimulate
photosynthesis

photosynthetic
phototelegraph
phragmoplastic
phraseographic
phraseological
Phrygian bonnet
phthalocyanine
phthisiologist
phthisiophobia
phyllosilicate
phylogenetical
phylogenically
physical object
physical optics
physico-chemist
physiochemical
physiognomical
phytochemistry
phytogeography
phytopathology
phytosociology
piano accordion
piano reduction
piccaninny dawn
pick one's feet up
picoplanktonic
picture element
picture gallery
picture library
picture monitor
picturesquerie
picture theatre
picture-writing
piece of crumpet
pied flycatcher
pied kingfisher
pied woodpecker
pierced earring
piercement dome
piezomagnetism
piezoresistive
pigeon-breasted
pigeon-fancying
piggyback plant
pig in the middle
pile on the agony
Pilgrim Fathers
pilgrim's bottle
pillar and stall
pilot parachute
pincer movement
pinealectomize
pineapple fibre
pine carpet moth
pine lappet moth
pinkster flower
Pinkster flower
pinnated grouse
pinnatipartite
pin one's faith on
pin one's hopes on

pins and needles
pioneer species
piscicapturist
pisciculturist
piss and vinegar
pistachio green
pistilliferous
pistol-whipping
pit bull terrier
pitching moment
pituitary gland
placentiferous
placentography
placentologist
place of vantage
place of worship
plagiarization
plagiocephalic
plaguesomeness
plain chocolate
plain Dunstable
plain-heartedly
plains viscacha
plains-wanderer
Planck constant
Planck equation
plane-polarized
planetocentric
planetological
planet-stricken
planing-machine
planktological
plankton feeder
planktotrophic
planned economy
plan of campaign
plantation song
plant geography
plant pathology
plasmacellular
plasma dynamics
plasma membrane
plasmapheresis
plasmaphoresis
plasmodesmatal
plaster casting
plaster of Paris
plastic crystal
plasticization
plastic surgeon
plastic surgery
plate tectonics
platform rocker
platform sandal
platform tennis
platform ticket
platinocyanide
platino-iridium
platinum blonde
platinum metals
platinum sponge

platitudinizer
play a good stick
play a shell game
playback singer
play favourites
play for a sucker
play gooseberry
play it straight
playleadership
play the dickens
play the giddy ox
plea bargaining
plead not guilty
pleased as Punch
pleasurability
pleasure-ground
pleasuremonger
pleasure-seeker
plebiscitarian
plenary session
plenipotential
pleochroic halo
pleonastically
plesiomorphous
plethysmograph
pleurapophysis
pleurobranchia
plexiform layer
plough grinding
ploughing-match
plough the sands
pluck up courage
plug-compatible
plumber's friend
plumbosolvency
plum-in-the-mouth
plumose anemone
plunge grinding
plunge neckline
plural marriage
pluripotential
plurisegmental
plurisignative
plush-velveteen
plutocratizing
pluto-democracy
pluviculturist
pluviometrical
pneumatic drill
pneumatic-tyred
pneumatisation
pneumatization
pneumatologist
pneumatothorax
pneumoconiosis
pneumoconiotic
poacher's pocket
pocketableness
pocket expenses
pococuranteism
poet's narcissus

poikilitically
poikiloblastic
poikilocytosis
poikilothermal
poikilothermia
poikilothermic
point a finger at
point discharge
pointed blanket
point of station
point-policeman
point rationing
point-to-pointer
Poiseuille flow
Poiseuille's law
poison register
poke one's nose in
Polaris missile
polarizability
polar wandering
pole plantation
police informer
police positive
police reporter
Polish-American
Polish draughts
Polish notation
political novel
political trial
politicization
pollen analysis
pollen spectrum
polling station
polyacrylamide
polyalphabetic
polyautography
polybrominated
polycarpellary
polychromatism
polydispersity
polyelectronic
polyfunctional
polyglacialism
polyglacialist
polygonization
polygynandrous
polyhydramnios
polyisocyanate
polylingualism
polylithionite
polymenorrhoea
polymerization
polymorphously
polyneuropathy
polynomial time
polynucleotide
polyphonically
polyphosphoric
polypodiaceous
polyrhythmical
polysaccharide

polysyllabical
polytechnician
polytheistical
polythetically
polyunsaturate
polyvinylidene
pompano dolphin
Pontefract-cake
pontifical Mass
pontifical mass
pooh-pooh theory
poor man's orange
poor man's orchid
pop the question
popularity poll
popularization
populistically
porcelain shell
porcupine grass
pork-barrelling
porphyrization
porphyrogenita
porphyrogenite
portentousness
Port Jackson fig
Portland cement
Portland oolite
Portland powder
Portland spurge
positional play
position vector
positive column
posse comitatus
possessionless
possessive case
possessiveness
postacetabular
postal currency
posterolateral
posteroventral
postganglionic
post-industrial
postindustrial
post-infectious
postmastership
postmenopausal
post-millennial
postpositional
postpositively
postprandially
post-production
post-structural
potamoplankton
potash feldspar
potassium-argon
potato dumpling
potentiometric
potentiostatic
pounce commerce
powder magazine
powder one's nose

power breakfast
power frequency
power-political
practicability
practicalities
practical joker
practical nurse
pragmaticality
pragmatization
prairie-breaker
prairie chicken
prairie country
prairie rattler
prairie warbler
praiseworthily
prayerlessness
praying machine
preaching-cross
preaching friar
preaching-house
pre-adolescence
preadolescence
pre-anaesthetic
pre-appointment
pre-arrangement
prearrangement
prebendaryship
precalculation
precariousness
precatory words
precious metals
precipitinogen
precociousness
precommissural
pre-compression
preconsonantal
predaciousness
pre-delinquency
predesignation
predestinarian
predestinately
predestination
predeterminate
predictability
predictiveness
predisposition
pre-exponential
prefabrication
prefectorially
preferableness
preferentially
preferred share
preferred stock
pregermination
preglottalized
prehensiveness
pre-imagination
pre-impregnated
pre-incarnation
prejudiciously
premeditatedly

premenstrually
premillenarian
premonstration
prenegotiation
preoperational
preoperatively
preponderantly
preponderately
preponderation
preposterously
pre-publication
prepublication
prepunctuality
Pre-Raphaelitic
presbyterially
Presbyterianly
prescriptively
prescriptivism
prescriptivist
prescriptivity
presence of mind
presentability
presentational
presentimental
present oneself
preservability
president-elect
presidentially
presiding elder
press corrector
pressed for time
pressoreceptor
press secretary
press the button
pressure cooker
pressure vessel
pressurization
presumptuously
presupposition
pretensionless
pretensiveness
pretergression
prettification
prevailingness
prevailing wind
preventability
preventatively
preventibility
prevocalically
price-sensitive
prick and praise
prickly rhubarb
priest-in-charge
prima ballerina
primary feather
primary poverty
primary quality
primary teacher
primatological
primitive plane
primordial soup

Primrose League
primrose yellow
Prince Charming
princely States
prince's feather
Princess Regent
principal focus
principalities
principal parts
principal point
principledness
prinkum-prankum
printed circuit
printer plotter
printer-slotter
printing-office
prioritization
Priscillianism
Priscillianist
Priscillianite
prismatic layer
prison-breaking
prison sentence
prittle-prattle
private company
private inquiry
private patient
private service
private soldier
privileged debt
privileged deed
priviligentsia
pro aris et focis
probabiliorism
probabiliorist
probation order
pro bono publico
proboscidiform
proceleusmatic
processability
process control
processionally
prochlorophyte
procrastinator
Procrusteanism
procryptically
proctorization
procuratorship
prodigiousness
productibility
production line
production rule
productiveness
professionally
professionless
professorially
proficiency pay
profile machine
profitableness
profit à prendre
profitlessness

profligateness
progenitorship
progestational
prognosticable
prognostically
prognosticator
programme movie
programme music
progress-chaser
progressionism
progressionist
progress report
prohibited area
prohibitionary
prohibitionism
prohibitionist
projection lens
projection room
projection rule
projection test
projective test
proletarianise
proletarianism
proletarianize
prolocutorship
promise oneself
promissory note
promissory oath
prompt-critical
pronunciamento
proof-theoretic
propaedeutical
propagableness
propagandistic
proparoxytonic
propeller shaft
propenenitrile
proper fraction
propheticality
Prophet's flower
propitiatingly
propitiatorily
propitiousness
proportionable
proportionably
proportionally
proportionless
proportionment
propositionize
propraetorship
proprietorship
proprioception
proprioceptive
propyl aldehyde
propylene imine
proscriptively
prosencephalic
prosencephalon
prosopographer
prosopographic
prospectusless

prosperousness
prostatorrhoea
prosthetically
prosthodontics
prosthodontist
Protagoreanism
protectingness
protectiveness
protein plastic
protein therapy
proterogenesis
protest marcher
Protevangelium
prothonotaries
protistologist
protocanonical
protocontinent
proto-diasystem
Protogeometric
proto-historian
proton acceptor
proton-donating
protonospheric
protopetroleum
protoplanetary
protoplasmatic
protoporcelain
protoporphyria
protoporphyrin
protopresbyter
protospathaire
prototypically
protozoologist
protractedness
protrusiveness
proventricular
proventriculus
providentially
provincialship
Provisional IRA
provisionality
provost marshal
proximity talks
Prussian collar
Prutenic tables
pseudaesthesia
pseudarthrosis
pseudepigrapha
pseudisodomous
pseudo-catholic
pseudodipteral
pseudofracture
pseudomembrane
pseudomorphism
pseudomorphous
pseudoneurotic
pseudonymously
pseudopregnant
pseudoracemate
pseudorandomly
pseudo-rational

pseudoscorpion	purple swamphen	quaking pudding
pseudosymmetry	purposefulness	quality control
psilanthropism	purse and person	quantification
psilanthropist	push the boat out	quantitatively
psychedelicize	put a bold face on	quantitativist
psychoacoustic	put a good face on	quantity theory
psychoactivity	put a person up to	quaquaversally
psychoanalysis	put a person wise	quarantine flag
psychoanalytic	put a slight upon	quart and tierce
psychobiologic	putative father	quartan malaria
psychochemical	put it on the line	quarterbacking
psychocultural	put it to a person	quarter-binding
psychodramatic	put off the scent	quarter century
psychodynamics	put on a good show	quarter-gallery
psychogalvanic	put on a pedestal	quarter leather
psychogenetics	put on a poor show	quarter-pierced
psychographics	put one's faith in	quarter-pounder
psychohistoric	put one's hands on	quarter-section
psycholinguist	put one's money on	quarter stretch
psychologistic	put one's shirt on	quartette table
psychometrical	put one's spoke in	quartetto table
psychoneurosis	put on the market	Quaternitarian
psychoneurotic	put on the screws	quaternization
psychopannychy	put out of the way	quattrocentist
psychophonetic	put out to tender	Queen Anne's lace
psychophysical	putrescibility	Queen in Council
psychopolitics	put the blocks on	queening square
psychosexually	put the breeze up	Queen of the West
psychosocially	put the collar on	Queen's Attorney
psychosomatics	put the finger on	Queen's Champion
psychosomatist	put the kibosh on	Queen's evidence
psychostatical	put the question	Queensland blue
psychosurgical	put the screws on	Queensland hemp
psychrospheric	put the sleeve on	Queensland sore
psychrotrophic	put the tin hat on	Queen's shilling
pteridological	put the tin lid on	queen substance
pterodactyloid	put up a good show	quench-cracking
public defender	put up a poor show	quercitron lake
public interest	pyelolithotomy	questionlessly
publicity agent	pyelonephritic	question master
public nuisance	pyelonephritis	quiche Lorraine
public-spirited	pyramidologist	quick on the draw
puerperal fever	pyramid selling	quick-reference
puffin crossing	pyrenomycetous	quick with child
pugilistically	pyridostigmine	quiescent sheva
pugnaciousness	pyriform muscle	quincentennial
puisne mortgage	pyritification	quinquagesimal
Pullman kitchen	pyrobituminous	quinquedentate
pull one's weight	pyrogallic acid	quinquefoliate
pull the longbow	pyrometallurgy	quinquelocular
pull the strings	pyrometrically	quinquennially
pulmobranchiae	pyrometric cone	quinquepartite
pulmobranchial	pyrophosphoric	quinquesection
punctuationist	pyrotechnician	quintessential
punishableness	Pythagoreanism	quite something
pupil barrister	quadragenarian	quodlibetarian
pupillographic	quadrangularly	quotidian fever
pupillometrics	quadrantanopia	Rabelaisianism
purchasability	quadrant method	Rachmaninovian
purple amaranth	quadrate muscle	rack one's brains
purple membrane	quadrisyllable	radial symmetry

radial velocity
radiation frost
radiator grille
radicalization
radio announcer
radio astronomy
radioautograph
radiobiologist
radiochemistry
radioenzymatic
radio frequency
radiogenically
radiographical
radiologically
radio-resistant
radiosensitive
radiosensitize
radio-telegraph
radio-telemetry
radio-telephone
radio-telephony
radio telescope
radiotherapist
radius of action
Rafferty's rules
raft foundation
railway station
rainbow-serpent
rain pitchforks
rainwater goods
raise a blockade
raise an eyebrow
raise a standard
raise one's guard
raise one's voice
rambunctiously
rammelsbergite
rampageousness
ramshackleness
random variable
Rangoon creeper
rank difference
ranunculaceous
Raschig process
Rastafarianism
rate of exchange
ration strength
rat's-tail cactus
rat's-tail fescue
rat-tailed spoon
rattle one's dags
rattle the sabre
Rayleigh number
razor-billed auk
reaccumulation
reacquaintance
reactionaryism
reading-machine
read-only memory
read the riot act
read the Riot Act

reality-testing
realizableness
reaping-machine
reappraisement
rear projection
rear-view mirror
rear-wheel drive
reasonableness
reasonlessness
reassimilation
rebelliousness
recalcitrantly
recalcitration
recapacitation
recapitulation
recapitulative
recapitulatory
receiving order
reception class
reception order
recess printing
reciprocity law
recivilization
recoil particle
recollectively
recolonization
recombinant DNA
recommencement
recommendation
recommendatory
reconciliation
reconciliative
reconciliatory
reconfirmation
reconnaissance
reconsecration
reconstitution
reconstruction
reconstructive
record-breaking
recording angel
recording level
recoverability
recreationally
rectangularity
rectilinearity
recuperability
recurrence time
red-backed mouse
red-bloodedness
redeemableness
redintegration
redintegrative
redistillation
redistribution
redistributive
red-necked grebe
red precipitate
reductionistic
reed instrument
Reeves pheasant

refectory table
reference frame
reference group
reference level
reference-point
referentiality
reflectionless
reflectiveness
reflex klystron
reflexological
reformationist
Reformed Church
refractiveness
refractometric
refractoriness
refrangibility
refreshingness
refreshment bar
refugee capital
regardlessness
regasification
regeneratively
registered post
register office
registrability
registry office
regression line
regressiveness
regularization
regular octagon
regular soldier
regulator clock
rehabilitation
rehabilitative
reillumination
reimplantation
reinauguration
reindeer lichen
reinterpreting
reintroduction
reinvigoration
Rejection Front
rejuvenescence
relapsing fever
relational word
relativization
relaxation time
relentlessness
relexification
relief printing
relieve oneself
relinquishment
remain to be seen
remarkableness
Rembrandtesque
remedilessness
Remembrance Day
reminiscential
remobilization
remodification
remonetization

remoralization
remorsefulness
remuneratively
Renaissance man
renormalizable
reorganization
repetition work
repetitiveness
replaceability
replica plating
repolarization
reported speech
report progress
re-presentation
representation
representative
repressiveness
reprimandingly
repristination
reproductively
reproductivity
reprogrammable
repromulgation
repudiationist
repulsion motor
repurification
requisitionist
re-registration
reservationist
residentiaries
residual stress
resignationism
resignationist
resinification
resistanceless
resistlessness
resolving power
resonant cavity
resource centre
resource person
respectabilise
respectability
respectabilize
respectfulness
respect persons
responsibility
responsiveness
responsorially
restitutionism
restitutionist
rest on one's oars
restorationism
restorationist
restore in blood
restrainedness
restricted area
restrictedness
restrictionism
restrictionist
resurrectional
resurrectioner

retained object
retained profit
retention money
retinoblastoma
retirement home
retractability
retransmission
retransmitting
retributionist
retrievability
retrocognition
retrocognitive
retrodictively
retroductively
retrogradation
retroreflector
return envelope
return to nature
revalorisation
revalorization
revengefulness
Reverend Mother
reverification
reverse charges
reverse osmosis
reversing falls
reversing layer
reversing light
Revised Version
revitalization
revivification
revolving stage
rewardableness
Reynolds number
Reynolds stress
rheogoniometer
rhesus-negative
rhesus-positive
rhetoricalness
rheumatic fever
rheumatologist
rhinencephalic
rhinencephalon
rhinoceros bird
rhinoceros bush
rhinoceros horn
rhinosporidial
rhizocephalous
Rhode Island Red
rhopheocytosis
rhynchokinesis
rhynchokinetic
rhynchophorous
rhynchosaurian
rhynchosporium
rhyparographer
rhyparographic
rhythm and blues
ribbon-building
ribonucleoside
ribonucleotide

rich tea biscuit
rickety-rackety
riddle of claret
ridiculousness
right about-face
right about-turn
right ascension
right-hand drive
right-hand screw
right off the bat
rigidification
Ringer solution
ring in one's ears
ringmastership
ring the changes
ring the knell of
rise in the world
rise with the sun
Ritter's disease
river blindness
roadworthiness
roaring forties
roaring success
roast-beef plant
Robin Hood's barn
robin redbreast
Robinson Crusoe
robin's plantain
robustiousness
roche moutonnée
rocket larkspur
rocket launcher
roentgenograph
roentgenologic
roentgenoscope
roentgenoscopy
rogation flower
Rogation Sunday
rolling barrage
rolling chamber
romanceishness
Romanian stitch
romanticalness
roof of the mouth
roof of the world
root-mean-square
root of scarcity
rose leafhopper
rosette disease
rose-water still
Rosicrucianism
rostro-carinate
rostrocaudally
rotary printing
rough-and-tumble
rough breathing
rough greyhound
rough horsetail
roundaboutness
roundhouse kick
round on a person

round-the-houses
round the wicket
Rowland grating
Rowland's circle
royal abundance
Royal Engineers
Royal Sovereign
Royal Worcester
rubber solution
rubbing alcohol
rub the wrong way
ruddy sheldrake
ruddy turnstone
Rueping process
ruff and discard
Rules Committee
rules of the game
rumblegumption
Rump Parliament
run a person hard
run in the family
running account
running banquet
running bowline
running footman
running repairs
running rigging
run off one's feet
run one's own show
run the blockade
run the gauntlet
run the rule over
run with the ball
Rural Institute
rush one's fences
Russell paradox
Russianization
Russian scandal
Russian thistle
rust-resistance
Rydberg formula
Sabatier effect
Sabbatarianism
sabbaticalness
sabbatical year
sacchariferous
saccharimetric
saccharization
saccharomycete
sacramentalism
sacramentalist
sacramentality
sacramentarian
sacrament house
sacrament-money
sacrifice price
sacrilegiously
saddleback crow
saddleback gull
saddleback seal
saddle-coloured

saddle-grafting
saddle scabbard
saddle shoulder
saddle thrombus
safety-critical
safety engineer
saffron milk-cap
saffron-thistle
saleswomanship
saline solution
salinification
salinity crisis
Salisbury steak
salmon-coloured
saloon carriage
salpingography
salt of wormwood
salt-water taffy
salubriousness
salute the judge
same difference
sanctification
Sandemanianism
sandwich course
sanguification
sanguinariness
sanguinivorous
sanitary napkin
sansculotterie
Santa Gertrudis
saponification
sapphire quartz
sarcosporidial
sarcosporidium
satellite photo
satellite state
satellite State
satisfactorily
satisfiability
satisfyingness
satisfy oneself
saturated steam
saturation dive
saturnicentric
sausage balloon
sausage machine
savannah flower
savannah forest
savannah monkey
saved by the bell
save one's breath
save one's pocket
save the trouble
savings account
savings and loan
saw-scaled viper
saxifragaceous
say one thing for
scala vestibuli
scalogram board
scaly francolin

scandalization
scandalousness
scanning raster
scaphocephalic
scaphocephalus
scaphognathite
scared shitless
scaremongering
scarlatiniform
scarlet lychnis
scarlet tanager
scatterbrained
scatter cushion
scatter diagram
Schaumann's body
Scheduled Caste
Scheduled Tribe
Scheiner number
schematization
scheme of colour
Schering bridge
Schick-negative
Schick-positive
Schiff reaction
schismatically
schismogenesis
schistosomulum
schizonticidal
schizontocidal
schlockmeister
Schmitt trigger
schola cantorum
scholastically
scholasticized
schoolboyishly
school district
school-divinity
schoolgirlhood
schoolmasterly
schoolmistress
School of the Air
schoolteaching
Schottky defect
Schottky effect
Schottky theory
schreierpfeife
Schwenkfeldian
Schwyzertütsch
science fantasy
science fiction
scientifically
scientifiction
scientometrics
scintilla juris
scintillograph
scintillometer
scintillometry
scintilloscope
scintiscanning
sclerification
sclerophyllous

sclerotization	secular society	self-government
scobberlotcher	secundigravida	self-hypnotized
scolopophorous	securitization	self-immolation
scoop stretcher	seditious libel	self-importance
score points off	seedling blight	self-improvable
scorpion orchid	see something of	self-inductance
scorpion-spider	see the elephant	self-indulgence
Scotch asphodel	segmentability	self-infliction
Scotch attorney	segregationist	self-interested
Scotch baronial	Seidlitz powder	self-involution
Scotch woodcock	seismic sea-wave	self-ionization
Scott-connected	seismometrical	self-justifying
Scotticization	seismotectonic	self-limitation
Scottification	self-abhorrence	self-liquidator
Scottish-French	self-abnegating	self-management
scouring powder	self-abnegation	self-motivation
scoutmastering	self-abnegatory	self-mutilation
scrape ceremony	self-absorption	self-partiality
scrape-trencher	self-accusation	self-pollinated
scratch-brusher	self-accusatory	self-pollinator
scratching post	self-adjustment	self-possession
screaming eagle	self-admiration	self-preserving
screen printing	self-advertiser	self-proclaimed
screw propeller	self-alienation	self-propelling
scribbleomania	self-applauding	self-protection
scripturalness	self-assessment	self-protective
scritch-scratch	self-betterment	self-punishment
scrofulodermia	self-cancelling	self-reflection
Scroll of the Law	self-censorship	self-reflective
scroll painting	self-compatible	self-regulating
scrubbing-brush	self-complacent	self-regulation
scrupulousness	self-conception	self-regulative
scrutinization	self-condemning	self-regulatory
scurrilousness	self-confidence	self-repression
sea-caterpillar	self-consistent	self-respectful
sea gilliflower	self-controlled	self-respecting
seamstress-ship	self-conviction	self-restrained
seaside sparrow	self-correcting	self-revelation
seasonableness	self-definition	self-sacrificer
season cracking	self-defrosting	self-satisfying
sea stickleback	self-dependence	self-similarity
sebaceous crypt	self-destroying	self-subsistent
sebaceous gland	self-determined	self-sufficient
secondary cause	self-diffidence	self-suggestion
secondary radar	self-discipline	self-supporting
secondary umbel	self-effacement	self-sustaining
second blessing	self-effacingly	self-sustenance
second-handness	self-employment	selfwilledness
second language	self-estimation	semaphorically
second mortgage	self-evaluation	semasiological
second mourning	self-evidencing	semi-autonomous
second pendulum	self-exaltation	semicircularly
second position	self-excitation	semiconducting
second-rateness	self-experience	semiconduction
second thoughts	self-expression	semiconductive
Second World War	self-expressive	semi-convergent
secret dovetail	self-fertilized	semi-detachment
sector analysis	self-flattering	semi-diaphanous
sector scanning	self-fulfilling	semi-elliptical
secularisation	self-fulfilment	semi-fabricated
secularization	self-generating	semifabricator

semi-lunar valve
seminal vesicle
seminary priest
semi-occasional
semi-officially
semi-retirement
semispheroidal
Semitic-Hamitic
semnopithecine
semotactically
senatus consult
send of an errand
senile dementia
senior moralist
senior security
senior wrangler
sensationalise
sensationalism
sensationalist
sensationalize
sensationistic
sensitive brier
sensitive plant
sensory aphasia
sensualization
sentence adverb
sentimentalise
sentimentalism
sentimentalist
sentimentality
sentimentalize
separate school
septemdecenary
septuagenarian
sequaciousness
sequestrectomy
Serene Highness
sergeant-at-arms
sergeant-at-mace
Sergeant-at-mace
sergeant bugler
serial homology
serial symmetry
sericicultural
sericitization
series-parallel
serio-comically
serjeant-at-arms
serjeants-at-law
seroconversion
serodiagnostic
seropositivity
seroprevalence
serous membrane
serpentary root
serpentiferous
serpentine jade
serpentine rock
serum hepatitis
serve-and-volley
serve one's needs

serviceability
service ceiling
service measure
service-program
service routine
service station
servo-amplifier
servohydraulic
servo-mechanism
servomechanism
sesquialterate
sesquipedalian
sesquipedality
set oneself up as
set one's heart on
seven champions
Seven Last Words
seven-year apple
several fishery
several tenancy
sexcentenaries
sextuplication
sexual equality
sexual politics
seymouriamorph
shadowgraphist
shadowlessness
shadow quilting
shagbark walnut
shaggy-dog story
shake a loose leg
shake by the hand
shake hands with
shake one's elbow
shake one's sides
Shakespeariana
shamefacedness
Shanghailander
sharp as a needle
sharps and flats
shatter-brained
sheaf catalogue
shearing strain
shearing stress
shed the blood of
sheepdog trials
sheep's scabious
sheet lightning
Sheffer's stroke
Sheffield plate
shelf-catalogue
shell parrakeet
shepherd's check
shepherd's cress
shepherd's crook
shepherd's plaid
shepherd's purse
shepherd's staff
sheriff officer
Sherlock Holmes
shift character

shift end for end
shifting centre
shillingsworth
shilly-shallied
shilly-shallies
shilly-shallyer
shingle machine
shipping-master
shipping-office
ship's-carpenter
shock-absorbent
shock-absorbing
shock treatment
shooting-ground
shooting jacket
shooting season
shoot one's cuffs
shoot the breeze
shoot the chutes
shopping arcade
shopping centre
shore patrolman
shortlivedness
short-sightedly
short square leg
shotgun wedding
shot-hole fungus
shotten herring
shoulder charge
shouldered arch
shoulder-girdle
shoulder-height
shoulder-lappet
shoulder-length
shoulder period
shoulder season
shoulder stripe
shove-halfpenny
shovel and broom
shove one's oar in
show one's mettle
shrift-district
shrimp cocktail
shrinkage crack
shut one's eyes to
shut one's mind to
shutter release
shuttle bombing
shuttle service
sialolithiasis
Siamese fighter
Siberian weasel
sibling rivalry
sibling species
Sibylline books
sick and tired of
sickle-cell gene
side-of-the-mouth
siege mentality
Siemens furnace
Siemens process

sight liability
sigillographer
sigmoid flexure
sigmoidoscopic
signal strength
sign of the cross
sign of the times
silent majority
silicification
silicon carbide
siliconization
silk-stockinged
silk-tassel bush
silver-bell tree
silver pheasant
silver-printing
silver quandong
silversmithing
silver standard
silver sycamore
silviculturist
simple fracture
simple interest
simple interval
simple majority
simple-mindedly
simple pendulum
simple sentence
simplex tableau
simplification
simplificatory
simplistically
simultaneously
sindonological
Singapore sling
singe one's wings
single acrostic
single-breasted
single-handedly
single-mindedly
single standard
single-stranded
single suckling
singsong theory
sinking feeling
sin one's mercies
sins of the flesh
siphonapterous
siphonaxanthin
siphonoxanthin
sir-reverence of
sit at the feet of
sit in judgement
sit on one's hands
sit on the splice
sit on the throne
situationalism
situationalist
six o'clock swill
six-rowed barley
sixteen pounder

skate on thin ice
skeletal muscle
skiascopically
skimble-skamble
skin and blister
skin resistance
slack one's hands
slanderousness
slantindicular
slatternliness
slaughterhouse
slaughteringly
slaughterously
Slave of the Lamp
Slavonian grebe
sleeping beauty
Sleeping Beauty
sleeping lizard
sleeping-potion
sleep paralysis
sleepy sickness
sleeve-coupling
sleevelessness
slice of the cake
slide projector
sliding contact
slime bacterium
sling-back chair
slip-coat cheese
slipshoddiness
slip the painter
slope detection
slot television
sluggardliness
slumberousness
small-bourgeois
small intestine
small-mouth bass
small of the back
smelling bottle
smell of the lamp
smell of the shop
smell the ground
smoking concert
smooth flounder
smoothing plane
snaggle-toothed
snakebark maple
snapper sampler
snapping shrimp
snapping turtle
snatch one's time
snipper-snapper
snip-snap-snorum
snowflake curve
snowshoe rabbit
sociable plover
sociable weaver
social casework
social climbing
social contract

social democrat
social distance
social document
social drinking
social dynamics
social medicine
social mobility
social position
social register
social security
society of Jesus
Society of Jesus
sociobiologist
sociologically
socio-political
socio-religious
socio-technical
soda-mint tablet
sodium chloride
sodium lighting
soft-headedness
soil deficiency
soil exhaustion
soldier-termite
solecistically
solenoglyphous
solicitousness
solicitudinous
solid diffusion
solidification
solid injection
solifluctional
solitary thrush
solitudinarian
solubilization
solvent extract
solvolytically
someone or other
somewhere about
somnambulantly
somnambulation
somnambulistic
sonnet-sequence
soon afterwards
sooty albatross
sophistication
sophomorically
soporiferously
sordid dragonet
soreheadedness
soteriological
soul-destroying
sound as a pippin
sound generator
sound in damages
sounding rocket
sound-insulated
sound moderator
sound-symbolism
sound synthesis
source language

sourdough bread
south-easterner
south-eastwards
southern lights
Southern Paiute
Southern States
South Sea bubble
South Sea Bubble
South Sea scheme
south-south-east
south-southerly
south-south-west
south-westerner
south-westwards
Sovietological
space astronomy
space programme
space-reddening
space satellite
spaceship earth
space simulator
space telescope
space traveller
spacing machine
spaghetti house
spaghetti tongs
Spanish America
Spanish bayonet
Spanish bowline
Spanish dancing
Spanish Mission
Spanish needles
Spanish opening
spargefication
spark machining
spathic iron ore
spatial ability
spatialization
spatio-temporal
spatter rampart
spattling poppy
speak by the card
speak extempore
speak for itself
speaking skills
speak in tongues
speak like a book
speak out of turn
special edition
special effects
specialization
special licence
special partner
special pleader
special service
special verdict
specific charge
specific thrust
specific volume
spectacled bear
spectacle-glass

spectacularism
spectacularity
spectatorially
spectator sport
spectral series
spectrographer
spectrographic
spectrological
spectrometrist
spectroscopist
speechlessness
spellbindingly
spelling school
Spencer carbine
spermatiferous
spermatiophore
spermatization
spermatogonium
spermatophoric
spermatorrhoea
spermiogenesis
speromagnetism
sphere of action
spherical angle
spherical wedge
spheroplasting
sphincterotomy
sphygmographic
sphygmological
spinal puncture
spindle machine
spindle-shanked
spinning tunnel
spinous process
spin-stabilized
spinthariscope
spiny cocklebur
spiral cleavage
spirantization
spiritlessness
spiritual court
spiritualistic
spirituousness
spirochaetosis
spironolactone
spit and sawdust
spite and malice
spit in the eye of
splenic flexure
splice-grafting
splishy-splashy
split one's sides
split-skin graft
split the breeze
split the ticket
splitting field
sponge sandwich
sporadic E-layer
sporadic region
sporangiferous
sporangiophore

sporangiospore
sporotrichosis
sport-fisherman
sporting chance
sporting editor
sports medicine
spot commercial
spotted dogfish
spotted rat-fish
spread-eagleism
spread-eagleist
spreading adder
spreading-board
spreadsheeting
sprightfulness
spring mattress
spring training
sputter ion pump
squadron leader
squamocolumnar
square brackets
square-shooting
squatter pigeon
squeezableness
squelch circuit
squirearchical
squirrel-headed
squirrel monkey
stadial moraine
stadtholderate
stadtholderess
stage direction
stagflationary
stainless steel
stain-resistant
staircase shell
stalagmometric
stamp catalogue
stamp collector
stamped leather
stamped mealies
stamping ground
standard-bearer
standard candle
standardizable
standard-winged
stand corrected
standing-ground
standing orders
standing pillar
stand of colours
stand one's trial
stand the market
stand the racket
Stanislavskian
Stanley bustard
staphylococcal
staphylococcus
staphylomatous
starboard watch
starch hyacinth

star connection
stare into space
starfish flower
starlight scope
starting-handle
starting pistol
starting salary
starting-signal
start something
starvation diet
starve the crows
state an account
State education
state of affairs
State's attorney
State socialism
State socialist
stathmokinesis
stathmokinetic
static friction
static pressure
stationariness
stationary bike
stationary wave
Stationers' Hall
station-keeping
station pointer
statuary marble
statuesqueness
statutableness
steady from hare
steady the Buffs
steak and kidney
steal a marriage
steel engraving
steelification
steeplechasing
steeple-crowned
steering column
stegocephalian
Steller sea lion
Steller's sea cow
stellification
stentorophonic
stepped in years
stercoricolous
sterelminthous
stereochemical
stereoisomeric
stereometrical
stereomutation
stereo-plotting
stereoptically
stereoregulate
stereospecific
sterling silver
sternutatories
stertorousness
stethendoscope
stethoscopical
stibogluconate

stichometrical
stick-and-carrot
stick at nothing
stick in the mire
stick one's bib in
sticky-fingered
stigmatiferous
stigmatization
Stillson wrench
stilt sandpiper
stinging nettle
sting in the tail
stinking badger
stinking Willie
Stirling number
stir one's stumps
stirrup leather
stitchdown shoe
stochastically
stockbrokerage
stock character
stocking filler
stocking-masked
stocking stitch
stocking tights
stocking-weaver
stoichiometric
stomatogastric
stomatological
stone-cold sober
stopping effect
stopping-ground
storage battery
storage heating
storm and stress
storm in a teacup
stout-heartedly
strabismometer
strabismometry
straight-backed
straight driver
straight-haired
straightjacket
straight muscle
straight-necked
straight stitch
straight ticket
straining-frame
Straits Chinese
Strasbourg pâté
straticulation
stratification
stratigraphist
strawberry bass
strawberry bush
strawberry dish
strawberry leaf
strawberry mark
strawberry pear
strawberry roan
strawberry tree

straw in the wind
straw-splitting
stream function
street credible
street fighting
street lighting
streets ahead of
street-to-street
strengthlessly
strepsipterous
streptodornase
streptothricin
streptovaricin
streptozotocin
stress analysis
stress-breaking
stress fracture
stretchability
stretcher-party
stretch forming
stretching beam
stretching-bond
stretching-iron
stria atrophica
striated muscle
stridulousness
strike a balance
strike a bargain
strike a blow for
strike one's flag
striking-circle
string-coloured
strip-jack-naked
stroboscopical
stroke of genius
stroke of policy
stromatolithic
stromatoporoid
strong language
strong-man's-weed
strontium oxide
strophanthidin
Strouhal number
structural load
structuredness
strumpetocracy
strut one's stuff
stubble-burning
studentization
student teacher
student—teacher
studio portrait
stultification
stultificatory
stultiloquence
stumbling block
stupendousness
styloid process
subalternation
subatmospheric
subatomic level

subconsciously
subcontinental
subcontrariety
subcutaneously
subdisjunctive
subdistinction
subduction zone
suberification
subgenerically
subinfeudation
subinfeudatory
subjectability
subject-heading
subjective case
subjectiveness
subjectivistic
sub-lieutenancy
subliminal self
submerged tenth
submersibility
submicroscopic
submissiveness
subscribership
subsidiary goal
substance abuse
substantialise
substantialism
substantialist
substantiality
substantialize
substantiation
substantiative
substantivally
substitutional
substitutively
substitutivity
subtense method
subterraneanly
subterrestrial
sub-underwriter
subversiveness
successfulness
successionally
successionless
successiveness
Successor State
sucking-cushion
sucking stomach
suck the blood of
suck the hind tit
suction dredger
sufferance quay
suffice it to say
suggestibility
suggestio falsi
suggestiveness
suicide mission
suicide squeeze
sulfhemoglobin
sulphadimidine
sulphafurazole

sulphanilamide
sulphapyridine
sulphasalazine
sulphathiazole
sulphisoxazole
sulphonylation
sulphur dioxide
sulphurization
sulphurous acid
sulphurousness
summary offence
summation check
summer hyacinth
summer mastitis
summer quarters
summer resident
summer solstice
Sunflower State
sun in splendour
sunset industry
sunshine-yellow
superabundance
superabundancy
superadiabatic
superaffluence
superannuation
superannuitant
superb starling
supercargoship
supercelestial
superciliously
supercivilized
supercomputing
superconductor
superconscious
supercontinent
superelevation
supereminently
supererogation
supererogatory
superessential
superexcellent
superficialism
superficialist
superficiality
superficialize
superhelically
superhumanness
superimpending
superimposable
superincumbent
superinduction
superinfection
superintendent
superlapsarian
superlaryngeal
superluminally
supermanliness
supermarketeer
supermarketing
supermullioned

supermultiplet
supernaturally
supernormality
superoccipital
superovulation
superoxygenate
superphosphate
superpurgation
superradiantly
super-realistic
supersaturated
superscripting
superscription
supersensitive
supersensually
supersonically
superstitional
superstructive
superstructory
superstructure
supersubtilize
supersymmetric
superterranean
supervacaneous
supervisorship
supplementally
supplicatingly
supportability
supporting film
supportiveness
suppositionary
suppositiously
supposititious
suppressio veri
suppressor cell
suppressor gene
suppressor grid
suprachoroidal
supralapsarian
supramaxillary
supramolecular
supraoccipital
suprasegmental
supra-threshold
supreme pontiff
sure-footedness
surface blow-off
surface-printed
surface tension
surgeon general
Surgeon General
surgical spirit
Suriname cherry
Suriname poison
surpass oneself
surprise packet
surprisingness
surrender value
sursumvergence
susceptibility
susceptiveness

suspend payment
suspensiveness
suspiciousness
sustainability
sustained yield
swaddling-bands
swami jewellery
swamp sassafras
swan animalcule
Swan River daisy
swear like a lord
Swedish massage
Swedish masseur
sweet coltsfoot
sweeten the pill
sweet fenugreek
sweet galingale
sweetheart neck
sweetheart rose
sweet seventeen
swimming trunks
Swinburnianism
swine influenza
swinging-bridge
Swiss stone pine
sword of justice
sword-swallower
sworn to secrecy
symbolicalness
symbolo-fideism
symbolo-fideist
symmetricality
symmetric group
symmetrization
symmetrophobia
sympathetic ink
sympathicotony
sympathotropic
sympathy strike
symphysis pubis
symplectically
symptomatology
symptom complex
synaptogenesis
synchondrosial
synchronically
syncretistical
syncretization
synergetically
syngenetically
synonymousness
Synoptic Gospel
synsedimentary
syntax language
synthetic resin
syringe passage
Syrophoenician
systematically
system-building
system operator
systems analyst

system software
systems program
tabernacle-work
tableau curtain
tablespoonfuls
tabloidization
tabular iceberg
tachistoscopic
tacho-generator
tachygraphical
tachymetabolic
Taconic orogeny
Tahiti chestnut
tail-end Charlie
tailor-madeness
take a dim view of
take advantages
take a rise out of
take a slipper to
take by surprise
take delivery of
take farewell of
take fast hold of
take for granted
take holy orders
take in good part
take off one's hat
take one's chance
take one's choice
take oneself off
take one's flight
takeover bidder
take pleasure in
take possession
take precedence
take the biscuit
take the can back
take the edge off
take the gauge of
take the liberty
take the place of
take the trouble
take to one's legs
take to the boats
take up the glove
take up the slack
take up the torch
talismanically
talking machine
talking picture
tallow-chandler
tambourine dove
tangible assets
tank locomotive
tape reproducer
tapestry beetle
tapestry needle
tapestry-worker
tappity-tappity
tar and feathers
tarantula-juice

target audience
target language
tariff-reformer
taskmastership
Tasmanian cedar
Tasmanian devil
Tasmanian tiger
tassel hyacinth
tassel-pondweed
taste-blindness
tatterdemalion
tattersal check
tattle-tale grey
tautologically
tawny frogmouth
tea and sympathy
teacher edition
teaching fellow
tea-scented rose
technical hitch
technicalities
technification
techno-economic
technostressed
tectonophysics
tectonothermal
telangiectasis
telangiectatic
telautographic
teleconference
teleconnection
tele-evangelist
telegraph blank
telegraph board
telegraph plant
telemetrically
teleologically
telepathically
telephone booth
telephone kiosk
telephonically
telephonograph
telephotograph
teleprocessing
telescope-sight
telescopically
teletypesetter
teletypewriter
televangelical
televisionless
television tube
television-wise
tell it like it is
tell its own tale
telomerization
temporaneously
temporary tooth
temptationless
tenant paravail
tendo-synovitis
Tennysonianism

ten o'clock swill
tenore di grazia
tenure in capite
tequila sunrise
Tequistlatecan
teratogenicity
tercentenaries
terebinthinate
terebinthinous
tergiversation
tergiversatory
terminableness
terminal market
terminal string
terminal symbol
terminological
terminus ad quem
termitophagous
termitophilous
term of reproach
terotechnology
terra incognita
terra irredenta
terra ponderosa
terra sigillata
terrestriality
terrestrialize
terrible infant
territorialise
territorialism
territorialist
territoriality
territorialize
terror-stricken
terry towelling
tertian malaria
testamentarily
testimonialize
testing station
tetartohedrism
tetraalkyllead
tetrachotomous
tetracosactrin
tetractinellid
tetradactylous
tetraethyl lead
Tetragrammaton
tetrevangelium
Texas armadillo
text processing
thalamostriate
thalassography
thalassophobia
thanatological
that is news to me
thaumatropical
thaumaturgical
the age of reason
theatricalness
the Author of all
the beaten track

Thebesian valve
the bird is flown
the boy next door
theca folliculi
the Carabiniers
the child unborn
the Christ-child
the clean potato
the Emerald Isle
the English pale
the environment
the Eternal City
the facts of life
the far infrared
the fatal thread
the Five Nations
the Flowery Land
the frozen limit
the gate of death
the gentle craft
the great Author
the Great Divide
the Great Unpaid
the heart bleeds
the high command
the Hundred Days
the Incarnation
the Inquisition
the King's colour
the King's speech
the kiss of death
the laugh is on me
the life of Riley
the little woman
the Long Forties
the Lord's Prayer
the Lord's Supper
the Man Upstairs
the new celibacy
the noble savage
theocentricism
theocentricity
theocratically
Theodosian Code
the Old Dominion
theology of hope
the opposite sex
theosophically
the Philosopher
the public purse
the Queen's peace
therianthropic
the rich glutton
theriogenology
theriomorphism
thermal barrier
thermal imaging
thermal inertia
thermalization
thermal neutron
thermal printer

thermal reactor
thermal runaway
thermal springs
thermal storage
thermionically
thermochemical
thermochromism
thermodynamics
thermoelectric
thermo-junction
thermolability
thermomagnetic
thermometrical
thermophysical
thermoreceptor
thermoregulate
thermoremanent
thermotolerant
therocephalian
the roof falls in
the sinews of war
the Six Counties
the small screen
the sum of things
the two cultures
the vale of years
the whole shmear
the witch is in it
the world to come
thieves' kitchen
thieves' vinegar
thimble printer
thingification
things personal
think in terms of
think nothing of
thioglycollate
third-and-fourth
Third Programme
Third Secretary
third ventricle
thirteenth part
thirty-year rule
this mortal coil
thoracic cavity
thorny woodcock
thorough-lights
thorough-stitch
thought control
thoughtfulness
thoughtography
thought pattern
thought-reading
thousand island
thousand-jacket
thousandth part
threadbareness
three-card monte
three-card trick
three halfpence
three-halfpenny

three-letter man
threepenny nail
three-point turn
threshing floor
thrift industry
thriftlessness
thrombasthenia
thrombocytosis
thromboembolic
thromboplastic
thromboplastin
thrombosthenin
throne and altar
through-draught
through-ganging
through-passage
through-the-lens
through traffic
throw a veil over
throw oneself at
throw oneself on
throw overboard
throw the book at
throw the switch
thrust and parry
thrust reverser
thump the pulpit
thunder-bearing
thunder-blasted
thunderousness
thwacking-frame
thyro-arytenoid
thyroid hormone
thyrotoxicosis
thysanopterous
Tibetan mastiff
Tibetan spaniel
Tibetan terrier
Tiburtine stone
ticket-of-leaver
ticket-splitter
tickle the peter
tiddly-om-pom-pom
tie hand and foot
tilting furnace
timber carriage
time dilatation
time immemorial
time of one's life
time-travelling
tinhorn gambler
tintinnabulant
tintinnabulary
tintinnabulate
tintinnabulous
tissue-matching
title catalogue
title insurance
to a great extent
to a person's cost
to a person's face

tobacco-stopper
toilet-training
toing and froing
token-reflexive
tolerance level
tolerance limit
tolerogenicity
Tolman sweeting
Tom-and-Jerryism
tomato hornworm
tomfoolishness
tone separation
tongue-tiedness
tongue-twisting
to one's dying day
to one's own cheek
toothbrush tree
topgallant mast
topicalization
topochemically
topoinhibition
topologization
topotactically
topsy-turviness
topsy-turvyhood
torpedo-catcher
torpedo-netting
torsion balance
tortoise-beetle
torture chamber
to say nothing of
total abstainer
to tell the truth
to the bitter end
to the four winds
to the utterance
tough as leather
tower of silence
town councillor
toxin-antitoxin
tracheostomies
tracking weight
traction engine
traction splint
tractor-trailer
trade allowance
trade reduction
tradesman's door
trades unionist
trade-unionized
trading account
trading station
traditionalise
traditionalism
traditionalist
traditionality
traditionalize
Trafalgar chair
trafficability
traffic analyst
traffic calming

traffic control
traffic offence
traffic officer
traffic pattern
tragicomically
trailing vortex
training-school
traitorousness
transacetylase
transamination
transanimation
transcendental
transcendently
transcendingly
transconjugant
transductional
transempirical
transferential
transfer factor
transformation
transformative
transformer oil
transform fault
transfretation
transfusionist
transgressible
transitionally
transitiveness
transitoriness
Transjordanian
translationese
translatorship
transliterator
translocatable
transmigration
transmigrative
transmigratory
transmissional
transmissivity
transmit button
transmogrified
transmogrifier
transmogrifies
transparencies
transpeptidase
transpicuously
transplantable
transplendency
transplutonium
transpolitical
transportation
transportative
Transport House
transport-plane
transpulmonary
transsexualism
transsexualist
transsexuality
Transvaal daisy
transvaluation
transverbation

transversality
transverse axis
transverseness
transverse wave
transvesticism
transvestitism
trapdoor spider
trapeze harness
traumatization
traumatologist
traumatotropic
travel brochure
traveller's palm
traveller's tale
travelling wave
travel-sickness
traverse-survey
treacle mustard
tread the boards
tread under foot
treasure-flower
treat like a lord
tremendousness
treponematosis
treponemicidal
tricentenaries
trichinellosis
trichomoniasis
trichophytosis
trichotomously
trickle charger
tricontinental
Tridentine mass
tridimensional
tried and tested
trifacial nerve
trigger circuit
trigonocephaly
trihalomethane
trihedral angle
trihedral quoin
triiodomethane
trilateralness
trimethylamine
Trinitarianism
trinitrophenol
trinitrotoluol
trinkum-trankum
tripelennamine
tripersonalism
tripersonalist
tripersonality
triple acrostic
triple alliance
triple tonguing
tripperishness
triquetral bone
trisoctahedron
trisubstituted
trituberculate
triumphalistic

trivialization
Trivial Pursuit
trochlear nerve
troop the colour
trophoneurosis
tropical weight
tropic of Cancer
tropicopolitan
tropologically
trouble at t' mill
troubleshooter
trough of the sea
trouser-presser
true-lover's knot
Truman doctrine
trumpet creeper
trumpet-mouthed
trumpet pattern
trumpet-tongued
trussing needle
trustee process
trust territory
Trust Territory
truth-condition
try one's fortune
trypanosomatid
trypsinization
Tuatha Dé Danann
tubal pregnancy
tuberculin test
tumblification
tumbling-barrel
tumorigenicity
tumultuousness
tuner-amplifier
tunnel-visioned
turbogenerator
turf accountant
turkey-merchant
Turkish delight
Turkish slipper
Turkish tobacco
Turkoman carpet
turn a cartwheel
turn a deaf ear to
turn one's back on
turn one's girdle
turn one's hand to
turn on one's heel
turnpike sailor
turn up one's nose
turn up one's toes
turpentine-tree
turpentine weed
twiddle-twaddle
twingle-twangle
Twinkie defence
twistification
twist in the wind
twists and turns
twit in the teeth

two-backed beast
two-dimensional
two-pot screamer
tympanic cavity
tyndallization
type-psychology
tyrannicalness
ubiquitination
ubiquitousness
Ugandanization
ultimatization
ultimogeniture
ultracrepidate
ultrafidianism
ultramicrotome
ultramicrotomy
ultramontanism
ultramontanist
ultrasonically
ultrasonograph
ultrastructure
ultraviolation
ultroneousness
umbrageousness
umbrella bridge
Umklapp process
unacclimatized
unaccommodated
unaccomplished
unaccounted for
unaccustomedly
unacknowledged
unackowledging
unacquaintance
unadaptability
unadministered
unaffectedness
unaffectionate
unaggressively
unalterability
unambivalently
un-Americanized
unappetizingly
unappreciative
unapprehensive
unapproachable
unapproachably
unappropriated
unarithmetical
unartificially
unartistically
unaspiringness
unassumingness
unathletically
unattachedness
unattractively
unattributable
unattributably
unauthenticity
unauthorizedly
unavailability

unavoidability
unbearableness
unbecomingness
unbegottenness
unbureaucratic
unbusinesslike
uncertificated
unchangingness
uncheerfulness
unchivalrously
unchristianise
unchristianity
unchristianize
uncircumcision
uncivilization
unclassifiable
uncommissioned
uncommunicable
uncommunicated
uncompoundedly
uncomprehended
uncompromising
unconciliatory
unconditionate
unconfidential
unconfinedness
uncongeniality
unconscionable
unconscionably
unconservative
unconsiderable
unconsolidated
unconstructive
uncontaminated
uncontemplated
uncontemporary
uncontradicted
uncontrollable
uncontrollably
uncontrolledly
uncontroverted
unconventional
unconvincingly
uncorroborated
uncounsellable
uncountability
uncountenanced
uncourtierlike
uncrackability
uncriticizable
uncrystallized
undecidability
undecipherable
undecipherably
undecisiveness
undecomposable
undecompounded
undecorticated
undegenerating
undelightfully
undemonstrable

undemonstrated
undeniableness
underabundance
under bare poles
underbevelling
under command of
underdetermine
underdeveloped
underdiagnosis
underdispersed
undereducation
underemphasise
underemphasize
undergraduette
under-housemaid
underinsurance
underlineation
undermentioned
undernourished
under-occupancy
under-officered
underofficered
under penalty of
underperformer
underpetticoat
underpopulated
underprivilege
underqualified
underrehearsal
under-rehearsed
underrehearsed
under-represent
underrepresent
undersaturated
under-secretary
undersketching
understandable
understandably
understatement
understimulate
understrapping
undersubscribe
under suspicion
undertenancies
under the harrow
under the heel of
under the plough
under the wing of
under-treasurer
undertreatment
undervaluation
underwaistcoat
underworldling
undeservedness
undesirability
undestructible
undeterminable
undiminishable
undiscerningly
undiscontinued
undiscoverable

undiscoverably
undispatchable
undistractedly
undogmatically
undomesticated
undoubtfulness
undoubtingness
undramatically
undue influence
unearned income
uneconomically
uneducatedness
unelectability
unemphatically
unendurability
unenfranchised
unenlightening
unenterprising
unentertaining
unenthusiastic
unequilibrated
unetymological
uneuphoniously
uneventfulness
unexcitability
unexhilarating
unexpectedness
unexperimented
unextinguished
unfaithfulness
unfamiliarized
unfastidiously
unfatherliness
unfinishedness
unflappability
unflatteringly
unforeknowable
unforeseeingly
unfractionated
unfriendliness
unfruitfulness
ungenerousness
ungracefulness
ungraciousness
ungratefulness
ungroundedness
unhandsomeness
unharmoniously
unhesitatingly
unhistorically
unholy alliance
unhygienically
unhypocritical
unicellularity
unidentifiable
unidentifiably
unidimensional
unidirectional
unificationist
uniformitarian
uniformization

unilateralized	unparalleledly	unresponsively
unilluminating	unparallelness	unrestrainable
unillustrative	unparticipated	unrestrainably
unimmortalized	unpassionately	unrestrainedly
unimolecularly	unperceptively	unrestrictedly
unimpressively	unpersuasively	unrhythmically
unincorporated	unphilosophize	unrightfulness
unindifference	unphotographed	unromantically
unindifferency	unpleasantness	unsaleableness
unintellectual	unpleasantries	unsatiableness
unintelligence	unpleasingness	unsatisfaction
unintelligible	unpornographic	unsatisfactory
unintelligibly	unpracticality	unsatisfyingly
uninterestedly	unpraiseworthy	unscripturally
unintermittent	unprecipitated	unscrupulously
unintermitting	unprejudicedly	unshakeability
uninterrogated	unpremeditated	unshockability
uninterruption	unpreparedness	unshoe-the-horse
unintoxicating	unprepossessed	unsociableness
uninvestigable	unpresumptuous	unsociological
uninvestigated	unpretendingly	unsolvableness
union catalogue	unprinceliness	unsophisticate
union workhouse	unproblematize	unspeakability
Union Workhouse	unproductively	unspirituality
United Brethren	unprofessional	unspiritualize
United-Stateser	unprogrammable	unsplinterable
universal agent	unpropitiously	unstandardized
universal donor	unproportional	unstoppability
universalistic	unproportioned	unstraightened
universal joint	unprosperously	unstrengthened
universitarian	unprotestingly	unsubmissively
unknowableness	unprovableness	unsubstantiate
unknown country	unprovidedness	unsuccessfully
Unknown Soldier	unprovokedness	unsufficiently
Unknown Warrior	unquantifiable	unsuitableness
unletteredness	unquestionable	unsupercharged
unliterariness	unquestionably	unsuppressible
unmaidenliness	unreadableness	unsurmountable
unmaintainable	unreciprocated	unsurprisingly
unmalleability	unrecognisable	unsuspectingly
unmannerliness	unrecognizable	unsuspiciously
unmanufactured	unrecognizably	unsympathizing
unmarriageable	unreconcilable	unsystematized
unmathematical	unreflectingly	untameableness
unmatriculated	unreformedness	unthankfulness
unmeasuredness	unrefrigerated	unthinkability
unmerchantable	unregenerately	unthinkingness
unmercifulness	unregeneration	unthoughtfully
unmetaphorical	unreliableness	untouchability
unmetaphysical	unrelinquished	untowardliness
unmethodically	unrememberable	untractability
unmotherliness	unremorsefully	untranquillize
unnavigability	unremunerative	untransferable
unnecessitated	unrenounceable	untranslatable
unobligingness	unreproachable	untranslatably
unobstructedly	unreproducible	untransmutable
unornamentally	unreproductive	untransplanted
unostentatious	unrequitedness	untruthfulness
unpaintability	unreservedness	unupbraidingly
unpalatability	unresolvedness	unutterability
unparallelable	unrespectfully	unvanquishable

unvariableness
unvendibleness
unverbalizable
unvirtuousness
unwatchfulness
unwhisperables
unworkableness
unyieldingness
uproariousness
upside-down cake
up to one's neck in
up to one's tricks
up to the knocker
upwardly mobile
upward mobility
uranographical
urban guerrilla
urethral meatus
urinary bladder
use of the globes
user-orientated
user-unfriendly
uterine brother
utero-gestation
uteroplacental
utilitarianism
utilitarianize
utility program
utility routine
utility vehicle
utriculoplasty
vaccine-damaged
vaccine disease
vaccine program
vaccine therapy
vacuum abortion
vacuum activity
vaingloriously
valence grammar
Valencia almond
Valencia orange
valency grammar
Valentinianism
valerianaceous
valetudinarian
valetudinaries
vallate papilla
value judgement
vanilla essence
vanishing cream
vanishing point
vapour pressure
Varangian Guard
various reading
vasa deferentia
vascular bundle
vascular system
vasodilatation
vasomotorially
Vatican Council
Vaticanologist

vectored thrust
vector function
vegetable ivory
vegetable sheep
vegetationally
vegetationless
vegetative cell
vegetativeness
vegetative pole
velopharyngeal
velvet-painting
velvet tamarind
vending machine
venereological
Venetian carpet
Venetian School
Venetian window
ventriculogram
ventromedially
venture capital
Venus hairstone
verifiableness
verisimilitude
Verreaux's eagle
Verrocchiesque
vertical angles
vertical circle
vertical market
verticillaster
verticillation
vesicopustular
vesicoureteral
vesicoureteric
vespertilionid
vested interest
vestibular fold
vexillological
via affirmativa
vicar apostolic
vicar episcopal
vice-chancellor
vice-consulship
vice-legateship
vice-presidency
Victorian cycle
Victoria sponge
victoriousness
victrix ludorum
video amplifier
video frequency
video recording
video-telephone
Viennese coffee
Vietnamization
Villafranchian
villainousness
villein service
Vincent's angina
vindictiveness
vin doux naturel
vinho de consumo

viola da braccio
viola da gambist
violent profits
violet sea-snail
violetta marina
violino piccolo
Virginian quail
Virginian stock
Virgin Islander
virgin olive oil
virgin's garland
virial equation
virtual cathode
virtual reality
virtuous circle
visceral cavity
visceral pleura
viscerocranium
viscerotropism
viscose process
viscosity index
visible horizon
vision splendid
visiting fellow
visiting rights
visiting ticket
vitaminization
vitelline gland
vitelline layer
vitellogenesis
vitellogenetic
vitreous enamel
vitreous humour
vitreous lustre
vitreous silica
vitreous sponge
vitrifiability
vitriolization
vituperatively
viviparousness
vivisectionist
vociferousness
voice frequency
voicespondence
volatilization
volcaniclastic
volcanological
voltage divider
voltaic battery
volumetrically
voluminousness
voluntary-aided
Volunteer State
voluptuousness
vortex shedding
vouch to warrant
vowel gradation
vulcanological
vulgar fraction
vulnerableness
vulpine opossum

vulvovaginitis
wagtail warbler
waifs and strays
waiting problem
walk a chalk-line
walking catfish
walking funeral
walking machine
walking wounded
walk on crutches
walk one's rounds
walk the streets
walk with a stick
Walpurgis night
Walter Scottish
wandering hands
wandering nerve
want for nothing
wappenschawing
ward in Chancery
wardrobe master
warehouse party
war of attrition
warrantability
warrant dormant
warrant-officer
Wars of the Roses
war-substantive
wash and brush-up
washing machine
Washington clam
Washington lily
Wassermann test
Watch Committee
watch this space
water authority
water barometer
water bewitched
water-breathing
water chickweed
water chincapin
watercolourist
Waterford glass
water germander
water injection
water-insoluble
water on the knee
water pimpernel
water-privilege
waterproofness
water-repellent
water-resistant
watertightness
wattled lapwing
wave-mechanical
waw consecutive
waxen chatterer
weak-mindedness
weapons-carrier
weapon-training
wearing apparel

wear yellow hose
weatherability
weather balloon
weather-breeder
weathercockism
weather-cottage
weatherization
weatherproofed
weather prophet
weather station
wedding-garment
Wegener's theory
Weierstrassian
weighing-engine
weigh one's words
weight function
weightlessness
weight training
weight-watching
Weimar Republic
welfare benefit
welfare statism
well acquainted
well-documented
well-formedness
wellington boot
Wellington coat
well-maintained
well-structured
well thought out
Welsh clearwing
Weltanschauung
welter handicap
western hemlock
westernization
West Highlander
wet one's whistle
wet the other eye
whalebone whale
whaling station
what a vengeance
what countryman
what do you say to
what do you think
what-d'you-call-'em
what-d'you-call-it
what is your will
wheaten terrier
wheel balancing
wheel barometer
wheel-engraving
wheeler-dealing
wheel of fortune
wheel of Fortune
wheelwrighting
whiplash injury
whippersnapper
whiptail lizard
whistling eagle
whistling thorn
white blood cell

white butterfly
white chameleon
white Christmas
white corpuscle
white-headed boy
White Highlands
white horehound
white lightning
White man's grave
white merganser
white nickel ore
White supremacy
white-tailed gnu
whiting pollack
whittie-whattie
wholeheartedly
whole-tone scale
whoopee cushion
whortleberries
who the hangment
wide open spaces
widow bewitched
Wiedemann-Franz
wigs on the green
wild-goose chase
wild mignonette
wild snapdragon
wild strawberry
Wilhelmstrasse
William Morrisy
william-nilliam
will see about it
Winchester disk
wind and weather
wind-chill index
windfall profit
wind instrument
window dressing
window-envelope
windowlessness
window-trimming
Windsor uniform
Winebrennarian
winning-gallery
winning opening
winter daffodil
winter flounder
winter quarters
winter solstice
winter woollies
win the exchange
wish-fulfilling
wish-fulfilment
wishful thinker
wishy-washiness
witch-doctoring
witches' sabbath
with a good grace
with a heavy hand
with all reserve
with an even keel

with an ill grace
with a single eye
with a stick in it
with a vengeance
with a wet finger
with a whole skin
with difficulty
withdrawal slip
with effect from
with half a heart
withholding tax
within a cooee of
within an inch of
within the walls
with one eye shut
with one's tail up
without a murmur
without example
without more ado
without offence
without-profits
without remorse
without reserve
without scruple
with relation to
with the colours
Wittig reaction
woe worth the day
Wollaston prism
Wolverine State
woman about town
woman of fortune
woman of letters
woman of the town
woman-slaughter
woman's magazine
woman's movement
women's magazine
women's movement
Women's Movement
women's suffrage
wonder-stricken

woodchat shrike
wooden overcoat
wooden spoonist
woodland garden
wood strawberry
woollen-drapery
Worcesterberry
Worcester sauce
Worcestershire
word-internally
word processing
Wordsworthiana
worker-director
work experience
working capital
working classes
working drawing
working outline
working storage
working surface
work in progress
work like a charm
work one's ticket
works committee
world-weariness
worse than death
worshipfulness
worth one's while
worth's one's salt
worthwhileness
wring one's hands
wring the neck of
wrist-wrestling
writing cabinet
writ of tresaiel
xanthene colour
xenodiagnostic
xenophobically
xeroradiograph
xiphoid process
X-ray astronomer
X-ray department

yellow-breasted
yellow centaury
yellow oleander
yellow suckling
yellowtail scad
yellow toadflax
yeoman's service
yesterday's news
yoke-fellowship
Yorkshire chair
Yorkshirewoman
Yorkshirewomen
you bet your life
Young—Helmholtz
Young Pretender
you're telling me
you're the doctor
your little game
yours sincerely
Yours sincerely
yours to command
your university
youth and old age
youth hosteller
Zambianization
zebra angelfish
Zener breakdown
zenith distance
zero-derivation
zeta hypothesis
zeugmatography
zillah parishad
zingiberaceous
zooarchaeology
zoographically
zoological park
zoopraxography
Zoroastrianism
Zoroastrianize
zymogen granule
zymotechnology
zymotic disease

FIFTEEN LETTERS

Abbot of Unreason
a bone in her mouth
a bone in one's head
above the gangway
absolute alcohol
absorbent cotton
absorptiometric
abstracting from
acanthocephalan
accelerator card
accidental sharp
acclimatization
accommodatingly
accommodational
according to plan
accountableness
account rendered
accounts payable
acculturational
acculturization
a certain disease
acetic anhydride
acetyl coenzyme A
ace up one's sleeve
achlorophyllous
achondroplasiac
achondroplastic
acknowledgeable
acknowledgement
acoustic coupler
acquisitiveness
a crack of the whip
acrimoniousness
across the tracks
actinopterygian
action committee
action potential
activated carbon
activated sludge
active transport
act of contrition
Act of Parliament
Act of Settlement
Act of Toleration
Act of Uniformity
acupuncturation
acute rheumatism
Addison's disease
adenohypophysis
Adjutant General
administratress
Admiral of the Red
a drop in the ocean
adsignification
advanced studies
adventurousness
adverb of quality

advertisemental
Advocate-General
aerial torpedoed
aerial torpedoes
aerodynamically
affluent society
affranchisement
a fish out of water
African-American
African elephant
African mahogany
after first brush
against one's will
against the clock
against the grain
against the world
age of discretion
agglutinability
a gleam in one's eye
a glint in one's eye
agranulocytosis
agribusinessman
agribusinessmen
agriculturalist
a hair in one's neck
a hard nut to crack
ahead of one's time
a hundred per cent
Air Chief Marshal
air-conditioning
aircraft carrier
a kick in the teeth
algorithmically
alimentary canal
alive and kicking
all-accomplished
all along the line
all hell let loose
allotetraploidy
all over the place
all the night long
all the world over
a lot on one's plate
alphabetization
alternate angles
alternative fuel
alternativeness
aluminium bronze
aluminosilicate
a man and a brother
amaryllidaceous
a matter of course
a matter of record
ambassadorially
ambulance chaser
amende honorable
American cowslip

American English
Americanization
amicable numbers
a million dollars
amphiarthrodial
amphitheatrical
amusement arcade
anabolic steroid
anaesthesiology
anaesthetically
a nasty bit of work
ancient monument
ancylostomiasis
Andaman Islander
Anderson shelter
andromonoecious
androstenedione
angle of friction
angle of position
Anglo-vernacular
angular momentum
angular velocity
animal husbandry
animal magnetism
anisotropically
ankylostomiasis
annihilationism
annihilationist
annus horribilis
anomalistic year
anorexia nervosa
Antarctic Circle
antepenultimate
anteroposterior
anthropocentric
anthropogenesis
anthropological
anthropometrist
anthropomorphic
anthropopathism
anthropophagite
anthropophagous
anthroposophist
anthropotomical
anti-abortionist
antichristianly
anticlericalism
anticoagulation
antiferromagnet
anti-Gallicanism
antilogarithmic
antimonarchical
antimonious acid
antiperistaltic
antiphlogistian
Antiphlogistine
antisabbatarian

antisymmetrical
antitrinitarian
any port in a storm
apocalyptically
Apollinarianism
apophthegmatize
apparent horizon
appearance money
appendicularian
approachability
approbativeness
appropinquation
appropriateness
approximatively
apron-string hold
aqueous solution
arboriculturist
archaebacterial
archaebacterium
archaeomagnetic
archiepiscopacy
archiepiscopate
architectonical
architecturally
area linguistics
argumentatively
Aristotelianism
arithmetization
armed neutrality
armed to the teeth
armillary sphere
Arms of Patronage
arrest judgement
arterialization
artificial stone
artsy-and-craftsy
as a matter of fact
ascending letter
ascend the throne
asclepiadaceous
as dead as the dodo
as deaf as a beetle
as dry as a whistle
as dumb as a beetle
as easy as winking
as far as in me lies
as keen as mustard
ask for one's cards
a slice of the cake
as like as two peas
as long as your arm
asparagus beetle
a spit and a stride
as pretty as paint
assembly program
assimilationist
assisted passage
as sober as a judge
association book
associativeness
as sound as a roach
as the saying goes

astronavigation
Astronomer Royal
astronomical day
astrophysically
at a disadvantage
at all adventures
at close quarters
at cross purposes
Athanasian Creed
at heck and manger
atherosclerosis
atherosclerotic
athwart the hawse
Atlantic Charter
Atlantic pomfret
atmospherically
atomic structure
atrabiliousness
at rack and manger
at the crossroads
at the drop of a hat
at the first blush
at the instance of
Attorney-General
Attorney general
audience-chamber
Augustal Prefect
auricular finger
aurora australis
Australian crawl
Australian hazel
Australian Rules
authoritatively
autobiographies
autobiographist
autochthonously
autocorrelation
autocorrelogram
auto-destruction
auto-destructive
autogenetically
autograph-hunter
autographically
autolithography
autoplastically
autoradiography
autoschediastic
auto-suggestible
autotransformer
autotransfusion
autotrophically
autumnal equinox
auxiliary troops
aversion therapy
Avogadro's number
a wing and a prayer
awkward customer
Axminster carpet
bachelor's degree
background music
background noise
back on one's heels

back to square one
backward masking
bacteriological
Bahasa Indonesia
balaclava helmet
balance of nature
balance of terror
ballistic rocket
ballroom dancing
balsamic vinegar
Baltimore oriole
bargain basement
barking squirrel
barothermograph
Bartholomew fair
basal metabolism
basidiomycetous
basilar membrane
bastard mahogany
batch processing
batch production
Batesian mimicry
bathymetrically
bats in the belfry
battering-engine
Battersea enamel
bear away the bell
bear the blame for
beat all to sticks
beat a person to it
beaten at the post
beat the pants off
beat the tar out of
beat with the spit
beautiful people
beauty treatment
bed and breakfast
beefsteak fungus
beefsteak tomato
beer and skittles
be food for fishes
be food for powder
before the face of
before the letter
behind the scenes
be in at the finish
believe one's ears
Bell's inequality
below one's breath
below the gangway
bend someone's ear
beneath contempt
Benedictine rule
benefit of clergy
be one's own master
Bermuda triangle
Bermuda Triangle
beside the saddle
Bessemer process
between two fires
Beverley Minster
beyond exception

beyond one's grasp
bibliographical
bibliothecarial
bibliothecarian
bidirectionally
Bill of Exclusion
bill of mortality
bill of privilege
bimetallic strip
bind hand and foot
binocular vision
binomial theorem
bioavailability
biobibliography
biogeochemistry
biogeographical
biological clock
bioluminescence
biomechanically
biorhythmically
biosociological
biospeleologist
biostatistician
biostratigraphy
biotechnologist
birds of a feather
birthday honours
bishop suffragan
bite on the bullet
biting stonecrop
bituminous shale
black-coat worker
blackcurrant jam
Black Forest cake
black nightshade
black rhinoceros
black spleenwort
blackwater fever
black wildebeest
blameworthiness
blasphemousness
bleaching powder
Blenheim spaniel
blepharoplastic
blind baggage car
block signalling
blood-and-thunder
bloodthirstiest
Bloomsbury Group
bluegill sunfish
bluestockingism
blue vinny cheese
blunt instrument
board and lodging
Board of Ordnance
boatswain's chair
body-line bowling
bolt from the blue
bolt-uprightness
bonded warehouse
book of reference
Bordeaux mixture

Border Leicester
bore the pants off
Bornholm disease
born in the purple
borough surveyor
borrowed plumage
bottom-fermented
bottom of the heap
boustrophedonic
bowling analysis
Bow Street runner
bowstring-bridge
brachiocephalic
brachistochrone
brachycephalism
brachycephalous
brachydactylous
bradymetabolism
brake horsepower
braking distance
branchiobdellid
branchiostegite
branchiostegous
Brazilian nutmeg
breach of promise
bread of idleness
breaking of bread
break on the wheel
breath consonant
breathe one's last
breeding plumage
bricks and mortar
bring-and-buy sale
bring into effect
bring pressure on
bring to its knees
bristlecone pine
Britannia silver
British Standard
brittle fracture
broadly speaking
broad-mindedness
broken-heartedly
bronzed diabetes
bronze medallist
brothel creepers
brown rot disease
brushtail possum
Brussels griffon
bubble and squeak
building society
Burmese rosewood
burnet saxifrage
burning mountain
burn midnight oil
burn one's bridges
burn one's fingers
burst into flames
bury the tomahawk
business as usual
business studies
butter-and-egg man

butterfly blenny
butterfly flower
butterfly orchid
butterfly stroke
butter of almonds
by common consent
by fits and starts
by guess and by God
by hook or by crook
by process of time
by the grace of God
by these presents
by way of reprisal
cabbalistically
Cabinet minister
Cabinet Minister
cable television
calcium sulphate
Californian jack
call all to naught
call attention to
Calvinistically
candelabrum tree
cannibalization
cannot choose but
Canterbury bells
Cape Barren goose
Cape forget-me-not
Cape leaping hare
capillary action
capital gains tax
capitation grant
Capricorn beetle
captain's biscuit
captive audience
capture myopathy
carbonate of lime
carbonic acid gas
carcinogenicity
cardinal numeral
cardiopulmonary
career structure
carnal knowledge
carnivorousness
Carolina jasmine
carriage and pair
carriage forward
carriage release
Carrion's disease
carry conviction
carry the can back
carve for oneself
cash in one's chips
cask-conditioned
casting-director
cataclysmically
catch a glimpse of
catch-as-catch-can
catch one's breath
catch the fancy of
catechistically
categorematical

cathedral church
catheterization
Catholicization
cavity resonator
celestial sphere
cells of the brain
cellular blanket
Celtic spikenard
Centennial State
Central American
centrally-heated
centre of gravity
centre of inertia
cephalhaematoma
cephalochordate
cephalothoracic
cepheid variable
ceratobranchial
cerebrovascular
ceremoniousness
certified cheque
Ceylon satinwood
chamberlainship
change of address
change of clothes
change of scenery
change of the moon
Channel Islander
chanting goshawk
chapter and verse
character sketch
character string
charcoal biscuit
chargé d'affaires
charismatically
chattel interest
chattel mortgage
checking account
chemical warfare
chemico-physical
chemoautotrophy
chemotactically
chemotropically
chenopodiaceous
chess tournament
Chesterfieldian
Chian turpentine
chicken-breasted
chicken chasseur
chicken Maryland
chief technician
child of the manse
child psychology
Chinaman's chance
Chinese chequers
Chinese layering
Chinese whispers
chipping sparrow
chloramphenicol
chloroplatinate
chocolate mousse
cholangiography

cholecalciferol
cholecystectomy
cholera infantum
chondrification
choreographical
chorio-allantoic
chorio-allantois
choriocarcinoma
chorioretinitis
Christadelphian
Christian burial
Christmas flower
chromatographer
chromatographic
chronogrammatic
chronographical
chronologically
chuck in the towel
chuck-will's-widow
Church Catechism
Church of England
churchwardenism
churchwardenize
Churrigueresque
cigarette coupon
cigarette-holder
cinematographer
cinematographic
cinemicrography
cinephotography
cineradiography
circuit-training
circularization
circumambulator
circumferential
circumforaneous
circumgestation
circumincession
circumnavigable
circumnavigator
circumscribable
circumscription
circumspectious
circumspectness
circumstantiate
circumvallation
Citizen's Charter
civil government
civilianization
Clapham Junction
classical Arabic
classical ballet
classical guitar
cleansing tissue
clear a thing with
clear conscience
clear-headedness
clear one's throat
clericalization
Clerk of the Irons
Clerk of the Pells
clerk of the works

clingstone peach
close one's eyes to
close one's mind to
clotheslessness
cloud-cuckoo-land
cluster compound
coccolithophore
cocculus indicus
cochineal insect
cockneyfication
cock-of-the-plains
cocktail cabinet
cocktail sausage
co-consciousness
co-determination
codicologically
coequate anomaly
coextensiveness
coffee-table book
coherence theory
co-instantaneous
cold-bloodedness
cold-heartedness
cold obstruction
collaborate with
collaboratively
collared lemming
collared peccary
collateral issue
collective fruit
collector's piece
collegial church
collenchymatous
collision course
colonizationism
colonizationist
colour-blindness
colour constancy
coloured hearing
colouring matter
colour prejudice
combination laws
combination lock
combination oven
combination room
combination tone
combinatorially
combining weight
combustibleness
come back to earth
come down the pike
come down to cases
comedy of manners
come from nowhere
come home to roost
come into contact
come into one's own
come naturally to
come rain or shine
come the raw prawn
come to grips with
come to terms with

come to think of it
comfortableness
comity of nations
command language
commemoratively
commendableness
commentatorship
commercial docks
commercial space
commiseratingly
commiseratively
commissary court
commission agent
commit to writing
commodification
common gallinule
common knowledge
common-law lawyer
common logarithm
common merganser
common of pasture
common of piscary
commonplace book
commonplaceness
common sandpiper
common scrub-fowl
common twayblade
Commonwealth Day
communalization
communicability
communicational
communicatively
communistically
community centre
community charge
community leader
community spirit
community worker
commutativeness
companion-in-arms
companion ladder
company promoter
compartmentally
compassionately
compendiousness
competitiveness
compilation film
complementarily
complementarity
complementation
complex sentence
complicatedness
complimentarily
compliments slip
compositionally
compound machine
comprehendingly
comprehensively
comprehensivize
compressibility
computationally
computerization

computer program
computer science
conceivableness
concentric cable
conceptualistic
Concert of Europe
concert overture
concessionnaire
conchologically
condescendingly
conditional mood
condition-powder
condylarthrosis
confidence level
confidence limit
confidence trick
confidentiality
configurational
conformableness
confraternities
confrontational
congregationist
conical pendulum
conic projection
conjugationally
conjunctionally
conjunctiveness
connectionalism
Connemara marble
connoisseurship
connotative term
conscience money
conscientiously
conscriptionist
consecutiveness
consentaneously
consenting adult
consequentially
conservationist
conservation law
Conservative Jew
conservatorship
considerability
considerateness
consistory court
conspicuousness
constructionism
constructionist
consubstantiate
consumer durable
consumer society
consumptiveness
contemplatively
contemporaneity
contemporaneous
contemptibility
contempt of court
contentiousness
contingency fund
contingency plan
continuation day
contortuplicate

contraband of war
contraceptively
contractibility
contradictively
contradictorily
contrariousness
contrastiveness
contravallation
controllability
controversially
conus arteriosus
conus medullaris
convenience food
Conventicle Acts
conventionalise
conventionalism
conventionalist
conventionality
conventionalize
conversableness
conversationist
convolvulaceous
cool as a cucumber
cooperative farm
cooperativeness
co-precipitation
coracoid process
coral-root orchid
corbie messenger
cordon sanitaire
Corinthian brass
Corinthianesque
corno di bassetto
Corona Australis
coronoid process
corporate raider
corporation sole
correction fluid
correlativeness
correspondently
correspondingly
corroboratively
corrugated paper
corruptibleness
corrupt practice
corynebacterium
cosmic radiation
cosmochemically
cosmopolitanise
cosmopolitanism
cosmopolitanize
Cossack trousers
Costa Geriatrica
cost a person dear
cost-effectively
costermongerdom
costermongering
costoclavicular
cottage hospital
cottage industry
counsellor-at-law
counter-approach

counter-argument	cultivatability	deferred payment
counter-claimant	cultivation bank	deficit spending
counter-coloured	cultural attaché	definite article
countercultural	Cumberland sauce	definition in use
countercyclical	cumulative error	degenerationism
counter-evidence	curriculum vitae	degenerationist
counterfeitness	Curse of Scotland	deglamorization
counter-flowered	Cushing's disease	degree of freedom
counter-indicate	custos rotulorum	dehydroascorbic
counterirritant	cut-and-come-again	dehydrogenation
countermandable	cut one's eye-teeth	deindustrialize
countermovement	cutthroat weaver	delabialization
counterpart fund	cutting compound	deleteriousness
counterposition	cylindricalness	delightsomeness
counter-pressure	cylindro-conical	delignification
counter-question	cytogenetically	delirium tremens
county corporate	cytomegalovirus	deliver the goods
Court of Audience	cytophotometric	Della Cruscanism
Court of Chancery	Czechoslovakian	delta connection
Court of Requests	dacryoadenalgia	demagnetization
couteau de chasse	damp-proof course	demagnification
Covenant of Grace	dandelion coffee	dementia praecox
Covenant of Works	dandelion greens	Democratic Party
cover much ground	Dartford warbler	democratization
cover one's tracks	daughter element	demographically
craniologically	daylight robbery	demoiselle crane
crashworthiness	day of obligation	demolition derby
creation science	dead as a door-nail	demolition Derby
creature of habit	dead as a doornail	demolition order
credit insurance	dead man's fingers	demonologically
creeping barrage	deafferentation	demonstrability
creeping thistle	de-afforestation	demonstrational
creep to the cross	de-Anglicization	demonstratively
cribriform plate	Dean of peculiars	demutualization
crime passionnel	Dean of the Arches	demystification
criminalization	decalcification	demythicization
crissal thrasher	decarbonization	denitrification
criteriological	decarboxylation	dental hygienist
critical damping	decarburization	departmentalise
cross-connection	decartelization	departmentalism
cross-culturally	decasualization	departmentalize
crossing sweeper	decemnovenarian	department store
crossopterygian	decertification	depauperization
crossword puzzle	decimal fraction	dephlogisticate
crude turpentine	decision problem	dephosphorylate
crustaceologist	declamatoriness	depressor muscle
cry a person mercy	declination axis	deprovincialize
cry from the heart	decolourization	depth psychology
cry one's heart out	decommunization	deracialization
cryoprecipitate	decomposability	dermatoglyphics
cryptanalytical	decomposibility	dermatographism
crypto-Calvinist	deconcentration	dermatomyositis
cryptozoologist	deconstructible	dermatophytosis
crystalliferous	decontamination	desacralization
crystalline lens	decontextualise	descant recorder
crystallisation	decontextualize	descriptiveness
crystallization	decrement of life	desensitization
crystallography	dedifferentiate	desertification
cry stinking fish	deed of variation	desilverization
cry wolf too often	deep X-ray therapy	dessertspoonful
cubic centimetre	defencelessness	destabilization
cuckoo in the nest	deferred annuity	de-Stalinization

destroyer-escort	discretionarily	domestic science
destroyer leader	disenchantingly	domestic servant
destroying angel	disentanglement	domestic service
destructibility	disenthronement	domineeringness
destructiveness	disgracefulness	dominical letter
destructuration	dishabilitation	done like a dinner
detention centre	disharmoniously	don't you forget it
determinability	dishearteningly	doomsday machine
determinateness	disillusionizer	do one's damnedest
determinatively	disillusionment	do one's heart good
detribalization	disimprisonment	do one's level best
deuteranomalous	disinflationary	do the other thing
developmentally	disinterestedly	double-barrelled
development area	disintoxication	double-facedness
devil-on-the-coals	disobligingness	double indemnity
devil-worshipper	disorderly house	double or nothing
devitrification	disorganization	double pneumonia
Devonshire cream	dispassionately	double precision
dezincification	displaceability	Dow–Jones average
diagonalization	displaced person	downheartedness
diaheliotropism	displacement ton	down to the ground
dialectological	displeasingness	downy woodpecker
dialogistically	dispositionally	Doyenne du Comice
diamagnetically	disproportional	Dragon variation
diamondback moth	disproportioned	drain to the dregs
diamond crossing	disputativeness	dramatistically
diaphonemically	disquisitionist	dramaturgically
diaphototropism	disreputability	draught-excluder
diastereoisomer	disrespectfully	draughtsmanship
dichotomization	dissatisfaction	draw in one's horns
dictatorialness	dissatisfactory	drawn-thread work
differentiation	dissecting knife	drawn-threadwork
digestive system	dissimilarities	draw the curtains
dig up the hatchet	dissipationless	dream-vision poem
diocesan council	dissociableness	dressing forceps
Dionysian period	distastefulness	dressing station
diphenhydramine	distemperedness	drinking problem
diplomatic corps	distinctiveness	drogue parachute
diplomatic pouch	distinguishable	droit de seigneur
direction-finder	distinguishably	droit du seigneur
director-general	distinguishedly	drop one's aitches
disacquaintance	distinguishment	drugstore cowboy
disadvantageous	distractability	drunk as a fiddler
disafforestment	distractibility	dry distillation
disagreeability	distressfulness	dual carriageway
disappearing act	distress warrant	dual personality
disappointingly	distribution map	duchess potatoes
disarticulation	distributorship	dumping syndrome
discernibleness	district auditor	duple proportion
discerptibility	district heating	duplicate bridge
discommendation	district visitor	duplicitousness
discommodiously	distrustfulness	durchkomponiert
discomposedness	dithyrambically	Durham shorthorn
disconcertingly	diversification	dusky cranesbill
disconfirmation	dividend warrant	Dutch elm disease
disconfirmatory	Divisional Court	dynamic friction
disconformities	division lobbied	dynamic pressure
discontinuation	division lobbies	dysfunctionally
discontinuously	doctrinarianism	dyslogistically
discountenancer	dog's tooth violet	dysteleological
discoverability	dolichocephalic	early retirement
discovery method	dollar diplomacy	earnings-related

earth connection
earthly paradise
earth-shattering
Easter-offerings
eat a person's salt
eat one's heart out
eat the wind out of
ecclesiasticism
ecclesiasticize
ecclesiological
echocardiograph
éclaircissement
eclipse of the sun
eclipsing binary
econometrically
economic geology
economic history
economic warfare
ectoplasmically
efficaciousness
efficiency audit
egg-and-spoon race
Egyptianization
Egyptian vulture
eighteen-pounder
ejaculatory duct
elastic stocking
election address
electrical storm
electric battery
electric blanket
electric circuit
electrification
electro-acoustic
electro-analysis
electrochemical
electrochromism
electrodialysis
electrodynamics
electrofocusing
electrogenicity
electrolysation
electromagnetic
electrometrical
electromyograph
electronegative
electronic flash
electronography
electrophoresis
electrophoretic
electroporation
electropositive
electroreceptor
electrostatical
electrosurgical
electrotechnics
Eleonora's falcon
eleutheromaniac
elevated railway
emancipationist
embarras de choix
embryologically

emotionlessness
empirio-critical
emulsifiability
enantiomorphism
enantiomorphous
encephalisation
encephalization
encephalography
encephalopathic
enchondromatous
encomiastically
endoatmospheric
endocrinologist
endonucleolytic
enforceableness
enfranchisement
Engelmann spruce
engineer's yeoman
English basement
English Canadian
English sickness
enlarge an estate
enlarge the heart
enlightenedness
entente cordiale
Entente Cordiale
enterohepatitis
enterotoxigenic
entomologically
entrench oneself
entrepreneurial
entrepreneurism
environmentally
epidemic cholera
epidemiological
epifluorescence
epipalaeolithic
epiploic foramen
Episcopal Church
episcopalianism
epistemological
epistolographic
epitheliomatous
equalitarianism
equation of state
equatorial mount
equatorial plate
equidimensional
equinoctial line
equinoctial year
equiponderation
equiprobability
equity draftsman
Erlenmeyer flask
erythromelalgia
escalator clause
escape committee
eternal triangle
etherealization
ethidium bromide
ethnic cleansing
ethnocentricism

ethnocentricity
ethnolinguistic
ethnomusicology
ethylenediamine
etymologization
Eucharistically
eudiometrically
euphemistically
Europeanization
evaporating dish
evening grosbeak
evening primrose
everlasting life
everlastingness
every now and then
exasperatedness
exceptionalness
exchangeability
exchange control
exclamation mark
exclamatoriness
exclusion clause
excommunication
excommunicative
excommunicatory
excrementitious
execute an estate
exemplification
exemplificative
exercise bicycle
exhaust manifold
exhibitionistic
exoerythrocytic
exonerate nature
expanded plastic
expanding bullet
expansion engine
expeditiousness
experientialism
experientialist
experimentalise
experimentalism
experimentalist
experimentalize
experimentation
experimentative
explanatoriness
exploded diagram
exponential time
expostulatively
express delivery
expressionistic
extemporariness
extemporization
extension course
extension ladder
exteriorization
externalization
exterritorially
extracellularly
extra-curricular
extracurricular

extrajudicially
extralinguistic
extraordinarily
extraprovincial
extrapunitively
extravascularly
extrinsic factor
extrinsic muscle
eyebrow tweezers
facts and figures
falling sickness
fall into one's lap
fall on hard times
fall on one's sword
fall over oneself
fall to one's share
fall to the ground
false conception
familiarization
family allowance
famous last words
fantasticalness
fantasy football
Faraday constant
fashionableness
Father Christmas
Father of History
feast of trumpets
feast one's eyes on
feathered friend
feather hyacinth
featherlessness
feather one's nest
feather-top grass
featurelessness
federal district
federal land-bank
feel in one's bones
feel oneself into
feel the weight of
fellow Christian
fellow-traveller
feminine caesura
fenestra rotunda
Fermi statistics
ferruginous duck
Fertile Crescent
feuilletonistic
Fibonacci number
Fibonacci series
fiddle-patterned
fideicommissary
fifth-generation
fight like billy-o
financial wizard
find in one's heart
finishing school
finishing stroke
fire certificate
fire in one's belly
first concoction
first derivative

first-generation
first intentions
first lieutenant
fisherman's story
fissiparousness
fissure eruption
fits of the mother
fix a person's fate
flash photolysis
flathead catfish
flavourlessness
flex one's muscles
flibbertigibbet
flight attendant
fling to the winds
flirtatiousness
floriferousness
flowering cherry
flowering willow
flower of the hour
fluorescent bulb
fluorescent lamp
fluoridationist
fly at higher game
flying phalanger
Flying Scotchman
fly off the handle
folding strength
folie de grandeur
folk-etymologize
follow the hounds
follow-the-leader
follow the plough
follow the string
fool's watercress
football stadium
foot-pound-second
forage-harvester
for all it is worth
forbidden ground
force the bidding
fore-appointment
foreground music
foreign exchange
foreign minister
Foreign Minister
forensic science
foresightedness
forget-me-not blue
for goodness' sake
forked lightning
form a government
formal education
formalinization
formation flying
formularization
for old sake's sake
for old times' sake
for one's name sake
for one's occasion
forthcomingness
for the first time

for the time being
Fortin barometer
forwarding agent
Foucault current
foul-mouthedness
foundation cream
foundation stone
four-dimensional
Fourier analysis
four-rowed barley
fourth dimension
fractionization
fragmentariness
fragmentization
Frankensteinian
franking machine
franklinization
Fraunhofer lines
free association
freedom of speech
Free Will Baptist
freezing-mixture
French artichoke
Frenchification
French partridge
friction welding
Friendly Society
frigate mackerel
frog in the throat
from first to last
from hand to mouth
from the ground up
from thenceforth
from the shoulder
from top to bottom
front-end loading
front-line states
front-wheel drive
frost shattering
führer principle
full-bloodedness
full-dress debate
full-heartedness
fulminating gold
functional group
functionalistic
fundamental bass
fundamental note
fundamental tone
funeral director
funeral expenses
fungistatically
funnel-web spider
furniture beetle
furniture polish
furor academicus
fused participle
futilitarianism
gaiety of nations
gain one's colours
Gainsborough hat
galactic equator

galvanic battery
gammon and patter
gasteromycetous
gastro-enteritis
gastroenteritis
gastronomically
gathering ground
Gaucher's disease
gauge invariance
gaze at one's navel
gelatin dynamite
General American
General Assembly
general delivery
general election
general hospital
general practice
gentleman-at-arms
gentleman farmer
gentleman friend
gentlemanliness
gentlewomanhood
gentlewomanlike
geochronologist
geochronometric
geomagnetically
geomorphologist
German cockroach
German cotillion
germinal vesicle
gesticulatingly
get a person's goat
get into one's head
get off the ground
get one's dander up
get one's head down
get one's rocks off
get one's skates on
get on with the job
get out from under
get out of the road
get the hell out of
get the measure of
get the worst of it
get-togetherness
get to windward of
get up to mischief
Gigantopithecus
gingerbread-palm
gingerbread-plum
gingerbread tree
give a person a fit
give a person best
give a person fits
give a person hell
give a person rats
give a person time
give it some welly
give it to a person
give my service to
give oneself airs
give oneself up to

give one's heart to
give one's regrets
give the finger to
give the game away
give the show away
glacio-eustatism
glass of antimony
glass-rope sponge
Gleichschaltung
globigerina ooze
globular cluster
Glorious Twelfth
glosso-laryngeal
gluconeogenesis
gluconeogenetic
gnathochilarium
gnathostomatous
Gobelin tapestry
God bless the mark
go down in history
go for the big spit
go for the jugular
gold-beater's skin
gold certificate
golden delicious
Golden Delicious
golden handcuffs
golden handshake
golden parachute
golden retriever
golden saxifrage
gonfaloniership
go off the deep end
go one better than
go out of one's head
gossip columnist
go to one's account
go to the scaffold
Götterdämmerung
go under the knife
government house
Government House
government issue
government paper
Government paper
governor-general
Governor-General
go without saying
go with the stream
graceless florin
graduated filter
grammaticalness
gramophonically
grandfatherhood
grandfatherless
grand horizontal
grandiloquently
Grand Inquisitor
grandmastership
grandmotherhood
grandmotherless
Grand Pensionary

granger railroad
granite-porphyry
grant-maintained
graphologically
gravimetrically
gravitationally
grease the fat pig
grease the fat sow
grease the palm of
grease the wheels
Greater Doxology
great-grandchild
great vowel shift
great white chief
great white egret
great white heron
great white shark
greenery-yallery
green revolution
green woodpecker
grenade-launcher
Grenadier Guards
greyhound-racing
Grignard reagent
grind the faces of
grist for the mill
groom of the stole
groom of the stool
groves of Academe
growth regulator
grumble and grunt
Guards battalion
guest appearance
gunner's daughter
gynaecocratical
gynandromorphic
Habeas Corpus Act
hackney carriage
hackney-chairman
hackney-coachman
haemagglutinate
haemoglobinuria
hairy in the heels
hairy woodpecker
half as much again
half-heartedness
hall of residence
hallucinatorily
hammer and sickle
hammerhead shark
Hamming distance
hand in one's chips
hand it to a person
hanging wardrobe
hang up one's boots
Hanseatic League
happy as a sandboy
hard-heartedness
hare and tortoise
hare's-foot clover
hark who's talking
harlequin beetle

harlequin smiler
harmonistically
harp on one string
Harrogate toffee
harum-scarumness
harvest festival
has no business to
hatched moulding
Haussmanization
have a bone to pick
have a good mind to
have a good stroke
have a person's ear
have a screw loose
have a slate loose
have a thing about
have a way with one
have been known to
have by the throat
have had enough of
have lost sight of
have money to burn
have no truck with
have one's heart in
have one's mansion
have one's moments
have one's way with
have the best of it
have the breeze up
have the dingbats
have the last word
have two left feet
have what it takes
hawksbill turtle
Hawthorne effect
health insurance
hearsay evidence
heartbreakingly
heating engineer
heaven of heavens
heavy-handedness
heir presumptive
heliacal setting
heliocentricism
heliometrically
heliotropically
Hellenistically
helminthologist
hemicryptophyte
hemicylindrical
hemispherectomy
hemispherically
hendecasyllabic
hendecasyllable
herb Christopher
Herculean labour
Hercules' Pillars
Hercynian Forest
heritage highway
hermaphroditism
hermeneutically
herring-bone gear

hesitation waltz
heterochromatic
heterochromatin
heterogeneously
heteromorphosis
heteroscedastic
heterosexuality
heterotopically
heuristic method
hexachloraphane
hexylresorcinol
hierogrammatist
higher criticism
higher education
Highland terrier
highly commended
high-muckety-muck
Himalayan balsam
Hippocratic oath
Hispanicization
histochemically
histocompatible
histopathologic
historic present
historiographer
historiographic
hit below the belt
Hitler moustache
hit the headlines
hit the high spots
hit the right note
hobbledehoyhood
Hodgkin's disease
Hofmann reaction
hold by the sleeve
hold one's service
hold one's whistle
holocrystalline
holographically
holosymmetrical
Holy Ghost flower
Holy Roman Empire
Homeric laughter
Homeric question
homochlamydeous
homogeneousness
homomorphically
honey locust tree
honeymoon couple
hooded merganser
hope against hope
horned syllogism
Horner's syndrome
hornet clearwing
horse and hattock
horseback-riding
horse-mastership
horseradish tree
horseshoe magnet
horticulturally
hospital corners
hospitality room

hospitalization
hot on the heels of
Hottentot cherry
Hottentot's bread
householdership
household troops
housemastership
housewifeliness
how the wind blows
how the world wags
Hubble's constant
hudibrastically
Hudsonian curlew
Hudsonian godwit
humanitarianism
Hungarian millet
Hungarian turnip
hurdy-gurdy house
Hurler's syndrome
hyaloid membrane
hybrid perpetual
hydraulic cement
hydraulic mining
hydrobiological
hydrobromic acid
hydrocyanic acid
hydrodynamician
hydrodynamicist
hydroelectrical
hydro-extraction
hydrogen cyanide
hydrogeological
hydromechanical
hydrometallurgy
hydrophobically
hydrops foetalis
hydrostatically
hydrosulphurous
hydrotropically
hydroxylapatite
hygrometrically
hygroscopically
hypercatalectic
hyperchromicity
hypercoagulable
hyperconjugated
hypercorrection
hypercritically
hyperdisyllable
hyperextensible
hyperfunctional
hyperinsulinism
hyperlipidaemia
hyperlipidaemic
hypermetabolism
hyperosmolality
hyperosmolarity
hyperparasitism
hyperphysically
hyperrhythmical
hypersomnolence
hyperspatiality

hyperthyroidism
hypnotizability
hypocellularity
hypochlorhydria
hypochlorhydric
hypochondriacal
hypochondriasis
hypochromatosis
hypocrateriform
hypomagnesaemia
hypomagnesaemic
hypoparathyroid
hypophosphorous
hypopituitarism
hypostasization
hypostatic union
hypostatization
hypothetication
hypoventilation
hypovitaminosis
hypsometrically
hysteresis curve
hysterica passio
hysteric passion
hystero-epilepsy
hystricomorphic
I am not concerned
iatromechanical
ice-cream parlour
ichthyodorulite
iconometrically
identifiability
identity element
ideographically
idiomorphically
idiosyncratical
idioventricular
idols of the tribe
if it comes to that
ignominiousness
ill-favouredness
illimitableness
illustriousness
image processing
imaginativeness
immatriculation
immeasurability
immedicableness
immersion heater
immoral earnings
immortalization
immortification
immunochemistry
immunocompetent
immunodeficient
immunodepressed
immunodiffusion
immunologically
impassionedness
impecuniousness
impenetrability
imperative logic

Imperial Majesty
imperial mammoth
imperial quarter
imperishability
imperscriptible
impertinentness
implicationally
implicativeness
imponderability
importunateness
impossibilitate
impossibilities
impracticalness
impredicability
impregnableness
imprescriptible
impressionistic
improgressively
improvidentness
improvisational
improvisatorial
inacceptability
inaccessibility
inadmissibility
in a great measure
in a large measure
in all conscience
in all likelihood
inamissibleness
inanimate nature
in a person's hands
in a person's mouth
in a person's place
in a person's stead
in a person's steps
in a person's train
inapplicability
inapprehensible
inappropriately
inattentiveness
Inauguration Day
inauthoritative
in black and white
incalculability
incidental music
incoagulability
incognizability
incommensurable
incommensurably
incommunicating
incommunicative
incommutability
incomparability
incompatibility
incomprehending
incomprehension
incomprehensive
incongruousness
inconnectedness
inconsecutively
inconsequential
inconsiderately

inconsideration
inconsistencies
inconsolability
inconspicuously
in contemplation
incorrigibility
increasableness
incredulousness
in debt to someone
indecent assault
indeed and indeed
indefeasibility
indefectibility
indefensibility
indefinableness
indemnification
indentation test
Independence Day
indeterminately
indetermination
indeterministic
Indian liquorice
Indian rope-trick
indifference map
indigestibility
indirect address
indirect passive
indisciplinable
indisputability
indissolubilist
indissolubility
indistinctively
indistinguished
indistributable
individualistic
individualities
indivisibleness
Indo-Europeanist
indomitableness
indubitableness
induced reaction
industriousness
ineffaceability
ineffectiveness
ineffectualness
inefficaciously
inexcusableness
inexpensiveness
inexplicability
inextensibility
inextricability
infanticipation
infantilization
infant mortality
infernal machine
infinite regress
infinitesimally
in fits and starts
inflammableness
informal patient
informationally
information room

informativeness
infrastructural
infundibuliform
infusorial earth
ingeminate peace
inheritableness
inhomogeneously
inhospitability
injudiciousness
in mint condition
in monosyllables
in no condition to
in no shape or form
innumerableness
inoffensiveness
in one's hip pocket
in one's own person
in one's right mind
inoperativeness
inopportuneness
in pride of grease
in prime of grease
in process of time
in quadruplicate
inquest of office
in quintuplicate
inquisitiveness
inquisitorially
in recompense for
in remembrance of
inscriptionless
inscrutableness
insensitiveness
inseparableness
in seventh heaven
insignificantly
insinuatingness
insinuativeness
inspection cover
inspirationally
instantaneously
institutionally
instructiveness
instrumentalism
instrumentalist
instrumentality
instrumentation
instrument board
instrument panel
insubordinately
insubordination
insubstantially
insurance broker
insurance policy
insurrectionary
insurrectionist
intellectualise
intellectualism
intellectualist
intellectuality
intellectualize
intelligibility

intemperateness
intensification
intention tremor
interactionally
intercellularly
intercessionary
interchangeable
interchangeably
interclavicular
intercollegiate
intercolumniary
intercomparison
interconnection
interconversion
interdependence
interdependency
interdigitation
interdiscipline
interestingness
interfascicular
interference fit
interferingness
interferometric
interfoliaceous
interglaciation
interim dividend
interindividual
interiorization
interjectionary
interlaboratory
interlacustrine
interlamination
interlinguistic
interminability
interminglement
intermodulation
internalization
internal revenue
internationally
interosculation
interparietally
interpersonally
interphalangeal
interpolability
interpolymerize
interpretership
interprovincial
interrogatingly
interrogational
interrogatively
interrogatories
interscholastic
intersentential
intersubjective
intertanglement
intertextuality
intertransverse
intertubercular
inter-university
interventionism
interventionist
intestinal flora

in the altogether
in the business of
in the first place
in the interest of
in the last resort
in the melting-pot
in the nick of time
in the presence of
in there pitching
in the same breath
in the vicinage of
in the vicinity of
in the wilderness
in this day and age
in time of drought
intolerableness
intonation curve
into the Ewigkeit
intracellularly
intracerebrally
intractableness
intraculturally
intra-epithelial
intrafascicular
intrafoliaceous
intra-linguistic
intramembranous
intramuscularly
intransigentism
intraperitoneal
intra-subjective
intravascularly
intrinsicalness
intrinsic factor
introjectionism
introjectionist
introspectively
introsusception
intrusive growth
intussusception
intussuscipiens
inverse spelling
investigational
investigatorial
investment trust
invisible export
invisible import
invisible mender
involuntariness
invulnerability
ion implantation
ionization gauge
ionospherically
ipecacuanha wine
Irish Australian
Irish blackguard
Irish martingale
Irish Sweepstake
irrationability
irrationalistic
irreconcilement
irreconciliable

irreconciliably
irredeemability
irreducibleness
irreductibility
irreflexiveness
irreformability
irrefragability
irreligiousness
irremovableness
irreparableness
irrepealability
irreprehensible
irrepresentable
irresistability
irresistibility
irretentiveness
irreverentially
irreversibility
irrevocableness
irrigation canal
irrotationality
I shouldn't wonder
island continent
is no oil painting
isoagglutinogen
isoelectrically
isoimmunization
isoperimetrical
isophane insulin
isotope dilution
isotransplanted
Italian quilting
Italian vermouth
it's a free country
jackass schooner
Jack in the basket
Jack-in-the-pulpit
jack of all trades
Jack of all trades
Jack of both sides
jagged chickweed
Japanese anemone
Japanese current
Japanese lacquer
Japanese lantern
Japanese macaque
Japanese spaniel
Japanese waltzer
japanned leather
jeepers creepers
Jeffersonianism
Jehovah's Witness
Jersey lightning
Jerusalem cherry
jewel in the crown
John-Bullishness
Johnny Head-in-Air
joint and several
join the banner of
join the majority
Jonathanization
journeyman clock

judge and warrant
judgement debtor
judicial torture
judiciary combat
jumping-off place
jumping-off point
junction railway
junior barrister
Jupiter's distaff
jurisprudential
justifiableness
juvenile hormone
juxtaglomerular
juxtapositional
kangaroo closure
kangaroo justice
katathermometer
keep a low profile
keep an eye peeled
keep company with
keep friends with
keep off the grass
keep one's balance
keep one's counsel
keep one's pants on
keep one's shirt on
keep one's station
Kentucky warbler
Kepler's equation
keratoacanthoma
kick a person's ass
kick the tar out of
kick up one's heels
killer submarine
kilogram calorie
kind-heartedness
King of the Castle
King of the Romans
king's bad bargain
King's quarantain
Kirghiz pheasant
kiss the pope's toe
kiss the Pope's toe
kitchen-gardener
kleptoparasitic
knickerbockered
knick-knackatory
knight commander
Knight of the Bath
knight of the post
knight of the road
knights bachelor
Knights Templars
knitting machine
knock all of a heap
know a thing or two
know from nothing
know-nothingness
know one's own mind
know where to find
knuckle sandwich
Koch's postulates

kymographically
labourer-in-trust
labour-intensive
labour relations
Labrador current
labradorescence
lachryma Christi
lackadaisically
lactoperoxidase
lacto-vegetarian
ladder-back chair
ladies' cloakroom
ladies-in-waiting
Lagrangian point
laissez-faireism
laissez-faireist
Lakeland terrier
lance bombardier
landed immigrant
land-measurement
landscape-marble
language loyalty
Laplace equation
Laplace operator
Lapland longspur
lapsang souchong
larch needle-cast
lares and penates
Larmor frequency
laryngotracheal
last but not least
latensification
latent ambiguity
lateral thinking
Latter-day Saints
lattice constant
laughing jackass
laugh like a drain
laugh out of court
Law Commissioner
law of continuity
law of mass action
law of succession
lay down one's arms
lay one's finger on
Laysan albatross
lay up in lavender
lazy daisy stitch
leading question
lead up the garden
League of Nations
learning machine
learn one's lesson
learn the hard way
least flycatcher
leather breeches
Leather-Stocking
leave in the lurch
ledger-millstone
legalitarianism
legal separation
leg before wicket

legislatorially	linseed poultice	luncheon voucher
leg-of-mutton sail	liquid petroleum	lunisolar period
Leninist—Marxist	literary adviser	lute harpsichord
lenticular cloud	literary history	lymphadenectomy
lenticular gland	lithochromatics	lymphadenopathy
leopard-tortoise	lithonephrotomy	lymphatic system
lepidopterology	little chief hare	lymphocytotoxic
leptomeningitis	Little Englander	lymphocytotoxin
let a person blood	little girls' room	lymphoedematous
let daylight into	little or nothing	lymphogranuloma
lethargicalness	liturgiological	lymphoreticular
let it all hang out	live dangerously	lyotropic series
let one's hair down	live one's own life	McNaughten rules
letter of comfort	live over the shop	machiavellianly
Letters of Orders	live with oneself	machine language
leukaemogenesis	living daylights	machine-readable
level-headedness	living newspaper	machine washable
leveraged buyout	loan translation	macrocosmically
lever escapement	loaves and fishes	macrolinguistic
Lewis machine-gun	local government	macrophotograph
lexicographical	local oscillator	macroscopically
lexicologically	Loch Ness monster	macrostructural
lexicostatistic	loco-descriptive	magazine section
lexigraphically	locomotor ataxia	Magellanic cloud
Liberal Democrat	lodger-franchise	Magellanic Cloud
Liberal Unionist	logarithmically	magistratically
lichenification	logarithmic sine	magnanimousness
lichen substance	logical addition	magnetic anomaly
lick the trencher	logographically	magnetic compass
Liebig condenser	London shrinking	magnetic equator
lie in one's throat	Longer Catechism	magnetic termite
lie like a trooper	long-persistence	magnetizability
lie on the stomach	long-sightedness	magnetochemical
lie upon the wager	long-sufferingly	magneto-electric
life-everlasting	longsufferingly	magnetotelluric
life-threatening	look the other way	magnifying glass
lift coefficient	look who's talking	main half-breadth
lift up one's hands	lophobranchiate	maintainability
lift up one's voice	Lord bless my soul	maintenance dose
light-handedness	Lord Chamberlain	Maintenon cutlet
light-headedness	Lord High Admiral	maison de couture
light microscope	lord-lieutenancy	majoritarianism
light-mindedness	lord proprietary	majority carrier
lightning beetle	Lords Appellants	majority verdict
lightning strike	lords of creation	make a beeline for
light of one's life	lose countenance	make a clean job of
light-scattering	lose one's balance	make a conquest of
lignocellulosic	lose one's heart to	make a difference
lignosulphonate	lose the exchange	make a difficulty
like a dog's dinner	loudness control	make a good fist at
like a drowned rat	loves' young dream	make an example of
like a scalded cat	love's young dream	make an excursion
likelihood ratio	Lower California	make a person's day
like the clappers	lower one's sights	make a person sick
like thirty cents	lower yield point	make a poor fist at
lily of the valley	low-spiritedness	make a practice of
Lincoln Longwool	loxodromic curve	make a religion of
Lincolnshire Red	lues Boswelliana	make a stranger of
line-integration	Lulworth skipper	make a thing about
line of flotation	lumbrical muscle	make friends with
line of scrimmage	luminosity curve	make life easy for
linguistic atlas	lump in the throat	make light work of

make matchwood of
make mincemeat of
make one's manners
make out a case for
make shipwreck of
make short work of
make something of
make the best of it
make the money fly
malacopterygian
malaria parasite
malassimilation
malconformation
malconstruction
maldistribution
malice prepensed
malorganization
Malpighian layer
malpresentation
managed currency
Manchester goods
Manchester wares
Manchurian crane
Manchurian tiger
manganese bronze
manganese nodule
manganese-purple
manganese violet
mangel-wurzel fly
mangrove snapper
manic depression
manic-depressive
manifestational
manifestatively
manifest destiny
manneristically
manoeuvrability
manorialization
manslaughterous
manuscript paper
many a time and oft
maremma sheepdog
Marfan's syndrome
margaritiferous
marginalization
marine biologist
mariner's compass
mariner's portage
marine scientist
market potential
market socialism
marriageability
marriage licence
marriage payment
marriage portion
marshalling yard
marsh arrow-grass
marsh fritillary
martensitically
marvellous apple
Marxism-Leninism
Marxist-Leninism

Marxist-Leninist
Maryland chicken
masculinization
masochistically
mass observation
mass radiography
master-craftsman
master of beagles
Master of Misrule
Master of Science
material control
material culture
materialization
material science
mathematization
Matres Dolorosae
matriculability
matrix mechanics
mauvais coucheur
Maxwell equation
McNaughten rules
meadow buttercup
meadow soft-grass
meaninglessness
measurelessness
meat and potatoes
mechanical power
mechanistically
mechanochemical
mechano-electric
mechanomorphism
mechanoreceptor
medial malleolus
medical examiner
medical register
medieval history
medium frequency
medullary sheath
medulloblastoma
meet a person's eye
megachiropteran
megagametophyte
megalocephalous
megamillionaire
Meissner's plexus
melancholically
melissyl alcohol
mellifluousness
memorialization
memoria technica
mend one's manners
meningomyelitis
mental breakdown
mental defective
mentalistically
Mephistophelean
Mephistophelian
merchantability
merchant banking
merchant of death
merchant service
merchant stapler

mercurification
meritoriousness
merosymmetrical
merveille du jour
mesmerizability
messenger-at-arms
metagenetically
metageometrical
metal arc welding
metalinguistics
metallic circuit
metallothionein
metallurgically
metamathematics
metamictization
metaphysicality
metasomatically
metasyncritical
metempsychosist
methamphetamine
Methodistically
methods engineer
methylcellulose
methylphenidate
metropolitanate
metropolitanism
metropolitanize
Mexican-American
Mexican fruit fly
Mexican shilling
Mexican stand-off
mezzotint rocker
Michaelmas daisy
Michelson–Morley
microaerophilic
microanalytical
microangiopathy
microbiological
microcosmically
microcosmic salt
micro-electronic
microelectronic
microfilm reader
microfloppy disk
microfracturing
microgametocyte
microlinguistic
micromanipulate
micrometeoritic
micrometrically
micromillimetre
microphotograph
microphotometer
microphotometry
microprogrammer
microprojection
microradiograph
microscope slide
microscopically
microsporangium
microstructural
microtopography

microtrabecular
middle-age spread
middle-classness
middle-of-the-road
migratory locust
military academy
military attaché
military college
military honours
military service
military tribune
military two-step
millionaireship
Millionaires' Row
Minamata disease
mind one's P's and Q's
mineral charcoal
mineral dressing
mineralogically
mineralographic
miniature camera
miniaturization
minimal free form
minimum free form
minister general
Minister of State
minister premier
minority carrier
miogeosynclinal
miraculous berry
miraculous fruit
misappreciation
misapprehension
misapprehensive
misarticulation
misbecomingness
miscellaneously
mischaracterize
mischievousness
misconstruction
misdistribution
misintelligence
misproportioned
misrecollection
misregistration
mistletoe cactus
mist propagation
mistrustfulness
misunderstander
misvocalization
mite-borne typhus
mitochondrially
mixotrophically
mobile sculpture
mobile telephone
mock-nightingale
modernistically
modern languages
modulation index
moisten one's clay
moisture content
Moldo-Wallachian

molecular weight
molly cotton-tail
Molotov cocktail
molybdophyllite
moment of inertia
monadologically
monarcho-fascist
Monday fortnight
money for old rope
Mongolian hotpot
monkey orchestra
monkeywrenching
monochlamydeous
monochlorinated
monoconsonantal
monocrystalline
monodimensional
monographically
mono-substituted
monosyllabicity
monosymmetrical
monosymptomatic
mono-unsaturated
monounsaturated
Montagu's harrier
Monterey cypress
Montessorianism
month after month
montmorillonite
montmorillonoid
monumental mason
Moog synthesizer
moonlight lustre
mop the floor with
moral philosophy
moral psychology
Moral Rearmament
Moral Re-Armament
morning sickness
morphogenetical
morphographemic
morphographical
morphologically
morphophonemics
morphophonology
morphosyntactic
morphotectonics
Morrison shelter
mortise and tenon
mosquito-curtain
mosquito-netting
Mothering Sunday
mother of vinegar
motorway madness
mountain chicken
mountain-climber
mountain-folding
mountain gazelle
mountain gorilla
mountain hemlock
mountainousness
mountain panther

mountain railway
mountain ringlet
mounted infantry
mourning warbler
mousetrap cheese
mousseline glass
mousseline sauce
moustache-lifter
moustache monkey
moving staircase
much of a muchness
Muggletonianism
multi-articulate
multiculturally
multifunctional
multilateralism
multilateralist
multilateralize
multilingualism
multinationally
multi-occupation
multiple factors
multiple fission
multiprocessing
multiprogrammed
multitudinosity
multitudinously
murmur diphthong
muscovitization
muscular feeling
muscular stomach
musculoskeletal
musée imaginaire
musical director
musicologically
music to one's ears
musique concrète
mustard and cress
mustard-coloured
mutatis mutandis
mutton-leg sleeve
mutual induction
mutual insurance
mutualistically
myeloperoxidase
myenteric reflex
my learned friend
myoelectrically
myrmekitization
my sainted mother
mystery-religion
mythologization
naked as a jay-bird
nannoplanktonic
naphthalization
national holiday
nationalization
national product
National Lottery
National Savings
national service
national theatre

native companion
native cranberry
natural-coloured
natural language
natural religion
natural shoulder
natural theology
nature sanctuary
naughty nineties
nautical almanac
navigation light
near-sightedness
near ultraviolet
neat but not gaudy
necessitousness
necrobacillosis
necromantically
needle-and-thread
Néel temperature
Negro-Portuguese
neighbourliness
neoarsphenamine
Neo-Confucianism
neontologically
nephelinization
nephrolithiasis
nephrolithotomy
nephrosclerosis
neritic province
Nessler's reagent
nether millstone
network analyser
network analysis
network modifier
neurenteric cyst
neuroanatomical
neurobiological
neurodermatitis
neurodermatosis
neuroepithelial
neuroepithelium
neurohypophysis
neurolinguistic
neuropathologic
neurophysiology
neuropsychiatry
neuropsychology
neurosyphilitic
New Age traveller
New Commonwealth
New England aster
Newfoundland dog
New Frontiersman
Newgate Calendar
Newgate hornpipe
Newgate novelist
New Red Sandstone
New Zealand robin
nickel-in-the-slot
Nigerianization
Nightingale ward
night starvation

nineteen-pounder
nitrogen dioxide
nitrogen mustard
noble-mindedness
nobody's business
nomenclaturally
nomographically
non-attributable
non-attributably
non-availability
non-belligerence
non-belligerency
non-commissioned
non-committalism
non compos mentis
non-confidential
non-contagionist
non-contributory
nondescriptness
none the worse for
non-governmental
non-intelligence
non-interference
non-intervention
non-intoxicating
non-naturalistic
non-partisanship
non-prescription
non-productively
non-professional
non-profit-making
non-residentiary
nonsensicalness
non-significance
non-transferable
Norfolk dumpling
Norroy and Ulster
north-countryman
North countryman
north-countrymen
north-eastwardly
northern sea lion
north-westwardly
not anywhere near
not a proposition
not breathe a word
not care twopence
nothingarianism
nothing less than
not know from Adam
not much to look at
not once nor twice
not spare oneself
not the word for it
not unadjacent to
notwithstanding
not worth a button
nouvelle cuisine
now you're talking
nuclear emulsion
nuclear magneton
nuclear medicine

nuclear umbrella
nucleophilicity
nucleoprotamine
nucleosynthesis
nucleosynthetic
number crunching
numbered account
numerologically
numismatologist
Nuremberg trials
Nuremburg trials
nursery language
nystagmographic
obedientialness
objectification
objectivization
observationally
observation post
observation ward
obsidional crown
obstetrical toad
obstructiveness
obturator muscle
occasional cause
occasionalistic
occasional table
occidental topaz
occipitofrontal
occupation layer
oceanic province
oceanographical
ocellated turkey
ochlocratically
octocentenaries
octogenarianism
ocular dominance
odontoid process
odoriferousness
odour of sanctity
oestrogenically
official secrets
officina gentium
of foreign growth
of no consequence
of one's own accord
of one's own motion
of the first order
of the first water
of the same leaven
of understanding
oil a person's hand
oil of turpentine
old age pensioner
Old Commonwealth
Old Red Sandstone
old-womanishness
oligarchization
oligodendrocyte
oligodendroglia
oligohydramnios
oligomenorrhoea
oligomerization

oligonucleotide
oligosaccharide
omelette soufflé
omnidirectional
omnifariousness
on active service
on a person's track
once in a blue moon
on condition that
one-and-thirtieth
oneirocriticism
one over the eight
one's cake is dough
one's fingers itch
one's heart bleeds
one's heart breaks
one's mouth waters
one way or another
onomasiological
on one's high horse
on one's Jack Jones
on one's own ground
on speaking terms
on the back burner
on the foundation
on the ragged edge
on the right track
on the strength of
on the water wagon
on the wrong track
ontogenetically
on top of the world
onychogryphosis
open-heartedness
open one's heart to
operating profit
operating system
ophthalmologist
ophthalmometric
ophthalmoplegia
ophthalmoplegic
ophthalmoscopic
opinionatedness
opisthoglyphous
opisthognathous
opportunity cost
opprobriousness
optical activity
optical illusion
optically active
optical rotation
optic commissure
optimal foraging
optoelectronics
optokinetically
orange underwing
orange upperwing
orchestra stalls
orderly corporal
orderly sergeant
orders are orders
organizationist

organization man
organized labour
organogenically
organ-pipe cactus
orientalization
orientationally
original pravity
ornaments rubric
ornithorhynchus
orohydrographic
orthochromatize
orthodiagraphic
orthodontically
orthodromically
orthometrically
orthopaedically
orthopercussion
orthophosphoric
orthopsychiatry
orthostatically
Osgood—Schlatter
osmium tetroxide
osmotic pressure
osteochondritis
osteodystrophia
osteodystrophic
osteopathically
ostreoculturist
otolaryngologic
our first parents
Our Lady's psalter
outdoor pursuits
out of all measure
out of commission
out of one's senses
out of one's sphere
out of proportion
out of the picture
out of the running
out-of-the-wayness
outside interest
outsiderishness
ovarian follicle
overachievement
overambitiously
over and done with
overbearingness
overcarefulness
overcentralized
overconfidently
overcrowdedness
overcuriousness
overdevelopment
overearnestness
over-elaborately
overelaborately
over-elaboration
overelaboration
over-emotionally
overfamiliarity
overflowingness
overflow meeting

overforwardness
over head and ears
overmasteringly
overseas Chinese
oversensitivity
overstep the mark
overstimulation
oversusceptible
overventilation
overweeningness
Oxford marmalade
oxidation number
oxytetracycline
oyer and terminer
pacific blockade
packet switching
packing fraction
padder capacitor
padder condenser
Paddy's hurricane
painstakingness
painted terrapin
painted top-shell
painted tortoise
paint the town red
paired-associate
pair of compasses
pair of virginals
palaeencephalon
palaeoanthropic
palaeobiologist
palaeobotanical
palaeochemistry
palaeoecologist
palaeoethnology
palaeogeography
palaeogeologist
palaeographical
palaeohydrology
palaeointensity
palaeolimnology
palaeomagnetism
palaeomagnetist
palaeoneurology
palaeontography
palaeontologist
palaeopathology
palaeophytology
palaeostructure
palaeozoologist
palatine earldom
palato-maxillary
pale crêpe rubber
palynologically
pancreatization
pancreatography
panencephalitis
panophthalmitis
pan-Presbyterian
panselectionism
panselectionist
pantheistically

pantisocratical
pantothenic acid
paper-making wasp
papillary muscle
papulo-vesicular
parabolic spiral
paracrystalline
paradoxicalness
paragenetically
parageosyncline
paragraphically
paraheliotropic
parahippocampal
paralinguistics
parallelization
parallel parking
paralytic stroke
paramesonephric
parametric curve
paranitraniline
parasite fighter
parasiticalness
parasitic jaeger
parasitological
parasol mushroom
parasympathetic
paraventricular
parcels delivery
parchment-beaver
parchment-coffee
paregoric elixir
parenthetically
parfocalization
par for the course
Paris embroidery
parish communion
parish constable
parish Eucharist
parishionership
parliamentarian
parliamentarily
parliamentarism
Parliament clock
Parliament House
parochial school
paroemiographer
parrot-crossbill
parsonage teinds
parson's freehold
parthenogenesis
parthenogenetic
partial fraction
partial pressure
participational
particle physics
particularistic
particularities
Pascal's triangle
passenger pigeon
pass for sterling
pass in one's chips
passionlessness

passive immunity
passive-resister
pass one's eye over
passport control
pass round the hat
pass the hat round
pastoralization
past participial
paternoster lake
paternoster lift
paternoster line
pathetic fallacy
pathophysiology
patrimonial seas
patripassianism
pattern baldness
patterned ground
pattern practice
Patterson's curse
paulo-post-future
paurometabolous
pavement-pounder
pavement-toothed
pay off old scores
pay one's respects
peaches and cream
peacock pheasant
peacock's feather
Peano postulates
pebble prominent
pedogenetically
Pekingese stitch
pelican crossing
penalty shoot-out
pencil moustache
pencil sharpener
penetratingness
penetration twin
penetrativeness
pentaerythritol
pentanucleotide
people of the Book
Peoples of the Sea
people's republic
peppermint cream
peppermint-water
pepper saxifrage
peptic digestion
percentage point
perceptual-motor
percussion drill
peregrine falcon
perfect interval
perfectionation
perfectionistic
perfluorocarbon
performance bond
performance test
perfunctoriness
pergamentaceous
perianth segment
pericardiectomy

Périgord truffle
periodic decimal
perioesophageal
perioperatively
peripatetically
peristaltically
peristaltic pump
peritectic point
periventricular
Perkin synthesis
permanent magnet
permanganic acid
permissible dose
permselectivity
peroxosulphuric
perpendicularly
perpetual curate
perpetual motion
perpetuum mobile
per recte et retro
personal effects
personality cult
personalization
personal pension
personal pronoun
personal service
persona non grata
personification
perspectivistic
perspicaciously
perspicuousness
persuadableness
pessimistically
petition of right
Petition of Right
petits bourgeois
petrochemically
petticoat bodice
phaeochromocyte
phagocytability
phantasmagorian
Pharaoh's serpent
pharmacodynamic
pharmacogenetic
pharmacognosist
pharmacognostic
pharmacokinetic
pharmacological
pharmacotherapy
phase distortion
phase modulation
phenakistoscope
phenolphthalein
phenomenalistic
phenomenologist
phenylhydrazine
phenylhydrazone
phenylketonuria
phenylketonuric
philanthropical
philoprogeneity
philosophers' egg

philosophership
philosophically
philosophic wool
phonautographic
phonematization
phonemicization
phoneticization
phonocardiogram
phonologization
phonometrically
phonotactically
phosphatase test
phosphate island
phosphatization
phosphocreatine
phosphoglyceric
phosphonitrilic
phosphorescence
phosphorous acid
phosphorylation
phosphosilicate
phosphuranylite
photoabsorption
photoactivation
photobiological
photochemically
photoclinometry
photocoagulator
photoconducting
photoconduction
photoconductive
photoconversion
photodegradable
photodetachment
photodissociate
photoelasticity
photoelectrical
photoelectronic
photo-excitation
photofluorogram
photogoniometer
photogoniometry
photogrammetric
photoheliograph
photoionization
photojournalism
photojournalist
photolithograph
photolithotroph
photomacrograph
photomechanical
photometrically
photomicrograph
photomultiplier
photonegativity
photo-oxidizable
photopolymerize
photopositively
photopositivity
photoproduction
photoprotection
photoprotective

photoreactivate
photoregulation
photoresistance
photoresponsive
photoreversible
photosensitizer
photostationary
photosynthesise
photosynthesize
phototactically
phototelegraphy
photo-theodolite
phototopography
phototransistor
phototropically
phototypesetter
photozincograph
phrase-structure
phreatomagmatic
phrenologically
phreno-magnetism
phthisiological
physical culture
physicalization
physical science
physical therapy
physical torture
physico-chemical
physico-theology
physiographical
physiologically
physiopathology
physiotherapist
phytoagglutinin
phytochemically
phytoflagellate
phytogeographer
phytogeographic
phytopathogenic
phytoplanktonic
Pickering series
picket-pin gopher
picture magazine
picture-moulding
picture postcard
picturesqueness
pied-billed grebe
piezoelectrical
piezoresistance
pigeon guillemot
pigment printing
piliferous layer
pillow structure
pinking scissors
pin one's ears back
pinprick picture
pirate radio ship
pisciculturally
Piscis Austrinus
pitching machine
pitch the wickets
pitchy copper ore

pithecanthropic
Pithecanthropus
pit of the stomach
placenta praevia
plagiotropously
plain-spokenness
Planck's constant
Planck's equation
planetary nebula
planetary system
planimetrically
plantation crêpe
plant geographer
plasma frequency
plasmalemmasome
plasmal reaction
plasmodiophorid
plasmolytically
platform machine
platitudinarian
platitudinously
Platonistically
play a good game of
play a person foul
play a poor game of
play cat and mouse
play first fiddle
play first violin
play it for laughs
play off the stage
play the bear with
play third fiddle
play triumph about
Pleas of the Crown
pleasurableness
pleasure-cruiser
pleasure-seeking
plectonemically
pledge one's troth
pleiotropically
plenipotentiary
plethysmography
pleuropneumonia
plica circularis
plight one's troth
Plio-Pleistocene
plotting machine
ploughing engine
ploughman's lunch
ploughshare bone
plumed partridge
pluralistically
plurilingualism
plutocratically
pneumatic trough
pneumatological
Pneumatomachian
Pneumatomachist
pneumatotherapy
pneumonectomies
pneumonia blouse
pneumonic plague

pneumotachogram
pocket billiards
poetical justice
poikilothermous
Poincaré section
point discharger
point of no return
points rationing
point-to-pointing
poisoned chalice
poison pen letter
polar coordinate
polar flattening
polari-bilocular
police constable
police scientist
political animal
political asylum
political police
politzerization
polychlorinated
polychloroprene
polycrystalline
polydaemonistic
polydimensional
polyelectrolyte
polygenetically
polygon of forces
polygraphically
polyisobutylene
polyoxyethylene
polyphloisboian
polyplacophoran
polysomnography
polysyllabicity
polysymptomatic
polyunsaturated
polyvinyl acetal
pomatorhine skua
Pomeranian bream
Pontifex Maximus
poor boy sandwich
poor man of mutton
poor man's plaster
poor man's treacle
popular frontism
population curve
porcelain enamel
porcelain jasper
pork scratchings
porphobilinogen
porphyritically
porphyroblastic
porphyroclastic
Port Jackson pine
portmanteau word
portmantologism
portrait-gallery
portrait-painter
positional goods
position-finding
positive vetting

possession order
postage currency
post-consonantal
postoperatively
post-precipitate
post-synchronize
postulationally
postvocalically
potassium iodide
Potemkin village
potential energy
pottery-bark tree
poulter's measure
pour cold water on
poverty-stricken
powdering-closet
power-assistance
power of attorney
power-politician
power transistor
Poynting's vector
practicableness
praetorian guard
pragmaticalness
prairie-breaking
Prairie Province
prairie schooner
preachification
pre-acquaintance
pre-agricultural
pre-announcement
preapprehension
precancellation
precarcinogenic
precinct captain
precinct station
precipitability
precipitateness
precipitousness
preconceptional
predeterminable
predicamentally
predissociation
predominatingly
Prefect of Police
preference share
preference stock
prefiguratively
preformationism
preformationist
prehistorically
pre-implantation
pre-impregnation
prejudicialness
premeditatingly
premier minister
premodification
prenasalization
prenotification
prepositionally
prepositionless
prepossessingly

pre-professional
Pre-Raphaelitism
pre-recorded tape
preregistration
pre-reproductive
prerogative writ
Presbyterianism
Presbyterianize
prescriptionist
presence chamber
presentableness
presentationism
presentationist
preservationism
preservationist
presidentialism
presidentialist
presidents-elect
press conference
press correction
pressure casting
pressure chamber
pressure flaking
prestidigitator
prestigiousness
pretentiousness
preterimperfect
preternaturally
prevenient grace
price elasticity
prickly saltwort
prick up one's ears
pride of the world
priests-in-charge
prima ballerinas
primary election
primary evidence
primary industry
primary syphilis
Primitive Church
primitive circle
primitive colour
primitive groove
primitive streak
primitivization
Primrose Leaguer
principal clause
principal stress
print journalism
print journalist
prisoner of state
prisoner of State
prisoner's friend
private attorney
private language
private practice
private sentinel
privity of estate
privy councillor
privy counsellor
probationership
problematically

problem-oriented
proboscis monkey
procarcinogenic
processed cheese
procrastination
procrastinative
procrastinatory
professionalise
professionalism
professionalist
professionality
professionalize
professorialism
profibrinolysin
profile grinding
pro forma invoice
progenitiveness
prognostication
prognosticative
prognosticatory
programmability
progressive kiln
progressiveness
prohibitiveness
projection booth
projection fibre
projective plane
projective space
projective verse
prolate spheroid
proletarization
promiscuousness
promorphologist
pronunciability
Proper Bostonian
properispomenon
propheticalness
propidium iodide
propionaldehyde
proportionalism
proportionalist
proportionality
proportionately
propose marriage
propositionally
proprietary name
proprietary term
proprietorially
propylene glycol
propylitization
proselytization
prosenchymatous
prosobranchiate
prosopographies
prospectiveness
protection money
proteolytically
proteroglyphous
Protestant ethic
protestant flail
proto-historical
proton-accepting

protonephridial
protonephridium
protonotaryship
proto-scientific
protozoological
providentialism
provisionalness
provocation test
provocativeness
provocative test
proxime accessit
prunes and prisms
Prussian binding
Prussianization
Psalter of Cashel
psephologically
pseudaposematic
pseudepigraphal
pseudepigraphic
pseudo-Christian
pseudo-classical
pseudocoelomate
pseudohexagonal
pseudomalachite
pseudo-operation
pseudopotential
pseudopregnancy
pseudo-scientist
pseudo-statement
psychagogically
psychedelically
psychedelic rock
psychiatrically
psychoacoustics
psycho-aesthetic
psychobiography
psychobiologist
psychodiagnosis
psychodramatics
psychodramatist
psychodysleptic
psychoendocrine
psychogenically
psychogeography
psychogeriatric
psychohistorian
psychologically
psychometrician
psychopathology
psychophonetics
psychophysicist
psychopolitical
psychosexuality
psychosociology
psychostimulant
psychosynthesis
psychotechnical
psychotherapist
psychotogenesis
psychotomimetic
psychrotolerant
pteroylglutamic

pterygoid muscle
Ptolemaic system
public education
public ownership
public relations
public transport
publisher's cloth
pudding-pipe tree
pulchritudinous
pull a person's leg
pull by the sleeve
pull in one's horns
pull one's freight
pull one's pudding
pull one's punches
pull one's socks up
pullorum disease
pull the other one
pulmonary artery
pulmonary pleura
pulse modulation
punctiliousness
punctuation mark
punctus elevatus
punitive damages
purchasing power
pure mathematics
purple bacterium
purple copper ore
purple gallinule
purple moor-grass
purple sandpiper
purple sea urchin
purposelessness
push one's fortune
pusillanimously
puss in the corner
pussy-footedness
put a girdle about
put in one's pocket
put into practice
put one's back into
put one's finger on
put one's foot down
put one's foot in it
put on the buskins
put out of its pain
put out to pasture
put stuffing into
put the clock back
put the fluence on
put the helm aport
put the mockers on
put the squeeze on
put to one's shifts
put to the torture
pycnohydrometer
pygmy chimpanzee
pyloric stenosis
pyopneumothorax
pyramidal muscle
pyramidal orchid

pyramidal system
pyramidological
pyroclastic flow
pyroelectricity
pyrolytic carbon
pyrometamorphic
pyrophosphatase
pyrotechnically
quadragenarious
quadripartition
quadruplication
quantifiability
quantum increase
quarrelsomeness
quarterback club
quarterback sack
quarter-elliptic
quarter of an hour
quarter-repeater
quarter sessions
quarter-tonality
quatercentenary
quaternion group
Queen and country
queen of puddings
queen-of-the-night
Queensland maple
Queen's messenger
Queen's Messenger
quench hardening
questionability
quicker than scat
quick succession
quick-wittedness
quinalbarbitone
quincentenaries
quinquagenarian
quinquarticular
quintessentiate
quintuplication
rabbit-bandicoot
radioactivation
radio astronomer
radioautography
radiobiological
radiochemically
radio-controlled
radio-goniometer
radiogoniometer
radiogoniometry
radio-gramophone
radioheliograph
radioimmunology
radiolarian ooze
radiometrically
radio-protection
radio-resistance
radiosensitizer
radio-telegraphy
radio-telephonic
radio wavelength
radium emanation

railroad service
railway crossing
rainbow lorikeet
rain cats and dogs
raised-arm salute
raise one's hand to
raise one's sights
raise the siege of
raisins of the sun
range safety crew
rank correlation
Rankine's formula
rapid deployment
raspberry beetle
rational horizon
rationalization
rat-tailed maggot
rat-tailed radish
rattlesnake fern
rattlesnake root
rattlesnake weed
reactionariness
reaction chamber
reaction circuit
reaction pattern
reaction turbine
read-around ratio
re-advertisement
readvertisement
reafforestation
reaper-and-binder
reapportionment
rearguard action
rear its ugly head
rebarbarization
rebarbativeness
recarburization
receiver-general
receiver of wreck
reception centre
reciprocal cross
reciprocitarian
recitativo secco
recognizability
recollectedness
recombinational
reconcentration
reconcilability
reconfiguration
reconsideration
reconsolidation
reconstructable
reconstructible
reconvalescence
recoverableness
recreationalist
recrementitious
recruiting agent
rectified spirit
redaction critic
red-backed shrike
redemption yield

Redemptoristine
redetermination
red-headed wigeon
red-necked avocet
reds under the bed
reduce to silence
redundancy check
reduplicatively
red whortleberry
reed canary-grass
re-entering angle
re-establishment
reflexivization
reflux condenser
reformativeness
refortification
refracting angle
refractive index
refresher course
refrigeratories
regal walnut moth
regard one's navel
Regge trajectory
regionalization
regionary bishop
registered nurse
register tonnage
Regius professor
regression curve
regrettableness
rehearsal dinner
reimbursability
reincorporation
reindustrialise
reindustrialize
reinvestigation
relative address
relative density
releasing factor
relieving tackle
remand in custody
rememberability
remember oneself
Remembrancetide
remonstratingly
remorselessness
renal portal vein
render an account
renormalization
reopening clause
repeating circle
repetitiousness
reprecipitation
reprivatization
reproachfulness
reproducibility
Republican Party
required reading
requisitionally
rescue breathing
réseau ordinaire
resedimentation

reserve buoyancy
reserve currency
residence permit
residual current
residuary powers
resistentialism
resistentialist
resocialization
resonance energy
resonance hybrid
resourcefulness
respiratory tree
respiratory tuft
responsibleness
restrictiveness
resurrectionist
resurrectionize
resurrection man
resuscitability
reticular fibres
reticular system
reticular tissue
reticulocytosis
reticulosarcoma
retribalization
retroanalytical
retrogressional
retrogressively
retroperitoneal
retropharyngeal
retroreflective
retrospectively
retrotransposon
reverentialness
reversal process
reverse take-over
reverse takeover
revolutionaries
revolutionarily
revolutionology
revolving credit
rheumatological
rhinolaryngitis
rhinopharyngeal
rhombencephalic
rhombencephalon
rhyparographist
rhythmicization
ribbon cartridge
ribbon parachute
ribonucleic acid
Richardson's skua
riddle me a riddle
ride skimmington
ride the cushions
ride whip and spur
Riemann geometry
Riemann integral
rifle microphone
right-handedness
Right Honourable
right-mindedness

ring-a-ring o' roses
ring-tailed eagle
ring-tailed lemur
Rip-Van-Winkledom
Rip-Van-Winkleish
Rip-Van-Winkleism
rise with the lark
rising diphthong
risus sardonicus
ritualistically
road fund licence
roaring twenties
Robin Goodfellow
roche moutonnéed
rocket projector
roentgenography
roentgenologist
roentgenoscopic
Roger de Coverley
rogue and villain
Rolandic fissure
role-playing game
roly-poly pudding
romanticization
room temperature
Rossi−Forel scale
rotary converter
rotary egg-beater
Rotherham plough
rough green snake
roughly speaking
rough puff pastry
roundaboutation
round-shouldered
round-trip ticket
Rowland mounting
Royal Commission
Rubarth's disease
rubber fetishism
Rube Goldbergian
ruby anniversary
rudimentariness
ruler of the choir
rules of evidence
rumbustiousness
run a temperature
run interference
running headline
Russell's paradox
Russian dressing
Russian longhair
Russian roulette
Rutherford model
Rydberg constant
sabbatical river
Sabbatical river
sabre-toothed cat
sabretooth tiger
sacrifice market
saddleback shrew
saddle-stitching
saddling paddock

sado-masochistic
sadomasochistic
sage Derby cheese
sagittal section
sailor's farewell
sailor's pleasure
salamander-stove
salami technique
sales department
sales resistance
salicylaldehyde
salmon poisoning
salpingectomies
salpingographic
sancta sanctorum
sanctimoniously
sanguineousness
Sanskritization
sapphire wedding
saprophytically
satin flycatcher
satisfactionist
saturated diving
saturation point
savannah sparrow
save appearances
save one's longing
save one's own hide
scalene cylinder
scale of notation
scan-column index
Scandinavianism
Scandinavianize
scapolitization
scapular feather
scapulocoracoid
scarlet grosbeak
scarper the letty
scattering angle
scattering layer
scheduled flight
schillerization
schistosomiasis
schistosomicide
schizo-affective
Schmidt reaction
scholasticizing
school committee
school inspector
school-marmishly
schoolmastering
schoolmasterish
schoolmistressy
school of thought
schooner-frigate
Schopenhauerian
Schopenhauerism
Schopenhauerist
Schotten−Baumann
Schottky barrier
Schottky diagram
Schultz−Charlton

scientificality
scientistically
scimitar-babbler
scintillatingly
scintillography
scissors-grinder
sclerodermatous
Scotch Blackface
Scotchification
Scotch marmalade
Scott connection
Scottish terrier
scouring machine
scrape the barrel
scratched figure
scratch hardness
scratch one's head
scribaciousness
scribbling block
scribbling paper
scrivener's cramp
scrumptiousness
sculpturesquely
sea-island cotton
Sealyham terrier
sea oak coralline
seasick medicine
Second Adventist
secondary burial
secondary colour
secondary modern
secondary oocyte
secondary planet
second breakfast
second childhood
second-handiness
second honeymoon
second in command
second intention
second messenger
second secretary
Second Secretary
section sergeant
sector of a sphere
secular equation
secular humanism
secundogeniture
securities house
security analyst
security blanket
Security Council
sedan-chair clock
sedentarization
sedimentologist
see a person right
seek one's fortune
see the New Year in
seismic velocity
seismographical
seismologically
select committee
selenographical

selenologically
self-abandonment
self-advancement
self-advertising
self-affirmation
self-approbation
self-assuredness
self-capacitance
self-centredness
self-coincidence
self-complacence
self-complacency
self-confidently
self-consciously
self-consequence
self-consistency
self-constituted
self-containedly
self-containment
self-contentedly
self-contentment
self-cultivation
self-deliverance
self-deprecating
self-deprecation
self-deprecatory
self-destruction
self-destructive
self-determining
self-development
self-disciplined
self-dissociated
self-examination
self-explanatory
self-fertilizing
self-gratulation
self-gratulatory
self-gravitating
self-gravitation
self-importantly
self-improvement
self-indulgently
self-instruction
self-involvement
self-liquidating
self-liquidation
self-maintaining
self-maintenance
self-observation
self-opinionated
self-orientation
self-oscillating
self-oscillation
self-pollinating
self-pollination
self-portraiture
self-pronouncing
self-propagating
self-realisation
self-realization
self-referential
self-registering

self-reproachful
self-reproaching
self-righteously
self-sacrificial
self-sacrificing
self-satisfiedly
self-slaughtered
self-stimulation
self-subsistence
self-subsistency
self-substantial
self-sufficience
self-sufficiency
sell a person a pup
sell by the candle
Sellenger's round
semantic aphasia
semantic paradox
semicircularity
semi-crystalline
semicylindrical
semi-documentary
semi-empirically
semi-independent
semi-logarithmic
semi-manufacture
semi-Pelagianism
semi-permanently
semi-proletariat
semi-submersible
semi-transparent
senatorial order
Sendero Luminoso
send in an account
send round the hat
Seneca snakeroot
senior registrar
sense-experience
sensible horizon
sentence of death
sententiousness
sentimentalizer
separation order
septcentenaries
sequence dancing
sequestrotomies
serendipitously
sergeant-painter
sericiculturist
serjeants-at-arms
sero-sanguineous
serotherapeutic
serpentine front
serpentine stone
serpentine verse
serve the purpose
serve the stead of
serviceableness
service contract
service engineer
service industry
servomechanical

sesquicentenary	shuffle the cards	social causation
sesquioxidation	shut one's heart to	social character
sesquiterpenoid	shuttle armature	social Darwinism
session musician	Sibbald's rorqual	social democracy
set a high value on	Siberian mammoth	social geography
set one's sights on	Siberian pea-tree	social insurance
set the clock back	Sicilian defence	socialistically
settlement house	Sicilian Vespers	social ownership
settle on the lees	Sicilian vespers	social scientist
settler's matches	sickle-cell trait	social secretary
seven deadly sins	sick man of Europe	social structure
seventeenth part	sickness benefit	sociobiological
seventeen-tonner	side-splittingly	socio-culturally
sexagenarianism	side-stream smoke	socioculturally
sexual inversion	Siemens producer	socioecological
sexual selection	sigmoidoscopies	socio-historical
shaft horsepower	signal generator	sociolinguistic
Shakespearianly	significant form	sociometrically
shake the midriff	significational	sodium carbonate
Shannon's theorem	sign of the zodiac	sodium hydroxide
shape one's course	silage harvester	soft-centredness
sharp-wittedness	silkworm disease	soft furnishings
shear-thickening	silky flycatcher	soft-heartedness
shelter magazine	Silver Star medal	soft-shell turtle
shepherd's needle	silvery marmoset	soil association
sherbet fountain	Simmonds' disease	soil conditioner
sheriff's officer	simple structure	soil resistivity
shield cartilage	simply connected	solar prominence
shield-nose snake	simultanagnosia	soldier of Christ
shift for oneself	sing another song	solipsistically
shifting spanner	single-electrode	Solomon Islander
shift one's ground	single pneumonia	solstitial point
shift-terminator	sing the same song	solubility curve
shilling shocker	singularization	somatologically
ship of the desert	sin of commission	somatotopically
shipping tobacco	sintered carbide	sonoluminescent
shirt-waist dress	sister chromatid	sooty shearwater
shiver my timbers	situation comedy	sophisticatedly
shock excitation	situation ethics	soprano recorder
shoe-billed stork	situation report	sororal polygyny
shoestring catch	six-and-thirtieth	sorry for oneself
shooting gallery	sixty-fourth note	soul-searchingly
shopping trolley	skeletonization	sounding-balloon
shop-within-a-shop	skim the cream off	sound insulation
shorten one's grip	sleeping draught	source-criticism
shorten the arm of	sleeping partner	South Africanism
shorthandedness	sleeve Pekingese	south-eastwardly
shorthand typist	slender mongoose	Southern Baptist
short-headedness	sling the hatchet	Southern Comfort
Short Parliament	slip in the clutch	south-westwardly
short sweetening	slip of the tongue	sow one's wild oats
short-windedness	slog one's guts out	spaceworthiness
shotgun marriage	slotted armature	spaghetti tubing
shot-hole disease	Slough of Despond	Spanish American
shoulder holster	small-mindedness	Spanish bluebell
shoulder-shotten	smoke respirator	Spanish chestnut
show a thing or two	smooth breathing	Spanish-Colonial
show one's colours	snake in the grass	Spanish mackerel
shrinkage cavity	snap one's fingers	Spanish omelette
shrinking violet	snow scorpion fly	Spanish windlass
shrink-resistant	soaked to the skin	spark telegraphy
shrunk in the wash	social butterfly	sparring partner

spasmodicalness
spathose iron ore
spatial-temporal
speaker-listener
speak for oneself
speaking-machine
speaking-trumpet
speak of the devil
speak volumes for
special delivery
special interest
special pleading
special sessions
species richness
species-specific
specific disease
specific epithet
specific gravity
specific impulse
specific surface
speckled yellows
spectacled cobra
spectral tarsier
spectrochemical
spectroscopical
specular iron ore
speculativeness
speech community
speechification
speech pathology
speech stretcher
speech therapist
spelling checker
spermaceti whale
spermatogenesis
spermatogenetic
spes recuperandi
sphaerosiderite
spheroidal state
spheroidization
spherulitically
sphincter muscle
spike microphone
spill the blood of
spinifex texture
spinning machine
spinning process
spinning reserve
spinsterishness
spiral bevel gear
spiral stability
spiral staircase
spiritual courts
spiritual father
spirochaeticide
splanchnologist
splanchnomegaly
splanchnopleure
splendiferously
splenoportogram
splinter-netting
split infinitive

spoil a person for
spoilt for choice
spokeswomanship
spongioblastoma
spontaneousness
sporophytically
sporting picture
spotted redshank
sprain one's ankle
spreading factor
spread it on thick
spread one's wings
Sprengel air pump
spring snowflake
sprinkler system
spruce partridge
spur-of-the-moment
square the circle
squeeze an orange
squire of the body
stable companion
stadtholdership
stage management
stagnation point
stamp collecting
stamp collection
stand and deliver
standardization
standing ovation
standing rigging
stand-offishness
standoffishness
stand on ceremony
stand one's corner
stand one's ground
stand on one's head
stanhope phaeton
staphylorrhaphy
star of Bethlehem
starred question
Stars and Stripes
starvation wages
stasipatrically
State capitalism
State Department
State university
stationary point
stationary state
station-distance
station hospital
stationmistress
station-sergeant
statute merchant
statutes at large
statutory tenant
stealth aircraft
steal the picture
steamboat Gothic
steering compass
Stefan–Boltzmann
Steller's sea lion
stem-Christiania

stem-composition
Stensen's foramen
step on the toes of
stereochemistry
stereographical
stereoisomerism
stereoisomerize
stereologically
stereomonoscope
stereoselection
stereoselective
stereotaxically
stereotelescope
stereotypedness
stereotypically
steric hindrance
sternomaxillary
sternovertebral
steroidogenesis
Stevenson screen
sticking plaster
stick in one's craw
stick to one's guns
stick to one's last
stinkhorn fungus
stinking mayweed
stock and station
stockbroker belt
stocking stuffer
stomacher brooch
stone motherless
stop a person's way
stop-me-and-buy-one
stopping mixture
stopping station
stop the breath of
storage location
store-and-forward
stowage capacity
straddle carrier
straddle milling
straggle-brained
straight-facedly
straightforward
straight-grained
straight shooter
strain hardening
strait and narrow
straitlacedness
strait waistcoat
strange particle
stratagematical
stratagemically
stratigraphical
stratospherical
strawberry blite
strawberry blond
strawberry guava
strawberry perch
strawberry shrub
straw-necked ibis
stream of thought

street furniture	subterraneously	superstructural
street jewellery	suburbanization	superterraneous
strephosymbolia	subvocalization	supplementarily
stress corrosion	succession house	supplementarity
stress-dilatancy	succession state	supplementation
stretcher-bearer	Succession State	supply and demand
stretcher strain	successlessness	suppressibility
stretching-board	succinylcholine	suppressor T cell
stretch one's legs	succus entericus	suprachiasmatic
stretch receptor	sucking response	supraclavicular
stretch spinning	suck the hind teat	supradecompound
stretch the rules	suction dredging	supranaturalism
stretch to the oar	suction pressure	supranaturalist
stria gravidarum	sufficient grace	suprarelational
stricken in years	sulcus of Rolando	surface couching
strict Communion	sulphaemoglobin	surface-crossing
strict liability	sulphamethazine	surface integral
strike-slip fault	Sulphamezathine	surface printing
strike soundings	sulphate process	surgeons general
string along with	sulphinpyrazone	surrender to bail
string orchestra	sulphureousness	surreptitiously
string telephone	sum and substance	surrogate mother
striped squirrel	summer and winter	surveyor-general
striped trousers	summer complaint	susceptibleness
strongyloidosis	summer diarrhoea	suspense account
strontian yellow	summer lightning	suspension point
structuralistic	summer snowflake	sustaining pedal
structural steel	sunrise industry	Sutherland table
structurization	sunset provision	Swainson's thrush
struggle meeting	superabundantly	swashbucklering
stuckuppishness	superadditional	sweep second hand
studio apartment	supercavitation	sweet Fanny Adams
studium generale	superclustering	sweetheart plant
stump embroidery	superconducting	sweetlip emperor
Sturt's desert pea	superconduction	swimming-bladder
stylographic pen	superconductive	swimming costume
stylostatistics	superexaltation	swim with the tide
subcommissioner	superexcellence	swine erysipelas
subdenomination	superexcellency	switch mechanism
subintellection	superficial foot	switch-reference
subintelligitur	superficialness	sword-and-buckler
subject superior	superfluousness	sword-and-sorcery
sublapsarianism	superheterodyne	sword of Damocles
sublimification	superimposition	sycophantically
submarine canyon	superindividual	Sydenham's chorea
submarine chaser	superinducement	Sydney or the bush
subordinateness	superintendence	syllabification
sub-postmistress	superintendency	syllogistically
subreptitiously	superior numbers	symbolic address
subsequentially	superlativeness	symbolical books
subsidiary cells	supermarket cart	symbolistically
subsistence crop	supernaturalise	symmetricalness
subsistence diet	supernaturalism	sympathectomies
subsistence wage	supernaturalist	sympathetically
subspecifically	supernaturality	sympathicotonia
substance abuser	supernaturalize	sympathicotonic
substantialness	supernumeraries	sympatho-adrenal
substantia nigra	superordination	sympathogonioma
substantiveness	superplasticity	sympathomimetic
substantive verb	supersaturation	sympathy striker
substitutionary	superstitionist	symphonic ballet
substratosphere	superstitiously	symptomatically

synchronistical	tattersall check	the Antonine Wall
synchronization	tautomerization	theatre workshop
synchro receiver	Tay-Sachs disease	the back of beyond
syndical chamber	teaching machine	the Baltic States
syndiotacticity	tear oneself away	the better part of
synecdochically	tear one's hair out	the bird has flown
synecologically	technical school	the Book of Psalms
synergistically	technologically	the breath of life
syntagmatically	technostructure	theca cell tumour
syntectonically	tectonophysical	the change of life
systematic error	telegraph editor	the coast is clear
systematization	telegraphically	the common rustic
systemic grammar	telephone number	the Commonwealth
systems analysis	telephotography	the Devil's own job
systems operator	teleradiography	the Dircaean swan
systems software	telerobotically	the dreaded lurgy
tableau curtains	telescope-driver	the eleventh hour
table of contents	telescopic-rifle	the Encyclopedia
tachymetabolism	telescopic sight	the end of the line
tacit relocation	telestereoscope	the end of the road
Tahiti arrowroot	telethermometer	the eye of a needle
take a bit of doing	tell its own story	the Fatal Sisters
take advantage of	temerariousness	the fat of the land
take a lot of doing	temnospondylous	the four freedoms
take a person up on	temperamentally	the girl next door
take a poor view of	tempestuousness	the Good Shepherd
take at advantage	tempt Providence	the great assizes
take by the button	tenancy in common	the Gulf of Mexico
take exception to	Ten Commandments	the Heavenly City
take into account	tendentiousness	the herd instinct
take into custody	Tennessee marble	the King's English
take it on the chin	Tennessee walker	the late lamented
take it or leave it	tensile strength	the man in the boat
take knowledge of	tentaculiferous	the man in the moon
take one's cue from	tent-caterpillar	the Merry Monarch
take one's eyes off	teratocarcinoma	the more's the pity
take one's leave of	terebinthinated	the nine worthies
take one's own life	terephthalamide	the noble science
take one's stand on	terminalization	the Old Pretender
take service with	terminal moraine	theorematically
take some beating	Territorial Army	theosophistical
take the bloom off	terroristically	the powers that be
take the chill off	tertiary college	the Principality
take the long view	tetrabranchiate	the Queen's colour
take the shilling	tetrahexahedron	the Queen's speech
take the view that	tetrahydrofuran	therapeutically
take the wraps off	tetramerization	there is no saying
take to one's bosom	tetranucleotide	thermal analysis
take to one's heels	tetrasporangium	thermal capacity
take wooden money	tetrasporophyte	thermal velocity
talk a person down	tetrasyllabical	thermionic valve
talk a person over	tetrazotization	thermite process
tallow-chandlery	Teutonic Knights	thermite welding
tamper-resistant	text linguistics	thermochemistry
tan a person's hide	thalamocortical	thermodynamical
tangent distance	thalassographic	thermo-halocline
tank transporter	thalassotherapy	thermo-hardening
target indicator	thalidomide baby	thermomagnetism
tarpaulin muster	thanatocoenosis	thermoregulator
tarragon vinegar	Thanksgiving Day	thermoremanence
tarsometatarsal	thankworthiness	thermosensitive
tarsometatarsus	that's more like it	thermostability

the Scourge of God	tickle in the palm	trans-equatorial
the show must go on	tiddley-om-pom-pom	transessentiate
the Six Dynasties	tiger salamander	transferability
the soul of honour	tight corner tilt	transfer company
the sport of kings	tighten one's belt	transfer machine
the Supreme Being	till kingdom come	transfer-printed
theta-phi diagram	tilt at windmills	transfiguration
the Three Estates	time of ignorance	transfigurative
the three sisters	time on one's hands	transfigurement
the Twelve Tables	time-servingness	transformerless
the usual warning	tinkling grackle	transgressively
the vast majority	tip of the iceberg	transhistorical
the weaker vessel	tip over the perch	transhumanation
the white feather	titanium dioxide	transilluminate
the whole boiling	titanohaematite	transindividual
the witching hour	titrimetrically	transistor radio
the worse for wear	to a person's teeth	transition curve
thickheadedness	tobacco hornworm	transition metal
Thiessen polygon	tobacco whitefly	transition point
things of the mind	to be going on with	translatability
think for oneself	tocodynamometer	translationally
thinking subject	to have and to hold	translation loan
think on one's feet	tomographically	translation wave
think the world of	tongue-and-groove	transliteration
think twice about	tongue-depressor	translocational
thin on the ground	tonsillectomies	transmissometer
thin-skinnedness	too clever by half	transmutability
third-generation	too good to be true	transmutational
thirty-something	too hot to hold one	transnationally
this day sennight	to one's knowledge	transparentness
this-worldliness	top fermentation	transphenomenal
thixotropically	topographically	transplantation
Thomsen's disease	torque converter	transport number
thoracicolumbar	torsion pendulum	transposability
thorough-draught	tossing the caber	transpositional
thoroughgoingly	total abstinence	transpositively
thoughtlessness	totalitarianism	transprovincial
threateningness	to the effect that	trans-subjective
three-legged race	to the finger-ends	transubstantial
three musketeers	to the fingertips	transverse colon
three-ring circus	to the last degree	transverse flute
thromboembolism	to the manner born	tranylcypromine
throttle control	to the right about	trapezoidal rule
through-composed	tough as old boots	traumatotropism
through the green	tough-mindedness	travel allowance
throw in one's hand	toujours perdrix	travelling crane
throw in the towel	tout au contraire	travelling stock
throw one's hand in	tower of strength	treacherousness
throw one's tongue	Townsend current	treasonableness
throw the hatchet	toxicologically	treasurableness
thrust augmentor	tracheotomy tube	tree of knowledge
thrust oneself in	tracking station	trembling poplar
thrust to the wall	Trafalgar Square	triacontahedral
thumbnail sketch	traffic analysis	triacontahedron
thumb one's nose at	traffic engineer	trial by the media
thunderstricken	tragico-farcical	trial of strength
thyrocalcitonin	trailing arbutus	triangular trade
thyroidectomize	training college	trichinelliasis
Tibetan antelope	transactionally	trichloroacetic
Tibeto-Himalayan	transactivation	trichloroethane
ticket collector	transcriptional	trichlorophenol
ticket-splitting	transelementate	trick of the trade

trick-or-treating	ubiquitarianism	uncomprehensive
trifluoperazine	ultimate Frisbee	unconcernedness
trigeminal nerve	ultimobranchial	uncondescending
trigonocephalic	ultracentrifuge	unconditionally
trigonometrical	ultrafilterable	unconjecturable
Trincomalee wood	ultrafiltration	unconnectedness
trinitrotoluene	ultramicroscope	unconscientious
Trinity Brethren	ultramicroscopy	unconsciousness
trip over oneself	ultramicrotomed	unconsequential
tripping-circuit	ultrasonication	unconstrainable
trisyllabically	ultrasonography	unconstrainedly
trochlear muscle	ultrastructural	uncontroversial
tropane alkaloid	umbilical artery	uncooperatively
trophectodermal	unacceptability	uncopyrightable
trophochromatin	unaccommodating	uncorrespondent
tropical cyclone	unadulteratedly	uncorresponding
tropicalization	unadventurously	uncorruptedness
troubadourishly	unadvisableness	uncountable noun
troubleshooting	unalterableness	uncoupling agent
troublesomeness	unambitiousness	uncourteousness
truant-inspector	unanalysability	uncultivability
true-heartedness	unanswerability	undangerousness
trumpet daffodil	unapostolically	undefinableness
trustee security	unarchitectural	undemandingness
trust-investment	unargumentative	undemonstrative
trustworthiness	unascertainable	undependability
truth-functional	unassailability	under advisement
try anything once	unassertiveness	undercapitalise
trypanosomiasis	unattributively	undercapitalize
try-your-strength	unauthentically	under compulsion
tuberculization	unauthenticated	under correction
tuberculostatic	unauthoritative	undercorrection
tufted hair-grass	unavailableness	underdispersion
tungsten carbide	unavoidableness	underemployment
tunica albuginea	unbeauteousness	underestimation
tunica vaginalis	unbeautifulness	undergraduatish
turban buttercup	unbefittingness	underhandedness
Turkish crescent	unbeginningness	underinvestment
Turkish trousers	unbelievability	under lock and key
turn a blind eye to	unbelievingness	undermodulation
turn in one's grave	unbeseemingness	underoccupation
turn on a sixpence	unboiled lobster	under one's breath
turnover article	unbrotherliness	under one's girdle
turn the tables on	uncategorizable	underpopulation
turn to advantage	unceremoniously	underprivileged
turnwrest plough	unchallengeable	underproduction
Turpentine State	unchallengeably	undersaturation
turpentine still	unchangeability	under sentence of
tussore silkworm	uncharacterized	understandingly
twenty-four carat	unchristianized	undersubscribed
twenty questions	unchristianlike	under the aegis of
twenty-something	unchronological	under the baton of
twilight housing	uncircumscribed	under the cloak of
twin carburettor	uncircumstanced	under the counter
twin lamb disease	uncommunicating	under the open sky
two-and-thirtieth	uncommunicative	under the weather
two pair of stairs	uncompanionable	undesirableness
twopenny library	uncompassionate	undetectability
twopenny upright	uncomplainingly	undischargeable
two-up and two-down	uncomplimentary	undisciplinable
typographically	uncomprehending	undiscriminated
typolithography	uncomprehension	undisguisedness

undissemblingly
undistinguished
undisturbedness
unembarrassable
unemployability
unendurableness
unenlightenment
unequivocalness
unexceptionable
unexceptionably
unexceptionally
unexclusiveness
unfathomability
unforgivingness
unfortunateness
unfossiliferous
ungelatinizable
ungeneralizable
ungentlemanlike
ungovernability
ungrammatically
unhealthfulness
unimaginatively
unimprovability
uninformatively
uninhabitedness
uninhibitedness
unintelligently
unintentionally
uninterestingly
unintermittedly
uninterpretable
uninterruptable
uninterruptedly
uninterruptible
uninventiveness
unitary symmetry
United Provinces
United Statesman
universal bishop
universalizable
universalizably
unknowledgeable
unknown quantity
unlistenability
unmercenariness
unmetamorphosed
unmistakability
unmixed blessing
unmortifiedness
unnaturalizable
unnecessariness
unobjectionable
unobjectionably
unobliteratable
unobservability
unobtrusiveness
unorganizedness
unoriginateness
unpaintableness
unpalatableness
unparliamentary

unparticipating
unpatriotically
unpeaceableness
unperturbedness
unphilosophical
unphysiological
unpicturability
unpicturesquely
unpracticalness
unprecedentedly
unpremeditation
unprepossessing
unpretentiously
unproblematical
unprogressively
unpromisingness
unpronounceable
unpronounceably
unproportionate
unprotectedness
unprotestantize
unqualifiedness
unquestioningly
unreachableness
unrealistically
unrecommendable
unreconstructed
unrelentingness
unremittingness
unrepeatability
unrepresentable
unresistingness
unrevolutionary
unrighteousness
unsatisfiedness
unscholarliness
unseaworthiness
unselfconscious
unsensationally
unsentimentally
un-Shakespearian
unshrinkability
unsociable hours
unsophisticated
unspeakableness
unspectacularly
unspiritualness
unsportsmanlike
unstatesmanlike
unsteadfastness
unsubstantially
unsubstantiated
unsuperstitious
unsupportedness
unsuspectedness
unsymmetrically
unteachableness
unthinkableness
until such time as
until the present
untouchableness
untraceableness

untractableness
untraditionally
untransformable
untransmissible
untransportable
untreatableness
ununderstanding
unutterableness
unwholesomeness
up-and-comingness
upper atmosphere
Upper California
upper-middlebrow
upper yield point
uprighteousness
upside downwards
up the wooden hill
up to the eyebrows
use a person's name
usurp the place of
utility function
vacuum extractor
vacuum packaging
valence electron
valency electron
vandalistically
vanilla ice-cream
vanish into smoke
vanity publisher
variation method
varicella zoster
varicocelectomy
vascularization
vasculotoxicity
vasoconstrictor
Vater's corpuscle
Vatican roulette
vector potential
vegetable butter
vegetable garden
vegetable marrow
vegetable oyster
vegetable sponge
vegetable tallow
Velikovskianism
velocity profile
velvet copper ore
venereal disease
Venetian shutter
venographically
ventilation duct
ventriloquially
ventriloquistic
ventrolaterally
venturesomeness
Venus's hairstone
Venus's navelwort
verbal adjective
verbal diarrhoea
verbalistically
verbalizability
verdigris agaric

verge escapement
verificationism
verificationist
vertebral column
vertebrarterial
vertebrobasilar
verticalization
vertical take-off
vertical tasting
vertiginousness
very approximate
vesiculobullous
vestibular nerve
vestibulo-ocular
vestibulospinal
vestimentiferan
vibration damper
vice-chamberlain
vicissitudinous
Victorian Gothic
Victorian period
videoconference
Vienna schnitzel
Vienna Secession
vindicativeness
vintage festival
Virginia cowslip
Virginia creeper
Virginia opossum
Virginia tobacco
visceralization
viscoelasticity
viscometrically
visible spectrum
visiting fireman
visiting firemen
visualizability
vital statistics
vitamin B complex
vitriol of copper
Vitruvian scroll
vive la bagatelle
vivisectionally
Völkerwanderung
volume indicator
voluntary school
von Hippel-Lindau
voucher specimen
vouch to warranty
voyeuristically
vulnerabilities
vulturine parrot
wag one's finger at
waitress service
Walden inversion
walking delegate
walking dragline
walking sickness
walk in one's sleep
walk on eggshells
wallop in a tether
Wall Street crash

walrus moustache
wandering sailor
warm-bloodedness
warm-heartedness
warm-temperature
warning triangle
warrantableness
wash one's hands of
waste one's breath
watching-chamber
waterloggedness
Water of Ayr stone
water on the brain
water over the dam
water-resistance
water whorl-grass
weak interaction
wear the breeches
wear the trousers
wear to the stumps
weatherboarding
weathercock-like
weather forecast
Weber–Fechner law
wedge photometer
weeping capuchin
weighing machine
weighted average
weight for weight
well-conditioned
well-constructed
well-established
well-foundedness
well-intentioned
well-upholstered
Werdnig–Hoffmann
Werner's syndrome
West African teak
Western American
western red cedar
western sandwich
Westphalia bacon
wet from the press
wet the baby's head
whale acorn-shell
whatchamacallit
what's the betting
what's your poison
wheel animalcule
wheelbarrow race
whet one's whistle
Whipple's disease
whiptail wallaby
whirling dervish
whirling disease
whiskered auklet
whiskey-straight
whistle and flute
whistle-language
whistling kettle
whistling marmot
whistling thrush

White chauvinism
White chauvinist
White Cliffs opal
white dead-nettle
whited sepulchre
white embroidery
white maidenhair
white phosphorus
white rhinoceros
white sandalwood
wide area network
Wiener schnitzel
wild service tree
will-o'-the-wispish
willow ptarmigan
Wimmera ryegrass
Winchester fives
Winchester goose
Winchester quart
Winchester style
windscreen wiper
wipe a person's eye
wireless cabinet
wise man of Gotham
wishful thinking
witches' thimbles
with a difference
with a flying seal
with all one's soul
with bated breath
withdrawing room
wither on the vine
withholding rate
within arm's reach
within one's grasp
with life and limb
without ceremony
without question
without recourse
with reference to
Wittgensteinian
woman of pleasure
Women's Institute
Woodbury gravure
woodland caribou
woody nightshade
word association
word recognition
work double tides
work like a beaver
work like a nigger
work measurement
work one's arse off
work one's guts out
work one's passage
work one's tail off
world-historical
world literature
world without end
wormwood lecture
write oneself man
write-permit ring

writ of privilege
wrong-headedness
xanthine oxidase
xanthochromatic
xerographically
xeroradiography
xylographically
Yarmouth bloater
Yates' correction
yellow archangel
yellow cartilage

yellow pimpernel
yellow underwing
yeoman of signals
yield one's breath
yoko-shiho-gatame
you bet your boots
you'd be surprised
your corporosity
yours faithfully
Yours faithfully
you see what I mean

Yukawa potential
zenith telescope
zero-dimensional
zeugmatographic
Ziegfeld Follies
zodiac of the moon
zona fasciculata
zona glomerulosa
zona reticularis
zoogeographical
zygomatic muscle

SIXTEEN LETTERS

a barrel of monkeys
a bee in one's bonnet
ablative absolute
able-bodied rating
able-bodied seaman
a bolt from the blue
absentee landlord
absent-mindedness
absolute humidity
absolute majority
Abyssinian banana
academic material
academic parlance
acanthopterygian
accelerator board
accessory mineral
access television
accommodationist
according to Hoyle
account executive
accounting period
accumulativeness
acquaintance rape
acquaintanceship
acroparaesthesia
actual bodily harm
a day after the fair
addition reaction
address oneself to
adjustment centre
Adjutant Generals
administratively
Admiral of the Blue
adrenalectomized
a drop in the bucket
advantageousness
adventitious root
aeromagnetometer
affectionateness
affiliation order
a foot in both camps
African blackwood
Afrikanerization
against the stream
agent provocateur
a hard act to follow
Alexandrine verse
a lick and a promise
alienation effect
alimentativeness
all gas and gaiters
all girls together
alligator snapper
alliterativeness
alpine strawberry
alternative birth
altitude sickness

a matter of opinion
ambidextrousness
American football
American John Dory
American woodcock
amoebic dysentery
Anabaptistically
anaesthetization
anagrammatically
a nasty bit of goods
anathematization
ancient historian
angle of incidence
Anglo-Catholicism
Angostura Bitters
animal liberation
annual aberration
anomalistic month
answering machine
answering service
antagonistically
anthropocentrism
anthropometrical
anthropomorphise
anthropomorphism
anthropomorphist
anthropomorphite
anthropomorphize
anthropomorphous
anthropopsychism
anthroposophical
antibody-negative
antichristianism
antichristianity
anticyclonically
anti-inflammatory
antipathetically
any other business
a piece of one's mind
a play within a play
a plum in one's mouth
apophthegmatical
apoplectic stroke
Apostolic Fathers
appendicectomies
appreciativeness
apprehensibility
apprehensiveness
approachableness
a price on one's head
archaeo-astronomy
archaeologically
archaeomagnetism
archiepiscopally
Archimedean drill
Archimedean screw
areal linguistics

aristocratically
arithmetic series
ark of the Covenant
Ark of the Covenant
army of occupation
aromatherapeutic
arranged marriage
arteriosclerosis
arteriosclerotic
articulated lorry
artificial kidney
artificial mother
artificial person
a run for one's money
as clear as crystal
as flat as a pancake
a shoulder to cry on
as near as a toucher
a song in one's heart
as pleased as Punch
as right as a trivet
assembly language
assistant manager
associationistic
as straight as a die
astro-archaeology
astrometeorology
astronomical unit
astronomical year
astrophotography
a thorn in one's side
a tiger in one's tank
atomic philosophy
at one's finger-ends
at one's fingertips
atrioventricular
at short intervals
at sixes and sevens
attendance centre
attesting witness
at the best of times
at the end of the day
attract attention
audience research
auditory scanning
auricular witness
Australian salmon
Australopithecus
authoritarianism
autobiographical
autoimmunization
auto-intoxication
autointoxication
autolithographic
automatic landing
automatic writing
autopsychography

autoradiographic
Avogadro constant
a whoop and a holler
bachelor's buttons
background heater
ballistic missile
ballyhoo of blazes
banded rudder-fish
Bangalore torpedo
Barbary partridge
barren strawberry
basement membrane
bathythermograph
bear a great stroke
beat about the bush
beat the hell out of
beat the shit out of
beautiful letters
behaviour pattern
behaviour therapy
behind the curtain
bells and whistles
Benedictine order
Benjamin's portion
Bermuda buttercup
best bib and tucker
between cup and lip
between ourselves
between the sheets
betwixt cup and lip
beyond comparison
biblical theology
bicycle-repair kit
bill of indictment
bill of quantities
bill of sufferance
bill of suspension
binary arithmetic
biocompatibility
biodegradability
biological mother
biospeleological
biostratigrapher
biostratigraphic
biosynthetically
biotechnological
bird-eating spider
bird's eye primrose
bird's-foot trefoil
birth certificate
birth control pill
black ipecacuanha
black nationalism
blackpoll warbler
black swallowwort
blackthorn winter
blast from the past
blind-man's holiday
blind with science
bloodthirstiness
blood transfusion
bloody-mindedness

blot one's copybook
blow one's socks off
blow the whistle on
bombardier beetle
bone of contention
born out of wedlock
boroughmongering
bottleneck guitar
bowels of the earth
Bow Street officer
brachycatalectic
Bramley's seedling
breach of the peace
bread and circuses
breakfast-service
breaking-strength
breath of fresh air
Brewster Sessions
brigadier general
bright young thing
Bristol porcelain
broderie anglaise
bronchopneumonia
bronchopulmonary
Brother of Charity
Brownian movement
brushed aluminium
builders' merchant
bull in a china shop
bumiputraization
bureaucratically
Burkitt's lymphoma
bursa of Fabricius
buttonhole stitch
cabbage butterfly
Caesarean section
calcium carbonate
calcium hydroxide
calcium phosphate
California condor
Californian holly
Californian poppy
call a spade a spade
calligraphically
call into question
call over the coals
calorimetrically
Camberwell Beauty
campanologically
Canadian pondweed
cantankerousness
canteen of cutlery
Canterbury gallop
cantilever bridge
capital-intensive
capitalistically
capitalist roader
capital territory
capita succedanea
cap of maintenance
captain-generalcy
caput succedaneum

carbon disulphide
carbon microphone
carbonyl chloride
cardiac glycoside
cardiac tamponade
cardinal-grosbeak
card up one's sleeve
Carolina allspice
carrying capacity
cartel of defiance
cartographically
caryophyllaceous
case of conscience
cassette recorder
catachrestically
catalytic cracker
catastrophically
Catholic Epistles
celestial equator
celestial horizon
cellulose acetate
central processor
centre of buoyancy
centre of pressure
centrifugal force
centripetal force
Chamber of Horrors
chamber orchestra
Champagne Charley
champing at the bit
change the subject
chaotic attractor
characterisation
characteristical
characterization
characterologist
character witness
chattels personal
chauvinistically
cheap and cheerful
Chelsea pensioner
chemical engineer
chemical reaction
chemiluminescent
chemoautotrophic
chemoprophylaxis
chemotherapeutic
chequered skipper
child-molestation
child pornography
children of Israel
Chiltern Hundreds
Chinese artichoke
chipping squirrel
chlordiazepoxide
chocolate biscuit
chocolate soldier
cholecystography
Chorlton-cum-Hardy
chorographically
Christianization
Christian Science

Christmas cracker
Christmas disease
Christmas present
Christmas pudding
chromic anhydride
chromolithograph
chronicle history
chronobiological
chronometrically
chryselephantine
church-government
church membership
Church of Scotland
churchwardenship
chymotrypsinogen
cigarette-lighter
cigarette machine
cinefluorography
cinematographist
cinemicrographic
cineradiographic
circle of position
circumambulation
circumambulatory
circumflex accent
circumlocutional
circumnavigation
circumspectively
circumstantially
Cities of the Plain
civil engineering
civil libertarian
clang association
clear-sightedness
Cleopatra's Needle
clerestory window
clerk of the cheque
Clerk of the Closet
clerk of the course
Clerk of the Scales
Clifden nonpareil
climatologically
clinical medicine
clitoridectomies
close one's heart to
clothes-conscious
clove gillyflower
clustered columns
coals to Newcastle
cobweb micrometer
coca-colonization
coccolithophorid
cock and bull story
cock one's eyebrows
codlings-and-cream
cognitive science
coitus reservatus
collaborationist
collateral bundle
collateral damage
collective memory
collectivization

College of Justice
collegiate church
collegiate Gothic
colorimetrically
colour supplement
colour television
combinatoriality
combine harvester
come into question
come into the world
come out in the wash
come to a sticky end
come to one's senses
come to the surface
come with a wet sail
commander-in-chief
commedia dell'arte
commensurability
commensurateness
commercial school
commissionership
Commodore-in-Chief
common astrologer
Common Councilman
common ground dove
common-law husband
commonsensically
common silverbill
common stork's-bill
commonwealth's-man
communal marriage
communicableness
community college
community service
community singing
companionability
compartmentalise
compartmentalize
compartmentation
complemental male
complex conjugate
complexification
compound fracture
compound interest
compound interval
compound pendulum
compound sentence
compression ratio
computer-friendly
computer graphics
computer language
computer literacy
computer-literate
computer-readable
concentratedness
concentric bundle
conceptualizable
conciliatoriness
conditional offer
conditions of sale
conference centre
confidentialness

configurationism
conformationally
congregationally
congressionalist
connective tissue
consanguineously
conscience clause
conscience-struck
conscionableness
conscious subject
conscript fathers
consequentialism
consequentialist
consequentiality
consequent points
conservation area
conservativeness
considerableness
consignification
consignificative
consolation prize
consolidated fund
Consolidated Fund
consolidationist
conspiracy theory
conspiratorially
constitutionally
constitutiveness
constructionally
construction camp
construction site
constructiveness
consubstantially
consumer research
consummativeness
contact herbicide
containerization
contemporariness
contemptibleness
contemptuousness
conterminousness
continental crust
continental drift
continental quilt
Continental roast
continental shelf
continental slope
contour ploughing
contraction joint
contradictiously
contra-indication
contraindication
contrapositively
contrary to nature
contra-seasonally
controversialism
controversialist
controversiality
contumaciousness
contumeliousness
convalescent home
convenience store

conversationally
conversation card
conversion factor
converter reactor
cooling-off period
cooperative store
Copernican system
Copernican theory
copolymerisation
copolymerization
copyright library
Corinthian bronze
Cornish moneywort
Coronation Street
corporealization
corpus cavernosum
corpus spongiosum
correspondential
corridor carriage
corridors of power
corrupt practices
cosmical constant
cosmographically
cost an arm and a leg
costume jewellery
cotton-boll weevil
counsel of despair
counter-clockwise
counterclockwise
counterculturist
countercurrently
counter-disengage
counter-embattled
counter-espionage
counter-extension
counterfactually
counterfeit crank
counter-influence
counter-intuitive
counter-offensive
counter-signature
countersignature
countervallation
Countess Palatine
country gentleman
county councillor
coupling constant
Court of Cassation
Court of Exchequer
court of peculiars
critical pressure
Crookes dark space
cross-correlation
cross-examination
cross-grainedness
cross one's fingers
crossover network
cross-pollination
crowd the mourners
cruciate ligament
crustaceological
cryopreservation

cryptobranchiate
cryptogrammatist
cryptozoological
crystalloblastic
crystallo-ceramie
crystallogenesis
crystallographer
crystallographic
crystals of tartar
cudgel one's brains
culpable homicide
cumulative voting
curve of striction
Cushing's syndrome
cuticularization
cut one's own throat
cyanamide process
cylindro-conoidal
cytoarchitecture
damage limitation
dance upon nothing
Danish blue cheese
Darby and Joan club
dark red silver ore
Davy Jones's locker
day of retribution
Day of the Covenant
deadly nightshade
dead-stick landing
deafening silence
death certificate
death-watch beetle
Debye temperature
decaffeinization
decapitalization
decentralization
declaration of war
declassification
dedolomitization
defence mechanism
deficit financing
definite integral
dehumidification
delegitimization
deliberativeness
demilitarization
demineralization
demonopolization
demonstrableness
demonstrationist
demonstratorship
denaturalization
dendrochronology
denominationally
dental technician
denuclearization
deoxyribonucleic
depalatalization
depoliticization
depolymerization
depressed classes
depressurization

deproletarianize
deproteinization
deputy lieutenant
descending letter
desophistication
despecialization
dessertspoonfuls
desulphurization
desynonymization
detective fiction
detention barrack
deteriorationist
determinableness
deuterocanonical
developmentalism
developmentalist
devil's coach-horse
devil's paintbrush
devolatilization
diabetes mellitus
diacetylmorphine
diagrammatically
dialect geography
dibenzanthracene
dies non juridicus
differential gear
differently abled
digestive biscuit
digital audio tape
dig up the tomahawk
dihydroxyacetone
diminishableness
diminishing glass
diphthongization
dip one's pen in gall
direction-finding
director-generals
direct proportion
disaccommodation
disafforestation
disagreeableness
disappropriation
discombobulation
disconnectedness
disconsideration
disconsolateness
discontentedness
discourteousness
discreditability
discriminability
discriminateness
discriminatingly
discriminatively
disembarrassment
disestablishment
disfranchisement
dishallucination
disheartenedness
disincarceration
disincorporation
disindividualize
disingenuousness

disinsectization
disintegratively
displacement pump
disposable income
disproportionate
disputatiousness
disqualification
disregardfulness
disreputableness
dissatisfiedness
dissymmetrically
distance learning
distinguishingly
distributionally
distributiveness
district attorney
disvulnerability
diverticulectomy
divine proportion
division of labour
Doctor of Civil Law
dogmatic theology
dolichocephalism
dolichocephalous
dolphin of the mast
domestic politics
domiciliary visit
dominium directum
donkey's breakfast
dot matrix printer
double Gloucester
double-mindedness
double refraction
double summertime
double yellow line
dovetail moulding
downwardly mobile
drama-documentary
dramatis personae
Dresden porcelain
dressmaker's dummy
drinking fountain
Droit of Admiralty
droplet infection
dropped handlebar
drown the shamrock
drumstick primula
dry behind the ears
duchesse potatoes
dull as ditchwater
duplex escapement
duplicato-dentate
Dutch nightingale
dynamic viscosity
East Indian walnut
eastward position
eccentric anomaly
ecclesiastically
echocardiography
eclipse of the moon
economies of scale
ectopic pregnancy

effectual calling
efficacious grace
eicosapentaenoic
eigenfrequencies
Eisenhower jacket
elastic cartilage
election petition
electoral college
electrician's tape
electricity meter
electro-acoustics
electrobiologist
electrochemistry
electrodynamical
electrogenic pump
electro-hydraulic
electrolytically
electromagnetism
electromigration
electromyography
electronographic
electro-oculogram
electro-optically
electropneumatic
electroreception
electroreduction
electrostriction
electrostrictive
electrosynthesis
electrotechnical
electrotherapist
electroviscosity
elegant variation
elementary school
elliptic geometry
embarkation leave
emission spectrum
emperor angel-fish
empirical formula
empirio-criticism
employment agency
employment office
enantiodromiacal
encephalitogenic
encephalographic
encephalopathies
encyclopedically
endocrinological
endotheliomatous
enemy of the people
engineering brick
English breakfast
English galingale
enough and to spare
enterochromaffin
entertainingness
enthusiastically
entomopathogenic
entrepreneurship
environmentalism
environmentalist
epeirogernically

epigrammatically
epiphenomenalism
epiphenomenalist
Epstein-Barr virus
expectative grace
expressionlessly
express messenger
Expurgatory Index
extemporaneously
extension bellows
external evidence
external relation
exterritoriality
extracorporeally
extra-essentially
extra-illustrated
extra-illustrator
extraordinary ray
extraterrestrial
extraterritorial
eyeball to eyeball
Fabry-Pérot etalon
facsimile edition
faint-heartedness
fall a sacrifice to
fall by the wayside
falling diphthong
fall into contempt
fall into oblivion
false bitter-sweet
false chanterelle
Faraday dark space
Faraday's constant
farthingale chair
fashion-conscious
fashion jewellery
feasibility study
Feast of Orthodoxy
feature programme
federal territory
feeble-mindedness
fellow countryman
fermentation lock
ferroelectricity
festival of lights
few and far between
fibroadenomatous
fictionalization
field-conventicle
Fifth-monarchy-man
fight to the finish
fight to the stumps
figure of four trap
finisher of the law
finishing touches
finite difference
fire and brimstone
fire extinguisher
first and foremost
first conjugation
first past the post
first things first

first triumvirate
fissure of Rolando
five o'clock shadow
flat-bottomed boat
flexible response
flibbertygibbety
flight lieutenant
flight refuelling
Florentine mosaic
Florentine stitch
flotsam and jetsam
flowering currant
flowers of sulphur
fluorimetrically
fluorometrically
fluorophotometer
fluorophotometry
fluoroscopically
fluviolacustrine
fly in the ointment
foam extinguisher
football hooligan
for all one is worth
forbidden degrees
for the love of Mike
for what it is worth
Foucault pendulum
foundation course
foundation member
foundation-school
Fourier transform
four-leaved clover
fourth-generation
frame of reference
Freedom of the Rule
French Revolution
frequency changer
frequency diagram
frequency polygon
fresh off the irons
from cover to cover
from force of habit
from month to month
from pillar to post
from space to space
fruits of the earth
Fulbright scholar
full dress uniform
fuming nitric acid
funicular polygon
funicular railway
further education
future contingent
galactic latitude
gammon and spinach
ganglion-blocking
gardener's garters
Garter King of Arms
gastric influenza
gastro-enterology
gastroenterology
gastro-intestinal

gastrointestinal
gastroscopically
genealogical tree
generalizability
general knowledge
genetic profiling
Geneva Convention
genitive absolute
gentleman of virtu
Gentleman's Relish
gentlemen farmers
geochronological
geographical mile
geographical pole
geological survey
geometrical ratio
geometric tracery
geomorphological
get away from it all
get one's hooks into
get one's knife into
get one's own back on
get one's teeth into
get to the bottom of
get up with the lark
girdle of chastity
give a miss-in-baulk
give a wide berth to
give full weight to
give to understand
glaciolacustrine
glosso-epiglottic
glosso-pharyngeal
glossopharyngeal
glottochronology
glove compartment
glucose phosphate
glycerophosphate
go-aheadativeness
go all unnecessary
golden maidenhair
goods and chattels
grey marketeering
groom of the ladder
guerrilla warfare
guiding telescope
guilty conscience
gunboat diplomacy
gutter journalism
gynaecologically
gynandromorphism
gynandromorphous
haematologically
haematoporphyrin
haemochromatosis
haemodynamically
haemoglobinaemia
hairline fracture
Hallelujah Chorus
hand and glove with
hand in one's checks
hanging committee

hanging indention
hanging paragraph
hang in the balance
hang up one's fiddle
happy-go-luckiness
harmonic analysis
harmonic function
haul over the coals
have for breakfast
have it one's own way
Hawking radiation
head and shoulders
hearsay knowledge
heart-lung machine
hearts-and-flowers
Heath-Robinsonish
Hebrew Scriptures
heiress-portioner
heirs presumptive
heliocentrically
heliographically
hell and high water
helmeted curassow
hepatolenticular
herbaceous border
hermaphroditical
herpetologically
hetero-agglutinin
heterosuggestion
heterotransplant
hexachloroethane
hieroglyphically
higgledy-piggledy
High Commissioner
highfalutination
histogenetically
histopathologist
hither and thither
hold a person's hand
holding operation
hold one's head high
hollandaise sauce
Holy Innocents' Day
home away from home
horseback opinion
horses for courses
horticulturalist
hospital gangrene
hostage to fortune
household effects
household science
housemaid's closet
House of Delegates
human engineering
hundred-per-center
hyaline cartilage
hydrochloric acid
hydrodynamically
hydroelectricity
hydro-engineering
hydrofluoric acid
hydroformylation

hydrogen peroxide	implementiferous	indiscriminately
hydrogen sulphide	imponderableness	indiscrimination
hydrographically	impracticability	indiscriminative
hydrometeorology	improper fraction	indispensability
hydropericardium	imputrescibility	indisputableness
hydrostatic press	in a brace of shakes	indissolubleness
hydrotherapeutic	inaccessibleness	indoleacetic acid
hydrothermal vent	in accordance with	induction furnace
hydroxocobalamin	in a class of its own	induction heating
hygrothermograph	in all probability	industrial action
hyperbolic cosine	in and out of season	industrial estate
hyper-Calvinistic	in any shape or form	industrial injury
hypercellularity	inappreciatively	industrial school
hyperchlorhydria	inarticulateness	inegalitarianism
hyperchlorhydric	in a state of nature	inertial guidance
hyperchromatosis	inauspiciousness	inexhaustibility
hyperconjugation	incalculableness	inexplicableness
hypercorrectness	incipient species	inexpressiveness
hypergeometrical	incognoscibility	inexpugnableness
hypermetamorphic	incombustibility	inextinguishable
hyperoxygenation	incommensurately	inextinguishably
hyperparathyroid	incommodiousness	inferior meridian
hyperpituitarism	incomparableness	in flagrant delict
hypersensitivity	in comparison with	influence peddler
hypertrophically	incompatibleness	information booth
hyperventilation	incompletability	inharmoniousness
hypervitaminosis	incomplete symbol	inhospitableness
hypnotherapeutic	in compliance with	in huckster's hands
hypochlorous acid	incompossibility	initial consonant
hypochondriacism	incomprehensible	injection-moulded
hypocoristically	incomprehensibly	injured innocence
hypodermatically	inconceivability	inland navigation
hypophysectomize	inconclusiveness	in less than no time
hypophysiotropic	in connection with	innominate artery
hypsilophodontid	inconsequentness	in propria persona
hystero-epileptic	inconsolableness	insolubilization
hysteron proteron	incontestability	inspector general
iatromathematics	incontrovertible	inspector of taxes
iconoclastically	incontrovertibly	in spite of oneself
iconographically	inconvertibility	in statu pupillari
icositetrahedron	incorrespondence	institutionalise
identificational	incorrespondency	institutionalism
idols of the market	incorrigibleness.	institutionalist
illegal operation	incorruptibility	institutionalize
image intensifier	incubation period	instrumentalness
immature cataract	indecent exposure	insubstantiality
immeasurableness	indeclinableness	insufferableness
immunochemically	indefatigability	insufficientness
immunodeficiency	indefeasibleness	insulin treatment
immunodepressant	indefensibleness	insurance company
immunodepression	independent float	insurance premium
immunodepressive	indescribability	interpretability
immunosuppressed	Indian paintbrush	interpretational
impenetrableness	Indian restaurant	interpretatively
imperceptibility	Indian tragacanth	interpunctuation
imperfect cadence	indiarubber plant	interrelatedness
imperfectibility	indicator diagram	interrupted screw
imperial elephant	indigestibleness	intersegmentally
Imperial Highness	indirect evidence	interstitial cell
imperishableness	indirect lighting	interterritorial
impermissibility	indirect question	intertestamental
imperturbability	indiscernibility	interval training

interventricular	journeys accounts	Laplace's operator
intervocalically	judgement summons	Laplace transform
in the affirmative	jumping-off ground	Larmor precession
in the driver's seat	junior common room	laryngealization
in the first flight	junior high school	laser angioplasty
in the lap of luxury	junior management	last thing at night
in the ordinary way	junior technician	lateral malleolus
in the personage of	jurisdictionally	lattice leaf plant
in the pudding club	Justinianian code	lattice vibration
in the same measure	karyoplasplasmic	laugh one's head off
in the second place	keep an eye skinned	Laurentian Shield
in this connection	keep a tight rein on	law of gravitation
intracisternally	keep one's distance	law of least action
intracontinental	keep one's eyes open	lay hands on the ark
intracutaneously	keep one's head down	leaden fly-catcher
intraformational	keep one's trap shut	Leadenhall Street
intragastrically	keep under one's hat	Leader of the House
intramolecularly	keep your pecker up	learning resource
intransgressible	Kerry Blue terrier	leave the door open
intrapericardial	kick the shit out of	left-hand marriage
intraventricular	kill with kindness	left out in the cold
introspectionism	Kilmarnock bonnet	legal proceedings
introspectionist	Kilmarnock willow	legitimatization
inverisimilitude	kinaesthetically	lemon meringue pie
inversely conical	King Charles's head	lenticular galaxy
inverse square law	King James Version	lentiform nucleus
inverted pendulum	king's hard bargain	lesser of two evils
inverted snobbery	kiss and be friends	letter of attorney
inverted spelling	kitchen-gardening	letter of credence
invisible exports	kite's-foot tobacco	letters avocatory
invisible imports	kleptoparasitism	letters dimissory
invisible mending	kleptoparasitize	Levitical degrees
invulnerableness	knight-errantship	lexicostatistics
inward investment	Knight of Columbus	Liberal Christian
ionization energy	knight of the shire	Liberian calendar
irreclaimability	knock the socks off	life imprisonment
irreconciliation	knock the tar out of	lift up the heart of
irreflectiveness	knowledgeability	light-heartedness
irremediableness	knowledge factory	light heavyweight
irrepressibility	know the reason why	lignin sulphonate
irresistableness	know the time of day	like a bull at a gate
irresistibleness	know what one likes	like a Cheshire cat
irresponsibility	Krukenberg tumour	like a dose of salts
irresponsiveness	kulturgeschichte	like a duck to water
irretrievability	Kurrichane thrush	like a house on fire
irreversibleness	laboratory animal	like a shag on a rock
isoagglutination	laboratory school	like a ton of bricks
isoagglutinative	labouring classes	limited liability
isoelectric point	Labour of Hercules	limousine liberal
isolating barrier	Labrador feldspar	linen manufacture
Italian warehouse	lackadaisicality	line-of-battle ship
it stands to reason	ladder tournament	liqueur chocolate
Jacobian function	Ladies' Aid Society	listening gallery
Jamaica satinwood	lady of easy virtue	literary-critical
Japanese knotweed	Lagrange equation	literary executor
Japanese wisteria	laminated plastic	locomotive engine
Jerusalem letters	Lancashire hotpot	logarithmic curve
John Innes compost	landscape painter	logarithmic scale
Johnny-come-lately	language planning	loggerhead shrike
jolterheadedness	language-specific	loggerhead turtle
Joule's equivalent	lapis calaminaris	logical necessity
journalistically	Laplace's equation	logical operation

logical structure
loiter with intent
London particular
longitudinal wave
long-nosed potoroo
long-tailed jaeger
looking-glass carp
looking-glass land
Lord Chief Justice
Lord Commissioner
Lord Justice Clerk
Lorentz-covariant
Lorentz-invariant
lose one's bearings
lose one's stirrups
lost in the shuffle
love at first sight
love-lies-bleeding
lunar observation
lycopodium powder
lymphangiectasis
lymphangiography
lymphangiomatous
lyra glockenspiel
machiavellianism
macro-engineering
macro-instruction
macrolepidoptera
Macrolepidoptera
macrolinguistics
macrophotography
maestro di capella
magic chain-stitch
magistrates' court
magnesiochromite
magnetic meridian
magnetochemistry
magnetostriction
magnetostrictive
magnetotellurics
maintainableness
maintained school
maintenance order
Majorana particle
major-generalship
make an appearance
make both ends meet
make capital out of
make conversation
make no bones about
make no difference
maladministrator
malapportionment
malappropriation
Malayo-Polynesian
Malaysianization
malcontentedness
male-chauvinistic
male impersonator
malignant pustule
Malpighian tubule
mammographically

management buyout
managing director
Manchester cotton
Manchester School
mango-hummingbird
manifestationist
manipulativeness
man of distinction
man-of-the-worldish
maraschino cherry
marine-biological
marine scientific
market researcher
marriage articles
marriage guidance
marshmallow roast
marsupialization
masculine protest
mass spectrograph
mass spectrometer
mass spectrometry
mass spectroscope
Master in Chancery
Master of Requests
Master of the Horse
Master of the Rolls
master oscillator
material handling
maternal language
maternity benefit
matrimonial agent
matter of breviary
matter-of-factness
Matthew principle
Maxwell–Boltzmann
mayor of the palace
mealy-mouthedness
mean proportional
measurement cargo
mechanical stoker
mechanico-morphic
mechanochemistry
mechanoreception
mechanoreceptive
mechanosensitive
mediate inference
mediate knowledge
medical diathermy
mediocritization
Mediterraneanize
medium of exchange
medulla oblongata
meet one's Waterloo
melodramatically
melon-caterpillar
Member of Congress
members' enclosure
meningomyelocele
mental arithmetic
mental deficiency
mercantile marine
mercantile system

merchantableness
merchant-princely
merchant-venturer
mercurialization
mercury sublimate
meretriciousness
meridian altitude
meristematically
meritorious cause
mesembryanthemum
metabolic pathway
metabolizability
metallic tractors
metallocarborane
metallographical
metamathematical
meta-metalanguage
metaphrastically
meteorologically
methodologically
methylated spirit
methyl isocyanate
methyl salicylate
methylthiouracil
metropolitanship
metropolitically
Mexican overdrive
Michelangelesque
microcalorimeter
microcalorimetry
microchiropteran
microcirculation
microclimatology
microcontinental
microcrystalline
microelectronics
micro-electronics
micro-encapsulate
micro-engineering
micro-environment
microfiche reader
microfilamentous
microgametophyte
micrographically
microinstruction
microlepidoptera
Microlepidoptera
microlinguistics
micromanipulator
micrometeoroidal
micrometeorology
microminiaturize
microphotography
microphotometric
microprogramming
micropropagation
micropublication
microradiography
microsporidiosis
microtopographic
middle-aged spread
middle common room

middle distillate	mousseline-de-soie	navicular disease
middle linebacker	moustached guenon	Neapolitan medlar
middle management	move the goalposts	Neapolitan violet
midsummer madness	move with the times	Neapolitan yellow
militaristically	muddle-headedness	nearest neighbour
military hospital	mulberry-coloured	nearest one's heart
milking shorthorn	Müllerian mimicry	necessitarianism
mind-transference	mullion structure	neck-handkerchief
mineral chameleon	multibillionaire	negative eugenics
ministering angel	multicellularity	negative evidence
minor determinant	multiculturalism	negative feedback
minority movement	multiculturalist	negative geotaxis
mirror embroidery	multidimensional	negative instance
misanthropically	multidirectional	negative pregnant
misappropriation	multidisciplined	negative quantity
miscommunication	multifactorially	negative transfer
miscomprehension	multifariousness	negro-head tobacco
misinterpretable	multilateralness	Negro Renaissance
mispronunciation	multimillionaire	neo-impressionism
mission furniture	multiple exposure	neo-impressionist
mission statement	multiplepoinding	neo-Malthusianism
Miss Lonelyhearts	multiple standard	neo-scholasticism
mistaken identity	multiplicability	nepheline-syenite
misunderstanding	multiplicational	nephrocalcinosis
modal personality	multiplicatively	nervous breakdown
model aircraft kit	multiplier effect	Net Book Agreement
molecular biology	multiplying-glass	network structure
momentaneousness	multiprogramming	neurocirculatory
monarch butterfly	multituberculate	neurogenic theory
monetary targetry	municipalization	neurohypophysial
monkey-puzzle tree	mushroom-coloured	neurolinguistics
monkey's allowance	musical dramatist	neuropathologist
monoamine oxidase	musquash sealskin	neurophysiologic
monochromaticity	muster-mastership	neuropsychiatric
monocotyledonous	mutation pressure	neurotransmitter
monoethanolamine	mutual inductance	Newcastle disease
monopolistically	myasthenia gravis	Newcastle pottery
mono-substitution	myelographically	Newfoundland fish
monosyllabically	myelomeningocele	newspaper article
monotheistically	myricyl palmitate	newspaper English
Montagu's sea-snail	myrmidon of the law	New Zealand falcon
Monte Carlo method	myrtle-of-the-river	New Zealand rabbit
Monterey mackerel	nail to the counter	New Zealand thrush
montmorillonitic	naked singularity	nightingale floor
moral inspiration	nanophanerophyte	Nilotic crocodile
more often than not	nanotechnologist	Nirvana principle
more than ordinary	narcissistically	nitrate reductase
more than somewhat	narrow-mindedness	nitrogen fixation
morning-after pill	Nasmyth's membrane	nitrogen narcosis
morphic resonance	National Assembly	Nobel prizewinner
morphologization	National Covenant	no-claims discount
morphometrically	national football	no laughing matter
morphotactically	national minority	nonbiodegradable
Mother Goose rhyme	natural deduction	non-chronological
moules bonne femme	natural frequency	non-communicating
mountain bluebird	natural historian	non-contradiction
mountain-building	naturalistically	non-controversial
mountain-climbing	natural logarithm	non-destructively
mountain mahogany	natural marmalade	non-disjunctional
mountain reedbuck	natural resources	non-orientability
mountain sickness	natural scientist	non-participating
mountain tortoise	natural selection	non-proliferation

nonsense syllable
nonsensicalities
nonsensification
no questions asked
north-easternmost
north-east passage
northern hornworm
northwesternmost
north-west passage
notch-brittleness
note of admiration
nothing else for it
nothing of the kind
nothing of the sort
nothing to show for
not to be sneezed at
no two ways about it
nuclear chemistry
nuclear holocaust
nucleochronology
nucleophilically
nullificationist
nut milk chocolate
Nyquist criterion
oath of abjuration
Oath of Abjuration
oath of allegiance
obdiplostemonous
object complement
oblique ascension
observationalism
observationalist
obstreperousness
obstruction light
obturator foramen
occipital condyle
occipito-anterior
occipitotemporal
occupation bridge
occupation centre
occupation number
odium theologicum
oestrogenization
official birthday
official receiver
offshore islander
offshore purchase
oil of wintergreen
Old Contemptibles
old-fashionedness
old-fashioned rose
old Spanish custom
oligodendroglial
oligomenorrhoeic
on an empty stomach
on a silver platter
one of those things
one's better nature
one's gorge rises at
one's own resources
one way and another
onomatopoeically

on one's conscience
on one's own account
on pins and needles
on the front burner
on the right side of
on the stroke of one
on the windy side of
on the wrong side of
open-heart surgery
open the shoulders
operating theatre
ophthalmic artery
ophthalmological
ophthalmoscopist
opinionativeness
opisthographical
opisthopulmonate
opportunity State
opsonocytophagic
optical isomerism
optical pyrometer
oranges and lemons
order of Dannebrog
order of magnitude
Order of the Garter
organic chemistry
overplay one's hand
over-prescription
overreach oneself
overscrupulously
overshoot the mark
oversubscription
over the telephone
overwhelmingness
oviform limestone
ovigerous fraenum
oyster-shell scale
pachydermatously
padding capacitor
paired associates
paired comparison
pair of spectacles
palace revolution
palaeobathymetry
palaeocerebellar
palaeocerebellum
palaeodemography
palaeoecological
palaeo-equatorial
palaeogeographer
palaeogeographic
palaeogeological
palaeogeomorphic
palaeogeophysics
palaeolithologic
palaeontographer
palaeontological
palaeopathologic
palaeopedologist
palaeotopography
palaeozoological
palagonitization

palato-pharyngeal
palingenetically
palinspastically
pancreatectomize
Pantagruelically
pantographically
Pappenheimer body
para-aminobenzoic
paradigmatically
paradox of the liar
paraformaldehyde
parageosynclinal
paraheliotropism
parajournalistic
parallelepipedal
parallelogrammic
parallel tracking
paralysis agitans
paramagnetically
parameterization
paraphrasability
paraphrastically
paraprofessional
paraproteinaemia
parapsychologist
parautochthonous
parish councillor
parliamentaryism
parliamenteering
parochialization
parsimoniousness
partial involucre
particular estate
pass in one's checks
pass in one's marble
passive obedience
passive sacrifice
pass the time of day
pass to one's reward
Pasteur treatment
pastoral epistles
pastoral theology
paternoster-while
pathogenetically
pathophysiologic
patriarchal cross
patronal festival
pattern congruity
Pauline privilege
pay a compliment to
Paymaster General
peach-potato aphid
peacock butterfly
pearl everlasting
pebble spectacles
pedal steel guitar
peerless primrose
peine forte et dure
pellitory of Spain
Peloponnesian war
pendulum governor
penetration agent

people's democracy
peregrine praetor
perfectibilarian
perfidious Albion
perforation plate
performativeness
performing rights
periodical cicada
periodic function
period-luminosity
periodontoclasia
periphrastically
perish the thought
permanent pasture
permeabilization
permutation group
perpendicularity
perpetual spinach
perpetual student
persecution mania
Persian greyhound
personal computer
personal equation
personal property
personnel carrier
pertinaciousness
pervicaciousness
Peter Pannishness
petite bourgeoise
petitio principii
petrogenetically
petrographically
petroleum geology
petty bourgeoisie
Petzval condition
Peyronie's disease
phacoanaphylaxis
phalaris staggers
phallocentricity
phantasmagorical
phantom pregnancy
pharmaceutically
pharmacodynamics
pharmacogenetics
pharmacognostics
pharmacokinetics
pharyngalization
pharyngo-palatine
phenakistoscopic
phenolcarboxylic
phenomenological
phenylenediamine
philanthropinism
philanthropinist
philoprogenitive
philosopher's wool
philosophization
phlebothrombosis
phlebotomization
phlorizinization
phonetic alphabet
phonocardiograph

phonographically
phonograph record
phonophotography
phosphoglycerate
phosphoglyceride
phosphoinositide
phosphorescently
photoautotrophic
photochromoscope
photocoagulation
photocomposition
photoconductance
photodegradation
photoduplication
photodynamically
photoelectricity
photoelectronics
photofabrication
photofluorograph
photofluoroscope
photofluoroscopy
photogoniometric
photogrammetrist
photographically
photoheliography
photoheterotroph
photointerpreter
photokinetically
photolithography
photolitho offset
photolithotrophy
photoluminescent
photomacrography
photomicrography
photo opportunity
photoorganotroph
photoperiodicity
photopolarimeter
photopolarimetry
photoreactivable
photorespiration
photorespiratory
photosensitivity
photostereograph
photostimulation
photosynthesizer
phototelegraphic
phototherapeutic
phototopographer
phototopographic
phototrophically
phototypesetting
photovoltaically
photozincography
phraseologically
phycobiliprotein
phylogenetically
physical training
physico-chemistry
physiognomically
physiognomonical
physiopathologic

physiophilosophy
physio-psychology
phytopathologist
phytosociologist
pictorialization
picture frequency
picture-telephone
piezoelectricity
piezoresistivity
pigeon-woodpecker
piggy in the middle
pigtailed macaque
pillion passenger
pithecanthropine
pithecanthropoid
Pitman's Shorthand
pituitary extract
plagiaristically
plagiotropically
plain-heartedness
planishing hammer
planishing roller
planktonological
plankton recorder
plantation creole
plasma propulsion
plastic explosive
play fast and loose
play second fiddle
play second violin
play silly buggers
play the devil with
play the giddy goat
play to the gallery
pleased to meet you
plethysmographic
pleuro-peritoneal
pleuro-peritoneum
plunging neckline
plurisignatively
pluviometrically
Plymouth Brethren
pneumonectomized
pneumonoconiosis
pneumonoconiotic
pneumoperitoneum
pneumotachograph
poached-egg flower
pocket battleship
pocket calculator
poet-laureateship
poikilodermatous
poikilosmoticity
point of departure
point of reference
poke one's nose into
polarimetrically
polarizing filter
police dispatcher
police magistrate
policeman's helmet
police procedural

political economy
political hostess
politicalization
political offence
political refugee
political science
politico-economic
pollen mother cell
polychromatophil
polycondensation
polycotyledonous
polyelectrolytic
polygonal numbers
polymerizability
polymolecularity
polyoxymethylene
polyphyletically
polypseudonymous
polyrhythmically
polysomnographic
polysyllabically
polytheistically
polyvinyl acetate
polyvinyl alcohol
pommes allumettes
Pontifical Zouave
poor man's diggings
pop goes the weasel
poplar leaf-beetle
poplar lutestring
popular etymology
porcelainization
pornographically
portable computer
porterhouse steak
Port Jackson shark
Portuguese oyster
port-wine magnolia
positive definite
positive electron
positive eugenics
positive feedback
positive geotaxis
positive pressure
positive thinking
positive transfer
positivistically
posterolaterally
posteroventrally
post-modification
post-office bridge
post-reproductive
potassium cyanide
potential barrier
potential cautery
Poupart's ligament
poverty programme
powder metallurgy
powder-post beetle
power transformer
Poynting's theorem
pragmatistically

praiseworthiness
Prausnitz–Küstner
preaching-station
preamplification
preconsciousness
preconsideration
predatory pricing
predetermination
predeterminative
predial servitude
prelumirhodopsin
premeditatedness
premillennialism
premillennialist
Premonstratenses
Premonstratensis
preponderatingly
preposterousness
pre-revolutionary
prerogative court
prescriptibility
prescription drug
prescriptiveness
presensitization
presentationally
presentation copy
president-general
presiding officer
presignification
press into service
prestidigitation
prestidigitatory
presumption of law
presumptuousness
presuppositional
preterite-present
preternaturalism
preternaturalist
preterpluperfect
pretty as a picture
pretty-prettiness
previous question
prick in the garter
prickly glasswort
primary education
primary structure
primary treatment
Primate of England
prime-ministerial
Primitive Baptist
primitive lattice
primrose peerless
primus inter pares
Prince of Darkness
prince of the blood
principal section
printed circuitry
prior probability
prismatic compass
prisoner at the bar
prisoner's dilemma
private detective

private judgement
private residence
private secretary
probability curve
probation officer
probation service
problematization
proboscidiferous
process annealing
prochlorperazine
procurator fiscal
production number
product of inertia
professional foul
proficiency badge
progestationally
programmatically
programme company
programme picture
programme trading
progress of titles
Prohibition party
projectile anchor
projection welder
promenade concert
promorphological
pronounceability
pronunciation key
propargyl alcohol
propeller turbine
propelling pencil
propertylessness
property mistress
prophetic perfect
prophetic present
prophylactically
propositionalist
proprioceptively
propylthiouracil
proscriptiveness
proslambanomenos
prosodic analysis
prosopographical
prospecting claim
prosthaphaeresis
protected species
protection forest
protection racket
protective arrest
protochlorophyll
prototrophically
prototypographer
providentialness
Provident Society
proximity of blood
pseudepigraphous
pseudo-classicism
pseudocopulation
pseudoextinction
pseudomembranous
pseudomorphously
pseudoperipteral

pseudoperipteros
pseudoplasticity
pseudo-scientific
pseudoscopically
pseudostratified
psophometrically
psychiatric nurse
psychiatrization
psychic energizer
psychoacoustical
psycho-aesthetics
psychoanalytical
psychobiographer
psychobiographic
psychobiological
psychodiagnostic
psychogeographic
psychohistorical
psycholinguistic
psychologization
psychometrically
psychopathically
psychopathologic
psychophysically
psychophysiology
psychosomaticist
psychotechnology
psychotropically
pteroylglutamate
pterygoid process
pterygo-maxillary
public prosecutor
public-spiritedly
pudding in the oven
pull out of the fire
pull up by the roots
pull up one's stumps
pumpkinification
Punch-and-Judy show
punch-drunkenness
punctuationalism
punctuationalist
pupil-teachership
Purkinje's vesicle
purple granadilla
pursuit aeroplane
put a bold face on it
putative marriage
put heads together
put one's heart into
put out of one's mind
put the hard word on
put the skids under
put up the shutters
pyramidal numbers
Pyrenean sheepdog
pyrometallurgist
pyrometamorphism
quadraphonically
quadratic residue
quadricentennial
quadrupole moment

quality newspaper
quantificational
quantitativeness
quantity of estate
quantity surveyor
quantum chemistry
quantum mechanics
quarterback sneak
quarterly meeting
quarterly-pierced
quarter-partition
quarter-repeating
quasi-contractual
quatercentennial
Queckenstedt test
Queen Anne's bounty
queen-of-the-meadow
Queensberry rules
Queensland walnut
queen trigger fish
questionableness
quintessentially
rabbit-foot clover
radappertization
radial keratotomy
radiation counter
radiation pattern
radiation therapy
radiative capture
radiesthetically
radioactive waste
radioautographic
radio frequencies
radiogoniometric
radiographically
radioimmunoassay
radioimmunologic
radiolarian chert
radiolarian earth
radiosensitivity
radio-telegraphic
radiotherapeutic
ragtag and bobtail
Railway Institute
rainbow coalition
raise from the dead
raise its ugly head
raise one's glass to
raisins of Corinth
rambunctiousness
ramus communicans
rape crisis centre
rapid eye-movement
rap on the knuckles
rapture of the deep
raspberry vinegar
ratio cognoscendi
rat's-tail plantain
Rayleigh–Jeans law
razor strop fungus
reality principle
reap the whirlwind

recapitalization
recategorization
Received Standard
receive the spirit
receive the Spirit
receiving blanket
reciprocal course
reclassification
recoil escapement
recollectiveness
reconcilableness
reconstructional
recorded delivery
recording channel
recover the wind of
recovery position
recreation ground
recrystallizable
rectifying column
rectus et inversus
recurring decimal
recursion formula
red-breasted goose
red-light district
red-necked wallaby
Red Republicanism
red-throated diver
reduce to the ranks
reference library
refractory period
regal pelargonium
regent honeyeater
regimental colour
regiospecificity
Registrar General
registration mark
regular satellite
rehalogenization
re-identification
reign of terrorism
reincarnationism
reincarnationist
reintermediation
reinterpretation
relative humidity
relativistically
relieving officer
remainder theorem
remembrancership
remilitarization
remineralization
remote-controlled
removal of remains
remunerativeness
rend one's garments
renounce the world
reorganizational
repeating decimal
repertory company
replica technique
reprehensibility
representability

representational	rock with laughter	Schilder's disease
representatively	rococo embroidery	schismaticalness
representativity	roentgenkymogram	schistosomicidal
reproachlessness	roentgenographic	schizophreniform
reproductiveness	roentgenotherapy	schlicht function
reprographically	Rolando substance	Schmidt telescope
republican weaver	Roman Catholicism	schoolboyishness
request programme	roof over one's head	school-leaving age
requisite variety	roseate spoonbill	schoolmastership
re-representation	round-headed borer	schools broadcast
rescue excavation	roving commission	schools programme
réseau à l'aiguille	Rowland's mounting	Schweizerdeutsch
residentiaryship	royal Bengal tiger	science-fictional
residual activity	Royal Institution	scientificalness
residuary devisee	royal prerogative	scientific method
resist decoration	rub shoulders with	scientifictional
resolidification	rule of proportion	scintillographic
resolutive clause	run into the ground	scissors and paste
resonance capture	running on the spot	sclerenchymatous
resonance chamber	run off at the mouth	Scotch warming-pan
resource industry	Russian bagatelle	Scottish baronial
resourcelessness	Russian cigarette	scratch around for
respiratory tract	Russian Easter egg	screw dislocation
responsibilities	Russian wolfhound	scribble-scrabble
resting potential	saccharification	scripture account
restraint of trade	saccharimetrical	Scythian antelope
resurrection body	Sacrament Sabbath	searcher of hearts
resurrection fern	sacrifice bidding	search high and low
retail price index	sacrificial anode	seaweed marquetry
reticulate python	saddlebacked crow	secondary feather
retinoscopically	saddleback jackal	secondary poverty
retractile testis	saffron butterfly	secondary quality
retransformation	Saint-Simonianism	secondary rainbow
retransportation	sale and leaseback	secondary teacher
retrogressionist	sallow kitten moth	second-generation
returning officer	salvation history	second-handedness
reunificationist	same but different	second intentions
revealed religion	sanctum sanctorum	second lieutenant
reversing stratum	sanitary engineer	Secretary-General
revival of letters	sarcosporidiosis	Secretary of State
revolutioneering	Sardinian warbler	secret as the grave
rhabdomyosarcoma	satellite country	sectionalization
Rhenish stoneware	satellite station	sedimentological
rheumatoid factor	satisfaction note	see a man about a dog
rhinoceros auklet	satisfactoriness	see a thing through
rhinoceros beetle	saturable reactor	see off the new ball
rhinolaryngology	saturation diving	see the light of day
rhinopharyngitis	Saturday-to-Monday	segmentalization
rhinosporidiosis	saussuritization	segment of a circle
Rhode Island White	savannah woodland	segment of a sphere
rhynchocephalian	save out of the fire	segregationalist
rhythm instrument	save the phenomena	seismocardiogram
ribbon microphone	save the situation	seize the open file
ride the lightning	scaly-bark hickory	selection felling
ring-tailed possum	scare the pants off	selective realism
ring-tailed roarer	scarlet king-snake	selective service
ring the changes on	scarlet pimpernel	self-aggrandizing
rise from the ashes	scarlet rosefinch	self-annihilation
rise from the ranks	scarlet tiger moth	self-appreciation
river engineering	scenographically	self-condemnation
robin's pincushion	scentless mayweed	self-condensation
rocker-bottom foot	scheduled service	self-consistently

self-contemptuous
self-depreciation
self-depreciatory
self-dissociation
self-estrangement
self-flagellation
self-incompatible
self-inconsistent
self-opinionative
self-perpetuating
self-perpetuation
self-preservation
self-preservative
self-renunciation
self-satisfaction
self-sufficiently
self-transcending
sell a bill of goods
sell down the river
sell like hot cakes
sell one's life dear
semicircularness
semi-conservative
semidine reaction
semi-occasionally
semipermeability
semi-professional
semi-transparency
send in one's papers
send the hat around
senior common room
senior high school
senior management
sensationalistic
sense of direction
sentimentalistic
sentimental value
separate but equal
sequence of tenses
sergeant-majorish
Sermon on the Mount
seroepidemiology
serpentine marble
serpentinization
serve hand and foot
serve one's country
service reservoir
sesquicentennial
set little store by
set the kiln on fire
set-theoretically
seven-league boots
sewage irrigation
sex determination
sexual dimorphism
sexual harassment
sexual revolution
shake in one's shoes
Shakespearianism
shake the plum-tree
shearing strength
Sheehan's syndrome

shellbark hickory
shell transformer
sheriff principal
Shetland sheepdog
shifting keyboard
shiitake mushroom
shilling dreadful
shipping-articles
shirtsleeve order
shisha embroidery
shoestring fungus
shoestring potato
shortcrust pastry
Shorter Catechism
short-sightedness
shotgun formation
shoulder-of-mutton
shuttle diplomacy
Siberian purslane
Sibylline oracles
sick at the stomach
sick to the stomach
side-necked turtle
side-saddle flower
Sierra Leone peach
sight for sore eyes
signal-noise ratio
signal of distress
significance test
significant digit
significant other
silent dog whistle
silicoflagellate
silviculturalist
simple-mindedness
simultaneousness
singer-songwriter
single-lens reflex
single malt whisky
single-mindedness
sing the praises of
situations vacant
six and half a dozen
sixth-form college
size distribution
skeleton building
skirting radiator
slantindicularly
sleeping carriage
sleeping princess
sleeping sickness
sling one's hammock
slubberdegullion
small claims court
small is beautiful
small-still whisky
smell of the candle
smite hip and thigh
snakes and ladders
sociable grosbeak
social chauvinism
social conscience

social democratic
social-historical
socialist realism
socialist-realist
social morphology
social psychiatry
social psychology
social revolution
Society of Friends
socio-demographic
sociolinguistics
Socratic elenchus
soda-lime feldspar
sodium-vapour lamp
soil conservation
soldier of fortune
soldier's farewell
Solicitor-General
Solochrome cyanin
something chronic
something or other
sonoluminescence
soporiferousness
soprano saxophone
sound-conditioned
sound spectrogram
south-easternmost
southern hornworm
Southern Triangle
south-westernmost
sovereign pontiff
Sovietologically
space observatory
spaghetti western
Spanish influenza
Spanish toothpick
spark transmitter
spastic paralysis
spatio-temporally
speak with tongues
special constable
special intention
special plea-in-bar
specific activity
specific medicine
specific rotation
spectacled cayman
spectral analysis
spectrobolometer
spectrochemistry
spectroheliogram
spectrum analyser
spectrum analysis
speech physiology
speech recognizer
spendthriftiness
Spenserian stanza
spes successionis
sphaerocobaltite
sphincter control
sphingolipidosis
sphygmomanometer

sphygmomanometry
spick-and-spanness
spill one's guts out
spin polarization
spiny pocket-mouse
spiral divergence
spiral thickening
spirit duplicator
spiritual healing
spiritualization
spirituous liquor
spirochaeticidal
spirographically
Spithead pheasant
spit something out
spitting distance
splanchnocranial
splanchnocranium
splanchnological
splanchnopleuric
split personality
sporting of nature
spray steelmaking
square-shouldered
squeeze cementing
stag-horn calculus
Stammbaumtheorie
Standard American
standard of living
stand in the breach
stand up to the rack
stand widdershins
start withershins
state of emergency
State Scholarship
stationary motion
Stationery Office
statutory company
statutory holiday
statutory meeting
stay a person's hand
steganographical
Steinert's disease
stellate ganglion
stenographically
stepmotherliness
stepping-off place
step saver kitchen
stereochemically
stereocomparator
stereocontrolled
stereoelectronic
stereometrically
stereomicrograph
stereomicroscope
stereophonically
stereophotograph
stereoplanigraph
stereoradiograph
stereoregularity
stereoregulation
stereoscopically

stereospondylous
stereotactically
sterling balances
sternoclavicular
stethoscopically
Steward of England
stichometrically
stick one's chin out
stick one's neck out
stick-to-it-iveness
stinking camomile
stipple engraving
stock certificate
stock-gillyflower
stoichiometrical
Stonesfield slate
stopping distance
storefront church
stout-heartedness
stout trencherman
strain at the leash
strain every nerve
strange attractor
stratificational
stratified charge
strawberry blonde
strawberry clover
strawberry colour
strawberry tomato
strawberry weevil
streak photograph
strengthlessness
streptothricosis
stress relaxation
stretching-course
stretch one's wings
stretch the neck of
stretto maestrale
strictly speaking
strict settlement
strike a false note
strike all of a heap
strike an attitude
striking distance
striking platform
strip cultivation
strip development
stroboscopically
stroke of apoplexy
stroke of business
strolling players
strongheadedness
strong-mindedness
strong silent type
strongyloidiasis
struggle-for-lifer
strychninization
stubble your whids
stuff and nonsense
stuff of household
subcartilaginous
subconsciousness

subfractionation
subject catalogue
subjectification
submicroscopical
subordinated debt
subordinated loan
subordinationism
subordinationist
subscribe oneself
subscription book
subscriptionless
subsistence level
subsistence money
substitutability
substitutionally
substratum theory
succès de scandale
succession powder
sucrose phosphate
suffragistically
sulfaquinoxaline
sulphate-reducing
sulphur bacterium
sulphur butterfly
summer yellowbird
summit conference
sun-and-planet gear
Sunday observance
Sunday supplement
superaerodynamic
superciliousness
superconsciously
supercontraction
supercriticality
super-Dreadnought
supererogatorily
superessentially
superexcellently
superfecundation
superficialities
superficial metre
superintelligent
supernationalism
supernaturalness
superplastically
supersensitivity
superserviceable
superstitionless
supersubstantial
super-superlative
superterrestrial
supervacaneously
supervision order
supplementary arc
supply the stead of
support equipment
support stockings
suppositiousness
supposititiously
supranationalism
supranationality
suprasegmentally

supraterrestrial	tear limb from limb	the great outdoors
supraventricular	technical college	the great unwashed
surface chemistry	technical drawing	the higher command
surface-condenser	technocratically	the Holy Innocents
surface structure	tectonophysicist	the Holy Sacrament
surface-to-surface	teddy bears' picnic	the Holy Sepulchre
surrealistically	teeming and lading	the King's Serjeant
susceptibilities	teeter on the brink	the lady of the lamp
suspend disbelief	teething problems	the late Bronze Age
suspended ceiling	teething troubles	the life of the mind
suspension bridge	teleconferencing	the lion's provider
suspension-feeder	telecurietherapy	the Lord's Anointed
sustained-release	telephonographic	the Lords temporal
swaddling-clothes	telephotographic	the Maid of Orleans
Swainson's warbler	telespectroscope	the Metaphysicals
swallow prominent	temperature-chart	the name of the game
swamp honeysuckle	temperature-curve	theologian of hope
sweating-sickness	Temple parliament	the one and the many
sweat one's guts out	temple prostitute	theophilanthrope
Swedenborgianism	temporaneousness	theophilanthropy
Swedish whitebeam	temporary captain	the other way about
sweet vernal grass	tender loving care	the other way round
Swinhoe's pheasant	tender-mindedness	the present writer
Swiss cheese plant	tephrochronology	the Queen's English
switch-blade knife	terephthalic acid	the real Simon Pure
symbolic delivery	terminal guidance	there is no knowing
symmetry-breaking	terminal juncture	there is no telling
sympathectomized	terminal nosedive	there lies your way
sympathetic magic	terminal velocity	thermal agitation
sympathetic nerve	terminologically	thermal diffusion
sympathicotropic	terminus ante quem	thermal pollution
sympathoblastoma	terminus post quem	thermal radiation
symptomatologist	term of endearment	thermanaesthesia
synaesthetically	terms of reference	thermoacidophile
syncategorematic	terotechnologist	thermochemically
synchondrosially	terrain-following	thermodynamicist
synchrocyclotron	terrestrial globe	thermoelectrical
synchronological	territorial limit	thermogravimetry
synchronous curve	tertiary industry	thermomechanical
synchronous motor	tertiary recovery	thermometrically
syndiotactically	tertiary syphilis	thermo-multiplier
synovial membrane	testimonial match	thermoneutrality
tabes mesenterica	textual criticism	thermoplasticity
table centrepiece	thalamencephalon	thermoregulation
tagrag and bobtail	thalidomide child	thermoregulatory
take a rain check on	that makes two of us	thermostabilized
take a running jump	that will be the day	thermostatically
take in one's stride	the Age of Chivalry	the seals of office
take off one's hat to	the Alliance Party	the Seven Years War
take one's medicine	the ancient regime	the short answer is
take the gloves off	the Angelic Doctor	the Siege Perilous
take the measure of	Theatre of Cruelty	the sky is the limit
take the piss out of	the Bank of England	the sovereign good
take the sacrament	the Church visible	the story of my life
take to the heather	the Dark Continent	the talk of the town
take to the streets	the end of the earth	theta temperature
take up one's livery	the end of the world	the tender passion
take up the cudgels	the festive season	the usual channels
take up the running	the Flowery Empire	Thevenin's theorem
talk to a brick wall	the full treatment	the way of all flesh
teacher appraisal	the gift of tongues	the Way of the Cross
teaching hospital	the great majority	the whole caboodle

the worse for drink
thick as two planks
thick-billed murre
thick on the ground
thigmotactically
thinking distance
think nothing of it
think the better of
third conjugation
thirty-second note
this earthly round
thoracic vertebra
those were the days
thought-executing
thought-provoking
thousand-head kale
three-birds-flying
three-dimensional
three-halves power
three-quarter back
three wise monkeys
threshing machine
throat microphone
thrombocythaemia
thrombocytopenia
thrombocytopenic
thrombophlebitis
through passenger
throw cold water on
throw in one's chips
throw in the sponge
throw off the scent
throw oneself into
throw to the wolves
thumbnail scraper
thyroid cartilage
tibial tuberosity
ticket-of-leave man
tickle the ivories
tickle the midriff
time and time again
tintinnabulation
tintinnabulatory
tip a person a stave
titular character
to all appearances
to be reckoned with
toings and froings
tonic contraction
to outward seeming
topological space
torpedo destroyer
tortoiseshell cat
Tottenham Pudding
tourmalinization
tournedos Rossini
tracheary element
tracheobronchial
trackless trolley
traditionalistic
traffic policeman
traffic violation

tragi-catastrophe
train of carriages
tranquillization
transactionalist
transatlantician
transatlanticism
transcendentally
transcendentness
transcendingness
transconductance
transcontinental
transcriptionist
transcriptitious
transcrystalline
transculturation
transferable vote
transfer function
transfer moulding
transformability
transformational
transhydrogenase
transilluminator
transitional case
transitionalness
transition period
transitory action
transit passenger
translation table
transmethylation
transmigratively
transmissibility
transmission-gear
transmission line
transmission loss
transmutationist
transpeptidation
transportability
transportational
transposing organ
transposing piano
transubstantiate
transverse magnet
transverse suture
traveller's cheque
trente-et-quarante
triangle of forces
triangular number
triboelectricity
triboluminescent
trichotillomania
trick photography
typhoid condition
tyrant flycatcher
ultracentrifugal
ultracrepidarian
ultracrepidation
ultramicroscopic
ultrasonographer
unacceptableness
unaccomplishable
unaccountability
unaccustomedness

unacquaintedness
unaggressiveness
unanswerableness
unapologetically
unappealableness
unappeasableness
unassailableness
unattainableness
unattractiveness
unbelievableness
unchangeableness
uncharacteristic
uncharitableness
uncircumspection
uncircumstantial
unclaimed layaway
uncognoscibility
uncompoundedness
uncompromisingly
unconditionality
unconditionately
unconformability
unconstitutional
uncontradictable
uncontradictably
uncontrovertedly
uncontrovertible
uncontrovertibly
unconventionally
uncrystallizable
undemocratically
undenominational
underachievement
under a flying seal
underconsumption
underdevelopment
undernourishment
under observation
under pain of death
underperformance
under requisition
under-secretaries
understimulation
under the same roof
underutilization
undifferentiated
undiplomatically
undiscourageable
undiscriminating
undistinguishing
undistractedness
unecclesiastical
uneconomicalness
unenforceability
unenterprisingly
unentertainingly
unexperienceable
unextinguishable
unfashionability
unfathomableness
unfavourableness
ungovernableness

ungrammaticality
unhesitatingness
unidirectionally
unimaginableness
unimpeachability
unimpressibility
unimpressionable
unimpressiveness
unindividualized
unindustrialized
uninflammability
uninstructedness
unintellectually
uninterestedness
unintermittently
unintermittingly
United Free Church
universal compass
universal grammar
universalization
university member
university of life
unlawful assembly
unlawful homicide
unmanageableness
unmentionability
unmetaphorically
unmistakableness
unmodifiableness
unnoticeableness
unobsequiousness
unofficial member
unofficial strike
unoriginatedness
unostentatiously
unparalleledness
unpardonableness
unpassionateness
unperceptiveness
unperishableness
unpredictability
unprejudicedness
unpremeditatedly
unpresumptuously
unpretendingness
unprincipledness
unproductiveness
unprofessionally
unprofitableness
unpropitiousness
unprosperousness
unreasonableness
unreflectingness
unremuneratively
unrenormalizable
unrepresentative
unrespectability
unresponsiveness
unrestrainedness
unrestrictedness
unsatisfactorily
unsatisfyingness

unscientifically
unscrupulousness
unsearchableness
unseasonableness
unsentimentality
unsentimentalize
unserviceability
unsophistication
unsubmissiveness
unsubstantiality
unsuccessfulness
unsufficientness
unsusceptibility
unsuspectingness
unsuspiciousness
unsustainability
unsystematically
unsystematizable
unthoughtfulness
untranscendental
ununderstandable
ununderstandably
unwarrantability
up against the wall
upper middle class
upper pastern-bone
upper ten thousand
upward-compatible
urea-formaldehyde
ureterolithotomy
uroporphyrinogen
user-friendliness
user-programmable
uveoparotid fever
vacant possession
vacuum aspiration
vacuum deposition
vacuum extraction
vagabond's disease
vaingloriousness
Valdez Principles
value engineering
value-orientation
vanity publishing
vascular cylinder
vasoconstricting
vasoconstriction
vasoconstrictive
vectorcardiogram
vegetable gelatin
vegetable kingdom
vegetable sulphur
velocity of escape
velocity pressure
velvet revolution
Venice turpentine
venoconstriction
vent one's spleen on
ventriculoatrial
ventriculography
vermiform process
vertical thinking

vesiculopustular
vicarage tea party
vicar-generalship
vice-presidencies
vice-presidential
Victoria sandwich
victualling-house
vinaigrette sauce
viper in one's bosom
Virginia bluebell
Virginian cowslip
Virginian creeper
Virginian opossum
visiting lecturer
vive la différence
viviparous blenny
viviparous lizard
voice synthesizer
voltammetrically
voluntary patient
vote of confidence
vote with one's feet
Vulcanian Islands
vulpine phalanger
walking gentleman
walking on two legs
walking-stick palm
walk in the way with
walk the hospitals
war correspondent
wardrobe mistress
war establishment
warn off the course
war of the elements
warrant of fitness
washerwoman's itch
washerwoman's skin
waste-paper basket
water-intoxicated
water stick insect
way of looking at it
weaken the hands of
wear the petticoat
weatherproofness
weather-resistant
weather-stripping
weatherstripping
Weberian ossicles
wedding breakfast
wedding reception
week and week about
well-favouredness
well-proportioned
Welsh Nationalist
Wernicke's aphasia
Wernicke's disease
Wessex saddleback
western white pine
westward position
wet behind the ears
whale-headed stork
what the vengeance

Wheatstone bridge
wheel arrangement
whistle in the dark
white-eyed pochard
Whitehall Warrior
white information
white ipecacuanha
white iron pyrites
white-necked raven
white precipitate
White supremacism
White supremacist
white swallowwort
wholeheartedness
wooden-headedness

woolly rhinoceros
Wordsworthianism
working breakfast
working knowledge
worry oneself sick
wound tumour virus
xeroradiographic
xiphoid cartilage
Yankee jib topsail
yellowfin croaker
yellow phosphorus
yellow snapdragon
Yeoman of the Guard
Yeomen of the Guard
York–Antwerp rules

Yorkshire pudding
Yorkshire teacake
Yorkshire terrier
you know what I mean
young fellow-me-lad
young-gentlemanly
young grammarians
Zéphirine Drouhin
zigzag connection
zonal pelargonium
zooarchaeologist
zoological garden
zygomatic process
zymotechnologist